Music's Odyssey

Music's Odyssey

An Invitation to Western Classical Music

ROBIN HOLLOWAY

ALLEN LANE
an imprint of
PENGUIN BOOKS

ALLEN LANE

UK | USA | Canada | Ireland | Australia
India | New Zealand | South Africa

Allen Lane is part of the Penguin Random House group of companies
whose addresses can be found at global.penguinrandomhouse.com

Penguin Random House UK
One Embassy Gardens, 8 Viaduct Gardens, London SW11 7BW

penguin.co.uk

Penguin
Random House
UK

First published 2025

001

Set in 11.2/15pt Sabon Next LT Pro
Typeset by Six Red Marbles UK, Thetford, Norfolk
Printed and bound in Great Britain by Clays Ltd, Elcograf S.p.A.

The authorized representative in the EEA is Penguin Random House Ireland,
Morrison Chambers, 32 Nassau Street, Dublin D02 YH68

A CIP catalogue record for this book is available from the British Library

ISBN: 978-0-241-18301-4

Penguin Random House is committed to a sustainable future
for our business, our readers and our planet. This book is made from
Forest Stewardship Council® certified paper.

Contents

Preface and Acknowledgements

My aim in this book is to offer an invitation to the glorious long voyage of Western classical music for all who enjoy and love it, and who seek to deepen their enjoyment and love without getting bogged down in musicology and technicalities: an *invitation au voyage*, an entry to Aladdin's cave, an injunction to 'taste and see' re-angled for the sense of hearing in all its complex and various modes. Not historical; but broadly chronological and thematic, from the earliest adventures in notation up to the present day – some fourteen centuries of continuity and interruptions, revolutions and renewals, complements and contrasts – via many detailed descriptions of individual composers and individual pieces.

My guides are boldly stated in verse:

> I keep six honest serving-men
> (They taught me all I knew);
> Their names are What and Why and When
> And How and Where and Who.

Or, gentler and more subtle than Kipling's brusque rune, Virginia Woolf's aims in writing on writers for her 'common reader' – 'to say what I thought, and say it in my own way' – not to provide objective assessment, let alone scholarly or analytical accounting, so much as 'to enter into the mind of the writer; to see each work of art by itself, and judge how each artist has succeeded in his aim', sharing enthusiasms (and occasional aversions) by celebrating beauties, wonders, joys high and low and – touchingly – to testify 'before I die to the great fun and pleasure my habit of reading has given me' (in all this, for *read* take *listen*, *writer* take *composer*, and *her* as well as *his*!).

The pages that follow are the fruit of a lifetime's engagement with music, as a boy-chorister, as ardent if amateur piano-player (preferably in duets on one or two keyboards where the medium offers camouflage), as concert- and opera-goer, as avid consumer of recorded music, and, above all, as composer. Not deliberately, but unavoidably, my every reaction springs from the fact that I, too, however humbly, occupy myself with making sounds into shapes, forms, journeys, expressive of feeling and able to communicate it. As well as this primal source, my approach is born of a lifetime's teaching, whether institutional or informal, and of innumerable exchanges with countless friends, colleagues, pupils down the decades; sometimes extended and elaborate, often enough casual – 'the kindness of strangers' – things caught in passing, or from such revealing places as *Desert Island Discs* or *Private Passions*. Some material here is incorporated from previous publications sometimes almost unchanged; more often slightly, now and then extensively re-thought, and occasional pieces expanded way beyond their original size. Everything re-used has been consolidated into an organic whole; and there is far more new-written than old-recycled. 'Way beyond their original size' is a loaded phrase: *Music's Odyssey* was originally half as long again and was brought, with some regrets, to its present extent. The style throughout is inherently allusive, and I've tried everywhere to preserve, however elaborate the sentences, the intonations and rhythms of speech – spontaneous, improvised, natural as breathing.

Primary acknowledgements are due to Stuart Proffitt of Penguin, who offered the initial commission and has exercised unceasing attention, experience, skill, in the Procrustes' Progress of shortening the body to practicable size; to the late Sir Roger Scruton, who first published a selection of my writings on music and offered endorsement and encouragement all along the sometimes tortuous way; to Sir Noel Malcolm, who, much more recently, most generously undertook to do a final round of cuts himself; to Sally Farquharson, who typed chapter-by-chapter as they were written – *hand*written; to

Paddy Gormley, who resolved my ineptitude with computers with endless patience, goodwill and resource.

Many other friends, colleagues, ex-pupils have been helpful, either in general encouragement or in explicit response and commentary: Caroline Elam and John Drury; the late Bayan Northcott; the late Graeme Mitchison. My principal debt to professorial and other colleagues is to Roger Parker and the late Richard Taruskin – their reactions worth printing in their own right! Also to Arnold Whittall; Julian Rushton; John Deathridge; Martin Ennis; Jeremy Thurlow; Marina Frolova. Fellow composers – David Matthews; Colin Matthews; Julian Anderson; Howard Skempton. For definitions and the 'Technicalities' section, Martin Golding, Gérard Bricogne; Gillian Moore; Lorenzo Goehr; Oliver Soskice. For French connexions – Roy Howat; Roger Nichols; Jeremy Sams; Peter Asimov; for Austro-German, the late Michael Tanner; John Casey; Chris Walton; Kathryn Puffett; Richard Nickl; Jeremy Sams again. For medieval/Renaissance, Sean Curran; for J. S. Bach, Geoffrey Webber and John Butt. For general encouragement, most of the foregoing plus Paul Guinery; Ian Julier; Christopher Hum; Ben Harris; Dan Warburton; Janis Susskind; John Kerrigan; Jeremy Prynne; Robin Reeve; Peter Digney; Cedric Cullingford; Charles Hart; John Vallance; Eirik Lodén. At Penguin, I thank Richard Duguid for invaluable help with proofing.

Many books on music are referred to in the text. Some authors stand permanently in the background. I gladly acknowledge a mighty handful fundamental to my understanding, sometimes to my angle, down many decades: Tovey; Rosen; Taruskin; the Stravinsky/Craft *Conversation*-books; the chapters in *Man and His Music* by Wilfrid Mellers; the elegant composer-encapsulations in the old record-guide of Sackville-West and Shawe-Taylor. Other sources are too widespread and fleeting to be captured. My late beloved master Sandy Goehr disparaged the belles-lettres of LP sleeves and CD booklets; I've however always found them exceedingly informative.

An Autobiographical Introduction

A 'personal statement'; a bit of autobiography – my particular path to music; the 'growth of a composer's mind'. No immediate musical background; both parents loved music, though both trained as painters and were taken direct from the Royal College of Art early in the Second World War to join the camouflage unit in the Midlands, where I was born, October 1943, in Leamington Spa. Evidently I responded from the pram onwards to musical sounds, but only begin to recall rather later, after the war, when the young family relocated in Balham, South London: the wind-up gramophone, our precious handful of treasured 78s etched in the memory, complete with declining pitch and speed towards the end of each side – the *Blue Danube* in its entirety, the glockenspiely bit with the Pamina/Papageno duet from *The Magic Flute*, a flashing harpsichord (probably Landowska's *Italian Concerto*), Schubert songs (my father's favourite). And running in diminishing circles round the back garden singing Purcell's Trumpet Tune, timed to end with the smallest revolution – attempting to *be* a record.

I recall nothing of music at the local primary school. Very important, though, the local church choir, taking treble solos in standard hymns and carols, and piano lessons from the nice old Welsh organist, learning the usual simple pieces, a way into musical notation. An unexpected legacy paid for a sweet-toned upright piano, enabling me to practise at home; also to try out sound-effects, and even 'composition', manifested mainly in altering the exercise-material (*plus ça change*), though I can still, more than seventy years on, vamp the primitive 'overture' to an attempted 'opera' on *Pinocchio*. But my principal infantile passion was for machinery, above all clocks and clockwork. Every Sunday morning, a round bus-trip to gaze at all the clocks en route: ecstasy if we passed Big Ben as it struck midday.

Next landmark, Great Tom, St Paul's Cathedral's answer to Westminster. On a family holiday we'd made a trip to Canterbury. I was – aged five or six? – thrilled to bits by the Cathedral, caught the singing at a service, and afterwards the boys at play in their lovely purple and black on the grass especially reserved for them alone. I began to badger my parents, who investigated possibilities, starting with St Paul's because its education and lodging were provided free. And I succeeded at this first choice first go, despite only offering a hymn for my test – 'For All The Saints' – when all the other candidates seemed to have airs from *Messiah* and such. Misbelieved the good news when my parents announced it: first indication of diffidence/self-mistrust running the course of my life alongside exuberance and self-confidence, perhaps equally misplaced.

First evening away from home, first assembly of the newly united choristers: no instructions, just take your place and sing along, picking up by ear rather than reading the printed copies. When the voices divided into upper/lower – decani/cantoris as later discovered; I'd been placed in cantoris – remains one of the most vivid moments in my experience: dazzling, piercing, incandescent, inexplicable. Soon falling into routine, learning the ropes as Probationer (as such just missing the Coronation in 1953). A nervous, frightened little boy, not good at friendships, or games, only very gradually making good in this very special and intense atmosphere. Total saturation in the great Cathedral (and its environs, still largely devastated after the Blitz): hearing the Bible through aloud annually, the Psalms monthly, the principal offices daily: total saturation in Anglican church-music from Tallis/Byrd/Gibbons, via Purcell, to Wesley, the Victorians, Edwardians and Georgians, with advanced ventures into Vaughan Williams, Finzi, Howells. Broader repertoire included movements from liturgical works by Haydn, Mozart, Schubert, and the Brahms *Requiem*, Bach's motets and Handel's anthems. And, supreme climax, the annual alternation of *Messiah* with the *St Matthew Passion*, where the Cathedral Choir provided soloists – all us thirty boys in unison for the soprano arias – and massed voices from all across the diocese filled the space of transepts and dome, producing a monster sonority à la the Crystal Palace in Victorian days, totally inauthentic, unforgettably oceanic, engulfing, sublime.

Simultaneous was the discovery of altogether other musics via piano-lessons at the choir school. Easily most vivid and lasting, the impact of Debussy. I could learn to play the simpler numbers from *Children's Corner* and *Préludes 1*, and listen to the harder ones given by request every morning before choir-practice by the wonderful musicianship and indulgence of the organist, John Dykes Bower. Better still, his masterly way with the transcriptions for piano of Debussy's orchestral music which I began to acquire every Birthday and Christmas – *L'Après-midi*, the *Nocturnes*, above all *La Mer*, all known in this form before encountered orchestrally. DB's feeling for music so far off his natural habitat was quite uncanny.

And composing: copious and childish, closely reflecting whatever newly encountered in Debussy (even a piece called *The Sea*!). More to the point, an entire opera in full score, on Hans Christian Andersen's *Snow Queen*, libretto by one of my best friends at the still-alien choir school. I would wake in the small hours, steal from the dormitory to the little cupboard of a room where all the multiple copies of services and anthems were stored, write away for a few hours – Great Tom reverberating the times from nearby/above – then creep back to bed. A little later the same morning, the première, fresh from source, when DB would play the new stuff over, his musicality making it sound miles better than its actuality, and ask with a twinkle, 'I wonder, Holloway, *when* you can find the *time* to write all this *music*?!' Worthless rubbish, of course – I was not precocious; but evidence for sure of persistence and perseverance. With the same collaborator, a burlesque sequel was begun on an entirely original plot, but only got so far as its first act.

Aged thirteen-ish, voice-break; exchanging boarding choir school for day public school, living at home, with access to broadcasting and the dawn of the LP era: early to mid-teens. Standard repertoire slow-growing – my major thrills not yet mainstream classics so much as *The Dream of Gerontius*, *The Planets*, *Belshazzar's Feast*,

Sinfonia Antarctica. And somewhere/somehow, modern strains from
the continent began to infiltrate – from Debussy to Ravel and the
early Stravinsky ballets; Bartók a tremendous excitement; blown
asunder by a casually encountered Third Programme broadcast of
Erwartung, followed by immediate purchase of the only-available
atonal Schoenberg – lucky: Kubelik's Chicago Symphony Orchestra *Five Orchestral Pieces*, still the best recording of one of his best
works. Strauss' *Salome* and *Elektra* worked their intoxicating syrup,
the *Four Last Songs* their solace after many a nasty bout of mud-and-
scrum on the rugger-field. Enchanted by earliest encounters with
then-rare Mahler, survived a live 8th Symphony at the Albert Hall,
remained in love with *Wunderhorn*-works, in awe of Symphonies 6
and 9, reverent towards *Das Lied von der Erde*. Avid for Janáček and
Weill, Britten and Tippett: puzzled by neo-classical Stravinsky, then
intrigued and delighted by *Agon* – the crude first recording, specially
ordered from the USA, when the work was still very new.

Also becoming aware of living composers of a younger generation
and different tendencies – in the air and on the air – and then a particular connection via the music-master at school, where my father
was art-master. I was pretty miserable and isolated, not much good at
work, no good at all at games, crazy about cultural things shared by
no one, trying to compose – VW, Britten, Bartók, I suppose (it's all
gone into the incinerator, together with all the previous 'Debussy').
John Carol Case, the music-master, a fine singer – 'best Christ in the
business' – who also occasionally tried out something more modern
than *Let Us Garlands Bring*, and had retreated, groaning, from taking
on Dallapiccola's *Cinque canti* under the young firebrand conductor
John Carewe. JCC mentioned to JC his problem-pupil, son of the
art-master, mad about the new music – any ideas? The result, a benevolent dispensation; I was permitted, instead of compulsory corps
or its compulsory substitute (metal- or woodwork), to travel up to
central London every fortnight for an hour or so with this 'official
conductor' to the English avant-garde, the 'Manchester School' –
Alexander Goehr, Peter Maxwell Davies, Harrison Birtwistle – who,
vivified by Paris (Messiaen and Boulez), Italy, Germany, the USA,
were making waves in their native land.

Sessions with Carewe were more a matter of liberation and stimulus than actual teaching. He tried, heaven knows; but I resisted; and didn't either want or (really) need. Sufficient that we talked – music and other things; that I left loaded with scores, and came up now and then to hear his concerts – the Manchester threesome, *Pierrot lunaire* with his then-wife as *diseuse*, and – best of all – the first English *Marteau sans maître*. John's principal benefit, even so, was to get me into the Summer School of Music at Dartington, where his ensemble regularly performed. The True History of those remarkable years at that lovely place under William Glock's directorship has yet to be told: it was the leaven within the dough of British musical life, later raised to national significance when Glock headed Radio 3 and the Proms but already germinating in secret for four weeks every summer in the beautiful Devonshire terrain.

I attended several years in succession from 1958 on; sang in the chorus – *St Nicolas*, *Glagolitic Mass*, Bruckner's in E-minor; was exposed to Carter, Maderna, Nono; and blown inside-out by rehearsals for the first English *Oiseaux exotiques*. Also dutifully attended composition-classes. That first year they were led by Stefan Wolpe. At fifteen I was far the youngest in the group: he was unremittingly severe with my tepid VW/Britten/Bartók. Next year, Britten himself was there for a recital; much more kindly when shyly approached and questioned about his withdrawn Gerald Manley Hopkins settings by a tyro teenager also attempting the same poet. And the year after I think must have been when I encountered Luigi Nono. Exhorted by the fanatical devotion of a fellow-student (Bill Hopkins – no relation) I booked a private session and shyly showed my orchestral songs. Nono's response: 'You have talent but your music is historically impossible. There is a composer in this country who can help you.' We emerged, and the mæstro escorted me over the lawn to find and introduce Sandy Goehr. He and I easily agreed to meet when both back in London: I visited the boisterous household in Barnes many times over the next few years.

Between Sandy and John Carewe I'd had a few awkward sessions with Iain Hamilton – dully dutiful academic analysis, nothing whatever for my own compositional efforts however dim, when most they, and me, needed help. *Bei* Sandy things were quite different: prolonged wide-ranging exchanges about music and everything, just what a confused buttoned-up adolescent would thrive on. There was only a decade or so between our ages, but this son of a distinguished musician (himself a Schoenberg-pupil), married with a lively wife and three irrepressible daughters, and at the centre of the new music scene in the capital city was meat-and-drink to an inhibited schoolboy, struggling with rugger by winter, cricket by summer, awful O-levels and then A-levels all the year round. Our efforts to undertake exercises were completely futile; I simply couldn't or wouldn't be *taught*: we soon abandoned them. Many years later when I realized that Sandy had received no payment for our many hours together (my parents unable to afford) and tried to thank him, he laughingly dismissed my apology – 'I took no money because I taught you nothing: and I stole all your ideas.'

Meanwhile, troubled mid-teens, my life vitally nourished by broadcasts, LPs, concerts and operas; and all the time trying to compose – from Bartók into twelve-noterie into pseudo avant-garderie, all stillborn. Official piano-lessons no good whatever, nor school-music. I read omnivorously outside the curriculum, and was besotted by painting – I wanted most of all to be an artist and, among other efforts, twice executed gigantic murals on a blank wall of the school workshop: first, the Seven Deadly Sins (out of *The Faerie Queen* Bk I, set work for Eng. Lit.), hastily obliterated as 'indecent', replaced the next year by a procession of enormous colourful abstractions. These unreal (albeit realized) aims were inhibited by my father's proximity as charismatically creative art-master, and eventually died a natural death. In academic subjects I was poor at languages, bad at maths, and so hopeless in the sciences that after mock O-levels (under 10 per cent in both Physics and Chemistry) I was forbidden to proceed to the real exams. But I was good at History and bloomed at English under the inspiring incitement of a fiery Leavisite who trained me up hard for Cambridge entry. I won an Exhibition to King's before the dreaded A-levels fell due, and left school as soon as feasible, took a job at the nearby big department-store (selling towellings and buying books); then a happy month or so in the West Country, tutor to a lad only a couple of years or so younger, coaching him for his forthcoming exams in History, English, Religious Knowledge – I seem to recall we talked mostly about Hopkins and D. H. Lawrence.

Up to Cambridge autumn 1961 to read English. Music was far too precious to be spoilt by 'study' as represented by the provincial mediocrity of the Music Tripos in its then state. So I missed out on what it could do quite well – grounding in traditional skills, harmony and counterpoint (earlier Sandy, seeing a deficiency here, had sent me to his friend Hugh Wood for these, but it didn't work out well). To this day I cannot fill out a Palestrina-texture, harmonize a Bach-chorale or construct a tonal fugue. Cause for regret, even shame: yet undoubtedly this deficiency has proved positive by encouraging empirical usages in an idiosyncratic deployment of tonal means: I'd not have found them if trained to be 'correct'. As composer still for the moment – c.1962 – a bigoted little modernist: gradually, in a rather lonely/melancholy time, finding a few kindred spirits; otherwise, kept alive by Sandy in vacations and Dartington every summer. Enter the Classics. King's has a superb music-library and had then a record-collection already extensive and open to suggestion. I changed my scores and records three or four times a week, eagerly exploring music largely ignored by previous enthusiasms – Bach, especially cantatas; Mozart, especially everything; Beethoven, especially quartets; early Romantics, thence Wagner and Bruckner (not yet Brahms – tried and failed); Tchaikovsky ballets; more Mahler and Strauss, till joining up with previous thresholds around the early years of the twentieth century – Debussy, Ravel, Diaghilev–Stravinsky; Bartók, Schoenberg and beyond; Janáček and Weill. And countless innumerables to all sides of these main routes, ancient and modern. Some of these discoveries shared with a friend, most consumed in solitude. Live revelations from this time mostly in London: Cambridge yielded an unforgettable *Winterreise* with Britten and Pears, and the life-enhancing visits of the Chelsea Opera Group with *The Damnation of Faust, Benvenuto Cellini*, Act III of *Meistersinger*.

Composition began to lift during my undergraduate years.

Three performances stand out in particular: *The Leaden Echo* (still Hopkins) for tenor and ensemble; a constructivistic machine for a 'lunatic-lover-poet' phantasmagoria; and *Garden Music*, also for ensemble, very audibly responding to the unforgettable *Oiseaux exotiques* at Dartington, plus lots of Schoenberg and pure unadulterated Webern. Also, intimations of a possible Self: when later I began to give pieces opus-numbers, *Garden Music*, suitably pruned, became op. 1 though it was by no means the earliest piece to survive puritanical purges of earlier efforts. All these three were performed at the College Musical Society under my own nervous baton: I didn't dare the larger organizations. After two years' inattention, my English Part I was mediocre. Stripped of my Exhibition, disgruntled with the subject as it left close reading and began to tend towards generalities like 'Tragedy' or 'The English Moralists', I gave in and switched to Music for Part 2, since this third year dropped the disciplines (apart from a compulsory fugue), admitted 'Free Composition', and permitted close encounter with a set work (unfortunately in 1963 Britten's *War Requiem*, then new and sweeping all before it). My change to Music began very badly, with a change of Professor. The incomer, Thurston Dart, was determined to display muscle and wield the sceptre over his new kingdom. He summoned a meeting of all students reading the subject, asking us all, one by one, name/college/supervisor(s). Having only just transferred, I came up last. When, asked my composition-supervisor, I answered 'Alexander Goehr', Dart's wrath and contempt were terrible to witness. I was all for scurrying back to 'Tragedy' and 'The English Moralists' but was persuaded to stay by the effective intervention of the gentle old music-fellow at King's, who placated the monster, and supervised me himself – how to hone my Finzi and Howells – it being tacitly understood that I'd continue to see Sandy in the vacations. Prof. Dart was memorably checked a few months later when the Society for the Promotion of New Music held an out-of-town meeting in Cambridge, chaired by Dart with Goehr as guest-speaker, and my new *Garden Music*, already heard in London, was on the menu. The ensuing discussion saw the Tyrant as satisfactorily suppressed as the guinea-pig at Alice's Trial. And ironically, Dart only lasted two years in the Cambridge Chair, leaving for another where he'd be free to exert his sway: his successor-but-one at Cambridge was none other than 'Alexander Goehr' (I can still hear the tones of theatrical horror with which the despised name was uttered).

But I did poorly in my third undergraduate year too, and went down in 1964, four months short of my Majority, tail between legs, to live at home, take some grotty job so as not to sponge upon the long-suffering parents, and try to compose. A feeble idea, resulting in a feeble time. The job – writing correspondence-courses for emergent African countries (including an English Grammar in four volumes as well as companions to set-books in Eng. Lit.) was hackwork wretchedly paid. I got on my parents' nerves and my own; and dried as composer – even when managing to finish anything, it was tight and mean. Broke out of the mistake, after a couple of years of it, by re-embracing the call of academe. After much heart-searching for a genuine subject, I applied to Oxford to commence a Doctorate on the interconnections between Debussy and his adored-and-loathed Wagner. Admitted to New College for two fruitful if fraught years, getting composing again as well as progressing with the thesis. These years were unfunded: I put together what I could from various sources including two summers on the local dustbins and roadworks. The third year was rescued by Cambridge – a generous studentship at Caius, followed by a junior research fellowship there; then, as this was running out, by an assistant lectureship at the Cambridge Music Faculty – the Faculty I'd spurned as an undergrad. It was they who spurned me now! I only got this junior post at the fifth application, and then only when its first choice withdrew. 'Ironically' again, my tenure – up to full lectureship, readership, eventually Professor – is the longest-held in the Faculty's recent history.

Initial lecturing was gangling and stilted, relaxing into naturalness by abandoning the script and ad-libbing, eventually not too bad (with some awful moments). Evaded the dread harmony-and-counterpoint so far as I could; did my duties as examiner; and thrived upon composition-teaching, even before I got the post, and, briefly, after retiring from it. This was wonderfully rewarding (though here too, the inevitable awful moments): you learn as much as you give out, whether dealing with a natural talent like Judith Weir, Robert Saxton, George Benjamin (to go back to my earliest years), or in dealing with recalcitrance, lack of gift, sometimes almost psychosis, or simply (simply!) getting a choral-scholar to hone his Finzi/Howells. Every composer is different (but some are more different than others): the one-to-one relationship brings this out as nothing else within an institution possibly could.

My own composition reached crisis-point even before I got a job-for-life. It dried so completely that I'd resigned myself to being an academic (though no scholar), not a composer at all. A huge constructivistic/modernist monster that yet managed to hinge its architecture and its affect around a Brahms song – *First Concerto for Orchestra* – had burst out in initial violence then gone ominously quiet. An extreme without a future (though I did manage effortfully to finish it later). The future, when granted, was wholly unexpected. A commission for a new orchestral piece for the 1970 Cheltenham Festival found me empty and embarrassed. I resorted to making play with some favourite Schumann songs, a process of dreamy rumination that had begun already during my time at Oxford. Suddenly it came to the boil, rapid, spontaneous, fluent (albeit effortful), sure of itself (albeit radically uncertain within): freedom in one bound from the shackles of trying, even succeeding in a dreary sort of way, to be a 'modern music' composer. Dissatisfactions, strong but not daring to come forth, with most of the current music I'd been so committed to, suddenly focused, were faced, overcome, and seemed to dissolve into the thin air of chimera. If this had been the conscious aim it must surely have failed: it was all intuitive and desperate till resolved. Whatever subsequent difficulties, vicissitudes, changes of angle and direction, reversions and contradictions, my course as composer after *Scenes from Schumann* was set.

So too the year's work-pattern: teaching autumn through spring, climaxing in exams late June; summer devoted to composition – a natural rhythm – sowing and harvesting; breathing in, breathing forth – that usually worked fine, though the occasional sterile summer broke it badly. Odd moments throughout the academic year could be given over to orchestration and fair-copying; and sometimes, when a deadline pressed or a new piece could not be repressed, these somehow proved workable too. It resembled my practice at the choir school – composing in the small hours (but nowadays more like four in the morning); lecturing/teaching from 9 a.m. onwards; early to bed to ensure the continuation of stamina. The pattern continued till retirement in 2011; in the years since I've often felt somewhat shapeless/rootless/deprived – even futile – without it.

Thus the biographical background to this book: reactions to, experiences of, reflection upon a wide range of music over a lifetime devoted to putting them across, trying to enthuse and excite as well as to explain and expound; to light up, in all who cared to hear, my own loves, choices, valuations. Discriminations too – preferences and prejudices, limits and renewals, deaf-spots and some certainties that X or Y by so-and-so isn't worth the bother, and that P, D and Q are truly bad and beneath serious consideration. 'A judgement is personal or it is nothing.' Every observation here has been tried this way and that, and tested in a burning crucible of pleasure, delight, entrancement – of wonder and awe and adoration – by a composer who tries also to practise what he preaches.

The Shape of the Book

First, a Prologue: a bird's-eye view of Western Music's origins in monody – folksong and plainsong – across ever-unfolding expanses of vocal polyphony culminating, via countless accretions, in a mighty body of skill, knowledge, experience, usage, in such great masters as Lassus, Victoria, Palestrina, Byrd. This will not be a History: the story is told in specific works by specific composers across some four centuries of development; chosen for calibre – architectural/constructive power, expressive intensity; almost wholly religious – liturgy and motets; rarely secular. There are many omissions – this is an enthusiast's record of delighted discoveries, not a scholar's coverage; a journey of accidental encounters, not a map. Broad sweeps, homing in now and then upon an exemplary piece of music as a launching-point for further exploration.

The main problem in describing polyphony is its unmemorability: it's a texture, often of complex facture and expressive depth, enhanced by the wonderful acoustic structures for which it was conceived and which still suit it best in live performance. Yet even when the same melodic line runs through an entire Mass – as with the ubiquitous secular song *L'Homme armé* or the plainchant for a particular festival or the head-motifs from an individual motet, the sound is not memorable in detail; it doesn't do themes, let alone melodies in a later sense. You can't hum or whistle Machaut or Josquin, Taverner or Tallis! What one hears is a composite – a choral sonority in two to six parts (forty is a special tour de force) whose moment-to-moment interweavings and overall flux can be oceanic – one is engulfed in the texture/process/sonority, and sometimes drowned. Lifelines, thrown out by close technical description of how these polyphonic marvels are constructed, don't always help. Nor, oddly, often enough, does following the structure and content of the text. Only towards the culmination and close of these long centuries does explicit expression become audible, most movingly in setting the *Lamentations* and *Reproaches*. In earlier times it's hard to catch a change of intonation between *crucifixus est* and *et resurrexit*. The range of aching penitence, tender devotion, poignancy and exuberant rejoicing in Byrd's motets is something new.

For this earliest epoch, then, impressionism, evocation by description, avowedly subjective, subject, too, to ignorances and omissions that true scholars of this music and its composers will deplore – yet, I hope, helpful towards expanded horizons for the eager novice like myself; '*Ich kann nicht anders.*' Nor can I do much different for the changes that overturn the glories of polyphony at their apex – the birth of monody, the dawn of opera, the first flourishings of purely instrumental music, whether sacred or – principally – worldly. *Here* my confession is not of ignorant eagerness, as before, so much as to a lack of sympathy that, at worst, ends up in boredom, even resentment. This first drastic revolution/reversal in music's history can be seen initially as *merely* negative: acres of dreary recitative with routine conventionalized continuo accompaniment, fuller passages all scales and fanfares across a few primitive tonal relationships. I'll do what I *can* for Monteverdi and his consequences, then for the growth of concertos and trio sonatas and such. And there are pockets of delectation down the waste-decades: notably, the line of fantazia along the English seventeenth century, from late Elizabethan, through James, Charles, the Interregnum, to culminate in that dazzling treasure of ahistorical genius, the eighteen-year-old Purcell's collection of 1680.

And as continuo-culture enrichens, it slowly takes on new continuities, purposes, sizes, textures, harmonies, to replace the lost glories of polyphony, which couldn't possibly have achieved or even desired such results. Italian, German, English, Spanish, particularly French – the range between theatrical sublimity and intimate intricacy of Rameau, Charpentier, Couperin, justifies the loose term Baroque (impressionism again) at its great apogee: add to it Purcell – the model, thence Handel – the Handel of Old Testament oratorio (with one supreme Christian exception), and *Firework-* and

Water-Music, not those insufferably unbelievable *opere serie*: then throw in the irresistible variety and sparkle of Domenico Scarlatti. But all these are still treated in cameo rather than covered at length and in depth. My story *really* starts with J. S. Bach, contemporary with most of these developments (and exactly contemporary with Scarlatti and Handel). Indeed, I wanted at first to commence this book here – a friend wittily dubbed all prior to him as 'B.C.' – but was persuaded otherwise. He and Schubert are the twin centres – Sun and Moon – of my musical universe; here is the first composer I know well enough to try to write of at length. His achievement, unlike his contemporaries', extends far into the past, apparently superseded for ever by them; he revives the arts, textures, aims of polyphony, and takes them to an incredible consummation.

This was not thus understood until well after his death. Bach now appears as junction-point of all Western Music, at once the *goal* to which everything before – except the boring seventeenth-century blip – had tended; its *summa*, wherein everything before reaches comprehensive fulfilment with a richness of technique and expression unforeseen even by Byrd or Purcell at their most intense; a *synthesis* of styles, open to whatever comes his way, curious, energetically eclectic, choosing and creatively learning from all available idioms and practices; and a *completion*: there can be no other. All this was unknown at the time of his death and for long years thereafter. A century or so later, the picture has altogether changed (although before this, the principal prophets included some great composers – Mozart, Beethoven, Mendelssohn, Schumann): thence the wholesale enthronement by later German Romantics – Brahms, Bruckner, Wagner; and thereafter Universal.

Après-Bach – 'A.D.' – come individual sections on successive composers, continuing well into the twentieth century, and commencing with Haydn and the 'classical style'. To invoke this famous phrase is to encounter the second gigantic revolution/metamorphosis in Western Music's evolution – another drastic case of mature mastery thrown out the window in exchange for what, by comparison, seems unbearably flimsy, trivial, infantile. The story of how this new manner rapidly ripened into Viennese classicism; thence, with the sea-change wrought within the art's possibilities by Schubert, into the Austro-German mainstream all down the nineteenth century to its gigantification and decadence in Strauss and Mahler and its hoped-for reconstitution by Schoenberg, is told composer-by-composer. This river-run is powerful enough even to ingest the widest divergence from it possible from within it, the explosion of Wagner's mature music-dramas. Yet Wagner, too, is unimaginable without Beethoven and Schubert as direct forebears and an affinity with Bach, deepening all the way from loving archaism in *Meistersinger* to profound resemblances – of language, expressive intent, harmonic-polyphonic saturation – in *Parsifal*.

The unbroken Teutonic line is carried right up to the mid-twentieth century, with the deaths (on each side of 1950) of Strauss and Schoenberg. Then other very different nineteenth-century paths are explored: French from Berlioz (notwithstanding his debts to Gluck, Beethoven, Weber); via Bizet, Delibes, Chabrier, to Franck and his circle; Fauré, Debussy, Satie, Ravel: Russian from Glinka, via 'the Five' (Musorgsky to the fore); to Tchaikovsky, Rachmaninov, Scriabin. Back for other nineteenth-century nationalists – Chopin and Liszt the outstanding Romantic composer-pianists; Dvořák and Janáček; Symanowski and Enescu. Back yet again for another nineteenth-century line that I have to confess is another deaf-spot – Italian Opera from Rossini through Bellini and Donizetti to the mighty Verdi and the equivocally seductive Puccini. As with earlier such patches, I can only hope that my difficulties with this repertoire, honestly tussled with, might help some other listeners with theirs; and even, via such breast-baring breast-beating, confirm their pleasures for those who have no problem with this particular area of musical expression.

The Great Modernist Pioneers follow: Schoenberg and his principal pupils, already included in the Teutonic line, are now joined by Sibelius, Bartók, Stravinsky; also by such 'pre-moderns', late-flowering Romantics, as Elgar and Delius, the maverick radical Ives and his rugged companion Ruggles and the thoroughly commercial Gershwin. The 1940s/1950s are a watershed: many deaths, some in ripe or angry old age, some tragically premature; and one unique case, the remarkable renewal of Stravinsky for a further twenty or so years of surprises when he'd seemed to be worked dry. This decade, with all its paradoxical overlaps, marks another major swerve in Western Music's history, with the emergence of an ideologically committed avant-garde determined to erase the past and start all over again from square one.

And from this point on, my coverage will again be, as at the start, a bird's-eye view: broad sweeps and massive generalizations; only a few important individual composers are covered in the same detail as in the book's main body; otherwise, cameos – representative figures, represented by one or two salient works, right up to the present day. Some individual composers of stature had already proven themselves such even before the Second World War – Shostakovich, Messiaen, Copland, Britten. Their variously chequered careers are rendered continuous, to interlace with commanding new voices who begin to come into their own in the years following the war, among them Tippett, Carter, Lutosławski. Simply to drop these names alongside those already mentioned is to wonder at the width, if not always the depth, of an epoch that can embrace Britten and Shostakovich at one extreme, John Cage at the other, while also embracing the ultra-complexity of Boulez/ Nono/Stockhausen and their followers, the ultra-simplification of Reich/Riley/Glass and the subsequent clean-sweep of minimalism, holy or worldly; all these simultaneous with the mature experimental modernism of Carter, the mature idiosyncrasy of Messiaen, the polyglot euphoria of Berio, the quicksilver phantasmagoria of Ligeti, the stalwart and determined classicism of Robert Simpson and the lush neo-Romanticism of Nicholas Maw, the exquisite finish of Dutilleux, the inner stillness of Feldman, the maverick madness of David Del Tredici. Many others too; too many to name except, when this final chapter is reached, in passing: the bird's-eye view again. The past seventy years or so of Western Music are protean beyond any previous period; and it's all still in spate: there's no question whatever in my mind that the state of the art remains colossally vital: my closing section is not an Epilogue, still less a Lament: I would deplore any such intonation or intention.

Nevertheless, there *is* a Big Question: does all this creative ferment of heterogeneity have a centre? The ubiquity cannot be denied; nor, at its best, the calibre. Flux and contradiction, fertility interlocked with sterility, mediocrity, as always (but merely bogus and inept given such scope as not possible in the past), are also undeniable – quite apart from sociological concerns as to the present and future of the art which are not part of my brief. Answer came there, No! No centre. But could there be a synthesis? Here I live (and practise) in hope. Let's fantasize. After revolutions, destructions, replacement techniques and even languages on a scale unprecedented (just recall Music *c.*1600; again, *c.*1750; again, when Wagnerism eroded the language), comes a wearily tolerant stability – anything goes, everything is available and possible, neither better nor worse in an ever-expanding Past as well as a Present that includes the ends of the earth in ethnic musics and the untold resources of technology. The state of the art is more than simply eclectic; it is omnivorous, greedy, undiscriminating, promiscuous. As after such earlier times of flux the elements fertile in any innovation have survived, cross-bred, metamorphosed, borne fruit and even moved towards some sense of a common practice (think Music *c.*1550; again, *c.*1700; again, *c.*1780– 1830; again, as the 'poison' of Wagnerism bloomed afresh in those composers strong enough to transform it). The most recent instance is the conversion whereby the dead hand of classic twelve-note serialism comes to life in its begetter's principal pupils (to his consternation) – and even, sporadically, in Schoenberg himself: and is thence disseminated/re-applied/reinvented, in composers as diverse as Britten, Messiaen, Copland, Poulenc, Shostakovich, above all the *terra nova* of late Stravinsky, to reach a sort of universality – 'we are all serialists now'. But then music always has been reborn again, phoenix-like, out of its own substance. And the same goes for the 'culturalization' of – say – the irritating fetishes of symmetry and proportion in Bartók, or Stravinsky's manneristic tics and tricks of rhythm and articulation; and everything else pursued and captured in the twentieth century's first half – most of all, its exploitation of the octatonic scale as substitute for the diatonic. All this is now digested, assimilated, standard; as with tyrants of influence in the past – Beethoven, then Wagner – casting a long shadow till re-interpreted, and redirected to irrigate new soil. Revolution circles into evolution: the vital recharges the weak, the withered stalks are trampled underfoot. Yet the history of all the arts is also full of surprises: an apparent dead end sometimes turns out to be (think J. S. Bach *c.*1750–1820) sole entry into a verdant 'field full of folk'.

A note on method

As said before, this book is not *History*: it's *Appreciation*, partial and personal (though I've prefaced telegrammatic biographical sum-maries to locate individual composers in time and place, as well as making occasional overviews as Western Music undergoes a wind-of-change). Nor is its method methodical. Rather, I've tried to take deliberate advantage of what seemed to be happening involuntarily – writing in the spirit of, under the impulse of, in the tone of, each individual composer in turn: a bit of a chameleon-act. The treatment is consistently descriptive and evaluative, not technical or analyt-ical except when it sometimes *has* to be. Of course, the emotional power and intellectual might of music, in all its range, from titillat-ing to shattering and every detail of its actual facture, depend upon technicalities. I've employed them as sparingly as possible, when they become indispensable: the section on Some Basic Technical-ities (below) sets them out and defines them as clearly as I'm able.

Because not a history (though broadly chronological), this is a book for dipping/browsing/skipping. 'What does he have to say about . . . this particular Bach cantata, or Schubert song, or Beethoven quartet? About *Figaro* or *Wozzeck*, *Jeux* or *Pierrot lunaire*, *The Sleeping Beauty* or *The Miraculous Mandarin*, Musorgsky's *Sunless* or Fauré's *Bonne chanson*?' (etc., ad infinitum). And if any *particular* work is not mentioned, the parallels between it and those that *are* are full of sug-gestion and implication. For *comprehensiveness* is quite impossible. Most great composers are also greatly copious – Bach's work-list runs to some 1,130 items, there are 626 Köchel-numbers for Mozart, about 970 Deutsch-numbers for Schubert, to go no further. In only one instance have I been able to mention everything a composer wrote, because Ravel's output is so slim and choice. Elsewhere, throughout, drastic selectivity operates; by no means demoting what's not included, but going for perceived supremacy within the oeuvre – Mozart's operas and piano concertos, Brahms's chamber-music, Beethoven's piano sonatas and string quartets, for instance. Which doesn't mean to demean Mozart's supreme string quintets, Beethoven's and Brahms's symphonies, Bach's keyboard collections or major choral utterances such as the *Mass in B-minor* and the two *Passions*. God forbid! But limits must be drawn. My hope is that by intense concentration upon exemplary choices – 15 songs, widely different, from Schubert's *c*.600; some 20 cantatas, widely different, from Bach's *c*.200, and thus for every other composer (even Wagner, with just seven of his mature operas in play, four if you count the *Ring* as one) – the eager and curious reader/listener will be encouraged to explore further, according to pleasure, interest, predilection, reward. 'Go thou and do likewise.' My choices are 'touchstones' in Matthew Arnold's sense: emerald, sapphire, diamond – yet only a representative fraction of that immeasurable treasury, so readily reachable, of which they are part.

A *guidebook*. Suppose a first visit, only a week, to Florence or Bruges. What must absolutely not be missed? What is desirable yet alternative? What can surely be passed by on the other side? Let me be your Ruskin or Baedeker! A start, with hints for further discoveries – these things don't go away – you'll come again, under your own steam, venture wider, deeper, further; there'll be no limit to the riches, 'more of the same' or, sometimes, new and surprising. And then there are all those other towns, other countries, other continents. (Though sometimes this Baedeker will omit a large feature for its very familiarity.) And tastes change, develop, mature – previous loves can grow sated; epochs and manners once alien can become congenial; styles and gods once dauntingly difficult, even repulsive, can wax familiar and lovely. This, again, is an *invitation au voyage*; an 'Open, Sesame' to Aladdin's cave: 'take, eat'; '*servez-vous*'; 'oh taste and see'; 'enjoy' – such well-worn injunctions to ease, refreshment, nourishment, are my guiding lights.

Some Basic Technicalities

Sing or play a *note*: so far, so good – neutrality. Then another, higher or lower – immediately there is a relationship, tense/expectant or calm/consonant/resolving: the distance between the two notes is alive and pregnant with possibilities. Sound the two together (which begins to require a keyboard rather than two singing voices): the *interval* between them vibrates, tingling or grating. Sound a third pitch and the sonorous space begins to expand: harmony is implicit, even before all three can be sounded simultaneously. Play/sing the three notes in a different order, and *contour* begins to take shape; sound them again, varying their order, perhaps repeating the note that comes first to end with, and *motif* is implicit, thence *melody*.

Back to just a single pitch: vary its length: repeat it at random, with gaps for articulation and expectancy. Then not-so-random: the second lasting half as long as the first (or vice versa) – a third as long (or vice versa) – a fourth as long (ditto). Try these patterns twice, thrice, four times – with gaps or continuous: begin to vary and alternate the durational relationships. The bases of *rhythm* and *measurement* are here.

Combine changing the pitches (still only three) with playing about with the durations, and the fundamental constituents of organized music are in place: intervals in relation to each other, rhythmic pulse, harmony implicit if not yet actual, taking place in sound, in space and time. Folksong and plainsong can begin to burgeon.

Four notes will raise the stakes, five yet higher, six and more are already complex and dense with potential. Order and pattern suggest themselves: conjunct intervals form *scales*, upwards and downwards: gapped intervals make *arpeggio*-shapes: both are the nuclei of melody. In the conjunct scales some pitches sound out as more important than others, this note seems to need that one: it pushes up, it presses down; what follows it is completed-sounding, or incomplete, requiring more. The initially principal pitch can yield to another: such shifts can be stimulating/energizing or relaxing/reposeful; and ambiguous, subversive, contradictory, paradoxical, conflicting – all these are involuntary tributes to the sense that intervals lean, pull, attract, whether successive – contour, motif, tune – or simultaneous – harmony. The implications of just the two notes, whatever they be, that we began with, begin to be realized as more and more are included in: possibilities ramify.

A conjunct rise of five notes makes a scale: poising on the fifth, then descending, already begins to define a *key*. And so with a conjunct descent of five notes. Completing the ascent or descent with three further notes is to *hear* that the starting-pitch has been reached again at either higher or lower position – the *octave*: at which a continued ascent/descent will sound so consonant with the initial position as to be its replication. (From now on a keyboard will really be needed to show these things.) Sticking for a moment to the 'white' notes (literally, on a keyboard), beginning on middle C (heaven knows why the primal key is counted from C rather than A, making the scale run CDEFGABC upwards and CBAGFEDC downwards) we perceive that the intervals vary very slightly: upwards, the gap between the third and fourth notes is smaller; downwards, the very first move is the smaller: already a tiny discrepancy with enormous consequences to come.

A yet more significant discrepancy comes when only notes 1-3-5 are sounded (by now a keyboard is indispensable!): the *triad*. Try triads going up the scale – those on D-E-A (2-3-6) are otherwise from those on F (4) and G (5). (Roman numerals can be and are used just as frequently and normatively as Arabic – I to VII, and higher numbers as called for.) The formation is identical, the sound is definitely if indefinably different: *major* and *minor*. Those on 4 and 5 have the wider third of their two intervals below, the narrower above; those on 2-3-6 the other way about. This slight asymmetry is fundamental to all diatonic music, whether *modal*, as in folksong, plainsong and the compositional culture springing from them, or *tonal*, as in succeeding centuries of further compositional possibilities.

The triad on B (7) sounds anomalous – it is neither major nor minor, its two thirds, both narrower, make it symmetrical yet, curiously, imperfect. Its anomalous nature made it hard to accommodate: in the era of modality it was nicknamed *'diabolus in musica'*. And now for the *real* powers of darkness – the 'black' notes (literally black on any keyboard) have to somehow be fitted in and learn their places. Their names are *sharp* – ♯ – pushing up the pitch by the smallest interval in the system, the *semitone*, which in turn wishes to push up a notch further: and *flat* – ♭ – depressing the pitch similarly, and similarly wishing to push a further notch down. All this is as audibly appreciable to the ear as the pull of gravity to the feet. Beginning again on C for five ascending notes, but now flattening the third, making a *minor* scale: descend five from the C and flattening the third is more dramatic, producing an interval not yet encountered in the seven-note diatonic scale. Its first move is the smallest; its second, to the now A♭ note, is wider, with implications for both structure and expression, before stability is restored with the fourth and fifth rungs of the descent. Upwards and downwards from the keynote in the *minor* is thus more discrepant/asymmetric than anything in the *major*. These more acute intervallic pulls are *chromatic* – 'coloured'. If, beginning from C in ascent or descent, every black note is included with every white, the succession of semitones makes the chromatic scale as opposed to the diatonic: *not* opposed, of course – they fit into each other, creating means for boundless structural and expressive ends. Wider intervals than the semitone – the (whole) *tone*, minor and major *thirds*, the *fourths*, *fifths*, *sixths*, etc. – can be re-coloured by *diminution* and *augmentation*, these words meaning exactly what they say: all such formations, both melodic and harmonic, are rich and versatile, in grammar and expression: *Affekt*.

Concord and *discord*, *consonance* and *dissonance*; these terms are of course self-defining, and absolutely basic. It's important that they are not seen as antithetical and literal – 'beautiful'/'ugly' – as in their normative English meanings. Of course, a concord/consonance is rounded, pleasing, suggestive of fulfilment, repose, close – a triad: and a discord/dissonance is incomplete, displeasing, suggestive of dissatisfaction, restlessness, need to find closure – cadence. The discord's *cadence* is found in the consonance to which it relates, directly or obliquely: it confirms the triad of whatever key the music has reached, wherever it has modulated to in passing, or when it reaches its principal home. But *dissonance* is a rich and wonderful resource in music – it can be beautiful, beguiling, tempting, ravishing, just as easily as tense and demanding and incomplete. And *consonance* can sometimes be trite and commonplace.

'Poising on the fifth, then descending, already begins to define a key.' This fifth pitch can exert great power: it aspires upward, completing the ascending scale, with or without intervening notes, in positively triumphalist fashion: it pushes downward, or equally is pulled, by the initial note, again with or without intervening pitches, just as decisively. This shape – fundamental starting-point, the *tonic*; its replication an octave above or below; the fifth inside – outlines any and every key (still for now only C): the foundation-stone of tonality. Why 'tonic' God only knows, but the name for the fifth – *dominant* – is poetically and technically apt whatever its linguistic roots: it *dominates*, it cries out for conquest or resolution or answer in the home starting-point. *Cadence* – the great V–I, the primal urge to rise and sink, activate and repose, leave the shore then return to harbour.

The *subdominant* is second in importance and power – the triad on the fourth degree of the ascending scale or the fifth of the descending – still in C, so it's F. The name is deceptive; rather than 'under' the dominant, the subdominant is its mirror, relaxing rather than dynamic. This remains true even when it's used to cadence upon the tonic – the great IV–I, 'plagal' (as against the 'perfect' close of dominant-to-tonic V–I) – the 'Great A-men' that can be sublime, or ridiculous when abused (especially when the subdominant triad is minor).

The *mediant* – III: keys a major or minor third apart also relate closely to their tonic, though the connection is not so fundamental

as the dominant's or the subdominant's. The mediant is not just
the particular key on the third degree between I and VI, so much
as all positions at a third's distance: it can be reached within the
course of a phrase, a melody, a paragraph, as too in the broader
relationships within an entire movement. As tonal usages expand,
in Schubert in particular, mediant connections become as vivid,
expressive, structural, as any other, though never the bedrock which
remains I–IV–V–I.

Needless to say, all these primeval basics can be suppled, re-
angled, reinterpreted, reinvented in countless ways playful/joking/
teasing, serious/profound/subtle/paradoxical, obvious or mysterious, crashingly trite or ambiguous, veiled, indefinite. Also needless
to say, the basics remain the same whatever different pitch is used
as the key-note. A work in E♭ or D reproduces exactly the same
relationships to its dominant and subdominant and the lesser connections as in C-major or minor; and so with every other note.
C is for Conventional, its clear origin in everyone's experience
who's ever had piano-lessons. Interval relationships – pushes and
pulls, adventures close to home and far afield, attraction back to
starting-point – remain constant whatever the chosen key-centre.
Absolutely salient is *modulation*: moving from principal key with
all its inherent relationships, to another – close by, further away,
normative or surprising, equivocal, startling, disruptive – is of the
essence. For local expressive accent within a phrase of a melody;
for structure on a larger scale – clauses, sentences, paragraphs, to
the entirety of a complete movement within a work, to the entirety
of all that work's movements, be it a cantata, a symphony, a piano
sonata, an opera. The so-called 'abstract' nature of music without
texts, voices, story – 'music about music' – 'absolute music' – is completely contingent upon realizing these tonal relationships, dramatizing them, rendering them 'articulate', indeed having them speak,
narrate, be expressive; all these terms are metaphors from words and
language whose use, truly, is more than metaphorical. The potential for structure, journey, argument, utterance, building upon the
harmony latent within tonal relationships from their simplest to
their most rarified, is limitless. *Tonality* is the foundation, deep in

the fundamentals, of the edifice rising to the cloud-capp'd towers of Western Music. 'When we trace the slow and difficult evolution of our harmonic system, we cease to wonder that it was not evolved sooner and elsewhere, and we learn to revere the miracle that it was evolved at all.'

'Tonality' in the broadest possible application. It should not be narrowly defined by/confined to Western practice from approximately Bach to Brahms. *All* music is tonal, in the sense with which I began – a single note, neutral; another, an electric tingle; a third, a fourth, etc., setting up interconnective possibilities without end. Such relationships are still paramount in the most advanced music at the beginnings of modernism, *c*.1890–1914, when traditional Bach-to-Brahms usage seemed moribund to some of the epoch's best composers. Schoenberg's 'atonality', with its 'emancipation of the dissonance', still works as before: its sonorities are enhanced and expanded into realms hitherto unheard of: but not unheard. We have only one pair of ears; the human voice and the nature of musical instruments are equally founded in acoustic/physical facts that cannot change. Similarly with Debussy's enthusiasm for Oriental musics that 'make our tonics and dominants seem like ghosts', or Stravinsky's pulverizing and anatomizing rhythm into additive cellular organisms, or Vaughan Williams' 'emancipation of the consonance'.

We can only hear what they have cared to write with our ears, as they are, alert to what *must* be audible and interpretable, however new and arcane. They are 'all we've got', but they can be further stretched, sometimes painfully – 'it must be; but it's so hard' – than seemed possible to previous philosophies. We can learn to hear in as many ways as there are different musics to listen to. Admiration for the finale of Mozart's *Jupiter* or the first movement of Beethoven's *Eroica*, awe at the *Crucifixus* or the *et expecto resurrectionem mortuorum* of Bach's *Mass in B-minor* doesn't preclude delight in Chabrier's *España*, some rum-ti-tum from Donizetti, or a Piazzola tango. Our mental and cultural equipment for taking in the vast range of musical intonations and idioms down the centuries is identical for each case: so too our physiological equipment for interpreting and making meaningful how this note is linked to the next on the most minute and the most colossal scale (Webern to Wagner). Both can be taught by experience, wax elastic and tolerant, and may be expanded eventually to encompass the weird new world of microtones.

Brief definitions of other terms, common abbreviations, foreign words, etc. will be given as they occur in the text. A glossary of musical terms is given at the end.

CHAPTER I

'The Shock of the Old'

Western Music c.600–1600

The discovery and recovery of European music from the dawn of the Common or Christian Era – down the Middle Ages, up into the Renaissance – is a triumph of historical musicology. Beginning in antiquarianism, developing through the nineteenth and early twentieth centuries into genuine scholarship with marvellous collected editions, gradually coming to life in performance – initially pioneering and tentative, then ever more confident and assured, and in the post-war decades sweeping all before it – with a repertoire as vital as the Classics, the Romantics, and (hopefully) the Moderns.

'Old Music' or '*das alte Werk/Archiv*', etc., is now perceived, justly, as parallel and equal to what has been known and appreciated far longer: the epoch's architecture with its breathtaking feats of construction and proportion; the sculpture in stone and wood; the ironwork; the facture in jewels and precious metals; the illuminated manuscripts; the stained glass; the paintings. As, too, the literature of universal Latinity, thence the slow blooming into the vernacular in prose and verse: as, too, the slow emergence of the natural sciences from the gropings of alchemy, of astronomy from astrology, of mathematics from numerology: as, too, the evolution of civil society, law and order, Good Government in an Ideal City. All are organically intertwined: the 'Nature of Gothic' (as a more comprehensive Ruskin might have defined it): the 'Waning of the Middle Ages' as Huizinga had it: the 'Renaissance' (as envisaged by Burckhardt) – conditions of life spiritual, intellectual, sensual – auditory, tactile, visual, social, religious, philosophical: *Piers Plowman*, *The Divine Comedy*, *Gargantua and Pantagruel*.

The whole story is told with commanding brilliance and readability in Volume I of Richard Taruskin's *Oxford History of Western Music*, copiously illustrated in photographs and transcriptions. It's a demanding tome – the ability to read notation and master figures is indispensable; I feel that it's only open in full to a reader who already possesses the necessary basics. My attempt here misses out not just the historical scholarship, but also the nitty-gritty technicalities. I offer instead some names and dates with indications of their significance, plus descriptions of some of the actual music, as it occurs, gathered while listening to a fraction of this vast repertoire.

All this huge body of work – some eight centuries' worth, from Charlemagne's court and Pope Gregory's purported codification of the early Christian Church's plainsong, to the culmination of polyphony in Palestrina and Byrd and its 'replacement' around the turn of the seventeenth century by a different ideal of musical texture and procedure – is *functional*: inseparable in its time, though not in ours, from ritual centred upon all-embracing religious observance as professed and practised in the yearly and daily round of the great cathedrals, abbeys, monasteries. When secular, the music is equally functional – the songs and dances of the people, the elegant entertainments of the court. Only vestigially, towards the end of the great timespan, do any of these musics become 'art', to be played and (mainly) sung for its own value, as communal diversion for its performers and hearers, or for solitary meditation, still inherently religious in character. All this is mostly lost to modern conditions (except of course where the sacred repertoire is employed liturgically): contexts, settings, purposes, are all changed utterly: the concert-hall and recording-studio, thence the home, the car, the jogger's earphones, the gym-session, put original intentions at risk more surely than with any music from later epochs. The gain, however, is a widespread dissemination of untold glories hitherto barely suspected.

Vocal monody

Vocal monody is *fons et origo*. Monody both *sacred* – plainsong, free-flow arabesque albeit beautifully structured and contoured; and *secular* – rhythmic, strophic: monody is the basis for an astonishing flowering of polyphony. *Sacred* springs from the earliest written notations – gaunt and spiky, yet spritely too; long-linear, perhaps pre-harmonic, certainly pre-tonal, achieving massive feats of construction/engineering/proportion analogous to its contemporary architecture – the pointed arch, the vaulting, the flying buttress. *Secular* branches into a corpus of song-and-dance music ever more ambitious and wide-ranging. Sacred and secular interpenetrate without inhibition – hymns to the Saviour and his Mother can build upon profanities addressed to an ideal or an actual mistress; the war-song *L'Homme armé* is compositional ground for countless Masses. The best pieces achieve a balance of cerebral rigour – sometimes plain/square/didactic/mechanized, sometimes complex and ornate – with suavity, euphony, grace: both can touch the depths and hit the heights. Eventual emergence of affect – conscious expressiveness, a human countenance – whose chief means is the slow clarification and codification of the harmony that combinations of polyphonic lines inevitably produce.

Vital stages in this process are as important for music in particular as, in previous epochs of mankind at large, the gradual discovery of alphabets and writing. For centuries the actual rendition of chant and song was retained by heart in the mind and handed down by ear – the art of memory. Thence, inevitable with hindsight, *notation* – measurement of what had always been known, pitches, intervals, then durations of rhythms. Thus an act of reading supersedes an act of memorialization. Thus *composition* becomes possible. The archaic modes are rationalized and added to, enabling larger structures to be made even when setting the hallowed unchanging texts of Mass, antiphon, psalm, sequence. From monody, with or without a sustained drone to support, via 'primitive' doublings in parallel intervals, to free movement of parts – two, three, four voices – to polyphony often in five, six, eight parts; thence to harmony, founded upon the pulls and pressures of consonance and dissonance arising from the play of the contrapuntal parts; from *modal* thinking to *tonal*.

What follows here is a roster: a litany: names and dates (earlier on the latter are often speculative, sometimes the former too) and (irrespective of the technicalities, theories, treatises, which bristle with specialities) indications of each individual's output, importance, influence, and attempted evocations of their actual *sounds*.

Many of the special terms are piquant enough – quaint, droll, appetizing. All are readily defined in any good account of the period. I list some for the fun of it: *Forms, sacred and profane*: caccia, canario, cantiga, carol, coranto, saltarello, tordion, volta, domp, estompie, folia, frottola, lai, lauda, passamezzo, pavane, piva, roundeau, virelai. *Devices and techniques*: conductus, descant, gamut, gimel, solmization, hocket, intabulation, isorhythmic talea and color, mean, tactus, mensuration, trope, macaronic, organum, prolation, quodlibet, fauxbourdon, occursus, twinsong, pricksong, hemiola, sesquialtera, dragma. *Musica* of sundry natures – theoretica, poetica, ficta: *Masses* paraphrase and parody. *Names of instruments* to delight Christopher Smart and James Joyce: crwth/crowd, buisne, cittern, clarion, bandora, penocon, poliphant, stump, clavicytherium/claviorganum, cornemuse, lizard, crumhorn, dulcian/dolziana/douçaine/dulcimer, nakers/tabor, rebec, flageolet, gemshorn, kortholt, pochette, lirone, pandurina/angélique/colascione/mandora/orpharium (all varieties of lute), monochord, rommelpot, psaltery, racket, rauschpfeife, shawm, serpent, sordan, hurdy-gurdy, vilhuela, tromba marina (actually a bowed string-instrument completely unconnected with trumpet and ocean). So, to movements of style and practice – *stile antico/moderno/concitato/rappresentativo*; *prima prattica/seconda prattica*. So, to important treatises, e.g. *Musica Enchiriadis*, the *Dodecachordon*; and important collections, e.g. the *Roman de Fauvel*, the Old Hall manuscript, the Eton Choir-book, *Parthenia*.

So, to some actual makers, frequently composing both music and words, as well as crossing easily from sacred to secular. Sometimes these figures are corporate: courtly troubadours, flourishing in Provence from *c.*1100; the trouvères, their successors from the mid-century in northern France; in Germany the Minnesänger, aristocratic poet-musicians of the twelfth to fourteenth century, hymning Love as their name indicates; their fifteenth- to sixteenth-century continuation in the Meistersinger – civic/*bürgherlich*, again as indicated by their name. Some celebrated figures shade into legend rather than ascertainable fact: Adam de St Victor, with hymns and sequences dedicated to the glory of religion; Bernart de Ventadorn, with praises to his mistress; and, unique, the output of Hildegard, abbess of Bingen (1098–1179) – 'visionary, naturalist, play-wright, poetess, composer', who also involved herself in medicine, church organization, and wider fields of diplomacy. Her texts are ecstatic and intoxicating/intoxicated – 'writing, seeing, hearing, and knowing, all in one manner' – her own words: her music for them, if not a wishful fabrication, fails in intrinsic interest – an astonish-ing phenomenon, a psychedelic bore.

Intrinsic interest arises in the late twelfth century with the Notre-Dame composers centred upon the great church in Paris. Organa of heavenly length by the putative Leonin, then, rather later, Perotin (possibly two composers) – longer, richly lively sustained stretches of Gothic architecture in sound. Leonin's are in two parts, fast-moving over the slow drone of the chant. *Viderunt*, first of the two Perotin's two famous pieces, is in three parts over the chant. *Viderunt omnes* – all the ends of the earth shall see the salvation of our God; all the earth shall rejoice in him; the Lord has made known his salvation; before the face of all people he has revealed his righteousness. *Sederunt*, longer still, begins similar till the fourth part also waxes relatively active: *sederunt principes* – the princes sat and spoke against me; they persecute me unjustly; help me, Lord my God; save me for thy mercy's sake. Endless, nay interminable, jig-like rhythmic top voices, infec-tiously bouncy and cheerful, supported on long droning underlay, its text and its melody too drawn-out to perceive as a contour except when its pitch and syllable change. Hilarious, exhilarating, invigorat-ing; faintly ridiculous, utterly captivating: *les jongleurs de Notre-Dame*.
   Lively cheer chez Adam de la Halle (*c.*1240–80), best known for the *Jeu de Robin et Marion*, a pastoral 'opera' setting his own words to his own melodies or folk-tunes. More salient, though important more

for theory than practice, the versatile Philippe de Vitry (also a poet): his treatise *ars nova* (*c*.1320) is fundamental for advancing notation of pitches and (especially) of rhythm, thus enabling the first composer one can responsibly call great: Guillaume de Machaut (*c*.1300–1377), supreme master of the *ars nova* in music, also a considerable poet, setting his own texts in many solo and polyphonic songs. Most notable, however, for the isolated Mass (and a cheeky little pendant, the *hoquetus* – 'hiccoughing' – *David* for instruments alone). The Mass is gaunt and grim, 'burnt out' with inner fire, yet bracingly fresh and raw: important music – one can *hear* this. The *Kyrie*'s many petitions make this brief-texted movement as long as any that follow. One is conscious throughout of punctuation – acutely aware, after Leonin/ Perotin with their unchanging jig-trot, of the *lengths* of notes, from the longest-held to the liveliest flurry. The *Gloria* is more syllabic: long serious chords, twice, for *Jesu Christe*; no 'expression' for words subsequently set as deeply affective; long *Amen* on swinging rhythm; as the end nears, the bass also begins to sway. *Credo* – long serious chords for *ex Maria virgine* but, again, no affects for *crucifixus* nor especial change of mood and momentum for *et resurrexit* nor significant phrases like *et expecto . . . mortuorum*; then a wonderful communal fluorescence on an extended *Amen*. *Sanctus* – infectious hoquet for the song of the angels, returning in culmination, after the *benedicite*, for *osanna in excelsis*. *Agnus*: the gaunt jerky gaiety that prevails throughout the entire Mass is more disconcerting here when considered from a later view of these words' substance and tone – which is anachronistic, of course. Finally, the dismissal, out onto the streets of Paris. Where one might encounter the streetwise vitality of the *hoquetus David* – its hiccoughing interplay of the two treble instruments over the steady David-chant below is completely captivating.

Which prompts a brief secular excursion down to the south of France; Avignon, where the Great Schism of the Latin Church had placed a rival Pope since 1309. Towards the end of the century southern France developed an astonishing indigenous musical culture, its word-play and note-play of bizarre freakiness, its harmony weird, its rhythmic structure sometimes of a complexity not to be matched until the twentieth century – Elliott Carter's 'metric modulation' not merely mooted but put into effect; the effect often mind-boggling, dizzy-making, hilarious – lusty lewdness cheek-by-jowl with amorous sweetness. Some of these composers' names are as odd as their music – Vaillant, Pykini, Solage, Borlet/Trebol, Grimace. The dissonance and syncopation of one ballade in particular – *Le greygnour bien* by Matheus de Perusio – 'are so extravagant that the three parts often appear totally unrelated, and the composer seems to be attempting to cram into one piece all the notational subtleties and intricate cross-rhythms of which music is capable'. Thus David Munrow, introducing his pioneer recording *Late Fourteenth Century Avant Garde*, still yielding after nearly fifty years a riot of surprise and delight, for all that later renditions have sobered the squiffiness.

Back to Machaut the cunning subtle-constructor: *Ma fin est mon commencement*, an ingenious little thing whose text exactly prescribes its process, reversing backwards – *et mon commencement ma fin* – and tripling within: a display, a learnèd conceit, in performance delicious and delicate. Machaut the secular: *Lai de la fontaine*, an extended canonic sequence whose poem (his own) enchantingly interpenetrates carnal and spiritual: the rejected lover seeks solace in Trinitarian mysteries embodied in natural phenomena – a fountain, a brook, a canal, three distinct conductors of water yet the water is one – all this elegantly and beautifully mirrored in the canonic dexterity. The next named composer who has exercised real appeal for me is John Dunstable (*c*.1380–1453): English, and for ever associated with a tag – *'la contenance Angloise'* – that characterizes a new ideal of sweetness and light. 'An astrologer, a mathematician, a musitian, and what not,' said a contemporary: some of these inform his mastery of an isorhythmic structuring that can clank and creak: alongside lie grace, smoothness, euphony, tenderness, much admired and imitated on the continent. Two pieces can exemplify; both are addressed to an ideal female figure, one sacred the other profane, in words and music that have the apparent antitheses merge into one. *Quam pulchra es*: 'How fair thou art ... thy stature like unto a palm-tree: thy breast ... thy head ... thy neck ... come, beloved, into the fields ... there I will yield thee my breasts.' And *O rosa bella*: 'O lovely rose, do not let me die ... must I end wounded for my loyalty in love? See how I die every hour at her hands. Save me from languishing, O heart of my body.' Spare yet graceful; melodious; beautifully fashioned: in both pieces the fair new 'countenance' extends to the whole lovely body.

Dunstable has been called 'the transition from Middle Ages to Renaissance': Guillaume Dufay (*c.*1400–1474), 'the bridge between the Middle Ages and the Renaissance'. Take your pick! Again, hearing these remote strains, one senses the presence of a great composer; arcs of contour in euphonious harmony, serene implacability pervading the sometimes astounding feats of cerebration. Witness Dufay's *Nuper rosarum flores* – a celebratory motet for the consecration of the Duomo at Florence in 1436, a construction in music of proportional/mathematical precision to match Brunelleschi's dome, centred upon the dedication-antiphon *Terribilis est locus iste* – 'Awesome is this place' – fusing the new building here being consecrated with biblical measurements – the length, width, height; and temporal – fourteen days – of Solomon's Temple at Jerusalem. The text deploys further number-symbolism – sevens to represent the Virgin, Florence's Patroness, and fours representing the points of the Cross: deliberate conscious antiquarianisms in this new-made context. The upshot is a grim granite-like block of sonority that succeeds in containing and combining all this with virtuoso prowess, mitigated en route with exhilarating dancing syncopations, and a grand dome of solid *Amen* to close. Then the motet and Mass on *Ave regina coelorum* – the Virgin is paramount here. The motet, which Dufay desired to be sung at his death and in perpetuity ever after, also plays with his own name, in musical code. The personal presence of the composer, his pathos, his supplication, his cry not to be damned, alternate with radiant salutation to Mary's beauty and glory: all the musical material (still including the secret signature) is reworked into the Mass: touching evidence of mortality, fragile and fugitive, in alignment with the indestructible verities of eternity.

Two overlapping composers figure now: Gilles Binchois (*c.*1400–1460) and Antoine Busnois (*c.*1430–92). Both wrote for the Church, but are more valued here for their secular *chansons*. Binchois has some fifty-five, light in texture – three parts – delicate, tender, melodious. Busnois has some sixty-three, tending towards fuller textures and more elaborated length: equally appealing, beautifully attuned to such debonaire poets as Charles d'Orléans and Christine de Pizan. A welcome *intermezzo* of human appeal between the strenuous work-outs of the liturgy.

This is exemplified with forbidding splendour by the next self-evident great composer, Johannes Ockeghem (*c*.1425–97): his principal works ten Masses and the first-ever polyphonic setting of the liturgy for the Requiem. The *Missa prolationum* is a towering masterpiece fusing ingenuity, architecture and sonorous magnificence: a continuous canonic structure of the utmost severity that would take an engineer to detail in full, lies hidden within the flow of expressive-contoured polyphony that occasionally goes homophonic. Treatment of salient serious words is not yet affective/pathetic/madrigal-y, just *serious*: in the *Credo* at *qui tollis . . . sepultus est* (but no upward surge for *et resurrexit*), and again at *et exspecto*. The fine Requiem does not yet include the *dies irae* sequence that would offer more such opportunities. That Ockeghem can be sweeter and gentler is shown in his *Intemerata Dei mater* – sober, restrained, inward-turned, with a fine sense of choral 'orchestration' between upper and lower voices: constructivism with a human countenance.

The stature of Josquin des Prez (*c*.1450–1521) has never been questioned in his own day nor in ours – 'the central figure of the High Renaissance', widely disseminated by the rise of music-printing: supreme craftsman, standardizing previous techniques into flawless facture in some twenty Masses, some one hundred motets, as well as secular pieces. Like Palestrina later, a classic, a touchstone, whose perfection, manifest and not to be nay'd, can leave the willing listener a little cold. Take the *Missa 'Pange lingua'*: no longer any gaunt gawkiness – all is even, purposeful, smooth; but somehow the combination induces blandness. Then suddenly in the *Credo* a moment of solemn stillness for the *et incarnatus* through to the *crucifixus* that halts music and listener in their tracks. The contour of the old hymn omnipresent from start to finish, very audibly: here perhaps is the moment whereabouts the 'unmemorability' of polyphony (as mentioned before) begins to become memorable: witness the single melodic lines hauled up the whole choir in *Benedictus* – melodic shapes one retains as they continue in the ensuing two-part counterpoint. Josquin at his most heroic in the *Missa Hercules Dux Ferrariae*, where the same pros and cons apply. An eight-note cantus firmus derived from the august dedicatee's name is present throughout in long notes: against them, a continuous play of small conjunct figures effortlessly expanding, frequent scale-passages, much canonizing, every process, unlike the secret art of Ockeghem, explicit and audible: lucid, impeccable, dull. Josquin can be heard to better advantage in the exquisitely tender 'lament for the makers', *Nymphes des bois*. The invitation to the nymphs to deplore the passing of Ockeghem is built over the *Requiem*-cantus in Latin: towards the end his own name joins the mourners, plus the names of three other eminent equals, one of whom will also figure here.

Meanwhile, for this listener, further disappointments from some other famous contemporaries. Jacob Obrecht (*c*.1450–1505) – a Lego-composer, ingenious to the point of being arcane – *Missa 'Sub tuum praesidium'* strong, stiff, reliable, tedious: perhaps good performances might animate the bones. Heinrich Isaac (*c*.1450–1517) – 'one of Josquin's greatest contemporaries': the well-known song *Innsbruck, ich muss dich lassen* is charming, and the *Missa 'O praeclara'* has its moments – he thinks in sentences, an attractive light flow keeps things buoyant, occasionally breaking into croppy dance: but the *Missa de Apostolis* is rather a clunker.

Three younger contemporaries are more rewarding if less important. Pierre de la Rue (*c*.1460–1518): many Masses including a *L'Homme armé*. Its most memorable moment very brief, the *et homo factus est* in the *Credo*, a moment of ghostly gravity, supernatural indeed, in an overall context slightly sober and anonymous, though the ends of the *Gloria* and the *Credo* both burst into flowering vigour and the *Agnus* is lovely. The old song is audible all the way, which helps. But the prevailing impression – highly accomplished and rather dry. Nothing dry chez Antoine Brumel (*c*.1460–1520)'s *Et ecce terrae motus*: this twelve-part Mass is not so much an earth- as a sea-quake, in whose oceanic deployment of the twelve voices the listener, as no doubt the singers, must swim or drown. Harmony is the anchor, securing the mass of polyphony around slow-moving cantus firmus, with marked rhythmic articulation of the fluid blocks of sound. Simpler music, for all the complex textures, than severe strictness in the epoch's usual four or five parts: Tallis's *Spem in alium* on the horizon. Brumel's *Sanctus* is particularly resplendent, with a dancing *pleni sunt* and a bell-ringing *osanna*. Two-voice writing relieves resplendence in the *Benedicite*, then, for the *Agnus*, back to seraphic immersion.

Brumel's *Lamentations* consist only of two versets, each preceded by the traditional Hebrew initial: *Heth*, its text dealing in general destruction; *Caph* more particular – 'my eyes grow dim, my bowels tremble, my bile is spilt': then the closing plea, a mournful lilt on words that are going to become nearly as familiar as the texts of the Mass – 'Jerusalem, turn again to the Lord your God'. Another *Lamentations* sets all nine *lecti*, each with its Hebrew initial – the setting for six voices by Elzéar Carpentras (*c*.1475–1548), whose 'long and agonizing illness' can surely be sensed in the intensity of this superb music. The initials are set with rich-wrought polyphony: they are epigrams. The setting of Jeremiah is largely homophonic – grave, dark, warmly full, though movement can grow almost light and dancing: vocal scoring very varied, the duets especially good. Overall, a work of surpassing *gravitas*: noble, chaste without meanness: together with the smooth perfection universally attributed to Josquin come qualities that the Master of the Age seems to lack.

Enough for now of Masses, Requiems, Lamentations (there'll be plenty more): light relief in a secular diversion from around the same time. Clément Janequin (*c*.1485–1558): there *is* religious music, but his fame rests more securely upon nearly three hundred *chansons*, mainly playful/vivacious/frivolous; usually amorous, sometimes erotic, occasionally racy, even lewd – shepherds and shepherdesses in a pastoral world of thwarted or gratified licence, utterly captivating. Three special exceptions stand out, gigantic evocations of war (*la guerre*), of hunting (*la chasse*), and birdsong (*le chant des oyseaux*) – tours de force of onomatopoeia, inspiration and models across more than five centuries for Messiaen's spectacular *Cinq Rechants*. Musical content as such is slight in such pieces: their entertainment-value is high.

Return, refreshed, to holiness: the state of the art in England and
Scotland from the late fifteenth century till well into the next. The Eton
Choir-book is the fullest collection from this period to survive virtually intact (though there was attrition in later times): fifty complete
works and fifteen fragments, representative of style and practice by
minor English composers between the major oeuvre of Dunstable
and Taverner. Their names (taken from the superb complete edition
in three volumes of *Musica Britannica*) are often quaint and evocative: Browne, Kellyk, Lambe, Sturton, Wylkynson, Horwood, Davy,
Cornysh, Sutton, Hacomplaynt, Huchyn, Fayrfax, Hygons, Hamphon,
Banester, Fawkyner, Turges, Nesbett, Stratford, all yielding complete
pieces; some of these same names recurring among the fragments,
to whom can be added Brugeman, Sygar and Holyngborne. Their
lives are for the most part obscure, sometimes unknown – oh for an
Aubrey! What they have in common is idiomatic consistency and an
absolute devotion to the Virgin-Mother.

Dipping into these waters induces mingled responses. The idiom
is extreme, indigenous, parochial, analogous to the contemporary
architecture of Eton Chapel and its twin foundation at King's
College, Cambridge for extravagant ornamentation overlying functional plainness of actual structure. In the end, some disappointment:
this music is just not odd, strange, fetching enough: note-spinning
prevails, invention is pedestrian rather than extravagant; one hankers
for the bizarreries of Gothic and the 'fourteenth-century avant-garde'
of *ars subtilior*. The best piece in this curate's egg is Fawkyner's
Gaude rosa (no. 32), a long piece greatly helped by its poem providing metre, stanzas, rhyme: a hymn to Mary's youthful charm rather
than the Mother lamenting her Son or the triumphant Queen of
Heaven – equally devout, but gay and fresh in celebration. The first
stanza gives the tone of the whole – 'rejoice, rose without thorn,
virgin of the morning star, shining brighter than heaven' – though
the nature imagery doesn't recur in the ensuing thirteen terzettes.
Graceful melodiousness at last! Some sections get a bit stuck, but
flow and direction win: the reward, a long trio for upper voices that
can only be called delicious, and its ornamentation positively pretty.
A brief access of sobriety, then hilarity, then a longer stretch sweeps

one over the hills and far away with splendid vitality, to a resounding close.

All this has been by way of prelude to England's greatest early sixteenth-century composer for sure, John Taverner (1490–1545/6). His painful vacillation between Catholic and Reformed belief made the subject for a full-scale operatic treatment by the young Peter Maxwell Davies, himself impelled by notions of betrayal, of self and of others. None of this is reflected in Taverner's eight Masses and some thirty motets. Three examples. The *Missa 'Corona spinea'* reveals the calibre at once – straight in at the *Gloria* (no *Kyrie* habitual in the practice of the day): the play of six parts permits great variety of vocal 'orchestration': the norm is a free-flow of five around a slow-moving tenor, so when *Jesu* lands on six-part chords and *Christe* moves in six voices, we're alert to significance. The *Credo* is lightened with duets, trios, quartets, and the composer's remarkable feel for wide spacings – his *descendit* goes up and up and stays there. This high-point is surpassed in a beautiful trio on *sepultus*, a grand tutti for *resurrexit*, climactic sostenuto till *non erit finis*; *et exspecto* vivacious; *et vitam venturi* radiant. Longer duets in the *Sanctus*, including treble and bass together, with yawning gap between – the building invites and supplies resonant amplitude. For the *Benedictus* the trebles divide but there are never seven parts – the two trebles interlock like chimes over a deep two-part bass; a huge melisma on *Domini* – Taverner the ornate and extravagant, parallel with English Gothic building in its glorious prime. *Agnus* exudes radiant sonority, the top three voices in motion over the bottom three in slow sostenuto; for the last petition trebles and altos both divide over deep slow bass – angelic; for the closing *dona* the music goes fast, light, dancing; even the basses divide for a brief duet before the grand final tutti *pacem*. Glory of sonority, never previously a conscious aim, is paramount in Taverner, even if it wasn't *his* conscious aim either.

When not thus enkindled he can be dullish and greyish. The *Western Wind* Mass for four voices is relatively featureless, even when one recognizes the omnipresence of the old song forming its basis. On magnificent form, however, for the *Missa 'Gloria tibi Trinitas'* for six. Again no *Kyrie*: the *Gloria* gives special significance to *tu solus sanctus*, the closing *Amen* rejoices in exultant scales. *Credo* is particularly fine – *lumen de lumine* shines; a huge *descendit de coelo* both up and down; *et incarnatus* complex and ornate, thus enhancing the bare *crucifixus* – trebles in two parts over deep bass, sepulchral yet seraphic; broad confident *resurrexit* and a real take-off in all voices for *ascendit*; *ex exspecto* vital and joyous. *Sanctus* sumptuous à six; then two trios, resuming tutti for rich *osanna*. *Benedictus* a lovely trio then surpassingly lovely quartet; *osanna* returns, differently set, on the whole choir, with a grand fiesta close. *Agnus* again varies the densities and combinations of the 'orchestration'. Every element in this marvellous work is *melody*: it sings, it resonates in the mind as in the great buildings for which it was conceived: grandeur and awe are its aims, and they are grandly and awesomely achieved. And on a smaller front, this Mass is vital for yielding the fragment of contour derived from the plainsong *gloria tibi Trinitas* and featured at *in nomine Domine* during the *Benedictus* that provides the basis for a long series of fantazias upon it by many English composers well into the seventeenth century.

A handful of three further English composers of note, and one Scot, who overlap with Taverner at both ends of his life. The two earliest are also found in the Eton Choir-book: both escape its confines to achieve wider distinction. Robert Fayrfax (1464–1521): his principal output six Masses, notable for serene imperturbability, all relaxes no braces, soothing and smooth; on a generous scale, with big paragraphs, genial and harmonious. The ensuing composers elicit for the most part the same range of adjectival reactions: one traces the '*countenance Angloise*' – although not so marked as in Dunstable for whom the phrase was coined – a genuine national idiom. Thus with William Cornysh (*c*.1470–1523): suavely graceful; melodious; almost tuneful; these qualities retained even when rhythms enliven. His tone is *light* in both senses: in spirit, and in the irradiated textures – especially the cavorting stratospheric high treble parts. A fine *Stabat mater*, rich and ecstatic: an exceptionally intense long setting of *woefully arrayed* – piercingly vivid for Jesus' reproaches as he undergoes betrayal, torture, mockery, a base criminal death – 'my body blo and wan . . . thus naked am I nailèd . . . with pains my veins constrain'd to crake'. A handful of secular songs utter reproaches of another kind: they include several amorous *Adieus* and the enchanting *Ah, Robin*.

Next chronologically, a sole instance of the Scotch countenance, Robert Carver (c.1487–1546): different, and most impressive. One can drown in his Mass for ten voices – no themes, all texture, mass-effects of sonorous splendour; take the *et iterum* in the *Credo*, rocking across just two chords in a swaying hypnotic trance of considerable power, continuing thus till the end; and the grand *Sanctus* – slabs of angel-basalt layered edge-to-edge, rank upon rank. *O bone Jesu* in nineteen voices – a marvellous thing – a dense halo of charismatic sonority around the oft-invoked sacred name. *Missa 'Fera pessima'* (apparently the beast whom Jacob believed had destroyed his son Joseph) – amazingly prolonged riffs on certain words; intoxicating. Mass in six – even more cloud-capp'd wordless drifts in the *Sanctus* (if *Sanctus* it be: the text so engulfed in the waves of sound): *Agnus* more clearly shaped, dulcet and melodious. Mass in four all flowing contour, remitting for gentle *incarnatus*, all melody; darkening for *crucifixus*, *resurrexit* not so different, and one of Carver's rolling/riffing *Amens*. Distinguished composing: nor does he need nineteen parts to achieve it.

Back to England for John Sheppard (c.1515–1560). Here 'uneventful imperturbability', as previously encountered, is a positive: Sheppard's music, for all its seraphic tranquillity, is charged with inner life, reaching the outer surface in the many false relations.* *Media vita*: the text for this long meditation on life and death centres upon the agèd Simeon's greeting to the infant Christ, a paraphrase/extension of the *Nunc dimittis* with a touching additional prayer, not to be abandoned as strength fails his old age, for close.

Meanwhile, two continental contemporaries of wholly complementary countenance: one Spanish, one French. Cristóbal de Morales (c.1500–1553): *Missa Quaeramus cum pastoribus*: difficult to convey the different feel of this music from anything heretofore – an airiness to the flow of five-part polyphony, no longer gaunt/

---

* False relations are where major and minor thirds are placed closely together; and are sometimes simultaneous.

severe/constructivist – he writes *fast* music, continuously lithe and graceful, the tone blithe yet tender – it seems as though there are no minor triads, only major, and not a hint of the darker Spanish undercurrents encountered later, in Victoria above all. Perhaps it's the shepherds of the title. The happiest *Kyrie* ever? How, one wonders, will he do the affective words in the *Gloria* and *Credo*? *Qui tollis* is just as gay; the momentum winds down only slightly in the closing *Amen*. In the *Credo* it yields more for *et homo factus est*; but Christ is crucified and buried with almost hilarity: pace resumes, sweeping mysteries and promises up with brio, till, again, a more thoughtful *Amen*.

Claudin de Sermisy (1490–1562). Everything I've encountered by this Frenchman is special: he's best-known for secular pieces; my selection is entirely sacred, of which there's plenty. His *Leçons de ténèbres* reveal the darker strain seemingly absent from Morales: the usual Hebrew initials are dense little nuggets of intensity; the Lamentations they introduce show Jeremiah at his most bitter – anger, rancour, affliction, resentment, envy, desire for vindication and revenge prevail in these hard words. The composer doesn't 'madrigalize' – i.e. illustrate: he lets the notes do the work in sombre low pitches, marvellously sonorous – every note 'costs'; no routine. The closing appeals to Jerusalem that she return to her God withdraw into restrained melancholic introversion. One encounters the same demure yet charged quality, with the higher voices added, in de Sermisy's motets and Psalm-settings – limpid and fluid even when texts tend towards suffering and complaint: the setting of one line in particular stands out in the memory to represent it all – *pauper sum ego*: I am poor and in travail from my youth up.

(A general point, covering the entire span of music so far considered, and beyond, grows more particular with these two composers: futile regrets over the universal practice of intoning the opening phrases of the *Gloria* and *Credo* and other standard liturgical texts: 'Glory be to God on high'; 'I believe in one God'; 'My soul doth magnify the Lord'. For all that they utter the essence of everything else to come, they're never, till much later, set to composed music.)

*

To England again for a composer of international stature as well as national: Thomas Tallis (c.1505–85). An uneven output, at its best very fine; at its least, very pedestrian (this end shown at full disadvantage in his dreary keyboard pieces). A wide range from modest to complex: his melodies for congregational hymns are sometimes inspired in their simplicity – every music lover knows the one Vaughan Williams uses as the basis for his *Fantasia*, and its composer put several others into his seminal *English Hymnal* of 1906. Tallis's canticles and anthems in English and Latin – he was caught sideways by the Reformation – range from utilitarian to excellent, and the celebrated *Lamentations* are supreme. Each of its two sets commences with formality: here begin the lamentations of Jeremiah the Prophet – by implication an injunction to *hear*. Then the Hebrew initials, all five expressive wonders of delicate polyphony, *Aleph* particularly, introducing Jerusalem's desolate widowhood, painted plangent yet restrained. *Beth*, a little gem of concentration, develops the scene – she weeps by night, she cannot be consoled. Plangency mounts, growing minatory in reproach of friends and lovers now become enemies. This first set closes with the first appeal to Jerusalem to turn back to her abandoned God who has abandoned her: polyphony yields to homophony – part-writing becomes block harmony, the top voice set in apposition to the lower four, repeated notes insistent, almost fierce. The second set is immediately more urgent even in its formal opening, longer, more intense, flavoured with occasional piercing false relations – major/minor adjacencies or simultaneities. *Gimel* almost a fughetta, with exquisite overlapping contours, introducing Zion's exile among the heathen, finding no peace. *Daleth* is another miniature wonder – continuous melody on the middle voice, the others accompanying in antiphony, above then below, before all five conjoin: persecutors reproached – momentum quickens into fierce bitterness, then subsides into acquiescence. *Heth* another tiny gem, a lyric round for three voices, the other two holding the texture together. This procedure continues as Zion's enemies prosper in the face of her multitudinous iniquities. Homophony returns as her children are led captive while she impotently mourns. Direct into closing *Jerusalem* – the plea to turn and return, rising to greater intensity than the first set's; then easing into a deeper acquiescence, all tears spent.

I'm tickled and piqued by a judgement this marvellous work once occasioned: 'the two pieces can be recognized as the major achievement of a minor master of the highest order.' Mister Facing-Two-Ways! Recognition for sure in the enormous popularity of Tallis's *Spem in alium*, his motet in forty parts, finest fruit of a brief fashion for such sonic spectaculars (the most extreme is sixty), beyond Carver's *Jesu* and Brumel's earthquake, overwhelming when experienced live in the vast echoing spaces for which it was intended. It begins in imitative polyphony: but soon the eight choirs grow antiphonal, alternating counterpoint with massed chordal sonority. The text expresses unwavering hope in God, gracious even when angry, forgiving mankind its sins. 'Lord God, creator of heaven and earth' – and now the great moment: after the unbroken mass of voices, silence: they re-enter on an electrifying change of harmony for *respice* – be mindful – of our lowly estate. Another 'major achievement of a minor master of the highest order'?

So to William Byrd (1543–1623). Unquestionably a major master of whatever order. He and Tallis (with whom he'd shared a post at the Chapel Royal in London) were together granted the monopoly for music publishing in England. Its first production, the *Cantiones Sacrae* of 1575, contained thirty-four motets, by both men. After Tallis's death Byrd held the monopoly singly: three more collections followed, by him alone. He also collaborated with the younger John Bull and the still-younger Orlando Gibbons on an important collection of keyboard music, *Parthenia* (1612). Byrd remained faithful to Catholicism till the end and was saved from persecution only by royal favour. His Latin works remained 'closeted', being heard, at great risk, only in the privacy of families who adhered to the old ways. But he served his monarch in her role as head of the Anglican Church with no reservation or diminution of quality, and his longest work is the *Great Service*, setting all the canticles for morning and evening worship, plus the *Kyrie* and *Creed* for the Eucharist, in the vernacular. He also appears to have invented the verse-anthem, with instrumental accompaniment, for which every music-lover must be heartily grateful: its rich flowering down the seventeenth century culminates in the glories of Purcell. Byrd was also a master of purely instrumental composition (see later), and there is a fine handful of secular songs with viol-consort.

Every musical child used to come across Byrd's jolly little rhyme 'since singing is so good a thing, I wish all men would learn to sing'. Less familiar are some remarkable words that fuse compositional impulse with religious faith and sheer direct response to the rhythms and quantities of the language: 'as I have learned by trial, the most suitable of all musical ideas occur as of themselves (I know not how) to one thinking upon things divine and earnestly and diligently pondering them, and suggest themselves spontaneously to the mind that is not indolent and inert.' This all applies equally to his English output and the three Latin Masses – in three, four and five parts – that form the core of his achievement. The three-part Mass is a wonderful thing, notable throughout for fullness of sonority with such slender means. Sensitive and obedient – 'diligent' – to phrase-lengths of the texts, units of meaning, prose not verse rhythms: always perfectly articulated. Chamber-music, as of a viol-consort; play of homophony and linear points of imitation, as of instrumental give-and-take albeit always idiomatically vocal. Plain yet not austere: when florid/exuberant, still sober – no arching flights or flying arches à la Taverner. Salient words not *expressed*, as in madrigals, so much as *marked*: in the *Credo* one can't miss (after an under-madrigalized *descendit*) the beautiful melisma on *coelis* nor the changed mode for *et incarnatus* that immediately follows, nor the emphatic repetition of *catholicam et apostolicam ecclesiam* – Byrd the closet Roman. *Sanctus* and *Benedictus* radiate serene in-contained joy: *Agnus* serene in-contained entreaty.

The four-part Mass begins with a long *Kyrie* (the older custom of dispensing with a *Kyrie* now superseded), charged up with suspensions. In the *Gloria* the words *laudamus/benedicamus/adoramus* induce what are virtually trumpet-calls, *glorificamus* twice, upper and lower voices responding to each other in pairs, then all four for *glorificamus* again: such forthright deployment obviously not possible in a spare three-part texture. But three are used for a long stretch of *Domine Deus . . . qui tollis . . . miserere . . . suscipe* – every possible combination of three from the four. The *Credo* continues stalwart: more fanfares at *genitum non factum*, again at *et incarnatus* (somewhat unexpected, perhaps inapposite); again (eminently suitable) at *et resurrexit*: burst of frisky energy for *ad dexteram patris*: solidity for the one holy catholic apostolic Church. Passages concerning deeper mysteries are not especially affective – confident, rather than superstitious, the *et exspecto* and *et vitam venturi*. All this by way of exemplifying the truth of the composer's words about his craft and its sources. So the *Sanctus*, rapt and serene as in the three-part work, and indeed a long passage dispenses with the bass voice: all four for *osanna*, with exhilarating active leaps in the third, then, to end, one in the fourth too – marvellously vocal – 'singing is so good a thing'. The *Agnus* however *is* affective, with plangent suspensions predominating for *dona nobis pacem*.

Five voices permit more expansive melodiousness and harmonic richness, both palpable at once in the *Kyrie*; and variety of 'orchestration' as in the *Gloria*. Byrd is now building in paragraphs not phrases, and admitting more rhetoric even in music written initially for intimate surroundings; chunky for the *laudamus* . . . phrases, cooling into *gratias*; *Domine Deus* through to *miserere* a tender trio; *qui tollis* set twice, for two trios differently constituted. From *quoniam* on, celebratory syncopations, calming for a very brief and very beautiful *Amen*. The *Credo* eschews madrigal imitation: the descending phrase comes on *salutem* rather than *descendit*, the following word: *et incarnatus* a long paragraph in three parts; its *ex Maria virgine, et homo factus est* is particularly haunting; the 'unmemorability' of polyphony here wholly confuted – I recall exactly, some seventy years after singing these passages as a boy-chorister, this twice-repeated contour! Then *crucifixus* in five voices: such 'scoring' is expressive in itself. *Et resurrexit* triumphal, *et ascendit* pictorial; motion devolves for *mortuorum*, revives grandly for *non erit finis*: *et in spiritum sanctum* breaks into sturdy triple-time dance, persisting long until *per prophetas*. Acclamation as now expected for the Universal Church: the General rather than the individual Resurrection is bright, vigorous, charged with life-to-come, before a complete mood-swing to an exquisitely moulded *Amen*. *Sanctus* utterly magical: slow three-note figure exchanged across the parts, surrounded by suave comely contours of lyricism, all on the one sanctified word: for the next three, *Dominus Deus sabaoth*, strong block harmony. *Pleni sunt* ... is a trio, *osanna* a powerfully exultant tutti, recurring exact to close the *Benedictus*. First plea of *Agnus* a trio for upper voices, second plea a quartet, third plea is in five parts – again the 'orchestration' is expressive in itself: the Mass concludes with a surpassingly lovely *dona nobis pacem*. If only there were Masses by Byrd for six, seven voices, for double-choir in twelve, nineteen or forty parts! They would surely continue the upward trajectory in more than vocal resources.

Byrd's variety and calibre in the three collections of English motets and the two of Latin *Gradualia* are unparalleled in all the centuries of plainsong-to-polyphony. His choice of texts is protean, his response invariable – again we're reminded of those words 'the most suitable of all musical ideas occur as of themselves ...' in a range whose extreme edges touch desolation over the fate of Jerusalem (almost certainly code for the lost faith of his native land) to exultant thanksgiving and rejoicing, with every shade of the affective colour-spectrum in between, and all at the highest level of craft and art. Not till Purcell will he be equalled in variety and versatility, and not till Bach surpassed: the nearest comparison is more unlikely – Byrd's acute sensitivity to and depth of identification with the words he chooses, and his ability to match and enhance them, are akin, across obvious differences of genre, idiom, aim, to Schubert's.

Back to mainland Europe for mainstream composers whose dates cover more than a century, from the birth of Clemens non Papa in *c*.1510 (d. 1556) to include Palestrina (1525–94) and Lassus (1532–94) to the death of Victoria (b. 1548) in 1611. This, with Byrd, is polyphony's Golden Age, the perfected fruit of every growth preceding it.

All agog: but initial disappointment with Clemens. Motet and Mass *Pastores quidnam vidistis*: so smooth and equable, one wants to spice it up, even at the risk of histrionics or eccentricities. No response to the words – *et incarnatus*, the Mass's central moment, is so tranquil as to be tranquillized; and the same untroubling tone pervades equally the rejoicing words of the *Sanctus* and the fervent appeals of the *Agnus*. When momentum briefly enlivens the mood remains listless; one longs for touches of *musica ficta* – some leading-notes, please! – to cheer the prevailing passivity. Try motets – will he rise to more various texts? No: even when bewailing sin and suffering, or relating the repentance and forgiveness of the Prodigal Son, or hymning the lilies of the valley and the well of living waters, the same flow of listless sounds: Clemens appears utterly uninterested in/incapable of (do they correlate?) differentiation; in the end, of expression itself.

Giovanni Pierluigi da Palestrina: long seen as the epoch's summa, and never lost to sight in succeeding times. An enormous output – 105 Masses, some 250 motets, other liturgical music, madrigals both spiritual and secular. The key-work is the *Missa Papae Marcelli*, celebrated in fact and fantasy by indubitable connection with the Council of Trent (first summoned in 1545, its sessions continuing regularly until 1563). Injunctions concerning church-music had just been issued: 'the whole plan of singing in musical modes shall be constituted not to give empty pleasure to the ear, but in such a way that the words may be clearly understood by all, and the hearts of the listeners be drawn to the desire of heavenly harmonies, in the contemplation of the joys of the blessed.'

The legend is that the *Papae Marcelli* was the model Mass specially composed to answer every objection to complications and ostentation that obscured the sacred words and gave opening to Protestant scorn. Pope Marcellus's reign lasted only three weeks of 1555: Palestrina's Mass might have been written then or later – there is a tale of its being requested by and produced before a Papal commission in 1565 as evidence that sacred music could indeed behave as desired: but, equally, it could have been written well before this, indeed before Marcellus's supposed injunction ten years earlier. A further layer of uncertainty: despite the embargo upon using secular songs, often lascivious, as bases for liturgical music, the presence of *L'Homme armé* has been detected in Palestrina's model Mass! Fantasy becomes poetry in the legend that the composer, initially declining the pressing invitation on grounds of age, unworthiness and failing inspiration after the death of his wife, was visited in the night by, first, the old masters of polyphony who urged his mission to complete their work, to be the last link in the chain; then, by a host of angels who dictated the entire piece, all complete by the following dawn. This becomes the substance of the first act of Pfitzner's moving opera *Palestrina* (1912–15) – see later.

Even when the Mass is sung by mortals one must kneel before such serene perfection. Not a note out of place, consummate clarity and euphony, every word distinct – phrases in the *Gloria* and *Credo* often set several times to make assurance doubly sure: when rejoicing, unstrained; when sad/serious, no emotive coloration; and loveliest of all when able to float free as in the *Sanctus* and *Agnus*. Charles Gounod, master-composer of nineteenth-century religious kitsch, catches it well: 'This severe ascetic music, calm and horizontal as the line of the ocean, monotonous by virtue of its serenity, anti-sensuous; and yet so intense in its contemplativeness that it verges sometimes on ecstasy.' Just so: yet there are difficulties in gaining a hold on this music, and on Palestrina at large. The limits are, so to speak, so audible – what it does *not* do, or does not *care* to. It somehow eludes hearing in itself: the smoothness, serenity, horizontality, etc., etc. can leave one out rather than invite one in, let alone urge or tempt. Placid can become temperate, temperate tepid. Interesting, then, to see how Palestrina will fare in his collection of twenty-nine madrigal-motets or verses from the Song of Songs: the eroticism of these texts, however allegorically reconvened, is here dissolved into sweetness and light without a hint of sublimation. How will he fare with the *Lamentations*? Predictably perfect – calmly grave, serious, beautiful; a wonderful curve, towards the end, into muted elegy. But . . .

Palestrina's manifest technical perfection is central to European music at large: its consummation of what had preceded, the achievement of correctness and euphony in counterpoint that at the same time controls harmonic rhythm, all rapidly codified into rules for every student of composition down the centuries and insisted upon as recently in his teaching by Ligeti – as also in universities and conservatoires (though here it is nowadays eroding). Three interesting historical sidelights: Bach made his own performing version of another Palestrina Mass (*sine nomine*); Wagner his of the *Stabat mater* (remarkably faithful, though adding Romantic dynamics);

Bruckner's *Mass in E-minor* (1866) pays a debt of homage with generous interest: thus on to Pfitzner.

I've experienced comparable reservations with the next undoubted sixteenth-century giant, Orlandus Lassus, to be confronted after a brief diversion into a minor contemporary more immediately attractive, Paschal de l'Estocart (*c.*1540–90). The nineteen little numbers composing his *Octonaires de la vanité du monde* provide relief after so many Masses, Magnificats, Lamentations, Penitential Psalms: they are certainly not liturgical-for-usage, though neither are they madrigals for fun. The poems, each of two four-line stanzas, varying in metre, are by Antoine de la Roche-Chandieu: quaint, even bizarre; almost surreal, certainly metaphysical in analogy to such poets in seventeenth-century England – 'Morte est la mort' is Donne direct, though the general resemblances are to later more capricious poets like Francis Quarles, John Cleveland, Edward Benlowes – emblematic encapsulations of the world in all its beauty, allure, glitter and shine, as also its dangers, mud, stinks, ordure – the entire spectrum a metaphor for humanity vain, vulnerable, malicious, corrupt, with some kind of approach to an Eternity, only vestigially Christian, at the end. All below is folly, tedium, triviality, vexation: God alone is constant and wise. Conventional enough – but Paschal's settings continually illuminate with all the quirks, surprises, frissons missed in Clemens, Palestrina and Lassus. One hangs upon every word and every musical response to it: witty brevity, pungent concentration, tense intensity, piercing plangency. Setting mainly syllabic; texture mainly homophonic – and the harmony both melting in the mouth and biting into the flesh: timing masterly in a range from comic to acerbic, with constant veering of tempo, direction, mood: virtuoso composing, requiring virtuoso performance.

Lassus, alas. Standard stuff, no surprises, mastery complete and unfailing, the sense of a production-line – over two thousand works! No shock of recognition: if only the Masses lived up to their titles: *Osculetur me*; *Vinum bonum*; *Triste depart*, etc. The extended cycle of *Sacrae Lectiones ex propheta Job* sounds promising. He set these sublime words twice – as a young man before 1565 and as a mature master around 1580. The mature version seems improbably cheerful, even light-hearted, for such lacerating thoughts. Not quite 'goes to heaven on a jig' – never less than decorous, and does grow more reflective as it proceeds, but never for a moment penetrates the depths or achieves the heights of its texts. If the idiom of Paschal de l'Estocart could be amplified on a larger scale it would surely be capable of encompassing Job. Lassus's *Lamentations* fail better: one senses the great composer; imperturbability and unsurprisingness are virtues here; albeit negative, for the depths of these troubled/troubling words are not plumbed as by Tallis, or Couperin, or Stravinsky.

No such doubts over Tomás Luis de Victoria. His range is narrow – sacred works only (one cannot imagine him as a madrigalist): a priest, whose religious vision matches those of St Teresa, St John of the Cross, Ribera, Zurbarán. The 'Spanishness' of these writers and painters and Victoria's music is hard to quantify precisely, and impossible to miss. Take the *Responsories for Tenebrae*: eighteen pieces grouped in threes for Maundy Thursday, Good Friday and Holy Saturday, telling obliquely and incompletely the betrayal of Jesus, his arrest, trial, punishment, burial, from the Gospels, interspersed with prophecies from the Old Testament and reproaches and laments uttered by Christ himself. Each *respond* is quadripartite – i ii iii ii – and all are fashioned from closely related material constantly recharged over similar territory, usually for four voices with occasional duos and trios for variety. The formal structure of repetitions and the persistent re-use of severely limited material induce intense concentration from apparent poverty: dramatic, without rhetoric or artifice: all is essentialized; and it burns.

Wider ranges of intonation appear in Victoria's *Lamentations* and *Requiem*. In the former the hard, even harsh, edge of the *Tenebrae* is reversed to its antithesis: one could call this music exquisite were this not to evoke inappropriate associations of luxury and over-refinement. All is sombre sweetness: even the appeals to Jerusalem to mend her ways are withdrawn-in – passion not spent but saved. Occasional efflorescence from the prevailing restraint only emphasizes it the more. The *Requiem* (second of two settings) is immediately – six not four parts – more sumptuous: largely homophonic (separated by monophonic chant with wonderful shifts of the simple chords, as at the start of the *Libera me*. There'd been no *dies irae*; when the *Libera me* refers to the Day of Judgment with its fiery punishment, calamity, woe, Victoria's setting responds – vehement and turbulent – in sharp contrast to the studied neutrality, rich or chaste, that otherwise prevails: *requiem aeternam* and *lux perpetua* restore them – but Victoria is in essence no madrigalist.

He can, however, be joyous. Witness the two most celebrated of his twenty Masses, *O quam gloriosum* and *O magnum mysterium*, both of them closely wrought from their magnificent eponymous motets. The *gloriosum* is radiant: madrigalism perhaps enters after all in its response to the glorious kingdom wherein the saints rejoice with Christ; then calming for their white robes and following their steps as they follow the Lamb whithersoever he goeth. Motifs from motet permeate Mass throughout: one hears unity in heterogeneity, epitomized in the extra closing piece after the *Agnus* – holy is he who has stood fast, even unto death, for his God: he is founded upon a rock. Thus, too, with the *mysterium* motet, its text concerning the mystery of Christ's incarnation and birth. A gentler piece till its euphoric final alleluia, and the Mass accords with both moods: exultation in the *Gloria* and *Credo* – *et resurrexit* and *et exspecto* are as vivacious as any fa-la-la from this composer who never touched a secular text: and between the two exuberant outbursts of *osanna* the *Benedictus* is as fragile and tender as any amorous nymph or swain. The *Agnus* is surpassingly simple and lovely.

After the deaths of Victoria (1611) and Byrd (1623) the summit of plainsong-to-polyphony is passed: by 1600 one of Western Music's most drastic changes of direction is already well under way. Before turning to this mighty shift, a handful of further names; composers who still adhere to the old ways with individuality and calibre. In Portugal Duarte Lobo (1565–1646) and Manuel Cardoso (1566–1650): in England Thomas Tomkins, whose long life (1572–1656) contained the brief span of Orlando Gibbons (1582–1625): in Germany the complex case of Heinrich Schütz (1585–1672), whose output straddles and partakes of both cultures.

The two Portuguese are both well-represented by a fine *Requiem* each, both audibly in the line of Victoria's – severe, hard-edged, with some indefinable grain of individuality. Tomkins, however, is for the most part not distinctive: he's here because he continues so late the technique and idiom of his master Byrd: and just once he memorably hits the spot: *When David heard* – music as heartbreaking as its text – 'O my son, my son! Would God I had died for thee, O Absalom son, my son.' Some other anthems are almost as good – *Almighty God, the fountain of all wisdom* and *O sing unto the Lord a new song* sport an astonishing array of false relations. The shock of the old – how did early ears hear these piercing clashes – as beautiful? as audacious? as mistakes? Gibbons, in everything he touches, is the real thing – his madrigals, keyboard and consort-music will come later: of his church-music the verse-anthems are particularly fine. *This is the record of John* tells how the Baptist was questioned closely, acquitted himself well, and vindicated his role as solitary forebear. *O thou the central Orb* radiates God's lustre in terms almost pantheistic, and concludes with a Gibbons speciality, the elaborate *Amen*, this one perhaps the most beautiful of all. *See, see, the word is incarnate* tells the Redemption stage-by-stage, from Virgin-birth via miracles, resurrection (*preceding* Jesus' gory wounds), ascension, triumphant resumption of rightful place in heaven, telegramatically compressed in the words, in the music every phrase opened out into serenely ecstatic utterance – the 'peace on earth', Jesus' preaching, the injunction to welcome the hallowed guest, are particularly memorable.

Schütz is hard to position. At his birth (1585) Palestrina is sixty, Byrd in his late thirties, Victoria thirty-four, Gibbons two: at his death (1672) Monteverdi had departed nearly thirty years before, Corelli is nearly twenty, Purcell thirteen, François Couperin four, while Rameau (b. 1683), Handel, Bach and Scarlatti (all b. 1685) are imminent. Music has altered,

> Leaving the old, both worlds at once they view,
> That stand upon the threshold of the new.

German-born and resident most of his eighty-seven years, with two important periods in Venice (1609–12, studying with Giovanni

Gabrieli; 1628–9, to acquaint himself with the latest Italian music – his tombstone marked by his own request as one who brought Italian light to Germany). Schütz's output belongs equally with the Old – *prima prattica*, polyphony as followed throughout this chapter; and the New – *seconda prattica*, vocal monody over figure-bass accompaniment, soon to be explored. His large-scale *seconda prattica* music, including an opera on *Dafne*, was all lost in the depre-dations of war; but many madrigals published on the first Venetian residency survive, and his settings of German texts are infiltrated with Italian traits. At the same time his German sacred music lies in the direct line of his native traditions, where Schütz keeps up and recharges the archaic polyphonic skills in their newest manifest-ation before the overwhelming impact of Bach early in the century following.

But I fear that Schütz is a bore. The title *Schwanengesang* and the work's circumstances – a conscious summation and farewell, to be sung at his own obsequies – are promising indeed: but the text – Psalm 119, longest and dullest in the whole Psalter, doggedly set with utilitarian syllabic obedience, is only saved from being a trundle by moments of handsome splendour in the instrumentation, trom-bones especially. Another promising title, *Musikalische Exequien*, yields settings strangely light and un-searing for their dark texts, scarcely sounding their depths. The six works narrating episodes in the life of Christ are more compelling – *Seven Last Words* and *Resurrection History* strong, penny-plain, bread-and-butter: *Christ-mas History* charming with its generous yet delicate instrumental writing. Charm inappropriate for three *Passions*, a Luke, a John, a Matthew: extremely – exceedingly – austere, stripped to the bare bone; late survivals, of monody in the prevalence of unaccompan-ied unmeasured recitative, of polyphony in the choral writing (there are no instruments), achieving stark characterization and drama in crowd-scenes and moving directness in their meditative closes. This music's self-denial gives spiritual nourishment where richer fare would cloy.

CHAPTER II

A New Start

Every aspect of music's slow-evolving long-sustained glory thus far followed is overturned, as it were overnight, by what now appears (although it couldn't have at the time) the most drastic change of direction in the history of the art. New goals and ideals, with the techniques to implement them: a vision of origins, a back-to-basics, a clean start. For all these, the close-wrought textures and procedures of polyphony at its culmination would be useless: they were ditched. The new goal is secular, drama-and-word-centred: text is primal and primary, clarity of diction paramount – rhetoric and artifice in pursuit of truth and nature. Music completely subservient, willing slave to word and deed.

The technical means enabling this *seconda prattica* (the term coined in 1607) is keyboard continuo, harmony built up from the bass, realized in fundamental chord-progressions that for recitative, even for *arioso* and aria, need not be composed and notated in full: figured bass, shorthand for its executants, to whom the new skills became second nature, reliable, conventional, stereotyped whether pedestrian or inventive. The new genres were initially vocal – solo song and cantata, mainly secular; above all, the dramatic scena, thence opera at full-length; its first hero Monteverdi, preceded, and succeeded down the century, by congeries of also-rans. Instrumental genres developed later – chamber sonatas, concertos – whose texture and procedure also depend upon a foundation of figure-bass continuo: they reach maturity in Corelli and Vivaldi, and culmination in Couperin, Handel and Bach.

Seminal for *seconda prattica* is the Camerata, a group of aristocrats, intellectuals, scientists, poets, musicians, gathering in Florence in the

1570s. Several overlapping circles: their common pursuit a new ideal with ancient antecedents and justification – Greek drama reborn; on stage, in speech, song, movement. Speech *is* song – pitched declamation, readily audible and comprehensible, rendering with fidelity (albeit deriving from theoretical speculation as to what the Greeks actually *did*) human expression of the passions. Polyphony eschewed for its complexity and obfuscation of the texts; its replacement is *stile rappresentativo*, the solo voice reciting prose or verse, supported only by continuo as described. The result is, strangely, a reassertion of monody, now harmony-driven, completely different from the monody out of which polyphony slowly flowered. And everything redolent of the *prima prattica* seems old-fashioned, fusty, churchy – the rejection of Christian subjects and texts in favour of the myths of antiquity is also a strong motive, however implicit.

The three pioneering composers associated with the Camerata and first fulfilling its aims are Emilio de' Cavalieri (*c*.1550–1602), Giulio Caccini (*c*.1551–1618) and Jacopo Peri (1561–1633). From a shared context of elaborate stage-presentations with music for courtly occasions, mostly wedding-festivities, the first operas are born. Cavalieri's principal memorial is exceptional in being sacred: *Rappresentatione di Anima et di Corpo* ('Soul and Body portrayed'): the title promising indeed, the music – recitative variegated with madrigals, songs, dances – a desert of tedium. Of Peri's *Dafne* only fragments survive: his subsequent *Euridice* (1600) was rapidly assimilated and imitated in Caccini's to the same libretto: same norms, recitative predominating, and just as deadly dull. Life and interest quicken only with Monteverdi (who might possibly have encountered the collaborative *Euridice* in Florence).

Monteverdi

Claudio Monteverdi (1567–1643): born Cremona, trained in the old ways at its cathedral: *c*.1590 to Mantua with its sophisticated culture centred upon the Gonzaga court, head of its music from 1601, writing for festivities and celebrations, and madrigals for private cognoscenti. His first opera *Orfeo* (1607) retells the *Euridice* story and derives its libretto from the composite work of its predecessors. *Arianna* followed in 1608: the music for this full-length piece lost save for the heroine's famous Lament, reworked as a madrigal and widely disseminated. Madrigals continue down Monteverdi's life whatever the changes of career – eight books, and several posthumous collections. Personal tragedy and professional dissatisfactions bring about the principal change: he tries for the leading post at St Mark's, Venice, advertising availability and ability with the *Vespers* of 1610. Successful, he appears to have abjured the theatre, though gradually drawn back via dramatic madrigals and concerted pieces involving song and dance to tell a story. Tempted the whole way in old age: *Arianna* revised and replayed 1640; next, *Il ritorno d'Ulisse in patria*, completely new; *L'incoronazione di Poppea* (1643), the year of his death.

Orfeo

It is wonderfully felicitous that the earliest opera that still lives on the stage has the power of music – music's *new* powers, scarce called-upon previously – as its subject. Orpheus, son of Apollo the sun-god, god of reason/balance/self-knowledge, leader of the Muses; Orpheus the master of song who can tame the beasts and have the inanimate forces of nature – winds, waters, trees, even the rocks – melt to his strains; Orpheus who loses his love, perhaps punishment for his overweening, perhaps merely arbitrary; who seeks her amid the shades of the underworld, wooing its sullen guardian, enchanting its hapless denizens, persuading its dark ruler (himself moved also by his saturnine hold upon his ravished bride and hers on him) to release the dead into life; the awful proviso, the all-too-inevitable human weakness that compels Orpheus to disobey, the second loss of Eurydice, this time irreversible; and the *ending* – either happy; apotheosis, ascent to his father's mansions in exultant song; or torn to pieces by the beasts he'd once been able to charm into docility, his severed head floating down the stream of time, still singing. A parable of universal appeal concerning love and human nature, an allegory of music in general and opera in particular, its later manifestations both direct – Gluck, Liszt, Stravinsky, Birtwistle – or satirical – Offenbach; or metaphorical, as at the heart of many purely instrumental works, mainly (obviously) concertos, wherein a potent protagonist menaces, charms, persuades, conquers, the forces that would destroy him, compelling them into coexistence and harmony.

In Monteverdi's Prologue *la Musica* herself, after the bright rousing formal-festive toccata all on one chord, initiates: she invites the spectator in and tells what she can achieve with all her arts that can calm every troubled heart, enflaming the coldest with noble anger or ardent love: *thus*, she must tell of Orpheus. All this in flexible *stile recitato* punctuated with an instrumental ritornello heard six times, the last slightly extended to close. And used again to open Act I: pastoral setting, nymphs and shepherds, Orpheus in his felicity, Euridice too – free recitative, measured solo songs, duets, a trio, consorted madrigals, instrumental ritornelli either sweet-serious or gay-dancing – a mosaic of small nuggets making a lovely whole. Hymen blesses the pair for whom there is nothing further to be desired. So to Act II: Orpheus alone with male companions in complete contentment – delicious little ritornelli featuring different instruments in duet. His grandly masculine aria of confidence and prowess – my good times, after my bad – four stanzas, each repeating the first line of music with different words; vital energy of adjacent triple accents; recitative almost abandoned for continuous diversified measurement – lucky the handful of nymphs who incite this song and are privileged to hear it. Recitative again prevails for the Messenger with her dire news: Orpheus's questioning more and more urgent, her replies reluctant, then definite; her circumstantial account – the snake, the poisonous bite, the rapid dimming of life, nothing can revive, Euridice expires calling upon her lover's name. The continuo harmony intensifies to embrace such pathetic wrenches as E-major/G-minor and C-minor/A-major, expressive at once of the ill-tidings and the Messenger's compunction at being their bearer. Fine madrigal deploring the cruelty of fate, the avarice of heaven, the frailty of mortal bliss; heard thrice, interspersed with pathetic sinfonia and sadly duetting shepherds. The act closes with the ritornello that had punctuated Act I, with a strong effect of recalling a past now lost.

Act III commences with a serene sinfonia, but it heralds *Orpheus aux enfers*, and the style of the *stile recitato* darkens. Hope is his guide, yet even she can now advance no further – all hope must here be abandoned (the famous phrase is quoted). Charon, boatman of the underworld, is chary to transport a living mortal – a wonderfully surly sinfonia concludes his refusal. Orpheus woos him by music: he waxes lyrical and virtuosic, his florid song framed by instrumental refrains – two solo violins, in antiphony then in thirds; two cornetti, ditto; then his own instrument the lyre, represented by a harp; then a solo string trio, who eventually accompany the voice. But Charon remains churlish: Orpheus's repeated command/appeal – *rendetimi il mio ben*, give me back my good – ever more emphatic, falls upon ears indifferent, then deaf, then sleeping – beautiful sombre sinfonia renders the sleep. Orpheus resolves upon boldness – give me her back! yet again. Unaided and unchallenged he crosses the Styx; a chorus of spirits moralize – man undertakes nothing in vain; he conquers the stagnant waters and scorns the violence of winds south and north to achieve the farther bank. This act, core of the work, achieves the goals for *la Musica*'s potential at their most exalted.

Dare one say that the succeeding acts are slightly anti-climactic? Back, after a fine sinfonia, to recitative: Proserpina appeals to Pluto her Lord; he can deny her nothing – Euridice will (with the demanding proviso) be restored, spirits will effect the practicalities: a dullish stretch, Pluto a little flat after Charon, Proserpina colourless. Vigour renewed with Orpheus's triumphant song, over energetic walking bass with exuberant violins between the vocal phrases. BUT – doubts set in – does she follow? What are these noises? Do Furies snatch at my love? He turns to look, darkness envelops her, her lament brief and feeble – for all her great love she's lost him: all this rather inexplicit in the action and wholly underplayed in the music. It recovers intensity as the spirits, who at the moment of crisis could only say (via their spokesman) 'you have broken the law and are unworthy of grace', now moralize in the opera's most

extended madrigal – Orpheus conquered hell, his emotions conquered him: only he who conquers *himself* deserves victory. Act V
returns to square one with the first act's ritornello: all is the same,
yet utterly different. Echo both comforts and mocks the unhappy
hero with her plaintive repetitions of his words. The score now no
way so eloquent as earlier: wastelands of monody-to-come already
on the horizon. Grand solemn sinfonia for Apollo's descent, then
the recitative between him and his errant son continues, featureless,
till they at last rise to heaven together, singing. Robust cheery dance
and chorus of nymphs and shepherds round the piece off. Somehow
somewhere it's lost its heart: after the high point of Act III and the
rise to it in I and II, the close seems perfunctory and routine.

But that heart is convincing and stirring: a new spirit, a new
sound, a new goal, achieved. One-dimensional compared with what
came before and what will come after: yet its impulse for ever fresh –
evergreen like its composer's name: unexplored territory for music,
a gamut of human utterance from pathos to exultation. To be 'one-
dimensional' is its true character and quality – a positive. The formality of patterning, the decorum and neatness, the architecture of
inter-slotted units, the dictionary of affects – a geometrical game-
board, bright/clear/stiff – Uccello made audible – vivacious and
captivating, now and again moving, lacking in shadow, exciting in
colour, momentum, perspective. The promise latent and actual in
Orfeo is not fulfilled by Monteverdi's two late operas, still less in the
sandy deserts that follow him. His genius is more fully realized in
dramatic madrigals and in the celebrated *Vespers*.

First, though, an attractive antecedent; a precursor at Venice indispensable to Monteverdi's achievement there: Giovanni Gabrieli
(*c*.1556–1612). He studied with his composer-uncle Andrea, long
employed at S. Marco; went briefly to Munich to study with Lassus;
returned to Venice 1585, served as the basilica's principal composer
from the year following. Consolidator if not originator of the style,
idiom, techniques unique to the great building – continuo-based
recitative, florid declamation, polyphony gradually yielding, eventually succumbing, to homophony, employing the spatial layout

with forces choral and instrumental antiphonically disposed in music both lavish and showy, the wonder and envy of its day. His output largely sacred vocal: very significant, however, is the body of purely instrumental sonatas, sinfonias, canzonas. Two representative works – one of each. *Sonata pian' e forte* – grand formal antiphonal interplay of its double orchestra, with adroit use of what the title indicates – contrasting dynamics – vital to Monteverdi later. *In ecclesiis* – magnificent sober-sumptuous motet; occasionally scrumptious too, with juicy suspensions worthy of Purcell. Sudden juxtapositions of unrelated triads separated by silences or jammed close-adjoined; dramatic contrasts of tempo, orchestration vocal and instrumental, dynamics (as in the *Sonata*). Splendour and relish – no inwardness: 'expensive', glorifying the city's wealth and largesse rather than God's anger and mercy and Christ's sacrificial intercession.

Monteverdi's *Vespers* of 1610 – a hybrid: eight items from the liturgy of evening devotion to the Virgin, set with great resplendence for the full choral and orchestral forces at the disposal of S. Marco, interspersed with four antiphons for small vocal and instrumental groups, and a sonata, basically orchestral, save for the one constantly repeated line of sung text. The composite, published as a declaration of availability and suitability for the St Mark's post, works so well in performance that it has settled into a standard favourite with choirs and audiences alike. From the very opening, *Deus in adjutorium*, an *image sonore* of fresh bright vitality – the initial toccata of *Orfeo* magnified into festive celebration, made of prime colours, primitive, even empty, no harmonic movement whatever, sweeping the listener up into clouds of brio. Movement commences in no. 2, *Dixit Dominus*: 'child's-play', rondels of lively gaiety, repeated notes, declamations and exclamations, round and round till a dramatic change of mood and momentum for solemn invocation of Father, Son, Holy Ghost, then a serene 'as it was ... is now and ever'. *Nigra sum* – I am black but comely – first interpolated 'concerto'; strangely colourless setting of the ravishing words from the Song of Songs. Back to liturgy no. 3, *Laudate pueri*: same bright irrepressible energy as before, with comparable moments of magical quiet and a fine drifting-away *Amen*, polyphonic after so much homophony, the full double choir diminishing to leave only two solo voices in florid duet, very operatic. Next antiphon 'concerto' is *Pulchra es*, again from the Song of Songs, gentle and unerotic despite the words' evident inclinations: even when the beloved is 'terrible as an army arrayed for battle' the tone is submissive – very different from Monteverdi's *Madrigals of Love and War*. Main liturgy again; no. 4, *Laetatus sum* – cheery stride over walking bass, the plainsong that pervades every standard item in the *Vespers* most exposed here, contrasting with a fine flurry of chordal floribundance for *illuc enim* ('*whither* the tribes go up') and an outburst of scotch snaps on *propter* ('*for* my brethren's and companions' sakes'): why these insignificant words so haloed? For the sheer fun of it, here and throughout.

Next interpolation *duo Seraphim*: top calibre at last in this bravura echo-number with its delightful employment of spaces and distances between the two ululating angels, joined towards the end by a third voice to represent the Trinity, then briefly by the full choir. They resume the liturgy no. 5, *Nisi Dominus*: one drowns in the close-knit mesh of imitation on double chorus, ten parts in all; not quite polyphony as of yore – a texture like minimalism or Morton Feldman: then bright antiphonal patter between the mighty pillars of chord for all the forces; then dancing, till briefly quelled by sombre-sumptuous *Gloria*; then return ... 'as it was' ... to beginning, then soft prayerful *Amen*. Next interpolation, *Audi coelum*, a hymn to the Virgin that might have wandered in from *Orfeo* – the hero's scene with Echo. The poem's sweet infantine echolalia faithfully followed even at risk of ridicule: *gaudio/audio, benedicat/dicat, Orientalis/talis*, etc.; funniest of all, *remedium/medium*; cleverest, *maria/Maria*. Human love charges this charming music the more warmly that the erotic pulse was eschewed in the two antiphons from Solomon's Song: human – manly, chivalric, devoted. The choir joins the solo tenor – the hero – and his echoing double as *omnes – all* are invited to venerate: the two men return for a final joke – *Solamen/Amen*; then a beautiful close for full chorus. Liturgy 6, *Lauda Jerusalem* – extrovert energy and joy, frisky for God's wondrous prowesses – marvellous words from Psalm

147: he giveth snow like wool, he scattereth the hoar-frost like ashes, he casteth forth his ice like morsels, who can stand before his cold? The texture solidifies into grand *Gloria*, then re-enlivens into broad festive momentum.

So to the glorious *Sonata*, a purely orchestral piece of ostentatious splendour, displaying the players to be as versatile, virtuoso, articulate, as the singers who are confined to the ten syllables of the five-word plainchant *Sancta Maria, ora pro nobis*, interwoven now and again; a serious strain, never-changing save for the occasional hiccoughing hoquet, binding the variegated colours, speeds, characters, of instrumental invention. Grand slowing-down into close. Liturgy no. 7 returns, *Ave maris stella*: after a rich eight-part opening, regular stanzas, song-and-dance feel, choir alternating with instrumental ritornelli – strings, then brass, then winds: further stanzas for varying solo voices: all in all, a direct descendant of the earlier stages in *Orfeo*, a jigsaw-mosaic of decorous sweet-severe strains: formal, patterned, slightly stiff, wholly engaging. Final quatrain set to the same rich music as the first, then adding a fine short *Amen*. No. 8 is a full setting of the *Magnificat*, concluding the entire work which is solidly grounded in standard liturgical practice, for all its five additional diversions. After initial choral invocation a varied layout: one part always on long plain cantus; around it, decorative displays of singing, blowing, bowing. The simple plainsong on sopranos, then altos; tenors exuberant and vaunting, instrumental ritornelli; then the tenors go plain, joined below by solemn trombones, above by watery warbling recorders. Now the basses go frisky, with violins darting around, altos again holding firm to the plain long line. For the Lord's mercy, serene choral antiphony, three men's voices, three women's, finally all six together. The Lord's strength given in a delicious jig; his disposing the proud accompanied by two noble trumpets, vying then agreeing; two violins exalt the humble and meek. Only Orpheus with his double-harp is missing from this Guide to the Orchestra, doubling too as tribute to the Power of Music. All the forces conjoin in a spirited seven-part close. The composer manifestly enjoys enormously exerting all his resources – his players and singers, his technical mastery, his high spirits – in praise of the Mother of God, and his hopes, audibly confident, of winning the supreme musical position in his native territory. He got the job: the rest is history.

Madrigals, lute-songs, consort-music

After the preceding avalanche of sacred music, back to secular: the madrigal as it peaked in Italy with Marenzio, Monteverdi and Gesualdo; in England the solo song with lute accompaniment, its supreme master Dowland; and – a particular corner of delight – the line of consort-music cherished in late Tudor/early Stuart culture.

The madrigal: another lost world, rarified and sophisticated, a bloom of courtly diversion, to parallel the universal patronage of the Church. Three essential figures from the proliferation of practitioners. Luca Marenzio (c.1553–99): a small contribution to sacred music lies alongside an enormous corpus of secular, ranging from pastoral lightness to darker shades imbued with an undertow of eroticism that can even grow morbid: fluent ease and effortless mastery prevail: hugely influential in his own country and in England. This music gives delight and hurts not, unlike that of his contemporary and compatriot Carlo Gesualdo (c.1560–1613). Reception of Gesualdo's work is still inevitably coloured – will be for ever – by the sensational events of his life, murdering his wife and her lover. He was Prince of Venosa in southern Italy and the killing was recognized by aristocratic codes as honourable, not criminal. He lived on to wed a d'Este – this marriage also shadowed if not stained: the couple's only child died in infancy – and devote himself to the cultivation of his estates and the composition of music sacred and secular. It is facile yet unavoidable to associate his work with the passionate psychotic personality: wayward and freakish from the start, his madrigals develop through six volumes (from the 1590s to 1611) into extremes of chromatic excruciation and rhythmic/textural wildness: excesses of mannerist contortion, merely weird were they not so piercingly expressive. Such pieces as *Mercè grido piangendo* (Mercy! I cry, weeping), *Asciugate i begli occhi* (Dry your lovely eyes), and *Deh,*

coprite il bel seno (I beg you, cover your lovely breast) from Book V:
and from its successor *Tu piangi, O Filli mia* (You weep, O my Phillis),
Io parto (I leave), *Mille volte il dì moro* (I die each day a thousand
deaths), *O dolce mio tesoro* (O my sweet treasure), *Io pur respiro in così
gran dolore* (Do I yet breathe thus in such great woe) send tingles
down the spine and up into the scalp with their burning audacity;
and there are many more. Another from Book V encapsulates the
expressive terrain in its closing phrase – *che le dà morte e vita*/from
which comes death and life. The source of pain is actually his lover's
lovely breast; yet the nexus between the traditional conceit of dying
in orgasm, old as the hills, and the transcendent spiritual exaltation
of Isolde's *Liebestod* cannot be missed. Wagner comes to the ears, too,
in *Moro lasso!* from Book VI, Gesualdo's most celebrated number:
'I die, alas, of my grief; and she who can restore me kills me, ah, and
will not heal: woeful fate – she who can give me life brings, ah, my
death.' There is of course no direct link – Gesualdo's mannerist art
was lost down successive centuries and only in the twentieth appreciated as the wonder it is – but turn-of-the-screw harmonic tension
is employed by both composers to the same affect/effect.

The trouble with madrigals is that composers all seem to be
setting the same two poems, whether by an acknowledged master
or an epigone copyist. This applies even to Monteverdi, whose nine
Books are much more variegated: Marenzio and Gesualdo tread and
re-tread the same gamut over and over. The first poem goes: 'I burn
in torment, I freeze in longing! O cruel inconstant nymph, take pity
on my suffering, you who hold my life and my death in your merciless hands: O Love, take pity – I gaze, I sigh, I weep, I taste, I touch,
in vain: turn my bitter to sweet, my woe to joy, my death to life.' The
other poem – spring returns, flowers blossom, nymphs and zephyrs
dance, Cupid smiles, the Graces bless, etc., etc. – is just as frequent
and stereotyped.

The closing years of Elizabeth I's reign, that of her successor James
I, and the earliest of his son Charles I's, are without compare in
English culture. Drama at a high-point from Marlowe to Shake-
speare and Jonson with their coevals: the effusion of verse whether

heroic – especially in translation from the Greek, the Latin, the Italian – or in sonnets and smaller lyrics; and in devotional-meditational reflections of greater length. Prose, too, from virtuoso euphuistic play to the eloquence of the great preachers, paramount among them John Donne and Lancelot Andrewes; and Francis Bacon's ambition to systematize the entirety of human knowledge. Supreme in prose of course, the Authorized Version of the Bible.

While the political climate rumbled with mounting discontents civil and religious, the culture continued to burgeon, now attuned to 'these distracted times', now oblivious. The 'School of Donne' succeeds 'The Shakespearean Moment': the subtleties of George Herbert, so seeming-prosaic yet so high in aims and searching in depths, and the ecstatic abandon of Richard Crashaw at his best, quintessentialize Protestant and Catholic at their core: and the further range of this epoch is still wider – it can include debonair Cavalier poets and delectable Robert Herrick, and enthusiastically pursue the outlandish in the wilder flights of the 'metaphysicals' – at their most bizarre prophetic of the inspired 'nonsense' of Edward Lear and Lewis Carroll. All these meet at an apogee in the earlier work of Andrew Marvell, whose poise enables incompatibles to conjoin in perfect equilibrium. Prose too; Robert Burton's encyclo-paedic, almost Joycean *Anatomy of Melancholy* begets the beguil-ing quiddities of Thomas Browne. The whole half-century or so of English writing mirrors the country's wider status and nature: a wonderfully rich epoch, rounded and mature, to be tragically eroded by inner and outer pressures strong, confident, destructive, with God on their side as they despoiled his temples, curbed the arts of performance musical and theatrical, executed his anointed monarch and set up the Rule of the Saints on Earth. T. S. Eliot's sug-gestion that a Civil War is never ended comes to mind: England's culture – social, religious, artistic, ethical – has never fully recovered, and cannot forget.

The lost golden world, self-perfected and perhaps idealized, visionary, even delusory, is matched by its music, albeit no way on the same scale in quantity or stature as its literature. Music was intrinsic to religious services, to drama, to lyric verse, and the private delectation of all who could afford it in courts, palaces, mansions metropolitan and rural. No well-to-do household lacked its players and singers, who often also composed what they performed with such accomplishment. (And, ironically, the two most famous or infamous Puritans, Milton and Cromwell himself, were both devoted to the art.) Initially the professionals were mainly imported, principally from Italy: these foreigners often settled in a country that paid so well – in appreciation as well as lucre: they married, and begat equally gifted successors, taught the natives their arts on lutes and viols: England had never lacked singers, and such collections as the *Fitzwilliam Virginal Book*, the *Mulliner Book* and *Parthenia* attest to outstanding keyboard skills. In vocal composition, sacred – Mass and motet – and secular – madrigal – the English contribution is on a par with the continental. With solo song and music for instrumental consort, there is no continental parallel. Dowland's lute-songs and *Lachrimae* fantazias, the body of viol-consort work by the younger Lawes brother William, make ample compensation for the decades of recitative brought into the epoch by the barrenness of *seconda prattica* till a later English composer brought this, too, to its consummation by re-admitting music back on equal terms with the words it serves – Purcell.

John Dowland (1562–1626): his solo songs with lute (he was the outstanding exponent of the day, celebrated in foreign courts as at home) come in four volumes, dating from 1597 to *A Pilgrimes Solace* of 1612. Their range of affect is wide, but he'll always be most intimately associated with the melancholy that puns with his very name – *semper Dowland semper dolens*. Book I foreshadows his theme here and there – *Unquiet thoughts*; *Burst forth, my tears*; *Go, crystal tears*; *Come, heavy sleep* (inter alia): and one setting – *All ye, whom love or fortune hath betray'd* – strikes the authentic core in its notes as in the (all-too-conventional) words ... 'my woe wants comfort, and my sorrow end'. It prevails in the second book (1600) with several of the most celebrated songs – *I saw my lady weep*; *Sorrow, stay* – and *Flow, my tears* is the prototype pavane which generates the greater half of *Lachrimae*, the consort-collection of 1604. Long vocal lines, subtly and supply responsive to salient words and their quantity in measurement and accent, enhanced with syncopations, repetitions, echoes: to all these, the plucked accompaniments are sympathetically resonant, occasionally inserting a short phrase while the singer reflects. *Sorrow, stay* can exemplify. Its very first word is set twice, with plangent suspensions; *woeful* and *hence* are also soon repeated, as extra *poor* (not in the poem) prefaces the second *heart*; *pity* is set six times to an urgent mutter; *mark me not to endless pain*, the whole phrase repeated; *alas I am condemn'd* is heard thrice before its concluding *ever*. The rhetorical climax *down* comes four times, in syncopation, before its sense is given in full – I *fall*; then, again, a new direction – upwards for *down and arise*, to a sort of fanfare; a second time higher and the last syllable long-protracted till its decisive negation – *I never shall*: all this again, exact till the *rise* of the last *arise*, now doubled from its already considerable length first time round, the lute descending down down down, till again, *I never shall*, now devastatingly final.

Such observations can suggest paths into the entire corpus: and one mustn't forget that Dowland isn't always *dolens*: there's gaiety, good humour (and sometimes actual humour), playfulness, melodious sweetness, placid hymn-like beauty, and lyric ease sometimes magically simple – try *Come ye heavy states of night* from Book II. And in *The Pilgrimes Solace*, an extended sequence with descant and supporting bass for viols, on related religious themes – God's advocation via Job of patience, via David of hope; then the cripple by the pool awaiting Christ's healing, combining both Virtues. But the pearl of the fourth collection, and of all Dowland's songs, is surely *In darkness let me dwell*. Every aspect hitherto mentioned is intensified on a broader scale, shown at once by the lute's spacious introduction: every darkness-dwelling grief, banishing cheerful light, now focuses upon *music* itself – *my music* wrought now into *hellish jarring sounds* (these ugly consonant-choked words much repeated), leading the incarcerated protagonist to cry directly for death, even a living death; *till death do come* in actuality not metaphor or mere fantasy – nor, one senses, in mere poetic convention. Here the original text ends: the song, however, is rounded off with its first line repeated, ending mid-air for voice, on a suspension, resolved in just one short note as its accompaniment is withdrawn: simple, bold, telling, desolating.

This superb body of song wouldn't necessarily suggest Dowland's high calibre in purely instrumental composition. True, the *Seaven Teares figured in seaven passionate Pavans* that comprise the first half of *Lachrimae* launch off with *Flow my teares* from Book II, its eloquent melancholy widely popular – roll-call of the usual suspects – *flow, fall, forlorn, dark, despair, woes, never, sighs, groans, fear, grief, hopes extinguished, darkness-dwelling, contemn light* and – rather unusual – *night's black bird, singing in sad infamy*. The song's three strains distinguishingly shape the seven pavanes that ensue, warmly scored for five viols, progressively extracting more and more richness in what amounts to a variation-set (perhaps more exactly, a set of doubles) with their ever-more-depressive titles: from the original *Lachrimae antiquae* (the old familiar tears) via (all prefaced by the *L*-word) *antiquae novae* (new old tears), *gementes* (sighing), *tristes* (melancholy), *coactae* (enforced), *amantis* (the lover's), *verae* (true); to the eighth and most searching, *Semper Dowland semper dolens* – longer, more elaborate, a self-portrait in sound, as contained and elegant as Hilliard, as self-revealing as Schumann. The cycle can be extended with a ninth pavane, *Sir Henry Umpton's Funerall*, serious but *not* melancholic: and the collection as a whole is diversified with jollier dances dedicated to, though not portraying, personages of the day, known – the King of Denmark, the Earl of Essex – or unknown (Mrs Nichol, Mr Nicholas Gryffith, etc.) – one more pavane, two allemandes, the other nine all galliards.

So far as lute-songs are concerned, the period contains many slighter charms, and one very fetching figure with five books of ayres to his name, Thomas Campion. His songs are in no way up to Dowland's but they set his own poems, inventive and delicious in diction and construction far beyond the commonplaces that contented the superior composer. And Campion's two music-theory publications – *A New Way of Making Fowre Parts in Counterpoint*

(?1614) and the more important *Observations in the Art of English Poesie* (1602) – would not have lain within Dowland's scope.

Turning to the consort as self-sufficient medium the line is long and absorbing, involving some of England's principal composers continuously down more than a century, though mostly as a sideline to their more central work for cathedrals, churches and chapels. Its fountainhead is the *in nomine*, using the phrase setting these words – *in nomine Domini* – from the *Benedictus* of Taverner's *Gloria tibi Trinitas* Mass as cantus firmus – anchor, or magnet, round which the free polyphony of the other parts goes its ways – instrumental polyphony, though at first scarce distinguishable from vocal. As the genre develops, virtuosity grows too, eventually exploiting techniques, speeds, registers, that voices couldn't possibly manage. Whether routine (mostly), or special, or (sometimes) exalted, the corpus of viol-consort music, freed from the shackles of the *in nomine*, is a field of pleasure and reward for its players' enjoyment (as madrigals for their singers'), before that of its listeners: the vocal-as-the-instrumental diversions disappear with the gradual, then total, erosion of the culture that gave it birth. A sacred place however modest, even a sideline to Western Music at large, yet a reserve, nurturing noble game, preserved by noble men and women. Thomas Mace, writing his *Musicks Monument* in the 1670s when composition and performance of string fantazias was virtually extinct, eloquently describes and defends: 'so many Pathettical Stories, Rhetorical, and Sublime Discourses; Subtil, and Acute Argumentations; so Suitable, and Intellectual Faculties of the Soul and Mind; that to set them forth according to their True Praise, there are no Words sufficient in Language'.

Dowland's *Lachrimae* has already been described: with Byrd and Gibbons, the consort works lie peripheral to their vocal music for worship whether clandestine or open. Even so, calibre and mastery will out. Byrd's *in nomine* pieces are strong and subtle: besides them two high-points: a *Browning* in five parts, a riot of ingenious, invigorating invention, eighteen entries of the principal motif across all five parts, not quite a round or a fugue, on the lusty folk couplet 'The leaves be greene the nuts be browne / They hang soe high they will not come downe': and a very fine *fantazia* in six – long and varied, antiphonal trios both high and low then the full six parts rich and sonorous; then goes martial and chunky, thence into a triple-time dance with repeats, before slow juicy-grinding close over long-held bass-notes, worthy of Purcell.

The image of Gibbons as more sensitive and refined, even fragile, given by his verse-anthems and madrigals is belied by his tough stringy consort works – direct, sturdy, energetic, physical. Take the *in nomine* in three parts featuring 'the Great Dooble Base', or the one in five, a workout uningratiating in its severity. *Go from my window* recalls Byrd's *Browning*, the way the old song gradually infiltrates all six parts. Yet Gibbons can be dainty, even hilarious – a two-part invention suggests squirrels chasing each other's tails along the branches and across the lawn. And he can be earthy, as in two Sets embodying the *Cries of London* wherein *actual* voices are reintroduced to call their wares – fish, fruit, fowl, vegetables, salads, nuts, items of household utility, tobacco; a lost grey mare 'with a long mane and a short tail, she halts right down before and is stark lame behind'. Amid much more, poor Tom o' Bedlam, naked and a-cold, makes a brief appearance; also 'the poor women, we lie cold and comfortless night and day on the bare boards in the dark dungeons in great misery' – all intermixed with bacon, a fine washing ball, hot spice cakes, and so on and on. 'And so we make an end' – all five voices in semi-seria homophony. Thus the first Set; the sequel much the same, its diverse comestibles commencing with 'a good sausage'. Just one moment of pathos – 'the poor pris'ners of the Marshalsea'; and more close-wrought polyphony for the viols' continuity as the singers drift in and out: it ends on the monotone bell sounding 'Twelve o'clock, look well to your lock, your fire and your light, and so goodnight.' Piquant indeed that this second Set of *Cries* is founded around the *in nomine Domini* from Taverner's *tibi Trinitas Benedictus*!

English keyboard music of the epoch is extensive and testifies to ebullience and prowess in digital dexterity: acres of empty scale-practice, much naïve onomatopoeia evoking bells and

thunderstorms, interminable divisions on popular songs: the barren
fields occasionally bedecked with pretty wayside flowers – a *Prim-
erose*. The essence comes in *Parthenia* (1612), with eight pieces by
Byrd, seven by John Bull, six by Gibbons. Bull's are more remarkable for experimental chromaticism than musical content; Byrd's,
sometimes vapid and jangling, can rise to invention worthy of his
finest. The Gibbons are, at their best, supreme. Take the rich-wrought
nobility of the *Pavane for the Lord of Salisbury*: and whenever I play it
over (on the utterly anachronistic modern piano) the long *Fantazia*
in four parts in A-minor strikes me as the greatest keyboard polyphony before Bach.

Returning to the string consort: much minor music, enjoyable
enough – John Ward, Thomas Lupo, Thomas Simpson, John Jenkins
(who lived on till 1678): and one undoubted great – William Lawes
(1602–45), younger brother of Henry; both pupils of Coperario,
and William in the employ of Charles I's court. He fell fighting for
his King in the Civil War (Henry, a dull composer, lived on to see
the Restoration). William is prolific – perhaps over so: he begins
foppish, elegant, slightly silly; then rapidly develops into something rich and strange, individual, deep-searching though always
urbane, with splendours manifold amid the profusion, tempting
one to dub him the Haydn of the English consort, sometimes the
Strauss. Individual numbers are grouped into Sets, usually without
a fantazia – a dance-suite, in up to seven pieces united by key. Even
when apparently periodic and regular, the unexpected phrase-
lengths, the lurches and twists of the harmony, take these dances
beyond functionality – the dancers would stumble and trip. When
he does essay fantazia – free-flow of counterpoint (the familiar
Taverner *in nomine* sometimes figures), Lawes' linear mastery is pronounced from the start – active but spare; never dense – textures
open and athletic: occasional awkwardness, even gawkiness, sometimes moving into excruciated eccentricity, more often just *individual*. One senses that he's more at home the more parts he has to play
with – some moments of concentrated busyness can foreshadow
early Tippett. Outstanding, the *Sett à 6* in F: a seraphic *fantazy*, a
complex yet gentle *aire*, second *fantazy* energetic yet restrained till

a sudden stop and plangent close; second *aire* more formal and dance-like. *Airs for three lyra-viols* – grave, dark-hued, thoughtful though never melancholic à la Dowland; even when livelier, the same gravelly texture and sonority; then amazing chromatic dying falls, down into the black – Purcell not Dowland. *Humour* too – changes of mood/speed/direction positively feline. The *Sett à 6* in G-minor: its opening *Pavan* one of his supreme moments – compacted treasure, harmony drooping downward while textural layers ride upward: *Fantazy* leggy then jammy with exquisite excruciations, then layers piled-up as in the *Pavan*, here clearing and re-forming, thickening to a full slow close: concluding *Aire* simpler at first, till its end is just as jammy and odd, maybe more so. Best of all, perhaps, the *Sett à 6* in Bb. Prizes invidious for this music as for any other: all have deserved to win, and all shall have prizes.

Matthew Locke (1621/2–77): though no Lawes, a distinctive voice, late in the line (Jenkins, born some thirty years earlier, died a year later, and Purcell, last in the line, was born in 1659). His six *Suites* in four parts (1660) mostly comprise four movements, fantazias and dances. The voice is so quirky, so full of surprises, unpredictable changes of direction in speed, texture, character, as to invite the word *mad*. This for fantazias: dances of course more straightforward, yet equally full of quirks. Locke's chromaticism not languishing/piercing/passionate as in Purcell – more a matter of his innate oddness: there's plentiful strong rangy-leggy counterpoint à la Lawes, and a bluff sturdiness all his own.

Purcell

Purcell's contribution to the viol-consort is its ultimate crown. A compositional miracle, twelve fantazies in three or four parts; a thirteenth in five, its extra voice confined to the same single note repeated every bar; two *in nomine* in six parts and one in seven; all written *c.*1680 by a young man scarce out of his teens. More yet: it now seems that the two pieces using the traditional cantus firmus from Taverner might have been composed still earlier. For all his thorough-going alertness to the latest music from France and Italy, Purcell the ex-chorister was steeped in the long traditions of his own country, palpably learning from, adding to, benefitting and enrichening himself and them. The fantazies are treasure heaped high from a precocious genius comparable to Mozart's, Schubert's, Mendelssohn's – total mastery of a genre and an idiom already 'superseded' (save that the word is a betrayal, for this is a consummation and renewal in one). Inspiration bold and free, wanton inventiveness under masterful control, adroit in polyphony, rhetoric, shaping of journey and form. Above all, the harmony: even in three parts Purcell's notes can squelch; with more voices, more so; with all seven for just the last piece, the effect is spine-tingling. And utterly un-freakish – this isn't like Gesualdo, who's 'trying it on': Purcell's extremes are wholly lucid and grammatical, though just as justified and equally astounding.

Born 1659 of a musical family: manifesting exceptional promise from the start; chorister at the Chapel Royal, later at Westminster Abbey, succeeding his teacher John Blow in 1679; had already published some songs and was composing the string fantazies and anthems. Copious output – church-music, secular instrumental works, music for court and civic occasions, and, eventually prevailing, music for the theatre – masques and semi-operas and one actual opera, albeit modest in scale, and incidental scores for over forty plays, as well as isolated songs, dances, catches, glees, and 'whatnot'. Died 1695.

Soon after the old-fangled fantazias (which remained in manuscript until the twentieth century) come two substantial collections that reveal the young composer as thoroughly au fait with the newest music from the continent: twelve trio sonatas à 3, published 1683, ten 'Sonatas' à 4, written synchronously, but only issued posthumously (in 1697) by the composer's widow. Both ventures are commercial – Purcell is clued up to consumer-demand. In fact, the layout of all twenty-two works is identical – three individual parts, with the bass supported by continuo which also fills in harmony as needed. Not that these impeccable inventions need help: crystal-clear writing, full of varied delight, sometimes sounding the introspective depths that receded before the new foreign taste of the Restoration after the privations of the all-too-native Saints. There's also a handful of miscellaneous string-pieces: a couple of *Overtures* and a *Suite*, as French as the sonatas are Italian, and somewhat ordinary for this of all composers; some lovely pavanes, one in G-minor contemporary with or still earlier than the fantazias – its putative date 1677 (Purcell is seventeen or eighteen) – and worthy to stand beside them, as, too, the fantazia in three parts over a ground bass, with its boyish display of learnèd prowess. And one masterpiece, *Chacony à 4* in G-minor, where learnèd prowess is lightened with Lullyan leaven (easily surpassing the model). A strong piece, still stronger when given with full string forces – grand solemn weight, moments of contrasting energy or delicacy, a touching apparent farewell in triplicate before impetus in part regained, then *morendo al estinto*. I think the unattributed performance I've been hearing must be conducted by Benjamin Britten – the rapport is complete, and the care and love for every note of a precursor to whom he owed so much.

Purcell's reach is so wide that he comes under at least four heads: purely instrumental music, 'ancient' and 'modern': his large body of church-music which sustains the verse-anthem of Tudor and Jacobean usage, with generous assimilation of new French influences. A wealth of ceremonial work for royal or civic occasions – though sometimes invoking the Patron Saint of Music, Cecilia, at the annual festivities for her Company – which might willingly be dismissed as dutiful hack-work but for their often-inspired quality. Last, and most, his theatre-music, ranging from individual songs, dances, entr'actes, to full-evening-length stage spectaculars evincing a feel for story, setting, character as acute as any subsequent composer – the tragedy being that the theatre-culture of the day was simply not ready to take on such talents.

Purcell the Master of Ceremonies and Occasions. All twenty-four odes are on the face of it ephemeral, to be thrown away (unless frugally recycled) once the date has passed. There was no need for them, any more than for the Bach church cantatas, to be inspired: competence and punctuality sufficed. Instead, because both composers so overflow with musical ideas, they write occasional pieces which we would as little think of throwing away as a Holbein drawing. In a sense, Purcell's is the more remarkable victory for quality. Bach's texts often scrape the depths of lugubrious pietism, but elsewhere he sets fine specimens of German hymnody as well as passages from Luther's Bible. And, of course, he fervently believes every word. Purcell's odes not only have, in almost every instance, texts of McGonagall-esque badness, but dispiriting subjects too. Six celebrate Queen Mary's birthday (though she seems to have been unfeignedly beloved); five hail Charles II and three James II; and there are one-offs for other royal occasions and a few miscellaneous celebrations. The Mary works say 'Happy birthday' with many a lolloping trope, the Charles/James works say 'Welcome home, great sir'. Grovelling obsequiousness is the mode, with the royal personages regularly hailed as 'Caesar' and 'Augusta' and sometimes compared to Olympian deities. Topical allusion is sometimes made. The principal intonation is imperative – *Come! Rejoice! Hail! Sing! Now cease!* The void is total. One imagines Purcell's muse tucking up her sleeves with a groan at yet another loyal injunction, before getting down to duty. No time to wait for the fire of inspiration!

But celestial fire always waited for him. It is a measure of his disinterested genius that he could respond to these fustian occasions with the same enthusiasm he devoted to a subject that undoubtedly did stir his passions, music itself and its patroness St Cecilia, whose feast day was celebrated each year by the Musicians' Company with a specially composed ode. St Cecilia touches off the sublime every time. Purcell's five odes to music range from a ten-minute miniature, *Laudate Ceciliam* (uniquely not in English), to the most familiar of these (largely unknown) pieces, *Hail! Bright Cecilia* of 1692, at over fifty minutes the grandest in scale and in orchestra and in generosity of inspiration. The text, hymning music as 'Nature's Voice', 'the Soul of the World', tuning the 'jarring seeds of matter' into harmonious proportion, and featuring each instrument in turn in a sort of young person's guide, cannot hold a candle to Dryden's wonderful *Ode*, from which it obviously derives (would that Purcell had set that!). But it serves well enough; and even the crashing bathos of the last line praising the 'Patroness of Us [i.e. the Company] and Harmony' is transcended in the general splendour that closes a work remarkable among much else for its range of techniques and depth of expression, and for the boldness of its joins. Remarkable but not exceptional. The standard here is so high that I can detect a whiff of routine only in one (*Celebrate this Festival* – we can hear his muse's groan); and even this has unique beauties and audacities equal to anything in the others.

In a *valete* on concluding his admirable recording of Purcell's complete religious music – a treasury that embraces the darker, more introspective aspects of the composer's inexhaustible gift – Robert King writes, 'hardly a piece has gone by which has not left me amazed at the sheer originality and genius' of this body of work – sixty-five anthems, various sacred songs and scenas, a complete set of canticles and liturgies for Matins, the Eucharist and Evensong, as well as a grand *Te Deum* and *Jubilate* for state affairs, and solemn strains, choral and instrumental, for a royal funeral. There are perhaps only two duds, around eight rank as pretty fine, and nearly thirty-nine as supreme by any reckoning. The remaining twenty-seven or so are far from nugatory: as with Bach's cantatas and Schubert's songs, sheer quantity can embarrass the explorer, while quality is set so high that one doesn't know where to begin and how to choose.

In Purcell's religious music genres range from grand royal occasionals to intimate sacred songs, solo or concerted and dramatic scenas with one or more soloists. The main body, though, is for choir, with or without soloists, and organ with or without strings: the verse-anthem of late Tudor/early Stuart practice, elaborated, extended, adorned with mod cons from France and encouraged by Charles II's fancy for violinistic liveliness. Purcell is always good for good cheer: yet most of the corpus is severe, penitential, grim and grovelling. A high proportion is early. Even *very* early: one – *Lord who can tell how oft he offendeth?* – dates from his late teens. (The boy has talent! Bold assurance, especially of the harmony; declamation already masterly; inwardness deep and unfeigned, rendering acceptable the meditations of the heart; a mutely vivacious doxology with serene *Amen*.) Then as his principal concerns turn theatre-wards, the output of church-music dwindles, though not its quality.

On the large-scale: splendid *Te Deum* and *Jubilate*, originally composed for St Cecilia's Day 1694; a prototype, frequently revived down the following century to celebrate victorious campaigns in various wars. The most sizeable anthem as such, *My heart is inditing*, was written for James II's coronation in 1685 – a big ceremonial piece, perfect for the purpose, unimpeachable in facture, some sections of high inspiration, all in all somewhat penny-plain after terrific opening Symphony: not a work to charm or move, less still to cause unfathomable awe as so often elsewhere. Two bright Cheerfuls accommodated to Restoration taste, both familiar and deservedly popular. *O sing unto the Lord* – tip-top in every respect; 'The Lord is great', one of Purcell's most fetching numbers upon a ground bass, especially in the strings' continuation after the voices cease; sumptuous splendour unbound, yet strangeness too – 'O worship the Lord in the beauty of holiness'; winning ingenious euphony of final *alleluias*. *Rejoice in the Lord alway*: celebrated descending-scale 'bells' in the opening string sinfonia give this anthem its nickname (and sometimes the bells ascend too): Moderation (in the text) is observed, then high cheer resumes – 'again, again I say, rejoice', and the sinfonia is heard again, extended: 'be careful for nothing' seems to endorse the admonition to Moderation, but energetic momentum is retained till 'the peace that passes all understanding' is set with great tenderness, voices, then strings alone: so to resumption of 'rejoice, and again I say again, and again, rejoice' – immoderation wins.

Many other excellent anthems share this extrovert character, but Penitence and Mourning far outstrip, in number and in weight. First, another grand large-scale royal occasion, the music, instrumental and choral, for Queen Mary's funeral in 1695. The entity *Queen Mary's Funeral Music* is a tangled net involving also some older settings by Morley in traditional usage, and some later by Croft. Purcell's contribution, easily disentangled, is sublime. Instrumental comprises a *March* for four trumpets and optional drums, sounded as the funeral chariot processed the streets of London en route to Westminster Abbey, and a *Canzona* for the same forces, 'sounded in the Abbey after the Anthem' – fine serious movements, intonation just and right (though, piquantly, the *March* was redeployed later in 1695 into incidental music for *The Libertine* – Purcell the opportunist! But God is not mocked – *Thou knowest, Lord* from the burial-sentences was sung at his own obsequies later that same year in the same building he'd served so well.) The three settings of *Funeral Sentences* from the Scriptures are among his greatest: associated with them, *Hear my prayer*, apparently a fragment though complete in itself, is a masterpiece of construction fused with emotional intensity – in eight parts built on just two shapes, one of just two notes, the other a sinuous chromatic turn, the shapes woven criss-cross with breathtaking expressive power. The other three *Sentences* – *Man that is born of a woman*; *In the midst of life we are in death*; *Thou knowest, Lord, the secrets of our hearts* – though less amazing are scarce inferior: from sober, well-measured homophony to excruciating dissonances worthy of Gesualdo without his caprice, provocation, mannerist shock-tactics. Six further supreme-sublime *Penitentials*. *Who hath believed our report?* – extreme pathos and dolour for these woeful words from Isaiah; plangent flexible recitative shared between the four soloists 'stricken and smitten of God'; all four together for 'all we like sheep . . . he hath borne the iniquity of us all'; chorus takes up 'all we . . . we all': more recitative, ultra-expressive, for the lamb led to the slaughter . . . dumb – 'so opened he not his mouth'. 'Cut off from the land of the living' more metrical: an echo-song. To close, 'all we like sheep . . .' repeated, now on choir: no ameliorating *Alleluias*.

Another marvel: *Remember not, Lord, our offences*; intensity here hardens into continuity; no variety nor remission, just astonishing cumulating pain in the pleas to be spared, then calm patient supplication at 'be not angry with us for ever'; unreproachful acquiescent end – the music, not the words, promises deliverance, as 'spare us good Lord' returns in refrain. Another – *Let mine eyes run down with tears*: a Lamentation of Jeremiah – 'hast thou utterly rejected Judah? hath thy soul loathed Zion?' This alien-archaic stuff humanized by the music beyond time and place: the last section – 'do not abhor . . . do not disgrace . . .' – is especially searching, before a transition to hope, faith, patience – none of these *named* although powerfully *implied*, again as if the music brings into being the words that aren't present as such. Another – *O Lord rebuke me not*: guilt and suffering essentialized in marvellous notes – 'sore troubled' indeed – two clashing treble voices in utter supplication – 'O save me ... weary of my groaning ...'; scarce a ray of cheer, and after it 'O save me' again, again restores dolour. Another – *O Lord of hosts*; like *Hear my prayer* in eight parts, a miracle of compacted pathos nearly its equal; at the last pathos yields to confidence. Finally, an anthem, *Jehovah, quam multi sunt hostes mei*, that mitigates the torment by being more varied in texts and textures, tempi and moods. Its brief duration encompasses lamentation, exultant trust in the Lord's protection, defiance of his enemies whose cheekbones he'll smite and whose teeth he'll break, and a closing chorus of salvation and blessing. Within all this, an unforgettable still centre – *ego cubui et dormivi*; 'I laid me down and slept, and rose again: for the Lord sustained me': fourteen bars of rapt inwardness, the harmony sometimes so strange that Elgar, orchestrating *Jehovah* for a Three Choirs Festival, wondered if these might be misprints. No: it's correct: and can still awake disbelief.

From Purcell's many sacred songs just four (though 'all are delectable'). *The wakeful shepherd that does Israel keep*, a miniature for treble of the utmost tender sensitivity. *With sick and famish'd eyes* sets for once a great poet rather than the usual pietistic fustian that, admittedly, served the composer just as well as Scriptures. Here seven of the fourteen stanzas comprising George Herbert's *Longing* are used, but not set as a lyric, as the poem suggests; Purcell eschews the elegant formality behind which Herbert hides his anguish, in favour of continuous recitative of desperate plangency – all imperatives, exclamations, questions so urgent and piercing as to confirm this composer as one of the greatest masters ever of affective declamation. A final outcry before the heart 'dies' within its troubled breast can wring the spirit like Schubert or Wolf. *Close thine eyes, and sleep secure* also sets a poet of stature, though no Herbert – Francis

Quarles – in duet for high and low voices, placed far apart, in odd intervals over continuo doing what it can to bridge the void: a gem of purest water. As also the only such piece to be widely familiar, the *Evening Hymn – Now that the sun has veiled his light*, for solo treble: a beauty – long-spun melody over steady ground bass, involving response for, in bed, the body; for the soul, in God's arms: so, Soul, sings, to 'praise / The mercy that prolongs thy days' by its nightly refreshment. *Alleluia* to conclude in complete contentment.

Finally, two complementary scenas of fabulous histrionic immediacy – Purcell the nascent dramatist/character-depicter/storyteller to the fore, as eventually won out over church-music in his curtailed career. *In guilty night: Saul and the Witch of Endor*; in his desperation Saul comes to her – she can summon the spirit of the deceased prophet Samuel, who can resolve the King's cares of state and soul. Every stage electric – forsaken Saul's pleas and orders – the Witch's reproachful/resentful reluctance – her fearsome cries of *Alas!* as her fearful scruples are overcome. Samuel rises from the under-world sinister as Pluto its ruler: he can promise only more misery – imminent defeat in battle; then 'thou and thy son tomorrow shall be with me beneath'. All three voices join, as chorus, to close – just two words, oft-repeated – 'Oh! Farewell'. A wonder of the (under)world. And one of living daylight: *Tell me, some pitying angel: The Blessed Virgin's Expostulation*. Mary takes her boy to the temple, loses him, gives vent to her worst imaginings in music of wild abandonment. *À bas* Monteverdi! *This* is what *seconda prattica* can achieve extended to its full potential: what it was invented for. Four repeated cries of *Gabriel!* – where is he now, who once brought me tidings of ultimate joy? – are extra to the verse-scheme (by Nahum Tate, librettist of *Dido*): *Arianna's Lament* on steroids! – then a *further* four times: but 'he comes not'. Now less hysterical but no less urgent: the word here repeated over and over is *How* ('*How* shall my soul its motions guide? / *How* shall I stem the various tide?') – *how how how how*? The climax of poignancy reached with the second line of her closing couplet, 'I trust the God, but oh! I fear the child': music manifests what text only implies, the awe and dread that her infant's loss, only temporary, might be the eternal loss of the world's salvation that she, chosen to bear and nurture, has now suffered to mislay.

To the stage: the calibre of *Dido and Aeneas* has long been recognized, admired, adored. This miniature masterpiece is, wretchedly, the only theatre-work of this born theatre-composer that is completely viable on-stage: its fame and familiarity need no introduction nor case to be made. (And a word in passing for the admirable libretto, often mocked – neat, economical, now and then excellently sententious without being trite: 'Thus on the fatal banks of Nile / Weeps the deceitful crocodile. / Thus hypocrites that murder act, / Make Heaven and Gods the authors of the fact': eloquent when required; then when required, self-effacing, knowing only which words to retain – '... thy hand, Belinda ... remember me but, ah, forget my fate.')

    As well as *Dido* I would urge Purcell's three longest and most ambitious works in any genre; masque or semi-opera, mishmashes tricked out with picturesque outlandish clutter, among it some of his greatest invention – *Dioclesian*, *King Arthur* and *The Fairy Queen*. Fatal as Nile (the stultifying convention *Dido*'s modesty escapes) that, in stage presentations with music, the main action was spoken – instrumental music being confined to overtures, closes, entr'actes, scene-changes, dances; and vocal numbers to songs and ensembles peripheral to the principal characters. The sort of farrago acceptable to the times can be followed with increasing frustration through these three grand attempts to cope, override, transcend. *Dioclesian* (1690): its play derives from Fletcher and Massinger – a mishmash of pseudo-Roman history, with few opportunities for music, pretty well taken till the play is done and music can flower in the concluding Masque. Dryden's *King Arthur* had been written as a play in 1684 and adapted 1691 as 'A Dramatic Opera' with Purcell's active collaboration. Again a mishmash of pseudo-history, this time tinctured with mythology, Merlin and pagan deities involved as well as the Christian Arthur: ends with Honour herself, invoking St George as she instigates for Britain's 'fairest isle' the Order of the Garter. One doesn't know whether to laugh or cry at the unresisting imbecilities foisted by the going conventions upon poet and composer so akin in genius. The score abounds in splendid music: outstanding, the Masque of Coldness in Act III, and the marvellous chaconne in Act IV wherein the chaste King, forewarned by his Magician, is enabled to resist the lures of a pair of naked Thames-Maidens – 242 bars of sustained invention, the score's high point.

How will it be when Purcell collaborates with the greatest poet/playwright of all? *The Fairy Queen* (1692) derives from *A Midsummer Night's Dream*. Shakespeare's original is given, typically mangled and deboshed to the debased taste of the times: and here each of the five acts is crowned by a Masque wherein that taste's penchant for lavish spectacular is allowed its head as never before. Simply to enumerate the additional places and personages can indicate the ambition of the absurdities: Hymen and Juno appear; a drunken poet is scourged for his bad verses; Mopsa resists lustful Corydon (or is it the other way round, and does s/he resist?); Night, Secrecy, Sleep, Mystery, are personified; the Seasons appear; and two Chinese women, a Chinese man, then a Chinese chorus are added to the Indian Boy who occasions Shakespeare's quarrel between Oberon and Titania. (Why not a whole Indian contingent – and an Aztec/Inca scene, and one from the *Arabian Nights*?)

The finest music in this long evening is also its most extended: in Act II the Masque lulling Titania to sleep and penetrating her dreams; in Act IV the Masque of the Four Seasons culminating in Winter with his cavernous textures, descending chromatics, tingling suspensions. Finest of all, the *Plaint* in Act V, one of Purcell's supreme utterances, absurdly incongruent with its context, the triple marriage in 'Athens' of its Duke Theseus and the four lovers after their mismatchings are untangled, the whole under the benign patronage of Oberon and Titania, now reconciled. Why should Oberon request 'a sad song'? He surely receives it in this consummate expression of woe, abandonment, loss, matched only by Dido's lament. It doesn't sour the triple nuptials, and the long evening rounds off with lusty festivity, sometimes 'Chinese'.

These three sprawling hotchpotches of absurdity, for all their musical wealth, emphasize the contrast with *Dido* – its economy, compactness, speed; above all its complete inter-relevance of action, character, score. *Dido* also has absurdities: the subplot of witches is pretty silly – but their malevolence is germane to the plot, and they engineer the externals of its catastrophe. There is also the question of missing music here and there – not a major problem and easily solved with dexterous additions from other material from Purcell's copious theatre-output. More serious, the *internals* of the catastrophe: the heroine is presented and explored with subtlety, sympathy, and depth: her relations with her faithful women, particularly Belinda her confidante, are given in full. The missing complement is a comparable coverage of the hero. Aeneas, never granted an aria wherein to express his divided loyalties nor his single passion, can seem something of a lay-figure perhaps: certainly incomplete. His recitative is alive to every shade of Purcell's characterizing sensitivity, but he needs more *space*: and oh for two imagined duets – love ('one night enjoy'd') and betrayal ('to your promis'd empire fly, / And let forsaken Dido die') – that would express their emotions in articulated composed sounds! This might have been beyond the resources, indeed the decencies, of the School for Young Gentlewomen for which the work was supposedly written in 1689. They would not have been beyond Purcell's gift. As always, the old double-barrelled *Record Guide* of Sackville-West and Shawe-Taylor encapsulates best:

> it is difficult to contemplate his career as a whole without regret. His divine genius was largely frustrated by unfavourable circumstances ... Everything fitted Purcell for the rôle of a great English opera composer: a vividly dramatic imagination, a profound understanding of the voice, and a skill in setting English words to music which has never been equalled for variety and ease.

I would put it more crudely and provocatively: Purcell, together with Marc-Antoine Charpentier (who outlived him at both ends, born some fifteen years before, dying some nine years after), are simply the greatest composers between the dissolution of polyphony around the early decades of the seventeenth century and its reflorescence in the early eighteenth at the hands of Bach.

CHAPTER III

French Baroque Opera

To reach Charpentier one must first surmount Jean-Baptiste Lully (1632–87). Florentine by birth, in France from early teens until his death; accomplished player and dancer, rapidly successful at court, eventually holding down all the principal theatrical/musical posts in the capital; a power-freak, repressing with his monopolies all rivals who didn't toe the line. Power for positive too, codifying the form and conduct of French opera for nigh on a century to come; its origins Italian, its outcome wholly French – conventions, notation, idioms, choice and treatment of subjects all set in stone, awaiting the animating genius that could bring the statue to life. For Lully is another one-dimensional composer, tame in his music as violent and tyrannical in his professional and private behaviour.

The animating genius is Marc-Antoine Charpentier (1643–1704): youthful study in Rome; back in his native Paris, some success in the theatre, including collaboration with Molière, who'd already worked with Lully, whose restrictive practices nonetheless prevented Charpentier's free flight. Of two tragedies on religious subjects only *David et Jonathas* survives: his only full-length opera *Médée* (1693 – Lully safely disposed of) not successful; perhaps a one-off, for most of the copious output is sacred, and employment by the Church was the mainstay of his career. Like Purcell he excels in categories that seem, on the face of it, incompatible. Their stature is comparable, though after the deep strangeness of Purcell, Charpentier seems quite normal: *decorum vincit omnia*; to pair them is to emphasize Purcell's uniqueness. But *Médée*, even *David et Jonathas*, point the huge advantages for the Frenchman of the French genre: a coherent plot, flim-flammery kept to the periphery: a music-theatre whereby music and drama are fused and aimed along the same journey for the same purpose, and music is no adjunct – rather, the centre and *raison d'être*.

This said, one has in *Médée* to endure an extended Prologue of pure sycophancy! Royalty ordained this obsequious stuff wherein assorted rustics, then allegorical figures – Victory, Fame – hail Louis XIV's triumphs in War and (perhaps) Love. Charpentier does his excellent best: Purcell's effortless ease with such matters, and the lavish invention of which they are unworthy, are not so evident. Once the opera-proper commences, its libretto by Thomas Corneille, younger brother of the famous Pierre, is deft, fluent, apropos. Its source is Euripides' Greek and Seneca's Latin treatment of the subject (more recently the elder Corneille had produced his own version: the younger brother pinches some of Pierre's lines). Medea, having enabled with her black magic the hero Jason's exploits, notably in gaining the golden fleece, now marries him: the pair escape retribution for her crimes by fleeing to Corinth. Its king Creon allies with Orontes, ruler of Argos, against Medea's revenge-seeking compatriots, and promises his new ally the hand of his daughter Creusa in marriage. But Jason becomes enamoured of her: his wife suspects the truth. Creon encourages the affair; Orontes is naturally offended – he and Medea bond in outraged sympathy. Medea's black arts again a resource: hearing that Creusa is indeed, with her father's blessing, to wed Jason, the sorceress prepares a poisoned robe for the ceremony: for the time being, till she can bargain further, the poison lies dormant. Her bargain is that Orontes not Jason be the groom: only then will she permit to be valid the banishment from Corinth required of her. Creon tries his royal powers, easily vanquished by Medea's supernatural – first by turning his soldiers against each other, then dispersing them in pursuit of beguiling maidens, then by driving the King insane. Further negotiations: Creusa begs Medea to cure her father's madness; Medea agrees only if she, Creusa, will marry Orontes not Jason. Too late – in his madness Creon has slain the would-be suitor. The two women confront conflicted: *now* the poison is activated: Creusa dies in agony: Jason, witnessing, vows vengeance upon Medea, still his wife (and erstwhile salvation), but is overwhelmed by a further triumph of her malignity (however justly occasioned by his perfidy) – she's fulfilled her earlier threat and had their children murdered. She flies off on her dragon, leaving in her wake a trail of destruction – three of the four other principals dead, the innocent babes also slaughtered – possibly to wreak more havoc in another country; the palace of Corinth a smouldering ruin: Jason alone survives, though his life can't be worth living. (Though 'some say' the couple were later reconciled; and a further tradition goes that, dead at last, Medea married the shade of Achilles in the Elysian Fields!)

This tight knot of five people in a tangle of desires adverse, perverse, ardent, impassioned, or all these admixed, is presented at all points by Corneille with clarity, in plain speech unambiguous yet suggestive, powerfully heightened at crucial moments, unexaggeratedly eloquent without rodomontade; and always human – even the demonic urges prompting the heroine to unleash her fury are rendered comprehensible, even sympathetic. The music responds to everything with subtle flexibility, easily slipping in and out from recitative to *petits airs*, sometimes extended into arias, occasionally into duets: chorus as needed: instrumental pieces ranging from tiny moments of articulation/punctuation to full-scale action/dance, again as needed: an exploration of character, a narrative journey, an architectural totality composed of short views.

When the screw is tightened, Charpentier reveals his master hand. Acts I and II are rather a slow burn. Medea's rancorous power, always intensifying, reaches full extent in Act III in a superb accompanied recitative *Quel prix de mon amour, quel fruit de mes forfaits!* followed first by an explosion of rage – *c'est en fait* – then resort to her sorcery, calling up evil spirits to prepare the poisoned robe for her rival, then to wreak general havoc. Act IV's most remarkable music comes at its end as the horrors take effect – ravishing phantoms, soldiers distracted by ravishing them, the King rendered insane. The horrors culminate, after a furious orchestral interlude, in Act V with its succession of poignancies, pleas, lacerations, revelations, craziness, despair; to conclude with the diabolical heroine's

total triumph – up aloft, straddling her dragon, taunting her faithless lover, father of their children she's slain – 'You've still more to
avenge; here's the dagger that's snatched your children from your
love.' J. – 'I'll to hell to punish you.' M. – 'Poor fool, what can you do?
The skies are open to me. Farewell Jason, my vengeance is complete,
Corinth in flames, all dead but you, left alive to the solace of your
own self-destruction.' The dragon bears her off, demons break in to
fire the palace. The end is brief and furious, as, their work complete,
they vanish leaving behind an empty scene of destruction.

  This ending a shade cursory? One can easily imagine what
Purcell might have been capable of here, as in earlier places of
emotional extremity for all five of Charpentier's principals: recall
many such place in the Englishman's stage-spectaculars – recall
above all *The Blessed Virgin's Expostulation* and *In guilty night*. But
these lurid colours are not Charpentier's way: *decorum vincit omnia*,
and 'it is right it should be so': this masterpiece is all the more
firmly rooted in stable soil for the self-contained restraint of its
artistic manners.

Brief relief from classic tragedy: a precious corner of priceless
worth – the French line of *leçons de ténèbres*, born of the traditional
devotions for Holy Week, Jeremiah's penitential/reproachful verses
long-since applied to Jesus' Passion and set in choral polyphony by
some of the finest composers of earlier epochs. The French genre
and manner are different: concerted chamber-music, for solo voice
or duet, accompanied by continuo on clavecin or organ, with string
bass. Chamber-music: these setting are domestic and intimate
rather than public for church-usage: complaints of worldliness were
frequent – not so much a congregation attending a service, as an
audience attending a concert in order to relish unseemly displays
of vocal virtuosity. And indeed, the art of florid ornamentation here
reaches a peak hard to distinguish from contemporary practice in
opera. The results can be so delicate and lovely as to have the hearer
succumb in sheer ravishment, then to remember the subject and
purport of these texts in some embarrassment, before managing to
fuse aesthetic enchantment with religious devotion. Four figures

stand out. Michel Lambert (*c*.1610–96) is the prototype – plain, though already the finesse of declamation is in place; his range as composer is small. Charpentier again distinguished, as also his younger contemporary Michel-Richard Delalande (1657–1726). At their hands the scope of the *ténèbres* widens: in their settings of the traditional opening Hebrew initials and the closing appeals to Jerusalem to turn again to her God, lyricism stirs and blooms. The *trois leçons* of François Couperin are the crown-jewel. They are at once more self-contained and more continuous, this latter effected by some subtle joins. Set-numbers focus around the central *Recordare* of the second *leçon*, a sarabande in B-minor, whose long-spun vocal cantilena over the descending chromatic ground bass of the traditional *lamento* wrings the heart. However, the third *leçon*, with two singers, can arouse suspicions, for the tender loveliness of the voices overlapping Hebrew initials – on *Jod* at the start, on *Caph* even more, on *Lamed* more still, thence *Med* and *Nun* – sounds more like canoodling lovers than lamenting *dévotes*! And the closing duet on Jerusalem is yet more operatic, both singers achieving several high A's. Melted by such beauty, God would surely forbear.

Couperin will recur in a completely different context. For now, return to the stage. The Lully-line is established and continued. *Médée* was Charpentier's sole venture into it: other composers' operas almost always good, sometimes really fine: those I've explored and enjoyed – Henri Desmarest, Marin Marais, André Campra, Michel Montéclair, Jean-Marie Leclair, Jean-Joseph Mondonville. But the dominant genius of the epoch in his country, on-stage and in most other genres, is Jean-Philippe Rameau. Born Dijon 1683: organist in several provincial cities, including a couple of years in the capital before settling there for good in 1722. Famous at first as theorist – *Traité de l'Harmonie* 'epoch-making', followed by copious further writings. *Actual* composition, chamber-music, harpsichord-music, church-music. Late to the stage – *Hippolyte et Aricie* 1733 – he's fifty. Thereafter a stream of theatre-pieces tragic, comic, divertissements, opéra-ballets, consistently innovative and inventive – nearly thirty works, some lost, most survive intact, to be revived in modern times fresh as new. Creatively fertile to the end, dying in 1764 aged eighty-one.

Hippolyte et Aricie: the tragedy-proper is preceded by the inevitable Prologue, more coherently linked in to the main events than usual. A virile *ouverture*: Diana and her nymphs dance and sing – the goddess in a halo of flutes; one day in each year, Love is permitted in her woods that at all other times are devoted to Chastity. Cupid appears, also deliciously surrounded by flutes. They duet, equals in spriteliness. Then Diana grows serious, addressing the sovereign arbiter of Heaven and Earth: and Jupiter descends. He too admits Love is the most powerful god: Chastity must yield. He ascends, she submits: her votaries Hippolyte, son of the hero/ruler Theseus, and Hippolyte's love Aricie, are in danger: Diana must protect them.

Act I: Aricie alone: she's compelled by Pallas Athene's ancient enmity to Theseus to vow herself to a single life despite her love for Theseus' son. When Hippolyte appears they shyly avow their sentiment, before turning towards Diana's temple where she must renounce it. Recitative of supple expressivity: occasional *petits airs*: then ceremonial music for the priestesses – Love, your torments can't trouble our peace. Things quicken when Queen Phèdre enters, enraged to discover Diana's promised protection of the young lovers – it subverts Theseus' explicit, and her own secret, wishes – tremble at my vengeance! The priestesses are indignant, summoning up thunder – a splendid fizz and foam of scales and tremolandi: musically empty, but achieving its aim – we've been heard! our goddess descends! Tremble, sacrilegious queen! Diana protects *la liberté des coeurs*! – and the lovers enter the temple. Phèdre now confers with her old nurse/confidante Oenone: the queen admits Aricie to be her rival for her stepson, and expresses hatred, rage, jealousy. Arcas, a messenger, brings news of Theseus' death – following, hero that he is, a dear friend to Hades in hopes of rescuing him. Now your crime can be *légitime*, Oenone insinuates: Phèdre resists, but the old woman beguiles – you can make him King! Phèdre forebodes – if this doesn't suffice whom I love, Death is my last resort. This indication of repressed passionate cross-currents in her words always taken up and enhanced by their setting, already on heat even so early, ready to boil over and burn out when tempted and provoked beyond endurance.

Act II discovers the Underworld. Theseus is guided on his noble self-sacrificing mission by Tisiphone, a Fury: their dialogue, then duet, are almost comic in tone. Not so when Pluto is reached, enthroned and supported by the Fates: grand dark-strained music, strong in anger when Pluto calls for vengeance against any mortal who dares defy him and his mate, powerfully taken up by the infernal chorus. Marvellous trio of Fates – three male voices, unaccompanied, at once stark yet rich. And Theseus' ensuing monologue, appealing to his father Neptune to grant a second wish, reversing the first that permitted entry, to now permit exit from the regions of eternal darkness. The chorus say, in vain; but Mercury, who can dissolve all boundaries, appears, begging clemency in Neptune's name – Jupiter rules the Heavens, Neptune the oceans, you the shades – the happiness of the universe depends upon your common good will. These grand sentiments are also given lightly – Mercury is mercurial, and Pluto not so plutonic as before. He concedes: I release Theseus – perhaps his fate will be no kindlier for my kindness. Then he loses the light touch in the act's magnificent closing stretch, commanding his Fates to tell the hero his destiny. They reply in a trio of dire presentiment and astonishing enharmonic modulations: why hurry, *malheureux*? shudder with terror! You quit the infernal regions to find hell in your own home; a marvellous curtain, ruined by the later addition of brief, matter-of-fact practicalities between Mercury and Theseus as to the King's return-journey.

Act III opens with Phèdre's superb B-minor *Plaint* – my passion horrifies me, but my crime is thine – Love's vengeance. Oenone announces Hippolyte's arrival: the Queen trembles: her stepson all polite solicitude for the newly made widow. I am hateful to you, he claims; she almost betrays herself – hateful to me? How far from the truth! Slippery exchanges – I'll be your brother and support your son and his throne: no – I place all under *votre loi*. He – I count as naught: Aricie is my sole desire. Phèdre is aghast to realize her mistake: misalignments take off in a duo of strong sinewy cross-purposes: their unambiguous outcome – *ma rivale*! It's out, and he understands: she – strike my guilty breast! You hate me as I love you – *donne*! At this disastrous moment Theseus returns, not dead as we know and they don't, but able to be instantly deceived. The ugly wrong is fixed: Hippolyte too decent, Phèdre too willing, Oenone complicit, Theseus deluded: his son has attempted outrage. All this in tense, urgent recitative occasionally breaking into *arioso*, alive to every fluctuating nuance. And dispersed for now by bright irony: grateful for my safe return, says the King, my people come to render thanks. March and chorus of citizens and sailors, a *rigaudon aux tambours*, saucy song for *une matelote* – gay sturdy lightness in a dark context. Theseus thanks them, then remains alone to face the promised hell in heart and home. A son so guilty: favour must not be shown: punishment is ineluctable. Grand invocation to *his* father Neptune – hear my groaning, let your son importune you one last time: if you refuse, I am a parricide and you a perjurer. Marvellous *frémissant des flots* as *Neptune oblige*, a surging orchestral disturbance in which the god of the ocean makes his powers audible. Theseus' close is triumphant: blood-ties are in vain, my guilty son must die, my father will keep faith, gods must avenge kings.

At the start of Act IV Hippolyte is granted his moment – he's fled with Aricie to Diana's realm: ravishing *mélange* of *arioso*, recitative, aria, Rameau's exquisite instrumentation and harmonic sureness to the fore: then the lovers gently duet. The goddess of chastity and hunting is celebrated in jolly bucolic divertissement, orchestral dances and vocal numbers, perhaps a little o'er-prolonged, Rameau not here on top form, soon to be reached again. Up from the ocean rears *un monstre horrible*. All cry for help, Hippolyte is carried off, Aricie laments, and the chorus join in mournful eloquence, plain, severe, grand – *O disgrâce cruelle: Hippolyte n'est plus*. Enter Phèdre: what plaint calls me here? They repeat their second strain, adding to it – vain regrets! – and describe the disaster. It's my work, says the Queen: it's I who've caused the spilling of innocent blood; Heaven, what remorse! She vows to confess her guilt and Hippolyte's innocence. Vain regrets – *Hippolyte n'est plus*, with an extra wringing suspension on the *ly* of his name: another superb curtain.

In good classical tradition Phèdre's clarifying confession and

suicide have occurred off-stage. In Act V Theseus, who has witnessed them, prepares for his own. More magnificence: my son was
innocent, I am guilty: to Hell again? God of the Ocean, hide me
for ever from mortal sight. Neptune now *does* appear in person, to
prevent his son from suicide by drowning: your son is not dead –
Diana protects his life. Your punishment – too credulous, too ready
to fix and revenge guilt – you must never see him again. Further
magnificence in the King's stoical acquiescence and farewell. The
remainder of the opera removes to *jardins délicieux*: a happy ending
threatens, and it seems likely to go on for quite a time. Not happy at
once: Aricie, alone, laments her loss in a pretty little *plaint*. Shepherds
and their lasses dance. Diana descends – nice little ariette without
bass. Aricie – I've lost him; it's *irréparable*: but she doesn't seem too
deeply concerned; and anyway here he is, transported by Zephyr –
delicious little flight on the orchestra, too short. Initial incredulity
soon yields to acceptance: Diana will unite the pair, under the law
of the gods. Dances, choruses, a march, a closing chaconne, an *air du
madrigal*, sweet enough. But not enough to silence the disappointment: this happy ending seems unearned – unaffecting in itself, and
shallow after the depths previously plumbed, sure indication of a
masterpiece.

Two later stage-pieces, chosen to complement *Hippolyte* in contrasting fashion. First, *Les Indes galantes*, a spectacular *opéra-ballet* of 1735
(the last of its four sections added two years later). The gorgeous
exuberance and generosity of this work's terrestrial embrace is comparable to the near-contemporary (1750–53) frescoes by Tiepolo for
the Residenz at Würzburg, wherein the four continents, personified with their flora, fauna, attributes, are visited by Apollo on his
daily round of the heavens. The score's glory is its cornucopia of
abundance – a huge range of colourful invention vocal and gestural
(as the genre *opéra-ballet* indicates) – lyric, dramatic, ceremonial, in
all shades: and not forgetting the scenery and special effects – in Act
I a terrific sea-storm, in Act II the terrific volcano, which makes two
appearances, first in warning, second as terminal convulsion.

Platée – a *comédie lyrique* of 1745 – couldn't be more different.

Perhaps *ballet buffon*, as on the title-page, better suggests this piece's fusion, unclassifiable and unique, without forebear or progeny – a self-reflective *mélange* of singing and dancing, masquerade, serious and farcical, setting them all at sixes and sevens, lambasting with merciless parody: and leaving behind, after the hilarity abates, quite a sour taste. For Platée, though convinced of her irresistible charms, is *hideous* – vain, ludicrous, pathetic. The work was first played during festivities for the marriage of the Dauphin to the Spanish Infanta, known to be uncomely: the tactlessness cannot have been unknowing, but seems not to have caused trouble. Another layer is important, introducing in Acts II and III *La Folie* herself. She directs and dominates the denouement: hers in the biggest role; she is the real heroine, after the model of Erasmus in his celebrated encomium *In Praise of Folly*. Yet Platée retains our sympathy: she is ridiculous and pitiable; the grotesque action teaches her no lesson concerning vanity and o'erweening; she is utterly humiliated. But somehow we're on her side, intermittently and in the end wholly. This unique piece cuts deeper than one might think from its mere plot: the music's calibre is, of course, at once cause and effect.

Rameau's other stage-works are extraordinarily varied: the mystical hocus-pocus of *Zoroastre*, the pastoral delectation of *Zaïs* and *Naïs*, the tragic fervour of *Castor et Pollux*, and in *Dardanus* tragedy to nearly match *Hippolyte*. And finally, the fantastic wind-swept *Boréades*, his last, composed in his early eighties: a mechanical and perfunctory plot of small human interest or affective reson-ance. But did Rameau ever compose so rich a score? The level is consistently high – bold, dynamic, colourful (especially its instru-mentation), lyrical where needed, ditto with serious and search-ing. Above all, the fluidity of momentum, most obviously in the winds themselves – the Boréades: and elsewhere throughout. And the animation of his smaller units, themselves supple and diversified beyond his previous: grouped together in complement and contrast and continuity to make the whole. In his old age Rameau essays and conquers a new world.

*

Another switch of genre within the same epoch; two overlapping masters of the keyboard miniature. François Couperin (1668–1733): the outstanding member from an extensive family of musicians; from age seventeen till his death, organist at St Gervais, Paris; from twenty-five one of the organists to the King. Celebrated teacher as well as player – *L'Art de toucher le clavecin* (1716) combines both. His keyboard works are gathered in twenty-nine *Ordres*, each set comprising from four to around twenty little pieces, often given fanciful titles though all are dance-forms (with the occasional prelude) that sometimes remain purely abstract. Some fine chamber-music and church-music, notably the three sets of *leçons de ténèbres* for Holy Week, alluded to in the previous section: the focus here is on the *Ordres*. Couperin chimes with Domenico Scarlatti (1685–1757): also the most outstanding from an extensive family of musicians; Naples-born, appointed to the court there aged sixteen, then, within five years, extensive European travels – Venice, Rome, Lisbon, where he tutored the King's gifted daughter. She married the Spanish crown prince in 1729, and brought her teacher with her, as crown princess then Queen, first to Seville, then, from 1733 till his death, Madrid. Operas, cantatas, church-music, mainly early and un-special: Scarlatti's lasting fame stands upon the mountain of miniatures – some 550 harpsichord *essercizi*/sonatas for himself and his royal patroness, demonstrating their formidable shared technique and his unique flair and fantasy.

Both composers are 'Latin' and make the perfect complement to the contemporary harpsichord oeuvre of Bach. He, even when Italianate, is learnèd, didactic, exhaustive: he demonstrates how to *compose* as well as how to play, sometimes with a questioning research that can justly be called mathematical, even scientific – forty-eight preludes and fugues in all twenty-four keys, the *Art of Fugue*, in the *Goldberg Variations* the art of canon; even when dance-based, the contents are gathered into well-organized schemes. And the actual music is often dense, complex, profoundly searching, extending the edges of the known musical universe – even, sometimes, when dance-based, or in concertos designed to display performance-prowess. Bach is by no means averse to physical vitality, brio, wit, sparkle, delicacy; but these qualities are not what spring first to mind.

They do so at once chez Couperin and Scarlatti. Dean Sutcliffe, the latter's best commentator has, tongue-in-cheek, listed under the heading *Instant Latinate Essentials Generator* the stereotypical expectations that apply well enough to both composers:

1. elegance and grace
2. rationality and logic
3. Mediterranean, Classical
4. detachment, dryness, precision
5. joy and happiness
6. clarity, limpidity, transparency, lucidity
7. brightness and brilliance
8. lightness

Stereotypes, but with a base of truth: one can easily make exceptions: chez Couperin, detachment and dryness do not figure; chez Scarlatti 1 is infrequent; 2 is dubious; and the qualities of 3 seem better-attuned to later times – Mozart, Verdi, the latter half of Hugo Wolf, Ravel. And some further characteristics must be added – in Couperin, tenderness, deliciousness, sweetness whether gay or melancholy; in Scarlatti, ferocity, obsession, quiddity – the 'imp of the perverse', culminating in what the same commentator calls 'irritation'.

Couperin never irritates: he charms, cajoles, smiles. Take the first *Ordre*: even the allemande is titled *l'Auguste*, the sarabande *la Majesteuse*, the gigue *la Mylordine*, the first rondeau *les Sylvains*, the second *les Abeilles*, a second sarabande *les Sentiments*, a gavotte *la Bourbonnoise*, the third rondeau *l'Enchanteresse*: other movements are given only their dance-forms: and no fewer than six just their capricious titles – *la Nanette, la Pastorelle, les Nonètes* (in two halves, *les Blondes* and *les Brunes*), *la Manon, la Fleurie ou la tendre Nanette, les Plaisirs de Saint Germain en Laÿe*. This suffices to give the tone: there are twenty-eight more *Ordres* to come: one wants to list the contents entire – a mini-universe of pleasure, never less than delightful, of perfect facture with their exquisite play of ornament, and by no means, sometimes, lacking depth and inwardness. No. XIII includes *l'âme en peine*, XXV *la visionnaire* and *les ombres errantes*: VI the well-known *barricades mistérieuses*, enigmatic in its music as its title; VIII the longest single movement, a superb *passacaille* in B-minor. No. XI includes a burlesque play in five acts, its finale *désordre, et déroute de toute la troupe*: XIV presents various birds in love, in affright, in plaint, in triumph, and closes with *le petit rien*: but Couperin has plenty of *something*.

Scarlatti is never so refined. At best, the 'Latinate Essentials' prevail, as above. But there's a high proportion of sameness in his huge body of tiny pieces. He doesn't do *ordres*: at the most, a couple of sonatas might be paired major/minor, but there's no sense of larger balances, nor often of internal balances within the individual pieces. He can be scrappy, flimsy, perfunctory, threadbare: yet the verve, dash, wit, sparkle, spunk, are untrammelled and irresistible. The vivid daring of his discordant scrunches and percussive insistence anticipate such in Bartók and Stravinsky, equally exotic to Central European mainstream manners: they can jangle and exhilarate the nerves with another term used by his best commentator – 'delirium'.

And if one tires of the clattering harpsichord or the gentle clavecin, both composers' keyboard works have elicited some delectable orchestrations. Strauss paid Couperin several loving homages: a *Tanzsuite* (1922) and a *Divertimento* (1941) – this latter adopted from *Verklungene Feste*, a ballet composed just before – 'dance vision from two centuries with music after Couperin'. Tommasini scored some Scarlatti sonatas in 1916 for Diaghilev: the resulting *Good-humour'd Ladies* gave Stravinsky the impulse to turn to 'Pergolesi' for *Pulcinella* and the crucial shift in his style that ensued. And Casella's *Scarlattiana*, a divertimento for piano and orchestra of 1926, also pays homage in its own way. One wishes that Berio had gone further than simply to set six little encores for piano alongside six Scarlatti sonatas; a large-scale 'Scarlattiana' from Berio would surely be a thing of joy: they're made for each other.

CHAPTER IV
Handel

Georg Friderick (various spellings) Handel: born Halle 1685; intended for the law; music-study opposed by father, but immense innate gift soon emerged, with organist posts at the city's church and cathedral. To Hamburg aged nineteen as violinist in the opera-band; his own first two operas produced there 1705; a third followed after he'd already departed for four years in Italy – Rome, Florence, Venice – fruitfully experiencing their diverse musical riches, opera to the fore. Back in Germany 1710, accepting post in Hanover with its direct links to London, first visited that same year, preceding removal there 1712, which remained permanent: naturalized English subject by Act of Parliament 1727. Huge success, prodigious output, fluent in music for public occasions, flourishing under royal, civic, aristocratic patronage. Opera to the fore, principally under his own steam being his own impresario and manager – some thirty-five works between 1711 and his last in 1741. Rather earlier, after several disastrous financial mishaps, had begun a shift towards oratorio, gradual then decisive: some twenty, all save three on Old Testament subjects, with strong narrative/character-driven impulse carried over from his operatic output. Two exceptions are classical – *Hercules*, *Semele*; the third, uniquely, is mainly New Testament-based, theological/meditative, without narrative – *Messiah*. Last years shadowed by poor health and eventual blindness: died 1759.

Four connections, comparing and contrasting Handel with pre-cursors and contemporaries so as to concentrate in this exceptionally protean figure what is essentially Handelian. First and clearest: his compatriot and exact contemporary J. S. Bach. The most striking complement lies in subject-matter and its treatment. Handel is at core operatic – stage-based, dramatic, virtuosic and showy, commercial entertainment; plots drawn from romance, chivalry, history, Renaissance epic; his idiom is hearty, robust, straightforward, unexploratory, direct, diatonic; above all a melodist, endlessly rich and fertile; his nature is wholesome, pagan, extrovert. If 'religious', his music is festive and ceremonious: when he treats biblical subjects on a larger scale their sources are almost all Old Testament. Jehovah but one God, albeit the true one, amid the Dagons and Baals and Molochs; the Israelites the one true people, beset with Philistines and Ammonites. He eschews theology and the New Testament except once, greatest of all, *Messiah*. Bach is Christian to the core: when not liturgical – Masses, *Magnificat* – the *Passions* and cantatas centre upon Christ the Redeemer, salvation from guilt and suffering, contrition for sin, abasement in unworthiness, eventual heavenly reward. Their music is introverted, deeply troubled, probing, searching, groping; its technique built upon contrapuntal mastery beyond compare, with especial intensity of chromatic harmony achieved via complex interweaving of polyphonic lines – ultra-detailed and intricate, the polar opposite of Handel's broad brush which, sweeping all before it, is often skimpy, even perfunctory, in detail. These Bachian traits turn naturally towards exploration of the ultimate reaches of music's possibilities in its epoch, in a spirit at once scientific – discovery, demonstration – and didactic: everything the art can do, laid out schematically, for teaching, to learn from: and at the same time infused with passionate expressivity. All this absolutely alien to the essential Handel: unneeded by it, perhaps repugnant. Bach *can* be robust, earthy, extrovert – this comes to the fore in dance-suites for keyboard or orchestra (and can invade the church-music too): he can relish virtuosity and displays of prowess – again, keyboard pieces whether sacred (for organ) or secular, especially in concertos. And he can be as routine *sometimes* as Handel is *often*: the jog-trot/'sewing machine' of Bach on a dull day (or in a poor performance) can equal Handel on autopilot. All this is epitomized by their respective choral-writing: massive diatonic homophony; and when fugal, loose-weave, open, full of air; clarity and splendour perfect for either huge echo-y interiors – St Paul's Cathedral, the Crystal Palace – or

festive outdoor events: vis-à-vis dense chromatic interweave, sometimes very difficult to sing (Handel is always a joy for the chorus,
even when the Israelites mourn), the complex totality easily lost in
a jungly mush when the building can't take it, and in the open lost
on the air. But both composers are uninhibited and unabashed in
borrowing or stealing, then transforming material of their precursors and contemporaries; and flagrant in self-recycling.

Next connection, another near-exact contemporary, though
not compatriot: Rameau. Here the complementary focus *is* the
musical stage. French Baroque opera, Rameau its greatest exemplar,
benefits enormously from its solid ground in Greek tragedy, then
Seneca, then Racine's essentialized bare-to-the-heart reworkings:
these facilitate a *Médée*, an *Hippolyte et Aricie*, a *Dardanus*, and so
on to Gluck's *Armide, Alceste, Orpheus and Euridice*, the two *Iphi-
genia* pieces. The basis for Handel's operas is Italianate: we groan and
yawn under the subjects, the characters, the crippling conventions,
the uninvolving complications and entanglements: the music itself
can be wonderful, the works themselves are lost below the horizon –
acres of tedium, concerts in costume, performers not personages: the
dramatic coherence and human profundity of Greek mythology set
alongside the flimsy inflections of history and romance: rock-solid
fundamentals beside froth and bubble.

The third Handelian nexus is wholly Italian: Arcangelo Corelli's
life (1653–1713) overlaps Handel's for three decades. The importance
of his relatively limited oeuvre – nothing vocal, all instrumental, four
collections of trio sonatas, a set of twelve concerti grossi – can hardly
be exaggerated: he established the genres of sonata and concerto,
he consolidated the pre-eminence of the violin-family, he solidified
functioning tonality, he was seen as the embodiment of stylistic perfection. The oeuvre was disseminated all over Europe, reprinted and
played again and again. It's a vital model for Purcell as, later, for the
French Baroque: witness Couperin's admiring words – 'delighted
with the sonatas of Signor Corelli, whose work I shall enjoy so long
as I live' – and their result in his *L'apothéose de Corelli*. Bach learnt
deeply from him; Handel's own concertos and other instrumental
music are inconceivable without him; and in modern times one of

Tippett's greatest works, the *Fantasia Concertante*, pays homage in its glorious enrichment of Corelli's original.

Finally, Handel and Purcell. The parallel here is not contemporary – Purcell was born twenty-six years before Handel, and died when the Saxon was ten. The connections are of genre, culture and musical type. Handel settled in England aged twenty-seven (and was naturalized thirteen years later): his easy adaptation to English musical requirements, expectations, genres, idioms, owes greatly to his greatest predecessor. Church, court, aristocracy, the gradual discovery and exploitation of a paying bourgeois audience: both composers produce to the manner born exactly what's right – for birthdays and coronations and deaths of royalty, celebrations of victories in war and subsequent peace, civic and mercantile festivities, public and private – music for fireworks and water-revels: natural laureates, absolutely un(en)forced. Both mirror the wider styles of their time and place – *urban* (specifically London) – in architecture, clothes, manners. *Pastoral*, which both handle beautifully, is fancy-dress holiday, rustic or courtly; comic or amorous, all evincing tender feeling for nature. Purcell is still 'Stuart', whether new-fangled and Frenchified to the taste of Charles II, or harking back to Charles his father. Handel is Palladian/Augustan – symmetry, normality, nothing eccentric: formal, cheerful, splendid, showy, expensive. He has no significant intercourse with the greatest in contemporary letters – Pope and Swift – yet is wholly at home with the culture of its time in his adopted land. In instrumental music both share the common Italian influence embodied in Corelli, the style, sonority, forms, formulae of trio sonata and (with Handel) concerto grosso: both manifest an unfailing sense of display and entertainment, revelling in the brilliant gifts of their performers, beginning in their own performing prowess. A divergence – the final flowering of the English viol-fantasy in Purcell is completely foreign to the Saxon. More generally, neither the survival and continuation in most of Purcell's church-music of the preceding century or so in the English sacred tradition, nor what goes with it – his remarkable intensity and inwardness – apply with Handel: his church-music is, by comparison, a shade perfunctory. But when Purcell's puts on a

public accent – the big *Te Deum* and *Jubilate*, for instance – the result
is so Handelian that the Saxon Englishman must have known and
learnt from the native.

Above all, they both show a natural bent for the stage: born
dramatists-in-music, innate feel for pacing, story and character, total
understanding of the singer and the voice. Both suffer comparable
constrictions just where they might bloom most fully: English 'opera'
simply not yet ready for Purcell's gifts; result, cumbersome dodos
filled with marvellous music. Handel's equally Italian-based opera,
also filled with marvellous things, vitiated by irksome stiffness, dead
conventions, unreal tangles of plot and personage in which one
couldn't give a damn who loves or hates whom – especially when the
principal roles are performed in travesty! Both are masters of vocal
rhetoric in all its ranges, from pathetic to heroic. Purcell's way with
his native tongue is miraculous: Handel's with his adopted *can* be
awkward, insensitive, clumsy, and is *always* generalized not particular. Both suffer from British fustian: the texts for Purcell's Odes and
'semi-operas' are sad stuff: just as awful, the biblical poetastry that
Handel is so often faced with when he turns to dramatic oratorio
in English. Whenever they're given poetic calibre they rise finely.
Dryden – used by both composers, sometimes, whatever the missed
chances of fuller collaboration worthy of the genius of all three. For
Handel, Milton, whether mangled (*Samson*) or realigned (*L'Allegro*
and *Il Penseroso*, with a reversion to British fustian in *Il Moderato* that
thankfully has no deleterious effect on its musical setting); Congreve;
with a few lines from Pope (*Semele*). Alas no Shakespeare for either:
but the Authorized Version when used direct always arouses the best
in both composers. Oratorio doesn't yet figure for Purcell, though
he could have, and wonderfully. Handel's later turn from opera
to oratorio (often with powerful operatic residue) brings out his
greatest qualities, in solo-writing and, above all, in the writing, almost
non-existent in the operas, for chorus. His Old Testament subjects
are treated with the depth, breadth, grandeur, they require, equal in
weight and value with the Greek tragedies of the French Baroque.

Main conclusion: the illuminating contrast between Purcell's endless originality, daring, plangency, penetration – protean,

dazzling, ear-stopping – and his incredible contrapuntal prowess, vis-à-vis Handel's bluff *ordinario* (a favourite tempo-indication) – carefree and free, machine-made of tropes and commonplaces, churned out by the kilometre. Yet he too can frequently touch the sublime, achieving, as Beethoven famously remarked, the greatest effects by the simplest means – common chords, motor-rhythms, well-worn clichés, all producing juxtapositions that can take the breath away or – as George II hearing the Hallelujah-chorus from *Messiah* – compel the listener to stand erect in awed astonishment.

The delights of Handel's *Fireworks-Music* and *Water-Music* need no introduction nor exegesis: no composer has better understood the tone, level, spirit, of such public festivities, nor provided exactly the musical invention to suit. The same goes for such ceremonial pieces as the Utrecht *Jubilate* and the Dettingen *Te Deum*, the eleven Chandos Anthems, and the anthems for Coronations – open spaciousness, unsurpassed of its kind. The spirit is not inward, contemplative, searching – one has only to think of Bach's church-music. Handel is untroubled, unfraught, guilt-free; faith is confident, not requiring enquiry that could shake its foundations before reassuring them. Neither the indignation of the Prophet nor the angry pulpit of the Preacher is needed: even in Lamentation Handel's tone is sober. The earlier *Dixit Dominus* already shows this, for all its differences – a product (1707) of his Italian sojourn rather than his English domicile – this magnificent work, his masterpiece in the genre, evinces exuberance over all things.

I've made apologia for bypassing the Italian operas that form the main bulk of his lifework. Their admirers make the best defence: I confess to frustration, annoyance, eventual indifference, despite some of the richest treasures from his copious store. Preference goes to the operas in English on classical subjects; to oratorios on dark Old Testament subjects wherein the treatment retains considerable residue from the long operatic experience; a unique pastoral *intermezzo* of unparalleled felicity; and finally, two supreme heights of the genre, covering the Old Testament promise and its fulfilment in the New.

*

Acis and Galatea: serenata of 1718 for Cannons, the future Duke of Chandos's grand new palace north of London, later memorably lambasted by Pope – 'lo, what huge heaps of littleness around . . .', etc. No jealous rancours sully Handel's delectable piece, unwontedly compact and without a single lapse. Direct from the lovers' pastoral pleasures to the dramatic nub wherein their joys are destroyed by a jealously amorous monster. *Wretched lovers! Fate decrees no joy shall last*: at first plangent minor with suspensions, then growing chromatic and imperative as *Quit your dream* is worked in: ending in peremptory block chords – *Behold!* Heavy momentum sets up the cause – *the monster Polypheme*: his busy figure set across the long-sustained *wretched lovers'* motif with telling cunning. Freeze: silence: then *staccato* ejaculation syllable by syllable: *see-what-am-ple-strides-he-takes*: then, still separated by silences, *the mountain nods . . . the forest shakes*. Momentum resumed continuous as *the waves run frighten'd to the shores*, rumbling away in the bass while upper voices bark out *hark: how the thund'ring giant roars*, eventually uniting all voices as the one-eyed monster rears up to declare his rage, then his desire for Galatea. Laying down his pine-club, he calls for reeds wherewith to fashion a pipe, and, with its tweeting recorder descant, serenades her in the irresistible *O ruddier than the cherry*. The next high point is the score's finest number, a trio for the heroine with her fair and her hideous lovers. A pang of regret for the potential quartet, wherein the two shepherds' implicit rivalry is also worked in, gives way before Handel's fluent mastery: only Mozart could have done this too. *The flocks shall leave the mountains, / The woods the turtle-dove, / The nymphs forsake the fountains, / Ere I forsake my love*: Acis and Galatea languish in ravishing suspensions, caressing the *dear smiles* of their mutual affection over a gently walking bass, which bursts into action for Polyphemus's explosion – *Torture! fury! rage! despair! No, no, I cannot cannot bear*, then towards the end *Fly swift, thou massy ruin, fly: Die, presumptuous Acis, die*, he sings alone, seizes a rock (the 'massy ruin') and hurls it at his rival. Exquisite expiring recitative from Acis – *Help, Galatea!* Then as he sighs to the gods to *take me, dying, to your deep abodes*, the bass descends eight semitones before the pathetic close. Sarabande chorus of mourning, dulcet, not wringing its hands, reminiscent of the cupids who close *Dido* (Rameau also comes to mind, the chorus lamenting the death of Hippolyte, not yet written): *the gentle Acis* – pause – *is no more*; coming the third time it broadens further still – *no ... more ... no ... more*; beautifully repeated in the orchestra's coda.

Semele (1744) is one of Handel's most perfect works. The story of Jupiter's infatuation with the vain mortal beauty, Juno's jealousy, the girl's desire for equality with the gods, her inevitable destruction, is well known and well told. After a rather standard first act things begin to soar. Juno's awakening rage at her husband's flagrant infidelity yields a terrific accompanied recitative invoking Saturnia: *Seize and destroy the cursèd Semele! Let her fall! fall! fall! Rolling down the depths of night* – literally rendered in baroque rhetoric of malign power. *Sleep* will be the weapon: Semele takes it, all unawares, in her hauntingly beautiful *O Sleep, why dost thou leave me?* Soon after comes her lover's celebrated *Where'er you walk*, its words taken from Pope's *Summer* pastoral, a seraphic foretaste of *Waft her, angels* eight years on. Act III's high points are richly various. *Sleep*, now personified in Somnus, his sonorous lethargy hypnotically conveyed by an orchestral prelude: commanded by Zeus to wake, his *leave me, loathsome light! receive me, silent night!* – marvellous lullaby of inertia, completely traumatized, every phrase slightly different within an overall effect of seamless sameness. Semele's four arias: *Myself, I shall adore*, apogee of narcissistic coloratura: *Thus let my thanks be paid*, self-love incarnate in languid sensuous siciliano: then, feeding her lover-god's advances yet fobbing them off, *I am ever granting, you always complain; I always am wanting, yet never obtain* – Handel's gift for characterization nails the eternal wheedle, and intensifies it in the orchestral coda: *No, no, I'll take no less* catches perfectly her vanity and folly; also, in the middle-eight, her imperious sexual hold over the intoxicated god. But now the inevitable come-uppance: she's tempted his fire and it will consume her.

Handel is always great with ineluctable fate. Jupiter – *'tis past recall, she must a victim fall*: but does not eschew a touch of tender almost-humour, promising his victim *my softest light'ning and mildest thunderbolt*. Realizing too late the consequence of her folly gives the heroine a fifth high point – in *vain* (her vanity) she implores pity – *O help! I can no more*: her voice collapses into flat monotone for the last four words; the orchestra eloquently expresses their pathos. Chorus expresses *terror and astonishment!* They are, as before, observers and commentary, outside the action – clear indication of Handel's future way forward, opera into oratorio, later also incorporating motet. Age-of-Reason nostrums: *Nature to each allots his proper sphere, / But that forsaken, we like meteors err, / And all our boasted fire is lost in smoke* – trite commonplaces, given weight and depth in this inspired setting: the sostenuto chromatic descent towards the end as smoke conceals the sacrifice particularly fine. Handel flourishes upon such situations, and such words.

Turning to the Old Testament oratorio (often now staged), I'm drawn by two dark heroes – *Saul* (1738), *Jephtha* (1751) – and a sublime heroine, *Theodora* (1749).

Saul is an Old Testament tragedy of personality, here darker and without happy issue, explored with the same combination of opera, oratorio, motet, by a composer whom the theme must have touched to the core. Again some highlights: in Part I, threatened by Saul's jealous madness, David answers in the sublime *O Lord whose mercies*: he begs the Lord *the busy fiend control* and *heal his wounded soul* – music's mythic power revived as with Orpheus and through-out Handel's oeuvre. In vain: the opening of Part II exposes the dark matter to light in a magnificent stately statement, orchestra in dotted rhythm then repeated chords over strong walking bass; chorus in long-note exchanges on salient opening word *Envy*, then severally, with motion, for *eldest born of hell*, joining in pairs for *cease in human breast to dwell*, severally again *for ever at all good repining / Still the happy undermining! / God and man by thee infested, / Thou by God and man detested!*; duetting again for *Most thyself thou dost torment, / At once the crime and punishment*; full choir again for *Hide thee in the blackest night! / Virtue sickens at thy sight!*; separate-voiced single notes on *hence, hence, hence*, while the orchestra rushes up in sickening scales; ending with a return to opening text to texture, two more *hence*, and a closing tutti *cease in human breasts to dwell*, twice. These simple mechanics show Handel's masterful manipulation of choral-writing at its most potent. Part III begins with another moment of superb dark introspection, Saul's recitative *Wretch that I am, of my own ruin author! Am I become coward? not so! If Heaven denies thee aid, seek it from Hell!* So to the Witch of Endor. After his foretold defeat and suicide comes the Dead March – grand simple play of *sonorités opposées*, brass full and rich, flutes high and flutey, both with drums, and all in the major. One of Handel's greatest choruses follows – *Mourn, Israel, mourn thy beauty lost: thy choicest youth dead, thy fairest hopes cross'd*: especially moving, the reiterated *mourn*; the silence; the unaccompanied setting, gapped thus: *thy choicest youth – on – Gilboa slain*: four bars stupefied orchestral coda. And despite another triumphal end, the work's heart of envy, insanity, defeat in battle – not to mention the death of David's beloved Jonathan – obliteration, lost in oblivion, the actual close is ambiguous: after loud choral rejoicing, an orchestral withdrawal by *diminuendo* – a subtle unobtrusive question-mark.

Jephtha: a more pathetic and human Old Testament subject, also poised, differently, to bring out the composer's deepest impulses. Again, magnificent inspirations alongside efficient humdrum, which fairly describes most of Part I. The turning-point occurs halfway through Part II when the consequences of Jephtha's rash vow – victory granted, to sacrifice the first person who'll greet his homecoming – are revealed: it's his daughter Iphis. His ensuing aria, *Open thy marble jaws, O tomb*, begins with one of Handel's mighty unisons: jagged, palpitant, shuddery; harmony when granted is tensely chromatic; the middle-eight more linear and sustained. The frightful vow is disclosed and must be enacted. Which introduces one of the score's and its composer's highest flights: a quartet – the mode now is distinctly operatic. Protagonist stands firm, reiterating over and over *recorded stands my vow in heav'n above*, then *I'll hear no more, her doom is fix'd, is fix'd as fate*, while the various pleas of the other three characters come and go, in vain. Jephtha has the last words, capped by the orchestra in stern unison. A magnificent piece.

Returning, Iphis has heard of the vow and accepts the consequences – her life is the price of her country's victory under her father's leadership – in an exquisite air of contented resignation – *Happy they*: no repining, *sinking in the arms of death* with strong fragility and fragile strength. He answers in tenebrous recitative – *deeper and deeper yet*: what pierces deepest is his child's goodness – *it pierceth a father's bleeding heart*. Does Jehovah sleep? No: heav'n heard my thought . . . *It must be so*: but my pangs *lash me into madness . . . tomorrow's dawn . . . I can no more!* This is worthy of Verdi's darkest male broodings. As Jephtha stammers to a close, another supreme chorus of bafflement in the face of fate's inescapable workings, and eventual resignation to them. *How dark, O Lord, are thy decrees*: slow dotted rhythm in the orchestra, harmonies as vagrant in obscurity as in radiance for *Zadok the Priest*; chorus mournfully drooping or else in block chords. Thence to flowing triple-time and two-part canonic writing, developing into a sort of round, uncannily serene for these words – *All our joys to sorrow turning . . . / As the night succeeds the day.* Now a vigorous *ordinario* fugue on *No certain bliss, / No solid peace, / We mortals know / On earth below*: it cadences into slow seriousness to proclaim the maxim that must be still ever obeyed. It is taken from Pope's *Essay on Man – Whatever is, is right*; and set with brusque peremptory rhetoric, hammered home whole or broken, some twelve times. Pope's maxim, on the face of it facile, even complacent, is given weight and profundity, the Palladian platitude wholly subsumed in this music's hard-won yea-saying renunciation. The structure, tone, texture, are those of a motet: one of the clearest places in all these works where the three separate genres – motet, opera, oratorio – meet and merge.

Whither after such? Part III begins with Jephtha in deep despair – *hide thou thy hated beams, O Sun*, a fine recitative into the justly adored *Waft her, angels* – dulcet chains of ascent, wafting the willing innocent sacrifice *far above your azure plain*: subtle reuse of these melismas in the voice-part of the middle-eight on *reign*; Iphis will *reign* for ever in her native heaven. She is demure, resigned, ready, bidding the priests not to fear to execute their unfamiliar office. She continues with *Farewell, ye limpid springs*, a muted slow siciliano bidding goodbye to the beauties of the world below, then opening out into steady common-time over walking bass – *Brighter scenes*

I seek above: placid perfection of the orchestral coda. The chorus retains the state of rapt acquiescence – *Doubtful fear and rev'rent awe*: the people bow to the law informing the sacred vow: whatever is, is right. Yet woe will out, distress is also voiced: the Lord will hear our prayer, and *thy determin'd will declare*. Might the outcome be altered . . . ?

It is: cheery sinfonia-dance blows away the woe (maybe too easily). An angel wafts downwards, declaring in recitative God's *true* intent: the maiden is to be sacrificed in a higher sense, *dedicated*, virgin-pure, to God's service. The angel's air promises a happy future in the virgin-choir; and, in the middle-eight, her immortal fame. In one wonderful page – *for ever blessed be thy holy name* – her father gives thanks. Chorus responds, hymning the *theme sublime of endless praise*, and invigorated for fugal celebration of God's ways, *just and righteous*, and his *enduring mercies, ever faithful, ever sure*. 'Whatever is' is still latent in the background, not needing to be spoken directly. The work could end well here: a more modern sensibility could have closed it with still greater weight with the maxim itself. As it now stands, the remainder reverts to moral-taking words set to humdrum music. The lesson of obedience really is trite, after the story wherein it is learnt has been explored so deeply! Everything after *ever faithful, ever sure*, though agreeable enough, is rum-tum-tum and rhubarb.

Theodora has no Old Testament origin: rather, it is a concoction involving Christians and pagans at odds in ancient Rome, rolled up with conflicts of love and duty; oblique and convoluted, will-ingly bypassed. The tortuous plot can be ignored: unignorable, the great chorus ending Part II, wherein religious and human concerns interact. The deception whereby Christian Theodora might have escaped shame has been rejected – she and her pagan lover will die together, a mutual sacrifice to both opposing ideologies. But how does this occasion the oratorio's finest music? Why now the chorus of Christians, *He saw the lovely youth*? Explanation doesn't cover the inexplicable that the words alone don't present directly. The Christians pray for their beloved Theodora's deliverance. In the un-divulged background they refer to the Widow of Nain (Luke 7:11–16), where Jesus bids the only son of his mother, 'and she a widow', to rise from the dead. *He saw the lovely youth, death's early prey*: a dulled funeral march with its dumb-speaking gapped orchestral rhythm, over which the voices' eloquent phrases interweave till a climactic *alas! too early snatch't away* and the single setting of *He heard a mother's fun'ral cries*. Slow minor lament yields to imperative fast major – *Rise, youth, he said*: rising scales enact the miracle. The ludicrous last line, *lowly the matron bow'd and bore away the prize* (in Luke's Gospel simply 'and he delivered him to his mother') has to be forgiven for the glorious flow of fugal felicity it inspired in the composer who takes it on. Handel declared this chorus 'far beyond' *Alleluia* in *Messiah*. Again, opera/oratorio has wholly devolved into motet.

Part III, as elsewhere in these works, is anti-climactic: loose ends are tied up, and the music tends towards routine.

Relief from dark biblical subjects with their almost operatic format, in *L'Allegro, il Penseroso ed il Moderato* (an eighteenth-century amelioration): serenata/cantata of 1740. Milton's linked diptych presenting the two eternally prevailing types, its ultimate source Democritus' laughing and weeping philosophers, is ingeniously cut up and re-spliced for maximum contrast and complement in a formalized argument. The music audibly flourishes upon these celebrated words: there's scarcely a duff moment: it reveals Handel the Pantheist Humanist, the thoughtful but untroubled lover of nature and of humanity in all its phases. No overture: straight in: *L'Allegro* (henceforth <u>A</u>) banishes *loathèd Melancholy* in fine serious-stern recitative – interesting, that its first ten bars contain, in the three possible diminished sevenths, all twelve semitones. *Il Penseroso* (henceforth <u>P</u>) answers: *hence, vain deluding joys*. Thus the argument is formally set up: subtle, that <u>A</u>'s first music be dark and minatory, <u>P</u>'s bright and gay. <u>A</u>'s first air invites Euphrosyne – *come, come, thou goddess fair and free*: <u>P</u>'s first prefers another deity – *come, rather, goddess sage and holy: Hail divinest Melancholy*. The contrast/complement thus established persists, chorus and four soloists exchanging roles with facility: most numbers are mercifully compact, all are freshly

inventive in characterization. A's *Haste thee, nymph* tenor air taken
up by a chorus of *Laughter holding both his sides* are particularly vivid
and visible, equally so the tenor's dance-number on the *light fantastic
toe* – again, the chorus continue. P's turn in a slow serious soprano
recitative invoking Milton's *pensive nun, devout and pure*, leading
to her air *Come, but keep thy wonted state*, a noble number, further
enhanced in its orchestral coda. The serious mood continued in recitative, voice now bold in ascent – *there, held in holy passion still*; and
descent – *with a sad leaden downward cast*: she now resumes her air
to further words invoking Peace and Quiet, then the Muses singing
round about Jove's altar: climax, long-held soft high B♭ – ecstatic:
again the chorus resume, and a sober unison orchestral coda. Such
linked continuities are as vital to the work's conviction and calibre
as the contrasts upon which it is equally based. A banishes the music
of the spheres – *Mirth, admit me of thy crew* (Liberty too is invited) –
in scampering hilarity that might be merely naïve, nay idiotic –
see/hear *then to come, in spite of sorrow / And at my window bid good
morrow*, and its later echo on high violins – were it not so irresistible. P's turn again – *Contemplation* invited, with Philomel and her
nightingale: *Sweet bird, that shun'st the noise of folly*, soprano and flute
perfectly paired, all delicious delicate flutter: very long, unusually
in this work; its plainer middle-eight presents a grand rising of the
moon *to her highest noon*: the da capo gratefully varies the two birds,
vocal and instrumental. This music is as 'imbecile' as A's receding
mirth: they balance out. A again invokes Mirth, now to preside over
hunting, with splendid lusty horn obbligato. P responds in a meditative evening-scene, the dull boom of the curfew represented by
deep pizzicato. Handel is sensitive to Milton's *strangeness*, desiring
a place where *gloomy embers through the room / Teach light to coun-
terfeit a gloom*. The soprano soloist continues the thoughtful vein
in broad lyricism – *Far from all resort of mirth*, with its remarkable
melisma on *save* [i.e. *except*] – *save the cricket on the hearth*. Her air
now presents the bellman's drowsy charm with daring bareness: as elsewhere, Handel can pare down with extraordinary effect – the texture
empties again for just two bars in the orchestral coda standing in
for absent and superfluous da capo. Now a more pensive A: *Let me*

wander, not unseen – slow gentle siciliana, pastoral cast of plough-man, milkmaid, mower, shepherd – till he's diverted by *new pleasures*, albeit still relatively sober and pastoral. Now, however, an unwonted trespass into P̲'s territory – grand accompanied recitative evoking *mountains, shallow brooks and rivers wide*, and resplendent *tow'rs and battlements*. Laughter reassumes the land – *Let the merry bells ring round*: a carillon to hand, youths and maids *dancing in the chequer'd shade*: chorus also imitate the bells, *and young and old come forth to play*. As daylight fails, motion broadens: beautiful creeping to bed, *by whisp'ring winds soon lull'd to sleep* – winding down, slower, softer, lull'd to sleep, slumber deep, the orchestral coda a temporary truce in *L'Allegro*'s pensive close to Part I.

In Part II the same paired mingling antithesis as before. P̲ kicks off, banishing *vain deluding joys* in recitative, inviting studious night of philosophic contemplation, Plato to guide; this introduces an air, *Sometimes let gorgeous Tragedy* – with stately suavity she comes *sweeping by*, dignity personified. The tone continues in P̲'s next, a long elaborate air, cello obbligato florid as the voice – *But Oh, sad virgin, that thy power / Might raise Musaeus from his bower* – a fine number, often omitted. Solitary meditation banished by morning and *Populous cities*, cheerfully hailed by A̲'s bass soloist, taken up by A̲ in chorus, refreshed and invigorated after the deep slumber closing Part I. *The busy busy busy hum of men* holding their high triumphs infectiously rendered; almost an Alleluia-chorus in brief: then the ladies, a dainty middle-eight in triple-time; then the men return. *Populous cities please me then* – Handel the townee, avid and eager as the countryman. Hymen now appears in a tenor air. Contemplative solitude soon resumes – *Hide me from day's garish eye*, invoking bees, sleep, dream – another pearl of price. But A̲ resumes city-pleasures: to the theatre, lively and pompous: *knowing*, too: Milton refers to learnèd Jonson and natural Shakespeare: Handel the impresario who'd tasted fortune and bankruptcy must have smiled and sighed. The order of the numbers around here varies from score to score and performance to performance: perhaps this responds to a sort of merger between A̲ and P̲ for *Ever, against eating cares / Lap me in soft Lydian airs*. Music the object now – *many a winding bout / Of linkèd sweetness long drawn out*: quite so! No composer ever more suited than Handel to demonstrate this, and reveal *the hidden soul of harmony* with the simplest means. *Orpheus himself may heave his head*, and Pluto's ear be won over, with *such strains*. But it's A̱ for sure who continues: *These delights if thou canst give / Mirth, with thee I mean to live*. The chorus lustily take up the soloist; a brave pair of trumpets crown the vow. P̱ is now due to reassert the inner life: the cloister calls, *casting a dim religious light*, in recitative followed by solemn homophonic chorus evoking *the pealing organ and full-voic'd choir* at their *service high and anthems clear* – opening for organ improvisation between the choral phrases. P̱ is dissolved into ecstasies that *bring all Heav'n before mine eyes*. Also a vision of what's to come – *May at last my weary age*, a very fine piece, all acquiescence without tragedy. At the last, Wisdom, Knowledge, Experience *do attain / To something like prophetic strain*. The P̱ chorus sing in plain serious fugue: *These pleasures, Melancholy, give, / And we with thee will choose to live*, balancing A̱'s earlier bargain. Now to resolve.

Il Moderato (henceforth M̱) has occasioned the mirth of the Cheerful and the contempt of the Pensive. Both are mistaken. The concept shouldn't be mocked, nor its verse despised. A neutral personification of the Middle Way, equipoised without compromise between two rejected extremes, is fruitfully explored by Handel's librettist Charles Jennens. Of course, he's no Milton: he provides what's required, and the composer's response is ardent. It begins with a recitative inviting *Temperance, Health, Contentment, Frugality, Chaste Love, by Reason led*. M̱'s first air continues the sagacity – *Keep, as of old, the middle way, / Now deeply sad, not idly gay . . . / Easy, cheerful, and sedate*: this sober/sensible language – Moderation's *native lustre* – is matched in the setting: bass solo leads, chorus follows in *company serene*. Now a soprano M̱ – *Come, with gentle hand restrain* – urges again that extremes be shunned – *prudent keep the golden mean*. Not a Miltonic virtue! Pope would certainly better have expressed what oft had been thought: but the sentiments, pure Augustan, are deeply felt and unimpugnably authentic. A recitative hammers the platitude home, each extreme deplored in turn – *frantic mirth and childish play*, or *lifeless, ever musing, moping, dreaming*. It opens the next air,

Each action will derive new grace: *they are order, measure, time, and place*, interestingly rendered in interlocking hemiola; not the usual 2 + 2 + 2 in triple-time (3 + 3); a real 9/4 athwart the pulse – *due proportion* embodied with smooth naturalness. Now comes the crown jewel of *Il Moderato* and of the work as a whole: duet for soprano and tenor with obbligato oboe and bassoon, *As steals the moon upon the night*: *Truth* and *Reason* expel fumes clouding the mind, *restoring intellectual Day*: one of Handel's supreme lyric utterances, rapt and seraphic in total tranquillity. So to the concluding apostrophe, balancing those previously uttered by *L'Allegro* and *Il Penseroso* in words not unworthy of the Milton they echo: *Thy pleasures, Moderation, give / In them alone we truly live*: a solid *moderato* fugue, not one of Handel's greatest, just right for here, *in them alone* oft-repeated without didactic emphasis: placid, rock-certain.

This adorable work wherein a great English poet is matched with a great naturalized-English composer, makes a rewarding comparison with a later masterpiece with a parallel provenance: Haydn's *Seasons*, its composer inspired by encountering his predecessor's choral works in England, the text, translated into German from James Thomson's *Seasons* (completed 1730), itself strongly Miltonized. Haydn's Deity is explicit; Handel's, his presiding ideals being Reason and the Golden Mean, more a sense of 'dim, religious light'. Yet both works share a reverent joy in, wonder at, gratitude for, natural beauty; and celebrate humanity's submission to the cycle of birth, growth, decay, rebirth, expressed with contentment, acceptance, cheer, normality; and endless exuberance of musical invention.

Oratorio and motet: Old Testament promise; New Testament fulfilment

Israel in Egypt (1739) is very original in being almost completely chorus-grounded: recitatives and airs for the soloists are easily outnumbered by the choir's contribution, which carries the weight and makes the basis of the work's grandeur. And it is very *unoriginal* in the high proportion of self-adaptations and outright thefts from other composers, senior and contemporary: the work is a *locus classicus* for this common practice, Handel its principal practitioner. Deplored in the era when originality was a touchstone, better understood after an era of eclecticism, influence, imitation, or what Stravinsky dubbed 'kleptomania' – encapsulated in Eliot's 'minor poets imitate, great poets steal' – a return to vindication of what, in between, was regarded as flagrant. Later in Handel's own century it was remarked of this very work that 'he takes pebbles and converts them to diamonds'.

Part I: *Israel* originally opened with *The Ways of Zion do mourn*, a funeral anthem for Queen Caroline (1737), adapted to become 'the lamentation of the Israelites over the death of Joseph'. Since the first sustained music in the oratorio is also a chorus of lamentation, the double-dose was wisely seen as too much: and with the absence of overture, the immediate plunge from plain recitative – *Now there arose a new king over Egypt, which knew not Joseph; and he set over Israel taskmasters to afflict them with burdens; and they made them serve with rigour* – is immediately electrifying. The ensuing chorus of affliction is one of Handel's finest: double choir, skilfully deployed, flowing motion with gapped sighs, long-breathed crying unto God under the rigorous bondage, which cry eventually rises up to God. Brief recitative introduces Moses and Aaron, who initiate signs and wonders.

The remainder of Part I graphically depicts the seven plagues. First, water into blood – *they loathèd to drink of the river*; gawky fugal first half, second all slithery, the chromatics of each infiltrating the other, all convincingly slimy. Now for frogs, alto solo; they hop visibly: it modulates into the third – *blotches and blains broke forth on man and beast* – not distinctive visually, and the number ends with a coda of jumping frogs. Such relative cheer is quelled by a stern call-to-order: *the Lord spoke the word*, introducing the fourth (though the plagues' order in Exodus is mutated for artistic purposes) – *all manner of flies*: virtuoso fizzy zizzing for the violins as the double-chorus bounce the nasty insects to and fro. The plague of locusts is included here rather than later, making effective culmination as they *came without number and devour'd the fruits of the ground*. No need to halt the momentum with tedious negotiations between Moses and Pharaoh – plagues follow headlong: hailstones, *fire mingled with the hail* is positively exuberant, as though these destructive freaks of nature were admired and relished. Not so the next, *a thick darkness over all the land, even darkness which might be felt*: magnificent opening, orchestral then choral homophony, after which the massed voices disintegrate into broken phrases of measured recitative, reiterating the same words, bemused, lost in the obscurity. Vigour returns for the destruction of the first-born – a sturdy choral fugue set against mighty smiting for the orchestra; later the roles reverse: the strength of Egypt graphically emasculated in the closing bars. Plagues completed, a celebration. *But as for his people*, prosaic introduction to suave melodious continuation, *he led them he led them* [the same words come and come] *forth like sheep* – great arc of graciousness, generous contours, more momentum for *silver and gold*, back to solid introduction initiating further ample arches: it comes and comes till the glorious triumphal end – *there was not one feeble person among their tribes*. Nowhere in Handel shows better how he achieves 'the greatest effects with the simplest means'. *Egypt was glad when they departed* not on the same plane: the Israelites' satisfaction somewhat stolid till – great effect, simple means – the two slow-motion closing chords on orchestra alone. The Red Sea is rebuked with grandeur – *and it was dried up*. The passage through the deep, and the waters returning to overwhelm the Egyptian pursuit – not one left (second-born and feeble as they now are) – are rendered with splendid turbulent energy in this closing sequence of five successive choruses, closing with solemn thanks and confirmation of faith in Moses and his God.

Part II: the exodus is complete, the shouting remains: *Moses' Song*, twenty-three numbers of almost unalleviated triumphalism. The first chorus setting off the victorious trail begins with another of Handel's greatest/simplest moments – stately *pomposo* succession of common chords in uncommon juxtapositions, followed by plain double-choir homophony – *and spake, saying: I will sing* – vigorous fugue setting long notes across purposeful activity – *the horse and his rider hath he thrown into the sea*: the busy texture coalesces into

exclamation so vehement as to be aggressive. Next, duet for two
trebles – *The Lord is my strength* – turns exclamation into exuberance, florid and solid. Next, one page for all the forces vocal and
instrumental that gets Handel's simple splendour in a nutshell –
He is my God, and I will prepare him an habitation, my father's God
just once, grandiose block chords for contrast. Music like this has
one understand Samuel Butler's exaltation of Handel far above all
other composers. Perhaps not, however, for the celebrated duet for
two basses that follows, *The Lord is a man of war*, in Victorian performances often rendered by the massed men of the already vast choral
body – two hundred to each part! Even with just two, the crowing
tone – *Pharaoh's chariots and his host hath he cast into the sea ... his
chosen captains are also drowned in the Red Sea* – is gloatingly offensive, though the rhetoric is terrific.

Triumphalism continues rampant: even when the level is high,
as the next double-chorus, *the depths have covered them*, for all its succession of well-judged contrasts of speeds and textures, spirit and
flesh are repleted. Notwithstanding the grand-grind dissonance on
the first syllable of the fourth word (*and in the greatness of thine excel-
lency*), nor (after a relatively dull fugue on *thou sentest forth thy wrath,
which consum'd them as stubble*), nor the tremendous voice-writing
for the gathered waters (standing *upright as an heap*), one is sated
at the insistent victorious vengefulness and vindication. Welcome
relief with a treble solo extolling the winds, though these too prove
destructive not refreshing – the Egyptians sink *as lead in the mighty
waters*. Another one-page wonder, *Who is like unto thee, O Lord among
the Gods?* has one exclaim the same in reference to Handel himself.
But it introduces another rather routine fugue wherein the wretched
Egyptians, having been drowned in the sea, are now swallowed up
by the earth. Followed by a suavely gracious duet, sensuously singing
the Lord's mercy: the work's best number not choral. Now comes
its best of any description. The double-chorus, *The people shall hear*,
is truly awesome: primitive triumphalism subsumed into compunction: the people hear, and fear, sorrow seizes hold of them: all this
forms a first paragraph of incomparable grandeur. Which now *melts
away*: all the inhabitants of Canaan melt away for bar upon bar,

the cause only given once to close this second paragraph – *by the greatness of thy arm*. Third paragraph alternates bare unison – *they shall be as still as a stone*, with overlapping rising figure – *till thy people pass over, O Lord, which thou hast purchasèd* – endless flights of angels, implicitly consolidating the first Covenant binding God to his Chosen People. This is the work's heart, for Tovey the greatest single movement in all Handel's works. Hard to disagree, though its composer himself indignantly preferred another (see *Theodora* above). *Israel in Egypt* might well end here. Instead, another chorus resuming triumph/victory with muscular prowess: one senses a coronation is being celebrated, or at least a Lord Mayor's inauguration, rather than the Lord of the Covenant. Moses' sister, the prophetess Miriam, leads the Israelites in a cantus firmus dominating in all voices successively the energetic bustle all around, working to a recapitulation of the horse-and-his-rider from earlier.

The Old Dispensation is succeeded by the New: *Messiah* was conceived from the start as *Israel*'s continuation and consequence. Composed between 22 August and 12 September 1741 (and with no recycling – all material new), astonishing even for this speed-merchant: first performed in Dublin the following spring: back in England it was soon established as a national treasure, much revived by its composer in endlessly different versions pragmatically altered to suit changing circumstances. Later in the century it was given 'additional accompaniments' (sometimes of high inspiration) by Mozart: ever-expanded down the nineteenth century, culminating in the mammoth performances mounted in the Crystal Palace, although the work was ubiquitous the length and breadth of the land, especially in the North; a staple ingredient of the British Way of Life. In recent times, stripped down to its authentic speeds, instrumental and choral forces, and character, it is no less popular or revered: the apex of the genre. Text from both Testaments, ingeniously put together by Handel's trusted librettist Jennens, tells the Messiah's role in three parts: first, the prophecies of his coming and their first fulfilment in the Christmas story: second, Christ the 'Suffering Servant', concentrating upon his Passion (though not a narrative à la Bach) and, by implication, his Resurrection, culminating in *Alleluia*: third, Christ's own prophecies fulfilled, culminating in his Return. Rock-solid scheme, seen through by the composer with the visionary inspiration implied by the composition-dates. There's scarcely a dud number in the fifty-or-so total: even with no plot or characters, a strong sense of ongoing narration and, in the arias, of characterization, wherein contrasts and complements are human, not didactic/theological. Yet the idiom often remains operatic – no need to relinquish what he'd required and employed for a *Giulio Cesare*, a *Rinaldo*, a *Rodelinda*, an *Ariodante*.

Part I: Attention alerted (after usual-ish overture) by the first recitative, employing the contour-setting *comfort ye* throughout on the orchestra, however much the tenor's text changes: *saith your God* – it's God's voice speaking the comforting three-note phrase. Heard again, now clear and confident, in the first chorus *And the glory of the Lord*, with declamation low then high on long monotone set across a sturdy minuet – *for the mouth of the Lord hath spoken it*. Every aria is top-drawer: finest so far, *But who may abide the day of his coming?* – melting grace enclosing a middle-eight of angry *refiner's fire*. The Christmas story keeps it up. Old Testament prophecies come to light – good tidings to Zion; *arise, shine, for thy light is come* – and dark, *even a darkness which might be felt* (chiming with the thick dark plague in *Israel*) in the superb recitative preceding the superb *People that walkèd in darkness* with its creeping/groping unison, long vocal phrases on *death* (the shadow of) while the orchestra struggles upward and downward back to its initial note. Prophecies substantiated: *For unto us a child is born*, with its exuberant vocal fanfares on *Wonderful! Counsellor!* This *everlasting Father,* this *Prince of Peace,* is also a man of war, as the *real* trumpets and drums confirm. Delicate grace ensues in the *Pifa*, the shepherds' siciliano serenade. An angel appears with *good tidings of great joy*: suddenly he is joined by his heavenly companions, *praising God and saying* – glorious chorus, its trumpets now celestial not military, '*da lontano e poco piano*' – *glory in the highest, peace on earth* – lovely play of animation in the heights and stillness in the depths. *Good will towards men* waxes fugal and human, the angels' vanishing re-ascent at the end graphic, at once naïve, amusing, touching. Soprano air with obbligato violin *Rejoice greatly* very fine, brilliant in outer sections, languishingly inviting – *he shall speak peace* – in the centre. Yet surpassed by the alto's *He shall feed his flock*, the ultimate pastorale, with its inspired change halfway through, changed words – *come unto him* – set to the same music: repose after labour and heavy burdens personified in the music, even unto embodying the Messiah's meekness and lowliness of heart. *His yoke is easy* – not so easy for the choir! *His burthen is light* – just so: the music bubbles with charm and high spirits, most unusually pushing the sopranos up to a momentary high Bb – easiness and lightness personified in turn, before, at this close to Part I, weight and effort are recalled.

Part II, again following the New Testament's fulfilment of prophecies and promises made in the Old, presents Christ the Suffering Servant. From the very start, an intonation not yet heard: *Behold the lamb of God* – stately serious dotted rhythms, against them a Handel speciality, long sustained last word of *that takest away the sins of the world*. Alto air, *He was despisèd*: again the orchestra recalls the vocal shape throughout, however the text changes: affective chromatic harmony for *acquainted with grief*, with play of major/minor, escaping each time to major. In the middle section *He* (never named) is subjected to physical tortures and the mental torment of mockery and shame: his Passion anticipated. The ensuing chorus *Surely he hath borne our griefs and carried our sorrows* is grand, a choral sequence, at first on the same implacable dotted rhythm, broadening out for his wounds and bruises, returning for his chastisement, opening up into *And with his stripes we are healèd*, fugue on a favourite baroque tag affective of suffering, achieving cheer out of pain in *All we like sheep* with its alternation of confidence and waywardness – *we have turnèd every one to his own way*, errant and astray, *turnèd* every direction, not without humour, till the devastating adagio close – *and the Lord hath laid on him the iniquity of us all.*

More Messiah-mocking: remarkable and effective that the Passion story is not told direct – present, powerful, by implication and analogue. Yet *He trusted in God that he would deliver him* has the spite and viciousness of the crowd in Bach's *St John Passion. Thy rebuke hath broken his heart* – heartbreaking recitative: *Behold and see if there be any sorrow* a miniature pearl of pathos; recitative *he was cut off from the land of the living*: aria of comfort and reassurance *but thou didst not leave his soul in hell*. Simply listing this sequence is to realize its origin in, its dependence on, the composer's long experience in opera, now essentialized and intensified into this *Sacred Oratorio* (as *Messiah*'s title-page declares). Thus, stage by stage (albeit in church or concert hall) to triumph and rejoicing. *Lift up your heads* an echo-chorus – imperatives, questions, answers, bounced between upper and lower voices, then their roles reversed, then all joining in the unanimous answer to *Who?* – *He is the King of Glory*. Then *all the angels of God* add their adoration.

Now the work seems briefly to lose the thread, straying like sheep each to his own way. Bass air *Thou art gone up on high* a touch routine, chorus about the great company of the preachers rum-tum. Even the celebrated *How beautiful are the feet* seems misplaced. Go forth, preach *glad tidings of good things*: but what are they? There's been neither Crucifixion nor Resurrection: the plot has indicated Ascension, and jumped to the Apostles and their mission – *their sound is gone out into all lands*. But why *Why do the nations?*, the famous bass showpiece querying the peoples' vain imaginings? *Let us break their bonds asunder* cry the chorus; *and cast away their yokes from us* – strayed in from Part I of *Israel in Egypt*. *Thou shalt break them*, famous tenor showpiece of anger, revenge, punishment, breaking them (who?) with rods of iron, dashing them in pieces (why?) like a potter's vessel. Thus – but not cogently – into *Alleluia*: ultimate triumph of Handel's greatest effects with simplest means; basic tattoos and fanfares, commonest common chords, long declamatory single-note unisons extending in broad cantus firmus from basses to high trumpet: sober homophony, soft for *the kingdoms of this world ... is become* – then blazing forth into *the kingdom of our Lord, and of his Christ* (the first time the title-protagonist is actually named). This passage only the once: after it, all the ingredients in place *for ever and ever* – fugue and tattoo and long-held single-note motif worked up in unforgettable resplendence: an Archetype.

Part III – 'Christ's Promises fulfilled – his Return': and first, his Rise – glorious soprano air *I know that my Redeemer liveth*: all Handel's ardent amplitude and grace, rising visibly at the second setting of *for now is Christ risen, for now is Christ risen from the dead* (the first setting had been understated). The orchestra's lulling dotted-note figure seems to be suggested by mention of *worms* who *destroy this body*: later it becomes an image for repose – *the first fruits of them that sleep*. From here on, Theology takes centre stage: Pauline theology. *Since by man came death*, grave: *by man came also the resurrection of the dead*, triumphant. *For as in Adam all die*, grave: *even so in Christ shall all be made alive*, exuberant. The mystery of transformation *at the last trumpet* yields the instrument's showpiece bravura obbligato to the bass aria: *the dead shall rise incorruptible, and we shall all be changed*. A very Pauline conundrum for its middle-eight – *this corruption must put on incorruption; and this mortal must put on immortality*: Handel manages, just. A sweet canoodling duet dispatches death's sting and grave's victory: the ensuing chorus of thanks feels a little routine: soprano air *If God is for us who can be against us?* copes manfully with Paul's jaw-breaking vocabulary – *who shall lay anything to the charge of God's elect?* etc. So – because it comes next rather than because it makes cogent consequence – to *Worthy is the Lamb*. These ultimate choral numbers, with sturdy *Amen* to conclude, are slightly tame and very standard: far from adding further to *Alleluia* – impossible anyway – they actually detract from it.

A Note on Gluck

Christoph Willibald Gluck: born 1714 into a family of gamekeep-ers serving minor Bohemian royalty; studied law then music at Prague: to Vienna, then Milan and Venice, where his earliest operas produced with success. Vienna again, and a few years in London, encountering Handel; often travelling the continent, touring with an opera-company: eventually its director. More permanently back in Vienna 1752 – many stage-works, conventionally adapted to the taste of the time. Turning-point, collaboration with librettist Ranieri de' Calzabigi: together they engineer the celebrated reform of the genre, *Orfeo* (1762) its first manifestation, *Alceste* (1766–7) and the famous Preface its polemic vindication. Despite acclaim, Gluck moved in 1772 to Paris, potentially a more fruitful ground for the new ideals. Despite polemical squabbles, acclaim here too, its high point centred around the two *Iphigénie* operas – *in Aulis* (1771–3), *in Tauris* (1778), and the French revision of *Orphée* (1774). His last Parisian venture, *Echo et Narcisse* (1779), a failure: he returned to Vienna, dying there in 1787.

Gluck is vitally important as – more than its reformer – the second founder of opera, reaffirming, albeit with no historical connection to the Camerata and Monteverdi, the genre's first principles – classical subjects, truth to nature, primacy of words, purity of purpose. Reform consists in ridding the genre of stulti-fying conventions that had gradually accrued and hardened across the century-and-a-half since its earliest exemplars, seen at their apogee in the essentially Italian art of Handel. Abuses to be dis-carded: primacy of singers and scenery; perpetual back-to-square-one of the da capo structure, inhibiting dramatic momentum; plots, anyway idiotic and incoherent, failing to purposefully interact with the score. (That all this had been already achieved in Charpentier's

Médée and several pieces by Rameau seems somehow not to figure.) Gluck's neo-classical music-theatre influenced Mozart for certain, Beethoven possibly. Berlioz adored him for the stance and the music too; Wagner admired the force and cogency of the theory, and also paid the practical homage of staging the Aulis *Iphigénie* (Dresden 1847) in his own 'critical' version. Admiration for the stagecraft continued into the twentieth century with Mahler then Strauss. Tovey devoted a fine essay to the music as such.

But the music as such is the sticking-point. Gluck's is so threadbare, flattened, lacking in surprise or personality, restricted in affective range, in melody, in harmony, in counterpoint, in colour: in effect, dull. The stagecraft is unimpugnable: I recall once seeing *Idomeneo* and *Iphigénie en Tauride* in the same few days. Gluck's work gripping in timing, pacing, articulation: Mozart's, musically an incomparable masterpiece, didn't come to life in any of these respects – a 'concert in costume' by one of the two greatest dramatists-in-music, who'd not yet found the ideal means-and-ends for his genius. Gluck's admirers claim inner fire with an exterior to match Winckelmann's ideal of 'noble simplicity and calm grandeur'. I hear only frigidity. Let us explore!

Orfeo ed Euridice presents much bother over versions – the Vienna original being in Italian, the Paris revision in French. The consensus seems to favour the latter, except when it's been too fussed-up, but returns to the former for its more coherent tonal scheme, spoilt in the later substitution of tenor for castrato in the hero's role (itself often famously taken by a contralto). This account follows Vienna mainly. Overture absurdly perky, irrelevant, trivial. The pastoral chorus mourns Euridice: Orpheus plangently interjects with standard pathos, rousing to reproach the cruelty of fate. Amor answers in a neat little minuet which then turns gigue-wards – through the power of love you will gain her again. The bargain is made – Love will see you righted. So far, no thrills. Which do materialize when the Underworld is reached – Furies with their stark jagged ferocity, including rendition of Cerberus barking. Orpheus strikes his lyre and sings. They dance long and stormy, ending after a long diminuendo in a surprising major. He pleads, they stamp *No!* thirteen times, but are eventually half-placated. His grief explains his need, his music defeats them – permission granted to enter and retrieve Euridice. Elysian Fields another good moment, with famous flute solo and lovely scoring all around: the ballet-music retains calm serenity, undifferentiated and finally insipid. Orpheus's greeting to the pure clear sky is justly celebrated – oboe sings, flute flutters, strings ripple and purr. The Blessed Spirits do not have to be won over by his art: they appreciate without reluctance: but only *she* can restore his life. Euridice is completely uncharacterized – interminable dull recitative, then a feeble little duet, cover the crucial situation: *he* mustn't see her, and must not explain the bargain: *she*, ignorant, complains of his apparent indifference: both are in distress that cannot be resolved, though could certainly be expressed in music less wooden. The crisis – he turns to look, she dies again, all in very ordinary recitative. So the *che faro/j'ai perdu*, the oddly suave-bland air of his second loss. *Que faire?* To Hades again? No! – I'll kill myself. *No!* Amor prevents, and in a trice all is happiness – he's passed the ordeal, Love is stronger than Death, she lives again, re-restored to him in a pastoral landscape as blissful as Elysium below. All the closing music as commonplace as the overture beginning the work. 'I neither see, nor feel, nor hear' the quality that has Tovey call *Orfeo* 'one of the most intense of all music dramas'. Let's try another: *en Aulide*.

I follow Wagner's masterly 'reform' for the production he directed shortly before his long exile from Germany. He cuts extensively to reach the core, elides and joins with unerring instinct, intensifies, sometimes providing new material entirely within the spirit, even the letter, of an original he clearly admires. Witness the return, after storm, of the fine pathetic strains with which the opera opens, tactfully and unobtrusively extended to run into the same material for Agamemnon's first words pleading with Artemis/Diana to relent, still the storm, permit his fleet to sail on to Troy. No irrelevant perkiness here – this overture already germane to the situation. The angry goddess demands a victim, to be named this very day. Calchas, priest of her temple, has been told that the victim must be Agamemnon's daughter Iphigénie. He too pleads, they plead together, in vain. Agamemnon queries – how can a goddess require a father to sacrifice a daughter? He won't obey: he heeds '*le cri plaintif de la nature*', which speaks truly to his heart – a fine passage highly praised by Berlioz. But for the most part the music is stiff and pedestrian. With her mother Clytemnestra, Iphigénie is already arrived, to be married to Achilles. Her father spreads a deceitful rumour that Achilles is faithless. Believing this, Clytemnestra urges their daughter to return home. Achilles, ignorant of the false charge, meets his bride and is hurt to be received with disdain. When enlightened, he repudiates the slur, and the couple are reunited. Wagner has cut huge swathes of recitative (and *ballet* – so much for reform): what remains, though purposeful, is mostly humdrum and unmemorable.

Anxiety continues. Achilles learns that Agamemnon still suspects his loyalty to his affianced, yet has ordered ceremonial as if in preparation for their nuptials. His real intention is quite other: to sacrifice Iphigénie in propitiation of the angry goddess, thereby gaining favourable winds for his war-fleet. The Greek hero confronts his King and remonstrates – cardboard recitative then almost buffo duet, the King's vacillating anguish barely even attempted. Striking, though, Clytemnestra's vision of the imminent sacrifice, her husband's knife at their daughter's throat: not striking *musically*; rather, for its oddity and gestural quality. Elsewhere, conventionality and sometimes blandness. The people angrily demand the sacrifice proceed. Achilles challenges them, though Iphigénie is willing to make the placatory offering. Crucial moment; anger appeased, bloodshed averted: Calchas proclaims that the goddess has relented, her wrath reversed by what she has perceived of human calibre – Clytemnestra's tears, Achilles' valour, Iphigénie's nobility. The score's finest moment here: all these three, plus Agamemnon, in a quartet of relief and harmony, serene to start, ending in rejoicing. Then plenty of festive dancing and, to close, a big chaconne, all cut by Wagner's reforming shears. His performing version improves the sense of the plot throughout; pacing is tightened, characterization sharpened. When he infills, he's got the idiom and temperature just right: if fustian or cardboard needed, he provides, and there's life in it; yet he doesn't interpose himself. And Diana's intervention, not in Gluck, is inspired – a real denouement where the original was funked or fudged, using the good fragments from it, and its one fine number complete: then straight into a brief-but-judicious festive close that reintroduces the principal motif from Gluck's overture with mastery.

Wretched Iphigénie: having nearly lost her life in Aulis, she's put to a still severer test *en Tauride*. Gluck's treatment of the sequel is surely his finest work, achieving its goal, limitations overcome and stretched into strengths. It needs no Wagner's reforming hand: and Berlioz's words *glow*:

> I read his scores time and time again, I copied them, I memo-rized them, they robbed me of sleep, made me forget eating and drinking: I was utterly enraptured. And on the day when, after much anxious expectation, it was granted me finally to hear *Iphi-génie en Tauride*, I swore on leaving the theatre that in the teeth of Father, Mother, uncles, aunts, grandparents, friends, I would become a composer.

Yet reservations continue, and prevail. There are striking moments in Act I – a *real* overture to what it initiates, all sweet placidity – distant storm discerned – it nears, it explodes in rain, hail, wind, soon to be mirrored in the heroine's opening recitative – in my heart the turbulence continues. A comparable effect comes early in Act II: Orestes challenges the gods in stern recitative, collapsing exhausted into deceptive tranquillity – *le calme rentre dans mon coeur*, with its famous antithesis of the words in their pulsating *sforzando* accompaniment, a complex effect achieved with masterly simpli-city. The Furies mime their menace with crashing hammer-blows, naïvely illustrative and absolutely right. Their voices torment him with imminent punishment; he cries out in anguish; the shade of his murdered mother appears as they exclaim *il a tué sa mère*. All this is classic art. But the gradual *éclaircissement* with his sister comes in many pages of neutral recitative. Music revives as Iphigénie's priest-esses bewail, and rises to what heights Gluck can command with her

O malheureuse Iphigénie that so especially fired Berlioz. The women join, the number dies down – the affect is marmoreal – static – a frieze. But the work's climax, Diana's appearance in Act IV as *dea ex machina*, is completely non-numinous: how could the composer be so dull to the opportunity? She settles every tangle and sorts the destinies of her votaries with the brisk dispatch of an efficient committee chairman; and the close in general rejoicing is as commonplace as could be.

All-told, a greater feel for timing and pacing, and a far higher rate of musical interest and value, in Tauris than in Aulis. But how can Gluck be said to have reformed opera? Opera had already been reformed, along much the same lines, by composers incomparably stronger. In the face of *Médée*, *Hippolyte et Aricie*, *Dardanus*, *Castor et Pollux*, the Gluckian corpus shines dim and wan – next stop Mozart.

CHAPTER V

J. S. Bach

Born 1685, into an extensive musical clan widespread in Saxony whose accumulated skills and experience he inherits and harvests: early education subject to ill-temperament, early life to many bereavements – death of mother in 1694, of newly wed father the next year. Early employments as organist witness to remarkable gifts widely acknowledged from the start: Weimar 1703; Arnstadt; Mülhausen 1707 (his first marriage in his first year there); Weimar again 1708–17, ending in undignified dismissal; Cöthen 1717–23, where his first wife dies and he re-marries (1721) – many children with both spouses, with awfully poor survival rate. In 1723 to his ultimate employment as cantor of the Thomaskirche in Leipzig. This position inaugurates astonishing industry: as well as the projected three cycles of weekly cantatas to cover the Church-year, the *Magnificat* (1723), *St John Passion* (first version 1724), the *St Matthew Passion* (first given 1727). Alongside this, copious production of purely instrumental music: *sacred* – for his own principal instrument the organ, of which he was recognized without dispute as a master: *secular* – concertos for various solo and duo combinations, particularly the six *Brandenburgs* from the Cöthen years; suites of other pieces for klavier, solo violin, solo cello; works of teaching and learning – the two books of twenty-four Preludes and Fugues in all the twelve major and minor keys (Book I 1722, Book II completed 1742) – 'well-tempered' (i.e. to consolidate practical playing and intervallic character).

Altercations with authorities civic and ecclesiastical: but recognition in wider spheres, and enthusiastic adoption by a learnèd society for whom musical composition was a branch of scientific investigation, in which direction his comprehensive contrapuntal and proportional explorations had always tended. Withdrawing from functional work for the Church-year into monuments of abstraction – *Goldberg Variations* (published 1741) and *Musical Offering* from the same year, both of them ultimate pinnacles of canon till joined in 1748 by the canonic variations for organ on *Von Himmel hoch*: ultimate exploration of fugue in *The Art of Fugue* (not quite completed). A late summa of a different kind, *Mass in B-minor*, put together from recycled cantata and *missa brevis* material into a vast composite without any realistic possibility of performance whether secular or liturgical. Died 1750 aged sixty-five.

'The difficulty of writing anything on Bach remotely worthy of its subject', remarks one of his best biographers. The very name has always been symbolic/emblematic: a *stream*, in both senses: it flows, ever strong, natural, fresh, nourishing, fertilizing: and it *streams*, copious and universal, like the *omnes generationes* of the Bach family down the seventeenth and eighteenth centuries in their corner of Germany, then, subsequently, thanks to their greatest manifestation, copious and universal in the musical culture of every time and place.

Exceptions to his stature and nature are few and perverse. There are of course reservations, adversions, resistances: but it's difficult to think of any composer, performer, lover of music, for whom Bach is not the Grand Central meeting-point/exchange-rate/gold-standard/source-and-goal. He represents music itself at its essence: what it *is*, what it is *for*.

That he was 'forgotten' for many years after his death is at best a simplification, at worst, a Romantic falsification. It is true that the goals and idioms of music altered drastically: the ideals of opera, then the sonata-structure/process initially so dependent upon its tropes, are different from, even antithetical to, everything Bach stood for, thus permitting him to be perceived as an old fogey – *superseded*. (See, here, the introductory remarks to Chapter VI, page 172.) But Bach the pedagogue, supreme master of counterpoint, was never forgotten: and the apparently dead letter is a living presence in the greatest masters of the new impulse. With Haydn contact is minimal. With Mozart, certain and significant: the antiquarian

interests of Baron von Swieten led to performances of Handel with
Mozart's additions and embellishments, and Mozart's transcriptions
of fugues from the forty-eight and elsewhere in Bach for string-trio
or quartet, some with his own newly composed and very sympathetic preludes. Antiquarian interest quickened to living enthusiasm at Mozart's well-known encounter, Leipzig 1789, with the
still-performed Bach motets – 'a revolution and crisis in Mozart's
creative activity' – witness the chorale-prelude for the two armed
men in *The Magic Flute*, the two late fantazias for mechanical organ,
then the *Requiem*. Beethoven's early training included Bach's forty-
eight fugues: its delayed impact is explicit in the last piano-sonatas
and string-quartets, most especially the C#-minor. For Schubert,
a blank: correspondence of 1824 makes cryptic reference to an
exchange of 'the Bach fugues': the composer of the closing stretch
of the F-minor fantazia for piano-duet is a supreme contrapuntist;
its actual workings are not Bachian at all.

   Thus, the revelation of Mendelssohn's celebrated revival of the
St Matthew Passion in 1829 – two years after Beethoven's death, one
after Schubert's – for all the appeal of righting a wrong, has been
overdone. Thereafter Bach is canonical; there is no composer in
the Austro-German line for whom he is not epicentral: Bruckner's
baroque polyphony; Wagner's Nuremberg chorales and 'music
of the future' chromaticism (see below, page 448, for the 'elective
affinity' between Wagner and Bach, Schubert as fulcrum); Liszt's B-
A-C-H-ian ravings and his surprisingly straight piano-transcriptions
of organ-works; Schumann's more sober devotion in spirit and letter,
as well as Mendelssohn's; Brahms's total absorption – in motets
where Bach's are the audible model, in orchestral and chamber-
music where the close motivic working pays a different kind of
homage – and not forgetting the Bach-origin of the chaconne-base
for the 4th Symphony's finale. Brahms awaited each latest publication of Bach's complete works, inaugurated in 1850, with the eagerness of any reader of Dickens, or for the next instalment of a modern
thriller.

   So it continues: Mahler's declaration that 'there is no more
harmony, only counterpoint'; Max Reger's declaration that he is

Bach's sole authentic continuation (with massive organ-donation to prove it); Schoenberg's worshipful stance, epitomized in the halo around the B-A-C-H motif in his *Orchestral Variations*, readily apparent elsewhere – and not forgetting his scrumptious full-orchestra scoring of a couple of chorale-preludes and the 'St Anne' prelude and fugue. Webern's Bach-transcription, the six-part ricercar from the *Musical Offering*, lies at the other extreme – skeletal, analytical; the close-work of his own composing is comparably complementary. And not to forget Berg's inspired incorporation of Bach's *Es ist genug* into his *Violin Concerto*. To the same broad area belong Busoni's monumental homage to the *Art of Fugue* in his *Fantasia Contrappuntistica*, and his piano-transcriptions, many and thrilling. Outside the Germanic line, the canonic ubiquity doesn't hang so heavy: Bach is Cod [note to reader: Cod is correct] in academic French pompiers like Gounod and Saint-Saëns when on their best behaviour; a living presence in Franck, dissolved in Fauré; for Debussy, surly boredom (save unstinted pleasure in Bach's command of the 'divine arabesque'); for Ravel, no use whatever, but no resentment.

Nor is he much use for the Russian nationalists, whether provocatively anti-learnèd like Musorgsky or besotted with Romantic rococo like Tchaikovsky. But Bach is vital to Chopin: the affinity, within utterly different aims, genres, idioms, is clear – contrapuntal subtlety; delicacy of ornamentation; chromatic inflection sometimes so intensive as nearly – but never quite – to subvert grammar; purity of line. Not much use for nineteenth-century Italian opera's earlier phases: but Verdi – 'how lucky you Germans are, still the sons of Bach'! The composer of the *Libera me* fugue in the *Requiem* and the closing fugal reconciliation in *Falstaff* was no mean contrapuntist. His library included the *Mass in B-minor*.

The great Moderns are Bachians to a man: Stravinsky's wistful wish to have been cantor to a small German municipality in the eighteenth century; and the music from *L'Histoire du soldat* (sardonic 'wrong-note' chorales) via the *Violin Concerto* (two beautifully wrought homage-paying central arias), through to the end, sounds for itself. Hindemith's succession explicit and emphatic – 'back to Bach'. Bartók's three compositional Gods – Bach for counterpoint, Beethoven for structure, Debussy for sonority. Ruggles and 'dissonant counterpoint'. Other instances could be multiplied.

This all suggests that the stream can flow in many directions, fertilizing all it encounters. The source himself is protean and eclectic. Bach was endlessly curious, about his forebears in his own culture, and new developments, even if they induced scorn, pity, contempt. He begged, borrowed, stole, with avid intake; learning, transcribing, arranging, adapting, imitating, improving, paying back the debts with compound generosity, from Palestrina and other earlier masters, to his contemporaries and juniors. As well as every possible Germanic, there are French and 'English' suites, Italian concertos, and occasional touches of Polish, Hungarian, Croatian. He would have embraced Russian and Spanish for sure, possibly Indian and Chinese! In addition to all this openness to external stimuli, Bach is a tireless recycler of his own music, instrumental and choral, sacred and secular: this activity culminates in the *Missa Parodia* known as the *Mass in B-minor*. (Parody in the technical sense – largely made of pre-existent music.)

Bach's all-embracing inclusiveness receives its mirror-reverse in the extraordinary variety and extent of imitations, transcriptions, reworkings, homages, transformations, that his music has inspired. Some have already been mentioned. Other orchestrations range from lurid to sober – Stokowski's D-minor toccata and fugue in *Fantasia* (how good to know that this wretched piece is probably spurious!); Respighi's *Passacaglia*, the pact between Elgar and Strauss that each would score a major organ-work with the advantages of the modern symphony orchestra, resulting in Elgar's splendid C-minor prelude and fugue (Strauss reneged). Very different visions of Bach inform Percy Grainger, Heitor Villa-Lobos, Charles Koechlin, Dmitri Shostakovich (olden style, twenty-four preludes and fugues in all the keys) and Conlon Nancarrow (new style, studies for player-piano that take polyphonic complexity onto a new planet); and many others. And endless recreation in jazz and popular music – enough simply to mention Dave Brubeck and Les Swingles.

Bach's monumental late contrapuntal compilations make a

special category. *The Art of Fugue*, whether completed in style with scholarly mastery of strict idiom and technique à la Tovey or with free fantasy à la Busoni: the *Musical Offering* with its problematic 'non-performance' puzzle-canons: the canonic variations upon *Von Himmel hoch*, marvellously reinvented in Stravinsky's orchestration: the endless transcriptions of a handful of *Goldberg Variations*. The present writer has contributed in his own way to this hoard: *Gilded Goldbergs* for two pianos, a vast odyssey venturing down the centuries via, inter alia, Dowland, Schubert, Grainger, Enescu, so far as Nancarrow, before pulling in to harbour – dream-montage upon the great Original: and more recently a new version of the *Art of Fugue*, and a new take on the *Musical Offering* that incorporates realizations of the canons into the structure given by the three mighty ricercars, adds plentiful new invention devoid of scholarship or pastiche, and ends in 'awed silence'. Which is where I should leave off and *begin*.

The church cantatas

The church cantatas are the heart of the corpus: Bach's working life was to provide and perform them even before he arrived in Leipzig, where, once established, he aimed to compose three cycles covering weekly services and special days for the entire ecclesiastical year. This wasn't achieved in full: some earlier works were revived; and from the totality many have been lost. Confronted with the 199 that survive, the mind boggles. There are inevitably stretches of routine – yet Bach's routine is superior to most of his contemporaries at their best: and when he is on top form he is without compare, touching greatness again and again. The compositional inventiveness is as remarkable as the range of subject, content, and the depths and heights of affective expression.

Having listened in early life to as many as I could encounter when performances and recordings were rare, I heard the entire body again a few years ago, jotting down copious observations and reactions. From this total exposure I have chosen for here 19 individual works to represent the 199, as differentiated as possible though all of supreme quality. The two great *Passions* and the big *Mass* have been shyly bypassed: their place as pinnacles of Western art is undisputed and immovable; no lover of music doesn't know them; they will survive the passing of the Faith which gave them birth and suffuses their every note. They shine in the background, summit of the Church's year, commemorating the Crucial Event – the 'Common Epoch' in the world's history, as the foreground of weekly services and one-off occasionals is partially – in every sense – here explored. The choice is entirely personal; the intention entirely to whet curiosity – a way in, inviting further exploration, along similar lines or by way of fruitful deviation. By no means dissenting from them, I've mostly avoided overlap with some outstanding previous discussions, notably Joseph Kerman's on no. 78 and some illuminating pages in John Eliot Gardiner's *Music in the Castle of Heaven*, and Richard Taruskin's provocative stance in his six-volume *History of Western Music*.

Cantata 6: Bleib bei uns, denn es will Abend werden

A gem of intimate inwardness perfectly attuned to its source in the episode where the sorrowing disciples on the road to Emmaus encounter their risen Lord, at first unrecognized, then revealed: imagery of loss and recovery centred upon day lost to night as inner illumination is vouchsafed. First chorus – 'abide with us, for it is toward evening and the day is far spent' – funeral sarabande foretelling the grander such closing both the Matthew and John *Passions*, especially the latter. A patient repeated note underlies the plangent three-oboe choir; later the lines begin to intertwine and exchange roles as the chorus-choir takes up the sarabande. The same two-phrase text is reset at walking-pace, in a web of expressive polyphony underpinned by long single notes for *blieb – bei – uns*, passing from voice, rising too to the violins, as if this simple figure were also uttering its pleading imperative. The sarabande returns curtailed to round off the first number. The ensuing aria, alto with oboe da caccia, is also Passional: 'Son of God, let it not displease you that you remain our light before darkness falls' – fluent, graceful, from stock at the highest level. As also no. 3 – perfect *Hausmusik*, cello piccolo at its exercises, continuously busy over steady/sturdy bass; between them boys or girls sing a familiar chorale to a newly appropriate text – 'remain with us, Lord, as night nears: let not the brightness of your word be quenched among us in these troubled times.' No. 4 is a plain bass recitative – 'darkness everywhere: whence? because neither great nor small proceeds in the right path: thus you have cast down their light.' No. 5 is a lovely tenor aria with full strings – standard perhaps, routine not (Bach's 'standard' always special by any other's standards): 'Jesus, may we be guided by you from sinful paths: let the illumination of your word keep you ever alive in our thought.' Close with chorale; plain, simple, perfect – 'show your might, Lord of Lords; shield your poor Christian folk, to offer you eternal praise.' Whatever one's beliefs or unbelief, the meaning is universally germane and cannot be missed.

Cantata 12: Weinen, Klagen, Sorgen, Zagen

A wonderful opening sinfonia, florid oboe cantilena supported with gapped sighs on violins in two parts and violas in two parts continuous, over two chords per bar, separated by silence, in the bass: as if to 'demonstrate' divisions – crotchet, quaver, semiquaver, demi-semiquaver, from the bottom upwards: sixteen bars of perfection, in proportion and in *Affekt*. It could continue for ever, *Leid ohn' Ende*, though poised to introduce the first chorus – 'weeping, woe, care, distress, are our Christians' daily bread' – gravely intense sarabande over the immemorial lamenting ground bass, five descending semitones, framed by open octaves, cadencing upon itself, heard twelve times underpinning the sarabande on strings; across it the chorus's wailing phrases with their astonishing dissonant suspensions. They come together for *Angst und Noth* (anxiety and need), then separate to intensify the grind. A middle section flows free of tension – 'these are the signs Jesus bears' – before resumption, complete and exact, of the unbearable burden, borne by lamenting bass, dance stateliness, wailing voices. This outer section will be re-used for the *Crucifixus* of the *Mass in B-minor*: the original is surely preferable in its purity of intention. No. 3 is a very expressive accompanied recitative – 'we must through much tribulation into God's kingdom enter': the alto's drooping phrase on *Trübsal* dominates this seven-bar epitome of suffering. It introduces her aria with oboe obbligato, another marvel of expressive floridity that would grace a *Passion* – 'cross and crown, struggle and reward, are fused; Christians at all times undergo persecution; their comfort lies in Christ's own suffering'. Cheer ensues, sturdy/resolute/stalwart/determined: the bass soloist, strings in supportive agreement, takes the Open Road – 'I follow him for good and ill, for living and dying; I embrace his shame and suffering; I will not leave him': contrast – right thing in right place. More special, no. 6: again strong purposeful bass, sustaining suave tenor solo – 'be true; pain will pass; after rain blessings bloom; keep faith!' A soft trumpet floats in and out, with subtly unexpected gaps and overlaps with the singer: itself a voice, albeit wordless; every congregation would recognize *Jesu meine Freude*, and possibly hummed along internally. And certainly joined in singing the concluding chorale with the corporate sense that all is for the best – 'What God does is well done: I stand firm [despite *Weinen/Klagen/Sorgen/Zagen/Angst und Noth*]: God the Father holds me in his paternal arms; I yield myself to him.' The solo trumpet, more normally instrument of warfare, rage, revenge, or of festivity, celebration, triumph, floats serene and effortless above.

Cantata 21: Ich hatte viel Bekümmerniss

After intimacy and brevity, a large-scale, even grandiose cantata, of equal calibre across a wider range – *per ogni Tempo* – for all seasons.

Part I begins in similar distress to Cantata 12, to end, solace granted, in a triumphant paean of praise, joy, exultation. Sinfonia: another exquisitely wrought oboe cantilena; here its florid solo-line is matched with the first violin's, equally decorative; inner strings sustain; all over a gently walking bass: to introduce the chorus with its insistent gapped stammer *Ich – ich – ich*/I – I – I – 'I bore great affliction in my heart'. The walk resumes, now more of a patient trudge, supporting close-worked vocal entries periodically punctuated by the upper orchestra – dense, endless, issueless, till checked

by silence and massive setting of the word upon which structure
and sense pivot, heard only the once – *aber*/but: movement resumes
spirited, energetic, almost gay: '(*but*) your comfort quickens my soul'.
Now follows another soprano/oboe aria from Bach's deep wells of
living water, plangent, and unusually abbreviated – 'sighs, tears,
distresses, angsts, fears, sufferings, gnaw my clammed-up heart: I
feel only sorrow and pain.' An accompanied tenor recitative grows
querulous – 'Why have you abandoned me in my need? Do you no
longer acknowledge your child? Do you not hear the lamentations
of your faithful?' This introduces a superb aria laden with passing
false-relations in the strings, active high, middle, low – 'bitter tears,
stream forth without cease'. The complaint is momentarily dispersed
in a short burst of athletic protest – 'stormy waves will overwhelm
my enfeebled frame; the ship shivers, the anchor plummets, I stand
on the brink of hell'; then the streams of woe recommence. Soloists
then chorus ask questions: 'why so distressed, oh my soul?' – slow
and strongly plain: 'why so unquiet?' – *spirituoso* (Bach's instruction)
yet anxious and urgent, halted by slow cadential 'within me'/*in mir*,
set only the once. A euphonious largo enjoins, long suffering – 'wait
upon God: I will yet give him thanks'; lively again, soloists first then
full choir, in fugal setting of 'that he is my very help and my very
God'. Close of Part I on a firm *tierce de Picardie*.*

Part II begins with accompanied duet recitative, then aria, for
soprano and bass. She is cast as Soul, he as Comfort, personified
in Jesus himself. Their recitative is plain till a beautiful *arioso* on
Jesus' last words promising sweet release from earthly pains. The
aria (accompanied only by continuo) is deliciously operatic; almost
coy: *She* – come my Jesus, restore me with your grace: *He* – yes I
come and restore you with my grace. The voices curl and canoodle;
when the Soul sings '*nein, ach nein, du hassest mich!*' and the Comforter responds, '*ja, ach ja, ich liebe dich*' one pictures Zerlina with
Don Giovanni or the Count with Susanna. Such profanity is lost
in the glorious number following: soloists, then chorus, in celestial rounds upon rounds centred upon the binding chorale. First

---

*   *Tierce de Picardie* – the major third in the triad, after the minor.

round, soprano, alto, bass reiterate 'be at peace, my soul', swinging up and down the scales about a thousand times, while tenor holds the central melody – 'what helps us in our heavy sorrows, our *weh* and *ach*? We but make our suffering the heavier.' Now lower voices, on the scales with more internal motion: to 'be at peace' is added 'for the Lord has dealt well by you', a thousand times, while soprano takes the chorale – 'you are not abandoned: think not that he who sits in God's bosom is wholly free of hunger [rather Brechtian!]: times alter: to everything its due end.' So the circulating planets rotate into their preordained peaceful stasis. Next a tenor aria with continuo only – 'Rejoice! Change *wein* to *wine* [no kidding! it works as well in English as in German]: my soul burns with the pure flame of heavenly joy.' Rather *ordinaire*, this vintage; mercifully short, the temperature is not lowered, and the flame of heavenly joy burns bright again for the close, soloists then chorus, a magnificent festivity whose words are biblical not fustian. Trumpets and drums set off in a slow bright opening – 'the Lamb, slain for us, is worthy to receive Power, Riches, Wisdom, Praise, Glory': then a vigorous fugue upon a subject of virile potency, soloists first, then full chorus – 'Glory, Honour, Praise, Might, be to our God from Eternity to Eternity, Amen, Allelujah!' Prompt ending, almost brusque: no waste: perhaps standard practice, but in Bach's hands powerful, indeed masterful.

Cantata 101: Nimm von uns, Herr, du treuer Gott

Now for some excoriation. Cantata 101 a towering masterpiece; very various, though all its numbers save one are closely bound to the *Vater Unser* melody – the Lord's Prayer. The opening chorus a complete chorale-prelude upon it – 'Take from us, O true God, the harsh chastisement we have deserved for our numberless offences: preserve us from war and pestilence, fire and great troubles.' Textures alternate between intense density – three oboes and upper strings in six parts, a cornetto doubling the soprano on the chorale melody with a single flute doubling at the upper octave; the choir's lower voices in three independent parts doubled by trombones; all over a strong independent bass-line – and extreme bareness, wherein the music's workings are, so to speak, X-rayed. The dense passages contain some of the most extreme dissonance Bach ever wrote, grinding away in daring suspensions of unbelievable tension before their resolution: while the bare passages contain some of the most angular and awkward – overlapping three-note 'sighings and groanings that cannot be uttered', but *are*. This music is tragic and elegiac beyond mere contrition: mankind on an inexorable treadmill. What follows can only be called light relief: no. 2, tenor aria with violin solo over pizzicato bass – *Hausmusik*; delicate, almost dainty – 'do not deal with us as we have earned; let the enemy's sword repose; hear our petition, so we not vanish, like Jerusalem, on account of our sins.'

No. 3 returns to the *Vater Unser*: a most original little number alternating the cantus, gracefully melodized over a dance-like bass, with free recitative. The soprano must split herself between two textures and two texts:

CHORALE: O Lord God, in your faithfulness . . .
RECIT: Our land will rest in peace whatever threatens it:
CHORALE: . . . Appear, with comfort and salvation:
RECIT: You can restrain the enemy: punish us not at the time
    when we are weakest . . .
CHORALE: Dwell with us in your goodness:
RECIT: . . . give us to strive only for the right [enjambing with
    last line of . . .]
CHORALE: Your fierce anger will stay far from us.

No. 4 is a bass aria: he gives the *Vater Unser* melody phrase by phrase, and sings freely in between, accompanied by the three oboes with bassoon continuo, a remarkable and memorable sonority, the three reeds pursuing each other in close imitation like squabbling rats/cats/squirrels; they are chordal for the Lord's Prayer, eventually singing it themselves in four-part quasi-choral block-harmony: 'Why such rage? Such over-zealousy? Desist, we beg; let your fatherly tenderness forbear; our flesh is weak.'

No. 5, like 3, alternates chorale and recitative, this time for tenor, who sings both:

CHORALE: We are wholly corrupted by sin ...

RECIT: ... even the most devout lament it ...

CHORALE: The Devil plagues us ever more ...

RECIT: ... yes the evil one, ever the murderer, would annul our salvation and devour us like a lion.

CHORALE: The world, our very flesh and blood, seeks always [here a hair-raising modulation] to entrap us.

RECIT: On the narrow path of life lie so many hindrances to virtue:

CHORALE: You Lord alone know of this wretched condition:

RECIT: help, helper of the weak: you can strengthen us.

CHORALE: Ah, let us trust in you.

No. 6 is a miracle of ingenuity and beauty; a 'quartet' for the soprano and alto with a flute and an oboe, all over an equally expressive and characterful bass-line. The *Vater Unser* is threaded in and out of all four 'voices', who otherwise go their own dulcet way, sometimes florid sometimes plain, sometimes clashing in piercingly ravishing chromaticism, sometimes sweetly lilting. The whole is in sicilienne movement, spun out to heavenly length with the utmost, albeit unobtrusive, mastery in the teeth of a pietistic truism: 'Bethink you, O Father, of Jesus' bitter death; his wounds ransom the whole world: grant me such compassion; I bethink me of Jesus' bitter death.' Plain strong chorale to close, confirming in plain strong apparency the tune, and its missing words, that has been present, explicit or subliminal, from the grinding opening to the miraculous 'quartet': 'Lead us aright; bless our city and our country; grant at all times your holy word; protect us from the Devil's murderous trickery; give us the sacred hour when we will abide beside you for evermore.'

Cantata 105: Herr, gehe nicht ins Gericht

'Enter not into judgment with thy servant, for in thy sight shall no man living be justified.' The opening chorus sets these words with unforgettable intensity: two suspension-charged lines strong in doubled timbre, first violins unison with an oboe and a horn, seconds with an oboe, over a pounding bass, patient violas holding the middle: choral entry, weighty *Herr* exchanged in all four voices, the next words with more motion, only yielding the last, the once, on a half-close – *Knecht*/vassal. Again, prolonged and more venturous tonally, every part alive with chromatic sighs; a third time; a soft instrumental coda of exquisite sonority. Now vigour gives the reason – *denn*/for replacing *Herr*/Lord – 'for in thy sight ...' – to initiate each entry of a fugue, close-worked, marvellously sustained and prolonged, with towards its end a telling play of dynamics – everyone *piano*, then *pianissimo* – before *forte* restored in a final broadening. An alto recitative acknowledges guilt, beseeches penitence, offering free confession in sure belief that the Lord's judgments are just. Next is a soprano aria – 'sinners shiver and quake, blaming each other and denying their own fault, yet ill-at-ease with their own conscience' – trembling dialogue between the singer and the oboe, accompanied by a shimmer of pulsating dissonance on violins over pulsating violas – no bass to this beautiful number; it floats on for ever, worth every second. Next, an accompanied bass recitative, wave-like upper strings topping pizzicato bass, elaborate and tight-woven, worthy of a *Passion* – 'happy the man assured that his debt of guilt is full paid by Jesus' atonement: God will hear him at the hour of death; and when the mortal remains are borne to their grave, God will open to him the portals of Eternity' – on which word the singer opens them up himself. Now comes a relatively jolly affair: robust horn solo entirely doubled by first violins, they florid in ornament while the horn remains simple – a memorable coloration. The tenor soloist does his best to compete, disavowing Mammon's worldly riches for the companionship of Jesus' poverty. Doth he protest too much? The endless repetition of *so gilt der Mammon nichts bei mir* (fourteen times) and *ich finde kein Vergnügen hier* (ten times) is comic, and the overall feel is comfortable and easy-going. The closing chorale restores gravity – a wonderful piece on the *Jesu, der du meine Seele* melody, in four plain choral parts, accompanied and punctuated by the upper strings recalling the earlier repeated-note shivers in gradually lengthening rhythmic values – semiquavers, triplets, quavers, triplets reduced to long-plus-short, and lastly, after the chorale's final phrase, regular crotchets. Again the bass has dropped away. It is difficult to square the moving effect with the conventional words, reiterating quietening of fears in promise of eternal life: the *music* displays poetic fantasy of a high order – very expressive harmony too. It must have bemused its original congregation, already at sea in the complete chorale, however familiar.

Cantata 106: Gottes Zeit ist der allerbeste Zeit

Aka the *Actus tragicus*. An early cantata of intimate delicacy belying its profound handling of weighty content: greatly helped by the choice of texts, all biblical, no pietistic fustian – a personal anthology of related thoughts as revealing in its way as the choices made by Brahms for his *German Requiem*. Opening 'Sonatina': background, a dulcet pair of violas da gamba over gently pulsing bass; above, two recorders – preferably flutes! – in near-unison, splitting heterophonically into strange, clashing overlapping echoes. It leads directly into a long and various number, sectional but continuous. The choral opening – 'God's time is the best of all' – continues the same refined formal momentum: it then animates into triple measure – 'in him we live, move, and have our being' – euphonious courtly dance – 'so long' (the word is long-sustained) 'as he wills'. This cadences into a serious adagio with four-part chromatic harmony – 'in him we die at the due time – when he wills'. Which cadences in turn into a slow tenor aria (the individual emerges from the corporate) – 'Ah Lord! Teach us to keep in mind' . . . repetitions, hesitations . . . 'that we must die.' The lesson is gently insinuated and insistent, till 'so that, so that, so that' and, just once, 'we become wise'. Cadence into animation, contrasting confidence, almost perky: the bass enjoins discipline and readiness – 'set thy house in order!' A frisky flute responds in a texture now bare after previous fullness – 'for you must die and not continue living' – set many times, with a long melisma on *lebendig*, then a shorter, then the single final injunction, and the flute to wrap it up – almost a gigue. Cadences into an andante, grave again. The lower three choral voices in angular yet unanguished counterpoint over a walking bass, deliberately archaizing for 'it is the ancient covenant: man, thou must die.' As they round in to close, the missing soprano is introduced over continuing continuo – '*ja, ja*, oh come Lord Jesu'; many verbal repetitions, the *ja ja*'s on the edge of comical, though also surpassingly tender. An unobtrusive indication of a significant reorientation, whereby the New Testament enters to fulfil the Old Dispensation. Upper instruments now return, harmonizing a chorale – 'I have cast my care upon God', devoid of its words, present by association and implication. Lower chorus voices creep in with the ancient covenant: the soprano continues her pleading – 'oh come!' – and keeps at it across continuing instrumental chorale and vocal bargain – 'man, thou must die' – in ever-inventive new conjunctions: one is dazzled even with such understated docility. Last line of wordless chorale, last extended *sterben* on lower voices, last suspiring soprano, left dangling up high as every support, instrumental or choral, drops away beneath her. 'Come, Lord Jesu!' – a delicate coloratura on the Saviour/Lover's sacred name three bars before the end; in the penultimate bar that name alone; in the ultimate, a notated silence unique in Bach. An astonishing stretch of music, its disparate speeds, textures, texts, materials – six in all – bound into one with control at once supple and hard as iron.

It is enough: *consummata est*: but there is more. Alto solo over running bass – 'Into thy hands I commit my spirit, for thou hast redeemed me, O Lord thou God of Truth.' Other words of Jesus from the Cross are added by the bass soloist – 'today thou shalt be with me in Paradise'. When the alto resumes she now sings, in long notes against the bass-line's continued activity, the chorale 'In peace and joy I pass away': with her re-entry re-enter the violas da gamba, forming a five-part texture of lambent lucidity. The bass singer sticks to 'today with me in Paradise', the continuo continues to wander and support, the alto sticks to her hymn – 'my heart trusts: safe and still in God's keeping' [at this point the male singer expires]: 'Death is become my Sleep'. To end, an enchanting 'musical snuffbox': the closing chorale is a miniature march led by the pair of magic flutes who prettily decorate between the vocal phrases – 'Glory, Praise, Majesty ... be to God the Father ... and to the Son ... and to the Holy Ghost ... holy strength ... gives us Victory ...' thence to a lively coda – 'through Jesus Christ, Amen' – cheerful *fugato* joined in its later stages by the flutes and the violas, broadening into soprano long notes as it winds down. The last *Amen* on choir only, the last words, wordless, its soft echo on only the treble instruments. A pearl of great price.

Cantata 71: Gott ist mein König

Another very early work, this lies at the opposite extreme: festive, extrovert, wholly this-worldly. Its exceptionally large orchestra lies in complete antithesis to the *Actus tragicus*'s chamber-privacy, its stiff formality to that work's intimate individuality – the council election at Mühlhausen in 1708 wouldn't require such: yet this work is also of the highest calibre. Its choir is divided into small ripieno and large pleno. The orchestration is resplendent – three trumpets, with drums; two flutes with solo cello their foundation; two oboes with bassoon for theirs; full strings; and solo organ, independent of its continuo function.

No. 1: the full forces used already in first bar and again in the second and again the third – 'God, God, God, is my King' – first with salvo of trumpets and drums, second the softer oboes, third the still softer flutes. Such terracing retained throughout with effect both naïve and ingenious, splendid and smile-inducing. God's Kingship decisively declared again; then the smaller choir completes the words – 'of old: the help that is done upon earth he doeth himself.' Large and small continue to alternate, and the close repeats the timbral de-crescendo twice, down from trumpets, via oboes, to flutes.

No. 2 is a complex chorale-prelude, solo soprano decorating the melody, free tenor solo interleaved on a different text, a steady ground bass (very Purcellian) for the organ's left hand (and feet), the right interposing little decorative twiddles of great charm. The interleaving runs thus:

> *CHORALE:* I have fourscore years: why should thy servant serve
>   longer?
> *TENOR:* How should I bear my life further, my sour steps
>   dragging towards old age?
> *CHORALE:* I will return, to die in my own place –
> *TENOR:* Grant mercy for my sin, save me from disgrace, so I may
>   bear . . .
> *CHORALE:* . . . near my parents' grave.
> *TENOR:* . . . with honour my grey hairs.

Both finish together, 'hairs' misrhymed with 'grave'; and the obbligato has the last word with its longest break, as if it too has a word of its own – wry and droll. Seriousness follows: full chorus accompanied only with continuo, in the old-fashioned *stile antico*, close-woven counterpoint, suiting the words – 'so your age be as your youth, God is with you in all you do' – a fine number in its quiet solemn manner.

No. 4 takes its words again from the Psalms – 'the day is thine and the night also: thou hast made light and sun; thou hast set the borders of the earth' (Bach omits the next phrase 'thou hast made summer and winter'). Delectable tripartite setting of an august text, a sarabande for bass soloist with the two woodwind groups, cello always bottom to the flutes, in alternation or combination for night and day: lively middle section without running continuo for setting up the borders, then exact return of the sarabande. (Pity about summer and winter; he would have done them so well.) In no. 5 the alto formally congratulates the Great Maker – 'through your strength . . .' – salvo of festive *vivace* applause for trumpets and drums . . . 'our borders' (slowish) 'are maintained; peace must flourish despite the surrounding horrors of war . . .'; one bar's applause, again *vivace*; andante resumes – 'let crown and sceptre tremble; salvation comes from your strength alone' – with hefty melisma on the *schafft*: and the closing *Kraft* another vivacious salvo to round the lovable absurdity off.

But no. 6 is a marvel, with its richly variegated employment of the entire forces, slow and soft over the solo cello's continuous semiquaver arpeggio patterns: the orchestral bass treads stealthy staccato, the bassoon hiccoughs the gaps, the pairs of flutes and oboes talk to each other, as the full choir, with strings, sing another verse from the Psalms – 'deliver not the soul of thy turtle-dove into the hand of the wicked' – in block harmony with just one moment of florid polyphony. The combination of the separate layers, vocal and instrumental, is unsurpassed in all Bach. Now to end, festive splendour matching the opening – 'crown with blessings the new dispensation! Let peace, calm, well-being always obtain! Happiness, health, victory rejoice you, Joseph! Thus all lands will continue in happiness, health, and victory.' Grand slowish common-time, curiously called *arioso*, twice alternates with fast triple-time, its first go in block chords, its second fugal and greatly extended; the third go of the slow common-time enhanced with long-held notes for the tenors. The work concludes with the same timbral diminuendo as closed its first number: tutti crowned with trumpets; the bass runs down and out; a rising fourth on the two oboes in unison, then the same on the flutes. No grand blaze of the lavish forces: it's as if the young composer were thumbing his nose. Yet, earlier, civic pomp and pride celebrated without an iota of irony. And the whole lovable work is so fresh and full of music: he's trying things out and delighting in the tiniest details – catch the snatches of obbligato organ's right hand in the finale's second bout of common-time, echoing its role in no. 2; and the solo cello's six quadruple-stopped chords amid the bustling melee. It doesn't dig deep: guilt and contrition are conspicuously absent, and not missed.

Cantata 131: Aus der Tiefen

Full abasement, however, in another early cantata, 131, also for Mühlhausen, the year before (1707), a masterpiece to stand with the *Actus tragicus*; and, like it, greatly helped by a preponderance of biblical texts. One sometimes wonders, encountering the best of these early works, what was lost later when Bach embarked on his Leipzig cycles: these are more mature, rounded, masterly, yet somehow less personal; they can now and then indicate routine, even drudgery. One can forget how young he was – at Mühlhausen he was aged twenty-two, his second Weimar post held between the ages of twenty-three and thirty-two. The precocious individuality of the cantatas from these positions compares with the young Mozart, Schubert, Mendelssohn. *Aus der Tiefen* exposes invention of the highest order wholly devoted to the deeply felt articulation of the emotions expressed. The opening is a slow sarabande chorus, oboe and violins in mournful yet elegant exchange – no second violins, though violas in two parts. Voices enter piecemeal and fragmentary before coming together in full harmony, spacious then compressed – 'from the depths I cry to thee, Lord'. The tempo grows lively but not the mood – 'Lord, hear my voice: let your ears consider the voice of my complaint' – this last word marked with expressive sighing gaps. The close-worked texture gradually accumulates tension, twice strangely disintegrated by play of dynamics in antiphony across instruments and voices, the same affective complaint broken into panting fragments – *fle-e-e*, then a prolonged further *e* before the second syllable *hens* is granted (*flehens*/beseech), and a gradation of *forte*, *piano*, *pianissimo*, *forte* again. A third time, antiphonal between oboe and strings, closes into an andante *arioso* for bass in dialogue with oboe over imperturbably wandering bass-line – 'if you reckon our sins, Lord, who shall stand?' Threaded across, sopranos deliver line-by-line a chorale – 'have mercy on me, so sin-laden: free the heart you have redeemed on the Cross, that I not drown in my guilt for ever': absorbing contrast between their long-sustained lines and the wiggly circularity of the bass's melismas on *furchte*/fear, faithfully imitated by the oboe.

Solemn tutti – 'I wait for the Lord' – twice separated by unaccompanied vocal flourishes: it introduces a marvellous slow fugal setting – 'my soul waits; I hope in his word'; the texture composite of long-note chromatic descent, the two-part violas in interlocked stammer, the oboe and violins interlocked in busy semiquaver patterns, often producing fascinating dissonances. The section is prolonged – finely sustained, proportions just-so: a lovely touch, the bassoon on continuo given a little solo break in the penultimate bar. Next is another aria – tenor now – with chorale – the alto's turn. *He* and continuo lilt in graceful sicilienne – 'my soul waits [long literal held notes or extended melismas on this salient word] upon the Lord more than them who wait from morning watch to evening watch'. *Her* chorale concerns the sinner – 'eaten by conscience, long-lamenting, longing to be washed clean like David and Manasseh of old'. Finally, the chorus returns – 'Israel' – hailed thrice in solemn chordal invocation, releasing a vigorous plea for hope, polyphonic, occasionally coalescing into block harmony – 'hope in the Lord, for with him is plentiful grace and redemption'. Thence into an allegro – 'and he shall deliver Israel from all his sins' – close-wrought, without clot, of different speeds and motions (and at its start another moment of unobtrusive glory for the bassoon). The last three bars, adagio again, and a startlingly dissonant cadence, as if to subvert the Lord's plenty and remind the listening congregation of the nagging conscience, or indeed the wood and nails of the Cross.

Cantata 161: Komm, du süsse Todesstunde

'One of the top ten – top five? Utter inspiration and perfection in every way – even to its words, when vindicated.' Thus I scribbled in midst of re-hearing all the cantatas, endorsing the experience of nearly sixty years' exploration.

Opening, alto aria with two flutes over continuo bass – 'Come, sweet hour of death, that my spirit may taste honey from the lion's jaws: ease my parting; tarry not, last light, so I may embrace my Saviour.' Across the soloist's suave intensity and the flutes' sensuous delicacy are placed the stark line of the familiar Passion-chorale; on organ right hand, without words, but everyone would know them; their absence possibly compels the congregation to recall them: the combination sets up richly ambiguous discrepancy.

No. 2 an unusually expressive recitative for tenor, bidding farewell to the world's delusory allure – 'its sugar but poison, its joyful light a comet, its roses thorns pricking our soul: Death's pallor is my rosy dawn, when the sun rises to reveal the wonder and glory of heaven. Though I sigh, I welcome in the depth of my heart the hour of parting' [the cantata's title]. Declamation folds into *arioso* as the functional bass begins to flow, up from the cello's bottom strings, retouching the low C five more times before ending on it – 'I desire to be soon by Christ: I desire to depart this wicked world.' No. 3, his aria, follows, with full strings – fine austere outer sections, the middle more intimate and ornate, in continuo too, with extensive melisma on salient words. But *all* the words are salient here: whatever their quality as 'literature' it is the *feeling* – sentiment, emotion – that convinces and moves – 'my longing is, to reach the Saviour, to be soon with Christ: though, dying, death renders my body to ash and earth, my soul will blaze in pure radiance like the angels' – remarkable especially, the melismas on *zermalet*/crush and *prangen*/shine, gleam, glitter, blaze.

The fourth number is a seraphic alto recitative accompanied, delicately, with full orchestra. First, chordal and formal – 'the end is nigh; farewell oh world; my solace, soon in Jesus' arms to die.' On this word the continuo initiates a dying descending scale, which the voice takes up – 'he is my gentle sleep': the continuo in turn imitates her, then the flutes in overlap, the bass again, as she sustains *Schlaff* for so long as she can. Again, ending on cadential dissonance, resolved in the same words twice more, in chromatic two-part writing. Formal recitative resumed – 'the cool grave will I deck with roses; with Jesus I will awake [sudden surge for her and all the instruments]: he'll lead his sheep to sweet heavenly meadows where death cannot part us.' Now the full texture glows, shines, twinkles – 'so break forth, joyous day of death; strike, you passing bells!' – an *image sonore* employed in several other cantatas that allude to the *Stundenschlag*/passing bell – plucked strings, high reiterated single notes on the winds. She invites the delicate tintinnabulation over and over: charming simplicity, when she stops, of the four closing chords, flutes still on top, strings all still pizzicato.

No. 5 is a chorus of lulling gentleness – Elysian Fields. Strings sing and lilt, flutes decorate and whitter in thirds, catching the echo of the passing bell left on earth below. The chorus also sing in thirds, women, then men, then all together with delicious harmonic tingles – 'would that I repose my body this night with the earth all around; that the soul, the body's guest, rise to undyingness, clad in sweet heavenly joy.' Yet more delectable the orchestra's little interlude here, before 'Jesu come and take me!' much-repeated, then, just once, 'this shall be my last word!', and equally delectable instrumental coda.

But: the last word is still to come, and it's an odd one. The Passion-chorale again, plain four-parts in choir and strings, flutes unison on a decorative descant generous in subtleties, beauties, surprises. Principal surprise, the harmonization of the chorale's penultimate line into E-minor, the tonic, pre-empting the close two bars later into A-major, only granted, as if grudgingly, by the flutes suspended until the very final G♯. Perhaps something in the text can explain – 'the body, sure, will be laid in earth consumed by worms, yet shall rise beautifully transfigured by Christ: it will shine like the sun and live without woe in heavenly joy and pleasure. How can death harm me?' The value of this work, as of many others, does not lie in the texts that have brought about its outer forms. Whether from the viewpoint of a believer or merely the literary angle, their vapid, morbid, unnatural, sentimental awfulness is subsumed utterly into the music's treasury of lyric efflorescence.

Cantata 67: Halt im Gedächtnis Jesum Christ

Marvellous first chorus on its telegrammatic text – 'hold in remembrance Jesus Christ, who is risen from the dead', round and round, from the very first bar, with the long *halt* on the horn, then figuratively literal, *long* in all the parts, the motif heard – *seen* – from ever-fresh textural and harmonic aspects, full of air and spring, with magnificent modulations – a summons, a command, accepted with enthusiastic cheer, impossible to resist – the bright al fresco orchestra, strings topped by two flutes, two oboes, and that invigorating horn. No. 2 is a tenor aria with oboe and strings – 'my Jesus is risen: why am I still afraid? Faith acknowledges his victory, yet struggle and strife persist: salvation, appear!' The mixture of trust and mistrust is subtly built into the music's alternations of confidence and sighing. No. 3 is a recitative containing a chorale:

the alto soloist continues to voice disquiet even after she has invoked the chorus in full certainty of the Resurrection, ending in resolute *Alleluia* – 'my enemies still threaten my peace. If yours was the victory of old, fight beside me now: yes, we know that you, Prince of Peace, will fulfil your promise.' No. 4 is the work's glory, matching its first chorus: the keyword *Friede*/Peace has just been heard: it irradiates the next section, a composite number oddly headed '*aria*', in fact an extended scena set in the Upper Room wherein Jesus appears to his disciples with just four words, reiterated four times – 'Peace be unto you.' He is the bass soloist; the three higher choral voices represent the bass-less disciples. Vibrant vibrating string ritornello, disappearing into stately courtly triple measure for the three woodwinds (the horn is resting), for 'Peace', four times – celestial regal radiant tranquil assurance. Ritornello again, the disciples added – 'well with us, Jesus helps us resist and quieten the fiend's anger': voices as nimble and athletic as the strings (including the continuo bass-line) – only the first violins' brilliant upward scales aren't vocalized too – 'Satan go, go, go, go!' Courtly winds return, fascinatingly spaced, taking a different harmonic turn after Jesus' phrase given twice, his third iteration. Ritornello third time – 'Jesus brings us peace, and quickens us in our weariness, body and soul' – closer-worked texture, then again yielding to the dulcet dance, re-angled tonally, for the Lord's four further utterances of his four-word mantra. In the fourth ritornello his voice (always on the same words) thrice alternates with his disciples' – 'Oh Lord, help us drive our way through death into your glorious Kingdom!' For the final round of stately courtliness the woodwinds are magically doubled from the fourth bar on by the strings: four times the same words, surrounded now by this glowing halo of sound. Jesus' last utterance – the twenty-second – takes him for the first and only time to the movement's key-note in the bottom register – A; yet he seems to float weightless and transparent. After this, the closing chorale *does* seem to come down to earth: the melody is square and honest, the words prosaic (they invoke Jesus the Prince of Peace): but the horn recovers, to play the tune.

Cantatas *50* – Nun ist das Heil *and 118* –
O Jesu Christ, meins Lebens Licht

Two free-standing anomalies, completely contrasted except in mastery and inspiration: a battle hymn of triumph and vindication, a song of mourning and contrition. Cantata 50, a mighty torso, first chorus – double choir – of cantata otherwise lost celebrating St Michael and his Angels' victory over Satan – 'Now is the salvation, power, Kingdom, might of God manifest in his Christ: for he is destroyed that reviled us day and night before God.' Power and might manifest, force and energy unsurpassed, the hammer of Righteous certainty down-and-outcasting the Old Accuser, from the weighty principal fugue-subject to the grinding chromatic descent halfway, and the close where Satan himself seems to bewail his precipitate fall and his everlasting fate. The two choirs are set against each other in antiphony, bouncing the heavy ball with effortless ease: now and then they unite in one mass. The orchestra also bounces: three tiers of upper instruments in threes, oboes, strings, trumpets (with their companionable drums) in and across the texture: when all the forces unite the effect is overwhelming. A triumph of architecture and facture: a machine of computer-generated intricacy, yet organically alive in every detail.

O Jesu Christ is a motet with orchestra, sole survivor of an otherwise lost funeral-cantata, or perhaps a free-standing motet for an out-of-doors ceremony: combining grief, contrition, solace, with unsurpassed intensity – 'Jesus Christ, my life-light, treasure, comfort, protection; I am on earth but a guest, my sin lies heavy upon me.' Comparable to its sibling, the first chorus of Cantata 101 – also a chorale-prelude with sonorous brass doubling the voices – for its inexorable pressure: but the dissonances here do not grind and bruise: the overall sonority and feeling are tender, dulcet, nobly sweet, warmly rich.

Six superb works follow for solo voice without chorus (save sometimes for a closing chorale): one all rejoicing, the others plumbing various circles of yearning, grief, excoriation, death-wish.

Cantata 51: Jauchzet Gott

This is a cantata of exhilaration with brilliant trumpet, soprano agile and exuberant to match, with double-concerto for violins thrown in. 'Praise God in every land, all creatures in heaven and earth: we likewise offer our tribute, since he is steadfast in all our woes' – all energy, no rum-tum or sewing-machine: the extroversion mitigated in the ensuing accompanied recitative, the trumpet silent, a tone of expressive inwardness – 'We pray in the temple where God's honour dwells; where, new each day, our faith is rewarded.' The plain pulsing strings drop away as the soprano waxes delicately ornate in phrases belying her words – 'though our weak voices fail before his wonders, yet our slender tribute pleases him'. It would be a churlish deity not to be enchanted by this ravishing music: the solo cello from the continuo responds in a lovely envoi.

No. 3 is a long aria, the cello continuing melodious throughout this epitome of contentment – 'Lord, renew your goodness each morning: thus a thankful mind and a pious life show us to be children of your fatherly concern.' No. 4 is composite: first the double-violin concerto as mentioned, surrounding the singer's chorale – 'All praise to God Father, Son and Holy Ghost! His promise of grace will burgeon within us, so we trust him with unstinting consciousness (*Sinn*): our faith ensures our goal: thus we sing *Amen*': seraphically on and on – 'heavenly length' – never a dull or perfunctory bar. It yields into the second section, devoted entirely to *Alleluia*, soprano now vying again with the restored trumpet in joyous altercation, infectiously high-spirited, sometimes positively farcical as voice and instrument strive for and achieve their highest note, the four syllables *al-le-lu-ja* wittily separated, trumpet clearly spelling them out too. His note eventually goes one tone higher: but she can out-run him – her final burst of melisma would tax any operatic soubrette, and must surely have been way beyond the powers of any boy-treble.

Cantata 54: Widerstehe doch der Sünde

This requires no instrumental obbligati, only strings, for the contralto soloist: she must be deep, gravelly, dramatic, melodramatic –
Medea, Ulrica, Clytemnestra, Jocasta – for this grim compelling
piece. Its very first chord initiates a chugging grind of suspensions
on upper strings in four parts (thick divided violas), the violins in
obsessive slow-motion, over heavy pounding slow-change bass:
exactly attuned to the excoriating text – 'Be steadfast against sin, lest
its venom strikes you down.' The salient syllable of the salient word
widerstehe several times cruelly prolonged – the persistence, the *stay*,
within the resistance that *must* stand fast against evil. The middle-
eight scarcely remits – 'Let not Satan deceive you: who dishonours
God's glory bears a deadly curse.' Then exact return of the opening
section. This entire number recycled nearly twenty years later for
the aria in the *St Mark Passion* (see pp. 161–4) reflecting directly on
Judas's Kiss – 'False world, your wheedling kiss is poison for the
pious: your tongues are thorns, your words carry destruction.'

Next, in the cantata, a vehement jagged recitative, well-suited to
its implacable words – 'the way of sin seems beautiful till, too late,
remorse and woe afflict the soul. It may seem like gold, but once
within its grasp, an empty shadow, a whitewashed grave. It is like an
apple of Sodom – who tastes it cannot enter God's Kingdom. It is
like a sharp sword [here the continuo bass runs wild] that pierces
body and soul.' The closing panel of this compact triptych is called
aria: difficult to imagine anything less song-like in all Bach's work.
Violas initiate, violins join, a fierce chromatic syncopated fugue, in
which the singer and the bass equally partake as it drives forward,
propelled by semiquavers as strenuous as those in *Jauchzet Gott* are
gay and exhilarating. When the bass also takes them, it's a rumble
of tumbrils, electric, hair-raising – 'Whoever sins is of the Devil: but
should a man break the fetters with true devotion, Satan can no
more prevail.' The fugal devices are ingenious, various, admirable,
masterly: but this music isn't about music!

Cantata 55: Ich armer Mensch, ich Sündenknecht

This solo tenor cantata manages to make abasement and contrition intensely lyrical, the more pathetic for the grace, elegance, ease of utterance, as well, of course, as total mastery of facture. An unusual sonority – no violas, therefore no middle – the tenor is set at high tessitura, amid first and second violins, a solo flute and solo oboe. The opening number shows at its most seductive the line of beauty's artistic victory over the grovelling text – 'I, wretched slave to sin, I enter God's presence, with fear and trembling, to face judgment: he is righteous, I am not; wretched man, slave to sin.' Now comes an agonized recitative worthy of a contrite Peter – 'I have gone against God and not followed the way he ordains. Whereto? If I took the wings of the morning for flight to the ultimate ocean, the hand of the Almighty would track me down and scourge me with the thongs of sin: though I bedded down in hell, his wrath is there; earth shields me not; if I rise to heaven, there dwells he who judges me.' The ensuing aria with flute obbligato, no. 3, is as dangerously attractive as no. 1, in both decorative near-prettiness and woeful plangency, D-minor with acute chromatic inflexions – 'Have mercy! Let my tears melt you, reaching your heart: for Jesus' sake let your angry zeal be quenched: have mercy!' Solace follows in the sober diatonic sanity of a fine string-accompanied recitative, in which violas *do* momentarily appear – 'Mercy! Yet I comfort me: I would not stand trial, I would to my holy Father's mercy-throne, would recall to him his Son, the suffering, the redemption, how he ransomed my offence: and beg his forbearance. Henceforth I will sin no more: thus God will re-admit me to his grace.' After which the plain full-choir chorale seems inconclusive: strong, simple, perfect in itself as always, it leaves unquieted what the final aria, especially, has disturbed – 'though I abandoned you, I yield myself back; your Son has atoned for us through his sufferings and death. My guilt I do not deny; your mercy is greater than the sin that engulfs me.'

Cantata 56: Ich will den Kreuzstab gerne tragen

The same reservation, perhaps superficial, applies to this celebrated *Kreuzstab* cantata, four interconnected numbers that have one on one's knees, closing then with a chorale that for all its sterling character cannot consummate what has preceded. No. 1, upper strings, the three parts all doubled by oboes in unison throughout with one tiny exception. The solo bass carries the burden – 'I will bear the cross gladly: it comes from God's dear hand. It guides me through my torment [here, as the bass launches a long melisma on the first syllable of this crucial word *plagen*, the three oboes have their single undoubled phrase, answered by the oboe-less strings, equally brief; extraordinarily telling] to God, in the promised land.' A seamless stream of sighing affect – long aspiring rise, little sighing falls, worked with acute sensitivity to every passing chromatic inflection: the voice-part a miracle of expressiveness, combining both shapes in endlessly renewed metamorphosis/evolution. As well as on *plagen* the singer has two long melismas on *tragen*/bear, taxing the voice to its limits of breath-control as well as controlling the emotions that would overwhelm it. Spent for now, the momentum broadens paradoxically to embrace faster detail – syllabic setting in triplets of 'I will lay my sorrows in the grave: my Saviour himself will wash away my tears'; given in several bouts, the principal motion retreating to a vestige, resumed between each time ever more delicate, exquisite, sensitive, the last consummate in shapeliness. It leads to a reprise of the orchestral opening.

Now a recitative of equal calibre: over solo cello figuration, plain arpeggios, outlining the harmony as in a well-tempered prelude, depicting the protagonist's passage through world, life, time – 'My wandering is like the voyage of a ship; affliction, Cross, need, the waves surrounding me, and death affrights me daily: my anchor though, which holds me fast, is the mercy by which my God often rejoices me. He calls me thus – "I am with you: I will never abandon or neglect you!" And when the raging shall subside [the cello here descends low to join the motionless bass-line] I shall step out of the ship into my city, that is the heavenly city, whereto I with the faithful through much travail will come.' Sober declamation after earlier excruciation and effort, with decoration only for *vieler Trübsal*/deepest sadness. Brighter and cheerier, the ensuing aria with oboe obbligato – 'soon soon will my yoke be lifted.' Not, however, that technical demands upon the soloist are lightened: the yoke itself, then the lifting, tax his brio as heavily as *plagen* and *tragen* before. The middle-eight varies the tone – 'he gives me strength to fight, the power of an eagle so I can fly free of this world. Oh might it be today!' – and here a slight urgency can be sensed in the six settings of this plea, especially the repeat of *heute*/today at the fifth: the brief anxiety is forgotten in the long cheery da capo.

Next, an accompanied recitative, firm plain string chords – 'I stand ready and prepared, my eternal bliss to take, with longing request, from Jesus' hand. What happiness will be mine when I see appear the gate of peace.' And now, the supreme moment: reminiscence of the opening – one bar of its sighing, sinking motion suffices – then two further settings of 'I will lay my sorrows in the grave ...', the first transposed and adjusted from one of the previous, the second a variant of the previous final time, beautifully reshaped to end high rather than in the depths. The closing chorale is not *de trop* musically, but its words do disappoint – 'come, death, sleep's brother, guide me; take my ship's rudder, bring me to harbour. Some there are who will fear thee; but in thee I delight: for through you I come to behold the lovely Christ-child.' We want the Son-of-Man, and God-his-Father, to be at once Pilot and welcoming host on the secure shore.

The *Kreuzstab* is at the summit: a nonpareil of beauty and expression devoted to difficult territory – gladly bearing the burden, willing endurance of affliction, submission to woe, in the sure hope, nay belief, that a loving Saviour will guide the weak sinner through the threatening water to the promised end: all this without morbidity, masochism, creepy language of guilt, sickness, corruption, worms, dragons, Old Satan, etc. Elegiac yet serene, stoicism patient and acquiescent; everything musicalized, fused into the notes with unparalleled intensity and mastery. Every listener can see, hear, feel, with unwithholding empathy.

Cantata 82: Ich habe genug

Thus too with the other celebrated cantata for solo bass, *Ich habe genug,* justly beloved as the high-point of many tender death-devoted lullabies. In the opening aria the obbligato oboe *sings*: the violins murmur and soothe, violas and continuo bind; the voice is largely syllabic and plain, blossoming into coloratura for *Freuden/* joys – 'I ask nothing more: my Saviour, hope of the world, I take to my arms. I ask nothing more: I have seen him; in faith my heart embraces him. I long to depart this day in joy. I ask no more.' Thus to the sublime lullaby *schlummert ein* – 'sleep, weary eyes: world, I depart, you have nothing my soul requires. With you, only woe; *there* lies sweet and utter repose. Sleep, weary eyes.' Strings only: they cease for the parting, stealing in again for the ultimate tranquillity: antithesis of the *Kreuzstab*'s initial tortuousness – smooth euphony, close intervals, nothing angular. The oboe rejoins for the closing aria – 'I rejoice me in my death: would that death come now – thus will I escape all that binds me to earth below. Gladly I die: would it were now.' This is equivalent to the cheerful number in the *Kreuzstab*: *there*, a shaft of gaiety and energy within the prevailing gravity; here the up-beat ending, emphatic and positive, particularly the final orchestral tutti, *forte* and *fort*, with pronounced *tierce de Picardie*: just possibly this closing number lets the overall level down a notch.

Cantata 199: Mein Herz schwimmt im Blut

This work's title, with texts to confirm, gives hostages to the mocker; and, as always, is transcended by composition of a high order; one senses that Bach's inspiration flows from sources deeper than the occasion, the function, the obedience to his creed and the words in which it is formulated. 'My heart swims in blood, for my brood of sins makes me monstrous in God's holy eyes. My conscience pains me, my sins are hell's hangmen', etc. This horrid stuff yields a singularly expressive accompanied recitative, prefacing an aria of profound plangency – a dictionary of affect – 'dumb sighs, silent cries, must tell my sorrow, for my mouth is sealed. A well-spring of tears bears sure witness to the repentance of my wicked heart – a pool of tears, my eyes hot fountains – ah God, who shall make peace with you?' The oboe obbligato seems to utter the words the soprano claims to be locked: they vie with each other to excel and outdo – a spiritual and physical 'anything you can do I can do better'.

Now is another string-accompanied recitative, again very expressive, not a hint of routine or withdrawal – 'but God must be merciful, for I abase myself – "God be merciful to me, a sinner": yea his heart is softened, and my soul speaks' – to give voice to the work's heart, a long stately sarabande/minuet, ceremonial and melodious, suave and rich, Handelian in generous amplitude – his *Largo* or Purcell's *Fairest Isle*: 'deeply abased, brimful with contrition, I lie before you, dear God. I acknowledge my guilt: have patience, have patience!' It *unrolls* like a magnificent carpet, phrase upon phrase, *la longue ligne in excelsis*: nearly expires in a broken cadenza, then recovers imperturbability for a da capo that, for once in a while, is really welcome.

Next a tiny recitative – 'and as I rue with woe, this word of comfort falls' – leads into an aria with solo string obbligato across which the soprano sings a chorale – 'I, your troubled child, discharge all the sin that lies within and terrifies me so, into your capacious wounds, wherein I find relief' – tender/sturdy church-*Hausmusik*. And the work concludes in a jolly gigue with oboe and full strings – 'how joyful my heart [the heart that formerly swam in blood]: God is assuaged by my contrition and sorrow; he will no longer banish me from a place in *his* heart.' A comparison occurs, for the whole of this text and many such other, with the poetry of Richard Crashaw, notorious for such language and often reviled for it. At his best this seventeenth-century Catholic convert is a great poet on a different plane from the gunk favoured in the Protestant culture of Bach's time and place; at his worst they are not dissimilar. Crashaw's imagery is consistently erotic and sado-masochistic; so too is the imagery Bach favours, to which he adds an excretory emphasis alien to the gentle Englishman who ended up serving the shrine of Our Lady in Loreto. Counter-Reformation meets Reformation!

These persistent themes – the leper-house, the whole world a hospital, the worms of corruption, the discharge of inner pains, the capaciously erotic wounds, the sweet relief of the Saviour's kiss or else the kiss of Death – the whole kinky sado-masochistic caboodle – have to be faced up to, and faced down.

Cantata 198: Lass, Fürstin, or Trauer-Ode

Cantata 198 is in a category of its own. This large-scale work of superlative calibre was composed for an Occasion – the funeral of a much-beloved and admired Electress, Christiane Eberhardine, in 1727. The gravity, of the opening chorus in particular, has always tended to rescue the piece from its original once-only circumstances: five of the ten numbers were adapted by Bach himself, with newly written texts, for the St Mark Passion known to have been given in Leipzig on Good Friday 1731. There have been many reconstructed versions, mostly convincing in performance, sometimes deeply impressive: the scholarly reasoning is various as to interpolations and adaptations from elsewhere in Bach's output, and how to solve the missing Gospel narrative itself, with its associated chorus-music, and to provide suitable chorales. This account will focus upon the original Trauer-Ode, with cross-references to the Mark Passion wherever they occur.

A special sonority from the start – opening number: rich, dense but not thick, transparent yet veiled, choked: made possible by the full and unusual orchestration – pairs of flutes, oboes, violas da gamba, as well as full strings, and the continuo enhanced with two lutes. No horns; and no trumpets and drums: these bucolic or festive instruments equally unsuited to a Passion or a Funeral. As well as sonority, the first chorus is a fusion of feeling and compositional profundity: huge spans of harmonic/melodic tension, yet formal, even decorous, without the bitterness of the opening chorus in the St John Passion or the endless tragic trudge and multilayered complexity of that in the Matthew. Yet equally with these, a procession to Golgotha that cannot be erased by the music's original words and purpose – 'Let, Princess, one more ray gleam from starry Salem: see how we gather for your memory in floods of tears.' The eventual text in the Passion, exactly fitting metre and quantity in the

German, runs, 'Go, Jesus, to your suffering! I will mourn you so long as your consolation is granted me and my absolution sure.' Upon the four layers of sound in the orchestra is superimposed the chorus in four parts: yet due to antiphonies, echoes, rhetorical rests, the texture is full of air and space: the key is B-minor, always a good sign.

No. 2 is obviously too occasional to be recycled – 'Saxony and Meissen are numb with dismay; so too Prince and country, nobles and burghers, all folk, when your death became known.' A fine accompanied recitative, rich three-part string chords in little heaving sighs twice rising to a more explicit gesture of grief. It introduces no. 3: soprano aria – 'silence, you gentle strings; be dumb: no sounds can express the distress: oh word of sorrows'. In the *Passion* the same music is placed after Jesus has indicated but not named the man who will betray him: hence its words – 'He comes! He is here! Ah my Jesus he seeks you: flee, my Salvation; leave me in bondage in your place.' A fine aria with florid solo violin, not sounding the depths. Which *do* sound in the *Ode*'s next number: far the most striking of the many funeral-bell evocations throughout the cantatas. The solo alto sings a measured recitative, in parlando declamation – 'Resonating bells penetrate our bodies; their fearful tintinnabulation each day fills our ear, witness to all Europe of our woe.' Even newly texted, this music cannot sustain legitimate life in a Passion – no church-bells in Jerusalem yet. The sound is astonishing: flutes reiterate single notes high and staccato, oboes sustain a long, slowly shifting wail, the standard strings pluck pizzicato in semiquavers, the unusual strings – violas da gamba – pluck in quavers, the continuo bass plucks in crotchets – an eleven-bar 'sound-sheet' worthy of Ligeti or Reich or indeed Sibelius; fascinatingly cut off to close, layer by layer – flute 1, flute 2, oboe 1, oboe 2, first violins, second violins, voice, violas standard and gambas together, leaving only a deep bass plonk to end.

It introduces no. 5, the alto's aria, featuring the pair of violas, with continuo on the lutes, in lovely flowing euphony; gentle, almost amorous – 'how placid her passing! How courageous her struggle with victorious death.' In the *Passion* the same music is accorded a significant place at the Last Supper, after Jesus' consecration of the bread and wine; its new text – 'I do not forget you, my Saviour [the *nicht* endlessly repeated]: I contain within me your body and blood: my trust in you is firm.' The last syllable of the last word, *gericht*, is perhaps the longest sustained unbroken note in all Bach's works – in the *Ode* the syllable is *starb*. No. 6, however, remains un-recycled: another lovely thing, recitative with measure accompaniment featuring now the two oboes d'amore warbling in sixths and thirds and sighs over gently arpeggiated bass – 'She lived the art of holy dying; death could not daunt her: blest! the spirit who trembles not when the creator summons!' Nor can the *Passion* use the choral fugue that follows, in olden-style strictness whose severity is mitigated by placid pacing, the instrumental doubling of the voice-parts imbuing the sound with a silver-grey sheen. Polyphonic texture yields here and there to melodious homophony, irrigating learning potentially dry, and to a delicate episode of trio sonata for the two flutes, bass'd by the love-violas in unison – 'You, great woman, exalted ruler, defender of the faith, model of a great soul.' End of the *Ode*'s first part.

Sermon. Then Part II commences with a tenor aria deemed Passion-worthy. Gracious ease, elegant flute solo with subsidiary oboe, strings lightened of their bass-line: nothing special; for once in a thousand the extravagant imagery and diction of the words suggest more than Bach's setting provides – 'the sapphire dome of eternity [as, much later, Shelley's memorial to Keats] lead you, great Lady, up from our base place, effacing sordid earth. The gleam of a hundred suns [Hiroshima, later still?] turning our day to midnight, yea darkening our sun itself, encircles your transfigured head.' In the *Mark Passion* the aria is placed after the disciples, including Mark himself, desert their master. The new text speaks of Jesus the Comforter, abandoned, taken, innocent, to receive skewed judgment and eventual death-sentence. Next in the *Ode*, no. 9, bass recitative whose words resume specific locality and provincial fustian – 'what wonder! 'tis your just reward, model of all rulers! Now you are clad in pure innocence not proud purple: you scorn what you have discarded.' Thence into melodious *arioso*: seven mourning rivers are named, ornaments of 'the terrain that [return to declamation, with enchantingly spaced harmony on the four woodwinds] grows powerless since losing you'.

This introduces no. 10, closing chorus of the temporary original and should-be-permanent adaptation – 'Yet, O Queen, you are not dead: we know your worth: it will live on until the world comes to its end: write, poets! [compose, composing mortals!]: we would read the repute of her people and her perpetual virtue and praise.' This is effortlessly transformed by the skill of Bach's poet-collaborator Christian Picander into a *tombeau* for Christ himself – 'I will gaze at your grave, with heart grateful and rejoicing: here is your epitaph – my life comes from your death; I have buried within me my sins and your self.' The music common to both profane and sacred exequies lies in complete contrast to the sublime death-dance sarabandes concluding the *John* and the *Matthew* Passions with tragic mourning charged with consolation and hope. This too is a dance – light, though not frivolous; enchantingly melodious, simple, gentle; almost a folksong. As such, the perfect complement to the complex chromatic gravitas and weight of the opening chorus (to either text); most especially in the memorable phrases of choral unison under the main motif, now on flutes only, windows in the otherwise tutti texture of all the forces all the time that yet retains the work's veiled dove-grey sonority. 'The work's'? *Which* work's? There's surely no doubt that Christiane must lose her last four letters, change her sex, and be superseded in eternity by Christ.

Magnificat

As with the *Mark*, rather than the two complete *Passions*, so, now, for Bach's Latin *Magnificat* rather than the mighty, if problematically uneven, Latin *Mass in B-minor*. The *Magnificat* is flawless, perfect, compact and written in-one, for whatever purpose, rather than cobbled-together for none. And because of its text, a *happy* work – felicity prevails from the start, there is no grovelling in sin and corruption: it is *festive* without civic or ducal obligations; and *various*, because the song of the Virgin's joyous acceptance of her destiny changes mood and stance for every one of its ten verses. Bach binds the varieties together within strong yet liberating symmetry by, when reaching the standard *Gloria*'s last words 'as it was in the beginning is now and ever shall be' setting them to a condensed reprise of how it is at the opening, the resplendent chorus with trumpets and drums, a sort of sacred *Brandenburg Concerto*, the Virgin's 'magnification' of the Lord made corporate, communal, universal. *Et exultavit* – 'and my spirit has rejoiced in God my Saviour' – vigorously sturdy submission, with full strings, succeeded by graceful humility with oboe d'amore – *et respexit*: 'for he hath regarded the lowliness of his handmaiden', soprano exchanging with oboe their shapely phrases, culminating with exquisite overlapping in the closing bars. Which don't close. Bach has ingeniously reversed the words – 'for behold, blessed shall call me' – and suddenly full chorus and orchestra (except trumpets) burst in upon the solitary maiden's prayer with *omnes generationes* – all epochs of humanity to come, thronging at the threshold, with just these two words, endlessly repeated in thrilled and thrilling gabble, bounced across the five-part choir, orchestra doubling, bassing, topping, till its activity freezes into solid detached chords and the voices pile up all the generations in a five-part round ending on sustained dissonance before the combined forces release, then romp to the end.

Bass solo, with continuo only, proclaims 'he that is mighty hath done me great things, and holy is his name' – bluff and hearty, right thing in right place, soon eclipsed by the *et misericordia*, using both soprano soloists (each had been heard separately, for *et exultavit* and *et respexit*) in lilting siciliano of refined and stringent sweetness, the strings muted, their violins doubled by silvery flutes. Stravinsky's admiring observation, that Bach, unlike his contemporaries, can always surprise with the unexpected note, is delectably exemplified here: indeed, some of the vocal contours and intervals are almost Stravinskian. Power now: full chorus for *fecit potentiam* – 'he hath shewn strength with his arm' – virtuoso vigour in part after part, tenors first, then altos, then basses, then sopranos, capped by trumpets, all over a strongly emphatic figure, bar after bar, on continuo. The first salient word, *dispersit*/scattered, emerges clear from the melee in a penultimate dispersal over all voices: the other salient word is heard only once on a curt dissonance – *superbos*/the proud. Motion grinds into seven tremendous slow bars completing the verse – 'in the imagination of their hearts'.

Straightforwardness for the other male soloist, tenor, with virile athletic violins in unison, for *deposuit* – 'he hath put down the mighty from their seats'. The corresponding phrase 'and hath exalted them of low degree' isn't really expressed by the setting, bar the aria's sole long-held lowish note on *humiles*: the accents of humility have been heard to perfection earlier. Now another delight: *esurientes* – 'hath filled the hungry with good things' – this alto aria with two duetting flutes is delicious enough to eat, daintily posed on its dinky pizzicato bass. Again, the corollary – 'and the rich he hath sent empty away' – is not expressed by any change in the music's character. Now the *Magnificat*'s heart; *suscepit Israel* – 'he hath holpen his servant Israel in remembrance of his mercy' – ravishingly dulcet three-part writing for the higher voices of the chorus over a continuo lightened of its weightiest bass. The voices intertwine like some extra number from *Così fan tutte* – the *Rosenkavalier* trio on the far horizon? – sinuous yet chaste, amorousness implicit, and kept well-regulated by the oboes in unison, singing out in long notes the timeless *Magnificat* plainsong. The re-entering male chorus banish this all-female vision. A deliberately stolid fugue, basses first, tenors next, before the women's parts join in succession: no orchestra (continuo excepted): consciously archaic for 'as he spake to our forefathers, Abraham and his seed for ever'. Plain polyphony solidifies for broad chordal close, and the orchestra rejoins for the *Gloria*: triple invocation; to the Father – voices upwards from depths to heights in ceremonial ascending triplet scales; to the Son – choral entries skilfully staggered; to the Holy Ghost – down the scales from top to bottom. The three trumpets plus their drums crown the Trinity with their first entry since scattering the proud in the imagination of their hearts. A firm dominant cadence prepares the aforementioned reprise – as it was so is it now and shall be evermore. Perfect end to a lovable work perfect in all its parts, neatness and propriety raised to the summit for God's magnification: D-major, key of joyous celebration – an earlier version was set in the less brilliant-sounding E♭ and included interpolations, special to Christmas, of inferior quality.

Conclusion: Heaven and Earth

Albeit universal, Bach is also human (though one recalls that graffito from the Sixties declaring 'Bach is God') and doesn't extend to the utmost of his divine creator's range. What he clearly *does* contain comes in three main categories. In secular instrumental music – suites, partitas, concertos, for keyboard, solo violin or cello, orchestra – physical energy prevails; the robust body-rhythms of this dance-based corpus, its cheerfulness, with outbreaks of festivity; its tone of small-court ceremonial, provincial-town society, family comity, though in no way lacking tenderness, lyricism, inwardness, is fundamentally extrovert. In religious vocal music, the range is infinitely wider and deeper: from epic in subject and scale (both *Passions* and the huge *Mass*) to small-scale devotional intimacy (particularly in the earliest cantatas – from Weimar and Cöthen) and plenty in between, including the four Leipzig Masses and the vast corpus of church cantatas. Here the scope is a great as the music: occasions brilliant or funerary, spiritual utterance in many shades – strenuous battle-pieces wherein Satan is routed and the City of God rises bright and strong, theological dialogues (between Hope and Fear usually) of exquisite feeling, images of expectant virgin-brides and contented mothers, renditions of sin, guilt, unworthiness that can attain tragic expression. And, third, his works of learning: literally educational in little musettes, passepieds, minuets, marches, etc., for his own children, from which they (subsequently everybody) can progress to little fugues and inventions in two, then three parts; thence to ever-more ambitious compilations of theory and practice, the two incomparable volumes each of twenty-four preludes and fugues; thence to quasi-scientific demonstration – e.g. the *Goldberg Variations*; thence visionary speculation – the *Musical Offering*; the *Art of Fugue* – wherein a mortal maker renders his ablest homage to the author of the celestial motions. All three aspects interpenetrate without incongruity, strain, imbalance, to achieve flawless integration.

So what does Bach seem not to have? For people who dislike

this music, it is deficient in wit, lightness of being, surprise, grace, charm, elegance; and wholly lacking sensuousness, hence sensuality, hence eroticism and passion. Both charges can be contradicted. Think of the sheer deliciousness of some of the three-part Inventions, the sheer delicacy of the French Suites: then the positively Stravinskian mental agility combined with sparky fun in some of the fugues from the forty-eight (e.g. A-major, Book I; F-major, Book II, and many such numbers from the enormous collection of organ music (especially when played on dulcet period instruments sporting tinkling *zimbelstern*). For charm, elegance, grace (abounding, actually, throughout the oeuvre, often in unlikely corners), one need go no further than the arias and ensembles in the *Magnificat*, whose melting suavity would enhance any operatic stage. Surprise? Well, not like Haydn, but occasionally a touch of feline teasing not a thousand miles apart.

True, there is nothing sensual/erotic as such. But every lulling invitation to death as sweet welcome repose is implicitly as amorous/ ecstatic as Isolde and Tristan on their flowery bank: every writhing worm of contrition eating into the soul foretells Tristan's delirium, Amfortas's torment, Parsifal's empathetic anguish. In such places Bach's affective vocabulary, chromatic in contour and harmony, is way outside the norms of his epoch. One would say 'before its time', and 'only fulfilled by Schubert, then Wagner, then Wolf', except this way of thinking ahead is so pointless. Bach has already realized and fulfilled to the full in his own idiom, and with his own time's characteristic subject-matter, aspects of music intrinsic to its nature and possibilities, whether the context be erotic admission of guilt, amorous longing for heavenly repose, voluptuous submission to punishment, or a Hymn to the Night, an Invocation to Frau Venus, or a Poem of Ecstasy.

Only rationalist bigots are fooled by the superficial repulsiveness of the bloody pietistic metaphor overloading the texts Bach sets with such zest into thinking that this is what they're really about. Musical utterance has been traducing and transcending its texts and pretexts these eight centuries or so! And this process (inevitable, in fact, and probably for the best) decidedly includes most great song, opera; oratorio even, when its words are not from the Bible. In Bach, all this interpenetrates, too, with the aspects of his output that don't divide opinion. His celestial mechanics are earthy, robust, dance-y, as well: the *Goldberg* canons, intricate cerebrations, alternate with exuberant virtuoso display and cheery dances; each half contains a melodious cantilena of searching expressivity, the first calm, the second twisty with passionate sin/guilt/voluptuousness; and the penultimate quodlibet invokes warm family togetherness with the riotous good humour of a Brueghel. Every note, here and everywhere, is absolutely practical. The *Art of Fugue* is laid out as didactic demonstration, but lies naturally under the fingers at the keyboard in the most normative and grateful manner; the canons in the *Offering* are set out as puzzles, but they, too, are essentially performing music once solved. And it all *sounds* so marvellous! It is *actuel*. Bach's quest for the inexpressible/inextinguishable/unattainable is not an assault on the heavens or a theoretical abstraction; he finds everything needful to hand at his feet, on the fruitful earth.

A Note on Vivaldi

Antonio Vivaldi: born Venice 1678, studied for the priesthood, ordained, but obtained dispensation from office because of ill-health: instead, devoted most of his life to the Ospedale della Pietà and its celebrated female choir: for these, plentiful sacred vocal works. Secular works: countless sonatas and concertos for all instruments not just his own (far-famed as a violinist); productive and successful also in opera (more than fifty). Died impoverished in Vienna 1741, having moved there to mend his fortunes, but failing to find patronage. Largely forgotten for many decades, till the gradual revival in the early twentieth century burgeoned into the huge popularity he now enjoys.

Vivaldi and J. S. Bach are alike in industrious copiousness, whether serving their respective institutions or for wider dissemination (only difference, Bach doesn't do opera). But their artistic aims and natures are absolutely antithetical. Bach inward, searching, aspiring to heights achieved with fervour and exultation; probing depths with anguish, excruciation, even morbidity: prodigiously learnèd – composition a branch of knowledge, almost science – comprehensive compilations of fugue, canon, variation: music as theology – the entire Church-year covered instrumentally and chorally. Vivaldi, even when the music is sacred, is the opposite of introspective – extrovert, bright, brisk and clear, tinkly and cheery: 'light music' – one could even say slight – which would be to miss the pleasure and the point. He surpasses Bach in his feeling for instrumental colour – concertos for every conceivable instrument relish sonority and character beyond any other composer of the epoch save Rameau. Witness the *Four Seasons* with their enchanting evocations of birds, beasts, insects, the times of day as well as of the year. The old canard that Vivaldi wrote the same concerto five hundred times can't survive the most casual exploration.

And Bach himself was enthusiastic: he made ten concerto transcriptions from the Italian master, and there are traces elsewhere in his work, even in the *St Matthew* and *St John Passions*.

CHAPTER VI

Another New Start

'The Classical Style'

The phrase 'the classical style' has come to stay, thanks to the commanding stature of Charles Rosen's marvellous book of that name which, building upon the insights of its precursors (notably many brilliant scattered observations of Tovey), has erected a Greek Temple outstanding for nobility and elegance as well as beauty, humour and humanity, height and depth, comprehensive and coherent, setting the most elevated standard imaginable for generations to come: the centre of the art.

Nonetheless 'style' is not quite the *mot juste*. Nor would 'idiom', nor even 'language' be right. Rather, it's a matter of musical texture and procedure: the achievement of the Viennese masters – Haydn, Mozart, Beethoven – is to invent, effect, consolidate another mighty revolution in how music is conceived and constructed, comparable in radicality to its precursor, the change from elaborated polyphony to simplified accompanied monody already described. Which of course is inseparable from a revolution in the techniques and goals of music itself: social/functional, yes; but also, and more important, the exploration of qualities innate to the art, the liberation of its self-sufficiency and autonomy – for performers and performance as always; and now to be heard and listened to and sought out for itself; in a dull and forbidding word, 'abstract'.

Again, the initial sacrifice is cruel. The glories of the Baroque in the hands of its great masters now go for little or nothing: the range of the French – lyrical/tragic/heroic/festive grandeur à la Rameau, delicate intricacy/intimacy à la Couperin (whether whimsical or, as in his *ténèbres*, pathetic). The magnificent dark expressivity of Charpentier; sparkle and fire à la Scarlatti, grandeur and broad humanity like Handel; above all the sublime fusion in J. S. Bach of the entire range of *Affekt* with unsurpassed contrapuntal and harmonic learning – all these are dispensable for the new aims; indeed in their earliest phase irrelevant, even inhibiting. Counterpoint as its own end would be an impediment; textures based upon figured-bass building up the substance from below, usually not composed/notated in full, its conventions so universal and well understood, are simply inapplicable except for recitatives, which remain utilitarian throughout the new manners/techniques/goals. The new can't use the old even at their peak of perfection. And indeed the skinny poverty of the nascent classical style is pretty pathetic – baby out with bathwater – humdrum, routine, dull, vacuous, mediocre; experimental 'historical interest only' – as in the earliest phase of *seconda prattica* before it gradually matures into blooms and fruit; copious and wasteland-ish after the glorious harvest of the polyphony it seemed to supersede. What's lost in this later revolution is for a long time far more apparent than what's gained.

The vital activating texture and procedure in the classical style is *Sonata*: simply described, a structure of dynamism employing the power of key relationships, above all the primal tonic/dominant – home key and its closest relative – at once friendly and inimical, welcoming and challenging, demanding closure at close quarters and over time/space/duration, so alive that it can generate tension and release, by means of well-aimed cadence, sufficient to make an entire section, an entire movement, an entire work. Establish its key: move away from it with purpose: return to it: stop. Start again: move further; play, invent, surprise, explore, draw out implications – in a word, 'development'. Return to the home key by means obvious or subtle: restate the initial material, redirected with art to subvert dominant tendencies, homing everything in on the home key: stop. A structure, a journey, a demonstration, an argument. On this fundamental basis are built the glories of the new ideal whether brief or vast, demanding or diverting. Of its nature the material to make such structures and processes has to be simple, primal, clear-cut, even naïve. Ironically (as they say) the basis of the new idiom lies firmly in the clichés and routines of *opera buffa*, in all its threadbare poverty. There's no place – no use – for any baroque forms or techniques, and the texture cannot be half-improvised by the conventions of continuo: every note must be exactly composed and notated, to be played exactly as written (save in ornaments and cadenzas, obviously).

Such a bare-bones account omits richness, depth, density, felicity of actual invention. Naturally a great and important style cannot do without these things! Expeditions to further keys than the animating tonic – dominant – tonic are of course permitted: contrasting themes/characters/moods become part of what's expected: the underlying foundation is so strong, the framework so flexible, that a sonata movement can contain opposites as well as it can complements. The structure's procedure is, in the end, as supple, comprehensive, profound as what preceded it, able to express everything that music can, using all the means needed, inventing material of ever-greater complexity alongside the naïve formulae so indispensable to it too, embracing the most extreme apparent discrepancies, disturbances, fractures, destructions within its overall coherence. Eventually, as the sonata matures, it can incorporate what it had, in feckless youth, to jettison – the principles and practice of contrapuntal working, most notably the jewel in the baroque crown, fugue: already in Haydn, both before and after its fascination in Mozart both for archaic severity and intellectual gaiety/energy, culminating in its astounding reclamation and reinvention in late Beethoven.

Crucial, and absolutely new, is the idea of *development*: statement of thematic material establishing principal key, the move to its dominant, preparations for its return, and material re-angled for confirmatory closure can expand to cover large and adventurous expanses. The texture and procedure for such sizes is development – varied repetition; contrasting ideas, similarly treated, manipulated, mutated, even transformed into an end result almost beyond recognition though every step be comprehensible and apprehensible – meldings and mergings – ingenious – affective – diverting – dislocating – re-forming, organic as a living organism.

The ultimate perfection of such means/ends, still always within the primal basics of its simple origins, achieves the same level of integration as what it apparently supersedes, what it had spurned.

Above all it's a matter of *proportions* – perspective, relationships in space and time, scenery and landscape disposition, terrain and journey across/through it, embracing an enormous range of emotional expression: imagery from nature and also from the human body, brain, soul. Imagery from architecture – both the individual building in all the relationships of all its parts; and from buildings in context, city or country, their juxtapositions however bold, their contrasts and complements fusing into integration. The classical style, or 'sonata principle' as it used to be called, isn't so much 'frozen music' as architecture liquified, made lambent, supple, flowing, dynamic, transparent, communicative.

Haydn: the musician's musician

Franz Joseph Haydn, born 1732 in Lower Austria to humble origins. Showing musical tendencies he was sent, aged eight, as a choirboy to St Stephen's Cathedral choir in Vienna: after this, he eked out an exiguous livelihood in the capital, teaching himself with determined assiduity the basics of his art, composing for church, keyboard, and for string quartet in its earliest primitive stage.

First appointment, music director to an aristocratic family, in 1759; the next, two years later, permanent and final, to the fabulously rich Esterházy dynasty, where he served willingly and faithfully down the following three decades and more, organizing opera, music for the liturgy, orchestral and chamber works for the family's lavish set-up in the middle of nowhere – 'there was no one to guide me, and I was forced to become original'. Less viable output too – over a hundred pieces for the baryton, a string instrument which can be plucked as well as bowed, to satisfy his insatiable employer besotted with the thing. But Haydn's principal genres during the Esterházy years are keyboard sonatas – wherein one can most easily chart the evolution of the sonata principle from puerility to virility:

symphony – from lightweight divertimenti to an engagement with
the current move of *Sturm und Drang*/Storm and Stress – intense
expression and experiment that could produce such middle-
period (early 1770s) masterpieces as the *Lamentatione*, the *Trauer*,
the *Passione*, whose titles speak for themselves: and, above all, string
quartets – from earliest serenade pieces via the six of opus 20 (the
'Sun' quartets of 1772) and the six of op. 33 – 'written in a quite new
and special manner' (1781), opening up over the next twenty-two
years thirty-three further quartets, culminating in 1802, then the two
fine movements of another the following year that he lacked the
strength to complete. These purely instrumental genres advance in
maturity, scope, mastery, as the first peak of the new texture-and-
procedure known as Sonata: alongside them, a choice and copious
output of piano trios whose more intimate genre permits invention
of ravishing sensibility: the body of piano sonatas is equally fine.

His fame spread from the remote swamps of Hungary to embrace
all Europe: his music was in demand in every musical centre: 1785
the *Seven Last Words* for Cadiz Cathedral; Paris commissioned six
symphonies in 1786; London a first further set of six in 1791–2, and
another 1794–5; Haydn's residence in the English capital was a
personal and artistic triumph of a new kind. He'd been freed from
the Esterházy position in 1790 and was thus able to follow these fulfilling invitations in his own self-effacing yet realistic manner – he
knew his own worth.

Late excursions into unexplored territory – the Esterházys
retained his employ only for an annual memorial Mass – six further
settings crowning many previous; but absolutely fresh. The two
great oratorios, both to texts originally English, and inspired by the
previous Teutonic master who, settled in London, had invented and
consolidated the genre – *The Creation* (1798), after *Paradise Lost*, and
The Seasons (1801), after James Thomson.

Haydn's unaffected admiration for the younger Mozart (whom
he outlived for some twelve more composing years) makes a
touching tale: awkward, rather, the edgy relationship with the
youthful Beethoven, who unwittingly inherited the sonata/
symphony/string quartet mantle and took the 'classical style' to its

unsuspected furthest apogee. This Haydn–Beethoven line is direct: Mozart, though of course within the style and culture and epoch, is really a different kind of composer (see later). But later underestimation of the older master – even patronization or condescension, as Mozart's supremacy in opera and concerto (neither are great genres for Haydn) waxed ever clearer, while Beethoven's turbulent power swept all before it – meant that Haydn could long be belittled as a mere precursor. The authors of *The Record Guide* felt compelled to open their entry on him with a challenge – 'Haydn was one of the greatest composers who ever lived': and Tovey's seminal introduction 'Haydn the Inaccessible' forms the background and springboard to the following essay that, also, would put this indispensable composer to the forefront as second to none.

The current picture of Haydn is something like this: a great inventor, intelligence, humanist, wit, who works with juvenile diligence to master every available old technique while simultaneously eager to embrace and advance every new, forced by the isolation of his employment to 'become original', quivering for a time to strains of emotional turbulence which immeasurably deepened his art, then learning to wear it lightly with tropes and timing from *opera buffa*, before broadening with maturity and age into the expression of social, ethical, religious values with genuinely popular appeal – all held together in a balanced synthesis that embodies to its fullest in music, and perhaps in all the arts, the concept of Enlightenment. The musical character is perceived as sunny, energetic, impersonal, normative, unbowed by angst, cheerfully pious, a life-enhancer: *Laus Deo*.

Such a 'Haydn the Accessible' is certainly not wrong. It is the basis of the affection in which he is held, especially in the country which took so immediately to him and his music in the 1790s. Yet he is not, and probably never will be, a wholly popular composer like Mozart, Beethoven, Tchaikovsky, and now Mahler and Shostakovich. Not even an ampler grasp of his true size and scope will bring this about. There is something inherently unembraceable. Even in minuets his good humour can frequently not be quite what it seems;

the *innocentamente* of his variation themes and finales is definitely not to be trusted; the unmistakable *affettuoso* of slow movements can also be austere, even chilling; and the cerebration of sonata-allegros is sometimes so urgent as to drive out immediate musical pleasure. 'Haydn the Repellent'? There is also, alongside the upfront straightforwardness, an emotional reserve or veiling which invites another sobriquet: 'Haydn the Withdrawn'.

Such qualities have never alarmed professional musicians – performers, connoisseurs, academics, analysts, perhaps composers most of all. From the discriminating appreciation of his middle life and the wide dissemination of his old age, Haydn has enjoyed the praise of fellow practitioners. Testimony from the greatest of his immediate successors is more in works than words: Mozart and Schubert, very different kinds of composer from him and from each other, are audibly saturated in Haydn as source and example; Beethoven, audibly the same kind of composer, owes enormous and quantifiable debts (which are fully repaid). The early Romantic generation had little regard, as they had no use, for Haydn's particular mastery. But even as the Romantic century advanced and his repertoire was contracted and his style patronized, his stature for the chosen few remained unimpugned. To the avid creativity as well as the nostalgic historicism of Brahms, Haydn stood in parity with the other three Viennese masters. 'I want my ninth symphony to be like this!' he exclaimed, playing the andante of Symphony no. 88 'with wallowing enthusiasm'. More surprising is the cordiality recorded by Cosima Wagner in her husband's conversations: a few favourite symphonies and quartets were often piano-duetted or played live, eliciting joy and reflection (sometimes profound). What must surely be the same largo ('of Haydn's G-major symphony') 'is one of the loveliest things ever written; and how wonderful it sounds!' On 19 October 1873, R. takes 'infinite delight' in the 'masterly art' of the 'London' Symphony: 'Haydn, spurred on after Mozart's death by Mozart's genius, became the true precursor of Beethoven; varied instrumentation, and yet so artistic; everything speaks, everything is inspiration.' On 3 February 1874, R. 'plays the *andante* (G-minor) from another [Haydn] symphony, explaining its beauties, above all its concision – everything expresses something, no arabesques, the two themes circle around each other like sun and moon.' (I think Cosima might mean the C-minor/C-major andante of no. 103; there is no G-minor slow movement in the Paris, Oxford or London sets likely to have been available at the time.) 'How wonderful it sounds.' Another master of the large up-to-date orchestra, Rimsky-Korsakov, actually placed the 'primitive' Haydn at the summit of this branch of the art.

The last Romantics, like the first, felt least rapport. For a Delius, a Debussy or a Rachmaninov, such music has nothing beyond dead formulae. Mahler, notoriously contemptuous of eighteenth-century development sections, invoked Haydn for association in the principal subject of the 4th Symphony's first movement and, still more, its tick-tock accompaniment. But then we learn of his loving revival of a Haydn opera; of his inspired performance of *The Creation*, and of a 'London' symphony that the critic Eduard Hanslick found 'incomparable'. Strauss's feeling for the epoch was confined to a periwigged and chocoladed Mozart – Haydn's lack of sensuality and dinkiness had no appeal. And for Schoenberg the evolutionist, Haydn is merely the first in a Viennese classical package that awards him no distinguishing features. But his progress with moderns and post-moderns has been triumphal. In his old age Stravinsky's listening included the quartets and symphonies in its very select company; Britten used to curl up in bed with pocket scores of the quartets. Their attitude can characterize at the highest level the prevailing view. As appreciation has widened, from Tovey (who as usual implied it all) into Rosen and Webster, with Robbins Landon for voluminous documentation, and the advocacy of performers like Brendel and Schiff, rather than sloggers like Antal Dorati and the Aeolian Quartet (though some old-stagers – the feline Beecham, the granitic Klemperer, the sinewy yet singing Hans Rosbaud – remain unforgotten, and Britten's *Creation* from the 1966 Aldeburgh Festival is the single most inspired Haydn performance I've ever encountered), his standing in general has never been higher. And in particular, among composers, there is scarcely a dissenting voice. Here is Ligeti, in hospital between revising his Violin Concerto, studying the late quartets in depth – 'from Haydn you can learn how to achieve the clearest effect with the simplest means – when having to choose between a more ornate structure and a skeleton, Haydn always chooses the skeleton, never using one more note than he needs.'

Yet even here, amid his loyal subjects, Haydn remains oddly shadowy and elusive. Acknowledged by all, he is still without influence. Of the Viennese pack, Beethoven hung like a thundercloud over his progeny from Schubert to Schoenberg, emphatically including Brahms, Bruckner and Wagner. Mozart's influence has been a complementary rebound all the way from Tchaikovsky's *Mozartiana* to Stravinsky's *The Rake's Progress* and beyond; but more often he has been made to embody an attitude rather than a style, as in the ideal posited by Busoni's 'Young Classicism' or the very different versions invoked by Ravel in his two-hand Piano Concerto, Strauss in his wind sonatinas, Messiaen in his *Sourire*. Whereas, apart from Robert Simpson, possibly Elliott Carter and a facetious tootle from Vaughan Williams ('Haydn to the rescue' from a temporary impasse in composing *his* 9th Symphony), Haydn has had no progeny and has received only little, rather cursory homage – from a distinguished French handful (including Ravel and Debussy) for the centenary of his death in 1909, from six British composers (including George Benjamin) for his 250th birthday in 1982, and for the bicentennial of his death in 2009 I completed the transcription of all the string quartets from op. 20 to op. 103 for piano-duet that had partially begun in the nineteenth century. He appears to be unsusceptible to 'recomposition' à la Stravinsky (except, appropriately, for certain Haydnesque features of Stravinsky's *Symphony in C*): no doubt because he has already done it all himself.

For no composer before, and none again till modern times, has been so self-conscious. The former image was one of innocence, unaffected simplicity, cheeriness, whether of a 'Papa' or child-like ('Haydn is like a child, for there is no knowing what he will do next' was Keats's reaction when his friend Joseph Severn played him symphonies on the piano in Rome in 1820). It accompanies a sonorous stereotype of C-major openness, music of clear outline and definite goal, unsullied by self-expression, stilted heroics, lachrymose pathos:

music in a pristine state. This picture has now been enormously amplified, and partially reversed. Haydn is now seen as a sort of scientist or doctor of music: knowledge is explored and exploited, experiments are undertaken, both these things sometimes without the alleviation of aesthetic charm. There is little reliance upon moulds or self-evident formulae: despite the fertility there is great care not to do the same thing twice, which can produce dryness but never routine like Mozart on an off-day or sleepwalking like Schubert, let alone the trickle or gush of a Vivaldi, Raff, Martinů or Henze. Rather than child-like and spontaneous, Haydn is 'artificial' – deliberate, quizzical, critical; even (dread word) 'ironic', inasmuch as he can achieve his complex ends with hackneyed material of no intrinsic worth.*

This expanded view of Haydn fulfils a modernist dream of the composer as craftsman, an impersonal maker of functioning objects. So conspicuous a devotion to the craft of composition is valued both for itself and as a stick with which to knock expressionist splurge and impressionistic haze, equally with avant-garde pseuderie and the blackmail of 'commitment'. Further aspects yet are so alien to previously received notions of him that they are still coming into focus: Haydn the mannerist, the whimsical, the Shandyan; Haydn who teases – not always in fun; less cat-and-mouse, more tigerish – his material, his forms, his players, his listeners. Just as he leavens his learning with 'obsequious' acknowledgement of licentious infringe-ments on the local scale, so on the large, whole movements, whole works even, can be sarcastically subversive – not with the tedious doctrinaire 'absurdity' of Dada and surrealism but, rather, within the synthesis and integration that remain so paramount that he has always to be called one of their greatest exemplars.

All this could make him into a somewhat forbidding icon

---

* Irony – most debased of critical terms, requiring forcible retirement. 'Saying one thing to mean another' produced profound effects in literature from Greek tragedy to Jane Austen, Henry James and beyond. In music, so abused by Mahler, Shostako-vich, Stravinsky – cheap material carrying genuine emotion, or playfully inverted – that it has worn threadbare. In general, 'ironic' connotes little beyond 'sarcastic', 'piquant', 'coincidental'.

of 'the right attitude' to the materials of music and their proper deployment – the master of small points in a comprehensively cogent musical speech so well understood that allusions, jokes, surprises, ambiguities, subversions, ironies become normative too, and confounded expectations as expected as straightforward fulfilment of the rules of the game. Which suggests not so much an icon as a sacred cow, ruminating the cud of every correct notion in cultural studies at large; the composers' composer or musicians' musician yielding to the analyst's, the academic's, the historian's. Which is as boring as Dada without the fun. If there is an angle from which this complex figure can be seen steadily and whole, it must surely be in the idea of music's intrinsicality; whatever else might or might not be present, music as music, unsullied or compromised by extraneous matter, autonomous. Haydn leads more directly than any other composer to this easily uttered but endlessly slippery idea.

He is the purest of all composers; his art has the fewest external referents, is more completely about itself than any other. Bach is rightly regarded as the supreme celestial mechanic; but possibly the most characteristic, certainly the deepest, aspect of Bach is his weaving a tissue of messages and meanings soaked in *Affekt* way beyond the norms of his epoch, evincing a personality of morbid inwardness wholly compatible with his robust functionality, vigorous physicality and learnèd 'science'. Mozart is always opera *manqué*, his articulation and phrasing vocal, his setting theatrical, his forms and processes not organic but, rather, whisked on and off like prefabricated flats. He doesn't argue, or build, or grow; he sets out the sections in finely judged symmetry/asymmetry and sends them through a constellation of closely related keys. Interest derives from the fine draughtsmanship which distinguishes high calibre from routine, sensuous pleasure from his perpetually fertile melodiousness.

Beethoven is music made from music for sure, supreme in the processes of development as argument and journey, and also in extracting the ultimate potential from his thematic material. As Wagner remarks, he is, in this, the fulfilment of Haydn. He raises the temperature and the voice, enlarges the durations and the difficulties; the strain waxes heroic-pathetic, with a rhetoric of struggle and victory aimed at more people, in bigger rooms, aimed at Humanity en masse. He has something important to tell them. Put in words this message tends towards inert abstractions like 'brotherhood', the 'ideal feminine', 'freedom', but what he really has to show that is so important to him as to compel audiences ever since into feeling that it is also important to them, is, of course, his notes. And Sonata's greatest victor has imbued his actual notes with a new tone – ethical, moralistic, idealistic, 'improving'. Music, as it were, returns to church (albeit secular, non-denominational: First Church of God Pantheist) after a few generations at court, at the theatre, in the market-place.

Schubert, by contrast, is all voluptuous hedonism and 'amorous propensity', driven by a libido which is wholly compatible with such complements as great stillness, great radiance, or temper tantrums of extraordinary violence, and severity pushed towards unsurpassed extremes – as in the *Winterreise* songs which so signally disconcerted his circle of friends. And so to the first Romantics, to Wagner, late Romantics, Expressionists, Degenerates: a tale of degradation – the wholesale invasion of music as a medium of sociability and intellectual exchange, by subject-matter, story-telling, atmosphere-painting, message-bearing, capable of gushing over into autobiography both lubricious and spiritually ostentatious, the confessional quadruple *forte* and sextuple *piano* (both are to be found in the first movement of Tchaikovsky's *Symphonie Pathétique*), which have become for its average lovers what music is expected to be. Thence to the modernist reaction which gleefully topples the rotten tree.

Haydn alone gives no handle: there is nothing to latch on to, biographically or in subject-matter. *Sturm und Drang* of course; 'Farewell', *La Passione*, the *Lamentatione*. But what are they beside a Bruckner 9th, a Mahler 10th, an Elgar 2nd or Sibelius 4th? Nor do any quartets reveal the secrets of sickroom and convalescence, let alone an *Aus meinem Leben*, an *Intimate Letters*, a *Lyric Suite*. His operas, for all the musical value, do not apparently live as drama, nor is he, like Mozart, an instrumental dramatist via the concerto. When he does produce

an instrumental scena the result is stilted or parodic, or both. The
primal archetype for his melody is often neither vocal (like Mozart
again) nor instrumental, but rather a sort of fabrication which can
cope equally well with values from a semibreve to a demisemiquaver
in one long line, throwing in plentiful turns and graces, with triplets
and other divisions en route. Haydn the Artificial.

Onomatopoeia does figure of course, both in early symphonies –
Le matin, Le midi, Le soir – and in the two late oratorios: whether
juvenile or mellow the result is so one-dimensional and panto-
mimic as to seem naïve even when manifestly sublime – a classic
instance of naïve as opposed to sentimental art. Unlike the, in some
ways, comparable Brahms there is no body of secular vocal music
to suggest by analogy any interpretation of his favourite turns of
phrase. (Who could find Brahms impersonal anyway? The character
is almost palpable in his textures, harmonies, contours, procedures.)
Neither affects, nor onomatopoeia, nor a clear projection of personality (though they are not exactly lacking) provides the clue to
his core, as they can with every other composer, even when, as with
Stravinsky, such things are deliberately eschewed. Even while practising with consummate perfection the art of music as amicable intercourse, the doors are closed. Haydn the Impenetrable.

This music is pure because it cannot be translated. Despite one's
ready recognition of a ragbag of tropes and types – snippets of
nonsense from opera buffa and pathos or elevation from opera seria,
tags from textbooks, snatches of folksong 'from Croatia's woods and
fields' or urban serenade from Vienna's back alleys, opening and
closing gambits from contemporary cliché – it owes less than any
other to metaphor, simile, association. Haydn doesn't seem to invest
his artistic capital in such stock; he does not fully ally himself with it.
Other composers inhabit; Haydn is aloof. Then to proceed to build
entirely from such material, and entirely upon points of grammar
and proportion, would seem a flagrant courtship of dryness. 'Music
as music', upon which he is so single-mindedly fixed, is, artistically,
a dead letter – mere grids, blueprints, engineers' working drawings.

He is music's supreme intellectual. Yet every lover of Haydn recognizes within the cerebral power many characteristics difficult to

name without absurdity, so wholly are they musicalized. But the
risk is worth taking. The range is enormous. High spirits, all the way
from physical brio and athletic bravura (Tovey makes the connection with the cerebral power: 'his forms become the more subtle as
his animal spirits rise') to jokes, puns, games of sometimes surprising
intellectual and even expressive weight, profound in their ambiguity,
exploratory in their paradoxes, witty like the metaphors in metaphysical poetry, touching on rarified places which no other means could
reach. (When unambiguously farcical, as in *Il distratto* and other
mid-period symphonies, the effect is quite different – *simply* silly; it's
a pity that this side of Haydn receives disproportionate emphasis.)
There is serenity and hymn-like calm; Enlightenment openness,
sage and humane; radiance without shadow – like tempera, pure
colours on a white base. Their opposite – twisting strangeness, contortion, mannerist extremity – is almost as frequent, and this too
is shadowless in that it is never morbid. Compare Bach with his
worm-gnawed chromatics of sin, guilt, corruption; the hectic consumptive flush of Mozart in G-minor; the driving *Tod* tarantellas of
Schubert (to go no further than composers who overlap Haydn's life
at both ends). Rather it is part of his unceasing exploration of yet
another aspect of music's extent that fascinates him for a moment or
a movement, something he can *use*, as he *uses* stale old contrapuntal
routines both for earnest and for effervescent purposes. Then there
is deep still contemplation, simultaneously remote and glowing,
giving utterance to an extreme of inner solitude paralleled only in
Bartók and possibly Kurtág: a bare space wherein something exceedingly quiet, intense and private is apprehended with a nakedness
beyond sensuous beauty, making music an object of both meditation and solace, worked out in a dream realm of punning harmonic
labyrinths. Into this, cheerfulness is always breaking, for these pools
of loneliness are always adjacent to the body-rhythm of a minuet or
appear within the tearing energy of a finale.

   The tone of voice ranges similarly from such confessional impersonality to the late development of a successfully common-touch
lingua franca in the oratorios and last Masses, whether raptly devotional or ceremonially jubilant, with a repertoire of moods between

the two that satisfactorily renders whatever it sets out to and wisely
evades characterization (those three Archangels! *The Seasons'* Hanne,
Lukas and Simon!!) – though the birds, beasts and insects are vivid,
and the injunction to the whales to multiply touches the depths.
But a further secret side of Haydn gives tongue with extraordinary
passion – such places as the wild improvisatory gypsy flourishes of
the first violin above the chorale on the other three strings in the
second movement of the String Quartet op. 54 no. 2; or, in the mis-
leadingly titled *'Allegretto'* of the Piano Trio no. 44 in E-major, the
uncurling of the melody above and then below the gaunt stealthy
bass, in octaves then thirds and tenths, till the tension is so great
that the movement literally breaks apart before snapping shut like
a slap in the face. Utterance of such unsullied-by-*espressivo* intensity
makes the Romantics seem extrovert, showy and babyish, whatever
the higher pitch of their anguish or the urgent pressure of their
engagement. Just as startling is Haydn's mastery of the Primeval,
not so much in *The Creation* itself as in the powerfully pregnant
slow introductions to eleven out of twelve symphonies, and, most
particularly, the 'London', no. 104. When the *fortissimo* tutti falling
fourth of bar 2, answering the rising fifth of the opening, is replaced
in bar 15 by a *pianissimo* falling fifth on strings alone, the space and
mystery evoked are as vast as such effects in Bruckner, though the
actual duration is tiny.

Mendelssohn's famous declaration that music sets up resonances more definite than words receives a supreme testing in
Haydn's instrumental works. A couple of further concrete instances
might extend the sense of a language in use, of which both arts
partake. The first is comparatively early – the *'Affettuoso e sostenuto'*
movement from the String Quartet op. 20 no. 1. What is it? Certainly not a melody: rather, a themeless continuum, momentum,
texture, not quite homophony; not quite polyphony either, making
a dense serious sound, sometimes close-spaced, sometimes wide,
often peculiar, with perverse interlocking and crossing of parts, arbitrary doublings, passing chords that if lingered on would be solecisms or even Stravinskyisms. Everyone plays all the time almost
without exception, in even quavers almost without exception; the

only rests come with the first violin solos, which also produce the only decoration, at the double bars and for the three bars in the second 'half' which lead to the 'return'. For 'half' it is not: despite the impression of unbroken tranquillity, the larger structure and the smaller phrasing are asymmetrical and unpredictable (except for the movement's one weak link, soon rectified). From start to close the listener glides on an imperturbable loop of endless melody, renewing itself out of its own motion – a gentle, modest ancestor of the *Tristan* Prelude and the obbligato recitative from Schoenberg's op. 16. In *mood*, however, this movement achieves an encapsulation of *largo religioso* feeling without any hint of *'religioso'* sanctimony: everything inheres within the notes.

Next, a middle movement from the end of Haydn's quartet-writing life: the andante from the String Quartet in F-major, op. 77 no. 2. Again, it is a matter of an ongoing momentum: but here textures, spacing and density are perpetually changing and the whole movement is melody-led and propelled by a walking bass; their combined impulse is so strong that both continue to be felt even when either surprisingly ceases. The melody (essentially 'three blind mice' with twiddles) is a sort of *faux naïve* Lego, whose every link can be used to make a different thing. It is at once genuine-simple and true-complex in its tone – how serious? how light? – as in the apparently artless, actually ultra-experienced twists and turns of its perpetually reinterpreted harmonizations. The crunch comes at the climax, where it makes its most elaborate reappearance. The spacing is marvellous – low viola on the march bass, high cello on the melody, first violin delivering a decorative descent of arpeggios and scales in staccato demisemiquavers (with second violin confined to occasional help filling out cadences). Instead of rounding off, it opens out. Taking up the bars of bare minims earlier in the movement, all three lower strings hold broad chords, but violin 1 continues its brilliant *essercizi* as the accompanying trio become explicitly military, even peremptory, then urgent, then in *crescendo* to *fortissimo*, as the solo violin flourishes cadenza-like on D-major triads then scales, the last being joined by violin 2 and viola in an upward rush of parallel first-inversion chords. It ought to be commonplace; in fact, it is tense and electric, creating an effect of extraordinary liberation – a tethered eagle unleashed. Yet the great bird is left in mid-air, and the movement's only silences follow (still perceived in measure), with one slashing dominant, brutally banal; then the resumption of the opening melody, richly harmonized in four parts in sonorous, low-position *pianissimo*, winding down via its internal self-recycling in ever-new textural subtleties and harmonic/ rhythmic inflections to close in a brief coda-ish extra. The feel of the movement altogether is haunting yet ordinary, obsessive yet open, short-circuiting yet free: persistent in dogged stoical trudge, genial but not wholly amiable, as much defiant as cheerful.

How are we to take music that seems to evoke such ambiguities and contrarieties as these, but that certainly supersedes their merely verbal expression – that offers, in its own intrinsic terms, a play of mood, as of material, simultaneously so straightforward and so ungraspable?

Things as remarkable, and extremely various, could easily be multiplied from the quartets between op. 20 no. 1 and op. 77 no. 2, as well, of course, as from his other greatest genres – mid-early and very-late piano sonatas and symphonies, and the fascinating treasure-house of piano trios. But how would such adjective-laden prose-poems as they might well elicit (I wrote many such in the course of preparing this chapter) square with the claim that Haydn is concerned more purely than any other composer with music's intrinsicality? Painting can more obviously than music be at once abstract and concrete. In the landscapes and still lifes of William Nicholson, says Merlin Ingli James,

> Horizons fall at endlessly surprising intervals and angles across the canvases; objects are unexpectedly aligned or misaligned with each other, placed with odd centrality, or half-dropped off a canvas's edge. Viewpoints are often unusually high, or low; boldly frontal or oddly oblique. As purely formal arrangements of tone and colour, the works have great individuality and sonorous beauty. These very formal and perceptual paintings are also, of course, highly metaphoric.

It would be idle to ask further: metaphors of *what*? This is the area at the heart of all the arts where structure and process fuse inseparably into expression; the total result is an emanation, however direct or oblique, from the life of the unique individual who is doing the making and summoning into being.

Music is about notes, whether the upshot is Tristan's delirium, Tchaikovsky's floods of passion, cardiac convulsions in Mahler and Berg, or any sonata, trio, quartet, symphony by Haydn. If it's not good composing, neither is it good expression of an emotion, or depiction of a character, or evocation of sunlight playing on the waves and all the rest. If 'words, not ideas, make a poem', how much more true is this for the relatively unconnotational art of music? It is not passions, neuroses, concepts, pictures or any other extraneous intentions that make a piece of music, but pitches, rhythms, durations, timbres, in all their infinite potential for organized combination.

Yet music *does* render all those extraneous things. If it were indeed just 'pure music', something – the main thing – would be missing (as in Mondrian, or Nicholson *fils*, when the viewer hankers to see apples, boughs, faces). So, what is abstraction, and how can unmitigated concentration upon the process of composition be at the same time a quest for what Debussy called 'the naked flesh of emotion'? It must be that the materials of music themselves not only convey passions, pictures and so forth, but that they actually are passionate and pictorial – intrinsically, of their nature. The 'extras' inhere; they are of the essence too. The problem is to reconcile music's natural tendency towards extra-musical content with the impulse to make pattern, argument and structure that are equally intrinsic to the art. And Haydn is poised right at its centre: because of the exceptionally nice balance he strikes, he compels one more than any other composer to ask what music actually is.

If there is, fortunately, no answer, further parallels from painting can again shift the ground. 'Significant form' was the once-familiar phrase coined to indicate the composition of a picture to be its own subject in the teeth of its ostensible replication of a nude, a landscape, a still life. Music as its own subject produces for Haydn a representation of itself – the disinterested exploration of compositional possibilities, the posing of difficulties, the pleasure and astonishment of their resolution – with 'sonata', 'double variation' and all the rest of his composing kit for playing field or chessboard. Its material is the mass of sonorous actualities available to him – clarinets here, no trumpets in Lent, etc., etc. – together with, of course, shapes and gestures that have been used over and over again and are dense with associations. The rest is all specific and particular: invention, resource, experience and experiment, intelligence focusing hard and fantasy flying free, the dispassion and involvement, amusement and interest, the piety and warmth of heart, the essential strangeness and solitude, and all the other traits of personality and character with which this individual human being will perforce infuse almost everyone in the succession of musical objects he makes.

Confronted by this oeuvre, discrepancies between abstract and concrete seem factitious. One could even sophistically claim that Haydn's very concreteness makes him so abstract, and vice versa. Moreover, his awareness of such sophistries is a part of his genius. He is as consummately in control of such questions about how music is doing what it is doing as he is of the materials and processes of a particular piece. There is an omniscience to his art that surpasses even Bach's, who knew everything about the science of music but was, one senses, unconscious of what his music was saying through its extraordinary transcendence of its stylistic norms and ostensible aims. Bach is the profounder artist; Haydn is the greater realist. None of which renders him any more graspable. Haydn the Ambiguous to the last. And how appropriate for Haydn the Ambiguous that his most inspired movement, 'The Representation of Chaos', should be simultaneously the representation of Order in a perfectly formed introduction-sonata, the weird contradiction expressed in sounds that sometimes come from some chuckling Biedermeier serenade (bars 28–31), sometimes grope into Bruckner at his creepiest (bars 32ff.), sometimes heave and pant with the sheer physical strain of giving birth (bars 26–7, 48–9), touch upon the metaphysical without strain throughout, and for the final ten bars (till the cadence) stray into the 'music of the future' fifty years before its time. But Haydn is the music of the future still. The true extent of his greatness is for the connoisseur a well-kept secret, for the larger public a ticking time bomb that has yet to go off. When its hour comes, the explosion, rather than a Big Bang, will be a still small voice telling of the strange within the normal, the vast within the modest, the dark within the bright and vice versa: the essence of human experience in essentially musical terms.

Mozart

Wolfgang Amadeus Mozart – born Salzburg 1756 into musically cultivated family – no early obscurity or struggle – an infant prodigy in performance and composition alike. With his elder sister, exploited by ambitious father from the age of five for a dazzling succession of successes Europe-wide: Austria, Germany, Paris, London, Holland, etc. Return to Salzburg aged ten – a year there, then three more in Vienna, another back home: then Italy – Rome, Bologna, Milan (several times); learning from all he encountered, composing copiously (often to prestigious commissions and general recognition of exceptional powers). Home again for some five further years, with intermittent foreign trips, principally Paris again, and Munich for *Idomeneo*. In 1781, aged twenty-six, he kicked off the irksome, patronizing patronage of his repressive employer, the Archbishop of Salzburg, to attempt the perilous life of a freelance musician in the capital. Initial success as player and teacher: the composing output plentiful in every going genre, now universally acknowledged as supreme, not then so widely appreciated as to lead to the court or church appointments necessary for livelihood – a sorry story of disappointments, debts, desperations, mitigated by occasional exceptional triumphs abroad, most notably *Figaro* and *Don Giovanni* in Prague. At home, no such surety, though *The Magic Flute* was playing to enthusiastic audiences even as his health, and seemingly career, declined. He died December 1791, aged thirty-six.

Mozart's present universal popularity would have surprised the taste of 1891. Early in that century he was taken by Hoffmann as a harbinger of Romantic daemonism, but as the Romantic epoch blossomed (with Hoffmann one of its key sources) Mozart was seen rather as an island of innocence before music realized its full powers. Between the summits of Bachian polyphony and Beethovenian symphonism came 'Papa' Haydn and the infant Mozart. Schumann's well-known view (incomprehensible to us) of the G-minor Symphony's carefree gaiety reaches a climax in Mahler's notorious contempt for classical formulae. Though his supremacy in opera was never doubted, vicissitudes of taste lost *Idomeneo*, *Così fan tutte*, even *The Magic Flute*, for many decades. These works, unsurpassed in their respective genres, all had to be revived in the twentieth century.

In fact, Mozart is a stranger composer than his apparently complete centrality would suggest. He lies athwart the main lines. On one hand there are the affect-and-image-makers – Bach, Schubert, Wagner – with their baroque continuity of texture and primacy of expressive meaning. But his native place would appear to be on the other – the thematic development and tonal argument whose focus is in the Viennese classical style and the sonata principle. At heart, though, Mozart is not like his two peers Beethoven and Haydn. He is not by nature an arguer or a developer. His starting-point is the conventions, routines, givens of material and form that make the going commonplaces of his time. His instrumental works 'go through the motions', shifting prefabricated musical units across highly formalized perspectives of key and texture; construction and proportion are what concern him, not logic or journey, or organic growth. They are at their greatest when most is in play, above all in the mature piano concertos with their extraordinary abundance of themes (far more than required by Haydn and Beethoven, whatever the genre). But in symphonies and chamber-music the result is often neat and dry. Only when these genres are infused with a vocal/dramatic element does Mozart take wing.

For what stirs his depths is virtuosity and display, wowing the aisles and bringing the house down. Though this also accounts for the quality of the piano concertos and those movements in chamber-works which seem to be rendering an operatic scene, it reaches its native land in music for the human voice. And vocal means the gamut of human expression, placed in an operatic context. Church-music only comes to life when charged, sometimes flagrantly, with theatrical fervour. Mozart's religious and ethical aspect lies altogether elsewhere, in pieces for Masonic rituals that culminate in the sublime *Funeral Music*, and only reach a larger public, as it were, surreptitiously, via *The Magic Flute*.

Another difference between Mozart and his classical peers is that his catalogue is full of oddments – bits and bobs that he touches with the highest flights of fantasy. Who but Mozart, commissioned to write something for a glass harmonica or a clockwork organ, would have bothered to turn these unappealing tasks (we have his word for it) into one-off masterpieces, or lavished his genius upon arias for insertion into other composers' operas, or transformed routine serenades and divertimentos (sometimes) into inspirations that belong with his greatest work? Two isolated piano-pieces stand with his highest and deepest inspirations – for the latter, an adagio in B-minor, for the former a rondo in A-minor, exquisite in poignant facture worthy of Chopin. Uninspired pieces are also, of course, numerous: Glenn Gould compared Mozart on an off-day to an interdepartmental communication. That such music shares the same lucidity and command as his greatest work makes his greatest vulnerable to easy-listening muzakization, as invited by not much of Haydn's, and almost nothing of Beethoven's. A high percentage of Mozart's bicentennial popularity is fuelled by the wallpaper quality which can debase him into a rococo successor to Vivaldi.

The core of the output, its animating *coeur*, being operatic, it follows that the 'abstract' genres suiting him best are posited upon display, prowess, projection: hence his supremacy in concertos – prin-cipally for his own instrument and performance, the piano; then for favourites like the clarinet and the violin/viola concertante; the horn, the flute-and-harp, even the solo violin, are relatively negligible. The comparable element prevails in the greatest chamber-works: as noted earlier, 'Mozart is always opera *manqué*', his articulation and phrasing vocal, his setting theatrical, his forms and processes dramatic. The greatest chamber-works all *project*: the eloquent protagonist of the clarinet quintet, the amorous duetting of first violin and first viola in the andante of the C-major String Quintet K. 515 and the two right hands in that of the F-major Piano-Duet Sonata K. 497, the trio of first oboe, clarinet, basset-horn in the adagio of the 13-Wind Serenade K. 361, all four winds in the larghetto of their quartet with piano in Eb K. 452: four of his greatest masterpieces. The solo keyboard sonata – so unlike Beethoven – is not essentially his; nor, despite some marvellous exceptions, is really the string quartet – so unlike Haydn as well as Beethoven! The string quintet's greater richness and – paradoxically – intimacy yield the deeper rewards. And the piano needs an orchestra to talk with. Arguably – I await execution – neither does the symphony suit him so exactly and perfectly as his two peers, unsurpassed in this genre – and this despite such magnificent utterances as the *Prague*, the G-minor, the *Jupiter* finale. Sonata is not, *au fond*, Mozart's forte: he doesn't argue, or build, or evolve: rather, setting out the sections of his sonata first movement in finely judged symmetry/asymmetry, sending them through a constellation of closely related keys – a slight sense of sleight-of-hand/ vamp-till-ready – stage-scenery shifted here and there till the design is complete, keeping going by mechanical routines that can sometimes be brusque, even perfunctory. The balancing compensation is the constant surprise/delight of new material – something that those mighty non-theatrical developers Beethoven and Haydn don't vouchsafe – when in doubt, another delicious new idea – opera/character/projection, not process/argument/journey. And the basis of all his ideas is always melodic – as, again, not *bei* Haydn and Beethoven – except, obviously, for figuration and scales and virtuous look-at-me/ listen-to-me stuff, whether keyboard or vocal. Vocal is the word; everything in Mozart is composed upon, phrased by, the voice.

Mozart is music's completest eclectic: as Hermann Abert's marvellous book (my review of it was headed 'the best book about the best composer') shows in exhaustive detail, he assimilated everything he encountered with rapidity, understanding, resourcefulness, flair: there's nothing he cannot *use*, transforming it all into a personal version of the universal and generalized idioms, procedures, routines, clichés of the common practice of his age. Mozart the boy prodigy toured the length and breadth of musical Europe, responding eagerly and fruitfully to everything he encountered, absorbing matters of technique, style, expression, mastering every instrumental and vocal advance, early learning to sharpen inborn taste and discrimination, transforming all he assimilated with natural avidity, taking everything thus devoured further, higher, deeper, *more* – be it tricks of the trade, routines and tropes, virtuosity, individual and corporate, or notable individuals' personal traits. This receptivity, so fructifying to his eclectic nature, continued into his brief, supercharged adult life. He responded equally to ephemeral phenomena and to the complex challenges presented by outstanding creative personalities: the living – Gluck, Haydn the two principal composers, as well as J. S. Bach's sons Carl Philipp Emanuel and Johann Christian – and eventually, the grateful dead: Handel and J. S. Bach himself.

All these contacts and contexts are fully explored by Abert, but nothing surpasses the detail with which Italian opera, Mozart's most celebrated genre, is filled in. Phrase after phrase one has whistled or hummed for decades, treasuring its especially Mozartian contour (not just from his Italian operas, but from the whole range of the output) turns out to be a standard turn, even a cliché, from his numerous predecessors in this field. Or, less often, something rather unusual that one's delighted ears have remembered. Mozart now emerges as a crowning synthesis of a whole voluminous and voluble tradition – greatest by far among figures by no means negligible, and far more ignored when Abert first researched them than nowadays, when the precursors of baroque and rococo are exploitatively gleaned. If the idea of plagiarism – the dismal climate that has eventuated in the notion of 'intellectual property' – had existed in his day, Mozart wouldn't have had a leg to stand on! The fact that he invariably enhanced what he 'stole' or 'borrowed' or 'remembered' would not mitigate the offence. He emerges as the most flagrant cribber, in this epoch of common property freely exploited, since Handel, the most notorious of all.

And yet he is also so utterly special and himself. Salieri's wry tribute at his premature death – 'It's just as well – if he'd lived we others would all be out of a job!' – speaks (if inadvertently) for every contemporary in its implicit acknowledgement not merely of Mozart's technical supremacy and easy copiousness (these were taken for granted in the culture) so much as of the extra, the *je ne sais quoi*, transcending common practice to produce something unique and celestial.

Operas

So to the core of the corpus: opera. Mozart is innately and naturally theatrical: character, situation, emotional particularity are crucial to him as not for Haydn, and for Beethoven still less. The basis is *buffa* – 'comic'; from this an enormous range of human conditions can ramify, including the 'serious' in all its aspects. Actual *seria* pieces are all impaired, even stilted, though sometimes containing some of his sublimest music. But the genius for *buffa* is ample enough to embrace a love-sick adolescent boy, a love-lorn aristocratic lady, a love-crazed virago, a lust-driven seducer hell-bent and defiant to the last. Canonical – the summit of Parnassus – stand the three Da Ponte collaborations in Italian, with the German *Singspiel Magic Flute*, *Idomeneo* (*seria*; Italian) and *Seraglio* (*Singspiel*; German) only a little below (if at all).

The path to the summit is full of delights and surprises. Not counting two extras, indispensable classics only since the Second World War, there are sixteen theatre pieces before *Figaro* in 1785–6: they range from full-length operas (four *seria*, four *buffa*) to shorter serenatas, occasional works; even a school show in Latin (*Apollo et Hyacinthus* – first in the long line, written at the age of eleven). One, *Zaïde*, though unfinished, is so substantial and inspired that it's not possible now to imagine doing without it. *Thamos, King of Egypt*, also impressive, only ever consisted of incidental choruses and orchestral interludes; two others, both begun in the wake of *Idomeneo*, are too fragmentary for rescue.

The journey can be undertaken with wonder and delight, commingled with many a yawn. At the very least there is the reward for diligence in watching the prodigious boy then teenager learning the ropes – not just how to master the conventions, get the things moving, build through complement and contrast, characterize, but how to cope equally with singers' recalcitrance, vanity, stupidity as with their spectacular endowments; how to respond at speed to challenges and emergencies of every kind (including positives, like some exceptionally accomplished instrumentalist); how to get on with and if necessary around his librettists. Plus plentiful exposure to the messy machinations endemic to theatrical life, then as now, but then compounded by the politics of Court, Church, Nobility at the heart of the *ancien régime*.

From the vantage point of the later masterpieces it's obvious that his comic genius will be Mozart's most fruitful way forward. Not, though, to the young composer hungry to succeed and bursting with ideas. For him the greatest aspiration was *opera seria* in all its frigid panoply of unreal people in stilted situations exercising impossible clemency or villainy. Of course, the characters and situations of comedy are just as stereotyped to begin with; but it's with them that the future lies. Or with a mixture. And while there's no doubt that there's more pleasure and value in Mozart's earlier stage endeavours on the *buffa* side, and that all the worst longueurs are *seria*, what one sees is the progressive breakdown and intermingling of these seemingly watertight separations. Ahead by a very few years lie the coexistence in *Figaro* of high and low equalized in the exigencies of desire and the cunning needed to fulfil it; the tragic nobility and the rustic peasantry who dance obedient to the tune of master and man in *Don Giovanni*; the invasion in *Così fan tutte* of absurdity and parody by real, sharp, painful emotion. All this is being tried out in the earlier pieces; sometimes the connection is tenuous: more often it is so strong as to induce a shock of precognition.

From the eleven-year-old's first efforts through to *Zaïde* (1779–80, aged twenty-three/four) Mozart is learning the ropes. Plentiful promise of what's to come: the audaciously extended finale to Act II of *La finta giardiniera* (surpassing – in scale – the celebrated Act II finale in *Figaro*): in *Zaïde* the experimental melodramas, mix of speech and music, indicate a path not taken; the heroine's *Ruhe sanft* aria is justly famous; and the ensembles evince the prodigy now to be master of all he surveys.

Idomeneo and *Die Entführung* are the complementary twin-peaks of Mozart's earlier operatic output, one a heroic *seria* on the grandest scale, the other a small-scaled *Singspiel* (i.e. in German, not Italian, and with spoken dialogue rather than sung recitative between the musical numbers) – of consummate wit, brio, finish. *Idomeneo* (K. 366) was a commission for Munich in 1780–81: Mozart immediately considered a recast into German, and later (1786) revised the work for a revival in Vienna. It then fell into oblivion in the nineteenth century, to be rediscovered in the twentieth, and is now seen as among his very greatest compositions, a regular though not absolutely standard in the repertoire, and by no means without its problems.

Idomeneo, King of Crete, out on stormy seas returning from the Trojan War, vows that in exchange for safe return he will sacrifice to Neptune the first living being he encounters on his native strand. Who of course turns out to be his beloved but unrecognized son, Idamante. The situation at court is already troubled by a love-triangle: Idamante loves Ilya, a captive Trojan princess; but is pursued by a Greek princess, Elettra, with wild abandon and jealous hatred of her rival. To escape execution of his rash vow the King intends sending his son, with the wrong woman, to safety abroad: in these arrangements Ilya inadvertently reveals her affections – another reason to separate them. All is thwarted by Neptune's rage at the vow's evasion: he sends a monster to the island, accompanied by a tempest, and Act II ends with scenes of communal terror. At the start of Act III relative calm is momentarily shed as the young lovers finally confess their feelings in a duet. But the ensuing quartet is altogether tragic – the conflicted love-triangle (Elettra joins in), plus the father's compunction even as he urges his son's departure that will desolate all but Elettra (and probably her too). The action now opens from close encounters to wide open spaces in the presence of the priesthood and populace of Crete. Idomeneo is compelled to confess his promise and to fulfil it: steps to the sacrifice commence, Neptune's temple aside the sea-god's oceanic realm the appointed place. The King prays for remission: news is brought that his son has slain the monster and will return to willingly embrace his own death: Ilya interposes her own body in his stead: angry Neptune is moved to mercy – the old King must abdicate; the young pair, united, will reign in his place – and all ends in rejoicing save for the spurned and embittered Elettra, whose fury penetrates like a thorn in the flesh (and we know that her later story will end badly).

A familiar tale told via standard conventions, whose music continually breaks the bonds. Such numbers as Elettra's two tirades and her rival's lyric aria in Act II with four concertante wind-instruments surpass in richness anything in Mozart's subsequent operas: the quartet, too, is supreme among his ensembles. There's a lavishness from the twenty-five-year-old, a careless generosity that later, with experience, he spreads more sparingly. And the chorus-writing is unsurpassed elsewhere, even by the two mighty incomplete Masses (C-minor and *Requiem*). The panic terror as the monster threatens tingles the spine; the grand ritual solemnity of the scene in the sea-god's temple shakes the soul as no *Sanctus* or *Credo* – astonishing music – among the greatest he ever wrote: that can sometimes seem to be actually *the* greatest – promising future developments *in potentia* that never came to be. Yet there is a stiffness, a lack of tension, an element of deadness in the drama as a whole, that is utterly *un*-Mozartian. Seeing *Idomeneo* in the theatre is like going to a concert. Gluck's two operas upon the same theme – the inadvertent sacrifice of a beloved relative – *move* through pacing and momentum, despite their comparative musical meagreness.

That Mozart's gift for comedy is more innate and natural to him than for these grand, lofty, tragic subjects, whatever depths he plumbs (and whatever their happy *deus-ex-machina* endings), has already been suggested, and is confirmed in full by his next work, *Die Entführung aus dem Serail* (henceforth *Seraglio*) – a *Singspiel* written for Vienna in 1781–2. It again was long something of a Cinderella until its widespread recognition and acceptance from the mid-twentieth century. Characters and setting capitalize on the fashion for all things Oriental, exotic and amorous: the story is slight and silly, the music is utterly fresh and delicious, enhancing and transcending its occasion, and occasionally finding within it some unexpected depths. Mozart's letters while composing *Seraglio* reveal how he felt for and with these cardboard cut-outs – the palpitations of the young hero in love, the sadistic rage of the eunuch (presumably) who would thwart him: and somehow the imbalances and incompleteness of the action and its actors are lost to the score's overflowing effervescence.

There are two shortcomings: a clear weakness that the benevolent barbarian Bassa Selim is confined to speech alone: but *too much* music is the problem with the heroine's notorious showpiece *Marten aller Arten* (tortures of all kinds will not prevail against my virtue and fidelity) – a colossal virtuoso concerto – four obbligato instrumental soloists as well as the soprano – decidedly not among Mozart's best. Far more valuable the delicious Vaudeville to close, wherein every character signs off appropriately in couplets, clear forerunner of the epilogue to *Don Giovanni*.

Both these 1780–82 works, flawed yet full of marvellous music, foretell what is to come: and with hindsight what is to come will more fruitfully be 'comic' not 'serious'. In the Da Ponte operas that commence some four years later, *buffa* and *giocosa* (humour) are the prevailing intonation; into these, currents of pathos, melodrama, even tragedy, can be subsumed, and are. Meanwhile an *intermezzo*, slight, even trivial, yet musically of the highest order. *Der Schauspiel-direktor* (K. 486) – *The Impresario* – a *jeu d'esprit* satirizing and parodying opera-singers and their manager, received from their composer (present only by implication – insignificant, a mere flunkey) a score utterly discrepant, brimming with top-notch invention (as well as fun), not least in the superb Overture, superior musically to any of those for the greater works. A court divertissement, by definition ephemeral – what a waste! – originally intervolved with an equally temporary piece by Mozart's bête noire Salieri, whose subject, *prima la musica poi le parole*, was to blossom some 150-plus years later into Strauss's last and finest opera *Capriccio*. Mozart's contribution in 1786 was, after the aforesaid Overture, just four vocal numbers. Impresario Frank and his factotum Buff are forming a troupe: two speaking actresses are engaged, then comes Mme Herz, all pathetic, and Mlle Silberklang, all brilliance though not without pathos. Their rivalry

over who shall command the highest fee turns into a slanging-
match over who can produce the highest note, thence a contest
between their respective prowess with *adagissimo* and *allegrissimo*.
A trio develops wherein the tenor Vogelsang keeps the peace (just):
the three's genuine warmth in praise of their common art moves
well beyond parody/satire. Trio becomes quartet when Buff joins:
all four agree to split their differences when Herr Frank threatens to
abandon the enterprise altogether if they won't. Mozart's parodies
are acute, indeed lethal: yet there's no doubt that music wins over
words. And the next word-and-music is *Figaro*, already commenced
when the *jeu d'occasion* interrupted it, and completed later the same
year. *The Impresario*'s idiom and manner are posed between *Seraglio*
(they share the same librettist) and the parodies and rivalries of *Così*
to come: and musically it is as rich as either or both.

But *Figaro* (K. 492) is the real thing at last: plot and characters
wherein Mozart's gifts for such find their fullest scope for utterance
and expression. Here's a précis demonstrating the perfect balance
of symmetry and asymmetry. Aristocratic male/female leads Count
Almaviva and his Countess (only once named – Rosina); their
plebeian maid- and manservants, engaged to be married, Figaro
and Susanna: marked 'gender' sympathy between mistress and maid,
mirrored by male-to-male complicity plus suppressed sexual rivalry
between master and man. 'Forbidden' desires; explicit, the Count's
for Susanna; latent, perhaps, between Figaro and the Countess.
Figaro as Mercury-cum-Master of Ceremonies – cum Conjurer/
Manipulator. The delicate tender/tactful exploration of every fluctuation of the two pairs' relationships and of the cross-currents
between each possible pairing (not forgetting class-barriers, their
proprieties and transgressions, which *they* never do). Cherubino –
ravishing study of adolescent amorous ardour and waxing male
sexuality, completely without lubriciousness (think of Octavian in
Rosenkavalier!): Cherubino equipoised between his panting worship
of the Countess and his knockabout flirtatiousness with Susanna,
wherein he rhymes with Figaro, and will one day be a seducing
seigneur exercising his *droit*, like the Count. Even little Barbarina
has her part in these interconnections worthy of Laclos and Austen;

erotic object-ette of Cherubino (well-suited in age-and-stage) and
the Count (just one more in his list of 1,003 conquests); her single
cameo of an aria as expressive of character as anything from the
major figures.

Secondary one-dimensional roles are all also very strongly
present without a false move: and the plot truly needs them – they
aren't peripheral, except the Lawyer: even Antonio the drunken
gardener is indispensable as a necessary cog in the comic machinery; and the ageing enamoured Marcellina, her shuffling ex-lover
Bartolo, crafty insinuating Basilio – stock figures, all, of *commedia
dell'arte* – actually help articulate the structure and advance the plot
('His mother!?' 'Yes, and I'm his father too'). It's a pity that the individual solo numbers at the start of Act IV are almost invariably
omitted, the work being already so long. Not that great musically,
they expand its human and social scope, and fulfil an architectural/
pacing scheme – five arias in a row commencing with Barbarina's
(a gem: never omitted!) and ending with Figaro's diatribe, believing
himself about to be betrayed by his bride; then hers, which he takes
to be the living proof of his bitter words, though she actually sings
only of her new husband – before the fastest-moving and easily the
most complicated imbroglio, set to the work's most densely concentrated music, in which tangles, mistakes, disguises, faults venal
or venial, are committed, exposed, condoned, forgiven.

The entire plot could be told thus, instancing its interlocking ingenuity and complexity. I'm not going to here: it's familiar
enough in essentials, and until the imbroglio of Act IV easy enough
to follow. Thereafter I and many others can still be baffled by who
is in who's clothes imitating whose voice, mistakenly misidentified
or accurately surmised but ignorance feigned, etc., etc. – to all of
which the music is obedient in every note, from mockery bitter or
hilarious, rage feigned or real, cross-dressing and crossing the class-
barriers, deep currents of desire disguised or transposed before the
explicit heart-on-sleeve/heart-stopping discovery/denouement. But
to thus reduce to algebra would be like *Emma* without the novelist's
actual words. In Mozart as surely as in Wagner after him the heart of
the tale, its events and personages, lies in the music itself. A truism,

obviously: and for sure the original Beaumarchais play and even Da Ponte's purposefully simplified transposition would make effective sense without a note of music beyond the 'diegetic' strains of Cherubino's serenade and the chorus and dances for the Marriage itself. Mozart's omniscient self-transformations into every aspect of every character make a *dramma per musica* fully as mature as the more elaborate intellectual and 'cultural' ideal of the *Gesamtkunstwerk*: without the latter's heavy paraphernalia; still wholly within the conventions of the genre, and not requiring the music of the future and a special new species of tuba.

Figaro is the summa of integrated human-compositional-architectural perfection. None of its successors equal, let alone surpass, it, though its immediate successor, *Don Giovanni*, is yet more celebrated – from the start iconic and archetypal, like *Hamlet* or *Faust*. Unlike the others it remained constant in the repertoire throughout the nineteenth century, stripped of the apparently facetious 'morning after' Epilogue to close in well-deserved retributive hell-fire. Even before the cheeky homage paid to it in the epilogue to *The Rake's Progress*, the coda was restored, recognized as inseparable from, indispensable to, the paradox of a *dramma giocosa*, the opera's description on the title page.

Puzzles, inconsequences, loose-ends, redundancies, disappointments abound in *Don Giovanni*. Everyone questions Don Ottavio, procrastinating wimp without Hamlet's reasons, feeble foil to the virile all-conquering hero. And everyone agrees upon the strengths – the Commendatore's murder at the very start of the action, his petrification into a living statue come to claim supper and vengeance at the action's close; the vengeful woman, seduced and abandoned by the libertine but still painfully obsessed with him, desire, even love, strong as death. Between these extremes of *seria*, the *buffa* – the hero's and manservant's burlesque episodic (mis)adventures, notoriously none of them successful. Any number of such mock-heroic diminishments could occur: they are not organic, are indeed haphazard, almost arbitrary: structure (such as it is) is additive – events repeat without accumulating to culminate in the inevitable fatal close. On a disgruntled day one can feel that Act II has nothing vital

to add, till the Statue and the Supper: that the terrific close of Act I
has finished the piece off save for this 'promised end' prophesied at
the Overture's opening.

Set-piece character-arias for the women are marvellous – raging
love-driven Elvira (Elettra from *Idomeneo* on acid): Anna her faithful,
patient, father-fond complement: the peasant-couple and their interrupted nuptials are deftly drawn: Leporello the resourceful manservant full of life: the Commendatore comes to death, then to
life, in a few economical strokes. But the two principal men don't.
Ottavio the dummy has been already mentioned: but Giovanni
himself is also a man of straw, curiously uninhabited and inexpres-
sive. It's oft-remarked that he has no real music of his own – his
single number, the 'champagne aria', is hardly a highlight! – maybe
an inwardly searching, confessional-revealing piece à la Verdi would
be outside the work's, and the period's, manners. Above all there is
no continuous interaction of the kind that keeps *Figaro* perpetually
volatile. Master-and-Man come closest to a relationship: then, again,
think of Figaro and the Count – three dimensions, not one.

Interaction *does* occur in the opera's two greatest individual
numbers – the wonderful quartet in Act I, the superb sextet in
Act II; yet both are redundant dramatically! The latter is unarguably the greatest number in the work, arguably the greatest in all
Mozart's operatic achievement. Yet the four people in the quartet,
the six in the sextet, are exactly where they were at the end as at the
start. Compare the 'recognition' sextet in *Figaro*, with its rapid succession of revelations, misapprehensions, teasings, bickerings, recon-
ciliations (albeit with a muffled undercurrent of baffled rage): the
plot and its characters have *advanced* during and by means of this
ensemble – the principals' relations are radically altered: they, and
we, are somewhere else.

Don Giovanni all loose ends: *Così fan tutte* (two years later) tight as
a seatbelt: formulaic, a board-game, a machine, an equation – 'loves
of the triangles' *à quattro* rather than in threes. If one merely read the
scenario then the libretto in full, one could be excused for dismissing *Così* as mere algebra, inhuman and frigid. Beethoven notoriously
declared it unworthy of Mozart and demeaning of Women (which

didn't prevent his ripping off rotten the canonic trio wherein, their original pairings resumed, the lovers toast each other – with the angry exception of single disappointed Guglielmo, who's not come out so well from the swop – into the high-minded exaltation of the canonic quartet in *Fidelio*!).

Elsewhere, the paired male pawns are not deeply differentiated: ardent amorous tenor, gruffer basso harder to move and please: together they complement the cynical manipulative bachelor who sets up the situation, a wager over woman's innate fickleness. The pert knowing/conniving/encouraging maid-confidante whose bottom he pinches is straight out of stock; musically too. The two girls are more distinct, though distinctly types not individuals: Dorabella lighter, more easily seduced from the faithful path; Fiordiligi more passionate, adamant, falling (eventually) from a nobler stance and a greater height. Neither is three-dimensional like the Countess/Susanna/Cherubino, nor so etched in their single unchanging humour as Elvira or Anna. The machinery is mechanical, the denouement as disappointingly perfunctory as the Overture.

The enterprise invites parody, uncalled-for elsewhere in the canon except for obvious purposes in *The Impresario*: and the invitation is accepted. Which makes for stiffness in the arias, none save one among the composer's greatest. The exception, too, is only partial: Fiordiligi's *per pietà* rondo with the obbligato pair of horns (again, not lost on the composer of *Fidelio*) ends as vacuous as it commences beautiful. The work's musical glories lie in ensembles, of the essence with a cast of six – two sisters, two suitors, the male and female exhorters – in a great variety of pairings, triplings, quartettings and sextettings; and of emotional temperature from pathos mock or real to bluster, importunity, anger, ardour, persiflage. The finest individual moment, crisis of the long journey by which the prevailing artifice gradually breaks down the most resistant girl and most persistent wooer – little broken phrases for the two voices beneath an exquisitely poised cadential melody for oboe – four bars of seraphic beauty that would be as moving, and in the same way, as the Count's *perdono* in *Figaro* and his Countess granting him the mercy he craves. But the context of *Così* overall not exactly sullies as, surely, diminishes such intimations of deeper undercurrents. The more consistent glories are the ensembles: now in one affect such as the famous farewell trio invoking calm sea and prosperous voyage, wherein for once the cynic can join the sisters' melting harmony and the dulcet orchestra without distancing irony; or in multifaceted ambiguity like the succession in Act I of trios, quartets, quintets and a single sextet – prodigies of invention and ingenuity, subsuming algebra and parody and opposites into complex human unity 'as if by magic'. Act II has nothing to compare save the precious four bars in which Fiordiligi succumbs to the wrong/right man's beguilements.

Let's dispose of *La clemenza di Tito*, written later in Mozart's final year for a Bohemian coronation: throwback to *opera seria* at its most routine, whose dead-duck nature had been so superseded in his operas from *Idomeneo* on. The name-part's fearsome clemency, formalized into formula by Pietro Metastasio, had already been set some forty times, variously adapted. Unlike most of Mozart's now-canonical operas, *Titus* was popular in the nineteenth century and fell out of favour as these others returned to it. In recent decades it has been apologized for/explained away to some effect; but neither in story nor score can it compete, though the villainess-heroine Vitellia's principal number is strong, and the strange glacial chill, frozen as Rome burns, of the Act I finale is not quite like anything else in the output, foreshadowing the frigid neo-classicism of Cherubini or/and Spontini (*Rienzi* on the far horizon).

He is on course with its predecessor. 'The difficulties of *Fidelio* are very instructive', wrote Tovey. Substitute for these the lacklustre, the loss of vital comic impulse, the tiredness of *Titus*, to turn back 'to the almost nonsensical *Zauberflöte* and observe how perfectly the comings and goings of Mozart's music explain themselves'.

Music begins naturally on the rise of the curtain, and stops naturally with the exit of all the characters except the youth who is lying unconscious. He revives, wonders where he is, hears a distant piping; and the approach of the bird-catcher Papageno explains the piping and is accompanied by the orchestral introduction to his song. Later on, three veiled ladies give the hero a miniature portrait of the princess he is to rescue. He gazes at the portrait and falls in love; the orchestra heaves two sighs and Tamino's love-song begins. The scene darkens, the Queen of Night appears, enthroned among stars, pours out her woes and promises her daughter to the hero. She vanishes. Daylight returns. Tamino, wondering whether it was all a dream, is encountered by poor Papageno who, punished for his lies with a padlock on his mouth, can only sing *hm, hm, hm*; another perfect occasion for music, worked up in a quintet in which the three veiled ladies remove his padlock and instruct him and Tamino how to set forth on their quest. And so from point to point the happy nonsense proceeds, always right and effective in matters the mishandling of which may ruin the finest story.

Let me attempt to continue Tovey's incomparable start through to the end. A complete change of scene – 'a splendid room in the Egyptian style, with carpets, divans, etc.' A blackamoor, raging with lust, pursues a hapless white girl; slaves fetter her; enter the birdcatcher – where am I? He addresses the heroine; but, confronting the villain, each is flabbergasted by the other's bizarre coloration, and the little trio ends as a comic duet upon further nonsense-monosyllables, and their frightened flight in opposite directions. But Papageno at once re-enters as the girl recovers from her swoon. They discover themselves to each other in spoken dialogue: Pamina, still unnamed, already drawn to the still-unnamed Tamino. The bird-catcher sadly regrets the lack of a partner for himself. Cue for music – delectable duet praising mutual faithful love. Exeunt. Finale: a Grove with Temples, one dedicated to Wisdom, another to Nature. Sweetly solemn strains as three 'Genii' – boys to match the three veiled ladies of earlier, who had promised this guidance – lead Tamino in, and commend him to be steadfast, obedient, silent. To his anxious enquiry – will I find Pamina here? – they can only repeat the injunction, adding that if he manifests courage he will surely gain the victory. Left alone, he boldly attempts one Temple, to be sternly repulsed by voices from within; again with the second;

so he tries a third (Virtue? the libretto is often vague in specifics). This third time (everything in the work comes in Masonic threes) an agèd Priest appears. Their long dialogue is perhaps the high-point of accompanied recitative in all opera. The grave old man questions, the impetuous young man rebels – all he's heard so far of Sarastro, leader of this high-minded commune, is bad: for now he cannot be disabused. Recitativo grows metrical and melodic with the Priest's departing words – when you are fit and ready, friendship's hand will permit admission to our sacred order. The orchestra heaves two poignant sighs, and Tamino is left alone in spiritual and physical darkness. The Priest's final rune is sung twice by the cellos, as a male chorus within reply to the hero's anguished questions – 'soon, or never' will he find Enlightenment; and promise that Pamina still lives.

Rejoicing, he takes up the flute the ladies had given him (Tovey's précis didn't mention the magic musical gift that provides the work's title, nor the set of magic chimes presented to Papageno); his playing alternates with his singing: wild animals, literally enchanted into tameness, creep from the boscage to listen. The flute's last phrase coincides with the bird-catcher's pipes, heard answering. Tamino rushes off in search; Pamina and Papageno appear, searching for him; further exchanges of flute and pipes at least show that Tamino still lives. They would rush away in search but are apprehended by the menacing blackamoor, now naming himself – Monostatos – summoning slaves to chain the pair till, recalling the bells, Papageno starts up a tinkling carillon that sets slaves and their master off into a grotesque and harmless dance. As they dance off the two halves of the as-yet-separated pairs sing their second duet, hymning harmony, human sympathy, mutuality, without which is no joy on earth.

Distant chorus (for the first time full, including women's voices) proclaim the entry of Sarastro. Papageno whimpers in fear, Pamina is steadfast in urging The Truth come what may. The Leader and his retinue now appear – he in a triumphal car drawn by lions. Pompous choral tribute to their Leader's wisdom and benevolence, as yet unproven and apparently, from the Queen of the Night's testimony, false. Pamina pleads with dignified self-possession – my escape was compelled by the lustful Moor's pursuit. Sarastro answers in noble strains – I cannot free you yet. *She* – but heed a daughter's tears. *He* – don't mention your evil mother to me – you need a man's Reason, not a woman's Folly and Falsehood. At which controversial point Monostatos enters with his captured prey Tamino. Hero and heroine instantly recognize each other as the right other; the chorus briefly wonder; the Moor wheedles and cringes before his master, to be tricked into a bastinado, rather than his expected congratulations, for reward. Such further evidence of Wisdom and Benevolence is hailed chorally; a few bars of recitative foretell the sacred rites to come, and the chorus burst out again in praise of such Godlike Virtue. End of Act I.

'And so from point to point the happy nonsense proceeds'; and it's abundantly clear by now that sublime elevation can coexist alongside pantomime gags, and deep feeling – amorous, humane, pathetic – alongside cosy cheer, truistic platitude, unrestrained lechery: and that an apparent glitch in story and character whereby good and bad forces, darkness of Night and brightness of Sun, appear to have got confused, even reversed, can be completely overridden.

Shall I continue point to point for Act II? The point is made; but the interest can be prolonged and the pleasure is irresistible. Happy nonsense now grows more serious and ethical as the Trial for the noble hero and his plebeian counterpart approaches. A ravishing little Masonic-non-military march opens the Act: Sarastro's spoken declaration of proceedings is punctuated by the ritual thrice times three chords on solemn Masonic winds: he invokes Isis and Osiris to guide the heroic pair, echoed by the male chorus after both stanzas of his noble aria. The two men-at-trial are led in: silence is enjoined – cue for music! – two priests briefly warn against women's wiles. On cue the three ladies of early in Act I reappear, re-urging the Queen's cause. Tamino preserves his silence, Papageno of course can't restrain his native babble. Disconcerted in defeat, the ladies prepare to disappear on a note of mocking reproach, and the light-footed quintet suddenly erupts into a violent outburst from the angry male chorus. The ladies cry out thrice in woe and sink into the ground: Papageno also thrice cries *woe* – no hope for him now. Cue for speech: priests escort the two towards their ordeals.

With Shakespearean fluency we're in a garden: Pamina sleeps, Monostatos hovers with intent. Cue for music – a sparkling little Turkish number, feather-light with piccolo, as he renews his assault, to be foiled by the Queen of the Night herself. The Moor she easily dismisses; but with her daughter matters are no longer straightforward – Pamina's loyalty now lies elsewhere. A hint of prior events between Night and Sun drops casually into their spoken dialogue, going as naught in the opera itself, but waxing evermore significant in later variants and *hommages*, from Goethe's sequel and Hofmannsthal's gigantic elaboration to Tippett's *Midsummer Marriage* and Bergman's enchanting film. Mother gives daughter a dagger, commanding her to slay Sarastro and thus restore the domain of Darkness – cue for her second aria, a splendid set-piece of thunder-and-lightning flim-flam with its notorious high F's. She sinks to earth, Moor and maid are again left to speech – yield to me and I'll save you! Never! Never? – then die! Sarastro opportunely comes upon the crisis and averts it, filling in a bit more missing background. All this too silly to be sung: music resumes in his second aria, its key right outside the work's principal tonal areas, celebrating the peace to be found in this sacred place – as in his first, noble, grave, and as notable for its deep notes as the Queen's two aria's for their high.

From exalted to low: Papageno's Trials, part 1 – there he is, tantalized by the unappetizing guise of his heart's desire as a withered old crone. For once *not* quite cue for music from their dialogue: the boys and their trio come from nowhere, bearing a table spread with refreshments plus the flute and the carillon. This delicious fleecy sicilienne, another sharp-keyed number in this E♭/C-centred work, seems to have strayed in from *Così* or the *Seraglio*. The two men (Tamino is also on stage) are left with foods, wines and their respective instruments. Papageno the earthy partakes and relishes and cannot keep silent, Tamino abstains (apart from a few notes on his magic flute): his locked lips taken by poor Pamina, when she now arrives, as evidence that he no longer loves her. Now, again, 'a perfect occasion for music' – her heartbroken aria of desolation, ending with an invocation to death, closing with three bars of orchestral coda to melt the heart of a stone. She wanders off and the two men resume one-way discourse by speech and dumb-signs.

In a vault of a Temple (Abstinence?) the chorus of Priests again invoke the Egyptian gods, binding the noble youth to their precepts and promising a good outcome. Sarastro is also present: in a brief spoken scene he sentences the lovers (Pamina has returned) to a 'last farewell'. A touching trio ensues, beautifully poised between the three voices, expressing perplexity and forbidding on her part, stalwart steadiness on her lover's, with Sarastro as a sort of maître d'/ compère – the hour is nigh, it must be farewell till we meet again – another number that might easily fit mood- and idiom-wise, into *Così* or even *Giovanni*. Back down to low-life: Papageno's Trial by hunger and thirst. Granted an enchanted goblet of wine he breaks into women and song for his second aria, bird-catcher turned girl-catcher, straight from the woods and fields of *Völkisch* Austria or the taverns of working-man's Vienna. Its ritornello employs the magic bells: as its third stanza ends, they yield once again the old crone. More pressing this time, she warns that unless he embraces her, he'll never gain his goal. Muttering escape-clauses he does so: she's instantly transformed into his heart's desire and counterpart, the bird-girl Papagena; and as instantly whipped away. He's not yet worthy – further trials are in store. All this is spoken, of course.

For no particular reason the finale begins here – by definition continuous music with no further speaking. I've never understood quite why it always feels absolutely right, though odd, that this long ensuing stretch of through-composed music should begin in the middle of nowhere/anywhere. No cue for music serves just as well as a '*Fanget an!*'. Dulcet wind-strains: the three boy-genii hail the rising sun – earth would be a heaven were it not for Pamina their ward's distress, bereft of Reason in the torments of Love. She joins in, bearing the dagger given her by her mother – she'd fain perish at her own hand. The boys forestall the deed – he still loves you – more we cannot say, than that he will be true unto death: all four treble voices blend to celebrate the mutuality of two loving hearts.

From dulcet suavity to solemn grandeur: trombones to the fore, a chorale-prelude – Lutheran and Catholic style, material, technique for this Masonic Brotherhood centred upon Man and Mankind. Two armoured male figures guarding a Pyramid sing the chorale in unison at the octave, Stravinskian unison non-legato on the trombones doubled by winds adding two further higher octaves, while the strings weave a stealthy web of dissonant dragging counterpoint: he who can overcome the fear of death will reach Enlightenment. As it closes, Tamino declares his readiness to face the ordeal. As the threshold is crossed to enter the Pyramid, he hears Pamina's voice – stay! The three male voices blend in trio – the two warriors now humanizing almost into skittishness – and the principal couple is permitted to embrace at last, in a radiant exchange of four-bar phrases, absolutely simple, absolutely unforgettable. She continues alone in *arioso*: as she ends, the three men steal gently in – the power of Sound will guide us beyond the power of Death. And so to the Trials: by fire first, Tamino leading, playing his magic flute, accompanied by soft brass and drums. Fire safely traversed, the lovers sing in rapt gentle tenths and sixths that water may equally prove harmless; the flute-led march again, a concentrated encapsulation of the quietly triumphant rapture, then the scene is flooded with brilliant sunlight and the off-stage chorus – now, again, including women's voices – hail the noble pair and invite them to enter into the reward they have so-hard earned.

Papageno's last Trial still looms. In a nearby garden he tootles his five-note pipe with comic desperation, calling by her name the pretty little wife he'd only glimpsed for a moment before she was snatched from him. Major turns minor; the music briefly foretells Mozart's last, only a few months on, the *Lachrymosa* where his work on the *Requiem* breaks down, as the poor bird-man prepares to hang himself. Delaying tactics – he gives Fate three (of course) chances – three piping tootles – 'nobody comes'. He steels himself to die – farewell, false world! – as the three boys step in – stay! be sensible! He's scornful, till they remind him of his other instrument, the bells. What a perfect fool I am! how could I forget? He sets them chiming, himself singing a little invocation; the boys turn him around, and there she is, young and willing and waiting. Their nonsense-duet – as though he still had a padlock on his tongue and can only stammer *Pa . . . pa . . . pa*, which she obediently imitates – is the happy outcome of his two duets with the exalted P-heroine in Act I, both commending married felicity. Now at last it's come to be the right P-girl: they count their forthcoming offspring with the glee of Leporello enumerating his master's conquests.

The abundant prospect closes in noisy jubilation, to be followed at once by its opposite, a soft, choked march – Monostatos and the three ladies, hushing each other as they essay a desperate last assault upon the reign of Light. The Queen of the Darkness is with them, now indistinguishable from her servitors till they join in a foursome to pray that her powers bring about imminent revenge. Instead, with brusque suddenness and brevity all five are overturned by thunder and lightning. They scatter into the depths, their power destroyed for ever. All is done save the shouting: light floods in; a strange two bars of clashing descending suspensions open out into ceremonial pomp as Sarastro declares the banishment of superstition and falsehood. Not of women per se: two loving pairs are united, and the choruses that follow are again *full* – at first slow, serious, Handelian; then gay, *brioso*, Haydnesque (with plenty of magic flautism in the scoring), containing a more lyric strain, then ending bright and loud: as voices cease the flute-motif comes softly for four bars, then a further eight of orchestral tutti rounds off 'the happy nonsense' in the most satisfactory manner imaginable.

All in all, a shining paradigm of how in opera the 'exotic', 'irrational', 'imbecile' can be of the very essence of the genre. Not so much 'folly to be wise' as Wise to be Foolish. Erasmus would have smiled approval: the next great landmark is *Parsifal*.

Church-music

With two outstanding exceptions Mozart's music for the Catholic Church is disappointing – written by rote, part of an employment he left early and willingly, then later re-sought of necessity. Neither Haydn's unquestioning faith nor Beethoven's mighty metaphysical struggles are apparent in the amiably accomplished anonymity of Mozart's Masses, Vespers, Epistle-Sonatas, etc. Two operas touch realms of religious sublimity way beyond most of the church-music, for all their pagan provenance: the ceremonial parts of *Idomeneo* and the hymns to Isis and Osiris and Enlightenment in *The Magic Flute*.

The two exceptions in his liturgical work are fortuitously both unfinished. Both were unwontedly personal, though hardly in a Romantic sense: the *Mass in C-minor* (K. 427), a wedding-gift for his bride Constanze (and including a starring role for her soprano voice); and the *Requiem in D-minor* (K. 626), his last composition, widely seen as his own swan-song (he sang fragments to his amanuensis on his deathbed). Both are instinctively/unaffectedly/unashamedly operatic in idiom and technique.

How to round them off rightly has exercised musicians ever since that troubled demise. Rescue-work on the mighty *Mass*-torso had been begun by its composer himself, transforming it into an oratorio, *Davide Penitente*, for which some fine new numbers were added to the re-texted liturgical sections. It has long seemed plausible to take these additions back into the Mass they might have come from. This has been effected with loving skill by the scholar-pianist Robert Levin: he also adapts further fragments and sketches, to make a performing score completing the familiar liturgy with the size, splendour, high inspiration of what Mozart left. Yet the whole remains uneven: the opening *Kyrie*, the *Domine Deus* and *Quoniam* from the *Gloria* extend our sense of Mozart's compositional range and powers: the *Incarnatus* from the *Credo* is a delectable operatic lollipop for Constanze: but the *Sanctus* is routine, and its *Osanna* recalls the dire 'all legal devices considered' fugue for two pianos in the same key written at the same time, also for his bride, wooing her with polyphonic prowess (she was fond of counterpoint). Above all, the heart of the *Mass* fails to convince. Just where, in the *Credo*, the central mysteries of the faith approach and are then uttered, the music fails to express them. This is not a concert-work for all its worldly charms. Mozart was a devout Catholic despite his Masonry. As Levin says, it is odd (to say the least) to omit or eschew, for whatever reason, 'the Crucifixion, Resurrection, and the hope for the Life to come'. His attempt to fill the void is valiant; but there's a lot of rum-ti-tum, and another dire fugue to cap the one closing the *Gloria*, that couldn't have pleased even Constanze. No question of operatic idiom here – 'churchy' in the worst sense.

The *Requiem*, unfinished for well-known reasons, is equally uneven. Mozart's setting of the *dies irae* sequence is inspired, hell-and-heaven-driven, fire-scorched with anger and fear, touching upon new depths of pathos in the chromatic harmony marking its passages of pleading and submission. Elsewhere, though, the music can be pedestrian, even wooden: the work's incompletion has remained a problem unresolved by any of the frequent attempts to solve it (including Levin's, the best yet). Performances would gain by respecting the work's incompletion, breaking off where its composer did, towards the end of the sequence, with comparable effect to leaving the unfinished last contrapunctus from Bach's *Art of Fugue* hanging in the silence – same key, same thoughts lying too deep for tears.

Apart from these two monuments, Mozart's deeper religious and ethical aspects lie altogether elsewhere, in pieces for Masonic rituals culminating in the solemn sections of the *Magic Flute*. They reach their apogee in the unique *Masonic Funeral Music* (K. 477), surrounded by a flotilla of exquisite miniatures charged with inspiration and feeling in the same mode of archaizing seriousness – the motet *Ave verum corpus* and then two very late fantasies for mechanical organ (KK. 618, 594 and 608) – and touched with sweet lyric tenderness in another one-off, the Adagio and Rondo for Glass Harmonica with flute, oboe, viola and cello (K. 617). Who but Mozart would have bothered to turn these humdrum commissions into mini-masterpieces of the highest order? Or lavished his genius upon insertion-arias for other composers' operas sometimes as good as those in his own, and transformed routine bread-and-butter Serenades into inspirations belonging with his greatest work? – for Eight Winds in Eb and C-minor (KK. 375 and 388), for Thirteen Winds in Bb (K. 361), the astonishing Eb Divertimento for String Trio (K. 563). Another pair of works in his favourite key stand at the peak of his achievement in chamber-music – the aforementioned Quintet for

Piano and Winds K. 452 and – more perfect still – the *'Kegelstatt'* Trio for his three favourite instruments, clarinet/viola/piano K. 498 – both combinations unique in their day, the former to be imitated by Beethoven, the latter by Brahms (cello replacing viola). Also sharing the peak, the four original String Quintets (the fifth is a transcription of the C-minor Wind Serenade): again an unusual line-up, yielding with Mozart the genre at its apogee.

Piano concertos

But the core of Mozart's instrumental oeuvre lies in the more standard genre of piano concerto: some twenty-one (not counting arrangements, fragments, single movements, and the works for two or three keyboards), dating from 1773 to the year of his death. Their design is pretty standard. First movements always the longest and most elaborate: an orchestral exposition preparing the soloist's entry; who then takes over with a mixture of new ideas and material already displayed, discussing, conversing, challenging, exploring potentialities singly and in company, taking the thematic matter on a journey that culminates in recapitulation of the opening, leading this time to the formal half-close indicating a cadenza – supposedly improvised, nowadays usually employing Mozart's own – formulaic and unsurprising: the orchestra, with or without soloist, rounds off. Second movements are slow – adagio, andante, andantino, larghetto: in a closely related key (often the minor in a major-key work, and vice versa): cantabile and affettuoso. Finales are mostly a rondo, sometimes a variation-set: simpler, high-spirited, resolving and dispersing anything previous of tension or strenuousness: in several instances interpolating a slower episode – e.g. a minuet – by way of contrast before the inevitable rush to the finishing-line. With a few exceptions Mozart's piano concertos are designed for himself; his prowess as player and improviser as well as composer are on display: and even the grandest and most symphonic have a quality of chamber-music not found in the actual symphonies where there is no protagonist (even when that protagonist is first among equals).

Space doesn't permit the detailed work-by-work description

this oeuvre deserves. As with Bach's cantatas, Haydn's quartets, and plenty still to come, I have set down my thoughts on every Mozart piano concerto, which will here be squeezed into thimbles, leaving just three in full as exemplars.

First of the great works – K. 271 in Eb-major/Salzburg 1777 – begins with a quiet revolution: piano answers orchestra at the very start, then comes orchestral exposition, then exchanges begin – modest tonal adventures, the small wind-section – two oboes, two horns – modestly soloistic: already the process is that of stage-flats in motion. The C-minor andantino passionate and intense – muted violins in close imitation, across which the piano spins a pathetic cantilena, operatically heart-broken, explicitly operatic at the emphatic V–I gestures with which each paragraph is marked off. Middle-section in relative major (i.e. the home key of the work as a whole); less troubled: return of the minor takes opening material to new places; its highlight the soloist's right hand in brief canon with the first violins, leading to a searching cadenza, absolutely non-perfunctory (for once), more pleading still in its broken pathetic phrases, till the loud stagey V–I ends it, like slamming a door. And the rondo-finale is pure *opera buffa*; then detouring into a *menuetto – très galante*; subtly scored when the orchestra joins the soloist – inner strings muted and singing, outer strings dry pizzicato: for its last phrases all the strings sing, piano ripples, and the winds unob-trusively bind the texture: resumption of *presto* takes some new directions before hilariously disappearing to *pianissimo* preceding another *forte* operatic close.

KK. 413–15 (nos. 11–13) are all written for Mozart's first Viennese appearances in 1782–3. All three are small-scale and can plausibly be performed as chamber-music. K. 414 in A is the most attractive, already giving to this key the special character later to bloom in two major clarinet works, Quintet and Concerto, from his prime. KK. 449 and 450 (nos. 14–15) of 1784 are richer and more surprising; and their woodwinds are now indispensable. The heart of both is their central andantino and andante respectively – the former is a lovely creature, delicate in ornamentation, sensitive in harmonic inflexions: the latter a gem of hushed inwardness, opening into turbulence, even panic, before calm is restored. The same year also yielded the rather neutral K. 451 in D (no. 16) and the heavenly K. 453 (no. 17) in G, so ardently appreciated by Myra Hess's audience at a wartime National Gallery concert. Also two others – K. 456 in Bb and K. 459 in F (nos. 18–19): the first dullish as a whole, remarkable for a shift of key and time-signature in its finale, Bb to B♮, duple to triple, most unusual for Mozart – an exciting passage, all too brief. The second's strongest movement is also its finale, a riot of brio capped with contrapuntal prowess.

With K. 466 – D-minor, of 1785 – we leave *Figaro* for premonitions of *Don Giovanni*, not written till 1787. This marvellous concerto is a touchstone for D-minor key-characteristics, far older than Mozart, established iconically by him in these two works and the *Requiem* and pursued down the ensuing century via Beethoven's and Bruckner's 9th Symphonies (and not forgetting Brahms's symphony-like 1st Piano Concerto and significant places throughout Wagner), and into the twentieth century with Mahler's 9th, early Schoenberg, *Wozzeck* and Britten's *Sinfonia da Requiem*. K. 466 requires a fuller orchestra – single flute, two each of oboes, bassoons, horns, trumpets, drums – indispensable to the work's sonority, power and the nature of its materials. Opening, an obscure syncopated texture on strings, without themes: when these begin to focus, march-like – not military so much as to the Scaffold or Judgment Seat, with a driven quality threatening *dies irae*, all febrile tension and agitation even when more lyrical, and still sensed in the relative balm of the relative major. The solo-writing is tumultuous whether muttering or exploding; the progression through 'stage-flats' of keys is dynamic rather than processional; and the ending is astonishing – a winding-down, a burning-out, anger to ashes, the entire forces involved in the descent to a cowed *pianissimo*. Now the *Romanze* spreads serene lyric suavity: but it too contains a turbulent middle-eight in G-minor (another key celebrated in Mozart's oeuvre, of course, for its very particular affect, in this case peculiar to him): piano storms, winds wail, strings merely kick off the others with a brutal initial chord for each phrase. As this section closes, their stabs grow more continuous, calming into peaceful return of the opening plus seraphic new coda.

But vehemence immediately restored in the finale: soloist launches, orchestra replies, trumpets and drums cutting through on strong accents with puncturing punctuation. Chromaticism abounds: not decorative; rather, demonstrative and emphatic – tuneless chromatic scales ascending and descending in slow motion above the seething momentum below. Relative F is reached: not kindly major, but F-*minor* with its notes alien to, inimical to, the home key. Then suddenly the home key's major is granted, and the Vision of Judgment goes briefly all genial and *buffa*. Lost for the moment in the return of the D-minor opening stretch; then, as the recapitulation develops, the brioso major material comes, after a rhetorical little cadenza, in the *tonic* major – its F♯ as alien to D-minor as A♭ had been. Yet even in the major the mood can still seem tense and driven: only towards the very end real good humour really breaks in, a cheerful military tone replaces the minatory as the instruments of war – trumpets, with drums in support – intone softly, four times, their innocent little triadic tattoo.

Though fully equal in calibre, the next three works must necessarily be summarized – 1785–6, nos. 21–3, KK. 467 in C, 482 in E♭, 488 in A. The C-major concerto's glorious andante was made so famous by the film *Elvira Madigan* (1967) that it gave the work a nickname à la Haydn: an utterly special utterance – the choked throb of muted middle strings over a pizzicato bass, together supporting the airy melody on first violins; an atmosphere of erotic intensity, further intensified, when the winds enter, by the melody's downward plunges and grinding suspensions in the harmony that would give pain were they not so pleasurable. Then the same material on the piano, vocal beyond the voice's range, right hand duetting with itself in high treble and low bass as the left continues mid-register pulsating accompaniment, opening out into an episode of airborne lyricism before foreclosing in the consummating, concentrated, concluding eleven bars. In the E♭, clarinets replace oboes for the first time, tingling the sonority throughout: the heart here is the gorgeous *menuetto* interpolated into the rather rum-tum hunting finale. For the A-major, clarinets have come to stay – this is *their* key after all; their warm suavity pervades the entire course of this adorable work. Yet its most memorable key is a rarity – F♯-minor for the adagio, a sicilienne fusing deep pathos with melting Neapolitan sensuality.

The year 1786 also yields a pair – K. 491 in C-minor, K. 503 in C-major (nos. 24 and 25) – so outstanding and so complementary that they must be described in full. The C-minor fields the longest duration and the largest band – oboes *and* clarinets, with the single flute, and pairs of bassoons, horns, trumpets, drums. The exposition commences on a complex first idea – no tootling formalities – a soft unison line – severe, even grim – on strings, chromatic and rhythmically jagged: its loud restatement, tutti and harmonized, with minatory tattoos on brass and timpani as the violins seethe – sense of a 'C-minor *Requiem*'. When lyric ideas arrive they are all pathetic, pleading, yearning, albeit graceful – many woodwind solos and full wind-writing, but no longer serenade-ish (there *is* a superb Wind Serenade in C-minor – K. 388 – itself uniquely severe for a function ostensibly diverting). All phrases last longer than expected; size is always implicitly still larger than actually stated; and the tuttis are heavily scored and dense. In the work-out section, far-out tonal divergence beyond any other concerto, the materials intensively explored, each motif split and anatomized: as it advances, four *roars*, each of three bars, on successive dominant ninths, winds sustaining, strings heaving in thick double-stops, piano answering in arpeggios up the chord (though without the ninths): each cancels out its predecessor, harmonically speaking – an effect of power thwarted hard to parallel in the epoch's going idiom. Absolute independence of the wind-writing – a new realm of importance and individuality: at one point the grim opening motif is given to the fragile single flute. Marvellous coda over tonic pedal, the timpani *rolling* for the only time (I think) in any of these works; pairs of oboes and bassoons throwing a fragment of the opening theme at each other, not in play, piano arpeggiating away without look-at-me brilliance, all in a quiet, choked dynamic still charged with unspent energy, till the last three bars go softer still.

After such disturbance, the larghetto's main melody is serene. Piano announces, orchestra responds, then joins, differently voiced in every phrase. The first of two serenades returns from relative major Eb to the work's main key C-minor – a wind-ensemble, led by oboes, accompanied by bassoons decorated by flute; piano answers, with string support. Curtailed reprise of opening melody. Second wind-serenade, in Ab, led by clarinets – a melting paragraph, again answered in both its halves by the soloist; its beautiful continuation and 'elimination' on strings – oboes now permitted to rejoin the wind-band – leads to the reappearance of the opening strain in full, then extended into what amounts almost to a third wind-serenade – meltingly lovely parallel and contrary-motion thirds on clarinets and bassoons, answered by oboes and first horn, over the second horn's deep pulsating bass, while the flute flutters upwards above: pianist answers. Same again, pianist's right hand replacing the fluttering flute, who now plays cantabile with the clarinets: the exquisite passage prolonged with further piano cantilena and sustained winds over a gently clucking bassoon, the strings now giving a more continuous, though still discreet, support three octaves deep. Mozart's sense of instrumental texture and voicing in such places is perfect.

The finale is absolutely on a par (not always so): a set of variations, the theme necessarily more regular than the material of the first movement – not urgent or driven, but sharing its C-minor colour, and its poignant chromaticism. After four very varied variations (double-variations – first half, its varied repeat; second half, ditto) turning up the tension, comes a wind-serenade in Ab, clarinet-led, piano-answered – relief light, not trivial; followed by something severe, even demanding, but not heavy – pure chromatic polyphony for piano alone in each half, followed by choral repeat over energetic rumbling left hand (always the double-variation pattern). This grimm-ish section again induces a wind-serenade, now in C-major (untouched in the work as a whole heretofore) – oboe-led, answered by flute, then (double-variation pattern as always) soloist's version in answer. Now the theme returns as at the start (though differently scored and including the piano as not before) – sense of running down – business concluded – then a cadenza opens out a final variation that extends into a quite sizeable coda – 'finale' (not so-designated), a lively yet melancholy gigue, pervaded by plangent chromaticisms and poignant dissonances, stabs and prickles, almost obsessive in its insistence on avoiding cadential relief, lean and urgent for all its course, brass-and-drum-less till they rejoin for the very last powerful punctual bars.

A hard act to follow. But Mozart's next, K. 503 in C-major, also of 1786, makes a magnificent complement. Here more than any other is the masterpiece of architectural proportion, of building by tonal relationships in actual time. Its materials, then, are necessarily rather neutral: there's not the loving lavishness of its C-minor companion; this wouldn't suit purpose and nature in any of its movements. The first is a grand allegro maestoso with more than a touch of Handel: material plain and formal, employing a large band (though no clarinets – too alluring for this monument of Portland stone). No themes, just building-elements; very soon a minor-ish tinge to the triumphal major, then a repeated-note motif always driving the rhythm forward, then scale-practice, then a grand stately close on the dominant, followed by what might barely be called a tune, led again by the three-note up-beat – a clockwork nursery-ditty which, in the event, proves potent and adaptable enough to open out the most magnificent spaces of stage-flat tonal perspectives in all these works. The ensuing andante *is* perhaps a little chill – marmoreal without the inner suppleness of the slow movement in K. 453 – 'patience on a monument', no Hermione – perfectly executed; Canova in sound. The finale begins rum-tum *ordinaire*, till it gets going, ticklish and delicious with piano and woodwinds' melodic exchanges in the middle, where some beautiful *non*-pathetic chromaticism brings a flush to the stonework – Hermione breathes. When rum-tum renews, some darker shadows occasionally obtrude before the eventual inevitable triumphant ending.

All this doesn't appear to support my claim for K. 503 as Emperor of the Mozart piano concertos to the C-minor's Queen! The piece's statuesque formality, serious plainness, neutrality of material, deliberation, pomposity, maybe dryness, perhaps pedantry – even, on a dull day, coldness – are all *purposive*. An impersonal work, without

the well-curbed but unmistakable impress of inner turmoil experienced elsewhere; non-subjective, non-affective – *unexpressive*, as
in Milton's 'harping in loud and solemn quire / With unexpressive
notes . . .'. Processes, proportions and the musical substance suited
to set them forth are in themselves expressive even without affective
appeal. (We adore the Queen in all her grace, beauty, abundance: to
the Emperor we bow the knee in veneration.)

Together the C-minor and the C-major really *are* impossible to
surpass. What follows is an inevitable let-down – K. 537 in D (1788)
is as dull as its sobriquet the 'Coronation' unfairly suggests. It simply
has nothing to say worth hearing – Glenn Gould's put-down of an
off-day Mozart – 'interdepartmental communication' – comes again
to mind: consummately competent, every routine in place, no joys
or surprises whatever beyond the mild outbreak of counterpoint for
the pianist in the finale, a timid echo of the superb polyphony in
the C-minor's equivalent place. With relief to K. 595 in Bb, Mozart's
last piano concerto, written in the last year of his life: Princess to
the Queen and the Emperor (and in no way related to the Coronation) – a gracious work of effortlessly limpid lyricism not without
touches of wryness, even acidity. The first movement sets off bold
modulatory explorations in a variety of 'wrong' keys as cheeky as
Prokofiev, before a finely poised glide back home: the other movements not special; by now, the last year of his life, Mozart's deeper
musical impulses lie altogether otherwise, whether in a sublime
jeu d'occasion for glass harmonica or the hell-bent *dies irae* of the
Requiem.

Mozart's curtailed lifespan doesn't admit a putative 'later style':
this facile concept has anyway passed its sell-by date. There is certainly an 'autumnal' feel, palpable yet indefinable, to this last piano
concerto and the two clarinet works, Quintet K. 581 and Concerto
K. 622: the *dies irae* sequence in the *Requiem* trembles plangently
upon the verge of new worlds harmonically; the heroine's and the
three boys' music in *The Magic Flute* shows a new slender frugality:
and his assimilation of J. S. Bach might have developed from initial
awed amazement – 'here's something we can learn from!' – to a

characteristically ingestive incorporation by one supreme eclectic magpie of another. But one doesn't sense the imminence of a Future, as in Beethoven's final string quartet *after* the 'late' ones; let alone Schubert's 'open Sesame' to a new musical universe as *his* early extinction neared. And there are signs of weariness and emptying-out in the drear tedium of the last opera, written to order and without love. Mozart's oeuvre feels perfected and rounded-out; it would surely have been 'more of the same' – to which no one would say no.

Where do the limits lie in this supremely equipped and finished artist? Busoni, revering him as a Godhead, produced some forty aphorisms for the 150th anniversary of Mozart's birth in 1906. They remain subtle and suggestive: from unconditional accolade – 'up to now he is the most complete manifestation of musical gifts . . . his short life and his fertility lift his perfection to the rank of the phenomenal . . .' – to the wary – 'he dares nothing foolhardy . . . he sets himself tasks to tax his strength to the utmost limits, but no further . . . his resources are extraordinarily abundant, but he never uses them all . . .' – to give just the hint of a reservation:

> he bears all characters within himself, but only as a presenter and portrayer . . . he disposes of light and shadow, but his light does not pain and his darkness still shows clear outline . . . he stands so high that he sees further than all, and sees everything, there-fore, somewhat diminished . . . his palace is immeasurably large but he never steps beyond its walls – through its windows he sees nature; the window-frame is also her frame . . . joy is his most out-standing feature; his smile decks with flowers even what is most unpleasant.

Perhaps Haydn's deceptively plain tributes say more with less? To Mozart's weighty father Leopold, 'I declare to you before God [no mere cipher for Haydn] and as an honest man [ditto] that your son is the greatest composer I know, either in person or by repute': and after Mozart's death, 'I have often been flattered by my friends with possessing some genius, but he was much my superior.' But there's no need to go that far: it's not a competition: they are first-equal, and thus so among many others. No best, there is none.

Beethoven

Beethoven is the archetypal model for heroic genius locked in struggle, eventually victorious, with daemonic internal forces and with external circumstances, compelling the outer world from indifference, via toleration and accommodation, to adulation amounting to worship. The terrible personality, compounded by the wretched misfortune of early deafness (by his closing years – he was only fifty-six when he died – almost total), and the humiliation of his amorous hankerings, make him in every respect the counter-pole to his contemporary Goethe (into whose lifespan Beethoven's sits): equally an archetype and model, serene, balanced, successful in love, life, art, attentive to his own applause even as he willingly receives universal veneration.

This challenging image has always appealed to mankind's instinct for rebellion, revolution, defiance – a Promethean grappling with Fate and Destiny, emerging bloody and unbowed against dictators of every hue, totalitarian, democrat, liberator, oppressor, and ordinary humanity at large. This strain in Beethoven's work can repel – heroic triumphalism sometimes touching bombast; emphasis upon big blank pieties – Liberty, Brotherhood, Unity, etc.; alongside the melodramatics and pathos of his affective strain. On a bad day, in the wrong mood, such music – the sonatas *pathétique* and *appassionata*, *Coriolan* and *Egmont* overtures, the *Eroica* finale and 5th Symphony *in toto*, *Fidelio*'s celebratory bits, the 'Ode to Joy' concluding the 9th Symphony – hectors, bullies, coerces, tyrannizes.

This music invokes Abstractions in a negative sense. But Beethoven is the supreme composer of this word positively understood. No composer before or since matches what Stravinsky sought and found the *mot juste* for – his 'might'. Which can of course be another type of tyranny: all down the successive century Beethoven's example and his practice loom large, a challenge that must be taken on whatever the unlikelihood of success; or else, if possible, be ducked or transcended. His achievement – to realize with astounding 'might' the dynamism latent in the sonata principle from simplicity to epic exploration; to reinvent fugue, reinhabiting both letter and spirit of J. S. Bach – remains as startling now as ever it was when even cultivated musicians could shake their heads and say 'Beethoven is ripe for the madhouse'.

Perhaps the achievement is better understood nowadays? *Abstract* as a living thing – the power to make and shape, welded from strong fundamental materials and evolving by statement, development, counter-statement, into architecture, argument, journey, arrival, across an expressive terrain ranging variously joyful in energy, euphoria, brio (not without humour) to darkly meditative, exploratory, passionate, melancholic even unto tragic. Everything is contained within the notes, the processes, the structures, the devices – the very forms are expressive in themselves, needing no other connotation than notations on the page, translated into sounds on the air/ear, thence direct to the heart, brain, soul, of the listener. This is what *abstract* in music means, and Beethoven's is its utmost fulfilment.

Ludwig van Beethoven – born Bonn 1770 into a family of musicians in the Elector's service: early promise as keyboard-player (also viola and organ) and composer. Aged seventeen to Vienna, hoping to study with Mozart: thwarted by death of his mother. Returned to Vienna aged twenty-two to study with Haydn; remained there for the rest of his life. Lessons with the old master ended in rancour; yet there is a symbolic rightness in even such fugitive connections with the two great peers whose achievement he continues, crowns, transcends.

Between the temporary and the permanent Viennese journeys, unremarkable earliest instrumental pieces had also yielded an exception, the prophetic flash, aged twenty, in the inspired cantata on the death of Emperor Joseph II. His published op. 1 consists of three piano trios, variously and strongly characterized, bold and provocative (especially to Haydn), fiery and young-masterly in the going idiom, already pushing at its edges. Next early works: ten piano sonatas, opp. 2, 7, 10, 13, 14; two cello sonatas, three violin sonatas, three string trios – the main body of his work up to the turn of the century. The piano sonatas chart the progress most clearly: written for himself to display his formidable prowess as player, both technical and expressive. All three of op. 2 'lay down the gauntlet' – fire and dash in first movements, depth of utterance in second, energy and grace in finales. Taken together the six works of opp. 1 and 2 show a *big* composer: ambition, vaunting, not a dull bar: the op. 3 cello sonatas consolidate – grand slow introductions, then just the two movements, but wide in scope. Op. 7 as op. 2, but more so in every respect: evidencing the power of the young composer's execution – brilliant virtuosity; searching and lyrical; playful/abrupt/teasing; menacing and dangerous. Also his *rests*! The silences can be as expressive as the notes. An enormous variety of forms, textures, moods – inventiveness in all these: *reinventiveness* – no sense of filling out forms and formulae. Extension of the range of feeling even as the instrument itself extends its compass high and low. The third of the three op. 10 sonatas can exemplify all this at its best.

First movement: *presto*: a soft but dynamic off-beat start: staccato octaves descend, rise fast and steep to an accented unison dominant, long-held, poised and tense. Soft answer, smooth descending parallel chords, the dominant ringing above, to reach abrupt tonic. Repeated loud and high, as a sort of carillon, the dominant now far below in the bass: tonic again. Reopening, soft and now syncopated: the precipitate ascent extended to high major third of home key: dynamic pause on it, now reinterpreted as dominant of B (relative) minor: right hand sings lyrical theme over the left's arpeggios – regular, then expanding – losing lyricism and recovering energy, ending on a trill into dominant of home key, now an established move – A. A jingly little idea derived from the opening, then bare staccato octaves: again, an octave higher and in A-minor; abrupt cut-off (but no pause): and now the very opening's off-beat start fuels a longer paragraph built upon the first four notes: high and low converse: modulations, soft and softer, in converse too, till crescendo to powerful r. h. chords over powerful scale-descents in the

l. h., through four notes extended unbroken to piano's lowest A: dominant come to stay, this time.

But isn't all this a bore?! It takes longer to read than to hear, redundant anyway compared to the physical particularity and pleasure of the actual thing. The point is, that such facts as the music's material and its course yield will always, at every moment, be followable, intelligible, assimilable, self-explanatory (sometimes in retrospect if not immediately): coherent, communicative in the language of what it's communicating: the music's processes, sounds, facture, its actuality in sounds-in-time, *are* its content.

But I will try with the other movements complete. No. 2 *largo e mesto* (sorrowful). D-minor, not agitated/turbulent *dies irae* so much as dark, inward, brooding, tragic-hued. Opening paragraph thick throbbing chords – just once nearly *Tristan*-esque – supporting a coiling belt of even-paced melody: two halves, second rising to a peak before rapid descent into home tonic. A more florid strain, thinner texture, taking the key out of home, again peaking before descending to cadence. Pleading gestures, peremptory/brusque response; these repeated, the reply-gesture emphasized thrice before again calming: half-way half-close – this too is a sonata-movement. Restart in relative major F – growing intensity of uncoiling melody, thickly scored as originally; the punctuation-places where melody rests, l. h. throbs on unchanging harmonies, r. h. in flights of agita-tion, thrice over dominant pedal, guttering and whimpering out; sudden renewal of energy, again running into the ground, for recap-itulation of the opening. Its second phrase moves elsewhere, the can-tilena is foreshortened to close, the pleading and its curt riposte also curtailed. The movement might have ended here, in balance with its first half, now home-key secure. Instead, a powerful coda, all the way from *pianissimo* to *fortissimo*, l. h. building upon gist of opening melody, underneath return in the r. h. of agitated movement on purely arpeggiac outline of the harmony till, at the top, back to tonic-dominant-tonic, the flight/flutter is restored, this time declin-ing easily and unbroken to the bare low key-note. Coda of coda: desolate further take on the opening, high suspiring sighs, low full cadences, return of low full thick chords: two *mesto* tears: the second an octave above; answered by tonic D four octaves below. Emptied-out, passion spent: Beethoven's profoundest movement in all this earliest phase.

Third movement *menuetto* – 'Beethoven the Charmer', a sweet gracious thing after the vehemence of the first and the brooding sadness of the second – euphonious and graceful, though not without athleticism and D-minor-ish tinges. Trio is stormy – a storm in a teacup; l. h. in dialogue with itself below and above the even momentum of the r. h. No repeats; rather it boils up to the *menuetto*'s reprise. As the movement proceeds, abrupt surprises, changes of direction, mood, texture, the feline quality beginning to show its claws as well as its playfulness, all in polar opposite temperature to the *largo e mesto*, though closing with an echo of that movement's ending. *Finale* – rondo – is positively feline – tricks and teases, false starts, deceptions – before getting going on a lyric torrent of motion.

Works with orchestra in this first period are less exuberant and less bold – even timid, conservative, 'inhibited' – 2nd Piano Concerto (composed before the first) in 1798; 1st Symphony, completed 1800. Beethoven is learning the ropes even while trying them for suppleness and strength: modelling on his masters – classic instance the Quintet op. 16 for four winds and piano in E♭, clearly imitating Mozart's masterpiece for the same forces in the same key. This process is at once Resolute, Independent and Beholden. Its climax, the six string quartets, op. 18, completed 1800: a graduation exercise and a prophecy: but 'nothing like the sun' (thinking of Haydn's op. 20 which really had lit out the new territory) – disappointing as a totality and often surpassed by previous works in this same epoch (not least the remarkable three string trios of 1796–8, op. 9). Sometimes strong, deep, individual; sometimes dependent upon the decorums to the extent of mousiness, even academicism. 'Beethoven the Charmer' is best exemplified in the Septet op. 20, also completed in 1800. Latest (till Schubert's Octet) in the line of *ancien-régime* divertimento, utterly pleasing, no disturbances: its composer came to resent the delightful piece's popularity and turned his back on it;

but such aristocratic strains with their successful intention-to-please are by no means lost in the storms, stresses, revolutions of later, often recurring in surprising guises and contexts right up to the end.

Beethoven the Un-charmer: signs already in this earliest phase of bad things that will burgeon later – overkill, bombast, staginess, pathos, lachrymose rhetoric, 'heroism'. The *Pathétique* Piano Sonata in C-minor op. 13 of 1798–9 already foretells some of these – a blow-up of Mozart's sonata in the same key, exaggerating yet diluting the model with poorer material, way under the calibre of what precedes and follows it in the same decade. Changes to come can be focused around two exactly contemporary works (concluded 1800) on an ambitious scale – the 1st Symphony op. 21 in C is wholly within the mould: the Piano Sonata in Bb op. 22 begins to burst it – first movement magnificently open, grand, *brioso*, heroic, wholly without bombast or overkill; a searching slow movement with some fine cloudy, erotic dissonances: a *menuetto* ostensibly demure and 'charming' but with claws, and a tumultuous trio; a long finale, relaxing yet tensing, sometimes densely, to relax again, almost teasing towards the end, though always retaining the sense of wary electricity.

Full flush of young maturity, c.1800–c.1812

Many more piano sonatas and much more chamber-music, including five further string quartets; theatre-music including initial, interim and ultimate versions of his only opera; piano concertos nos. three, four and five, one for violin, one for piano trio; an oratorio and a Mass; six further symphonies. This incredible prodigality set against the physical and spiritual crisis of his thwarted personal life and the encroachments of deafness, movingly recounted in the 'Heiligenstadt Testament' of 1802, heroically overcome in the course of the decade and subsequently. Some notes:

Second Symphony op. 36 (1801–2); the ultimate Haydn/Mozart orchestral piece, bold and confident as the first had been inhibited: 3rd Piano Concerto op. 37, written just before, fulfils the Mozartian mould and begins to extend it beyond the *ancien régime*. Prime

classicism at its apex – the three *Razumovsky* string quartets of 1805–
6, op. 59; the *Archduke* Piano Trio op. 97 (1813): serene muscular-
expressive hugeness without straining – 'energy divine'. Bursting the
bonds, not without effort and cost – the *Eroica* 3rd Symphony op.
55 (1803), with its celebrated dedication to Napoleon, withdrawn
in contempt when the liberator became the tyrant: 5th Symphony
op. 67 (1807–8) – struggle and victory, darkness to light: 5th Piano
Concerto op. 73 (1809), the *Emperor* – unattractively boastful, assertive, bullying – as if indeed Napoleon were again the dedicatee – he
should've been: 7th Symphony op. 92 (1811–12) – 'apotheosis of the
dance' (Wagner)/'Beethoven is now fit for the madhouse' (Weber) –
apotheosis of dithyrambic energy, whether crazed or sane, utterly
intoxicating. Heroic idealism with a strong remit of sentiment,
pathos, rodomontade alongside deep feeling and high inspiration
in all these, never more so than *Leonora/Fidelio* (1805–14). Mirrored in
the piano sonatas – angry violence of the *Appassionata* op. 57 (1805)
and the *Waldstein* op. 53 (1803–4): why such rage?

Alongside these large searching works, their complements – lyric
piano sonatas of the highest calibre, the two free-standing string
quartets – the *Harp* op. 74 (1809) so airy, the *Serioso* op. 95 (1810)
so inward; 4th Piano Concerto op. 58 (1805–6); 4th Symphony op.
60 and the Violin Concerto op. 61 (both 1806), the Cello Sonata
op. 69 and the two piano trios op. 70 (all 1807–8) – works wherein
'Beethoven the Charmer' takes pleasure and delight in euphony to a
new plane. Unique here, the *Pastoral* 6th Symphony op. 68 (contemporary with the embattled 5th, 1807–8) and the 8th Symphony op.
93 (contemporary with the drunken 7th, 1811–12). Both can be seen
as throw-back works. The *Pastoral*, for all its fling into the future –
Mendelssohn, Wagner, Mahler – a descendant of Haydn's *Creation*
(somewhat) and *Seasons* (greatly): the 8th a return to the eighteenth
century – Haydn/Mozart/Serenade (clearly in the delectable minuet-
and-trio) – wit, brio, concision, elegance – till the colossal fling into
the future when the finale begins to grow and grow and grow.

Two exemplars from this mixed cornucopia. First, the Sonata for
Violin and Piano in G op. 96: dating from 1812, year of Europe-wide

ructions, this is a lovable creature from the author of unlovely *Coriolan*, *Egmont*, *Prometheus* and *Wellington's Victory*. The first movement begins in exchanges between the two instruments of simple gracious phrases – euphoria and tranquillity – on the verge of naïve, but don't be fooled. Gradual animation; move to the usual unusual key (Bb), mild adventures, exploring the material with some new ideas and keys, but the same temperature: return unobtrusive/undramatic; soon some new directions and a new light-glow of Eb major before everything recurs in the home key: some further Eb coloration, and the closing G-major/Eb-tinged diminished sevenths take it into shadows seemingly far from home, but home is a near neighbour after all – the movement disappears, till a sudden good-natured up-rush to a loud end.

Eb fulfilled in the second movement – adagio, all outward sobriety and inward exaltation, succeeded by the third – playful G-minor scherzo enclosing a trio as euphoric as the first movement: the scherzo's return ends in the major to introduce the finale, variation-set on a dinky little tune recalling Haydn in *innocentamente* vein, reaching in the eighth variation some mysterious contrapuntal places before closing in a witty imitative contest for both instruments to reach their highest note: gravity resumes – soft whimsical exchanges, evermore curtailed, till a sudden stampede to a *fortissimo* conclusion. Maybe on a 'lower level' than what precedes (a frequent feeling throughout the classical idiom, that grows to fearsome proportions in Schubert and his successors), this finale is, nevertheless, just the job – right thing in the right place: and, as indicated, it resolves without fuss this modestly perfect work's principal contrasts, tonally and in mood, in textures of pellucid felicity, piano and violin effortlessly balanced in evenness of tone.

The Piano Trio in Bb op. 97 – the *Archduke* – also dates from 1812, adding only one instrument to op. 96: but a bigger contrast could hardly be offered – the sonata's playfulness, gentleness, compactness, the trio's grandeur, spaciousness, ambition – Beethoven's process at their prime peak before the troubles, and their resolution, of the last phase in piano sonatas, and variations, huge works for chorus and orchestra, and the final string quartets.

There is no more compelling demonstration in all Beethoven's oeuvre of the making-process: direct statement of simple material, so plain as to be basic, stage by audible stage broken down, re-assembled, followable as the well-marked map of a bold and successful voyage, erecting a structure-in-time of the utmost splendour. The moment of recapitulation in the first movement, hitherto the hub of any sonata-shape, is here so unobtrusive as almost to pass unperceived; somehow the tonic is re-reached undramatically, inevitably, yet surprisingly, before one knows where one is, till one *does*. And all this wonderful first movement is a demonstration, which would be didactic, nay pedantic, were it not so riveting: process becomes expressive in itself, irrespective of thematic nobility, beauty, interest, which here are not in themselves so remarkable – indeed rather *neutral* (though not commonplace).

After the scherzo, the third movement, *andante cantabile, ma però con moto*, takes the wonder into yet further places. I can't forbear a detailed account of this extraordinary creation: the reader must sink or skim. A set of variations: theme a noble hymnic sarabande in D-major, on piano, sonorously spaced though soft, the strings answering first half with a sigh before joining the first half's repeat: second half ditto, except the full-scored repeat is foreshortened and the sigh comes at the end. Four variations follow, then an enriched restatement of the theme, and a coda so extensive as to be a sort of epilogue, balancing what precedes and fully as important. Variation I opens out the harmonic framework into wide-spaced arpeggios, pedal-sustained, on piano: no *theme* – strings hold the bass, then the middle parts, in octaves with slight rhythmic impetus, like brass and woodwinds unobtrusively binding an orchestral texture. They return to action for var. 2 – again an outline of its harmony rather than the theme itself, in figuration exchanged bar-by-bar, accompanied by dry chords from the piano: in the repeats the keyboard doubles the string-figuration at the octave. Lovely as the theme is, it's its structure that matters more – skeleton not body, bone-structure behind the face. Thus, too, with the next two variations: var. 3 choppy chords and repeated notes and still no theme; var. 4 rustling piano l. h. momentum, r. h. singing syncopated cantabile but still

barely a theme, while strings sustain. In the first half's repeat both
the pianist's hands rustle, and the strings have still less, if possible,
of the theme: the second half retains this double-pattern.

Back to the theme in same block chords as it had first been heard.
But now modulation is immediate, and there's no repeat. The second
half is subject to comparable rerouting: in place of earlier deep-
breathed sighs, the phrase breaks off, thrice, before swelling up into
what should be its full-close. Now the miracle begins. It comprises
just a tone, two notes, one thrice and longer, the other, subsidiary,
just once and short – the penultimate phrase of the main melody
now dangling bereft of its close; on violin, echoed by cello, taken
up in repeated chords by piano, thence in a hushed tutti expanded
through arc upon arc of melody-less harmonic motion, strings in
octaves on the motif as it slowly creeps up through the altering
harmony on piano, in itself completely basic, nothing unusual let
alone *outré*; yet the combination effecting a sense of serenely confident airborne infallibility. First wave cadences into second, where
the strings answer each other in quasi-canon then begin to sing
independently, cello first, violin answering: this dialogue continued, piano's triplet accompaniment gradually assuming melodic
contour too; ending in three overlapping gapped sighs, strings versus
keyboard: singing resumed, led this time by violin, cello answering,
on melodic fragments that didn't appear in the melody itself upon
which these variations have been based. The beatific vision fades,
suspires; an enquiring chord turns into link for finale – a rondo,
the enquiring chord the home key, but with flattened seventh that
sets off the easy-going jog-trot principal theme at an angle, soon
'corrected'.

There's nothing to say, really, about this rondo; it speaks for
itself (as really, of course, do the preceding movements): amiable, a
bit garrulous: a furtive chromatic patch, recurring now and again,
recalls the chromatic patches in the scherzo. For the final stretch, the
easy-going jog-trot in 2/4 turns to 6/8 presto, beginning in A-major
complementing the D-major of the andante but soon veering home-
wards to end in a high-spirited gallop. Again, as in op. 96, this finale
is not on the same level as what's gone before; but, again, it achieves

the appropriate lowering of tension (down from sublimity in this case) without lowering the threshold.

1815–23

The years 1812–16 are not literally without music, but nonetheless represent a biographical and stylistic/technical/expressive crisis within Beethoven's artistic nature. Compelled by circumstances to relinquish performing he survived through private patronage, often generous and disinterested (for the great man was also a beast who bit the feeding hand) and much-haggled-over payments from publishers. A disastrous family epoch too (for the invincible man was also a mass of paranoia and vulnerability). Total deafness by 1819. Gradually, ultimately complete regeneration.

First, a one-off, no masterpiece in itself but touching evidence of inner sensibility, and of vital importance, beyond its intrinsic value, for a stream of music to come that moves clean contra to sonata-style and procedure and aim. *An die ferne Geliebte*, a cycle of six linked songs for voice and piano, op. 98 of 1816; a sweet demure work whose intimacy can be compared to its profounder sister the piano sonata in E♭ of 1809 – *Les Adieux*. The importance to Schubert in the endeavour as a whole is most specific in the third song; the fifth uncannily anticipates Mahler's earliest *Knaben Wunderhorn* settings with piano; the sixth is vital for Schumann, applying the generic theme of distance from the beloved and ultimate reunion, and using its melody as a consistent reminder of his own situation in some of his greatest pieces. And the notion of linking lyrics into a continuity of contrasts – a cycle wherein the circle is closed by the opening returning, is seminal throughout the Romantic epoch.

So to the final piano-works – five sonatas and a variation-set, composed between 1815 and 1823, thus overlapping with the 9th Symphony and the *Missa Solemnis*, with a few bagatelles thrown in for fun. The sonatas opp. 101, 109 and 110 are gentle creatures: witness their performing-instructions in German, indicating xenophobic prejudice against the current craze for Rossini, and, more interesting, new expressive requirements of the instrument, the player, the composer himself – *mit der innigsten Empfindung/* with deepest inward tenderness; and the same with a significant addition – *gesangvoll*/songful. Between them comes op. 106, known as the *Hammerklavier*: which merely means the keyboard for which it and all its companions were written, but has taken on connotations of power, might, force, strain; and in the gigantic closing fugue, of Hammer Horror at maximalist Gothic extravagance. This amazing movement is preceded by pages of free-association/stream-of-consciousness, perhaps the most extraordinary music Beethoven ever wrote. They are transitions from the huge preceding adagio – back to Italian; *appassionato e con molto sentimento* – an unfolding of endless melody touching depths and heights unreached heretofore (till arguably spoilt by a fudged climax on a diminished seventh). Before the adagio, there'd been a wry, sardonic scherzo, parodying the colossal dynamism of the first movement. The work is as a whole awesome, not lovable.

Beethoven the Charmer returns to the fore in the Sonata in A♭ op. 110 (1821), most consistently lyrical of all these five sonatas – *amabile* is the performing instruction, true indication of character throughout. First movement – *moderato cantabile molto espressivo*: hymnic opening, simple and euphonious, pausing on its dominant, continued, singing over conventional accompaniment, breaking out as it cadences its first period into delicate arpeggios; concluding in luminous broken octaves between the hands, extended coda-ish to close/open into the relative minor version of the opening – just its first half – now taken upon further-ranging adventures – lyric, then the arpeggios return; second half is similarly explored; broken octaves glide poetically and cleverly from a long way away tonally into home – a curtailed recapitulation of all these constituents plus some new ones. The second is a fast scherzo in duple time and relative minor; for the trio F's 'other' relative major, D♭, runs away with itself; scherzo repeated; coda freezes into loud full chords and empty full silences, diminishing to F-major as dominant of B♭-minor for an operatic adagio with recitative; a bold modulation underpins a pulsating high repeated note, descending and slowing to wrench the tonality back to dominant of home key, but A♭-minor for the passionate *arioso* that now begins – marked *dolente*, almost Bellini-esque *bel canto* over pulsating left hand, rising high, suspiring upon soft bare unison; preluding a fugue in the major. Even-flowing 6/8, bell-like subject in fourths answered with regular entries; not a hint of Gothic horror – euphonious and equable. Its first stage climaxes upon dominant seventh, transformed into G-minor for a return of the *arioso*, still more operatic, passionate with sighs and tears, disintegrating into sad little gasps, then off-beat low unisons and chords, losing all sense of pulse – a little sister to the comparable page of flux introducing the fugue in the *Hammerklavier*. Here the fugue is resumed in G-minor with its subject upside-down (which sounds absurd in words – Humpty Dumpty; in sounds, absolutely recognizable and intelligible). Flow quite soon checked by, paradoxically, a faster notation in a slower tempo. The subject (now right-way-up) bounced around between the parts before re-emerging powerfully in the bass, ascending via mid-register to sing out resplendent on the top – the *amabile* hymnic nature of the first movement's opening blooming and fulfilled in triumph without bombast or strain, ending in a shower of Ab-major from the top of Beethoven's *Hammerklavier* to the bottom, and back again, the instrument's new sustaining-pedal catching the tonic chord in all its octaves in resonating radiance.

For me, op. 110 is the most perfect of these last sonatas: the last of all, C-minor/C-major op. 111 (1822) remains problematic and unloved, though as always one has to bow the knee. C-minor is often a bad sign in this composer – cue for melodrama, histrionics, false pathos, rodomontade, amply fulfilled in the corny gestures of the *maestoso* opening – Liszt on the horizon – and furthered with the ensuing allegro's melodrama soon replaced by pathos, both equally cardboard. The power is undeniable, but one submits resentful and unwilling, muttering inwardly 'come off it ... cool it ... stop faking'.

The movement's quiet close in the major heralds another world; the celebrated *Arietta with Variations*, a tour de force of metrical/geometrical construction fused with deep simple expression, each successive stage opening out rhythmic diminutions from initial becalmed stasis to motions reminiscent of Jelly Roll Morton or Art

Tatum. This process spends itself, to restart as low, soft, syncopated throbs over a tremolando bass: ascent in sixths to delicate tintinnabulation still clearly catching the theme even as it dissolves into the ether: thus far both halves, low to high; the closing dissolution ends on a middle trill; fragments of theme sound below then above, now losing identity as trills take over, ascending, left alone up on high, joined by the bass abysms beneath – freakish piano-texture unconvincing in even the most accomplished performances. Mood and movement now resemble the *arioso dolente* of op. 110 – repeated chords underpinning gapped sobbing melody – in E♭, relative major of first movement's C-minor, soon swinging round home for the return of theme in C-major, richly voiced over the left hand's quasi-tremolando, towards its close expanding into areas of ecstasy, dispersing on dominant, bass now relinquished – a texture of high trill, melody below, l. h. oscillation, gradually re-descending even while the treble remains celestial: cadential melodic winding-up: when done nothing remains but a lovely cloud of soft high thirds, descending in sixths, crescendo to middle C, loud; the theme's first three notes – answered two octaves deeper – dominant up in high register – again, an octave higher yet – cadence over the theme's first two notes the other way round – closing chord, twice short and high, once soft and middle, stop. A clockwork Paradise heard in a Vision by a deaf musician.

As a totality the final five sonatas form an amazing bouquet of highs and lows, deeply and exaltedly uneven – even flawed. The keyboard work written alongside takes only the best, better still, and eschews the shortcomings, and comprehends the entirety of the vision into an epitome; the 33 *Variations on a Waltz by Diabelli*, op. 120 (1819–23). Again, this has been so wonderfully described by Tovey and Rosen that 'there is nammore to seyn' – simply an index to indicate the work's range. After Diabelli's tinkly little dance the set commences with a grand serious march (i) and ends with a delicate minuet (xxxiii): between comes the cornucopia of hugely various (it *is* a variation-set) compacted treasures – a whole made of thirty-three objects. Such are Beethoven's strictness and regularity that listeners can never lose their whereabouts in the theme, whatever the diversity of its treatment and the extremes of the contrasts and juxtapositions: exciting virtuosity and brilliance – (vi), (x); elfin delicacy à la Mendelssohn-to-come, sometimes with dark undercurrents – (xi), sometimes (ii) airy and free; Brahmsian warmth (viii, virtually a *Liebeslied*-waltz *avant la letter*); gruff abrupt doggedness, sometimes bizarre (xii), sometimes good-natured as in the famous take-off of *Don Giovanni* (xxii); tumults and storms (xvi), (xvii) and whirl-windmills (x–xiii); gently luminous pearls (xxvi) and sparkly diamonds (xxvii); athleticism (vi) and dancing grace (vii): calm lyricism and searching harmonic exploration (iii–iv); (xiv) a sort of funeral march in the major to complement (i); (xx) a half-way catch-breath caesura, long, slow dark-brooding harmony anticipating Musorgsky's *Catacombs*. Schumann is often prophesied – *in der Nacht* (xxvii) or in a whirlwind of dream-flights (x) or in droll humour/humoresque vein (ix), (xxviii). C-tonality consistent throughout: in C-minor a 'slow movement' – (xxix), (xxxi); culminating in the third of these, a profound and exquisite outpouring of ornamented cantilena poised between the past – the 'dark pearl', no. 25 in Bach's *Goldbergs* – and Chopin-to-come. A fughetta (xxiv), calm and thoughtful; a full-scale fugue (xxxii) dynamic and powerful, the only variation to change key – Eb – and to extend the theme's shape, else-wise always identifiable, culminating in a dissonant flourish and three mystical harmonic moves, dimming from *fortissimo* to *pianissimo*; to reach C-major again for the aforementioned *menuetto*, with its delicious/delicate/dainty coloration – a Tchaikovsky musical snuffbox completely unanticipated yet wonderfully felicitous after all that has come and gone before. Variation proper completed, a coda yet more delectable – Windsor Forest under Herne's Oak on Midsummer Night. It darkens and de-spangles, comes almost to resemble the end of the arietta in op. III; then re-animates – up/down/up and down simultaneously, coalescing in the middle as it disappears – gone – till the sudden loud last chord wakes the listener to earth.

Diabelli, impresario and publisher as well as provider of the theme, announced his surprise catch thus: 'We here present to the world Variations of no ordinary type, but a great and important masterpiece ... such a work as only Beethoven ... Beethoven and no other, can produce. The most original structures and ideas, the boldest musical idiom and harmonies, are here exhausted ...' And so on, ardent for his commercial concerns but by no means cheap or foolish: one might even think he's said it all in a nutshell.

The last quartets

Before examining Beethoven's last quartets, two mega-works: huge efforts, five years in the making (1819–24), overlapping with the six consummating piano-works, overweeningly ambitious in size and scope; both in D. The 9th Symphony op. 125 – three magnificent orchestral movements in D-minor, a choral finale in D-major ultimately remaining something of a stumbling-block for some: its idealistic brotherhood-of-humanity strains the listener's faith as it does the vocalists' stamina; on a good day, sublime; on a bad day leaving one out in the cold. Ditto, *mutatis mutandis*, with the *Missa Solemnis* op. 123. Again, on one's knees in awe – a position where one can also see the feet of clay and even pull the leg – tremendous, heaven-storming, sublime high and low, sometimes surpassing everything in sight, sometimes straining credulity beyond its tolerance, altogether difficult to love or enjoy. Ravel's quip, 'I'd rather have written *España*', and Debussy's snide reference to '*le vieux sourd*' come to mind: they should be banished by its composer's own testament – 'from the heart, may it go to the heart'.

The last string quartets, five or six in all, the number depending on separating the *Große Fuge* from Beethoven's original intention, as the finale to op. 130, or retaining it there: op. 127 in E♭; the B♭ op. 130; op. 131 in C♯-minor; op. 132 in A-minor; op. 135 in F; the said *Fuge* is op. 133; its replacement finale is the last music Beethoven wrote. As with the last piano sonatas, the totality is absolutely transcendent and extremely uneven. Op. 127 is flawless – the ultimate four-movement classical work. So too is op. 131, the ultra-classical work that breaks all the classical norms, arguably (which always implies unarguably!) its composer's single greatest composition.

Opp. 130 and 132 are problematic: both veer from sublime to ridiculous; in the Bb the crazed disparities between bursting stop/start first movement, the trivial little dance *alla tedesca* (German and Italian now fuse), *Cav*(atina) with its (*Pag*)liacci sobs, open question of choosing between the wild volcanic turbulence of the *Fuge* or the tame palliating substitute finale; in the A-minor the pious emotional blackmail of the *Heilige Dankgesang* third movement. Op. 135 is also perfect, and turns a corner – a lightening, a smile, a cheerfulness – brief, witty, deft, unstraining – more than a nod to Haydn – almost a divertimento – the dark questioning prefacing its finale – '*must* it be? it *must* be?' facetious – a private joke concerning payment – publisher? landlord? – and is anyway blown away by what follows. Hans Keller used to claim this lovable work – the last issue of Beethoven-the-Charmer – as isolated forerunner of a putative '4th Period', terminated by death the year after its completion: a nourishing thought.

Op. 131 in C♯-minor is the greatest of these great works – on the grandest scale, plumbing depths and scaling heights that can sometimes seem without parallel elsewhere, and no lapses as arguably flaw op. 130 (that trite *alla danza tedesca*, that tearful *cavatina*, that monstrous fugue or its trivial substitute finale) and op. 132 (the pious sublimity of the *Heiliger Dankgesang* with its factitious intromission of *neue Kraft*). Its plan – seven movements, played without break, intimately related by common sources sometimes subliminal sometimes explicit, is apparently just as anti-classical as its siblings: yet, properly apprehended, op. 131 manifests the 'classical style' at its apogee. The journey is initiated by another fugue, here germane and seminal to the whole structure: *adagio ma non troppo e molto espressivo*. It could scarcely be more unorthodox than to begin with a slow inwardly searching fugue. But already there are signs: the expressive subject centres upon an accented dissonant note – D – due to become crucial to the quartet's intervallic feel and its structure of keys: and the fugal answer is already unusual – subdominant not dominant – its accented dissonant note thus providing A, the other pivot. Both alien notes are then naturally subsumed into the intense yet even polyphonic fabric closing on the bare octave tonic C♯, after a touch of C♯-major.

It glides effortlessly as leading-note to no. 2 *allegro molto vivace* in D-major: apparently a scherzo, light, lilting, dancing: but soon showing itself to be a sonata-movement, moving to the dominant A for 'second subject'. A and D, the two notes from the fugue-subject and its answer, now hinge the structure, these fundamental keys coloured by the C♯-major that had precipitated the change of mood, tempo, coloration and key. Without break into no. 3 *allegro moderato* – brief link, brusque then scattering then brusque again, then more scatter, sudden adagio, operatic cadence that turns the direction, via D dominant seventh, to the A-major of no. 4 *andante ma non troppo e molto cantabile* – a set of variations upon a harmonic base rather than a treble melody, so regularly adhered to for its earlier stages that the listener – the composer! – is never lost in these double-variations however greatly the textures change. The first five range from near-*opera buffa* (parodying the all-conquering Rossini?) to stealthy creeping counterpoint, a tranquil adagio enlivened with bizarre pizzicato plinks (high) and plonks (low), then a strange stretch of overlapping double-stopping without precedent in the literature – almost athematic/arhythmic, yet always the contour of the theme can be discerned in all its regularity. Now for the heart: variation 6, *adagio ma non troppo semplice*, in 9/4, pulsating chords with the first beat silent, initially no melody whatever, till – first beat restored – violin 1 begins to sing. The first-half variant retains the full nine beats, chords placed high and sonorous, bass-less now because the cello is put onto a sort of buzzing wiggle, accenting each second beat of the composite triple-time (nine crotchets in three groups of three) – bizarre buzz undermining soaring songfulness. Violin 1 climbs even higher, till a sudden silence and another loud annoying buzz from the cello. The irksome insect continues to puncture – subdued but not suppressed – as the other three instruments resume their exalted flight, and the pattern continues thus (with a couple of angry answer-buzzes for violin 1 thrown in) for the remainder of the double-variation which, again, as always, stays wholly anchored in the regularity of the theme through all these vicissitudes.

As this section winds down, the close harmony opens in a succession of measured solo cadenzas, each answered by the other three players awaiting the outcome – violin 1 first; viola; cello; violin 2; violin 1 again, closing on a succession of trills while the other three exchange arpeggios that gradually, for the first time, take the harmony away from home. The movement seems to have disintegrated . . . for now comes the opening of the opening theme, fast and absurd, in C-major, getting idiotically stuck after three bars on the same two notes like an old-style gramophone-record, till haring off in a flurry of trills into main key and tempo. In both these the first half of the main theme returns richly scored; violin 2 and viola singing in octaves in the middle register, cello chundering harmony on bass, violin 1 continuing to trill above and below and inside the principal melody-line. After this first strain, disintegration again – violin 1 trills above, modulating arpeggios exchanged below by the other three, issuing this time in F-major for return of same thing – idiot version, fast, of the theme's first three bars, locking on the fourth, stuck in the groove on the same two notes till rescued by the others in the dominant of home key A, released into virtuoso flourish across four octaves, to pick up fragments of the theme's second half in heartfelt dying falls – the last bar of which even resumes the pizzicato of earlier, then fierce and humorous, now soft and (if a plucked string can be) tender; as up-beat – pause but no break – to the fifth movement, *presto*: a tearing scherzo, humorous but mirthless (or is it full of mirth – aggressively so – but humourless?): in E, relative major of the work's overall C♯-minor, lost to sound since the opening fugue, closes with three emphatic concluding chords, immediately followed by three unison G♯s – third of E-major, dominant of C♯-minor and tonic of no. 6 – *adagio quasi un poco andante* – link-page in G♯-minor – not *quite* dominant of C♯. A profound moment of inward expression, led by viola, answered by first violin, then all three upper strings in dialogue, over the cello's continuity, in contours already reminiscent of the fugue-subject in the first movement and in the finale to come, for which this prepares in a closing-twist to its major – the true full dominant, barely encountered before, of the whole work's home key: cadencing into no. 7, *allegro* in C♯-minor – again; at last! A tremendous explosion of energy and power entirely without the droll-mechanical impetus of no. 5. It's a sonata: displaced from the first-movement position occupied by the fugue: absolute contrast of texture and procedure, as of mood, tempo, temperature; yet increasingly cognate with each other in shared motivic/thematic contours becoming increasingly explicit throughout the finale's furious course. Dramatic, not melodramatic – a brusque terse key-note, long pause, a fierce unison figure already reminiscent of no. 1. A galloping motion sets in that will prevail almost continuously, through soft and loud, lyric and dynamic, thick and thin. A softer configuration, introducing a note of pathos, still further recalls the fugue-subject heard so long ago: its tail is taken up in imitation before galloping resumes with violin 1 *below* the other three instruments on the opening subject. Contrast in relative major and temporary remission of tension – long-held chords, violin 1 singing in descending scales, then a penetratingly expressive high repeated note, soaring aloft as viola answers, then violin 2. Motion temporarily ceases till ferocity resumes; opening motif in unison, then galloping without theme.

Now a new texture: four-note ascending scale in long notes, gallop continued in counterpoint, these two interlocked ideas bounced between the four players, the scale extending to complete an octave, climaxing in unison return of opening, gaps and all, but shifting up its position, then cutting it to its first half against continuous running quavers, building through the keys – including D and A, old familiars – to reach dominant, insisted upon even as the bristling texture declines in volume to reach a muttering stasis in three-bar periods, breaking the powerful four-bar pattern elsewhere. Utterly athematic here, for four times three spasms of exhausted whirring on a dominant minor ninth, diminishing to *pianissimo* for the third, swelling on the fourth to *fortissimo* and tonic, four-bar phrases, and the opening theme's return, realigned to close rather than commence its statement, its gaps filled with athletic upward arpeggios, tonic and dominant, twice, while violin 1 continues the whirring oscillation with its prominent A♮. Galloping resumes, against long notes passed from cello to viola to violin 2 to violin 1, who takes them into the pathos-inflected idea. Next landmark D-major – the other maverick note – and actual

change of key-signature: again, galloping motion is remitted for
long-held chords supporting singing descending scales, again the
intense repeated notes – as before, violin 1 answered by viola, violin 2
answered by 1. The repeated notes grow more and more intense and
held-back and the key swerves into C♯-major for the same music.
Motion solidifies, texture after wide-spaced voicing coalesces into
close-position harmony, galloping softly resumes, reintroducing the
opening motif in the home key.

This is a recapitulation! At first direct, albeit elided, then literal,
then deviating and extending. Its first long paragraph cadences
into the start of the next – long-held scales return, now descending in five-note steps – violin 1 perilously playing octave double-
stops, cello overlapping, the others galloping: then viola and cello
together while violins continue the momentum. Another disappearing disintegration – four bars of mutter and rapid upward scales not
expressive/singing, in D (again), cadencing loud and brusque into
C♯-minor: exactly repeated, the tonic now retained and reinforced,
soon to reach reopening in home position – rough unison – but
dominant not tonic: a bar's silence.

Coda: combining both principal ideas, the first reduced to an
echo in the bass, the second, downward-drooping pathos, extends
in octaves on first violin; viola, violin 2 keeping up momentum
without galloping. The deeply expressive descending four-notes of
contour from the first movement fugue soon grows into a whole
octave descending scale, its chromatic inflexions prominently featuring A and D. It ends in tight close position diminished seventh,
almost motionless for four bars though the cello rumbles on in
the opening motif. Motion picks up, long singing notes in turn
for cello, viola, violin 2, violin 1, resumed fragments of first motif
and galloping momentum, now always winding down into what
might have been F♯-minor but by the time a *poco adagio* is reached,
reached also is the unambiguously tonic major, even though its
dominant is not sounded. The final exchanges of the broken
gallop – violin 1, violin 2, violin 1 – are marked *semplice*, under-
lined with the long notes on cello and viola, gaps in the texture
filled in by dying fragments of the once-so-living opening motif.

Tempo primo on a bare C♯/G♯ fifth proclaims without emphasis the promised end: then a sudden precipitate upward lunge from the bottom of the cello to the highest possible C♯ on violin 1 – from *pianissimo* to *fortissimo* in four bars: three slashing *fortissimo* chords (viola with *quadruple* stops!) of tonic major to close. The defiantly positive upsurge reminds me of some words of Chekhov (already coughing blood) – 'the older I get, the faster and stronger does the pulse of life beat in me.'

But all this is redundant to what the music *does*, concrete and exact, precise in every calculation and proportion, yet physical and sensory, touching heights and depths of what cannot be uttered, with entire linguistic coherence. A grammar of *Affekt* without needing words.

Schubert

I vividly recall the sense of pain, outrage, contempt, during that silly game on Radio Three (the BBC's classical musical station) some years ago where well-known musical personalities eliminate their unfavourite composers, upon hearing how rapidly Schubert went to the dogs. These things are supposed amusing: but the unseemly glee with which he was dumped, not funny in itself, caused a kind of spiritual contusion that can still be felt now and then.

For Schubert surely is at the very heart of music. More; a definition of what he is, an account of what he did, in music, are tantamount to a description of music itself in its most normative and widely shared sense – what it is, how it works, what it is *for*. No composer is less dispensable, more essential and intrinsic. 'Essential' meaning closest to the art's grammar, syntax, language, which he employs with extraordinary purity and exactness even while they undergo in his hands the most radical extensions ever made by one individual. Their purpose, of course, to expand, deepen, intensify expression: to which the same superlative applies – no other single composer has added so largely to what music, in its innate nature, not foisted upon it, can *say*. This is just as essential and intrinsic as the linguistic usage. They can't be separated: the wider key-relationships, the major/minor ambiguity, the enharmonics, the enhanced dissonances – equally with the exploration of the most basic facts of diatonicism, and every motive, melodic, rhythmic, textural element; all this is in such perfect fusion with the affective ends that he has to be called Apollonian, whatsoever is being expressed – amiable/convivial, frenzied, doom-laden, *Angstvoll*, erotic, pantheistic, radiant, desolate, God-forsaken, weary-unto-death, furious, frustrated, fragmented, nihilistic, nostalgic, or just *cold*! Many more words could be thus adduced, for Schubert covers a wider range of emotion than any other composer and most other artists in any medium; but they would be mere signs and ciphers apart from the way their every nuance within the comprehensive coverage is imprinted into the notes.

This composer is *sui generis* in every way. Relatable by audible, ascertainable influence to such manifestly indebted successors as Schumann, Brahms, Bruckner, Mahler, Dvořák: and by elective metaphor, transcending 'history', to Bach before and Wagner after, through emblematic encapsulation of emotion within nuggets of melody and harmony, woven into continuity by ostinato-like momentum: yet the sheerness of the self-contained phenomenon is still more extraordinary when such gigantic ramifications from it are taken into account.

Considering his supreme greatness, Schubert has not done too well in musical literature. He falls off the end of *The Classical Style* and slips between the mountain-cracks in *The Romantic Generation*. Taruskin's new *History* has some characteristically brilliant details, but can be no more comprehensive than Rosen. Best, still, though inevitably specialized, is Tovey's study of 'Tonality in Schubert', written for the centenary of the composer's death. Let's hope that by 2028 this dearth will be reversed.

Franz Schubert, born Vienna 1797, son of schoolmaster cultivated in domestic music-making: thorough early education in theory and playing – violin, viola, piano: composing away all the way. Chorister in the Imperial Chapel 1808, ending 1813, by which time he'd already begun writing songs as well as copious chamber-music, the earliest symphonies, much church-music.

Celebrated breakthrough with two Goethe-settings, aged seventeen: abandons teaching for freelance way-of-life, convivial but insecure, among circle of like-minded friends and contemporaries: shared tastes, pleasures, sensibilities, quivering to new impulses in literature and music which he alone was able to focus/articulate/notate in a copious spate of high calibre *Lieder*. Also copious in chamber-music, orchestral, religious and (without success) in the one genre that could have kept him housed and fed – opera.

Landmarks of *c*.1820–25: 1819 *Trout* Quintet; 1820 *Quartettsatz* (first movement of an unfinished string quartet); 1822 first two movements of 'Unfinished' Symphony and the *Wanderer-Fantasie* for piano; 1824 the *Rosamunde* String Quartet in A-minor, and *Death and the Maiden* in D-minor; the year before, the song-cycle *Die schöne Müllerin*; and perpetual output of individual songs. In 1822–4 personal crisis, marked in words by a somewhat-contrived over-literary effort entitled *My Dream*, and an all-too-genuine confessional poem 'My Prayer': recognition of illness, probably syphilis, likely to prove fatal before many years were out. Mid-1820s three gigantic sonata-works in C: the *Grand Duo* for piano-duet (but a symphony lurks within the homely necessitous medium); *Reliquie* Piano Sonata (unfinished); 9th Symphony, 'the Great'.

In the three years remaining, 1825–8, plentiful output in all genres – landmarks, the huge G-major String Quartet (1826), big piano sonatas and many precious miniatures, and much functional dance-music for solo piano; piano-duets large and small; a sizeable Mass; and always the profusion of *Lieder*. The last year or so is miraculous – abundant even beyond previous years, and virtually all at the tip-top of inspiration, consolidating, enhancing, deepening, and (right at the end) advancing visionary new territory: three last piano sonatas, two piano trios, string quintet, *Fantasie* for violin and piano, *Fantasie* for piano-duet; *Winterreise*, the second song-cycle, subsequent songs with intimations of new worlds; nothing for orchestra save initial sketches for a tenth symphony. And a large-scale Mass.

Can't hope to keep up with such profusion! I will concentrate upon the domestic genres: some masterpieces for piano four-hands: then move on to the heart of the corpus, the songs. First, though, the shape of the output as a whole.

Song is the centre: the brief lyric for the single singer plus piano accompaniment in the domestic setting more important even than symphony, solo or duetted piano-music, chamber-music, let alone opera or Mass. But Schubert is also vitally important, and great, in the evolution of large-scale wordless forms. He turned his fertility and originality in a new direction, the fantazia of linked movements, with transformation of themes, as in the *Wanderer-Fantasie* (1822) for solo piano, bold if a bit hammy; the *Fantasie* for violin and piano (1828), a mix of divinely inspired with distressing triviality and routine – both these works centred on material taken directly from the *Lieder*; and the *Fantasie* in F-minor for piano-duet (also 1828), its fusion of form and content at the highest level of inspiration. This 'side-stream' influential down the rest of the nineteenth century – for Wagner (atmosphere; 'endless melody') via Liszt (transformation of themes)'s excellent transcription of the *Wanderer* into a piano concerto; also for Schumann and Brahms; all four successors uniting in such tours de force as Schoenberg's 1st Quartet and 1st Chamber Symphony, where the goal of total integration – four movements in one, one movement in four, and complete interdependence of all the thematic material, is achieved (and hence serialism . . .).

Mainstream output of sonata-works, for solo piano, string quartets and the quintet, piano trios, symphonies, juvenilia and adolescentalia – learning the trade from Haydn and Mozart – home quartet-playing, school orchestra. Astonishing Great Leap Forward, the two movements of the B-minor symphony that remains for ever 'Unfinished' (1822). Enter Beethoven – Schubert's obsession with his overpowering neighbour, in particular the 7th Symphony: Schubert's own 'Seventh' (as his '9th' is still numbered on the continent), one of the three enormous ventures of 1825, all in C-major, colossal in length and in strain, wherein he undertakes to expand his forms and processes to unprecedented 'heavenly lengths'. Ultimate destination here is Bruckner, whose symphonic problems and solutions are astonishingly prefigured – the contour of the themes, the audaciously individual harmony, the process-filled repetitions, the ostinato textures – even, sometimes, the orchestration – as well as the vastly extended sizes. But Brahms, via Schumann, is heir to this aspect of Schubert equally with his fantazia-side: thence Dvořák, Elgar, Mahler, Franz Schmidt. Fusion of song-impulse and material into symphonic procedure and form is vital to all these successors, however different among each other. Sometimes Schubert uses an *actual* song here too – the *Rosamunde*-theme (not exactly a song, of course) and *Die Götter Griechenlands* in the A-minor Quartet, *Death and the Maiden* in the D-minor: more frequent and important, song-like lyrical invention, incompatible with the stringent economy and relevance of the classical style.

Analogous to the larger chamber-works, a body of solo piano sonatas very mixed in quality – sublime to absurd, often within the same work – sublime winning in the last of all. More analogous to the *Lieder*, many miniatures for solo piano – *Impromptus*, *Moments Musicaux* – some not so miniature – sonatas in disguise? – though never the range or depth of the greatest vocal settings. And not to forget his evocatively titled sets of keyboard dances – functional, churned out by the metre in both senses – unassuming, good-natured, tuneful and danceable – *valses nobles*, *valses sentimentales*, *Hommage aux belles Viennoises*, etc. – unpretentious overflow from his foaming cornucopia, prototypes for the Schumann fantasy-cycles of the 1830s (as well as giving Ravel the title for his most perfect piece).

Opera and Mass – the two largest musical genres – are not mainstream for Schubert. Worldly ambition compelled both, without success: in the operas (all fifteen, many unfinished) lie lovely and characteristic things, lost in preposterous stories: he evinces no talent for narrative pacing, for individual character or characters in interaction on-stage, whereas the songs abound in vivid balladry and searching psychological depictions both empathetic and acute. Masses, too, lost in preposterous stories? For these, the ex-chorister can draw upon a strong traditional local heritage culminating in

Haydn. Schubert's evince loads of skill and fluency, much routine (especially those *et expecto fugato* sections) with much grace and euphony; also, some moments of visionary awe that make the listener quail (again Bruckner on the horizon); but they are not where the value presses. Neither church nor theatre contains him so suitably as the domestic chambers wherein his greatest music opens up whole new terrains for musical expression.

Piano four-hands

The generous extent of Schubert's output for piano-duet shows him at his most convivial and sociable. This and the songs were the staples of innumerable Schubertiades: the modest domestic medium – two friends at one keyboard – symbolized in the D-major Rondeau *notre amitié est invariable*, where the players cross arms in fraternal complicity for the main tune's final appearance. To this entertainment-category belong endless *marches – grandes, militaires, héroiques, caractéristiques*; plentiful *polonaises*; sets of variations on his own or others' themes, and the *divertissement à la Hongroise*, a massive rave-up lasting over half-an-hour. Often in this area the invention is high – Schubert is almost incapable of dullness even when perfunctory – the marches especially are chock-full of strong material, with ineffable melodious trios to mitigate the military/ heroic masculinity: try the Eb-minor, op. 40 no. 5, a genuinely serious utterance, and not unique – though more usually the tone is jocular and catchy. Going up a notch, there's a group of smaller pieces for the medium which achieves perfection in its own terms: the Sonata in Bb and the Variations in E would make a lesser composer's name. The Rondeau in A (1828) is perhaps the ultimate model for how to score delicately and subtly for a texture that lends itself to crashing and tinkling – it also boasts lovely material, beautifully worked, and some of his best-ever changes of key and layout.

And there are four blazing masterpieces wholly transcending the medium's humble nature – the inherent domesticity that still keeps it off the recital-platform. Schubert's keyboard-writing here is more idiomatic and grateful than in the bigger solo piano music, often extremely awkward to execute and not sounding too convincing even when the notes are safe. (Some of the songs too, even some of the greatest, have exceedingly tricky accompaniments.) The extended possibilities for sonority, range, power, complexity of layout, equally with greater variety and delicacy of touch and voicing, exactly suit the nature of two of these works without any sense of straining the medium beyond what it can enjoyably take. The other two open up another question-mark – the sense of a frustrated orchestral composer, hearing nothing live beyond the earliest symphonies, making the best of it – possibly applicable to *Lebensstürme* (1828), certainly to the aforementioned *Grand Duo*, conjacent to the Grand Symphony and the equally powerful/ambitious/ heaven-storming unfinished solo piano sonata, all three in C. The two keyboard-works in this triptych *do* burst the medium, and can produce a pounding crash-and-clatter sonority in the effort to render their genuine weight. Highly inspired, they also manifest problems of form-and-content that would need extensive detail to gauge aright. *Lebensstürme* is different: a single-movement sonata-allegro of the highest order, one of his greatest inspirations, passionate and impetuous as the title – probably not his own – indicates – Life Storms – a driving rhythm – 'Desire knows no Rest' – its astonishing harmonic and contrapuntal tortures and hair-raising modulations (Bruckner not so much on the horizon as beating down the door) contrasted with ethereal lyric consolation, almost chorale-ish though always driven by pulsing syncopated *Hauptrhythmus* – as it were 'good Liszt' (if that were possible): and the four-hand lay-out always clean and clear however tumultuous. *Lebensstürme* doesn't *need* the scoring for orchestra that the *Grand Duo* cries out for (the job in both cases is tempting and has been attempted).

Nor does Schubert's masterpiece for piano-duet, the *Fantasie* in F-minor, one of his last works (1828) and one of his greatest. (It too has been orchestrated and it sounds all wrong from the very second bar, where the melody is given to the wrong instrument – and continues all wrong all the way.) I've already referred in passing to the three fantasy-pieces: the category indicates freedom and suppleness, which by no means means looseness, wooliness, slack: his earlier classical forms can be stiff; later they encounter problems in the move towards new sizes and procedures not fully realized in the cut-off life (as Tovey reminds us, *all* Schubert's works are early). The *Wanderer* remains unique – a fling into the Future, the song at the heart, motifs from it yielding material for all four linked movements, culmination in a monster-fugue several years before Beethoven's two: rather an awful piece, actually, though exceedingly significant historically. The violin/piano *Fantasie* also song-centred – the variations on *Sei mir gegrüßt* contained within its huge continuous baggy sprawl – introduction divinely dictated, allegro tinkly and protracted, variations ever more showy and facile, magnificent return of the opening, vapid *allegro molto*, one more go at the song, *presto* dash to finishing-line. The F-minor piano-duet *Fantasie* has features in common with both but gets everything just right, upon material of the highest order, working at high intensity to create new forms, textures, continuities, which, unlike the *Wanderer*, did *not* have a Future. Its principal extra is the strong baroque presence – as in Mozart's two sublime late fantazias for clockwork organ (both also in F-minor), a wholly un-pastiche recreation of techniques from the Past gives an extraordinary charge to the Present. Over discreet accompaniment the exquisitely sensitive fragmentary melody, all repeated notes and internal echoes/repetitions, plangently unfurls, its supporting harmony acutely attuned to its every inflexion: again, in octaves, taking a still-more-poignant colouring. The top player's lower hand assumes the harmonic support, now unbroken; below and above, fragments of melody converse; the stab of coloration, more acute and prolonged, breaks off: to the major – as so often in Schubert inexplicably sadder still; close into returning F-minor, forceful and emphatic; the bass sounds out a five-note shape that will come to dominate everything later – initially disguised in treble-register decoration, gradually more and more stark: stops for now at the dominant – suddenly soft, the E♮ of C-major becomes F♭ of D♭-minor – opening melody now set in this key beautifully and smoothly gliding by enharmony (F♭ = E♮; E♭ = D♯); in one deft bound, dominant of A – so to A-minor for the forceful music again, the five-note motif disguised then open – an exact repeat A-major third above; another sudden soft, magical enharmony – G♯ to A♭ – and we're back in F-minor as thought we'd never left. Opening melody returns in opening key, without the plaintive coloration, closing into gentle F-major, a sort of coda to this first section. Under a high tremolo the five-note figure grows lyrical rather than peremptory, opening out in warm euphonious imitation, reaching the treble as the high tremolo also becomes cantabile, closing on even chords over deep bass and low chromatic murmur, stilled into two bars of harmonic stasis, only the deep bass retaining motion, *ppp*. At the third bar the chord begins to repeat and swell, at the fourth its tonic and dominant notes are raised by a semitone – C and F to C♯ and F♯ – the third (A) remains constant – modulation as *not* by the book – into *Largo* in F♯-minor.

Grandiose baroque formality now, almost pompous – double-dotted rhythm, rhetoric on stilts and in periwig – deep low octaves answered by high trills; then taken over below – stately plump splendour, soon in triplets before double-dottedness resumes, ending on a powerful dominant – C♯-major. Now lyricism in F♯-major: against throbbing accompaniment shared between the players' inner hands, their outer exchange operatic declarations, impassioning to a dominant close; a hushed echo; resumption, ghost-like and very soft, of baroque panoply, trills and all. The triplet-bars when they return are now in broken figuration; double-dottedness returns *ff* and continues longer, through some grinding harmonic wrenches (Schubert *must* have known those Mozart fantazias, also in fantasy-baroque idiom, where some extreme scrunches are perpetrated). Comes out all right in emphatic dominant C♯-major.

To F♯-minor tonic for *Scherzo* and *Trio* – virile and vigorous invention, regular in phrase-lengths though not in modulations (as usual): the chunky piano writing – double octaves to the fore – variegated with passages of delicacy, showing again that the Cinderella-medium is just right for Schubert's keyboard imagination. Trio in D, marked *con delicatezza* – almost elfish though it too can evince weight. Full repeat of scherzo, exploding as it ends into its dominant C♯, enharmonically transformed – C♯ to D♭, B♮ to C♭, F♮ and A♭ remaining constant, for *Finale* in F-minor, reached by fierce IV–V in dramatic pause: return of the opening, gentle and plaintive as before – an exact return, albeit compressed of its previous expansiveness till, at reaching F-major again, action begins.

The five-note figure, previously warm and cantabile, now pervades every part of the texture with forceful emphasis: this is the place in a fantazia for a contrapuntal workout: here, not quite fugal; rather, a cantus firmus, the unchanging five-note shape put against wriggly chromatic counter-subjects, equally tortuous and ingenious and always driven by the inexorable cantus firmus – well-named – beginning in tenor, answered by soprano, moving to bass, answered by alto. Tenor again, now soft; bass, now beginning to expand, then fragmenting, imitations gaining upon each other in overlap. Loud and powerful again in bass, under high treble tremolo, with grinding quasi-canon and crowded tenor triplets. Bass takes over triplets and tremolo as pedal, the other parts exchanging positions: then bass pedal begins to pound and rumble as the motif itself thickens into chords. Climax on diminished seventh; texture continuing thus for six bars, ending on sudden *piano*: exact repeat but tensely soft till crescendo and the chords re-baroqued – dotted rhythm – to reach tonic *ff* – motif crashed out in bass, imitated in gapped tenor and chordal alto under soprano whirl: this texture also climaxes upon a diminished seventh: and then again – this time surmounting it to rise to dominant, up high over furious dissonant thunder down low. Dramatic bar of silence: the opening accompaniment, reverted to opening tempo (inevitably in the excitement and strain of the workout the speed has accelerated, though unmarked in the score): the plangently stuttering melody commences, achingly reharmonized after its second phrase: the ache persisted upon, swelling to apex – decline – cadence. Angry chords slam the doors – is the listener safe within the Biedermeier parlour, or brusquely ejected? Precipitate bass plunge, two bars' grinding penultimate dissonance, final prolonged chord soft, in a sonority way beyond a single player's capacities, to end.

Perhaps this great work is not absolutely flawless. His rough sketches indicate that Schubert at one point intended a march-section in D-major (no doubt to complement the F♯-minor of the scherzo); and it's possible to regret the absence of the real songful slow movement at which he was natural and supreme, in the F♯-minor largo – though this is balanced by the gentler lyricism of the opening and its return. But perfect in every respect – utterly felicitous from A to Z – is the set of Variations in A♭ (1824). Eight variations, the last extended into a full-scale finale: the rest remain close to the theme's ground-plan, though often diverging into harmonic adventures of great and mysterious beauty. Theme itself a demure creature: its first half repeated; its second twice as long and already embracing internal contrasts to be exploited later to the full as the piece unfolds. (Recommended in performance to repeat the second half too – easily done with a few simple adjustments: every player will want to play it twice, every listener twice to hear.) Var. 1 opens out into graceful triplets: var. 2, though still mainly soft, sets out over a wave-formation of semiquavers, in the second half reaching middle then top, with some bold passing dissonances and a characteristic dynamics-trajectory from *pp* to *ff*, down to *p*, up to *ff* again – Schubert's dynamics can verge upon the expressionistic even when content and context tender and playful. Playful the word for var. 3; slightly slower – imitative cantabile over ballet-music accompaniment, *con delicatezza*, straight out of, or into, Delibes and Tchaikovsky. Var. 4 restores vigour – loud then soft give-and-take between the parts; in the second half energetic semiquavers reduced to an obedient Alberti-bass – in the middle of the texture, for under it the *secondo* player's left hand chuckles and gurgles, while the *primo*'s right hand becomes positively frisky, till initial energy and vigour restored. Var. 5 is a complete contrast to this and to everything so far: in A♭-minor: Alberti-tenor and double-bass bass, velvety and gentle, over which the minor inflexions produce a lovely new light upon the major melody as first encountered. The theme's mild adventures in its second half become, in the minor, harmonic enhancements of great boldness and penetrating beauty – even reaching A♮-major without jar or judder before gliding effortlessly back to home.

Var. 6, *maestoso*, restores the major in heavy chords and weighty figuration for its first half: its second in complete contrast – the figuration goes high and delicate, the chords melt into delicious repeat-pattern, every half-bar, the dotted rhythm occasionally featuring in the theme now persistent, lightly accented, half-staccato half-slurred; the moment of ultimate bliss the turn towards subdominant. After sensuous delight, grinding severity – second half of second half, heavy octaves in thirds against treble in harsh suspensions: at one point F G♭ E♭ E D D♭ so synchronous as to be almost simultaneous. This eases into brief return of delectation, then brief resumption of the variation's opening manner, grand *maestoso* to end. Var. 7 is the work's core, a mysterious still centre, *più lento, con sordini*, before the extrovert gaiety of the finale. Dissonances here positively Purcellian, dynamics positively Schoenbergian – *fortissimo crescendo diminuendo piano* in just five beats (sonority the more striking as such extremes are required with the muting pedal still down). What Schubert can permit by way of suspensions and wrenches passes belief: as always, absolutely within the framework of the theme, and absolutely grammatical in themselves. The result isn't in the slightest eccentric, freakish, experimental – simply (simply!) an intensification borne of some innate potentialities of tonal harmony, pushed to their edges for expressive ends – Schubert the expressionist, again – always inward-contained, never provocative, flagrant, ostentatious.

The screw is loosened, a dominant seventh plus flattened sixth prepares var. 8, a long, lolloping sicilienne/gigue, cheerful and animated: well-behaved to begin with, then, as the framework of the theme begins to expand, not without further bold adventures in modulation and some strong dissonant suspensions, both these recalling their cousins earlier in the work. Eventually all clear: the piece romps to an unsullied diatonic close with whooping horns taking over the gallop-motion (but no temptation to orchestrate such consummate four-hand keyboard writing) – bright animal spirits, good will to all men – his convivial circle – and all *belles Viennoises*, without strain or shadow. Already, in 1824, in the knowledge that life-expectancy likely to be short.

Mid-1820s – Grand Composite Symphonic Work in C

A Frankenstein monster fabricated of body parts from the sonata for piano named *Reliquie*, because it remained unfinished, the *Grand Duo* for piano four-hands and the 9th (or 7th, to taste) Symphony. The first movement of the sonata is boldest of all: the symphony's is magnificent but problematic – slow introduction superb, its return at the end unconvincing even when its unsuccessful orchestral balance is adjusted: some glories, including the inspired soft trombone passage, not germane to structure/argument: and the orchestra of his time can't manage remote keys so crucial to Schubert's practice, easy on a keyboard. The *Duo* gets the two together – an 'orchestral' work in convenient four-hand keyboard medium that the composer could actually *play* and actually *hear*.

As it proceeds, the *Duo*'s modulations grow so hair-raising that even Bruckner might have taken fright at such harmonic wrenches (were they not so much within his still-more-audacious scope). The sonata's first movement is more daring yet – an extraordinary emanation, monothematic and monolithic, complex but primevally simplified, raw and cooked, grimly severe in triumph, often crumpled in defeat, surpassing lyricism undercut with disquieting subcurrents, ambiguous to the last; the ambiguities would be vacillating were the purposes not so sure.

The sonata's andante is simple, and shares something of the first movement's gauntness: at its centre one of the earliest of Schubert's increasing tendency to alarming outbursts of violence. The unfinished scherzo, the lovely complete trio, the hapless unfinished finale, seem to indicate that, as so often throughout his oeuvre, the composer himself was defeated by his new discoveries. The *Duo*, however, endures to the end. Its scherzo is Schubert's most Beethovenian: a whirl of athletic gaiety, its actual material not all that catchy – this in complete contrast to the symphony's. More so still, their respective trios – in the *Duo* a tight ghostly affair in the minor, treble and bass heaving in imitation, joined yet kept separate by a pulsing syncopated inner-voice – Schubert at his severest: the trio of the symphony being truly joyous, the apotheosis of angelic goodwill towards men. And the *Duo*'s finale – perky, droll – (funny to realize that the indebtedness to it of Brahms's piano-quintet finale extends way beyond the close resemblance of their opening themes): for this finale verges upon the ridiculous – saved by its energy ('eternal delight'), some as-usual-astounding jerks of modulation, and a dangerous daring in deconstructing its own materials from near the start to the devastating conclusion where the first two notes of the rondo-tune wax minatory, and eventually smash jocularity to smithereens.

So to the symphony's second half. One of the best orchestral scherzos ever – huge, genial, abundant in marvellous themes at once jovial and jocose, Olympian yet peasanty/rustic/bucolic: Earth and Parnassus join in the dance. *Dance* above all – a fast supercharged *Ländler* folkdance, both rough and graceful. Towards the end of first half, arpeggio-figures in broad phrasing begin on all the strings, four octaves deep, *pp*: from D, dominant of dominant in this C-major movement, D's two minor relations F♯ and B, to close in G preparatory to repeat. In the much longer second half these arpeggios sweep all before them with irresistible athletic prowess: and for all its earthy vigour, this *Ländler* is a sonata-movement too. And the trio seems to be set in a village inn, or perhaps a Viennese tavern when the new wine is brought in each autumn from the surrounding countryside: in A-major, bright after C: woodwinds prevailing in warm rich layers of doubling: outdoor feel as well as the snug within – a sort of heavenly barrel-organ of wonderful euphony: the *Ländler* rhythm kept up by the strings, and in the second half some gorgeously opulent modulations beyond the range of any townee or peasant, however merry – café-music celestialized.

The symphony's finale is colossal: in size, in reckless boldness, in uncurbed exuberance: if it had but been heard soon after its composition, even Beethoven, with hearing restored, might have said 'Schubert is ripe for the madhouse' (and of course the string-players at Mendelssohn's early attempt to launch the work in England simply declined to submit to such insanity). Energy – eternal delight – boils over, whether explicit in the tumultuous whirl of motion, or latent and repressed in the tremendous repeated-note passages that sound like a genial version of the stone guest's summons in *Don Giovanni* taken far further. *Colossal*: yet the proportions are just: especially for the gigantic coda; where one might have thought composer and his material had spent their all, comes, instead, *neue Kraft* from the same ingredients, churned up in different ways: orgiastic, nay apocalyptic, crashing through the gates of excess to storm the palace of fulfilment, if not exactly of wisdom.

Lieder

The main problem with the German *Lied*, of which Schubert remains at once pioneer and fulfilment, is: how can such, on the whole, morbid, trite, sentimental subject-matter and, on the whole, mediocre verse, be reconciled with our estimation of an art-form capable, in his hands, of expressing with the utmost invention, mastery, intensity, beauty, an incomparably wide and deep range of emotion?

Consider first the alleged mediocrity of most of his texts, both in content and in diction. It is fundamental to the *Lied* that the poem's quality *as poem* rarely signifies. Whether an accredited Great – Goethe, Schiller, Heine – or middling, plain bad or merely feeble, the text is pretext for the release of feeling: that is, the reason, even excuse, for writing music. What it's saying – its subject-matter – will attract and stimulate: its imagery and metaphors will suggest musical shapes and figures within the overall mood and tone: the stanzaic pattern will give form and direction: the words themselves – rhyme, rhythm, quantity, accent – suggest contour and character for accompaniment as well as voice; the sentiments uttered, the feelings expressed, whatever their nature, touch upon what the composer wants to say, and can. In all this, literary quality is not the prime concern: indeed, high literary calibre can be inhibiting, and unresisting mediocrity of thought and its utterance can even be positively stimulating. For in every good song, despite the poem's originating indispensability, then the collaboration and fusion that bring about the outcome, music wins: it is no longer the poet's contribution that we primarily listen to and most value.

There is also the problem of the *Lied*'s remoteness in sentiment and sensibility. For all the currency of the most familiar, the terrain of Schubert's songs as a whole can feel as remote as the way of life that gave it birth and saw it to maturity. There's a parallel with that twin peak of nearly subterranean musical achievement, the two hundred-odd church cantatas of Bach, where the ideology, spirit, language, in which the texts are couched, to which the music is bound however greatly it transcends them, are still further sunk beyond possibility of retrieval. Six hundred-odd songs! Brahms claimed to be able to learn from any of them. But as Tovey sensibly glossed, you'd have to be a Brahms to learn the lesson. Doubtless the vital life of these lost summits of Western culture lies in the several complete recordings of the Bach cantatas and the wonderful set of all Schubert's songs issued by Hyperion Records under Graham Johnson's masterly guidance. Yet Schubert remains his own best interpreter: the copious corpus of songs shines bright across the sentiment-and-sensibility divide, and the language, foreign in several senses – the superseded conventions, the alienating thoughts, feelings, passions, proclivities. Also through much fustian, bombast, tacky sentimentality, naff narrative, insipid prettiness, poetic corn, didactic prosiness. Among all this stand lyrics and ballads by acknowledged masters of the German tongue as well as translations from, inter alia, Shakespeare, Pope, Scott, Byron (alongside inevitable reams of Ossian). But in effect there's no difference: here the pristine naïveté of Müller, the cosy verses of Schubert's social circle, the morbid effusions of Mayrhofer, etc., etc., are on an equal with Goethe/Schiller/Heine.

Through all this literary matter, occasioned by it and consuming it utterly, burns the compelling intensity and unlimited beauty of – throw caution to the winds! – the most *original, fecund, inspired* composer who has ever existed. *Original* because so unbeholden: no composer before or since has had in his gift a larger admixture of absolutely new things that music can embody and express. *Fecund* because so frequent, with such protean variety (obviously not every one of the six hundred will be equally new, beautiful, profound, but the proportion of quality is high, there is plenty to cherish on the lower slopes of Parnassus, almost nothing is wholly untouched by his powers). *Inspired* because he is the composer closest to music's intrinsic nature; he combines consummate purity of grammatical usage (even when such usages had scarcely been touched on, or touched off, before) fused with an unprecedented reliance upon total expressiveness; objective and subjective are held in such equipoise that they lose their customary polarity.

Whereas in instrumental forms the output, however treasurable or astonishing, remains with his death at thirty-one understandably 'unfinished', in songs Schubert is from his mid-teens onwards the flawless master of a hitherto unsuspected realm. There were *Lieder* before, but the genre was minor, even puny. With Schubert it becomes for all its brevity and the humbleness of its performing resources and domestic circumstances, as significant as symphony, concerto, sonata, opera, oratorio, Mass. This is major art with modest means – not watercolour as opposed to fresco or oil-painting – because the emotional range is so wide and so deep. 'All human life is here'; within this lyric/narrative genre any and every shade and degree of feeling can be contained, uttered with comprehensive psychological penetration, breathtakingly direct in the physical appeal of its sheer loveliness, in its workmanship subtle and far-reaching beyond analysis or any other description. 'Size matters': the actual dimensions (together with the lurking cosiness of the genre, the remoteness in culture and sensibility, and the frequent triteness of the mere words) are subsumed in the grandeur of the *real* content.

The pattern is thus: schoolboy attempts, often bold and gauche, trying things out, discovering, learning the ropes: sudden surprise of genius in two celebrated Goethe-settings of 1815, aged seventeen – *Gretchen am Spinnrade* and the *Erlkönig*. Thereafter, copious song-production, for the delectation of his amiable circle, sometimes achieving wider circulation; and always accompanied by equally copious output of chamber and orchestral works, church-music, and the vain pursuit of operatic success. First Müller song-cycle *Die schöne Müllerin* 1823; early 1827 twelve further Müller-settings comprising Part I of *Winterreise*, completed later that year with the other dozen: late 1828 seven settings of Rellstab and six of Heine, published posthumously as *Schwanengesang* but incontestably *not* a cycle, with an extra item to avoid the unlucky thirteen.

No possibility of covering six hundred-plus! I've made a bouquet of fifteen relatively unfamiliar individual songs chosen to indicate something of Schubert's vast variety in subject-matter, expression, technique, form; the two *real* cycles are so well-known and well-covered as to be left well-alone: the last songs, equally famous, are so special and new, on the threshold of mortality and immortality, that some are again discussed in detail.

SONGS OF CONTENTMENT, FELICITY, PASTORAL OR DOMESTIC

Das Lied im Grünen (1827): the pleasures of the open air in a green countryside, evoked in a *moto perpetuo rondeau* – one of many songs with continuous motion from start to finish, whether for a furious ride or, as here, a gentle ramble. Stanza upon stanza list the modest raptures, three melodies alternate, making the rondo-shape, modulations mirror moments of inward-turning or opening up to the skies, a single brief shadow of minor presages the time when life will no longer bloom – so don't miss it in its springtime.

Der Winterabend (1828) – rapt calm unfolding of the sad/happy long winter evenings – day with its too-much bright and noise has faded into grey and stillness: I sit alone, sole companion the moonlight shimmering on the familiar furnishings; even take up the now-idle spindle, causing no disturbance – silent come silent go – *her* spindle – long ago – vanished felicity – leaving me to sigh, to muse, to doze. A song of ravishing inward joy notwithstanding passing shadows, the vocal melody first sung by the piano over an unceasing chordal accompaniment that can curve into echoes and anticipations of the poem-as-sung while pointing the harmony with consummate delicacy, swelling again into singing between the stanzas. Modulations to close-related keys, some brighter, some not so much darker as more reposeful. Loveliest of all, the two closing lines, set twice with further repetitions after the first, many after the second – *und Sinne*: brood, contemplate, muse – where piano tenderly descants voice in counter-melody: after the voice ceases, the piano sings upon just one note – a bar where it is key-note of the brightest foreign key before, without modulation, becoming the third of the home key, to commence a third time the old familiar thoughts.

LOVE: SENSUOUS, SENSUAL, LONGING, TORMENTED, SUFFERING, AFFLICTED

Suleika 1 (1821). This marvellous song is all anticipation: begins uniquely – the amorous breath of wind from the East (this is Goethe in Oriental mode, or his anonymous female collaborator) whispers up from the bass of the piano, swelling to a burning/yearning dissonance (a dominant eleventh, if the sound needs a name), relaxing and expectant for two bars' wait-for-it establishing key, a treble momentum that will persist unbroken till the last stanza, and bass pulse-rhythm that drives the music inexorably forward, however gently. The opening waft of air is never heard again though its impulse is always felt. Resemblance to the initiating momentum in the 'Unfinished' Symphony is remarkable – it was 'finished' the year after the song, and must surely signify the same impulses. When Suleika enters she has no melody as such – rather, a line poised beautifully upon the pulsations below, responsive to every inflexion of the words, opening out now and again onto wider intervals, sustaining high, sinking low, for the first three stanzas. The fourth – the wind whispers to me a thousand greetings from my love – gives a hint of horn-calls within the texture, the voice-doubling first horn an octave above; then – as, always *pianissimo*, this erotically charged sonority continues – the piano's top o'ertops the singer – the tremolo motion unceasingly somewhere in the texture; as, too, when the driving-pulsation rhythm returns for stanza 5 and the volume is permitted to swell to *ff* for the climax on *Vielgeliebten* – the man I *really* love. This is a full close in the dominant: the V-note persists unbroken for the remainder of the song – two further stanzas, set whole, repeated, then broken down – only the quatrain's first two lines – true message, breath of love, life new-quickened – then the fourth line just once – only his breath can give it. From the dominant climax, ten bars' down-winding over the unceasing pulsation, to home key and a slower tempo. Rich Brahmsian viola/clarinet register (he audibly adored this music), the pulse now steadied into even repeated notes, on dominant till end, in the right hand a new rhythm, also persisting all the way, that gathers the horns into a glowing bunch, the voice focusing the text with the same expressive care, peaking at the characteristic touch of minor: stanza-repeat exact save that horns are now clarinets, up an octave. For the fragmentary third setting they've retreated to warm lower register: above them, a single tolling note: all still over the regularly pulsing bass.

Delphine (1825): another superb song in comparable emotional territory, with less whispered secrecy, more explicit desire, and, if possible, still greater rapture – the voice-part like an unleashed kite in a blue sky. Touches of horn-call spacing and persisting pulsing rhythm remembered from *Suleika 1*; extra here, the piano's left hand in sinuous counter-song with the vocal line. No need for details all over again: go listen!

Daß sie hier gewesen! (1823): another East wind, fugitive and evasive as in *Suleika 1*, warm with Eastern promise. Here the ghostly trace of the beloved's fragrance tells him *daß sie hier gewesen*, that she has been here: the tiny middle quatrain reverses the fragile confidences – tell her that I have been here: the closing stanza combines the two – can Beauty or Love remain hidden? Fragrance and tears tell me she has been here. Enormous intensity in a song barely two pages long and never rising above *piano* save for one stabbing accent. Dissonances worthy of (very prescient of) Wolf, remote from home key, support spare almost parlando setting of the first stanza – title-phrase, its last line (*without* exclamation-mark!) begins a two-bar couplet – four notes of downward scale: answer, rising, on tonic at *last* (literally); twice, the second concluded as voice breaks off – breaks down – by piano alone; but its commentating/collaborative accompaniment only manages the falling scale before also falling silent. Stanza 2 identical musically till, at this same place, the bar previously silent is extended upwards, twice – all

three or four descending notes of the scale. Voice, commencing third
stanza, picks up the identical sequence: at its top, the single *sforzando*, only the dominant seventh of home key, nothing like so dissonant as the song's rootless opening: which now returns for the
last stanza's third line – longest-held note on *Düfte*/fragrance, as the
sighing suspension mounts on the piano, intensifying on the next
noun *Thränen*/tears. Now the key-words are set twice, identically, *very*
far from home: dissonances rock, gradually re-reaching the latter
stages of stanzas 1 and 2 as the last lines of 3 are set again – the key-
words and their music twice, exact, as before. The piano's continuation is permitted this time to rest: until (the final note intimates)
it all starts over and over again.

    Du liebst mich nicht (1822). Another song driven by an all-
pervading rhythmic shape from which it cannot escape: and, here,
a range of modulations as wide as the world yet imprisoning rather
than liberating – one could almost call it a *de*-range – cruellest
most when towards the end, after *chemins perfides*, treacherous ways,
the tonic major is reached. My heart is broken, you love me no
more – plainly set; and you've had me know it – identical save the
heightened note on *du*: tho' I begged and entreated my urgent love,
you love me no more – the voice begins to rise, the harmony to
modulate, the rhythm persists: still further harmonic wrenches –
for all that the music remains soft, the register subdued to mid-
keyboard, the pressure intensifies – you told me unmistakably, in
words, you love me not: thus must I yield stars, moon, sun, since
you love me no more – anguish, still contained within the unforgiving rhythm, rises: no break, this time, into continuation – what for
me blooms the rose, the jasmine, the narcissus? You love (furthest
key) you *love* (second inversion of home key) me not: these words
again, twice, from another alien key, to home second inversion – all
this *fortissimo* irrupting from a dynamic that's only heretofore been
pp to *p*. And this second home-cadence reaches the bitter irony of
the tonic major for repetition of stars, moon, sun – *pp* to *ff*, deepest
bass note on peak of dissonance; repeat for roses, jasmine, narcissus, music identical; dissonant peak melts away as before, voice
sustains, rhythmic pattern broadens, voice and accompaniment

pulling apart – *liebst*: *nicht*: *liebst* are sustained, but accents only on the shorter *du*: *du*. Cadence in the major for shortest note-value possible, and suddenly soft. *Piano* opening, when first heard already roaming, new-adapted to close the case – this is not a snake-biting-tail circle able to start over again: the close is inexorable.

ARCHAIC MYTHOLOGY

Classical Greece as important to Schubert as Ossian is, and very much more conducive to great songs. *Memnon* (1819). Mysterious veiled tranquillity swathes the inner anguish of the quivering soul entrapped within implacable stone, permitted one hollow moan every new day when the rays of dawn strike him. Piano introduction renders this almost visually – solemn slow march in velvety middle register, tonality major but dark, a tattoo of soft triplets heard as from within the living statue, as the song proceeds binding it all together, on-beat and off-beat. Voice given no melody as such – recitative – declamation, in which the imprisoned soul mutters his fate, rising to despair when realizing that what to his ears is pain is to all others' harmonious. The captive figure now speaks for the poet unable to utter freely – even in dumbness the vocal line grows eloquent. Stillness begins to seethe tho' still soft, the four-note tattoo pervades the bass, ending in stark articulation beyond the voice's blocked powers. The closing stanza – oh to be at one with the Dawn, far above the hubbub; to shine, a pale star, from realms of love and freedom, upon the emptiness below: the hollow summons-figure now subsumed into continuous momentum, the voice more sostenuto, with strange wide intervals and cadential decoration, the piano's left hand singing deep below – not a glint of the starry heavens as so beautifully evoked in many Schubert songs elsewhere. The close of *Memnon* returns to veiled velvet middle and deep on the keyboard, its harmony at repose, even the continued motion hypnotized and hypnotizing – acquiescence and renunciation, till the next day dawns.

An Schwager Kronos (1816). Could hardly be in greater contrast, this proud display of energy, bravura, pride: Get along, Time,

sluggish coachman – no holding back whatever the bumpy road –
struggle uphill, onwards in strife and hope – vast mountain vistas
arise before the spirit, promising life eternal: here's an inviting inn
and a pretty girl – share your fresh healthy youth with me! Down,
down; the sun sinks; before you vanish, before mists seize me, an
old dotard, snatch me up, drunken and blinded with your last rays;
let me storm Orcus' dark gate; toot your horn, coachman Time – let
them know I'm coming, order a hot welcome. Songs with piano can
and must be freely transposed to accommodate different voices: but
this is an ur-D-minor piece, miniature pendant to Mozart's *Giovanni*
(whose terminal defiance it emulates) and *Requiem* (whose *dies irae*
threatens): stormy D-minor Beethoven – Brahms – Wagner to come;
most of all Bruckner, whose scherzos (in any key) pound away on
obsessive ostinati, as here. Schubert's sticks pretty close to tonic,
dominant, relative major till, exhorting the sluggard driver to be
up, a lurch via a neutral new key into a brilliantly different one for
the glorious prospect of the world at the traveller's feet: still further
for the mountain ranges, back to dominant for eternal life. More
relaxed, less unremitting, for the inn and the girl – a touch of tune
for the voice, of waggishness for the piano's bass – D-major, then F-
major, relative of returning D-minor, *ff* for furious hurry to catch the
setting sun before it sinks: back to opening, fading into soft repeated
diminished sevenths at the foreseen onset of old age. Sparks fly at
glimpsing the sea of fire within Hell's gate (Wagner surely remembered this bit when Siegfried's forging his sword also makes the
sparks fly – same key, too). As Hell's jaws open wide, superb (=
proud) move to permanent D-major, fanfares ablaze – the coachman's horn apocalyptic. Triumph persists to the end – the rider's
hope of Hell's hospitality more a command than a request.

    Gruppe aus dem Tartarus (1817, after a first, failed attempt the
previous year). A terrifying masterpiece, unique in the canon. Begins
at a distance from the frightening scene – Hark! the groanings of
the damned! – tremolo unison rising semitone-by-semitone over the
omnipresent tonic to first dissonance, diminishing as dominant to
all this again, up a semitone, diminishing again to commence a third
assault, where the voice enters, clinging to the unchanging note as

the semitones inexorably rise to next dissonance – the turbid ocean of damnation – remaining here briefly as it cadences, then on in slowed-up harmonic movement (momentum always tremolando, though the left hand now pulsates rather than rumbles), arriving on the last *Ach!* at a vehement allegro – severe, gaunt, baroque-ish dotted-rhythm pattern, voice broader above, telling of agony-distorted faces, cursing gaping-mouthed, hollow-eyed, straining towards the bridge over one of Hell's rivers whereby, perhaps, they arrived, by which they certainly can never leave. Motion near-ceases for this though its pulse still sensed; voice crawls up in semitones, wholly unmelodic, the long notes permitting every harmonic grind to hurt. Half-motion returns for the bridge of tears – grim texture, internal octaves hollow, *pianissimo* after *fortissimo*, voice swelling into momentary melody as the vision dims. Soft and anxious, the damned souls enquire of each other whether and when their torment will end – low mutter creeping up by semitones as piano hammers out the merciless repeated notes in octave unison, the bass jacking up the harmony to the crack of doom till – Schubert the grammarian even as he imperils all the laws – dominant of what can and must, only now, be heard as the main key is reached, emphasized and battering, for the hideous mirth of the answer: *Eternity* is their punishment – brilliant fanfares in the major – an irony more terrible than the defiant triumph closing the entry to Hell in *Kronos*: Eternity swings above, breaking Saturn's scythe in twain. An anti-modulatory lunge lurches the key up a semitone: it slides back almost at once for the second setting of the divisive scythe, and, cadencing, immediately detumesces, down the minor scale inside the repeated home-note over and under, down another octave, as at the start but now without tremolo, lasting two bars, *pp diminuendo*, ending short – silence – the bitterest twist of all, a high arpeggiated minor chord – here's your answer.

PANTHEISTIC ECSTASY

Two wonders – *Im Walde* (*Waldesnacht*) – 1820; *Auflösung* – 1824. The first a tour de force of continuous momentum, whirring in one fixed position or moving slowly or with breathtaking rapidity through the keys, a killer for an accompanist's right hand, essaying often awkward layout virtually without relief for six minutes encompassing a timeless torrent of outpouring rapture. Night-ride into dark forest, fitfully illuminated by dawn then night again, as if days swallowed up in the whirlwind rush, driven by God's wings, the creative breath of the Spirit – impelled from within, above, ahead, behind. After the piano's introduction, already curving in a bold arc between alien keys, the voice enters in broad but broken phrases, gradually coalescing, sometimes expressively contoured though never a conjunct melody: more like 'endless melody' à la Wagner, who must have known this song even if he didn't (so to speak). The opening tremolo in both pianist's hands now given only to the right, while the left marks a speaking bass, sometimes doubling voice, sometimes holding the harmony, and always urging forward. Voice rises and falls in octaves up from, back to, its unison with the deep dark bass, while the indefatigable right hand continues to whirr and whirl. Slight change of texture for the glowing red of dawn – whirr/whirl descends, l. h. dry staccato, imitated by voice, twice: previous continuity briefly resumed, then the flames begin to throw up sparks as if summoned upwards to rejoin their divine origin.

Mentioning God brings the otherwise unbroken momentum to a momentary break – repeated chord *p* swelling to *ff*; just four beats, a solid cadence (though we're miles further on from home-key opening); apostrophe to the Divinity again, a tiny transition, and the long journey resumes. Gentle, now, *very* soft, the perpetual motion higher, the l. h. doubling voice at the unison, previous heavy bass lost to sight and sound – a very *lovely* sound, intensified when the single melodic strand divides into two and the harmony becomes more stable – a lyric oasis, ending in re-descent of texture to nether regions, and a piano epilogue/link to – turbulence renewed – r. h. arpeggios, l. h. tremolos: life presses – fierce strong impulses struggle with what curbs them, to transform into the fullness of love's fulfilment: the breath of Creation fills the sails of the soul – back to gapped phrases, rising and rising, the more melodious over another staccato bass-pattern, now syncopated and always forward-pressing:

many verbal repetitions needed to encompass the music's huge scope; modulations ever more hair-raising – the Spirit speaks. The end of this amazing section resets the poem's opening line, very soft, to resumed voice-plus-left hand octaves, voice taming piano's conjunct motion into leaping ninths – rushing wind, God's wings. Through all this the harmonic rate slackens, to an actual return of opening music, and its words again, compressed as it continues, crowning the structure with new directions and greater boldness for the singer (but no relief for the pianist's suffering r. h.) even as the poem's final stanza, setting out from an almost-identical first couplet – *kühler*/cool night becomes *dunkel*/dark – open up the closing thought – free from constraints the mind hears the song of the spirits in the breezes – calm spacious ending, harmony slowing down (though momentum not relinquished till very last chord), words deep in the voice, longer and longer sustained notes, and, after traversing the tonal spectrum, a drawn-out Amen cadence to, at long last, cessation in *ppp* sustained major.

Auflösung is comparable – less wild and dithyrambic, yet more ecstatic. First stanza is all imperatives – 'Hide you, Sun; my rapturous fires out-do you: sounds, go dumb; flee, springtime beauties; I would be alone!' Deep soft bass tremolo, right hand in upward curl of arpeggio, descending in a quiver of diminished sevenths to re-opening over which voice sings in arching curves, down the arpeggio, up with ardent athleticism to the glow of rapture, long-sustained for the wholeness of being through which the rapture burns. Again for silencing sounds and banishing spring, with opening-out expansion to new key, up a semitone, for 'leave me alone', set twice. There is only one further stanza, the same length, but its setting fills the remainder of the song. 'Gentle strength wells up from every secret place of my soul, swathing me in heavenly song': and now, imperative again: 'Dissolve, world – go down – never no more sully the sweet celestial chorus.' Or as Schoenberg put it (setting Stefan George some eight decades later in the same loved-and-hated Vienna), 'I am but a spark of the sacred flame, but a rumble of the holy voice.' Texture continues – upward flourishes over static but tremolando bass, voice's arcs more joined-up: slow harmonic movement, beginning to quicken as the salient 'heavenly' reached, heard twice: change of texture as the last imperative – *Geh'unter*/Get down! – arrives; both hands tremolo, stabbing *fortepiano* accents on every main beat, as voice declaims its command, before resuming previous texture as the key homes in to restart, equalling the poem's final line – athletic from the word go, opening out into pure physical ecstasy for the sweet ethereal chorus: again, exactly repeated till expanded, yet more extravagant for the same closing climactic two words. As if the sounds being summoned are now, indeed, joining in. When the huge flight lands, the piano, already diminuendo, reaches the highest register of the whole song and remains up aloft, softly tremolando, the l. h. deep in the abysm, all the resonance between somehow lingering in the spectral memory. Into this vibrating void the voice repeats the imperative twice in a low mutter, then a third, with a long-held major third: *Geh'unter, Welt!* Resolution achieved, the right hand sinks to rest, and the rest is silence.

BALLADS

Many; much long-drawn-out tedium, Ossian to the fore; some cele-brated Goethe-settings, and this, which represents this genre at its most compelling – *Der Zwerg* (1822). Another song dominated by continuous tremolando – here *literally* uninterrupted – and an ostinato rhythm, at once driving forward and anchoring deep: also some of the key-changes that could be heard as mere habits – idiosyncratic tics of style – were they not ever-renewed in perpetual changes of angle and colour. Coloration of this macabre Gothic tale is cold sea-grey, as it might be on a winter crossing between Cornwall and Brittany with doomed lovers aboard – again, if Wagner didn't know this song when evolving the colour of the sea-music in *Tristan*, he should have.

The difference from previous ostinato-driven songs already described is that this is a story, a situation, with characters who speak – akin therefore to Schubert's most celebrated ballad *Erlkönig*, and many others. Unless *Der Doppelgänger* is a ballad of sorts, this surpasses them all. Setting, twilight on the open sea, land receding, weather calm; on the open deck, the Queen and her Dwarf – tranced monotonous surface of the water, tiny hints of internal melody within or above the even tremolo: below, the depth of the left hand on its obsessive downbeat tattoo. The bass thrice describes a downward chromatic curve before returning home; the voice outlines the minor triad, gradually filling in all the notes of the primal fifth as though outlining the primal source for tonality itself as in Bruckner; a little link, here inconspicuous, is destined for later enormities.

Stanza 2 begins the same, then as the Queen gazes up into the vault of heaven and the blue receding hills, the phrase lifts too, just a notch, remaining up for the salient word – *hinauf* – and broadening out as the poem invokes the Milky Way. A lurching modulation induces direct speech – she cries out to the stars – 'you've never betrayed me: you tell me I shall die soon; and in truth I die gladly' – stern declamation over the fateful bass-rhythm, ceasing as the word 'die' is reached. Another modulation, fatefully easy, to unison the tremolo: voice in muttered parlando, unison with piano left hand, as the Dwarf steps to silently tie around the neck of his mistress the red silk cord that will fulfil her fate – creepy music of insinuation and repressed menace, the more so when repeated, tremolo now harmonized, voice moving independent of the speaking bass – the hideous creature weeps as though his sorrows would blind him: 'He speaks' – modulation – then back to bare octave tremolo, bass and voice unison, up a semitone – 'you bear the blame for your suffering, for you have forsaken me for the King' (like the Queen mysteriously unnamed and unexplained): growing strong and angry, the speaking bass now heavy, the voice denunciatory – 'only your death can revive my life' – literally *Freude*/joy – doubly emphasized – 'though I shall ever hate myself as the cause of your death, yet die you must – grow pale for an early grave.'

Drama is perilously near melodrama here: when the prevailing ostinato-tattoo, reminiscent from the start of 'Fate' of the opening of Beethoven's 5th Symphony, is hammered out outlining a tritone, one can smile, or even laugh outright (as I well recall, including this song in a lecture, when this passage was reached): but mirth is

stifled as this inadvertent moment glides ineluctably by – the pallor
of the early grave – into reopening in tonic major, as often, uncannily more sinister than the initial minor. A sort of recapitulation, all
majored – 'full of youth and life, she lays her hand on her heart, her
eyes o'erflow with heavy tears as she would pray'. Here the majored
recapitulation deviates wonderfully at her last words: 'may my death
bring you no sorrow', she says, or rather *cries* – sudden sharp accent
as the red silk cord is pulled tight; the alien note persists as the bass
slowly reinterprets it – the Dwarf kisses her blanched cheeks, his
senses fade, fate resounds in the bass, a prolonged harmonic homecoming: 'he gazes upon her as death seizes her, he lowers her into
the sea' – *Meer*; tonic first inversion achieved; 'with his own two
hands' (climactic dominant – these hands that did the deed): home
minor re-reached, last singing out the ur-melody, voice declaiming primal matter – 'his heart so burns for her' – set twice – 'such
burning longing' – and a third time yet more burning: as it cadences,
home key reached in root-position, suddenly *pp*, exactly as at start –
the place thereof shall know them no more. As the narrator holds
one melody-less intonation, set only once – 'no coast will ever see
him ashore' – it's as though Dwarf and vessel, as well as Queen, have
sunk deeper than plumb-line sounded – bare A tremolo in four
octaves, bare A-minor chord (bare A-major would be beyond irony).

SONGS OF CALM

Two songs of utter stillness after all this disturbance, perpetual
motion, obsessive driving rhythms, perturbation whether erotic,
fearful, or even psychotic. *Meeres Stille* (1815 – this is a second, final,
version). Enchanted becalmed motionless sea-surface with undercurrent of anxiety – no breeze ruffles the glassy water, the calm is
uncanny, even sinister: not a wave stirs. Schubert's momentum-
machine here solidified into thirty-two slow chords, one per bar,
gently rolled but otherwise without other movement, the blueprint
for a Bach prelude, in simple yet mysterious modulation out from
C to Sea, back again to a C without harbour in sight or hope. Over
this, voice declaims in soft recitative, no melody but shapely and

sensitive, in plain contour, eschewing all decoration save two brief ornamental turns, and requiring enormous artistry from its singer because stripped bare of all allure.

Nacht und Träume (1822). 'Hallowed Night sinks; dreams float moonlit into the silent hearts of mankind, who cry out when day dawns for their return, Return, oh Dreams!' Motionless as *Meeres Stille*, though the slow-moving harmony is laid out in gentle continuum of pulsation, never leaving the tenor/bass register of the keyboard; overall effect of both the motionless and the moving song is mesmerizing, tranquillized – indeed traumatized. One bar establishes key and motion: the piano's top for the next three outlines a melody not heard again in either voice or keyboard. Singer floats in on exquisite long-drawn phrases; repose is endorsed with only close harmonic coloration, then completely othered with bold non-modulation for second stanza, direct to G-major from B-major (if original key is performed): what elsewhere in Schubert is often a judder or jolt here deepens the calm: two bars' pure G – mankind listens with *joy*; pure C-major for two bars on this vital word; the words set again, *joy* now arriving on the returning G-major: the simplest and most poetic perfect cadence V–I in all music? It takes boundless daring, purity of heart, inner confidence, to do something so apparently artless. One bar of diminished seventh effects a return to home key's neighbours; an exact recapitulation save syllabic adjustments due to changed text – last three lines of first quatrain equal last three lines of the second (its first having been set twice in the G–C excursion as described). Piano demurely demurs from playing its introductory melody as epilogue – voice's melody has sung its all: coda of simple oscillation between home and diminished seventh over tonic key-note, twice, ending on full tonic chord, the third at the top as if inviting the singer, whose first note this had been, to re-enter the hallowed space.

RELIGIOUS SONGS

Religious songs – not including ballads, etc., where a religious setting is evoked, such as *Die junge Nonne*; or hymnic deistic splurges like *Der Allmacht* – comprise one tiny instance, a precious gem of refined, interiorized devotion so modest it doesn't even fill one page of print: *Vom mitleiden Mariä* (1818). After the preceding excitations and eventual repose, this response to the Virgin's suffering at beholding her Son's on the Cross comes in surprising contrast. Archaizing austerity, yet a sweetness within the spare three-part texture – voice and both piano's hands absolutely equal, in even minim-crotchet motion with occasional quavers, fuller harmony (still in only three parts) at the piano's tiny interlude when the voice pauses for breath after each stanza's first couplet (three stanzas, musically identical). The second half of each verse is a tercet, extended, by the composer's setting its last line twice, into a quatrain: piano's three-part four-bar-close begins as voice ends; between verses 1 and 2 it's a link, after the third it's equally serviceable as an ending. Somehow the modest decorum of this lovely little song entirely forgoes expression of the poem's grisly references to Christ's bloody wounds, the thorns piercing eyes, ear, brow, bone, brain, and his mother's keen stab of empathetic identification, by holding it all in the balance of its masterly control of dissonance-within-euphony. Especially delicate, when sung by a woman, the interplay of her line with the piano's top – sometimes above sometimes below her; and, *very* occasionally, coinciding.

SONG-CYCLES

The two Müller-cycles have been so much written-on, and are so familiar, that further description would be redundant. They remain at the pinnacle of the genre; unsurpassed; unsurpassable. Here, only a brief reminder, placing them in this wider context of Schubert's *Lieder* as a whole, and that within the scope of his symphonic, piano and chamber music. For the third so-called cycle I will revert to some detailed descriptions, attempting to evoke, maybe even to capture, the outer features, if not the inner essence, of this extraordinary final harvest.

Schubert first came across the poetry of Wilhelm Müller in 1823. The *Schöne Müllerin* cycle was the immediate result of his enthusiastic response, but he waited until February 1827 before setting the twelve poems that comprise Part I of *Winterreise*. This was published later that year with the promise of a 'second half' because he had meanwhile found another source with twelve additional poems, not so much following on as interspersed among the original set. This *Fortsetzung der Winterreise* was composed in October 1827. A case has recently been made for using Müller's final order, as somehow being what Schubert might really have meant, given the chance. But he did have the chance and chose not to take it. And, in fact, the psychological curve described by the composer's own ordering of the journey, however fortuitous, is strong, convincing, and by now seems unshakeable and inevitable.

Die schöne Müllerin told a story in its protagonist's own voice – a novelette of calf-love in a series of vignettes picturing his rising exaltation, his gradual disappointment, his jealousy, despair and final suicide by drowning (in the last two songs the young man's voice yields to the voice of the brook). *Winterreise* is like an alternative continuation. The same situation – rejection in love – lies behind it (though now without any circumstantial detail) and the voice is the protagonist's throughout, with no other angle upon the experiences and feelings undergone. Here, instead of turning to the maternal lullaby of the flowing water, he ventures again out into the world, a wanderer as he'd been at the start of the earlier cycle. But now it is winter, no stream could receive him, they are all frozen over, so he has to keep moving on, propelled from within, no destination, homeless everywhere, rejected of men. And rejected by the girl; the cycle's paramount event, over before it begins, burns itself into everything that follows. Instead of plot there is a succession of images – the weathervane, the frozen stream with the turbulence beneath its surface, the frost that turns his black hair to white, the last leaf in the tree, and so forth – each an emblem of inner state mirrored in outward appearance, in naïve pathetic fallacy as sharp and simple as a folk-ballad. The cycle's journey, therefore, is not so much chronological or topographical as, rather, a progress of images and mental states in a descending curve of desolation, mitigated by memories of warmth and greenery, by deceptive gleams of hope or hints of renewed strength, collapsing eventually in self-abandonment and loss of reason.

In this music the domestic, sometimes overly cosy aspect of Schubert is entirely absent. The *Winterreise* songs are often severe to the point of harshness. Warmth is used only to heighten the contrast, and in the final stages the full textures of 'Das Wirtshaus' and 'Die Nebensonnen' are as demoralizing in their delusiveness as the 'Leiermann' in its naked exposure. Late in 1827 he told the members of his friendly song-circle 'I will sing you some songs that will make you shiver' and then went through all twenty-four 'in a voice vibrant with emotion'. When his friends were puzzled and unenthusiastic he declared: 'I like these songs more than all the others, and you will get to like them too.' He was right.

The circumstances of *Schwanengesang*'s publication are well known; Schubert's idea of two groups of songs, seven Rellstab settings and six Heine, all written in August 1828, knocked into an awkward whole after his death that December by a publisher who threw in the pretty 'Die Taubenpost' (Seidl) to avoid an unlucky number, divided the fourteen into two unequal halves (1–6; 7–14) and gave it a lachrymose catchpenny title because the Seidl song was its composer's last.

The title has stuck and, more unfortunately, the sense that this miscellany must be respected and made somehow to cohere. Attempts to find in it a story are patently forced; as also attempts to fuse Heine and Rellstab into an emotional entity. So long as artists of high calibre persist in performing *Schwanengesang* as a whole it is best taken just as another group from the great body of Schubert songs: a group of remarkable quality, gaining in poignance by the clear achievement of extraordinary new territory just as he was about to die.

The Heine settings are astonishing, vast in scope though small in compass, and intense in emotion beyond any individual song in *Winterreise*. Heard successively their very intensity can induce claustrophobia. Though actually the songs are highly differentiated there is not in effect enough contrast, except with 'Fischermädchen' (last and subtlest of innumerable lilting 6/8 ditties), which fits ill with the inwardness of 'Ihr Bild' and 'Am Meer' and not at all with the volcanic 'Atlas', the veiled then suddenly naked 'Stadt', and the cataclysmic 'Doppelgänger'. After this last, the charm of 'Die Taubenpost' can easily lead to its underestimation; but 'Doppelgänger' also suffers from this absurd juxtaposition. The Rellstab songs are slighter. 'Liebesbotschaft' is the last in a long line of gentle pastorals, 'Abschied' of his bright energetic chatterboxes, 'Frühlingssehnsucht' and 'Ständchen' are also familiar types, and the lightish vein of all four reaches here its ultimate delicacy of handling. The others are darker, moving already towards Heineland though with nothing of the same concentration. 'Kriegers Ahnung', a scena in several sections, uncannily forecasts Wolf's soldier-songs from the Mörike book and Mahler's settings of *Wunderhorn* poems about soldiers and their woes. 'Aufenthalt' strikes deeper, a supreme example of Schubert's enormous melodic control, here grim and urgent, here more lyrical (and once briefly pretty), passing through harmonic shifts that can still be hair-raising. And 'In der Ferne', though quite different from them, touches equally with the Heine settings upon worlds unknown. The bathetic pathos and rhythmic stiffness of the verse are transcended in the hieratic setting, its first two stanzas in the minor with simple chordal accompaniment (but what chords!) and echo-bars, transformed into one vast arc of major (where as so often the mere *words* of the last stanza have to be set twice to fulfil the size of the musical design), incorporating the echoes into the progress, breaking the chords into a dark shimmer, discovering key-shifts whose aching beauty and grammatical sureness have never been equalled by any composer, before or since. This song more than the others prepares the listener for the Heine settings that (after the incongruously cheerful 'Abschied') follow. There is no sense of a whole in all these parts. If only singers, accompanists, impresarios, record companies, were not hidebound in their servitude to the mere *name* of a swansong that doesn't exist! No sensitive artist would choose these fourteen songs by deliberate design: too much respect is paid to accident and convention.

*

Leaving the old, both worlds at once they view
That stand upon the threshold of the new.

Edmund Waller's lovely words can be employed again, to characterize Schubert's Seven Last Songs. 'Der Atlas' – he sings in his own
person: 'I, wretched Atlas, must bear an entire world of woe; unbearable; my heart breaks within me: *proud* heart, it's your wish – to be
endlessly happy or endlessly wretched; now endless wretchedness
is your lot.' Grim grinding utterance of gigantic yet choked power
worthy of an Alberich; or Wotan in pain, his light double. First
stanza persistent right-hand tremolo, mid-low pitch (the piano-part
all in bass clef), over heavily marked figure in the left. Voice joins
in near-unison, rising above the tremolo for its closing word *Leibe* –
the *body*, its shoulders unbowed by the load they carry, its heart
broken within – to a horrendous modulatory gear-change and a
triple *forte*. The new key, now major, is retained for commencement
of stanza 2, where tremolos cease, replaced by heavy oom-pah-pah
accompaniment, each first beat accented. Over this the voice goes,
freer and cantabile; a ray of light for *endless joy*; declining sadly
into *endless woe*, heard twice, swelling up again for the proud heart
in its self-elected punishment – this passage the key back to home.
Compressed resetting of first stanza's first two lines, their repetition
enhanced with a colossal third setting, as if Atlas attempts to heave
off the mountainous weight of sorrow: another triple *forte* – rapid
crumple – epilogue, piano alone, tremolo and weighty bass, soft
with diminuendo, till last-minute crescendo towards loud defiant
closing chord.

'Ihr Bild', her picture. Utter contrast – still, spare, inward beyond
intimacy. Two unharmonized notes open the brooding meditation;
voice in unison with bare piano octaves – 'in dark dreaming I gaze
at her picture': piano – harmony at last – half closes, half opens
up: chorale-like setting in tender major – 'the beloved countenance
begins to come secretly alive' – a sort of Amen-close, Quaker in
demure contained piety. Now the song begins to stir harmonically,
still within the same absolute textural simplicity, moving flat-wards,
voice always not independent, clinging for support to the parlour

harmonium – 'a wonderful smile played upon her lips' – a tender
little hopping-gesture in the piano: then harmonium again – 'her
eyes shone with tears of woe' – eyes virtually identical with lips save
for one crucial passing chromatic intensification: piano again, again
the hopping – a gulp of choked reaction; this time echoed slow and
low, twice, the second restoring home-tonality without its defining
third. Third stanza defines it; first half of first stanza repeated, exact
save for the ongoing text – 'my tears, too, flowed down my cheeks':
the third is *minor*. Thus for the second half – exact repeat of music,
text ongoing to close – '*ach*, I cannot believe you are lost to me!' –
this time major *ach*ing in the full major harmony, more *ach*ute than
in the bare minor unison. But the coda to stanza I, which had been
major too, is now minor though the chordal voicing is the fullest in
the whole song: minor is sadder still, after all. A world of loss in a
drop of dew: infinity in two minutes, and two pages.

'Das Fischermädchen'; light relief – 'last of innumerable 6/8
ditties' and one of the sweetest – grace and tender eroticism in the
lilting tune and its lightly sonorous accompaniment, the middle
stanza elegantly modulating up a third, still more adroitly returning home for the last. A very different sea-picture conjured by
'Am Meer', another two-page wonder to stand with 'Ihr Bild': the
fisher-girl's dark double, amorous charm rankled and curdled to
erotic poison. 'We sat by the lonely fisherman's house as the sun
shed its dying rays over the glittering sea; silent and alone: mists
arose, water surged, the gulls flew here and there; tears dropped
from your love-filled eyes.' Thus the first half: beginning on soft
but burning dissonance, resolving to major, twice: voice enters
unison with richly scored accompaniment of solemn simplicity –
no longer Quaker grey so much as plum/cerise/violet. 'Silent and
alone.' Now the mists arise – to the minor, tremolando, voice now
alert and independent: motion stagnates; she weeps – her tears
fall with unbearable plangency, piano echoes *ppp*. The second half
repeats the first's music unaltered till three-quarters through: 'I
saw those tears fall on your hand; sinking to my knee I drank
them from your white hand.' Half-way – this is where in verse I
the mists arose: here, to identical music, 'Since that moment my

flesh is consumed and my soul dies of longing.' Last quarter, same music as before fundamentally, but wracked up to excruciation strangely resembling the last cry of pain-wracked Atlas – (since then) 'I am by that wretched woman's tears' – voice and piano top in operatic thirds – two tenors – then the same plangent phrase, twice, as for the tears the first time, now setting *vergiftet/* poisoned: a delicate little decoration on the voice's last *Thränen* – tears, matching the one in each stanza's first half: piano epilogue to match its prologue – soft burning dissonance cadencing to even-softer resolution – major! – twice, the closing one softer yet. It *is* a touch operatic; it's set in a *scene*, there's a whiff of melodrama. But no great interpretation of this song can fail to recognize and elicit the authentic anguish burning within both its over-warm first halves and the agitations of its second, that twice bursts up to the surface in unforgettable cries from the heart.

'Die Stadt': 'Music of the Future' – not so much Wagner's as late Liszt, late Brahms, Busoni, Sibelius? Britten? Debussy's *Voiles*? – in the atmospheric swirls of vapour, and Mahler in the funereal tread (albeit in triple time) of the earthbound contrasting strain. Begins as a *bagatelle sans tonalité*, only the single diminished seventh floating up in soft arpeggio, down in two answering chords, all over a soft bass-note octave tremolo. Voice enters as the tread commences – low dense chordal funeral march, no independent melody: on the distant horizon a misty apparition, the town with its towers shrouded in twilight. Opening texture returns, this time continu-ing unfaltering – eleven bars of the same diminished seventh in the same pattern over the same left-hand shudder, the voice outlin-ing the same chord in gradual descent, with a few passing notes to relieve the hypnotic monotony: 'Damp breezes riffle the grey water as with mournful strokes the boatman guides the boat.' Last verse set to the same thick heavy complementary strain, now loud and strong, the vocal intervals more heroic, a flattened inflexion – 'The sun rises once more, radiant from the ground, and shows me the place' – flat-tened inflexion – 'where' – heroic climactic high note – 'my loved one' – diminuendo and cadence – 'was lost.' He's drained and spent, but the mists survive: first five bars return exact, the diminished

seventh refusing to resolve, down to the sixth bar, formerly tremolando, now still – void – extinction.

'Der Doppelgänger'. This celebrated creation will remain for ever
awesome beyond words. Completely original texture and procedure
for the *Lied* – parlando/recitativo for the text almost throughout,
over a sort of chaconne/ostinato four bars long for the accompaniment (another that barely rises into the treble clef). The four-bar
ground is first heard by itself; its two-part writing, doubled in two
or three octaves where possible, bound by an inner dominant pedal,
already evokes a unique atmosphere, setting the scene as if in the
night-deserted streets of 'Die Stadt' 'where I lost my love', seen from
afar off. As the chaconne repeats, then begins to diverge, the protagonist speaks, describing the empty silence – 'and in this house my
sweetheart dwelt' – regular pattern extended by an echo on piano
of the voice's last phrase with a flicker of added dissonance – first
intimation of a Double. He continues – 'she has long departed, but
the house stands here still' – same music again, and again the echo
of the voice's last words – 'on the selfsame place'.

Now the chaconne begins to grow – first seven chords identical,
but accented, no longer legato, and overall crescendo to expressionist
fff on the seventh, on the eighth, shattering Neapolitan dissonance also *sforzando*, is then held motionless for a whole further bar,
breaking the so-far regularity. 'There's a man there too, staring up,
wringing his hands in anguish.' Chaconne resumes, exactly as this
second half had – soft, separated, accented, swelling up to a still-
acuter version of the dissonant eighth chord, voice emphasizing the
single crucially changed note by rising to it at the top of its register –
highest note in the song – on *Gestalt*/shape/form – 'I shudder when
catching his face – the moon reveals to me my own' (shape/form/
Gestalt): upon this dissonance the extra motionless bar again hangs.

Now things really move: an accelerando as the chaconne resumes,
soft but rapidly swelling, sometimes more fully chorded and always
rising semitone by semitone, doubled in three octaves, hung
upon the unchanging internal pedal-note. 'You Double, blanched
comrade, why' – first alien arrival, a pure minor triad so remote in
key as to sound like a dissonance – 'why *ape* [*äffst*, on this chord] my

love-sorrows'; the alien key stays – tonic/dominant – 'which I suffered on this very threshold?' The build-up retains the nine-bar pattern, its last, extra bar the most bloodcurdling wrench of all, cadencing into first inversion, sure sign of homecoming (but *this* is no home) – 'so many a night in times long past' – cadence almost casual after such wracking torments. At the voice's last word the chaconne re-begins as at the start (save only the first chord, its bare fifth now enriched with its minor third), till its fourth bar, startlingly major, the enriching major third clearly audible for all the duskiness – before slipping down with magnificent disregard for 'forbidden' parallel octaves *and* fifths, to root-position tonic major with its flattened seventh compelling resolution upon subdominant minor, and thence back to pure tonic major in an Amen plagal cadence more terminal, despite the triple *piano*, than a perfect. Voice throughout this continuation and close has grown ever higher in broken phrases of recitativo to reach the climax on *Gestalt*: thence through the direct address to the Double who is also himself – oneself – myself – you. The word-setting is almost monotone, slightly melodizing then rising for the 'many nights in times of old' to an arch of expression at last released, especially by the melisma on *alter*/old – that seems to bring the uncanny experience into frightening close-up, before the coda distances it into the remote past, unreachable and irredeemable.

And so to 'Die Taubenpost', added to the unhappy baker's dozen making up the so-called cycle. With Heine, Schubert at last found a poet of elective affinity and equal calibre. Seidl is no Heine! The pretty little conceit also contains a belovèd's house, to which the lover sends out his pigeon a thousand times each day – the carrier's true name is *Sehnsucht* –longing/desire – Schubert's consistent muse from earliest to – literally – last (October 1828: he died the next month). The music is carefree and delectable, with complementary excursions to remote keys bewitching as any, not least in their effortless glide/slide back home: cunning as serpents and sweet as doves: the last word from the supreme composer of amorous libido – 'Desire knows no Rest'.

CHAPTER VII

Early German Romantics

Weber

Carl Maria von Weber: born 1786; scrappy education among theatrical folk; studied with Michael Haydn late 1790s, thence to Vienna; outstanding pianist, and from 1804 employed on and off as musical director in small-town operatic positions – more important, Prague 1813, then Dresden 1816. After earlier operatic ventures, devoted himself mainly to instrumental works: 1821 *Der Freischütz* in Berlin made him a celebrity; *Euryanthe* commissioned for Vienna 1823; Covent Garden commissioned *Oberon* the next year; against doctor's advice he visited London to direct its première, dying there June 1826 – before Beethoven and Schubert – aged only thirty-nine.

Lovable and lamentable Weber, inventor in music of enchantment, magic black and fairy-gold, by melodic refinement with harmonic subtlety to match, and a sensitivity to timbre like no composer before, although also evinced in several *concertante*-works, slight in themselves – for clarinet, bassoon, horn, viola – most especially the charming chivalry of the *Konzertstück* for piano – though at its fullest and most prophetic in orchestral contexts. Which principally means the three main operas: digging deep into folklore and balladry and – maybe not so deep – into dark places of the psyche; opening up new areas for music in subject-matter and feeling – Gothic, Romantic, picturesque, evocative, affective – archetypal and seminal for a subsequent century and more of German music, also for French and Russian. Whatever Wagner, Berlioz, Tchaikovsky, Mahler achieved later in this terrain, Weber had defined it first. Here

I will attempt the three full-length operas in turn: their mingled flaws and glories will explain the *lamentable* as well as the *lovable*.

Der Freischütz

Der Freischütz is sole survivor in the repertoire. The familiar legend tells of magic bullets bound to hit their mark and gain their marksman's wishes, their potency granted by bargaining with devilish forces. Setting, the human landscape of pastoral and forestry, church bells and hunting horns up-hill and down-dale; maidenly innocence all in white, robust masculinity shaken by and vulnerable to black impulses. Light and Night in conflict and eventual resolution amid resonant, pantheistic Nature both benign and fearsome – forest raptures, terrors, mysteries: simple pieties; true love tried and tested from within and without; love triumphant in the end; salvation in the faithfulness of a true woman – all this the archetype of every trope in German Romantic opera, from the very start enjoying recognition, acclaim, widespread and enthusiastic dissemination.

Equally seminal and pregnant is the work's musical idiom: tropes invented or consolidated here for sinister/anxious/terror/storm/supernatural events; for weddings and hunting; pious strains for upright folks' life by day equally with spooky strains for dark doings deep in the woods; dulcet tenderness for the injured heroine equally with stalwartness for the hero however irresolute, a pert cheekiness for her maid; bland cantabile for the hermit *ex machina* who unties the knot at the end, to the Devil's own music – spoken not sung, but memorably characterized. Weber's style at once aristocratic – elegant, dapper, Beau Brummel; yet indefinably vulgar, Cockney, sentimental – Tom Moore: refined and bumptious; and unfailingly fluent, graceful to the voice and the ear. Also so modern, setting the new feeling and subject-matter on its course for the rest of the nineteenth century, yet also clear heir to *Fidelio* – heroically self-sacrificing devotion, and the *affettuoso* determination, of Leonora: and to *The Magic Flute* – darkness vanquished by light; domestic bliss desired, attained, celebrated; popular folkloric strains. Heir, above all, to Haydn's dictionary of pastoral as realized in *The Seasons*: most memorably (and remembered), the unforgettable C-major resplendence in *The Creation* when light bursts upon the darkness, reproduced in *small* in many places throughout the opera, to culminate in the all-illuminating finale.

The Overture, written last as usual, a standard epitome of key-moments and salient motifs in the action to come, put together with a flair anything but standard: new worlds shudder and shimmer into being; these sounds intimate a fresh primal scene. Commences with virtually a Haydn symphony's first movement slow introduction: long-held unison, swelling to a questioning three-note motif; bare soft violins alone: the same two elements return in dominant, to answer: expectant silence: tonic restored and momentum set up, gentle background on strings, till ready to support entry of lustrous glowing soft horns – a pair, answered by another, then all four – celebration of primeval diatonicism in music's fundamental key – C – and all *Rheingold* implicit. The passage is rounded off as the strings die down: horns are replaced by clarinets in their lowest register, the chalumeau, with its unique dark, throaty timbre, inside shivering string tremolos, the darkening harmony underpinned by off-beat drum-beats plus pizzicato double-basses on tonal music's most ambiguous chord the diminished seventh, soon to be abused into wearisome commonplace, here thrillingly strange: high cellos intimate the human accent – fearful, yearning, loving, uncertain. This fused composite image peaks and fades: the *vivace* begins in C-minor, agitated and nervy, stormy and energetic as it whips up, rounding off by-the-book in relative major of tonic minor – an excellent sonata-exposition. Now things deviate: the four horns blast a summons, answered by solo clarinet *con molto passione*, telling of hopes and terrors to come, before a more stable lyric theme telling of their assuagement and appeasement. The Overture's remaining course froths up all these elements (save the horn quartet) into a skilful potpourri – patchwork, eventual decline-and-fall into the menacing chalumeau/thudding pizzicato diminished seventh shudder, before the fiery commonplaces of a brilliant C-major apotheosis foretells the opera's Happy End.

But the work's largest stretch of inventive genius comes at its

Unhappy Middle, the celebrated scene in the Wolf's Glen where evil bargains are struck and magic bullets forged, and Weber touches heights and depths of evocation previously untrod. The action prior to this scene closing Act II is simply told: a shooting-match on the edge of the great Bohemian forest. Max, a forester, is defeated; a fight threatens. Another forester, Caspar, who lies in fief to the Dark Huntsman Samiel, suggests mockingly that Max engage supernatural forces to ensure victory next day. He is rebuked by Cuno, head-forester, father of Max's betrothed Agathe: if Max again fails in the match he will not gain her hand in marriage. Max broods on his lack of luck; Caspar gets him drinking, offers help, proves his efficacy by a magically aided shot: all this observed by Samiel, invisible. 'My bullet was magic – you too can benefit – come with me to the Wolf's Glen at midnight.' His need is to replace himself by Max as forfeit to the dark forces; Act I ends in Caspar's exultant certainty that it will go his way.

The crucial Act II takes place the same evening at the head-forester's house. Cousin Ännchen attempts to cheer Agathe, alarmed at a falling portrait, then by the local Hermit offering her white roses against an unspecified danger. Comforted, Agathe expresses her joy at her lover's return. Joy turns to fear when Max urges a night-expedition to collect the stag he'd shot earlier. This is the immediate context for the act's finale; an extended trio – for heroine, alarmed by hero's need, on what seems like a pretext, to set out, by night, to the forest and its notorious Wolf's Glen; her confidante adding agitating information; the hero evasive yet determined, knowing full well what is at stake – the magic bullets for next day's shooting-match that will gain or lose his lover's hand. Heroics for Max, tenderness and apprehensions for Agathe, soubrette cluckings for Ännchen: no rest for the huntsman by day or night – Max's pretext; ending for all three in mutual mistrust and incomprehension, for all the euphoria and optimism of the music itself. Straight from full warm Eb-major to dusky F#-minor for this seminal fount of German Romanticism. Décor and atmosphere as in the contemporary paintings of Caspar David Friedrich. Setting, a craggy forest glen surrounded by high mountains; a cascade; a blasted oak on whose twisted branches an

owl perches; a few rank scattered pines. The sick moon casts a lurid
light on all these, and on Caspar, placed with a skull, a crucible, a
bullet-mould, an eagle's wing, within a circle of black stones, getting
down to the job.

An invisible chorus wails '*Uhui!* Death will tomorrow claim
for our Master another sweet bride.' They specify lurid *Macbeth*-
witches' ingredients for their nasty brew. Dusky shudders over soft
heavy bass, punctuated with *fortissimo* yelps from the woodwinds,
accompany their incantations. In the distance midnight chimes, but
a loud tritone proclaims Satan rather than Jesus. Caspar, preparations done, brandishing the skull, summons Samiel, to the quivering tremolo diminished sevenths already heard in the Overture.
Samiel, the Devil's Representative, appears; Caspar, his minion, pros-
trates himself, promising another victim in his place: Max. Grant
him the magic bullets: six will find their target, the seventh will
slay. Samiel vanishes in thunder, as also the skull: a glowing hearth
appears: Caspar swigs deep in relief, and awaits his date: owls and
other baleful night-birds circle around as the fire burns up. To the
horn-blast from the Overture Max appears, high up the gorge.
Spooky rustlings from the boscage (*pianissimo* string tremolos)
don't daunt – *ich muß*; and he begins to clamber down. Caspar,
aside, thanks Samiel, and, aloud, welcomes the substitute bond to
the work they will share. Max fears slipping in his descent and is
terrified by the apparition of his mother's ghost, veiled in white as
in her coffin, warning him, by gestures, to flee. Caspar mocks: the
figure is replaced by Agathe's, apparently about to throw herself into
the cascade. Max now *must* – *muß* – follow and save her: he reaches
ground intact: the two men are now aligned for their deadly task.

The moon darkens, with further *Macbeth*-ingredients for the
chorus the busy preparations resume, their only illumination the
fire, the owl's eyes, the phosphorescent glow of the decayed oak-
tree. For the casting of the seven bewitched bullets, musical illustrations precede the numbering, accompanying what's seen before
it is announced, then each number is echoed by demon-voices off-
stage. At *Eins!* the crucible bubbles up in a greenish flame (to a
whizzing black-magic foretaste of Mendelssohn's *good* fairies). For

Zwei! night-birds flap out of the forest menacing and baleful (Berliozian stuttering woodwinds). For *Drei!* lower strings heave on a heavy double-dotted rhythm as a wild boar crashes out from the trees across the stage. At *Vier!* a very baroque hurricane develops the double-dottedness in thick contrary-motion thirds and furious scales, breaking the tops of the pines and rousing the fire to angry sparks. For *Fünf!* a tremendous *Schwager Kronos* galumphing as horses are heard straining under whiplashes, and four fiery wheels roll across the scene. Horses and hounds come into sight for *Sechs!* – misty huntsmen, riding and on foot, pursuing the stag, singing an uncouth hunting chorus – grim mirror of Autumn's gaiety and extroversion in *The Seasons*, and the wild chase of the Dead Huntsmen in Schoenberg's *Gurrelieder* already on the horizon. As Caspar terminates the nightmare vision with second shouted *Sechs!* total darkness obliterates all, the scene intermittently lit by flashes of lightning, sulphurous flames from below the ground, and flaming meteors in the surrounding hills: the C-minor first tutti from the Overture now achieves its fore-destined place. At Caspar's screech, through the thunder, of *Samiel! Hilf! Sieben!* the F♯-minor in which the finale began returns: Samiel declares his witness, Caspar is thrown headlong, Max falls senseless. One o'clock chimes afar, the orchestra temporarily subsides to a soft low unison tremolo, bursting out anew, tutti *fortissimo*, as Max convulsively regains consciousness; full low *pianissimo* F♯-minor chord as Act II ends. *Locus classicus* of International Gothic, though also as utterly of its nation as of its time: naïve and direct, even 'artless', as folklore seems – yet great art too, in every aspect technical and imaginative.

Act III doesn't hold the same heights or depths. Next morning Max has used three of the magic bullets, so hard-earned, out hunting, and has only one left (the other three went to Caspar). Agathe is distraught by a nightmare in which, as a white dove, she'd been shot. Ännchen attempts diversion; bridesmaids arrive; merry peasantry. Then another bad omen – the arrival by mistake of a funeral, not a wedding, wreath. Something more appropriate is made from the Hermit's white roses. The shooting-match – white dove chosen as target – Max takes aim – Agathe cries out 'the dove is me!' Hermit stage-manages: Max fires his last magic bullet, Agathe and Caspar fall. Initial consternation – he's killed her! – but it's only the evil one who's felled; he dies inveterate; Max confesses; Hermit blesses; the work ends in happy resolution. Nothing here achieves the heights as the depths Weber has plumbed in the dark places of Act II. The plot's spasmodic agitations and contrived ameliorations are not con-solidated in a musical plausibility that only the composer is able to provide. Yet the power of *The Creation*'s C-major breakthrough after the Hermit's so-near-yet-so-far B-major can illuminate the factitious close of *Der Freischütz* with moving effect: and the opera as a whole remains germinal for everything that follows.

Euryanthe

Euryanthe was written 1823 for Vienna, to story and text by the poet-astress Helmina von Chézy that have become notorious for hapless imbecility in a field strewn with plentiful comparisons before and since. But is the fault hers? Weber accepted the project, seemingly without quibble, and for all his dramatic acumen swallowed it whole, pouring into it his ripest powers: *Euryanthe* is his most ambi-tious effort, his 'heart's blood' Wagner called it; and for Tovey 'both a more mature work of art and a more advanced development of Wag-nerian music-drama than *Lohengrin*'. This gallant apologia is hard to endorse. *Euryanthe*'s best music is indeed wonderful, but the opera's incoherence, overlying a fundamental shallowness, makes it impos-sible to take their fusion seriously: the shallowness and 'imbecility', not being merely on the surface, impede access to the music's expres-sive intentions: music is deprived of its potency, its *raison d'être* in a theatrical composite, when we are unable to identify with and feel for and empathize with such absurdity of event, character, emotion. If, as Joseph Kerman insisted years ago, 'in opera the composer is the dramatist' it is Weber we must blame for the disaster-area that has kept *Euryanthe* from the stage ever since she first graced it: and this in spite of Weber's greatest inspirations, and the piece's epoch-making significance as the first-ever thorough-composed German Romantic opera – that is, without speech as in *The Magic Flute*,

Fidelio, and in his own *Freischütz*, or secco recitative as in the Italian; and a rudimentary system of leitmotifs later to burgeon, bloom, fruit, ramify, rampage, in Wagnerian music-drama.

What Wagner owes to *Euryanthe* is, above all, that fundamental of all German opera since *Die Zauberflöte*: the placing into different 'worlds' of contrasting characters who form a black-and-white moral equation. Euryanthe the chaste is lovingly joined to Adolar the brave. Lysiart (jealous for Euryanthe) and Eglantine (jealous for Adolar) join in a loveless bond to bring the fair couple, objects of their love thwarted and turned poisonous, down to their own state of hell. Lysiart is the disaffected element in the King's chivalrous court, where love and virtue are celebrated. Eglantine is the serpent at Nevers, seat of the virtuous love of Adolar and Euryanthe. So long as each paradise has one fair and one foul, there is stasis. When disaffection from the first travels with evil intent to the other, the two dark ones infallibly find each other out and join forces to extinguish the two lights. They discover the canker in their seemingly perfect love – Euryanthe's weakness and guilt over the secret of Emma's tomb; Adolar's too-little faith, his over-impetuous readiness to believe ill – an unexamined mistrust which the plot against the lovers subtly plays upon, blowing it up into open repudiation. So now the true lovers are self-exiled in the desert, love dead between them; and their real knowledge is won, but too late. However, through legitimate coincidences and suspensions of disbelief the evil pair are exposed even as they turn in hatred to each other, having wrecked the objects of their true though illicit love. All is explained and reconciled: the wicked are vanquished; the canker healed; the hymns to love resound again and now ring true.

This summary sketches some conventional but realistic possibilities in the plot of *Euryanthe*. The actuality is unmotivated and unclear, bungled in crucial respects and impeded with every kind of local ineptitude. Act I unrolls in dream-like lethargy. In Act II (although it contains the central dramatic flaw) things are moving at last. Here also Weber is at the height of his powers, and such things as the orchestral introduction, Lysiart's invocation to the powers of vengeance, Adolar's love-song, Euryanthe's marvellous cry for justice when first accused, and the big ensemble soon after, show the richest blossoming of his genius both as musician and dramatist. Here alone the entity lives up to the claims made for it. We are swept on, over and past the flaw, and it proves hardly to matter. The first half of Act III is equally inspired, even after the plot has sunk into ineptness that no sympathy can find the sense of. The music eventually loses its grip as well: the tedious *pas de cinq* and the rustics tripping it to three verses of *Ros' im Mai* (pretty enough in itself) dissipate all tensions. Neither story nor music recovers, and the dénouement, if not so absolutely null as the winding-up of the end of *Der Freischütz*, is badly timed and perfunctory. It is Wagner's genius to have grasped the potential richness and truth of this material. He takes the moral equation and the defining of character by place, and makes them really telling: in *Tannhäuser* as Venus and her Venusberg versus Elisabeth and her Wartburg – both actual places, visible from each other; and states of mind in the protagonist, whose oscillation between the two generates a moral conflict of some power; then something really profound in the complex geo-psychology of *Parsifal*.

Lohengrin of course offers a direct comparison. In taking virtually the same plot as *Euryanthe*, Wagner at once pays homage to the work that most directly showed him what to do, and gives it such a trouncing that it will never recover: the guileless heroine wickedly impugned; the 'dark' couple, whose conspiracy against virtue is confounded by their unresolved dissensions and mirrored in the crucial failure of trust within the 'light' couple; a background of chivalry, a judging King, a chorus for celebration, astonishment, denunciation. Some features are adopted wholesale: an invocation to night and vengeance (Act II of both); a *coup-de-théâtre* lifting of the mask (Eglantine in Act I, Ortrud in Act II, respectively); a big ensemble of perplexity (Act II of both). And Wagner's music, patently steeped in Weber, has expanded it into something larger, cruder and incomparably more vital. Weber still has the virtue of his rather slack, closed forms, as well as the new range of possibilities of running them into each other, but there are jolts in his pace and lapses in his quality. The contrast between his inspired and his pedestrian moments helps define Wagner's surer sense of pace and continuity of style (although heaven knows Wagner's early works have their *mauvais quarts d'heure*, and lack the delicate bloom and distinction of Weber's melody and the incomparable refinement of his instrumentation).

Above all, Wagner knows so much better (as composer to his own dramatist) what he is doing and how and why. For instance, the nearly fatal slowness of Act I of *Euryanthe* is *used* in Act I of *Lohengrin* to make the tableaux whose cumulation makes the dramatic and musical architecture so strong. And Wagner has learnt from the spectacular collapse of Weber's Act III as much from the almost complete success of his Act II. In fact, there is a sense in which, in his absorption in the pioneering work, he has imitated too well. The unsatisfactory dénouements of all three of the pre-*Ring* operas reflect the abject inadequacy of Weber's, while the vagueness at the centre of *Lohengrin* – the lingering sense that it is 'about' much less than its gorgeous trappings would warrant – seems to be the last vestige of the 'unresisting imbecility' of *Euryanthe*. This witlessness will perpetually vitiate the beauty of the music or unman it by forcing enjoyment of it to be entirely disassociated from what it expresses. This is why it is wrong to prefer it (with all its beauties) to *Lohengrin* or even to *Tannhäuser* (with all its longueurs).

Oberon

Oberon, Weber's swansong alas, was commissioned for London in 1825, then postponed till the following year because of difficulties over its libretto. The composer, already a sick man, died and was buried in the capital shortly after conducting the première: his venerated remains were loyally and lovingly transferred to Dresden in 1846 under the aegis of his successor there as musical director, then in the mainstream of German Romantic opera – Wagner.

Oberon's embarrassments have continued ever since. After the tragedy of Weber's most ambitious and prophetic endeavour, *Euryanthe* – an imbecilic farrago of culinary flim-flam, barest ghost of plot and personages, merely providing an excuse for lavish scenery, costumes and effects, and the prowess of marvellous singers and dancers and a virtuoso orchestra: all this the shaky scaffold for a score both exalted and enchanting. Christoph Wieland's original poem *Oberon* (1780) sets a tale of fidelity in love from medieval chivalry in a succession of exotic locations, ranging from fairyland, Baghdad, Tunis, via rocky seashore and sterile desert, to end at Charlemagne's Court in a blaze of reconciliation uniting Orient and Occident, fairy royalty and human lovers. The question posed – whether man or woman is the more constant – is instigated by the quarrel between Oberon and Titania familiar from *A Midsummer Night's Dream*: Sir Huon, one of Charlemagne's paladins, must undergo impossible ordeals, as too must Rezia, daughter of the Caliph of Baghdad, seen by Huon only in a magic dream, till – and despite temptations and attempted deviations on both sides – constancy wins (whether the man's or the woman's is firmer not made clear). I hope this tangled account of the main outline indicates the arbitrary nature of what Covent Garden confronted Weber with! Wieland's poem had delicately balanced Enlightenment values and picturesque Orientalism/medievalry with gentle irony and iron control beneath superficial frivolity. Planché's libretto dissolves all this into a mishmash of commercialized opportunism.

Confusion is worse compounded by the old English vice upon which Purcell's most ambitious attempts to fuse music and drama had foundered a century-and-a-half before – that the core of the *story*, even when so exiguous as in *The Fairy Queen* or in *Oberon*, its indirect successor, isn't expressed in and carried by the music. Thus opera's *raison d'être* and glory are demoted to decorative divertissement. The sick and needy composer did what he could: the picturesque elements are indeed delectable; and whenever an opportunity rises for character and situation to be explored deeper he rises to it with power undiminished.

Shown at its most resplendent in the heroine's celebrated scena *Ocean! Thou mighty monster* [all titles given in the fustian English Weber had to set, rather than the German translation in which the work is more familiarly staged, or at least recorded]. Shipwrecked, cast up alone on a desolate shore by night, Rezia apostrophizes the turbulent waves in stately recitative then surging *arioso*: during this, abandoned hope is reborn as light breaks over the sullen sea-surface – yet another remake of the C-major birth of light from *The Creation*. And it culminates in salutation to the rising sun directly prescient of Brünnhilde's hymn on awakening from her long sleep – the high bright exposed major third is almost a quotation *avant la lettre*, then the Ur-trumpet almost Brucknerian as, alas, the fiery orb sinks back into the mighty monster Ocean, Rezia's hopes extinguished with it. Rescue is of course at hand: her cries of joy, her enthusiastic handkerchief-waving as Sir Huon nears in a final burst of glorious sunset foretell Isolde's rapture as her lover keeps his tryst near the start of *Tristan* Act II, though not, here, Wagner's actual musical substance.

Power can also be manifest in miniature. Best and loveliest the succession of sound-images commencing the Overture. The magic instrument of *Oberon* (its prototypes the flute from Mozart, the trumpet from *Fidelio*) is a horn – lyric-poetic hero of German opera; of German Romantic music *tout court*. Its solo – his solo! – is the work's first sound: just three rising notes, a soft summons, over-heard from infinitely far away. Then soft tender-yearning strings: the summons again, again the strings, joined and intensified by the horn on an inconspicuous inner part: rapt tempo-less trance on strings, irradiated with a delicate flicker of fairy woodwinds – next stop, Mendelssohn's fairies from 1826; after that, Berlioz's in the enchantment-sequences from *The Damnation of Faust*. The strings grow more affective: pause: a demure little march-tattoo on brass, *pianissimo possibile*, answered with elegant flourishes on strings, who can leap athletically while remaining soft and light. The toy militia yield to a lovely string-strain led by cellos answered by violins: another pause, now quivering with anticipation (during it the violins must silently remove the mutes): a sharp tutti crash: and the *allegro con fuoco* begins.

Most of these ingredients recur at salient moments in the entertainment to come. The horn-call, gentle or commanding, is used throughout as magic rescue from threats and dangers (like the bells in *The Magic Flute*), equally with the promise of joys and fulfilment; and even becomes basis for an entire dance towards the end. The fairy-flicker returns to evoke the realm of Oberon and Titania; the miniature march, all-but-forgotten, heralds in full-brass brilliance the joyous finale at Charlemagne's Court where the lovers' tribulations, human and supernatural, are resolved (that one can't remember, nor needs nor cares to, whether it's Rezia or Huon who wins the fidelity-wager, is inadvertent acknowledgement of the piece's frivolity). The *allegro con fuoco*, the Overture's main body, after its introductory Cornell-showcase of pre-echoing treasures wrought of commonplaces transmuted into precious matter, is a potpourri of further places to come – the optimistic embarkation that ends in shipwreck; the lyric centre of Huon's bravura aria – 'a gentle ray, a milder beam / Broke sweetly in life's broader stream / And lent its lustre soft and fair / To temper glory's crimson glare' – is heard: and Puck (also engaged in this mishmash)'s call to his spirits of earth, air, sea, fire before the storm; the mermaid's chorus; the exultant closing stretch of Rezia's *Ocean! Thou mighty monster*. The storm itself, and her salute to the sun, are absent from this opening epitome: its Overture is virtually sole memento of *Oberon*: what ensues survives only in continually renewed attempts, never catching on, to readapt, reshape, rescue the wreckage.

Other highlights of the piecemeal melange that follows include its prevailing 'Oriental' coloration – at one point employing an actual Oriental melody – delicate and sensitive, sometimes foretelling Bizet, even Chabrier, alongside the fairy-strains foretelling more certainly Mendelssohn's; thence the mix of both in Tchaikovsky's *Nutcracker*. Another parallel with Mendelssohn comes in *Oberon*'s sea-music – the three other finely evocative concert-overtures, *The Hebrides*, *The Fair Melusine* and *Calm Sea and Prosperous Voyage*. By comparison, Weber's ocean is somewhat formulaic, indeed dry – canvas and plywood absolutely threadbare in content, absolutely right for their theatrical function. Wagner's seas and storms are of course heralded by both these early Romantic pioneers (and not forgetting what his river-music owes to *Melusine*): the tremendous physical immediacy of sea and storm in *The Flying Dutchman* is incomparably more intense, though still retaining a whiff of paint and canvas as well as salt and spume: thence the lightning and thunder of *Die Walküre* – with plenty of Wolf's Glen thrown in – where nature's manifestations are psychologized into character and situation – Siegmund's plight, Wotan's rage – with ends as well as means far beyond the earlier composer's range. But Weber showed the way: and if this 'lovable and lamentable' master had been spared to exert his full powers upon subjects suited to them, he might well have taken it too.

Mendelssohn

A question still hangs over Felix Mendelssohn, music's eternal representative of youthful brilliance, gaiety, grace. How was such sunniness so ineluctably transformed into dutiful facile routine? Felix was felicitously named; blessed at the cradle with every talent personal, artistic, social, born into enlightenment, affluence, comfort, unthwarted by struggle with circumstances, unbruised by struggle within the temperament. Descriptions of him as a boy, from the family circle right up to Goethe himself, sound an angelic chorus: 'that beautiful youth, with his auburn hair clustering in ringlets around his shoulders, the look of his brilliant clear eyes, the smile of innocence and candour on his lips'. Yet also a proper boy: after serious grown-up music-making, the twelve-year-old makes for the garden, 'clearing high hedges with a leap, running, singing, or climbing up trees like a squirrel – the very image of health and happiness'. When not composing, or playing (a very accomplished pianist), or drawing (a very accomplished draughtsman) or writing very intelligent and lively letters, he was a vigorous and skilful gymnast, a tirelessly enthusiastic swimmer, an accomplished horseman, a winner at chess.

This angelic boy and omni-gifted youth matured into a generous, enterprising, diligent citizen of music. All descriptions agree as to his fineness, distinction, the expressive mobility, the sweetness, intensity and power of the mature man. Behind the face lies infinite tact and address, charming the high society of three countries emphatically, including 'our own dear Queen', and not averse to elegant misbehaviour in the best circles. Domestic Mendelssohn, loving and simpatico, devoted to his beautiful wife and five beautiful children. More important, Mendelssohn the indefatigable performing musician, organizer, musical educator, establishing foundations and principles in concert hall and conservatoire that remain intact to this day.

But even such superhuman indefatigability must tire. Later reports speak of growing 'irritability', 'distrustfulness', 'fretfulness', 'morbid conscientiousness'. One life-long friend, writing in February 1846, says frankly, 'I thought he did not discriminate between his impulse to work and to create.' By August of the following year Mendelssohn says to a visitor three times in as many days, 'I shall not live to see it' ('and the glow faded from his face, and the sad, worn look came back which it pained the very heart to see'). Early that November the most attractive human figure among all the great composers was dead – victim of a noble nature, instinct with generosity, a highly-strung nervous constitution and a Protestant work-ethic laid over a vocation to higher tasks entirely the fault of his fathers.

The shape of the oeuvre, with salient titles, dates and other significant milestones, is thus: born Hamburg 1809 to a distinguished Jewish family (his grandfather the philosopher Moses Mendelssohn); copious boyhood composing – 1821–3 string symphonies; 1824 1st Symphony for full orchestra; 1825 Octet; 1826 *A Midsummer Night's Dream* Overture; 1827–9 large-scale string quartets showing knowledge of Beethoven's last, almost contemporary; 1829 milestone revival of Bach's *St Matthew Passion*; 1830 *Hebrides* Overture and 'Reformation' Symphony; 1831 'Italian' Symphony begun (completed 1833), 'Scottish' Symphony begun (completed 1842) – both indicating something of his eager European travelling; 1832 *Die erste Walpurgisnacht* (tinkered with on and off for a further decade); 1834–6 *St Paul* (a New Testament oratorio); 1838 Violin Concerto (completed 1844); 1839 D-minor Piano Trio, and conducts première of Schubert's 'Great' C-major Symphony; 1840 *Lobgesang* (symphony with choral finale); 1841 *Variations Sérieuses* for piano; 1843 incidental music to *A Midsummer Night's Dream*; 1845 C-minor Piano Trio; 1846 completion of *Elijah* (Old Testament oratorio); 1847 two movements of the String Quartet in F-minor, sketches for *Loreley* (fairy-tale) and *Christus* (*not* a fairy-tale); died November that year.

More than any other, the lovable best of Mendelssohn's music, mostly from the younger end of his life, embodies youthful grace, sweetness, freshness, eagerness: high-spirited yet refined, elegant without over-neatness, impeccable yet intoxicating, imbued with ardent Romantic feeling. The Octet shows all these: a new world of sensibility and texture, the outer movements buoyant and fiery, their brio at once physical and intellectual (the way the finale incorporates and combines with the scherzo preceding it); the andante charged with blushful melting tenderness, the scherzo itself, with its fleet effervescence, a weightlessness never heard before, nor equalled in these respects by any composer since (including its own). In the *Midsummer Night's Dream* Overture the eighteen-year-old's new sensibility expands into congenial Shakespearean territory to miraculous effect. Again, as with the 1st Symphony for full orchestral forces, after the thirteen miniatures for strings alone, the orchestra follows string-sonority. And what an orchestra! It makes Weber's otherworldly music from the same years and culture appear one-dimensional and generalized by comparison. Mendelssohn's fairy-apparitions are so specific, and he penetrates deeper into *good* white magic: Weber and what grows from him surpasses him in the *black*. From the first gently radiant wind-chords we are transported to a realm of delicate evanescence. Strings enter, turning major to minor: then momentum begins, violins in four parts shimmer and skitter in playful staccato, soon underpinned by light pizzicato; winds twice stop the motion with a soft-sweet-piercing dissonance – then suddenly the whole orchestra blazes out *fortissimo* with bright festive royal strains for Hippolyta and Theseus. Flickering momentum renewed in backdrop to amorous strains evoking the quartet of human lovers, whose cross-purposes and reconciliation form one strand in the play to come. The two returns to the enchanted woodlands are varied and enhanced with isolated notes, very soft, in woodwinds and drums, gradually outlining non-thematic shapes, coalescing into flickers of tattoo; the first return also varied by soft long-sustained notes in unexpected places on unexpected instruments, which sometimes suddenly blast forth *con tutta la forza*; the second return continues the same game, now only soft-held-long but including wondrous exposed entries of the ophicleïde – sole surviving moments of glory for this short-lived descendant of the eighteenth-century serpent, something between tuba (brass) and double-bassoon (wooden), well-worth retaining just for these brief appearances. In between and in-and-out of fairy-continuity, the play's and the overture's other three strands – Athenian royalty, human lovers, rustics complete with ee-yaw-braying donkey for Bottom 'translated' by his ass's head – interweave with felicitous skill. Only Puck is missing – but the feel is Puckish throughout. Proportions are perfect, and all the musical material from the top-drawer. The 'Amen-cadence' within the opening chords that return to close the piece – so sanctimonious in so much nineteenth-century music to come, are also here imbued with the same delicate judiciousness – even its more dangerous version, from IV minor to tonic major. Danger averted, the vision passes into the distance; overheard, glimpsed down the wrong end of a telescope – crystal-clear yet unfathomably mysterious – through a glass lightly, uncanny without shadow.

The miracle of 1826 was renewed seventeen years on in the incidental music for the play 'commanded' by the King of Prussia in 1842 (alongside scores for Sophocles and Racine) and composed in 1843. By now Mendelssohn, still barely middle-aged, was yet far from the precocious genius of the Overture. In the years between these two involvements with Shakespeare comes the principal output, with all its routine as well as its treasures – an overall trajectory, with exceptions, from genius to talent. Even the justly beloved Violin Concerto, perfect of its genre – perhaps the best-ever – shows some signs of slackening. The last major instrumental piece, the String Quartet in F-minor, written in distress at his adored sister Fanny's death and under the shadow of his own mortality, is a strong piece opening up potential new ground. But only the incidental music from these last years recaptures the youthful brio of ease, the precocious genius, of Mendelssohn's teens. A delicious scherzo – less feather-light than of old, more solid and rustic: if Puck is absent from the Overture he surely figures here – and indeed the celebrated tour de force for the flute ending this delightful number – '240 intelligible syllables at the uniform rate of 9 to a second' – introduces his first appearance in the play. The four further purely instrumental pieces are equally good: the plangent agitations – *allegro appassionato* – rendering the lovers' exhaustion after quarrelling and getting lost and re-found to each other in the wood – ending then on a droll little entry for Bottom and his mates; the lovely *Nocturne* wherein the lovers sink into reconciling sleep; the *Clowns' Dance*, perfectly gauged for rustics to entertain their courtly audience; the all-too-hackneyed *Wedding March* – splendid if one can hear it freshly – just right in its confident, slightly bumptious mock-heroic brightness. And the two songs with soloists and chorus – *Ye spotted snakes*, sung by her fairy attendants to their Queen Titania, with Oberon, also reconciled after civil strife, closing the finale in final benison – a new vocal line to combine with the fairy scamperings from the Overture, ending with Puck's spoken Epilogue and the same magic woodwind chords, closing casements revealed seventeen years before, still tinct with enchantment nearly two centuries later.

Scanning the body of Mendelssohn's oeuvre of those seventeen years a consistent pattern emerges. On the one hand, 'pure' music – the *Variations sérieuses*, the two piano trios, the Violin Concerto – which merges into wordless evocations of nature, sea-scapes especially – *The Hebrides*, *Calm Sea and Prosperous Voyage* – which merge into the two titled symphonies evocative of place on a broader scale – the 'Italian', the 'Scottish': these in turn overlapping with the supernatural/fairy-tale/lightly mythological, the Shakespeare-music most directly, and the *Walpurgisnacht*. On the other, his elevated-ethical public endeavours: two large-scale oratorios – *St Paul* (in German: Christian) and *Elijah* (in English: Judaic), together with such analogous things as the 'Reformation' Symphony for the 300th anniversary of Luther's Augsburg Confession – purely orchestral; and the symphony-with-voices to mark the 400th of Gutenberg's invention of printing, the *Lobgesang*. (*Christus* and *Loreley*, both on

the stocks at the time of his death, retain the pagan/Christian dichotomy.) Simply to lay this out thus is to see where the truest value lies.
His picturesque, delicate, magic-fairy subjects, for all the seeming
lightness, outweigh the high-minded heavy-duty subjects equally
in the calibre of their invention and in the pleasure they yield. The
Importance of being earnest, the Joy of being unconfined. A detailed
glance at some of the successes will, I hope, confirm and consolidate
this judgement.

Die erste Walpurgisnacht and St Paul: a pious mausoleum of what
Charles Rosen memorably dubbed (claiming Mendelssohn as its
inventor) 'Victorian religious kitsch', vis-à-vis a pagan Cantata, equally
neglected, setting Christians against Druids in a tulgey Nordic dark
age when the two faiths were in direct conflict. Goethe's ballad, later
reworked in Faust Part II, takes place on the last night of April, a
spring ritual devoted to the renewal of fertility by diabolic means. As
the poet wrote:

> it seems that long ago pagan German priests and patriarchs,
> driven from their sacred groves as the new Christianity was com-
> pelled upon the people, retreated as winter ended to the wild
> inaccessible Harz mountains to offer prayer and sacrifice by fire
> to the Old Gods. Their doings were disguised with masks and
> repellencies to frighten Christian spies: thus protected, their
> pagan devotions continued intact, till the later revelation's in-
> evitable conquest.

Tannhäuser's tussle between Venus and the Virgin is prefigured, as
also the pagan/Christian undercurrent of Lohengrin, in the baptized
Jew's surprising masterpiece of Teutonic Druidism, first mooted
while travelling in Italy in 1831 and brought to fruition some twelve
years later.

This splendid piece ought to displace Elijah from its perch, as
well as dreary Paul (where one waits, chafing and in vain, for how
the composer will deal with 'it is hard for thee to kick against the
pricks'). Walpurgisnacht's overture depicts 'bad weather' – born of

experience in another of its well-travelled composer's European adventures, a severe Swiss storm witnessed the year he began the cantata – thence the passage to spring: exactly analogous to the bipartite Introduction in Haydn's *Seasons* depicting just the same transition, though in thematic contour recognizably overlapping with the 'Scottish' Symphony. Serious summons on horns and bassoons quieten winter's rage, only to flare up anew and fiercer: called again to order, subdued, yielding to dulcet strains on woodwinds while strings still mutter discontentedly below. Enter Spring – tonic major and change of tempo, gracefully interwoven descending figure on upper strings alternating with flute, then clarinet solos introduce – no. 1, Mayday chorus led by a Druid, calling the people to uplift their heart in observation and praise in the old ways for Spring's renewal by fire. In no. 2 an old woman warns what the folk have to fear if the Christians catch them: in no. 3 a Druid priest, plus male chorus, urges the other tribesmen to persist – 'the woods are free!' – a fine piece, demonstrating, with *Paul* and *Elijah* in mind, that Pagan tunes are just as good, indeed better, than those of Christians and Jews. In no. 4 Druid guards keep watch as preparations for the rites get under way – light scurry not a thousand miles distant from the woods of Athens in the *Midsummer Night's Dream*, all muted and *sotto voce*, fading into no. 5, recitative for Druid guard – 'we'll frighten those Popish Christians with spikes, pitchforks, rattles, fireworks' – introducing a choral march, same words, a martial mutter à la Berlioz (who'd been spell-bound by the entire work at its première), complete with spikes, pitchforks, rattles and screech-owls. No. 6 is the high-point: loud 6/8 hunting-horn tutti after the preceding muttered animation – exactly the same juxtaposition as in the Wolf's Glen from *Freischütz*: the entire Pagan populace on the offensive, men first, then women, then combined, in a magnificent orgy of energy, boiling up, via sudden alternations of very soft, to a climax of howls and expletives making the liveliest Pagan pages of *Elijah*, the High Priests' invocation to Baal, seem by comparison demure and timid – those ferocious descending trombones cutting down through the surge and flicker of the urgent tarantella above! It boils over into no. 7, wherein a Druid priest exhorts the excited folk to preserve a pure heart – 'They [the Christians] can't quench our Light even if they quell our old ways.' His unction is as urgent as that of the new ways, and shares the same musical idiom – 'Victorian religious kitsch', righteously reinforced by the chorus at the close. No. 8 presents the enemy: a Christian guard and his men, straitly deploring the stench of sulphur. Links direct into no. 9, finale, wherein the words of no. 7 return, its music exhausted: 'we'll still have our Light, as the flame cleanses the smoke of the fire into hardness.' Victory to Paganism? Certainly in quality of invention: the Pagans easily win for vitality in this conception prophetic (via Goethe) of Nietzsche and (via Mendelssohn) of Wagner and even Richard Strauss: the distinctly 'Victorian' A-men cadence celebrating the Light which can't be wrenched from them can only sound ironic after the Death of God.

One of the three other outstanding overtures, apart from the *Dream*, belongs with it to Mendelssohn's gentler supernatural side – *The Fairy-Tale of the Lovely Melusine*, adroitly alternating liquid strains for the beautiful mermaid (decidedly not lost on Wagner when coming to characterize his Rhine-daughters some twenty years later) with bright stiffly chivalric strains for her knight-in-armour. *Melusine* is an inland freshwater sister to the two seascape masterpieces preceding it. *Calm Sea and Prosperous Voyage*, after two poems by Goethe (set as such by Beethoven) is the slighter, made from many of the same ingredients as the *Hebrides* – they share deep calm, then energy and brio; but no storm here, nor awe before a mysterious natural wonder: a voyage, extrovert and optimistic, with a touch of festive pride and pomposity – burgher/merchant relatives of royalty/aristocracy in the *Dream*, including a foretaste of its insouciant Wedding March; then, after the noisy acclamation is done, three bars of thoughtfulness renewing the deep calm of the opening, the entire orchestra (minus piccolo) reducing from *fortissimo* to *pianissimo* in yet another A-men cadence, expressive of grateful relief rather than sanctimonious unction.

    The Hebrides – Fingal's Cave; prototype of all sea-pictures and among the greatest, comes two years after the *Calm Sea*: a work of

high inspiration, easily combining evocative Romantic depiction
with clear classical form and procedure, by-the-book yet fancy-free,
fusing mystery and suggestion with structure/process/argument.
Every note, from stormiest blast to the most delicate nuance, is
exact with, between these extremes, some of the warmest middle-
richness textures to be found before Brahms; and the material itself
eschews the touch of commonplace slightly infiltrating *Melusine*
and pervading Mendelssohn's other well-known overture *Ruy Blas*
(fustian blarney, enjoyable as such). Every phrase is distinctive and
distinguished, from the initial momentum-motif, jotted down in
sight of Fingal's Cave itself, that then germinates the piece's principal substance, to the fine strain of middle-richness, as mentioned,
for 'second subject' (to revert to the textbook). Momentum alternates with long-held single notes and octaves, usually on winds
and particularly tingling on a pair of soft trumpets: clarity and
economy sometimes open out vistas of shimmering emptiness,
recalling the same, in wholly different context, from the *Dream*
overture. Here the bare middle follows upon great ferocity, culminating in themeless fanfares/summons/tattoos: elsewhere on the
edge of festive pomposity, now strangely evocative – worldly connotations lost in the seascape void; the composer daring to court both
bathos and bareness to bring the scene so sharply alive to ears and
eyes. Then a scherzando; fairies robust – not airy-fairies; muscular
tritons with conches, however playful; Celtic not Mediterranean.
So to 'recapitulation', with 'second subject' in tonic major, its deep
calm enhanced without underlining, raised to a single, then a pair
of clarinets, echoed in divided violas as the piece seems to dwindle
into placid extinction. Not so: the 'coda' builds up in renewed agitation, boiling over into a splendid storm (its techniques, as its substance, not lost on the composer of *The Flying Dutchman*), crowned
by the wonderful ending, simultaneously both loud and soft – the
whole orchestra's short sharp chords, except for the sustained *pianissimo* octave on two soft trumpets, subliminally perceived as the
chords subside to reveal the two clarinets eliminating the principal motif from start to finish; the first clarinet high-ish, the second
low-ish, overlapping a low flute rising through it on a reminiscence

of the second subject, as soft oboes take over the soft trumpets and the sharp orchestral chords reduce to *pianissimo* unison string pizzicatos plus soft drum-taps. By such dry punctilious exactitude magic is made. Work of this order is not achieved without enormous expenditure of nervous energy, however invisible. Work with another weighting – debilitating grind, also born of nervous energy all-too-visible, was Mendelssohn's destiny. Infelix Felix – he worked himself to death.

Schumann

Schumann is probably the most lovable of the great German masters, simply because his music is inextricably involved in first impressions: many children learning the piano will encounter early the pretty little pieces from his *Album for the Young*, moving on with enhanced delight to the easier numbers in *Scenes from Childhood*. Then, after headier teenage intoxications, the taste recoils to discover his two greatest contributions to the world hoard – the body of solo piano works with which he began, and the body of songs that overlapped then wholly took over.

The twenty-four piano works present a cavalcade of dancing, dreaming fantasy, peopled by lovers real or imagined, heroes of music and literature living and dead, brother warriors in art against the philistines. Creatures of the night from Gothic folklore and daemonic emanations from the subconscious coexist with glittering ballrooms and enchanted palaces. All is born of his own divided personality, its zigzag oscillation between euphoria and melancholy, never so vividly contrasted as in the eight movements of the *Fantasy Pieces* op. 12 – Evening – Soaring – Why – Whims – In the Night – Fable – Dream-Perplexities – End of the Tale. Such contradictions are scarcely integrated by constructing a hopeful middle way – 'Meister Raro' (formed of his own and his Clara's first names) – to bridge the sometimes frightening discrepancies.

Clara it is, of course, who inspires Robert's next phase: their tortuous courtship ending in 1840 with marriage, releasing the glorious effusion of song, words explicit at last after lurking encoded so long. The highlights are *Myrthen* (a garland of twenty-six, many-mooded for many poets); *Frauenliebe und -leben* (infinitely chalorous account of the course of a marriage); the two cycles to Heine texts, the op. 24 *Liederkreis* and *Dichterliebe* op. 48, charting every nuance of youthful passion, from shy rapture to heartbreak and renunciation, defiant, stoical, nostalgic; and, greatest of all, the other *Liederkreis* (poems by Eichendorff), encapsulating in twelve brief songs a whole dictionary of romantic themes – nature welcoming and solacing, or menacing and uncanny; love and hope; exile and loss; medieval balladry and folktale set in deep Germanic forests, ecstatic renewal by the surging sap of spring. In rendering these states of mind, body, soul, no other composer can compare for impulsive immediacy. Schubert's range is broader, his depth more profound. Schumann, within narrower confines, reaches the most secret places with the most intimate touch. Chopin seems by comparison salon-bound, even at his most delicate: counting countesses, calculating subscriptions (that peremptory 'Pay up! Get out!' concluding the Barcarolle!); while Liszt is all too obviously a figure of limelight even when ostentatiously avoiding it.

The question of Schumann's subsequent output remains open and somewhat divisive. To those for whom he blooms early, the later work is a gradual victory for Meister Raro, wherein spontaneous invention is swamped by respectful/respectable submission to 'bourgeois' music-making in 'official' genres: symphony, chamber-music, opera, oratorio. For the defence, the later work expands in mastery with these newly acquired genres, opening up altogether original glimpses into further territory. All can agree to cherish wonderful moments, sometimes complete movements, in the four symphonies and the copious chamber-works. Some of the later songs reflect the earlier with a paler, altered light, as moon the sun. A few larger pieces escape ossification completely. But much gives hostages to fortune. And in the end, one never senses that, as in Schubert, this composer is untimely cut off with indescribable potential riches still to yield. In Schumann the feeling of dilution, then guttering out, is palpable and unmistakable.

But wherever its centre is located, this body of work has moved music-lovers in a unique manner, and always will. And the roster of composers touched by it speaks for itself: audible successors – Brahms, Tchaikovsky, Dvořák, Elgar, Mahler, Strauss, Wolf, Pfitzner; less immediately apparent (spirit over letter) – Fauré, Ravel, Berg, Britten. Not even Wagner has so wide a catchment; and his influence was more often a disadvantage, sometimes a downright disaster. Schumann's is wholly benign, fertilizing further beauties wherever it alights.

Note his suggestiveness, his hints of incompleteness, his open-endedness, his penetrability. Most other composers are fully rounded-out: addition, alteration, interposition, interference, 're-composition', would be unthinkable: there are no entry-points. (The great exception is J. S. Bach – wholly completed in every detail, yet infinitely adaptable and reinterpretable.) In Schumann this is true not just when he is, as so often, open-ended: the same suggestiveness is also found in his fully formed statements.

This most personal of composers is speaking to only one person: Clara, of course – then also *you* or *me*. The listener, and especially the player, seems to be being personally addressed in phrase after phrase. When Schumann takes on more public forms, this precious, indefinable intimacy recedes into the background, or goes missing altogether. This must underlie one's dissatisfaction with the symphonies, let alone the later cantatas such as the *Scenes from Faust*, quite apart from their sometimes-tired material and often stilted processes.

Schumann's intimacy is partly a matter of secrets, ciphers, coded messages – of which he is, with Berg, the world-master. (Again, compare Bach – for all his inbuilt play of symbolic numbers and proportions, Bach's music is never elusive or arcane.) But it's mainly a matter of his characteristic musical material in itself: it is instinct with charged-up, one-to-one communication. Every musical person (not only composers!) must feel this quality – not unique to Schumann, but most clearly to the fore in him, and listen in response.

*

Robert Schumann: born 1810 into bookish circumstances – father published and sold them, his shop full of music too. Early promise as pianist: intended for the law, but music and letters won. Lessons from piano-pedagogue Friedrich Wieck; hopes for career as virtuoso dashed by equivocal hand-injury 1832. By then he had encountered Wieck's gifted daughter, Clara; by 1836 the pair knew they were destined for each other despite her father's violent opposition. Copious composing, almost all for solo piano; also important as a writer on music; 1833 founds influential *Neue Zeitschrift für Musik*, championing favourite causes and defying the philistines. Defying her father, marries Clara 1840, releasing a torrent of *Lieder*. After the ardours of courtship and eventual fulfilment, the succeeding years troubled: crises mental and physical (probably originating in syphilis contracted as a student) together with un-fittedness for career as conductor – Dresden, Düsseldorf. Attempted suicide by drowning '*im Rhein, im heiligen Strome*' 1854; sent to private asylum, where he died two years later.

His music after the glory-years of piano- and song-cycles makes a long story of decline, rhyming with the personal demoralization that closes in tragedy then pathos. The young David combating the Philistines, evinced also in his fiery youthful journalism, grows flaccid with middle-age: the ardent wooer turns aberrant husband; the impulsive eagerness of 'Florestan' and dreamy inwardness of 'Eusebius' (his personifications for the two extremes of his personality: active/dreamy) mutate to merge into 'Meister Raro', voice of mediation and middle-way that can end in mere mediocrity. It used to be the consensus that the great Schumann consists in the wild/tender, intimate/abandoned, impulsive-unchained/secret-speaking works of his twenties and early thirties rather than in the public/formal genres that he then began to favour. This view has been vigorously challenged in recent years, in eloquent words and performances, but the pendulum swings ineluctably back, and comes to rest where the gold lies.

The heart of the corpus whence the blood circulates: the great piano-cycles and song-cycles of Schumann's younger years. *Abegg Variations* op. 1 (1830) opens the *Fabel*: a miniature world in eight minutes. It's all here, already, implicit: the imaginary girl's name (place) making a cipher-contour in five pitches; the sublimated-Schubert waltz theme on the shape; the intricate piano-writing that follows, its full range from delicate/fragile to lumpy-gallumphing-barnstorming heroic. Var. 2 with '*il basso parlando*' (then the melody raised to soprano) telling of secrets shared or undivulged; the volatile deliciousness of Var. 3; the dreamy romance of Var. 4, dissolving half-way into figuration preparatory to *finale alla fantasia*, growing from demure *Fischermädchen* 6/8 to a whirlwind of animation, cut off by the conceit of spelling the salient letters by elimination rather than by sounding them; so to the soft *vivacissimo* descent from sparkling heights to soft-as-possible depths of the keyboard, à la *Kreisleriana* to come.

Papillons op. 2 (1832): more of same, doubled in length, enhanced with yet more fanciful play of invention; and the dedicatees – Therese, Rosalie, Emilie – presumed real rather than dream-figments. Next in this line *Carnaval*, where similar scheme and material return on a yet-more-extensive canvas; and their further excursions in the ballroom scenes and fantasies in most of the *Novelettes*.

Meanwhile, serious business: to succeed as a virtuoso pianist, composing for his own repertoire big works without fancy dress. There are nine such – sonatas, variations, studies, and a grand fantasie – sizeable, difficult, ambitious, unlovely. The *Études symphoniques* have their moments, lost to memory in the interminable jog-trot finale. The *Fantasie* op. 17 is another matter, unquestionably a major work (dedicated to Liszt), important in itself and deeply significant for its composer – autobiographical beyond the fantasy self-projections of the *Davidsbündler* or *Kreisleriana*, rife with coded messages, their substance centred upon the quotation from Beethoven's *An die ferne Geliebte*, alongside explicit homage to Beethoven in heroic vein, and a secret programme of withdrawal into mystic innerness as voiced in the quatrain from Schlegel prefacing the slow lyric-meditative finale. Admiration and recognition must be acknowledged, but the work remains obstinately unlovable: also undistinguished in its actual musical elements by comparison with the successions of more fantastical fantasies – less inspired, less personal, for all the composer's personal investment. Not simply near-duff, like most of the *Études symphoniques*, but surely not from Schumann's top drawer. Yet the *Fantasie* is hero, or victim, of a consensus; Charles Rosen's enthusiastic appreciation puts the case at its most persuasive.

With relief we return to Schumann's pure gold, a treasury of imagination released and abounding. We left fantasy-land with *Papillons* in 1832, and re-enter in 1837 with the *Davidsbündler*-dances (op. 6) and the *Fantasy-pieces* op. 12: *Kreisleriana* op. 16 and the *Novelettes* op. 21 follow next year; the *Humoreske* op. 20 and the *Faschingsschwank aus Wien* op. 26 in 1839: three smaller pieces from the same store overlap the big ones – in 1838 *Scenes from Childhood* op. 15; from 1839 the *Blumenstück* op. 19 and the *Arabeske*. The following selection is based upon personal predilection; and upon the desire to rescue some Cinderella-music, just as good as the familiar, from their ashy neglect. Then *Carnaval* op. 9 – no Cinderella, and actually composed alongside the dullish abstract works of the mid-1830s (1834–5) to close in a blaze of exuberance.

Davidsbündler: a song-and-dance suite, the dances mainly waltzes. No scenario, no titles, but in the first edition individual numbers are assigned 'F.' or 'E.', and sometimes both – Florestan or Eusebius, united as the Brother-band of David, contra Philistines, under a motto from Clara. There are also occasional 'stage-directions', also omitted in later editions – between nos. 8 and 9, 'here Florestan stopped, and his lips trembled convulsively'. But words are, throughout, altogether too gross a medium for this variously intimate and boisterous music, all of the highest inventive power – *papillons* of flesh and blood, alive with quivering sensitivity. Never more so than when the sequence-proper closes, Florestan and Eusebius united in its principal key, B-minor. An Epilogue then opens up a new realm of tenderness and intimacy in alien-but-aligned C-for-Clara; the delicate heterophonic hesitation-waltz, almost too fragile to play, gradually dissolves and disappears down to the depths of the keyboard – outside and beyond the framework of the whole while yet consolidating it, putting it into exquisite retrospect – 'quite redundantly Eusebius added the ensuing, but spoke with his eyes great happiness'.

The eight *Fantasiestücke* do have titles. *Des Abends* – exquisite layout between the hands and the pedal, catching the melodic contour, on top, then, slightly displaced, on inner-parts, ravishing touches of dissonance opening up distant keys – nuances of nightness – before a coda, more formal and gently clinching, ending on the piece's highest note, seemingly opening up a further dimension. *Aufschwung* – uplift, flight, soaring: just what it says – from initial release of energy, then cantabile buoyed up with figuration; opening returns, now earthed into dissonance, moving this time into broader singing, rising scales in close imitation, down depthwards, gradual invasion by the opening salvo over the later continuous bass-energy till it explodes into a 'recapitulation' – round again till given emphatic closing cadence resolving the dissonance till now left open. *Warum?* Why? – a tiny lyric, two treble voices tenderly duetting; later joined by a third in the bass, briefly, twice. Delicate subtlety, in the second half, the same pleading-questioning motif over and over again, each repetition with tiny variants curving back to their source in the opening duet, now foreshortened and closing resolved yet still questioning. *Grillen* – whims, caprices, fancies: hefty waltz-strain, lusty and vital, answered with lyricism, then returning – sense of questioning and dialogue here too: centre lower, richer, almost chorale-like, with continuous placing across the missing first beat – later a problem in Schumann, here essential to the forward momentum even when energy is subdued before returning in full, lusty vigour.

In der Nacht – turbulent whirlwind of spookiness and alarms, passionate fragmented cries, later calmer and more sustained, then muttering *sotto voce*, boiling up, with the opening section's return, to the same climax in two spasms, placed higher and at once quenched; close still alternating mutter with appeals, ending suddenly loud. *Unheimlich* – uncanny. *Fabel* by contrast homely and familiar. A slow introduction says 'listen to a winter's tale'; this injunction alternates with its lively telling, gay and spritely though not without darker undercurrents. The energetic sections put the 'exercise' nature of the Paganini-studies to poetic purpose. End – 'there, the tale is told': twice, as during, but their order reversed; then a third, extra – 'so it was' – and very quiet confirmatory close of the storybook. *Traumes Wirren* – dream-disorders/ perplexities – fire-flickers worthy of Liszt; a more solemn chordal strain in the centre. *Ende vom Lied* – what it says (my edition glosses the German into 'the upshot of it'): hearty plainspoken march, mock-pompous then brightly festive, with a terrific chromatic bubble-up, as though parodying the *Tristan*-motif *avant la lettre*. After return of the bluff stuff, a soft recession into the distant past, the heroic-narrative contour stealing in from the bass upwards – the upshot? – from depths to a surface still viola-tessitura, then down again to end the song in deep slumber.

The *Novellettes* are as neglected as *Kreisleriana* familiar: there are eight. No individual titles, the generic appellation suggests the tone; fantasy, soaring or dark-wards, is replaced by gaiety, exuberance, celebration in ballroom or boudoir or on the open streets; but absolutely no decline of Schumann's fantasy-invention. No. 1 makes the perfect entrée – a sturdy march enclosing impulsive tender song-section; march briefly continued, then lyrical descending overlapping scales, almost ecclesiastical; snatch of march, more impulsive ardour, a rainbow of keys, march to close. No. 2 is yet another *Traumes Wirren* whirligig containing a graceful, delicate, volatile intermezzo. No. 3 – *leicht und mit Humor*: a spritely scherzo, charged with good-humoured energy interfused with – fused with – delicacy: then its intermezzo comes *rasch und wild*; but its untamed nature remains exuberant rather than the driven intensity of *Kreisleriana*'s finale at its central climax. No. 4 is a ball-scene – *sehr munter* – a waltz number, initially cheerful as indicated, growing more impassioned in questions-and-answers between left hand and right – him, her – and Schumann's syncopations, later to become compulsive, still under expressive control. Back into public view; the waltz's new continuation takes off *brillante alla* Chopin. A glimpse of High Society, sparkling diamonds and champagne – almost hectic – a scene from Balzac, seen from the outsider's viewpoint – consumptive Chopin, syphilitic Schubert, Schumann, Chabrier – masters of the dance, in all its glamour and sparkle, outmatched only by Tchaikovsky (who was merely gay).

No. 5 is another brightly lit dance-scene, not so hectic – *rauschend und festlich* – festive and intoxicated? The Italian directs *pomposo e brillante* – true enough; the touch of pomposity is unmiss-able, as too the stylish elegance and a dash of gallantry. First trio contrasting – rich warm viola-colouring in sixths and thirds. The opening returns. Another intermezzo contrasts differently – waltz-motion lost; instead, a quiet throbbing strum accompanying a plain not-quite melody on just three notes, first in treble then in alto, the treble and tenor combined. The loud festive opening creeps in soft, low, distant, then piles up in a rapid crescendo to its initial flourish of bravura. Another episode is new – terrific energy in its short-repeated rhythm – animal pounding, sometimes relegated to the bass before bounding upwards again: fragments of opening ritornello, eventually all of it, then another trio/intermezzo, viola-coloured in sixths as before though the material is different. This time it winds down to an expectant pause: resumes in one voice; two a sixth apart; three, two sixths apart; four, three sixths apart – a sound as strange and beguiling as its description is off-putting, and not lost on Debussy, who virtually reproduces it in his *Study in Sixths* nearly eight decades later. So into the three-note melody, and ending on it, as the vital ball-scene is forgotten – just a surreptitious whisper in the bass – on an almost religious note to close. This is clearly a more extended and elaborated *Novellette*: quite a sizeable form built of self-contained mosaic-sections (and reaching its apotheosis here in no. 8). Next is simpler: no. 6, another *munter scherzo*; *sehr lebhaft, mit vielem Humor*: its lively emphatic opening is succeeded by a hymnic chordal strain, dissolving in cheerfulness, laughter, a skip and a jump. After its second round, vivacity is replaced by lovely lyricism; then fairy-lightness à la Mendelssohn. Volatile interplay between all these elements – this piece is not so simple as its sibling no. 3. The opening is lost to sight and sound, but the skip-and-jump is worked in to alternate and react with the hymnic strain and the lovely lyricism. Another disappearing ending, this one quizzical, with a whiff of violins' open strings. No. 7 is the set's shortest and simplest – an extrovert quick waltz, infectious and without shadows: ardent singing trio, in its second half the melody transferred to alto, then bass: the waltz-return so drastically curtailed as to give an effect of foreshortening that's almost visual.

So to no. 8; this is much longer – several *Novellettes* in one – a complex masterpiece of copious material in many textures, moods, speeds. Begins with another *In der Nacht*, impassioned turbulence of accompaniment, voices above, below, middle, picking up the call from each other. Surge reduces to staccato chopping, then treble and bass resume in full power together. Trio 1, though, is graceful, saucy, flirtatious, winning. Three quizzical notes reopen the night piece, identical at first, then growing to strong thematic simplification, the outer voices in canon, the surge in between, till ending, again identical with first round. Trio 2 is all sturdy peasant robustness – a quartet of al fresco horns joyously invoked; but instead of climaxing it sinks – the lusty rhythm retained as background to the fading recession, eventually just as bass to a long cantilena – *Stimme aus der Ferne*; voice from afar – here only mooted, incomplete and half-closing on a semi-colon; *Fortsetzung*; continuation; the distant voice now near, tenderly sung in full, gently peaking, breaking off in a sigh; and the quieter half of Trio 2 returns, over its lively rhythm, declining into another version of the same half-close – immediately taken up as opening and motto for *Fortsetzung und Schluss*, a mosaic of repeated interlocking segments, many with their own distinct middle-sections, embracing a wide variety of colours, textures, moods. Broader continuity erodes sectionality, the feeling darkens, the tessitura and dynamic sink; then begin to tense and strain, up to a passionate reappearance of the *Stimme*, now in the very same room: its quiet echo is marked *Innig*/heartfelt; it fades; dance-mosaic softly resumes – a kaleidoscopic re-throw of the coloured constituents, broadly in reverse order, ending with strong emphasis where it began.

The *Humoreske* is another tip-top cycle-sequence, relatively neglected albeit just as good as any of these marvellous works. Also sort of more-of-the-same: moods, materials, techniques, inventive and fresh at the highest level throughout; and, again, with features new and unique to it. But I must, as the Gospel enjoins, pass (reluctantly) by on the other side, to reach the *Faschingsschwank aus Wien* ('Carnival-jest from Vienna'): in effect a ninth *Novellette* extended after the example of the eighth to make what amounts in size, structure and stature a five-movement sonata, the classical order reversed.

Thus it commences with a rondo-'finale' – ebullient and sweeping, a sublimated waltz brought out from the shadows of the ballroom into the bright light of the open streets: energy alternates with ardent cantabile – the quieter strain after the brief return of *brioso* opening shows Schumann's predilection for effacing the first beat becoming chronic – twenty-three bars without one, another seven, then another (then thirty-two bars exactly repeated): here it still works – the impulsive rhythmic emphasis of the main rondo-waltz is felt strongly enough to carry the long suspension. Second episode all swings and seesaws; the third is a splendidly vigorous Viennese barn-dance – Schubert on octane; it builds up to explicitly and provocatively quote the *Marseillaise*, forbidden by the authorities in the city at this time; and ends in a brief turbulence, opening out into the fourth episode, a delicate swinging between full chords high and low, borrowed, even its key, from the trio of the scherzo in Beethoven's Sonata op. 31/iii. This dulcet moment is followed by a strange snaky chromatic link into the main rondo-material, much-curtailed, then a return of the quieter strain with suppressed first beats, foreshortened and winding down almost to stopping-point; two lulling suspensions on a dissonance, then winding up with sudden renewed ebullience to a brilliant end that still manages to suppress the main beat, twice, at the penultimate moment.

The second movement is a *Romanze*: one precious page of tender plaintive questioning – as it might be, *Warum?* passed through the *Scenes from Childhood*; consolation in a gentle hymnic middle-section that also could be related. (*Scenes* had been composed the year before.) No. 3 is a *Scherzino*: two precious pages of dainty festivity that can wax boisterous, even rough – Bottom and Puck both present in this epitome of Weber's magic in *Oberon* and Mendelssohn's in his *Midsummer Night's Dream*. Delicate and mysterious alternate with rambunctious – strange stases and silences very like the Mendelssohn – suddenly grotesque – uncouth upward chromatic slither to a brusque end. No. 4 – *Intermezzo*: another *In der Nacht*/start of the eighth *Novellette*; turbulent surging, in the middle, deep gapped bass, passionate calling by the right hand. When right and left parley in imitation, the resemblance to the *Novellette* is still more marked. No. 5 – *finale* in first-movement sonata-form, marked *höchst lebhaft*/maximum vitality and vividness. Also very Mendelssohn-ish – Mendelssohn with higher blood-heat and sperm-count: bubbly euphoric brio alternates with aspiring lyricism, both extrovert. Seems towards the end to be heading for one of Schumann's animated disappearing-acts; then boils up for resounding cadential chords and a very orchestral fanfare. Florestan to the fore.

Carnaval – '*scènes mignonnes sur quatre notes*' – returns this section to where it began – *Abegg* and *Papillons* – a private dream-world populated with lovers, real or imaginary, brothers-in-art, enemies of art; and taking that world to its all-time apex, justly familiar, cherished, adored. There were to have been twenty-six numbers, as in Schumann's first song-collection *Myrthen* – one for each letter of the alphabet – *Lettres Dansantes*. Eventually there were twenty – plus or minus, depending on how they're counted. And on whether the '*quatre notes*' printed as 'Sphinxes' are played or not. Three shapes, spelling out names and places half-divulged, half-concealed; the first and third give four pitches, the middle just three. They should be divulged not concealed: their penetration of the work as a whole is so clever, subtle, poetic. The *scènes mignonnes* are titled, rather than numbered. *Préambule* is just what it says: heroic opening, more march than waltz, animated scurry, waltz/*valse* reached and confirmed, vigour enclosing frolicking caprice; ends in a whirl of syncopated euphoria. *Pierrot*, a wistful sad/happy cameo, interrupted by the same three-note figure like a rebuff – 'come on!' – or a reproach, finally bursting into jocular indignation before a soft ending. *Arlequin* redeploys the same idea – a frisky waltz with peremptory interruptions, five-note descending scale, this time ending the piece on the threshold of *valse noble* – elegant, coolly impassioned, no interruptions.

Eusebius – Schumann's moody/dreamy/introspective persona – a cameo of exquisite tenderness with remarkable fluidity in the rhythms of its melodic contours – septuplets before regular quavers, then a five and three pattern: second half opening up the upper octave over wide-spaced chords in the left hand, and hints of inner voices in this most inward of music. *Florestan* follows, alter ego of his creator's divided personality, all fire, impulse, overflow: and an impetuous waltz – marked *passionato* – keeps checking itself, holding back before rushing on: first such curb incomplete, second starts again then completes the phrase – from *Papillons*, and thus marked, with a '?' in the score. The piece starts on a dissonance, ends on it too, reiterated with crescendo and fragmentation of melody as introducing – *Coquette* – just as she says: she'll flirt with both sides of the composer's nature, subtly suggested by *Replique*, wherein what had been her first phrase is now the second – in reply. Here be *Sphinxes*, either silent/conceptual, or heard as intervallic sources for what's to come.

Papillons – *scherzissimo* in right hand, horns (so marked) in the left. *Lettres Dansantes* – anagrams of girls and places, Sphinxes at work and play, in presto waltz. *Chiarina* another *valse noble*, *con amore*, *appassionato*. *Chopin* – a wonderful miniature portrait/homage: agitato nocturne, even with its repeat only twenty-six bars long/short; as it flashes past we almost see the suffering visage. *Estrella* a third *valse noble*, this one turbulent and unquiet. Then the intoxicating bounce and bubble of *Reconnaissance*: Sphinx-shape growing into continuous melody, deliciously 'scored' for the right hand's upper fingers singing, lower fingers doubling in staccato, all over light, jaunty accompaniment in the left: middle-section the accompaniment more throbbing, and the soprano and bass sing to each other high and low.

Pantalon et Columbine – an excited chase around the *commedia dell'arte* stage, with delightful little close – he's caught her. *Valse Allemande*: another *valse noble*, this with a touch of coquette in the opening bars, of heroic in the second strain, the whole closer to the letter, not just the spirit, of Schubert than elsewhere: it encloses *Paganini*, another composer-cameo, as diabolically virtuoso/bravura as Chopin's was inward and agitated. *Aveu*; as it were on from *Reconnaissance*: more passionate; parlando, almost panting. *Promenade*, grandest of all the *valses nobles*: fascinating play with different layers of dynamic and register – generous opening gesture *mf*: secret *aveu* (so secret the melody-notes are in small print) *pp*: *f* then *ff* to face up to the crowded ballroom and brazen it out. Towards the end the three layers fuse.

Pause – anything but! Return of the whirl from end of *Préambule* straight into finale – *Marche des Davidsbündler contre les Philistines*. A march in triple-time, related to the opening but not the same – more chunky too – these striplings have muscle (unless it's Goliath we hear first). March yields to waltz, the bass bangs out a '*theme du XVIIième siècle*', the military and the dancers confront, collide, collude, characters from earlier reappear and are roped onto the barricades – nobody explicit (certainly not Chopin nor Paganini) – generalized waltz/*valse* shapes and sense of the dancing letters derived from the Sphinxes; ever faster and faster – like Alice, the music has to go ever faster in order to remain on the spot; ends in a burst of firework chords all over the keyboard.

Lieder *of 1840*

Schumann's song collection and cycles of this 'year of song' raise the matter of a different kind of unity from the simply narrative. There *are* narrative cycles: *Frauenliebe und -leben* is a special instance – the dramatization of lyric moments from a domestic saga – courtship, marriage, baby, loss. And the two Heine-cycles, *Dichterliebe* and the *Liederkreis* op. 24, are clearly in direct line from the two Schubert cycles, in particular *Die schöne Müllerin* with its story-telling directness. The great difference lies in Schumann's oblique presentation. Schubert's narrative links together lyric moments, easily followed. In Schumann the story is 'between the lines': chronology, even events, are only implied by lyric occasions, never told direct. In op. 24 this is so rarified that we lose all sense of the latent tale behind the successive expressions of emotion.

What compensates for the lack of line is a much more

deliberate and, so to speak, 'silver-age' self-consciousness about structure – in key-relationships, and, in *Dichterliebe*, by internal cross-reminiscences – as compared with Schubert's Shakespearean prodigality and careless ease. Op. 24 shows this in its almost obsessive simplicity of key-movement in a brief cycle – nine songs; linking them unbreakably into a single span (despite the sometimes shocking transpositions in older editions, that can still jar in many modern performances). This unification is very successful – the simplicity is subtle, strong, deep: successful above all in the way it works *instead* of a direct, coherent narrative: it permits elisions and shifts of focus, in the shadowy events and personages, by being in itself so structurally expressive.

The op. 24 *Liederkreis* shows the way forward to the op. 39 – the Eichendorff-cycle – where there is not an iota of story. The unity of these twelve songs is *poetic* – of mood, feeling, situation, imagery: and *musical* – of key-sequence and subtle, unobtrusive motivic transformation between the individual items. We feel them to belong to each other, to be juxtaposed, contrasted, inter-remembered, absolutely right and inevitable in their place, as surely as if the cycles were advancing a chronological narrative with protagonist and other personages.

More of this, in detail, later, when both *Liederkreise* are reached. Meanwhile, a collection that's neither narrative nor coherent in these subtle new ways: *Myrthen*, twenty-six songs, one for each letter of the alphabet, wrought into a fugitive myrtle-wreath as wedding gifts for Clara, presented to her the day – night? – before, after long unjust 'cause and impediment', their longed-for nuptials – 12 September of the *Wunderjahr*. A garland; a miscellany: though sensitively shaped around contrasts and complements, including a vestigial overall key-scheme, and despite autobiographical undercurrents sometimes revealed by an alphabetical correspondence, *Myrthen* is no narrative. The gender and angle of the poems require two singers at least (they are not specified); and to hear the opus is to enjoy a succession of gems loosely strung upon the theme of marriage, and some of them among his most precious, rather than a Unity.

The texts come from six well-known poets and one

unknown – Julius Mosen, immortalized in *Der Nussbaum*. Five
are from Goethe's *West-östlicher Divan* (cod-Persian with a Weimar
heart); three by Heine (set extensively of course elsewhere in 1840);
five from Rückert; two translations from Byron's English (though
one is a *Hebrew Melody*), two from his Irish chum Tom Moore and
eight from the Scotch of Burns. The collection begins and ends in
Rückert – the celebrated *Widmung* – a rapturous Dedication – 'You
my Soul, my Heart, my Joy and my Sorrow – my Earth where I
live, Heaven whereto I aspire, the Grave in which my despair lies
buried.' Beautiful key-change, and accompaniment from exuberant arpeggios to throbbing chords with hint of an inner voice as
it expands – 'You are Calm and Peace: that you love me gives me
my value' and, as we return softly to initial key and texture, 'You
my better I' (nearly Martin Buber): so to a return of the opening,
taking a new turn upon some of the same words, emphatic chords
breaking the momentum – 'my Good Ghost, my Better Half!' –
then a quiet coda, piano only, that already hints of pain and sorrow
to come.

The other four Rückert songs, not so utterly lovable, occupy a
similar area of ardent intimacy: nos. 11 and 12, *Lieder der Braut*, say as
much; their music already that of *Frauenliebe und -leben*. The final
two are just as lovely in a more generalized love-language: no. 25
Aus den östlichen Rosen – almost monotone voice-part over light
luminous figuration, the piano's right hand interjecting tiny sighs
more speaking than the singer, both blooming together for the final
line, set twice – 'so heaven may lighten my night'; then the piano's
counter-melody repeated an octave lower as a coda, and the closing
arpeggio returning to the song's opening descending arpeggio with
added upward gesture to close. No. 26 *Zum Schluss*/To Close itself,
rapt/plain/hymnic, seems a little po-minded – *Schwester-Braut*/Sister-
Bride might raise eyebrows for Robert and Clara, untroubled by
Siegmund and Sieglinde.

All three Heine-settings are special. No. 24 *Du bist wie eine Blume*
is justly celebrated – twenty bars of rapt concentration, broadening
from repeated to single chords for the voice's salient phrase and
highest note – '*betend, daß Gott dich erhalte*' – 'pray that *God* preserve

you' – topped by piano with gentle answering emphasis, the piano also stealing the last word in the song's richest harmonies and most expressive melodic contour. Just as lovely is the Cinderella of the three, no. 21, *Was will die einsame Thräne?* – utterly simple tenderness pared down, as of the Schubert/Heine *Ihr Bild*, light-version, with a touch of bucolic when the poem speaks of the solitary tear's shining sisters, and a climactic dissonance on *Qualen*/sorrows, similarly poised to pierce-with-joy as in the sixth song of *Frauenliebe*. No Cinderella is *Die Lotosblume* – no. 7: the creature so quiveringly evoked herein rises from her shy avoidance of the sun to unfold – *blüht und glüht und leuchtet*/blooms and glows and shines – under the warmer rays of her lover the Moon. The piano's chords float arhythmic and rootless, outlining then enclosing then supporting the vocal line over a bass left hand, deep-sustained save for just two faster notes, passing but infinitely suggestive. Bass ceases altogether as the Moon emerges: both hands take the chords into a gently dissonant higher region, gradually intensifying, growing faster, descending, till – she blooms into fragrance, and weeps, and trembles – the climactic last line – 'with love and love's woe' – a diminuendo, echoed by accompaniment, re-echoed by singer.

Only one of the Goethe-settings reaches the calibre of those of Heine and Rückert: no. 9 *Lied der Suleika*, the more meditative cousin of *Widmung* and sister to several in the courtship-and-marriage cycle. Perhaps it's a finer song because its poem is by Marianne von Willemer, not the Meister, in their unattributed collaborations. The others – nos. 2, 5, 6 and 8 – also come from the *West-östlicher Divan*: poky patches of pseudo-Oriental wisdom, drinking-songs, whims and irks. Far more attractive Schumann's responses to Burns, characterizing Highland types male and female, married, pining, widowed: eight in all, almost all tip-top. Take no. 4, *Jemand*/Someone, with its desolate simplicity – Gretchen abandoned without the consolation of spinning, or the desolate girl of Wolf's *Das verlaßene Mägdlein*; with a more surprising glimpse into the future as love's protecting power is invoked, the harmony intensifies, and Mahler's *Urlicht* steals into the memory from things-to-come. No. 10 – the *Highland Widow*: defiant urgent galloping regret for bonny Donald, perished at Culloden. No. 13, another strong sturdy song, extrovert rather than lamenting: 'my heart's in the Highlands' – with, unlike any others of the eight, a tinge of Scotchness in the melodic shape. No. 14 – *Highland Cradlesong* – a tiny nugget of gentleness, over a drone-bass that may convey a hint of bagpipes? The up-beat drone-fifth lasts a mere quaver; the dominant sets in for all three stanzas, renewed on surprising off-beats, delivering the low tonic just twice, *en passant*; the little piano interlude between the stanzas – then closes the lullaby with simple rightness.

No. 20 is another pearl – *Weit, weit*/Far, far – her handsome lad is far away, leaving her, probably for ever, with child (the German translation omits Burns' explicit stanza): piano right hand's plaintive phrase, retreating then simply to shadow the voice, coming alive again and eloquent in the left; then as the singer re-enters, o'ertopping her with poignant descant: this thrice for the three verses (it would have needed five to tell the whole truth), then a coda, intensifying the pain, before guttering out in nerveless staccato.

The two Tom Moore songs make a pair: nos. 17 and 18, Venetian flittings – the youth guides his gondola to his lover's balcony: lagoon-lapped night-assignations, languorous then crisp for both identical strophes. Then Ninetta in the Piazzetta, eloping with her lover disguised as a gondolier, a gay little cameo strayed from *Carnaval*, light as air. Depths had been sounded earlier in no. 15, a plangent *Hebrew Melody* from Byron, supposedly sung by Saul in his melancholia, begging young David to tune his harp to a dark strain; but actually in effect reading, then sounding, like an impassioned love-lyric. Harp evoked in the simpler arpeggios of the middle section, background to the singer's calmer sostenuto; then after the return of the anguished introduction for piano alone, the voice re-enters on large strained leaps – descending ninths, ascending octaves. The outer sections – to open, to close – foretell in sinister chromatic contours the quietly menacing dusk of '*Zwielicht*' in the Eichendorff *Liederkreis*. Then for the final line the poet/composer/protagonist's crucial choice – 'break, heart, or be healed in song' – is set to an adapted augmentation of the piano-harp's principal shape, forcibly positing a coda descending into depths of saturnine darkness, with a perhaps annealing close into the major.

Next comes this profound song's silly complement: no. 16 *Rätsel*/Riddle; the English original attributed to Byron (true author Catherine Fanshawe) plays on the letter H, neatly Germanized with the additional fun, not possible in English, of H being B in German musical spelling. A bagatelle, it earns its place merely by contrast-in-context, unlike the single song by the Unknown, *Der Nussbaum* – no. 3 – which has always been precious to lovers of this composer and to its performers. Who cares that this poem is flimsy: it doesn't impede the music, and says what the composer wants to say, and his female subject too – blissful anticipation as the foliage of the walnut-tree whispers of her imminent bridegroom. Exquisite interplay over transparent arpeggio-figuration in the left hand of the right, eliciting then doubling the girl's voice, answering with what it had begun with, suggesting endless circularity, before pointing a new direction, light-and-shading the not-quite unison: till in the coda the singer sinks to a near whisper as her tree-accompaniment rustles on a drone with only three notes left of the already fragmentary melody. Would that there were more Mosen and less *West-östliche* Goethe!

The *Liederkreis* op. 24 is actually the first sustained product of Schumann's 1840 efflorescence of songs – nine Heine poems, whose subject is as much – if not more – an account of how life/love/hope/fear/loss are transformed into artistic expression – than a subjective, obliquely told narration of an affair. The summary final poem is explicit:

> Let this book be a shrine to bury my songs; and would my love too / On love's grave grows the flower of peace – / Others may pluck it; for me it blooms only after I'm dead and gone. / These songs, born of my burning passions fierce as Etna's lava, now congealed: / Yet love can revive them; and will, when you, my dearest distant love, receive them.

The balancing equation-equivalent act of sublimation couldn't be clearer; the composer's immediate self-identification also.

After the riotous burgeoning complexity of the solo piano years the immediate contrast is striking: op. 24's material and its treatment are simple, stripped, severe – purity and plainness of diction, in notes that *speak* – *lettres* no longer *dansantes* so much as walking, waking, dreaming, thinking, hammering, listening, asking, objecting, loving and hating, exploding with rancour, bursting up like a volcano, or drifting peacefully down the Rhine whose crystal depths conceal treachery, night and death. Also, there is a deliberate paucity of ample vocal melody: it's piano-music still, in this new bareness – the voice-parts often contained within the accompaniments – subtly not *quite*; the deviations sensitively nuanced; and the one exception, no. 7 *Berg und Burgen*, an entire vocal span of great beauty, carefully placed for maximum contrasting effect.

This plainness in musical idioms is fastened into a cast-iron key-scheme; basic and telling. Take the gap between nos. 2 and 3: magic power of soft full major after fierce E-minor; and the other same-tonic-minor to major between nos. 4 and 5. Elsewhere, almost as basic, dominant-to-tonic for nos. 3–4, 6–7, 7–8, 8–9; major to relative minor for nos. 1–2, and the same key albeit a total change of momentum and mood, for nos. 5–6. All these fundamental relationships are contained between the outer songs: nos. 1 and 9's unity of key. If any of these are disregarded, woe betide! The immediate wrongness will strike every first-time hearer even without the awful gift of perfect pitch.*

Bound into the cast-iron construction of this brief cycle is an almost obsessive sense of rhyming – later, such interconnections are hinted and suggested; here they are hammered home in the likeness of nos. 1, 2 and 4, all sharing the same melodic contour and accompaniment-types. The two longer cantabile songs, 5 and 7, seem

---

* Yet performers who tinker with the keys are outvied by the grotesque absurdity of some old standard editions of Schumann's work, which printed the concluding song in Volume I – favourite Schumann *Lieder* – and the other eight in Volume II, where they 'end' on a repeated '?' in the text (though this was added by the composer; Heine's poem lacks it) and the most-audible-imaginable semi-colon in the music, crying out for what must ensue.

to rhyme less obviously but just as surely. The closing song seems a
sort of summary, including the near-citation of preceding textures
and shapes without ever actually quoting, the effect being to lay the
whole to rest, not just the pain and stoic acceptance of its question/
semicolon prelude. Plentiful further internal riveting strengthens
the single shape made of nine separate sections: no. 1: each morning
I awake asking, will she come? Each evening I grieve; each night I lie
in sleepless woe: all day I wander around half-asleep. No. 2: I burn
with impatience to see her again – stir yourselves, lazy hours – you've
never been in love. No. 3: alone under the trees with my sorrow.
Birds sing golden words – 'she sang them here all day long'. *Ach!*
Don't tell me! No. 4: place your hand on my heart, my darling: you
hear a knocking? Knock, knock, knock, night and day. Finish the
job, evil carpenter, let me rest in peace. No. 5: Fair cradle of my woes,
I must leave you, where I first saw her. If only I'd not! But I never
sought your love – yet you speak harshly, you banish me – my heart
is sick, my mind touches madness, I must depart, to reach, wearied
unto death, a cold distant grave. No. 6: wait, wild sailor! I'll soon be
aboard. But first, farewell to two treacherous women – Europa and
her. Let me write it in my blood. And another – Eve, bringing death
into the world; and another, Eris, mother of discord: curses on you
all; all women! No. 7: mountains and castles reflected clear in the
Rhine's mirror; we glide in gentle rapture, light plays gold on the
waters, my feelings re-awake: I know that under its friendly surface
lie darkness and death. You, river, are her image – lovely to look at,
softly smiling, treacherous within. No. 8: at first I near despaired – I
will never bear it: at the last, never ask how, borne it I have. No. 9: I
would bind this little book with myrtle, roses and cypress – a grove
for my songs. Would my love might be buried too! Once my songs
burnt fierce as Etna; now they lie congealed and dumb: yet if love
rears its head they will flame up anew. So be it; my little book will
reach you from beyond the gave; all passion spent, its pale words
will look into your peerless eyes and whisper of my wistful yearning.

Huge matter, dense gravity, lie latent within these poems and
their setting: the fusion is red-hot: it desires to, needs to, *must*
burst – à la Etna – before the garland of myrtles and roses can grant

assuagement. The Heine *Liederkreis* is still relatively neglected among the Schumann cycles. It is as great and important as the other, if not so loveable: its stripped ferocity of content and its embodiment preclude adoration.

Next, though not next-composed, come *Dichterliebe* and *Frauenliebe*: but I will alight again at the other *Liederkreis*, Eichendorff's. For Rosen, Sams and Johnson already say it all for the two most familiar song-cycles, the latter pair in continuous notes, the first more sporadically, with a sensitivity and precision of observation moving in itself.

   Liederkreis op. 39: twelve songs to poems by Eichendorff: a dictionary of early German Romantic themes and affects, without protagonist or story – moods and images tell their own tale. Nature, mysterious whether benign or uncanny, prevails almost throughout. Other subjects flicker up and fade out – exile, alienation, foreignness, strangeness: aspects of love – tender devotion, rapturous secrecy, explicit ecstasy: undercurrents of pain and anxiety, and their ambiguous intermingling with states of hope and joy. Nine of the twelve are set in forests, which their music evokes when hunting-horns are mentioned. Distances and perspective constantly shift: two songs present actual personages in a narrative, one direct, the other oblique. All this is conjoined in an unobtrusive weave of musical connections motivic, harmonic, accompaniment-patterns, within a grid of closely related keys subtly both symmetrical and asymmetrical within the cyclic circularity – foretellings and recallings; memory in every dimension of time and space.

   Some details of individual poems and their setting. *In der Fremde*: exile, oblivion, far from home, father and mother long dead, soon I too will be forgotten, the lovely lonely forest will rustle above my unknown resting-place: plangent melodious melancholy, F♯-minor mirroring the F♯-major homecoming – all joyous exaltation – of the cycle's closing song.* *Intermezzo* – in A, relative major, balan-

---

*   All keys given here as in the original: naturally singers will need to transpose in
     accord with their individual ranges, but if transpositions are inconsistent, alas for
     Schumann's expressive and telling care.

cing the A-major of the penultimate song: I carry your lovely image in my heart; my heart sings its secret inward song, winging its way to you: voice and piano right hand intertwine in echo, anticipation, response; ending in exquisitely wrought coda for piano alone, two voices interfused. *Waldesgespräch* – words in woods – E, dominant of preceding A, and an excursion to C unmatched elsewhere. More extended, and characterized – a narrative episode, not a solitary mood-piece: the knight riding late through the woods encounters the lovely bride – he will protect her from the treachery of men (here the plunge into the alien key): They have broken my heart – hark, the hunting horns – fly me – you know not what I am. So fine-arrayed (back to home key), so seductively beautiful ... now I know you – the bewitching Lorelei! (Now she sings in his key) – Yes, 'tis I; my castle from its high crag looks deep into the Rhine: it grows cold and late; you'll never escape my thrall. Obliqueness of speech and event rendered in a setting without ambiguity – direct and dramatic, till, as the horn-calls recede into infinite chivalric remoteness, music seems poised, in key and contour, for what's to come later.

Meanwhile, another intermezzo – the G-major of *Die Stille* – the Quiet One, gentle dominant to the Lorelei's dangerous C: secret happiness, silently kept to myself; if only I were a little bird I could fly over the seas and reach my heaven! So to the still centre, B-major *Mondnacht*. Yearning requited: as heaven condescends to kiss the earth so the earth aspires to reach the heavens: breezes ruffle the foliage, night is starry-bright; my soul spreads wide its wings, spanning the silent terrain as though it were winging home. A celebrated high-point of early Romantic utterance, so rapt on its pedal dominant, with some exquisite suspensions and one famous tingling clash – granted four times in a single night – as hardly to define, its key – E – till – right at the end the piano's coda – dare one say disappointingly? – homes in on a subdominant move that – dare one say? – breaks the spell.

The B-pedal becomes actual key for *Schöne Fremde*, another seminal song, this time unimpugnably flawless, with its inviting suggestion of an inexplicable happiness to come, vaguely intimated in fantastical dreams born of the half-perceived presence of ancient gods in the ruined precincts of some lovely foreign holy place. Its rustling, hinting momentum, at once shy yet impetuous, is stilled in the cycle's still centre to which B-major has been dominant up-beat – the E-minor of *Auf einer Burg*, modally inflected in plain quasi-choral imitative counterpoint, voice almost entirely doubling chorus top-part with telling touches of deviation, the polyphony coagulating into grinding dislocated suspensions frozen into the stonework. The old knight stationed at his castle look-out many hundreds of years as his hair and beard matt and mix. The forest is still; the birds sing: down from remote past to a distant miniature of the present – sunlit wedding-party sailing down sunlit Rhine – musicians play cheerful, the beautiful bride weeps.

This song's closing *tierce de Merovingia* links direct, as its dominant, to A-minor for *In der Fremde*. Motion and emotions are resumed; and from here on the listener becomes more clearly aware of the subtle peripheral-vision filaments of motivic contours, harmony, patterns of figuration weaving a web of inter-reference across songs with ostensibly little or nothing in common: a unity subliminal, not imposed – casual, even accidental, in an inexplic-able/illogical fashion absolutely right. I hear the brooks, the forest-murmurs, the nightingales – I see the moonbeams, the distant castle; but I am lost in this foreign place, this foreign present – as though (don't look for explanation or logic) my love awaited me still in the rose-filled garden – yet she is long-since dead. The accompaniment's alternation of bare octaves and pitter-patter vamp-figures gives a new texture and tone to the cycle, even as its A-minor rhymes with the A-major behind and still to come, and is also anchored firmly with its dominant to each immediate side. Next being *Wehmut*/Melan-choly: given a further new texture – rich, warm, hymnic, quickened by internal echoes and counter-melodies as though the piano were singing too; I can sing as though I were happy, but the tears well up from within – so with caged nightingales when spring comes – all are glad, no one feels the pain deep inside the joy.

Wehmut's comforting fullness at once dispersed by the gaunt texture of *Zwielicht* – direct from its first bare note to E-minor from the major, thus rhyming with the previous sinister twilight in the forest when the young knight encountered the Lorelei. *This* twilight is only inhabited by off-stage shadows and furtive menaces: the world grows grey and frightening – watch first for your favourite deer – huntsmen are around, horns and voices resound and re-echo. Trust not your best friend at this hour – his countenance smiles, his thoughts are malign. Tomorrow will raise new-born what now goes wearily to repose: but in the night much can be lost – watch out; be alert and cheerful! Fascinating sinuous-sinister chromatic figures in one and two parts, at first floating rootless, then over deep displaced bass-notes that in the third stanza leap syncopated and tipsy before, finally, settling solid on-the-beat bass to regular repeated chords, the singer at last casting his line free and independent: the gnomic last words a low recitative mutter, closed with secco chords as soft as they can be played. *Im Walde*, initially the bright twin to this creepy vision, follows – in A, the key-circle now palindromically complete at this penultimate song; a merry wedding party, birds singing, lusty huntsmen with their horns; then suddenly, all vacant, silent, night rapidly advancing; the forest rustles, my heart shudders to its depths. Gay hunting 6/8 on the horns; but already even in the singer's first line, the tempo holds back: *brioso* and tentative continue to alternate till the sudden emptiness, then the oncoming darkness prevails, and the heart's shudder takes the voice to its deepest possible note. Then, by wonderful means innocent of logic/order/reason, F♯-minor, relative to the A-major just left in the dark, is majored – a bright new tonal coloration for the miniature – over in a flash – transport of delirium that rounds the ring; *Frühlingsnacht*: birds return, flowers bloom, spring is here: I laugh, I cry – it must be a dream – old miracles shine renewed in the moonlight; moon and stars declare, woods whisper, nightingales sing it – she is Yours!

I've tried to emulate, by keys, key-words, indications of mood/momentum/coloration, of continuity and contrast, of forward and backward glances, subtle inter-motivic connections, the fusion of poetry, music, feeling, time-place-space, imagery visual and conceptual whereby this heavenly work *works*. Not so much through its machinery as in its inner impingement upon the outer senses – mainly auditory, from blasting hunting-horns to thoughts too mute and secret for utterance – visual (most often) and with a touch of touch perhaps (no. 5), certainly a whiff of fragrance (no. 12) – though no *taste*! All this in a special manner that remains almost without parallel; if not, maybe, absolutely unique. Unequalled, before or since.

Schumann and Mendelssohn compared

Encapsulating notes comparing and contrasting Schumann and Mendelssohn: contemporaries, born (M. 1809, S. 1810) into rich culture of literature and music, ardently influenced by the new currents in early German Romanticism, gifted performers, family men, making their way in musical careers among friends, supporters, brothers-in-arms; and with close personal ties (see Schumann's loving tribute on Mendelssohn's death in the *Album for the Young*).

Mendelssohn's lineage runs from late (at the time recent) Beethoven, through Weber, to the rediscovery of the Baroque, Bach principally but also Handel. Schumann's also involves Beethoven, though his principal precursor is Schubert; he also reinvents Bach in his own manner; but is more involved with his contemporaries, who also take arms against the philistines – Paganini, Chopin and Hoffmann's fictional 'Kreisler'; final salute to the future in recognizing the genius of the young Brahms.

Schumann aspires the hard way to classical forms and procedures, with varying success: Mendelssohn, innately a formalist (Debussy scoffed 'that elegant notary'), whatever the inspiration from travels, seascapes, Shakespeare, Goethe. Both peak early and manifest clear, albeit bumpy decline, losing the 'first fine careless [Mendelssohn *careful*] rapture', and fall into routine and mass-productions. Too-early deaths, Schumann's a descent into deep disturbance and eventual insanity, with physical origins in venereal disease; Mendelssohn's from sheer overwork, nervous strain and the self-imposed demands of a fine, generous, public-spirited, conscientious man.

Schumann undoubtedly the greater composer – reaches heights

and depths, agonies and ecstasies unknown to Mendelssohn and with far greater boldness in language, form, technique. In his great media – piano-and-song-cycle – flawless, and even in his awkward orchestral writing, more daring for all the faults. Wittgenstein's well-known *mot* seems made to point the contrast: 'Within all great work of art there is a WILD animal: tamed. Not, <u>e.g.</u>, with Mendelssohn.'

CHAPTER VIII
Later German Romantics

Brahms

Johannes Brahms: born Hamburg 1833; early promise as pianist – double-bass-playing father tried to push his son as a prodigy, but wiser counsels prevailed; instead, played to entertain clientèle in the low dives of the great port. Deliverance aged twenty; concert-tour with a violinist friend, encountering important musicians, including Liszt, and especially Robert and Clara Schumann, who recognized and generously saluted the enormous talent. Intermittent employment as conductor of small-court orchestras and a ladies' choir back home. First visits Vienna 1862; settles there for good in 1869, aged thirty-five. Frequent concert-tours, composing holidays in Italy, Austria, Switzerland (but – averse to the sea-crossing, declined England). Died Vienna 1897.

Brahms is a complex composite composer; many aspects and angles compose, and contradict, the finished outward form with its appearance of roundedness, at once ostensibly 'conservative' – committed to the past, continuing the line of his great Viennese predecessors in an oeuvre purely instrumental, eschewing 'the music of the future' that beat so powerful and seductive all about his present – and 'progressive' despite this image of reaction; willy-nilly innovatory, even radical, with a future vital for Schoenberg (who first thus dubbed him) and thence a major path down twentieth-century music at large.

Coming after Mendelssohn and Schumann, the young Brahms is a 'sum of the parts'. He inherits and amalgamates both: Mendelssohn's (neo)classicism, formal perfection, artistic stance and goals in general – though not in particular (no fairies, no land- and seascapes). And, from the direct contact with Schumann, the fiery early Romanticism, soaked in literature – Hoffmann, Jean Paul; the dictionary of moods and affects in Schumann's *Lieder*. There were tender *hommages* to the master and his wife in two early sets of variations upon Robert's themes; and life-long devotion to Clara after her husband's pathetic end. From both composers, veneration for Bach, opening up access to further Baroque masters, and back beyond them to earlier styles and techniques.

But Brahms's most important forebears are Beethoven and Schubert. His 'Beethoven-problem' – the long struggle, the eventual resolution – is familiar. Schubert, on the contrary, is not challenging: Brahms has innate affinity with his lyricism whether in *Lieder* or as interfused into purely instrumental music. The mature Brahmsian oeuvre unites these two vital predecessors 'over the head' of what had developed in the intervening generation. He learns fast: *late* Beethoven taken head-on in the three huge piano sonatas completed before his twenty-first birthday (which are also pervaded with stormy Romantic overdoing): back to *early* Beethoven in the two orchestral serenades; harking thence to Mozart, thence Haydn – Brahms appreciated both at their true value in the epoch of their underestimation. Beethoven meets Handel in the grand variation-set for piano: Schubert always and everywhere – the original version of the B-major Piano Trio of 1854 is stuffed with quotations, severely suppressed when revised in 1889; the 1st String Sextet (1860) evokes spirit and letter with no such self-consciousness. Bach always and everywhere – pastiches and exercises, spirit and letter – a would-be *Goldberg* canon in an early set of piano-variations later marked with its composer's heavy-pencilled question-marks; a lumbering fugue in the B-major Trio's first movement, also deleted in the late revision along with the Schubert-allusions.

Back beyond Bach and Handel to older severity and disciplines, pursuing contrapuntal studies with rigour, composing a *Missa Canonica* to prove it. The mature all-together Brahms is probably the most learnèd and scholarly of all the great composers. Mendelssohn had his fugues, Schumann his fughettas and canons, on the side.

In Brahms this way of thinking is germane to everything he wrote, and his historical view is much longer and wider – also from the Baroque, Domenico Scarlatti and François Couperin (whose twenty-seven books of clavecin *Ordres* Brahms co-edited); further back in his own tradition, Schütz and Isaac; further back, all over Europe, for vocal polyphony; and saturating everything past-and-present, folksong. In this matter of inheritance near and distant, Brahms makes an illuminating comparison/contrast with Bruckner – nine years older, dying the year before (1896), centred upon the same city. Both are heirs equally and crucially to Beethoven and Schubert, both are masters of strict contrapuntal training. This nexus, merely stated for now, will be explored later in full.

As with Schumann and Wagner, I admit to a long, difficult journey before the stature of Brahms became clear. With Wagner, greatness was obvious; the problem, merely that greatness's size! With Brahms the difficulty was one of tone and content – particularly since I'd already succumbed to the 'poison of the music-drama' (and had had no trouble at all with Bruckner). As an enthusiastic teenager drunk on Debussy, Mahler and modernism, the classics seemed simply boring. As teens turned to twenties, they marched in in full regimentals, followed by the metal-clad Romantic heavies, Bruckner and Wagner. Brahms had no place with either; he fell between the intellectual energy, social grace and physical vitality of classical Vienna, and the mythological-heroic sublimity and sheer sonorous magnificence of his contemporaries. He appeared merely stodgy, musclebound, without wit, brio or charm; sentimental in expression when not, unconvincingly, uplifting.

To the stiff priggish Leavisite that I was, wholesale appropriation of Nietzsche's gibes – 'he cannot exult'; he reveals 'the melancholy of impotence' – was all too easy. And I recall a spasm of genuine prudishness when first hearing the celebrated *Four Serious Songs*, the master's penultimate opus. The first three seemed dull brown, as usual, but the last was positively offensive. It sets the famous passage from 1 Corinthians 13. First comes plenty of beefy twenty-fingered piano-writing, rendering tongues of men and angels, sounding brass and tinkling cymbal, etc. with singular ineptness. Then when apostle and composer see through a glass darkly, looking forward to full face-to-face knowledge, the speed and mood change completely: over gentle piano ripples the voice swells out into a waltz-melody whose character – oleaginous yet beery – becomes more and more pronounced, culminating in a saucy little barmaid twiddle in the final phrase. After briefly returning to full speed to set up the three cardinal virtues, Love (Charity) is awarded the palm to a return of the slow waltz, piano now crooning along with voice, oozing with unction – 'the Grease of God'. The callow ear, attuned to the neon-lit alienation of Mahler and Strauss's purposeful vulgarity, missed out on the tone of this typical passage of Brahms (written when both his juniors were getting into their stride). For him, strains of salon and beer-hall can express exaltation, idealism, piety, absolutely without irony. As the *jongleur* juggles before the Virgin because it's what he does naturally and best, so Brahms hymns Love in a waltz. He'd long before bound them together in two sets of *Liebeslieder* waltzes, composed for drawing-room pleasure and set (with one exception) to *vers de société* of amorous triviality.

As an ex-chorister, I should have trusted appetite and scorned supercilious superiority. Like most cathedral choirs, mine did a few numbers from the master's *German Requiem*, unsuitably masquerading as Anglican anthems. All three were keenly relished, and they all contain waltzes. One, 'How Lovely is thy Dwelling-Place', could go alongside the *Liebeslieder* in style (though of course longer, more various and elaborated). It portrays the delights of the celestial mansion with unabashed worldliness – one seems to tread on carpets, sit on sofas, glance through the potted palms at Johann Strauss and his band – though strenuous counterpoint cannot be kept out of the middle section. In the other two the waltz-nature is not explicit. Indeed, 'Behold All Flesh' is no dance, but a funeral march in triple-time. Yet a lilt gets in at the sighing figures later accompanying the words 'and lo, the grass withereth, and the flower thereof fadeth'. The central section, concerning the patient husbandman, is a gentler, subliminal *Liebeslied* waltz. And then, after the march's full-scale return, the Lord's word blows away soldier-trudge or ballroom-lilt in a vigorous common-time fugue. But they return when the Last Trump sounds, again in triple-time after a spooky march for 'Here on earth have we no abiding place'. It certainly doesn't sound like a waltz to start with, nor yet for 'Death where is thy sting?'; but when it reaches, 'Hell, where is thy victory?' there's a hoofy lurch to the triple-time that brings connotations of rustic rather than urban dance-floors.

Brahms, though one of concert-giving's safest staples, is by no means set in stone. The thick veil of classical sobriety and emotional reserve conceals some surprises. It is, of course, a metaphor: the disguising beard (actually grown quite late in life), the cigar, the coarseness, the brusque ill-humour with which he fended off interference and, possibly, the urges of Eros; in musical terms the muscular effortfulness, the unconcealed cerebration, the Old Master-ishness. Beneath all this beats a maiden's tender heart, a vulnerable openness to feeling that, so often thwarted, dignifies without hardening over the decades into autumnal stoicism which, disdaining equally the consolations of religion and the high-noon apotheosis of Wagnerian redemption-by-love, can yet declare to strains of sublimated beer-hall that, of the three virtues, Love abideth foremost.

   Paradoxically it was when young in years, and fully beardless, that his composition was most heaven-storming. One pities the audience, the piano and the pianist when the three early sonatas are undertaken, let alone the colossal 1st Concerto. But there is a magnificent bravado to the ambition here that later retreats as if it had singed its hands; and, in the concerto at least, the themes and their deployment are so inspired that I sometimes find myself calling it his greatest work. The 1st Symphony, originating in this period, completed in maturity, still reveals fissures that are not so much healed as evaded in its triumphalist finale. Other pieces athwart the same biographical fault line resolve it with marvellous powers of integration – the Piano Quintet with its struggle to find the right format (the 'interim' two-piano version best realizes the physical weight), and the 3rd Piano Quartet with its turbulent emotional resonances from Goethe's *Werther*.

And, meanwhile, the true Brahms, lyrical and Schubertian rather than Beethovenian and dynamic, had come into being; first in such enormous but non-barn-storming works as the other two piano quartets (though it's true that Schoenberg felt compelled to make his glorious Technicolor orchestration of the first because it was usually played so clumpingly); and then in the long catalogue of instrumental masterpieces, both chamber and (once the first symphony was out of the way) orchestral. And the point about the true Brahms is his ability to subsume the mental power and physical muscle – his heritage from the other two 'great Bs' Bach and Beethoven – into a stream of songfulness learnt from his two adored Schu's (-bert and -mann). Brahms's formidable synthesis of B and B enabled him to achieve what neither Schu had managed – the wholly successful fusion of lyric song and structural argument.

To mention song is to recall that *Lieder* form the largest part of his output (though one wouldn't credit it from the same old handful endlessly repeated in recitals and recordings): as in the precious late harvest of piano miniatures with which he withdrew from the world, Brahms the beardless is revealed in his songs with touching frankness. Sometimes it's direct – there's a song about a girl's rosy cheeks which almost brings a blush to one's own. More characteristic, however, is obliqueness, even evasion, under whose cover he can give voluptuousness, flirtatiousness, or longing and despair, or melancholy acquiescence in disappointment (a sort of written-out detumescence) their various voices.

This music could be called repressed were it not for the juicy *jouissance* of the actual notes. For all his self-abnegation Brahms is almost visible in these densely sonorous yet delicate, elusive, ambiguous intimacies, with or without words. He yields nothing in confessional confidences to those composers who bare their privates in public as a way of life. Yet the mighty brainpower, suitably subtle to work on the smallest scales, is still at work, in play. His treatment of the only high-calibre text in the *Liebeslieder*, its epilogue from Goethe, can crystallize everything. While the four voices sing its long arching lyric phrases, the accompaniment sets up a typically complex waltz *à deux temps* over that most intellectual of devices, a ground-bass, taken straight from the composer's most directly personal work, the *Alto Rhapsody* op. 53, whose text (also by Goethe) begs a merciful dispensation from the Father of Love to the misanthrope lost and alone in the barren wasteland. Never explicitly a self-expressive composer – let alone an autobiographer like Mahler and Strauss – Brahms nonetheless involuntarily lays himself bare with touching frankness. The life *is* the work, the work the life: the following account will attempt to intertwine them into one.

It's worth remembering that the first great composer with a 'Beethoven-problem' (unless one counts the man himself) was Schubert. Brahms's inheritance, via Mendelssohn's relatively lightweight and Schumann's more effortful burden, is intimately bound up with the biographical fault line already mentioned: the key event in his emotional life, when only in his early twenties – the anguish over and powerlessness to assuage Schumann's debility and death; his love and care for the widowed Clara, and anguish and powerlessness to express and fulfil his undoubted love; his reluctance (or perhaps a stronger term) to commit to any other woman or be contentedly 'married to the single life'. Deep disturbance, high aspirations, producing a yield of five masterpieces (one perfect, the others magnificent even in their flaws), with sometimes near-explicit personal content, and many mutations of genre indicative of uncertainty within masterful assurance.

Thus a projected D-minor Symphony of 1854–5 yields material for both the 1st Piano Concerto (1856–9) and the *German Requiem* (1863–7): an earlier try at a piano quartet in C♯-minor (1855–6) only reaches fruition in the completed work – in C-minor – of 1875; a string quintet in F-minor of 1862 is reworked before completion into a sonata for two pianos, before the eventual compromise – strings for lyricism, piano for power – in the Piano Quintet (1864): fifthly and most famous, the long gestation of the 1st Symphony – initial sketching 1862 or earlier still; eventual completion 1876. The greatest music in these great works evinces a nobler aspiration, a higher ambition, a flight nearer the sun, a gauntlet laid down in challenge, that arguably raises them above everything – manifestly more mature, more resolved, more masterly – that follows without birth pangs as the fault line is resolved and the composer settles into acquiescence. Very significant that the mature Brahms avoids Beethoven's other supreme genres except the symphony; no further piano sonatas after 1853; the three string quartets – eventual product of much inhibition – decidedly not of his best.

A smile and a scowl from Brahms's earliest take on his classical inheritance. The smile is delightful – the 1st Serenade (1859–60), originally for nonet à la Beethoven's Septet and Schubert's Octet, then reworked for orchestra. No. 1 is rustic al fresco: drone-bass on open fifth, carefree horn solo, clarinet answers, a tutti gradually emerges and keys begin to radiate. Development surprisingly strenuous, even intellectual, with wide modulations opening up large spaces: a Czech feel – Dvořák must have loved and might have signed it. Further adventures in the recapitulation, which eventually winds down from blazing triumph to a gentle close and a coda ambiguous and fragmentary. Nearly six hundred bars: some serenade! No. 2, a scherzo in D-minor, subdued ancestor of its obstreperous descendant the 2nd Piano Concerto twenty years on, and far more engaging. Again, festive triumph is touched only to be relinquished: a close in a riot of celebration is held in reserve.

Meanwhile no. 3, *adagio non troppo*, is all dulcet tenderness, redolent of early German Romantic woodland-scapes and prophetic of those to come in Mahler: they have Hoffmann and Jean Paul in common. Touches of march, passages of intricate closework, don't break the spell – radiant, heart-on-sleeve: Brahms not yet a bear: unbearded, sweet as a heroine from Walter Scott. No. 4 owes the clearest debt to Haydn and Schubert: a first minuet, demurely feline, encloses a second, Mozartian: then enters early Beethoven for no. 5, a scherzo of lusty exuberance, cheery horn solo over vigorous purposeful bass, hearty and extrovert as an all-male sports pitch. Sets the mood for no. 6, *rondo finale*, its prevailing idea a riding-motion, all physical energy; its second lyrical, wide-eyed and open-armed. Again, as in no. 1, the development is surprisingly intensive, tonally rangy, full of contrasts, surprises, changes of colour and angle. Also as in no. 1, a boil-up then a decline into fragmentation, before, at last, the promised riot, not evaded this time, to close: clear dry-run for the 2nd Symphony's finale in the same key. Otherwise than there, the gaiety and freshness of this serenade (its companion from the same years, though more subdued – its orchestra omits violins – is just as cherishable) are absent from the mature composer.

Lost, too, are the grandeur, vaulting ambition, determined assault upon the sublime, of the 1st Piano Concerto. Here is the aforementioned scowl, as of an angry Jove. First movement *maestoso* – the *mot juste*: powerful aggro in these craggy, jagged themes and ferocious trills: soloist pitted against orchestra, not a hint of *conversation* à la Mozart. Then balm, lamenting consolation, remote shimmering oscillation – plangency and vulnerability, polar opposites to the opening paragraph's menace, now virtually forgotten till a rude reminder, uncouth as a beast scrumpled upon itself, trills bristling. Long decline, diminishing in dynamics and scoring (though retaining *dies irae* trumpets and drums), down to *pianissimo*, into which – at long, at last – the soloist is given a contrasting tone in a noble, tragic-hued Bachian sarabande: so different that, once more, one can forget how the work began. Till it reminds us, more furious than ever. Another sarabande, rich yet sober, serious not solemn – also for soloist initially, then this time taken up, rather than denied, by the orchestra. The textures become delicate, refined and passionate as Chopin: every ounce of energy drains away, castle and its intruder in an enchanted sleep, till . . . Call to order! – tumultuous resumption of Stern Realities, the same constituents re-combined, intensified – the piano's re-entry electrically unexpected, mood-and-texture swings drastically between warmth, fragility, brutality, to end in blustering battle, smashing and battering through to close, in custom-hallowed key, on Judgment Day.

Comforting contrast needed, and found in the following adagio: its intonation is indicated by the words *benedictus qui venit in nomine Domine*, associated with Schumann in his breakdown: they exactly fit the contour of the opening melody. The serenity, religious without piety, is slightly lost in a middle section whose materials seem not to come, unlike any others in the work, from the highest levels of inspiration. But the *rondo finale* is splendid throughout, in energy, size, scope: superb virile themes, Beethoven to the fore (the form is modelled on the finale of his 3rd Piano Concerto), till Mozart takes over for a coda, in the major, of pure *opera buffa*. Before this, the commanding presence of the two B's is already invoked in the first movement: the cadenza – *quasi fantasia* – begins Bachian, then the piano subsides into almost vocal melody in reminiscence of the solo quartet's written-out cadenza in the finale of Beethoven's Choral Symphony, so close as to be explicit. A second cadenza occurs in the *opera buffa* coda; here too the resemblance to the 9th Symphony is unmissable. Bach and Beethoven combine in this wonderful work that, for all its problems, its composer never surpassed: in it he earns his place – the third of 'the three B's'.

The early phase of Brahms's output is generous too in fully achieved music that escapes the biographical fault line altogether. Alongside the complex mutations of the *Requiem*, the D-minor Concerto, the C♯-minor Piano Quartet, the Piano Quintet, the ongoing struggle with the C-minor Symphony, stand such untroubled feasts of abundance as the first two Piano Quartets (G-minor; A-minor) and the 2nd String Sextet: also the monumental *Handel Variations* for piano, and many songs, including his only cycle, equally monumental, *Die schöne Magelone*, fifteen settings of Ludwig Tieck, a fine work, unjustly neglected. Orchestral mastery is reached in the *Haydn Variations* (*St Anthony Chorale*), written first for two pianos, scored with a felicity not encountered since the Serenades and not always after.

First harvest

Thus on to Brahms's first harvest: before its fullest maturation – both of them principally instrumental – intermezzo with voices: complementary works, both from 1869, that reveal the composer's nature in its darker and its lighter aspects. The *Rhapsodie* for contralto solo, male chorus and orchestra, is a personal confession – 'my bridal-song' – and he is purported to have slept with a copy under his pillow, if not between the sheets. It sets three stanzas from Goethe's

Harzreise im Winter, written to comfort a disturbed soul – spiritual brother of the troubled composer and any others who suffer alike. Setting, a barren winter mountain-scape: immediate background of dark meditation – all our ends are predestined: some tear swiftly down the path of joy; but he who is crushed by woes strives in vain to escape his fate – the journey blessed by Fortune is easy, is princely . . . but . . .

And now the stanzas Brahms sets: but who is this who turns aside? His way is lost in the thickets, he leaves no traces, the barren places consume him. Who can heal his smart, when comfort turns to poison, he who from Love's fullness has drunk only Hate? The mocker mocked, the self-adorer spurned by his self, self-consumer of his woes. Father of Love, is there no melody in all your Psalter his ear can hear? Solace his wounded heart with healing music. *Il meurt de soif auprès de la fontaine*: open his blinded vision to the thousand freshets all around the parched spirit in the desert place. Goethe's poem now goes on to open up the scene – give joy to the lusty huntsmen, bless the Solitary till summer's return, light his way through dark, dangerous terrain, raise him into joyous gratitude. Behold the glory of the mountains aloft and ahead. Brahms's setting manages to suggest this glimpse of hope without overdoing it.

Dark brooding scene-setting, shuddering tremolandi over heaving melancholy bass: muted strings rise effortfully, plunging collapse on woodwinds down a diminished seventh: the paragraph suspires in sighs. Pause. The contralto soloist – not quite the protagonist? – asks the question – who is this? – but it *is* herself – Brahms the stripling, unprotected by manly beard. The orchestral introduction recurs exactly under the continuing words – the grasses swallow him, leaving no sign – this time ending in a semicolon; singer suspended over a gaping void, hollow tritone deep below; then her anguished D-minor ninth before cadencing onto dominant. Tonic – C-minor – re-reached for paragraphs of *arioso* – who/what can heal the woeful one, riven by self-hatred and hatred for all mankind: warm ample curves of comfort. Then eking out, momentum suspended, strings vanishing leaving woodwinds as the singer projects evermore-extreme vocal leaps – the fullness of Love, lost in Hatred;

love which hatred has denied. *Arioso* returns, continuing, ampler, curving up into a contour of woe before returning to its opening – same text, same setting though modified and intensified, same extreme vocal intervals to end. Orchestra rounds it off: clear cadence into tonic – every sense – C-major for the entry of the male voices, supporting the female soloist: hymn-like solemnity/serenity in block harmony over plucked accompaniment (cellos pizzicato), evoking the psaltery – David's harp comforting dark-depressed Saul. Beautiful strains, consonant after the preceding tension, though with just a touch of dissonance on *erquikke*/refresh: and just a touch of unction inextricably melded into the intonation, deeply affecting nonetheless. The texture lightens as the contralto begins her pleas, men's voices answering, to open the sufferer's eyes to the myriad streams all around. Her lovely phrase taken up by oboe: as the men close on the thirsting one in the wasteland, violins take it up further, a heart-swelling five bars closing in resumption of the C-major prayer, now fully scored. The plea again, woodwinds led by flute – two bars only: its *words* aren't again heard, only the *erquikke sein Herz*, over and over: first time halting the flow; next time extended and with more internal vocal movement, the pleasure/pain dissonant suspensions lingered over; then, diminishing, just *erquikke*, twice, men only, then a third time joined by the contralto: silence: calm soft broad full-orchestra completing the phrase, giving the imperative verb its subject – *sein ... Hertz*: an Amen-cadence absolutely without unction.

So to the *Rhapsodie*'s exact contemporary and exact complement, the *Liebeslieder* waltzes, for four solo singers and piano four-hands: eighteen in Book I, another fifteen in Book II. But there is a closer connection than sheer antithesis when the closing number is reached, setting Goethe again. The other poems are all German adaptations of folk-dance songs from the Polish, Russian, Hungarian; slight, amorous, slightly silly, wholly delightful: and Brahms has lavished upon this froth some of his most spontaneous invention, and, in the second collection, some of his most winning and unobtrusive cunning.

The waltzes are fun to hear and to play on piano-duet alone

and this medium is quite self-sufficient: but their fullest richness can only be appreciated with the vocal quartet thrown in. Vocal and keyboard layout are varied and resourceful from start to finish, with solos and duets to break up the ensembles. And the verses so untrammelled and frank – Women, oh Women – what joy you bring! If it weren't for Women I would have been a monk! (no. 3): no. 16 more accordant with the facts – Love is a dangerous trap, a deep well: wretched fellow, I fell in, can't see or hear, only think on my joys and bemoan my woes. No need for details – 'all are delect-able': the first book is lighter, the *Neue Liebesliederwalzer* are more intensively worked, with an overall key-scheme, interconnections across some numbers, developments, and some fine-wrought *serioso* counterpoint, though never drying the cornucopia of tunefulness and lilt. So to the *Envoi* for Goethe: Enough, Muses! In vain would you show how pain and pleasure alternate in the loving heart: you cannot heal love's wounds, but your benign care brings our only relief. The first six notes of the vocal line setting *Ist auf deinem Psalter* from the *Rhapsodie* form a two-bar ground bass, heard four times before the harmony begins to move. A fascinating texture – deep ground bass three slow beats per bar; voices, after lovely intro-ductory curve for *primo* pianist, in flowing nine-in-a-bar, second pianist continuous cross-rhythm, faster – eighteen quavers per bar, grouped in six times three, and staccato quasi pizzicato to resemble the actual pizzicato of the cellos in the orchestration of the *Rhap-sodie*'s Hymn. After the introductory curve, the four singers enter as chorus – *Hush!* – then expand in ample arches of mellifluous polyphony modulating over the unchanging ground bass, closing in the return of the piano's opening. Wider modulations do now compel the bass to shift, and the staccato quavers become *legato* and *espressivo*, the voices continuing ample and overlapping in imitation. Climax – quavers stop, then piano ceases, voices swell *a cappella*: return of opening key, the psalter-scoring, the six-note ground bass twice more, the 'choir' curving in gratitude to the kindly Muses and their balsam. Dulcet calm rapture as the ground bass is grounded, the double-tempo *'pizzicato'* gradually easing into *'arco' legato*; tenor solo answered by piano *primo*; soprano solo answered by *primo* out-singing her: domesticity exalted, consecration of the house, *luxe/ calme/volupté*, Viennese version.

Mature harvest

Brahms's maturity yields an ample harvest: middle-aged, Old-Masterly, youthful tensions resolved, lifestyle confirmed: the bulk of the oeuvre, carefully cultivated, nurtured to fruition. Not quite, perhaps, fully fulfilling the enormous potential of what precedes. Haydn, Beethoven, his contemporaries Wagner and Bruckner, deepen, extend, explore, evolve: Brahms fills the moulds – so richly that complaint would be ridiculous though reservation remains. Polemic dismissals – 'a Jewish csárdás-player' (Wagner): the 'melancholy of impotence' – 'he cannot exult' (Nietzsche), the bitter execrations of Wolf, the snide sneers of Shaw – are lost down the stream of time: yet a scintilla remains – the over-warmth, nearly glutinous and syrupy – 'Smharb'; the hint of self-pity alongside the robust stoicism; the tendency by which cerebral power of a high order can become stodgy and muscle-bound; its complement, the cosy cushion. All these characteristics, contradictory yet fused, are variously inherited by his successors, to be sorted, or remain unsolved in their turn – by Elgar, Reger, Schoenberg.

Meanwhile, what a harvest! Once that damn first symphony was behind him (1876) the second followed within a year – the 1st Serenade on a higher plane – and the finale proving that Brahms *can* exult! Its dilute double the Violin Concerto (1878), the symphonic summit of the 3rd Symphony (1883) – perfection; the 4th Symphony (1884–5), three magnificent movements compromised by the jocose galumphing scherzo: in both works, an absorbing motivic integration across the movements making the whole greater than the sum of the parts. The saggy self-indulgence of the 2nd Piano Concerto (1881) a test case, flabby after the burning intensity of the first, saved at the last minute by the wickedly voluptuous Hungarian finale: back to top form in the Double Concerto for Violin and Cello (1887).

Two overtures, one festive and splendid, the other 'tragic' and dull; four smaller works for chorus and orchestra, the Hölderlin/

Schiller/Goethe settings magnificent, the biblical one an embarrassment. The three violin sonatas (1879, 1886, 1888); the two later
piano trios, together with the 1891 rewrite of the first; the two string
quintets, 1882–3 and 1890 – the second intended as a farewell, a
'retirement' until reinvigoration by the beguilements of 'Fräulein
Klarinette'. The aforementioned reservations do apply here and
there – the over-muscular outer movements of the 1st String Quintet,
the ugly textures of the C-minor Piano Trio, the over-strenuous 3rd
Violin Sonata – always alongside mitigations of beauty and distinction. Two chamber-works succeed in every detail on a level of consummate felicity: one dark and turbulent, one all sunshine for all
its rainy origins.

The C-minor Piano Quartet op. 60, with its shadowy references
to Goethe's *Werther* and his fate, is the most fully achieved fruit
of Brahms's biographical fault line, going back to the troubled
1850s, when it was in C♯-minor: resolved now, a semitone lower,
and uncompromisingly tragic – no triumphant finale: perhaps with
the 3rd Symphony its composer's most perfectly integrated work.
The first movement is remarkably ingenious: the second subject of
a sonata exposition is a set of variations; the development another,
on first-subject material; the recapitulation resumes and resolves the
dichotomy with ever-varied textures and temperatures, from passionate and vehement and complex to gracious, pellucid euphony;
one of the most intricate sonata-movements ever written; and on
tip-top material. The scherzo, also C-minor: a pell-mell whirl, angry
and aggressive. No mitigating lyrical trio: the scherzo – no joke –
repeated exact till, where the first time the turbulence had momentarily abated, the assault is upped – all strings in three-octave unison,
piano pounding the harmony, to a blazing close in the tonic major.

Balm in the heavenly andante that follows – in E-major. The bold
key-contrast would have been natural enough in the work's original
C♯-minor: just as telling in its final context. Endless melody, long-
breathed (though it can be broken down into distinct clauses and
phrases, all beautifully articulated). And amorous – celestial salon-
music euphonious even when encountering melting suspensions
and tingling dissonances: ends upon one of the most perfect perfect

cadences imaginable. Back to C-minor for magnificent sonata-finale, one of the few that resolve the 'finale problem' – what can follow? – with abiding conviction and rightness, retaining the calibre of what precedes and bringing it to consummation. Surging energy un-enforced, passion unrestrained, till quietening into a chorale *without* religiose tincture. Development, all cloudy ambiguities, drifting modulations, mysterious journeys, until the chorale's return; it now does wax rather 'Victorian' – choir and organ, though maybe a hint of tongue-in-cheek – and anyway forgotten in the sinister disintegra-tion that ends the movement and the work. Their crashing C-major tutti call for the word so often misapplied as to lose its meaning – tragic *irony*. Would one could say the same of the triumphant C-major close of the C-minor Symphony.

A complete complement in the romantic-bucolic comedy of the 1st Violin Sonata. Brahms's inheritance from Schubert in taking one of his songs as basis for a purely instrumental piece is here realized to perfection: the violin's first phrase begins with the repeated two notes, a slight catch-of-breath between, a lilting lisp, that opens his *Regenlied* ('Rain Song') op. 59: in the sonata it pervades the first movement, is transformed almost unnoticed in the middle, then comes to the fore in the finale.

The first movement is all ease and flow: graceful curves of melody, soon expanding into effortless cross-rhythms capable of great com-plexity across the bar-lines, yet natural as flying. Textures come and go (not so good when the violin's pizzicato has to emulate a guitar); tensions mount and are surmounted, prior events return, reinter-preted, contradictions are resolved, all is serene and euphonious. The second movement introduces songful new material on a horn-call motif, growing plangent, then martial, even severe: the *Regenlied* source subtly subliminal throughout, to emerge direct in the finale, beginning as a virtual transcription of the song though omitting its rather clunky opening bars and its contrasting second stanza. Rain-patterns persist almost unbroken until the rondo's first episode, introducing the theme from the andante, soon transporting it to pastures new. A variation-set, miniature as that in the Piano Quartet's is extensive – eight brief entries, the basic shape always recognizable in all its transformations. Rain resumes, hesitant flurries, vagrant modulations, till the return of the opening – not in full: cunningly compressed, with new twists and turns gently winding down in warm sweetness: a sense of epilogue, to the movement itself, to the work as a whole, merging its contrasted materials into compatibility. Sense now of the epilogue to the epilogue, slowing still further, swelling from *piano* to *forte* in ample contour, to close in a IV–I cadence – the great A-men without a hint of blandness or unction. Brahms's most contented work? *La vie en rose*; it might be Fauré.

Late harvest

'Retirement'; revivification; retrospect; summa; farewell. The marvellous vitality of the 1890 2nd String Quintet that had his friends exclaiming 'Brahms writes like a man of thirty' was intended to say goodbye to composing. The artistry of the clarinettist Richard Mühlfeld reversed this premature impulse, yielding four further chamber-works – the Clarinet Trio (with piano and cello) and Clarinet Quintet, both 1891, and the two clarinet sonatas (1894). A late harvest of solo piano miniatures had been prophesied by the Eight Pieces op. 76 back in the 1870s: in the 1890s come four collections, opp. 116–119, comprising twenty items in all. House-in-order: fifty-one exercises for piano published 1893; seven volumes of *Deutsche Volkslieder* – forty-nine German folksongs – published 1894: summa – *Four Serious Songs* on biblical texts (1896): farewell – eleven chorale-preludes for organ, also 1896 though some probably composed earlier.

The Clarinet Trio in A-minor can epitomize this late idiom: dark warm coloration – 'autumnal'; material familiar yet newly angled; concentrated and compressed with Old-Master experience: less lovable than the Clarinet Quintet, and just as fine.

First movement densely wrought and complex, richly 'orchestrated' though never thick, even when exploiting double-stopping on the cello and the clarinet's deepest chalumeau – its lowest note C♯ conveniently the major third of the home key: a dark-hued palette with moments of sunny radiance. The second surpasses it in velvety

ardour: here the concentration of Brahms's late style is positively
elliptical; what formerly required expansiveness here compressed
into nuggets of intensity, always lyrical – expression embodied in
high specific gravity, suppressed eroticism fuelling the sonority from
within. The work's second half, an intermezzo marked *andantino
grazioso*, a lively finale with Hungarian flavouring, makes a composite, balancing the first half's weight – simplicity and openness after
involution. The *andantino* demure, playful, songful, dancing: here
and there it comes so close to the *miaou*-figure in Fauré's *Kitty-Valse*
as to suggest that 'Fräulein Klarinette' (Brahms's sobriquet for the
player who inspired all four pieces) is a teasing feline. But nothing
could be more Austrian than the rustic *Ländler* within the waltz/
Valse.

The finale's vigour can occasionally grow stormy: at one point it
alludes unmistakably to the 4th Symphony's chains of descending
thirds, before coming to a robust close. As a whole the work's trajectory moves from strong and intricate, via intimate and amorous,
to delicious flirtatiousness, then sturdy heartiness: its unmistakable
unity fuses opposites, even contrarieties.

Last thoughts

The late piano-pieces explore such places, singly and deeper. The
four collections – opp. 116–119 – perhaps intended to be played item-
by-item though each opus makes a satisfying whole. This is complex
music, equally in its technical facture, subtler and more compressed
than ever; in its harmonic/melodic/motivic intensiveness; and in its
range of *Affekt*, sometimes so inward-turned and secretive as to seem
furtive, morbid, kinky, and sometimes abandoning concealment in
unabashed frankness of utterance. This is the Brahms of eager acquiescence in Max Klinger's fascinatingly dreadful etchings inspired
by his music; of ardent youthful Romanticism via Schumann out
of Hoffmann and Jean Paul, gone rancid, overripe; weird beyond
the dreams of the French, Belgian or Nordic *fin de siècle*, overlapping with the more extreme shores of German and Viennese expressionism; the Brahms who is deathwards turned with a purpose as

undeviating as Tristan's wildest ravings; the Brahms who renounced the joys of Eros and Agape as well as the consolations of religion.

There are twenty little pieces in all; three titled *Capriccio*, fourteen *Intermezzo*, and a single *Ballade, Romanza, Rhapsodie*. It is fair to say that the less extrovert, the more inward-turned, the better the music: the *Rhapsodie*, last of all, is a crasher: so is the *Ballade*, and some of the *Intermezzi* (op. 116) nos. i, ii, iii; op. 118/i). The remaining fourteen pieces are dark pearls of dense-wrought introspection and consummate/cunning mastery: Brahms the miniaturist, joining hands across the centuries with the Bach of the *Orgelbüchlein*, and across the pavements of Vienna with Wolf's *Italian Songbook*, exactly contemporary.

Most nascent piano-learners encounter op. 117/i, the lovely lullaby inspired by Scots balladry – 'Balou my boy, lie down and sleep / It grieves me sore to see thee weep' – whose rhythm it preserves. This *intermezzo* makes the perfect introduction to these late works, simple yet suggestive: outer section with the melody contained within the cradling descant, flowering into liquid decoration on its return till briefly admitted to the top part, the whole exquisitely spaced, sonorous yet full of air; and the middle section introducing the late works' darker side, ambiguous and elliptical. Op. 117/iii is also Scots-inspired – after a German version of 'O Waly, Waly' – also an a–b–a form but more complex and varied – almost a miniature variation-set: a subdued searching unison; again, lightly harmonized; answering continuation in unison; again, up an octave, harmonized with syncopation: first strain, on inner part, more amply scored, twice; second strain, unison then with syncopated harmony, exactly as before. Middle section, magical transparent opening-up of keyboard resonances high and low after the middle-close register so far – ghost of melody, implicit not actual, within the melting figuration and pungently clashing false-relation dissonances suggestive of a further role for *Fräulein Klarinette*. The opening section's return oblique in very soft, very dense three and three bars reproducing – perhaps unconsciously – a special place in the andante of Schubert's last piano sonata – as introduction to opening theme on inner voice, contour identical but harmony re-angled; then again,

as before exactly; the answering unison and its repeat with syncopated harmony, again exact; coda, broadening out the first theme
and bringing it to rest.

Several other beauties with the same mix of subtlety, delicacy,
warmth, ingenuity: op. 119/ii, another compressed variation-set,
putting its shy stammering little idea through a range of keys and
textures before, for the middle eight, transforming it into a waltz as
delectable as any in the *Liebeslieder*: once in a while, volatility and
legerity – op. 119/iii, as fleet and airborne as what follows (the aforesaid *Rhapsodie*), is for most of its length fat and galumphing: op.
118/v a study in repression – every up-beat a six-note chord, every
down-beat only two notes; op. 118/iv, an extraordinarily ingenious
and fugitive canon, initially just across the two hands, later in four
implied parts with rhythmic displacements and harmonic slithers,
almost Escher-like in double-meaning.

None of these call for the words 'morbid', 'decadent', 'psychopathological', nor bring Krafft-Ebing to mind, let alone Freud. Here
are three that do. Op. 117/i: Bb-minor: no melody; rather, its vestige
in broken contour amidst delicate figuration occasionally plunging
deep into the keyboard – a pedal-effect impossible to imagine
orchestrated: contrast, sweetly harped chordal luminosity, with its
own contrast, a dark passage of sinuous, serpentine chromaticism.
The opening returns in bare octaves, then figuration between the
hands in chromatic contrary motion – left rising, right falling –
coalescing in exchange of soft acrid dissonances and a weary smear
of iridescence before resumption in full, taking new turns, up to a
climax, down to the chordal contrast, now effaced not luminous,
and broadening over a long dominant pedal with a semitonal limp,
più adagio, to reach a broad cadence.

Op. 119/i: B-minor: a haunting, crepuscular study in stacked
thirds; again only the shadow of a melody, held at the top line of
each bar, with touches of canon below now and then. Duskiness
grows more glowing in contrasting lyricism, still essentially athematic, rising to plangent climax, descending *Tristan*-esque, rising
again to rhyme with first climax, this time interrupted, broken off
into yearning gestures rapidly sinking bass-wards. The stacked thirds

move upwards in thick superimpositions, then thin to re-reach the opening – as before, but decorated with inner-part triplets: coda – an epitome: semi-staccato after the choked sostenuto; gapped after the unbroken flow; half-spoken, eloquent in understatement, *piano* then *più piano*, till cadence from the densest-yet stack of thirds – a dominant eleventh.

It's not inadvertent that corporeal and emotive imagery comes so naturally, trying to evoke this music: breathe, choke; feel, touch; sigh, yearn. Such imagery extends inevitably into the sexual, thence psychosexual, then psychopathological, in op. 118/vi. Eb-minor; general indication *andante*, *largo e mesto*: particular instructions within the first few bars *p sotto voce*, *perdendo*, *pp una corda*. A doleful little doodle on only three notes, unharmonized till the left hand creeps in from miles below on dusky diminished sevenths in arpeggio – up, down (*perdendo*): r. h. resumes the doleful circular figure an octave lower; this time the l. h. arpeggiates from its start, outlining a descending bass: r. h. up the octave again, the figure now doubled in thirds with bitter-sweet chromaticisms, and the lower octave overlaps them. Overlaps continue, with aching suspensions, exchanged between both hands, rising and rising, the deep bass touched in intermittent lightness, caught by the pedal; suspensions descend; back to opening phrase, now dominant minor and darkly doubled two octaves apart, with its own dominant fifth held as tolling pedal. Dominant seventh without its comforting major third returns to Eb-minor and the opening: doleful obsessive phrase in upper octave, now joined as it closes by slithery creeping left hand, opening into dissonant arpeggios under the phrase's repeat at lower octave: then the continuation in thirds, its overlap, and their superimposition up-up-down, and closing into darkly doubled dominant, exactly as before.

This time it slides into Gb-major for the middle-eight: a choked muffled march (albeit in triple time) – initially *sotto voce* but rising to *forte*, then *fortissimo*, *più forte*, *fortissimo crescendo*, to a terrific double *sforzando* that Tchaikovsky or Mahler would certainly have marked *fff*, for all that it collapses in two bars to *p* then *pp*. The nature of this march is equally volatile: initially stealthy, wary, circumspect;

the first phrase ends on bare trumpet-and-drums tattoo, continued in the second, now building to the first *forte*: the third continues upward modulations and dynamics and registers till the first *fortissimo* – return of the piece's opening motif – the three-note doodle – at same pitch, now fully harmonized as dominant ninth on F, thence on Bb, to cadence in Eb-minor, and 'scored' with maximum weight and force. March resumes, compressed, modulating, growing in volume till second *fortissimo* and thence biggest climax of all, the convulsive *sff* (*fff*), again on the opening three-note motif at opening pitch, harmonized this time as dominant on Ab – two-bars' worth, unmissably directed at a cadence on Db. But this note isn't one of the opening's three-note circle, and it is absolutely denied the place it's screaming out for, either in motivic contour or in tonal resolution.

Instead, a detumescence: Eb-minor, soft, the obsessive circular motif, the crepuscular diminished sevenths, return – cold coming – at the lower octave; answered with exquisite sublimation by the continuation, formerly in thirds, now opened initially into sixths before reverting to thirds, the dissonant suspension-overlaps now more meltingly, piercingly silver-sweet still, curling up in fascinating two-part sinuousness (C# against Cb!) to decline to low, dark return of opening three-note figure, doubled now in three octaves, in home key, with dominant pedal. As it closes, the register ascends in a broad hemiola, harmonically neutral, to reach the phrase's original tessitura: but here, fully scored, doubled by left hand two octaves lower, then in three octaves as the right adds 'registration'; and fully harmonized, swelling over its first two bars from *pp* to, on its third bar, another *sff*: broad hemiola, diminuendo, as the piece reaches home, home harmony deprived of its bass tonic till the soft slow Eb-minor arpeggio sustained by the pedal to resonate under its top note, the solitary Eb of the concluding bar.

Consummate concentration in almost all of these late fruits – a lifetime's experience, knowledge, craft, distilled; every note thematic, choked intensity, powers thwarted to let loose equally with desires acted upon or unacted; purple silk-damask shot through with eroticism the more compelling for being so oblique and metaphorical:

the proximity of Klinger and Sacher-Masoch behind, Klimt, Schiele and Schoenberg to come, only adds to the allure.

So to an area of pastoral, fresh and unsullied by undercurrents of the *fin de siècle*. Brahms's life-long involvement with German folksong also comes into consummatory focus during his final years.

'Put thy house in order'; 'be someone on whom nothing is wasted'; or, as Brahms put it himself, 'the serpent eats his own tail'. German folksong was a lifetime's preoccupation – from 1858 come twenty-eight *Deutsche Volkslieder* and fourteen *Volks-Kinderlieder*; from 1894 the gathered-in harvest of the years between: seven books of further settings. Volumes 1 to 6 for voice and piano, vol. 7 with chorus. To hear them though is a revelation: love of your own country's folksong is generally associated only with obvious nationalism, or else late-Romantic and early-modern nostalgia for simpler times. While Brahms's attitude is clearly nostalgic, his actual use of such materials is more akin to the former. German folksong proves fundamental to his musical language at large – a stimulus, both as profound quickener of feeling and as source of motif and contour; a compositional norm to which his own *Lieder* are directly related and, from them, the endless wealth of themes more-or-less folk-like in the orchestral and chamber-works. These manifest an extraordinary fusion of lyrical and analytical powers; I have tried to show how he subjects his material to the most far-reaching motivic treatment, while always retaining a strong sense of its melodic origin and continuing melodic presence, often with something of almost vocal immediacy. Through all its complex and subtle metamorphoses, the primal melodic contour is always palpable in a facture of cunningly organized overlapping phrase-structure, whose simple source lies in German folksong.

The actual arrangements are perfect instances of art conceal-ing art. It seems at first that anyone could have made them, and one must hear other folksong settings to realize how good Brahms is at this possibly humdrum but surprisingly tricky task. He elects for the opposite of a personal interpretation, as found so success-fully in the Britten folksong arrangements; there, we are touched by the personal involvement and delighted by the cleverness of the treatment: our pleasure and admiration are directly akin to our feeling for Britten's own original composition. What is Brahmsian in Brahms's settings comes only slowly to light: behind the scrupulous abnegation, the tenderness of the involvement, as well as the simple rightness of harmony, texture, extent of variation or (more often) of non-variation, reveals mastery and affection in equal measure. The songs do not receive a personal interpretation even where his known feelings are expressed, because he has identified his own self-expression so fully with the folk-material that it becomes his expression too. Hearing his voluminous folksong arrangements gives a clue to that sense of fulfilment that glows from all his oeuvre in spite of personal melancholy – rounded homogeneity, a relationship of goal and source, a gather-in of every thread and scrap into a fully uttered whole, a triumphant reconciliation of heart and mind.

The man and the music

Brahms is all one; from the fiery youth convinced that even to conceive, let alone write such a piece as Bach's D-minor Chaconne would drive him mad with 'extreme excitement and emotional tension', to the early-old man who could pen such a thing as the Eb-minor *Intermezzo* from op. 118, at once so unabashed and so shameless in the unguardedness of its psychological and physiological self-portrait. His entire oeuvre offers such points of entry. Behind the impersonal lies confession, just as his angelic young face lay behind his shapeless and aggressive beard. His music is as charged with implicit meanings, private but scarcely hidden, as Wagner's is with explicit meanings, brazenly trumpeted forth.

The direct influence of both sides in the great nineteenth-century divide in German music was pretty disastrous. Only Dvořák and Elgar benefit directly, to palpable advantage. Otherwise, the dead hand of Brahms produces stodgy academic corpses in symphonies and chamber-music as surely as the dead hand of Wagner produces the wreckage of hapless music-drama. These great composers need to be transformed utterly for their implications to become fruitful – the seminal presence of Wagner in Debussy's *Pelléas* a perfect example.

Even when the succession is within the same musical culture, the original must be subverted as well as revered. 'Brahms the Progressive', as described by Schoenberg and manifested throughout his work in all its phases, is a transformation as well as a continuity.

But the Wagner/Brahms polarized polemic is a factitious affair – historically/aesthetically/stylistically significant, of course; but not rich in *content* the way that such suggestive ahistorical twinnings as Wagner/Verdi or Wagner/Tchaikovsky are: mere ideology – no illumination by way of mutual definition. The complement with Brahms that suggests such richness is with Bruckner.

A note on Johann Strauss

But first, a waltz-divertimento – a cameo for Johann Strauss II: a master of popular art at the highest level, endlessly fertile within the strict confines of his dance-forms; principally the waltz, in its Viennese version, with Schubert in the background, then Joseph Lanner and his own father, Johann Strauss I: functional music to move to, though in the end good enough to be listened to; developed into suites and chains of contrasting numbers, quite extensive, and introduced by poetic preluding of high imaginative calibre – those to the *Blue Danube* and the *Emperor Waltz* outstanding – before being exalted into opera and symphony by his admiring peers and juniors.

Johann Strauss is a mediator: every musician, whatever their polemical differences, agrees to admire and to love his art and craft. When no one could or would play the 'crazy' *Tristan* prelude in Vienna, Strauss – so the story goes – put it on with his band, without accidentals (it is in a sort of sublimated *valse*-rhythm after all). The *Ländler*-waltz element in *The Flying Dutchman* – the sailors on board and the girls on shore in Act III; in the *Ring* – Mime 'deceiving' Siegfried; in *Meistersinger*, the apprentices' dance; in *Parsifal*, the Flower-maidens: all this shows that the lesson of the master was not lost on the Meister. With Brahms, waltzes prevail throughout the oeuvre – direct as in the *Liebeslieder* and the waltz-set for solo piano; indirect as in many – most – of the chamber-music; sublimated as in the

Requiem, the 4th Symphony's chaconne-finale, the last of the biblical songs. He once copied out the opening of the *Blue Danube* into an autograph book, superscribing his signature with 'would that he had composed this'. Mahler's music is waltz-saturated, from early songs through the symphonies to the 9th and 10th. Strauss (Richard) is *besotted*, unable to keep waltzes out even of *Elektra* let alone where they are germane – *Rosenkavalier, Intermezzo, Arabella* : in his version even Nietzsche's Superman ends up waltzing – perhaps it was this extreme incongruity that occasioned the well-known *bon mot* 'if Richard, then Wagner; if Strauss, then Johann'. So to the 'Second Viennese School' with their loving transcriptions of the full orchestral waltzes for small ensembles to grace their charity-concerts: let alone the huge waltz-component of Berg's *Three Orchestral Pieces* and *Wozzeck*, and the last of Schoenberg's *Five Orchestral Pieces*, a sort of celestialized transcendental Swedenborgian *Invitation to the Dance*.

Bruckner/Brahms nexus

Comparisons/contrasts/complements, to distinguish and define:

- Near contemporaries; Bruckner born 1824, Brahms 1833; fellow Viennese (Brahms, north German by birth, settled permanently in Vienna from 1869).
- Neighbours and uneasy 'rivals' in the same close-knit culture; Bruckner dies 1896, Brahms attends his funeral and is dead within the next half-year (April 1897).
- Bruckner a fervent unwavering Catholic with rock-like peasant faith, dedicating the 9th Symphony to 'der liebe Gott'. Brahms a stoic Protestant agnostic: Gott not mentioned in any religious work, nor any article of belief beyond generalities, though he was soaked in the Bible, Old and New Testaments, all the way to his very last work: the Biblical Songs. Bruckner composes Masses, motets, a *Te Deum*, a 150th Psalm: Brahms composes 'secular' choral-and-orchestral works of profound, searching thoughtfulness,

from the *German Requiem* (eschewing the Liturgy: it is a personal florilège of biblical texts) to the smaller pieces for choir and orchestra setting Goethe, Schiller, Hölderlin.

- Sad story of their respective amorous/erotic/sexual hankerings: Brahms yearns and renounces, with the one central relationship withheld; Bruckner embarrassingly entangled with a succession of chambermaids, and has to be rescued again and again by his friends.

- Bruckner a celebrated virtuoso organist, though no important compositions for his instrument: Brahms a could-be career pianist, clearly formidable in his prime, but not taking that path: important piano oeuvre from very start to near the finish.

- Bruckner just the one chamber-work, admittedly superb – a string quintet: Brahms's are central, copious, high calibre – three piano quartets and three piano trios, seven duo-sonatas, horn trio and clarinet trio, two each of string quintets and string sextets, a clarinet quintet, and the three admittedly not-so-great string quartets (he claimed to have destroyed many others).

- Opera absolutely unimaginable for either: the mind boggles! Brahms's *Rinaldo* – a concert cantata – proves the point.

- *Lieder*: Bruckner none; Brahms copious from start to finish – songs form the largest item in his output, and he is soaked in literature, especially poetry, whereas one imagines that Bruckner could scarcely read.

- But *musical* learning common to both: Bruckner's obsessively thorough training in all possible skills and techniques, Brahms's scholarly interest in the past, evidenced by his eager anticipation and absorption of every new volume of the complete Bach edition as it came out. Bruckner appears not such an eager Bachian: his archaism is older, running back through traditional church-idioms to Palestrina and thence earlier still.

- Symphonies: Brahms cast as upholder and continuation of classical goals, with Mendelssohn and Schumann added

to the Haydn/Mozart/Beethoven line. Bruckner cast as the
symphonist needed by the Wagnerians – mighty constructions without programme let alone words, but open to the
size, orchestral sonority, formal openness of symphonic
poem and music-drama. Equally, behind both lie Beethoven
and Schubert: Brahms and Bruckner continue from, diverge
from, reinterpret, realize further, fulfil their dual symphonic
heritage in contrasting, complementary, discrepant ways.
Brahms's four come amid plentiful other genres: Bruckner's
nine (eleven, if No. o and No. –1 are included) form the
backbone and body of his oeuvre.

What is the 'idea' of the Symphony – especially sonata first movements, their processes and techniques; their means; and hence
their ends – for each composer? Bruckner's 8th, his last fully-
completed (1884–90) could be placed alongside Brahms's 3rd (1883)
and 4th (1884–5) as basis of comparison: *not* competition, so much
as an attempt to define by differentiation the conception and the
workings whereby these contemporaries, neighbours, formed from
the same musical ancestry, achieve such divergent, fruitful results in
the epoch's most important instrumental genre.

Bruckner

Anton Bruckner, born 1824; early music experience in rural Austria
centred upon the monastery of St Florian, becoming its organist
1845. Immediate musical background, *a cappella* church-music –
severe and chaste, or with orchestra, florid and baroque in the line of
Haydn's Masses: his third setting, the *Mass in E-minor* (1866), gets the
two sources together – wind-band, no strings, and an individual recreation in nineteenth-century idioms of Palestrina. But unlike every
other nineteenth-century Austro-German composer from Mendelssohn onwards, not J. S. Bach-centred, though certainly not ignorant
of him. From 1855 cathedral organist at Linz: from 1868 Professor of
Harmony at the Vienna Conservatory. He remained in Vienna for

the remainder of his life; trips abroad as organist; visits to Bayreuth as avid enthusiast for Wagner. Died 1896.

Symphonies 1–4

Eager insatiable appetite for learning, avid submission to strict repressive disciplines in harmony, melody, counterpoint. Piquant that his master in all this was Simon Sechter, who'd briefly coached Schubert in his last-gasp desire for contrapuntal training. Sechter also taught 'form' and 'orchestration': Bruckner's earliest symphonic efforts were written under his guidance – the Overture (i.e. sonata first movement) in G-minor; F-minor student symphony (1863); thence the 'Nullte' (i.e. nought) in D-minor (1864); and breaking free in Nos. 1 and 2 (1865–72). There's lots of life, character, quality here – No. 0 should certainly be in the canon; and some prototypes established that will last him to the end. Numerous rewrites of these works and most of those that follow – a tangled tale.

No. 3 is a crunch and a crisis. Two gigantic influences on this D-minor symphony, second of three in this loaded key (No. 0 and No. 9 also); Beethoven's last, inescapable: and the huge impact of Wagner, its dedicatee. Endless revisions – the first, 1871 version full of quotations from the Meister, later mostly deleted: in the end no one version is quite right of this problem-work, ambitious and unlovable: a breakthrough, but also a bore (though with marvel- lous things), and in this respect comparable with Brahms's 1st; after confronting their Beethovenian dragons, the gates open upon free access to what is exactly appropriate for what follows – in Bruckner's case, his right scale, type of material, textures and procedures for the facture of the mature Brucknerian symphony. Which also involves his astonishing affinity with the large-scale Schubert, whether of symphony or chamber-work, most particularly the three enormous C-major works of the mid-1820s – Symphony, *Grand Duo* for piano- duet, *'Reliquie'* Sonata (unfinished) for solo piano, that Bruckner couldn't possibly have known – though there's the tempting tale of his playing as a young man some then-unpublished Schubert four- hand works with an old lady who'd played them as a girl with their composer himself. Sadly, this proves to be mythical: it *ought* to be true, but the remarkable compatibilities between the two genuine Austrians are an Elective Affinity, not an Historical Fact.

Bruckner's 4th Symphony (1874–8) is also a problem. 'Four is a bore' – it's incomprehensible that this 'Romantic' symphony is its composer's most popular. Except for the wonderful opening, it's his least distinguished, as it now stands. The original version, virtually unknown, is something else: unpublished and unperformed in his lifetime (first publication 1975) it treats the same material better throughout when the material is common to both versions: the scherzo and trio are quite different, and superior: and the finale is daring beyond belief – fantastic boldness of its perpetuum mobile in quintuplets – Bruckner reaching out to Janáček and Stravinsky: if it could have been heard when it was written . . . but, it wasn't. Finales are his Achilles heel in every subsequent symphony but one.

Symphonies 5–9

Bruckner is now on course for five further symphonies. The exception is in 1878 – the String Quintet, a glorious work with obvious problems of texture and stamina, crying out for a full orchestration – except for the stretches where it sounds so well on the five string-instruments.

The 5th Symphony (1875–6) is the vindication of all the laborious years of training on Sechter-principles: they flower in a superb display of polyphonic prowess, culminating with his only completely successful and convincing finale, a succession of fugues crowned with a chorale. Convincing and successful too in its experiments with internal integration – the transformations across the movements, scherzo's material formed of the preceding adagio's, the whole-scale transference of material from the first movement to the last, wherein it finds resolution and fulfilment. But the first movement also contains some really dumb stuff – hostage to the hostile. The 6th Symphony (1879–81) is Bruckner's Cinderella: its adagio is his noblest yet, and the coda to its first movement is unsurpassed by anything later until the 9th; a wonderful ocean of pulsating pattern, athematic, almost minimalist, moving through a shifting iridescent rainbow of keys – Wagner on acid. Many fine things elsewhere, but the finale lets it down – Cinderella needs her Prince, both to champion the work and to save it from itself. The same goes for the 7th (1881–3): the golden lyrical breadths and depths of its first movement sweep all before them; as, too, the scherzo, a propulsive streamlined steam-train. The adagio pays tribute to two of Bruckner's three princi-pal influences: its double-variation scheme, alternating very slow, sonorous, noble (also incorporating the *non confundar in aeternum* from his own *Te Deum*, used to make the magnificent climax) with a more flowing lyric melody for contrast, is borrowed directly from the adagio of Beethoven's 9th: the coda was added, or adapted, on hearing the news of Wagner's death – an unforgettable solemn salute that requires no specific quotation from his hero's works. (The third principal influence, Schubert, is by now so integral to Bruckner's forms and procedures as to transcend mere resemblance.) But after these three perfect movements, the finale is so runtish as to be almost ridiculous; its unwontedly frisky opening stretch is delightful – would that it carried through to what ensues . . .

The vicissitudes of the 8th Symphony show that this apparent *naïf* is, after all, extremely conscious of what he is doing: Bruckner's obsequious rewrite of the first movement after its initial rejection turns something already so strong and confident into something supreme of its kind – though if we didn't know of the rewritten version and had only the original, we'd scarcely be able to fault it: beneath an outward diffidence veering often to crippling self-doubt, lies a total confidence in his own language, technique, structure, even as they grow ever-more bold, making him one of the most original composers who ever lived. Yet this first movement is also his most 'classical', the fulfilment and vindication of the new impulses brought to the symphony by Schubert, fused with the heritage from Haydn and Beethoven. Every constituent is present in its first version; the revision takes all the same material, in much the same order, and shakes it up as in some gigantic mixer, to produce a result uncannily identical but different, a mutation, that would be a traducement were it not so right. '*Un*justified criticism', although vindicated by the upshot. Bruckner doesn't 'develop': he juxtaposes his elements across a tonal/spatial terrain of enormous extent: as if a gigantic kaleidoscope were shaken to realign the unchanging constituents in ever-new figurations, or a mosaic were constructed where, instead of postage-stamp-sized marble bits, great chunks of rock are the medium's means.

A blow-by-blow account could describe and account for every detail in the architectural journey: it surely speaks for itself – juxtapositions and superimpositions, textures sometimes triumphal, sometimes grinding; or their opposite, unstable, feeble, drained-out, skeletal. The moment of recapitulation, unmistakable *bei* Brahms, is in Bruckner secret, almost unnoticed – missable. It culminates in an infernal machine from which there's no way to escape. Dead awed silence. The drums resume the roll, still on tonic C, now very soft and separated by silences though the pulse is still felt. Coda: main theme twice on strings, soft, ♭-oriented, very dissonantly harmonized but closing on a brief C-major; answered by solo clarinet and soft drum-roll: again, third time, harmony now omitted till end of the phrase, its most dissonant chord, sustained as the theme disintegrates between first violins and clarinet, till settling for long-held C-major *ppp*, violins exchanging fragments of theme, drum-rolls shorter: four bars of this. Then the sustained major tonic is relinquished – bare tonic and dominant fifth, not even a minor third – four bars; four more, the drum's beat without roll, the strings pizzicato save viola's muttering semitonal descent down to their bottom string, all that survives of thematic matter. The last bar, which might have been the first of another four – eight – sixteen, is indeed terminal; the machine stops.

No question that this bleak, remorseless end is truer than the first version's blaze of C-major glory. The composer had done that before, notably in his 7th: the tragic intensity of the revised 8th's first movement extends his vision. Otherwise its original composition would seem unimprovable, except that what he then did with it is greater still. (Compare Brahms's so-called 'Tragic' Overture: comfort and ease all the way! *His* tragic vision is expressed in the C-minor Piano Quartet.)

The second movement, *scherzo*: a propulsive engine of extrovert energy. After an introductory two bars the one-bar ostinato sets in, topped by feathery momentum on violins – a sturdy shape; persisting, present or implied, for the entire outer sections of the movement, in and out of many changes of key, and with instrumentation ranging from muttered flutterings to brazen brilliance. The trio brings out Bruckner's Schubert-strain – Schubert's harmonic fluidity, not his melodic fecundity: a tender, graceful four-bar figure on strings; Ab-major, already characteristically tinged with chromaticism in the melody of its first bar, in the harmony of the next two; and the answering phrase is already in Cb-major. So it goes on – enharmonic shine, every two bars somewhere different, modulation made sensuously palpable, brightness visible, crowned at its apex with fanfare on all three trumpets, relaxing into angelic afterglow, horns in dulcet duo, and harp arpeggios – this and the next movement the only appearance of harps in all Bruckner's work. Second half yet sweeter and more tender – an almost pleading quality on the strings' beginning, but answered by horn-quartet in robust rustic mode: return to opening, curtailed and taking evershifting new harmonic turns, the harp joining at the peak, E-major. Sudden *pianissimo* for the returning horn-duo in Ab, this time succeeded by an extra four bars where they underpin a flute solo straight out of Youth's Magic Horn. Scherzo repeated, exact, in full.

The following adagio deserves fuller description. As with the first movement the consequences of the initial paragraph unfold gradually, stage by stage fulfilling their potential, by long continuities or sudden contrasts, with episodes that might at first acquaintance seem inorganic, all making for the long-withheld goal, a huge slow build-up on the return of the main theme to reach, at heavenly length, its crowning consummation. It comes in successive waves, but a background of sextuplet semiquavers is unbroken all the way. First wave, main theme on second violins, harmonized by winds, the firsts in answering descant, both over the initial throbbing pulsation on cellos. When the new single-note motif begins to heave, richer brass support the intensifying harmonic movement and the descant grows more pressing. Second wave begins *fortissimo*, then *pianissimo crescendo*, on the ecclesiastical ascent, the sextuplet figuration – now busy not neutral – on upper strings. In the third and fourth bars, a clear annunciation of an actual Wagner quotation, Siegfried's motif on his own instrument, the horn, though using all four for sonority – first time, not fully defined, second time unmistakable, third time climactic – busy figuration on all the strings four octaves deep, opening theme over drum-roll on all the brass save for the four horns, now in answer on fanfare-shape without outlining the hero. Third wave a wonderfully beautiful ten bars of lyric remission (sometimes unforgivably cut, from scores and performances, the initial damage alas sanctioned by the composer himself); back to *pianissimo*, throb/pulse renewed, phrases from opening pages, twice, with overlapping echoes from woodwinds, clarinet ascending, flute then oboe descending, first violins taking over the figuration high and low; third repetition gives the moving half of main theme only, twice; fourth repetition augments it to cover a whole four bars, declining from *forte* to *pianissimo*.

The fourth wave crashes in on tutti orchestra, just two bars and the next downbeat: pulsation up high on woodwinds, all strings on figuration, reverting to powerful after its floating quality in the preceding lyric oasis; backdrop to Proclamation, magnificent on three trumpets, taken over by woodwinds and violins as it ascends beyond the trumpets' range, for the quintuplet turn. Fifth wave, another oasis: again soft and lyrical, strings only – first violins singing – *sehr gesangvoll* – twice giving the lovely descending contour from the opening pages, now also incorporating the quintuplet; violas resuming figuration, the other strings sustaining harmony, no longer throbbing and pulsing. After four bars all thematic content is relinquished: a *diminuendo* to *pianissimo*, on four-note shape, treated sequentially, rising and swelling in volume over eight bars into the sixth wave: re-entry of some winds but still without theme – building over a bass now activating momentum as figuration stops: two bars: two more with superimposition of peremptory ejaculations from the three trumpets, answered by three oboes – a moment pre-empting Janáček, in dissonance too, as also its abrupt cut-off end. Pause for breath. Resumption – seventh wave – again suddenly quiet, athematic still, figuration resumed in violas, broad expressive shape above, then at double-speed on horns, violins in fragmented answer, swelling over six bars to the eighth wave – re-entry of trombones, moving up in parallel-triad procession, taken higher on horns and a trumpet, while violins trill and woodwinds hammer out sextuplets on repeated notes, primitive survivor of figuration once lacey – another Janáček moment. At the top of the ascent, two bars' harmonic stasis, with stuttering trumpet, though momentum inexorable to ... Climax, the third arrival: long-prophesied from way back, deferred over and over throughout the eight waves of journey towards it, and worth the wait: the view is wonderful.

Not even three harps suffice for audibility; but the tinkling triangle and sounding cymbal-clash can certainly be heard as the immense augmentation of the Proclamation at last crowns the Edifice, its quintuplet now the very cornerstone. This huge moment is placed upon a second inversion of Eb: previously its harmony had not shifted at the close; now it 'resolves' at the fifth bar onto a blinding Cb-major, second crash of percussion to confirm (and in some unguarded performances the poor harps left exposed on their upward arpeggios as the mighty woodwind/brass chord is ceased). How will the movement's true key recover from such conflicting tonal pulls? Somehow it will, and does. The Elevation returns in Ab, mounting to the Benediction with multi-divided strings and harp arpeggios from Db-minor in well-attested steps to F-minor to close on an expectant C-major – *diminuendo* – pause. A fragment of the secondary thematic area – the fluid cello lyricism – begins in Db, on violins, unharmonized, for a bar, answered by a liquid clarinet solo, moves easily by IV–V to reconfirm the Db as I/tonic for the coda.

Initial texture of throbbing-pulsating returns: the thematic shape now in harmony on three horns, just one further liquid clarinet solo, then its four-note descent taken up by violins, growing into expressive non-thematic counter-voice as the horns continue to sound the motif. All passion spent: this entire stretch of coda is fixed upon stable tonic or dominant bass – twenty bars on Db, four on Ab, eight more on Db, one more that closes the period into the opening of another. The horns leave the main motif and well up into mellifluous euphony, as if it were festive celebration recollected in tranquillity from the next valley, while first violins continue to caress and extend the clarinet-idea, and the pulse/throb is renewed piece-meal, and the tubas sustain the tonic. Horns grow bucolic to reach the dominant, first violins still playing with the four-note descending scale, pulse/throb replaced by single short chords, and the tubas silenced. When tonic again reached, the lower strings' single short chords become pizzicato, the horns cease, replaced by their deeper brothers the Wagner-tubas, still recalling the opening thematic shape; the first violins still toy with the four-note descending scale. For the very end they rise to the higher Db and broaden the rhythm to climb down the entire scale. In all this coda, thematic content is a mere vestige: the material's potential has been comprehensively exhausted; nothing remains but the movement's tonality itself.

Alas, the finale: never more problematic than here, after the three preceding movements whose calibre so requires a *finis coronat opus*. This colossal affair begins splendidly; quite ingenious – a section of Sechter close-work with very un-Sechter harmony: but for most of its inordinate length, it is desultory inconsequential stop/start upon indifferent material, as though to illustrate his detractors' complaints. The opening impetus long since forgotten: when it at last resurfaces, unwelcome possibly, unconvincing for sure: at such insistence and length its initial power now counterproductive: ends without issue, leaving the horns stranded in mid-air, a triple *forte* call for help, but unavailing. Plenty more desultory inconsequentiality. Deliverance in sight with, after another long pause, a *pianissimo* dominant drum-roll. Things are going to accrue, albeit not without prevarications even so late in: one of them, the huge unconvincing return of the first move-ment's main theme. Long pause as the drum on G self-extinguishes. C-minor coda commences; violins in upward-arpeggio figuration, the opening chorale slowed down, soft, solemn, a gradual swell through the keys: F-major for massive return of scherzo ostinato-figure extended to fill two bars of common time, then put across itself in canon. C-major with trumpets and drums: final two pages superimpose main figures from the three *great* movements, the first's and the adagio third movement's smoothed out into pure white-note diatonicism, the scherzo's always diatonic anyway, in an orgy of learnèd yet futile grandiosity that leaves the listener cold.

And leaves the lover of this incomparable composer all the more grateful that his final, and greatest, symphony lacks a finale. Bruckner spent his last years attempting it: copious sketches survive and have been handsomely published; there have been several shots at a realization. Some individual moments, undoubtedly from his own hand, are dazzlingly audacious even by his own standards – music of the future anticipating Schoenberg via Mahler's apocalyptic unfinished 10th. But it's clear that such visionary moments, and the more humdrum bits, and the acres of blank five-staved paper, could never have added up and consummated the movements already completed. And if Bruckner couldn't do it, no one could. There's an inbuilt unconscious self-fulfilling desire at work here, comparable to Schoenberg's long obsession with an 'Act III' for his *Moses and Aaron*; the completed three movements/two acts are self-sufficient, unsurpassable, terminal. It's significant that though these three movements of the 9th Symphony (1890–96) are still more advanced and extreme in every respect than any music of his heretofore, Bruckner showed no impulse to subject them to the diffident self-criticism that, when voiced even by supporters, had caused him to withdraw his 8th and overhaul it before it could be performed.

One might even venture to speak of a new confidence in the 9th – its size and scope beyond all previous; its emotional range wider, its originality in every parameter – form, melody/harmony/rhythm, scoring – without hesitation or flaw or mannerism; its actual *Stoff*, the material itself, far richer. The 8th was dedicated to Emperor Franz Josef: the 9th is dedicated to God himself: Caesar had been duly paid: now he renders his tribute to the King of Kings, whose Kingdom is not of this world. The greatest of all symphonies? Haydn, Beethoven, Schubert, with archaic counterpoint and modernist Wagner thrown in, fused into living expression with incandescent ardour of an erotic/spiritual volcano, perfectly proportioned in the large as in the tiniest detail; a Gothic cathedral with futurist technology, as though one of Achilles Rizzoli's fantastic dream-designs had actually been erected.

Its compass is so generous that it can embrace the demonic without fear. The scherzo is a vision of Hell, all the more coruscating for being a blown-up country dance – a day's release from their endless toil for enslaved Nibelungs. Its trio, however, is quite opposite – new in Bruckner, fast, light, sparkly – fairy-music by Mendelssohn that embraces Berlioz, Tchaikovsky, Bizet more still, Janáček most. Bruckner was no doubt as ignorant of these composers, before and after, as they of him. Before it, the peerless first movement: adjectives fail. And after it, the adagio: Stravinsky, no Teuton, singled out late in life a particular passage where the angular main theme is pitted against itself in naked near-atonal counterpoint as among the most inspired music ever written. He'd not have cared with such close affinity for the transforming evocation of the 'Dresden Amen', as enhanced throughout *Parsifal*, that permeates Bruckner's third movement; nor its warmly glowing lyrical periods – Schubert on marijuana; nor, maybe, for the movement's apocalyptic climax culminating in the most hair-raising dissonance yet written, bowdlerized in early prints and performances to a feeble diminished seventh – which is then left to resonate unresolved in an appalled silence before the long-drawn coda can exorcize it and cadence it to rest.

Bruckner the unreadable

It remains with Bruckner exceptionally hard to understand the discrepancy between 'the man who suffers and the mind that creates'; and harder yet to imagine what might be contained in the spaces between. Bruckner as man and artist remains unreadable. The life is notorious for its profusion of anecdotes emphasizing the unlettered *naïf*, cross between village idiot and holy fool. Some of the stories are harmless enough – 'why are they burning that woman?' (on opening eyes, hitherto shut, upon the closing scene either of *Die Walküre* or *Götterdämmerung*); tipping Hans Richter a florin after he'd conducted the 7th Symphony – touching, raising a slightly pitying smile. Others are hair-raising. Positively twisted is the character that emerges from the account of an unholy fascination with a sex murderer: Bruckner avidly attended the trial (where his excitement embarrassed his well-wishers), failed in eager efforts to witness the execution, but succeeded for compensation in ordering from

a restaurant close to the court-house a schnitzel off the same veal
that provided the murderer's last earthly meal – after which the
composer stayed up all night to pray for his soul.

And the love-life (rather, the absence of) could come straight
out of *Psychopathia Sexualis* (first published 1886, between the 7th
and 8th symphonies): the tragi-comedy of Bruckner's indefatigable
infatuations with young girls, often nearly resulting in marriage.
One might ask, repressively, what light this shines on the music?
only to be confuted in the simplest way: 'He was always ripe for
infatuation and his emotions caught fire very quickly ... many
melodic passages in the symphonies owe their inspiration to some
pretty face that took his fancy.' Or, more directly, 'Come sit down
[he said to a beautiful sixteen-year-old whom he'd pursued around
the town of St Florian], and I'll tell you about the Ninth.' Everything, yet nothing, is 'explained' by such equations as these and,
elsewhere, anecdotes recalling numerological and other fixations.
Such a colossal drive to create will find a way, though the culverts
be never so cracked, crooked, cramped, curious, crabbed. Another
reminiscence makes quite clear what is anyway pretty evident, that,
despite taking precautions in his late sixties against his wet dreams
being found out, his physical chastity was unimpugned. And still
there is no connection. E. M. Forster's little tag does not apply: the
mind and the man, though certainly in communication, do not add
up. Within a droll little oddity, girt about with textbook psychoses,
lies one of the mightiest music-machines ever known. One has to
leave it at that.

When the impossible question – 'Who is your favourite
composer?' – comes up, my instant unthinking answer is 'Bruckner'.
When compelled actually to think *why*, I'm at a loss for words. What
can be said about music which in its every detail, whether normative or idiosyncratic, so exactly reaches the places that seek sustenance and irrigation; that discloses the potential heights that daily
life never touches, even as it similarly plumbs the depths; that seems
to say Carry On Living, the earth is firm, the heavens secure, God
is Good?

Bruckner/Mahler nexus

Fifty years ago, Bruckner and Mahler could be widely bracketed together as symphonic mastodons, inordinate in length, loudness, portentousness and tedium. Such distance from the truth now seems unbelievable in itself. Mahler, the more variegated and seductive composer, in tune, by the prescience of his electric nervous sensibility, with the anxieties and confusion of modern times, came well ahead in the race: from the 1960s onwards, his music swept the world like a great tsunami. Bruckner's present popularity, which will probably never be so extravagant, is possibly built on solider credentials. His high position is less dependent upon a particular zeitgeist. He is the tortoise who stays the course. As the Mahler wave recedes, the dry land of Bruckner emerges confirmed and defined.

Though they overlap both biographically and in some shared influences (Wagner, Schubert, Beethoven), they could not be more different as artistic types. And while the astonishing growth of Mahler's fame has been inseparable from the vehement and passionate inner life to which each song and symphony added a further instalment, Bruckner's oeuvre – confined equally to a handful of genres – is adamantine in its impersonality, never more freed from programmatic or self-expressive narrative than when he absurdly tried to claim its presence.

Perhaps the linkage of their names, a commonplace before either composer was well known outside Austria, still denigrates the older man. They are polar opposites. Mahler is a Modern: from the 1960s onwards the ambiguous friction of virtuosity, histrionics, hysteria, heartache, searing lyricism, nostalgia and undercutting irony has accorded with the zeitgeist and moved into centre-consciousness. In characterizing Bruckner every one of these words could be reversed. He has no hysteria or histrionics – whatever the psychopathology of the man, the symphonies and sacred choral works that form the great bulk of his output are impersonal and non-self-expressive, monumentalized almost into implacability. And though he can convey angst, irrupting above all in the searing lyricism and still-startling dissonances of the 9th Symphony, the pang of personal feeling is burnt out from them; their emotion is set in stone, not in the deliberated manner of twentieth-century objectivity, à la Stravinsky, but because this is how they are. And there is absolutely no irony, no nostalgia, no world-weariness.

Nor, of course, is there virtuosity. He is utterly not a wizard or a showman. No one would now accuse Bruckner of deficiency in technique. Virtually every passage of every work bristles with his hard-won learning, displayed with naïve pride and open mastery. His singularities of structure and procedure – the stops and starts, the reiterations, the self-interruptions, the colossalism so repugnant to early hearers (and not only those duty-bound to hostility like Brahms and his henchman Hanslick, who termed Bruckner 'a symphonic boa constrictor', but moving even the sympathetically disposed to make huge cuts in the composer's supposed better interests) – all these are now understood, and valued as the very constituents of an astonishing originality which, overcoming outward diffidence, had no choice but to be Itself with a granitic inevitability that can still, for all its manifest mental power, be fairly called primitive.

Equally, there is no call now to 'correct' the wonderful orchestration, once routinely castigated as 'organistic'. An obvious resemblance remains in the way that ranks of woodwinds, strings and especially brass (in single families and as a full chorus) are juxtaposed in antiphony and combined in mass. But far more striking is the way he eschews mixing, concentrating instead upon bold naked purity of timbre, a sonorous ideal at the other end of the range from the Wagner orchestra to which he also owes so much.

The influence of Wagner can be misrepresented. That he didn't miss what he *needed* from Wagner, the audacity of theme, size, volume, space, harmony, is audible enough. What is not so often said is that, as with Wagner's orchestration, the use of what he took could hardly be more different from his hero's. Chez Wagner, the musical speech is nothing if not emotive. It raises the temperature for love, pain, yearning, baleful broodings, heroic exaltations, and all the rest. It is always libido-driven, erotic, even carnal. Bruckner takes over and, indeed, intensifies the language, but, as with any self-expression, Eros and Longing are burnt out as if by the purging fires of the Holy Ghost. The contrast of musical imagery from below the belt and above the forehead propelling the story and subject of *Parsifal* so grossly that it can still sicken the unattuned admirer simply doesn't arise for the non-dramatic, non-psychological, essentially meditative and architectonic symphonist.

Which is, of course, to imply that Mahler as symphonist *is* dramatic – exhibitionist, even; psychological, essentially dynamic, formally episodic and picturesque, perhaps opportunistic, even random, always narrative whether with or without texts and programmes: above all self-confessional and autobiographical.

Mahler

Gustav Mahler; born 1860 in rural Bohemia; early privations, particularly the death of his brother Ernst, make lasting impression – as, also, the domestic and military and klezmer musics of the region. Youthful promise as pianist – to Vienna Conservatoire 1875 – shares lodgings with Hugo Wolf and Hans Rott; transcribes Bruckner's 3rd Symphony for piano but is not his pupil. *Das klagende Lied* written 1878–80 for a competition – the jury (with Brahms on it) rejects it.

Commencement of career as one of the epoch's greatest conductors, begins 1880 with modest provincial posts, then 1885 second conductor at Prague, 1886 second conductor at Leipzig. Copious composing (some lost), including first settings of poems from *Des Knaben Wunderhorn*, 1883–5, and *Songs of a Wayfarer*, born of an unhappy love-affair, first of several: its songs, and his woes, permeate 1st Symphony completed 1888. The year before, reworking of Weber's unfinished opera *Die drei Pintos* and conducts his first *Ring*-cycle. First major post, the Budapest Opera, 1888; 1889 death of both parents – he himself in perpetual ill-health.

Resigns Budapest post 1891 after ructions, to become principal conductor in Hamburg. Many *Wunderhorn* songs, now with orchestra rather than piano: they infiltrate successive symphonies – No. 2 (1887–94), No. 3 (1895–6); No. 4 (1899–1900) born of No. 3; and a touch remaining in No. 5 (completed 1902), also prophesied in No. 4.

Life-appointment as music-director of the Vienna Opera 1897 (for this, the prime musical post in the world, the Jewish composer converted to Catholicism), and the next year, of the Philharmonic: this latter troubled from the start, terminated with his resignation 1901. Purchases plot of land and begins to build a house 1899: two further *Wunderhorn* settings. Meets Alma Schindler 1901, marries her the next year, which also sees birth of first daughter; their second the year after. *Kindertotenlieder* 1–3 1901, 4–5 1904; also from this time, five other Rückert settings. The *Kindertotenlieder* infiltrate the 6th Symphony (1903–4) – life and art inextricably connected. The 7th begun 1904, completed the next year – it shows the influence of Mahler's sympathetic encouragement of the young Schoenberg's radicalism.

Iconic exchange with Sibelius in 1906 on the nature of the Symphony by its two greatest living exponents. A marital crisis resolved pro tem with 8th Symphony (1906–7). Trouble at the Opera – release from contract 1907, and appointed to New York: this same year domestic woe – death of his eldest daughter. Hard duty in NY autumn–winter–spring, back to Austria for composition each summer. His 9th Symphony 1909–10: an iconic consultation with Freud, temporarily resolving marital troubles with Alma, consolidated in triumphal première of the 8th. No. 10 begun, health ever-more dodgy. Fourth season in NY, strenuous as always; friction with the orchestra; returns to Europe in state of collapse, dying in Vienna May 1911, two latest major works unheard, a third left unachieved.

Ten symphonies (one uncompleted), all variously uneven and problematic except for the unique perfection of the 4th, which ends in a song: four song-cycles with orchestra, as well as four free-standing orchestral songs, of flawless perfection (maybe just one exception), interposed among and intimately related to the symphonies – the greatest work of all, *Das Lied von der Erde*, is a fusion; a song-cycle actually entitled 'Symphony' on the score. This intermix remains without parallel; only Schubert and Brahms resemble it at all, and not much. No opera, despite his being the outstanding opera conductor (and sometimes director) of the day, and despite an evident vein of drama and melodrama in the personality;

no chamber-music beyond an adolescent and uncharacteristic piano-quartet movement; nothing for keyboard despite manifest powers as a player; no other orchestral genre outside symphony, or vocal outside song (taking the choral element in three of the symphonies as essentially part of the orchestral fabric).

Yet before any of this interfused oeuvre, *Das klagende Lied*, a one-off, that would seem to be of all genres the most fruitful for his multifarious and steeply channelled gifts. Mahler is stylistically and spiritually a throwback to the earliest and freshest impulses of German Romanticism: Schubert above all, Weber not much less, Mendelssohn, Schumann, the earlier Wagner of *Tannhäuser* and *Lohengrin* before music-drama set in. For Bruckner he showed generous loyalty but there's no affinity in compositional type; towards Brahms he was cool if not wholly negative. Ever eclectic, he owes more to Tchaikovsky and Berlioz, even Bizet and Massenet. Mature Wagner is different: completely au fait with post-*Rheingold* harmony, texture, orchestra, Mahler nevertheless doesn't depend on it, nor much resemble. For any mainstream Austro-German composer who'd fully assimilated mature Wagner, the possibilities are: more music-drama – recipe for disaster unless re-angled and other-directed – Strauss, thence Zemlinsky, Schreker, Korngold: or quintessentialization, as in Wolf's *Lieder*. Mahler's *Das klagende Lied* realizes a potential 'Third Way' in a single bound. This product of his late teens is a hybrid: at once song-cycle, narrative choral cantata, opera *manqué*, with more than a dash of symphonism. A dark archetypal fairy-tale from mythical/chivalric German forests, told as a folk-legend – Mahler's own text, in the spirit of the Grimms' tales and the lyrics and ballads of the *Knaben Wunderhorn*.

Part I *Waldmärchen/Forest Legend* was omitted when he revised the work for its belated première in 1901: it is in no way inferior to the two parts he retained, and is indispensable for the piece's full scope to be understood. Nine six-line stanzas, sometimes employing a questioning refrain: i) the proud beautiful Queen rejecting all her suitors; ii) only the knight who can bring her the red flower deep in the forest can bring her love to bloom; iii) two brothers undertake the quest – the elder dark, rankling, envious; the younger fair and gentle; iv) in the forest their ways part; v) the younger finds the flower, plucks it, tucks it in his hat, lies down under the willow to sleep; vi) the elder storms over hill and dale in vain – at evening happens upon the willow, under it the sleeping youth, visibly successful; vii) the narration, heretofore direct, now turns oblique – you lovely birds – your music should waken the poor knight whose red flower shines like blood; viii) direct again – he's seen it all, he draws his sword – he laughs, the other smiles; ix) oblique again – why so dew-heavy, flowers? why so sad, winds? what do you mean? The refrain for this last stanza runs 'in the forest, on the green glade, grows an old willow'.

Part II: *Das Spielmann/The Minstrel*: five stanzas, six lines each, with refrain constant, ringing the changes upon *Leide!* and *Weh!* – sorrow and woe: i) by the old willow deep in the wood where ill-omened birds flutter lies a fair young knight covered by leaves and blooms; ii) a wandering minstrel passing this place spied a little bone – picked it up – fashioned from it a flute – its music will be passing strange! In iii) he sets flute to lips and – wonder – it sings of itself a beautiful strain, yet so sad – *ein klagende Lied*; iv) the sad song itself – the bone now speaks – 'hear my lament – for a flower my brother slew me – here in the forest my young body rots – he woos a beauteous bride'; v) the minstrel wanders the world everywhere letting the sad song be heard and asking what it might mean – I must hie me to the royal palace and the royal bride: *O Leide! Weh! O Leide!*

Part III: *Hochzeitsstück/Wedding-Piece*: seven six-line stanzas, all but one with refrain either of *Leide/Weh* again, or *Freude! Heia! Freude!* – joy – which from first brilliant festivity grows ever more sinister and malapropos. Off-stage carousing, festive and chivalric – close shades of *Euryanthe* and *Lohengrin*: i) the high castle shines, the gay music sounds, the gallant knights, the gracious ladies, throng – what's afoot? ii) you don't know? I can tell – today the Queen's pride will be brought down – she marries today – *Freude! Heia!* iii) so why is the King so dumb and pale? He notices not the festive throng, the splendour, the beauty – what troubles him? What does the minstrel here? *Leide! Weh!* For iv) the song of the bone, text exactly repeating Part II/no. iv; v) angry, the King (now evidently the elder brother) leaps up and seizes the bone flute, places it to his mouth, hears aghast the familiar story (no refrain here, the sole exception) – the wings of death o'ershadow the proceedings; vi) the flute continues, through the bone addressing its brother direct – dearest brother, you struck me down, now you play upon my body – why did you give its young life over to death? *Leide! Weh!* vii) disaster, ruin, shame – the Queen lies prostrate, trumpets and drums are stilled, the gay folk flee in terror, the lights extinguish, the proud castle collapses: 'what's left now of the Wedding Feast' (a line that could have come out of Heine via Schumann's *Dichterliebe*); and a final *ach Leide!*

The music for this dark tale takes indirection far further than its text: the story unfolds in shifting layers of unreal time, in a manner already explored by the play of memory between the lovers in Act I of *Tristan* and in Act III the hero's relentless self-analysis, or the superimposition of past, present and future-to-come in Act I of *Parsifal*. The chorus and the three soloists are not identified with any particular role: focus continually shifts, and the orchestra is as vocal as the vocalists. Rate of narration is equally fluid, from spell-bound protraction to drastic rapid action. The entire work is set in a fascinating dream-scape. Its range of musical idioms and moods runs from traumatized woodland tranquillity saturated with horn-calls and bedecked with birdsong – the nature-sounds from *Rhein-gold* and *Siegfried* turned around backwards to evoke their sources in Schubert, Weber, Schumann – to the raucous riot of off-stage festivity heralding the off-stage band in Berg's *Wozzeck*, even as it recalls the directly comparable set-up in Act II of *Lohengrin*. The gamut of lament – *Leide! Weh!* – runs from innermost sorrow to hysteria rendered with vivid modernity prescient of what will soon scorch its way all the way to expressionism. The overall trajectory is compelling, convincing, compulsive. And all this is composed by the teenaged poet-composer with mature mastery comparable only to the teenaged Mendelssohn and Schubert.

All these references to forebears might suggest an epigone as well as a tyro. But even when virtually quoting, or using stock stereotype material, the sound-world is original and authentic. Mahler's subsequent course remains thus: simultaneously unmissably eclectic and utterly unmistakable as himself. The marriage in *Das klagende Lied* of subject-matter, content, material, idiom and genres is so natural and so consummate that one senses his real genius lies here: a wonderfully promising world opens up that he does not pursue. Perhaps the worst consequence of the work's rejection, which he claimed condemned him to 'the hell of theatrical life', is his own: it also condemned him to pursue that wobbly quarry, the Symphony. Why was Mahler so enslaved to the Symphony as genre and goal? His obstinate adherence now appears retrograde, in the face of its wholescale and brilliant dissolution at his hands.

The first four symphonies are so deeply involved with his songs as to be known as the *Wunderhorn* Symphonies; and Symphony No. 1 takes the *Wayfarer* cycle as prime material for extensive elaborate treatment far beyond simple citation. This beautiful cycle is also set to Mahler's own texts, à la Müller/*Müllerin* – folk-imitation, *faux-naïve*, as perfectly apt to his purpose as the *Wunderhorn* poems. These four symphonies also declare poetic/autobiographical/metaphysical programmes, explicit or implicit. That of the 1st is a throwback to Jean Paul, favourite of Schumann and the young Brahms. The opening is magical – an evocation of forest dawn, on from *Das klagende Lied*, complete with cuckoo, whose call emerges into a main theme direct from the second *Wayfarer* song. Next comes a splendid rustic scherzo using an earlier *Wunderhorn*-setting with piano, *Hans und Grete*. Then a bizarre funeral cortège, the animals escorting their enemy the gamekeeper to his grave accompanied by a skeletal canon on *Frère Jacques* initiated by strangulated high solo double-bass, then an outbreak of the village klezmer-band from the composer's childhood; a trio transcribing virtually intact the lovely consolatory close of the *Wayfarer*-songs; then the march returns, *Frère Jacques* still in doleful canon, suddenly swamped by klezmer gone berserk, and ending with a juxtaposition of expiring cortège with aching nostalgia from the wandering minstrel; as up-beat to explosive start of finale, later all histrionic appassionato until terminal bombast all-too-prophetic of Soviet Realism in music.

It is a miscellany that doesn't add up: first in a life-long problem, still more marked in Symphony No. 2: death-rites to commence, resurrection to terminate, protagonist the 'hero' from the 1st Symphony. Between these extremes come a delectable *Ländler* dance – Dvořák cubed; a brilliant orchestral scherzo hugely developing and extending a *Wunderhorn* song and throwing in an apocalypse to boot; then an actual *Wunderhorn* song, heartfelt and sublime; *Urlicht*/Primeval Light – the soul's cry of need, from deepest woe, for the certainty of ultimate restoration to the light of God whence she came. And thus to the vast theatrical finale in the Last Days of Mankind, beginning with the apocalypse again, opening out into Judgment, sole survivor, empty desolation – a Berliozian fresco of virtuoso flair, ending with a Liszt/Hollywood closing chorus sending up *Urlicht* rotten, to close in the strains of *Hansel and Gretel* gone bloated and kitschy. It brings the house down every time: the implication of showmanship is deliberate.

Despite Mahler's ambiguity about programmes – constantly declaring, then withdrawing – Symphony No. 3 is pretty explicit and greatly helped by its ambitious scheme: the Great Chain of Being; in the huge first movement, all the way from rocks and stones animated by Pan, creative juices rise, the life-force flows, Spring triumphs over Winter, the resurgent Folk over the moribund Old Regime, Summer marches in, Pan in the vanguard – a colossal fresco longer than most classical symphonies in itself, this first movement. As previously, the smaller numbers that follow are adorable and superlative – no. 2, *What the wildflowers tell me*, an exquisite minuet with delicately wrought *scherzando* sections; no. 3, *What the woodland beasts tell me*, a fine-grained yet lusty scherzo with achingly nostalgic interludes featuring a solo flugelhorn – both these movements grow from already-written *Wunderhorn*-songs. The fourth movement is an actual setting – *What mankind tells me* – Zarathustra's 'Midnight Song' from Nietzsche – awakening from deep sleep to a world of suffering that must be overcome and banished in favour of eternal renewal – the music as awesome as the words.

The fifth movement, *What the angels tell me* – back to the *Wunderhorn* for a harrowing yet tender account of Peter's betrayal, contrition and Jesus' forgiveness – the disciple represented by the contralto who's just delivered the 'Midnight Song', the angelic trio by a girls' chorus, the bells implied in the poem by a boys' (Mahler changed his first title to *What the morning bells tell me*, because Midnight is superseded by Dawn, before censoring his programme altogether). So to no. 6 – finale: *What love tells me*; purely orchestral again; or rather, metaphorically, on harmonium – an adagio of sanctimonious unction, masterfully written, especially in the way it gathers up material from previous movements: without bombast, undoubtedly sincere; but this very sincerity has an element of look-at-me grandeur about it: *What God tells me* was its alternative title. And in the original scheme this movement would have been followed by a seventh – *What the child tells me* – another already-extant *Wunderhorn* setting whose ultimate destiny is to close the next symphony.

And it pervades its opening movement too. Yet Symphony No. 4, equally as hybrid as its predecessors, benefits from the absence of any programme except implicit, even fugitive. A Poetic Symphony of the highest order, no message or proclamation, no narrative, no 'hero', no Resurrection. Something fragile and unutterable concerning the Celestial Child, innocent and natural, out of Blake, Philipp Runge, Wordsworth 'trailing clouds of glory' 'trembling lest it grow impure', aspiring to regain the heavens whence it came.

The work is still a sort of suite, but the balance of its four movements is perfectly judged: no lapses of level or continuity: nor of taste – its musical fabric is of the highest calibre from start to finish, and its craftsmanship wonderful.

The opening movement: a complex tissue of intensive motivic-work on attractive *Wunderhorn*-ish material, with also something unexpected – more than a touch of Haydn in the opening theme, more still in its tick-tock accompaniment straight out of the andante of 'The Clock' Symphony No. 101. The second theme is irresistibly ardent: lyricism almost effusive were it not so open and inviting. Both themes, and several others, continuously evolve variants, counter-subjects, new offshoots, with generous profusion keeping many voices in play: and before either is heard comes an opening tinkle of jingle-bells, returning as punctuation all through the movement's extraordinarily fertile adventures. They will prove their meaning in the song-finale – already composed, for the third symphony, wisely deferred to a better destination in the fourth.

Particularly exciting, two central climaxes poised in rhyming equivalence across a crucial middle-space. The first disintegrates into a trumpet tattoo that will with hindsight – perhaps foresight – open Mahler's next symphony all by itself: it disappears, is answered by a sardonic snarl, and from the scattered fragments the Haydn-esque opening theme reassembles itself, distorted and dislocated: pause: then it's resumed from where it had been cut off, casual, cheeky, cocksure, without a care in the world – one of the most ingenious recapitulations in any first movement by anyone. It soon builds to the second climax, this one given its head, to plunge into the ardent lyrical period at full throttle. Even after all this the material continues to generate fresh invention all the way to the long-drawn nostalgic farewell that suddenly revs up to close boisterous.

The second movement is a slowish scherzo – *ohne Hast* – droll, humorous, bizarre, gruesome yet cheery – 'death strikes up' on the harsh violin solo tuned up a tone, the instrumentation acrid and linear throughout – a sort of X-ray revealing the fantastical inventiveness of Mahler's inner parts – his later revaluation of Bach – 'no more harmony, only polyphony' already prophesied. A more lyrical trio gives Death a break: just when it dies muttering away, a rapturous renewal; the scherzo's return, complete with fiddle, takes ever-stranger new directions.

The third is loosely a variation-set, over a bass rather than on a melody; a wide range of moods, textures, tempi – celestial tranquillity (as it were *What love tells me* from the 3rd Symphony, without its sanctimony); elegy/yearning/lament/passion (as it were the voice of the bone from *Das klagende Lied*, taken further): more motion and extended continuity, beautifully flowing: *Klage* renewed, yet more strained and unrestrained: back to geniality in a succession of brief linked *Ländler* – *andante* on solidly singing cellos; *allegretto* on rustic violins; *allegro*, now in duple time, on *scherzando* woodwinds; *allegro molto* involving nearly the full orchestra, plus glockenspiel, boiling up and over in just five bars when the brass enter, plus a cymbal-splash, and at once cooling into first tempo and texture yet more celestially tranquil than before, dying away into the distance in home key of G till a huge long-held up-beat opens up a panoply of the heavens in E: trumpets blaze, timpani bang out the theme-bass pervading the whole movement, all four horns (there are no deep brass in the entire work) whoop out a new thematic shape already extant – destined to be the main motif in the ensuing song, revealed in a moment of vision, not yet recognized for what it is. Long, slow, soft fade, re-achieving G via a magical route involving C-major and F-major: an unstable tonic, however – the movement had in effect closed before the visionary outburst: it wavers long, indecisive, to close on an uncertain dominant.

The song commences in the tonic – G – with the theme just blazoned forth now easy-going on clarinet before the soprano takes it up. A *Wunderhorn* poem, *Das himmlische Leben* – 'Life in Heaven', evoking the joys, the frolics, the sticky blisses, the eventual repose, of Paradise as seen through the senses of a child. Peaceful at first, growing frisky, with running figures from the first movement and a refrain invoking St Peter's benign onlooking taken from the music for his betrayal and contrition in the *Wunderhorn* choral-song from the 3rd Symphony. Now things begin to bustle, and the sleigh-bells from the first movement show what they promised there: St John yields his lamb to the butcher, St Luke slaughters his oxen, wine is free, angels bake the bread – other bits and pieces of material from the first movement, and the refrain from the 3rd Symphony: a brief reminder of initial indolence for all the good things from the heavenly vegetables, lively again for the heavenly fruits, slow refrain again for Martha-the-Cook. Just seven more bars' bustle, orchestra alone, showing in retrospect that the B–F♯ fifth on which, with jingle-bells, the entire work had begun before it swung round to G with the entry of Haydn's 'Clock', is going to prove dominant of its final key E, as heralded huge at the slow movement's end, now returning *ppp* on the double-basses' lowest note, low harp gently tolling, *Sehr zart und geheimnisvoll bis zum Schluß*/very tender and secretive/mysterious till the end. Over the gently tolling bass the earlier vocal melodies combine and expand in an interlude preparing for the soprano's entry with the closing stanza, as sweet-sated and reposeful as she earlier was all avid and agog; no earthly music can compare with our heavenly – as her eleven thousand virgins dance, St Ursula smiles (lovely expansive phrase): no earthly music can compare with ours (another, still more rapturous, as the bass briefly shifts the key to G♯-minor) – St Cecilia herself leads the angel-music; and all things awaken to joy. Or rather, sink into blissful slumber, down from the soprano's higher to her lower register, soon echoed by the cor anglais, four times, each retaining the initiating grace-note wherewith this motif had opened the symphony, right down to low harp, almost recommencing the *Frère Jacques* march in Symphony No. 1, right down to double-bass's bottom open string E – an audible image of repose, closing this book of Innocence Regained after Experience Lost that might have been dreamt, worded and illustrated by Blake.

In the supposedly more 'classical' symphonies of Mahler's middle-period – 5, 6, 7 – the divisions, discrepancies, lapses, lie deeper and more troubling than earlier, for all that they relinquish pro-grammes up to a point, and eschew voices altogether. As always when he embraces text to compose songs the results are, with one exception, peerless. The two *Wunderhorn* settings from this time are magnificent: *Der Tambourg'sell/*The Drummer-boy, a vignette from Housman or Kipling: he awaits the gallows for some unspeci-fied misdeed, bids farewell to all ranks of the regiment he's served devotedly, with unforgettable plangency and pathos: *Revelge/*Reveille – off to the wars with dare-devil cheerfulness; battle-scene; total victory only Death's; returning home as clattering skeletons, rank on rank, led by their drummer past the dwellings of their sweethearts to whom they'd waved their insouciant farewells at the start.

The five Rückert settings: their dark pearl the world-weary song of abandonment and loneliness, relinquishing the hurly-burly for an interior space of interior solitude; their clear pearl, the waft of lime-scent evoking her dear presence: both these songs are fine-spun and intimate, foretelling the still-sparer evocations of similar feelings in the *Das Lied von der Erde/Song of the Earth*. *Um Mit-ternacht/*At Midnight, however, ends grandiose and somewhat bombastic; valuable more for its opening evocation of desolation, midnight physical and spiritual, despair and anguish: right back to *Das klagende Lied*. The apotheosis – yielding to God's love and care – complete with chorale and cascades of scales and arpeggios from piano and harps, is magnificent in its way; but the religiosity prophesies a major disaster-area to come, aberrant as *Das Lied* is consummatory – Symphony No. 8. The remaining two Rückert settings are love-songs for Alma. *Liebst du um Schönheit* is somewhat insipid; *Blicke mir nicht in die Lieder!* is Mahler's sole dud in this genre. But the *Kindertotenlieder*, also setting Rückert, are flawless; in their spare-etched linearity, combining tenseness with relaxation, the very emblem of grief; delusory hopes alternate with apprehensions only too real; loss is evoked by elusive apparitions of the departed children; bitter self-reproaches precede eventual consolation, perhaps just as elusive/delusive as the apparitions and the hopes. For the poet, all-too-actual; for the composer, an empathetic fiction, playing with, tempting, Fate, setting such words when his young children enjoyed perfect health. As everyone knows, Fate took up the challenge. All these songs are related to the middle three symphonies not in direct re-usage as earlier, but by parallel and analogy rather than quotation: and of course in autobiography when Fate strikes.

The 5th Symphony is a five-movement 'conventional' symphony, without any specific programme, though beginning with a sort-of-protagonist's funeral-march (the main motif already complete in the first movement of Symphony No. 4, as if growing from its predecessor as No. 4 had from No. 3): and a general trajectory from gloom, strain, dark, to a breakthrough for Light and Triumph in the finale, thwarted earlier, granted victory in the closing pages (this finale also employs as its main motif another old *Wunderhorn* song). In between, an endless, mirthless scherzo that 'comes and comes and comes' – next stop, Shostakovich; and the tacky-sentimental *adagietto* – Massenet on a bad day; the finale's rejoicing triumphalism also foretells compulsory Soviet strains that found here a perfect prototype.

The 6th is the only symphony with four purely instrumental movements (even the first originally had five). The 'Tragic' Symphony – as autobiographical as Strauss's contemporary self-projections in *Heldenleben* and *Domestica*: Alma-theme in the first movement, their children at play in the scherzo's trio; culminating in the gigantic finale and its three hammer-blows – literally struck with a hammer – later changed superstitiously to two; symbolizing three strokes of Fate in his tormented self-fulfilling life. The totality is integrated with hammering over-insistence, as if in answer to 'just criticism' for the suite-like *Wunderhorn*-symphonies; as if, also, in pre-emption of Mahler's famous response, several years later, to Sibelius's severe ideal of what a Symphony should be – 'no, no, the Symphony should be like the world, it should contain everything' – Mahler's 6th tightens, excludes, concentrates, to the pitch of obsession. A very powerful work that can sweep all before it, or else sound merely OTT, protesting too much, histrionic and hysterical, grossly over-orchestrated, exhibitionistic. Easily its best music, the remote alpine heights that give remission from the grim march (*Revelge* is very close) or the cloying effusive Alma in the first movement; and the other-worldly andante that comes second or third in the symphony's ordering (still an open question from the composer's time onwards – albeit long-since resolved: it should come second).

Symphony No. 7 is not so much a suite as a hotchpotch, very uneven, not adding up or making overall sense – as programme, life-saga, poetic vision – any way. If only Mahler had relinquished it as a symphony and cut the work up into its constituents! The extraordinary first movement, his closest approach to his great opposite Strauss, could stand self-sufficient as a tone-poem self-portrait: *Don Gustavo*. Second – *Nachtmusik* – returns, enhanced, to a *Wunderhorn*-world with Schumann thrown in, music of forest, hunt, Rhine; third – the *Schattenhaft*/Shadowy scherzo – a night-march of spooky equivocation; and fourth, an amorous Southern serenade with mandolin and guitar – could make a fine three-piece suite. The fifth movement, the big *pomposo* finale, masterfully composed on mediocre material, which in context so signally fails to make any sense of what precedes it, could be rescued by standing alone as a sort of *1812* or *Meistersinger*-prelude (audibly its model) concert-piece.

Late works

The problems of the gigantic 8th Symphony are unique to it – the 'Symphony of a Thousand', storming the heavens with eight soloists, full chorus plus choirs of boys and girls, organ, enormous orchestra, setting the Latin *Veni Creator* in Part I, the closing scene from Goethe's *Faust* in Part II – look-at-me Masterpiece – Important, Pretentious, Significant; composed with colossal skill and euphoric exuberance – a resurgence of love for, confidence in, Alma (they wouldn't last); duff from bar one – that organ-entry! The *Veni Creator* can just about take the treatment; most of the *Faust*, after a magically evocative start, is dull and interminable – all those saints, male and female: then moving fluently, facilely through variegated circles of sonority and texture to close in 'religious kitsch' *in excelsis* for the *Chorus Mysticus* (its words already pretty bogus). Bombast Suprême. Yet prophetic too, here and there, most particularly the lively agility of the boys' and girls' choruses, a foretaste of the transparency of *Das Lied von der Erde* – Mahler's unsullied calibre in orchestral song, here fused with symphony in ways quite different from those of the *Wunderhorn*-works. An idiosyncratic and personal contribution to the Orientalism already so native (so to speak) in the French and Russian music of the epoch (though soon to be embraced by Strauss, Schreker, Schoenberg, Webern, in their various manners). Six poems taken from an anthology of German translations pre-dating Fenellosa and Ezra Pound, *Die chinesische Flöte/The Chinese Flute*: Mahler's embrace of Eastern aesthetics and spirituality more compelling, albeit not accompanied by actual conversion, than his Catholicism or his Goetheism. He even added words of his own to the final *Abschied*/Farewell as if to confirm his identification.

Two soloists alternate in the six songs that also make a quasi-symphonic entity. 'First movement', the tenor's *Trinklied vom Jammer der Erde*/Drinking-song of Earth's Sorrow, invocation to wine and music with heroic-defiant refrain as the goblet is again drained, dark is life, dark is earth. Between the bravura, antithetic glimpses of otherwise: the first lyrical and affirmative – the firmament eternally renews its blue, the earth its blossoming spring – how long can *you*, puny man, scarcely lasting a mere hundred years, claim to rejoice in your trashy earthly existence? The second vehement and shrill – see there, on the graves in the moonlight, a gibbering ape, howling down the sweet scent of humanity. *So*: drink to the lees: dark is life, dark is death! – superbly taut euphoric virile superbia.

'Second movement' the contralto's *Einsame im Herbst*/Lonely One in Autumn: slowish, aimless, pallid – *ermüdet*/wearied is the performing instruction: wandering lines on muted strings, underpinning a desolate solo oboe, soon joined by a clarinet, reminiscent of the desolate opening of *Um Mitternacht* before apotheosis took over. Here, no such thing: the voice steals softly in to introduce the title-word – *Herbst*: autumn mists drift over the lake, down the scale; up it for the next line – the grasses sparkle with frosty rime: these scales so exposed that their major/minor clashes really hurt. 'Wearied' etiolation alternates with impassioned appeals to lost happiness, vitality, love, that can verge upon the fulsome, especially when yearning bursts its bonds – I come to you, give me rest – always mitigated and 'corrected' by *Kindertotenlieder*-like linear sparseness: after the plummiest outcry of all, the victory for empty *Klage* is total.

The scherzo of the 'Symphony' is formed of a composite: three songs of a lighter cast – iii) the tenor evokes Youth; iv) the contralto evokes Beauty; v) the tenor invokes Drunkenness. Mahler here taps a vein of sheer prettiness, new in his music, perfect for its context. 'Youth' conjures a jade/porcelain world of graceful artificiality: gaily-clad friends sit, sip, chat, versify; the bridge to their little pavilion is mirrored in the water in a perfect bow – perfect too, the delicate whimsical Orientalia, exquisite mingling of pentatonic and diatonic – land of smiles. 'Beauty' is more thoughtful: a scene is set, young girls down by the river, plucking flowers, gently bantering – still more pentatony between delicate fluttery chromaticism. Same combination for second stanza – sunlight, waters, breezes, fragrance. Now languor livens: a glittering orchestral tutti introduces a royal Chinese march for the handsome young horsemen – just as pentatonic – cantering by on their lively steeds in the lustiness of their youth. One especially – how his horse's mane flutters, his nostrils steam. Sudden abrupt curtailment of excitement: back to opening scene – girls, water, sunlight; but something has changed – the loveliest girl looks long and longingly after the prince of her heart; her pretended indifference cannot conceal the pain of her passion. Long, lovingly drawn-out envoi, tender and refined beyond belief, blown away by 'Drunkenness' – *Der Trunkene im Frühling/* The Drunkard in Spring: a bibulous riot, also conspicuously penta-tonic; satyr-annexe to the desperate drinking of Earth's Sorrow, in one part of its title; in the other, prophetic of Spring's return as the earth blossoms anew in the finale-to-come. Harsh/raucous cameo of intoxication, textures and harmony lurching about in almost expressionist fashion, going sweetly, squiffily sentimental when the drunkard addresses the birdie on the tree and understands its message – Spring is here! – a moment of rapt tenderness; then drinks deep, staggers off to sleep, crying out to be drunk for ever.

The sixth song is the 'symphony''s finale: *Der Abschied/* The Farewell, a composite movement much longer than what precedes, centred upon another of Mahler's funeral-marches (as irresistible to him as the waltz to Richard – or Johann – Strauss). First section sets scene and mood over deep bell-like single-note tolling, with gong, a plangent oboe melisma, punctuated by stabs from a pair of horns gradually transforming into a sobbing descent as violins steal in to overlap and exchange phrases with the oboe; flute extends melisma into fearful flutter of a twilight bird. The sun sets, the earth exhales, the moon rises, the brook sings, weary mortals wend home, birds fall silent, the world sleeps – all this, sensitively phrased recitative over the deep tolling bass, with a solo flute in arabesque sympathy, the other figures gradually creeping back in; growing sustained and lyrical for nine bars evoking the rising of the moon – one of the most beautiful haiku in all music. More continuous for the stream – tolling bass replaced by irregular rocking on just two notes, oboe then singer added, drifting above. Brief orchestral spasm of passion amid the prevailing cool, during which a solo horn first announces the four-note main motif of the work's closing stages – a moment easily missed by performers and listeners alike. Return over the rocking motion of calm – brief angst – all desires are now stilled? – yes; the birds are silent, the earth sleeps.

Restart: I alone wake; I await my Friend, to share this beautiful evening, and bid him a last farewell. Recitative over deep bass note, sustained now, not tolling, flute melisma above: then more continuous motion, developing the four-note motif, first unobtrusive, that will dominate the song's closing pages. 'Where are you? – you leave me solitary too long. I wander alone, drunk with the love, beauty, life, of this wonderful world' – wonderfully rendered in fluid transparent textures equally free and daring in harmonic as rhythmic flexibility.

Restart: noises of birds, insects, small creatures, scuttling down for the night – worthy of Ravel's *L'Enfant et les sortilèges* in another aesthetic altogether – subside to introduce a monumental cortège on previous materials, now further developed, continuous not fragmentary, slowly mounting to a huge climax over the opening toll-bass-note-with-gong *fortissimo* not *pianissimo*. It expires, the *Einsame* remains, not now alone: during the funeral march the Friend has arrived; return to recitative over static sustained bass – with gong now to mark the bars – as he dismounts: they exchange the cup of farewell. He speaks – his voice veiled: he asks where he goes and why it must be thus. Deeply self-expressive, Mahler himself replies – 'Thou, my Friend, in this world my luck was not good. Where do I go? I wander the mountains, I seek rest for my lonely heart' – plangent *arioso*, recalling nothing so much (particularly if *Das Lied* is given with baritone rather than contralto, as Mahler sanctioned) as Jesus' *arioso* in the *St Matthew Passion*. Disappears on another shriek of a clarinet night-bird, followed by timorous cheeps on a flute, then bassoon, then cor anglais.

Restart and finish: the ostinato rocking resumes, the voice resumes cool and impersonal, flute melisma above: 'I make for my homeland – I shall roam no more – my heart is still, awaiting its time' – and so to the close, its words added by the composer to the German/Chinese of heretofore, greeting the earth's renewal in green and bloom as the eternal distances shine everywhere blue, *ewig, ewig/* for ever – the four-note motif now leading in the voice through phrase after phrase of luminous fluid transparency, gleaming and glinting and glimmering with harps, celesta, mandolin, gradually thinning, subsiding, vanishing; not without touches of kitsch (*non-religious*), redeemed and transformed utterly by the rapt authenticity of their context as the song of the earth sinks back into the earth from which it was born.

With the 9th Symphony problems of calibre again loom acute. The first movement is one of Mahler's greatest creations – perhaps the finest individual thing he ever wrote: consummate, consummating, consuming its hearers and its self: it extinguishes everything and everybody in sight, in sound. Were he not so hung up on 'the Symphony' he'd have had the courage to end here, where the work ends. Unfortunately he was, and it doesn't. The following three movements are not only redundant but also bad – Shostakovich again in the second, the parody *Ländler* and the third, the hectic joyless scherzo: then in the banal/sentimental main strain of the fourth, the closing adagio – another resemblance, in this case perhaps source, the last movement of Tchaikovsky's *Pathétique* – till, too late for redemption, the moving weariness as the long listless lines linger and fade into the dying horizon.

The importance of the 10th is that it would promise to be the one symphony where the whole is greater than the sum. At first sight its scheme seems to be another hopeless attempt to 'be like the world and contain everything'. But, rather, it is a synthesis and crowning glory of the symphony as extended and dissolved in all the ways already described: a cycle is embraced within a symphonic frame; there are motto motifs and material is reworked from movement to movement; there is song-like material and leitmotivic development; elements of programmatic and poetic meaning; 'the world, everything', but within the artistic bounds of what a symphony can hold. There are imperfections, of a very unusual and circumstantial kind; but the work is rescued by a plan that is extremely strong without being imposed like a grid upon material that seems ideally not to call for it.

The following examination of the work, with some details of its realization, tries to account for the very high evaluation I place on some music that, considered intrinsically, can hardly deserve it. The point is that the circumstances of the work's incompletion rule out an intrinsic view; and the overall conception is so coherent that it can carry the patent weakness of some of the material and the deficiency in its treatment. It is another five-movement scheme: *adagio*; first *scherzo* (half march, half *Ländler*); *Purgatorio*; second *scherzo* (wild and impassioned) fading, then cut short, direct into – slow introduction – *allegro* – slow epilogue.

In the opening adagio the tortuously criss-crossing material on the strings, with the very full harmony needed to render it bearable and beautiful, is inter-broken by the dispassionate *Stimme aus der Ferne* of the opening viola melody, and with material whose relative light-heartedness can turn febrile within a few bars. It is full of extraordinary touches, and the climax is in a class of its own for its power to singe and terrify. The viola melody tails off under long, wispy violin notes; suddenly an immense chorale-like block of common chords rears up, then the main theme's first phrase collapses onto a single, high, trumpet note, around which a horrible dissonance builds up on the full orchestra, layer by layer. It is cut off as if by a switch leaving the trumpet alone, like a voice from a cloud. Then the chord, now simultaneous, rams down again, all the violins enter screaming at the top of their range; and the cloud slowly disperses, revealing a land of lost content into which the movement gently subsides. The dissonance, though it has a long ancestry (back through *Erwartung*, *Salome* and *Elektra*, the adagio of Bruckner's 9th, *Parsifal*'s Kundry, the *Tannhäuser* Bacchanal, *Tristan* Act III, the *Faust-Symphony*, poignant stabs in Chopin, Schumann and Schubert, the frightful outburst before the recitative in Beethoven's choral finale), is in this context perhaps the most painful moment anywhere in the orchestral repertoire. What horrifies is, first, its seeming gratuitousness – a mere scream, out of all proportion, imposed upon the movement rather than, as in the Bruckner, growing inevitably out of a grinding progress which is bound to end in a terrific unresolved dissonance – and then its sadistic deliberation: blow by blow the noise is built up as if the constituent ingredients of anguish were being meted out and analysed.

Serious trouble starts with the second movement. Its character is

a *pastiche-et-mélange* of 6's scherzo, 7's finale and the middle movements of 9; there is even a flicker of 3's scherzo, as well as the harp
glissando from the rondo-burlesque of the 9th. Material is poor-
ish, its working patchy: the symphony's overall shape requires a
movement of this type, and there's no doubt that Mahler would
have intensified it into something resembling the scherzo in the 5th
for its riot of detail. The third movement – the *Purgatorio* – seems
when first heard to act as an intermezzo between the two scherzos: a
Wunderhorn-song-without-words – a lyrical episode like the *Blumine*
second movement in the earlier version of the 1st Symphony. This
comparison, however, shows how the *Purgatorio* is in fact (unlike
Blumine) the indispensable hub of the whole scheme. The seemingly
insignificant little lyric should be compared rather with *Urlicht* in
Symphony 2 and *Das himmlische Leben* in 3 and 4; it is great with
meaning too big for its modest scale and requires an enormous
area for its potential to be fully deployed. To find it trivial misses its
purpose as well as its poignancy. For this 'intermezzo' colours and
pervades everything subsequent to it: a ubiquitous presence in the
second scherzo, it provides the main theme of the introduction and
the thematic substance of the allegro in the fifth movement; even
with the return of the climax of the opening movement, the finale is
now *Purgatorio*-facing, and the passionate up-cry and down-sinking
of the last pages are absolutely direct from the source there, though
the transfiguration also is absolute. The source necessarily gives the
simplest statement of the simple material, in order that its manifold
transformations can make an immediately telling impact.

    The 4th movement is a second scherzo whose character is amply
indicated by the composer's anguished scrawled words on his
sketch – 'the devil dances it with me – Madness seizes me, accursed,
destroy me! that I may forget I exist, that I may cease to be, that . . .'.
The musical idea is marvellous: the three sharp chords again and
again punctuating its course, setting it differently, while clearly connecting it, to the unforgettable dissonance of the adagio. In itself
the material is not of the first quality. So closely made from the *Purgatorio*, and with strains '*von der Jammer der Erde*' running through
it, it is almost a parody movement, with the rondo burlesque from

the 9th as immediate prototype for shape and character, until the wind-down, fade-out ending whose prototype is that of the scherzo in the 6th. But the thing lives a life of its own, unlike the second movement: there is only one bad sag, and the stretch to the close is very good.

The last note, the sudden thwack on the big unstrung drum, obliterates the double bar, hanging the music open-ended over the silence before the next thwack, the first note of the finale. This is tremendous; thereafter the thwacks come too often, too predictably when not expected (though admittedly this deflation of hope is part of Mahler's rhetoric). This introduction plainly recreates that to the finale of the 6th; the fascination here is in the completely different use made of the *Purgatorio* motifs already so brilliantly exploited in the previous movement. It raises itself out of the depths for the famous flute melody, and so into the allegro on the same themes from movement no. 3, whose realization, with the ending, is the greatest triumph of Deryck Cooke's pioneering 1964 restoration. Glancing from the pitiful threadbare sketch to the realized full score is again and again to acknowledge his empathetic yet non-obtrusive rightness. But later the texture goes too slack. The trouble lies in the sketch's actual length; there is not enough allegro, the movement seems to run into the sand, so that the climax comes from nowhere – an accidental rather than deliberate surprise. The dissonance from the climax of the first movement is as unnerving as it was there, but in a different way. There it was an unprepared outburst, extremely theatrical no doubt (like the similar gesture mid third movement and at the start of the finale of Symphony No. 2) but authentically terrifying. As the shudder died down one asked why, and had to wait four movements for the answer. Here the moment unnerves because the sketch is still such a blueprint of Wagnerian 'great-moment' or 'turning-point' combination of themes. The music to which the opening viola melody evaporated just before the outburst in the adagio is now given *tutta forza* on all violins, against which the horns blare the main rhythmic tag of the *Purgatorio* material. Now the dissonance comes back wedge by wedge, each sharpened with the same rhythmic tag. The single trumpet is left hanging, while two others snarl out the allegro's main motif in its form closest to the *Purgatorio*. The entire chord rams down and again the single trumpet is left hanging; under it, the horns give out the opening viola melody (complete, rhythmically more emphatic, and no longer a distant murmur but beginning as powerful summons – all four, *forte* – then fading gently until only the first plays *p diminuendo*); the hanging trumpet simultaneously descends as the violins did previously. All this is effective indeed, and there can be no doubt whatever that fearful symmetry is established across five movements. But the apocalyptic character of these pages cannot conceal the fact that the execution of the idea is painfully bald. The sound is so *dangerous*: the scaffolding will be removed and the walls will not hold; the plaster will crack and the wound will not be healed.

Dangers of another kind threaten the ensuing slow epilogue. In the first movement the opening viola-melody had led to the main theme in F♯-major; in the fifth the same melody now leads to B♭-major. The symphony originally ended in this key: it is one of its simplest and greatest inspirations that F♯-major finally becomes the ultimate goal. But some of the means necessitated to effect this end are really wonky, even as one's heart is in one's mouth over the perilous balance of art and life involved. It is inevitably so moving; but is it good music? The return of the flute-melody from the introduction runs perilously close to the commonplace. Its accidental near-banality is a sort of revenge on Mahler for his lifetime of successful skirting around deliberate near-banality. Here is another disconcerting quality in this symphony, that having been taught by this same composer rightly to distrust the sentimentally easy flow of feeling, one then has to accept it head-on in his last testament. For this flute melody and its later flowering are not 'ironic' – they are heartfelt; witness Mahler's agonized appeals to Alma scrawled on the sketch – 'you alone know what it means – *ach! ach! ach!* Farewell, my lyre, farewell' – they rend the heart: but art is unforgiving. The only solution is to take the base metal and turn it to gold.

This had already begun even before the allegro, and the

characteristic interruption by the drum; now in the epilogue, with no drum to cut it short, it flowers gorgeously then fades out, flames up in a last cry of passionate ardour, then fades richly and fully away in the right key. The use of both *Purgatorio*-motifs, still recognizable but by now transformed utterly, in the last sixteen bars, restores the gold-standard – very simple, no *simplesse*, disaster averted, all falseness purged from notes that, without the spirit, would be trite: no ultimate desolation; a Happy Ending.

'If a composer himself has forced on his listeners the feelings which overwhelmed him then he has achieved his object. The language of music has then approached that of the word, but has communicated immeasurably more than the word is able to express.' I can't now remember who said this so well. The significance of the *Purgatorio* in the 10th, its place at the centre, its powers of pervasion and transformation, its ability to gather the scheme together as a whole; all this is at once deeply poetic and symbolic, and quite undefined. Herein lies its expressive power; the *Purgatorio* is vital just where the 'burial' and especially the 'resurrection' of 'the hero' or the hammer-blows that 'fell him as a tree is felled', all creak. In the 10th, Mahler has got poetic and formal scheme, *Wort und Ton*, into just balance. The musical fabric acts as carrier of the poetic idea – he no longer has to *resort* to the word to realize the music's full suggestion; the music is complete without it but completely upholds it and contains it as a vital but inexplicit (indeed inexplicable) element in the total significance.

And yet its greatness is ultimately inherent rather than actual; for of course its greatness could only be fully embodied in its detailed execution. *Pace* everything, for long stretches this score doesn't sound like real music; compositional foreground and background are in the same plane. The overall scheme and its great focal points are a thrilling conception, yet as the climax of the fifth movement shows, there is a painful absence of flesh. The different state of this movement and the first is clear, though even the adagio, almost completely orchestrated by the composer, comparatively often played and recorded as it is, has an indefinable aura of unrealization. But there is something special about this sketch-bareness: the naked exposure of the lines, particularly on the quadruple woodwinds; the 'unnatural' distinction between lines and supporting harmonic masses – such accidental features have authentic aesthetic quality, and open up possibilities excluded in works of high compositional finish. It would be absurd, in normal circumstances, to take this the way of Henry Moore and actually *prefer* the pregnancy of incompleteness to the barren perfection of a fully worked end-product. In music the sketch as such has no aesthetic value; but occasionally, through some accident, value is forced upon it. Mahler's 10th is one such; the loss of its fully worked completion the most crucial in modern times.

Mahler/Strauss nexus

Contemporaries: Mahler born 1860, Strauss 1864: top-level careers as outstanding conductors, opera especially: as composers they seesaw – Strauss an early brilliant subverter and shocker who soon became recognized, celebrated, enormously successful; Mahler, despite isolated triumphs, widely regarded as producing empty, unoriginal, pretentious, 'conductor's music', advocated only by himself and small circles of enthusiastic devotees – an attitude that persisted for decades after his premature death in 1911. *But* as the Mahler cult swelled from the 1960s on, Strauss's standing diminished; then bounced back, so that by now they stand equal, albeit in different genres and areas of content and expression: they still make an extremely expressive pairing for contrasting artistic types/aims/achievements.

Mahler's sources lie in Schubert/Weber/Schumann; folksong/military strains/klezmer; Italian heart-on-sleeve opera; Bachian polyphony. Strauss's lie in Weber/Mendelssohn/Schumann/Brahms; an idiosyncratic take upon baroque/rococo, from Couperin to Mozart. Both have Beethoven in common, up to a point, and Wagner in a big way – both soaked in him as conductors: with Wolf of the first Austro-German generation to be *post-Wagnerian* in assimilation as well as by date.

Genres: Mahler – symphonies and song-cycles *only*; single exception the early cantata, though so prophetic, *Das klagende Lied*. Strauss – symphonic poems; operas mainly; songs on the side; concertos early and late; plenty of miscellanea.

Both unparalleled masters of the epoch's mammoth orchestral forces and its heaven-storming aspirations. Mahler is all spiritual striving – mystical/transcendental/apocalyptic – torments and ecstasies of a suffering soul; Dostoevskian confession; life-and-death struggle; triumphs and defeats; farewells to life. Strauss does have something of these for sure – *Death and Transfiguration*, the *Alpine Symphony*; but his great strength lies in humorous-sentimental parody cast in narrative and/or depiction of character – *Till Eulenspiegel*, *Don Quixote* (and especially Sancho Panza). They meet over *Zarathustra* (in characteristically contrasted ways) – Strauss's *Also sprach* and Mahler's 3rd Symphony both use Zarathustra's 'Midnight Song'; but they don't meet over Christ – no 'Resurrection' or 8th Symphony for Strauss.

Mahler certainly has a strong parodistic urge, tending towards the grotesque, uncanny, sinister, subversive rather than Strauss's genial/droll – in the 4th Symphony scherzo spooky, in the 7th Symphony scherzo frightening, in the 9th and 10th malign and diabolical; and a strong sentimental side, with or without parody. Both share a tendency towards bombast, overkill. Mahler doesn't do erotic/voluptuous/sensuous-sensual-sexy, which Strauss is so good at – *Salome*, *Rosenkavalier*, or even the near-parody of Dulcinea in *Don Quixote* and his own wife in *Heldenleben* (compare the treatment of Alma in Mahler's 6th) or cheeky/passionate/seductive as in the succession of Don Juan's lovers. Strauss excels in *narrative*, Mahler does *programmes*.

But both are total self-projectors and autobiographers in music. Mahler presents an ongoing serial of his life from symphonies nos. 1 to 10 and including the song-cycles. Strauss is always present in various guises – the great swashbuckler Don Juan, the great mischief-maker Till, a double self-portrait in Don Quixote and his Squire; even before the gross outrageousness of *Heldenleben* – himself as culture-hero routing all opposition and spreading his works as the fruits of peace; and the *Symphonia Domestica* – himself as perfect bourgeois husband-and-father, equally effective in bed and over the breakfast coffee-cups – compare Mahler's version in his 6th Symphony – 'scenes from a marriage', complete with blows of Fate.

Strauss said, 'I want to set myself to music'; and 'if Alexander the Great or Napoleon why not me? I consider myself just as interesting.' Mahler simply *is* Napoleon, Jesus, Zarathustra, Faust – the Hero, the Protagonist, felled and resuscitated, felled again, risen again – Suffering Servant and Triumphal Victim/Victor, representing Mankind, led, not followed, by the *Ewig* (*ewig, ewig*) *Weibliche*/Eternal Feminine. (He's more assuming than Strauss, actually: Mahler's chutzpah is universalist.)

Unbelievable fluency, mastery, assurance, confidence – supreme technicians, masters of vulgarity, clichéd, shopsoiled bargain-basement dregs: absolutely without inhibition, scruple, shame – yet sheer genius and daring and originality alongside; dazzling, stirring, thrilling; and sometimes moving, occasionally deeply. Corny and Cornucopian.

Strauss

Born 1864: father an outstanding horn-player, contemptuous of the 'new music' (i.e. Wagner) he executed so well. Early promise like Mendelssohn/Weber/Schumann/Brahms/Bruch; *Wind Serenade*, 1st Horn Concerto; obediently hostile to Wagnerian music-drama and Lisztian programme-music, at both of which he was to excel.

Beginnings of outstanding conducting-career 1885; converted to the advanced currents in German music, not excluding Berlioz, but mainly Liszt and Wagner – soon to be hailed as 'Richard the Third – there can be no Second': triumphant succession of symphonic poems, putting this dubious and impure genre onto a new footing: *Macbeth* (1887–8) a curate's egg; *Don Juan* (1888–9) all daring, swashbuckling erotic exuberance; *Tod und Verklärung/Death and Transfiguration* (1889–90) all onomatopoeia and uplift;

Till Eulenspiegel (1894–5) all cheeky brilliance; and revealing a conspicuous gift for narrative, character, parody, depiction of *things*; *Also sprach Zarathustra* (1896) similar virtuosity in covering metaphysics and mystery-mongering; *Don Quixote* (1897–8) narrative, character, parody, depiction of *things* taken to their height; and in *Ein Heldenleben/A Hero's Life* (1898–9) taken over the top – the Hero is himself, the Hero's Life his own victories and defeats, his own works, his own personal life; taken to excess in the *Symphonia Domestica* (1903), which throws in baby, bathwater, bed-&-breakfast, and the *Alpine Symphony* (1911–15), which throws in a mountain, an organ and sixteen off-stage brass to amplify the already gigantic forces on-stage.

Meanwhile, opera: Wagner straight – *Guntram/Parsifal* (1892–3); its failure prompts Wagner parodied yet vindicated – *Feuersnot/ Meistersinger* (1900–1901). On course with a pair of lurid expressionist extremes, of the utmost boldness, flair, brilliance, cutting deep for all their shallowness: *Salome* (1904–5); *Elektra* (1906–8): *succès de scandale* with the first, enabling the building of his super-bourgeois villa.

Volte-face? 'Parody and sentimentality are my *forte*', put into practice well before this admission was made: the *real* Richard Strauss maybe, after all. *Der Rosenkavalier* (1909–10) – blown-up operetta, chocolates and spun-sugar from a 'Mozartian' never-never baroque/rococo Vienna – *succès fou*, at once and ever since. *Ariadne auf Naxos*, originally (1911–12) combined with Molière's *Bourgeois gentilhomme*, spoken, to conclude; revised with a new Prologue (and dropping the play) 1916: the play's incidental music worked up as a purely instrumental suite 1919.

The Great War and a last assault upon the grand-slam Sublime: *Die Frau ohne Schatten* (1914–18). What next? This is when he actually declares to his celebrated librettist (from *Elektra* onwards) that, in these terrible times, parody and sentimentality are his way forward – after all *this*, goodbye to all *that* – and abandons Hugo von Hofmannsthal for a while, for an *Intermezzo* (1917–23) to his own text: prosaic contemporary setting, dramatizing a marital riff, himself and his wife on-stage undisguised and unabashed: oddly linking this middle-aged high Romantic to the new and alien aims of the young post-war generation; and in its way a real triumph.

Interwar decades: after the *Intermezzo* a rapprochement with Hofmannsthal: back to highfalutin mythology – *Die ägyptische Helena* (1923–7) – and sentimental old Vienna – *Arabella* (1930–32), garrulous dilution of their *Rosenkavalier*. After Hofmannsthal's death in 1929, a succession of collaborations: with excellent Stefan Zweig *Die schweigsame Frau* (1933–4), adapting Ben Jonson's *Silent Woman*; with mediocre Joseph Gregor *Friedenstag* (1935–6) – ersatz *Fidelio*; *Daphne* (1936–7) – lyric/bucolic tragedy; *Die Liebe der Danae* (1938–40) – 'cheerful mythology', on a theme inherited from Hofmannsthal.

No large-scale non-operatic work of significance during the interwar decades, unless the preposterous ballet *Schlagobers* – *Whipped Cream* – to his own scenario (1921–2). But, all his life, Strauss a copious composer of *Lieder*, with piano, with orchestra, and often orchestrating songs originally written with piano only: variable, often routine, sometimes achieving high calibre. As the 1930s decline and darken, Strauss is more and more on autopilot: tireless fecundity, but the *music* is tired: occasional joys and newness, like the wit/speed/sparkle of *The Silent Woman*; the best of *Daphne* – her sundrenched expanses of pantheistic lyricism; Danae's shower of gold shows the old conjurer can still conjure magic. Then there is the question, still veiled in uncertainty, of his awkward, ambiguous relationship with Nazi musical officialdom.

Renewal and 'Indian summer': his last opera, *Capriccio* (1940–41) – renewed calibre of collaborator Clemens Krauss – is a triumph: everything meets, purified and refreshed – his 'Wagner' meets his 'Mozart' in a felicitous marriage of artifice and heartfelt testament. It liberates a succession of purely instrumental works that revisit his teens – Weber and Mendelssohn to the fore, with the intervening experience worked in and lightly worn: two 'sonatinas' (but they are gigantic!) for wind-band (1943–5): concertos for horn (No. 2 1942), for oboe (1945–6), for clarinet and bassoon (1947). Not so lightly worn, *Metamorphosen* for twenty-three solo strings (1945): Wagner and Beethoven invoked, and employed, to mourn German *Kultur* amid the wreckage: a hot-air balloon, tour de force of technique and stamina, somehow too sumptuous, too luxurious even in its grief, to move the listener to *real* tears. No such problem with the final four orchestral songs, summatory climax and adieu to the lifetime of *Lieder* – spring, summer, autumn, sleep (he'd always excelled at berceuses), farewell. Though after completing those *Four Last Songs* (1948) he sketched a fifth and began work on a little opera for children, *The Donkey's Shadow*; a few numbers managed before his death September 1949.

The British problem with Strauss, since it's a problem of our own self-definition or self-understanding, will never end. Who was it said, 'I never feel happy about pleasure'? – some famous or nameless genius of the national character. Yet this ambiguous discomfort about Strauss isn't merely prudish, priggish, prissy. Something in it isn't wrong, though not exactly right either. But – for our good and to our loss – such crashing plenitude of grossness and vulgarity sticks in our Pre-Raphaelite maw.

Take *Schlagobers*/*Whipped Cream*. What could be more utterly dreadful than this tasteless ballet about sweet-tasting goodies, this preposterous celebration of conspicuous consumption set in an all-too-*haute-bourgeoisie* patisserie? Completely lacking in the aristocratic finesse, and the romantic splendour, of its unacknowledged source in Act II of Tchaikovsky's *Nutcracker*, temporarily culminating in a girlie-routine à la Busby Berkeley for the 'Waltz of the Whipped Cream' before settling down with a comfortable porcine grunt to its true dialectic: class warfare between privileged pralines and proletarian buns, located in the lugubriously overstuffed stomach of a greedy schoolboy – could tackiness go further? Tactlessness too, as hyper-inflation loomed in the countries for which it was written, where even a humble gobstopper could cost a million marks.

Strauss's tastelessness and tedium remain stumbling-blocks. The first is all-permeating, inseparably part of the very definition of his genius. The second is less forgivable: would-be sublimity (*Die Frau ohne Schatten*), sentiment (*Arabella*) and fun (*Schweigsame Frau*) are accompanied by stretches of note-spinning routine that sometimes almost engulf the whole work. But let us continue to indulge, forgive and explore him, to be open to the amplitudes of a composer who can still, for all his familiarity, surprise and astonish.

Symphonic poems

Some pairs of complements from his mid-twenties to his mid-eighties, chosen to show him at his peak. First, the two best of the symphonic poems with which he shot to fame. Strauss's *Don Juan* is neither Mozart's *Giovanni* (*ancien régime/droit de seigneur*) nor Byron's (satirical/self-deflecting): his source is Nikolaus Lenau's unfinished play *Don Juans Ende* (1844) – a Faustian Quest for the Absolute via erotic conquest, life drunk to the dregs in the face of death. Three excerpts preface the score:

> I would square the immeasurable magic circle in a storm of pleasure, to die at last of a kiss. Oh that I could fly everywhere where beauty blooms; adore; achieve; a moment only of victory ...

> ... endless variety, endless renewal – every beautiful woman is different ... my love is boundless and ever-changing, springing ever new, knowing nothing of regret or backward-turning. Onwards and Upwards ...

> ... beautiful was the tempest that drove me: its force is spent: all is silent, all hope and desire quenched. Did lightning from the heavens I despised strike my lust-for-life, making my world a sudden dark desert? Maybe; maybe not: for sure, the fuel is consumed, the hearth cold.

Thus the tone: for shape, a sort-of-sonata with episodes: for idiom and technique, an electric 'skin-tight' fusion of Berlioz, Liszt, Wagner, with an orchestral virtuosity never heard before, from the very first rush up into impetuous main theme and first paragraph, racing to embrace a more expansive contour before renewed impetus, to open out into relaxed ardour on a violin solo; heralding Episode 1: its prima donna takes up the brief expansive contour into rolling periods of generous ardour – a sequence-machine à la Liszt, of incomparably greater compositional prowess: how he keeps it Onward and Upward! – till the inevitable moment of satiation and disgust, unmissably graphic: first, at apex of ardour . . . the texture disintegrates . . . second, a softer but harsher repudiation. Immediate signs of recovery: drastically foreshortened return of opening 'exposition' to introduce – Episode 2: exchanges between Juan's appassionato strings and a timid fluttering solo flute. He manages to still her fears: a long, tender love-scene ensues, led by broad singing oboe solo. This affair doesn't end in disgust – rather, a sad weariness, the gratified animal with a pang of regret – and again almost *visible* in sound – the reposeful warmth and euphony taking on a tinge of bitter aloes before again relaxing.

Not for long: Juan's on the rampage again. Brilliant of Strauss to hold back the hero's most celebrated theme's first appearance to this relatively late moment: virility incarnate on four unison horns: irresistible. Anxious oboe reply: the horns swell in anew, taken up by trombones, continually redeployed surrounded by rushing-motions and little fanfare-figures from earlier. Then all lights up – bright, carefree, playful *giocoso* – even including a glockenspiel solo on the horn-theme. Things get strenuous: polyphonic workout: another collapse, worse than the previous – deep shuddering drum-roll, bitter, soft, muted brass chords, flecks of once-insouciant vitality dispersing on flutes, then clarinets, then bassoons, a choke of muted strings, wistful flickers of past loves.

This lull ends with a short, sharp, soft chord on brass now unmuted over drum-roll, now un-menacing: a 'recapitulation' in the sort-of-sonata: the Don's initial up-rushing figure softly up the strings in turn – cellos, violas, violins; fragments of previous themes, gradually coalescing and uniting to bring back the first theme in all its first confidence: splendid polyphonic mishmash, everything in play, crowned with return of the four horns on their horny theme, now doubled with high cellos for extra sonority: then high on orchestral tutti. Range upon range of singing phrases, through the keys, a cymbal-crash on the remotest: a temporary stasis, then hurtling recklessly towards jubilant self-destruction – '*lachender Tod*'/ 'laughing death'; stringendo towards maximum volume over dominant pedal; cut-off; long silence; chill non-resolution to IV-minor, the full orchestra clammed from bottom to top except a pair of trumpets stabbing a dissonant minor sixth. The winds gradually removed from top to bottom as violins descend in shivering tremolando; a sound-image of ashes on a cold hearth, ashes at a cold heart. It disappears in a wisp of smoke up the violins rapid scale to E-minor: the A-men cadence without an iota of warmth let alone unction. Over the tonic pedal on drum, low-voiced dissonance on winds, then a pair of expressive bassoons, fading away as low violas shudder in tremolo; a very quiet, dry close: bare and pizzicato, plus drum and double-bassoon and trombones to help: *Alles endet*.

Till Eulenspiegel shares some characteristics – brio, confidence, swagger – with *Don Juan*, though the two protagonists are complements; Till is Juan's Leporello, even his Sancho Panza. The rogue and his pranks originate in 'early middle-low German folklore', gathered together in a chapbook in 1515; he exposes vices and mocks hypocrisy, and rather than ending up on the gallows, dies of the plague. *Eulenspiegel*/Owl's Mirror – has also a scatological connotation – *ulen*, to sweep; *Spiegel*, a mirror, but slang for hindquarters; the combination can mean 'wipe-arse'. Strauss's portrayal is fully aware of the double-sense; he never minced his words. Rondo is as absolutely suited for the anti-hero's episodic pranks as sonata is for the hero's amours: and the composer's command of his material, its pacing and placing, and his orchestration, is still more stunning. New for *Till* (not needed in *Don Juan*) are mischief, parody, anarchy, mayhem, and the sheer *thinginess* of depiction – the motifs depicting objects and actions in the *Ring* – sword, spear, forging and hammering, the Tarnhelm, etc. – become in Strauss's hands several degrees cleverer, more palpable, more vivid, even as their actual *meaning* is demoted.

Wagner glints from the very opening in Till's first theme, a wicked re-use of the principal motif in the *Tristan* love-duet (Strauss had conducted his first *Tristan* in 1892): just four bars of introduction that say 'hear an old story of one Till Eulenspiegel' before he himself leaps into the scene in the famous horn-solo – the composer's tongue-in-cheek tribute to his horn-playing father? – with its cunningly displaced accents and vertiginous descent to the instrument's near-bottom note. Twice; then taken up by other instruments; peremptory half-close; portentous pause on V: Till's opening '*Tristan*' phrase again, now fully in the present, in his own Tale, its cocky snook exactly suited to the shrill piccolo clarinet.

Market-day in picturesque main square of some medieval German Burg. Till rides his horse into the bustle; dismounts, wanders about with an air of disingenuous innocence – his '*Tristan*'-motif, just its first three notes, spun out into continuous motion on flute – as near to whistling in any score before actual whistling in Britten's *Albert Herring*. Tiny hint, *en passant*, of the trouble he's always courting, cheeking the upright Authorities who'll get him in the end. For now, tingling expectancy and mock meekness – sudden rush up a normal clarinet – all Bedlam let loose, stalls overturned, fruit and veg, hens, ducks, geese everywhere, market-women screeching – depicted with skill and glee, first raucous and dissonant then, after a silence, in bemused overlaid five-finger exercises up and down the scale – easing into casualness – he's disappeared unobserved to find the next prank.

A church procession, plump and satisfied – two bassoons unison with divided violas plus touches of clarinet; just right. '*Tristan*'-Till insinuated unctuously into the bass then reaches the top: ineffably complacent close. Slithy chromatic turns, rather nasty – he's thumbing his arse (or sticking out his Speigel, more likely). A solo violin skitters down nearly four octaves – 'it wasn't me – who're you blaming?' and, all genial again, he's after the girls. '*Tristan*'-Till gradually yielding to/combining with horn-Till in conjunctions and transformations as ingenious as they're witty: tender/amorous too, when he goes a-wooing, dapper and gallant as his Master, then waxing plump and pressing as Falstaff in love. Sudden cut-off leaving only the four horns suspended in mid-oration. Rebutted, or sated, or impatient, he escapes, with a rude sign, to the next prank. See the learnèd Doctors of Law, Philosophy, Theology, Astronomy, Medicine, Musicology, their procession as dry and jerky as the Prelates' was full-fat warm. From the near-start it incorporates Till-shapes; and in this clever work's most cunningly wrought music – appropriate as ever – the horn-motif is piled upon itself in spiteful close counterpoint, with fascinating virtuosity in the rhythmic dislocation of the initially regular pedants' march. It tangles magnificently into knots: then with one bound our hero is free, laughing all the way to the next – busyness calms into a gentle pastorale, the 'Tristan'-Till singing clear and open through flowing figuration on woodwinds and strings in graceful overlap – an oasis of gentleness, heralding Till's horn-theme again, as at first, incorporating the 'Tristan'-Till too, boiling up to a Grandiose Moment – powerful brass in augmentation on 'Tristan'-Till, a whirling momentum above, trumpets' tattoo penetrating and binding: same, treble and bass swapped about. Then diverts to a hop and a skip, briefly quietening for Till's whistle on flute, then re-amassing with mounting zest and invention, culminating in a fizz of ferocious Lord-of-Misrule defiance, a blast of Church and/or Civic Authority, now wielding its strength; then sharp cut-off leaving only dampened drum-roll. Terrific summons from the Powers-that-Be, alternating with the piccolo clarinet's contemptuous/indifferent thumbs-up: these alternate several times, the menaces undiminishing, the rude gestures growing shorter. The slithery chromatic turn from way back and not heard since now returns – his foretold fate now coming true, or wiping his arse to mock, insult, outrage his judges. A choked string tremolo – they're shocked: a verdict – guilty: a sentence – the gallows – very loud thumbs-down on brass; the piccolo clarinet cocks a last defiant snook, right up to its top, joined there by harsh high oboes and cor anglais, which descend slowly right to the depths of the orchestra – don't miss the last twitch of life on solo flute – horrid graphicness, yet also funny.

The thumbs-down dissonant note held throughout the execution; then, as the corpse is left dangling, this note resolves to home key and momentum is stilled. One bar of silence: another tonic chord, very soft: silence. Epilogue – the very opening again, after its third bar tenderly expanded: the 'Once upon a Time' feeling perfectly evoked (Strauss had conducted the première of *Hansel and Gretel* in 1893, the year before beginning his *Till*). Warm string-writing yields to woodwinds as sweet in nostalgia as, just before, they'd been scrawny for the gallows. Long-held remote triad very soft; sudden resumption of loud orchestral tutti, principal lively tempo, some main material including 'Tristan'-Till, to a perfectly comic-timed End. Till lives, to perform all his tricks anew. And Strauss's next prank goes up in the world – date with the cosmos, eternal recurrence, the great bell of midnight, Zarathustra and Superman. Then Don Quixote and Sancho; then Himself as Hero.

Operas

Salome, famously infamous from its première onwards and quite soon settling into a firm if always special place in the repertoire, is, with *Elektra* a couple of years later, Strauss's furthest venture into modernism. Important for subsequent Mahler, crucial to emergent expressionism and atonality: Schoenberg's two pre-Great War one-acters and his *Five Orchestral Pieces* – expressionism and atonality at their pinnacle of extremity – would not have been possible without Strauss's previous opening-out of the terrain; nor Berg's two post-War operas; nor too such analogous undertakings as Bartók's *Miraculous Mandarin* and further stage-works more directly of Austro-German culture. The only composer not to follow the lead was the leader himself. 'A superlative has no future': Strauss realized this early: as time elapses the distance between his goalposts diminishes – the two discrepant limits have more in common than anyone could have seen at the time.

Strauss the pragmatic craftsman, the earthy realist, the businessman, always produces exactly what's called for in each situation. Wilde's play is an *exercise de style* – lurid treatment of a peripheral Gospel-episode, ingrown late child to a long literary line evoking antiquity in decadence; closest behind, Flaubert's *Herodias* telling the same events, which Wilde's version virtually plagiarizes. Its diction is flashy and meretricious, its treatment of the subject trifling and sensationalist, its 'moral' facile and cheap. All this, together with the story itself, is just up Strauss's *Straße*: setting of scene – clichéd Orient with its well-known depravities; rendition of character and

caricature; steering a narrative; depiction of *things*; evading any sententious sermonizing: Wilde's *Salome* is made for him – the affinity
is as perfect as Maeterlinck's *Pelléas* for Debussy, Büchner's *Wozzeck*
for Berg, Melville's *Billy Budd* for Britten. The heroine's succession of
tributes to the Baptist's physical attractions – 'thy body is like unto
the lilies of the field . . . thy hair unto clusters of black grapes . . .', etc.,
mounting in rapture as their object's repudiations in vehemence,
to climax in what she'll eventually get – 'thy mouth is like unto a
pomegranate sliced with a silver knife': then later, the accumulation
of marvels Herod presses upon her if she but desist from the only
treasure she really wants – 'beggar's largesse' – white peacocks, jewels
beyond compare, half his kingdom, the veil of the Temple. All such
is a gift to Strauss's particular mercantile literalism, as the Dance of
the Seven Veils would be to most composers in general. And when
Wilde goes high-poetic – 'the moon is like a woman arising from
the tomb' (in the first scene); or portentous pseudo-profound (in the
last, when she's kissed the pomegranate mouth) – 'the mystery of
love is greater than the mystery of death' – these too are just his style.

So to the story: immediate setting, Tetrarch Herod's court,
his nagging spouse Herodias, Salome her daughter by a previous
match; courtiers, slaves (later an executioner); wider context of
fractious dogmatic Jews: distant sense of alien Roman rule: and,
down a deep well where he's incarcerated and invisible, but all-too-
audible, Jokanaan – John the Baptist – interrupting and articulat-
ing every earlier phase of the action with prophecies of doom. Swift
momentum from the start: Narraboth, a young guard, extols the
Princess's charms and is warned to beware by Herodias' page: the
moon looks especially sinister tonight. The Prophet's voice is heard:
Salome, escaping to the open terrace from her stepfather's unwelcome attentions, listens and is fascinated: playing upon Narraboth's
infatuation she persuades him, against stern prohibition, to have the
captive brought up from his incarceration. It is done: more tirades,
more vehement still when she tells him who she is – *ich bin Salome* –
and proceeds to extol his physical attributes. Narraboth kills himself
in despair. Jokanaan descends to his dark well with a parting curse;
the royal couple emerge on to the terrace.

Herod is all nerves: seeing the blood – 'he was comely' – and the malign moon, shivering in an uncanny wind felt only by him. The voice from the depths is again heard: Herodias winces – the denunciations are mainly directed against her; but Herod claims this man is from God. The Jews object, and bicker over points of belief. Two pious Nazarenes describe some of Jesus' recent miracles. 'What – he's raised the dead!?' Herod, tetchy/itching credulous/incredulous, calls for diversion: music; then for Salome to dance for him, promising lavish rewards. 'Anything I ask, Tetrarch? You swear your oath?' She knows what she desires and accepts the invitation despite her mother's urgent objections. Dance of the Seven Veils. It succeeds to perfection: Herod is intoxicated. The inevitable contest of wills ensues: his offers pile hyperbolically higher: she stubbornly holds out – 'I want the head of Jokanaan.' 'Well said, my daughter,' says her mother as the Tetrarch crumples – 'give her what she asks – she's truly her mother's daughter' – and sets the order in motion. The Executioner descends, the Princess hangs panting over the edge of the well till he reappears bearing the severed head on a silver salver. No one sees this; we're seeing the sound – one of the greatest passages of orchestral exaltation ever penned. It leaps off the pages of the full-score to the eyes as, from the pit of the theatre, it assails the spirit; these millions of notes making a teeming froth of multiform invention equal or superior to contemporary parallels in Schoenberg or Berg, for which it is the prototype, and far more intense than anything comparable in any other composer of the epoch. Incomprehensible that Strauss, the ultra-practical, should at the climactic crunch, the perfect cadence into the work's principal key C#-minor when Salome reaches the word *kiss*, should trust her main motif to the celesta, undoubled by any assistance from woodwinds, brasses, strings. The celesta – gently shining creature employed elsewhere for what it was invented for – sugar-plum icing, nimbus, sensual allure, halo of dim religious light! She apostrophizes her trophy in a long scena: the onlookers look on more and more aghast, occasionally muttering horrified reactions. Culmination, the Kiss, memorably represented in Beardsley's famous drawing; and a final burst of fulfilment – 'I have kissed thy mouth – it was bitter: they say love is bitter; but what of that – I have kissed thy mouth.' The malign moon illuminates the lurid sight. Herod, jibbing at last, commands his soldiers to crush Salome to death: it is done, in a sudden brusque termination, over in a flash after the long expanses preceding, in an absolutely alien key.

It's kitsch, it's exploitative, it's machine-made and thoroughly commercial. Also decidedly not profound or elevated: attempts to claim it so are misguided and apt to rebound. It is what it is – '*ich bin Salome*': gold and slag in red-hot fusion, unfazed by questions of taste, decorum, context, morality – calibre, even. In its own kind, a territory of its own, the best ever. Strauss and his brother-enemy-rival-complement Mahler are the greatest masters of the most highly developed means yet produced by Western musical culture, the symphony orchestra at its apogee of size, complexity, efficiency, prowess, pride. It's not their fault that their supreme command of high and low ended up in Hollywood.

Elektra takes *Salome* to yet further extremes: Strauss begged his librettist for more of the same, before retreating into reactionary rococo – *Rosenkavalier* and *Ariadne auf Naxos*. The most perfect result of this recoil, incidental music to *Le Bourgeois gentilhomme*, a suite of nine movements for *small* orchestra worked up from the incidental music to Molière's play, originally the entertainment commanded to close the eponymous gentleman's festivities after the serious opera and the comedy relief, before the fireworks. The Molière was dropped when *Ariadne auf Naxos* was elaborated into the complete evening, with its new Prologue setting backstage context for one of Strauss's conspicuously successful minglings of high and low: the *seria* of Ariadne's abandonment on the island, love-lorn, awaiting only death, interwoven with the capers of clowns and soubrette from the *commedia dell'arte*, compelled by shortage of time to play simultaneously not successively, piquantly interacting to mutual advantage, closing to the troupe's sympathetic satisfaction with Bacchus' arrival and the triumph of love reborn. The small orchestra for the *Gentilhomme Suite*, as for the opera – two each of woodwinds and horns, one trumpet, one trombone, fourteen strings, timpani and percussion; harp and a prominent concertante/continuo piano – is at the opposite pole from *Salome* and *Elektra* and Strauss's concurrent work on the still-more-extravagant *Alpine Symphony* and *Die Frau ohne Schatten*. It enables textures of a refinement and precision unique in his output. And the whole *Suite* Strauss's cleanest, most delicious work, detail and observation at their keenest, invention prime and fresh, nothing gross, coarse, exaggerated even when parody and caricature are involved. Even when depicting *food*, plain or fancy, the touch is light, sure, flawless. One recalls the terms of his admiration for Bizet's orchestration – the 'wonderful economy, and how every note and every rest is in its proper place'. He himself would not again regain such an ideal till the music of his final decade.

Le Bourgeois gentilhomme is significant in musical history too. 'Neo-classicism' – particularly a rejigging of the eighteenth century from Bach to Mozart – a principal strand in the 'music of the future' after the Great War, already flourished before it. It had been foreshadowed in such discrepant forerunners as Brahms's *Handel Variations*, Wagner's Lutheran chorales in *Meistersinger*, Tchaikovsky's ballets, *Mozartiana*, *Rococo Variations*, Chabrier's *gallanterie* in his *Suite pastorale*, and much else. The '*Mozartiana*' in *Rosenkavalier* is a direct harbinger. The *Bourgeois gentilhomme* music, originally of 1911–12, fits alongside such contiguous ventures into pastiche, imitation, re-composition, arrangement, impulses of reaction and renovation, whether weary or vital, as Reger's variation-sets on themes of Telemann and Mozart (both 1914), Ravel's *Tombeau de Couperin* (1914–17), Debussy's last sonatas (1915–17), Respighi's *Ancient Airs and Dances* (1917), Prokofiev's *Classical Symphony* (also 1917) and Stravinsky's *Pulcinella* (1919–20). What begins in playful fun-and-games grows serious, for all its frequent frivolity, as the long nineteenth century sags and implodes under its own weight; and the twentieth edges or protests into sharper definition. A large theme for later.

BETWEEN TWO WARS: INTERMEZZO TO CAPRICCIO

The very title – *Intermezzo* – of his next opera – his eighth – indicates that Strauss is on vacation/off duty from Hofmannsthal. Potentially

embarrassing, the piece is a distinct success: an intimate marital mis-
understanding, from the life, to its composer's own deft libretto,
which puts himself and his wife on the boards (the husband in the
first production actually wore a Strauss-mask): her harmless infatuation with a silly young aristocratic go-getter, his spot of bother with
a singer – Mitzi Meier! – stormy explanations, loving reconciliation,
Domestica twenty years after: fresh, funny, fast, innovative alike in
subject-matter and its treatment, and in its musical speech. Not so
with *Schlagobers*, composed alongside – a deplorable enterprise, this
ballet, also to his own scenario, as already described. But both these
works of the early 1920s show Strauss to be thoroughly au fait with
contemporary life – telegrams and anger.

Thereafter, Strauss is on autopilot: a couple of undistinguished
piano concertos – left-hand only, for Paul Wittgenstein; civic pomp
and circumstance for Vienna, Munich, the Olympic Stadium at Berlin,
the Imperial Dynasty of Japan: choral music with and without orchestra; songs with orchestra and piano including one first-class group –
Three Hölderlin Hymns of 1921 with soprano and orchestra – the *Four
Last Songs* already on the horizon. And six successive operas which
I've sketched in already. Millions of notes from this unfailingly fluent,
hard-working professional; vitality, energy, mastery unbounded; but
tired for all the unweariedness – lonely flickers of real calibre and
freshness: the precious silver half-hour or so of real calibre in *Arabella*
amid the desert wastes of note-spinning – where the sisters sing
together, or – best of all – where the heroine sings alone; the intermittent delights – especially its fleet-footed Overture – of *The Silent
Woman*; the ecstatic/pantheist close of *Daphne* – another *Liebestod*
wherein the heroine sings alone as her lover the Sun transforms her
into a laurel; the shower of gold in which her lover Jupiter descends
upon *Danae*. But in general, there'd be every justification for writing
Strauss off as a spent force well before 1940, until the marvellous reju-
venation effected by Clemens Krauss and *Capriccio*.

Its roots do, however, go back to the principal collaborator.
Strauss writes to Hofmannsthal (16 June 1927): 'the other day I
heard *Meistersinger* again – a tremendous work. Ever since I've
been unable to shake off the urge to write a work of this type some

day – unfortunately, needless to say, at a respectful distance.' Hofmannsthal replies to his request for a 'Meistersinger No. III' with one of the finest letters in the correspondence (1 July 1927), an evocation of Nuremberg as celebrated in romantic literature, and the culmination of this celebration in *Meistersinger*, whose 'indestructible truth' is that it 'brings to life again a genuine, complete world which did exist – not . . . imaginary worlds which have never existed anywhere'. He claims *Rosenkavalier* as a descendant of *Meistersinger*:

> Just as in the former opera the Nuremberg of 1500 is the true vehicle of the whole thing and that which gives life to the characters, in the latter it is the Vienna of Maria Theresa – a complete and real and therefore convincing city-world composed of a hundred living interrelations . . . from the palace through the backstairs . . . to the peasant in the farmyard.

Hofmannsthal's letter contains two points which extend the connection to cover subject-matter. First, resignation: Sachs, 'the ageing artist between desire and resignation', must surely recall the Marschallin; for all the differences between her poignant renunciation of her young lover and Sachs's noble relinquishment of his hopes for a young bride, the motif is the same. Second, class: 'the fine intermingling of the world of the knight with the world of the burgher' is as true, *mutatis mutandis*, of *Rosenkavalier* – compare the nuptials of Junkers Walther and Octavian with merchant-daughters Eva and Sophie.

A more general connection, concerning the artist's appearance in his own work, can be made between *Meistersinger* and Strauss at large (although not now including *Rosenkavalier*). One can take Walther and Sachs as self-portraits of the artist in fiery youth and rounded maturity; Walther routing his critics; Sachs teaching Walther how, by combining their prescriptions with respect for the traditions, to shape his visions into art. The analogues in Strauss are *Ein Heldenleben* (self-portrait of the artist as virile musician routing his critics), *Symphonia Domestica* (self-portrait of the artist in virile maturity), *Intermezzo* (scenes from married life). In old age Strauss's tendency to self-portraiture is diffused into such character-pieces as the 'convalescent' and 'merry workshop' sonatinas; something of a specific self-portrait (the artist as man of energetic *savoir faire*) is seen in the heroic Theatre Director in *Capriccio*. *Capriccio* also provides idealized (not self-portrayed) creative figures in its Poet and Composer, both of them derived from the composer in the Prelude of *Ariadne*. The fault of *Meistersinger* and its descendant *Rosenkavalier* is disproportion between form and content. In both a slender story is mercilessly prolonged, and musical invention better suited to a number-opera is given relentless music-drama treatment with the result that romantic comedy and operetta, respectively, become inflated beyond what these genres can properly take. This is not to deny the wonderful beauty and resource of Wagner's score, nor the gorgeous opulence and affecting poignancy of the best things in the Strauss. The disproportion is unacceptable only in their would-be comic aspects, the unfunniness of Beckmesser's and Ochs' discomfiture and the exaggerated crudity of its depiction in music. Hofmannsthal realized something of this. He expresses it in a remarkable letter to Strauss (11 June 1916) which, perhaps regrettably, was never sent. Strauss, he says, had in *Rosenkavalier* 'wholly failed at certain points to enter into my ideas, and treated quite a few things in the wrong style altogether ...' He instances the chorus of Faninal's servants in Act II, 'written only to be rattled off in burlesque fashion, i.e. in the transparent Offenbach style. What you did was to smother it with *heavy* music and so to destroy utterly the purpose of the words ... The fun of this passage has simply ceased to exist.' He complains similarly of the end of Act I and of the Baron's exit in Act III. In only one work, he says, has Strauss achieved the right style – the incidental music for *Le Bourgeois gentilhomme*. This music and *Ariadne*, the opera which originally formed the conclusion to the same project, have this *Meistersinger–Rosenkavalier* nexus as their background. Strauss to Hofmannsthal (September 1916):

> Your *cri-de-cœur* against Wagnerian 'note-spinning' has deeply touched my heart, and has thrust open a door to an entirely new landscape where, guided by *Ariadne* and in particular the new

Prelude, I hope to move forward wholly into the realm of un-Wagnerian emotional and human comic opera ... An amusing, interesting plot, with dialogue, arias, duets, ensembles or what you will, woven by real composable beings à la Marschallin, Ochs, Barak ... I promise you that I have now definitely stripped off the Wagnerian musical armour.

Capriccio seems just round the corner with this prescription, although the path there was long and arduous.

Meanwhile, their *Ariadne/Bourgeois gentilhomme* project, as already described, and particularly the discovery in its new Prologue of a new fluidity, speed, naturalness. *Capriccio* is a late second brew from this rich mixture. The *Meistersinger–Rosenkavalier* nexus is still behind it, both as modified by *Ariadne* and directly, as in the letter of July 1927, which made the nexus clear. What *Capriccio* has lost from its prototypes is their sense of the larger social whole – 'a genuine, complete world which did exist', 'composed of a hundred living interrelations' – and the wider class ramifications, 'the fine inter-mingling of the world of the knight with the world of the burgher', 'from the palace through the backstairs world of the footmen to the peasant in the farmyard'. It replaces these by unity of class and place; the rich specificities of Nuremberg in 1500 and Maria The-resa's Vienna have now shrunk to a country château, with Paris in the 1770s (Gluck versus Piccini, the new fashion for chocolate, old Goldoni, etc.) indicated by a skilfully suggestive sketchiness. A complex structure of social interconnection is no longer implied; instead, we have the polite mingling of those socially 'possible' or plausible in an aristocratic salon. Of course, authenticity of detail is not here of primary interest. This setting in time and place has been chosen because of its suitability to sustain a sentimental fantasy of aristocratic elegance and refinement, justifiable because it will elicit from its composer what he is able and wishes to do.

Capriccio returns to *Meistersinger* for a feature which the altogether more full-blooded and straightforward *Rosenkavalier* has no place for: the disputation upon art-forms, the public tradition versus innovation, etc. One feature among many in *Meistersinger*, in

Capriccio this has come so far to the fore as to embrace both plot and subject-matter, which have no existence outside it. The work is a conversation-piece, a disputation upon a question moved, whether *Wort oder Ton*/Words or Music, should take priority. The characters are both allegorized and reduced to typical expressions of a point of view, so that the events, such as they are, count as allegory and as argument as well as plot. Comparison of *Capriccio* with the allegory-disputation aspect of *Meistersinger* produces the interesting points of contact shown opposite.

Thus *Capriccio* flowers from *Ariadne* and *Le Bourgeois gentil-homme* in musical style, and in subject from Strauss's wish to do a *Meistersinger III*, and, obliquely and at a great distance, from *Meister-singer* itself. The deficient form-to-content balance of *Rosenkavalier* is resolved; *Ariadne* had been on the right lines, but, in spite of his promise, the 'Wagnerian musical armour' only gradually fell from his later operatic ventures. In *Intermezzo* Strauss took the direction indicated by *Ariadne*'s Prelude towards lightness, dexterity and conversation, but after it *Die ägyptische Helena* reverts to heaviness. The best parts of *Arabella* advance further towards parlando and lyricism, while *Daphne* almost overdoes the latter, ending with a soprano concerto closer to Glazunov than the *Liebestod*. These, and the other operas of the 1930s still more so, are tired in inspiration in spite of passing beauties. In *Capriccio* quality is restored, and lyricism and parlando are allowed to flourish throughout, while lightness, whose lack Hofmannsthal had so deplored, is achieved and sustained. It says 'Open Sesame' to the grace of Strauss's last concertos and songs.

There is, even so, something elusive, even shifty, about *Capriccio*. At first acquaintance the music seems undistinguished, in two senses – lacking quality and fineness. When with familiarity what seemed boring is no longer so – when one grows into loving the work – the music is undistinguished because it lacks differentiation, everything merging into everything else, nothing separately and distinctly glimpsed.

The central thematic mesh concerns music and words (characterized by Flamand, a musician, and the poet Olivier) and their

Meistersinger

Sachs
maturity, experience, artistry

Walther
youth, callowness,
impetuous lyrical feeling

Eva
muse: inspiration
Prize Song, inspired by Eva and composed by Walther for the purpose
of winning her hand; helped and given justification by Sachs. Wagner
identifies both with Sachs and with Walther, as his youthful and his
mature selves; they combine to put pedantry to rout and conquer the
heart of the people.

Capriccio

Flamand (music) $\rightarrow$ (incomplete without each other) $\leftarrow$ Olivier (poetry)
Both are youthful, ardent, lyrical

La Roche (director)
'midwife', Sachs-like, to poet and composer
experience, *savoir-faire*, solidity, worldliness

Clairon (performer)
secondary muse through which
things must pass

Countess (opera)
muse, inspiration

'Prize Song' (the Sonnet) inspired by the Countess as muse of opera,
composed by poet and musician, both seeking her love, in an unwilling
collaboration which makes an involuntary unity greater than either taken
separately. Indeed after it is written, they can no longer be separated.
Strauss's identification is rather with the director than with the poet or
composer the man who speaks of 'human beings ... who resemble us
and speak in our language ... Let their sorrow move us and their joy
fill us with gladness.'

losing their differentiation in opera. Words and music are brother
and sister, as the composer tells us very early on: so are the Count
and Countess, he representing the rationality of words ('Opera is
an absurd thing'); she, music as the language of the feelings ('Secret
emotions rise in my heart, though their meaning evades me'). These
characters' motifs lack distinction in both senses – they are tired
little scraps of tune, and they are extraordinarily undifferentiated
one from another – and the result is that Strauss can effect with
them continuous states of reference, light, easy-going, lacking any
'identity card' denomination, and corresponding perfectly to the
subtleties of the situation – the tail-end of what Wagner invented
for the *Ring*.

This norm would not be enough to sustain a whole opera.
Vigour and variety are provided by the Italianate and French
elements – the harpsichord dances; the Italian duet (inferior to
the aria in *Rosenkavalier*); Clairon and the Count; *buffa, seria*
(*Ariadne*) and *Bourgeois gentilhomme* in La Roche – and two sustained melodies give the work body, the Sonnet with its stiff five-
bar phrases, and the easy flow of the song theme which runs
through the texture at various points and finally flowers in the
interlude before the last scene.

Thematic undifferentiation provides a clue to another of the opera's
felicities – the contrast between formality and flow. The three
dances, the Italian duet, the contrived symmetry of the Sonnet
are played off against the contentious shapeliness of the ensembles, the so-called Fugue and the Laughing and Quarrelling Octet.
The sparkle of these ensembles puts them in a class of their own
in Strauss's output. It is wonderful how, so late in a lifetime of bad
habits, he could suddenly concentrate himself like this to produce
real energy, not just an inexhaustible spinning of notes, and real
wit, not just rib-tickling fun, yet lose nothing of his genial expansive flow.

Between these opposites come the 'shapely sprawl' of the undifferentiated thematic norm, which seems a blur of unpunctuation
until familiarity brings out its subtleties. And finally, the superior
powers of spontaneous shaping over a large scale, which we see in

La Roche's harangue, and (after the slight tiredness of inspiration which ensues is overcome) the triumphant succession of pleasures, from the goodbyes, through the servants' chorus, the scene with the Prompter, the interlude, to the last scene. In this succession all vestiges of Strauss's rather factitious music-drama are abandoned. It is virtually number-opera.

The last scene, however, restores symphonic flow to build the most perfect of his soprano monologues. The end of *Rosenkavalier* Act I surpasses it in richness and intensity of content, but such 'red corpuscles' (Strauss's own phrase) would be out of place in *Capriccio*, whose essence is that it presents everything diluted and muted. The familiar sentimental treatment of time passing, beauty fading, the mirror, the uncertain heart and the great lady in the rococo décor are here given a final exquisite refinement.

Further felicity is found in the unforced pointedness of many little touches of characterization and structure; the three beginnings, the sextet for the audience, the 'real' sextet for the stage and the final start as the Director wakes up; the skill of the diversified entrances; the cleverness whereby the conversation-piece builds up by twos and threes until an ensemble is called for, after which a big monologue shows to best advantage; the delights of the characteristic exits, Clairon and her couplets, Flamand's last words to be *Prima la musica*, the Poet's *Prima le parole*; the Director's leave-taking. 'See that I get effective exits in my part ... a really striking exit makes a great success ... the last impression a figure can cut ...' as he fades out into the night for Paris.

These unsophisticated and charming touches are continued in the servants' scene – 'They'll shortly be bringing domestics into their operas' – and the Prompter, who has, it seems, controlled the whole performance up to now in his sleep, but must wake to leave the final decision to the Countess. And, of course, the famous trivial ending as she yearns for an ending which will not be trivial – a delicate version of the close of *Ariadne* whose tongue-in-cheek suited Strauss so much better than exaltation or gravity: 'Supper is served'; no decision made; the only possible decision. These things are pure poetry, in the tradition of the Nightwatchman at the end of *Meistersinger* Act II, and a worthy appendix to that supreme touch.

The most successful joke is the central one, that of making the events we see into the work we are seeing. The initial idea, to make the opera the characters plan be Strauss's own *Daphne*, would have been an echo of the idea of *Ariadne* without its point. The eventual solution, that from the very beginning the whole work has been bringing itself into existence without our realizing it, is in a different category from those painfully excogitated 'works of art about themselves' and other comparable frigid self-reflexivities, which have provided so much gratuitous tedium in the arts of the twentieth century. In *Capriccio* the idea is so spontaneous and natural, its execution so easy-going and unpretentious, that there is no temptation to force upon it what it clearly eschews. It's simply a good idea, the happiest of the work's countless felicities; *c'est cela* – it's simple, charming and right, with no labour and nothing to investigate.

There's an intriguing undercurrent to *Capriccio*'s charm and rightness. Strauss's collaboration with his librettist, the conductor Clemens Krauss, is charted in detail through their correspondence from inception to happy end. It reveals a strong urge of bile and rancour on the composer's part that the urbane and cultivated writer has to placate, repress, excise. Strauss *yearns* (his own word) to denounce the degeneration of operetta, vaudeville, commercial music, in his own lifetime – this 'artistic liquid manure' (his own blunt Bavarian vernacular) – and has it in most particularly for Lehár and *The Merry Widow*. Krauss has to exercise all his tact and diplomacy to avoid any such contemporary references: they remain latent, even unsuspected, in La Roche's great tirade and in flickers of the ensembles to each side of it; and are, of course, the stronger for remaining so. On the other hand, the inspired *trouvaille* by which the piece's entire structure and meaning are poised upon self-reflexivity – an opera about its own events, bringing itself into being by retrospect and in prospect – is entirely the composer's. The librettist recognizes the felicity immediately; and their collaboration proceeds thereafter smoothly and amicably. The Strauss/Krauss correspondence, at least as absorbing as the more famous exchanges between the composer and Hofmannsthal, has been published in German and deserves to be in English.

Songs

In 1964, for the centenary of Richard Strauss's birth, his publishers issued the complete songs with piano in three volumes, completed by a fourth containing some twenty orchestrated versions from the master's hand, together with the four sets with opus numbers and the *Four Last Songs* without opus, making another fifteen in all that were, from the start, written for voice and orchestra. All are rarities in concerts except, of course, the Last Four, rightly hailed as the crown of his achievement in lyric writing and perhaps of his oeuvre as a whole.

The song with orchestra, one of the loveliest concert genres imaginable, has a small but choice repertoire. Romantic predecessors include Berlioz's *Nuits d'été* and Wagner's *Wesendonck* set; the heyday comes with Mahler, Diepenbrock, early Schoenberg, Chausson's *Poème de l'amour et de la mer* and Ravel's *Shéhérazade*; after-comers include Berg's *Der Wein*, Barber's *Knoxville*, Schoeck's *Lebendig begraben*, Britten's *Nocturne* and *Serenade* – not a dull or duff moment.

Strauss's contributions are well up to this standard. In his songs with piano the threads of tinsel amid the gold can be off-putting. Accompaniments tend to be sufficient but routine: the endless inventiveness of Brahms or Wolf, let alone Schubert, simply doesn't form part of Straussian economy, except in that fascinating anomaly *Der Krämerspiegel*/The Shopkeeper's Mirror where he lavishes ideas both tart and lyrical on a *jeu d'esprit* lambasting grasping publishers, in a project doomed from birth to be only circumstantial. He rescued only its closing arc of melody to form the glorious orchestral interlude in *Capriccio*. Elsewhere, too, the sketchy keyboard textures audibly cry out for the orchestration that often followed, sometimes immediately, in some cases many decades later. Here he, of course, is a consummate master. Not just perfunctory keyboard parts but musical ideas themselves that can seem hackneyed and lazy take on richness and resonance, realizing compositional potential in such a way as to give new meaning to the term 'threadbare'. Take the Christmas song *Die heiligen drei Könige*. On piano, the slow sustained background is ineffective, the onomatopoeia of bellowing bullocks and crying child obvious; on orchestra the illustration is naïve rather than cheap, and the final transfigured processional has a fairy-tale shimmer that transports everything to a higher plane.

Strauss's songs are almost wholly purified of dross and slag. Not of kitsch, vulgarity, sentimentality, erotic exhibitionism, stylistic provocation: if these too were purged, what would be left of him beyond Mendelssohn and Schumann doused with attar of Wagner and Liszt? This puzzling composer's well-knit surface conceals paradoxes as glaring as those his contemporary Mahler reveals; *bei* Strauss vulgarity, banality and all the rest are fused into creative powers of a high order, for manifest unambiguous benefit all round. He himself realized this and said as much with the same blunt realism that informs the music: 'Must one become seventy years old to recognize that one's greatest strength lies in creating kitsch?' (though many years earlier he'd already adumbrated a future for 'sentimentality and parody' as his prime urge after the Great War).

The range of the songs is broad and contains surprises. Erotic lyricism predominates, together with tender domesticity, parenthood, a famous and tacky hymn to mutual marital masochism (*Befriet*), songs of nature in storm and repose, and the consummation of all these themes, bound into nostalgia and farewell in the *Four Last Songs*. But there is also *Der Arbeitsmann*, a grim piece about the working man under the hoof of capitalism whose harsh, almost Weillish orchestration was only rediscovered and published after the 1964 collection. There are the three Hölderlin *Hymns*, ecstatic pantheistic/patriotic utterances calling for a superhuman combination of radiance, delicacy and blockbuster power in the doughty soprano who takes them on. The pagan element, revealing the Dionysiac fury beneath the composer's Bavarian phlegm, appears in several songs, culminating in the marvellous *Frühlingsfeier* – rites of spring – admittedly another orchestration of a piano original, though it's hard to believe, hearing the orchestra's seething frenzy, that the piano was anything more than a stopgap.

Unwonted excursions from soaring soprano to the deeper voices produces the best of all (always excepting the Last Four): a pair for deep bass, op. 51, studies in introspection, weariness, ageing, touching on facets of his style untried elsewhere. And still finer, the pair of songs for low voice (male or female), op. 44. The first, *Notturno*, explores (for around fifteen minutes) a death-haunted psychological landscape of alarming desolation, anxiety, morbidity – all expressionism is here, latent and actual, in the last year of the nineteenth century. The second, *Nächtlicher Gang*, is fantastic – nearly forty pages of orchestral score, boiling up and over with fiery intensity. It is most regrettable that, *still*, the wobbly stature of Richard Strauss is not more securely anchored by wider dissemination of a genre in his enormous output set consistently at such a high level. There is no room in his songs with orchestra for the longueurs and lapses of the operas, or the legerdemain, persiflage and bombast of the symphonic poems and programmatic symphonies.

'Dying will be just as I composed it in *Death and Transfiguration*,' said Strauss towards the end. He had already made the connection in the first-written of what turned out to be four final songs with orchestra (a fifth remained unfinished), in which music's greatest bourgeois-materialist, having toyed on-and-off all his life with matters spiritual and metaphysical, eventually achieves them, with wonderful beauty, within his own eminently realistic terms. Eichendorff's *Im Abendrot/At Sunset* evokes a long, loving companionship, the partners compared to a pair of larks still soaring upwards as the world darkens beneath. Their course is run, their natural end approaches, unargued, acquiescent. As the poem's last line – 'is this perhaps death?' – fades from the voice, the horn essays an answer with the transfiguration motif from the symphonic poem composed nearly sixty years before. The orchestra then broadens into a tranquil coda above which the ghosts of the contented birds still softly chirrup on a pair of piccolos.

Strauss completed *Im Abendrot* in May 1948: it is rightly placed last in the group though the other three songs were added later.

They set poems by Hermann Hesse – *Frühling/Spring*; *September*; *Beim Schlafengehen/Going to Sleep*. Mood and idiom of all four are familiar and well-loved, as befits this evocation of summation and adieu. But while the Eichendorff setting and the song of falling asleep could, save for their mellow burnish, have dated from prior epochs of Strauss's style, the other two Hesse settings unobtrusively float free. Their harmony, constantly shifting and glancing, achieves a subtle final consequence of his earlier preoccupation with dissonance sprinkled over a consonant base – best known of all in the silver-rose music from *Rosenkavalier*: the alien notes are no longer 'applied': they now work within the texture like leaven, to produce an elliptical late style comparable, *mutatis mutandis*, to Fauré's: its further possibilities still remain to be explored. And the orchestration here, from this commander of the juicy tutti, has a new transparency, translucency, evanescence – the opening of *September* especially – it seems to hover in mid-air. Strauss had always been lord of long, arching, almost instrumental soprano lines: they were never so sinuous, graceful, lissom, contoured, as here. Thus in the *Four Last Songs* youth, freshness, renewal, lie alongside experience, nostalgia, farewell.

Wolf

In February 1903, after some six years of hapless delusion in a Vienna asylum, Hugo Wolf died. He'd been born forty-three years before, to grow up into that neurasthenic culture later explored by Freud. As a student he was close friends with two other unstable young geniuses, the upwardly mobile Mahler and the wretched Hans Rott, who killed himself after Brahms had dismissed his compositional efforts. (The old master had snubbed the other two also, but both were robust enough to survive, Wolf repaying the insult with some of the most vituperative music criticism ever committed to print.)

Already, at eighteen, Wolf's internal pressure was shown in a heaven-storming string quartet with its stern motto, 'Thou shalt renounce!' Five years later a hell-bent tone-poem after Kleist's

Penthesilea, covering the Amazons' war-march upon Troy, the heroine's dream of an erotic rose-feast, ending with a huge finale appetizingly headed *Struggle, Passion, Frenzy, Destruction*, which, despite overloading and imbalance, reveals an unmistakable feel for large-scale orchestral thinking. Its only try-out was such a fiasco that the humiliated twenty-three-year-old never returned this way.

This debacle sent him on a route, unique in the epoch of gargantuan orchestral blockbusters, concentrating mainly on songs for solo voice and piano. His creative pattern is still the most extreme of any great composer. Auden could have written an essay along the lines of his diagnosis of Nathanael West and *Miss Lonelyhearts*, called 'Wolf's Disease'. Long periods of melancholic sterile depression were succeeded by bouts of exultant creative potency; revenging make-up for lost time.

The dates tell it all: after a few earlier songs of no great moment comes a single setting of Mörike (16 February 1888); six days later, he's off! – forty-three settings of Mörike by 18 May; in August he turns to Eichendorff, but after three days returns to Mörike for the remaining few, completing his first great collection. From 11 October 1888 to 15 February the next year he turns to setting Goethe; then, temporarily spent, waits till the autumn of 1889, when he turns for two months to German translations of miscellaneous old Spanish poets. Then another two-month gap with relaxing orchestration, till spring 1890 when a further two months completes this *Spanish Songbook* and rounds off the *Goethe*. Early that summer come six songs to poems by Gottfried Keller: then in the autumn he dips, with unwonted temperance, into a collection from the Italian, composing just seven before turning to other projects, then adding a further fifteen late in 1891.

Stagnation sets in with a long-baffled search to find an acceptable opera-text, composing which would gain him fame and glory, like his fatal hero Wagner, and the handsome royalties and universal delight now being earned by his old friend Humperdinck's *Hansel and Gretel*. His violent jealousy of the gentle master of fairy-tale is an early sign of the eventual breakdown in which even the vast master of myth and romance was denounced and demonized for standing in his way. There's no evidence from the eventual upshot of these operatic ambitions that Wolf had a particular gift for the genre. *Der Corregidor*, to the same story of Alarcón that later yielded Falla's *Three-Cornered Hat* ballet, is sadly laboured; its successor, *Manuel Venegas* (also after Alarcón), was not taken far enough for one to judge. But at least the first opera broke the four-year barren spell: when it was out of the way Wolf was back on course, completing the *Italian Songbook* with twenty-two more songs in thirty-seven days over the turn of winter/spring 1896. Soon after come evermore disturbing signs of incipient insanity. Yet some of a handful of late (soon to prove last) songs, so skimpy compared with the generous bouquets of earlier, reach still more exalted heights and depths: two on translations from Byron and three (a fourth was abandoned) on translations from Michelangelo.

The end was in sight. His final collapse was precipitated by his old friend Mahler's rejection of *Corregidor* for the Vienna Opera. Manic work at its successor didn't assuage the slight. Soon he was declaring wildly to anyone who'd listen that Mahler had been sacked; that he, Hugo Wolf, was director of the State Opera, where his own work would shortly be mounted. The following events, grotesque and pitiable, became the main source for the composer-hero's spectacular mental breakdown in Thomas Mann's *Doktor Faustus*.

Wolf rarely writes *tunes*! The exceptions, all excellent, show that he can; but usually his voice-parts are syllabic, in speech-rhythm, intertwining with the piano's right hand in serpentine collusion, sometimes strained, even freakish, mostly of great and subtle art. There's a sense of the piano-accompaniments coming first, almost complete without the voice – except that the intertwine is eventually inseparable: even if voice came last, the first impulse to set the poem, and the music's word-suggested shapes, are paramount. Compare Schumann's songs, where vocal melody is almost always contained within the piano-parts: and Schubert's, almost always voice-led, and always melodic except for moments of declamation or recitative, and whose accompaniments, however simple, do not contain the vocal line.

By general consent the *Mörike Songbook* represents Wolf's gift at its most attractive. Many are long enough to be mini-scenas, like *Auf einer Wanderung* with its kaleidoscope of synesthetic mood-states: there are ballads – comic (the pair of storks with their pair of babies), Gothic (the lake-sprites who invade dry land); macabre (the demonic *Feuerreiter*); lyrics and character-pieces tender, delicate and humorous; songs of guilty eroticism (two entitled *Peregrina*), of gentle mysticism (the two addressed to a Christmas rose); of pure rapture (the song of the earth at midnight, the elegiac ecstasy of the Aeolian harp); and many more: all in all a dictionary, illustrated in full colour, of German Romantic themes.

And, by common consent, the *Italian*-book represents his 'Mediterraneanizing' at its best – forty-six miniatures with scarcely a less-than-inspired number (I think there's one), distilling an essence of his already concentrated idiom into consummate essentiality, be the tone mocking, flirtatious, mournful, defiant, or so ardent that passion almost breaks the consciously set limits: Wagner in a nutshell of diamond.

Between come Eichendorff, Goethe, Keller and the *Spanish* collection. I will try to do justice to these too, though it will be clear where the affections and loyalties lie.

The *Mörike Songbook* has always been Wolf's most popular. In personal terms an efflorescence into full powers after years of frustrated toying and waiting, it represents in wider terms the full flowering of the *Lieder*-tradition originating in Schubert and continued in Schumann, so enriched by saturation in high and late Wagner that the longer songs can seem, in their dense, quasi-leitmotivic texture, a distillation in minutes of hours of music-drama, while even the shorter are permeated by Wagnerian harmony and vocal procedure. Wolf pays such extreme attention to verbal quantity and meaning as to lose out on sheer vocal beauty, losing felicity and ingratiation in a pyrrhic victory for words over music. This would have been incomprehensible to his precursors; often offended his contemporaries; and can still disconcert listeners even now. Needless to say, the best of his songs overcome such objections with ease and beauty: nowhere more so than here.

The fifty-three songs are decidedly not a performing entity: more an anthology, loosely circling around many overlapping themes. Apart from three deliberate pairings the only significance in their ordering is one of category, not performance. It is curious that the obsessively vigilant Wolf should leave completely open the large question of what follows what. In fact, there is so much music, so diverse in subject, level, tone, that the model of Schumann's Eichendorff-*Liederkreis* – non-narrative/non-protagonist garland held together by contrast or continuation in a musical frame of key-relationships and subtly perceived motivic cross-connections – could not have helped. This account will group the fifty-three songs into categories independent of the published order.

Types: first, humorous – an area that gives hostages to Wolf's detractors for all its evident importance to him: nine in all, ranging from thumbnail sketch to full-fledged comic/satiric episode owing too much to the unfunny idiom invented by Wagner for Beckmesser. Most rescuable, *Jägerlied*/Huntsman's Song, frisky 5/4 metre, dainty as a bird's footprints in the snow: *Der Tambour*/The Drummer-boy – sweet, the homesick lad's wistful wish for his mother's cooking and his missing girl. Which already suggests a category containing some of Wolf's best: character studies. Two contrasting instances: *Das verlaßene Mägdlein*/The Forsaken Servant-girl – her plight rendered in bare textures handled with rigorous simplicity, an *image sonore* of numbness, weariness, loss, her underlying sexual pain explicit in a brief outcry, instantly stifled. But let loose in *Erstes Liebeslied eines Mädchens*/A Girl's First Lovesong – 'of an intensity that would lacerate a block of marble' wrote its startled composer having just composed it. He is alive to every stab and spasm of the poet's imagery – 'what's in my net? I'm scared to look – an eel, a snake? It's living in my hands, it twists and turns, it pierces my breast and bites my heart, it coils around inside me, it will kill me with rapture, with anguish.'

The heart of the *Mörike*-book comprises songs of love, loss, memory, rumination, from relatively extrovert to deeply inward, philosophical, metaphysical – some fourteen in all. The range can be measured at once, placing the collection's opener, *Der Genesene an die Hoffnung*/Convalescent's Ode to Hope – grandiose invocation, sickness and vulnerability, conquered by heroic stamina, sinking childlike into Hope's maternal embrace – alongside *Fußreise*/A Walk – sane and healthy, an open-air stroll of untrammelled optimism. Two songs from this lifelong insomniac evoke sleep: *In der Frühe*/In the Early Morning ends upon radiant morning-bells bringing relief and release: *An den Schlaf*/To Sleep welcomes sleep as immemorially equated with death, both enjoined in erotic bliss; still more deeply probed in the two wonderful numbers entitled *Peregrina*. But some of this type court sentimentality, sogginess, tackiness – the gooey *Verborgenheit*/Seclusion, the unctuous *Gebet*/Prayer.

Two extended master-songs in this same area deserve extended description. They stand together as the *Songbook*'s highest achievement – lyric abandonment and fluid spontaneity casually yet masterfully controlled, in a complex fusion of past/present, loss/gain, bitter/sweet, anguish/ecstasy.

No. 13 *Im Frühling*/In Spring – an ultimate embodiment of nostalgia:

Here I lie on the hillside, my spirit soaring with birds and clouds, open like the sunflower, yearning to be at one with my inexpressible love and hope. What do you want of me, springtime? When will I be content and fulfilled? Nature's ardour penetrates my being, I sink unconscious, hearing only the murmurous bees; my thoughts wander here and there; a longing, half pleasure half pain, arises, for I know not what. Heart, what memories do you weave in the golden-greeny twilight – old days without a name?

Autumn melancholy within the golden renewal of spring, at once impetuously flowing to rise to a passion of lyrical yearning, then tranced into sweet rapturous stupor – the murmurous bees almost put the song to sleep: the little piano interlude that follows revives momentum, tessitura, volume, and the opening's return, giving the whole long song a quasi-symphonic feel – a 'recapitulation' indeed, albeit on the tonic already, to be subtly evaded after the voice's last questing words, wherein the lulling rhythm at last solidifies to close, broad and full, on a dominant that keeps the quest and the question posed, as of to recommence the seasonal cycle. No. 11, *An eine Äolsharfe/ To an Aeolian Harp*, is comparable in scope and size brought about through continuous gentle momentum over its considerable length – becalmed, gradually impassioned, into grief and longing, re-calmed and cadenced, the solo piano a long evanescing epilogue *ppp dolcissimo* with little swells, then quadruple *piano* as the title-harp fades, and a *diminuendo* even from *pppp* as the sound disappears into the ether. Mörike's epitaph from Horace – your loss gives you no respite by starlight or sunlight – is retained by Wolf, and implicit within his setting of the actual poem. It begins in recitativo – the mysterious harp who sounds unaided by human hands is addressed and asked to begin its

> music wrought by airs from the hills where the boy so dear had dwelt – how sweet you press upon my heart as the sadness of my loss swells and dies in the strings' invisible music. Sudden, vehement, the harp cries plangent, renewing the sweet pang within my spirit as the wind shakes the full-blown roses, scattering the petals at my feet.

Every fluctuation in these two masterpieces is rendered with urgent fidelity – the wild passion within the dreamy-drowsy nostalgia, pantheism, youthful bitter-sweetness of the first, every impulse of distress and grief in the second as the wounded instrument seems to utter the very motions stirring the poet-musician's soul at the thought of the beloved lost younger brother lives and dies in his memory (we don't learn the actual biographical reference in the poem nor, of course, in its setting).

No. 15, *Auf einer Wanderung/On a Journey*, is far the most complex: the almost indolent transparency of its two companions is replaced by a rapid tempo, kaleidoscopic multicoloured metamorphoses of a short motif put to developmental whirlwind worthy of a Haydn quartet, in the language and technique – leitmotivic interweave – of late Wagner, known so intimately to Wolf since early youth. It's as though in sequel to *Fußreise* – a good day's stride duly rewarded:

In the rosy glow of evening I arrive in a friendly little town;
and just at this moment, an open window, rich flowers and their
scents, garden bells, a human voice; a choir of nightingales heightening the roses into a tremble, the sky into radiance [a moment
of synaesthesia]; I gaze amazed, penetrated by joy. Somehow, how
I don't know, I found myself outside the town gates: how bright
the world! Behind, the buildings in a golden haze; above, the sky
in purple tumult; before, the murmuring stream; down below in
the valley the clacking mill . . . I'm drunk and disordered – kissed
by the Muse with a breath of Love.

Every turn of the chromatic sense-impregnated poem is faithfully caught in this tumult of sound, always forwards-constructed
throughout all its tonal adventures, yet capable of such extreme
contrasts within a few bars as the *ppp* for the nightingales and the
Tristan-esque upboiling of libido waxing the roses into still fierier
blushes, *fortissimo*, calming at once into the rapt moment of contemplation and the inexplicable transition from sensual riot of
town-centre to extramural quadruple *piano*. Thence the gradual
broadening till the Muse is invoked in fervent apostrophe: so to
resumption of excitement after the voice is stilled, even softer and
lower till, at the close, the echo of her blessing, and a quiet, plain,
almost formal close after all the tumult. (One trusts he wasn't apprehended as a drunken vagrant, found a nice B&B, and didn't suffer
the insomnia of *An den Schlaf* before proceeding the next morning
on his further *Fußreise*.)

One miniature after the three mighty ones is so special that it too
deserves detail: it also serves a link to a further area of the *Mörike*-
book's totality. No. 39, *Denk' es, o Seele!*/Think on This, My Soul!
The runic little verse comes from Mörike's novella *Mozart's Journey
to Prague*: during a halt en route the composer is recognized, persuaded to stay for a bit and make music for a wedding: after his
journey is resumed the new bride picks up an old songbook with
these lines within – she senses that, however inconsequential and
oblique, they foretell his early death:

A young fir tree grows green, a rose-bush blooms – in what forest, in what garden, who can say? Think on this, my soul: already they are destined to adorn your grave. Two black colts graze the meadow, trot briskly back to town: they will tread slow bearing your dead body – maybe, maybe, even before the bright iron I see glinting on their hooves is loosened and lost.

A unique little miracle, this succession of unrelated images, their inner connection implicit and devastating, perfectly matched by Wolf's acute sensitivity and precision – a snatch of rhythmic octave, a poignant chromatic phrase: again, both: a gay/gaunt lilting little sicilienne for the fir and the rose, darkening over the bare octave for the shadow of the grave, into which the music sinks: starts again, same ingredients, the young horses inducing a touch of frisk into the sicilienne till it is again checked – this time darkening the lilt too – by the thought of the corpse they will bear when fully grown. The oblique time-image – this'll happen before the bright horseshoes are cast – produces dramatic tremolos that really work without strain: the opening returns, its lilting bass and affective answer now more than halved, and the bass losing the lilt by suggestion of a march, which then turns actual and funereal in the tiny coda – a Mahler funeral march squeezed into a musical snuff-box. Apparently slight, even trivial – a riddle, *faux-naïf*, a fake folksong – that is indeed, after all, the opposite of all these things – ridden with portentous significance, ending miles on from where it began though still so brief as to be a miniature; life, death, eternity seen down the wrong end of the telescope, a vision worthy of Emily Dickinson.

This exquisite epitome opens up a small group of songs to simple lyrics. Several precious stones among them – the rapture of spring-awakening in *Er ist's!*, the rapture of lovers' impetuosity, abashed or unashamed, in *Begegnung*, the pang of homesickness in *Heimweh*. Most lovable, *Der Gärtner* – the young gardener, adoring from his low station the loveliest princess on her snow-white steed – oh for a secret token, a feather from her cap: and if you want a flower, take a thousand – the potentially tragic lilt and trot of *Denk' es* transformed into pure delight, with an undertow of hopeless yearning that yet retains hope.

Another category altogether: songs of the supernatural – pantheist, mythological, Christian, fairy-folklore. Fourteen in all ranging from a couple of long, slack, rhetorical blockbusters – *Karwoche*/Passion Week; *Wo find' ich Trost?*/Where Shall I Find Solace? – to an intense-wrought miniature of unbearable pain – *Seufzer*/A Sigh – spiritual anguish epitomized, guilty self-torment burnt into Gothic gauntness. Its polar opposite *Zum neuen Jahr*/ Hymn for the New Year, a delicious *scherzino* of holy hilarity. Two wonderful songs evoke the Christ-child direct. *Auf ein altes Bild*/ On an Old Picture: summer landscape shimmers in green haze, the Virgin sits by the cool water, on her lap the Child innocently plays; in the forest the wood of the Cross already waxes green, alas. The old painting is framed by quasi-archaic plainsongy contours, modally harmonized, the voice now mirroring now moving gently counter; at the core, though not the centre, the single stab of dissonance on the poem's last word *Stamm*; then the framing tranquillity is resumed as if there were no change in our perception of the tranced heat-haze: the piano epilogue echoes, then resolves in radiant major: tender piety utterly without unction; as though this fiercely anti-clerical composer were indeed as devoted to the faith as his pastor-poet. Companion-piece *Schlafendes Jesuskind*/Sleeping Christ-child, also originates in a painting (not imagined but actual, a work of the seventeenth-century Francesco Albani, which Mörike had seen reproduced in a journal). 'Heavenly son of the Virgin! you sleep in weightless dreams upon the wood that will bear the weight of your woeful body, as yet but a pillow placed by the pious painter with prophetic/symbolic fantasy. Yet but a bud, your Father's flowering glory yet but faintly foreshadowed – what images press behind your brow, your dark lashes?' Solemn hushed chorale-like strains, not so much the sanctimonious harmonium as an orchestra of muted strings or flute-tones reaching the entire tessitura; in rapt contemplation, deep, almost traumatized, tranquillity, the free-floating voicepart poised with infinite flexibility and sensitivity in, out, across the procession of slow chords that gradually bloom into melody, both coalescing together in the little knot of consciousness troubling the infant brow behind its untroubled sleep.

These two balance another precious pair wherein Christian feeling and imagery, now unspecific, overlap with pantheistic nature-mysticism, opening a path into magic, myth, fairy-tale. *Auf eine Christblume I*/On a Christmas Rose I – hovers delicately between all these realms: its imagery, mainly pantheist, can embrace the Virgin, and the five wounds of Christ's Passion as well as the season of his birth; and the poem ends with an elf pausing at midnight to glance at the Christmas rose before skipping hence to dance in the moonlight. The mixture of fervour and whimsy sounds distasteful, till words and setting alike hold the contrarities in suspension, creating a kind of asexual, areligious zone hard to define or parallel – fragile, fugitive, delicate, exquisitely tender and acid-sweet – perhaps Richard Dadd without the undertow of malevolence and madness? A long song that needs and earns its length – very various in texture: from almost motionless diatonic opening, gradually stirring into chromatic life; then twinkling semi-staccato right hand over sinuously curving left, while the voice in blanched monotone parlando; then declining into rapt slowness as the flower is addressed, intensifying differently (textures directly prophetic of the third Michelangelo setting) till the tintinnabulating twinkle, tinglingly dissonant in high treble momentum as the voice 'secretly' (*heimlich*) evokes the midnight elf gazing entranced then vanishing him(it)self into a closing quadruple *piano*, on which the palely ravishing spun-silk creation might well recommence. Instead, *Auf eine Christblume II*: in the dead winter earth sleeps a living chrysalis: but the butterfly will never taste the winter bloom's sweet nectar. Yet who knows? Its spirit might, after summer has passed, intoxicated by your fragrance, return unseen? One of the precious few songs in the *Mörike*-book whose accompaniment lies entirely in the treble clef: a single very expressive motif is slipped with consummate skill through a gentle dazzle of chromatic changings, seventeen in all, foreground and backdrop in one to the voice's subtly poised half parlando. As it ceases on the last question-mark the eighteenth repetition of the motif gives it straight, for the first and only time: the nineteenth reverts to iridescence, the twentieth and last extends it upwards into dying intangibility.

Yet another type is all playful – elves, butterflies, bees, a water-sprite:

and two open into grand mythology – *Gesang Weylas*/Weyla's Song: the sea-goddess sings broad and sublime over bardic harping from the piano: *Um Mitternacht*/At Midnight grander still – the Song of the Earth, Erda herself, primeval Ur-slumber of untroubled serenity, a huge arc of unbroken melody unequalled in all Wolf's output.

Finally, three extended ballads. One hilarious – *Storchenbotschaft*/ The Storks' Message: working in German and English, the euphemism that these birds bring the babies – in this case, twins. One delicious – *Die Geister am Mummelsee*/Ghosts on Mummelsee: spooky royal water-sprites at their funeral games, the waters of the lake glowing and sparkling with greenish fire. And, longest by far, *Der Feuerreiter*/Fire-rider, telling of the skeleton horseman who sniffs out, perhaps initiates, every nearby conflagration, inciting the populace to frenzies of panic till exorcized and reduced to ash: a tour de force for singer and pianist, almost breaking the domestic medium asunder in its hectic maelstrom of invention.

I curtail Wolf's next three songbooks to mere mentions. Eichendorff doesn't show him to advantage except once, though one of his greatest – *Das Ständchen*/The Serenade, beautifully evoking via the present a long-lost past. Goethe too can bring out Wolf's less cherishable aspects – fifty-one settings, only a handful yielding delight. The pathos of the celebrated lyrics from *Wilhelm Meister* – the wretched old harpist, Mignon the waif – somehow fails to move, though one feels it ought. Positive aversion to the many songs from the *West-östlicher Divan* – cod-Persian, wine/women/verse/spurious 'wisdom': cod-Coptic runes racy/salacious/raucous. Slight rise in the love-sequence for Hatem and Zuleika: decisive fall in the drinking-songs, sometimes downright repellent. Worse yet, the draughty corridor housing colossal plastercasts from Greek antiquity – *Prometheus*; *Grenzen der Menschheit*/Limits of Mankind – ranting and raving from a cardboard Wotan, all plasticene over a hollow core. *Ganymede* effects a partial rise: one would if one could adore this sumptuously upholstered go at the pantheist-erotic with its merging of youth-and-age, creator-and-created in rosy baroque clouds of scented tumescence … but somehow the deed is weaker than the will.

Greater regret bypassing the *Spanish Songbook*, forty-four settings of German translations from varied sources plus some original poems purporting to be traditional folk-material: for Wolf a first move, whether or not deliberate, to obey and fulfil Nietzsche's injunction for music to escape the fogs, metaphysics, psychological gropings, spiritual strivings of the damp North, to 'Mediterranean-ize' – become direct, passionate, full of blood.

The collection begins with ten Sacred Songs. Four concern guilt and redemption – fervent, ground-down with suffering and pain, expressed in a language of advanced chromatic dissonance poised between Amfortas's spiritual and physical agony, and the excrucia-tion of Webern's sacred songs still to come, born of the same Viennese culture as Wolf's a few years further along. Four concerning the Christ-child are gentler. In the two final songs the Saviour himself answers the Sinner's tortured questions and gives comfort: the close of *Herr, was trägt der Boden hier?*/Lord, What will Grow in this Soil? – 'Lord, for whose adornment are these wreaths woven? The thorns are for me; I give you the flowers' – is heartbreaking. Does the set of ten make a cycle? Their keys make a structure, their internal contrasts an architec-ture of meaning. Unlike Wolf's collection otherwise, the sacred songs are an entity, greater than the sum of their parts. And a most unlikely achievement: this is surely *not* what Nietzsche meant when urging the Mediterraneanization of music! Emphatically it 'falls at the foot of the Cross'. Unexpectedly, Wolf here realizes profound Christian values, in music comparable to all but the very greatest from the epochs of Belief. And it *is* Spanish and not *Carmen* – the Spanish of El Greco, Zurbarán, St John of the Cross and St Teresa.

Nietzsche's prescription is fulfilled in the thirty-four Secular Songs, but not always to their advantage. Explicitly 'Spanish' numbers with guitars, castanets and such, can be delicious – *Klinge, mein Pandero*; *In der Schatten meiner Locken*; the extra-ravishing *Auf dem grünen Balkon*; the extra-delectable *Wenn du zu den Blumen gehst* – really do make a Viennese counterpart to Bizet and Chabrier. Elsewhere rage, rancour, jealousy, mockery, scorn, vituperation, produce harshness and fakery, all flouncing gesture, unattractive and unconvincing, despite the invention richly wrought, its intricate artistry the most elaborate in the composer's output. Friskiness and flirtation yield more fun, and the tendency towards eroticism, dark or jubilant, is ever-compelling, culminating in two songs where undercurrent reaches surface. *Komm, o Tod*/Come, O Death and *Bedeckt mich mit Blumen*/Cover Me with Flowers – the sweet torments of love-death as enhanced in *Tristan* Act II, to which these palpitating songs pay inevitable tribute. The *Liebestod* predominates in *Geh, Geliebter*/Go, Beloved, a torrential outpouring of passion, last and longest in the book.

Before Wolf's final renewal, a kind word for the pearl of his Gottfried Keller songs: *Wie glänzt der helle Mond* – 'How cold and far the bright moon; yet further, my lost youth [it is an old peasant woman speaking]: soon I'll be journeying to Paradise, I'll see the Virgin-Mother and sleeping Child, I'll see God the Father feeding the Dove with celestial corn . . .' and so on, in high, bright, cold piano chords for the old woman's present and past, warmer harmony and a singing bass for her Paradise-to-come, tender onomatopoeia for St Peter at his celestial shoe-making.

Wolf's final Italian strain truly achieves the aesthetic/expressive goal implied or explicit in Nietzsche's call to Mediterraneanize music: passion direct and undilute, contained within lucid objectivity of idiom and facture: tight without meanness, light without shallows, clear yet deep, gay however melancholy; elegant, compact, perfected. Yet there's a paradox: the composer himself admitted that 'a warm heart beats in the little bodies of my newest children of the South, who cannot, despite appearances, deny their German origins . . . yes, their hearts beat in German, though the sun shines upon them in Italian.'

There'd been a forebear in his *Italian Serenade* for string quartet, then small orchestra, of 1887: a charming little thing, more beholden to Eichendorff than the Mediterranean. Settings of poems from German translations of Italian bits-and-bobs began with the first twenty-two in 1890–91; then comes the painful protracted block; another twenty-four were granted at last in 1896; and there's an Italian coda the following year in the three completed Michelangelo-settings; after which, the ultimate *nulla*. The forty-six songs make a Dictionary – a Symposium: miniatures; mostly just two pages short, a few rather longer, and some only the single page: covering Love in all its Aspects; from sublime/expiated/quasi-sacramental – whether ecstatic or tinged with guilt and pain – to pathetic/wistful/droll/comic/absurd to scorn/rage/repudiation/spite/hatred and including also calmness, gentleness, tenderness, easy-relaxed voluptuousness, amorousness – Love without agonies and ecstasies – to end in a final firework of spitfire triumph.

This is the celebrated *Ich hab' in Penna*: the female country-cousin of Don Giovanni enumerates her conquests: here and there and everywhere a lover, and *ten* in Castiglione – the climatic admission followed by a virtuoso piano-coda calculated both to tax the fingers and bring the house down. Its complement, the equally celebrated celebration of little things in the *Italian*-book's first song – the pearl, so costly yet so small; the olive, so good for all its tininess; the rose, so fragile yet so sweet to smell – exquisitely sensitive miniaturized delicacy, epitome of the nature and quality of what is to come. Between tender secrecy and triumphalist blaze come the other forty-four songs, assembled by their composer neither in performance-order nor by subject. As with the *Mörike*, I will attempt to sort by character and content. And as there, so here: let's get straight comedy out of the way: twelve in all, often testing indulgence and patience. At their best – suiting the *Italian*-book in general – dealing with the small: undersized swains, alarmed by insects, inadequate on their violin, serenading ugly as a donkey, mean with the victuals or greedily overeating. Humour and tenderness in plenty, often touching, always fine-wrought: just once, exquisite – *Mein Liebster singt*: the girl lies weeping but must conceal her pain from her mother as her lover's voice is heard from outside – a unique number, a 'Chopin' mazurka for accompaniment; within or against, the voice declaims the text without melody, playing scrupulous attention to every verbal nuance; foretaste of the *Italian*-book's glories to come.

Before then one must clear the ground of indignation, scorn, curses, hatreds – eleven in all, mostly all gesticulation and exclamation. Undoubtedly Wolf can etch these states with acid economy: the upshot is uncharming. But his great subject is love – not treated edgily, even derisively – love reciprocal and sustained, expressed in some twenty songs ranging from serenade and lullaby, morning, noon and night, gay and free, rapt and inward, demure and devoted yet sometimes veering extravagant and hyperbolic. Take *Ihr seid die Allerschönste* – you are loveliest of all, fairer than Maytime flowers, than Orvieto's cathedral, than Viterbo's fountain – even Siena must bow before you; drunken hymnic rapture, sumptuous textures, voluptuous harmony. Take *Und willst du deinen Liebsten* – 'if you would see your lover die, bind not your hair; let it down free in threads of purest gold': a single ostinato pattern, one bar's length, three notes only, warmly harmonized in harp-spread chords slowly expanding or enfolding upon themselves, accompanies the voice's expressively contoured recitative. After the besotted imperative – 'let your hair down' – the texture changes, the harp-ostinato in diminution to half-bar's length, right hand only, over the left's gentle rippling: an arc of rainbow enharmonics, glowing and shining, all Brangäne in a thimble – only six bars – as the intoxicated boy hymns his girl through her beautiful tresses – Mélisande in a dewdrop.

The *Italian*-book's two greatest love songs, *Wenn du, mein Liebster* and *Wenn du mich mit den Augen streifst*, both comprise a singing piano right hand in octaves, intertwining with a sinuously expressive syllabic voice-part in not-quite duet, not-quite counterpoint, nor yet quite heterophony but in all things utterly mutual, over a throbbing pulsating syncopated left hand, initially strummed, in both songs gradually enfiling to chords full but never thick, supporting the single span of fused music and words to the top of its curve. Succeeded in the first by a triumphal blast ending in one of Wolf's danger-signs, an *fff tremolo*; in the second an epitomizing epilogue, the strummed bass now yielding an inner voice as the singing voice ceases, to close soft and bare on a naked fifth, though still supporting the comfortable glow of the major third on which both voice and vocal right hand had begun. There's no question that this is the superior of these two outstanding songs – the other, composed later, over-does it – over-kills the thing it over-loves: when you, my love, ascend to heaven, I shall meet you, heart in hand; we will embrace and fall before our Lord who, seeing our love's woes, will join us for ever, two hearts in one, in paradise surrounded with celestial light.

Maybe the extravagance of this religio-erotic fantasy – the Blessed
Damozel is tasteful by comparison – has influenced its setting.

Wenn du mich induces no qualms: when you gaze and laugh, then
glance down, I beg a sign so I may quell my unquiet heart when it
would nigh burst my breast, when it would break, with its weight of
joy. Just as extravagant, but no extraneous props – angels, paradise,
God-the-Father: passion uninhibited yet contained in miniature –
twenty bars – and proportioned with exact precision that intensifies the intensity: eight bars to set a first half: return to opening,
more fully 'orchestrated' and already on the move melodically, then
harmonically, roving with purpose to a first mini-climax, descending, renewing to a second, a third-voice and singing right hand
alternately submerged and re-emergent – till the fourth (singing
piano victorious): another eight bars in all. Cadence into four bars;
encapsulation, as described. These two songs composed as though
to fulfil another of Nietzsche's observations – that Wagner is, paradoxically, the master of the miniature: secret places, known only to
the few, where he is 'worthy of admiration and love by virtue of his
inventiveness in small things, in his elaboration of details . . . our
greatest musical *miniaturist*, who compresses an infinity of meaning
and sweetness into the smallest space.' Wolf achieves throughout his
body of songs, and nowhere more than the 'less' of the Italians, what
in his (possible) mentor is merely a provocative paradox.

Wagner certainly looms large behind and within Wolf's subsequent Italian songs, setting German translations of three poems
by Michelangelo. 'Of course the sculptor must sing bass,' said the
composer: it seems just as ordained that he employ the accents of
Amfortas, Titurel, Gurnemanz. Not yet in the first song – more the
intonation here of the Old Harp-player from the Goethe-book – a
dark retrospect ending in a blaze of triumph ostensibly undermined,
even denied, by the brooding introspection that precedes: 'often I
think on my past life, before my love for you: no one knew me, each
day was lost. I thought to live only for my art, escaping the press of
humankind: and now all men speak my fame, in praise or blame:
all know I am that I am.' The magnificence of the *sprezzatura* quite
outweighs the initial groping sadness and diffidence – superbia in

superb confident rhetoric, the concluding fanfares, and a *ff tremolo* that, for once, falls the right side of bombast.

Especially since it is at once followed (for these three songs make a distinct mini-cycle) by one of the bleakest in a repertoire that includes Musorgsky's *Sunless* and Schubert's *Doppelgänger* (clear parallels both). A vision of catacombs, valley of bones, *cum mortuis in lingua mortua*: all created things must end: time flies, beholding that all passes – thought, speech, joy, grief. The absolute gauntness of the piano-part – Fafner slow-motion writhings, then Alberich dark-brooding doubled thirds against which care-laden Wotan declaims; with, on the first *Alles* – everything – one of the most excruciating major-minor clashes in all music, no less for being soft and *gedämpft/* muted – Wolf's instruction. Motion now sets inexorably in, over an ostinato bass gradually expanding the intervals in Amfortas-contour of grind in which *Schmerz* and *Wonne* – pain and joy – cannot be distinguished, climaxing after this last word in a virtual quotation from *Parsifal*. 'And our descendants vanish like daylight into darkness, like dust in the wind' – thus, too, the music thins and expires – always the piano taking over the singer's bare near-recitative into ampler expression, eloquent beyond words however brief, the left hand (but how one wants this music on the orchestra!) also 'speaking'. To reach the song's core, five bars of simplicity, plain and harrowing – 'once we too were men, happy, sad, like you'. From this impasse the music recovers direction with difficulty – one senses a clash of gears, however reluctant to admit it, in the four bars setting 'now we are lifeless, made of earth, as you see', and the two piano-only bars that ensue, leading back to an exact repeat of the opening lines as not in the original poem. The piano epilogue restores confidence: all now in dusky lower-middle register; the right hand Alberich thirds droop, the Amfortas left hand curves upwards then collapses, each bar. Then collapses only, then augments the subsidence to end upon the bare fifth of the key that, omnipresent from the start, has never yet been stated till the end: termination of the line. 'I'm literally afraid of this composition', wrote its composer a few days after writing it, 'because it makes me fear for my own sanity.' Perhaps he *knew*: 'Wolf would indeed be incurably insane before the year was out.'

The third Michelangelo song is in no way so extreme. If anything, its idiom and rich-wroughtness are Spanish rather than Italian (let alone Russian): or even German – the *Peregrina*-pair from the *Mörike*-book reflected down the nine years since. The sculptor's homage to a beautiful, highborn Signior is decorously transposed to a Mistress:

> Does my soul sense the desired light from God who created it, or does it shine from another beauty, breaking into my heart and awakening my memory in this vale of sorrows? I know not: nor what I feel, what I desire, what will guide me – these are not mine to possess. Only by another's grace can it be granted me: I dwell on this since I saw you, torn between a yea and a nay, a sweet and a bitter: and thus, dear Signior/Lady, I blame your eyes.

Richly packed, deeply moving chaos of a song, after the compaction of the Italian book as such, and the gaunt essentiality of *Alles endet*. Further *Parsifal* and harp-player, up from the depths till the sound – *Klang* – is reached, heralding the dream-vision filling the tormented heart, love-music of such ardour it well-nigh bursts, before the desolated 'I cannot tell.' Thenceforth it only renews in two spasms, both times swelling from soft to very loud, then collapsing – 'it is not in me: how may I attain it?' After which the music collapses completely: opening fumbling resumes briefly, then collapses too, linking none-too-expertly into a return of the ardour, also cut off before it can bloom, into a formal apostrophe to the dedicatee's eyes: then beautifully epitomized in four bars' epilogue for piano, that cannot succeed in summarizing and crowning what cannot be summarized and crowned: what it senses, feels, longs for, lies not within it.

Wolf destroyed as unworthy a fourth Michelangelo setting, and had intended further. Two other songs from the final phase are notable: setting Byron: an ice-cold invocation to the Moon, *Sun of the sleepless*, who 'shines not, warms not, with its powerless rays'; and its warm glowing counterpart *There be none of Beauty's daughters*, billowing on swelling summer seas in a tranced memory of Brangäne and her mistress from *Tristan*.

CHAPTER IX

Wagner

With Schoenberg, Wagner is the most disturbing and divisive composer in the history of the art: Schoenberg the Ultimate Jew, Wagner (for all the persisting ambiguity over his paternity) the Ultimate Aryan. They upheave music's very nature, making first a chaos then, hopefully, a new order, after which nothing can remain unchanged, to which nothing subsequent can remain indifferent, love it or loathe it. Both composers follow a Calling – Moses, Messiah – *chosen* for a Task whose necessity or inevitability occurred to no one but themselves, then undertaken with a gigantic surge of theory, explaining and vindicating the reformatory zeal and the cleansing artistic vision. Both claim as by right a keystone position in the art of their time, culture, nation, tradition: even while churning all this inside-out, they 'fulfil' it to the heights, widths, depths. Both are monsters of ego, Romantic self-expression taken beyond anything heretofore: art is born of the life, inner and outer, however impersonalized and objectified the upshot. In pursuit and conquest of a Vision that anyone in their senses would declare impossible, both push a complex and riotous language of chromaticism to unheard-of extremes; paralleled by unprecedented demands upon players, singers, venues and circumstances, resources, audiences – upon music itself.

To accomplish the Mission and realize the Vision in practical terms, to persuade or coerce the Folk to accept, love, revere, enjoy, was as arduous a goal as actually to write the music (and stories and words). Both composers encountered enormous resistance, at the time and ever since. For Wagner, Unconditional Surrender and Total Victory (which will never be Schoenberg's destiny, for reasons explored in a later chapter). 'We are all Wagnerians now' (though an anti-Wagnerian stance will never be quietened, and has some passages of legitimacy). The generation of composers succeeding him, however different and sometimes averse, all registered the impact and coped to the best advantage they could: Wagner's influence permits figures so diverse as Debussy and Sibelius to become themselves, as well as enabling clear direct-line admirers from Strauss to Elgar to enrich their art. 'Do likewise' or do unlikewise; either way the influence is equally potent: and thus with later generations – in the polemically anti-Wagnerian polar opposite Stravinsky, an uneasy similarity, the all-controlling personality manipulating history in its own image: with the wholly dissimilar case of Britten, the comparable culture-hub centred upon the individual genius, his place, his library, the Temple-enshrining model performances of his works, shares a Wagnerian footprint.

And the Folk have flocked: despite all excesses and unlikelihoods and impossibilities, Wagner's operas have never been more in demand, esteemed, studied, *enjoyed*. The Vision *was* and *is* pragmatic after all: singers *can* sing it (in the end) and can still be found (despite the 'shortage' of Siegfrieds and Isoldes): if an instrument was missing from the desired orchestral sonority, invent it (the resultant Wagner-tuba a resounding success): if the ideal theatre for presenting the unheard-of demands doesn't yet exist, design it, fund it by means fair and foul, and discover in the process the perfect acoustic. He even survives a universal plague of abominable productions; and, more important, political smirch by association with the ethos and iconography of the Third Reich.

Sources musical, dramatic, theoretical

Discussion of Wagner's ten canonical operas will be thematic and broadly chronological: there's no space here for details of plots and characters; I'm taking it that they will be broadly familiar. If not, they are readily accessible, and can easily be consulted.

The sources for the oeuvre of the man whom Auden called 'the greatest artist who ever lived' are deep and diverse. In *opera* he is the ardent heir to Weber – the breakthrough *Freischütz*, *Euryanthe* the noble failure; thence Weber's Gothic successors Marschner and Lortzing – fairy-tale, picturesque medievalry, aristocratic chivalry, rustic settings. Heir too to German opera's earlier idealistic/ethical strain, supremely embodied in *The Magic Flute* and *Fidelio*. A very different close background, Grand Opera in the spectacular French mode, its greatest example Rossini's *Guillaume Tell*, and including also Spontini, Auber, Halévy and the admired-and-despised Meyerbeer – the Paris success the young Wagner hankered for and came to execrate produced direct emulation in his *Rienzi* – 'Meyerbeer's best opera': its lasting influence is still patent in the melodrama and terrific stage-effects of *Götterdämmerung* and survives, just as powerful and more profound, in *Parsifal*. Then there is Italian *bel canto*, a vocal ideal Wagner located principally in Bellini (for whose *Norma* he provided an extra aria) and never relinquished, whatever his later very different demands on his singers: the mature idiom still retains many a surprising Italianate melodic turn, mediated via Chopin and Liszt as well as direct from his own experience as opera-conductor.

Add to the already eclectic mix what might seem incompatible, even contrary: the vital impact of Austro-German symphonism – structure and journey, development and argument, organic and evolutionary. Here Beethoven is paramount: Wagner the teenager copied the 5th and 9th Symphonies in full-score and made a piano transcription of the 9th, the work most germane to his language and aims. The inevitable next step, after the *Ode to Joy* – heroic/idealistic/rabble-rousing, addressing Humanity at large, introducing a voice, then voices, then Mankind, into the hitherto purely wordless genre of the Symphony – has to be . . . me, Richard! Not forgetting, however, his generous appreciation of Haydn – Wagner's recognition, within the formality, of maverick wit, the mastery of organic growth from small highly characterized cells (so unlike Mozart): and the emergence of Cosmos out of Chaos in the Introduction to *The Creation* (with *Tristan*-esque harmony unmissably prophesied).

He is not averse to learning and stealing from contemporaries: Mendelssohn for land- and seascape evocation – delicate watercolour draughtsman, as against Wagner's boiling oils: Berlioz – revelation of the modern orchestra, and of music's capacity to render gestures, frisson, electric nervousness, ardent eroticism, palpitating atmosphere, at its most catching in *Roméo et Juliette*: Liszt for some innovative harmonic explorations that Wagner wished their originator hadn't blathered about to an uncomprehending wider acquaintance. These benefactors are, like Meyerbeer, subject either to unlovely abuse or outright denial of debt or theft: the case of Liszt, everprincely in support both moral and practical (giving the première of *Lohengrin* when Wagner was exiled as well as indigent, and eventually becoming an ungrudging father-in-law), is particularly shameful.

Last and most, Schubert's songs. *Tristan* was once naughtily nutshelled as '*Lieder* louder': seriously, a matter of encapsulating an action, a motion, a place, a force of nature (most often *water* in all its varieties, from calm to tumultuous) into a musical impulse, an invention that then comes to contain *Affekt*; to be an emblem of emotion and feeling – to be a symbol, that utters and communicates, is understood with or without words – the essence of the leitmotif as container of *content* – semantic – as well as its limitless usefulness for producing ongoing texture, process, momentum. Schubert's way of fusing this into his astonishing harmonic vocabulary is analogous to Wagner's, whatever the historic actuality of how well or little the latter knew the body of Schubert's six hundred songs. And there is another, maybe non-historical, nexus with just these same matters in Bach – the endlessly affective harmony, the transmutation of momentum and imagery (quite often watery here too), via metaphor/emblem/symbol, into form and structure. How a-historical? Birth and boyhood in Leipzig; how much might the young Wagner have known of the city's principal cantor more than half a century before: certainly not the two-hundred-odd church cantatas. As with the Schubert connection, this is an elective affinity rather than a checkable influence: the nexus between the three is one of compositional type and type of mind – music as patterned fusion of its actual material means with representation of objects, persons, feelings – natural, innate, instructive, over and above 'history'. Though, of course, Bach's actual presence in the *burgherlich* chorales and counterpoint of *Meistersinger* is palpable, and is intensified in the polyphonic chromaticism of the processional-ritual element in *Parsifal*.

So to *words*: philosophy, religion, world-drama, world-literature. Wagner was an omnivorous reader, autodidact and didactic; and everything he consumed nourished him with rich substance. From his immediate native culture Goethe and Schiller, Hoffmann and Heine, the fairy-tales of Tieck and the Grimms, the whimsies of Jean Paul, the mystical pantheism of Novalis. Philosophy and religion are more problematic; essentially a home-brew originating in the Young German movement of his student days, right through to the ambiguous intellectual and personal relationship with Nietzsche; its crucial centre, discovering an affinity with Schopenhauer's philosophy – denial of the will, self-transcendence, the vital place of sexuality, informing the complementary worlds of *Tristan* and *Meistersinger*, the means – 'now at last I understand my Wotan' – to resolve the *Ring* that these two works had interrupted. World-drama the inspiring backdrop – Greek, tragic and comedic; Shakespeare, Calderón: Greek and Latin Epic, Homer and Virgil: mythology Norse and Icelandic, Teutonic/Burgundian: legend and romance, Teutonic, Celtic and French. These latter yield actual plots, of course, but (more indirect) the Greek theatre is a prevailing presence, and Shakespeare perhaps more still, though still more oblique (but not forgetting that *Das Liebesverbot* derives directly from *Measure for Measure*).

Cosima Wagner's riveting *Diaries* record the table-talk reactions of her husband's avid reading: his library at Wahnfried provides concrete evidence. Had he not been first and foremost a dramatist in music, Wagner might have been a classical scholar, a philologist of the German language, an anthropologist, a social and political commentator (with active, life-endangering engagement in revolutionary movements), as well as some sort of philosopher and some sort of poet. His large corpus of writing includes a notoriously unreliable autobiography, notebooks and diaries not intended for publication, together with works of theory concerning his aims and intentions that were made public – *Opera and Drama* principally. Unquestionably indispensable to the formation and eventual composition of the mature music-dramas: difficult to swallow whole, intermittently profound amid the turdge; sometimes illuminating, even stirring, even amusing, amid the tedium. The best of his later published writing concerns his incomparable insight upon the practicalities of conducting and staging. 'Silence was hard for Wagner': he held forth and freely emitted his opinions upon every conceivable subject – art and religion, politics and the state of contemporary civilization, the relations of the sexes, vivisection, et al. ad infinitum: most notoriously his views of Judaism and its interconnection with music. And – of course – correspondence, running into many thousands of letters whether private (often revelatory) or intended for open publication.

His sole deficiency appears to be visual: reaction to painting and architecture is relatively infrequent and rather trite, and its visual aspect remains the underdeveloped element in the dream-vision of the *Gesamtkunstwerk*, the fusion of all the arts mooted in *Opera and Drama*. Otherwise, Wagner is a sort of *Gesamtmensch*: all sources and resources within and around him are employed to foretell, vindicate, realize, consummate the comprehensive 'art-work of the future' – like Mahler's vision of the Symphony – that it, like the world, contain everything – applied to the musical stage.

Juvenilia and immaturity

Wagner's juvenile dramatic efforts included a tragedy so bloody that most of the cast had to reappear as ghosts to prevent the action guttering out. *Die Feen/The Fairies* (1833–4) was his first opera to reach completion. To his own libretto (always, from the start), after *La donna serpente* by Gozzi. Ada, immortal princess, loves Arindal, mortal prince. Her bargain – for eight years he must not ask her name and nature. The period is nearly elapsed when he succumbs, to lose her and be compelled to return to chivalric reality – his kingdom is under threat and he must defend it. He vows never to curse the wife who's abandoned him. She tests him further, in an illusion of destroying their children and leading his enemies in battle. Unaware of the delusion, Arindal curses her: she is turned to stone for a hundred years. But by supernatural means he wins her back; employing an enchanted lyre he sings a song that erodes the stone: conditions and chimeras and curses banished, the lovers live happily together for ever after: music and love have combined to make Arindal as immortal as his Ada. Elements of myth, chivalry, fairy-tale, foretell *Tannhäuser* and *Lohengrin* (more particularly, with the theme of the Forbidden Question – who and whence are you?): curse, and long slumber till awakened by love foretell the *Ring* (with a hint also of redemptions-to-come). The actual music foretells nothing – an amalgam of Weber and Mendelssohn (the opening 'magic' woodwind chords very close to the *Midsummer Night's Dream* Overture): fluent and faceless, prophetic only in its already expert orchestration and its vast lengths not yet able to be filled with the invention that would justify them.

Das Liebesverbot (1835–6) – to his own libretto (1835) after *Measure for Measure*, whose powerful plot is swivelled around to concentrate on and celebrate licence and abandon in the face of hypocritical repression – the theme for the actual 'Ban on Love' itself is the work's most memorable idea. General idiom Italianate with a vengeance: a long score, maddeningly noisy and busy, with welcome pools of relief for Isabella and Mariana sometimes foretelling the comparable idiom, in riper shape, for tender moments in *Tannhäuser* and *Lohengrin*. And the overkill achieves masterly fulfilment in the bustle and energy of *Meistersinger*; while the sexual tussle in and around the prohibition of sexual pleasure is re-explored and given its quietus in *Parsifal*.

Rienzi (1837–40), to his own libretto after Bulwer-Lytton's novel, is a massive false-direction; Wagner's true direction was hindered by its massive success. For the Paris Grand Opera super-spectacular it ticks every box: bold and fearless, in its way masterly, never less than theatrically effective and musically competent, now and again stirring, thrilling, even moving.

Romantic operas

The canon commences with *Der fliegende Holländer/The Flying Dutchman* (1840–41): from the very first notes on the right lines

musically and in narrative and human theme – Gothic psycho-
drama with mystic and religious undertones that set up reverberating concerns recurring, and deepening, throughout Wagner's entire
subsequent oeuvre. The hint of the hero as Wandering Jew, under a
curse till absolved, develops into Kundry: the same guilt-wracked hero
seeking forgiveness and redemption through the love and sacrifice
of a pure woman rhymes with Tannhäuser and Elisabeth: in *Lohengrin* Elsa's erotic yearning, wistful and wishful, and its fulfilment by
magical apparition of the Right Man, clearly foreshadowed in Senta's
Ballad, emotional and musical nucleus of the earlier work. Here still
a slightly shopsoiled trope – the heroine, means of salvation, plunged
into boiling seas, raised on high in triumphant mutual transfiguration
with her man: the cliché achieves quasi-religious stature at the close of
Tristan, and world-renewing apotheosis at the end of *Götterdämmerung*.

The music of *Dutchman* is very uneven: but its architecture is
absolutely sure: the huge three-act structures of the *Ring* after *Rheingold* clearly mooted; and, like *Rheingold*, the earlier work is best in
the original unbroken arc with its bold, simple, inspired transitions
from one sphere to another (whose power is dissipated by later exigencies dividing the continuity with intervals). This massing by
terrains of scoring and sonority as well as of place again foretells
Tannhäuser, and *Parsifal* still more: Act I, the male sphere – ship/
sanctuary of Monsalvat; Act II the spinning girls in their chamber/
the Flower-maidens in their garden – into both all-female domains
the male protagonist intrudes; Act III, communal dancing and
singing before the all-male double chorus of sailors living and
dead/the all-male Grail community, ending with terraces of full
mixed choirs. More complex, use of place as psychological indica-
tor: setting of sea/ship/anonymous crews from which individuals
emerge – Daland, the Steersman, the Dutchman himself: in *Tristan*
Act I, sea/ship/anonymous crews, background to the not-yet-lovers'
smouldering discontents, purveyed by their respective confidantes
and eventually confronted face-to-face, the surroundings dissolving into hallucination, only to haunt the subsequent act where the
lovers are, at last, actually alone *à deux*: the complex obliqueness of
the later presentation depends upon the directness of the earlier.

Clarification in reverse, vital to Wagner's later strategies, is employed with naïve power in *Dutchman*: music whose meaning only dawns retrospectively – *present* it first, *understand* it gradually: here at its most effective in using the work's opening horn-call, signifying the vessel and its accursed owner, as refrain of Senta's Ballad telling the legend; and in the Overture's encapsulation of the entire tale with its redemptive ending (admittedly this only achieved after several subsequent revisions) – a fully-integrated epitome, rounding the circle.

'The music is very uneven': its stylistic range is from undigested Italianate to Weber loudened and coarsened, with Beethoven's 9th thrown in from the very start; plenty of Lisztian religious kitsch; Mendelssohn's 'Scottish' Symphony and *Hebrides*, on octane, for the stormy seas. The weakest bits – especially Daland, and the central couple where they go into roulades – easily outweighed by the strengths – Senta's Ballad, Erik's Dream – and the sustained fury of the double-chorus of phantom and living ships' crews achieves a raw demonic vehemence refined but never surpassed in any later work. The Dutchman himself is one-dimensional, ham-and-corny, yet deeply identified-with, penetrated, thence projected outward, the prototype of several future protagonists wracked with guilt and torment. All in all, *Dutchman* is Hell-bent and crude as Hell, vital and unfailing in effect, blazing with suddenly unleashed genius whatever the inconsistencies, driven by obsession so forceful it can sweep aside all cavils and carry all before it.

Tannhäuser (1842–5: enhancements for Paris 1859–61) is a far larger and more ambitious venture, less surely attained: not on a tight trajectory – distended and slack, some of the music sheerly poor, even bad: the problems recognized by Wagner when overhauling the piece for Paris in the wake of *Tristan*: the superb calibre of these revisions rocks the boat; and the trouble remains unresolved even after *Parsifal*, telling a comparable story in incomparably greater depth: 'I still owe the world my *Tannhäuser*,' he told Cosima a fortnight before his death.

Connections with *Parsifal* are manifold: protagonists torn between sacred and sensual love, a struggle of flesh and spirit; both heroes undergo a purgative pilgrimage, vividly depicted, to be, in the end, redeemed; Tannhäuser's agent the love of a pure woman – Elisabeth, almost Maria-the-Virgin, while in *Parsifal* the hero himself is the redeemer. Terrains – Venus and her grotto of carnal bliss, placed in apposition to the Wartburg, seat of chaste courtly love, both visible from each other, Tannhäuser oscillating between the two; flesh and spirit, Venus and Maria: in *Parsifal*, nature, the swan-lake with its healing waters, the Grail-ceremonial, vis-à-vis Klingsor and his girls, and Kundry as unwilling emissary. Each aspect of the linked dichotomy is characterized by complementary musical idiom – open/diatonic/unsullied/frank and fresh; nature, shepherd-boy, huntingmen, stately ceremony, Wolfram and Elisabeth: as opposed to Venus and her sirens – luscious/chromatic/intoxicatingly coloured (especially after the post-*Tristan* enhancements for Paris): the same dichotomy, enormously intensified, fuels the diatonic/chromatic extremes of *Parsifal*. Venus's gratifications palling, the sated hero cries aloud for deliverance: but, later, oppressed by decorous Christian pieties, infiltrates them with pagan joys: ostracized by the ensuing outrage, he's sent off to beg the Pope's forgiveness, which, denied, sets him clamouring anew to be released from chastity, crying aloud for re-admission to the carnality he'd renounced: all this a directly narrative version of what, in *Parsifal*, is present obliquely and internalized, though clearly dependent upon its prototype in the earlier work.

The central song-contest in *Tannhäuser* obviously foretells *Meistersinger*, originally conceived as satyr-play to the earlier work's tragedy, Elisabeth–Eva the inspiring muse and prize whatever the drastically different outcomes. All three – *Meistersinger, Parsifal, Tannhäuser* – abound in splendid ceremonial processions, their timing and pacing completely different and absolutely right, emphatically including the touch of vulgarity in the earliest – showy, blatant, expertly stage-managed. Elsewhere *Tannhäuser*'s vulgarity can embrace the sheerly awful – the end of Act II; yet this follows direct from the magnificent Italianate ensemble wherein guilt/shame/accusation/plea for mercy/resolve to seek it are expressed by the entire cast plus chorus with a fervour worthy of Verdi. Earlier still, the contestants' songs preceding Tannhäuser's interruption perhaps *need* to be dull in order to precipitate it. Wolfram's celebrated 'Star of Eve' song in Act III is a sweetly insipid affair that surely wouldn't pass Venus' criteria (a hint, with Wolfram, of the renunciation theme – he, too, loves Elisabeth, but in secret – so strong and poignant for Sachs and Eva later). More important, the opera's closing agon between the doppel-image of Love Goddess/Virgin Muse is miffed and muffed for all its frenzy. Pilgrims and Huntsmen are from stock; their best music pertains to the hero's solitary pilgrimage in the purely orchestral tone-poem early in Act III, narrating the fruitless quest to Rome for the Pope's pardon.

Troubles arise because of the altogether superior calibre of the rewritten Venusberg music. It swells up out of the original overture; a Bacchanal of amazing richness and erotic charge – Wagner's only choreographed ballet (as required by the conventions and expectations of the Paris Opéra) – an orgy of pagan imagery – bacchantes, satyrs, fauns, in wild abandon; fluttering cupids discharging their arrows of desire; a *tableau vivant* for the Rape of Europa ... ; matched in every respect by supercharged music; then its post-coital withdrawal into gorgeous seductive languor. The ensuing dispute between the Goddess and her devotee is more astonishing yet: the original words (with some additions) are reset in a style of ripe *chaleur* surpassing *Tristan* Act II and anticipating Kundry (perhaps surpassing her too): this music expresses and embodies the pleasures of the senses uncurbed by any vestige of guilt or tinge of morbid spirituality – carnal delight that, indeed, is its own spirituality – Venus the 'child of nature' like Lulu, undivided in religious devotion to sexual joys. Tannhäuser's song, unaltered from the original, sticks out like an embarrassment – though this is maybe appropriate to the situation. For sure the return to 1843 after the headiness of 1861 produces a *coup de théâtre* of enormous emotional impact as, the argument completed, released from thralldom, he cries out his thanks and praise to God for the wonders of his mercy, ultimately to be denied him by God's representative on earth.

All in all, the power of *Tannhäuser*, as with *Hamlet*, to excite disturbance is greater than its power to understand this disturbance's causes and constituents. Thus to excite but not illuminate makes the work at once the most challenging and the least satisfying of Wagner's first three canonic operas. Neither *Dutchman* nor *Lohengrin* take on so much; and both are in their very different ways the more rounded works of art. The world is still owed its *Tannhäuser* – the debt is paid with generous interest in *Parsifal*.

Lohengrin (1845–8) is the ultimate – longest, greatest, last – German Romantic opera: fairy-tale shading into myth, legend, romance, medieval/chivalric setting à la Walter Scott, with Burgundian roots: supernatural dark and light forces in conflict à la *Freischütz*; added to these, all-too-human rancour/envy/love and hatred à la *Euryanthe* (to which it is at once homage and critique): wish-fantasy fulfilled then betrayed by what's not so much false within as weak, doubting, wavering. The intertwined motif of the identity that must not be divulged – that if revealed brings ruin to the most ardent couple; and the question that must not be asked and *is*, and *does*, brings for the first time a Classical element into Wagner's work: not as yet the agon and catharsis of Tragedy; rather, the echo of two tragi-comedies of love undone either by overweening – Semele determined to aspire to her god-paramour's stature; or pitiable longing – Psyche's fatal desire to see and know hers, Cupid. The same motif in *Die Feen* doesn't yet have such resonances.

Elsa is the Pure Maiden rather than Redeeming Woman; the Saviour by whom she is at first rescued, at last forgiven, is, unlike Tannhäuser and even Parsifal, a man undivided, the knight in shining armour, perhaps too good to be true. She is wrecked by curiosity, the worm in the bud: prompted by the sheerly human jealousy and rage of Ortrud, exploiting Elsa's doubts with subtle insinuation, goading her to mistrust her deliverer, to ask the forbidden question – his name and origin – thus losing him, thence herself, for ever. Ortrud's Count Telramund is the dark shadow of this radiant hero: black and white are compellingly marshalled for the inevitable outcome. Yet the work's ending is ambiguous and inconclusive: young Gottfried restored from swan to his mortal form and his kingdom, but Elsa (presumably) expires; Lohengrin, now named and placed, must return whence he'd appeared, leaving the kingdom to likely chaos and defeat; Telramund has been slain but Ortrud lives on, in thrall to her potent pagan religion. Though no Tragedy, it is not a Happy End.

Lohengrin is a clear ancestor of *Parsifal* (though in literal fact a descendant – his closing narration divulging name and nature reveals that Parsifal is his father!). Wagner's last work can re-employ actual material from the earlier; most simply, the swan, translated from a lovely poetic picture into symbol/emblem, first intimation of guilt and shame, first step of a Pilgrim's Progress towards self-knowledge: more complex, the Grail, in the flawless Prelude to *Lohengrin* high in the heavens, descending in ever-growing splendour to touch the world below, re-ascending to the heights – wonderful and one-dimensional. The *Parsifal* Grail is a remote presence, and the *Parsifal* Prelude touches upon sin, suffering, expiation, atonement: such troubled content, foreshadowed in *Tannhäuser*, is scarcely present in the fairy-tale with the unhappily-ever-after ending.

The score's salient characteristic and chief glory is its radical diatonicism – radiance unsullied, dulcet euphony, for a larger orchestra than hitherto, used with consummate art as the Prelude immediately shows. Such stretches as the King's Prayer in Act I, the earlier phrases of the principals' love-duet (before things begin to go so badly wrong) and Lohengrin's farewell, are instinct with this newly freshened musical language, at its boldest and brightest in simpler, purely ceremonial places – the dawn fanfares and entry-music for retainers and knights in Act I, the thrilling congregation to the judgment-oak in Act III, the resplendent fanfares throughout. This brilliance and clarity are somewhat counterbalanced by a prevailing rhythmic squareness that veers between hypnotic and plain stodgy: Wagner's verse-metres are the cause – long regular lines, faithfully set, almost all in common time. His next work will rectify this with the discovery and exploitation of short, brusque, alliterative trenchancy. *Lohengrin* doesn't yet employ leitmotifs: reminiscence-tags like the Fatal Question show that the idea is nascent, poised to expand in the next work to all-telling explicitness. And the next work is equally or more so still a celebration of radical diatonicism in all its unsullied radiance. But the difference is vast: the Rhine flows between the last German Romantic opera and the first music-drama. Yet *Lohengrin* and *Rheingold* have as much in common as what utterly differentiates them.

Music-drama: theory into practice

In *Dutchman* and *Tannhäuser* Wagner had touched upon his core: what, with mature powers (as yet only nascent), he would eventually be supremely endowed to realize, here only in fits and starts, although often compelling. In *Lohengrin* he achieved the consummation of German Romantic opera, which, by definition, is not compatible with the kind of psychological exploration by means of myth and legend understood, with hindsight, to be the goal and the nature of the mature music-dramas. After *Lohengrin* come Wagner's years of exile, dire financial distress and domestic disorders, brooding, theorizing and formulating – a creative blockage perilously akin to sterility; writing the text for the new-mooted work but still unable to take the plunge into its music, the logjam broken at last by the famous waking dream of submersion into a rush of ur-*wellen* waters gradually focusing into E♭ arpeggios, prefiguring the start of the tetralogy's actual sounds. (Sympathetic response lends poetic credence if not total credibility to the self-mythology of this tale, as to others in Wagner's symbolic fictions: true in a deeper sense: all poets feign!)

Salient dates: completion of *Lohengrin* 1845–8; political exile 1849, texts for *Siegfrieds Tod* 1848, of the entire tetralogy 1851–2; music of *Rheingold*, *Walküre* and first two acts of *Siegfried* 1853–7. *Tristan* pushes the *Ring* imperiously aside August 1857; Act I completed by April the next year, Act II by March 1859, Act III that autumn. Throughout this emanation from the depths *Parsifal*, whose story he'd first read in 1845 in connection with Lohengrin his son, was constantly on his mind. But next after *Tristan* comes *Meistersinger*, first mooted in connection with *Tannhäuser* – its comic 'parody' – a draft libretto from that period reworked, greatly enriched, 1860–61, the score completed 1864. That year the interrupted *Ring* resumed, scoring the previously sketched first two acts of *Siegfried* by the next year, composing Act III 1869–71: *Götterdämmerung* overlapped, eventually finished 1874. First Bayreuth Festival with first complete *Ring* cycle 1876. *Parsifal* text perfected after several earlier drafts 1877, its music completed 1882.

These astonishing facts and figures speak for themselves. The

account here will stick to chronology, splitting the *Ring* into everything *pre* and everything *post* the interruption of *Tristan* and *Meistersinger*, thus following the evolution of Wagner the composer as,
through deepening continuities or startling contrasts, and a fusion
of both into yet deeper richness, his music reaches its consummation. There'll be no heavy weather of biography or theories: rather,
concentration on what the works are doing and how they do it. So
far as the *Ring* is concerned, there are several basics to grasp and
remember. First, the backward growth of the texts, from the initial
Siegfrieds Tod, approximating to the eventual *Götterdämmerung*, seen
to require a first prequel to recount the hero's youth, then another
to present and explain the human pre-history, then a Prologue to
explore and present the entire saga's primeval origins, its setting in
a world-cosmography, the mesh of bargains and betrayals between
gods and destiny that sets the action, from its timeless context, off
on its course in time. This retrospective process is counterpointed
with the forward growth of the music, from *Lohengrin*-soundalike
Rheingold to *Tristan*/*Meistersinger*-charged *Götterdämmerung*.

Next, the dramatic shapes; they evince marvellous powers of
clarification and compression of extremely complex raw material
into massive architectural blocking: after *Rheingold* (itself a marvel
of articulation in one unbroken span) the three-act articulation
around essentials, often told in duologue (*Siegfried* entirely so),
paced by long, slow build-up elaborating a situation in all its causes
and their ramifications, all its doubts and fears, the tension released
in sudden drastic, decisive action, sometimes violent, that takes the
whole edifice/journey into a new place on a new plane. Paradoxically,
Wagner is a master of what can be omitted or implied as well as what
must be presented: never apologize, *always* explain: the expansion
from one evening to four is to show as well as to relate: his unique
genre owes as much to epic as to drama: music is always the means.

Hence, next, the widening scope of Wagner's purely *musical*
invention, in all its parameters, especially harmony and orchestration. Lengths hitherto loose and unearned – longueurs, *mauvais
quarts-d'heure* – are now fully occupied and justified – 'not a stone
out of place' as Loge says, proudly contemplating newly finished

Valhalla. Achieved by means of the leitmotif; every one at once one of these building-blocks, and a container-emblem in sound of demonstrative and/or expressive meaning – object, place, person-age, desire/wish/intention, emotion: a gradually expanding quasi-language given with dictionary-like orderliness, spelt out step by step, 'line upon line, precept upon precept' into a sonorous tissue of symbolic semantic *meaning*; its actual substance based in age-old musical tropes of action and *Affekt* and natural phenomena germane to the art since time immemorial, now applied to tasks never before demanded of it. Simultaneously in the small, respond-ing to the text's every passing play, fluid and versatile, yet hard and adamant; and in the large the means of building unprece-dently monumental sizes without danger of implosion. *Rheingold* already the longest unbroken span of music yet written, soon to be outdone by the vast three-act structures/journeys that succeed it. Furthermore – consequent, and still more important – the texture of interwoven leitmotifs acts as commentary: the orchestra can know more and understands better than the character singing, and can tell the audience so that it knows and understands also, involv-ing it in arguments/desires/impulses, conscious or unconscious, as never before – an extraordinarily daring and successful transform-ation of the Greek chorus into a sort of communal memory-bank/time-capsule. At its greatest – the colossal 'rhymes' across the four last-composed acts, from Brünnhilde's awakening, via the Norns, Siegfried's Rhine-journey, Waltraute's narration, Siegfried's death as he relives Brünnhilde's awakening, her concluding peroration – as if the Alps were nodding to the Andes and the Himalayas, as depicted by a super-Altdorfer.

The speed and sureness with which these unheard-of objectives are achieved up to the first two acts of *Siegfried* – after the logjam, the watercourse so full and free – confirm that this apparently crazy project is exactly tuned to what Wagner came into the world to do and *can*: the gifts, the limitations too, are equipoised for just this outcome: the tetralogy's further four acts, and the three further operas, are not so immediately inevitable, though in the end they are a part of the same great trajectory.

It is a wonderful thing that a man no longer young should not
only produce the seven most voluminous, highly-organized and
in all respects revolutionary works of art extant, but produce
them under the necessity of constantly inhibiting the impulse to
write the sort of melody that came naturally to him.

The caveat in Tovey's superlative can be related to the reservation in
Auden's (not given complete when cited earlier): 'the greatest artist
who ever lived – but for tragedy only.' Not just melody: the sort of
music 'that came naturally' must be transcended and transformed.
For melody: Wagner's tunes tend towards the commonplace – so
no more 'Star of Eve' and 'Here Comes the Bride'; instead, 'endless
melody', born of gesture and declamation, pregnant phrases, unforgettable in contour, encapsulating semantic meaning and emotional
Affekt. His attempts at sonatas and symphonies were mediocre – but
symphonic process and momentum can fuel his enormous continuities: he doesn't do polyphony – but the cross-cutting interpenetration of leitmotifs as required by text/character/situation effect a sort
of substitute that exactly suffices. And – *pace* Auden – he doesn't do
comedy but he can do a *Meistersinger*! Equally 'a wonderful thing',
the perfect if serendipitous timing, to leave the *Ring* when its first
flush is spent, and story and meaning alike require a new slant on the
familiar material as well as much new; then returning after *Tristan*
and *Meistersinger* have, through their complementary necessities,
enriched his language beyond all possible anticipation, feeding this
enhancement back into the initial impulse, now wholly recharged:
then in *Parsifal* learning in turn from the *Ring*'s last four acts.
    Some interconnections of subject-matter: in some respects the
Ring lies outside Wagner's principal preoccupations; no concern
with carnal/spiritual struggle – love here is clear and clean –
Siegmund and Sieglinde (for all that they become known to each
other to be twins); Siegfried and Brünnhilde (for all that their love
goes horribly wrong till wonderfully righted). Other loving relations
are just as direct – Wotan and his daughter, relinquished with heart-
rending pang as world-order ordains; Wotan and his hoped-for heir/
fulfilment/redemption, till their ugly spat destroys his authority for

ever; even Fricka and domestic decorum; and *everyone*'s lust for the
gold – libido embedded into a ring.

Some further parallels: Brünnhilde the all-comprehending/all-
forgiving Woman who not only redeems the erring hero but, doing
so, cleanses a corrupt old regime, rhymes with Senta and Elisabeth
and takes them higher and deeper: Siegmund the suffering outcast
develops directly from Tannhäuser, thence grows into Parsifal; and
can be related obliquely to Walther, rejected then accepted by Nuremberg's song-makers' guild and small-town society. Parallels between
dark forces of pure malignity à la Ortrud and Telramund are not so
salient: *Schwarz*-Alberich has his own integrity (and justice on his
side) – dark sibling to Wotan – *Licht*-Alberich – sharing the same
fatal knot of weakness, lust for gold/power/women, and the shabby
tricks they both are prepared to perpetrate to get their will. Mime,
Hunding and Hagen are as human in motivation and consequent
action as the brother-giants Fasolt and Fafner – ardent and generous/
actively greedy, later passively retentive; or the siblings Gunther and
Gutrune, variously victims to the lures of the flesh, however feeble.
(And the characterization of Mime resembles nothing so much as
Beckmesser's.) The cast for the entire tetralogy is not so large as that of
Meistersinger: whether gods, dwarfs, giants, water-maidens and norns,
or mere mortals, the impulses are all human. Unlike *Tristan* with its
sense of *sententiae* – questions mooted as to the nature of Love and
Death, rehearsed between superhuman archetypes without individual
personality: still more with *Parsifal* – every character a cipher, a figure
in an equation, the hero himself a cut-out, not a person; a generality,
a composite – a 'representative man'. This is no reservation, let alone
criticism of those great works: it is how they are; *es muß sein*: but comparison with a Fricka, a Loge, a Mime, let alone with larger characters,
is as revealing as with a David, a Magdelena, a Pogner, a Beckmesser.

The strongest link with *Parsifal* concerns Siegfried's moral education (though certainly not his sentimental education) – a journey
from callow ignorance, oafish obstreperousness, pure foolishness –
chasing bears, shooting swans – to mature manhood made wise by
empathy with suffering via mother then lover, to eventual compassionate embrace of the globe as well as (or instead of) the girl. Parsifal

achieves this goal: Siegfried's journey is cut off just as he's poised to grow into moral stature matching his physical prowess. Parsifal ends up as Redeemer – Wagner's sole male in this role. Siegfried defaults: the Redeemer's role is given to Brünnhilde: hers is the principal moral education in the entire oeuvre. Since she has undergone so much more suffering and betrayal than any other personage, her progress is the longest and most comprehensive: she must learn, obey, acquiesce, undergo, understand, forgive to become wise/compassionate at last, then strong enough to hold up the action, in both senses, and resolve it: she contains the ultimate consciousness of every person and every deed, knows how it came about and why it must be so: from this position of commanding clarity she can effect transformation. 'Redemption to the Redeemer' is as apt for Brünnhilde as for Parsifal.

Thus, the *Ring* relates in circumferences rather than right-angles to the rest of the oeuvre. It is also somewhat outside the nexus of the other works, before, during and after, in its actual idiom. Direct connections are mostly incidental: for sure the triadic diatonicism of *Lohengrin* is continued, celebrated, enhanced, in *Rheingold*, and the chivalric strains of the Gibichung court in *Götterdämmerung* descend direct, greatly enriched, from such in *Tannhäuser* too – *Siegfrieds Tod*, if composed when first projected, would have come next after *Lohengrin*. Connections between the love-music for Siegmund and Sieglinde in Act I of *Walküre* and the lovers in Act II of *Tristan* are slight, and there's no *Tristan* idiom whatever for Siegfried and Brünnhilde. *Siegfried*'s first two acts compare with *Meistersinger* throughout for energetic bustle, purposeful or pointless: and Wagner's sturdy-burly work-songs are generic from start to finish – sailors in *Dutchman*, Sach's shoe-ing and Siegfried's forging, close to Kurwenal's loyal tunes and the sailors' disrespectful ones in *Tristan*, and even to the Grail-Knights in *Parsifal* when after-communion communality waxes hearty.

A new appreciation of the *Ring*'s facture came about for me very recently. After a near-lifetime's involvement, initially reluctant, even rebellious, I listened to the tetralogy in a different way, following text only, in a new translation presenting it as a work of 'literature' in its own right, rather than following the orchestral scores constantly interested in and absorbed by a detail in second clarinet, fourth horn, violas (etc.), only occasionally glancing at the sung words in their fustian 'English'. Going for the text – character/situation/argument – *first*, putting *music* last, was to try to imagine the position of the poet-dramatist Wagner before Wagner-the-composer took over; to see what confronted him, as musician, when he embarked on his task. Result, a wholly new angle upon his genius as architect, constructor, agonist, wordsmith: his mastery of pacing and placing had never seemed greater. From the dialectic of *Rheingold* and its open-ended consequences, to the one-to-one/one-by-one duo-confrontations of *Walküre* with their further consequences, via the comic-epic duos of *Siegfried* – never more than two persons (including dragon, wood-bird, Earth-mother) on-stage at a time, ending (for now) in mutual erotic resolution; to the busy plot-workings of *Götterdämmerung*, crowded with new characters in new places, turbulent in action, speeded up with tense compression (for all its vast scale), violent with betrayals, oaths, murder-plot, actual murder, complex resolution – the massing and blocking so sure, the motivations so compelling, the arguments so riveting, the tying-up and un-tying of the knots so complete: an achievement of 'world-drama' up there with its models and successors – Aeschylus and Sophocles, Shakespeare, Calderón, Goethe and Schiller, Ibsen; and whatever reservations about the verbal idiom – stilted diction, creaky alliteration, cranky neologisms etc. – convincing in these respects also. All this prior to the music, which – it goes without saying but cannot be emphasized too strongly – is its *raison d'être* and goal, performing the real task of embodiment, expression/utterance, fulfilment, justification.

An ancillary side-effect was to vindicate certain places where the dramatic relevance has sometimes seemed a little strained – those stretches so mocked by the work's denigrators and sometimes by its champions (and performers even to the extent of their being cut) – Wotan's 'monologue' (to his attentive but silent daughter) in *Walküre* Act II, the question-and-answer game between Mime and the Wanderer in Act I of *Siegfried*, the Norns' prologue to *Götterdämmerung*: all three fell into place as high-points, necessary and inevitable. Each is telling 'the story so far', already known, wholly or in part, to the audience if not to all the participants: each gathers in the threads, rehearses the themes, presenting the familiar in a new light, while simultaneously carrying the action in new directions towards unforeseen outcomes. Wagner is here the equal of not so much the dramatists as the great epic-writers of antiquity and after – the Homer, Virgil, Milton, Tolkien of the outer life of war and peace, and those writers who chart interior journeys of self-exploration and self-discovery – Proust, Mann, Freud, Joyce.

Interregnum: *Tristan* and *Meistersinger*

Wagner's breaking off the *Ring* to undertake and complete two other projects of the highest calibre, difficulty, originality, is surely without parallel in any other artist. As in everything, his apparent foolhardiness turns out to be wise and well-founded – there's a happy hand guiding everything he essays. The *Ring*'s first, fine, impulsive rapture lasts till exactly the point where, impulse for now spent, it needs to rest, draw breath, recharge before moving on into deeper, more complex places: Wagner's instinct for timing is as uncannily sure in the outer circumstance of his works' creation as in their internal workings.

'Why *Tristan*?' There are biographical factors – it remains a moot point whether Wagner's relationship with Mathilde Wesendonck fuels the opera or the opera fuels the *affaire*: she certainly provided poems he set to music, two of the songs explicitly designated 'studies for *Tristan and Isolde*', trying out material later taken to its apogee in the opera's second and third acts. Also practicality: the need for a money-maker – small cast and chorus, relatively small orchestra, compact action (only one evening!) with no expensive effects. This aim, however, can be discounted as hopelessly unreal, and is gleefully abandoned as the project burgeons into its full nature, demanding in every aspect beyond any previous opera; including its demands upon music itself.

Subject-matter and themes – courtly love from the old Celtic romance, blown apart from within; the terrain of *Tannhäuser*, losing altogether the earlier work's conflict between sacred and sensual love; instead exploded into the mystic night-religion of Novalis, with a whiff of Buddhism – world-creation from the originating breath, world-relinquishment to attain Nirvana: and not a hint of Christianity. Human love physical, metaphysical, psychological: exploration from initial embargo by code, propriety, infringement of forbidden relationships, plus internal boundaries of repression: the Epic of the Interior, braving the emotions, the calls of the body, with the fearlessness with which the hero of the sagas confronts flames and dragons. These internal bounds passed, the lovers can rampage through the main courses, thence nooks and crannies of the psyche, unto extremes of being where, indifferent or impervious to all perils, they fuse into each other and are lost to normality and reality. Their mutuality inter-animates them into one person – 'no more Tristan, no more Isolde': erotic love is spiritualized – 'spilt religion' indeed – round an immense gamut embracing day and night, love and death: the opera remains for ever the summit of Romanticism, in all its aspect, in all the arts.

The lovers are not betrayed by something false, or, as with Elsa, something merely weak, within. Rather, the real world cannot contain such a state: ecstasy, like the superlative, has no future. The plot's expedients require envy – the lovers in heedless affection call Brangäne 'envious watcher' as she mounts guard during their tryst: her motivation in substituting love-potion for death-potion is inherent to plot and subject-matter, in no way personal. Melot, a mere cipher, enviously betrays Tristan to King Marke. Love-as-death, timeless conceit for sexual joy, is first rendered actual, then metaphorical in the end – a *Liebestod*. Before this ultimate draught of spilt religion the work's trajectory of endless desire, endless consummation till its hideous interruption, has moved from celebratory to terrible – Tristan's delirium in Act III a flow chart/case history of disturbance, pain-wracked and personality-wrecked, disintegrated into nerve-ends of suffering, strains from childhood and boyhood unlocking layer upon layer from the past, interfused with confused pressures from what we/he have seen and heard in the acts preceding. His ancestor is Tannhäuser, his descendant Amfortas, who both sin in the flesh. Tristan has not thus transgressed: his only disobedience is to overturn an injunction to conduct Isolde safe to her new, older husband: but he *has* obeyed Venus/Frau Minne, goddess of Love-strong-as-Death. A salient foretaste of *Parsifal's Liebe als Qual* – love as torment: at one stage Wagner intended Parsifal, on his long road of atonement for what he'd never committed except in imagination, to pass Tristan stricken and demented on his pallet, and – comfort? counsel? heal? Take up thy bed and join me on my pilgrimage?

Other thematic connections: Renunciation – Marke and Sachs: the 'arranged' husband, not pressing his 'rights' (this is gently yet unmistakably insinuated); the lonely widower still very audibly in his prime: both must needs renounce the maiden of their dreams in favour of the ardent younger man: unbearably moving *bei* Marke, lyricized and bluffed away by Sachs though the heartache stabs. This theme is varied with profound *Affekt* in Wotan's relinquishment of his daughter, and disappears into the mists in *Parsifal*, where renunciation becomes quite another thing. More oblique, Isolde as Redeeming Woman: unlike Elisabeth, let alone Brünnhilde, Isolde has nothing to forgive; she must simply acquiesce in, embrace and transfigure the metaphor of Love-Death into an actuality: a Happy End of sacramental import.

The *musical* embodiment of outer story and inner content is found in *Tristan's* radical chromaticism, exploited with radical intensity and – paradoxically – total rationality, lucidity, control: Wagner's take on his material is quasi-scientific – an investigation, an experiment, on an enormous scale, at the same time white-hot, searingly harsh and sensually beautiful, encompassing extremes of emotional utterance without parallel, tensions strained and extended to their utmost until resolved.

Pro and contra Wagner

Some wider thought occasioned by the big woolly words that inevitably arise in thinking about Wagner's oeuvre, and *Tristan* in particular. It's extremely important to try to rescue great art-works from the ideas and beliefs that helped them into being: and, by extension, from their creator's character and biography (despite our insatiable and all-too-human appetite for anecdotes and our fascination with every aspect of any outstanding creative individual).

There are three temptations that commentary on Wagner and his oeuvre finds hard to resist: to be seduced by the altogether extraordinary personality and biography; to become enmeshed in the coils of his published theorizing and reported opinion on a wide range of subjects, out of his depth, whose extreme sensitivity shows no sign of diminishing; and then, even if the art-works undoubtedly born from his life and thought as well as from the springs of imagination are kept 'clean', to be hung up on the 'issues' they raise, which can obscure, even obliterate, concentration upon the meaning inherent within narrative, situation, character, utterance and – paramount – the actual facture by which the poet/dramatist/ composer brings all this into artistic being.

Precisely because their invitation is so apparently ample, we shouldn't be overawed or beguiled by big abstract nouns like Love, Death, Renunciation, Redemption, Transfiguration, Transcendence. 'When I hear such words I reach for my gun.' Or, as F. R. Leavis said in relation to Dante Gabriel Rossetti's splurgy poetic vocabulary, it is 'beggar's largesse'. Or as Philip Larkin said of some of his peers, 'I am not going to fall on my face every time someone uses words such as Orpheus or Faust or Judas.' Or – ultimate purist – Mallarmé's celebrated injunction to Degas when the painter turned poet, 'poems are made with words not ideas.' Paintings are made of painted paint, music of composed sounds.

Which is not to say that the music of Wagner is not, also, inspired by and saturated in such overweening concepts – more so perhaps than in any other composer of major stature, and never more so than in *Tristan*. But they'd be as naught – beggar's largesse – if he'd not succeeded in embedding them deep into the actual stuff of his musical invention, the opposite of abstraction, conceptualization, woolly vagueness; the specific notes.

How he did this, how these sounds work, remains the boldest individual achievement in the entire culture of Western Music. It also remains contentious still, long after the Wagner-wars are over and the oeuvre's become a recognized cornerstone of operatic repertoire as well as common intellectual and cultural 'heritage'. Whether superficial or deeper, anti-Wagner polemic on the technical level has always been concerned with alleged abuse against the very nature of music itself (as I said, I'm keeping the art-works away from all ideological and biographical consideration). From whatever position of purism – classical ('a harmonic hooligan'), neo-classical ('shapeless, formless, without measure'), or postmodernist blasé ('too Freudian, too knowing, too explicit; everything *under-lined* and hammered home') – the objections focus implicitly upon the way that this composer, through claiming somehow to be more than merely a composer, compels music to attempt matters that music intrinsically cannot do – or if it can, shouldn't. At its simplest this is the endeavour to represent objects, places, persons, psychological impulses; at its worst (or, at least, most tendentious) the desire to express the big words like Transcendence that make even so ardent a Wagnerite as myself react negatively – concepts that move beyond the social/familial/amorous/ambitious preoccupations of humanity at large (and so comprehensively understood or explored with the microcosm of the music-dramas) into a sphere that should properly pertain only to religion.

Yet Wagner of course *does* succeed in imbuing his actual unmetaphysical notes with resonances from such dubious matter. He musicalizes the extra-musical. Which ought not to be possible either as an undertaking or technically – but there it is, he's done it. What we'd all like to know is, *how?* If this can be answered we might perhaps be able to say *what* it is, and what it *means*. I'd like to concentrate simply and briefly on the problems and solutions of Wagner the *composer*, thence Wagner the dramatist-in-music, rather than add to the confusion and hot air of Wagner the metaphysician (let alone the dangerous ideologue). But this is by no means to deny that 'other' Wagners do get in eventually, and that to get them in might have been a main, even a primary, aim of his work (though if it were, I would have to claim that they need protecting from it).

After these warning-signals, the music itself. The nub of Western Music is harmony – journey, argument, arrival, tension-and-release;

how to open, to continue, to interrupt, develop, to close; the balance of suspension and resolution. By common consent *Tristan* is pivotal in all this tradition of exploiting music's powers of inhalation and exhalation, intensifying them beyond anything imaginable before (and very little since, most of it by Wagner too, or in his wake). The opera's initial moves set up huge implications, of size, of trajectory, of emotional expression – impulses with consequences, issues requiring resolutions. The entire fabric of the ensuing three acts can be heard as the realization of these opening moves – a complex, richly ambiguous cadential idea spread wide over a structure lasting a whole long evening, which needs this amount of sonorous time-and-space for its full purport to be unwound, then resolved.

Is the Prelude to Act I in A-minor, or C; or even A-major?* Its ultimate goal – the end of Act III – is none of these; untransposed, it heads with surprising yet consummatory conviction for B-major. But its immediate resolution, at the start of Act I, is C-minor; the act's eventual harbour is C-major (with a powerful penultimate A-minor too). Simply to measure this one main journey through Act I, charting the delays, extensions, interruptions, evasions, frustrations, feints whereby C is dangled, denied and finally achieved, with all their mastery of musical grammar and their range of expressive nuance from irony and scorn to wild excitement, would show the inextricable linking of compositional prowess with dramatic pacing and human utterance of the highest order. Then there'd be all the further subsidiary strands in all their interwoven complexity (even though Act I is far the most 'straightforward' of the three). With such grasp of the composition in one's hands – whether intellectual/analytic, or, as in the theatre, by sheer intuitive gut-response – it might then be permissible to begin on the impalpables and conceptualities.

Just to make this chart would be sufficiently interesting; to elaborate it to its fullest reaches of significance would take years of labour. Fortunately, neither is necessary: Act I of *Tristan* has already

---

*   A-major is the chosen key with which Wagner closes his exquisite concert-ending (rarely performed) for the Prelude.

done it for us in the most succinct and elegant manner imaginable. And so with Acts II and III. A first, practicable line through Act II might again centre in concentration upon its breathing. The enormous span of love-duet is articulated around some five perfect cadences (sometimes vulgarly given a more carnal name). Their effect is extraordinarily powerful, at once reposeful and arriving, yet opening up new, larger vistas, after the normative language of Act I in which expectation and closure are constantly thwarted, and before the delirium of Act III in which tonal usage is strained, dissipated, exploded. After such conspicuous perfect-cadencing, the cadential interruption when the lovers are discovered and ecstatic night yields to cold dawn is overwhelming; an aching bruise only pacified in the closing stretch of the *Liebestod* at the end of Act III, whose whole course recapitulates the final stage of the love-duet, sweeping grandly on over where it had been so painfully cut off.

Another Act II exploration could focus on the beautiful and profound effect of the exchanges between the lovers after King Marke's reproachful monologue. After the ocean of a-periodic music with its amazing spans of free-prose and apparent improvisation (derided by Stravinsky as 'the slagheap of art' but more justly characterized by another Wagner-derogator, Nietzsche, as the precious jewellery of a musical miniaturist 'who compresses an infinity of meaning and sweetness into the smallest space'), elements from it are drawn in, realigned, combined with material from all the cognate Wesendonck-settings save one, to fashion another stanzaic, almost strophic, song. Formality is made from flux, absolutely without formalism, in this almost courtly *invitation au voyage* which plumbs the depths without seeming even to try to. Then, again, it doesn't full-close, opening out instead upon yet another interrupted cadence, gentle as the cut-off of the duet was violent, when the lovers' shared private ritual lifts its eyes, via their kiss, to face the consequences of their action in its wider social context.

The two most important architectural features of Act III are self-evident: the emblematic combination at Tristan's death of material from crucial previous places – the three signals with which Isolde summoned him to join her near the start of Act II, the 'death-devoted heart' motif, and the opening moves in the Act I Prelude – and the massive symmetry, already mentioned, set up by the *Liebestod* recapitulating the close of the Act II love-duet under guise of contrasting mood, tempo, texture, then sweeping it over the interruption into fulfilment and quietus. What this 'means' is Transcendence (*hélas!*). But the big woolly concept cannot be actualized without the meticulously planned and flawlessly executed mechanics of the compositional small print (which, sometimes, can be so fluent that it seems to run on auto-pilot: Wagner himself scribbled on the rough sketch of the *Liebestod* 'now the children can finish this!').

The other most conspicuous feature of Act III, however, is complexity incarnate, requiring bar-by-bar description/analysis, and occasionally note-by-note, to do it justice. This is the interweave of motifs from all over the opera, from recent bleeding ecstatic past and distant painful buried childhood past, penetrated with the shepherd's ubiquitous present-tense piping which elicits all the traumatic matter of Tristan's delirium in all its mesh of interconnection, tight and loose. The impeccable control with which extreme states are rendered with extreme means – X-ray, fragmentation, pulverization, cross-copulation, disintegration and reintegration – make evolution audible, even visible – a sonorous/verbal fusion over the edge of sane utterance, laid out with uncanny lucidity.

Some processes in Act III would be easier to illustrate, for instance showing the stages whereby its four-note opening motif, derived directly from the third Wesendonck setting and so completely different in effect from the four-note shape at the opera's very opening, nevertheless eventually merges indissolubly into it. This too would be a demonstration of evolution in action, interestingly different from its sources equally in Beethovenian development and Bachian spinning-out. And here too the purpose of the exploration would be to show how the conceptual, impalpable, 'extra-musical' is achieved by purely musical means. Which in turn suggests another whole field for fruitful investigation, concerning the nature of the utterance-potential innate in all musical patterning with or without texts or subject-matter, the quality whereby melodic contour, rhythmic propulsion, harmonic direction, timbre and all the further interlinked parameters of composition contain and convey meaning. But this would take more than a lifetime! And, again, is not in fact necessary: great works of music achieve this already, with precise exactness combined with the highest degree of expressive communication.

Virginia Woolf, an unlikely Wagnerienne, visiting Bayreuth for *Parsifal* and *Lohengrin* in 1909, encapsulates it beautifully:

> it may be that these exalted emotions, which belong to the essence of our being, and are rarely expressed, are those that are best translated by music; so that a satisfaction, or whatever one may call that sense of answer which the finest art supplies to its own question, is constantly conveyed here. Like Shakespeare, Wagner seems to have attained in the end [she refers explicitly to *Parsifal*] to such a mastery of technique that he could float and soar in regions where in the beginning he could scarcely breathe; the stubborn matter of his art dissolves in his fingers, and he shapes it as he chooses.

Comedy

Why *Meistersinger*? is harder to answer: autobiographical links exist (including an endearing account of Wagner's youthful prank which stirred the townsfolk of Nuremberg to riot; after it, walking the tranquil streets under the light of the moon): but the work is not born, like *Tristan*, of direct art–life pressures that cannot be restrained. Like *Tristan*, however, *Meistersinger* was intended to be a nice little earner while the inordinate requirements of the *Ring* awaited their hoped-for destination: again, the enterprise turns out hopelessly beyond practicality. But there doesn't appear to be an imperative – do *this*; *now* – yet, as always in his course, to turn at this moment to *Tristan*'s utter complement is absolutely the right decision. One can't imagine *Meistersinger* later; and for all its interconnections with the *Tannhäuser*-tale, he couldn't have done it earlier. The last four acts of the *Ring* needed renewal and enrichment equally from the chromatic saturation and emotional density of *Tristan* and from the huge unfolding paragraphs, the polyphony, the combination of close detail with broad spaciousness, the ceremonial, of *Meistersinger*; which then go on to fuse and concentrate in new ways in *Parsifal*.

It is commonplace to counterpoise the two 'interregnum works': death-devoted/life-affirming; morbid/healthy; psychological/psychotic/metaphysical vis-à-vis social and sociable, communal and *Völkisch*; with musical idioms to match. True, if trite, and movingly illustrated in the beautiful moment where Sachs refers Walther and Eva to the ill-fated lovers of legend and says that he, Sachs, won't be so foolish as poor old King Marke. *Meistersinger* concerns *humans* – no gods, dwarfs, giants – and deals in relationships within an actual society at an actual place and time – Nuremberg 1550 – in a structure of civic burgherdom – customs, crafts, métiers, beliefs and practices, extended familiarity – within which individual families are explored with almost novelistic care. Hofmannsthal's marvellous letter to Strauss urging him to abandon the mythic/legendary/saga aspects of Wagner, says it best: 'the truly decisive element, which governs all the others, is Nuremberg: Wagner's opera brings to life again a genuine, complete world which did exist, not imaginary or excogitated worlds which have never existed anywhere.'

Yet, unique though it is in the round, narrative, character and thematic links backward and forward are suggestive as ever. Most obviously, centring the action upon a song contest – in *Tannhäuser* courtly and exclusive (and with a disastrous outcome), in *Meistersinger* populist mingling with aristocratic (though the *Volk* have the Vote) and ending well. Sachs as Wotan as much as Marke – the ageing man sadly ceding the woman he loves most; Brünnhilde the actual daughter, Eva as daughter-figure passing into a girl potentially *en deuxième noce* with a widower. Walther is generic young male lead – cross between Sigmund and Siegfried his son, and Parsifal, with a dash of Lohengrin thrown in: their musical characterization has much in common. All in various fashion attain the heroine; only Walther is allowed to retain her (this is a comedy).

Meistersinger is human above all at its core – the emotions,

desires, their fulfilments and thwartings, between the four principals. For it *is* a foursome – an Eternal Quadrilateral rather than the
Eternal Triangle. Eva is angled between *three* men, and the exploration and rendition of their pains and privations are unsparing: the
equation-nature of the human intricacies is worthy of *The Golden
Bowl*, except that instead of James's claustrophobic void, Wagner's
is set amid a populous context rich in incidental detail as background to the foreground's close observation: Eva's growth from
girl to young womanhood via love-at-first-sight for Walther then
realization of Sachs's feelings for her; and her need to sympathize,
and pass; Walther's youthful headstrong pride and scorn tamed and
disciplined; Junker and Burgher in balance as the Wheel of Fortune
circles: Beckmesser addled, fazed, shamed, ruined by his legitimate
and understandable ambition to raise himself in city-status, to excel
as poet-composer, Master-songsmith, and thus win Eva the prize
in undoubted love for her – justice to Beckmesser as not shown in
the work itself. Which is rich in subsidiary characters outside the
Quadrilateral: David and Magdalena, secondary young couple also
eventually conjoined in marriage; the moving role of Pogner, Eva's
father, tender-loving yet also ambitious and canny on her behalf;
assorted Masters, named and unnamed; prentices and their girls;
the crowd, whether riotous as the close of Act II (and not forgetting
the exquisite cameo of the Nightwatchman) or celebratory as at the
close of Act III. Which opens to their broadest the resonances of
specific time and place – 'the Nuremberg of 1500' (Hofmannsthal's
dating somewhat out), the moment of Reformation, a new dawn
for city and fatherland and their glorious culture, criss-crossed with
idealistic hope concurrent with the work's composition for a united
Germany, not to be sullied by jingoism or the bad associations that
inevitably accrued to the work in the 1930s.

Several other features make for *Meistersinger*'s unique place
in Wagner's oeuvre. The Act II imbroglio is worthy of Shakespeare, Molière, Goldoni, Mozart/da Ponte – the lovers' attempted
elopement, the disguises and costume-swapping, thwarting of
unwelcome serenaders, the frustration of all concerned by Sachs's wise,
good-humoured curmudgeonliness. This area of crossed-purposes, the

foretaste of communal disorder to come: its 'madness' produces, the morning after, the work's deeper wisdom – resolution, independence, toleration, acquiescence. Unique and dead-central, the theme of artistic debate – *ars antiqua* vs *ars nova*, tradition vis-à-vis innovation; no mere gratuitous dialectic – it is inherent in words/ action, profoundly embodied in personages, and direct begetter of the work's musical idiom. Nothing elsewhere in Wagner calls for archaism – here pastiche, imitation, learnèd tropes and curlicues, are all achieved with loving skill – the 'Haydn' his friends recognized as it was coming slowly into existence (this too is unique, till *Parsifal* also took its time). Above all, the 'Bach': for all that the real-life J. S. Bach never visited Nuremberg and flourished a century-and-a-half after the action portrayed, he is the presiding genius of the work in all its church and ceremonial aspects, and presides too over such feats as the combination of themes in the Prelude to Act I, and its return in Sachs's closing peroration to 'holy German Art', and plentiful less-ostentatious polyphonic delights in small details. Another huge one: Bach would have been proud of the riot-scene's massive and masterly choral-and-orchestral fugue on Beckmesser's poor little ditty. Sheer joy in good craftsmanship befits the work's subject and doesn't apply to any other (except Siegfried forging his sword): Wagner-the-Brahms, its culmination the famous quintet in Act III (unique too, and dead against his theories, to have such an ensemble): its intimate domestic joy matched by the public choral affirmation of the great chorale out in the open meadows later on Midsummer Day. Elsewhere and throughout, *Meistersinger* is – again unique to music-drama if not to its precursors – a number-opera: story and setting require actual *songs* at every level, Prentice to Meister to Junker: Guild and their processional marches, work-songs, prize-songs for the hero and his shadow-brother, Walther's (as Beckmesser slinks off humiliated, ungenerously unforgiven by the work itself) eventually taken up as communal climax to balance the chorale. Sachs's superb monologues are also, just as his cobbling-songs, number-set-pieces. And Wagner-the-poet is at his most ingenious in this work: Beckmesser's hapless misunderstanding of Walther's text for his prize-song, surreal/Dada-esque *avant la lettre*; Walther's own impromptu embroideries upon it in the contest itself are quite glorious for the purpose.

Some reservations: its length – isn't it too long? Especially Act I: we treasure every leisurely move, but the whole is incommensurate with what's happening, what's being said – do the situations need all this? Act II is compact, ingenious, shapely, fleet, as indicated: Act III is superbly sustained for all its considerable duration and has the greatest set-pieces. Yet overall, a sense of slight ado about not particularly much. And isn't it too unfunny? Its humour can be laboured and laid on too thick. Which goes straight to the real criticism, Wagner's treatment of his bête noire, trouncing his own handling by the spiteful critic Eduard Hanslick. First of all, not that entertaining; second, cruel and gratuitous; third, not that convincing. There's malign brilliance in his 'mad-scene' when Beckmesser is surprisingly possessed of the new song – by Sachs! – that promises to gain him the prize, acclaim and Eva – an extraordinary venture into onomatopoeic cartoon-comedy music. But what's it all about? Compare the similar characterization of Mime in *Siegfried*'s first two acts – however repulsive, a real personage, germane to the developing plot, is being presented and probed with something like empathy, even sympathy. The treatment of Beckmesser is petty, vindictive, born of personal spite – an unwonted intrusion of *mere* autobiography, as demeaning to the author as to his victim: it leaves a bitter aftertaste even as festive acclamations rend the skies, with wedding-bells to follow.

A more generous treatment, remembering the Eternal Quadrilateral – three men painfully involved with the same girl in desire, need of love, jealousy, resentment – would show nobility commensurate with the work's general warmth of intonation. And – to cavil like Beckmesser himself – surely he must be a Master too? A fairer view of the Old/New debate would have him capable of a decent traditional song to balance the revolutionary strains of Walther's novel one in Act I. More speculative, Wagner is suppressing the Beckmesser within himself. These astonishing works are composed as much by a scrupulous, fault-finding Marker as a songfully outpouring Walther: such intricate detailing as the overlapping arpeggios of the *Rheingold*-prelude, or the calling-up of the winds or the patterns of forest-murmurs, wouldn't be possible without the penny-pinching pedant in Wagner: nor, on a higher plane, would the exhaustive exploitation of all its harmonic consequences from the opening of the *Tristan*-prelude.

And isn't Walther's prize song just a tad naff? Its gradual coming-into-being is magical: later it has to be heard so often that, for all the lovely extensions, last time round it can pall, even irritate – especially when the tenor isn't sweet-toned and is tending to tire. And – parting shot – isn't the contest itself rigged? If this were football or athletics, there could be grounds for an investigation!

Ring resumed

Armed with all the new resources learnt from *Tristan* – not to mention the revelation from reading Schopenhauer that deeply informs these two works and allows him to exclaim 'now at last I understand my Wotan!' and reshape Brünnhilde's closing words to utter these insights – Wagner resumes the *Ring* at just the point where action and meaning go deeper and more complex. These enrichments of thought, idiom, technique, would have been inapropos for the Epic's earlier stages: its later are unimaginable without them.

Siegfried Act III, the first composition after the interregnum, shows immediately the way old familiar materials are recharged. Soon after the turbulent prelude, the troubled places Wotan the Wanderer now reaches – consulting the Earth-Mother, mother of his Valkyries, as his deep-laid plans fall apart and his centre cannot hold, hearing again and understanding for the first time her prophecies of twilight and doom, able now to lightly cast them aside – employ every discovery of harmony, polyphony, orchestral subtlety and power and motivic interweave from the intervening years. As Act III develops, always via two-person encounter – Wotan's riveting tussle with Siegfried, apple-of-his-single-eye, closing with the tetralogy's second principal symbolic action, sword shattering spear, reversing its first; thence Siegfried's ascent through the flames to discover, not a man, nor his mother, but his destined bride, the first woman he's ever seen – the hugeness of the resources Wagner now commands, the daring to be spacious and empty after such weltering complexity, come into their full scope – the slowing-down of the harmony, the massiness of the scoring, for Brünnhilde's hymn to the sun after her long sleep – all these renew contact across abysses of time and change with the open diatonic ease of *Lohengrin*. Now a parallel of theme with the young Parsifal's 'sentimental education' – apprehension, fright, terror, flight from the mother-woman (in sober genealogical fact his aunt ...) before the hard-achieved joyous outcome denied Parsifal with Kundry. The two long wooing-scenes, difficult for both participants, are triumphs of sensitive and acute psychological strategy, stage by stage reaching in *Parsifal* mutual repudiation, in *Siegfried* mutual acceptance: in both 'a fact of life' – sexual attraction – forms implicitly the principal content; origin of guilt and woe, or gladly accepted, obeyed, exultantly relished.

For some early commentators, notably Shaw, the *Ring* should have ended here, the blaze of mutually consummating C-major its apex. Such optimistic shallowness is oddly oblivious of massive Unfinished Business with plentiful signals of things-to-come. And it ignores the well-known fact that Wagner had begun with the End – *Siegfrieds Tod* – and worked backwards to reach it via previous action that explains and justifies it. *Götterdämmerung* is of course the true apex: the story takes all the saga's themes, narrative and psychological, into new places: some of its personages are familiar, others unknown; one of these – Hagen, inheritor of ancient resentment from his father Alberich – becomes the principal manipulator of the action, which is unprecedentedly rapid and forward-driven: yet the retrospectives down the tetralogy's course, to its origins deep in the Rhine and the primal wrong born of illicit lusts, cover ever-wider vistas, recapitulations and interlocked developments articulated by a score by far Wagner's busiest, densest, most interwoven and wrought – as if *Tristan* and *Meistersinger* were superimposed. *Götterdämmerung*, not *Rienzi*, is 'Meyerbeer's best opera': for the paraphernalia of Parisian Grand Opera, all spectacle and show, 'effects without causes' makes a startling comeback (not that it had ever been entirely eschewed). *Pace* 'Reform', Wagner is far too pragmatic to jettison what the work needs as its plot rapidly advances and closes in; be it Rhine-panorama, Oath-swearing – Siegfried and Gunther blood-brothers for ever, then Siegfried and Brünnhilde, unfaithful man and betrayed woman – or Vassal-summoning, trio of Vengeance, hunting-scene, funeral procession; so to the ultimate super-spectacle of the Grand Finale involving Fire, Water, the Heavens and the Earth – Effects with Responsibilities: Wagner, heir to the Baroque and sire of cinematic animation. Messiaen used to claim to his class that *Götterdämmerung* is the greatest score ever composed.

Apotheosis

Parsifal, last in Wagner's gradual fulfilment of projects, all save one conceived in the 1840s, and linking back as described in story, theme, character, to his first three canonical operas. More significant still, the relationship to the exception, *Tristan*; *Liebe als Qual*/love as torment, its ultimate rendition still more agonizing than before. Both these works are founded in French-Celtic romance rather than Teutonic myth-legend: epics of the inner life, their victories psychological; though not forgetting in *Parsifal* the hero's progress to self-overcoming and self-knowledge comparable to Siegfried's and, unlike his, achieving completion.

Two terrains visible from each other: Monsalvat, sanctified, dedicated to chastity, devoted to service; all-male, ritual and ceremonial, centred upon the Grail: Magic Garden, voluptuous, hedonistic, devoted and dedicated to sexual delight; all-female (save its madame, a male eunuch). The contrasting places of story and meaning, remembered and deepened from *Tannhäuser*, were surely further inspired by Wagner's residence in Sicily during *Parsifal*'s composition – the shrine of Monreale perched high above Palermo, city of the plain. Between the two places the four central characters are strung: Amfortas, rescued from Garden to Grail, bearing a carnal wound which cannot be healed until touched by a vaguely promised Redeemer; his double, Klingsor, punished for overweening, would-be-holy, unable to restrain nature; so, carnally self-mutilated, setting up the alternative location where nature is given her head, all the while plotting the revenge that will regain him power in the Grail's domain. Parsifal, their foil, confronting identical temptations but resisting; growing from ignorant, uncouth lout via two moments of agonizing insight that pierce him with their identity – in Act I, Amfortas's pain-wracked body; at the work's living dead-centre, mid-point of Act II, his own painful sexual prompting, the carnal act desired by nature, denied by culture, to achieve by long, suffering expiation the compassion that will enable him to heal the wound, re-sanctify the Grail's stricken community, and – wider implications beyond the work's veneer of Christianity that has proved problematic and divisive from the start – renew the sterile Waste Land with good Easter growth rather than the artificial *fleurs-du-mal* of Klingsor's realm, which he had destroyed *en passant* after failing to enjoy its bowery blisses. Finally, Kundry, the emissary between the two worlds, servile and cringing albeit surly and froward in the holy terrain; in the unhallowed, seductress-in-chief, simultaneously avid and self-loathing: she is being punished down the centuries for mocking Christ on the Cross; she can only be redeemed by being denied what she both loves and hates; her will and her body in thrall, she can only submit until the unlikely event that we will see coming to pass, wherein her erotic wiles are rejected.

In this astounding farrago of four interlocked psychological mazes the Eternal Quadrilateral of *Meistersinger* turns on its dark side, and the problematic Christianity recedes to take its due place in a more extensive and comprehensive pattern. One must get over the ambiguity of the work's final words and intended message – 'Redemption to the Redeemer'; it's Parsiflage: back to Nietzsche and his contempt for Wagner's cowardly submission to the Cross. The work's *human* content, within a frame of Romance and Religion, is richer and, dare one say, truer – homecoming, righting of wrong, lessons in love beyond sensual gratification, empathy with and compassion for all sorts and conditions, nothing human alien;

then restoration of fertility to the withered body and spirit. Back to Blake! Contrarieties harmonized – evil flowers of concupiscence/ benign flowers of sacrifice; chaste knight of the Grail/luscious houris of the harem; Parsifal's, Kundry's, Amfortas's severed sex annealed (but there's no salving Klingsor) – the complete interfusion of carnal and spiritual so artificially and harmfully dichotomized by Christian piety; the divine image merging genders into a unity; the Marriage of Heaven and Hell. Such stuff, virtually inexpressible in itself – unlivable, not to be borne; yet the fusion of it all into its music gives it utterance.

The *music* bridges the extreme discrepancy, intrinsic to the work's subject-matter, between tortuous chromatics of sin/guilt/shame/ anguish and radiant diatonic euphony for the Grail, the Eucharist, the Good Friday meadows, the Baptism. This latter aspect can verge here and there upon blandness; paradoxically, the Flower-maidens' music mixes gorgeous chromatics of sinuous languor with dia-tonics of teasing flirtation – interfusion of opposites again. After the thematic profusion necessitated by *Götterdämmerung* with its vehement, hurtling action, *Parsifal* is spare and economical – the opening unison line in its major then its minor statements contains the germinal seeds of virtually all the work's material, 'good' and 'evil', endorsing the sense that the four characters fusing the central Quadrilateral are 'prints' of each other. The strengths and beauties of the score's greatest pages are supreme beyond anything else in Wagner's oeuvre. Granted, it is a work of old age – the colossal creative vitality needed for Act I of *Götterdämmerung* would not be appropriate for Act I of *Parsifal*, equally huge. Rather, it is a master-piece of narration – Gurnemanz relates the story, turns the pages, like the Evangelist in Bach's *Passions*; from his narration, embracing dark past, sad present, hoped-for future, characters step forth on cue, till the turning-point where the unnamed youth who shoots the swan is yanked unceremoniously onto the stage; action has seam-lessly commenced. Ceremonial processions here and in Act III are more magnificent and fraught with meaning than heretofore. Klingsor, opening Act II, is a bit hammy, his music a bit *réchauffé* (though revealing his and Kundry's place in the central foursome):

the Flower-maidens are ravishing, Kundry's first enunciation of the anonymous youth's name, and the initial courses of her desired-and-detested seduction produce some of the most beautiful harmony ever written. The sonority is a miracle throughout – Debussy described the *Parsifal* orchestra as 'illumined from behind'; it is of course Wagner's only work actually composed with the blended clarity of the Bayreuth acoustic in mind – subtly mixed colours, shot-silk, nuance upon nuance; then warm and ample for grandeur, piercing for naked timbres.

Up to the crucial kiss all is secure; after it, the Kundry/Parsifal debate can feel laboured and overlong; then the act's ending is terrific – effects *with* causes. And Act III is perhaps Wagner's single most perfect achievement: the prelude up to the mysterious knight's disarming is matched in exaltation only by the (very comparable) adagio of Bruckner's 9th Symphony; the Good Friday flowers and Parsifal's coronation – rebirth made audible (save only in the prosy words of old Gurnemanz); superb funeral-procession; thoroughly satisfying return of Spear to Grail and healing of the Wound. After which, the closing terraces of chorus and orchestra singing 'Redemption to the Redeemer' sound decidedly religiose: lovely, dulcet, the right thing in the right place – theatre church-music – a prop, like the tacky fluttering dove usually dropped from productions nowadays: by the time this efficient, suitable, predictable finale gets to flow, everything's over bar the sequences. Virginia Woolf again:

> *Parsifal* seems poured out in a smooth stream at white heat; its shape is solid and entire. How much of the singular atmosphere which surrounds the opera in one's mind springs from other sources than the music itself it would be hard to say. It is the only work which has no incongruous associations.

And (later): 'Perhaps music owes something of its astonishing power over us to this lack of definite articulation; its statements have all the majesty of a generalization, and yet contain our private emotions.' Remove her 'perhaps' and 'something'; the insight is certain and central.

*

Wagner did not now manage to sort out *Tannhäuser* as hoped: in a sense *Parsifal* effects just this. Very interesting, his declared late aim of writing symphonies: they were to be short, light, playful – not Beethoven's 9th Symphony, let alone Bruckner's. Haydn is the model – we recall his deeply appreciative remarks to Cosima concerning the 'masterly art of the London Symphony' and how 'everything speaks, everything is inspiration' – though all four movements were to be in one continuous span, foretelling Schoenberg's similar goals. And as foretold in his own *Siegfried Idyll*, at first intended only for private domestic performance then circulated to a wider public under financial pressure. The piece's intimate tone is belied by its relative length, its formal shaping is felicitous, as is its command of colour and mood with the handful of instruments, at opposite end from the colossal forces required by the *Ring*. But it's from the tetralogy's middle operas that the *Idyll* derives most of its material, discovering therein altogether different possibilities and combinations, alongside strains from the real-life little Siegfried's nursery and nursery-rhymes. The late sketches intended for symphonies have been realized with sympathetic skill by Matthew King. But Wagner's *opus ultimum*, *Der Nachmorgen*/The Morning After – fifth-evening sequel to the *Ring*, beginning as an excellent April Fool spoof, has yet to be written.

The 'long century' just traversed, from earliest German Romanticism to the death of Strauss in 1949, implies from now on a 'perpetual present', wherein references to 'things to come' run alongside subjects already past. Wagner comes at the end in the long Teutonic nineteenth century, though his life and work lie in the middle, because he is its epicentre. This shifting of chronologies will prevail, of necessity, from here on until near the end of the book. Before that, there'll be many returns to earlier times and places to retrieve their own individual continuities and characters, and present them intact, rather than mushing up every composer, country, culture, in confusing chronological exactness.

CHAPTER X

The Non-Teutonic Nineteenth Century

Two early-Romantic pianists – Liszt and Chopin

I have to admit to shortcomings, inadequacies even, with the two outstanding pianist-composers of the mid-nineteenth century from the edges of Europe. A matter of taste and sympathy. Not in Chopin's case *dis*-taste and *un*-sympathy: 'I see not feel' that this is often great music, high in its genre, achieving perfection with mastery, in every detail realizing to the utmost a rarified refinement of spirit, elegance and polish, and entertainment; containing and controlling depths of passion sometimes almost morbid, astonishingly original despite its clear ancestry and palpable influences – from the *bel canto* of his beloved Bellini to the fusion of surface urbanity with internal turmoil in his revered Mozart, and gradually taking on the harmonic/polyphonic extremes of his admired J. S. Bach. With Liszt, it's another thing altogether: here I *do* experience *dis*-taste and *un*-sympathy for what I perceive to be fundamentally shallow and flashy; poor composition upon inferior materials.

Of course there is more to Liszt! Chopin's oeuvre is almost wholly devoted to his own instrument: Liszt's embraces just about every genre going – only chamber-music is almost entirely lacking. As well as the enormous body of solo piano music and the two concertos (three if *Totentanz* is included) there are two extended programme-symphonies with voices – *Faust* and *Dante* (already I'm sniffing a whiff of aversion), and the thirteen symphonic poems – *Tasso, Mazeppa, Orpheus, Prometheus, Hamlet, The Ideal, From the Cradle to the Grave*, etc. (aversion thickens) – whose historic importance cannot be exaggerated: songs, cantatas, organ-works, an oratorio, a Mass – even the substantial fragment of an opera *Sardan-apalo*, recently realized with skill by a Cambridge musicologist and performed to acclaim. His catalogue is reckoned to be the longest of any composer's in *Grove's Dictionary*. In addition, the personality so vivid, the life so colourful, the nature so generous, handsome, princely: among the sullen, solipsistic, variously refractory compositional geniuses of his day – Berlioz, Schumann, Chopin, Wagner – Liszt shines disinterested, selfless, spreading intercommunication and understanding, sharing discoveries, disseminating and inseminating: a fertilizing bee: Liszt the Catalyst. Most of all for the greatest and littlest genius of all, Wagner, to whom he freely gave not only the most celebrated harmonic progression in all music, as well as endless encouragement, coverage, support moral, artistic and financial, but a daughter to marry.

But: the music itself! Amid the prolific rubble of grandiosity, pseudo-profundity, sheerly awful slag and debris, lie freshets of lyric purity and nuggets of gold, together with interesting discoveries destined to burgeon beautifully and richly in more discriminating hands. The output, from small to colossal, has ardent advocates; I'll leave the defence to them: what can't be impugned is the greatness of the *man* and the wonderful inventiveness of his keyboard writing.

The Piano Sonata of 1852–3 is justly regarded as his masterpiece for his instrument. Opening, a soft descending unison scale, twice, separated by quasi down-beats: an important communication is announced – jagged rhetorical gesture – the piece's principal motif; impassioned flourishes: a 'speaking' bass-figure, later very significant; fiery work-out/work-up to crashing quadruple octaves: quiescence – repeated note, the opening scale underneath; builds to a grandiose sarabande-idea, all stops out, quietening into a moment of *religioso*. More limpid: delicate quasi-recitative figures, down to the parlando bass-figure, soon transformed into songful 'second subject': repeated more decorated, gradually incorporating the principal motif, very expressive and pleading under trills: more fire and athletics, delicately diminishing to further lyricism under twinkling right hand: strenuous again, going crazy as opening descending scale re-reached: down to sarabande low/loud/thick – just its first phrase, twice; more recitative; sarabande's next two phrases; more recitative; dramatic pauses between all these. An interim: several themes in play – main motif and the second subject now reverted to its origins as parlando bass; another *religioso* moment, before extensive paragraph on second subject now lyricized: a Consolation. More sarabande, now given continuity, firing up *con passione*, incorporating opening, to *fff* climax, declining via delicate enharmonics to second subject, fragmented and broken off; preliminary preparations for reopening on the initial descending scale, now to introduce 'Diabolical Fugue' – on principal motif plus speaking bass – a display of virtuosity and sparkling energy showing off Liszt's powers of thematic transformation at their least contrived and most convincing. Things fire up again with the descending scale, ending on an abrupt hectoring question. Answer, the *grandioso* sarabande: then second subject yet again, phrase-by-phrase, ever more insistent – the composer can't develop and get it to *grow*, or doesn't want to. Final hectic bravura build-up to *fff furioso prestissimo*: sarabande on full organ: huge dominant seventh: dramatic silence. Consolation: second subject again de-lyricized to its original muttered bass, under steady right-hand chords: disintegration and elimination: the opening scale descends, diminishing, to the piano's deepest depths: answered by an angelic choir in the empty empyrean, then the keynote, B, low and soft as possible. Every motif, every gesture, every happening innately theatrical, hammy, ostentatious, the masterful legerdemain of a consummate conjuror – one hundred per cent sincere/genuine; one hundred per cent bogus. Next stop Mahler's 8th. Terminus, *Rhapsody in Blue*.

Chopin is something else. Fryderyk Franciszek Chopin: born near Warsaw 1810; his father originally from France: in the Polish capital, a child prodigy as pianist and composer – many smaller pieces and two concertos before, news of national unrest reaching him while abroad, his compelled self-exile to Paris 1830: from henceforth Frédéric François (though it appears he never fully mastered spoken French nor felt himself fully at home in Paris; in his person and in his music always the Pole). Soon in great demand as teacher of, player to, the aristocracy; the darling of the salons: he didn't care to perform much in public – intimate drawing rooms and intimate gatherings at his own residence. Cordial association with the city's musicians (including Berlioz), writers (including Heine), painters (including Delacroix, who portrayed him with memorable penetration). Abroad too: the friendly admiration of Mendelssohn, the unstinted endorsement of the two other most celebrated contemporary composers for the keyboard, Schumann and Liszt.

A stormy affair with George Sand precipitates a rich chapter of new work. During their stay in Majorca 1838–9, Chopin's delicate health first becomes apparent. The couple remain close yet apart for the next few years, his creative powers unimpaired even as his body declines. Income from lessons tails off: financial necessity impels a tour of Great Britain in 1848, taking him as far afield as Glasgow and Edinburgh. Back to Paris greatly weakened: died October 1849 aged thirty-nine. Many causes have been mooted; tuberculosis remains likeliest: it fits – the image of consumptive genius, feverish and denied repose, burnt out from within (Keats, Emily Brontë, D. H. Lawrence) finds in Chopin its archetypal exemplar.

The oeuvre comes in distinct genres, almost all miniature: nocturnes, waltzes, polonaises, études, preludes, scherzos, mazurkas, ballades. Four sonatas on a grander scale (one for cello and piano) are atypical and often unconvincing, though the whirlwind dust cloud closing of No. 2 in Bb-minor remains astounding: and there's a handful of attractive Polish songs. Native accents clearly prevail in the dance-types of polonaise and mazurka: the charming nocturnes of the Irish composer John Field provide a prototype for Chopin's own: and he treasured the melodic breadth of Italian opera, in particular the 'long long lines' of Bellini. Of the masters he revered above all Bach and Mozart: their presence can be felt behind many points of refinement, and sometimes of learning, throughout the oeuvre. But above all he is original. There is no precursor for the two sets of études (1830–32, 1834–7), opening up new worlds for the piano and for musical expression, fusing technical problems for the fingers with challenges for the composer into poetry belying and transcending both. Nor for the preludes (1838–9), encapsulating twenty-four moods with concentrated essentiality. A new language is born fully formed and perfect – an infant, yet pregnant with future life. Waltzes tend to be vapid and pretty, redolent of the salons they so pleased: this feel can also colour the nocturnes: and the polonaises can suffer from a complementary trouble born of the same cause – in this case barnstorming showiness. But the scherzos blow the mind with the same characteristics: their inner turbulence can break forth into explicit violence. And the mazurkas – all fifty – make a kind of compositional diary, with some his profoundest discoveries on this small scale and within the given dance form.

Greatest of all, the four ballades (1835; 1839; 1841; 1842–3). *Ballade* – the very word opens up the mysterious art whereby the atmosphere and mood of a tale are evoked without the need of personages or actions. The musical materials of these four pieces, already distinct and distinguished, are then subjected to some of the subtlest transformations in the repertoire, revealing now and then a homage to the spirit (not the letter) of J. S. Bach as surprising as it is profound. One recalls Busoni's passing fantasy that a particularly involuted prelude from the forty-eight is Bach's prophecy that one day a Chopin will come to be!

His supreme masterpiece, the Barcarolle in F♯-major (1845–6), makes in effect a fifth ballade: but now there's no longer any sense whatever of narrative, however latent; atmosphere is all. Two spacious introductory bars of radiant descending suspensions over dominant pedal; never heard again, diminishing, held shining, cadencing out into the lagoon, barcarolle-motion in left hand, to support supple sinuous-sensuous singing phrases in parallel thirds, never quite coalescing into continuous melody. The second phrase curves higher, the next opens thirds into sixths and insinuates hints of an inner voice that will figure vitally later; the fourth opens up into light play of sparkle, calming and broadening, half-closing into IV: two bars combining treble sparkle with alto cantabile, two more of wait-for-it, ending on trills: back to main key and replay of main theme, now ornamented. From its third phrase different, more richly harmonized and 'orchestrated', the note of passion sounded, ending in a rising clench of full chords over V pedal to re-achieve

F♯-major – poised, then plunging: but receding immediately to close upon the minor.

Texture now thinned to one part, a wandering line, then octave unison into A-major: one bar till-ready on vestige of the ever-present barcarolle-lilt; over it the right hand sings in two voices, the little shape insinuated earlier now coming significantly to the fore, in top voice then in secondary, with an occasional splash of luminous spume from the plashing gondolier-pole. The third phrase introduces an expressive dissonant note in the top voice – once, only half a bar; second, prolonged for the whole: then a ravishing 'lift' to the replay of this A-major paragraph, singing up the octave with enhanced texture over the same bass except for its more continuous motion within the lilt. The upper octave means that the significant little insinuation-figure can answer itself descending down three voices, and the poignant dissonance be yet more pronounced. Now a simpler strain – no polyphony – euphonious and Italianate, caressing graceful and cool up to a *ritenuto*, a *diminuendo*, a cut-off. Seven bars in-between, the first simply a one-note trill, then some exquisite chromatics, without theme though retaining the gist of the lilt, dissolving down to C♯-major – V – on which come six bars of delicate fine-spun decorations where, only time, the lilt is lost – adrift in freedom on the waters.

Sudden *crescendo* – back to purposeful goal-oriented voyage. The first material returns amplified – bass barcarolle-motion in octaves, treble melody enriched: a return to the first restatement rather than the actual opening, the note of passion more pressing, the upward clunch of chords over V now triumphantly permitted to close in the higher position – home key: but on the simpler, Italianate, strain, now gorgeously sensual, developing thrilling harmonic intensifications that 'lift' the piece into a new plane. At climax it swells rather than, as before, diminishing, and the trill, formerly a disappearance, is now the means of grand reattainment of F♯-major: right hand, over barcarolle-base now more sonorously spaced, brings out the polyphonic exchanges of the salient little figure initially so shy. Up an intensity-notch, still over tonic pedal supporting the same material with ever-increasing levels of dissonance – close your eyes and you might be on the stony rise to Golgotha rather than on the level waters of the Venetian lagoon – wracking excruciation, every wince and grimace exact, logical, grammatical, culminating in a *sforzando* scrunch and a firework of *fioritura* that, with the sustaining-pedal down as indicated, has all twelve semitones in simultaneous play, though the harmony's basic nature is never in doubt. The polychrome spume of phosphorescence clears, leaving only the undoubted key-note as motion resumes: two bars' gentle spangle, then two of a completely new idea on the familiar rhythm – simplified into an almost benediction in the left-hand chords, as the right delicately descants in patterns of light demisemiquavers, right up to the top possible F♯ and down to the lowest. The gondola's wake?

This makes a *crescendo* rather than a *diminuendo*. The vision isn't allowed to recede into magical distances: instead, the *fortissimo* four-octave-unison ending – up the fourth, down the fifth – V–I – get that! and that! it's ended; we're in F♯; applaud loudly and pay as you leave: a deplorable concession to the public, sullying its composer's finest creation, until this moment, one of Romanticism's finest *quarts d'heure*.

Chopin's influence is noted here and there in the ensuing pages: mainly upon successive piano music of course – it is vital to Scriabin, to Fauré, to Debussy (who dedicated his own études to Chopin's memory). There's also yards of dreamy flim-flam giving hostages to the non-fortune of those who discern the sources of such vapidity in the master himself. More speculative but very suggestive, the possible influence upon Wagner – perhaps via Liszt, intimate with both. Surely, hearing such things as the *Tristan* love-duet and the Flower-maidens in *Parsifal*, one can scent traces of chromatic magic across the vast distance of genre and aim?

Two Romantic nationalists – Dvořák and Grieg

Antonín Dvořák; born 1841 to rural innkeeper/butcher: early delight in village musicians; learns violin; aged eight becomes chorister in the village church; much violin-playing; from twelve studies music theory. To Prague 1857 – study and playing, discovering the classics: from 1859 makes exiguous living as viola-player; composing away: 1862 on, violinist in the orchestra of the National Theatre; further study and much composing – good contact with Smetana (some seventeen years older). From 1870 on his music begins to get around, 1873 leaves the orchestra for church organist post: marriage. Impresses Brahms 1875: his recommendation leads to government assistance; also – 1878 – to an important German publisher: the *Slavonic Dances* an immediate universal hit: invitations to England and Germany to conduct his own work – particularly popular in England – fifth visit 1886. Successful also at home – aged fifty, professor at the Prague Conservatory (and Hon. Doc. at Cambridge). The next year (1892) an offer from newly established New York Conservatory that cannot be refused – incredibly generous working-arrangements and free time, and the salary some thirty times what Prague paid. His four years there a great success: remains in touch with homeland through a Czech community in Iowa. Nor is England forgotten – ninth visit 1896. He'd returned to Prague the year before: 1901 appointed head of the Prague Conservatory: died Prague 1904.

Shape of the oeuvre: nine symphonies (their initial numbering complicated and confusing): no. 1 – 'The Bells of Zlonice' 1865; nos. 2–4 1865–74; no. 5 in F 1875; no. 6 in D 1880; no. 7 in D-minor 1885; no. 8 in G 1889; no. 9 – 'From the New World' E-minor 1893. Concertos, notably for violin (1880) and cello (1895): symphonic poems (all 1896): overtures, *Slavonic Rhapsodies* and *Dances*, *Legends*, miscellaneous bits and bobs: *String Serenade* 1875, *Wind Serenade* 1878. *Orchestral Variations* 1877; *Scherzo capriccioso* 1883. Piano-music neither here nor there except the lovable piano-duet *Slavonic Dances*: Chamber-music copious and variable, the best of it tip-top. Many songs and duets with piano: many choral works with orchestra, principally *Stabat Mater* (1877) and *Requiem* (1890): some ten operas, principally *Rusalka* (1900).

Very copious, very uneven: a handful of diamonds amid the useful hearth-warming coals. Dvořák perhaps the most conspicuous instance of a substantial composer who adds nothing to the course of music. Progress, Innovation, Significance, Importance simply don't figure: he is 'merely' a very good composer. Almost always appealing and enjoyable, often routine and sometimes empty, now and again reaching greatness. Without him the art would be defrauded of much pleasure but would scarcely be different.

Yet he is a composer to cherish: genial, warm, cheerful, good-humoured, generous and abundant in good ideas drawn from music's well-springs: a natural, naïve not sentimental (though charged with ardent feeling), a master yet absolutely non-intellectual, let alone learnèd. The closest parallel is Schubert, for the cornucopia of lovely material without let or hindrance: but Schubert is a BIG composer in some big areas, greater still in the vast range of his smaller. Neither can be claimed for Dvořák. Yet the negative positives accumulate: 'not intellectual nor learnèd' – when he tries, the result is touchingly unconvincing – but he's often ingenious, sometimes brilliant: untroubled, but a vein of melancholy, elegy, thoughtfulness, even touching upon tragedy: not erotic – Oscar Wilde's notorious reference to the scarlet sins of Dvořák's music couldn't be more inapt. On the contrary, health and sanity from the heart: not a hint of the morbid, let alone the degenerate: unprofound, but can cut deep without trying and maybe not meaning to be: but not shallow either; nor trivial or cheap even when setting out to mine a popular/lucrative vein as in the *Slavonic Dances*, which in actual fact, paradoxically, are his most perfect and individual creations – pure melody filling the given dance-forms, no trouble from symphonism or grandiosity, extremely varied with endlessly inventive accompaniments and marvellous harmonic colouration, absolutely right whether rich or simple; and, when orchestrated, clear/full/delicate/fiery with that indefinable Eastern European quality in the sonority, ample without an ounce of sludge, and many particular touches of felicity unbeholden to anything or anyone before.

How to discuss such directness that always speaks for itself? The symphonies make an interesting story: do Dvořák's nine make an alternative – a middle way – after Beethoven, after Schubert, between Bruckner and Brahms? One would wish so and welcome it. The genealogy and chronology are interesting. Seminal, the gradual dissemination of Schubert's 'Great' C-major Symphony

(1825); better-known from the start, Schumann's 2nd, also C-major and audibly indebted to Schubert's (1845–6): Brahms's 1st in difficult gestation from the early 1860s to its eventual première in 1876: Bruckner's No. 0, 1863–4, No. 1, 1865–6, No. 2, 1871–2: Tchaikovsky's first three 1868–75; Balakirev's 1st (also in C) begun 1864, prolonged through crisis after crisis, not complete till 1897. Dvořák's nine run analogously, from 1864 to 1893, and yield telling parallels.

His 1st Symphony, composed aged twenty-three, is a remarkable document: 'The Bells of Zlonice' – the village where the family lived during his early teens: no bells, nor illustration otherwise, nor narrative; born, rather, of youthful seething, with a scope and breadth and command of huge, slow-motion harmonic trajectory that calls Bruckner to mind, and, beyond him, Elgar and Sibelius. Not yet his distinctive melodic warmth and abundance – material rather neutral; it's the *size* that impresses, and the amplitude with which it is filled out. The finale almost quotes the Schubert source, then towards the end the intervening Schumann – all three in C. The finale of Dvořák's 2nd Symphony (the following year, 1865) is equally strong on 'go' – it comes and comes – the gumption is terrific, the material unmemorable. Unlike the scherzo – original and authentic. No. 3 also Schubertian – his 'Italianate' side, Rossini-frisky; also garrulous, also indistinctive – almost boring. The 4th overlaps with the 3rd (1873–4 the both): the first movement indicates clearly an alternative way from Schubert to either Bruckner's or Brahms's; second movement, enter Wagner, very specifically the Pilgrims' March from *Tannhäuser* with *Lohengrin* audibly among the chorus. Good rough scherzo and bucolic village-band trio. Finale so near to the Bruckner finale-problem inherited from Schubert that one longs for him to achieve success. Its actual material more Tchaikovskyan. It labours and keeps going – and coming – with exhaustless exuberance: but not quite, not yet up to it.

No. 5 (1875) – enter Mendelssohn; into the lovely pastoral material that can also take both grandiose and strenuous in its stride, vistas of seascape, emptying-out, stretching horizons as in Mendelssohn's two ocean overtures; similar windows open up in the finale, which closes with triumphal return of the first movement's material, à la Bruckner. Very Brucknerian, the *furiant scherzo* strongly resembling Bruckner's only fast 3/8, the scherzo of his 9th: Dvořák's trio then hints Mahler. And the andante second movement is a gem, especially its middle section – tender Slavonic Dance music, early Janáček plainly in view. With No. 6, enter Brahms: especially his 2nd of 1877: Dvořák's is three years after; both are in D, and burgeon-out from pastoral material; both are their respective composers' best yet. Dare one say that the homage flowers more fluently than the original? Dvořák's first movement is unlaboured where Brahms's, in the return to recapitulation, heaves and feints; the awkward double-return in his noble adagio is avoided in Dvořák's lovely slow-movement, admittedly slighter. The two finales make the connection clearest, and here Brahms remains unsurpassed – Dvořák hammers and hammers away well before the end whereas Brahms gets his ship into harbour with a burst of exuberance unique in his oeuvre. The best movement in the Dvořák is the third, a terrific *furiant* with an adorable trio – the first piccolo solo in any symphony? – and the heavenly arcs of string arpeggio-melody that follow.

The 7th Symphony (1884–5) is masterly from A to Z: this is of all Dvořák's nine symphonies the one that puts him justly into the company of the other grand '9-ers', Beethoven, Schubert, Bruckner, Mahler. Tovey's old programme-note is so good that I forbear to trespass: both for details and in generalities he remains unsurpassed – for instance on 'the long meandering sentence that ramifies into countless after-thoughts' in the first movement's development and still more the trio of the scherzo: 'if they alone were preserved as fragments of nineteenth-century music they would prove to a future civilization that Dvořák was a great composer.' The fruitful fusion of terse, concentrated with richness, variety, 'ramification' in the 7th remains unsurpassed. The 8th (1889) is altogether lighter: opening with a fine slow introduction, recurring half-way through the ensuing allegro, *very* Schubertian, ending a trifle overblown. Re-enter Schumann for the second movement, followed by a taste of Mahlerian klezmer, before the movement seems to lose its way: re-enter Tchaikovsky for no. 3, a graceful melancholic/

elegant *valse*; middle strain a Slavonic Dance; sudden fast spritely coda in duple-time. The finale is all pageantry: fanfares, a pomp-and-circumstance march at first soft then brilliant – entry of the royal couple in a Tchaikovsky ballet; then procession of the Three Kings with their camels; then a Persian market with bellowing bulls. Royal heralds summon a retreat, back to soft start, pomp-and-circumstance diminishing not advancing, an ache of nostalgia yet more redolent of Elgar, who must have known and relished this work, so germane to his own idiom and orchestral usage. Then the music revs up again – not great, but not too long – and including a moment of bravura for trombones that reappears in Elgar's *Cockaigne*. And the celebrated 9th – 'From the New World' but sketched out in the Old, and entirely of it in material – is disappointing, despite some unforgettable themes. First movement work-out by machine: second, after the glorious opening chords and one of the world's finest tunes, doesn't seem to know what to do or where to go. The scherzo begins well – very Bruckner-ish – and has delicious moments, lost in re-use of first-movement theme without convincing point; still more uncompelling in the finale, where it's joined by the adagio-theme too, obtrusive rather than organic: a quite pretty nostalgic fadeaway; then an ending of utter bombast.

Other miscellaneous orchestral works avoid such troubles. The *Symphonic Variations* of 1877: a most ingenious piece, on a theme so plain and naïve, then so naïvely treated, as to seem a non-starter. But this apparent artlessness is deceptive – without any of Brahms's old-mastery or Elgar's broad human canvas, these variations can stand alongside the *St Anthony* and the *Enigma*. Dvořák wrings from his severe little shape a surprising variety of characters and moods, ending with an extended finale, a fugue that might go into *Svanda the Bagpiper* combining polyphony with polka; then gets a bit empty and too-prolonged; a pretty oasis; then empty and noisy again to conclude. But the *Scherzo capriccioso* of six years later is flawless: a light-hearted piece from a dark epoch in his life: Slavonic Dance material worked with symphonic length and elaboration, wide range of keys, textures, moods – from gay ebullience to meditative introspection, and a lovely harp-and-horn romantic glade before the exuberant end that doesn't outstay its welcome: a masterpiece, that ought to figure more frequently in orchestral concerts.

Then the *Slavonic Dances* themselves – two sets (1878; 1886) each of eight numbers, with not a duff bar. Material pure gold and silver, ranging from pastoral to passionate, daisy-fresh to melancholy languor, outdoor jubilation to haunted ballroom, tavern to salon, amorous yearning to circus-raucous, tearing haste to urbane suavity, grandeur to impudence. The second set mounts higher and delves deeper than the first: melodic material yet more appealing, harmony richer, and several beginning to develop at greater length while never losing the basic dance-plan. Take the 7th – a presto whirl taking off into something virtually symphonic. And the 8th – a slow waltz aching with nostalgia, episodes of ballroom vitality in surprising keys; especially as scored, with the soft singing trumpets and the delicate single notes on glockenspiel – early Mahler with no undercurrents of angst or irony: also Brahms in *Liebeslieder*-mode, Tchaikovsky in salon-mode, Johann Strauss at the Prater, Richard Strauss anywhere, Lehár ... any would have been proud to sign it, and it is better than any at what it's doing. There *is* a Dvořák-shaped space and the *Slavonic Dances* occupy it with joy.

Edvard Grieg: born Bergen 1843 of part-Scottish ancestry: taught piano by his mother: aged fifteen went to study at the Leipzig Conservatory – course interrupted by illness, resumed, completed 1860. Composing – songs, piano-pieces, and in 1864 a symphony. That year, engagement; marriage 1867. Emboldened by friends in the common search for a national culture at home: often abroad – composing mainly miniatures, and some more ambitious ventures – Piano Concerto 1868 – culminating in the invitation from Ibsen himself to provide incidental score for *Peer Gynt*. Widespread recognition, plentiful composing: mainly chamber-music and piano – ten books of *Lyric Pieces* (1867–1901), and songs always, and some fine late Psalm-settings for chorus. Many Norwegian folksong arrangements, peaking in *Slåtter* (1900). Died 1907.

A tiny figure: I recall the life-sized full-length bronze statue outside the Grieg Centre adjoining his fairy-tale cosy-cottage at

Troldhaugen (in its grounds the enchanting little composing-hut with its soothing views over woodland and fjord) being hugged by a stream of Japanese tourists queuing up in turn to be photographed with the composer, all of them taller than him, in piquant contrast to the determined but utterly implausible efforts indoors to Beethovenize the national treasure into comparable stature. A tiny composer: but a permanent niche – this fragile snowdrop can manifest fibre if not muscle. Debussy's famous gibe – 'a pink bonbon stuffed with snow' – will always stick. But what a nice thing to be! We all know the sort of music Debussy means – pale, wimpish, neat and trim, vapid – some of it indeed by Debussy himself. Here are two instances where Grieg transcends the pretty and shows his fibre.

Slåtter – seventeen transcriptions for piano of traditional Norwegian fiddle-music, mainly wedding marches, which can surprise in their pungency, even anticipate the altogether harsher treatment of their folk material by a later generation, notably Bartók, Stravinsky, Falla. Not much pink bonbon and dinky snowdrop in these astringent and tangy little numbers. *Haugtussa/The Mountain Girl* (1895–8): cycle of eight songs for soprano and piano: a sort of *Schöne Müllerin* from the girl's viewpoint, with strange supernatural/primal undercurrents: she's in love, her boy abandons her, she seeks the solace of the stream. These songs' unrelieved strophism – many verses to an unchanging melody – can become slightly irksome: take no. 2 – here up on the hillside at ease – but suppose a bear should happen by – a fox – a wolf – a handsome young boy? – all to the same strain. But the final song, its poem equally additive down five stanzas – you rippling brook (the adjective *does* change each time), here will I rest; here will I dream; here remember; there forget; here weep – compensates with subtle/delicate/unobtrusive variants; and in the last stanza the piano's echoes of the singer, amid the rippling flow of the accompaniment, overlap as though to enact the merging of the love-lost maid and the welcoming waters in the drowning that, in text alone, remains inexplicit.

Still more than Dvořák, Grieg is 'historically unnecessary': his achievement is tiny, incomparable to the German *Lied* in his songs or the piano-oeuvre of Chopin, Schumann, Brahms. Yet a vital line of liberation flows from him, to Delius then Grainger, thence up the nooks and crannies of a twentieth century spurned or ignored by Official Progressive Modernism. And where would Gershwin's harmony be without Grieg's?

Nineteenth-century France

Hector Berlioz

Life and works are so intimately interlinked as to be one and the same. Hector Berlioz: born La Côte-Saint-André, Isère 1803; destined by doctor father for this career. To Paris 1821 for further studies, soon abandoning medicine for music; and already composing – 1824 *Messe solennelle* (lost, presumed destroyed, discovered and performed late twentieth century). Seminal exposure to Weber's *Freischütz*, Beethoven's symphonies and quartets, in his mid-twenties above all to Shakespeare – blown away by Harriet Smithson in *Romeo and Juliet* 1827: 1826 studies at Paris Conservatoire, winning the coveted Prix de Rome in 1830 at the fifth attempt. Meanwhile, *Huit scènes de Faust* 1829, overtures and an unfinished opera, the *Symphonie fantastique* 1830 and its sequel *Lélio* the year after. Returns to Paris 1832 and marries Harriet 1833: makes living by his effervescent journalism: also concert-giving: many grand projects aborted/abandoned; some songs make it, and *Harold en Italie* (picturesque symphony with viola obbligato) 1834. *Benvenuto Cellini* 1836–7, its première in 1838 a flop. *Grand Messe des morts* (*Requiem*) 1837; *Roméo et Juliette* (sort of choral symphony with operatic elements) 1839 – a generous gift from Paganini the year before had enabled this mighty creation to come into being (the solo part in *Harold* had been intended for Paganini's prowess). *Grande symphonie funèbre et triomphale* (grand patriotic ceremonial) 1840; 1841 *Les Nuits d'été* (intimate song-cycle, orchestrated 1856). Separated from Harriet 1842; next few years extensive foreign tours as conductor, and little composing – some overtures, and 1843 his Treatise on Orchestration. Commences *La Damnation de Faust* 1845, large-scale cantata with the *Eight Scenes* of 1829 as its nucleus – concluded 1846: further touring embraces Russia and England. *Te Deum* 1848–9; 1850 parts of what eventually becomes *L'Enfance du Christ*, completed 1854. A subject from the *Aeneid* mooted to Liszt and the Princess Wittgenstein 1855 (Virgil had been a boyhood passion before Goethe and Shakespeare knocked him for six); the next year they urge him to realize the idea – libretto of *Les Troyens* begun, score completed 1858. In the following years, very ill and spent; endless frustrations over potential production of his summa; composing now sparse; *Béatrice et Bénédict* 1860–62. Final years are desolating – no more composing, some successes abroad, *Trojans* given in Paris, mangled to a pulp; death of second wife 1862, and of beloved only son 1867; concerts abroad – despite ill-health and depression the old spark could still flash: death early 1869. As well as the lively journalism, the *Memoirs* (begun 1848, published 1865) present the character in all its volatile lovability, however heightened into romantic fiction.

Berlioz is one of those maverick composers who never quite settle into indisputable, unassailable evaluation. Certainly he is not, as Stravinsky lethally observed of Liszt's orchestral music, 'only kept alive by perpetually renewed neglect'. The stature is unimpugnable, and the best works are kept alive by continually renewed performance. But his unevenness – and now-and-again sheer badness – can also not be denied; around the round-figure anniversaries, claims mount *triomphales* rather *funèbres*: yet the unanswered questions don't go away, and must be tackled, maybe resolved. Does Berlioz require rescuing from his defenders?

England and Germany have long embraced this turbulent and contradictory musician. He was treasured as a conductor and composer in both countries while still struggling against impossible odds in his own. The first collected edition of his works was German; the second, employing high-calibre German printing, has been largely directed by British scholarship at its finest, under Hugh Macdonald's expert guidance; David Cairns's biography is recognized even by Berlioz's fellow French as outstanding; the best analytical writing on the music is by another English scholar, Julian

Rushton; and Colin Davis is only the most recent of its many superb British champions in live and recorded performance, following a tradition at least as old as Hamilton Harty and Thomas Beecham. However, if not 'perpetually renewed neglect', Berlioz certainly depends upon a periodic clarion-call that urges resounding, indeed hyperbolic, claims, often accompanied by gleeful attempts to downgrade a perceived Teutonic stranglehold, contemporary with his oeuvre, from late Beethoven via Bruckner and (mainly) Wagner to early Brahms. But the need to emplinth him in the Panthéon can backfire. Cooler appraisal shows him vulnerable to virtually every variety of legitimate criticism. And on every scale. The frequent solecisms in details – the placing of a harmony, the curve of a countermelody – don't irritate merely the squeamish grammarian: such fine points make the sensitive listener wince as the princess feels the pea through eighteen mattresses; their cumulative effect can undermine whole stretches of even his finest pieces.

The opposite fault is of course the gigantism – ambition, length, performing-forces, and the almighty noise they make under the able command of a general who is also a stirring rhetorician – but often rendered by mediocre ideas handled so laboriously that, again, the scrupulous listener senses not the eighteen mattresses beneath so much as the brontosaurus in the bed itself. For me, and many others, things like the *Grande Messe des morts* and the *Te Deum* are unambiguously monstrous – '*grotesques de la musique*', in Berlioz's own excellent phrase – and frigid to boot, for all the blasts of hot air. But what about the blockbusters composed from the heart? Take *Roméo et Juliette*. Purely orchestral movements (with the slightest touch of voices now and then) of the most ardent inspiration and emotional authenticity – love-lorn Roméo all alone as guests pour in for the Capulets' ball; the love-scene that unfolds as they depart; the gossamer toughness of the 'Queen Mab' scherzo; the fugal lament accompanying Juliette's cortège; the electric 'choreography' of the tomb scene, animating every frantic or pathetic gesture of the lovers' cross-purposes in death – are framed between a sort of résumé or index of what's to come plus an aesthetic credo. To close, an operatic scena of reconciliation ensures by its fustian grandiloquence upon pedestrian material that the marvellous preceding music goes clean out of one's mind. The rationale behind the hotchpotch can be explained, even vindicated, by the loyal Berliozian – we can be made to see exactly what he was doing – but the knowledge cannot make the thing work. Hugh Macdonald ingeniously postulates a 'Four Scenes from Shakespeare's *Romeo and Juliet*' as the living original from which the eventual monster grows, escalates and eventually spins out of control, by way of analogy with the birth of the evening-length *Damnation de Faust* from the earlier *Eight Scenes from Faust*. But if this is so, why does Berlioz not have the artistic taste – the *sense* – to retain the quintessence, the salient episodes that really fire his ardour in all its incandescent truth to authentic inspiration, rather than building the laborious Wooden Duck?

The other multi-media hybrid, *La Damnation*, is equally contrary to artistic sense, but comes off gloriously (Berlioz is nothing if not inconsistent!). Just the once, its conception, pacing, trajectory are almost completely sure-footed; and the music (save the concluding depiction à la Gustave Doré of Hell – cackling demons and smashes on the tam-tam; and of Heaven – harps and haloes) is consistently on the heights over a wider range than usual of tones and textures. Which decidedly cannot be said for the operas on which he set his heart: *Benvenuto Cellini* near the beginning, *Les Troyens*, with *Béatrice et Bénédict*, at the end. In all these, places of characteristic piercing tenderness or infectious brio and vivid coloration are embedded in acres of plasterwork almost – surprising in this of all composers – 'without identifying characteristics'. Their speed and vivacity are at the farthest extreme from Wagner's deliberated slowness: but Wagner always has momentum (despite the occasional dead patch) whereas Berlioz dances eloquently, pathetically, furiously, on the spot and the plot is always stalling. The music in Berlioz's operas doesn't tell the people on the stage what to *do*; it tells of feelings but issues no instructions as to dramatic expression or action. Wagner is always exact in stage-terms, rhetoric-and-gesture specific; *then* the commenting and interpreting orchestra can convey the emotion with which the viewer-listener can identify.

So what stand unmarred by such damaging flaws? As well as his marvellous overtures, Berlioz excels at orchestral songs. The *Nuits d'été* are consummate in their evocation of fragile romantic mood-states; a further handful of supreme songs with orchestra ought to be as well known and loved as this celebrated cycle, as also many isolated lyric and dramatic pieces for chorus with instruments. Every time I hear *Tristia*, a triptych consisting of a funeral march for Hamlet, a death-scene for Ophelia, plus, typically, something else that doesn't really fit, I melt with ruth at the exquisite sense of timbre, contour, nuance, the intensity yet chastity of expression, the sheer specialness of this on-the-edge genius, revealed in such places all naked and uncompromised by dross.

Bombast and bunkum: solecisms or plain mistakes that any capable hack could be taught to avoid; yet the inspired utterance, the unmistakable genius, of a composer who is certainly a great one. His permanent place among the Immortals depends upon a balancing act between these extremes which duly, and indeed humbly, acknowledges the shortcomings with the sublimities. This is what criticism is for; what criticism *is*. Where is Hector Berlioz, not in a hierarchy so much as where is what he's at, what he does? What he is? This phenomenon? This music? All-out claims deny such attempts at just definition. They also do him scant justice and even harm his cause. By taking the worst in him as seriously as the best, they don't take the greatest in him seriously enough.

More detailed notes on some of the indisputable *splendeurs*, big and small (with observations to the side upon some *misères*). *La Damnation de Faust*: not quite opera (as stage productions prove), certainly not oratorio despite an Easter Hymn near the start and an ending in Paradise – still best described as a *Légende dramatique en quatre parties*. A 'concert-opera'; its venue, the platform crowded with players and singers; its scope, their infinite power of suggestion, movement through time/place/space way beyond the resources of a stage, realizable by film-technology not even a speck on the horizon when the composer, and his poet/dramatist, wrote. (Compare Wagner – the realistic man-of-the-theatre; unprecedented demands, but achievable in actual designs, machines, buildings, technology, etc., of the day however they push beyond.) And in the *Damnation*

Berlioz's way with story, characters, narration, timescale and pacing, viewpoint and attitude, so bizarre elsewhere, is vindicated by almost total success.

The *Eight Scenes* of 1829 were in fact mainly songs: Mephistopheles' Serenade, Marguerite's ballad of the *King of Thulé* and her love song *D'amour l'ardente flamme* (combined with soldiers' chorus). *The Song of the Flea* and *The Song of the Rat*; two dances, for peasants, for sylphs; and the Easter Hymn. The Big Faust goes thus: Part I, Plains of Hungary; Faust alone at sunrise in open countryside, winter yielding to spring. He sings in character – lovely pastoral strain, linear and suave – nature renews, the world shines, my soul expands – *delicatissimo* evocation of fragrant breezes. He rejoices in his solitude, then falls silent: the orchestral textures begin to be penetrated by two elements alien to him as to each other – sounds of peasants rejoicing and soldiers on the march. First to reach the fore, the peasants' round-dance with tra-la-la refrain over a drone: Faust delights in their simple happiness. The scene shifts to 'another part of the plain' and the military signals near – what are these sons of the Danube to me, with their fiery pursuit of glory? – answered immediately by a fully caparisoned *Marche Hongroise* of the utmost dash and brilliance. It brings Part I to a resounding close. Much-criticized for irrelevance, it actually fulfils a strong, coherent balanced design and meaning – dancing peasantry, bravura soldiery, the hero betwixt and between, unable to belong to either. Now the story begins.

Part II: North Germany, Easter Morning: Faust has returned home, is alone and pensive in his study, joyless, weary of life – the mood exactly reproduced in soft sad wandering counterpoint – no direction, no aim: till one is found – in recitativo he bids farewell to his futile existence and prepares to quaff Life or Death from a crystal goblet of poison – checked at the crucial moment by the sound from the Cathedral and its choirs celebrating the Saviour's Resurrection on this holiest day of all. *Stage* religious music suits Berlioz perfectly, whereas the real thing – the *Requiem*; *Te Deum* – eludes him: Faust's boyhood raptures revive within him – his voice indoors – inside his soul – joins with the external choir's: as their hosannas fade, he determines to *live*. *Fine feelings!* exclaims the sudden stranger, unceremoniously introduced with brusque fierce gesture (trombones, piccolo, cymbals) and accompanied by upper strings *tremolando sul ponticello* (the mean, tight buzzing quality opposite of string tone in its natural beauty), as Mephistopheles – for it is he – ironically admires his newest victim's sensitive reactions to sacred sonorities. The bargain with Faust is soon sealed. You want proof? Just follow me! I consent.

They whirl off together into the air, and are rapidly deposited among the students in Auerbach's Cellar, Leipzig (not quite North Germany, but who minds) and plunged straight into the noisy hurly-burly of all-male drinking. Its hearty extroversion yields a solo turn – Brander's song of the fat rat poisoned by the spiteful cook who laughs her victim to scorn even in its death-agonies. Students bawl out a mocking A-men chorus (Mephistopheles: 'listen carefully – you'll hear bestiality naked!' Berlioz's *real* attitude to ecclesiastical music): again, context makes good; the contemptuous parody is not prolonged too long before the fiend's diabolic gesture introduces his ironic compliments and the way in for his own entertainment – the famous *Song of the Flea*. Students guffaw appreciation but fastidious Faust is disgusted. So the evil genius whirls them away through the air to something lyrical and lovely – woods and meadows on the banks of the Elbe. His cantilena suggestive of ease, happiness, vague promises of voluptuousnesses and blisses to come richly accompanied only with soft brass, bassoons below to mark the rhythm. Faust is lulled to sleep. In his dreams, gnomes and sylphs sing and dance in enchanted rounds of melody introduced and punctuated by flecks and flickers of woodwinds and horns remembered from Berlioz's belovèd Weber; the white magic of *Freischütz* and *Oberon* taken yet further, peaking as his dream produces the desired name – Marguerite! – in a full-choral apostrophe to the beauties of nature, then a blithe rondelle, then gradual dispersal under silky-silvery scales on strings. Faust reiterates the magic name; Mephistopheles insinuates 'soon he'll be mine', before thanking and dismissing his pretty minions – '*heureux Faust – dors! dors!*' their fading farewell. All this is so enchanting that one can't imagine its being surpassed until it *is*, in the succeeding *Dance of the Sylphs*, graceful and airy over its unfaltering pedal-note, harp harmonics making the ghost of a bass, the supernaturally pretty tune on violins vying with Mendelssohn on fairy ground, and maybe going one or two better in the exquisite wind-down – flutes, both harps, finally a soft-headed drum played as softly as possible. Faust sleeps, alone.

Then abruptly awakes – what a dream! where is she? take me! The obsequious false-friend obliges. But the story now goes on hold for an elaborate extended choral finale; soldiers off to victory in war or love or both; students lustily yawping their old Latin *chansons-à-boire*; then the two strains (Faust and Mephistopheles joining with the students) combined – a Berlioz speciality – culminating in enormous exuberance, gradually receding into both distances, down to the bottom note of long bassoon solo ending the story, half-way, on a semi-colon; poised upon a crucial place. And again the apparent gratuity of Berlioz's presentation is wholly convincing, if slightly self-indulgent.

Part III begins with an echo – brass and drums in the orchestra, answered by brass off-stage, sound the Retreat. This one *isn't* quite convincing – to allow the change of scene? A shift in the narration? Faust, alone by evening in Marguerite's bedroom, singing tenderly of his love, his sympathy for her suffering, before exploring 'with passionate curiosity' everything in the maiden's chamber. With his now-familiar peremptory gesture enter Mephistopheles – 'here she comes: hide!' Faust – '*calme-toi, mon âme*'. Thinking herself alone, she muses over her dream-lover, never to be seen in this life; introduction to her ballad of the King of Thulé – the golden goblet bequeathed by his adored Queen, treasured beyond all else, cast into the sea as his own end approaches, faithful unto death. She sinks into profound melancholy. Mephistopheles invokes his spirits of flame – *feux follets* – wonderfully evoked by staccato woodwinds topped with three piccolos, then fizzing strings – and surely not lost on the composer of Loge. *Go on! dance! lead her into temptation! If you fail, I'll quench your lights!* Now another ballet-number, *Menuet for Will-o'-the-Wisps*, worthy of Tchaikovsky at his best, at once robust and fragile till broken in on by inexplicable gigantic crescendos for the full orchestra hitherto only used in sensitive and sometimes hilarious sections: these fairies have teeth and muscles after all. The last two of these explosions are crowned with cymbals and a triangle: then follows a helter-skelter presto sort-of-polka; the two speeds then bizarrely fragmented in alternation; a declining trill on violins introduces Mephistopheles as hurdy-gurdy player, for his *Serenade with Wisps* – expostulating, mocking, humming along – don't trust him an inch, he'll do you wrong, men are fickle aye; when the fatal moment comes, resist with all your might till he proffers the nuptial ring – derisive sarcastic advice that happens to be exactly appropriate, albeit not-to-be-heeded by the infatuated girl – set to a sparkling catchy waltz with strings' pizzicato marvellously imitating the flickering twilight. The fire-sprites scintillate into thin air; the lovers are left alone as they imagine (though presumably – it's not explicit – the evil genius is on the lookout).

To a snatch of *Thulé* Marguerite wonders *Is it he? Can I believe my eyes?* before Faust hymns his adoration, calling her by her name. She responds with his; they alternate closer, and join in duet (the tenor touching several soft high B's and a single soft high C♯ if he possibly can): it fades upon his repeated *viens!* and her *je meurs . . . tout s'efface.* Before the inevitable can transpire, the full orchestra bursts into their intimacy, closely followed by its impresario Mephistopheles – danger is at hand, the neighbours are alerted, they've called for Marguerite's old mother. The lovers vow to meet again – the only hour Faust has wished to 'stay awhile, thou art so fair!' (though this famous desideratum wasn't mentioned in the earlier diabolical bargaining). Angry neighbours besiege the house; while vowing eternal devotion, the lovers must part and flee, Mephistopheles gloats on his victim's imminent perdition – trio with chorus, more conventionally operatic both in idiom and intention than anything elsewhere in the work; also in its actual pacing – this stretch alone could make plausible sense on the operatic stage. (It's also the work's weakest music.) Cut off as though by the Curtain at anxiety's tensest point.

Whatever next? is precisely what does *not* come next – clumsy or clever, according to taste. Part IV begins altogether elsewhere, with the score's most beautiful lyric number, Marguerite's Romance: *D'amour l'ardente flamme* (its words originally *une amoureuse flamme*) plus cor anglais obbligato setting up the melodic line in expressive conjunct intervals and the one huge leap – *consumes* (my happy days, devoured by love's ardent fires) – quintessential Berlioz, as of the *Nuits d'été* songs – closest there to *le spectre de la rose* for inner intensity and contained passion, winding down as she despairs of ever again exhaling her soul in his kisses ... as steals from the distance the Retreat that had opened Part III, a powerful poetic moment, all the more so for, as well as the contrasting idiom and the play of memory (ours, hers?), its mysterious inexplicability – why do the soldiers retreat again? – and then the students steal in too with their Latin ribaldries. Marguerite's joy is also in retreat; he'll never return: as fragments of the Romance return on the cor anglais, fading before its aspirant interval-leap – *hélas*. The hardest retreat of all is her lover's. We never see her or hear her again.

Total reversal and an intonation not encountered before. Faust summons all his substance for a grand *Invocation á la Nature*, a superb last-minute apostrophe, recreating all that's noblest, finest, deepest, highest in his flawed and multifarious being. He yields his jaded body upon Nature's nurturing breast, to revive his powers and live again: he invokes her wildness – over one of Berlioz's splendid tumultuous rhetorical basses; 'your storms, forests, rocks, torrents – let me unite my voice with yours, let me merge into a vast Empyrean where there'll be only the Universal Soul of well-being.' His evil genius has overheard and reverts to mordant reality – Marguerite is in prison, the sentence already passed for causing her mother's death at Faust's instigation, knowing or ignorant that the sleeping-draught to keep the old woman out of the way of her daughter's pleasures went a bit too far. Hunting-horns punctuate the tense dialogue: 'How can you get me out of this?' 'I've the power, but what's my payment?' 'What do you require?' 'From *you?!* Only a signature on this old parchment – I'll save her on the instant if you sign and vow to serve me afterwards.' 'What do I care for tomorrow?!' Faust signs – a *softissimo* double stroke of tam-tam and big drum – the hunting-horns resume, ever softer and softer, then cease. In the silence, Mephistopheles calls for his horses. Another silence. Galloping motion softly starts, builds, cuts off. Giour the stallion appears,

Faust is commanded to mount and gallop off, quick as thought, to escape the course of Justice.

But the ride is Hell-bent, no longer earthly – *la course à l'Abîme* – an astounding tour de force of Gothic terror; the apotheosis in all the arts of this odd European craze that began in playful fancy à la Strawberry Hill, peaked in the novels of 'Monk' Lewis, Mrs Radcliffe, Maturin, and was laughed out of its gloomy cloister by Northanger and Nightmare Abbeys well before Berlioz takes it to this present apogee. Faust and his Master rush headlong on black steeds – Giour and Vortex – to energetic *moto perpetuo* on violins over purposeful pizzicato bass, the bare combination supporting a wailing irregular solo oboe-line of surpassing originality, without identifying antecedents. Faust briefly bewails his abandoned victim – she is as though personified in a chorus of women peasants praying to the Virgin at a wayside Cross. Then to the Magdalen, to make the point acuter. Faust – watch out for the women and children! Mephistopheles – what the hell! Onwards! As the little chorus seem to invoke Marguerite closest of all, the crazed riders scatter them in terror. The uncanny naked texture – 'speaking' oboe, busy energy (now in two parts, second violins joining firsts) over the propulsive business-like bass – is joined by deep notes, soft but raucous and uncouth: two bassoons, two trombones, about as low as they can reach, coalescing, with addition of tuba and clarinet, to become chords; the perpetuo is intensified with added pulsation – Faust perceives huge, phantasmargoric night-birds – twitching high woodwinds thrown in – their cries, their rending wings – the *black* magic from *Freischütz* gone ballistic. Before we audience perceive it, Mephistopheles hears the bell marking the prisoner's execution: Afraid? Shall we return? Texture and momentum collapse as the bell *is* sounded. No – I hear it! Onwards! Ride resumes, as before yet extremer, bass marked by drums when they can, *all* the strings doing the energy, the hapless solo oboe all-but-drowned, giving up as three low clarinets and four bassoons take over, the Devil whips up the horses, his victim sees dancing skeletons with horrible smiles hailing them as they pass. So it grows, a colour/texture crescendo as well as in mere volume, underpinned by rolls on one then two drums, joined by a tam-tam roll executed by three players (two to beat the instrument, one to suspend it). The horses are terrified, the earth trembles, the heavens roll, it rains blood. Mephistopheles now reveals himself – 'in a voice of thunder' he calls upon his infernal cohorts to sound the trump of triumph – he is ours! Mine is the Victory! – as Faust yells in horror and they plunge into the abyss of . . .

Pandemonium: terrific black grandeur – the score's great music is done with; nothing remains but the shouting – but what shouting! Demons and Damned exclaim in an invented language of hellish nonsense: Mephistopheles' Princes hail their Emperor in French: questions and answers confirm the legitimacy of Faust's fate: wild, primitive, exultant chorus and dance breaks out – polka, waltz, polka; then brief return of the mighty opening chorale, rapidly diminishing to stillness; an empty page of aftermath: somehow back from the underworld to earth's surface: 'Hell is stilled, no howls of demons or cries of tormented souls reach us; deep below, a horrid mystery is fulfilled . . .' And so to . . .

Paradise. Celestial chorus, women's voices only (plus optional children's choir) sing pious words to pious music. Word of explan-ation/exculpation – *elle a beaucoup aimé, Seigneur!* – momentarily penetrates the dulcet weave, resumed as a solo soprano sings just the name 'Marguerite' over and over, supported by her sisters – 'love led her astray – come, take the crown your error nearly lost you; dry your tears; forget your terrestrial sorrows: hope; smile in happiness!' Purest icing-sugar on the triple-decker-cake of sweetly innocent/art-istically knowing kitsch, letting down lightly, appropriately, beauti-fully, the work which of all his output contains the most integrated and various, as well as nearly the best, of Berlioz's grandiose vision.

'Nearly the best'; this wobbly ideal is achieved in another all-evening effort, inordinately ambitious, here and there touching sublimities unparalleled, alongside much perfunctory infill of disconcerting competence: the whole a mismanaged chaos even the composer's most ardent apologists can't explain away. *Roméo et Juliette* really *is* a hybrid: symphony, song-cycle, cantata-oratorio, opera-mime – elements of all these, mashed together in admired disorder, with a little sermonette on the greatness of Shakespeare thrown in. Lost in this colossal grotesque is a modest, putative original. Mercutio's evocation of Queen Mab; the Ball at the Capulets; the balcony-scene; the tomb-scene – these four all stand out as the best of the eventual mastodon: it might well be worth trying to reconstitute this core of pure gold and drop the encumbering dross – it would save time and money. Within the eventual *Symphonie dramatique* these four movements can broadly be discerned. But this plan is not what the listener perceives. Here is what we actually get.

Part I *Introduction*: street-brawling between Capulets and Montagues – splendid vigorous fighting *fugato*, Berlioz at his fieriest: then the magnificent wordless rhetoric for the Prince of Verona's intervention – commanding recitativo on heavy brass imposing civic and familial order: the muttering factions disperse. In a *Prologue* the contralto soloist, supported by harp and small chorus, sets context and introduces the young people whose love crosses the ancient family feud. They tell the story to come, up to the balcony-scene, with a sort of sonorous index of principal motifs – an idea as original as it is bizarre. Follow, solemn *Strophes* wherein she generalizes about young love under warm southern skies, and hails Shakespeare who holds the supreme secret of its expression. The soloist is supported now by a few woodwinds, and, in a second stanza, by a long-breathed counter-melody on the cellos. The index resumes in recitative, foretasting Mercutio's Queen Mab speech and the deaths which will unite the warring families in shared grief.

Part II, Romeo alone, in his love-melancholy, evoked with exquisite sensitivity and expressiveness – the Berlioz of the songs, here unlimited by stanza-shape, metre, poem-length, *words* – supple paragraphs of beautifully controlled, purely orchestral free-flow. Into which steal distant strains of festivity – we perceive them as *he* must, insinuated on a drum and a tambourine almost subliminal through the trembling string tremolandi. Now a more song-shaped melody on the oboe representing him and his longing – serenade-like with pizzicato guitar accompaniment. The oboe peaks and declines, the festive sounds advance to the fore, and we are amid the joyous riot of the ball-scene at the Capulets – a tour de force worthy of Weber's

Invitation to the Dance which Berlioz had orchestrated in 1841, and the Chabrier *Fête polonaise* that was to succeed him. All three are waltz-dreams: here, something of a whirlwind/stampede, climaxing in the brazen superimposition of Romeo's oboe-song, blasted out on full winds – wholly losing its former introspection (though he still remains a Montague among the Capulets) – against a background of busy sparkle enhanced now with several harps – at least two, but '*on peut doubler ou tripler chaque partie de la Harpe*'. The triumphant combination is followed by prolonged development whose brilliance takes parallel places in the *Symphonie fantastique* to new heights – recession and proximity, in the midst of, outside and left out of, successively and simultaneously rendered, over heaving chromatic bass.

Part III consists only of the celebrated Love Scene. Nocturnal stillness of the Capulets' garden, sound of straggling male revellers, praising the entertainment, wishing each other goodbye, dreaming of love-making – 'what mad words, what lovely girls, tra-la-la.' As they recede, the garden begins to burgeon for what (with *Tristan* Act II) is surely the most perfect love-scene in all art. Unlike *Tristan* it proceeds uninterrupted – these lovers' nemesis comes later. This scene is a complete arc of ardour, velvety rich in themes and their orchestral vesture, rising to incandescent passion that eschews Wagner's erotic carnality (which, nevertheless, owes so much to this source in Berlioz, characteristically disparaged later ...) – somehow chaste, pure, *dis*passionate even in its utmost intensity. Now and again the 'voiceless' wholly orchestral movement breaks off into agitated recitativo-parlando, so urgent as to imply the former presence of a text later removed – perhaps direct from the balcony-scene in the Shakespeare: then the measured waves of melody resume – 'a full but soft emotion / Like the swell of summer's ocean' – then another passage of almost stammered 'speech' – then melody resumed yet more ardent than before, but fading sooner, disintegrating, halting, pausing, disappearing, ceasing altogether. If Berlioz had composed nothing else his seat in the Panthéon would be assured by this love-scene alone.

And not alone: for Part IV begins with another wonderful

success that couldn't be more different – the orchestral scherzo emulating the fun, nonsense, gaiety, brio of Mercutio's Queen Mab fantasy. Singing and character are equally abandoned, and wisely: Mercutio had figured only in the Index when pale love-lorn Romeo was twitted by his mates – *mon cher, dit l'elégant Mercutio, je parie que la reine Mab t'aura visité!* Cue for this delectable sparkler, beginning in suspended animation, ambiguity, pauses, silences, question-marks, before animation sets up, feather-light and springy, arrested again, and again, then at last truly commencing with the ultimate flower of the Weber/Mendelssohn fairy scherzo – all birds, bees, dragonflies, sprites, sylphs, *courants d'air*. The trio is slower, a gently melancholic strain on cor anglais, flickers of main scherzo occasionally to keep momentum in mind, and a clear high haze of violin harmonics to keep the texture heaven-bent. Scherzo resumes still faster, issuing in soft gay bravura for the horns; hunting the silver thimble or the milk-white unicorn rather than fox or stag. Suddenly the texture explodes, then vanishes: then, most enchanting of all, the hunting-motif on successive solo woodwinds sets up in a round underneath a tinkling ostinato on high harps with a twinkle of tiny tuned cymbals and a gently vibrating momentum of upper strings, while cellos pursue the quarry and deep, honking bass-notes are exchanged between a horn and four unison bassoons. This miniature episode is followed by the scherzo's return, epitomized, winding down into doubts, shadows, quivers, silences. Three more bell-tinkling-cymbal strokes, two harp pings, then the entire orchestra recovers speed and energy in a rush to the finish. Who can care that the movement's light-weighted brilliance, enshrining a minor character, overbalances the structure of the work as a whole, threatening the incoherence later achieved all-too-well by other means.

Before this ultimate *artistic* collapse, crisis of the *plot*, told obliquely in a mix of media that suggests ballet, then cinema, better than narration with words or by music alone. Juliette's funeral procession – fine-drawn orchestral threnody in Berlioz's introspective idiom for comparable places of brooding/groping in *Faust* and *Harold*. Threaded through it, the chorus of Capulets intoning on a monotone the instruction to strew flowers for the

dead maiden. As voices move into harmony the monotone is transferred to upper strings: the procession liquefies into smooth flowing
linearity – 'follow to the tomb our adorèd sister' – building strongly
in return of counterpoint as free and expressive as Berlioz's parodies,
elsewhere, are deliberately crude – proving (as if he needed to) that
he *can* do the real thing. The chorus broaden and cease, the *fugato*
lines gently dissolve: all that's left is the monotone, now deprived
even of its verbal rhythm, tolling soft and high over a murmuring
buzz of tremolando *pppp*.

Now for ballet-mime: Romeo at the tomb – 'delirious joy, despair,
last anguishes and deaths of the lovers' (the composer first saw the
play *'avec la dénouement de Garrick'* and follows it here). A frenzied
allegro agitato e disperato implodes, suspiring onto an extraordinary
page of long chords – slow and soft but timeless and unmeasured,
surrounded by silences, echoing between three low trombones,
all the woodwinds, four horns, all the strings: a solo oboe now
sustains, joined by two flutes – a fast, then slow Introduction to
Invocation, wordless aria of rhetorical magnificence sung by the four
bassoons, an English and a French horn in cholesterol-rich unison
over throbbing/pulsing lower strings and the occasional muted
drum-roll. Ballet and wordless ballad now yield to pure mime –
every gesture vivid, albeit unchoreographed, as every spasm of a
Petrushka or a sacrificial Virgin, illustrating the quoted words beginning this paragraph turn by turn. This isn't quite *music*: its gestural
content is electric, galvanic, spasmodic – Berlioz has invented, for
tragic histrionics, the technique of Mickey-Mousing: onomatopoeic
imitation and underlining of every movement and facial expression. Its compositional content is astonishing rather than good – or
indeed bad – simply astonishing.

But what happens now is astonishing merely because it *is* so
bad – in miscalculation, in actual musical substance. This huge
bombastic operatic finale commences well enough, with agitated
Capulets wondering about the as-yet obscure and unexplained
events – till – *Ciel!* – they arrive *au tombeau. Morts, tous les deux; et
leur sang fume encore! Quel mystère affreux!* Cue for the Fat Friar to
explain, deplore, urge forgiveness and reconciliation; an *Air* wherein

unctuous platitudes are succeeded by trite exhortations. Capulets and Montagues can't yet acquiesce in peaceful coexistence – too many old scores unsettled in this dark double-chorus, re-using their fight-music from the *Prologue*. The Padre quiets and shames them – does not this grand love cast out hate? His confident periods, mediocre and boring and anonymous; also competent, confident, credulous – Berlioz must have thought this the right note to sound. Gradually the tribes come round to right reason, and Lorenzo instigates a solemn *Vow*: by all that's holy, pardon's the word to all: the rolling tune is tub-thumped in mighty choral uplift to subscribe to the sentiments – *amis pour toujours*: a blaze of banality worthy of the Meyerbeer it resembles.

How to balance the pros and cons of this composer, more unevenly gifted than any other of clear stature? He achieves flawless perfection in lyrics: every song of *Nuits d'été* (as orchestrated; the piano-writing is inept) a gem of exquisitely poised sensitivity and sensibility – *brioso* spring freshness, aching pangs of absence, the fragrant romance of the rose, muted elegies of grief, a sortie out onto the open sea to *L'Île inconnu* where delusive happiness might still abide. Yet even here, it's parts, not a whole; the six songs don't connect, and the three slow, sad ones in succession can drag; and the cycle ideally requires several different vocal types and ranges, though not satisfactory when actually performed thus. One only has to remember Schumann's Eichendorff *Liederkreis* to see how a cycle of discrepant story-less moods can bond into a unity beyond the sum of its parts.
    And the Gothic dinosaurs are utterly unlovable – *Requiem*, *Te Deum*, *Symphonie funèbre et triomphale* all contain flashes, sometimes sustained stretches, of genius; but in the end they loom as dire as the heavy national/civic/ecclesiastical architecture that makes their contemporary visual and ideological counterpart. The two self-projecting Fantasy Symphonies – one directly from his own life (the *Fantastique*) the other (*Harold en Italie*) as clearly a heroical romanticized self-portrait, mix breathtaking inspiration with breathtaking bathos, and sweep all before them. The sequel to the first – *Lélio* – plunges into flagrant preposterousness – a

dustbin for gathering in waifs and strays with nowhere else to go; and, as always, some wonderful flashes. Plentiful other odds-and-ends, from bizarrerie like the *Hymn for the Railroads* to poetic pieces of a high order like *Tristia*. *L'Enfance du Christ* – a characteristic melange of flair and miscalculation, this oblique take on the tale of Herod's murderous paranoia, the Nativity, the Flight into Egypt: some strong moments (Herod's insomnia), some absurdities, music mostly tired and pale and sometimes interminably prolonged outside the story-line (that hospitable family entertainment!): at the end, a new simplicity and tenderness very touching in itself yet perilously nearing vapidity.

Finally, the operas, *hélas*. I've already tried to indicate that Berlioz's sense of characters alone, characters in interaction, dramatic timing and pacing, is non-operatic, and best-realized in the 'world-theatre' of the concert-hall. All three operas are problematic onstage. *Benvenuto Cellini* comes off best – the score bursts with vitality, the awkwardnesses (and the ham-fisted ending) can be lost in the riotous teeming invention. Riotous! Best crowd-scenes outside *Meistersinger*? *Béatrice et Bénédict* is sad: would-be sparkling wine gone flat. And *Les Troyens*. I'll be guillotined down a dark alley for saying so: this cornerstone of the composer and the Berliozians is a cardboard turkey rather than a wooden horse – long and boring for the most part, ending with a disastrous misfire to make the close of *Benvenuto* seem resourceful. Berlioz had spent his all: the score, however brilliant, is burnt-out, a dry husk, a tinkling cymbal. As ever, some magnificent exceptions – Cassandra's role in the Troy acts; in the Carthage, the septet, the duet, Dido's wild self-abandonment: and one of the two greatest ballet-*spectacles* in the entire repertoire of this obligatory French speciality, up there with the *Bacchanale* Wagner added to *Tannhäuser* for its Paris production – Berlioz's *Royal Hunt and Storm* wherein the Carthaginian Queen and the Trojan Prince acknowledge and consummate their love. *Here* Berlioz surely wins – Wagner's *Bacchanale* is simply a divertissement, for all its alignment in imagery to the dramatic situation: in contrast the *Hunt and Storm* is the crucial turning-point of the whole opera. But the whole does not live.

Bizet and Delibes

After this ever-divisive giant, a succession of smaller yet surer French charmers.

Georges Bizet; born 1838, studied at the Paris Conservatoire, though principal influence extra-mural, from Gounod. Mini-masterpiece, Symphony in C, aged eighteen (1855), 1858–60 residence in Rome as prix-winner. Destined from early on for opera – grand projects mooted, or unfinished, or thwarted. Principal surviving landmarks: *Le Docteur Miracle* (1856), sparkling operetta; *Les Pêcheurs du perles* (1863) – another Orientalist fantasy – eternal love and fidelity, jealousy and vengeance – and revealing his gifts for orchestral colouring and melodic abundance shining bright and warm above the absurdities: which win out wholly in *La Jolie Fille de Perth* (1866), a preposterous farrago *very* after Scott, whose music is far better than its libretto deserves; *Djamileh* (1871–2) – a delectable one-acter, story (again Oriental) slight, music top-drawer; *Carmen* (1873–5) – deservedly the most popular opera in the repertoire. Death, June 1875, shortly after its first, unsuccessful, production, before his heroine began her universal conquest.

Other notable pieces: a handful of fine songs, interesting solo piano music and the delectable *Jeux d'enfants* for piano-duet; incidental music to Daudet's *L'Arlésienne* (1872), originally for small ensemble perfectly suited to the occasion, blown up for full orchestra in two Suites – their intrinsic calibre survives the inflation, but one misses the masterly instinct for timbre revealed everywhere in *Carmen* and his own orchestration of *Jeux d'enfants* (five of the original twelve) as a *petite suite*. His most celebrated music is so familiar and well-beloved as to be beyond further description; I'll aim here to help three others over the stile into open countryside: two other stage-works, one big, one small, that deserve to be up there with *Pearl Fishers* and *Carmen*; and, to start, the twelve piano-duet miniatures of *Jeux d'enfants*, epitomizing Bizet's gifts within the modest confines of the drawing-room. *Jeux d'enfants* comes first in a long lovable line of French keyboard-music devoted to children, and sometimes for children to play: Fauré, Saint-Saëns, Debussy, Satie,

Ravel, Poulenc, Mompou. Even Stravinsky's little piano-duets, one set with simple *primo* the other with simple *secondo*, veer into this charmed circle. Analogous to Musorgsky's *Nursery* song-cycle; but, even at its most *enfantine* the naïve is *faux* – always seen from the grown-up's sophisticated perspective: *not* condescending, always affectionate, irredeemably adult. Musorgsky's unique miracle is to have penetrated the child's viewpoint and to render it from within, as we'll see later.

Bizet's contribution is decidedly too hard for any but infant prodigies to play. All are gems of invention, elegance, tender expression, refined lay-out, never less than pretty, often more; and fraught with originality mostly unobtrusive sometimes bold. *The Swing*'s indolent melody sings in the tenor, surrounded below and above with dainty arpeggios (very difficult to play daintily), with harp-like spread chords to bind the airy texture: runs the gamut from *ppp* to *ff* with lovely modulations en route: hardly *enfantine*! *The Spinning Top* is also difficult to play – a bright whirring whirl, twice stilled in mysterious soft stasis before motion resumed. *The Doll*, tenderness embodied, a sweet ache of nostalgia that could have come straight out of or go straight into the *Arlésienne* music. *The Merry-Go-Round* – another whirler, this time a *moto perpetuo* – a well-developed gigue/scherzo of infectious brio; towards its end the roundabout is wittily checked, resuming soft, fast disappearing. *Battledore and Shuttlecock* is marked *andantino molto* (surely unique?) – quintessence of delicacy, fragile as a spider-web, watchful as the spider who spins it. Over wary accompaniment-figures, ascending then descending scales flutter up/down, neither chromatic nor diatonic nor modal – Bizet as original here as Musorgsky, though always within rather than without the law: poised as on a knife-edge. Utter contrast, *Trumpet and Drum*, a toy march with tin soldiers – sabres, kepis, twirling mustachios, twinkles and winks, miniature fanfares: something between *Godunov*'s chiming clock and Tchaikovsky's *Nutcracker*, worthy of both.

The generous toy-box reveals another jewel of delicacy and precision, *Soap Bubbles*. Over spare accompaniment, an unbroken arabesque melodic line on its tiny unchanging rhythm, fine as an Indian silk, fragile and diaphanous as what it depicts: a perhaps conscious, more likely inadvertent homage to Schumann's *Prophet-Bird*, equally a thing of fantasy, visibility evasive, existence perilous. *Les Quatres Coins* – a game of puss-in-the-corner that *must* have been known to, delighted in, by Tchaikovsky doing Puss-in-Boots for the fairy-tale divertissement in *Sleeping Beauty*. Captivating felinity, sniffing, cornering, teasing, biding its time, pouncing, triumphantly catching, whether it's cat and mouse or a gang of excited kids. *Blindman's Buff*, another game needing cunning – timing – waiting; brilliantly gestural, piano four-hand textures (as in all these pieces) just perfect; graceful courtly 'wooing', more and more pressing till the sudden rush towards victory, and the sudden demure close. *Leap-frog*: another bold number, in the combination of oblique and straight harmony by which the game's physical motions are imitated – quiet creepy passage towards the end, after the most exuberant climax – slow descending chromatic progression above; below, the previous leap-frogging motion locked into virtually atonal rising scales, the combination over tonic pedal anchoring the strange sound in the home key, poetically wobbling and eroding at its edges.

After all this strenuous play of cunning or rough-and-tumble, tenderness to match and outdo the *Doll*: *Petit mari, petite femme* (only Louisa May Alcott could translate this – my edition calls it *Playing House*) – meltingly tender duet (each player's right hand) giving husband's and wife's voices in alternation, curving and gradually peaking to gentle climax, relaxing into return of opening, *petite femme* again leading, joined now by her *petit mari* in counter-voice. Could be tacky; saved by melodic and harmonic distinction that has to be called aristocratic, and the unfailing felicity of the texture: even on piano-duet it recalls Strauss's commendation of the orchestration of *Carmen* – 'wonderful economy: every note and every rest in its proper place', which goes too for every note and every rest in this, as in the other eleven of these pieces in a medium so easily thick and crashing, or thin and skimpy. Finally, *Le Bal*, a *presto galop*, not without several lapses into delicacy – *aussi pp que possible*, and some very remote keys – before romping to end in maximum *in*delicacy, *fff furioso*.

*

Now two non-repertoire operas, one full-length the other small. *La Jolie Fille de Perth* comes three years after the *Pearl Fishers* and some eight before *Carmen*. That its so-called plot is lost beyond recall from start to finish should be no disadvantage for an operatic culture which can swallow middle-period Verdi without demur. I remember Scott's original novel as one of the Northern Wizard's best, concretely localized in Scotland's prettiest town and his own convincingly invented past; its characters less cardboard than often, its story less dependent on improvisation and coincidence. But one would read it in vain to make sense of the unresisting imbecility offered to Bizet, with its chaos of misapprehensions and disguises, its ham and cod that passeth understanding, its lame-duck verses. Nor is there any discernible nub of emotional truth allowing one to become genuinely involved, as with Rigoletto and his daughter, Azucena and her mixed-up babies in *Trovatore*, the Duke caught between lover and husband in *Ballo*, even the hapless goings-on in *La forza del destino*. For sheer preposterousness, the close, in which Bizet's heroine, literally maddened by her absurd context, is shocked back to sanity via a pre-Freudian reconstruction of an earlier trauma (one of several), takes the prize. This is the climax of a succession of incredibilities that begins with some of the principal characters' names – Simon Glover, a glover; Henry Smith, a smith; Mab, Queen of the Gypsies – then proceeds from implausibility to implausibility as though there were no tomorrow.

Its only match is Chabrier's *Le Roi malgré lui*, an opera I would defend to the hilt, against all common sense, for the musical treasures surviving triumphant against an ocean of impossibles. *La Jolie Fille* is comparable in other ways, too: both works sank after mild initial success, and both have been hacked around without mercy in vain attempts to render them stage-worthy. Chez Chabrier the plot has been completely rewritten, twice, in order to rescue the huge, gorgeous, teeming score; chez Bizet a work that even in its fullest version is not long has suffered the death of a thousand cuts.

Also in common with Chabrier is the benign influence of Berlioz; not the ghastly Victorian Gothic of the *Requiem* and other such flummery, but the exquisitely sensitive volatile musician who composed 'with the point of a needle'; mercurial moods and textures, melodies bursting with gaiety, or saturated in amorous languor, or penetrated by noble melancholy, pungent and unclichéd in harmony, in a sharply etched orchestration of primary colours, every instrument, and every instrumental combination, retaining its unique unmistakable timbre. This Gallic quality reaches a first zenith in both successors' evocations of Spain – *Carmen* and *España* – before achieving still more vivid countries of the mind in Ravel and Debussy; but already in Bizet's 'Perth' and Chabrier's 'Poland' it is fully in place.

Unlike *Pearl Fishers* or *Carmen*, whatever their advantage in viability, *La Jolie Fille* doesn't have a single dull bar. The charms begin before the curtain rises in a delicate orchestral prelude, then continue without stint, from an anvil-song for Henry Smith at the opposite end of the world from Siegfried's – let alone the anvil-chorus in *Trovatore* (or is it *Ballo*, or *Forza*, or *Rigoletto*? Who cares?) – to tender music for the lovers, however criss-crossed, lilting grace for the seductive, pleasure-loving Duke, a drinking-song and carnival chorus among the best of their kind, and plenty else. Lovers of the minuet in the second *Arlésienne* suite will find its original here, subtly diegetic to accompany the Duke and the Gypsy Queen in their mutually deceptive *amours*. Smith's aria of desolation at his girl's presumed unfaithfulness, and the subsequent sextet with chorus, cut deep; and so out of the confusion via the mad scene (delectable) and dénouement already mentioned.

Only Catherine's disabusal and the happy conclusion are a bit perfunctory. The composer's suspended disbelief collapses here; he rounds the thing off with the Valentine's Day strains heard earlier. This born dramatist doesn't hang around wasting time even in so undramatic a work as this.

Djamileh, however, is completely viable; a mini opal of Orientalism, sadly neglected: for unlike *La Jolie Fille* this is not a lost cause, only to be rescued – if at all – by drastic readjustment. Plot slight and silly, after a tale by Alfred de Musset: Haroun, indolent young aristo, living for pleasure, changing one slave-girl for the next each month, purchased at the market in Cairo by his servant Splendiano.

The most recent, Djamileh, has broken the pattern by falling genu-inely in love with her master. She bargains with Splendiano, aware that he fancies her too, to deceive Haroun: let her appear among the next month's recruits: if she can re-win her first choice she'll be happy; if this fails, Splendiano can take her. It transpires as she desires – she dances by moonlight, Haroun is re-enchanted, she swears her true love, preferring slavery to liberty. Rejecting her at first, he is then moved by her depth of feeling: *amor vincit omnia*.

The highlights of this delightful score begin with its *Ouverture* – Orientalized trumpet and drum with 'Ketèlbey' counter-strain – in an Egyptian market-garden – before *fortissimo* return. Chabrier must have known this music – there were eleven performances in 1872 before it disappeared. The languid hero's first number is set between a distant chorus humming to a soft drum-beat, both stanzas closed by a delicious twinkling chromatic descent, during which he smokes his hookah; when he sings, a liberated/libertine Don José, at ease in his own skin. The next bits not so special, even when he arouses himself to exclaim, no woman lasts for me – it's Love – *j'aime l'amour; l'amour!* (But when not so special, think back to the acres of card-board in *Les Troyens* or *Beatrice et Bénédict*!) Next opal, the heroine's lyrical *ghazel*, sung to Splendiano's lute; the exotic strain in Bizet, first encountered in the oboe-melody of his 1855 symphony's slow movement, reaching its flower here in a superb isolated song with piano, the 'farewell of the Arabian hostess'; and thus on to the deline-ations of *Carmen*. Djamileh's next solo is quite different – a *Lamento* with striking dissonance near the start – this must have raised the eyebrows that condemned the score as 'Wagnerian'. Next highlight, the Oriental Dance with chorus, sinuous arabesque, insinuating equivocation between major and minor, over a pulsating drone-bass, the work's longest number till its Finale – 'recognition-scene' explanations, Haroun's feigned rejection and eventual acceptance of Djamileh's genuine love – duet 'caressed Love's divine radiance', a lovely amorous barcarolle, the ambiguous ending – all joy for two, the down-and-outer for contriving Splendiano, who didn't intend any such result, passing disregarded by the music itself.

*

Léo Delibes: born 1836, studied at Paris Conservatoire, subsequent career divided between church organist and worldly theatre composer. Some success with operas, especially the last, *Lakmé* (1883), staple of French Orientalism, love and death across racial divide, story as imbecilic as the music delightful. The best of him goes into ballets – *La Source* (1866) – only a few numbers, rounded out later to form a shapely suite: *Coppélia* (1870) after Hoffmann's famous tale of the mechanical maiden who comes to life: *Sylvia* (1876) after Tasso. These two lovable and distinguished scores put the genre, previously humdrum and mediocre, onto a new artistic footing: the two full-lengthers remain foundation classics, familiar to all devotees of the ballet. *La Source*, provenance provisional, scenario as preposterous as any in this world of muslin and flim-flam, its music as enchanting.

Tchaikovsky's imagination for what ballet-music can do was transformed by his contact with Delibes; and contact with *Carmen* (he saw it first in Paris in 1876) transformed his entire subsequent life and work. The impact was overwhelming; he identified wholly with the motif of Fate's influence upon its victims' loves and death, as he equally treasured the unstinting generous intensity with which these are rendered in Bizet's score. Not to mention its wealth of melody, its centring upon dance-rhythms, its consummately rich and clear orchestration. *Carmen* from soon after its poor start received accolades from other composers: Chabrier's *España*, and his everything else, take off from Bizet's opera and Bizet in general; Mahler declared that he took pleasure in something new every time he conducted it; Strauss said if you want to know how to orchestrate, learn from *Carmen* rather than Wagner.

Which opens up the opera's important symbolic place in European sensibility and thought and its wider repercussions. Nietzsche's intoxication with it is famous: *Carmen* becomes key symbol-banner and weapon in his campaign to demolish everything he understood by 'Wagnerism': decadence in the spirit and the flesh, the mind and the body, through submission to morbid psychopathologies; in the music itself, bombast, pretentiousness, histrionics, lack of rhythm and colour, 'endless melody' without tunes, degeneration of shape and form in endless improvisation, obscurity instead of illumination. Their antitheses – vibrancy, immediacy, sensuous actuality; dancing; clarity of outline; eschewing portentousness – while still acknowledging the power of Destiny over human life; and, above all, direct frank acquiescence in the centrality of erotic passion, and direct frank expression of it. Thus the polarities: Nietzsche's ambivalence over his former idol is something else, yet inseparable – the polemic is for ever ambiguous. But *Carmen*'s importance is fixed: the opera, as embodied in the sensuous actuality of its notes, becomes the iconic touchstone for a new current of thought and feeling at large, summed up in the splendid word 'Mediterreanization'. Through innumerable variations, transformations, reorientations (often literally) it comes to alter music's course in the following decades as fundamentally as does Glinka's *Kamarinskaya* (discussed later).

Chabrier

Emmanuel Chabrier: born 1841, destined for the Law, career in civil service, always crazy about music, composing whenever he could: almost bohemian lifestyle despite the job; friends with painters (including Manet – he was the first owner of *A Bar at the Folies-Bergère*) and writers (including Verlaine, with whom he collaborated on a pair of unfinished operettas). Mad about Wagner – hearing *Tristan* in Munich in 1879 precipitated decision to devote himself wholly to composition; trip to Spain 1882 yielded *España*. Pinned highest hopes on grand serious opera, but the essential genius quite other – a mighty handful of light music, top of its kind: songs, piano music, orchestral miniatures. The stage ventures on which he set his heart mix perfect attainment of realistic goals – operetta; with opera, pursuit of delusional grandeur; heartbreaking waste of much marvellous music. Died 1894.

Music of such pungent definition has never lacked discriminating admirers. But they have not necessarily seen him straight. Ravel and Poulenc do; their delight has no axe to grind. For Ravel, modern harmony began with Chabrier, without whom his own mature style would hardly have been possible. Ravel acknowledged his debt without false shame, and Poulenc, whose use of the earlier composer amounts now and again to pillage, shows the same frankness. But Debussy's praise – 'so marvellously endowed by the comic muse' – is disingenuous, as is Stravinsky's a generation later. For both, Chabrier was an instrument with which to beat the dreaded or detested Wagner, as Nietzsche had used *Carmen*. Such cultural polemic greatly distorts the art-works thus employed as ammunition. Chabrier would not have understood; for him Wagner was the biggest treat that music could offer. As a young man he had copied out the full score of the overture to *Tannhäuser* 'to learn the orchestra'. His first *Tristan* ('I've waited ten years for that A on the cellos!') precipitated the determination to abandon the civil service and, aged nearly forty, launch upon the precarious career of a full-time composer.

The truth is that Debussy and Chabrier are the only French composers individual enough to take on Wagner and survive. But Debussy's secretive nature compelled him to cover his traces, and eventually to turn against his early love. Chabrier, however, declares unambiguous affection everywhere, even when he mocks. His quadrilles 'on favourite motifs from *Tristan and Isolde*' (entitled *Souvenirs de Munich* because that is where he saw it) express at once engaging disrespect and genuine devotion to the epiphany that had changed his life, while in the late *Bourrée fantasque* the yearning Wagnerian harmony is completely interfused with the acrid sparkle and pounding rhythmic vitality that are literally all his own in as much as no outside references are needed to set it going. 'Wagner's music belongs to him,' he wrote, 'one shouldn't steal from anyone even if one is the poorer for it.' In the end he gets it both ways; the benefit of the greater richness shines out over an area far removed from the Wagnerian aesthetic.

For Chabrier celebrates in music of unfailing elegance the delights of the vulgar and the sentimental. Relish is paramount; there is no alienation or slumming. He evokes with vibrant colours and pungent flavours the pleasure of the senses, and expresses with tenderness the affections of friendship and love. His vision of the good life (the bourgeois version) resembles the achievement in painting of his friend Manet and its continuation in the *plein air* joys of the Impressionists. Like them he is not hung up on fake seriousness or the need to grapple with great subjects (except sometimes: see later). His contribution to the gaiety of nations accords exactly with his gift and how he employs it. Even its most ardent defenders can be known to groan, if pushed too far, at ritual pieties extolling French culture, so light, gay, refined, yet tough beneath the sparkle, all elegance and clarity, none of that Teutonic bombast, ostentatious brainwork, turgid texture, emotional overstatement. So what! one can say – to hell with *la clarté* and *l'esprit français* – I want music that gropes the depths, scorches the nerves, exposes the soul, brings me to my knees! Then the spirit can jib, and the flesh cry out for sensory materialist refreshment, diversion, amusement – colours, tastes, smells, sights; feelings meaning *touch* – the *feel* of furs, silks, ivory (to go no further): heady rough red wine from the Auvergne or champagne from the bar at the Folies-Bergères. No composer can satisfy such hankerings so well as Chabrier. He was one of those composers who are born fully themselves. It's all here already *in potentia* – the succinct melodiousness, the wit, energy, high spirits, the amorousness and underlying melancholy, the idiosyncratic pianism, the piquant and original harmony – not just in dabs and flecks, more a manner of thinking – that so attracted Debussy and so helped Ravel, and after him Poulenc, to achieve their own unmistakable styles.

His are shown at their most multifarious in the ten *Pièces pittoresques* for solo piano (1881): *Paysage* – him from the start, the curve of the melody, voicing in octaves, accompaniment above, then inside, a touch of *Tristan*, rapid rise to a peak; volatile changes of texture, dynamic, key; range of mood from tranquil to ecstatic, irregular phrase-periods, inventiveness and resource in every detail (and he's always very detailed) over far longer span than seemed at first intended: Chabrier's countryside is immense and populous. *Mélancholie*, however, just two pages of sensitively contoured cantabile: again his special spacing – opening up high, answering phrase in a lower unison, two octaves apart; again his resourcefulness – cleverness even (though this has the wrong implication) as the

theme develops in canon worthy of the late Brahms intermezzi, culminating in one bar of off-beat suspiration then a glorious spread
of peacock-tail chromatic iridescence before the close. *Tourbillon* –
whirl of lusty rusticity – *Sous bois* its opposite – murmuring
woodland haze, redolent of bodily and mental ease in the green
glades of Courbet or Corot: over deep ostinato-figuration bass,
treble harmonies grow more and more in clashing dissonances that
yet retain the sense of overall indolence and well-being, arching high
under the canopy of foliage, curving low to conclude nourished and
resolved. A piece without which, no Ravel.

Mauresque – what it says; a contribution to French Orientalia as
sharp-etched and sensuous as any of Bizet's. *Idylle – avec fraîcheur
et naïveté*: another pastorale, this one with a dinky touch of the
eighteenth century; amiable tune over ingenious accompaniment
suggesting tambour and double-bass: a walking-number, amble not
stride, broadening towards the end into pure harp-writing, rather
Aeolian than earthy – look at the view! *Danse villageoise*: earthi-
ness again, more vigorous than *Tourbillon* – macho, strutting, genial.
Then *Improvisation* from a different world – Chopin; Schumann; *fantasque et très passionée*, a tourbillon of introspective angst, complex
cross-rhythms and high dissonance-level, sometimes near-bursting
its bond (he was a notorious destroyer of pianos when he improvised): an unusual aspect of his nature, and just as genuine as the
more customary.

Menuet pompeux is home territory: lustiness not countrified;
gone city-wards; a *Bourgeois gentilhomme* with double chin and a
perruque; then in the trio essaying graceful dance-steps which, surprisingly, conquer the bearish bonhomie to achieve delicacy and
poise. Return of the *menuet* triumphantly *pompeux* as before, then
the piece slithers away as though to say 'Look at me! I'll make it!'
to conceal inner doubts that he won't, before sudden precipitate
loud end. Ravel appreciated such subtle uncertainties beneath the
veneer well enough to orchestrate Chabrier's piece (1918), having
already imitated it some twenty-three years before in his own
Menuet antique. Scherzo-Valse; just what it says. Socially somewhere
between three stools – rustic/bourgeois/aristocratic. Royalty playing

milkmaids? Irresistible, whatever. Chabrier orchestrated four of the *Pièces pittoresques* (not including the *Menuet*) to form his *Suite pastorale*: but we want all ten. His other notable solo piano work is the *Bourrée fantasque* of 1891, already described; this wizard of a piece also calls for scoring; he began it himself, abandoned it and I picked it up myself in 1993, in homage.

So to his keyboard music for four hands, at two pianos and at one. The two-piano piece, *Trois valses romantiques* (1883), is a knock-out. The *valses*'s titles are not given in the printed score – inauthentic (just hearsay)? suppressed? They add to the flavour, as one plays them, and for the listener. No. 1 *The Woman of Pleasure* – *très vite et impétueusement* – a volcano of enjoyment and relish, sweeping all before her, coquettish, inviting, abundant in give-and-take (one hears/sees both from the very first page); prink't with characteristic stings of harmonic acid amid the warmth; marvellously laid out across and between the two pianos (there's an orchestration by a German friend/champion of the composer which gets it absolutely wrong, the other two *valses* too). She's followed by no. 2, *The Fat Frau*; again one can almost see her, sprawled in the pinkly illuminated window of a seedy bar in Antwerp or Amsterdam. Begins hearty and buxom, soon turning playful, coyly inviting, suggestive, insinuating; then surprisingly refined, even hesitant, till her native vigour reasserted – an almost circusy middle-section; then return to opening salvo; its playful continuation now wheedling, whimsical, flirtatious, before – does the client pass by on the other side! – closing defiant gesture – a V-sign and a muttered expletive. 'And now the story really begins': the last is far longer and in every way richer. No. 3, *The Beautiful Jewess*, transcends waltz/*valse* into something serious, even grave. Bare soft low unison opening, answered by modal strains up full and high, prophetic of chastely sweet archaic moments in Debussy and Ravel (Ravel and a pianist-friend played the *Trois valses* to Chabrier in the year before his death, in the terminal dementia of tertiary syphilis). Low and high continue their thoughtful exchanges, gradually swelling to three gently climactic suspended dissonances, then easing into a waltz-motion at last – still serious, using the bare unison opening to gradually exfoliate into melodiousness, more fully 'orchestrated', growing in a grave ardour, picking up momentum, developing beautiful new curves of expressivity in ever-varied textures, aching with nostalgia poignant almost to painfulness, building on through wave upon wave till climactic return of the gaunt opening unison, now crashed out *ff* five octaves deep. After this high-point, downwards cantabile canon which both Brahms and Poulenc would have been proud to have written (and Poulenc nearly did), vanishing into a shimmer of tremolos in duple time on a wide-spaced added sixth; thence return to triple time, and the sarabande-like modal music from earlier, and an exquisite chromatic/pentatonic alternation as the beguilingly lovely subject takes her veil and her leave.

A cheeky satyr-pendant is provided by the *Cortège burlesque* for four hands at one piano (1871). Modest in length, goal, medium, yet perfect of its kind – Chabrier linking four-hands with Schubert in gregarious musical sociability. Brief, riotous, characteristic in every detail; the acrobatics of the outer sections – with a wickedly winking *Tristan*-chord – and the warm geniality of the middle-eight with its generous, ardent climax.

Chabrier's songs range wider than the usual agenda for this category-evading composer might suggest. Alongside the celebrated *bestiaire* – little pink pigs, gross pompous turkeys, silly cloned ducklings, crackling cicadas – come songs of sentiment from flirtatious to passionate, glowing evocations of nostalgia, character-sketches saucy, sexy, wistful, droll; and occasional OTT outbursts of pure delirium, like the comedy-duo for the *opéra-comique* usherette and her young man the draper from the market, or the crazy waltz-sequence entitled *Ivresses!* Sometimes slight, sometimes rampageous, always vivid and vital.

Extending the resources: the *Ode à la musique*, for solo soprano, women's chorus and piano, written for a friend's house-warming in 1890, orchestrated the next year. This paragon of tender amorous domesticity hymns '*musique adorable*' ('the composer's Credo', said Debussy) in a six-minute swoon of gentle ecstasy. Ecstasy tumultuous and torrid burns unbridled in *La Sulamite*, also for solo soprano – the Sulamite herself – her female supporters, and with orchestra from the start (first version 1885, reworked 1892). Never can the Song of Songs have deviated so far from the Christian allegory imposed upon it by decorum and prudishness. This torrent of sensuality unleashed can be disconcerting unless the listener is able to abandon all reserve, like the Sulamite herself to her Solomon:

> *Ah! ton amant vers toi tend les bras!*
> *A l'amour ne résiste pas, à l'amour ne résiste pas,*
> *Ah! viens! viens! viens!*

Again, Debussy patently loved this piece, remembering its earlier gentler phases in his setting only a few years later of Rossetti's *Blessed Damozel*, but eschewing the subsequent onset on the wilder shores of love.

Chabrier's purely orchestral repertoire consists of just two pieces, both winners. *España* needs no adjectives – a centre point in the long tale of 'Spanish' music by French composers from Bizet to Ravel and Russian from Glinka to Shchedrin, fresh as a daisy, tart as gazpacho from its launch in 1883. The *Marche joyeuse*, five years later, is better still: 'impossible to have more gaiety, verve, life', wrote a critic at its première. *Ça suffit* – only needing to add wit, timing, good-natured trickery and surprise, subverting 'expectations' (in the opposite sense from what Hans Keller used to require from any good composing).

Finally, the tragi-comedy of his operatic aspirations, *L'Étoile* (1877) and *Une éducation manquée* (1879) present no problems – operettas both, they fit unproblematically between Bizet's *Docteur Miracle* and Offenbach, with Arthur Sullivan to the surprising side, in a living tradition of high-quality light music as imperishable as the heavy of the epoch. *Le Roi malgré lui* (1887) is an operetta *manqué* – an inordinately huge affair – '*cette opérette colossale*', as Reynaldo Hahn said – upon an impossibly intricate and contrived 'plot' – 'a negative tour de force to invent such a confusing story with so few characters in it', said Harry Halbreich; crammed full of inspired music in his most fertile and ardent mode – surpassingly brilliant for the *fête*

polonaise – a 'ballroom scene to end all ballroom scenes', to the surpassingly tender retrospective Venetian love-music. Many attempts
to salvage the sunken treasure, but the cause is lost beyónd the plummet's sounding.

So to 'serious' subjects, swallowed whole by the gormless public
of the epoch; and, sadly, by this highly intelligent composer, so
credulous and naïve: one expects him to have known better. *Gwendoline* (1885), a romance of crossed lovers between enemy nations,
native Anglo-Saxons and invading Viking Danes, would seem to
invite obvious Wagnerism; it resists, to fall into altogether other
troubles – plausibility, for a start. The score is, again – once we've
got past the rampaging Overture, the only bit that's ever (now and
again) played – stuffed with good music. Sometimes – I stick my
neck out – great music; the wonderful *Epithalame* celebrating the
marriage of the miscegenating lovers, with double five-part chorus
(Gwendoline's treacherous father to one side). It'd make a welcome
change from the wedding-music in *Lohengrin* (equally doomed plot-
wise!); and is miles better music.

Briséis: only one act completed, in his last years, before he became
incapable of composition. Another dead duck strung between two
cultures: here, Paganism declining on its way out, versus Christianity arising on its way in (the libretto is loosely after Goethe's *Bride
of Corinth*). The completed act contains some of Chabrier's richest,
ripest, roundest invention, lavished upon an obvious non-starter. His
Ode à la musique makes the fairest conclusion – ardour unto ecstasy
in a context of unidealistic realistic contemporary urbane domesticity, familial affection, humanity à la Vuillard, Bonnard, Renoir,
Manet, Monet.

Franck

Once so sure of his place among the Immortals, esteemed by composers and critical taste, beloved by players and audiences, César
Franck appears nowadays to be almost universally reviled. Of the
late handful of indubitable masterpieces, only the Violin Sonata
still enjoys the affection, admiration and performances previously

accorded the Piano Quintet, the Symphony, the Symphonic Variations for piano and orchestra, and the two sizeable cycles for piano
alone. Organists still adhere to the chorales and other products of
this master of the instrument, the sole composer since Bach to give
it genuine oeuvre till joined by his successor Messiaen. There was
never much of a future for Franck's two operas; but what about a
likelier genre in the two oratorios? And, above all, that towering
final incandescent String Quartet, masterly and masterful, adored by
Proust and principal model for the symbolic Septet in his novel? The
present consensus is that Franck is merely thick, cloying, glutinous,
too sequential, too chromatic, stiff in rhythm and phrasing, mechanized in form and process – especially in the 'motto' idea, laboriously applied, whereby all of a work's themes transfer and transform
across all its movements. Principal bugbear remains an uneasy proximity of erotic fervour – so unabashed as to cause the discreet epi-
curean Saint-Saëns to blanche in disgust – with fervid religiosity, all
incense and unction. All this is true and obvious – to the sympathetic let alone the hostile gaze. Yet the joy Franck's music can give
is, with every reservation fully acknowledged, absolute and special.

The life-pattern is unusual. Belgian-born (Liège, 1822), he went
at thirteen to study in Paris, settling permanently in 1844; from 1853
onward he was organist at the church of Sainte-Clotilde. He made
his way with humble diffidence, slowly achieving calibre, never
celebrity, except within a close circle of younger enthusiasts who
revered his art and his personality alike. Unfortunate circumstances
ensured the abject flop of the two 1870s oratorios, *Les Béatitudes* and
Rédemption. Only in 1879, with the Quintet, did the circle expand: all
the remaining masterpieces date from the subsequent decade – *Les
Djinns* in 1884, next year the Variations, the Violin Sonata the year
after, from 1886–8 the Symphony and the symphonic cantata *Psyché*,
from 1889 the Quartet. He died in 1890, some six months after a col-
lision with a Paris cab: the principal successes were posthumous.

Between an astonishing early Piano Trio (in 1840, an isolated harbinger of things to come) and the works of the 1870s, lie deserts of
copious mediocrity; *Les Éolides* (1876), with its unexpectedly delicious depiction of buffeting, scent-bearing breezes, retains appeal.

But what of the oratorios? *Rédemption* is probably by now past redeeming. Here Franck for once completely fulfils the negative stereotype in a pious orgy of sanctimonious blandness. Awful words don't matter when set to inspired music, but here they are entrusted, frequently and at length, to a speaker, their direness undisguised.

Are the *Béatitudes* just as lost a cause? The scheme is dangerously schematic: each of Christ's eight pronouncements ('Blessèd be the merciful, for they shall obtain mercy', etc.) is illustrated in scena or sermonette or both, then concludes with Vox Christi uttering the sacred words surrounded by an oleaginous halo. Towards the end Satan emerges as counter-protagonist. Having done his damnedest, energetically supported by his infernal cohorts in four-square choruses straight from the pantomime, his voice alternates, then combines, with Jesus' in an ultimate struggle between darkness and light, bizarrely homoerotic in feel and sonority, before he is vanquished, leaving the way clear for celestial alleluias to fill the empyrean till the end of time. The text is fustian *in excelsis* (and its English, in my old copy, reaches unearthly realms of badness beyond the skill of the most devoted parodist). Yet ... the felicity, the radiance, the sheer beauty of the composing transcends this sorry stuff and elevates it to the same level, as music ever has and ever will transform duff conceptions and naff words: the heights are conquered and possessed by its sheer innate power of being. Lovers of Elgar's late oratorios should love *Les Béatitudes* too. *Gerontius*, uneven masterpiece set to another text of dubious worth, makes a closer comparison still. Franck's diabolic chorus is barely more absurd than Elgar's; his celestial serenity a good deal more convincing.

But, of course, it is in their purely instrumental works that both composers attain a quality uncompromised by their religious convictions. By these – a mighty handful in both cases – they are second only to the very greatest. And if you are still put off by Franck's glutinousness, try *Psyché*. Already in the *Éolides* and the *Djinns* (another lovely piece, totally neglected, from the best period), he'd essayed this vein of exotic/oriental luxury with success. In *Psyché* the eroticism of the pagan tale is imbued with the frank sensuality of the instrumental works and the rapt fervour of the Christian. Eros, the joyous reconciliation of the lovers at the end, will surprise and delight listeners who can't stand the Symphony or the Quintet. I spare the listener the perfervid reek of incense emitted from his Catholicism to go direct to its pagan complement. The text of *Psyché* is almost as bad – by Sicard and de Foucard (who they? Cousins of Flaubert's Bouvard and Pécuchet?): harmless frothy poetastry, completely suited to Franck's purpose. But the music is divine and so uninhibited in its eroticism that one seriously wonders at, worries for, this composer's inner life! Yet – so blameless: innocent, unknowing, utterly unsalacious – in a word, *frank* – and pure as a cerise bonbon stuffed with driven snow.

The Symphony remains the crucial test-piece for Franck's cyclic system – themes from individual movements recycled across the whole entity – at its most insistent. But 'this wonderful and most lovable' work (see Tovey's ardently sympathetic description) needs forbearance: Ravel complained of its 'abominable' orchestration, and even when this charge can be lightened, the music and its processes can wax turgid, clammy, browbeating, hectoring.

No such qualms with the *Symphonic Variations* for piano and orchestra (1885), one of its composer's three absolutely unflawed achievements and which also extends his range into unexpected humour, gaiety, fun. Everything is unlaboured; even the scoring is clear, lucid, sometimes even sparkling. Unobtrusively, too, an intellectual tour de force worthy of Schoenberg, though its subtleties and ingenuities are lost in the varied and delightful succession of events on the surface (as things should be, naturally): at once a variation-set and a sort of three-movement symphony, superimposed and interflowing: we perceive a continuity of contrasts – this, then that; no, not that next, but this; next; next – all adding up to more than the sum of its parts. (True also, still more, of the Violin Sonata the following year, 1886, another flawless achievement, whose universal popularity (unlike the *Symphonic Variations*, once a favourite, now sadly neglected) is never in doubt, even extending to performances on cello – passable; and flute – ridiculous.) Felicity, grace, elegance, ease – *bonheur en rose*: it could almost be by Fauré: when erotic, not frenetic – the temperature higher than chez Fauré (the ladies' man in real life of course, unlike the saintly 'Pater Seraphi-cus'). First movement perfection – languor and happiness without ooze or sleaze – sensuous not sensual: the way the home key is avoided, apart from a brief alighting early on, until after the climax, towards the end, is masterly. Harmony that could, intensely used, tear lovers asunder or bind them inseparable in *Tristan* Act II, here glows acute yet relaxing; piano-writing is ample yet open and airy, violin sings free: that climax, when it comes *tutta forza*, remains lyrical for all its power. The second movement, an agitated impas-sioned allegro, strong and tensed without strain, even in the trans-formation of material from the first (the work is, of course, cyclic) from languid and supple to muscular and regular; close a bit barn-storming but still within the parameters. Now a *recitativo-fantasia*, different again use of first-movement material; piano touches darker depths of erotic expression still without murk or biliousness, violin answers in free flight of improvisatory flourish: they join, rising via wild access of passion to a calm even broad-note melody, translu-cently accompanied, exciting up to operatic declamation – '*dram-matico*'; as it simmers down, the first movement briefly looks in, before the third resumes '*molto largamente e drammatico*', lending to a *fff* climax wherein the texture remains clean and clear; it soothes, sweet and sad – '*mesto*' – as preparation for the finale.

The world's best-ever canon? Extraordinarily felicitous and unforced – euphonious and athletic – *mens sana in corpore sano* – radiating well-being spiritual and physical. The piano-part looks lumpy, and certainly requires enormous hands; in the right pair it is both sonorous and transparent. Violin sings linear throughout – in the whole work there are but three double stops (one sets off the dramatic entry in the third movement, the others concluding the second) – and no pizzicato whatever. The canon unrolls excel-lently, yielding to a softer strain on broad calm melody from no. 3, not in canon; then canon resumes, peaking in exhilarating overlap-ping peals of the bells of St Clotilde's. Maybe the reintroduction of main theme from no. 1 is a wee bit stilted: not so the main theme from the third movement coming now in minor, out of canon, building rapidly from very soft to chunky *energico*, piano alone, its motif derived from and reintroducing the *drammatico* from the third movement as just the right thing – twice – second time '*grandioso*', ending in bells and the broad-note melody from earlier in the third movement, equally convincing – especially in not going on too long, winding down as its closing notes transform into the enchantingly engineered return of opening canon, exactly as before, till it closes into the great bells of St Clotilde again, now in home key, ending the whole work in joyous mutual peal, underpinned with piano's chunky *energico*, never once played as such by the violin, though audibly derived from canon-tune's third bar. A happy vindication of the cyclic principle without tears, for a domestic medium used without strain, and though large in conception, even heroic, not all that long.

In the String Quartet, however – Franck's last work (1889) the principles are taxed to their utmost, the timescale is huge, and the medium itself strained to its limits, perhaps beyond. These problems combine to conspire to preclude performances and popularity of what, nevertheless, is far his greatest work, on a different plane even from what precedes it in his late flowering, making his 'early' death all the more regrettable.

First movement, magnificent main theme, presented in vast, ever-expanding paragraphs of massive 'organ'-sonority: it can sound well on the quartet – it *does* sound well; but can't be called idiomatic and must be an enormous strain on the players, as on the medium itself. This is all by way of introduction to an extensive allegro, full-blooded, full-bodied, rich in activity, with occasional oases winding down into a fugue, then resuming more fiery than ever, stretched between climactic fervour and lyric withdrawal, sinking to an eventual tranquillo, all passion spent: almost a complete work in itself, though clearly indicating 'further business'. The ensuing scherzo, a whirligig of speed and legerity, the Zephyrs from *Psyché* in full play: its trio hints momentarily at the first movement, the scherzo's return is re-angled, to disappear in a perfumed twang. Third movement – a hymnic *larghetto* that, again, requires powers of sostenuto and intensity imperilling the medium. Chez Franck with this mood and idiom, unction threatens: it nears, but is avoided absolutely; this music is sacrosanct without becoming sanctimonious, effulgent without effluent – Communion wine *premier cru*. A sudden storm of passion blows up from nowhere, alarming in its erotic charge. Momentarily it subsides only to surge up again into a huge climax, followed by gentle decline into rapt shining third return of main theme, breaking off into stammering hesitation . . . shall we do it again? . . . *can* we? . . . heaving up into *another* huge climax, then down, down, down, into a rather regretful coda, brief after the vastness, in which one suspects that the Celestial Bridegroom wants to get it up a third time (or is it a fourth?). Such a thought doesn't traduce César Franck or his *larghetto*: I'm not putting words into his unworldly mouth: this is manifestly what the music is saying.

Finale, furious allegro, beginning with rough peremptory call-to-attention (distantly derived from material in no. 1), framing naïve recall, after Beethoven's 9th, of previous movements' themes; in reverse order, first the third's, then the second's, then the first's main, opening idea, very slow. Which, when speeded up, proves to be inner part for the finale's *real* main motif. As this *allegro molto* gets going it incorporates the rough opening: then goes remote and mysterious, nearly losing momentum, till picking up again with rough-music flourishes and a strong new theme over surging bass, ever more chunky and strenuous, exploding in forceful repeated double-stop chords, then hurtling on with late-Beethoven violence, for all that the first violin's struggling octaves transform the music first heard remote and mysterious. Many contrasted adventures, all the material in play, work up to principal theme *fff* 'recitando', the work's most strenuous sonority yet. But there's further to go, more to come. Further adventures far and wide, every familiar constituent in unfamiliar alignments and perspectives, everything at work/at play longer than the listener might think possible or bearable, were it not so compulsively compelling.

Another lull, miles from home. He's spent now, surely? No: the slow-down and halt are to introduce the opening the second movement scherzo, in finale tempo and notation; twice, alternating with its unaccustomed new context. At the third attempt, Franck with genius incorporates the alien material and its new context into ongoing resumption of the broken finale – its main theme and the scherzo-stuff combined in fluent counterpoint till – not too far on – the second *coup de théâtre*, vindicating the seeming naïveté of recalling the earlier movements' themes at the finale's start – the climactic return of the whole work's huge structure-process, triumphant return of slow movement melody, its triple-time grouped here into three-bar phrases, riding the storm much as, in the finale of the Symphony, its slow movement tune climactically triumphs, 'climax climaxorum', and much more convincingly achieved, really justified and *earned*. The strain on the listener's credulity is, merely, that the medium can't bear the message adequately.

Mahler would have brought in a choir here: Franck, innately equally melodramatic, has to make do, after the *larghetto* melody has sequenced itself up to massive chords now knocking hard at the door of the home key, with a few further sidesteps – principal theme in several 'wrong' tonalities, cooling down all the way, pausing several times on a question-mark, reaching harbour gently and, after everything, themelessly; till a last-minute stampede to the close, almost perfunctory, on the rough music that the work's final movement has derived from its first.

Not till Schoenberg's 1st String Quartet (1904–5) would any chamber-music be so intensive as this. It brings to mind heavy-laden works for heavier forces – Bruckner's 9th (1890–96) and Mahler's (1909–10): all four are in the same key.

L'école de Franck, *or The Curse of Franckenstein*

In the immediate circle of the Pater Seraphicus, and the entirely compatible shadow cast by Wagnerism over the French music of the last quarter or so of the nineteenth century, come two antithetical major masters, Chabrier and Debussy; one commanding commandeer of ideology, d'Indy; and three smaller figures of very particular calibre – Duparc, Chausson and Dukas. (Another major composer of the culture and the epoch, Fauré, escapes its dangers altogether.)

Summarizing life and work together at the start of each will show the extent of the overlap. The Impresario is the oldest. Vincent d'Indy, born Paris 1851, intended for the Law, took to his real drive, music, and studied from twenty-one at the Conservatoire – everything with Franck, performance as well as the theory and practice of composition. Copious throughout his long life in every genre – stage-works from operetta to '*actions musicales*' à la Wagnerian 'music-drama'; much piano music, some songs, much chamber-music; orchestral works including symphonies and symphonic poems. An autocratic aristocrat, in person and personality. Mission, to spread the gospel of Franck, still-living embodiment of music's ethical/spiritual greatness as prefigured in Beethoven's symphonic and Wagner's operatic oeuvres: Bach evidently too Protestant for this high-tory Catholic patriot (though one wonders how he could explain both the religion and the politics of the chosen touchstones). In this spirit he co-founded in 1894 (Franck now dead for four years) the Schola Cantorum explicitly to foster these ideals so debased elsewhere (i.e. the Conservatoire), and directed it from 1900 until his death in 1931.

Difficult to love this forceful and rebarbative figure, so admirable, indeed noble. Difficult to love his music too: the most appealing is *Istar*, a set of orchestral variations depicting the beautiful Houri's gradual unveiling herself by putting the theme naked at the close; and the *Symphonie sur un chant montagnard français*, a welcome blast of fresh air. The career is unimpugnable – a Success. The other principals in *L'école de Franck* are variously doomed to suffer the Curse of Franckenstein; blighted even to tragedy in their lives, their art to a greater or lesser degree unfulfilled: yet in the few pieces that escape, something burns almost as precious as in any of their taskmaster's.

DUPARC

Henri Duparc, born Paris 1848; as a boy taught piano by Franck, later becoming his pupil for composition: sadly truncated creative life – a rather constipated symphonic poem *Lénore*, various other bits-and-bobs; but his fame rests firmly upon a handful of published songs with piano. Others were destroyed, and from 1885 onwards he was

smitten with an unexplained nervous ailment, intermittently composing in the long years till his death in 1933, burning the results as
they were written.

Thirteen songs with piano (for all that their sometimes sumptuous overwriting suggests orchestration, Duparc's later instrumentations are curiously ineffective), of which seven are peaks of the
repertoire, three fair-to-middling and three (un)arguably flops, albeit
clearly by the same composer, and here and there closely related to
the triumphs. No composer of stature reposes upon a yield so slender.

Flops first: *Le Manoir de Rosemonde*; music as stilted in heroic
defiance as its poem – 'You can follow my blood trail, bitten by
love's voracious tooth, throughout the world, if the pursuit doesn't
weary you; and find that far, far off, I have died without discovering
the blue abode of Rosemonde.' Franck's *Chausser maudit* has heavily
hit this bombastic effort, though its penultimate dying fall indicates potential distinction and individuality. *Testament* surges and
billows on 'the black wings of remorse, withered by your beauty,
scorched by your eyes, swallowed by the abyss' – splurge and fury
signifying nothing much here, that will elsewhere be charged up to
reach heights not depths. *Sérénade florentine*, however, is unpretentious and unexaggerated: slight but not a flop – a sweet love-song,
deftly tender à la Fauré.

The first range of *suprêmes* are also love-songs. Perhaps greatest of
the four, *Elégie* is also something else by virtue of its text, a French
version of Tom Moore's verses on the death of his countryman, the
Irish patriot Robert Emmet:

> Oh! Breathe not his name, let it sleep in the shade,
> Where cold and unhonour'd his relics are laid.

The rest easier given in a translation of the translation: 'We weep
silent as the dew, but our silent tears will keep his memory green in
our hearts.' But the musical language and feeling are more amorous
than patriotic: the distant model for momentum and texture
is *Träume* from Wagner's *Wesendonck-Lieder*; a closer cousin lies
nearer to hand in Fauré's *Après un rêve* – pulsing repeated chords

under a two-note descending lament, now and then burgeoning into counter-melody to the voice's beautifully shaped parlando: the harmonic control is consummate. With night dew and silent tears, the accompaniment begins to ripple and the two-note figure to intensify, underpinning a sustained climactic arc as erotic as elegiac – they have loss and longing in common; and a quick end reaching tonic major consonance-cadence only at closing time.

The other three are unambiguously songs of loss: *Soupir* – 'Never to see or hear her again, to wait for ever, to stretch out one's arms, to weep, to love her ever more tenderly – in vain – for ever.' An exquisitely spaced, gently dissonant accompaniment, missing each first beat except in the bass: voice, when it enters, on a characteristically not-quite melody. Harmony grows quite *Tristan*-esque as the song expands, to end with exact repeat of first stanza, then two bars of repose – '*toujours*'. *Extase* is similar in momentum, but different in shape, posing the poem between a piano prelude – an arch of cantabile rather than a brief expressive figure much repeated – which then returns, an octave higher, before the singer repeats exactly the same music to the changed words: first, 'on a pale lily my heart slumbers, sweet as death – exquisite extinction, perfumed by my belovèd's breath'; second, 'on her pale breast my heart slumbers, in a sleep sweet as death'. The piano then gently closes, alone, this ravishing erotic lullaby – *Tristan* Act II for the salon, not so close as Wolf's directly comparable *Bedeckt mich mit Blumen*: Wagner refracted through Franck. And, most beautiful of these four, Duparc's, *Chanson triste*. And not so sad! 'Gentle summer, moonlight sleeps within your heart; let me drown me in your radiance – I will forget all my grief when you soothe me in your arms – you will comfort my troubled head – I will in your eyes drink so much love that, perhaps … I shall … be well.' Not so sad indeed: and the muted rapture of the setting settles any doubts: this song is as explicitly fulfilled in tenderness as any in Fauré's *Bonne Chanson*. Especially subtle, the intermittent little 'catch' in the rippling accompaniment, gradually taking on the role of another voice amorously entwining with the singer's till, poem complete, the piano has a few bars' coda with both parts in play.

Two longer, more ambitious *mélodies*, hovering on the cusp of top-calibre. *Lamento* sets Théophile Gautier – *Au cimetière* – already used by Berlioz in *Les Nuits d'été*. Duparc tightens his structure, and his intensity, by cutting the text by slightly over half, producing 'more of same'. Its burden goes –

> Do you know that whitened tomb where falls the shadow of a yew? From its darkness comes the sound of a dove, pale and sad in the setting sun. One would say the departed soul sang from below in sympathy. Nevermore will I return to that grave when evening falls, to hear there the pale dove's plaintive song from the branch of the yew.

Verse 1 in parlando, the voice introduced by fine richly sonorous lamento-chords from the piano, recurring to close, and start verse 2, musically identical. For verse 3 ('Ah! Never-more . . .') the calm solemn texture enlivens with subterranean turbulent figuration and expressive inner parts occasionally overlapping the now-eloquent voice: the lamento-figure is worked in, the modulations enrich the luscious melancholy, the dove's pallor and the saturnine yew are forgotten; the song closes as it had opened, once again plain chords, no busyness. The stature of *Phidylé* is harder to ascertain. Stretches of this *mélodie* are sublime: its climax can, under unfortunate fingers, approach the ridiculous.

Finally, two triumphs and one more dud, placed here because its failure defines and enhances the nature of the successes in others of these songs. *La Vague et la cloche* is a preposterous affair. The poet, knocked out by drink, dreams of drifting off, rudderless, goalless, onto a dark turbulent sea –

> at the height of horror, suddenly everything changed: the black chaos of the waves sank away – I was alone in an ancient belfry, astride a rocking bell, convulsively donging it till it made the fabric quake. Why doesn't my dream tell me what God purposes with all this din and toil, the futile life of mankind?

The sea-section is all bombastic surge, the bell-sequel builds up a three-note ostinato into a frenzy of menace that wouldn't hurt a bat; the eternal question is suitably heroic/rhetorical rodomontade, and it all signifies nothing much. Yet the same means are employed to grand effect in the first of two Baudelaire-settings, *La Vie antérieure* (Duparc's poets not named for the most part because they are – for the most part – poetasters): an apex of romantic exoticism, nostalgically hankering for the impossible Ideal – the anterior life, 'prior to this dull Now, set amid vast porticoes tinged by the setting sun, harmonized by the music of the sea-swell mirroring the heavens; the life of voluptuous calm, azure-tinted, fanned by naked slaves solicitous only to enhance the secret grief gnawing at my being.' Stately processional opening paragraph evokes the grand porticoes; the surge of sea mirroring the music of the skies is rendered in complex figuration and enrichment of harmonic movement towards a brilliant virtuoso flourish – '*there*! it is there I have lived' – heroic declamation over pounding repeated chords, entirely without bombast, indeed rapidly diminished in volume even while intensifying into deeper poignancy exactly capturing the poem's secret melancholy, longing, loss. Even before the singer ceases, the piano has begun to uncurl the longest line in all Duparc's *mélodies* – fifteen bars of epilogue encapsulating in a nonpareil of nostalgia the complex ambiguous emotion.

Another celebrated poem yields another perfect match; Baudelaire again: *L'Invitation au voyage*. Baudelaire's associated prose-poem doesn't name the '*pays superbe, un pays de Cocagne*' as a transfiguration of the prosaic flat-lands of Holland into a terrain of magic: content, rather, to suggest 'the Orient of the West, the China of Europe'. The poem itself, a quintessence, is still less specific – all is generalized into rapture, indolence, ease – '*ordre et beauté / Luxe, calme, et volupté*' – these last two words also occur conjoined in *La Vie antérieure*. The real canals of the Low Countries are exoticized into an imaginary East, the land of smiles, Wonderland. Subtle of the composer to set the famous motto to a stilled monotone – one note for its first line, another, lower, for its second, the words murmured, almost whispered, inside the luminous wide-spaced harmony that gently fixes and stills the song's initial motion, an effortless gliding, as shining and even as the melody unfurled in the voice. Wisely, Duparc omits Baudelaire's second stanza describing the interior furnishings of the barge: more would clearly be less. Baudelaire's third stanza thus makes Duparc's second: outdoors still as the declining sun bathes fields, canals, cities, in hyacinth and gold. Initially identical to the first: as the light brightens even as it deepens, the texture quickens and rises, the low sonorous bass is lost, the figuration sparkles rapid and high (another place where the composer's own orchestration absolutely fails – in his original, piano swathed in pedal resonance is just right), till at the word *lumière* the deep fundamental bass is resumed, sounding on from this glorious moment all the way to the end and its second setting of the motto – voice as before on monotone murmur/whisper, now surrounded with delicate high filigree new to this second stanza, together with fragments of melody from the first in the pianist's left hand, all over the softly renewed resonating depths, gradually then lifted as the delicate arpeggio-patterns decline, coalesce, disappear upwards to the song's highest chord, undernourished by the depths till they are softly touched in for a fourth time, *ppp* echo of the *ff* climax as if it could go on reverberating for ever: as perfect a fusion of word-image-emotion-sonority as music can show.

CHAUSSON

Ernest Chausson, born Paris 1855 of well-to-do family; trained to the Law, coming relatively late – mid-twenties – to music; composition lessons with Massenet, moving on to Franck, more congenial to his earnest/serious nature. Close friend of the young Debussy, several years his junior (there's an enchanting photograph of them in boaters, and their ladies with parasols, al fresco á la Monet with picnic on the banks of the Seine). Together they struggled with the overwhelming impact of Wagner: Chausson lost, Debussy won (but Debussy later lost his old fellow-fighter's friendship: Chausson could not tolerate Debussy's profligate lifestyle). Output small and

distinguished: a single Symphony (1889–90) inevitably Franck-
ian, though with its own freshness; chamber-music; some attractive songs with piano, and, with orchestra, the *Poème de l'amour et
de la mer* (1882 onwards), whose closing number, *Le Temps des lilas*,
perfectly captures the lavender nostalgia of the epoch, whose most
extended expression comes in the opening volumes of Proust. One
perfect piece, the *Poème* for violin and orchestra (1896); the only
completed opera *Le Roi Arthus* (1886–95) wherein his struggle to
banish Wagnerism is manifestly unsuccessful. Tragic death in a
cycling accident 1899, aged forty-four.

(A few salient early dates for Debussy here, to compare with
his immediate contemporaries within the same musical culture:
born 1862; early piano lessons: Conservatoire 1873 – brief contact
with Franck's class not congenial – he studied else-wise: wins Prix
de Rome 1884, returning to Paris 1887: at work on his opera after
Maeterlinck's *Pelléas et Mélisande* throughout the 1890s, overlapping with Chausson's on his Arthurian venture at one end, and at
the other with Dukas' *Ariane et Barbe-Bleu*, also to a Maeterlinck
original. Debussy of course becomes something quite Other: for
later.)

Chausson – well-named – was more Ernest than his friend, a
slow developer prone to doubts and scruples, German-facing, more
bound to tradition. And he's not in the same league: there's too
much conscientious homework and dutiful piety. The bolder, leaner
spirit with his utterly original way of hearing was able to embrace
a liberating range of exotic influences, thus severing himself from
his immediate origins even while retaining their loving tincture,
transformed into something strange and new. Any young composer
in *fin de siècle* Paris was fated to be in thrall to Wagner. Chausson
made the obligatory pilgrimages to Munich and Bayreuth to soak
himself in *Tristan* and *Parsifal* well before they crossed the Rhine. As
with Debussy (who joined the sacred trail rather later) the struggle
to compose their respective operas is the struggle to slough off the
overwhelming, irresistible seduction of these omnipotent origins.
The correspondence of the late 1880s and early 90s vividly recounts
the conscious need to escape the 'poison' of 'Old Klingsor, alias

R. Wagner'. Debussy, fleeter of foot, gets away. Chausson, for all his alerted-ness to 'that frightful Wagner who blocks my path', falls in the attempt to flee and is caught up in the spokes.

Le Roi Arthus and *Pelléas et Mélisande* are both close variants upon Wagner's *Tristan* in story. Chausson's plot (his own libretto) is more literally related. Its source is also Celtic, its core also an adulterous triangle wherein the older husband is deceived by his beautiful young queen and his most devoted knight in a context of chivalry dishonoured. For Marke/Isolde/Tristan, substitute Arthur/Guinevere/Lancelot. Betrayal is brought about by the lovers' envious rival (Melot/Mordred) and, more subtly, by what lies within, whether death-devoted affinity or something rotten with carnal desire. Guinevere has no maid to correspond with Isolde's crafty confidante Brangäne who sets the entire machinery in motion: but Lancelot's faithful Lyonnel exactly matches Tristan's Kurwenal.

Yet in purely musical affinity, *Parsifal* looms far larger than *Tristan* in both *Arthus* and *Pelléas*. True, Chausson's opera evokes all Wagner's mature oeuvre, even including the resolutely *bürgerlich Meistersinger* and the epic-fairy-tale *Ring*, sometimes so explicitly as to make one smile. Debussy's fastidious care to cover his Wagnerian traces ensures that his opera is less prone to inadvertent reminiscence; the cost is a certain pallor that, of course, is inseparable from its unique mastery of atmosphere and suggestion. Perhaps just because *Parsifal* tends in this direction already, its magical refinements of harmony and texture can be sensed at every evasive passage of *Pelléas*: while the choral finale of *Le Roi Arthus* takes the closing pages of *Parsifal* as its unambiguous starting-point for a closure of ethereal radiance quite different in effect, and surely its composer's finest quarter-hour.

Another composer, of lesser note, whose trajectory overlaps: Albéric Magnard: born Paris 1865; Conservatoire 1886, pupil of Massenet, from whom, like Chausson, he deserted to align himself with Franck and, later, with d'Indy: a strong personality evinced in symphonies, chamber-music, and, among three operas, *Guercoeur*, saturated in Wagnerism; but never quite achieving full artistic contour. Met heroic death, defying the advancing enemy early in the Great War (September 1914).

DUKAS

Better known than Magnard, Paul Dukas: born Paris 1865 into prosperous Jewish banking-family: Conservatoire aged sixteen, overlapping with Debussy (three years older); not a Franck-pupil, though within his influence. A failed Prix de Rome entrant; takes up career as composer and critic. Slow worker, inhibited, if not silenced, by diffidence and perfectionism. His Symphony (1895–6), inevitably shadowed by Franck's, not quite yet itself: this happens the next year (1897) with *The Sorcerer's Apprentice* – still very living, this unforgettable telling of Goethe's ballad, whose popularity at the expense of his other music came to resemble the later case of Ravel's *Boléro*. Big serious d'Indy-esque piano-works. Opera *Ariane et Barbe-bleue* (1899–1906); parallel with Debussy's *Pelléas*, which was eventually produced 1902 – same general musical ambience, same particular librettist. This also with his next sizeable piece, *La Péri* (completed 1912) – a ballet in exotic/erotic subject unfortunately not taken up, as wished, by Diaghilev – lost as the lustre of Stravinsky's *Firebird* (1910) swept all other such colourful ventures to the side. (Here Debussy too is a loser; his directly comparable erotic/exotic ballet *Khamma* (1912) sank without trace; then in 1913 his masterpiece on a contemporary theme, the ballet *Jeux*, was blown away in the scandal over *The Rite of Spring*.)

Like Duparc, Dukas lived long, though not in depressed isolation: an outstanding teacher at the Conservatoire. Messiaen – himself to become such for later generations – pays ardent homage to the man and his music. But in his last years he composed virtually nothing, though possibly destroying more substantial works than the few he let pass. He died 1935.

Ariane et Barbe-bleue is Dukas' most sustained and impressive achievement. Maeterlinck's symbolist adaptation of the timeless tale was, unlike his *Pelléas*, intended for music: the two have more in common than the fleeting appearance of Mélisande among the serial bigamist's previous wives. Act I: Ariane, latest conquest of mysterious Duke Bluebeard, arrives at his castle with her Nurse. Already we sense, in off-stage peasantry voicing their hatred, the sinister power he never manifests directly. Ariane has been given keys to seven locked doors, with licence to open the first six – the seventh is prohibited. She despises the permitted, but the Nurse opens them one by one, revealing Bluebeard's treasury – successively amethysts, sapphires, pearls, emeralds, rubies, diamonds – gorgeous opportunity for any composer in music's most opulent epoch. Of course, only the forbidden door interests her: when opened, it reveals treasure human not jewelled – the song of Bluebeard's five previous wives (Mélisande among them – Dukas cites her motif from Debussy's opera), welling up from deep down. Bluebeard appears, to prevent his newest bride descending to join her predecessors. The angry peasantry break in: she assures them that she has come to no harm.

But in Act II she has joined her sisters in the vaults: she urges them to seek freedom. They are weak, cowed, craven; Bluebeard has broken their spirit; they desire only to remain in servitude. Despite this, Ariane leads them up from darkness into light . . . (here Act III begins) . . . and in their tyrant's absence they begin to relish their release, spreading wide the wealth he has hoarded. Returning, he's set upon by the peasants and brought into the castle, wounded and enchained, for what the folk take to be just retribution at the hands of his victims. Not so: the women tend his injuries, indulge and pamper, even flirt with him. Even Ariane, the New Woman, comes to feel compassion for the failed male. She frees him, and sets out, with her Nurse, into pastures new, the wide-open world, inviting her five sisters to accompany her.

Obvious problem, the denigration of the male principle/principal. Bluebeard's role is minuscule: Ariane dominates vocally and dramatically; even the Nurse and the five wives have more to sing, though the part for the populace is nearly as exiguous as the off-stage sailors in *Pelléas*. The imbalance of vocal timbres is as unfair to the music as the ideology, implicit or explicit, of the story. Clearly conscious, perhaps intentional; but the listener resents the loaded scales; we tire, and so does the poor soprano.

The music, though, is often fine enough to still the doubts: lingua franca vintage 1900 plus/minus: Russian; Franck/Chausson/d'Indy: much whole-tonerie, but not à la Debussy, surprisingly absent apart from the homage implied by the quotation; some Wagner – Wagner Debussy-fied rather than direct form source: Messiaen prophesied (he loved his old teacher's work); and, overall, a very telling comparison with Bartók's treatment of the same tale, only a few years on from Dukas' and springing from many of the same stylistic elements. All in all, a noble work, the emanation of a distinguished mind: but one's pleasures, and loyalties, remain firmly located in *The Sorcerer's Apprentice*.

Italian opera

My problems with Italian opera are fundamental: I've always found its conventions limited and futile, its plots a succession of 'unresisting imbecilities' and its music uninteresting. Musically I am a Hun – 'Bach to Brahms', with a twentieth-century extension for Strauss, Mahler, Schoenberg and his great pupils, and a special cathedral dedicated to Bruckner. But also a listed Francophile – Bizet, Chabrier, Fauré, Debussy, Ravel, Messiaen, all rank high in the Pavilion of Pleasure: and a Russophile – Tchaikovsky, Musorgsky, Rachmaninov. I came early to Bartók and Stravinsky (and as a composer, though a convicted kleptomaniac, owe more to these two than to any others). I came late to Sibelius but early to Janáček. Much American music I love – Ives, Copland: admire – Ruggles, Carter, Crawford, Nancarrow, Feldman, Del Tredici: and worship – a special shrine for Gershwin. The post-Second World War avant-garde at its best – some Boulez, most Ligeti, Stockhausen in moderation, Berio for fun – isn't accounted alien. And I am English to the core, blood and bone: the Tudors, the Jacobeans, Purcell; Elgar; on a good day Delius, Vaughan Williams, Holst; Tippett and Britten; with Percy Grainger (not quite English, of course) as perpetual source of refreshment and surprise.

Excepting Berio, not a single Italian; and they only do *opera*; when at its peak – Mozart, Wagner – the art's most complex and significant genre. All my life I've wrestled and prayed with this endlessly rewarding fusion of sight/word/deed into music, their combination continuing to evolve within and quicken mind and spirit with no depth unsounded. How to take seriously the 'unreformed' opera of Rossini, Donizetti, Bellini, Verdi, with its ice-cream tunes, rum-tum accompaniments, raucous orchestration, formal routines – all those cabalettas and cadenzas evincing craven submission to mere vocality – its slavish stage-craft, its ludicrous plots?

I exaggerate the caricature: time has mellowed but not fundamentally changed the attitude. 'I see not feel' the irresistible brio of *Viaggio a Reims* and the grandeur emerging fully formed in *William Tell*, the affecting pathos of *Lucia di Lammermoor*, the fine-spun melodic finesse of *Norma*: and in Verdi, of course, the fire, fervour, fertility; the Shakespearean humanity; the way that the crude earlier habits, conventions, idioms, scoring, etc. are gradually, down his long career, infiltrated from within, understood, *used*, eventuating at last into living substance. Then there's Puccini: no cavil with his orchestration (consummate); reservations, sometimes drastic, concern the frequent squalor of plot and subject-matter, the mix of sadism and masochism, the emotional manipulation (unfailingly effective) that has its victims wringing their Kleenex and calling out for an ambulance.

Here follow brief outlines for three of these five composers; with a few jotted thoughts en route, and rather more for Verdi and Puccini.

Gioachino Rossini: born 1792; teenage ease, gaiety, sureness of touch already, viz. the delectable sonatas for strings (1804 – aged twelve). Opera first phase – *farse* and *buffa* with some *seria* elements: highlights *L'italiana in Algeri* (1813); *Il turco in Italia* (1814); *Il barbiere di Siviglia* (1816): their animal spirits, the unstoppable fizz of felicitous fun, rapidly swept the continent. Second phase – subjects growing serious, sentimental/fairy-tale/heroic; sources from antiquity and the Old Testament, Shakespeare, Tasso, Racine, Scott: highlights *Otello* (1816); *La Cenerentola* (Cinderella) (1817); *La gazza ladra* (1817); *Mosè in Egitto* (1818); *Ermione* (1819); *La donna del lago* (1819); *Semiramide* (1823). The least living part of the oeuvre now: if *Otello*, Verdi; if Babylonian/Egyptian, *Aida*; if Moses, Schoenberg; if Cinderella or the Lady of the Lake, Tchaikovsky.

Opera third phase and last – two Specials amid several *réchauffés*: *Il viaggio a Reims* (1825); tied to its one-off Occasion, the coronation of Charles X of France at Rheims that year; no plot whatsoever – vaudeville/revue – and as such liberated and original, brimming with the verve of Phase One on a new level of intoxication and absurdity: transformed three years later into *Le Comte Ory* with some good new additions, but the best material recycled from *Viaggio* is compromised, even spoilt. And *Guillaume Tell* (1829); French Grand Opera (in French, for Paris, though subject Swiss and original play – Schiller's – German); a different world, large-scale, cutting deeper into plot and characters, richer in harmony, texture, orchestration, achieving real romantic sublimity, most especially in the closing scene as, after the storm, sunlight shines out over the newly united motherland; hugely admired by, and not lost on, Berlioz and Wagner.

Tell might have been the mighty Opening: instead, there followed the debased grand spectaculars of Auber, Halévy, Meyerbeer, so deplored (again) by Wagner and Berlioz. Rossini at the peak of powers and fame, not yet forty, on the threshold of a new kingdom: a combination of circumstances – mainly the frenzied overworking that had produced so much so rapidly – excited a nervous collapse. Decades of ill-health and depression ensued; with, except the *Stabat Mater* (1832 six numbers; in 1841 all ten), virtually no composing at all. Late 1850s health, spirits recover, and with them music – 'sins of old age', miscellany of songs, choruses, piano-pieces, etc. full of spritely invention, gracing the last years of, by now, a celebrated wit, wag, host, gastronome, *bon vivant*. One work of size from this time – *Petite Messe solennelle*, with harmonium and two pianos (1863–4), scored for full orchestra 1867. He died the next year.

Next in succession Gaetano Donizetti, 1797–1848: the exemplar of the Italian Opera Machine; facile and copious, amiable and empty:

the going-conventions of the genre do most of the work – sixty-five operas! Subjects mainly romantic/historical – *Lucrezia Borgia*, *Anna Bolena*, *Maria Stuarda* and such. Three touchstones: *L'elisir d'amore* (1831) for the quintessence of the comic/sentimental vein; *Don Pasquale* (1843) for lightness of touch in the purely comic; *Lucia di Lammermoor* (1835) for its pathos and fragile beauty, overcoming propensity to laughter or self-parody in the famous mad-scene with flute and glass harmonica; and the fine sextet, prototype of Verdi's subsequent mastery of the operatic ensemble. Thence to Vincenzo Bellini, 1801–35: consumptive master of the chaste, long-spun-out singing line epitomized in *Casta diva* from *Norma* (1831), deeply admired by Wagner and seminal for Chopin. Every other parameter is primitive – harmony, rhythm, counterpoint, orchestration, characterization, plot. His last opera *I Puritani* (1834–5) shows great advances in all these except the last – the story is as preposterous as ever.

Verdi

Giuseppe Verdi, fulfilment of the genre: born 1813; juvenile experience as church organist, formal musical training from age twelve; aged nineteen turned down by the Milan Conservatorio; studies privately while continuing to try for ecclesiastical appointments. First opera and first marriage 1836 – the opera successful, the marriage tragic, wife and both children dying within the next few years. Other early operatic performances dismal failures; first real success *Nabucco* (1842); thereafter a pretty steady succession of new works (often revised later) with intermittent flops and mounting hits: highlights *Macbeth* (1847); *Rigoletto* (1851); *Il trovatore* and *La traviata* (both 1853); *Un ballo in maschera* (1859); *La forza del destino* (1862). Recognition both national – 'Viva VERDI' taken up from 1859 as coded clarion-call for 'Vittorio Emanuele Re d'Italia' – and universal, Europe from St Petersburg to London, and the New World. Last and greatest works: highlights *Don Carlos* (1867, revised 1884); *Aida* (1871); *Requiem* in memory of Manzoni (1873–4, its concluding *Libera me* dates from a corporate tribute to Rossini, 1869); the 1881 revision of *Simon Boccanegra* (originally of 1857) introduces Arrigo Boito as collaborator – he'd mooted an *Otello* in 1879 (the project was completed 1886), and Boito also wrote a libretto for a further Shakespeare adaption, *Falstaff*, composed 1890–92. *Te Deum* and *Stabat Mater* (1895–6), joining two previously isolated smaller choral numbers of the late 1880s to form *Four Sacred Pieces*. Died 1901 aged eighty-seven.

Un ballo in maschera can stand for all Verdi's operas till the great final four. Its action is incredible, ludicrous, laughable, implausible: the work is redeemed through the blazing intensity by which its music charges up plot and persons, and the standard idioms and conventions it continues to employ, into something compelling and convincing. Verdi is always able to find the core of emotional truth within the stilted, fustian, trite, clichéd, absurdity of every situation the libretto offers: incredibility is silenced: the authenticity of the music burns away disbelief.

Ballo's background is absurd enough. Desperately short of time to fulfil a contract for Naples in 1857, Verdi abandoned his long-held yearning for a *King Lear* to take up an earlier libretto (already set by another back in 1833) concerning the assassination in 1792 of Gustav III of Sweden. To show a monarch's murder on-stage was completely unacceptable to the censors: they insisted upon placing something so sensitive in a remote time and place – seventeenth-century Pomerania at first; then, after a failed attempt upon the life of Napoleon III, fourteenth-century Florence, and not a king but a duke. Verdi demurred, was sued for breach of contract, the case settled out of court. The subject was permitted to stand so long as the action was removed from Europe altogether. From various possibilities, the eventual choice of seventeenth-century Boston is surely unlikeliest of all: most modern productions restore action and character to whatever historical accuracy can be mustered. But authenticity in this sense is as remote from *Ballo*'s true value as Boston from Stockholm.

Plot is preposterous: but its telling is always plausible whether pathetic, painful, melodramatic, or just hilarious: and characterization is masterly and unforgettable throughout – we can see and feel for Oscar the lively young pageboy (a trouser-role), his counterpart the baleful Ulrica, the feckless Riccardo, his faithful counsellor Renato, whose wife Amelia dangles between the two, equally with the jolly pair of conspirators. Crucial scenes – marital embarrassment under the shade of the gallows, prolonged denouement and death at the masked ball itself – are strong and deep-searching. Everything in the score is tight, sure-footed; continuity and pacing excellent, always on the move even when slowing for a set-piece: an overall integrity of aim always concentrated upon the object.

But how often, and how much, would one wish to hear this music as *music*, like a Bach cantata, a Haydn quartet, a Mozart quintet, a Beethoven sonata, a Schubert song? And where's the value of the preposterous story (even when returned to Gustav III and 1792 Stockholm) in the face of the manifest human plausibility of a *Figaro*, or the comprehensive psychological grasp and depth of Wagner, whatever the distance imposed by legend/romance/myth? Or am I applying the wrong expectations?

Some brief reflections on four later operas. Their plots in full are easily accessible, though not always easy to comprehend. That of *Simon Boccanegra* is the most tangled of all; oblique, and cursed with a difficult time-lapse during which identities, even names, seem to get lost to their own confusion as well as the listener's. There is some superb music amid the debris. *Don Carlos* is Verdi's largest and most ambitious canvas, and as such, a Sacred Cow to the devotee: but very uneven, ranging from sublime to ridiculous; and confused, perhaps compromised, by conflicting versions and whether it goes best in French or Italian. *Otello* has the same grandeur, scope, ambition, with a plausible if painful plot, convincing characters and music at consistently high voltage. Pacing is marvellous throughout, and extraordinarily varied: the trajectory of Act I, from cataclysmic opening storm via delicious flickering bonfire of thanksgiving and relief, to intimations of malign motivation, a drinking-song whose forced brio carries it forward; an ugly fight checked by Otello's commanding re-entry; to the clear, starry night under whose radiance he and Desdemona renew their tender earliest vows, culminating in the Kiss.

In Act II the manipulative machinery instigated by Iago rapidly advances: his celebrated *Credo* unveils his real not his pretended motivation. Highlight of Act III, the greatest tragic ensemble in all Verdi's oeuvre, as the contradictory strands weave together towards full utterance: foreground of seven principals at sixes and sevens, all upon a musical basis simple in itself – Verdi is no Teuton: the complexity lies within the situation. Aftermath, Otello's delirious collapse in sight and hearing of all, The Lion of Venice abject and humiliated, Iago triumphant and crowing – a marvellous curtain.

Act IV is virtually perfect: classic essentiality reaching the core with frugal restraint and not a false touch for Desdemona in her distress – woodwind *tinta*, cor anglais, hollow low clarinets, lachrymating oboes – the pathos of Ophelia, Barbara, Willow Song – bare high flute and cavernous bassoons – the moment of major amid prevailing minor heartbreaking, as too the farewell to Emilia – the *Ave Maria* well on the right side of religious kitsch. So, to Otello's stealthy entry and the double-bass's bottom string *ppp* – 'the most terrible moment in all music-drama'. Dreadful scene between the two: and the inevitable end is nigh.

As well as the storm, the Kiss, the ensemble, the Willow Song, the score abounds in incidental felicities of a high order: take the suggestiveness of Iago's lying evocation of Cassio, asleep at his side, murmuring words of gratified desire for Desdemona that rebound with creepy erotic beauty upon Iago's own ambiguous sexuality: such moments place Verdi among the subtlest of operatic psychologists. Yet Iago's *Credo* ... high ham corn and cod, right for the purpose but as shallow musically as the nullative emptiness of the words. And the moment of the murder – after the frisson of genuine terror as the murderer first enters his wife's bedchamber, this diminished seventh *fff* tutti plus syncopations! 'Old habits die hard'; such crudity suspends involvement; all is externalized. Then, as so often, the tedious and superfluous explanations after the catastrophe: as at the very comparable juncture near the end of *Tristan* we want to cut the fuss and go direct to what will *truly* explain, with or without words – the *Liebestod* that recasts the lovers' earlier duet; the Kiss that reunites his victim with her slayer, victim of himself. That Otello's jealousy is so easily roused, so discrepant, so absolutely wrong, is never explored: his trouble is innate, and fundamental.

Falstaff: to my knowing and unwilling loss I can't join the universal chorus of acclaim for and delight in Verdi's last opera: the miracle of such creative self-renewal in old age, in a new area hitherto unventured, is prodigious; the calibre in small and large is twenty-four carat; the invention, the pacing, the characterization, the zest/wit/speed, the humanity – all is beyond praise let alone cavil. Highlights: the imbroglio closing Act I, four women in triple-time, four men in common-time, one young lover in a rapt world of his own, is breathtaking: the scene at Herne's Oak in Act III – midnight, woodland magic, fairy-music, mischief and comeuppance afoot, teasing and exposure, young love tenderly victorious, acquiescence all-round, forgiveness, geniality, humanity, uniting all ten principals and the chorus in the closing fugue. But 'I don't feel it here', as Dr Leavis used to say, clutching his heart. There's too much fuss and bother.

Recognition and respect from without the charmed consensus melts into genuine liking and love when *Aida* hoves into view. From a distance the sonorous *tinta* of this work is dominated by memories of the Triumphal March. Close to, it's the subtlety and delicacy of the sound, in harmony, melody and (above all) scoring, that captivate. The plot mixes familiar elements with depth and passion, eschewing the commonplace; and the characterization matches in both power and sensitivity. Set-pieces occur naturally, growing out of plot and character as they ramify.

Act I prelude, later seen as depicting Aida herself: Radamès' hymn to her beauty and his love for her, *Celeste Aida*, is a joy: the trio for him and the two women, unconscious rivals for his love, is fine – very ingenious, to hinge upon *ritorna vincitor!* with its different meanings for all three: Aida's characteristic music deepens her depiction at every recurrence: and the first finale is a riot of rampant Orientalism, with touches of solemn Masonry and some delicious dances. Act II the situation between heroine and rival further explored before the second finale already looms. This is *it*: Verdi's here equals Wagner's flair for big processions, simultaneously pompous and genuinely grand: then more exotic dances, almost up to Tchaikovsky. But this lavish finale also contains continually advancing matter vital to the plot and its personages. Amonasro's number very lovely, and some of the other vocal writing worthy of the *Requiem*. A grand ensemble – OK; Triumphal March return, just right; slightly flat end. Act III concentrates upon plot – conflicting loyalties, personal, familial, patriotic: betrayal is mooted, then escaping the nets: musically sufficient – not especially memorable, after the delicate initial soundscape evoking the River Nile under starry night-sky – enchanting.

Then Act IV rises to the heights. Amneris in confusion and perturbation – the *non* love-duet between her and the man who prefers her rival yields slightly stock invention for the work's tensest situation. Amneris in abjection and abasement is its strongest study, especially here, her passions tearing her in every contrary direction. So to the final finale, the double scene, lovers suffocating below in their tomb, Amneris without, distant priestesses at sacred songs and dances. The lovers' duet is celestial indeed, with its strange intervals at once tortuous and serene; the rejected one prays in contrition, and every stylistic trope and cliché in Verdi's output is transcended. Amneris has the final words, very strong even as she mutters and gutters out – a close with no concession to any audience whatever, let alone that gathered in Cairo to celebrate the opening of its opera house, coincidental with the completion of the Suez Canal.

No problem with the *Requiem*, the greatest Italian opera of all, a blazing masterpiece on a different level; not a duff, routine, perfunctory bar. A hallowed text, of course, some of it great literature as well as living liturgy; and no bother with plot, characters, stage-effects, etc. The idiom is indeed wholly operatic and therefore very stagey/rhetorical/characterized: Verdi speaks his native language and has no need to don respectable robes for religious intent. The *Requiem* is recognizably the work of the same composer who had written *Rigoletto* and *La traviata* and was to go on to *Don Carlos*; but the invention is consistently higher, deeper, more intense, more exalted, more beautiful, more moving, more believable; and there's much in it, the bold choral-writing above all, that he doesn't even touch upon in his stage-works. Moments in the very late *Four Sacred Pieces* recapture something of the *Requiem*'s fire; one of them, the *Ave Maria* on a 'scala enigmatica' set as a competition, tried in quizzical curiosity, has a harmonic daring strangely reminiscent of, and resemblant to, Bruckner's unaccompanied motets. And the most surprising piece in Verdi's output, the String Quartet of 1873, is a thing of delight. Would that he had written more music right outside the habitual genres that engaged him all his life, and possibly entrapped him.

Puccini

Generally perceived as Verdi's successor, Giacomo Puccini, born 1858 to a line of church musicians in Lucca: *Messa da Gloria* (1878–80) a contribution to what was expected of him; but soon drawn to opera; studied at Milan Conservatorio with Ponchielli, composer of *La Gioconda*. His own first operatic efforts *Le Villi* (1883, with several subsequent revisions) and *Edgar* (completed 1888, again several later revisions): the first succeeded, attracting the support of Italy's principal music publisher Ricordi; the second flopped, nearly losing him Ricordi's backing. Vindication with *Manon Lescaut* (completed 1892, again with later revisions, as by now seemingly inevitable) – his first national then international hit, repeated crescendo with the triumphs that ensued: *La bohème* completed 1895; *Tosca* 1896–9; *Madama Butterfly*, first version 1901–3, second 1904. Increasing difficulty in finding subjects to fire him up, and a nervous fastidious perfectionism, slowed the rate of later pieces: *Girl of the Golden West* (1908–10); *La rondine* (more an operetta) 1914–16; the *Trittico* – three unrelated one-acters all intended for the same evening – *Il tabarro/ The Cloak* 1915–16; *Suor Angelica* 1917; *Gianni Schicchi* 1917–18. Back to full-length on unprecedented scale and grandeur, *Turandot* (1920–24); its culminating love-duet incomplete at his death in 1924 (a spacious version by Franco Alfano, junior operatic colleague, was almost immediately reduced to something almost perfunctory; a later completion by Luciano Berio betrays Puccini's intentions and sketches into cheap political correctness and post-modernism).

Manon Lescaut displays a richness of musical treatment never surpassed later as Puccini comes more completely into his mature manner, even habits. *La bohème* is the perfection of romantically treasured daydreams: the gaiety and freedom of the *vie de bohème*, camaraderie of the struggling poet, painter, philosopher and musician starving in their garret; the tart with a heart; the fragile doomed consumptive heroine; the picturesque background of 1830s Paris. Pacing and timing flawless, orchestration refined, emotion tender and true: composer and subject ideally matched. With *Tosca* doubts and reservations begin to assert themselves; elements of manipulation, emotional blackmail, cruelty, exploitation – Scarpia's bargain with Tosca, gratifying his lust to save her lover, whose groans as he's tortured punctuate – puncture – the ugly scene; her impulsive murder of her tormentor; the unbearable tension intensified when her lover's faked execution turns out to be real; the ludicrous curtain where she plunges to her own death from the ramparts of the Castello Sant'Angelo. Joseph Kerman's notorious dismissal – 'a shabby little shocker' – has stuck. Is it so unfair? Certainly, the *noun* is apt: *Tosca is* shocking, the masterly craftsmanship, equally with the composer's all-too-evident involvement with every excruciating sado-erotic twist, justify the judgement. And this despite some unforgettable music: from the very start, a world of evil in a single brusque chord-progression; the *Te Deum* wherein the seducer's feverish anticipation interpenetrates the pious church service; the turning screw of the off-stage torture. Most memorable of all, the lull between the cruelties, the opening of Act III, all the bells of Rome, the shepherd-boy's innocent freshness, Cavarodossi awaiting execution charged with recall of happier days with his adored Tosca.

Butterfly is more manipulative still, the erotic sado-masochisms yet further to the fore: an unbearable affair, not nearly enough mitigated in the music's frequent beauties, refinements, subtleties, with colours borrowed from appreciation and appropriation, both sensitive and adroit, of parallel French Orientalism, some of it – Ravel's *Shéhérazade* – exactly contemporary, some – Debussy's goldfish and pagodas – not yet written. But 'Kleenex at the ready' for a weepie that can leave the listener/viewer nauseated rather than cleansed and purged. It hits below the belt; it's unfair; it exploits. *La fanciulla* – the girl from the golden West – and *La rondine*, the girl who renounces – can safely be bypassed, and the consummate *Trittico* left for later. *Turandot* renews the problems, acuter than ever. This horrible fable has every ingredient calculated to erect Puccini's proclivities – a pathetic female victim self-sacrificed to the insensible object of her abjection, balancing the Ice Princess with her insatiable demands for men's bodies, not to gratify wholesome carnality, rather in revenge against the sex whose alleged cruelty her own easily surpasses; then her submission at the challenge of a *real* man. *Amor vincit omnia* in this unreal warfare – victorious over herself as the composer fails to be, unable to write the love-triumph for reasons possibly psychological. New in the mix, the exceedingly undiverting trio of drolls Ping, Pang and Pong. Familiar to it, the command of pacing and placing, the orchestration more resourceful than ever, a wider range of harmonic colouration creatively responding to early Stravinsky and even atonal Schoenberg. And one or two marvellous lyric moments – notably the celebrated *Nessun dorma*, poised at Puccini's favourite point, blissful anticipation of sexual conquest – which will ensure *Turandot*'s rapturous reception so long as opera survives.

But his finest achievement is surely the *Trittico* – so far as I'm aware, without precedent or successor: an excellent idea, three self-contained one-act pieces, unconnected and totally contrasted – a dark melodrama, a religious weepie, a satirical comedy – in a single evening. A long one, and expensive (the casts scarcely overlap): rarely given as intended, and only the comedy enjoying the independent life that the other two equally deserve. The complete threesome is a unity of complementary discrepancies: each item enhances the others. It deserves a detailed account.

Place and mood evoked with skilful simplicity for *Il tabarro/The Cloak*: barge moored on the Seine, hooters from others in passing, sultriness, nascent passions sulkily repressed, Michele the owner, his pipe gone out, brooding into the sunset, his much-younger wife Giorgetta's concern for the stevedores. Is she growing indifferent to *him*? Handsome young Luigi, older Tinca, Talpa older still, Michele's crew, will all want refreshment. Luigi strikes up a vivacious drinking-song, taken up by his padrone's wife and crew. When she invites Luigi to dance with her, inconspicuous insinuation of a sharp gapped little phrase in the bass that will later turn to menace. Before this surfaces, endless varied diversions and delays until at last: the long-deferred colloquy between husband and wife. This *is* the work's emotional core, the more affecting since we know what separates them. The scene's construction is equal in compositional cunning to its placement in the melodrama: a sort of chaconne, the shape gone-through over and over, ever more plangent and enriched before its dying falls and re-resumptions. Prosaic words at first – why not in bed? Aren't you sleepy? – then about keeping Luigi on, and the troubles with the other crew. Michele now draws nearer to his wife as the chaconne burgeons – you love me no more – why? Her response is cold, her reasons factitious: burgeoning more tender still – we were so happy ... our baby ... This *does* move her – and indeed his next reminiscence would melt a heart of stone. The chaconne's last time rises to contain her anguish. A new motif accompanies a further recall – Michele holding mother and child lovingly enfolded in his cloak – *il tabarro*: a saturnine little figurine, then some creepy dissonant chords, very soft. Husband and wife are also granted a passionate duet, further transforming and intensifying the river music, disturbingly moving because *we* know where *she* stands and will soon know where *he* does. He begs her to return to him – 'tender is the night' (to almost violent version of the river-sounds): she demurs – we've changed ... and I'm sleepy: church bells as the emotion drains away; and suddenly, when she's gone below, the softly spoken *Sgualdrina*! You *whore*!

Stasis: lovers pass: distant bugle call from some barracks. Michele soliloquizes (to the saturnine figurine): nothing ... silence ... she's awake – she's waiting ... Who? He's sure there's a lover; but who? He runs over his crew, rejecting all, including Luigi. Whoever it be, I'll crush him to death. All three prevailing motifs intertwine with surging chromatic turbulence below then above. He collapses, overcome. Finale: *allegro vivo agitato*, saturnine figure to the fore, as he lights the fatal pipe, taken by eagerly expectant Luigi as his mistress's signal: he leaps aboard, is recognized, seized, gripped by the throat, divested of his knife, confession extorted, stifled to death:

things slow and quieten, the cloak-chords hover and enclose. The gapped bass dominates the denouement: Giorgetta, almost flirtatious rather than discomposed, sits beside her husband, unwisely referring to an old saying of his – everyone bears a cloak, sometimes a thing of joy, sometimes of woe. 'And sometimes of crime: come in under my cloak' – opening it out to reveal Luigi's corpse, and thrusting her face against his as the orchestra explodes *tutta forza*.

Suor Angelica, the perfect complement, begins with distant convent bells and closed curtain. It rises to reveal a clear spring evening, the stage still empty, the voices of nuns at prayer in the chapel – *Ave Maria*, muted strings, gentle diatonic dissonances, hint of plainchant, Debussy's Blessed Damozel hovering near. The tone enhanced and deepened down the story's vicissitudes – the harsh old Aunt with news of Angelica's shameful baby, dead two years since, the girl's anguish, the celestial vision of the little boy, holding out his hand to his mother as she expires. Potential 'religious kitsch' – so near, positively courted and embraced – yet so far. We are genuinely moved, stirred, transported, not exploited, manipulated, seduced (whether willing or reluctant). The *truth* of this piece must lie in the notes themselves – pure, clean, simple, *sincere*.

From its tumultuous opening to its gleeful triumphant close *Gianni Schicchi* blows away all such scruples. Its uniqueness in Puccini's oeuvre, and its intricate imbroglio, deserve a detailed account in imitation; alas, an epitome must suffice. It dramatizes an episode mentioned by Dante in passing (*Inferno* XXX line 32): the note for this single reference gives the opera's gist: On the death of the rich, miserly Buoso Donati his son Simone accedes to Schicchi's idea (he's famed for his mimicry) of impersonating the dead man and dictating a new will in Simone's favour; but cunning Schicchi directs all the most valuable items to himself. Puccini's skilful librettist amplified this hint, providing a troupe of six further avaricious relatives (a seventh, Rinuccio, the romantic tenor lead, is relatively disinterested, the eighth is but a small boy); and has Schicchi's trick hinge upon threats of disclosure – the punishment for false testimony is amputation: he has them in the grip of his unmaimed hand; they are powerless to protest. Romantic interest is provided by Rinuccio's ardent infatuation with Gianni's daughter Lauretta, unable to marry without the dowry her father's scheme will provide.

Florence 1299: old Buoso's death-chamber, with clear view from the window of the tower of the Palazzo Vecchio where justice is done: the room crowded with relatives concealing their hopes of lucre beneath hypocritical lamentation. All set for the ensuing brouhaha, brilliantly etched with wit and speed, greed, pomposity, hypocrisy equally with tender young love: the cheeky cunning of Gianni's manipulations has one breathless with admiration. The model is *Falstaff* (and there are several close parallels of phrase and situation). Model and homage share masterly timing and characterization throughout, with endless tiny touches of delicious detail. One common feature is the solicitous separation of the young lovers from their importunate surroundings – Fenton and Nannetta, Rinuccio and Lauretta are twins under the skin. Above all, the rounded portrayal of the title-figure in each work: we see and feel these marvellous, larger-than-life anti-heroes, and relish their every rascality. Neither Verdi nor Puccini essayed comedy/farce elsewhere, yet it's as though they'd been at it for years.

Nineteenth-century Russia

'The Mighty Acorn' – Glinka

'His music is minor, of course, but he is not' – thus Stravinsky characterized his compatriot and artistic ancestor Mikhail Glinka. Born 1804, comfortably off – bit of a dilettante, no need to work for a living. Extensive European residence – Italy, Austria, Germany – picking up a musical training here and there. Return to St Petersburg 1835: two operas foundational to the Russian repertoire – *Ivan Susanin* (originally *A Life for the Tsar*) 1836; *Ruslan and Ludmilla* 1842. Off from 1844 on further European travels; most importantly Spain, producing two orchestral diversions – *A Night in Madrid* and the *Jota aragonesa*, whose dry, bright slightness inadvertently invents the 'Spanish' music later reaching its apogee in *Carmen*,

Rimsky-Korsakov's *Capriccio espagnol*, Chabrier's *España*, Debussy's *Ibéria*, and almost every piece of Ravel, before returning to its mother-country via Albéniz, Falla and Gerhard.

But the one that matters most is *Kamarinskaya*. This orchestral miniature, alternating two folk wedding songs, written in 1848, is simplicity itself – a brief introduction to a slow melody in unison, followed by three varied harmonizations, then another bit of preluding: then a snatch of fast dance tune, six bars long (really only three, since each half comes twice), much repeated with varying harmony and instrumentation, gradually modifying rather than transforming: then, with a key-switch, the slow song returns three times; then a return of the fast dance, extended to allow further variants – melodic, harmonic, instrumental – but still basically repetition, soon returning to the opening key, and working up to a loud whirling climax, after which it fragments and stops. The hidden point is the connection between the two tunes.

Whether or not he knew it, Glinka's unpretentious little piece (six minutes short) amounts to a total subversion of every hallowed mid-European tradition. No development, no form except naïve alternation, only one modulation, then back, and a texture consisting of nothing save slightly varied repetition. When a more deliberately nationalist generation of Russian composers sought to throw off the shackles of Teutonic practice, the perfect model lay to hand in their own backyard. Even Tchaikovsky, for all his later disdain for the provinciality of the nationalists, paid tribute in words – *Kamarinskaya* is 'the acorn from which grows the mighty oak of Russian music' – and in the rather bludgeoning adoption of the '*Kamarinskaya* method' as described, in the finale of his 2nd Symphony. And for the nationalists it is fundamental. All their great orchestral achievements adopt the mosaic, repetition-based, anti-developmental procedure, whether the scale is small or large, whether the work tells a tale or simply works out its own processes – Balakirev's marvellous 1st Symphony and equally marvellous tone-poem *Tamara*, Borodin's 1st and 2nd Symphonies and the evocative miniature *In the Steppes of Central Asia*, Rimsky-Korsakov's *Russian Easter Overture* and *Scheherazade*.

When, from the 1880s onwards, Russian nationalist music, intertwined with Wagner, took Paris by storm, the *Kamarinskaya*-method made new conquests. Stravinsky's *Rite of Spring* is the perhaps inevitable fulfilment of some six decades of treating native folk-material to circular restatement with ever-altering harmony and orchestration. Less predictable is Debussy's contemporaneous Diaghilev ballet *Jeux*, where, because it retains the symbolist/impressionist aesthetic of erotic suggestiveness – glinting half-lights, mysterious glowing shadows – the mosaic construction is softened, and the continuous re-colouration of its constituent fragments is 'lit from behind like *Parsifal*' (his own description) rather than exposed to Stravinsky's direct, unambiguous glare.

It is paradoxical that this iridescent late bloom of art nouveau should be so close in actual building to another seminal Stravinsky masterpiece a few years on, the *Symphonies of Wind Instruments* dedicated to the memory of the composer of *Jeux*, whose surface – pungent, lapidary, abrasive – and character – ritual litanies of dance and chant grinding up against each other like shingle under surf – couldn't be more different. The next advance from this is both radical – the Varèse pieces of the interwar years, crystal-hard, implacable, brief yet vast; thence the ever-more gigantic block repetition rituals of Messiaen; thence Birtwistle's take on all three composers (not forgetting Tippett's later journey, where earlier bounding/boundless lyricism is segmented by bollards, breakwaters and pillboxes) – and (on the face of it) conservative – Stravinsky's own subsequent life-long practice of borrowings; which disguises a geometry of proportion, a balance of iteration and variance whatever the stylistic surface.

Glinka's modest *Kamarinskaya* lies behind all these, however great the distance. And it can be related to something quite other. The course of Sibelius's output, from an early epic like *En Saga* to the oeuvre's ultimate climax in *Tapiola* some thirty years after, takes the same principle down a very different route, though just as extreme. His characteristic method is to begin with hints and fragments, then gradually to coalesce them via many slow-rotating cycles of varied repetition, to divulge their full nature and interrelatedness only as the music ends. 'Teleological *Kamarinskaya*'; combining the power of obsessive circling with the sense of inexorable movement towards a revelatory goal.

And what is minimalism – the predominating face of serious classical music for the past few decades – but another version of the same thing? Stravinsky and Sibelius, apparent incompatibles from the frozen north, lie equally behind the entire tendency, whether cunning (Reich), naïve (Glass), sentimental (Adams), commercial (Nyman), soft (Pärt), hard (Andriessen), mystic (Tavener) or just ornery (Torke). That humble acorn has fathered not the mighty Russian oak so much as a world forest stretching into three centuries so far, with no sign of decay.

'The Mighty Handful'

Back to the source: The Five – the Kuchka – a group of composers united by the idealistic and ideological determination to found a Russian National Music, freed from the tyranny of the Austro-Germanic tradition (though not averse to influences from Schumann, as well as Liszt and Berlioz). A mixed egg, this 'famous five'; one outstanding genius, Musorgsky; two composers of cherishable gifts and the occasional hit, Balakirev and Borodin; Rimsky-Korsakov the brilliantly endowed ultra-professional, fatally facile; and the forgettable and forgotten César Cui.

Mily Balakirev; born 1837; to St Petersburg aged eighteen, charged up with idealistic aims for a national music, much encouraged by Glinka, to whom he's a clear heir in composing as well as attitude. From 1861, the gradual formation of the group, of which he was, with the critic and literateur Vladimir Stasov, the artistic and spiritual mentor. Composition always tortuous: 1871 a breakdown – major retreat into religious mysticism: a minor job on the railways: gradual return to composition from the mid-1870s onwards, achieving a mighty handful of important works: later life, gradual return to the earlier disturbances: lived on, mainly in obscurity and neglect, with a slight recrudescence towards the end, dying in 1910.

His masterpiece is *Tamara*. The wild, remote semi-Oriental Caucasus impressed and excited Balakirev in the early 1860s; he collected some of its songs and dances. *Tamara*, composed alongside *Islamey* for piano, began, like it, as an Oriental fantasy without story, then gradually grew towards a symphonic poem inspired by and illustrating the celebrated ballad by Lermontov. His breakdown compelled abandoning the work in the early 1870s; well-wishers urged its resumption; by the late 1870s it reached something like its final form – original songs-and-dances material contained within an Introduction and Epilogue evoking the legend's time and place. Work still dragged on till 1882. Dedicated to Liszt, consistent inspiration in his symphonic poems; the result is, rather, a latent ballet that would surely succeed triumphantly when actually danced, as it was.

A deep gorge, dark swirling waters below, high rocks above, and perched on them a tower whose light lures the lonely traveller. Its inmates, under the sway of the beautiful Tamara, siren of sexual desire and fulfilment, enticing every male passer-by for a session of passion; then, when she's used him up in one abandoned night, her cohorts laying on lavish songs, dances, wines, viands, come dawn another corpse is tumbled into the turbid waters. All is still, save the seductive voice – her farewell; then as a new night comes, her irresistible call goes out to the next eagerly answering victim.

Mysterious low muttering: harmony then a theme slowly emerges – Tamara's voice sounding out as dusk thickens. Same again, the melody developing a touch of Oriental ornament: a third start, more pressing – harp up to the heights, soft trumpets: a fourth time *animando* and crescendo. Now the music goes indoors, a 12/8 whirl of energy working up to first climax, rapidly down to soft drum tattoo, background for more languid dance-figures, further relaxing into dulcet melody on clarinets, with added ornamentation when repeated. A passage of plucking pizzicatos, return of animation, the two previous dance-movements skilfully intercut till their identities begin to merge. Lots of untuned percussion – instructive and seductive for later-comers, not least Rimsky in *Scheherazade* and Ravel in *Daphnis*. Sense of a new start, initially more restrained, soon boiling up more passionate than before, then reserving its full strength till releasing it in a Grand Slam (plus tam-tam) – possibly cut off too soon? – declining into nostalgia and regret, calming for

slow apotheosis, return of introductory tempo and mood, intensified with fine hymnic harmony – twice, second more acute than
first. A moment of chromatic recession, closely recalled in Stravinsky's *Firebird*; then back to the opening murmur and rustle deep in
the waters below.

I've mentioned three composers for which this piece in the archetypal *fons et origo*, and could adduce others, notably *La Péri*, Dukas'
ballet of 1912. Where would they all be without *Tamara*? All are ballets.
How does Balakirev fare with a large-scale form? His 1st Symphony,
completed after protracted struggles – some thirty years – in 1897
is successful on a large scale, without narrative or self-portraiture to
help it along. Again the orchestra is exotic – harps, lots of percussion,
special effects; but the material is sober and purposeful, till Tamara
and the Caucasus cannot be kept out. First movement, especially, a
triumph of resource with its five-note figure deployed in five hundred
ways. The scherzo is, so to speak, 'Mendelssohn-heavy' or 'Oriental
Bruckner' till the Tchaikovskyan trio: when the scherzo returns it
builds into a terrific new coda. Third movement another archetype –
Eastern languor, indolent ease embodied in melody, harmony, texture;
mood, momentum: it sags in the middle, goes briefly and unconvincingly melodramatic, then recovers and surpasses its opening in its
coda – ballet music after all, pure *Swan Lake*, all harps, gauze, flutters
and tutus. The finale isn't quite on the same level – a bit *ordinaire* till
Prince Igor looks in; never less than proficient, and sometimes more –
the closing polonaise and rousing end: it's by no means inferior, and
doesn't let the work as a whole down with an anticlimax.

Alexander Borodin, born St Petersburg 1833, died there 1887. Drawn
early to music, but studied medicine; principal career as distinguished
chemist, music remaining 'private passion' on the side. Hence the
sporadic oeuvre, littered with incompletions and completions by
other hands after his death – *Prince Igor* with its famous Polovtsian
dances – three symphonies, two quartets, a handful of lovely songs,
and another miniature archetype almost as seminal as *Kamarinskaya* –
In the Steppes of Central Asia (1880): middle of nowhere, unaccompanied woodwind solos answer each other; a soft procession from the

far distance slowly approaches, characterized by plaintive, haunting, repetitive melody, gradually and beautifully harmonized, suddenly full, bright, confident, then back to melancholy with chromatic inflexions, 'Glinka'd' with alternative instrumentations and harmonization; hypnotic. The caravan disappears into the distance, leaving behind only a solo flute. Russian folksong encounters the Orient – steppe/desert – the two cultures fraternize, escort each other on the endless way, disappearing fused and merged – an allegory.

Borodin's symphonies, once perhaps too popular, are now largely neglected. Though not so unfair as the ignorant ignoring of Balakirev's 1st, this is a pity. Borodin's 1st Symphony, completed 1868, is a bit dry and chewy, with moments of freshness – a 'kikimora' scherzo; touches of 'magic harmony' that runs all the way in Russian music from Glinka's *Ruslan* to *Rite of Spring* in a finale audibly close to Schumann's *Rhenish*. The extant movements of the 3rd Symphony, seen to completion by Glazunov, are diluted Kuchka stock-pot written by robot or computer (and not completely unattractive, actually). The 2nd Symphony (1874) remains the most alive, particularly the first movement, strongly bound together with its hammered-out opening motif, not forgotten by Messiaen. And the *prestissimo scherzo* with its lovely trio remains vivid: but the promising lyric material for the slow movement doesn't quite kindle, then over-blows; and the finale goes on a bit. What all three symphonies taken together show is how near naturalness and nationalism can approach the academicism they aim to expel. Borodin's beguiling gift of melody is at its lovely best in the 2nd String Quartet: the famous 'Kismet' melody of the *notturno* survives kitsching, all the three other movements are a pleasure. And the Polovtsian Dances from the opera are strong enough to endure anything.

The Kuchka member who matters most, however, is Modest Musorgsky. Born 1839: 1852–5 cadet in the army, 1856 joins a regiment: 1858 meets Alexander Dargomïzhsky and Balakirev, and studies with the latter: nervous disorder compels his leaving the army: musical studies continued, composing begins. Meets Rimsky-Korsakov (five years his junior) 1861; 1863 enters Civil Service; 1865 death of mother – heavy

drinking – *delirium tremens* – composing and decomposing. Leaves
Civil Service 1867 and makes precarious 'living' by musical means.
Drinking: 1878 job in another department of Civil Service, again
abandoned 1880. Subsidized by friends to finish the two massive ongoing operatic projects. Seriously ill by 1881; dies 28 March.

Canon: 1867 *St John's Night on the Bare Mountain* (incorporated later
into *Sorochintsy Fair* 1874–80, unfinished). First song of *Nursery* cycle
1868; Act I of *Marriage* – left incomplete, superseded by the idea of an
opera on *Boris Godunov*, first and best version finished 1869 – remod-
elled (and compromised?) 1871–2; versions by Rimsky-Korsakov –
by which *Boris* achieved wider fame – 1896 then 1908. *Nursery* cycle
returned to 1870, completed 1872; this year also sees mooting of opera
Khovanshchina. *Sunless* song-cycle 1874, *Pictures at an Exhibition* same
year (Ravel's orchestration 1922); first thoughts of *Sorochintsy Fair*. *Songs
and Dances of Death* 1875 (completed two years later); Act I of *Khovanshchina* completed, Act II begun: on into Act III the next year (Shostakovich's re-scoring completed 1958). Work on *Sorochintsy* intermittent
up to the end. As well as the sketchy state of much of this output, a
litter of aborted projects great and small – operas on *Oedipus in Athens*,
Salammbô; the Five's communal *Mlada*; orchestral bits and pieces;
choral work; including *The Destruction of Sennacherib*, after Byron; individual piano-miniatures; and some marvellous isolated songs outside
the three cycles.

Musorgsky wrote to Rimsky-Korsakov in 1869:

> Let me tell you, dear Korsinka, that the act of creating carries in
> itself the laws of beauty, whose tale is told by inner criticism, not
> outer; and whose consequences are determined by the artist's
> instinct: where either of these two elements is lacking, there can
> be no artistic creation. For artistic creation implies both, and the
> artist is a law unto himself.

One can imagine Korsinka's cavils. Compare Debussy:

> no one [save Musorgsky] has given utterance to the best within us
> in tones more gentle or profound: he is unique, and will remain

so, because his art is spontaneous and free from arid formula. Never has a more refined sensibility been conveyed by such simple means; it is like the art of an enquiring savage discovering music step by step through his emotions. Nor is there ever a question of any particular form; rather, the form is so varied that by no possibility whatever can it be related to any established, 'official' form, since it depends on and is made up of successive minute touches mysteriously linked together by means of an instinctive clairvoyance.

Setting *Marriage* the composer wrote: 'Throughout I try as hard as I can to note down clearly those changes in intonation which crop up in human conversation for the most futile causes, on the most insignificant words, changes in which lies the secret of Gogol's humour.' And – 'If I have managed to render the straightforward expression of thought and feelings as it occurs in ordinary speech, and my rendering is musicianly and artistic, then the deed is done.' (The deed *was* done: Act I of *Marriage* was completed in twenty-seven days.) And again: '*Marriage* is a cage in which I have to remain imprisoned until I have learnt my lesson ... What I should like to do is to make my characters speak on the stage exactly as people speak in everyday life, without exaggeration or distortion, and yet write music that will be thoroughly artistic.' Again, in December 1876:

I feel inclined to prophesy: and what I prophesy is 'the melody of life, not that of classicism'. I am at work on human speech. With great pains I have just achieved a type of melody evolved from speech: I have succeeded in merging recitative into melody ... I should like to call it 'well thought-out, justified melody'. Some day, all of a sudden the ineffable will arise against classical melody – arise unexpectedly, intelligible to one and all. If I succeed, I shall stand as a conqueror in art – and succeed I must.

The cage did indeed prove a prison; but, liberated from *Marriage*, the freedom of *Boris* did indeed succeed with sure-footed rapidity. Musorgsky's determination – stubborn/perverse/wilful, the defiant anti-intellectualism of a very intelligent and sensitive man – places anti-classicism/anti-Teutonic 'rationality' far beyond the needs of his nationalist companions and his own compositional requirements. (The comparison with his non-nationalist compatriot Tchaikovsky is illuminating and will be developed later.) Meanwhile, the comparable 'problems' (if problems they be) with other 'eccentric' composers who follow their instinct, break the rules and sometimes receive 'correction' (if correction it be): Berlioz (who can't be corrected – see Tovey on the 'problem' – any good student could do it better; but when 'corrected' it's just not right); Janáček; Ives. No problem either, nowadays, with the well-meant re-writings in Musorgsky's case: the Originals are what we want and what we have. What *are* they? How do they *work*? What *is* this unique music of 'minute successive touches mysteriously linked together by instinctive clairvoyance', so lovingly recognized by Debussy? Their innate *nature*, so hard won, that couldn't be other (though moments of mere uncouthness and inadequacy remain, mainly in the scoring of *Boris*, which sets up unworthy hankerings for the brazen brilliance of Rimsky-Korsakov's). Musorgsky's rightnesses, and what he *did* achieve in the teeth of his chaotic lifestyle, his alcoholic self-destruction, his chaos of impossible undertakings, are shown clearest and deepest in the three song-cycles, the piano-cycle, and whole stretches of the opera that is 'all his own work'.

SONG-CYCLES

Nursery: three detailed descriptions from the sequence of seven mini-masterpieces must suffice to convey its unique flavour. The texts (the composer's own) are as idiosyncratic as their settings.

No. 1: *With Nanny*. Penny-plain declamation – tell me, nanny, the story of that dreadful bogey-man – first fuller, dissonant chord – in the woods: how he prowled around the forest glades: how he brought the children to his den: how he crunched – it crunches – their bones – second crunch – and gnawed – third crunch – their bones white and dry. How the children cried and how they screamed – vivid rapid chromatic descent – so loud. Pause. Plain chord – continuing – Nanny dear, I can tell you why bogey-man ate them all up. Pause. Serious – they were naughty and wouldn't do what daddy and mummy and old nanny said. Piously saucy/pert/naughty chords – that was why he ate them, wasn't it? Long pause. Or – oh I know – tell me all about the King and Queen – the ones who – harmony and spacing more luminous and open – who lived across the sea and had a splendid castle: stab of dissonance – but the King – grimace – was lame and always limped – (second limp, then four more): when he stumbled (he stumbles) – then (flump) a mushroom grew – little pause – and the Queen – droll semitones in left hand – always had a cold: when she sneezed (she sneezes) everything was smashed (it smashes). Pause. You know, dear Nanny – penny plain – I don't want to hear about the bogey-man. I don't like him – pause – No – tell me a funny story, please.

No. 3: *The Beetle*. Tearing little introduction, then under-pinning Mischenka's first words – Nanna dear, oh how horrid, darling Nanna – evens out into a sort of Cossack trepak – I was playing in the sand by the beech-trees – I was building (more lyrical) a lovely house with sticks Mummy cut for me – I had to get it finished, a real house (getting excited) with a roof on it – when – *then* – (collapse of texture onto low dull rumble) – there settled on the roof a beetle (long beetly chord over the rumble) – enormous! Black, and frightening. He twiddled his whiskers – dreadfully – and all the time glared straight at me (dissonant busy wait): I was terrified: he buzzed (low trills, harsh though soft right-hand figure) – fiercely: then he spread his wings out and I knew he meant to fight me (the trills double and rush fiercely upward): then he flew and hit me bang on the forehead! Treble texture now calms and hovers – Oh Nanna I dared not move – I sat – and held my breath. Then I just peeped with one eye nearly shut – and – listen what happened, Nanny. Pause. Momentum resumes, very gentle: the beetle lay on his back, with his nose turned up and his legs all folded: he wasn't horrid, he didn't twiddle his whiskers, or buzz, and his wings were all trembling. (More hesitant) – did it kill him, or was he pretending? (Louder, more urgent) – what was wrong with him? Tell me, Nanna – what was wrong? He tried to fight me, and knocked himself down. Receding, winding away – Was he really dead, that beetle? Dying away, on unresolved gap suspended in mid-air.

No. 6: *Hobbyhorse*. Lively riding-motion trepak, encouraging nonsense-syllables, mini-climax suddenly calls a halt – *prrrrh* – and a recitativo invitation to his little friend – Vassya, listen, will you come and play this evening? Not too late, mind. The ride resumes – growing hectic, dangerous, ending in an onomatopoeic tumble – oh my leg, oh it hurts, awfully! Affective harmony introduces strains almost Schumannian as Mother comes to the rescue – Darling! What a nasty fall! Be a brave boy now, don't cry, get up again – there, there. Look – in the bushes – do you see the bird? What a pretty little bird! What feathers! See? And now (echo of the tender phrases) all right? All right? All right! Off we go again – I've been to town, Mummy: and now I'm back home. I must get on quick – hop hop – Vassya's coming round – I must get on quick: and the miniature epic again disappears high up at the top of the piano.

Absolutely unaffected, without whimsy, archness, cuteness, coyness: on a knife-edge of sheer awfulness, but every danger not so much avoided as simply not present. *Simply*: Debussy again: 'all these little dramas are set down, I repeat [earlier – 'never has a more refined sensibility been conveyed by such simple means'], with the utmost simplicity.' A miracle. The children of this Nursery include Satie, Yniold the little boy in Debussy's own *Pelléas*, *l'enfant* in Ravel's fairy-tale of the naughty child made good, Flora and Miles in Britten's *Turn of the Screw*, and *enfantine* songs and piano-pieces by Poulenc and Mompou. Not one of these is less knowing, more genuinely innocent, than their prototype.

Sunless – adult in introspective desolation comparable with, equal to, Schubert's Heine songs, the dark side of Schumann, Wolf setting Michelangelo. *Songs and Dances of Death*, grim implacable realism – could be described in as much detail as Musorgsky's *enfantines*. Both these marvellous later cycles are highly influential with future composers: in Janáček, Katya's suicide by drowning, and Katerina's in Shostakovich; for Debussy, bell-sounds, water-evocation (and one blatant theft); for Ravel, the textures and pulsating pedal-bell of *Le Gibet*: and many more. By rejecting 'learning', 'classicism',

Teutonic 'pedantry', Musorgsky attains what Debussy struggled to achieve in his last years – 'the naked flesh of emotion', concealing nothing, revealing all. The same stance informs the best music in the operas.

Before they're reached, a promenade into pure diversion. *Pictures at an Exhibition* is so familiar as not to need description: the music does it all. We see, feel, hear the Gnomes, the Vecchio Castello, Bydło, the lumbering wagon drawn by powerful oxen across the interminable steppe, wheedling-needling, whining-whimpering, groaning-grumbling Goldenberg and Schmuÿle, the children playing in the Tuileries, the bustling market in Limoges, the ballet of new-hatched chickens, the house on chicken's legs: we shudder in the Catacombs, we wonder at the Great Gate of Kiev. The idea of linking all these pictures by reflective Promenades, constantly varied, is ever-fresh and felicitously executed. *St John's Night on the Bare Mountain* makes an earlier (1867) more elaborate picture, extending into a complete tale, equally vivid – enough to be incorporated wholescale, by intention, into Musorgsky's last, unfinished opera.

OPERAS

First, his first. *Marriage* (1868): consciously a challenge, an experiment, to set Gogol's play word-for-word. The awful warning of Dargomïzhsky's *Stone Guest*, where musical interest, value, pleasure suspire in deserts of vast sterility, was not heeded. Act I completed rapidly in piano-score, then the impulse foundered for reasons pretty clear – word-for-word Gogol means total victory for verbality, and denigration of the music to gesticulation and underlining – phrase by phrase in spasmodic disjunction that drives the listener half-crazy. And perhaps is meant to: situation droll and farcical. Bachelor Podkolesin decides, at last, to marry. The marriage-broker, successful at last, vividly extols the charm of the chosen bride, and her dowry. Podkolesin still dithers, especially when his friend Kochkarov, astonished, tries first to dissuade, then takes over the matchmaker's function. Thus Act I. Musically, no structure beyond occasional retries of the opening, as a kind of ritornello: otherwise, the need to perpetually match every word is as exhausting to the listener as it must have been for the composer. One can imagine him, at the piano, improvising away, doing all three persons with well-attested magnetic brilliance, fragmentary musical images falling from his fingers to disappear through the cracks in the floor. But the venture had no future. It was left to a nonentity to compose the other acts.

It did have progeny: a possible – likely – influence upon Ravel's way with diction and verbal illustration in his equally droll-and-farcical *L'Heure espagnole*. And absolutely certain that the *Marriage*-methods impact upon the sustained grotesquerie of Shostakovich's early masterpiece *The Nose* – also Gogol. But no future for Musorgsky: *that* lies immediately to hand, in abandoning Gogol for Pushkin and *Marriage* for *Boris*. As well as Pushkin's play, much input from – inter alia – Karamzin's *History of the Russian State*, and also the composer's own documentary research – archival work like Wagner's for *Meistersinger*, Pfitzner's for *Palestrina* and Hindemith's for *Mathis der Maler*. Two versions of *Boris*: October 1868–July 1869 (orchestration completed December); second go, 1871–2, adding wholly new Polish act and in the last, the Kromy Forest scene, pointlessly 'necessitating' removal of some superb stuff in the St Basil scene and a bit of reshuffle with Boris's death, then the urchins' teasing the Idiot at the end. Kromy Forest is rum-tum hum-drum; the Polish subplot is tedious, redundant, musically undistinguished, but the later version also effects some successful enhancements, particularly to Act II, the work's greatest. All the problems surrounding this masterpiece are born of its composer's haphazard ways of life and work, as also of his alleged or actual deficiencies of technique.

The *action* need not be related: two crucial scenes can exemplify Musorgsky's wonderful way with *inaction* – the rendition of internal states, the fearful trembling conscience confronted by or evading its owner's guilt. Discussion of these will make more sense after laying out the story and its characters, implicit in what follows here.

Act II: its composer's high-point and a high-point in nineteenth-century opera and in all of opera's sublime and erratic trajectory. High strings introduce in bright mournful repetitive phrases Xenia's brightly sad little song, delicately underpointed by oboe, then strings again. Boris's daughter is singing of losing her fiancé; brother Fyodor, raising his eyes from his atlas, tries to comfort. Nurse sits silently sewing. The siblings' voices combine till distracted by the chiming clock whirring into action every quarter: over regular tritone tick-tock – subtle subliminal echo of earlier coronation bells – buzz of fast soft chromatics and, as Fyodor describes each move, the toy fanfares as the mechanical instruments activate and the figures animate like real people. Nurse looks up and intervenes as the per-formance ends – pull yourself together, don't think about him, we'll find another just as handsome, there's all the world to choose from. Xenia protests eternal fidelity: brushed aside by Nurse's promise of a nonsense-song, followed immediately by its fulfilment, a *capriccioso* tale of gnat, flea, dragonfly ending in the flea's tragi-comic death – all this directly analogous with the *Nursery*-cycle. Fyodor – really, Nanny what a song for now! He has one more appropriate – I'll sing, you'll join in. His contribution is more nonsensical yet – the hen hatching a calf, the piglet an egg; the sparrow and the owl: the village fire, the sexton and his mother who bakes him forty cakes each day, all swallowed down by the greedy watchman who also gobbles up two oxen and a cow and ten pigs and a bull yet still he's not full, and –

Boris enters as the hectic climax is reached, stopping the fun in its tracks. 'Am I the wolf who scares the hen?' Nurse apologizes. Fyodor returns to his atlas, Boris embraces his daughter: their tender exchanges show him to be all-too-human rather than – as well as – the inhuman monster we've already heard of. Left alone together, father and son talk over the mighty terrain, on the map, that they both rule, now and to come. 'You, my son, will inherit: work hard!' The boy resumes his study, the Tsar begins his great monologue as if unheard:

I stand supreme, after five years' untroubled reign: yet my soul is tormented. Nothing can heal my aching heart. My children – Xenia, my cherished – death, like lightning, strikes her beloved down. My heart is sick, my spirit wracked – I pray saints and angels release me from my torments – but God sends conspiracies,

plague, famine – all Russia groans, blames me – the name Boris is
hated. Even sleep abandons me – every night the child appears,
his face bloodied, begging for the mercy that was denied him: his
wound open afresh, he cries aloud. Oh God above, mercy!

All this rendered with the same astounding nervous intensity/under-
lining that accompanied every absurd gesture in *Marriage*, the same
psychological empathy that identifies with the child's every change
of tone in *Nursery*, every quiver of feeling in *Sunless*, every pang of
woe in the *Songs and Dances of Death*.

As his voice gutters out, Nurse's off-stage screech of grotesque
dissonant terror. Fyodor is sent to investigate, as an attendant Boyar
arrives to announce Prince Shuisky, craving audience. Before retiring,
the man whispers that Shuisky's coterie plot something, no doubt
bad. Fyodor returns with explanation for the unseemly screeching –
the parrot! Reluctant to trouble his troubled father further, the boy
is yet prevailed upon to tell the absurd tale of the wretched bird's
teasing and escape, savage scratching, everyone in a hysterical
tizzy – a brilliant mini-*Kamarinskaya*, alternating triple and quin-
tuple time, the same phrases given ever-permutating/varying harmonies, scoring, background articulation. 'My good son, how proud
you make me, telling the story just as it happened. Oh that I live to
see you Tsar, rightful ruler of this Empire: I'd gladly renounce power
and glory, crown and sceptre!' As he counsels caution and wariness,
especially where Shuisky is concerned – 'he seems so loyal, but he's
sly and false' – the man himself enters silently, overhearing – as unobtrusive as, at the Coronation, he'd been stentorian. Boris denounces
him to his face: Shuisky remains brazen and unabashed. The Tsar
exercises patience, sarcastically awaiting the news: in Poland, a Pretender, supported by King, Lords and Pope. His Name? Shuisky pre-
varicates, playing with his victim, before at last divulging the name
of the one who, likely, will rally the folk and rise successful against
the fated regime: Dimitri, the murdered Tsarevich. At this, Boris
dismisses the living Tsarevich despite the boy's protests – he wants
to share the danger he probably understands only too well. All this
somewhat humdrum musically, a low plateau between highs.

À deux Boris is again decisive with the Prince, ordering practical necessities – garrison the borders, etc. Confidence doesn't last: he's soon pressing his treacherous ally – 'who ever heard of buried children rising from their coffins against the Lord's anointed, confirmed by the people, crowned in the Cathedral by the Patriarch?' He breaks off in wild laughter, and berates Shuisky for not laughing too; then goes irrepressibly, wantonly on, retelling the circumstances – 'that bloodied body – that slain infant – that was surely Dimitri?' He begs, wheedles, implores the stony Prince – 'treason I can forgive, but if you try deceit your terrible death will make even Ivan shake in his grave!' Forced, Shuisky, as if reluctantly, in fact exerting compulsive power, recounts the infanticide – thirteen other little corpses, lying there on view with the royal one, all corrupting save him, his wound gaping, but smiling sweetly as though asleep in his cradle, one hand clasping a toy. Music wonderfully on course again – a shimmer of gentle supernatural radiance surrounding the unholy deeds told by the insinuating traitor, turning tight the tormenting screw.

It works. Boris chokes in anguish, dismissing Shuisky, who slinks out, watching significantly. Left alone, a terrible fit of convulsive trembling – a musical cardiac arrest, strings *sul ponticello* in hammer-twists of five-notes across the beat. 'Air! I'm suffocating . . .' then, as conscience smites, up strikes the chiming clock with its tick-tock tritone from the Coronation, its whirring chromatics, creaking sighs and, after a bit, the gay fanfares of its miniature instruments and animated figures: just as before when it failed to comfort Xenia – a quarter-of-an-hour ago? – so it cannot solace a human condition still worse – 'once stained, no escaping damnation: your soul will burn, your heart is filled with poison – it throbs within you, hammer-strokes ring in your ears!' Note Boris's language is now impersonal: it's the clock that's personified, its every movement, chime, tootle an accusation. A stroke of intuitive acumen and high genius, this return – the uncanny power of the pretty, decorative surface and the implacable machinery behind. No escaping this escapement! Infernal vengeance, the clockwork of destiny. He breaks off as does the chime – no quarter! The murdered boy appears in hallucin-ation, 'moving, growing, groaning', all this 'written on skin' with unforgettable authenticity, intensity, simplicity. His singing now breaks into inarticulate animal terror – 'go ... go ... leave me ... not I; others did it ... it was the people ...' Then as agitation peaks and dies, the slow spent calm closing seven bars of this amazing act which, in this final extremity, aspires to a condition *beyond* music altogether. The quiet closing bars contain the Tsar–murderer's plea to God, who desires not the death of a sinner, to grant his guilty soul forgiveness.

After the twaddling Polish act – Musorgsky's late concession to the factitious necessity of 'love-interest' and a leading female role – Act IV is on course again for the St Basil scene and the protagonist's collapse and demise. The starving, disaffected populace confront their Tsar outside St Basil's Cathedral, exchanging gossip and rumours – a dullish chorus, fair-to-middling. Full calibre suddenly restored in a sequence worthy of the greatest in the song-cycles and the opera's high-points: the Idiot sings his idiot-strain entwined around the wailing, nagging two-note horn ostinato, praying in moonlight for sunlight, cruelly mocked by street urchins, who snatch his precious silver kopek. The Idiot, too, lashes out at his earthly father, lamenting his coin: 'What makes him cry? The boys have run off with my kopek – command they be slain, like you murdered young Dimitri.' Shuisky wants him silenced but Boris protects the holy fool: 'pray for me' – and is rebuffed: 'I must not pray for Tsar Herod, the Lord will not allow it.' Then as the Imperial retinue moves on, the Idiot is left alone, resumes his lament, music as before, words extended now into a lament for Mother Russia in her eternal sorrow: 'weep tears of blood, soon comes the fire, then the dark, sorrow without cease for the wretched starving folk ...': song, then its orchestral echo, disintegrating before one's ears as the poor fool returns to mending his shoes.

Act IV Scene ii: a hall in the Kremlin: fine orchestral opening for the Council of Boyars to hear the Tsar's injunction concerning the Pretender and soliciting their loyalty. Enter Shuisky, detailing the Empire's dire state and reporting the dire condition of its Emperor – haggard, bathed in sweat, wracked with terror, 'recoiling from the ghost of the murdered boy, begging it be gone': and at this moment enter Boris, filling out the description with the actuality in every detail – their words overlap – forcing the incredulous Boyars to suspend disbelief. Boris pulls himself together. Cunning Shuisky introduces the ancient monk Pimen to testify to some important secret. 'Perhaps his message will console my suffering.' Pimen is admitted and permitted to tell his tale – oblique, long-drawn-out, chilly and mystically shining, the miracle of the murdered child transformed into worker of holy deeds unfolds, the monk-ex-machina as lethal as he is innocuous. Boris swoons; the shuddering strains of his terror before, when the apparition first haunted him, return; the living Fyodor is hastily brought in, his father bids him farewell and commends him to live and rule true and unbesmirched. 'Beware the Pretender, trust not the cunning Boyars, trust the simple wisdom of the folk, hold God and his Saints in reverence; keep your conscience clean; protect your sister, the angel we love.' As the litany continues it grows more and more ethereal and delicate – the guilty man addresses God direct, pleading the innocence of his children. A bell intrudes deep below the radiance – Coronation chords on their fixed tritone, denuded now of clangour, pomp, circumstance. 'Listen! The death-knell.' Monks off-stage acquiesce in the softest possible alleluia. The bell-knell again: the monks, nearer, continue in calm liturgical mode, singing of the defenceless child pleading in vain to be spared, while Boris mutters his acknowledgement of what he did. As the voices enter on their final phrase – 'there is no salvation' – he again rallies, would issue a last command, then gutters out into incoherence – 'Mercy! Death! Forgive me! See – your Tsar . . . ! Forgive, forgive . . .' – and dies in a long silence. The orchestra barely recovers, the Boyars whisper a single *Amen*, the curtain falls.

Incredible stuff – hammy melodrama *in excelsis* – somehow not quite *music*: as rhetoric/gesture/pacing and placing/rendition of character from without and within in its every living fibre of utterance at an extreme state, quite astounding. Exactly the same technique, even aim, as attempted without success for the *Marriage*-venture applied to grave/deep/serious/searching subject-matter, with all the empathy, to come or already achieved, of the song-cycles. 'Not quite *music*': *music* would be, weirdly, inappropriate, 'too much' as Blake said; detracting from whatever it *is*, in Musorgsky, that it *is*.

The question of choice between options when staging *Boris* is surpassed for thorniness only by Bruckner's 3rd Symphony. Musorgsky's second version is compromised dramatically and musically by the Rangoni/Marina Polish act and the episode in Kromy Forest. Then there's the Rimsky-Korsakov re-arrangement and re-scoring: undoubtedly more brilliant, brazen, sure-footed in sonorous splendour – it's the basis of the work's international success after its first airing in 1896 – Chaliapin unforgettable in the title-role; still more so in Rimsky's further treatment of 1908, which restored some cuts but also added further interpolations. (Inexplicably, both versions omitted the marvellous scene with the children and the clock.) An authentic score appeared in 1924: Shostakovich took this as source for his own re-orchestration in 1940: it makes a more authentic sound than his predecessor's. What the great work needs is merciless ditching of ersatz material, loving retention of every original feature, together with Musorgsky's later additions that do really *add*, in an overall sonority faithful to the best of his unique *tinta*, though helping it along where its ineffectuality can be an impediment.

Khovanshchina: this enormous piece was begun immediately after *Boris*, and is inextricably mixed up with *Sorochintsy Fair*: both are a textural tangle; the first is viable, the second not. Rimsky's version again cut-and-colourful. Diaghilev commissioned Ravel and Stravinsky to realize and score missing material for Paris 1913: Stravinsky's closing chorus is strong and true – an emptying-out desolation rather than an orgiastic blaze. Shostakovich's complete reorchestration of 1958 is faithful to spirit and style. No such thickets of choice as presented by *Boris*: the problems lie rather in the work's unevenness, even its grand spacious tedium.

Still more than *Boris*, *Khovanshchina* is grounded in genuine historical research. Result, a tableau-fresco of political and religious confrontation, impressively handled, intercrossed with a human story less than compelling. It doesn't call for a blow-by-blow account:

the work is disconcertingly smooth and professional – 'musical' even, as well as 'operatic'. Comparison might be with early Verdi for idiom and dramatic treatment, early Wagner for pacing, scope, length: fine strong moments lost in acres of slow-dragging near-or-actual monotony.

Sorochintsy Fair: a sad return to Gogol for a would-be merry/comic extrovert complement to *Khovanshchina*, undertaken simultaneously, continued after, but left far more fragmentary and chaotic: lots of attempts to complete it, but not even the most loving and authentic can disguise the plotless 'events' and the flavourless music. With one blazing exception – the wholescale incorporation of *St John's Night on the Bare Mountain*, fully worked up with chorus and soloists, but dramatically gratuitous, possibly opportunistic, certainly implausible. Breaks off into the Unknown ... Maybe this tragic figure had fulfilled whatever it was that lay so meagre yet so rich in his human and artistic nature.

Musorgsky/Tchaikovsky nexus

Musorgsky and Tchaikovsky make an illuminating couple to compare and contrast. Clearly the two outstanding composers of their culture in their time, their stance upon both could hardly be more different. Musorgsky: defiantly set against learning, grammar, finish and polish, decorum; despises the past and has no use for it; passionately Russophile, no farther horizons, the West the Enemy: empirical, intuitive, instinctive. Tchaikovsky: cultivated and polite, wants to please; fully trained as musician, one hundred per cent professional; Russophile up to a point, but with reservations; admires the Austro-German tradition and can, again up to a point, use it; and adores and venerates Mozart, 'the Christ of music', as the crown of a tender feeling for the eighteenth century in general. With contemporary music, a Westernizer – not Wagner or Brahms to be sure, but Italian opera, Liszt, Berlioz, in as much as they can be accommodated, and emphatically everything Parisian – the ballets of Delibes, that novel box of sugar-plums the celesta, and *Carmen* to drown in deeply, as Nietzsche later.

Chalk and cheese. Yet: Tchaikovsky's submission for most of his best and most individual music to the unabashed, unbridled subjectivism of emotional expression has an intuitive-instinctive-empirical strength and authenticity that couldn't have been achieved by way of his explicit artistic stance, training, goals. And Musorgsky's encapsulation-in-music, by means of impulsive grammar-less 'anti-music', of human utterance in all its variety – from infancy to old age, from Tsar to Idiot – achieves an objectivity, even (sometimes) a polish/finish, that justifies calling it 'classical' (he'd have hated this) in its own self-defining terms.

The two complement and round out each other. As with Carter and Messiaen, Britten and Tippett, arguably Stravinsky and Schoenberg, what a composer the fusion of the two would make! But I must stick to the Convergence of the Twain.

Tchaikovsky

Pyotr Ilyich Tchaikovsky: born 1840; early musical aptitude, continued when the family moved to St Petersburg 1848; but two years later entered Law School and in 1859 joined the Ministry of Justice. Always drawn to music, however, and from 1866 began further training at the newly founded Conservatoire; within five years appointed Professor of Harmony in Moscow. Composing flourished; encounter with nationalist circle centred upon Balakirev – climax of his involvement this way, his 2nd Symphony, the 'Little Russian' 1873: but the bent of his interests took him Westwards. From 1876, financial and emotional support from wealthy patroness Nadezhda von Meck – by mutual consent they never met. Disastrous marriage 1877, to quell rumours of homosexuality, major life-crisis, also cathartic, releasing the principal nature, curse and blessing of his genius – confessional operas and symphonies wherein self-projections achieve artistic relief, ballets where the troubles can be objectified into diversion and delight. Extensive European travels (and one visit to the USA) as his universal fame blossomed. Death in 1893 remains dark and divisive – a plot? A suicide-pact? An inadvertent misadventure with cholera-tainted water? The truth is established, but the rumours have hardened into legend.

Shape and highlights of the oeuvre: 1866 1st Symphony 'Winter Daydreams'; 1869 *Romeo and Juliet* fantasy-overture; 1876 *Francesca da Rimini* fantasy-overture; 1877 4th Symphony; *Swan Lake*; 1879 *Eugene Onegin*; 1882 *Serenade for Strings*; 1885 *Manfred Symphony*; 1888 5th Symphony; 1890 *Sleeping Beauty*; *The Queen of Spades*; 1891 *Voyevoda* – tone-poem for orchestra; 1892 *Nutcracker*; 1893 6th Symphony '*Pathétique*'. Many other operas; four orchestral suites and other overtures etc.; concertos for piano (two; a third unfinished), violin, cello (*Rococo Variations*); some piano-music, some chamber-music, many songs, some religious choral-music.

Dryden's rhetorical question – *What passion cannot Music raise and quell?* – can be answered by Tchaikovsky. Tchaikovsky is for some things the greatest of all composers. It's not just his melodic genius in itself so much as the musical utterance brought into being when this gift is given complete primacy in the music's total effect. For this, melody has to be suitably accompanied. He is not like Bellini, with the one element mature and the rest rudimentary. His music is very well-composed in every way required to give melody the lead. His command of form is commensurate in his best works with his demands upon it; he is a sure and individual harmonist; the orchestration is, of course, flawless and highly original; and indeed his actual *accompaniments* are inventive as well as appropriate. All these supporting roles subserve melody, supreme in every sense.

Melody is the means by which music exerts most immediately its power to 'raise and quell' the passions. More even than Handel, Schubert, possibly Verdi – the other supreme melodists – Tchaikovsky depends upon it, to liberate with incomparable generosity music's emotional potential. Above all he is audacious. He risks everything. But he has the resources – the range, copiousness and sheer genuineness to carry it off. The risk is greatest where he is most conspicuously at home, with the utterance of passion. The gamut from daintiness and charm, via ardour, yearning, voluptuousness to uninhibited eroticism is given so wholeheartedly as to sweep all before it. 'He never feared to let himself go,' as Stravinsky said. 'Prudes, whether *raffinés* or academic, were shocked by the frank speech of his music.' But this is by no means his only note; he excels also in urbanity and elegance, with melodies that embody with the utmost distinction an aristocratic *douceur de vivre*. This has its bourgeois level – suave still but not so polished – and its rustic counterpart – healthy, happy, exuberant. He also excels in gaiety and brio, wit and humour. Central again, the histrionics, the highly charged, the reckless abandonment to states of extreme tension, wild excitement, despairing hysteria. But even to denominate his melodic types like this is to simplify and limit (and omit); they interact and cross-fertilize with infinite variety. The wonder is that he could get such extremes together at all. There is a paradox; his control is so total as to be almost *dis*passionate. The propensity within to violent agitation is belied by the orderly life, the manifold scores (delivered on time), the obedience to the apparent constriction of exacting choreographic measurements, the reverence for the Apollonian equipoise of Mozart. But he has his own saving Apollonism: if the submission to the wilds of passion were technically incoherent, their interest would be psychopathological rather than artistic.

His liberation of music's power to touch and express, indeed to 'raise and quell', the secret life of its listeners, with melody as principal means, is the basis of Tchaikovsky's appeal. Mme von Meck imagined him to speak to her soul alone; the truth is that this intimate singling-out applies to everyone. It is open to obvious abuses. The charm can be (and frequently is) vapid; the glamour and romance can be debased into corn and cheap thrills; the bravura handling of raw-nerve emotion can be done by habit. Whereas an uninspired fugue or sonata is merely dull, fervour and passion by rote are unbearable. So he *has* to be inspired; when not, he is worse than dull.

More serious than such off-day lapses is the potential for cheapness that actually lies, by their very nature, at the heart of some of his greatest and most characteristic pieces. Take the love theme from *Romeo and Juliet* and the second subject of the *Pathétique* Symphony's first movement, the earliest and latest of their kind in his oeuvre. These marvellous ideas exemplify all the daring of Tchaikovsky's unprecedented reliance upon ardent expression. The opportunity they offer for sheer tackiness, both in performance and in subsequent imitation, is also unprecedented. Expression can be overdone in plenty of previous music; none before Tchaikovsky (and at his best) can be creamed with such ease. The dubious quality is not exactly 'in the notes'; but something in the notes, if not directly inviting a lubricious treatment, certainly does not decline it. After this the path lies broad and downhill towards sleazy sloughs of awful muzak-making, 'artistic' or commercial, ending up in the bog of Sylvichrino and Masturbani.

All in all Tchaikovsky opens up a Pandora's box of mingled boons and blains. His reward was to be for long decades the world's most popular composer; his simultaneous punishment, to be disapproved, even detested, for reasons that shift with the sifting sands of fashion. When the Teutonic hegemony still ruled unrivalled – Brahms and the Old Testament, Wagner and the New – his attempts upon the great forms were regarded with suspicion, and his ballet music (*not* a great genre) with disdain. Nor was he a hero for the Franco-Slavonic reaction. The new appetite sought exotic colour with a touch of the *outré* Russian nationalists, then French *plein-air* impressionists, then modern primitivity, thence modernism pure and simple: the anti-Romantic spirit of the age had in general no use for Tchaikovsky, in spite of Stravinsky's important defence both in words and in music. Nor did the bastions of high seriousness with which anti-modernists bore up the collapse of post-1900 Teutonry give Tchaikovsky an opening: Reger wasn't good enough, Mahler not yet seen to be good, Strauss had let the side down, and the radical advances of Schoenberg were simply beyond the pale. In turn Sibelius, successor to Beethoven in the symphony, then Bartók, successor to Beethoven in the string quartet, then at last the second Viennese group, were accorded the highbrow's veneration as the embodiment of past glories all set for the future. Plainly Tchaikovsky had no place here (in spite of the Tchaikovskyan element clearly audible in the earlier Sibelius and not lost when his direct influence is sublimated).

So from various exalted viewpoints he 'wouldn't do', even while he provided unmitigated satisfaction for the average music-lover. And since the 1960s this role has gradually been assumed by two rhetorical-confessional symphonists who both owe him an enormous debt. Mahler's is ambiguous, deploring and disavowing; Shostakovich's is direct and grateful (and of course he is gratefully indebted to Mahler too). The deification of this pair as the incarnation of middle-brow anguish and ecstasy has displaced those old warhorses, the last three Tchaikovsky symphonies. Other usurpation includes the enormously expanded popularity and dissemination of Wagnerian music-drama, the ever-rising stars of Strauss and Rachmaninov and the recent revival of late-Romantic 'degenerates' such as Schreker and Korngold who, perishing in alien modern times, only now receive the prize for their long sojourn in the cold.

All this is, broadly speaking, an extension and intensification of Tchaikovsky's native area of passionate expression: erotic throbs and thrills, self-exposing self-revelations, traumas and neuroses up on the rooftops in neon. He has been wholly upstaged at his own game. But in the general blow-up the core of his achievement – musical utterance via a genius for melody – has escaped. (Expressionism's means are harmonic, polyphonic, textural, timbral, and sometimes sheer volume.) And justice to the uniqueness and value of this achievement is still not so smiling as his case deserves. The charges against him that seem to have anything to them are defused if his genre-orientation is not only admitted but respected and loved. Everything in his work truest to his genius aspires to the condition of ballet. Here his central gift finds its exactly fitting form. It's not solely a question of function and style. It involves clarity of aim, a distinction and focus so physical that one can almost see them. *Atti e gesti*, Michelangelo's two inspirations, have never in music been so persuasive – Mozart's powers of operatic characterization are matched by what Tchaikovsky can evoke through stance and movement. Only Stravinsky (whose every bar Balanchine claimed he could choreograph) can touch him here; but Stravinsky is hardly a well-spring of original melody; his means are largely rhythmic.

This quality of melody-as-gesture can be found throughout

Tchaikovsky's work; in whole intermezzo movements and as elements of developmental movements in the symphonies, tone-poems and concertos; in plenty of songs and character pieces, not always by any means from his top-drawer. Also, more intermittently, in the operas – indeed the greatest music in his most popular opera, the letter-scene from *Eugene Onegin*, is a perfect instance, every phrase making a physiognomic and affective gesture of the utmost precision and sensitivity. The *Serenade* and *Souvenir de Florence* have it, and that other, much-despised Italian tribute, the *Caprice*, is among the clearest examples. When he's least like this he's at his least pleasurable and interesting; the heavy-duty stretches – mechanized developments, stilted joins, virtuoso display and operatic galley-work. And naturally when the work is an *actual* ballet, the result is the purest concentration upon what he does best with the smallest admixture of clutter and nuisance. The three ballets, whatever his doubts over the genre and ritual moans in *Nutcracker* over failing inspiration (always a good sign with Tchaikovsky!), are the summit of his work. To write a whole evening's worth of music based on the power of melody requires exactly what he had more than any other composer – a bottomless well of it.

But if this genre is still, even unconsciously, regarded with condescension, what is its defence? That on three occasions it has elicited such superb scores is vindication enough; in such hands at such a level the genre has a glory of its own. This was hardly true of earlier efforts, which teeter on the edge of absurdity and vacuity. The soppiness of *Les Sylphides* and *Giselle* seems to have no possible outcome. Only the full-length works of Delibes (much admired and heeded by Tchaikovsky) have artistic substance and some sort of aesthetic integrity. Then with Tchaikovsky the adequacy of the scenario, the classic status (whether from the start or reached later) of the choreography, and the calibre of the music, together raise ballet onto a different plane, a sort of feminine complement to the big serious genres of the late nineteenth century, with the composer as a sort of 'mistress' to the three most conspicuous late-nineteenth-century masters – Brahms for brains and culture, Verdi for broad humanity and Wagner for Wagnerism. There's not much reciprocity between them, but some indications of Tchaikovsky's attitudes and a more extended comparison, where fruitful, will perhaps help bring his greatness into clearer focus.

He aspired to Verdi's popular touch – the direct access to communal feeling, articulated by tight dramatic pacing and plenty of good tunes – as much as he aspired to be, above all, a composer of opera. Not, alas, the very un-Verdian kind of opera which he essayed but twice, with complete success – *Eugene Onegin*, intimate 'scenes from provincial life', at their heart two creatures of passion with whom he could wholly identify, and *The Queen of Spades* (also Pushkin), where he reaches regions of raw identification; but Grand Opera about Joan of Arc, etc. He didn't have a chance with this, but the clear-cut Italianate gestural character of the style certainly leaves audible traces. Brahms he simply despised. Hearing the new Double Concerto in Hamburg, his contempt was boundless for the German pedantry that constructs a tune by sticking one fourth on top of another (forgetting that many of his own finest are just as systematic). Nor could he be expected to feel, behind the apparent subservience to classical conventions, a glow at the core not so different in kind from his own; nor to get through the apparently graceless scoring to appreciate its cross-hatching polyphonic subtleties.

Wagner he predictably loathed, though he couldn't afford to despise him. Emerging from *Götterdämmerung* was 'like being let out of prison'. But Wagner's mastery of a very different kind of orchestral sonority was not lost on his avid professional ear, and there are stretches in the ballets (notably the depiction of Beauty's hundred-year sleep) where Wagner's way with time and space shows that the prison-sentence has not been utterly in vain. And it is in comparison with Wagner that the particular character of Tchaikovsky's genius can actually be more closely illuminated.

Wagner's realm is mythology, saga, high romance; Tchaikovsky's is Gothic legend, classic fairy-tale and nursery-land fantasy. Wagner's treatment of his stories is superhumanly vast and hieratic, his own texts are weighted with ideas, philosophies and interpretations, psychological exploration is everywhere latent, often explicit.

Tchaikovsky's treatment is gestural and mimetic, decorative and formal; there are of course no words, neither concepts nor declarations; depiction of character is by type, two-dimensional, not in-depth, and interpretation is uncalled for. Wagner's aims bring about his musical substance; his normal texture is a complex, omniscient interweave of nominating and commentating motifs, in themselves short and incomplete, then worked together in quasi-symphonic, quasi-polyphonic sequential fantasia to produce unprecedented duration, with an underlying massiness of architecture beneath the improvisatory flux. Tchaikovsky's aims bring about his musical substance just as exactly: and – as with Wagner – commensurate with his compositional proclivities – melodic, formal, shapely, articulated, closed, virtually without polyphony and only in exceptional passages developmental. Wagner creates size by an 'endless melody' of musical prose, Tchaikovsky by effortless extension of the single melodic line – 'musical poetry'. Wagner's motivic interweave is a means of bending time; the long reach into past and future brings them together with extraordinarily rich and powerful effect. Tchaikovsky's time is a perpetual present in which listeners can always know their exact whereabouts. So he fills a whole evening by addition – an expansion of what Schumann (a German he really liked) had achieved with the same kind of short complete song-and-dance-units in his larger piano-cycles. Tchaikovsky makes a mosaic, a cabinet of delights; Wagner an organism which can be excerpted only in painfully bleeding chunks. All in all, his medium is thick, Tchaikovsky's thin (no reservation is intended of either; all this attempts only definition).

Then there is the question of momentum. Wagner's is slow, even sluggish, gradually animating via long processes to a rich convulsive stream, oceanic and all-embracing, a rendition of the inner life. When physical he is primal, energetic, brutal – Mime hammering, Siegfried forging. True, the Flower-maidens waltz gracefully with Parsifal and the Apprentices lustily with their Fräuleins; but the general poverty of body-motion in Wagner can be obliquely adduced from Chabrier's burlesque quadrilles on themes from *Tristan*. Whereas Tchaikovsky of course is always utterly physical.

The whole body, not just the feet, wants to move – he's written the instructions, in the imperative and seductive mode. And while Wagner is metrically galumphing and not very various, Tchaikovsky's range is huge – *The Sleeping Beauty* in particular is a compendium of gestural and rhythmic models. The plentiful endowment is the reason he could fulfil the demand of tight choreographic lengths, and when, as often, he outran his choreographer Petipa's orders, the invention remains measured and shapely. Imagine Wagner attempting to fit into exact bar-counts, obeying specific instructions as to tempo, type, even timbre! And finally, their way with expression itself – after all, their principal goal. Here it is Wagner who issues the imperatives – be elevated! Be abased! Be overwhelmed! Though Tchaikovsky undoubtedly exerts all his powers to excite in his listeners what excites him, the element of dispassion, even of impersonality, keeps a distance: an Invitation to the Dance, for delight, rather than a Summons to the Temple, for ritual purgation.

A direct comparison where myth and fairy-tale, thick and thin, actually converge, can help fix the connection. The motif of the hundred-year slumber in *The Sleeping Beauty* – a virgin, protected from age and decay by the supernatural suspension of time and from casual marauders by a thicket of prickles so that only the Chosen One can penetrate it to wake her with a kiss and claim her as his own – is a clear double of Brünnhilde on her rock at the end of *Die Walküre*. (The only difference of story-line is that Brünnhilde is insured by flames not thorns, and that her sleep is a personal punishment.) Wagner's handling is reckoned, rightly, to be sublime and deep. The ancient motif is placed as half-way climax in his saga; destiny, with long tangled antecedents and a future perilously uncertain between salvation and destruction, is poised in vast expectation. Its human dimension is equally charged. The God/Father, as one link only of the intricate enmeshings in the consequences of his actions and hopes for their resolution, must sacrifice the part of himself he most loves. The Goddess/Daughter, discovering her own will in an impulse towards compassion that disobeys his, must descend from her pedestal and become a Woman, admitting Life and Love their fullest scope. In the face of such manifest grandeur (which cries out for these Archetypal Capitals) how can Tchaikovsky's handling hold a candle?

In *The Sleeping Beauty* the same motif, so close to its composer's inner desires, also makes at the heart of the work whose title it takes an extraordinary vastness and expectation. Life slumbers, waiting to be reborn into love. The apparatus of ballet – busy ceremonial, set-pieces of decorative display – is waived, to be reassumed, after the Prince wakes her, with enhanced magnificence and a wealth of invention that even Tchaikovsky never surpassed. Neither before nor after the crucial event is there much plot; character is the merest type; the simplification and flatness are total. But the overall impact is not small. Poetic meaning and artistic expression are anything but impoverished. And there is an extra dimension, which gives this genre its *raison d'être* as singing does opera (including music-drama) and accounts for the flatness and simplification in character and story – the riveting beauty of complex and demanding movements executed with grace, exuberance, apparent ease, individual physical prowess and disciplined communal pattern-making that fuses into an indivisible unity with the music. If the genre had not been so hidebound and hung-up on *divertissement*, Tchaikovsky might have matched his three actual ballets with further works of comparable quality on themes that appealed to the positive side of his histrionic powers – *Romeo and Juliet, Francesca da Rimini, Hamlet, Manfred, The Tempest* for a start. If he had, his theatrical oeuvre would be comparable to Wagner's in weight as well as value.

But all this is a historical conceit. The only contemporary Tchaikovsky *did* fall for in a big way was Bizet, chief weapon in Nietzsche's anti-Wagnerian persiflage: here the comparison is clearly direct and to the point. And so the summa of Tchaikovsky in his true genre is *The Nutcracker*, where the fairy-tale fullness of *Sleeping Beauty*, equally with the tragic melodrama of *Swan Lake*, falls victim to prettiness. Hardly any story survives this voyage from a Biedermeier Christmas, via a night battle between rats and toy soldiers, to the land of eternal meringues. But *what* prettiness! The music is indefatigably alive and (with one exception) all straight from the top

drawer. The battle, for instance, keeps up a prolonged sparky animation with at least as much brilliance as anything in the symphonies.
The transformation of the Christmas-tree from domestic parlour
to fir-forest deep in snow is one of the great Romantic moments,
the equivalent in this 'thin' medium of the great scene-changes in
the outer acts of *Parsifal*. (The one slightly duff number follows, a
snow-flake-*valse* where tinselly, wordless voices gormlessly reiterate
a less-than-inspired tune.) The total void, once the land of confiture
is reached, in such plot and characterization as have hitherto been
vouchsafed, is solaced by the sequence of character-dances familiar
in part from the *Suite* – 'light music' so distinguished that the adjective simply drops away. Then there's the celesta; then a glorious *pas-
de-deux* more fit for Faust and Helen, or Antony and Cleopatra, than
its actual occasion; then the best-ever final waltz. Maybe the 'content'
of most of this is akin to the paradise of sweeties and wine and
music rendered in the finale of Mahler's 4th Symphony, which will
be patronized by no one. But that *pas-de-deux*? The sheer hugeness of
the emotion released suggests what has perhaps been lost, or rather,
not fully realized, in his undertaking as a whole.

'What passion cannot Music raise and quell?' The phrase can
cover every shade, even the most sombre and disturbing, in the endlessly fresh world of exactly realized fantasy, poetically responsible
escape, and precisely disciplined self-indulgence, created from Tchaikovsky's frank and audacious exploitation of his unmatched gift for
melody.

After Tchaikovsky

> Only Russians can combine in themselves so many opposites at the
> same time.
>
> Dostoevsky, *The Gambler*

All three Russian composers to achieve prominence before the Great
War begin in faceless anonymity, masterly in technique, derivative
in idiom, academic in stance. Scriabin (b. 1872) begins in Chopin
before taking on Franck and Wagner with touches of Brahms and

Strauss; Rachmaninov (b. 1873) begins in Tchaikovsky; Stravinsky (b. 1882) in Glazunov for his Symphony in E♭, his teacher Rimsky-Korsakov in *Fireworks* and *Firebird*, his older contemporary Scriabin in earlier piano-pieces and right into the ground-breaking *Petrushka* and *Rite of Spring*. They are artistically bankrupt, or rather, heavily in debt, before slowly or suddenly enhancing or transcending their inheritance to become themselves. It's more than the traditional learning-by-modelling: compared with the defensive anti-cultural ideology of their predecessors in the Five – defiantly nationalist at a cost of narrowness, provinciality and, in Musorgsky's case, 'uncouth' primitivity and desolating incompletion – these new men manifest something of a cultural cringe.

Stravinsky's later course is altogether other. Scriabin and Rachmaninov make an illuminating complement: wonderfully gifted composer-pianists, moving from a shared common cultural background in divergent directions that yet continue to relate – Rachmaninov cool and contained, elegant and controlled even amid tempests of emotion; Scriabin refined and sensual, warming then burning then blazing with ardour personal and artistic, tending towards mystic ravings wherein self-expression and self-fulfilment will bring about a regenerated planet: the entire course of his brief life – he died in 1915 – is *vers la flamme*. Rachmaninov, though, is correspondingly heading away from initial turbulence towards Libra the Balance – the Golden Mean – fully achieved in the decade or so before his death in 1943.

Scriabin's early piano-pieces are wholly faceless, while always exquisitely laid out for the keyboard – Chopin, Chopin and again Chopin, adding nothing to the source: sole 'deviations' (to use Ravel's word for copying from the model) are matters of musical spelling and intricacies of technique, notably the incorporation of criss-crossing rhythmic pulses, that don't affect the underlying conventionalities – sweet and drippy, dramatic, elegiac, tragic and rhetorical. These emotive states eventually take over entirely. In the succession of ten sonatas running from 1892 to 1913 his forms, hitherto miniature – mazurka, prelude, nocturne, étude – expand; the piano-writing burgeons into an extraordinarily individual technique, the harmonic language into chromatic extremes way beyond its sources (Chopin again, Franck, *Tristan* and *Parsifal*) and the nature of the content – *Black Mass* (No. 9); *White Mass* (No. 7) – grows ever more urgent. Alongside these sizeable works for himself to play comes a series of more appealing miniatures; no longer generic (étude, etc.) and given poetic titles specifying their nature without equivocation; *poème Satanique*; *fragilité*; *poème ailé*; *ironies*; *desire*; *caresse dansée*; *étrangeté*; and the iconic *vers la flamme*. Wonderful subtlety and artifice herein, this claustrophobic hothouse microcosm where, like his own personally developed harmonic system, all is circular, self-referential, short-circuiting – aching perfumed erotic dissonance in search, in vain, for consummating relief by cadence. His *sounds* do it far better: but a few of the composer's self-fulfilling instructions to himself as performer, to the audience as auditors, can convey the scope and temperature of this body of music (all in his own original French): relatively ordinary – *avec douceur, avec élan, avec entraînement, étincelant, modéré*(!), *extatique, joyeux, languissant, murmuré, onduleux, vibrant, sombre*; hotting up – *inquiet, perfide, légendaire, étrange, impérieux, triumphant, ailé, avec ravissement et tendresse, avec trouble, comme des éclaires, avec une ardeur profonde et voilée*; extreme – *l'épouvement surgit, en un vertige, épanouissement de forces mystérieuses, avec une douce langueur de plus en plus caressant et empoisonée, avec un volupté douloureuse* (and also *radieuse*), *elle se méle à la danse délirante.*

Considering the central position of the piano throughout his output, it is all the more remarkable that Scriabin writes so outstandingly well for orchestra too. Chopin couldn't help him here, nor the other pianist-composers who go stodgy, lacklustre, inept when they come to scoring – Schumann, Liszt, even on a bad day or a poor performance Brahms and Beethoven. Scriabin's *Poème de l'extase* (1908) is an orchestral masterpiece, whatever reservations the puritan temperament might find in the piece's declared content – and this despite the evident fact that its characteristic textures and spacings have been conceived at the keyboard.

He had already written three symphonies. The first two are diploma-pieces without distinguishing features. They share a

disconcerting leaning towards C-major bathos: the first, overall in
E, turns to C for a choral fugue glorifying Art; the second, in C-
minor, ends with a march in the major best described in the composer's own subsequent view, 'instead of the translucence I desired, I
got only a military parade'. The third, *Le divin poème*, written alongside the *Satanic Poem* for piano (1902–4), doesn't wholly escape the
same charges. For all the Franck, Wagner, Strauss, together with a
first sprinkling of the notorious passional programmes and self-
commending performance-instructions (which already carry
Scriabin close to Messiaen), it remains at bottom a well-made conservatoire product.

Sampling this *Divin poème* is the best way to put the greatness
of *Le poème d'extase* in context. It too might fit the same description
(even down to the colossal C-major close) except for the miracle
which lifts it onto another plane altogether. Intended at first as a
fourth symphony, *Poème d'extase* was begun directly after, becoming
first a *Poème orgiaqie* before the definitive title was reached, late
in 1906. By then Scriabin had published the *actual* poem which
provides the score's overheated theosophical credo. This load of
sado-masochistic junk is a period-folly more amusing nowadays than
dangerous. Some specimens (from Hugh Macdonald's translation):

> The spirit of joy and hope / Gives itself to the bliss of love. / Amid
> the flowers of its creations / It abides in kisses, / In a plenitude
> of delight / It calls them to ecstasy. I call you to life / You hidden
> aspirations! / You, buried / In the dark depths / Of the creative
> spirit, / You timorous embryos of life, / I bring you /Audacity!
> / . . . the bites of panthers and hyenas / Have become but a new
> embrace, / A new torment, / The snake's bite / Is but a burning
> kiss / And the world resounds / With the joyful cry: / I AM!

The function of the words was to stimulate the music into being
by bites and caresses. They served the purpose. The resulting score
transcends dated mystico-erotic tat, embodying these 'godlike/
diabolic' impulses in memorable themes, gorgeously harmonized,
sumptuously orchestrated, worked into a thoroughly efficient shape,

its facture still somewhat overdependent on repetition and sequence, yet wholly convincing every time in strictly musical terms. Which by no means implies that one can't hear just what is flagrantly going on from fore to aft. The score doesn't need its *embarras* of French and Italian instructions/commendations; the entire vocabulary of amorous palpitation, perfumed ardour, mounting frenzy, culminating coming, is never ambiguous, least of all the victorious phallocentric theme played by the first trumpeter. No half-lit hints like *Jeux* or erotic insinuendo as in *Daphnis et Chloë* – for all its refinement the *Poème d'extase* goes naked, erect and proud.

It's built on a succession of ripples, waxing into wavelets, breakers, surf-splurges, culminating in one orgiastic roller-coaster before the hymnic close. First come longing (*languido*), dreaming (*suavamente*), skimming (*volando*); and the first imperious trumpet-summons. Then come amorous *délices*, a *très parfumé* passage growing via *ivresse* into *délire*; then the trumpet again, followed this time by a stormy episode of 'dark presentiment' with stabbing horn-chords and lurching trombone plunges, before the trumpet breaks through triumphant against a background of campanelli, harp glissandos and fantastical woodwind patterns, to achieve a half-way climax. The second half intensifies and kaleidoscopically re-juggles the same ingredients. The final stretch sets off *allegro molto, leggierissimo, volando*, soon overtaken and engulfed by the trumpet theme, now joined by all eight horns (the other four trumpets keeping up a brilliant high battery of twinkling triplets), the whole massive yet gleaming sonority underpinned by a Grand Organ. (At an early stage Scriabin also contemplated lighting-effects and a choral setting of the poem's climatic spasms – in the end reserving these extras for the next 'symphony', *Prometheus*, completed in 1910.) The climax breaks off *sur le point* for one last caress, before the overwhelming final Amen-cadence, powerfully appropriate for what has to be called a religious utterance in carnal guise.

Prometheus brings back the solo piano (though scrapping the Grand Organ) as well as adding chorus and a continuous play of symbolic-coloured lighting. Its harmonic language is more *outré*, its orchestration more advanced, but despite the insistent instructions – *de plus en plus lumineux et flamboyant*; *avec défi, belli-queux, orageaux*; *avec un éclat éblouissant*; *prestissimo, dans un vertige*, etc. – the wings don't lift, the fire doesn't blaze, as in its predecessor. Successor to all, the Great All itself, the *Mysterium* that obsessed the composer's final years, into which Divine Culminating Act many of the late piano miniatures would find a more expansive home. At his premature death, sketches for only the first stage – *Prefatory Action* – were achieved. The entire ultimate *Gesamtkunstwerk* would have out-vied Wagner by including dance and perfumes as well as play of light and inconceivably vast cohorts of singers and players: to take place in a specially constructed semi-spherical 'temple in the Hima-layas', mirrored in a lake to make the perfect sphere: clouds overhead would dangle enormous bells. As with Wagner the aim was regen-erative: unlike Wagner, however, Scriabin was no dramatist or poet – the texts are pure Theosophy-balderdash; and unlike Wagner he was unwise enough to give a term to the Vision's implementation – Mankind would arise transfigured and redeemed and enlightened after just seven days. Very much of its epoch, such overweening: compare the exactly contemporaneous *Jakobsleiter* of Schoenberg and the *Universe Symphony* of Ives, equally sublime/ridiculous, awesome and hapless; with their scarce-credible demands for and of performers, and their inevitable incompletion.

Mockery is invited, obvious, facile. Yet when Scriabin's '*Universe*' – an initial realization by a Soviet musician of what the composer had left – first appeared in the 1970s, the opening sounds wiped the smile from the face. Its sonorities are quite staggering: maybe he *could* have transfigured the world. Then after this opening, more of the same, less so, soon palls – 'enough, or too much' – and as *Universe* spins on and on one is too aware of the realizer's recourse to recyc-ling the composer's late piano pieces.

It is impossible to conceive further development along such lines. 'A superlative has no future.' But there is an absorbing little cluster of consequents to Scriabin's extremist aesthetic, retaining the mystical-erotic-constructionist aims (brought back to the solo piano), adhering to the spiritual in the drastically altered conditions of post-1917 Russia. Such virtually forgotten figures as Obouhov,

Krein, Stanchinsky, Roslavets, make a fascinating codicil to the colossal megalomania of their master, and can be just as impressive on their less vainglorious scale.

From directly similar context and background, Rachmaninov is something altogether otherwise. The nature of his oeuvre is marked by extravagant emotionality, Tchaikovsky taken over the cliff-edge – a torrential overflow of autobiographical confession, close to neurosis – and an actual nervous breakdown after the disastrous première in 1897 of the 1st Symphony (completed two years before, when aged twenty-two), resolved in composing the 2nd Piano Concerto (1901–2); the former nearly lost for ever, the latter nearly never found. Yet, already, the iron control that will command his pianism; a sense of mastering this red-hot matter, making a machine of it, manipulating, even exploiting, the melancholic lava-stream. He has something cool – *not* cold – at his centre.

Before these crucial landmarks, much solo piano music and the 1st Piano Concerto (1890–91), a trio in memory of Tchaikovsky (1893) and a one-act opera *Aleko* (1892): after them, two more one-acters, *The Miserly Knight* (1905) and *Francesca da Rimini* (1906); the 2nd Symphony (1906–7); *The Isle of the Dead* after Böcklin, for orchestra (1909); *The Bells*, a choral symphony on the poem of Poe (1913) and many songs. Alongside, what appears to be the polar antithesis, two magnificent sacred works for *a cappella* chorus, the *Liturgy of St John Chrysostom* (1910) and the *All-Night Vigil* (*Vespers*) (1915): a rich-layered world of resplendent choral sonority that could appear lush or indulgent but for the innate austerity, even chastity, of the Orthodox idiom.

He fled Russia after the Revolution to concentrate upon an international career as a fine conductor and one of the epoch's greatest pianists: tending towards residence in the USA, though building a family villa in Switzerland. Left Europe 1939; renting then settling in Beverly Hills, dying there 1943. His post-Revolution/Great War music shows, alongside the supreme performer's glamour, a slow growth towards deeper mastery, a stripping-down of the over-upholstered earlier textures that, sometimes, conceal emptiness. Landmarks: 4th

Piano Concerto (1920); 3rd Symphony (1935); *Variations on a Theme of Corelli* for solo piano (1931), *Rhapsody on a Theme of Paganini* for piano and orchestra (1934), and the *Symphonic Dances* for orchestra alone (1940). This later harvest reveals more and more closely his strange, contradictory nature: morbid, melancholic, death-devoted, yet elegant, dapper, velvet and satin, wit/sparkle/euphoria. 'Death-devoted' – the obsession with the *dies irae* plainchant; its pregnant shape, its dire words always implicit, is present in much of the output and sometimes all-pervasive. What does it *mean*? Especially what does it mean when, in the third *Symphonic Dance*, as well as the plainsong, whole stretches from one of the liturgical choruses in the *Vigil/Vespers* is reproduced verbatim and works to a terrifying climax – a bevy of blood-lust-maddened monks on the rampage? What does it mean? 'We will find out.'

This, however, is to begin at the end, with the last movement Rachmaninov wrote. Back to the *Dances'* first: an experiment – listening with an Innocent Ear as if one has never heard this music before; as if at the first performance in 1943, both in the context of world war and in the select microcosm of contemporary music. Three 'Symphonic Dances' – a contradiction in terms already. And No. 1 is marked, uniquely, *non allegro*, and never for a moment suggests any kind of dance whatsoever. A soft, shy, stuttering repeated note. As triads dissonant to it obtrude, it expands chromatically as its stammer is closed; the combination dies. Brusque reopening, hard and peremptory, introducing main theme, the triad from the start, now expanding into a wiry virile line with chunky chugging accompaniment, developed with enormous vitality and inventive-ness rhythmic and intervallic – complex music, on the face of it straightforward; and scored with a fierce edge, no stuffing, orchestral piano prominent: rhythmic dislocations and harmonic expeditions, all returning by variegated means to base, more muscular each time. Energy dies down leaving a themeless oscillation, oboe joined then by clarinet, background to a long melody on saxophone, its phrases answered in refrain: both grow longer and more expressive, melan-choly and spacious, looping upon itself apparently casually yet very subtly shaped, and very original – in emotional flavour too, as in texture and sonority; nothing quite like it anywhere though it seems to have existed since for ever. Taken up by violins and cellos, phrases and responses now joined into seamless long line, the accompanying figuration transferred to the piano as if to evoke an enormously enhanced Palm Court trio. When all the upper strings play together, *molto espressivo*, passion is not withheld – on the contrary, it is explicit and heart-on-sleeve; yet also cool, reserved, withdrawn.

This middle section fades: the opening material steals back surreptitious and altered, its bounding energy transmuted into a spectral outline. When energy is again turned on, the rhythm is triple not duple, though equally non-dance-like. The on going *non allegro* now fraught with considerable complexity both before and after an initially exact recapitulation: chunky clarity of outline yields to chopping chromaticism which coalesces in a mist of dulled tremolos and a shining ride to easy gentle openness – perfectly placed new idea, hymn-like on middle-range strings under a halo of piano, harp, flutes, glockenspiel, in gently sparkling staccato. The vision fades, the *non allegro* resumes on its initial non-thematic material, eliminated note by note till only one note left.

No. 2, however, is recognizably a dance: after a disconcerting opening salvo, acrid summons on muted brass – almost a snarl, borrowed from *The Bells*, given twice – a grimacing death-knell foretelling (with hind-ear) what's to come, a *tempo de valse* sets up with characterizing one-two-three accompaniment. A *valse lugubre* – elegant, suave, svelte, sensual/erotic, velvety, mournful, urbane – between worldly, warm-blooded Tchaikovsky and cool *café-chantant* Satie, and entirely its own thing. Seduction-waltz, hesitation-waltz, soft-shoe satin in darkling yet shiny hues. The temperature rises, arabesque flutters whirr and spin, the summons returns harsh and interruptive, the waltz (after a brief and perhaps pointless allusion to the first movement) resumes, ever more intensely charged; its curbed eroticism flows, ebbs, flows, the snarling opening twice cuts off pleasure before it resumes in a new place, not its old groove, mounting to ecstatic gestures of acceptance/abandon – unbridled yet always perfectly groomed – its decline then grows imperceptibly yet inevitably into a playful *scherzando* on the same motifs, whose

identity with the *Tristan*-shape, embedded earlier in the rich texture
complete with *Tristan*-harmony, is now subsumed into a whirlwind
tarantella of diabolic amorous itching. The excitement dies down
almost as soon as it arose, into all-controlled quizzical, enigmatic
eyebrows-raised close. 'What does it all mean?'

No. 3: and now the story really starts. Preceded by call-to-arms,
immediately succeeded by wailful descents in wonderfully original
harmony (this composer is up there with Weill and Gershwin, the
master-harmonists of the mid-twentieth-century mainstream) before
the whirligig is loosed. 'The Devil dances with me'; bells evoke a
Witches' Sabbath, and the main motif soon yields a tarantella distortion of – can it be? – it is – the *dies irae*. Everything works together
with transparent fluency, ease, invention, mastery; and the chanting
monks from no. 9 of the *Vespers* make their first appearance.

Cut-off: the wailing opening now openly recalling Tchaikovsky's *Pathétique* returns loud and grievous, inaugurating a slow
middle-section of complex and ambiguous allure, the plainsong
tag burningly expressive beneath waltz-strains and shivering, shimmering glissandi: all this but a prelude to a low-placed new motif,
initially unpromising, that in its slow burgeon produces the most
inspired music in its composer's output: veering between extreme
chromatic passion (but always so steely-cool-controlled) and easing
diaphanous diatonics (but so hot within): masterly paragraph-
building on material so potentially slippery, masterly the hand on
the temperature-controls where sleaze and gush lie so perilously
adjacent. When the music reaches *lamentoso* the heart burns, the
withers are wrung, the genitals quiver in anticipation. Wilds of
extravagant luscious abandon, yet so contained, so stylish, so inexplicable, that words fail. Wonderful wind-down into resumption
of *vivace*: tarantella with more than a whiff of sulphur, soon easily
exceeding its first run, recomposed with unflagging verve; a whiff
of Spain too, in the open strings down all the string body, plus tambourine; but not without delicacy amid the whirlwind.

As the *dies irae* grows more and more explicit, ending in a blaze
of fanfares and fireworks, we can half-anticipate what's coming
next – mad monks on the warpath, beards burning, cassocks hoisted,

chanting in bacchic tumult a mix of the plainchant with, from the *Vespers*, the Doxology and Hymn to the Virgin Mother of God who redeemed Adam from the sin of Eve: this reusage is astonishingly close to the choral original. *Night on Bare Mountain*, Walpurgisnacht, the orgy in the Venusberg all seem to get in too, at least by association: the pagan rout invades the Haunted Ballroom, the Dog-star is out, all Bedlam loosed: the scene ends in a wild rave, absolutely precise and punctual, beyond pleasure/pain, beyond good/evil – five stark final blows – D and A without a third major or minor, though major has prevailed heretofore; and the controversial overhang from the gong-of-death: whether the thing will be damped or left resounding after the rest of the sound is cut short; a cliff-hanger till the very last in every different performance.

The Innocent Ear's verdict after this anonymous first hearing says, not profound content-filled music like Bach, Beethoven, Bruckner; nor yet, like Haydn, Mozart, Schubert, music that takes its weight lightly: 'just' a wonderful piece. But what a 'just' – superb composing on terrific material, 'music about music', notes about notes, terrific notes for all their filthy-lucre contact with 'extra-musical' associations and the 'potency of cheap thrills' always in play. Impure and pure, ultra-affective yet paring its fingernails, right outside the official canonic mainstream of the progressive art of the twentieth century, here in 1943; but – with hindsight – a mainstream that rejects it is doomed to stagnate.

And 'what does it mean?' The vision that transfigures the close of the first Dance is a self-quotation from forty-five years before, the motto-theme from the 1st Symphony –'Vengeance is mine: I shall repay'; its recurrence here a closing of the circle, a goodbye, like Strauss a few years later (1949) quoting the *Verklärung*/transfiguration theme from his early tone-poem in a song towards the end of his life asking 'can this perhaps be death?' Alluding to *Tristan* speaks for itself – love/death inextricably fused. As does the *dies irae*; day of wrath, Judgment close kin to Vengeance; Rachmaninov's obsession with the motif is heard again and again all the way from that 1st Symphony, via the death-toll in *The Bells*, and the *Paganini Rhapsody* (to name but three) to its ultimate transformation in the impassioned middle-section of the final *Symphonic Dance*. And what about the mad monks on the march in the movement's crazed tarantella close? The words for the identical music in the *All-Night Vigil* read:

> Blessed art thou, O Lord: teach me thy statutes: The assembly of angels was amazed, beholding thee among the dead: Thou hast destroyed death, and sorrow, and raised Adam with thyself, and freed mankind from hell: Why do you women dilute the myrrh with your tears? cried the Angel: look at the tomb and understand – he is risen from the dead.

And the Doxology complete, using its first line as recurring refrain, ending 'Thou O Virgin, by giving birth to the Giver of Life, hast delivered Adam from his sin, given Eve joy not sadness: the God-Man thou barest has restored fallen mankind to life. Alleluia; Glory to Thee.'

All this quoted virtually exact, the 1915 *a cappella* setting transmogrified into the whirling madness of 1940, culminating in something near the Vengeance-motto of 1895, then the gong of annihilation. Rachmaninov in his summa is as covertly autobiographical as Mahler is explicitly in his; Tchaikovsky's 4th, 5th, 6th Symphonies the model for both.

The *Symphonic Dances*, with the *Paganini Rhapsody*, are Rachmaninov's summa: other milestones will have to be chipped. First, the 1st Symphony of his early twenties – deeply and obviously flawed, yet such a remarkable testament, so big with consequences, that it deserves to be his Op. 1 rather than its actual unlucky 13 – as if the baleful motto vowing vengeful repayment, also used by Tolstoy for *Anna Karenina*, were exacting its fee. The première was a disaster, the wounded young composer withdrew the score, which subsequently vanished: the second performance, after his death, was prepared by reconstructing the score from its performing material: and the work remains on the outer verge of the repertoire. Unlike its successor, No. 2, twenty years on, which also has its lapses yet sweeps all before it. So too with *The Bells*, symphony in all but name. At its best – first movement all sparkling gaiety – 'crystalline delight' as Poe's original English has it; and the third, scherzo of scampering firebells – 'a mad expostulation with the deaf and frantic fire' (Poe again). But the voluptuous ardour of the second movement – marriage bells – is already shot through with the inevitable *dies irae*: it penetrates the finale too, more appropriately – tolling death-bells, elegaic with an unconvincing interpolation of Gothic Horror, then resumption of mourning and melancholia, too easily succumbed to.

The complex juiciness of the choral-writing here contrasts sharply with the two works for unaccompanied voices written either side of it – lush luxury; austere restraint. The *All-Night Vigil* already mentioned is the later, the *Liturgy of St John Chrysostom* the earlier. Together they make the composer's most surprising venture. Written still within Scriabin's lifetime, while he was engaged with enlightening and redeeming the Universe via the most OTT resources ever envisaged, Rachmaninov turned to his Orthodox heritage and wrote for unaccompanied choir, eschewing the instrument of which his mastery was nonpareil and on which his career depended. Scriabin couldn't have done thus had he been spared many more decades. Rachmaninov's two cycles of liturgical devotion are masterpieces of imaginative choral layout, in an idiom at once austere yet sumptuously layered, grave and serious but sometimes buoyant, ecstatic, airborne. Their effect, with the right kind of singing and singers – basses with low Bbs! – and in an appropriate building – domed, cavernous, dim-lit, icon-filled – and, most of all, within their intended religious function, is jaw-dropping.

After 1917 Rachmaninov was an exile, a wandering virtuoso. Composition sparse at first, gradually picking up, eventually reblossoming. The concertos for himself to play were the staples of his fame and income. As models of their genre – 'black piano appassionato', Tchaikovsky's 1st Concerto the prototype – they remain unsurpassed. But what a type! The uncharacteristic 1st, the all-too-bedraggled 2nd (1891; 1901) are followed in 1909 by the 3rd, a big bad warhorse, all ostentation after its lovely first tune, unmistakable for any other composer. And the 4th (1926) is a disaster-area, its first movement tired and featureless, its second featuring only 'Three Blind Mice': the finale doesn't come to their rescue. Another ambitious effort of this interwar time, the 3rd Symphony, joins true gold with cheap Korngold. Altogether true, however, *Three Russian Songs* with orchestra (1926) – not folkloric: elliptical, passionate, dark.

The triumph of these uneven years is in effect a fifth piano concerto, *Rhapsody on a Theme of Paganini* (1934). There's an unexpected forebear three years earlier – *Variations on a Theme of Corelli* for piano solo: a dry run (sometimes excessively dry) for its full-blooded big brother, here and there directly prophetic – the central lyric oasis is in Db like the emotional heart of the *Paganini*, but can't yet wear it on its sleeve. The coda after the final variation is eloquent – brief, spare, suggestive of fullness, opening out from the theme towards what will bloom so ardently three years on. All in all, an individual angle on interwar neo-classicism; elegant archaism poised between Baroque theme and Romantic consequences.

The *Rhapsody on a Theme of Paganini* is the unexpected yet ordained masterpiece that fulfils all the preceding flickers of something new. On a different plane from anything before: brilliant in every parameter. Simplest of all, the piano-less start, 'prequel' to the theme (and entitled *Precedente*), wittily setting out its harmonic skeleton without harmony, or indeed theme, taken over by the piano for Variation 1 as the Paganini is permitted in its original violin-version, only beginning to come to life as soloist in 3. There are comparable felicities of sheer neatness throughout. The solo part hardly ever rampages/crashes/bashes/thumps: on the contrary; quicksilver sparkling clean as Scarlatti; wit, elegance, dexterity, adroitness, charm, play, all at top-invention. Var. 6 begins to explore deeper, preparatory to 7, slower, *dies irae* on piano, theme below, though its opening tag is mischievously insinuated higher now and again. Then the plainsong is forgotten for a while. Var. 8 is chunkier, 9 weightier and more driving, 10 a sort of march with the plainsong returning in unison octaves for the soloist, then aggressive syncopated chordal outbursts, then energetic glitter-work, self-disintegrating to end Part I.

Part II begins on a new note with var. 11, exploring lyric rather than athletic and playful potentialities – as up-beat, ruminative, cadenza-like, inconsequential in itself, dissolving in delicious delicate piano filigree plus harp glissandi; a touch of *de luxe* in the sound – to the *consequence*, var. 12, *menuetto*, art deco Ritz-rococo, rather resemblant of the Ravel of these years hinted in the *Corelli*, here fully realized. Var. 13 is chunky hairy-chested Brahms in his 2nd Piano Concerto; 14 introduces Rachmaninov's fingerprint trumpet-signal and opens out the so far mainly enclosed circle of the theme's harmony; 15, soloist alone, another mercurial Scarlatti-with-mod-cons, ending on a quizzical disappearing twang.

Part III commences more *serioso*, var. 16 closely foretelling the stutter opening-fan chords near the start of the first of the *Symphonic Dances*; then a surely deliberate allusion to the flutter-buzz accompaniment of *le café* from Tchaikovsky's *Nutcracker*. Still elegant/playful, but darkening towards melancholy. Var. 17, a magnificent deep grope into richly gaunt/gauntly rich strangeness: fascinating close harmony; bare wide intervals, ever more angular, on sustained woodwinds and brass, piano alone keeping the momentum slowly rolling. Complete in itself, yet actually up-beat to 18, the celebrated Db melody adumbrated in the Db variations of *Corelli*, the 'big tune' there relinquished blooming here with full rejoicing splendour, the inconceivable fruit of the wiry Paganini theme, though closely related by simple inversion, as audible as it is ingenious. Thrice: piano alone, beautifully laid-out, no fatty redundance: which is permitted when it accompanies the second go, melody on violins and cellos. The third go is the work's juiciest resemblance to the throbberama of the four piano concertos: finer in every respect, all the more for not milking the climax, instead beginning to decline almost so soon as peaking, soon embarking on a really marvellous swoon-down in which the orchestra gradually falls away leaving soloist alone, eventually plain, simple, chaste.

Part IV: new start. Var. 19 back to theme's basic outline, austere and twinkling. Animation sets in and grows all the way through the next variations: 22 is another march, building up up up from softest mutter, nearly choking on its own steam till chords give way to figuration, which in turn swells and engorges, issuing in barnstorming cadenza, mercifully brief, to complement the pearly earlier one in var. 11. Its provocative end is instantly mocked and subverted by the orchestra as 23 starts, and the finale – for so it essentially is – resumes more and more energetic and *brioso*; cascades of virtuosity brilliant then weighty, another very brief cadenza ('when in doubt, write a cadenza', but no doubts here), before resuming – 24 – in a whirlwind of velocity soon underpinned by the long-forgotten *dies irae*, grand and heavy on brass but not checking the momentum; nor, strangely, the mood; till the soft, neat, witty, deflationary close.

One would have to ask the 'meaning' of this too, though the question doesn't resonate like Vengeance and Vespers in the *Symphonic Dances*. The work completes the circle: the summa where Rachmaninov gets his entire endowment together, at the highest level, in the most unlikely synthesis of its time. Rapidly composed; for two pianos first, then the orchestration, after a four-year gap since the 3rd Symphony. 'I don't know how it happened. It must have been my last spark.' Weary, in failing health and strength, amid a world at war, his native country and culture lost for ever, the artistic climate alien and inimical: yet an affirmation of fire and energy, passion and surprise: absolutely without cynicism, irony, whinge, apology – utterly out of its time and place – and thus so for long epochs afterwards; and so outstanding in calibre as to be in the end a crucial element in how that time and place is defined and valued.

A Note on Ernő Dohnányi

Nineteen thirteen; return to the belle époque of marble staircases, deep carpets, plush curtains, gold-braided flunkeys. Dohnányi, four years younger than Rachmaninov, born 1877 into the same musical culture of superlative pianism and sound academic training in composition, where his 'true Penelope' is rather Brahms than Rachmaninov's Tchaikovsky. The *Variations on a Nursery Song* for piano and orchestra might well be in the background of the *Paganini Rhapsody* some twenty-one years later. They have much in common – stylish, witty, skilful, clever, sometimes luscious, 'naughty but nice'; though the Russian plumbs deeper depths than the Hungarian, whose piece is more of a *jeu d'esprit*. A very good one, that wears well though now sadly out of fashion. Dohnányi's dedication – 'for the enjoyment of lovers of humour and to the annoyance of others' – doesn't appeal so securely to an age soured by 'irony', whether sly and teasing à la Stravinsky and Poulenc, or harsh and strident à la Shostakovich.

Splendid baleful, portentous orchestral introduction, the nursery tune concealed within the wailing and fluttering between the brass's dire warnings, to emerge, innocent and mischievous as Haydn, on the solo piano, with whimsical little hesitations and a friendly bassoon counter-voice to close. Var. 1 is choppy, ending in glissandi down the ebony keys and up the ivories. Var. 2 is a march, alternating formal and jocose: 3 is a tongue-in-cheek homage to the Brahms/ Smharb who couldn't resist the sweetmeats of his adopted Vienna however gross: 4 is a cheeky number where the piano accompanies a duet of low bassoons plus double-bassoon/high flutes plus piccolo, joining ensemble to close. Var. 5 is gleaming and glittering, silky strings, harp and piano tintinnabulation, the theme on bells – a Christmas Tree. Var. 6 chuckles; 7 is a voluptuous waltz – Brahms again; very close to the ballroom sequences in the 2nd Piano Concerto finale, but not so distant from the *valse* in the second *Symphonic Dance* of Rachmaninov, without that piece's morbid, even menacing, undertones. The waltz is prolonged; and through it are discerned the nursery tune outline here and there: fading into 8, another march, sardonic almost à la Prokofiev. Var. 9 is a 3/8 scherzo very reminiscent of *The Sorcerer's Apprentice*, with a touch of *danse macabre* on the xylophone. Var. 10, the expressive nub, is a passacaglia, building with equal beauty and ingenuity from the theme, in minor, as bass, that couldn't have been anticipated from anything prior, to culminate via huge *crescendo-accelerando* in 11 – *Chorale*, somehow simultaneously paying tribute to *Hansel and Gretel* and J. S. Bach. Sure enough, the finale is a fugue: after silly jokes with scales in wrong keys, an excellent specimen, adroit straight or inverted, its harsh dissonant intervals curiously foretelling the fugue in the final of Bartók's *Concerto for Orchestra* thirty years later. Energetic athletic climax: theme again in all its *faux*-innocence, complete with languishing bassoon; tearaway coda – also very Bartók (all three piano concertos); surely Dohnányi's younger compatriot (by only four years) must have known this work, even if by 1913 his direction was already so alternative?

CHAPTER XI

Late Nationalists

Jean Sibelius

An Absolute of concentration and economy, all wrought of a single, simple phrase yielding variety enough to encompass stasis grinding or brooding, momentum in a sinister scherzo and a blinding snowstorm, convulsions of terror and panic, strangulated pleas as though for deliverance from fate, plangent yearning as though for deliverance from human feeling, awe before the power of nature at its northernmost point of intransigence and malignity, an eventual hymnic quietus unforgiving rather than consolatory, as though the termination of a life–death trajectory without a life-to-come. Sibelius's last major utterance *Tapiola*: 'not to be listened to alone'. How did this composer come to end up at such an Ultima Thule, this black hole towards which his previous output had ever tended, into which it plunges and is lost?

The rest is silence; after *Tapiola* what can be said? Except that, in the year following, the incidental score for *The Tempest* yields another Ultimate in the astonishing *Storm* prelude, followed by its strange further numbers: culmination in oddity, even freakishness, of the copious occasional and light music that sits alongside the craggy masterpieces of symphony and symphonic poem. Rumour and speculation about an 8th symphony fluctuate; only definite, a few desultory scraps, and the thirty-year silence.

My voyage to accommodate, let alone appreciate, this difficult composer was long and slow. Heady juvenile relish of his contemporaries had Sibelius appear unexciting – austere – forbidding – *noli me tangere*: the 'glass of cold clear water' that he posited for himself in conscious reaction against the age of conspicuous excess. Then a gradual realization of this music's specialness and stature: its power to express and move as well as its structural grandeur. Most of all, its unique stance in its time: upholding and extending diatonic tonality amid the general erosion – only few others, such isolated landmarks as Pfitzner's *Palestrina* and Vaughan Williams' *Tallis Fantasia*, upholding and extending classical goals amid their general neglect or abuse: *fons et origo* of a vital line down through the twentieth century, dull-seeming at first by contrast with the excitements and seduction of modernism; in the end just as exciting (maybe not so seductive); and just possibly more permanent. Because of his virtual abandoning of composition after 1926 Sibelius, though living on till 1957, belongs essentially to the maximalist era (see later) as, too, to the late phase of nineteenth-century nationalism: in the end, however, understood and valued as a composer for all times, seasons, countries.

'When I was a boy I thought I would invent an altogether new art – it would be half-sculpture and half-music' (Sibelius in 1890). Sculpture in three dimensions: add time as the fourth, translate into sonority, view and hear from all sides – always the same, every change of facet/angle/light upon unchanging mass of matter in sound and duration. The *subjects* of these objects are both physical and metaphysical: Nature, pantheistic and mystical without 'organized religion': the intellectual/structural/organic processes common to symphonic poems infused with land- and seascape or poetic symphonics ostensibly 'abstract': in both a strong but inexplicit element of autobiography. The resulting art-works are like works of nature – 'rocks, stones, trees'; waters, skies, clouds, swans and cranes, dawns and sunsets, thunderstorms and snowstorms: and their presiding deities, inimical, or merely indifferent, to puny mankind. No Eros: mighty visionary uplift, occasionally Triumph; no Consolation. Humanity enters via the Epic. The last words in his diary – 'what enormous musical possibilities the *Kalevala* offers' – might as well have been the first. With its larger-than-life heroes and heroines, its desperate deeds – slaughter, dissection, rapine – its magical journeys, its boisterous carousings; practicable and usable with its cycling stanzaic structures and the marked metrical rhythms, his country's national Epic is the foundation of his procedures and his idiom.

Influences from his own art are, of course, just as crucial: his own words can mostly say it all. Impact of Bruckner (3rd Symphony), Vienna 1890 – 'to my mind he is the greatest of all living composers'; 'you cannot imagine the enormous impression it has made on me.' *Kullervo* was conceived on this visit, and how one hears it. 'Empty' slowness and granitic 'primitivism' of material; all process and proportion; blocks of thematic matter; ostinati and diatonic pattern-making; primal. No use whatever for Bruckner's Catholic fervour or his sublimated-erotic harmony, nor his rustic Schubertian warmth and cheer. Bruckner's adagios are the heart of his content; slow movements in Sibelius can verge upon the slight, even the perfunctory.

Wagner: Bayreuth 1894 – 'heard *Parsifal*. Nothing in the world has ever made so overwhelming an impression on me. All my innermost heartstrings throbbed.' Until *Tristan* later that year '. . . nothing, not even *Parsifal*, made so overwhelming an impression. It leaves me feeling that everything else is pale and feeble by comparison.' Yet *Meistersinger* turns out to be his favourite Wagner work – 'surpassed all my expectations and completely bowled me over.' Oddly, considering his life-long involvement with Epic tales, characters, settings, the *Ring* doesn't loom large, but aspects that rhyme Wagner with Bruckner – the huge diatonic paragraphs, the ostinati, the ur-primeval motifs of *Rheingold* especially – are palpably not lost on him. *Parsifal* for ineluctable processional spaciousness, the filtered layered scoring, the intensely chromatic harmony from which the yearning, heaving *desire* has drained out: clearly audible. Not so clear, where desire burns brightest as *Tristan*: and of the still-more-favoured *Meistersinger*, not a trace.

Beethoven – 'the greatest composer of all, Beethoven did not have the greatest *natural* talent, but he subjected everything he did to the most searching self-criticism and by doing so achieved greatness.' A bit pro forma until one digs behind: 'how dreadful old age is for a composer! Things don't go so quickly as they used to, and self-criticism grows to impossible proportions': this despairing late cry reveals more of an identification with Beethoven than the partially condescending earlier remark. His presence in the Sibelius symphonies is more a matter of technique – the celebrated 'severity of form', the 'profound logic' that creates 'an inner connection between all the motifs' – than of actual sound.

Whereas resemblance to Tchaikovsky is paramount in Sibelius's first two symphonies and Violin Concerto – rhetoric, passion, melodic contour, harmony (with a touch of Borodin for sure, Balakirev perhaps), and the clear/full/direct primary-colour orchestration. Tchaikovsky is very soon assimilated and relinquished, but remains wholly incorporated deep within.

Mahler: definition by opposites, as illustrated in the two composers' famous exchange in 1907: Sibelius admires the Symphony in the phrases already used in connection with Beethoven. Everyone knows them, and Mahler's vehement rebuttal – '"No!" he said [Sibelius is reporting some twenty-five years later] – "the Symphony must be like the world. It must be all-embracing"' (often given as 'it must contain everything').

Palestrina: not Pfitzner's opera, though its remarkable congruity with Sibelius has already been noted. Both composers invoked 'the Saviour of music' in the same Great War years, and for just the same reason and purpose – an ideal of polyphonic purity, white-note modal/diatonic: in the opera, through an actual Palestrina Mass, imbuing its context with gentle radiance; in Sibelius's two final symphonies, via the textures and processes of any number of Palestrina motets.

Jean Sibelius, born 1865; early piano-lessons and attempts at composition; aged fifteen took up the violin; aged twenty tried the Law, abandoned next year for music – professional violinist. Aged twenty-four to Germany and Austria ('Bruckner the greatest living composer'); 1891–2 *Kullervo*, 1892 marriage to Aino, 1894 Bayreuth ('overwhelming impressions'), 1897 life-pension from the Finnish Government; splendid warhorses 1899–1903 – Symphonies Nos. 1 and 2, Violin Concerto, *Finlandia*: more on course, *En Saga* 1892 (revised 1901); *Lemminkäinen* cycle 1893–7. Full maturity: *Pohjola's Daughter* 1906, 3rd Symphony 1904–7, *Night Ride and Sunrise* 1907, 4th Symphony 1911, *The Bard* and *Luonnotar* 1913, *Oceanides* 1914. Growing international fame all these years, England and the USA especially; much travel – Berlin 1911, interesting contacts with the new developments there. Drinking and smoking problems all along, with crises health and marital. 'Late style' – 5th Symphony in three recensions, 1915/1916/1919; 6th Symphony 1923, 7th Symphony 1924, *Tapiola* 1924–5, *The Tempest* 1926. Crunch with Aino 1924 – 'either you or me' – resolved, but the Long Silence ensues. Rumours of an 8th symphony. Three decades of dumb depression, dying 1957 aged ninety-one.

Kullervo: a towering masterpiece, depicting the mighty hero, telling his deeds of prowess and shame – the male chorus narrates, two soloists take the two dramatic roles, and the orchestra is omni-present: youthful confidence, at extended length, despite youthful inexperience shown in the killing nature of the instrumental demands in all departments, though the overall sonority magnif-icent and sure. Idiom, an astonishing mix of Bruckner (as stated, Sibelius conceived the work in the light of a revelation from Bruck-ner's 3rd); Tchaikovsky and the *Karaminskaya*-method of cyclic repetitions; Wagner for the use of myth, saga, narration direct and oblique rather than actual musical language or method, except the long pattern-making over pedal-points, as Brucknerian as Wagne-rian; runic declamation and rhythmic chanting from the Finnish language itself. Also, parallels with music not yet written – to Janáček, to the Stravinsky of *Les Noces* and the *Symphony of Psalms*: these later composers could not have known *Kullervo* because of the embargo placed upon it after its première. Why did Sibelius withdraw it after this extremely successful event? For sure it repre-sents a route not taken, like Mahler's juvenile *Klagende Lied*, that seems in retrospect so natural and right: the ban – it wasn't heard again for another sixty-six years – seems to foreshadow the eventual self-destruction and silence.

Five movements: no. 1 – Portrait of the Hero in his youthful pride/glory/prowess – perhaps the work's finest for boldness, assurance,

complexity, pace: Bruckner to the fore. No. 2: a lullaby reverting
to Kullervo's boyhood – strange, tender-remote-gentle, withdrawn;
'Russian' in structure of cyclic rotations, and extraordinarily prescient of Janáček-to-come. No. 3 is the centrepiece, with narration on
the male chorus and dramatic presentation on the soloists, Kullervo
and his sister in her three guises. The initial runic 5/4 pattern persists
for 322 bars, in stark syllabic primitive chanting, setting out the
hero's journey by sledge, vivid in his blue stockings and yellow
hair, encountering a maiden and stopping his sledge to invite her
in. The unknown girl's response – may Death mount your sledge
and Sickness be your companion – doesn't promise well; he continues impetuously on, encountering another maiden and inviting
her to join him: she too declines; on he drives; his invitation to the
next girl is more seductive – share my apples, enjoy my nuts! She
vehemently objects and threatens – in your sledge is darkness. This
time he brooks no refusal and hauls her in. The seduction is told
obliquely yet incredible intensity is generated – emotional without
'expressionism', shockingly direct – wild – ice-cold yet red-hot; absolutely non-erotic. The deed done – ruined by silver, misled by gold –
she asks him his kin. Before divulging, he asks her hers. The frightful
truth also emerges obliquely: the maiden's Lament implicit in her
tale of leaving home seeking berries, losing herself, crying out for
mother, wanting to leap to her death, conceal a sister's loss of her
maidenhood at her brother's irresistible urge; and – inexplicit but
devastating, plunging only now to self-destruction.

This and the brother's tremendous outburst of guilt and shame –
no Siegmund! – would that I had never been born; Death and
Sickness did me wrong, not destroying me – are the work's high
points. But, forgetting all this, the fourth movement is all joyous
extroversion for orchestra alone, the hero in his prime, exalting in
battle – mostly energy and brio – though also beset with strange
threats and collapses – as if to say the dark past is known, that retribution awaits and will strike; and perhaps protests too much. For
no. 5 the male chorus again takes over to take the tale to a resplendent conclusion, Kullervo's apotheosis. But not before telling of his
pilgrimage to the place of outrage where the grass remains withered,

his expiation, his suicide on the blade of his own sword. Two vast dominant pedals, perhaps longer than any such in previous music, or later till minimalism: Kullervo's grand theme, not heard since the first movement, swells in magnificence as his nobler parts are exalted, before the sudden curt close.

'The way not taken.' The chosen path is, nevertheless, overshadowed by the size, nature, calibre of its tremendous beginning. And the next landmark in the oeuvre is in some ways a continuation – symphonic portrait of a hero from the sagas, telling of his great deeds, this time wordless – four symphonic poems – *Four Legends from the Kalevala* (also known as the *Lemminkäinen Suite*) – playable separately: and also, curiously, subject to their composer's self-suppressiveness. The first, *Lemminkaïnen and the Maidens of Saari* and the third, *Lemminkaïnen in Tuonela*, were composed 1895 but withheld until 1939: the second, *The Swan of Tuonela* (1893) and the last, *Lemminkaïnens Return* (also 1895), were permitted, and became repertoire-pieces from the start. But there is no perceptible difference of calibre, and the four *Legends* taken together make an impressive unity. The hero is first presented as the Finnish Don Juan – he seduces the entire female population of Saari with music of passionate erotic tension – no melody, just endless repetition and extension of the same phrase, keeping it up and up as fragments of gestural fanfare come and go, a seemingly random kaleidoscopic mosaic, rather Borodin-like and very Tchaikovskian – his late *Voyevoda*, a fine little-known orchestral telling of a *crime passionelle*, seems like the direct model: *Karaminskaya*-technique to the fore, modulations alter the colour, textures activate or cease in a *moto perpetuo*; whirring parallel tritones, seething chromatic scales – material almost non-existent yet compelling in effect and powerful in affect. The *Swan* a perfect contrast: Tuonela is the land of death, surrounded by black waters upon which the swan floats singing. Here the clear source is the prelude to *Lohengrin*, transformed and darkened and upside-down, building up from the bass not descending from the heights in banks of divided strings, and a very original use of the bass-drum as unpitched alternative to timpani. The swan's voice is given to cor anglais, with strong recollection of *Tristan* Act III for association rather than actual material, and to the start of that act for mood and atmosphere; occasionally also for sonority – string-lines drifting gently upward, ending in thin air. Paradoxical sense of lightening yet thickening, preparatory to the choked melody on massed strings over dense yet very soft brass and the hypnotic rhythm on two timpani (now introduced for pitch – a minor third apart): simple stroke (drum-stroke) of genius when they alone (helped a little by harp) continue the pulse under the return of the cor anglais.

Lemminkäinen in Tuonela: the hero must accomplish three mighty deeds in order to win the Maiden of the North. Two are done, one remains, but he is betrayed. His mother senses him to be dead: she descends to the realm of darkness to redeem him. With a rake forged by the mythic blacksmith god she gathers her son's remains, magically knitting them together to restore him to life. Back to the first piece – crepuscular string tremolos, overlapping and animating to underpin melodic phrases on the woodwinds – *Tapiola* clearly foretold, with *Parsifal* behind. Huge tension, huge climax, no resolution till, at last, relief in a magic soft shimmer (with tambourine, almost inaudible) and a sort of runic lullaby: *Parsifal* Tchaikovsky-fied, and a masterly close, harmony/gesture/texture/timing fused together like the hero's fragments. *Lemminkäinen's Return*: re-knit, the youthful hero returns home rejoicing: all animation and energetic virility, *ice-cold* version – no Straussian warmth for this Don Juan of the Frozen North. A clear heir to the extroversion of *Kullervo*'s fourth movement: and if that had flickers of disquiet across the brio, moments here are positively spooky, spine-tingling even before the chilling bells enter. Yet *moto perpetuo* never lets up, and after the sinister centre, *Return* is reached with a sweep and exuberance worthy of Berlioz, till the broad A-men close. 'A Short Ride in a Fast Machine' – a brilliant thing, by no means so one-dimensional as it might have been, considering the subject and actual musical means and material – 'made of nothing'.

Now – 1899–1903 – come the first two standard symphonies and the Violin Concerto: filled with echoes and derivatives, Tchaikovsky mostly, plus plenty of Borodin and an element of Balakirev, this Russian residue gone harsh and edgy or soft and corny. Material is

indifferent, even mediocre – histrionic, baleful, menacing; superseded stage-scenery left out in the winter cold, hotted up, milked
for all it's worth, and sometimes pumped up into bring-the-house-
down grandiosity prophesying triumphalist Soviet Realism or New
Deal uplift. Yet also prophetic of the great works to come, wrought
from very similar ingredients but 'understood for the first time': the
foretaste in the first movement of the 1st Symphony of the storm in
Tapiola, the breakthrough from the third movement to the finale in
the 2nd; and, most of all, the 2nd's first movement – its 'organicism',
whereby from material at first so neutral as to be uninteresting and
so disparately presented as to be desultory, shapes gradually focus
and eventually loom into clearer, larger definition and continuity in
a journey/structure almost as visible as auditory. All told, not good
music and often truly poor: but never without authority and power:
staples of the repertoire; warhorses; successful – even splendid – as
such. With hindsight, however, another direction not taken; this one
he was surely right to abandon.

The 3rd Symphony (1904–7) is a magnificent breakthrough,
and the 4th (1911) is the crucial central masterpiece. Born of a dark
passage in the composer's life – a death-scare brought about by
his excesses of drinking and smoking, threatening marital stability too: absolutely inexplicit/non-confessional in the work itself of
course – Sibelius does not do autobiography à la Strauss, Mahler
or even Elgar – but nonetheless permeating the work from within.
Much of it takes place 'inside' *Parsifal* – remember Bayreuth 1894, 'All
my innermost heart-strings throbbed.' In general, the atmosphere/
texture/sonority of the Act III prelude, that unforgettable depiction
of attrition physical and spiritual: in particular, the ur-resonance of
Amfortas's suffering from Act I, the sequential chromatic descent
over the cycle of fifths that expands hugely into the Transformation Music – an unforgettable sound-image remembered throughout this symphony: with further passing echoes and reminiscences
from early in Act III – Parsifal's weariness, the supreme moment
where he disarms, and a touch of Kundry. Even in the scherzo,
Sibelius's light-music side is taken towards dark places: its almost
dinky nature transmuted into sinister balefulness, harsh angularity,

edgy discomfiture alongside apparent geniality. Heart of darkness in what follows – third movement, *il tempo largo* – bare emptiness – the *oed' und leer* of the Act III *Tristan*-prelude, comfortless linear nakedness comparable to that in Mahler's near-contemporary 9th Symphony, occasional passages of incongruous richness, never sustained and fulfilled, melodic aspiration again and again thwarted till the last attempt, curving down from the heights to what will, with hindsight, turn out to be the main theme of the ensuing finale. For now, though, it precedes the end of the slow movement in uttermost desolation.

The finale commences in delightful exuberance, almost gaiety: but there are signs of trouble even within the brio – apparently casual semitone clashes in the bucolic material, innocent harbingers of excruciating dissonance to come. For now, a new tone, the *affettuoso* cello solo, then on violin, a sort of parlando-recitative, settling down into a gentle buzz of string-momentum: soon, the ice-cold tingle of *Glocken* – whether sparkly high glockenspiel or mid-range bells (depending upon different conductors' differing choices) their effect is anything but cheerful. Startling upward yelp of clarinet, like some great bird suddenly disturbed right under your feet. The disparate materials now begin to solidify, rocking upon tritonal conflict, growing almost hymnic. The opening returns, losing its initial *plein air* brio in a thick belt of woodwinds and brasses, drum-rolls, strings in rapid ascending/descending scale-practice. All material remains in play: *un*-play: tensifying once-frisky gaiety freezing as its potential for strain now takes over. Possibly the most excruciating dissonances in all music – *because* measured against tonal consonance: truly spine-curdling – 'all my innermost heart-strings throbbed'. This crucial passage issues in the Amfortas-strain on strings, broken by ferocious down-plunging major seventh on brass, the drums below on anything-but-resolving keynote. Amfortas-strings resume their lament, intercut by upper woodwinds' wailing raven-cry (fragments from an aborted setting of Poe's *Raven* are used in this finale). The bird of doom wins, supported soon by sour four-part harmony on the horns: is repeated higher and louder: strings resume their sequential chromatic syncopated descending lament, disappearing in a trembling ambiguous shudder. Raven on flute, descending seventh on oboe alternate, strings fragment the lament towards a solid, albeit *pianissimo*, perfect cadence – home key resolution achieved. Only strings now remain: four bars of chordal motet, *mf dolce*: two bars' silence; three of repeated A-minor minims; three more, separated by rests: no *ritenuto*, no *diminuendo* – *mf* to the last: one of the boldest and simplest endings ever, implacable and plain as the Great Bøyg's answer to Peer Gynt's question 'Who are you?' 'Myself': as close to self-expression as this composer will venture to approach.

Three tone-poems follow this ultimatum. *The Bard* (1913) is 'a mystery wrapped in an enigma' – baffling, elusive, made of next-to-nothing, fugitive beyond capture: one is, perhaps, tempted to call it epigonic, missing something rare and special. Not so with *Luonnotar* from the same year – a scena for soprano and orchestra telling of the world's creation, Finnish version. In some ways directly resembling *The Bard* – fugitive, mysterious, elusive, baffling, made of next-to-nothing; but here the minimalism is vindicated – 'the nothing that is not there and the nothing that is', wrought into a plangent visionary creation rendering creation itself. Sound-sheet background, including marvellous harp glissandi, against which, for once, a continuous plastically contoured expressive *line*: melodic or recitative or occasional crying out loud, the voice carries the content in a contour wherein every intervallic inflection tells ... of a maiden, daughter of the heavens, beautiful Luonnotar, wondering what her life might be, spent alone in the vast emptiness of space. The *Parsifal*-strain is intimated again in this amazing work, and grows very strong at its climax.

Wagner in *The Oceanides* (1914) is more unexpected – a distinct echo of the seductive invitation – *Komm!* – from the *Tannhäuser* Venusberg, *bei* Sibelius on ice, as usual. This curious work resembles both its predecessors, gone pallid and watery, ornamental and playful, involving seascapes and nereids at the opposite polar hemisphere from the Greek. Nothing happens: the waves begin to quicken: tuned steel-bars reminiscent of the *Glocke*/bells in the 4th Symphony finale, and more chilling still: is *something* going slowly to form and appear? Dissonant groundswell thickens, oscillating ostinati slowly grow into chromatic descent, then ascend to *fff*, down again, up again, an unlooked-for tremendous moment: the nereids sport in triumph on the great wave's crest: an instant total erasure – *fff* to soft in just two bars; and a quiet calm end. All in all, 'the nothing that is not there', as with *The Bard*; here, something within – 'the nothing that is' – that *The Bard* has not.

Interesting and significant that Sibelius's two supreme master-pieces, the 4th Symphony and *Tapiola*, both emerged (with whatever difficulty) unscathed, never needing revision (though he tried with the tone-poem). *Kullervo*, another high point, does need an overhaul for purely practical purposes: that it never received – perhaps for the best; it might have been spoilt. The 5th Symphony is his most extreme case (except for the enigmatic 8th) of 'justified self-criticism', resulting in radical rethink through three versions; an impressive record of self-appraisal to compare only with Bruckner. First is 1915; second the next year is interim; third version of 1919 is final.

Its eventual fusion of what had been two movements into a single continuity, from *moderato* into *allegro*, accelerating into *presto* then a whirlwind *più presto* is a tour de force of metrical engineering that has the hearer experience and feel its every metamorphosis on the pulses, in the bloodstream. Transformation of all the slow material into fast is compelling and convincing – especially clever, to appear to forget the opening fanfare-motif, holding back its return (after it has once effected the principal hinge joining the formerly separate movements) to be clinchingly climatic for the closing stretch. Every constituent in this double-single structure is subtly bringing to birth the Swan/Thor's Hammer theme to be explicitly revealed – revelation the *mot juste* – throughout the finale and as the whole symphony's ultimate goal. This powerful motif dates its first inspir-ation to 21 April 1915: 'today at ten to eleven I saw 16 swans. One of my greatest experiences! Lord God what beauty! They circled over me for a long time. Disappeared into the solar haze like a gleaming silver ribbon.' How the singing theme thus induced becomes the swinging theme of Thor's Hammer from the *Kalevala* is not clear except in the powerful energy of the motif itself. There had been an earlier vision too – the preceding April, when just commencing to sketch a new symphony – 'it's as if God the Father had thrown down the tiles of a mosaic from heaven's floor and asked me to determine what kind of picture it was.' And that September: 'for an instant God opens his door and *His* own orchestra plays *my 5th Symphony*'. James Hepokoski's outstanding introduction to the work elucidates these exalted utterances, then explains that the composer's visionary state encompassed eventually three further major works – the next two symphonies after the 5th, and *Tapiola* after them; and how the composer was long puzzled as to how to distinguish and disentangle them. Hepokoski then goes on to suggest that all four might well be named *Tapiola* – the forest; the place where its god dwells and reigns.

The 6th Symphony (1923) is the Cinderella for the general public: for some individual admirers, a very special work: I have to admit I simply don't *get* it. Between the beautiful opening – pure white-note 'Palestrina' string polyphony – and the inspired close comes insipid pattern-making on third-rate material, obsessively recycled to no compelling purpose. The second movement has a strange wistful/wry character of its own, but still not all that good – better, in the same vein, some of the *Tempest* music to come – the *Oak-tree* and *Ariel's Song*. And the 7th Symphony (1924) also compels reservations. For sure a remarkable intellectual feat: the compression into a single span of interrelated speeds and textures is astonishing: but the actual material, apart from a glorious motet of string polyphony and the noble trombone-theme, is a second brew from stronger originals in nos. 3 and 5.

So to the 'fourth *Tapiola*' from the following year, the work actually thus-named: where we came in, circle complete, the black hole towards which the entire oeuvre is headed, placed now in context of the complete journey. This great masterpiece is made by similar means from similar *Stoff* but better – the near-nothing of earlier better able to sustain an entire structure, charged-up to maximum from initial minimality. Harmony packed with the *Affekt* of late Romantic idioms and Wagner above all, *on ice*: pantheist mysticism, panic and terror, awe and wonder, eroticism possibly, all in deep-freeze, till the celebrated Outcry near the end explodes the glacier and the resolving consonance that fails to console.

Nielsen and Stenhammar

Two other distinguished Scandinavian composers overlap Sibelius – a Dane, Carl Nielsen and a Swede, Wilhelm Stenhammar. Carl Nielsen 1865–1931: two operas, three concertos, chamber and keyboard works; the core is six symphonies written from the 1890s through to the 1920s; the 1st (1892) Brahmsian; the 2nd (1901–2) '*The Four Temperaments*'; the 3rd (1910–11) is pastoral, the 4th (1914–16) '*The Inextinguishable*'; the 5th (1921–2) has no subtitle though representing the battle between anarchy, belligerence and destruction, and law-and-order, civil society and peace on earth; the 6th (1924–5) '*Semplice*' – a submission, it appears, in the face of contempt for contemporary culture at large – after a serious first movement, the other three are 'satirical', almost wilfully footling and inconsequential.

There is a problem with this composer so widely and justly admired. Undoubted authority and mastery, passionate advocacy for all the correct reasons – health and sanity, humanity, Man-the-Measure, nature and culture in equipoise – goals best reached when not declared outright. Nielsen's actual material, however, is often poor, and sometimes downright mediocre, the chromaticism unfocused, the diatonic featureless, the orchestration coarse: a surprising whiff of bad Shostakovich (excuse the pleonasm) can be smelled. In the 6th Symphony one sees what's being attempted – desperation, derision – but the satire is so jejeune – those rude slurps on the solo trombone in its 'humoreske' second movement! In the 5th the relegation of 'the enemy' to an angry military drum improvising as if at all costs to destroy the orchestra, rather than composing the conflict into the actual notes. And to call the 4th *Inextinguishable* is asking for trouble – optimistic uplift in unflinching cognizance and defiance of the dark strains in the outer world and the inner being, victorious over them with predictable triteness.

Happier when not thus fixed on the heights, the '*Espansiva*' – No. 3 – a generous invitation to the Pleasures of the Plains. The first movement – *allegro espansivo*: peremptory summons – I command you! When main theme obeys, irresistible energy and verve right up to *ffff*: recession into pastoral lyricism, with horn-call motif, though momentum not lost: a more rustic intonation introduces a brief fugue, soon blown away by swinging singing ending in a round-dance; end of exposition. Gentler strains, chirruping then waltzing, all the ingredients ingeniously in play: there's even a donkey hee-haw – then the tune on trumpets, then general dance. At last, a slackening – not for long, the pastorale with horn-motif, alternating with relaxed reminders of principal energy-motifs, everything in inventive reminglings: and suddenly we're in the thick of the action, wrenching towards main key, missing it by a mile, finding it, losing it again, till at last a resounding triumphal end. The second – *andante pastorale*: all strings in octaves for long-drawn modal line over a drone: the mood interrupted by strings now in passionate harmony: they resume, still more urgent, after the cool woodwinds have interrupted in turn. They come a third time, now underpinned by a drum-roll. Bucolic hunting-strains break in, slowly unwinding their horn into pure magic – twice. Ur-texture from the opening of *Das Rheingold* (same key) – deep bass drone, overlapping horn-motifs, woodwinds in gentle motion, and flute high above; muted first violins, seconds in imitation, sweetly flowing; a distant male singer in wordless cantilena, answered by a female, growing tenderly florid; him again; she now o'ertops him; brief interruption (nothing in particular, but just right): then the whole shelf of interlocking texture returns, foreshortened and enriched, the running material on violins present from the start and doubled by a flute and the clarinets; the voices also enter almost at once, male first female one beat later: the composite concentrated from twenty-nine to seven bars with no effect of constriction in the *Espansiva*'s most expansive and expressive passage. It's as though Nielsen were inspired by and trying to illustrate the famous description of the 'entangled bank' on the last page of Darwin's *Origin of Species*. Then just three more bars bring the movement to rest, low flutes adding a touch of chromaticism absent from the preceding diatonic purity.

Third movement – *allegretto* – a rather doleful musette, then rather strenuous, and as it develops, accruing overtones of sarcasm, bizarrerie, even unamiability, even menace – Pan the Dangerous, not the inciter to lascivious luxury. No. 4, the finale, is *espansiva* again:

full-fat, hearty meat-eating melody, continued with masterful easy
warmth, flowering into thoughtful places before returning brawny
in augmentation on heavy brass. Now more relaxed, pastoral, murmurous. Energy wells up again in a fugal stretch – up – down – out
into grandiose return of main melody, broadened, ending in hunky
self-confident Danish assertion. 'Man the Measure' far more enjoyable, and convincing, than in the symphonies that follow.

Wilhelm Stenhammar 1871–1927: noted pianist and conductor;
composer of operas and incidental music, two symphonies, two
piano concertos, six string quartets, notable for integrity and high
seriousness, indispensables guaranteeing nothing. Two works stand
out: *Serenade in F* for orchestra (1908–13) and a cantata *Sången/The
Song* (1920–21): both are special.

In the *Serenade*'s opening *allegrissimo* two musics alternate –
brioso and buzzy with burbling horns and dulcet suavity: then
solemn yet unportentous festive strains on multi-divided strings:
then superimposition, the chorale on winds, the busyness on strings:
a flicker of dulcet, a flicker of brio, a quizzical escaping close. No.
2: a *valse triste* with a foretaste of Rachmaninov's *Symphonic Dances*.
An answering section grows more distant and less urbane; eventually the two moods evolve into one, unfolded with mellifluous grace,
and leading direct into no. 3: the scherzo – fleet and light, strength-
ening into sinewy cross-rhythms, growing chromatic: the distant
festivities from the first movement return, their march/chorale
tempo set athwart the hunting-tempo – horns, then woodwinds, the
trumpets in splendour, then disappearing on woodwinds. A brief
contrasting *affetuoso*, then scherzo resumes, more brilliant, working
up to the festive processional now arrived at the forefront, peaking,
vanishing to no. 4: *notturno* – tranquil evenness, with fragmentary
memories of earlier joyousness from nos. 1 and 3 amid the nocturnal glades inhabited by amorous night-birds on solo winds. Mists
veil the moonlit scene; a breath of something more ardent: but this
isn't Respighi's Janiculum gardens nor *parfums de la nuit*: more like
the cool Nordic *Smiles of a Summer Night* à la Ingmar Bergman. No.
5 – finale: oddly Bruckner-ish slow introduction to lyrical allegro

with *scherzando* background; it goes dreamy, reanimates with pizzicato virtuosity and delicious slippery modulations; the opening
motif gradually infiltrated, ever more festive, heroic, martial; then all
gay and bubbling again, up to big broad climax; fade into summer-
night-smiles and strains of serious tender piety, till both dispersed
in turn by the elves and pixies of the *Midsummer Night's Dream* à la
Mendelssohn. A delight from start to finish – *Serenade* in excelsis.

The Song is weightier. Its poem was written, by a composer-friend,
to mark the 150th anniversary of Stockholm's Royal Academy of
Music, but the goal is not parochial; the Country, not the Academy,
is hymned – 'my song, my land – you land of my songs!' – with
memories of victories and defeats, of dark old gods superseded by
radiant new day which yet fulfils the vision of the Sagas. It's hard
to characterize Stenhammar's idiom here: a fingerprint, the closing
harmonies so often slid into an unexpected elision as to become
expected, sometimes resourcefully and movingly stacked up upon
themselves in terraces that descend (cadence) even as they rise. They
predominate in Part I: warm ample music, generous and eloquent
in fears and hope: shining pantheism infuses ardent patriotism; the
sap surges, unpriapic and unsensuous – 'desire springs free from a full
breast' – music of rejoicing, exuberant without excess, healthy and
sane. Orchestral interlude, religious without churchiness – 'natural
piety' translated into wordless sounds, analogous in tone and style to
Bruckner, Mahler, Elgar, grandly serious and gravelly. It leads direct
into Part II, as level and unhectic as Part I had been excitable and
volatile. Touches of Handel's and Haydn's oratorios – 'the Heavens
are telling' and the deistic moments in *The Seasons* come to mind.
Darker undercurrents encountered, evening out into the onward
flow: perfectly gauged quietening into high seraphic tranquillity
and a low quiet benedictory close. One for the Three Choirs Festival?

Janáček

Leoš Janáček: Czech successor of Smetana and Dvořák, born 1854,
son of a school-master: choir-boy, then music-teacher and conductor

of choral societies. Various German studies, returning home to teach and to collect Moravian folksongs. Third opera *Jenůfa* (1894–1903) initially staged locally: several times revised: after success in Prague 1906 widespread success in German-speaking lands precipitated – from his mid-sixties – a rich final twelve years; production of songs, chamber- and piano-music, orchestral, a full-scale Mass, and, above all, four further operas, all completely different from each other and from anything much by anyone else. Died 1928, aged seventy-four.

Broadly speaking, composers either want primarily to make shapes, patterns, forms, journeys, buildings, tables, gardens, mud-pies, whatever; or they want primarily to utter what wells up from within themselves, or from what is suggested within themselves by the impact of things around them. If Haydn is the ultimate instance of the 'pure' composer writing 'music about music' (though manifestly not deficient in humanity), Janáček can surely be seen as the ultimate composer of *Affekt*, in whom music becomes the medium for expression so immediate as to transcend the linguistic metaphor to become in itself the thing that feels and moves.

Suppose, when traversing the back routes of his loved and hated native land by coach or train, a vast pang of inarticulate emotion swells up around the composer's heart – 'my country'; suppose, thinking of his parents, his earliest memories, impressions, motivations, sensations, thought – 'my childhood'; suppose, reliving the deepest, tenderest, most painful intimacies, their mixture of harsh and delicate, tender and cruel, guilty and carefree, blighted and flowering, dampened and burning – 'my life'; suppose, then, the composer seeks to 'express' these feelings, to capture the unutterable, as music purportedly can, in a chord-sequence, in a turn of phrase, a rhythmic gesture, a timbral combination, how would he do so? *What* chords, intervals, rhythms, timbres? They would need to be precise, notated without ambiguity (let alone mistakes) as performance instructions to players; also to be accurate containers of the complex of emotions and sensations to be conveyed to the listeners, so that they understood aright. It would be Janáček's music above all, and in some respects his alone, that would be able to show how such things might be done.

But only if the means were sonorous – utterance, articulate or inarticulate, though not necessarily verbal. His *raison d'être* for writing music, and his main source of material with which to do so, is the sound of a human being in a condition of body and soul that compels such utterance. The human sound, whether heard or imagined, wrung from the depths, or casually observed in – as it might be – the vocal intonations of two girls chatting as they wait for a man who doesn't turn up. Here with something concrete to start from, Janáček speculates about their character, their lives, their futures; notates their conversation as if collecting a folksong, finds the clue to its rhythms and pitches; and eventually, from these, the harmony and coloration that will realize its latent musical life. According to Janáček himself, in 1928:

> Perhaps it was like this, strange as it seemed, that whenever someone spoke to me, I may [not have] grasped the words, but I grasped the rise and fall of the notes! I knew what the person was like: I knew how he or she felt, whether he or she was lying, whether he or she was upset. As the person talked to me in a conventional conversation, I knew, I *heard* that, inside himself, the person wept . . . I have been collecting speech melodies since 1879; I have an enormous collection. You see, these speech melodies are windows into people's souls – and what I would like to emphasize is this: for dramatic music they are of great importance.

The same eager appetite to record is applied to birds, beasts, the mosquitoes of Venice, the waves on the seashore at Vlissingen: there he is, notebook in hand, pencil poised, ear pricked. One feels he could have understood the language of rocks and stones and trees, and given contour to 'what the wild flowers tell me', so long as they spoke in noises not signs.

Thus far it could almost be the attitude of an ethnologist, a naturalist, even a speech therapist. But not quite. Janáček, in being after all a composer, can take the idea further: 'identical ripples of emotion compel rhythms of tone which accord with rhythms of colours and touch. This is the secret of the conception of a musical composition, an unconscious spontaneous connection in the mind.' After conception, however, the problems begin: continuation, for a start, then continuity into whatever forms and organizations such material will suggest and be able to sustain. The empirical approach – 'successive minute touches linked together by instinctive clairvoyance', as Debussy, in characterizing Musorgsky, also characterized himself – is all very well, but there has to be coherence and direction, however spontaneous, and logic, even grammar, however wayward or erratic. Janáček of course knew all this, and here too his solution is typically extreme. Strange though it is to think of him as a theorist of music, he attacked the aesthetic and linguistic problems with all his wonted assiduity, fervour and oddness for most of his life, alongside the composing or – more usually – in unconscious prophecy of it. The almost impossibly elusive current of utterance mooted above, equally with the prosaic chit-chat of daily life, and every shape of feeling in between, as it emanates in sound, were for him deliberated theoretical goals as well as artistic starting-points of tingling immediacy. He wishes by his notions of 'percolation', 'interpenetration', etc., to elaborate a thoroughgoing quasi-scientific dossier of affective usage wholly congruent with – indeed, inseparable from – his 'enormous collection' of human and animal sounds. Old Janáček hearsay – 'a chord that bleeds', 'a chord that makes you wring your hands' and so forth – can now be substantiated from what amounts to a composing-kit, however sketchy and in some obvious ways absurd. For Janáček even the most ordinary chord-connections contain an explosive emotional potential. Thus the VI–IV is 'like the swallow flying which almost touches the ground, and by that refreshing, lifts into the heights'; and the IV–III 'ruffles' the VII–I cadence 'as a breeze ruffles the surface of a fishpond'. If these bedrocks of tonal cliché can evoke such fantasy, the idea that more complex dissonances can cut, or be cut into, with a knife, like a knife, suddenly ceases to be so preposterous.

The aim is for music to achieve its purpose, the intense utterance of feeling, via the startling physicality of its every sonorous constituent. Together, they reach the auditor direct, circumventing formalist routines and play of conventions. Music's innermost meaning lies 'above', 'behind', 'beyond' the working relationships of its notes that make its intrinsic, non-referential grammar. This sense of what music can legitimately and naturally do leads inevitably to claims still more ambitious. Janáček would, one senses, have endorsed with enthusiasm these questions from the Shostakovich–Volkov *Testimony* that resounds with his own Slav urgency:

> Meaning in music – that must sound very strange for most people. Particularly in the West. It's here in Russia that the question is usually posed: What was the composer trying to say, after all, with this musical work? What was he trying to make clear? The questions are naïve, of course, but despite their naïveté and crudity, they definitely merit being asked. And I would add to them, for instance, Can music attack evil? Can it make a man stop and think? Can it cry out, and thereby draw man's attention to various vile acts to which he has grown accustomed? To the things he passes without any interest?

'All these questions began for me with Musorgsky', Shostakovich (or his ghost-reporter) continues. They are equally germane for Janáček. The problem is how, with such views of music as essentially a humanistic moral agent, can it be composed as an art, disinterested, uncommitted, as organization into grammar and form of pitches and durations and timbres?

Composers who put the *cri expressif* before all else usually have an internal music-machine to turn the wheels, which flows, courses, surges, spins: a force they can drive or be driven by – Schubert, Wagner, Tchaikovsky, Mahler. But when the utterance-type lacks this inner stream, or cannot reach it easily, cannot swim or finds it dammed, choked, frozen – Schumann, Brahms, Berg are instances – schemes and artifices are needed: games, codes, constructivist manipulations of material not 'naïvely' born from music in its primeval state. Though their eventuality appears spontaneous, its making has been contrived, even arbitrary. And when the utterer-by-instinct is by technique a stutterer – whether because the need for scaffolding or game-playing denies, in its defiance of naturalness, the utterer's 'from the life' directness, or through sheer lack of musical skill, or even talent, to match the sensitivity of the vibrations and the intensity of the vision – then there are radical problems for which only radical solutions will suffice. Examples of this are Musorgsky again, and Janáček – and indeed Shostakovich too, were it not for his being cursed, contrariwise, with one of the most facile music-machines ever known. (Instances of vision outweighing skill or talent would include very obviously a Gurney or a Satie, rather controversially a Berlioz, a Delius, an Ives.) What all these composers have in common, however different and mutually incomparable, is the primacy of expression. Each has his unique 'letter to the world', or, as Wordsworth said of the poet, 'he rejoices more than other men in the spirit of life that is in him'; he has a message and will burst if it is not delivered. They all stand at the polar opposite from the Stravinskian position which objects in sheer self-defence to music's capacity to say anything whatsoever outside itself.

It is not immediately clear how Janáček relates to these fellow-utterers. To Musorgsky for passionate commitment to naturalism, the expression of emotional truth via truth to human speech. But Musorgsky's manifest deficiencies in compositional technique and miraculous capture, in a handful of songs and some moments of opera, of exactly what he was after – exquisite musical precision in the teeth of incompetence – are like Janáček only in the upshot. For Musorgsky despised learning and training, whereas the youthful Janáček could not get enough. Then came the revealing moment (possibly apocryphal) when his youthful work was deemed 'too correct'; a judgement inconceivable chez Musorgsky, notoriously 'corrected' by an overseer who mistook empirical genius for ignorant ineptitude or wanton perversity. (The truth being, in Musorgsky's case, a bit of all three.) The mature Janáček offers a comparable mix, which has again involved well-meant and sometimes well-made improvements to scores wherein brilliance and clumsiness are often juxtaposed and sometimes combined. He was determined, clearly, that his music could never again incur the same charge!

The middle category can be discounted. Janáček did not need scaffolding to unbind utterance. He is, rather, the most urgent of all composers. Once he found himself, in late middle life, his sheer impetuosity precludes Schumann-esque letter-and-work-play as much as Brahmsian note-play, let alone the sedulous ramifications and sophistries of a Berg. What he shares with this composer-type is a more personal trait, the obsessive fixation upon an unattainable muse to whom every aspect of his art is referred. Yet while his mature musical speech is nothing if not obsessional, the two fixations do not go hand in hand. He would never chain in codes the fetishistic initials of names or events: blurting directness, not swathed secrecy, is his intonation. But neither does he contain a mighty machine like Schubert, nor the infinite interweave of Wagner's leitmotivic procedures, nor the melodic fertility (and sequential shamelessness) of Tchaikovsky, nor the improvisational splurge of Mahler. The native endowment is song-and-dance length, Dvořák as prototype, manifested in modest, blameless Slav-nationalist successes like the *Lachian Dances* (1888–9) or the faded lyricism of the *Idylla* (*Idyll*, 1878) and the *Suite* (1877). When he gets into being himself the lengths remain brief and the units become tiny, but the shapes are large, and the powers of driving continuity inexhaustible.

   The problem is to discover just how music as such can be reconciled with an aesthetic of unmitigated expression grounded in human utterance and guided by such peculiar theories (however well they worked for him in practice). His getting into being himself is a matter first of finding the right genre to take these overriding preoccupations – opera; then of finding what can be done with opera that squares with them, what can be put in and left out, what it can, when radically deconventionalized, astonishingly turn out to be able to do. The crucial leap, precipitated by the harrowing illness and early death of his daughter, comes between *Jenůfa* and *Osud/Fate*, the first a masterpiece in a received mould (Smetana not so far behind, except in stature), the second a Confession, of the utmost artistic oddity, an apparently unworkable maverick which, as it happened, prognosticates his late flowering into total idiosyncrasy. Once opera could be made wholly odd, other genres followed: song-cycle, string quartet, piano sonata and lyric (here alone are precedents, for this is what the small piano lyric had always been for), all the way to 'Concerto' (the two bizarre works of 1925–6), 'Symphony' (*Sinfonietta*, 1926) and 'Mass' (*Glagolitic*, 1926, rev. 1927).

'Unmitigated expression': Janáček places a higher premium upon this dangerous weapon than any composer before or since. Not that music before him had lacked the desire or the means, not just to be freely expressive but to encapsulate emotion within a sonorous image so fully that one has to say that this music means, or says, this thing. Its pre-Romantic history lies in tropes from madrigals and lute-songs, onomatopoeia and charged-up rhetoric from Monteverdi to Purcell, Charpentier, Rameau, the entire chapter of Baroque *Affekt* and its individual intensification in the hands of J. S. Bach. Nietzsche's notion of a 'lexicon' in Wagner of the most intimate, decadently perfumed, telling fragments, the miniaturist in him who palpitates with expressive life whereas the colossal remains still-born, simply brings into the open what had been achieved with consummate success in countless unflawed gems of Schubert, Schumann, Chopin, and was to flower further in Brahms, Fauré, Wolf, Webern.

As this latter list shows, it is a gift that lies at the opposite end of music's spectrum from opera. The phrase that speaks quietly, bearing a secret caress or a private message, is a creature of small spaces and small forces – song, solo piano, music for the chamber. Opera is, obviously, a collective genre that needs to raise its voice to cross footlights and be heard in the upper circle. The illusion of intimacy is one of its resources. That it can whisper was well known to such professional masters of the caress as Puccini or Massenet; their desired reaction is corporate, a unison 'oooh!' throughout the house. At the other extreme, the most famous whisper in all opera, the declaration of love in *Pelléas*, is overheard, not shared. Janáček's intimacy is as guiltless as Debussy of titillation, but otherwise resembles neither extreme. He is doing something else. Each individual within an attentive audience must feel that this music's utterance is directed to him or her alone. Even in communal scenes this tendency can be sensed; in monologues it is undisguised. In Wagner's monologues or duologues the audience is witness to a situation and its participants – this Wotan or Sachs, these two lovers, or two squabbling brothers, or two contrasted sisters (and so on). The presentation is detached, indeed objective, for all the nudging commentary in the orchestra's tissue of leitmotifs and the heated immediacy of the musical language in general. Whereas Janáček compels every hearer to identify with the single figure – the Forester, say – and with every person in a group as their turn comes – the circle of regulars at the village inn, or badger, vixen and dog-fox, owl in the forest. Nothing could be further from the various ways in which opera usually proceeds; different though they already are, Janáček is in contradistinction to them all; he makes *verismo* and *Wagnerismo* seem as stylized as aria and cabaletta. Music in Janáček's operas is his means of dissolving the distances and boundaries of convention, not of establishing them. And inasmuch as the same goes for concert music, thus far does he differ from all other composers.

Auden declared that in *Pelléas* Debussy flattered the audience, meaning (presumably) that, being given so little in the way of the usual vocal delights, their only compensation is the glow of cultural refinement their sacrifice has won them. Yet *Pelléas* is for the most part lovely to hear, if a little wishy-washy and deficient in dramatic momentum. These particular criticisms clearly do not apply to Janáček! But he is still more deficient than Debussy in grateful voice-centred lyricism, and can often be harsh, insistent, obsessive, tedious; even his brevity can seem aggressive because so foreshortened and brusque. Whole stretches – and one or two whole works – could fairly be called repellent for all his growth straight out of Dvořák and Smetana, and his non-relation to any of the commonly hated veins of 'ugliness' in twentieth-century music.

He neither 'flatters' the specialized susceptibilities of the refined, nor wows his audience *all'italiana* to bring down the house. In this genre of music more posited than any other on pleasing, he does not try to please. More often, he stings, shocks, burns. His music to go with the whip-cracks and chain-bearing in *From the House of the Dead* (1927–8) renders physical pain that makes the hearer wince; crueller still is the rendition in sound of mental and spiritual anguish. Compare the lashing in *Elektra*, the crushing in *Salome*, the torture in *Tosca*, or even such deeper expressions of psychological distress as the Kiss and its outcome in *Parsifal*, or Tristan's delirium. The audience writhes in its plush-covered seats with a groan of satisfaction. These places are protected, and distanced, by music, as surely as the padding and plush separate the soft body from the hard frame. Only such exceptional moments as Boris with the vision of the murdered boy, Golaud twisting Mélisande by her hair, Katerina Ismailova's song about the black lake in *Lady Macbeth of the Mtsensk District*, the music for the hanging of Billy Budd, dare go so naked as Janáček does by habit. While Berg's *Wozzeck*, enthusiastically hailed in the last year of Janáček's life ('a dramatist of astonishing importance, of deep truth ... each of his notes has been dipped in blood'), can seem altogether too well-dressed in interesting, absorbing, intricate, richly inventive *music*. And in Berg's *Lulu* the discrepancies between its gorgeous sonic opulence, its intellectual fascination and the moral then physical degradation of its characters can often be hard to bridge.

Be it unbearable physical pain or mental torture; or quivers, ecstasies, visions, desires, delusions; or merely some equivalent of the two girls waiting for the man to arrive (like the tiny cameo for the engineer and the young widow in *Fate* Act I), Janáček's unique grip upon utterance, from mind and spirit, in the body, via the voice, produces this 'intimate letter' from individual to individual that, so far from pleasing – flattering, wooing – his audience, is an exposure of them as much as of his characters. He strips the warm clothing of protective safety to reach naked empathy. To get 'into the skin' of, say, Katya's religio-erotic outpourings or Emilia Marty's 337-year-old weariness, he puts every auditor there too; singly – there is no plural.

There is also no space between the state of being and his rendition of it, whether it be just a flock of silly hens or the repartee of visitors at a summer spa – but it might equally be the farmer's decent son suffused with desire and shame, excitement and compunction – and correspondingly, no space between the music and its recipient. The only thing he does not express is *himself*; the absence of Romantic egotistic self-projection is remarkable. So too is the complete avoidance of preachiness; no judgements are made, no moral is drawn. The impulse is generous but by no means soft. Hard, if anything. Also furious and provocative; shocking in rawness; rude, embarrassing, button-holing, speaking too close in your face in public places; as excruciating, or as boring, as it would be in reality – the mad mother's accusations and leap from the balcony, the breakdown at the piano, the night of illicit romance and the subsequent admission wrested from guilt by the conniving elements, the night of icy sex in exchange for a much-desired document, the three prisoners' successive slow-motion monomaniac monologues for the first yet umpteenth time. These instances come successively from *Fate* (twice), *Katya Kabanova*, *The Makropulos Affair* and *From he House of the Dead*. 'Realism' – not so much an art-historical term as something the cat brings in, mangled and disgusting, a tribute yet also a victim for its unwilling owner to share – see, feel, smell, taste, with his/her own keen senses; added to which, the wholly human sense of what everything *means*.

Yet it is not so much an appeal to pious *Family of Man* humanity (too easily appropriating 'from the heart, let it go to the heart' as its motto), still less a compassionate weepy of emotive blackmail anticipating tendencies all-too-familiar nowadays. Janáček is *hard*. He presents documentation of people observed, caught, notated, collected. The truest alignment lies with the photo-document, akin to the work of August Sander, who plonked a specimen of 'businessman', 'architect', 'composer', 'peasant', 'artist' before his camera, squeezed the bulb, and gave the world the dispassionate image that makes the viewer weep. It's worth remembering that Janáček too began as a 'human naturalist' in observations from the 'field' that claimed quasi-scientific objectivity. For him this employment is without retirement. The humanity is boundless; the attitude towards its all-too-human manifestations is ardently unsentimental, most of all in its refusal to stereotype.

To achieve all this his actual music itself, if not exiguous, ought at any rate not to be given first place. In the old operatic debate *prima la musica, poi le parole*, Janáček would award the *pomo d'oro* to expression, rendered by natural human utterance. Which would imply that music as such must be thinned out – the Monteverdi/Musorgsky/ *Pelléas* aesthetic rather than the Mozart/Wagner/*Wozzeck*. In fact, it is anything but: rather, it is vehement, assertive, busy, gesticulatory, frantic, emotive and sometimes violently unrestrained. Simply on the practical level the orchestra has often to be curbed in order that the sensitive *parlante* of the voices that it ostensibly supports can be heard properly. Another kind of convention is at work, surprising but necessary, in this recasting of the genre that throws formality to the winds; for music undoubtedly comes first, possibly in spite of Janáček's wishes. He is in the end a *composer*, odd though this sometimes seems, and the composer in him cannot be prevented. It's not simply that the music is every bit as close-up as the life it renders – this is the first characteristic to strike every newcomer to it. It is something about his music itself. It can often be insufficient as such, yet it is the only medium that can carry his 'enormous collection' of human intonations, so spontaneously affixed to subjects and characters that it seems he might have collected these, too, at the bus stop or in the fishmonger's, or at his daughter's deathbed. It is the medium for his simultaneous detachment from and involvement with them all, and for his urgent concern to confront each single recipient in a physical encounter with what he has apprehended so acutely. It is the medium through which his recourse to the 'exotic and irrational' genre of opera (though his recasting of it is just as bizarre) can be rationalized and used, and its artificialities made real. It is the medium through which he can utter human speech. As this, it becomes great music like any other – albeit unlike any other in its premises and procedures.

With the benefit of outstanding Janáček scholarship both historical and textual (its first fruit lies in the series of superlative recordings under Charles Mackerras) the chaos over 'versions' that stood so long in the way of authentic Musorgsky – and can still bug authentic Bruckner – has been largely obviated. Thus the Anglo-Saxon embrace of this initially so localized music has given a picture true enough to need little or no exegesis. What we hear and admire is exactly what there is. His strangeness and extremity have become normative, his obliqueness direct, his foreignness native. This makes him difficult to write about further. His reception is both ardent and on-target; he is not misunderstood, and no longer a cause. That he remains resistant to analysis one discovers when banging one's head against his music in vain. He lays out his materials and his processes, however eccentric, so squarely and clearly that there is nothing that cannot be followed, and description or unknitting seems more than usually futile. Monumentalizing him is more attractive and more damaging. He has become the unlikely but perfect candidate in an epoch of fragmentation, alienating experiment, deliberate renunciation, even spurning, of liberal-humane themes, for music's continued concern with and expression of them without recourse to the bankrupt debris of late-Romantic *espressivo*. He is in his own freaky way a Modern, who retained pre-modernist values while driven to 'make it new' in idiosyncrasy and isolation.

Such is human nature that the moment anything revolutionary shows signs of settling into marble, an impulse of reaction sets in. Perhaps an attempt to work it out can help towards further definition of this strange and wonderful figure. The qualms begin with the element of wilfulness, deliberate mannerism, even affectation – the perversity, cussedness, going-against-the-grain, in all that he does. It is consciously contrary – he seems to be saying 'look how peculiar I can be'. Which is of course inseparable from his *genuine* strangeness whose authenticity and ardour cannot be mistaken. The choice of way-out subjects goes with the choice of way-out instrumental registers, voicing and spacing, odd habits of momentum and eccentric notations of both pitch and rhythm. It is as if burning sincerity *depended* upon being peculiar. When it works, his idiosyncratic vision carries music's empire into territory hitherto unsuspected. When it does not work, the result is merely eccentric without illumination.

And there is no difference. His manner is so all-pervasive that the stretches where he is tedious are indistinguishable from the stretches where he is electrically inspired. The pressure is as consistent as if he wrote always in *italics* or CAPS. Thus, initially at least, discrimination is disarmed. Recognition of the coexistence of inferior material indistinguishable from superior material, with plenty of infill between the two, is compounded by the unfamiliarity of the idiom as well as its gestural consistency. And that all of it is equally aimed at the utterance of burning human intensity makes it still more difficult. When everything depends upon the throb of committed subject-matter, making secondary the calibre of the materials and their workmanship, then tendentiousness looms. Because Janáček is manifestly, as artist and as exalted spirit, far above any low emotional blackmail, it seems mean to hold artistic scruples concerning the protagonists of *The Makropulos Affair* or amid the denizens of a prison-house. Like holding one's nose and passing by on the other side; like denying that in every living creature is a spark of God. But one has to acknowledge that, in taking on such subjects and treating them with such all-out sincerity, Janáček has deprived his listeners of their options.

Fate near the start of his maturity, *The Makropulos Affair* and *From the House of the Dead* at its end, show the difficulty most clearly. Between them comes the bulk of his mature achievement with its exact match of idiosyncratic music to the subject it sets, from the most intimate – *The Diary of a Young Man Who Disappeared* and the two programmatic string quartets (1923, 1928) drawn respectively from fiction and from life with equal immediacy – to the most public and ceremonial – *Sinfonietta* and *Glagolitic Mass*; not forgetting such joyous divertimenti as *Mládí* (*Youth*, 1924) and the *Říkadla* (*Nursery Rhymes*, 1925; rev. 1926). But the triumphant vindication of theory and practice alike, in all their peculiarity, comes in the two central operas, *Katya Kabanova* (1920–21) and *The Cunning Little Vixen* (1922–3). Their greatness silences reservations; the human tragedy with its blight upon happiness, tenderness and ardour crushed beneath the pitiless tyranny of propriety; and the animal comedy with its ecstatic cycle of endless renewal circumventing the vicious circle of ageing and death – manifest high peaks of the century's artistic endeavour, good deeds in wicked times, vindicating humane themes in an epoch of cynicism and mechanization.

So too are the three more awkward pieces, where greatness is flawed by his peculiarities outstretching their limitations, the inescapable obverse of his chosen manner. In all of them situations of extreme boldness are matched in music that appears to be on the point of fraying through sheer stress of wear. Sonorous images of unforgettable originality and intensity lie alongside stuff that sounds as if it was the first thing that came into his head in his tearing haste to get it down on paper.

In some ways *Fate* is musically the most satisfying. It shines with unforced surprise at what the new techniques can release, above all the way that the speech intonation of the voices grows into instrumental texture and thence into a continuity which can shape a whole act. Both in the 'photographic' reportage of its places – the sunny day at the animated spa, the storm raging while the apprehensive students gather round the piano to rehearse their master's opera – and in the 'reports' from a terrain of private anguish shot through with twisted disturbed states of being, Janáček is pushing to the ultimate from two opposing yet fused positions; the avid theorizing and the lacerating poignancy of his daughter's words notated as she lay dying. *Fate* is the first opera ever in the difficult new area set up by Janáček, where the music, though vehemently present, could not exist as such without the pressure of what has caused it, without which it would simply disintegrate. Which is more of a tribute than a qualm.

And *From the House of the Dead* is the last. (It is worth remembering that he neither saw nor even heard either work.) Every discovery so fresh and vivid in *Fate* – speech intonation filling out the entire instrumental fabric, violent foreshortening, quasi-cinematic flashback, intercutting, montage – here reaches the end of its tether. The three acts are articulated through sonorous imagery of unforgettable simplicity, sometimes sweet, sometimes exalted, more often naked, gawky, awkward and frequently pulverizing in its ferocity. The simplest and most memorable idea of all, the ur-*Klang* that, like the *Tristan*-chord, brings the whole work before one's eyes in a flash, is a chord of only three pitches but so spaced and voiced as to verge upon the physical pain it depicts.

The Makropulos Affair shows such worries more plainly. The electricity and shock inherent in story and situation go without saying. They produce awed astonishment at the boldness of treatment and breadth of understanding. But cavilling cannot be sopped. One is aghast at the really poor musical ideas upon which so much depends, especially the big primal melodic gesture manifestly intended to be the clue to the opera's dizzying subject; most of all when it is given in the fullest blaze of his orchestral heat an apotheosis that it cannot bear.

Such qualms, reservations, scrupulous attempts to sift chaff from grain, attempts to pinpoint the weakness with the greatness, are all very well. Then one hears Janáček again and falls to one's knees. He pulls and pulls your ears till you scream with the pain. Your art and your life fly about you in demented fragments; you are 337 years old and life has dried within you; you have murdered an officer, then a man who came between you and your girl, and then your sweetheart herself. You are exposed in all your human baseness. Yet you are not just told about the spark of God in every creature, you are made to feel its actual presence. You rejoice not with the stoical wriggle of the cut worm who forgives the plough but with the soaring flight of the freed eagle. Janáček, musical theorist, human ethnographer and composer, has brought all this about. There has never been anything like it, with or without music. 'What's music got to do with it anyway?' Though, more often than not, the music is fully up to the insistent demands he makes upon it. Never more so than in the pantheistic glow of his most perfect work, *The Cunning Little Vixen*.

The Outcast Victim: an un-historical excursus

Janáček's work can be seen as a precursor to a loose-knit sequence of five outstanding operas from the interwar years whose common theme is the Outcast Victim – rejected, despised, ostracized, hated, even crippled; whether guilty or innocent or an admixture of both, all these men and women are defeated and punished. The interconnections are so rich and interesting that it's worth pausing here to pursue them, in the light of Janáček as forerunner (though all five works figure in the sections below devoted to their individual composers).

Katya Kabanova (première 1921) and *From the House of the Dead* (première 1930) both derive from Russian originals, Ostrovsky and Dostoevsky respectively: in the first the victimized woman is driven to self-destruction after the briefest passage of passion outside her joyless marriage; the other is set in a prison camp where the dregs of the earth relive their terrible crimes. To them might be added *The Makropulos Affair* (première 1926), wherein a powerful central female figure is both victim and victor.

But Janáček is of an earlier generation and another intonation to the chosen five, though it's salient to recall his early and ardent recognition of Berg's *Wozzeck* (première 1925), first in the chain. Its source is Büchner's fragmentary play based upon the real-life case of the wretched soldier subject to fits, abused by superiors, abandoned by his mistress whom he is driven to murder before drowning himself. Next comes Shostakovich's *Lady Macbeth of the Mtsensk District* (première 1934), adapting a story by Nikolai Leskov, master tale-bearer of nineteenth-century Russia: here the title-heroine is the guilty party, though from the start, and even when she is twice led – to deliver herself from her joyless marriage – to murder, Katerina Ismailova has our sympathy, and by the terrible end our hearts beat with compassion for her fate even as she claims a third victim.

Lady Macbeth audibly/explicitly knows her *Wozzeck*. But obviously there is no connection whatsoever with Gershwin's *Porgy and Bess* (premièred the following year, 1935): its cultural soil is quite other – Broadway musicals, jazz, Black Shouts and Spirituals. Its source, DuBose Heyward's novel of 1925, takes place in the Charleston of the early twentieth century: and is for sure set among the scum – gambling, blasphemy, drug-pushing, murder; and the title-hero is a victim by virtue (several senses) of his crippled body: yet despite all this, Gershwin's opera is unique among these five, ending on a positive and affirmative note (but we also realize that Porgy's final blaze of optimism is due for disillusion).

No connection either with Berg's *Lulu* (incomplete work premièred 1937), though the opera's evocation of high bourgeois capitalism *c*.1890 is anachronistically saturated with American light-music of the 1920s and 30s (Berg told Gershwin, who'd been puzzled by his appreciation, 'music is music'). But these works' common themes prevail here *in extremis* – most of the cast come to Unhappy Ends, and Lulu herself is the ultimate Outcast Victim.

Peter Grimes, though perhaps ignorant of Lulu, knows his *Wozzeck*, his *Lady Macbeth*, his *Porgy and Bess* inside out – the influence, sometimes the actual modelling, are unmissable. The dates for Britten's masterpiece stretch these interrelationships a bit: Britten in the USA 1941, homesickness brought on by encountering E. M. Forster's radio talk on George Crabbe, seeking out Crabbe's poem evoking Suffolk and sketching in the character of the ostracized fisherman, rapid realization of its operatic potential, scenario by early the next year, thence full-scale libretto, a handsome commission, music 1944–5, thence the triumphant première that February. The Outcast Victim's latest manifestation, *Grimes* is surely the common theme's fullest and most explicit embodiment: the rough, surly, unloved antisocial protagonist, undoubtedly sadistic if not the actual murderer of his wretched apprentices, transformed into the Romantic Outsider; misfit, visionary idealist, deluded loner, eventually the sacrificial victim of upright/uptight small-town mores.

Parallels and rhyming across all these five operas (with the three of Janáček that can be seen as forebears) range from slight accidental echoes in large shared basics – oppressions, exploitation, violence, suicide, murder – and (except in *Grimes*) oodles of sex, whether squalid or (sometimes) exalted, with strong emphasis upon what it is to be a whole *man* and a real *woman*. They include formalities of architecture – passacaglia, variations and – principally – articulation by orchestral interludes: stage devices, especially on-stage pianos and dance-bands: different levels of intonation and idiom, parody and satire and light music cheek-by-jowl with dense, complex, advanced, serious composition; and several instances of direct resemblance – pursuit by the police or a vengeful crowd, the struggle with the door in a howling storm. All five in varying ways and degrees soften their original source even while scouring the soul with what they retain. One could make some fifteen or so boxes and see how many each work ticks. In the end, whatever the differences across boundaries of language, setting, culture, aim, they share the common pursuit and capture of their unifying theme. Which also links them across time and place, whether Suffolk *c.*1810 or South Carolina a hundred years later, or provincial Germany in the 1820s, provincial Russia of the 1830s, or the capitalist capitals of Germany, France and London at the height of the bourgeois era: as diverse as the period of their composition is synchronous – a period in part actually defined by their distinctive greatness.

Nationalism into modernism

Four Eastern European composers: an absorbing interconnection of parallels and diverging contrasts among contemporaries – Hungarian Bartók and Romanian Enescu born 1881, Polish Szymanowski and Russian Stravinsky born 1882: all steeped in their native country's indigenous musical culture; all poised upon Paris as cradle of the new (whatever the solid Germanic grounding of the first three). Stravinsky and Bartók are clearly 'modernists', inseparable from, indispensable to, some principal paths down the twentieth century; as such they will be reached here later, after the great divide of the Great War, for all their already imposing achievements during it and before 1914. The other two, coeval in time, are as clearly 'pre-modern' as Elgar, Fauré, Rachmaninov and the German and Austrian composers who continued to explore and expand their late-Romantic idiom into the 1920s, 30s, 40s, and in some cases beyond the Second World War. 'Modernism' is not a straight black line like the Mason–Dixon: it is jagged/zigzag/arbitrary; and all the more fascinating for its surprises and discrepancies.

George Enescu: born 1881; an infant prodigy, enrolled at the Vienna Conservatory in boyhood: then to Paris to continue violin studies and composition under Massenet, Gedalge, Fauré. Remained in Paris for the rest of his life, dying there 1955. One of the outstanding violinists of his day, also a fine pianist and distinguished conductor: as composer unique and special, only receiving due appreciation in recent decades. Karol Szymanowski: born 1882; taught music by his father, then at the Warsaw Conservatory: previous residence in Vienna: much-travelled, most influentially in Sicily and Mediterranean Africa. Back in Poland after the war: eventually Rector of his *alma mater*: concerned to consolidate a national music: last years shadowed by tuberculosis, dying in a Swiss sanatorium 1937.

Szymanowski is initially more Teutonic, imbued with the most lurid phase of Strauss and the most turgid of Reger, alleviated with erotic swooning from Scriabin, lightened towards colour, transparency,

refinement by the all-important influence of Debussy and particularly Ravel. A relatively brief period of high achievement from
around 1914 and the twelve years ensuing: all his best music is written
herein: piano-pieces and the three *Mythes* for violin and piano – *The
Fountain of Arethusa*, *Narcissus*, *Dryads and Pan*; the 3rd Symphony
on mystico-erotic Persian texts, already going a little splotchy; the
opera *King Roger* – Euripides' *Bacchae* reorientated into a confrontation between Pagan and Byzantine-Christian; the *Stabat Mater*, taking
up the Byzantine-Orthodox strain; best of all – flawless perfection of
his particular flavour – some ravishing songs with orchestra and the
adorable 1st Violin Concerto. Thereafter, a sharp decline in his nationalistic efforts – the 4th Symphony, the ballet *Harnasie* absolutely lack
the physical and intellectual might of their parallels in Bartók, and
the 2nd Violin Concerto a sad disappointment – distended, overwritten, under-characterized – after the 1st.

King Roger is his summa both for its textural and harmonic luxuriance and for its sonorous evocation of Orthodoxy, present at the
very start. Act I: Mass is celebrated in the mosaic-spangled Cathedral of Palermo – stage-religious music of dark veiled hypnotic
splendour – in the presence of the King and his consort Roxana.
At the service's end the King is asked to adjudicate on what to
do with a young Shepherd of seductive beauty who preaches an
Unknown God directly counter to Orthodox Christianity. Roxana
and Edrisi, the King's trusted Arabian Counsellor, advise an examination rather than outright imprisonment. The Shepherd is brought
in: the ecclesiastics are apprehensive, the Queen and Edrisi stirred,
at his honeyed gospel of pleasure and beauty. Roger too: he mitigates the death-sentence to banishment, then – to the delight of his
Queen and the horror of the deacons – aware of his own ambiguous
feelings, he changes his mind, inviting the young man to attend this
very evening a judgment at the royal palace.

Act II: awaiting the visitor, Roger voices to Edrisi his troubled
relations with Roxana: his earlier love has now grown tepid. Edrisi's
comfort is broken off by her voice singing an aria of intoxicating
ornamental/Oriental seduction, initially wordless; when words do
come they reveal her fascinated attraction to the new impulses and

the physical allure of the Shepherd who urges them. He is brought before them, and expounds his beliefs into a blasphemous declaration of his own divinity as Saviour and Liberator. The entire court falls under the spell, Roxana most of all; nor is the King quite immune. A dance of sensuous joy. Controlling himself, Roger has the Shepherd bound, but he breaks the bonds and freely leaves the palace, inviting all to follow. Roger appeals in vain that his wife remain: he is left alone with his faithful Counsellor. Still drawn by the powerful charisma, he abruptly decides to pursue the joyous throng.

Act III: just before dawn in the ruins of an ancient Greek temple, the King and Edrisi search for the rout. Edrisi counsels courage, Roger is in despair. He calls out to his Queen; her voice answers, mingling with the Shepherd's. She appears, and manages to persuade him into acceptance of what he already half acknowledges. He acquiesces: they prepare sacrificial homage at the altar: as the flames rise, the Shepherd appears, now undisguised – Dionysus, no longer the Unknown – the supposedly superseded God of abandonment to the senses. An ecstatic dance of satyrs and maenads: they vanish, Roxana among them. Dawn: Roger, left alone with Edrisi, mounts the temple steps to greet the morning light with an ecstatic salutation, offering his heart to Apollo, lord of moderation, reason, balance, fused with Dionysus, lord of primal bodily imperatives, combining to reassume their sway over a world gone grey with the breath of the pale Galilean's repressive puritanism.

Szymanowski's score has for background the Flower-maidens' and Kundry's blandishments from *Parsifal*, with elements from *Salome*, the Orientalism of *Prince Igor*, and 'the castle perilous' of Balakirev's *Tamara*. For foreground, a heady mix of Debussy's *Jeux*, Ravel's *Daphnis* and his *Shéhérazade* songs, most especially its third, *L'Indifférent*, with its actual coincidence of theme and subject; late Scriabin in general, *Le Poème de l'extase* and *Prometheus* in particular; and the post-*Rite* acts of Stravinsky's *Rossignol*, not least the nightingale's song itself, close prototype for Roxana's: plus the Orthodox strains analogous to Rachmaninov's contemporary *Vespers*. Yet the amalgam blends, at perfervid temperature, and the work as a whole exerts potent, if slightly sick-making, fascination, till the very close – which perhaps asks of music more than can be granted. Stay with the perfection of the 1st Violin Concerto.

Szymanowski closes a precious bejewelled chamber with no way out; Enescu opens the windows onto light, air, sky and sea. His trajectory is from normative of its time and place to something absolutely strange: initially the 'Romanian Dvořák' – the two *Rhapsodies* for orchestra that dogged his later years; then very Straussy and Scriabin-esque – symphonic pantheism, grandiose and overwritten, including wordless chorus (sign of the times); and also very French, taking aboard Debussy, Ravel (a close personal friend) and, more than either, his master Fauré, whose aesthetic of purifying, essentializing refinement he inherits and continues, ever more etherealized, supple, subtle, luminous, while not losing nostalgic intonations from his own country and his own boyhood – heard respectively in two masterpieces for violin and piano, the 3rd Sonata of 1926 and *Impressions d'Enfance* (1940). The closest parallel would be as if Bartók, after his prodigious early flowering, had not for the most part grown schematic and mechanical. A comparable heritage, chez Enescu, continues to burgeon with ever-increasing suppleness and luminosity. It is 'difficult' music in a sense quite different from the usual problematic strains of contemporary composition. Its passion is sublimated into dispassion, its tortuous processes, sometimes so subtle as to defy direct perception, in the end emerge crystalline. The overall effect is of rhapsodic improvisation yet the notation is obsessively meticulous. The later chamber-works especially are at once simple yet complex, straightforward yet elusive, inevitable yet unpredictable; and at their frequent best seem to me to belong easily with the century's highest compositional flights. Alongside such rarification, works of great strength and viscerality, some remaining incomplete: and perhaps such an oblique vision – for instance the weird and wonderful *Vox Maris/Voice of the Sea* – for orchestra, tenor and chorus, virtually wordless (on the go for some quarter of a century before completion in 1954) – could never have been realized in full, as with an Ives *Universe* or Grainger's 'free music'.

One substantial work stands fully extant, the opera *Oedipe*, first sketched before the Great War under the inspiration of a charismatic actor's assumption of the role, redrafted in 1921, fully worked and scored over the subsequent decade. This mighty piece, when fully encountered, weighed, assimilated, will, I believe, re-route the hackneyed highways of received twentieth-century musical history. The obvious point of comparison with *Oedipe* is Stravinsky's concurrent (1926–7) treatment of the same subject in *Oedipus Rex*. Both these 'outsiders' from the east of Europe, born within the same twelve-month period and settled in Paris, tackled Sophocles in the same decade. But here the similarities end. Stravinsky uses only the central action – the plague, the hero's vainglorious promise of deliverance, the process of revelation and fall by which it is fulfilled. This 'telegrammatically' (Stravinsky's word) brusque abridgement is emphasized by the music's manner: tight, grim, severe. A 'Cubist' assemblage of stolen goods ranging from Bach to Offenbach is held in a masterfully stylized vice; the whole is then distanced by an alienating spoken narration and 'turned to stone' (Stravinsky again) by the Latin language.

The resulting masterpiece combines liturgy and catharsis to unforgettable effect. It would be absurd to use it to knock Enescu's opera, or vice versa. What *Oedipe* has that *Oedipus Rex* abjures is the humanistic breadth to encompass the entire story from the protagonist's birth, his confrontation with the riddle of existence and his triumphant answer; and, after the grisly core, to add a further act of sublimely acquiescent apotheosis. Nor can Enescu's version be so easily placed in its musical manner. Stravinsky's is characteristically flagrant; he seems to be saying, 'Look what I can get away with!' *Oedipe* is entirely devoid of neo-classical references and only vestigially resembles the possible sources for antique subjects in his adopted culture. The touch of the commercial in Strauss's Sophocles-opera *Elektra* is never in question. Wagnerian leitmotifs are employed but Wagner himself is absent from the actual sonority and the large-scale rhetoric. Apart from a remarkable foretaste – in the scene where Oedipus encounters the Sphinx – of Messiaen at his most numinous, Enescu's music presages a future that has still not happened rather than recalling the past that has.

There is absolutely nothing cheap or showy in this work by a composer who was also one of the foremost virtuosos of his time. Here the comparison is with Busoni, who, also a lofty idealist, is not free from vulgarity when he tries to broaden the base of his appeal. Both lack the frank tackiness of Strauss, the inverted-comma sleaziness of Mahler, Berg and Weill, or Ravel's naughty commerce with the shopsoiled. But, unlike all these, Busoni's 'common touch' is unsuccessful, which both spoils the attempt to reach the folk and impugns the elevated stance. This Enescu retains, while never becoming tediously grey and high-minded. *Oedipe* achieves something very rare – distinction (in both senses) of utterance, which at the same time is charged with tremendous visceral directness.

The two works for violin and piano make an enticing entrée into the chamber-music. The 3rd Sonata, '*dans la caractère populaire roumain*' – spirit not letter of Romanian folksong, achieving an essence through extraordinarily refined and detailed interplay of the two instruments, nuance upon nuance, fantastically precise, arabesque, as if improvised, upon a motivic organization so subtle and complex as to be almost imperceptible, in a range from near-inaudibility to *fff* climaxes of passion unleashed without heaviness or rhetorical over-do. A sense of inner-lying illustration/ evocation without specifics: whereas *Impressions d'Enfance* is explicitly programmatic. Born of a visit to *Scenes from Childhood* and, unlike the Schumann, told for all its sophistication through the senses, feelings, perceptions of a child. The ten vignettes play continuous: *Ménétrier* – strolling fiddler, violin alone, jigging, whistling carefree: *Vieux Mendiant*, sad and weary, who seems to have heard the Debussy Violin Sonata somewhere on his travels: *Ruisselet au fond du jardin* – 'I can still see it – a small stream which tinkled softly at the bottom of our garden and sometimes grew into a little pond which shimmered in the light' – the advanced Ravel of *Miroirs*, the Szymanowski of *Mythes*, taken so far further that tonality and modality dissolve into atonality. *L'oiseau en cage et le coucou au mur* – *delicatissimo* imitation of the caged bird's song – Messiaen de-metalized and melting; then the artificial bird in the clock, including its works, infinitely remote descendant of the chiming clock in *Boris Godunov*. *Chanson pour bercer*, pristine folk simplicity – Musorgsky again, his *Nursery* not so far distant. *Grillon* – Chabrier's and Ravel's insects, rendered with onomatopoeic precision. *Lune à travers les vitres*, a rapt essence of late Fauré seeping through an as-yet-unwritten Ligeti étude. *Vent dans la cheminée*, just seven bars for violin alone, uncannily reproducing the soft crepitation of the wind in the chimney, continued stealthily swelling as the piano re-enters for – *Tempête au dehors, dans la nuit*, more and more tumultuous and menacing – the suite's longest section – extreme *complexité/complication* – dark and frightening – in the background *Gaspard de la nuit*: gradually opening out, obliquity and surprise all the way, powerfully peaking, declining, into the final – *Impression, lever du soleil*, also extended, transforming earlier themes into realm upon realm of ecstatic radiance. Literal perhaps, but no naïveté in this touching intimation of immortality.

These two make the best introduction to such later achievements in chamber-music as the Piano Quintet, the 2nd Piano Quartet and 2nd String Quartet, and Enescu's *Chamber Symphony* for twelve players, his last completed work, whose near-impenetrable subtlety – late Fauré gone further into tonal dissolve, upon etherealized Romanian intonations – is harder to grasp than anything serial, partial or total, from the same years. Diatonic through-and-through but scarcely tonal; heterophonic, acoustical, sometimes microtonal, exploring resonance with an exquisitely accurate aural imagination (his capture of bell-overtones *without* benefit of microtones in an earlier piano study is quite astonishing). Many inconclusions and completions – as if he too, like Edgard Varèse and Grainger, awaited the technology to realize his sonorous visions, though (unlike them) never yearning after electronic means. And often the completed pieces sound inconcluded too. An apparent blind alley that could yet open into pastures new; green, blue, fresh breezes charged with the light from the sea that never was.

Bartók

Of all the 1880s generation of modernists who, hailing from Eastern Europe – Szymanowski, Enescu; from Russia – Stravinsky; from the Mediterranean – Falla, Casella; and even Vaughan Williams from

England, make it to Paris as their Mecca, for its exciting antidote to stodgy Teutonia – Bartók, who looks to France rather than actually moving there, is intrinsically the richest in sheer musical endowment. With him the Austro-German strain – Brahms, Wagner, Strauss – is not relinquished: rather, it is fruitfully fused with Gallic tingles while escaping the struggling contradictions shown by its native composers. His compatriot forebear Liszt casts a benign light rather than, as on Busoni, an ambiguous shadow; the new impulses, from Debussy above all, liberate rather than limit; and as Bartók discovers, collects, catalogues, assimilates his native folk-music, and many others, this too is put to maximum fertilizing effect rather than narrowing him into ideological nationalism.

Stravinsky's comment – 'I could never share his life-long gusto for his native folklore. This devotion was certainly real and touching, but I couldn't help regretting it in the great musician' – is typically disingenuous: who, except Bartók, among all these composers, owed more to his country's folklore than Stravinsky, before he deliberately and provocatively relinquished it? No composer more than Bartók has ever made more creative use of work that, beginning scholarly/scientific/'disinterested', is soon taken out of the laboratory to enrich a personal idiom with all the ethnic vitality of the native soil. Another claim by Stravinsky is fairer: 'the composers of my generation, and I myself, owe the most to Debussy.' The younger men both evolve rapidly beyond imitation and dilution of an idiom that even endangered its creator with drowning-by-mannerism before his wonderful late renewal. Nor was Stravinsky's own achievement lost on Bartók. The influence of *Petrushka* and especially *Le Sacre* upon contemporaries and immediate juniors is almost without exception disastrous: Prokofiev's *Chout* (*Petrushka* mangled) and *Ala and Lolly* (*Rite*, gone wrong) are the most conspicuous. With Bartók, these seminal Stravinsky ballets fell onto fertile ground instead of scorching the earth and drying out the seed.

Béla Bartók: born 1881 on Hungarian/Romanian border; father an agronomist with keen musical interests; first piano lessons from mother. Composing away as a boy, and great promise as pianist. Various studies, concluding at the Budapest Academy aged eighteen. *Kossuth* 1903, aged twenty-two. Already collecting/ transcribing folk-music from 1904. Brief visit to Paris 1905, then close association with compatriot/contemporary Kodály, intro- duces him to Debussy's music. First marriage 1909, 1910 1st String Quartet, 1911 *Duke Bluebeard's Castle*: his folksong expeditions took him as far afield as North Africa. Great War–1919, two substan- tial ballets, 2nd String Quartet, two important sets of songs with piano. In 1923 divorces first wife and marries second. Interwar years, career as pianist and teacher, burgeoning international reputation as composer; fertile harvest, from *Dance Suite* in 1923 through to *Music for Strings, Percussion and Celesta* in 1936, contiguous with con- tinuing scholarly work on folksong. Deploring the European situ- ation, self-exiles to USA 1940; ethnomusicological work continues at Columbia University. Health, never robust, drastically worsens; handful of pieces to American commission prove to be his last; dies of leukaemia in New York 1945, aged sixty-four.

Already in the patriotic symphonic poem *Kossuth* the twenty- two-year-old composer's mastery of traditional means within on- going Habsburg practice is outstanding. The year before, he'd played his own piano-transcription of Strauss's *Heldenleben*: *Kossuth* is the direct outcome – a Hungarian Hero's Life, with a genuine protag- onist to celebrate rather than Strauss's outrageous self-portrait. And *Kossuth* carries conviction; unbeholden despite the obvious debt, in technique, idiom and colossal orchestral forces (eight horns, woodwinds and other brass to match); its battle-scene is cleaner than Strauss's; elsewhere its pastoral/elegiac strain is distinguished and distinctive; there's no Schlock-bombast-kitsch; and it's half the length. Well before Debussy's use of *Ein' feste Burg* (in *En blanc et noir* of 1915) to depict the Boche advance upon *La Patrie*, Bartók does just the same with the Austrians and their *Emperor's Hymn*. Indeed, this grotesque symbolic realism in sound, all wrong notes and mis- placed accents and exaggerated timbres, foreshadows an aspect of his music consistent throughout his oeuvre and natural to him – mockery, parody, distortion, malignity. Miles away from the aims and idioms of his mature achievement, *Kossuth* is far more than juvenilia:

in every circumstance (including homage to a national hero) it can justly compare with the *Kullervo* symphony of the young Sibelius.

Finest fruit of the next few years comes in 1908 – first bloom of perfection, the first, 'Ideal', of *Two Portraits* for violin and orchestra, with its serene triadic radiance and euphoric calm and its polyphonic, almost fugal texture. This movement is identical with the first of a two-movement Violin Concerto, published as such only in the 1950s: both second movements – they are different – fail to balance their seraphic companion: the other *Portrait* is a deliberate distortion and caricature of the 'Ideal' after the model of the Gretchen/Mephistopheles split in Liszt's *Faust-Symphony*. The second movement of the Concerto is no betrayal, but equally not a worthy mate to the lovely 'Ideal'. This gratuitous contrasting – beauty; its wilful perversity – already predicts trouble to come: both aspects of the single countenance are crucial to Bartók – it's as if he can't have one without the other: the wedge between them persists throughout most of his work, and is only healed (and only in part) towards the end of his compositional trajectory.

THREE STAGE-WORKS

Duke Bluebeard's Castle makes interesting comparison with Dukas' full-length opera of 1899–1906 (Bartók's is in one act), both based upon the immemorial fairy-tale best known in Perrault's eighteenth-century French version. Bartók's take, via his librettist Béla Balázs, withdraws altogether from a wider outside world (save for one magnificent moment), presenting the incompatibility of mature man and young bride; the forbidden mysteries behind the locked doors symbolize the internal secrecy and impenetrability of humanity at large, or imprisoned. The spoken prologue is mysterious and portentous: the music makes it fuller, deeper, more disturbing. As in Dukas, Bluebeard's role is pretty exiguous: Judith (as Ariane is renamed) carries the consciousness throughout all her ordeals, without even a nurse to activate her curiosity, let alone a bevy of house-hens to cajole and exhort. It can seem that the opera's principal protagonist is its enormous and fantastically coloured orchestra, depicting what each door releases with almost unparalleled evocative power.

First door, Bluebeard's torture-chamber; second door, his armoury, with blood-stained weapons; third, his treasure-chamber; fourth, his garden – jewels and blooms bloody alike. 'Almost unparalleled' – only the colour-crescendo at the centre of Schoenberg's contemporary *Glückliche Hand* (1910–13) surpasses this succession, which makes the cascades of precious stones in Dukas, lovely as they are, seem like paste, and the mystic play of lights in Scriabin's contemporary *Prometheus* (1908–10) seem like a fortune-teller's magic lantern slideshow.

With the fifth door the claustrophobic castle splits asunder to reveal Bluebeard's territories, as far as the eye can see, yet evincing his bloody clutch even unto the horizon. This magnificent heaven-opening moment – complete with organ, though the huge orchestra (here asking additionally for four each of on-stage trumpets and trombones) is already organ-like, and organum inspired (with help from Debussy's submerged cathedral) – is the work's centre and high point. All is now downhill towards elegy – darkness, failure, futility, despair. The sixth door reveals the most sheerly beautiful of all these marvellous cameo *images sonores*, the Lake of Tears, rendered in exquisitely refined timbral invention – fluttering flutes, one harp glissando, the other and the celesta arpeggios, two timpani and tam-tam *ppp* with gentle swell and decrease, string triads three octaves deep, muted and tremolando.

Bluebeard exerts a compelling erotic allure after each door is opened. At the grandeur of his glory at the fifth Judith murmurs that she is unimpressed: after the sixth, the Lake, their feeling becomes mutual – she desires him as he her: and here she puts the Forbidden Question lying latent at each previous door – who did you love before me? As with Psyche, Semele, Elsa in *Lohengrin*, her doom is sealed.

Troubles loom, for the protagonists' music as well as their situation. Before, though, the score's finest passage, wherein Bluebeard offers Judith the key to the seventh door and *tells* her what lies behind, and *she* has to be persuaded even before she knows, as previously, persuading *him* against his will. The libretto provides a subtle touch that music can't do – that Judith had herself taken from his treasure-chamber the crown, mantle, jewels which she now dons as Bluebeard's final and fairest Queen. The music is too large for the action – the Wagner-problem as perceived by Busoni – this wild passionate stuff renders the pair's *internal* tumult; nothing of it can be *represented* on-stage. She realizes her destiny and embraces it: the ultimate secret is revealed, three former wives, superb in beauty, sumptuous in accoutrement: not dead, as feared – simply struck dumb. As Bluebeard is at last struck eloquent – 'they brought me, in turn, all I possess; the first at dawn, the second at noon, the third at eve: you, most beautiful of all, at night. And now [as she trails silently after her predecessors] – now it is darkness for ever.' Enormous weight of emotion, deeply rendered in music, nothing to see.

The Wooden Prince: composed 1914–16, scoring completed 1917. The scenario for this ballet is as stiff, contrived, implausible as that for *Bluebeard* convincing and compelling: also the work of Balázs – an invented rather than a traditional fairy-tale, with consequent lack of resonance (compare the exactly contemporary Strauss/Hofmannstahl *Frau ohne Schatten*). It resonates, rather, and as always, with the composer's own complex and obsessive personality. A succession of bizarre impediments to an eventual union, set out with fearsome symmetry, utter implausibility and total inhumanity. Yet Bartók's score is fantastic. It opens on a rewrite of the *Rheingold* prelude, with more – eventually all – notes in play: a ravishing sound-sheet, foretelling Ligeti but with contours and themes. The ensuing action evinces Hungarian virility at its prime, the inflection rhythmic and intervallic very marked, melodic harmonic and orchestral potency of a high order. The enormous forces include saxophones (richly used), celesta *à quatre mains*, and a keyed xylophone, yet unlike Stravinsky's *Firebird* it's not 'all orchestration' ('I was prouder of the instrumentation than of the music'): actual *invention* is strong and intense, and would be so with 10 instead of 110 players. The score's 'wooden' aspect – parody, grotesquerie, caricature – as, too, its violence and cruelty – are more prophetic of the Bartók to come than its nature-music, gorgeously illustrative and pantheistically rich, or the fulfilment-love-music towards the end, a generous apotheosis before the return to the opening and a *ppp* close in pure C-major. The most potent music of its time in Europe? Anywhere, in fact, except perhaps Ives in America?

No: this dubious accolade must be accorded to *The Miraculous Mandarin*, Bartók's second ballet, composed 1918–19, scored 1923. In an upper room of a suburban slum in a great unnamed modern metropolis three down-and-out tramps, possibly pimps, use a young girl as decoy. The girl is reluctant but is forced against her will to blandish her wares from the window. The first client is a pathetic old roué, rich only in protestations of love and lust: when his lack of gold becomes clear he is roughly ejected and the girl returns to her place, enticing next a shy young lad to whom she's genuinely attracted: their brief timid togetherness can't survive; he too is penniless and thrown out without quarter. Again she returns to the window: a third client ascends from the street – an uncanny figure in middle-life, the Mandarin himself, frightening, awesome; inciting terror rather than desire, though prepotent beyond his predecessors. The parallel with the closing scene of *Lulu* – three clients, the third Jack the Ripper – is clear: Wedekind's play had been written on and off during the century's first decade. Man(darin) and girl struggle, with as much mutual repulsion as lust – both combine in electric tension: struggle turns into hunt, in which, as the quarry is cornered, the tramps re-enter to strip their victim of his evident wealth. Everything heretofore is shown in mime rather than dance – even pantomime: stage-directions are over-detailed; 'speech' as in silent movies is indicated; the girl's allure, the tramps' menaces, the contrasting mien of the first two clients, are all done in exaggerated gesticulation; only the Mandarin is balletic.

And now the story really begins. Having got hold of his money, the tramps want to dispose of the bizarre figure whose function is served. They try to smother him with pillows: in vain; his yearning for the girl keeps him alive through thick and thin. Their next attempt, triple thrusts from a rusty sword, also fails: he totters, but recovers to lunge out at the object of desire. They now hang him from the light-fitting: the light is extinguished, the suspended body glows green-blue yet refuses to die. Taken down (a Deposition?) at the girl's bidding, he renews his lustful quest; this time she yields to it and him; they embrace. Finally fulfilled: now the varied death-means can take their natural course – the sword-wounds bleed (and perhaps he is suffocated and his neck broken – the scenario is only implicit). The Miracle of the Miraculous Mandarin is done: he is permitted to die in a kind of inverted *Liebestod*; blood-'n'-sex trans-figuration given a lurid, macabre, post-Romantic, anti-Idealist twist of neck/pillow/knife.

This horrible affair inspires one of the early twentieth century's greatest scores. As with *Lulu* Act III, spiritual forces of enormous human suction are at work within the disgusting events amid the sleazy surroundings. Can the music of Bartók (and Berg) redeem them? Breathtaking opening; the violence and mayhem of rush-hour city traffic, rendered in orchestral furore first invented to depict primitive rituals, here thoroughly modernistic. Girl's seduc-tive decoy-call, beckoning oriental arabesques on clarinets. Old rake a grotesque gestural cameo. Young man presented in acrid-aching sweetly vulnerable tender-bitter mix of great appeal – too brief – not unlike his distant double in Debussy's *Jeux*. Mandarin's first music, when he's seen in the street, a bit *Chu Chin Chow*: when he first appears in the room his music is colossal – again, as in *Bluebeard*, too large for what occasions it – another version of decadence. The girl first dances with him in a lugubrious-erotic *valse* – an absorb-ent stretch of dirty-smeared satin; it then animates into glinting scintillation – *Jeux* on acid and gone round the bend into cubist, vorticist, futurist. Behind both scores lie the Flower-maidens from *Parsifal*: here their order is reversed, sparkly animation succeeded by swaying sensuousness. The *valse* hots up and up; and from now on the listener's ears are agog. The Mandarin's chase is a stampede – wild horses across the plains of Hungary, a Russian Revolution, a cannibalistic *Warriors* – way in excess of what's actually happen-ing. When he's smothered by pillows, an organ. When he emerges still living and lustful the music can scarcely be believed. When he's hanged one wants to call the police, the fire brigade, the ambu-lance. His dangling body glows with uncanny light – a wordless choir joins the forces. His eventual submission and fulfilment are beautiful at first, before thickening up to the sickening moment of consummation, its music explicit enough; for once the wordy stage-instructions are lacking. Not so when it's over – 'his longing is now stilled' and he can die – the music dies too, down to a slack, spent, emptied end, startlingly vivid.

The *Mandarin*, as with Bartók's other stage-works but far more so, is an extreme instance of means over ends. The score's power in violence and Eros, its fertility of invention, its kaleidoscopic lexicon of colour, tower over the wretched dramatic material they illustrate and express. This material in the two ballets, though not in the opera, is poor in itself – 'sorry stuff'; and, anyway, simply doesn't call for all these sophisticated, elaborate, lavishly expensive resources. What action would match the volcanic giganticism of this libido-and-blood-lust in music: what *could*? Yet Stravinsky's reservation about *Jeux* apply in a different context – 'an orchestral masterpiece only'. If only the *Mandarin*, and the *Prince*, were not attached to impossible stories and inappropriate genres, their fully developed language and technique might well have been the Future. But quite apart from some contras after such pros – the cruelty, the nastiness, the inhumane near-sadism of the subject-matter – there are limitations in the idiom itself despite its wealth – the obsessiveness, the dependence upon ostinato, the accumulation of density/volume/dissonance/orchestration. All are solved in some smaller works of the same years.

The heights are preceded by a rustic plain: *Two Pictures* (1910) for orchestra. The first, 'In Full Bloom', a ravishing Pissarro-Sisley shimmer-flutter, whole-tone-ish but not à la Debussy: this fragrant surface drawn with deep feeling, revealed when the bells begin to sound: Enescu's village scenes are close, and not all that far away, the miniature Delius. The second *Picture*, 'Village Dance', is rather standard, as such one of the better: amid the folksiness, a glimpse of remote tranquil desolation; towards the end, a touch of obsessionality; both these prognostic of the Bartók to come. The *Four Orchestral Pieces* of 1912 (scored 1921) raise the stakes. No. I is marvellous: analogous in sound and calibre to the best of contemporary Berg, Debussy, Vaughan Williams. No. II is a grotesque scherzo-waltz, perhaps the best of this recurring type: as often in his pre-war orchestral music, way too long. No. III is a lovely siciliano folk-waltz, rather Sibeliusy and very Janáčeky: the middle grows incon-sequentially turbulent and churned-up; the return of the siciliano is ravishing. No. IV, *marcia funèbre*, presents strong and feeble in close proximity: no real material – all gesture, tattoo, rhetoric – yet a vivid aural presence, with its acrid dissonances and penetrating instrumentation. The climax brings Ravel's song *Asie* so close one almost hears the absent soprano. The four pieces don't quite belong together despite interlinks, nor quite add up as the *Orchestral Pieces* of Schoenberg, Berg, Webern. But Bartók's own *Mandarin* is clearly visible in the near distance.

The 2nd String Quartet (1915–17): an uneven work; first movement long unwinding successor to the first *Portrait*, less radiant and expres-sive, more gaunt and austere, some of the harmony so chromatic as to verge on atonality. It's followed by a capriccio scherzo, becoming rather standard, with two early instances of frequent later occur-rences, Bartók's attacks of clustery buzzing insects and his obses-sion with sadistic semitones: nasty, brutish, and *long*. The concluding slow movement recovers, in spare intense dissonant counterpoint, bare and unforgiving – an inner world of blasted spiritual desola-tion and lonely self-communion, nascent before, here revealed for the first time in full. The composer's inner privacy, introversion with the palisades up, says *noli me tangere: keep out*.

But in ten songs with piano, synchronous with the String Quartet (1916) the guard is down. The five of op. 15 possibly set two poets, one of them possibly Bartók himself: a murky area, involving also a fervid episode with a young girl somewhere in the woods. The five songs of op. 16 raise the level – their poems by Endre Ady. This is 'war-music' in the sense that Pound's *Cathay* (1915) and Eliot's *Prufrock* (1917) are 'war-poetry' – remote from actualities that can barely be uttered, let alone adequately coped with: remote in place if possible and for sure in feeling – private, personal, internal; and in Bartók's case a release of erotic desire and its ecstatic fulfilment that are prohibited or punished in the three stage-works. Other 'war-music' is interest-ingly analogous: Janáček's *Diary of a Young Man Who Disappeared* (1917–19) can be compared also for its subject, however differently treated: Debussy's *Études* (1915) for their musical speech: if Bartók couldn't have known the new publications from Paris in war-time circumstances, the coincidences are all the more remarkable.

These ten songs as a whole make an astonishing harvest in themselves, as well as, evidently, *études* for or offshoots from the three concurrent stage-works: they are among the most advanced music of their time, and among the best. As also the two Sonatas for Violin and Piano (1921 and 1922): a culmination, a synthesis, a turning-point; distillation at maximum intensity and complexity of everything achieved in the peak-period, without the 'excessive dark', let alone the sheer morbid nastiness, that occasionally assails the stage-works, or the element of mawkishness that can, probably because of their words, sully the songs. A first summa, ending appropriately in the hard-won enigmatic resolution and peace of the weird-spaced C-major chord closing the 2nd Sonata.

Like all his coevals of the 1880s generation, Bartók is now faced with the problem of how to proceed – what to *do* – after earlier achievements whose possibilities seem to be exploited to the full. As in life generally so in the Arts, the 'war-to-end-all-wars' left an after-taste of futile negativity and a compelling need to begin anew. Renewal for Schoenberg and his pupils, for Stravinsky, for Bartók, whose pre-war harvest had been so ample, is made more complicated by the reaction from upcoming new generations, centred in Germany upon Hindemith, in France upon *Les Six* – a radical change in the air, rejecting the immediate past which had lost credence, foreshadowed already by such divergent portents as Strauss, Reger, Debussy (dying in 1918) and Ravel (caught *entre deux mondes*). Bartók's case is the purest because he doesn't do pastiche, play of styles, revivification of the Past, playful or profound, *Pulcinella*-like kleptomania. He does move towards a version of neo-classicism in response to Stravinsky's – he was bowled over by Stravinsky's *Concerto for Piano and Winds* (1923–4) – even while pursuing a lonely all-integrity furrow of his own: codification and quintessentialization of native folk-material; tightness of construction, symmetries paramount; even when content burns with personal urgency. To his famous mantra

'Bach for counterpoint; Beethoven for architecture and process; Debussy for colour' can be added the latest Stravinsky (after the earliest impact of Stravinsky's folklore/primitivity/maximalism/ machine-like) for pure 'civilized' baroque; folk-musics for material; nature for organicism, growth and form – shells, plants, insects, birds (Bartók the scientist, collector, collator); and nature-derived symmetrical constructions – golden sections, Fibonacci numbers, phases and spirals, fractals, etc., for patterns of relationship between the smallest detail and the overall shape and duration.

Bartók's interwar yield includes a cluster of solo piano works and two powerful concertos, another for violin, string quartets nos. 3– 6 and further chamber-music, and one masterpiece for a uniquely constituted orchestra (*Music for Strings, Percussion and Celesta*). This impressive body of achievement is acknowledged equal to anything else in its time: space precludes the detailed discussion it deserves. Its successes lie close alongside its faults – obsessive, if not fetishistic over-schematization that can issue in downright bullying – witness the horrible moment of 'parody' in the 5th Quartet's finale: a naïve little ditty crucified by wrong notes, mirthless, bitter, without point: or sheer perverse ugliness, as in the vicious attacks of stinging insects that infest, somewhere, almost everything he wrote, fast or slow.

These are mitigated by some smaller delights of folklore for voices and orchestra – *Village Scenes*, *Five Hungarian Folksongs*: and at their centre the *Cantata Profana* (1930), which excites no qualification whatever. Its source, a folk-legend from the Romanian, translated into Hungarian by Bartók himself and reshaped according to his needs – which, it scarcely needs saying, touches down deep to currents in his own personality, as well as to public patriotic sentiment all the more stirring for being non-specific. Part I is set amid primeval forests long ago: symmetric and asymmetric scales, 'acoustic' and derived from folk-modes, ascending and descending: double-chorus, overlapping and antiphonal, the layout and sonority masterful, *St Matthew Passion* an evident model, telling of the old man and his treasure – nine fine sons, strong and beautiful, taught by their sire not to trade nor plough nor handle horses or cattle, only to wander hill and dale hunting the noble stag. The hunt: belling horns, stamping strings, thudding drums tuned and unpitched, cries of *hi-ho*, clean-limb'd choral line after the crepuscular clusters earlier, as the nine lads hunt on, further and further into the endless forest, till, all of a sudden they encounter the haunted bridge, crossed heretofore only by stags: the boys cross it in heedless ignorance, and are transformed in turn. A magnificent volte-face not like anything else anywhere, as both choirs, surrounded by strings over a timpani/harp oscillation and underpinned by tam-tam, go quiet and mysterious, while brass, woodwinds and cymbals crash in puncturing punctuation, violently, four times (the poor horns have to undertake both the very soft and the very loud music): an extraordinary aural equivalent of a barrier confronted and surmounted; a portcullis – a guillotine – sharply descending. The nine young huntsmen are now transformed into what they'd hunted. The crashing is crushed and the opening scales resume, enhanced now by marvellous harp-writing, *ff glissandi* simultaneous from top to bottom and bottom to top, amid the orchestra's rustling *pp*. Nine beautiful stags, free to rove the boundless forest-lands.

Part 2 commences in dark brooding à la *Wooden Prince* and *Duke Bluebeard*: we return to the anxious father, unable to rest longer with no news, setting forth to seek his sons, rifle in hand, finding the bridge, following the trail of the noble nine-fold quarry, sighting them, falling to his knees to address their leader – the chorus now in eight parts, bristling with imitations and inversions without a scintilla of the fearful symmetry, if not downright pedantry, that vitiates the cantata's instrumental neighbours to both sides – the 4th String Quartet and 2nd Piano Concerto. The father's question not given, only his eldest son's answer, he of all the boys the dearest: 'Belovèd father, do not shoot! Or surely our antlers will pierce you, smash you to pieces down the rocks, grind your bones to powder and mangle your flesh to paste.' The tenor solo voicing the eldest stag rises to heights of searing intensity in depicting the destruction of his sire that are only matched by the guilty compunction of Kullervo on discovering his sin and the exaltation of the Young Man in Janáček's *Diary*: 'nought but dust shall survive thee, dearest loving father' almost bursts the work asunder as, too, the lungs of the hapless singer. The climactic cymbal clash with orchestra stacking up a minor third could be a quotation from Sibelius's early master-piece, except that it was unheard between 1892 and 1958.

The chorus now gives stage-directions, and the baritone the father's voice – loving, anxious, pleading: 'Oh darling children, come follow me home where awaits your good ...' and the salient word ... '*mother*.' In strains more lyrical and melodious than what's been required so far he evokes the paternal home where the mother waits, lonely and grieving – the lights are lit, the table laid, the glasses stand brimful with wine as her eyes with tears. Chorus introduce the son's reply: 'Dear father, return to our gentle mother! We cannot: never shall we return: our antlers cannot pass the narrow threshold: our bodies can wear only the wind and the sun, our slender legs cannot stand upon a hearthstone, our mouths can no longer sip wine from crystal glasses, only water from mountain springs.'

Part 3: As he reaches this last word the scene recedes into the music of the opening, now slipping away into remote epochs of time and events ... once an old man ... nine sons ... only hunting he taught them, no arts of domesticity or cultivation ... just as before: then, with no transition, to how the nine huntsmen wandered so far into the forest, were transformed into stags who will wander for ever ... their slender bodies ... their dainty legs ... their mouths ... for their antlers are too broad to pass through a human doorway. All this as before, word for word: the music, however, expands into euphonious serenity, a quiescence and acquiescence achieving the elegiac distancing of the long withdrawing closing stretch of *Blue-beard*. The tenor joins once more for the phrase about cooling mountain springs (the word *cooling* didn't appear before), beauti-fully 'majoring' the folk-mode in one last reminder of his previous anguish; and major prevails to the end as what's left of the orchestra gradually drops out, leaving only slow string scales, five octaves of D on winds, plucked out by the harp, and at last the chorus alone, a D-major first inversion with only one timid major third F♯; last note of all, a solitary drum, the missing deep bass tonic: perfectly judged close to a poetic/symbolic/epic/legend-ballad of the highest order.

The *Music for Strings, Percussion and Celesta* (1936) is another apex – a marvellous fusion of experiment and hallowed procedure;

the three succeeding movements all growing out from the opening fugue, all symmetry, all process, constructivism that all can perceive – even unconsciously; but it's hard to miss – fusing wholly with intense expressivity, imbued not just with rhetorical and structural power – climax, the furthermost outer pitch reached by the upper and the lower entries, plus cymbal trill to enhance – but also with strange shimmering ice-cold beauty as the celesta illuminates the asymmetrical return-journey. Bartók's compositional mantra, plus further rubrics of belief, is fulfilled here and throughout at the highest level, with no loss whatever, wherever, of passionate expressive weight, at its most compelling when as climax of the finale's close, the fugal subject receives climactic apotheosis.

Bartók's final European pieces comprise a palpable hit, *Contrasts* (1938) for clarinet (Benny Goodman), violin, piano (the composer himself), wittily mating jazz and Hungarian traditional music: a palpable dud, the *Divertimento for Strings* (1939): and a middling mixture, the 6th String Quartet of the same year – vicious in caricature, moving in the gradual efflorescence of the motto-theme initiating the first three movements to bloom as the entire substance of the fourth. Once arrived in the US he made a fine recovery, personal and artistic, in a new land alien in language and culture, generous yet unable to give him much of a livelihood. The genial accessibility of his American works, once held to be a compromise, is more fairly by now estimated as a mellowing: ripeness is all.

The first, *Concerto for Orchestra* (1942–3), is a triumph. Possibly its first movement creaks a bit – the phrases go up, answered pat by their inversion, in the allegro; but this can be enjoyed as wit, elegance, fun rather than the mechanical symmetries of earlier: and the dark brooding *Bluebeard* opening, then its soft tattoo on three trumpets, then the passionate string outburst, are inspired and unforgettable. In the ensuing allegro, a new warmth and euphony – sixths largely replace sevenths, tritones, clusters (though the up/down symmetries are in fourths): music yearning with longing for a native land lost beyond revisit but not beyond recall, undoubtedly influenced by his contiguous revision of his 2nd Suite from 1905–7 (arranged for two pianos 1941; orchestrated 1943).

Now comes a delicious serenade, 'jokes of the couples', systematic for sure; but not obsessive nor didactic – two bassoons in sixths, two oboes in thirds, two clarinets in minor sevenths, two flutes in fifths, two trumpets in seconds, all these couples in an unostentatious display of fresh attractive invention, nicely supported and framed by delicate accompaniments, begun and concluded with light drum-taps, which continue to mark the phrases of the brass chorale at the centre, before the couples resume, now as trios and quartets, schematically scored to have the incoming interval and instrumental pair heard first in a subservient role, the previous links greatly fore-shortened even as the accompanying textures are enhanced. Neat without fuss; and a gentle quizzical end, introducing the work's core/*coeur* ...

The third movement: *Elegy. Bluebeard*, suggested at the work's opening, now to the fore; darkly mysterious to start, before explicit reference to the Pool of Tears made audible and visible as Judith opened the sixth door of his castle. Poignant gapped melody on oboe, answered by piccolo as the oboe's gaps close, atop the shimmering waters; groping octatonic overlaps fade into the twittering piccolo solo; now the lament latent in the introduction to the first movement bursts forth tutti with passionate eloquence. A touch of acridity, a charged-up recitative on violas, then all the woodwinds, punctuated – punctured – by urgent chords, a snatch of Hungarian rhythm, harp glissandi, and a magnificent sonorous tragic climax, sinking back into initial darkness and the Pool of Tears, with stammering piccolo, into a calm close, almost '*religioso*' – a tone which becomes explicit in the 3rd Piano Concerto's slow movement two years later. A few dying shudders, the Hungarian horn, the piccolo stammer, a cadencing timp.

Fourth movement, *intermezzo interrotto* – interrupted intermezzo – tenderly whimsical foolish tune on a succession of solo winds: a deeper, more poignant strain in the ensuing melody on strings. Now the (in)famous 'interruption'; dry Rossini-like string accompaniment to insouciant clarinet jingle, greeted at its cheeky close by rude guffaws and lewd signs and disintegrating laughter, ending in burps and farts on slurping trombone slides, only to recommence in garish fairground scoring, soon jeered off only to resume differently, though equally trite, and be effectively quelled with hateful hate-filled mockery, emphasized with three cymbal-thrusts and a *fortissimo* tam-tam. The diabolic spectre is banished, the warmer string melody heard again just the once, the more whimsical tune on woodwinds reappears in fragments, dissolving in a flute-cadenza, and the intermezzo ends with its closing phrase thrice repeated in dialogue, a dying hint of the Rossini accompaniment, before its last three notes in well-timed close. There can be no doubt of the interruption's intentions: Bartók disingenuously identified the phrase with a well-known number from Lehár's *Merry Widow*, which it resembles almost exactly, then confessed that what he'd really had in mind was the endlessly repeated motif from the first movement of Shostakovich's 'Leningrad' Symphony (itself mocking the Lehár), hugely popular and overexposed in the heady days when the USA and Soviet Russia were still allies. Private sources testify to the rage, hatred, contempt with which he reacted to the broadcast and then transformed into his Interruption: a touch of envy too, perhaps; his own music's popularity was at a nadir. Best understood so long after the occasion as the last appearance of a strain persistent in his thinking ever since the Liszt-inspired distortions of the second *Portrait* some thirty years before, persisting in the often gratuitous moments of painful parody in interwar works, notably the 5th String Quartet finale, here finally vindicated, fully earned, redeemed by context – a bitter joke to balance the 'jokes of the couples': and, surely, fair comment – 'justified criticism' – of its source. The wry irony is that Shostakovich's symphony is, for all its crudity, engaged in the same battle against a common foe.

But now Bartók's finale rings with authentic, unforced, patriotic rejoicing, ending in a blaze of optimistic uplift bringing the house down every time, absolutely without cheapness, vulgarity, condescension. There had been bumpy moments earlier: the fugue on the opening horn summons, beginning in delightful energetic workout, goes acid and sour in a reversion to his interwar obsession with semitones, clusters, snarls and spite. But the run to the end is as exultant as the Janáček *Sinfonietta* it sometimes resembles.

The 3rd Piano Concerto is a thing of joy, more perfected than
the *Concerto for Orchestra* though not cutting so deep as its Elegy: it
is amazing to recall that it used to be patronized, if not downright
dismissed. A classical concerto ('like Mozart or Saint-Saëns' as Ravel
had wished for his Piano Concerto): not *neo*-classical – without academicism, yet observant of the genre's traditions.

The Viola Concerto from the same year (1945) is sadly incomplete, a second brew from the same ingredients. Not so the Sonata
for Solo Violin, completed the previous year, the last music Bartók
completed in every detail. A hard listen, rewarding the most intense
concentration, as exuded by the mental and physical strain upon the
player as s/he elicits that of the composer – a tour de force for all
concerned to surmount the difficulties, crack the secrets, penetrate to
the essence. Finest fruit of Bartók's veneration for Bach, in spirit not
letter; magnificent recreation of his great chaconne in the opening
movement, his solo violin fugues in no. 2. Then the third – *melodia* –
eases the tension in a line of limpid purity: not less intense; intense
in a different way – rapt inward self-communication that must also
communicate outwards, and does. The *presto* finale straightforward
after the earlier movements, its *moto perpetuo* alternating with robust
swaggering strain, all hussar/macho good humour without *bragga-
docio* forcing: genial virility, no bullying, no hectoring, albeit firmly
on top.

'There is so much more to say . . .' Bartók's words towards the end
are more than pathetic: his loss is tragic. The best in the last works
give the feeling, via its broadening bases, that the tight/mean/driven
countenance is finally turned away, leaving the other's warmth,
grace, charm, expansiveness. Which, as the Sonata shows, would
never renege on the commanding severity: his inner assurance and
outer austerity can meet in a smile. One senses that a second peak,
balancing the first of 1911–22, would have been actualized had he
lived only another few years.

Bartók's is the saddest of all the losses sustained by music
in the 1940s. Even as the war advanced then retreated and the
exhausted world faltered into a wary peace, the smaller world of
music lost a succession of variegated great ones. With the passing

of Rachmaninov (1943) and Falla (1946) two master-composers disappeared who altered nothing but simply added to the gaiety of nations. With the deaths in 1945 of Webern and Bartók, both clearly in their prime with plenty more to say, the loss is communal as well as individual. In 1949 the last giants of German Romanticism achieved death and transfiguration – Pfitzner at eighty, his single masterpiece *Palestrina* long behind him, Strauss at eighty-five, still refining his art into ever-more glowing farewells. The next year saw the loss of the wonderful old French magician Charles Koechlin, who will never achieve popularity but still awaits his due, and the fifty-year-old Kurt Weill, who now enjoys both. And in 1951 Arnold Schoenberg died – 'the solar plexus of twentieth-century music'. The jury is still out – will be out for ever – on his achievement as a whole. Stravinsky's phrase graphically conveys his unavoidable importance.

Stravinsky, coeval with Bartók in age, lives on to reinvent and renew himself yet again, and more radically than ever before, stirred, as are the emergent European avant-garde – the 'Holy Trinity' of Boulez, Stockhausen, Nono (aged between twenty-one and seventeen when the war ended) – by the guiding inspiration of Webern to create a new world from the debris. Messiaen is embarked upon his finest period: Tippett and Britten, very different composers, are entering theirs, Copland and Shostakovich are arguably past their prime. Bartók, of all these, his seniors, his contemporaries, his juniors (who owe him so much) was 'intrinsically the richest in sheer musical endowment'.

We have already touched the edge of the twentieth century's second half: all the composers here mentioned have been discussed or will be soon. But before I reach modernism, a breathing-space for an overview of the State of the Art between late Romantics and nationalists: after which, back again in time to gather in further composers who partake of both, in some cases straddling the divide, in others originating the completely New.

CHAPTER XII

'Portrait of an Age' c.1890–1914

'Maximalism' and Modernism

A stopping-point; a bird's-eye view of the period roughly after the nineteenth century but before the Great War, but with complex overlaps in chronology that reach both backwards and forwards even into the 1950s. The climax and fulfilment of High Romanticism was marked by the deaths between 1883 and 1897 of Wagner, Tchaikovsky, Bruckner, Brahms – Verdi lived later, dying aged eighty-seven in 1901 – and Wolf, of the next generation, effectively died compositionally by 1897. Composers in every musical culture born in the 1860s to 1880s are, however discrepant, concerned to realize a new vision of music's goals, techniques, sonorities, in the wake of their overwhelming predecessors. The mature collective achievement can simply be dubbed modernism, though individual descriptions are anything but simple. This is the epoch of so-called 'maximalism' – extremes, superlatives, hyper-everything: which includes contradictions, counter-currents, exceptions to the universal trends that are also vital to the total picture.

The richest period in all music's history? Certainly its most multifarious. After the explosion of the Wagnerian music-drama, the post-Wagnerian fall-out: debris, consequences, continuations; reactions against, repudiations of, the seismic phenomenon. After its prime exponent, the 'semanticization' of music's very aims and substance; the innate 'extra-musicality' of music's intrinsic music-ness, implicit from the origins, exteriorized down the Baroque, the classical, the early Romantic, made thoroughly explicit in Wagner, became the centre of just about every compositional endeavour as never before or since: together of course with the purely linguistic/ grammatical/technical means to achieve it. And a breadth of styles as never before – compare the simultaneous heyday of Beethoven and Rossini, of Wagner-Verdi-Brahms-Bruckner-Tchaikovsky – or since, as in the course of composition post-1945. If an epoch can embrace Satie at one end and Schoenberg's *Gurrelieder* at the other, the terrain must be vast! And the same with expressive goals and content: the same with everything.

Characteristics. Extremes of size: miniatures ('an entire novel in a sigh') and colossi, and everything betwixt. Extremes of forces: plenty for solo piano, songs with piano, chamber-music in traditional genres, especially string quartets, though maybe adding to them – the soprano in Schoenberg's 2nd; newly invented chamber-ensembles – Schoenberg's *Pierrot lunaire* and its immediate Parisian progeny in Stravinsky, Ravel, Delage. But the symphony orchestra is now normally triple woodwinds, plentiful brass and percussion, harps and celesta – and still more gigantic orchestral forces now become pretty normal too – Strauss and Mahler, pre-war Schoenberg/Berg/Webern orchestral pieces, Stravinsky's *Rite*: the paradox in Webern's case of vast forces used to miniature ends – his op. 6 orchestral pieces; and in his op. 10 the sense of vast forces conveyed by a handful of players – as, very different, the Schoenberg *Chamber Symphony* where fifteen players attempt to emulate the sonority of ninety. Opera, too, routinely expects these numbers – the massive demands of the *Ring* rather than the 'chamber' intimacy of *Tristan* or the 'Haydn' of *Meistersinger*. But then, contrariwise, the reduced instrumentation of *Ariadne auf Naxos* and *Le Bourgeois gentilhomme*.

Saturation in literature: after Liszt's pioneering efforts, this is the epoch of the Symphonic Poem: Strauss's triumphant succession – Lenau, medievalry, Nietzsche, Cervantes; Franck's and Saint-Saëns' contributions; Sibelius's Finnish mythology; Elgar's *Falstaff*. Obviously opera is, by definition, literature: this is the epoch of plays-into-music – *Pelléas, Salome*; plentiful other adaptations from Maeterlinck and Wilde – an eventual bloom from the same impulse in Berg's Büchner and Wedekind. Same with lyric poetry in French and German – an efflorescence of settings in both languages, often in cross-translation, now and then from the English – Debussy's Rossetti, Schoenberg's Dowson and MacKay. Oratorio is mainly out: large-scale works of calibre for chorus and orchestra tend to be secular – myth, fairy-tale – *Das klagende Lied* and *Gurrelieder*, Elgar's *King Olaf* and *Caractacus*, Delius' *Mass of Life*, Rachmaninov's *Bells*.

Major instrumental genres are just as saturated by text, narrative, extra-musical content: the Symphonic Poem intertwines with the Poetic Symphony – Mahler all the way from his 1st to his 10th; Strauss's *Domestica* and *Alpine*; Elgar 1st (slightly) and 2nd (very); the *Kullervo* and *Lemminkaïnen* symphonies of Sibelius; Glière's *Ilya Murometz*. With Elgar and Sibelius, 'abstract' and 'programmatic' completely intercross: *Falstaff* is subtitled a 'Symphonic Study in C-minor'; while what could be more evocative of landscape, saga-deeds/personages/moods, than Sibelius's symphonies from the 3rd to the 7th inclusive?

Which introduces depiction: painting, atmosphere, places, evoked and rendered in sound – not so ubiquitous as literature though still a significant *tendance*. *La Mer* – also described by its composer on the title-page as 'symphonic', and justly – Franck at sea: and also Debussy's three orchestral *images* evoking England, Spain, France; Ravel's Hellenistic Greece and ubiquitous Spain, Ives's *Three Places in New England*, Delius' *Summer Garden* idylls and his full-scale tribute to Florida in *Appalachia*. Debussy's fusion of word/image/sound in *L'Après-midi d'un faune* – text *illustrated* with *music* – remains unique – a precious distillation of the *Gesamtkunstwerk* ideal (and indeed at one stage intended to accompany '*poses plastiques*').

Overlapping with all these, autobiography: early Romantic self-expression à la Schumann now reaches centre stage, the artist's private/personal/intimate life rendered in the most public and sizeable genres. *Bei* Strauss oblique elements of self-portraiture – Don Juan, Till, Don Quixote and Sancho Panza – become unabashedly autobiographical in *Heldenleben* and *Domestica*. *Bei* Mahler the symphony as Confession – forebears, such 'darkness-to-light' scenarios as Beethoven's 5th and Schumann's 2nd; immediate prototypes Tchaikovsky's 4th, 5th, 6th – becomes Mahler's norm from his 5th to the end, after the poetic/conceptual schemes of his first four. Elgar and Sibelius more subtly and unobtrusively portray their own personalities and experiences – Sibelius in his 4th not so indirectly; and of course the finale of the *Enigma Variations* is a self-portrait as explicit and confident as any in Strauss. However, 'some do not': there are no French instances: this impulse would be repugnant, even alien, to the 'artistic manners' of Fauré, Debussy, Ravel.

Odd, therefore, that the epoch doesn't excel in concertos, where glamorous self-projection might be of the essence. After Brahms the genre retreats – the Elgar and Sibelius Violin Concertos aren't of their best: the Busoni Piano Concerto an extreme bizarrerie, and therefore characteristic of its time; none others of note spring to mind. But ballet flourishes as never before, to become as significant as any other genre. Dancing is as old as music itself: dance in opera has a long tradition – especially French, from Lully and Rameau to Saint-Saëns' *Samson and Delila* and beyond (and not forgetting the ballet-sequence Wagner felt incumbent to add to *Tannhäuser* for its Paris production); autonomous ballet scores are also initially French – Adam, Delibes – to culminate in Tchaikovsky, who owed them so much. But the early twentieth-century importation to Paris of Russian ballets, danced to the nationalists' scores, is a genuine new phenomenon. As the Diaghilev company began to commission more daringly, ballet comes to be a real attempt at a fusion of the arts in the wake of Wagner's – storyline and mime replacing words, of course; music and scenery/costumes on equal terms, fusing with the physical prowess and beauty of dancers male and female, soloists and *corps*. These new impulses are almost completely Franco-Russian, a principal factor in the change of taste and alteration of balance by which the Teutonic musical culture that had prevailed for some two centuries would be altered, perhaps for ever. Subject-matter and setting Oriental/exotic/supernatural – *Firebird*; folklore of city and showmanship – *Petrushka*; primitivism – *Le Sacre*; modernistic parody/satire/absurdist – Satie's *Parade*: the achievement already in place whereby Franco-Russian tastes and values and idioms would assume the Austro-Germanic centre from after the Great War. With an Austro-Hungarian annex – the three

Bartók stage-works, which owe enormously to Debussy and Stravinsky in Paris: absolutely symptomatic in content, subject-matter, with a hefty dash of expressionism thrown in for the sado-morbidity of the *Miraculous Mandarin*, and a touch of futurism in the modernity of its city-traffic evocations.

Another salient feature of the epoch, however, is barely French at all. Saturation in ideas, philosophies, beliefs, mysticism, magic. Christianity is in abeyance; nothing really of supreme calibre – *Gerontius* a curate's egg, Mahler's *Resurrection* ersatz, his *Veni Creator* 'religious kitsch'; Debussy's *Martyre de S. Sébastien* showy if not downright cynical: only the Fauré *Requiem* resonates authentic. But Nietzsche to the fore – Mahler again, Strauss, Delius, Diepenbrock. And esoteric weirdness: Swedenborg via Balzac seminal to Schoenberg in his Kandinsky-phase, thence *Jacob's Ladder*; Scriabin and Theosophy, thence his own role as self-confirming Messiah. Esoteric currents flicker and seduce – Pythagoras, the mystery of the Sphinx and the Pyramids, Golden Sections, Satie's queer invented churches (an exceptional French instance). Oriental influences for beliefs and practices as well as well-established colours and flavours: even *Tristan* and *Parsifal* had shown a Buddhistic tinge. The more familiar evocations of the East à la *Lakmé*, *Pearl Fishers*, Rimsky-Korsakov's *Scheherazade*, yield strange and wondrous fruit in the *Shéhérazade* songs of Ravel, Debussy's *pagodes*, *poissons d'or*, *le temple qui fut*, Delage's Hindu songs, Stravinsky's *Rossignol* and its amazing Chinese march: and in a wholly other culture become equally central in the Chinese texts of Mahler's *Das Lied*, the Tagore in Zemlinsky's *Lyric Symphony*, and settings by Schoenberg and Webern.

The generalization that embraces all the streams in every culture is the search for the New. The epoch is by definition 'post-Wagnerian': all its representative composers have a 'Wagner-Problem': how to take him, how to continue, what remains – after such a total achievement – to be done? Is anything left? Plenty, as it happens. Predictably the most direct response is dire – the sad case of August Bungert with his four-evening music-drama on the *Odyssey*; and there is Wagnerian dead-wood in some of the good composers of the time – the slack stretches of Strauss's *Guntram*, the bombastic aspects of Wolf,

Amfortas-of-the-Agony in *Gerontius* and the curse of the leitmotif in Elgar's later oratorios, the chorus-of-vassals in *Gurrelieder*.

How to escape the overwhelming influence if you truly revere and adore it? Use it to liberate aspects of your own individual style: Strauss everywhere, Mahler's subtle transformations of *Tristan* in the *Kindertotenlieder*, Schoenberg's in *Verklärte Nacht*, Duparc's in his songs, Scriabin's in later pieces large and small, Delius, Puccini, Rachmaninov. By parody: Strauss's *Feuersnot* and *Till Eulenspiegel*; and on a lighter note, the cheeky salon-send-ups of some French composers of the time – Chabrier's quadrilles on motifs from *Tristan*, Fauré and Messager collaborating to mock the *Ring*, Debussy going beyond mockery towards resentment in the *Golliwog's Cakewalk* (*Tristan* again); all these (even Debussy) combining sauciness with ardour, however ambiguous. More fruitful, where saturation in the original transmutes into the utterly Other – *Tristan* and especially *Parsifal* in Debussy's *Pelléas* and *Jeux* and Sibelius's 4th Symphony. If rejection is steadfast, unambivalent, wholesale, there is of course no 'Wagner-Problem'. But who did resist? Busoni's equivocation cannot conceal the debt that his rejection would deny. Fauré perhaps – but then one remembers the leitmotifs in his sole opera *Pénélope*. Ravel for sure – his instruction to play '*Wagneramente*' in his saucy contribution to *L'Evantail de Jeanne* makes a late addition to the line of French mockery. But even Ravel as a young man could tremble to the core at hearing *Tristan*.

By whatever means, with whatever attitude, it behoved Wagner's successors to move on from him. The Meister himself had said, '*Kinder, schäfft Neues!*' This epoch is more conspicuously devoted to onward exploration than any previous. The word 'New' rings out everywhere – 'new paths'/'new aesthetic'/'ars nova'. Mottoes from poets – '*il faut être absolument moderne*'; 'make it new' apply, spoken or tacit, to the musicians too. 'Progressive' is how Strauss hailed Elgar – his highest praise: the once 'music of the Future' as mooted by Wagner and Liszt is now the music of the Present. Even Brahms, widely seen in this time to be academic, old-fashioned, superseded, can be reborn as 'Brahms the Progressive' as Schoenberg's famous essay argued and his music put into effect.

The fabric – the actual *Stoff* of music – was perceived as thread-bare, worn-out, exhausted: 'degenerate' like a race, 'decadent' like an individual, 'debased' like a coinage, 'spent' like a lover or a penny. The cure is regeneration; renewal; recharge: by means of experimentation and exploration both technical, within the language, vocabulary, grammar; and in feeling, emotion, content, subject-matter. New. Modern. Dawn (especially as nineteenth century spun into the twentieth). Yet these vital new impulses coexist with every previous tendancy coming into its fullest bloom and fruition – indeed they are one and the same. And the next stage is also a degeneration/decadence/exhaustion. It's inseparable and inevitable that this amazing Tree of Life – 'the richest period in all music's history?' – should be simultaneously deep-rooted yet swaying and toppling; that it sports green shoots, ample boughs, withered twigs; that it buds, leafs, flowers, pollinates, ripens and bears luscious fruits and intoxicating poisonous berries; seeds within the generous plenty as it decays to nourish their new growth.

Every parameter of music to be rethought and remade. *Genre* least: it is still songs, chamber-music, poetic symphonies and symphonic poems, operas, for the most part. *Form*, however, is radically revolutionized; and *texture* and *process* inseparably. So too the basic elements – harmony, melody, polyphony, rhythm. All these of course proceeding from, dependent upon, inheritance from the past even as they are rethought and remade. More absolutely new is the isolation of and concentration upon *timbre* – colour – actual sonority as a goal in itself. All these meet and fuse in the search for revolutionary new *content* – expressive intention, emotion, feeling, meaning.

Extremes: the furthest edges, and sometimes beyond them, of human impulses, sensations, desires. *Eroticism* – gradually, then rapidly, more and more perverse and morbid; healthy 'Southern' sensuality/sexuality no longer celebrated as the norm; the potentialities for erotic depravity suggested in *Tristan* and explored more thoroughly in Kundry, Klingsor, Amfortas, developed still further; *psychopathologia sexualis* – Salome, Elektra, the woman of *Erwartung*, the characters in Schreker, Korngold, Zemlinsky; Puccini's 'sadistic' victimization of his heroines. *Hysteria and neurosis* – again from the extremes in Wagner – Tristan's delirium, Kundry's vacillations between abandon and salvation – where expression is pushed to its limits; over such limits, Mahler's 9th and 10th, the angst of expressionist atonality in the *Orchestral Pieces* of Schoenberg, Webern, Berg – the first of Schoenberg's *Five*, 'Premonitions', all fulfilled to the utmost. *Erotic/Exotic* – this is where France comes forward – the ravishing soft-porn of Ravel's *Daphnis et Chloé*; the 'horror' (his own word) between the three characters, their triple kiss in the Garden of Earthly Delights, captured in Debussy's 'thoroughly modern' ballet *Jeux*. Less dangerous, *Pleasure – volupté*, hedonism – a goal of sensuous/sexual blisses and refinements – Bilitis and Pan, or the faun languidly imagining his nymph – Debussy again; the consummate elegance, grace, decorum, of Fauré's amatory art, or the Eros exposed with animal heat and passion in the saintly Franck's Quintet, Violin Sonata, Quartet. Turning up the temperature further still, *Le Poème de l'extase* and other caressing phallo-triumphalist orgasms, solitary or shared, of Scriabin. But pleasure as the ultimate can be just as explicit with more modest intent – the motto for Ravel's *Valses nobles et sentimentales* – 'the delicious and ever-new pleasure of a useless occupation' – though the same general idiom, and some specific material from the earlier piece, is then pushed over the cliff in *La Valse* some eight years later. *Dark places of the soul* – Mahler again; Rachmaninov's 1st Symphony and Sibelius's 4th; Schoenberg's *Glückliche Hand*. What more could a world war of unprecedented proximity and carnage, with industrial-scale technology to furnish it, add to what was already being expressed without restraint in the musical culture immediately preceding?

The music of this epoch is at once esoteric, educated, ultra-sophisticated, 'advanced', elitist – the super-refined precious crest of bourgeois-mercantile civilization at its apex; and demotic – though admittedly its actual substance is not exactly geared to appeal to the working classes in cities, factories, mines, or on the land. But a genuine aim is to reach and express the People: celebrate them, give them a voice, use popular materials – songs, marches, dance-music: broaden the sights without debasing the standards of high art: the soldiers of the King and of the Salvation Army, the Cockney street-urchins in Elgar's *Cockaigne* (not to mention *Land of Hope and Glory*); the Mayday workers' choruses in the first movement of Mahler's 3rd Symphony; Ives's loving collages of hymnody, parlour-songs, marching bands, barn-dances. Celebratory as in those; or 'ironical' – twisted, distorted, parodistic – sometimes affectionate – the cliché-cheapo strain in *Petrushka* and thence in Debussy's *La Boîte à joujoux*: sometimes bitter, even painful – Mahler from first to last, thence *ach du liebe Augustin* in Schoenberg's 2nd Quartet, and so on to tavern- and militia-music in *Wozzeck*. Elgar, when asked why he didn't employ it, riposted 'I *am* folk-music.'

Real music of the folk, predominantly rural, is a vital component in these years: a revaluation of the spent coinage from fresh untapped riches, of Eastern Europe mainly, though including Russian, Finnish, English, Celtic, American. France notoriously doesn't possess such *richesses* of indigenous folksong: but most of the composers whose countries do made for Paris as the vibrant centre of everything new in music that excited them – even Vaughan Williams coming to learn from Ravel; more expectedly, Stravinsky, Enescu, Delius. When not actually settling in the city, these composers were alert and a-tingle to its new sounds and avidly assimilated them – Kodály and Bartók, Szymanowski; even some Viennese were not wholly untouched – Berg and Webern, though not their Master; Schreker for sure. Most of all, Spain: Falla (another adoptive Parisian) claimed that Debussy and Ravel had virtually invented his country's music: he inherited it from them.

Finally, *bad* music: the opportunities in this period for sentimentality, bombast, faking, exaggeration, bathos are commensurate with the flair, fluency and self-confidence that also characterize its greatest achievements. Cheap strains used for parody or pain have already been noted: *bad* music is inadvertent and there's plenty of it around – the saccharine would-be deeply-expressive and emotionally-true of Strauss's *Morgen*, and the *adagietto* of Mahler's 5th Symphony can stand for it all: in the same composers, would-be sublime/exalted-and-deep of Strauss's *Death and Transfiguration* and Mahler's 'Resurrection' Symphony: vulgarity and debasement perilously close to genuine value, sometimes with powerfully alienating effect – *Salome*, Mahler all the way. 'Religious kitsch' à la Mendelssohn and the closing terraces of *Parsifal* seems distant and innocent compared to such knowingness as this epoch can produce: 'Praise to the Holiest' in *Gerontius*, the religiose closing stretch of the *Alpine Symphony*, Mahler's *Chorus Mysticus* in the 8th.

Reactions: there is going to be a swing of the pendulum as extreme as what it's rebounding against: straws in the wind simultaneous with maximalism/Romanticism gone rotten, just as it also has within it the seeds, and some of the fruits/flowers/thorns, of the radical experimentation to come. 'Back to Baroque' and 'neo-classicism' are the watchwords of reaction against maximalism in all its excesses of idiom and intent, and will prevail in the interwar decades to come. Their forebears are Brahms's reverence for pre-classical techniques interfusing his reverence for the classical style; the living presence in Bruckner of Renaissance polyphony; the archaisms, pastiches, *hommages* so skilfully and lovingly used by Wagner to evoke sixteenth-century Nuremberg in *Die Meistersinger*; and Tchaikovsky's adoration of Mozart and his enchanting vein of rocoquerie in *The Sleeping Beauty*. These models lie variously behind the straws in the wind that will eventually blow up into a wind of change sweeping away all the clutter, debris, lumber, an epoch of conspicuous waste. Strauss's 'rococo' in *Rosenkavalier*, *Ariadne*, and, at its delicious best, in *Le Bourgeois gentilhomme*. Mahler's turn to linear leanness – 'there is no more harmony, only counterpoint': no fat, an X-ray clarity sometimes fleering. Very influential; taken yet further by Schoenberg's overlapping last tonal and first atonal works – of the former, the 1st Quartet, of the latter *Pierrot lunaire*, twin peaks of polyphonic prowess, chock-a-block with learning at once academic and intensely expressive/expressionistic. *Pierrot*, however, already has one pantaloon in a new place – reaction towards lightening, even divertimento, for all the gruesome traits still essential to its character: brilliant ingenuity and mordant wit fuse with black humour and morbidity to effect a tingling tribute to *commedia dell'arte* taken up, without the expressionistic props, in Schoenberg's *Serenade* (with mandolin and guitar) and on into the baroque dance-suites of his earliest serial ventures. And Webern – moving from

Wagnered Brahms in his op. 1 *Passacaglia*, via scholarly absorption in ancient techniques, to reinvent the canon and the motet.

Commedia dell'arte to the fore in Busoni's *Arlecchino* as well as *Ariadne auf Naxos*; but Busoni's 'Young Classicism' is very different, even with their shared veneration of Mozart, from anything of Strauss. Its goals – clarity, directness, objectivity, formality, in Busoni more will than deed – are all to be realized in the next generation, together with a revaluation and revival of Italian opera from Rossini to Verdi that did not, oddly, form part of Busoni's programme. Reger, too, worshipped at the same twin Godhead – 'Bach is the beginning and end of all music' – before moving on to Mozart, and declaring with Schoenbergian vainglory, 'I can say with a clear conscience that of all living composers I am perhaps the most closely in touch with the great masters of the past.' (December 1914, not a good time to be thinking such things: and prescient of another brash declaration, Schoenberg's in 1923: 'I have today discovered a method of composition that will ensure the supremacy of German music for a century to come.') Piquant that the Bachian component in Reger's voluminous organ-output is turgid in the extreme, and his Mozartian side so very un-Mozartian.

Diatonicism is at a premium in this the most chromatic epoch of all music's history. Yet here too there are both forebears and exceptions. Brahms of course with his persistence in using only 'natural' horns; Bruckner and his huge celebrations of the unadulterated common triad; *Meistersinger*, one of the grandest affirmations of 'the C-major of life', but also the diatonic islands within the surging chromaticism of *Tristan*, and within *Parsifal* the stage-psychological dichotomy between the 'good' holy-pure-sacred language of the Grail and its rituals and the 'evil' domain of its sorcerer, his sex-slave and their seductive handmaidens; and within the hero's divided breast. So to the prevailing white-note *tinta* of Pfitzner's *Palestrina*, and its usage in other stage-works for purposes of characterization. More central to its composer's innate idiom, the diatonicism of Sibelius throughout the period: his famous 'glass of cold clear water' in polemic opposition to the poisoned chalice of hot multi-coloured intoxication all around. Sibelius distinct too in his focus upon a classical ideal for the symphony – impersonal, architectural, all process and progress as the implications of its musical matter are explored and realized – though, as already indicated, he can be powerfully depictive/narrative too, and also autobiographical, just as Mahler can be 'all about' procedure and structure. A different voice altogether – 'see below'; the young Hindemith, rabidly expressionist in early youth, reacting against his young self to become the acknowledged leader of 'Back to Bach' in the Germany of the 1920s.

French and Franco-Spanish-Russian straws in the wind are pretty different; not primarily abstract, and never learnèd in polyphonic arts. The Latin/Slavonic nature of this epoch certainly excels in the multicoloured exotic-erotic opulence as described, and there will be the inevitable swing against all this after its hedonistic bloom-time; the swing is prophesied in some clear indications. Jean Cocteau's *rappel à l'ordre* of 1918, *Le Coq et l'arlequin*, banished the 'mists' of impressionism equally with the 'fogs' of Bayreuth – he might have added the tobacco-fumes of Brahms and the odour of incense surrounding Franck and his disciples. But all these had already begun to be banished anyway. Wartime Debussy, moving on from earlier rococo-baroquerie – *Suite bergamasque*, *Pour le piano*, 'Hommage à Rameau' – to pay explicit tribute to his seventeenth- and eighteenth-century compatriots as an act of patriotism in the three sonatas, to almost excoriate the hated Huns by name in *En blanc et noir*, to celebrate Chopin equally with 'abstraction' as in painting – banishing the picturesque subject-matter at which he'd excelled in earlier years – in the twelve *Études*. Ravel's French classicality innate from the start – *Sonatine* (1903–5) – again explicitly patriotic in *Le Tombeau de Couperin* with its *forlane, menuet, rigaudon* (1914–17). Both composers relinquish their previous sensuous-evocative triumphs to achieve such sacrificial severity. And their friend Satie never had them! He possesses the new attitudes and goals from the start – his chastity and simplicity are innate; he's all set to become eccentric uncle and mascot to *Les Six* after the war is over.

And Fauré: subtle/equivocal/stable throughout the turmoil: for piano nine preludes, thirteen barcaroles, thirteen nocturnes, six impromptus, *valses* and *valses-caprices* à la Chopin, a set of variations;

a corpus of chamber-music, fulfilling Mendelssohn and Schumann, rivalling Brahms. A *Requiem*, some incidental scores for the theatre and one opera of camerata-like restraint, nothing coloristic/evocative for orchestra. His contribution to the era's prevailing eroticism is contained – every sense – in the beautifully implicit Verlaine-songs: here too he follows in his own way a reaction, from their richness to the pellucid, austere, near-astringency of the later song-cycles – a glass of cool clear fresh water – and in the final war-time and post-war chamber-music a surviving yet newly made genuine classicism, overlapping with neo-revivalists who aren't genuinely classical at all.

Enter Stravinsky, managing a complete back-track from his sensational earlier successes: *Firebird*, 'Rimsky's best work' (or, as Debussy said, 'you've got to start somewhere'); *Petrushka*, where the phenomenon really finds itself; the *Rite*, which maximalizes every parameter; *The King of the Stars* that might have veered *vers* Scriabin. Instead, after 1914, he does a Satie – cubistic, parodistic, tight mean miniatures for piano-duet distorting and dislocating popular idioms, dangling their cheap ingredients in mocking distancing tweezers: then pungent folkloristic songs with instruments, woven together on a large scale for *Les Noces*, splintered and fragmented into the *Symphonies of Wind Instruments*, jazzed and fox-trotted in *L'Histoire du soldat*: come 1920 the 'new aesthetic' with a vengeance – literally, remembering his loathing equally of Boche and Bolshevism. Compare Bartók's reaction against, repudiation of, his earlier self: a climax of opulent richness in the three stage-works (1911–19); of advanced experimental modernism in the two violin sonatas (1921–2), before he also goes 'back to Bach' in a very different way. And Prokofiev, with the truly prognostic *'Classical' Symphony* of 1917, a 'sport' within a very different trajectory.

Between two worlds

Restrictions of space here entail drastic compression of twelve German or German-orientated composers, all valuable, some touching greatness, who begin in and cross over the post-Wagnerian terrain. Englebert Humperdinck and his adorable evergreen *Hansel and Gretel* – Wagner for *Kinder* of every age; Hans Rott, achieving at twenty a symphony his friend Mahler – 'What music has lost in him is immeasurable' – learnt (and stole) from, dying tragically at twenty-five; Alphons Diepenbrock, Dutch Mahlerian whose radiantly lovely orchestral songs setting Novalis, Hölderlin, Nietzsche, can bear the comparison; Max Reger, disconcerting mix of gross/turgid with golden syrup and shot-silk delicacy; Hans Pfitzner, achieving in the outer acts of *Palestrina* purity of intention and diction unique amid his countrymen's lurid excesses; Franz Schmidt, in four symphonies and a handful of chamber-works achieving a magnificent continuation of Brahms and Bruckner, resolving their factitious incompatibility; Alexander von Zemlinsky, Schoenberg's brother-in-law, inadvertent father in *Der Zwerg/The Dwarf* (adapting Oscar Wilde) of the 'Degeneracy' that reaches its apex in Franz Schreker's *Die Gezeichneten/The Branded Ones* on the same subject, the ugly man confronting the agonies of his sexual fate; Erich Korngold and the 'ultimate frabjous Schlock' *Das Wunder der Heliane*; Berthold Goldschmidt and the creepy kinkiness of *Der gewaltige Hahnrei/The Magnificent Cuckold*. With these last four, Degeneracy gets brutally entangled in the mounting horrors of interwar German politics: all four are Jewish, compelled into exile (unless, as Schreker, they happen to die in time to suffer nothing worse than execration and humiliation). Refreshment from psychopathetic morbidity with two further highly gifted Jewish composers: Jaromír Weinberger's *Schwanda the Bagpiper*, a Czech folk-fairy-tale of irresistible verve; the affecting lyricism and fervour of Walter Braunfels' *Die Vögel* (*The Birds*, after Aristophanes) – Braunfels alone managed to survive the Nazi years in Europe, in Switzerland, to be rehabilitated in his native land after the war.

Two others from this rich terrain are discussed at more length (though I would swear by *all* twelve) – one for his stature, still so underappreciated; the other for his singularity – before venturing back from its edges into the Austro-Germanic mainstream.

First Othmar Schoeck – 'The Last Romantic' – last most particularly in the great line of German *Lieder*-writers from Schubert through to Wolf, plus a handful of song-cycles with ensemble and one with orchestra that can stand, with Diepenbrock, as worthy successors to Mahler. His operas are not so much underrated as under-known: at least two deserve a place just below the century's finest. Born 1886; passed his entire life and career in his native Switzerland. Not, therefore, subject to the banning and exile of which some of these other composers were victims: his only entanglement with the Nazi regime is indeed rather shameful – to engineer for his last opera a Berlin première in 1941. Poetic justice: the plot was denounced by the authorities, the Swiss première two years later was a flop, and the work itself inferior. Died Zurich 1957.

Schoeck is a perfect example of a composer ironed-out by the factitious notion of 'historical necessity'. The course of twentieth-century music would be as unchanged by his absence as it is by his presence. Nevertheless, his music refuses to lie down and be flattened by the steamroller. With exploratory exposure, its fugitive subtlety lodges, its unobtrusive individuality unobtrusively deepens, and even alongside the adjacent giants – sometimes in contradistinction to them – his stature expands.

Clearly the corpus of over three hunded songs with piano, a handful of cycles with instrumental ensembles and one masterpiece with full orchestra will remain the touchstone of his achievement. Overall, they make a fifty-year journey from fresh tunefulness and relative conventionality into a refined distillation of essentialized simplicity devoted in the main to the exploration of pantheistic nostalgia. His poets earlier on are usually familiar German Romantics – Goethe, Eichendorff, Lenau, Uhland, Mörike. Later the Swiss predominate – Gottfried Keller, Conrad Ferdinand Meyer, the all-but-forgotten Heinrich Leuthold, drawn to his attention by his friend Hermann Hesse, whom he also set generously. The themes however remain constant: Romantic Germanic inwardness, grown sliver-thin with use – love/man/nature/gloom/despair/meditation on faith and doubt/recollection in tranquillity/death. Nothing could be further in matter and manner from the artistic concerns of the 1920s, 30s, 40s that are now seen to represent their times at their acutest, than this precious final distillation of a century of the German *Lied*.

The last of all, *Das holde Bescheiden/Sweet Acceptance*, forty Mörike settings lasting some two hours, composed 1947–9, is also the most beautiful.

Surprising that this piano-based composer should also write so well for instruments. Several cycles employ small ensembles in a fashion all his own. Circumventing the epoch's most influential precedents – Stravinsky's Russian songs from the Swiss period (raucous pungent primary colours that deliberately don't harmonize) or Schoenberg's *Pierrot lunaire* (fantastical chiaroscuro of dense yet melting polyphony), Schoeck deploys a rich yet transparent harmonic texture growing out of the piano's native resources of figuration, resonance, blurry yet luminous pedal effects. The piano usually remains centre as well as source of the entire sonority, as in the beautiful *Elegie* of 1921–3; with just string quartet the *Notturno* of ten years later is atypically lean and linear.

And there is the masterpiece for voice and full orchestra after the example of Mahler, Strauss, Diepenbrock – *Lebendig begraben/Buried Alive* (1926), a sort of *Song of the Earth* taking place six feet beneath. Keller's poems tell the unlucky protagonist's bizarre fate in his own words, from initial horror ('they've made a mistake!') and the panicking desperation of the attempts to attract attention and be released, via gradual acquiescence to eventual ecstatic abandonment – freedom at last – into a pantheistic compound of ocean, sky, eros and Helvetia. Schoeck's personal melancholy and sense of artistic isolation obviously found expression here: the result is a high pressure in the turnover of marvellous ideas unsurpassed in his output. Such places as the representation of the sound of the church bell resonating through six feet of earth and a sealed coffin, or the tender piety of the victim's blessing on his pathetic meal (the rose buried with him, eaten in darkness, never to know whether it was a red or a white), or the moment when the confining wood seems to transform into a lordly vessel cresting a warm swelling sea, are among the great well-kept secrets of twentieth-century music.

Still more surprising is that this introspective passivist was so ardently drawn towards the stage (five fully fledged operas, several other slighter or hybrid pieces). Only one fulfils the going notion (if there is one) of what might be expected from Schoeck's music. *Massimilla Doni* (1934–5), after the short story by Balzac, for all its play of subtle half-lights might well work more vividly in the theatre than can be imagined from simply listening (it was apparently one of the season's highlights at its first production, in Dresden 1937). It is like Henry James in music.

The biggest surprise of all from this master of the intimate nuance is *Penthesilea* (1924–5), a faithful encapsulation of Kleist's excoriating play. The opera's unleashed violence remains startling even in the epoch's wider context for such expression: on the more local scale it is extraordinary to compare the banked-down ellipses, the civilized compromises, the eventual acquiescent rapprochements with which the war of the sexes will be handled in *Massimilla Doni*, confronted by this all-out rendition of sexual attraction and repulsion carried inexorably to its bloody end. The obvious prototype is *Elektra*, a one-act trajectory alternating lyric episodes with crazed disturbance, moving swiftly to a crisis, resolved in a hymnic apotheosis-cum-*Liebestod*.

Yet even in *Penthesilea* Schoeck still strikes strongest as master of the consonance as much as of dissonance. His basis is always diatonicism, but the range of his harmony is enormous and his control of it covers every gradation of the expressive gamut. From pure triadic writing to triads with one extra note and so up via bitonality, 'tritonality' and the denser 'dominants', to something approaching the full chromatic, *Penthesilea* as a whole embraces the variety and modulation of intensity missing in consistently atonal music save when mitigated by expressive necessity à la Berg, and from neo-diatonic music save when enriched by alien chromatics. 'Radical diatonicism' and clean yet juicy smudginess, in dynamic equipoise.

'Parnassus has so many mansions.' Much the same *kind* of case, different only in particulars, could be made for many other names as for Schoeck's alongside or athwart the main traffic-routes of twentieth-century music. If the canon continues to ossify and diminish, anything to left or right will languish under-valued and under-loved, however special and – often – unique. Everyone will have their own candidates, and there need never be a full objective consensus. But we must keep everything good in play. At his best Schoeck is more than merely good: whether, most typically, in gentle contemplative beauty, temperate, welling deep and clear from music's unsullied springs; or sometimes, surprisingly, welling with equal authenticity from the fundamentals of erotic madness, frenzy, violence, despair, rage, his music can reach and sustain real greatness. And *Lebendig begraben* is a masterpiece of belated Romanticism, as out of its time – the 1920s – as Rachmaninov's *Symphonic Dances* and Strauss's *Four Last Songs* in the 1940s: and as indispensable to redefining it.

Ferruccio Busoni doesn't quite fit anywhere, but is perhaps best-placed here: despite completely different antecedents, origins, goals, he belongs principally to Germanic musical culture: Italian, Swiss, Finnish are marginal or fortuitous. Born 1866 of mixed Italian-German parentage: settled in Berlin for good 1894 till death in 1924, though travelling far and wide as one of the age's supreme pianists, and passing the Great War in Bologna, then Zurich.

A man of deep vision and broad culture, open to new impulses in all the arts. Witness the significant exchanges with Schoenberg in Berlin: his pianistic 'rendition' of the third of Schoenberg's *Three Pieces* op. 11, the first venture into atonality: the marvellous letter occasioned by the première – in his own home – of *Pierrot lunaire*; and his own nearest approach to Schoenberg's explorations in the 2nd Sonatina of 1912. His pupils at the Berlin Academy included Weill and Schoeck – both audibly beholden. His luminous writings on music focus around the *Sketch of a New Aesthetic* (1907): his aim, 'Young Classicism' – Bach for counterpoint and depth, Mozart for grace and lightness and proportion: anti Wagner and Wagner-ism but owes much to Brahms. His pianism in the mould of Liszt, revered as composer too. There's an analogy with most of this with Reger's exactly contemporary aims – Bach and Mozart and Brahms, return to 'classical' formality, retreat from confessional self-portrayal, lurid subject-matter, picturesque 'extra-musical' attempts in general. Both composers point to the change-of-air after 1918.

Principal landmarks: the Piano Concerto (1903–4): 'Brahms's

third', plus lavish dollops of Italianate ice-cream and a *chorus mysticus* to close – a gigantic barnstormer. Its gentle complement the *Berceuse élégiaque* of 1909 – a gem of subdued expression, study in silver-grey, commemorating his mother: transcribed by Schoenberg, conducted by Mahler: a successor in the same mode, not so fine, the *Nocturne symphonique* of 1912. *Die Brautwahl/The Bride's Choice* (1908–11): opera to his own text adapting a tale of Hoffmann – can't get much more German than this. Except *this* – *Fantasia Contrappuntistica* (1910) – vast extrapolation out of/conclusion to, Bach's *Art of Fugue*. *Arlecchino*, a one-act *jeu d'esprit* (1916) – 'Italian' in setting, subject, cast; but the text in German. And *Doktor Faust* at full-length – 1916–24, not quite finished at his death – is the ultimate German myth.

Doktor Faust, whatever its perceived unevenness, is Busoni's summa, into which he threw everything deepest, widest, highest, in his unique vision. The libretto is superb: from Wagner's example even while repudiating it; in the distinguished company of later composers writing their own texts – Pfitzner's *Palestrina*, Schreker, Braunfels, Strauss's *Intermezzo*, Hindemith's *Mathis der Maler*, Schoenberg's *Moses und Aron* – Busoni's is perhaps finest of all. The problem is the *music*. Words, deeds, thoughts, are always compelling and sometimes hair-raising: but much of the musical *Stoff* isn't up to them in distinctive invention; and everywhere (exceptions few and brief) his strange, grey, perverse off-focus notes; even when an idea is striking, it also proves hard to grasp – elusive – unmemorable. A high-profiled composer 'without distinguishing features' (as passports used to declare).

A very original and peculiar shape. First, *Symphonia* – crepuscular veils of shifting muslin, bells, voices singing Pax – this is music of the War – a drift of pastorale, a strain of hymnody (oddly close to Ives's 4th Symphony, roughly contemporaneous but of course completely unknown – including one phrase common to both works): mysterious and evocative. Some highlights and lowlights. Early on the raising of the demons sweeps all before it: a crescendo of texture, tessitura, momentum, from basso Gravis – swift as sand in the hourglass; Levis, as the falling leaf; Asmodus, as the rushing stream: each spirit now joined by an invisible chorus – Beelzebub,

as bullet from gun, Megäros, as tempest: the whole episode a thrilling recreation at the latter end of German Romanticism of the
Wolf's Glen in Weber's *Freischütz* at its dawn. All five demons have
failed: Faust in despair vows to return, wiser and better, to work,
humanity, God, when a sixth voice insinuates – soft, castrato high,
unsummoned, moving as quick as men's thoughts, calling Faust by
name though not divulging his own. It is of course Mephistopheles. This is marvellous – Busoni on top form. But quite soon comes
Busoni at his worst – dreadful faceless organ-fantazia, then neutral
military strains, for Faust's first Devil-inspired outrage, the scene
in the Minster where the brother of the girl he's seduced seeks her
seducer's death and gets his own.

     And so it goes, occasional highs amid plains of arid grey. Even
in the score's finest sustained movement, a purely orchestral *Sarabande*, localized lapses of harmony and textures can make the
listener wince. Elsewhere, we hanker for red wine, red blood, vitality
mental, spiritual and animal – a transfusion from Strauss, Schreker,
even Korngold: and Berlioz's treatment of the same legend always
the lamented missing background to Busoni's missing foreground.
Love-music for the Duchess of Parma, erotic evocation of Helen
of Troy, both woefully lacklustre. And then, the ambiguity of the
closing stages. Faust's magnificent bravura in the face of his fate – 'Is
there no mercy? Can I not repent?' No answer. 'So let me end my
work – let primal desire, driving force, fulfilling power, achieve their
highest goal: blood of my blood, flesh of my flesh, live through my
death: what I built cannot be straightened, what I omitted completed: I stand beyond time and law, at one with the eternal will' –
set to nondescript music crowned with a disastrous *chorus mysticus*
repeating the same words.

     There would have been further: the Busoni-scholar Antony
Beaumont has reconstructed an extended postlude to replace the
ending made by the composer's friend Philipp Jarnach for the
opera's première in 1925. It makes an interesting comparison with
Puccini's *Turandot*, also lacking its close at its composer's death (he
and Busoni both died 1924). Admiration grows over the years for
the distinction, skill, independence, with which both aftercomers

carried out their difficult task. Jarnach uses some Busoni-material, adds his own, doesn't truckle slavishly, and achieves genuine eloquence within a couple of pages, making the grindingly sardonic conclusion far more unnerving – Mephistopheles as Nightwatchman, stumbling upon Faust's corpse as the spirit of renewal born of his eternal will flees into the night, appealing to passers-by: 'Has this man met with an accident?' Beaumont's putatively more authentic close is colourless note-spinning.

Busoni: an enigma wrapped in a mystery: the Sphinx without an answer. Manifestly a charismatic mind and spirit – witness his letters and the *Sketch of a New Aesthetic*: the *Geist* is clear, deep, stirring. But rarely does the music lift to realize it: the wholes don't add up, the parts don't focus. For all the *man*'s personality, the *artist* is grey, neutral, colourless, elusive, evasive. Paradoxically all these negative qualities become positives in characterizing the one piece whose perfect realization places it among the epoch's most precious achievements – the *Berceuse élégiaque* wherein every note

> Shines with a mournful Light
> Like its own Tear,
> Because so long divided from the Sphere.

Arnold Schoenberg

'I come not to bring peace but a sword.'

'Somebody had to be me, and since no one else was willing, I had to take it on.'

'Today I have made a discovery that will ensure the supremacy of German music for the next hundred years.'

A *homo naturaliter religiosus*: fighting, struggling, seeking, striving: mythology of the creative artist *d'après* Wagner; philosophy *d'après* Nietzsche; mysticism *d'après* Swedenborg, Balzac, Theosophy; born a Jew, tried Christianity (Protestant), re-embraced Judaism. Christ into Moses, bearer of the Law and Saviour of Music: self-elected Chosen One – indeed elected of God. The provocative, combative personality ensures perennial problems: a riven heritage from the most contentious composer ever: he'll never be quieted and resolved – 'unto the fourth and fifth generation': 'there but for the grace of God goes God': the most divisive figure in musical history. The personality in actual life – an inspired leader and teacher/a horrible bully and control-freak – the contrarieties attested most painfully in the relationship with his greatest disciple, Alban Berg. So also with the music – power and genius of the first order; ditto the flaws. Yet the inheritance ('we're all serialists now') – a way of thinking about pitches and how they are and might be organized that no composer since can ignore, however they might resent/resist/detest, and though the resultant works still only half-live – even the better half – in public esteem, the inheritance cannot be overestimated. He has changed how music is heard, understood, created.

Arnold Schoenberg: born Vienna 1874 of humble Jewish parentage; learns violin as a boy and begins to compose dances, marches, etc., then art-music – songs and chamber. Converts to Protestantism 1898; *Verklärte Nacht* for string sextet, 1899; 1901 sketches *Gurrelieder* for gigantic choral and orchestral forces (fully-scored by 1911). Marriage 1901; hack-work scoring operetta, real work launched to its harsh reception by a hostile world. Beginning of friendship with Mahler 1903; career as outstanding teacher of composition commences with Berg and Webern, both taken on in 1904. His music rapidly more and more advanced, pushing over the edges of tonality in his 2nd String Quartet (with voice) and song-cycle *Book of the Hanging Gardens*, coinciding with a marital crisis – all this 1908. Painting occupies him as much as composition in the next tumultuous few years: the musical output includes the *Five Orchestral Pieces*, *Pierrot lunaire* and two one-act operas. In 1912 enormous success of *Gurrelieder* première (only recently completed): anything more radical merely an enormous scandal. Called up for the army, 1915 (aged forty-one), discharged the next year, called up again 1917: vast unfinished visionary oratorio *Jacob's Ladder* – text (his own) complete, music not – across these troubled years.

'Society for Private Musical Performances' founded 1918, to

evade public obloquy: it lasts till 1921. Gradually evolving the '12-note method', proudly announced that same year: 'today I have discovered ...', etc. Death of first wife 1923; remarries the next year. In 1925 (aged fifty-one) succeeds Busoni as director of composition at the Berlin Academy: moves to Berlin the year after. First major 12-tone monument *Orchestral Variations* 1928; 1931–2 libretto and music for *Moses and Aaron*. Doubly unacceptable – for his race, for his 'degenerate' music – to the newly powerful Nazis, 1933 flees Berlin; in Paris re-embraces Judaism; sails for the USA, ending up in Los Angeles late the next year, aged sixty. Teacher at UCLA and privately: composition still fluent; also theoretical writing and many trenchant essays on music and other subjects. Deteriorating health, financial insecurity after compulsory retirement at seventy (1944). At seventy-two, a near-fatal heart-attack: works inspired by this, by revelation of Holocaust horrors, by the creation of the state of Israel, by his unceasing search for religious enlightenment. Died 1951, aged seventy-six.

Gurrelieder – Songs of Gurre – will always inspire awe and astonishment at its size, spectacular lavishness of resources, over-the-top extravagance of idiom, absolute self-confidence, matching the tale told and the emotions proclaimed – eternal love/death of Tove and Waldemar; defiance of the cruel deity who can destroy half of this perfect pair; the curse-punishment for him who remains, to hunt for ever, by night, without reward; the long-distancing effect of placing living woes far down a tunnel of ancient past, with renewal amid blooming summer: a farrago of Gothic/Romantic themes set between the most evocatively crepuscular sunset and the most resplendently gorgeous dawn in all music.

Between them, the main body with its mixture of heady ardour curiously more Tchaikovskian than the expected *Tristan*; the delicately quivering-whirring wood-dove announcing the heroine's death, the hero's bombastic/histrionic curse-God-and-die; the wild excitement of the spectral night-hunt and the uncanny stillness when it is ceased at the quiver of first light: music of variable consistency and quality, sometimes intoxicating, sometimes less so, occasionally a liability – the dull stuff for the gob-smacked peasant affrighted by the ghost horsemen, the awful stuff for the Fool's wearisome jocular facetiousness (ironically the latest music in the work, composed after Schoenberg had utterly reversed his idiom and aesthetic – for *Gurrelieder*'s span of 1899–1911 virtually encompasses *Verklärte Nacht* of 1899 and *Pierrot lunaire* of 1912): and the oddly ineffective male-choruses, so over-fussed and woolly compared with the blazing simplicity of their prototype, the Vassals in *Götterdämmerung*. This anthology of variable calibre peaks in another late-orchestrated stretch, penultimate before the glorious dawn, 'The Summer Wind's Wild Chase', delirious counterbalance to the crazed night-hunts, its text of pantheistic ecstasy delivered in speech, not song, against the most extraordinary diaphony imaginable, in timbre as in arabesque and harmony.

Less grandiose, more consistently high-level, another early piece in received late nineteenth-century idioms, whose enormous popularity used to embarrass party-line progressives. *Verklärte Nacht/Transfigured Night* combines and integrates apparent incompatibles: a Strauss tone-poem illustrating every phase of a soupy text by a favourite poetaster of the epoch, Richard Dehmel; and a string sextet, fully worked with intensive thematic interweaving, in an idiom stemming from the love-music in Act II of *Tristan*, by no means excluding the lovers' 'envious watcher' Brangäne. The Wagner befits the situation: an unnamed woman confesses to her lover that she bears a child by another man; he assures her that the height and depth of their love will suffice to transfigure the shame; they walk on together into the night radiant with moon and stars. Potential tackiness, too, is transfigured in the music's intensity and range, from tentative foreboding via angst and guilty admission to solacing warmth and the transparent evocation of the magic illumination of nature, mirroring the mingling of the lovers' two-hearts-in-one. And Brahms would have been proud of the string sextet facture (and would have acknowledged the sentiments of the story if he'd dared). Already in this early masterpiece Schoenberg anneals the Brahms/Wagner divide, so factitious yet so damaging and inhibiting at the time. But *Verklärte Nacht* transferred on a large scale to a

huge orchestra is not such a joy: *Pelleas und Melisande*, completed
1903 in dangerous proximity to the première of Debussy's operatic
treatment of the Maeterlinck play that exercised international fascination in its day. Nothing could better illustrate what Debussy's
Pelléas is concerned to repudiate than Schoenberg's elephantine
mega-lump.

On course again within a couple of years for the first official
String Quartet, completed 1905 (there'd been an innocuous predecessor, more Dvořák than Brahms, from Schoenberg's early twenties).
This colossal work remains one of the peaks of the genre if not
of the repertoire: for, like Franck's final masterpiece, it strains the
medium to the uttermost over an hour's-worth of such intensity as
nearly to burst it, the players, the listener. Comparison with Franck's
String Quartet goes far further: both are audibly heirs to the most
strenuous medium-bursting aspects of Beethoven's last handful.
In both, tonal chromaticism is pushed to an intensity so heightened that it can scarcely be contained. The next step along the same
path pursues an identical goal: four-movements-in-one, continuous
intercross-referenced themes, density of working, chromaticism at
the edges of tonality: its intensity is enhanced by concentration –
less than half the 1st Quartet's length; and its layout for fifteen solo
instruments – woodwinds, two horns, string quintet – that squeezes
the epoch's normative giganticism into sometimes painful claustrophobia. Whatever its problems of balance, stridency, strain, the
Chamber Symphony of 1906 needs to be thus: Schoenberg's later
opening-out for full orchestra proves not so much a liberation as,
almost, a betrayal of the original intention where compression is all.
Some marvellous surging themes – as if Strauss's Don Juan were the
protagonist; new vistas opened up by chains of perfect fourths set
against-across whole-tone harmony; an omni-chromatic whirl; some
breathtaking feats of polyphony: as with Klaus Narr the Fool in *Gurrelieder*, the scherzo's wry sarcasms hurt and delight not, and one or
two stretches lose the lustre and go pedestrian/dutiful.

The next opus, the 2nd String Quartet, with soprano soloist,
of 1907–8 is iconic by virtue of the moment in the finale where
the singer's words, a setting of Stefan George's *Entrückung/Ecstasy*,

declare an 'air from other planets – I dissolve into sounds' as the baroque/classical/romantic tonality of at least three centuries melt into patterns of exquisite ecstatic euphony, to be known ever after as the origin of 'free atonality'. This phrase, much derided or deplored, serves well to define the nature and pinpoint the terrain here penetrated for the very first time, though sometimes glimpsed in Wagner and Liszt, even in Chopin, Schumann, Brahms – a moment as beautiful as it is important. Is the rest of the 2nd Quartet worthy of it? Born of personal crisis as acute as Beethoven's op. 130 or Smetana's 2nd Quartet, *aus mein Leben* – (from my life): but in its first movement somehow not getting high-calibre convincingness into the actual *notes*, those *töne* from other planets so compelling later: a really rather awful scherzo: and the first George-setting *Litanei* a drear, lugubrious affair: and isn't the long coda to the second setting a sad let-down after the voice has proclaimed herself a spark of the eternal flame – a long lapse into tonality restored that achieves, though it doesn't court, flabbiness?

This shadow of disappointment can be more clearly focused in Schoenberg's next significant work, again setting Stefan George, this time a cycle of fifteen songs with piano – *The Book of the Hanging Gardens* of 1908–9. Here we have the composer's own word, that he has achieved what he's long sought without knowing quite what it was. Difficult to equate with the curious greyness of the *tönen* – a sort of blanched wrong-note Brahms (in his *Lieder* with piano, not the orchestral or chamber Brahms), incongruent with the luscious exotic-erotic poems. The music emerges stilted – either gaunt and skeletal, or turgid and dense: either way misses the rich beautiful ripeness expected, hoped, desired. The 'pitch-deaf' 12-note sound of later, that continues still to be so problematic, is present already in these hanging gardens, which despite inaugurating (with the *Three Piano Pieces* op. 11 of 1909) the wholly 'free-atonal' years immediately following, now sound so inhibited.

For what characterizes what now ensues – a period of some eight years, 1909–17 – is an extraordinary efflorescence of vividness and intensification, originality, strangeness, whose rapid evolution is without parallel in music's history: some seven works, with or

without text, two for stage and one for a cabaret, exploring concept/
image/sight-and-sound/colour-texture-form, in absolutely new ways.
Some are miniatures for solo piano or small ensemble, some employ
huge forces compressed into a dense nucleus (the opposite of the
Chamber Symphony's big-in-little), one of the stage-pieces calls for
unheard-of effects in transformation and lighting only realizable
by later technologies. Of two unfinished ventures in these years one
so wholly transcends the conventional limits of concert-hall/opera-
house as to require completely new conditions, comparable to, if not
quite so extreme as, those needed for Scriabin's *Mysterium*.

Expressionism remains the encapsulating word: 'onomatopoeia of
the emotions': in music in particular (the phenomenon is general to
the mentality of the time but reaches its fullest fulfilment in music)
devoted to eliciting and obeying the flux of the feelings, the pulsations of body, the inner life of spirit as experienced down nerves and
senses: fidelity at whatever cost to pain, exposure to extremity, quivering immediacy of every impulse, psychological and physiological.
The Wagner of the romances rather than the myths is the principal
musical source – *Tristan* and *Parsifal* – though in Schoenberg's case
the urge is informed by contemporary explorations in literature and
painting, in scientific, or rather quasi-scientific, speculation, in mysticism, cabbalism, magic.

The first in this astounding shower of musical meteorites is
the closest to Schoenberg the painter – a lifetime's side-activity,
at its most active and nearest to the real thing during these years
with his association with the Blaue Reiter artists and Kandinsky.
Schoenberg's paintings are powerful, queer, horrid, and very bad:
his painterly vision in the *Five Orchestral Pieces* of 1909 evinces syn-
aesthesia across the sister arts of a high order: a specialized child
of the Wagnerian *Gesamtkunstwerk*, though there are no words, let
alone plot. Concept and imagery are deeply interfused, however,
and all five pieces originally bore titles. Like Mahler with his 'programmes', Schoenberg vacillated and eventually withdrew them:
but both have stuck.

No. 1: *Vorgefühle*/'Premonitions': ('Well, everyone has these,' said
the composer as he dithered) – peremptory spasms and twitches,

as arhythmic as atonal; jagged lurches, nagging tweaks, stammered iterations, shrieks and scuffles; with one celestial halo, four notes coloured by shining soft trumpets and celesta, before strenuous complexity sets in, the huge orchestra divided against itself in layer upon layer of turbulence at maximum temperature, all over a D-A drone with C♯, as if to declare continuity with the traditional tonality of Requiems, Tragedies, 9th Symphonies. The machine explodes and collapses into a rocking tick-tock, which in turn disintegrates and disappears even as the three-note drone swells to *fff*. All this in around two minutes: it probably took only two days to write.

No. 2: *Vergangenes*/'Bygone Times': total contrast, sustained lyricism, intense yet gentle, exquisite refined scoring; an ache of nostalgic yearning for a non-existent Past, poised upon the same D-A fifth that had figured throughout the premonitory terrors of *Vorgefühle*: at some four and a half minutes the set's longest piece – upbeat to the absolutely themeless/motionless/emotionless No. 3: *Farben*, a study in colours. This celebrated high point of textural imagination prophesies the wayward achievements of electronic music and their absorption *bei* Ligeti into living orchestral actuality. A lake, flat and still as morning light spreads over it, touching off layer on layer of depth, plane, tint, with an occasional sparkling glint of sun on a ripple, a ruffle of wind, and the unmistakable flicker, several times, of a rising fish plopping to the surface then descending. The technique is simply the changing timbral voicing of a succession of dully-shining chords. *Simply* becomes ever more complex as the technical idea is explored in a nascent polyphony at once frozen in stasis and breathing in organic flux. The four most complex bars – involving every player in the large orchestra except piccolos, harp, celesta (though this piece has no percussion) in precisely calibrated graduations of duration, pitch, articulation and (above all) nuances of softness – are more easily experienced than described, easier to imagine than to believe, to see than hear. The instruments omitted at this negative climax have been reserved for what follows, one of the flickering glints of light on the water's ruffling surface: which now stills again to the motionless changing chords of earlier, with a couple more flashing fish-leaps and the hint of something stirring in the depths. Three and three-quarter minutes.

No. 4: *Peripetie*/'Reversal', perhaps – the term for the sudden illumination, the turn of fate, upon which the tragedy hangs in Greek drama. Schoenberg's rendition is the first yet ultimate textbook example of 'expressionism' in music. Convulsion and hysteria reach their apogee in this terrifying piece, all gesture and histrionics. The texture fully atonal, athematic, arhythmic – flicks, jabs, jerks, bits, fragmented fragility or lunging vehemence, potent, gesticulation fantastical and grotesque, angst and tension pushed to the edge, collapsing into the strangulated twitching of a corpse. Duration two minutes. No. 5 has the only title not clear in itself nor clarified by the music. *Das obligate Rezitativ*/'The Obbligato Recitative' makes no sense as such; what Schoenberg meant by it is obscure; what he composed is neither obbligato nor a recitative by any stretch of sophistry. The piece is, rather, a stream of 'endless melody' – Wagner's term, carried to another ultimate, the complete antithesis of what's gone before, whether fragmentary and spasmodic or locked in stasis tense with internal momentum. Only the lyricism of the Past foretells this easy abundant flow of ardent lyricism, absolutely atonal and athematic: not arhythmic, however – the feel of a waltz is present from the start and grows more palpable all the way through massive climaxes, then a gently winding down/fading out end – three and a half minutes of endlessness.

More even than with Wagner, the charge of no melody is rebutted here: it's *all* melody; Schoenberg's fecundity repeats nothing – no sequences, no returns, no stanzas; an amplitude and fullness at the opposite pole from expressionist: dissonance and consonance lose distinction, all is richly euphonious, the notes so right that a wrong one sticks out as it would in Schubert. It is all flow: ebbs and falls, rises in waves and declines, and rich in polyphony, harmony, line above all, whether in the bass, the middle, or, sometimes, on top. One magic landmark when a near-orgasmic build-up is suddenly crowned by a soft-as-possible flutter of snow. The next stages are darker and oilier; from them arises a second crisis, this time taken to fulfilment's summit, complete with brief silence almost as explicit as *bei* Strauss before plunging home; and again; and a third time: after which, even-tenderer withdrawal, emptying out into bareness, all detail spent, before the darkly luminous closing chord.

If only these marvellous *Orchestral Pieces* had had the exposure enjoyed by *La Mer*, *Daphnis et Chloé*, *Petrushka* and the *Rite*, *Salome* and *Elektra*! They stand just as high in this epoch of music's coloristic climacteric. All five are quite new, quite different from each other despite inter-references, in their simultaneous unity-yet-variety giving the lie to the view that their atonal language can't cover a wide gamut of expression. Admittedly one doesn't look in the Schoenberg for joy, gaiety, well-being! What they abundantly yield are hitherto unexplored realms of feeling, realized in sonorities that can certainly singe and sear, but more often burn with surpassing beauty.

Next come two very different one-act stage-works. The first, *Erwartung*, was written at white heat directly after the orchestral pieces were finished (1909): the second, *Die glückliche Hand*, was begun the next year, then uncharacteristically hung fire, to be completed some three years later. In the gap come some other significant works, but the two operas go well together. *Erwartung* – expectation/awaiting – is a monodrama for a single character, a woman anticipating her lover's appearance by moonlight at the dark forest's verge. The text, written at the composer's prompting to a subject of his own making, very obviously overlaps with the pioneering explorations of Freud, contemporary in time and place: moonlight and a dark wood, but the setting might just as well be the psychoanalyst's consulting-room, the subject lying back on his couch letting her terrified and terrifying fantasies – or are they actualities? – loose. She gropes and searches in vain, every sound and sight a thing of alarm, she is lost and cannot return whence she came, dreading 'another woman', harbouring jealous rage at her man's possible infidelity, stumbling over his bloody corpse – or is it a figment of her hysteria? And is he really dead or can he be revived? And if he really is dead, did she do the deed?

Every fluctuation of her torrential articulacy or suggestive inarticulacy is rendered with quivering accuracy in this unique one-off whose relationship to its sources is nonetheless clear: without Tristan's delirious str eam-of-consciousness in Act III, without Kundry's madness, whether muted or frenzied, in acts I and II of *Parsifal*, there'd be no Woman in *Erwartung*: without Isolde's ecstatic closing delusion that her dead lover awakes to float with her into fragrant wafts of blissful love-in-death, Schoenberg's heroine would not imagine how her lover's corpse might still live and breathe; without Brünnhilde's cries for vengeance even unto her man's destruction, without Salome's orgasmic kiss to the lips of the severed head of the lover she's never enjoyed, the same goes (save the absence of the closing kiss). And then the final stretch of *Elektra*. All, including also Brünnhilde's immolation once her equilibrium is recovered, are essentially closing monologues for the heroine after the opera's main action has worked out and every other character fallen silent. *Erwartung* takes the culminating female monologue as its totality. The score remains an astonishment: but also – surprising and disconcerting – it can grow grey with age until the supreme exaltation of the final bars wherein the Woman acquiesces in and embraces her fate – everything that has or has not transpired – in that Wonder of the World, the concluding swoosh as the entire enormous orchestra disappears softly into the extremes of tessitura high and low while also holding the middle – again a sonority sought but never surpassed by electronic music.

The surprising greyness of *Erwartung* is pinpointed by the evocation of colour itself in the other one-acter of these astounding years, wherein a play of lights is accompanied by a timbral crescendo in the orchestra that burns and dazzles like a Tyger in the realms of Leo and Sol. The title – *Die glückliche Hand* – defeats translation: 'the lucky hand'; 'the fateful (or fated) choice'; 'the knack'? Scenario and text are entirely the composer's own this time: originally the piece was, like *Erwartung*, literally a monodrama – *the* Man, like *the* Woman. These unnamed archetypes remain but, though they don't sing, we do *see* other figures – one male, one female, plus an undefined monster; and a male chorus of smiths (at work but non-vocal) and twelve solo voices (six male, six female) who don't participate in the action, standing aside as commentators, commiserators, mockers, but who sing as part of the complex orchestral fabric.

Representative Man, symbolically defeated in every aspiration towards worldly success and love by forces from within and without inimical to his very existence. He enjoys one brief triumph – Man as Artist, creating a diadem of gold and precious stones in a Nibelheim-like smithy before, Siegfried-like, splitting the anvil and then tossing the artefact with contempt to the toilers – pearls before swine. The text is brief: more words by far are devoted to descriptions of scenery, stage-directions, and – above all – the lighting-scheme. A good case can be made for the lighting- and colour-effects as more important than the action and text; they for sure inform the music itself, indispensable to, inseparable from, its place as the summa of all such endeavours, including those of Scriabin, Messiaen, Stockhausen and Bliss, to infuse sound and light and colour with the utmost intensity of sensation – sensory, psychological, spiritual. From the very start we are in the world of artists – Böcklin, Klinger, von Stück: rear-stage draped in dark violet velvet, from whose gaps appear the six men and six women of the chorus, faces only, lit in green with soft red veiling – Klimt in the offing. When the conquering Artist/Siegfried tosses his precious creation to Nibelungs rather than Rhinemaidens, then resumes his puissant sword, all goes dark. A wind gets up, softly murmuring, growing ever wilder. Its accompanying light-crescendo goes from dull red, turning brown then dirty green, then blue-grey, then violet: this changes to an intense dark red, becoming ever brighter and more painful as it reaches blood-red, veering towards orange then yellow, eventually prevailing in glorious streams of sunlight flooding the entire space and the entire psyche. This yields finally to gentle blue-ish pleasantness. Painter-wise, a progress from Corinth and Thoma, via Marc and especially Kandinsky, late Gauguin, Malevich (but no black), early Matisse and Delaunay, culminating in Van Gogh. Schoenberg the composer achieves magnificently in sound what he can't begin to manage on canvas.

The music for this spectrum (the choices and orderings all his own) is indescribable: unconveyable except in its own terms. And the whole score, brief in duration, vast in scope, is a treasury of sonic wonders ranging from hair-splitting delicacies à la *Vergangenes* in the *Five Orchestral Pieces* to ear-splitting violence surpassing *Peripetie* in its gesticulatory vehemence. Altogether unprecedented is the choral writing for the twelve solo voices, mixing quasi-pitched speech – *Sprechstimme* – with fully-sung, in a fascinating close-weave of shot-velvet, presaging its more sparing use for the voice of the Burning Bush in *Moses und Aron* some twenty years on. There's also the new daintiness of the dance-figures by which the Woman as muse/seductress is characterized; the new rhythmic chunkiness of the work-music in the smithy – still virile and muscular here and when the Man's traitress lobs a monstrous rock on to him, though prophetic (with hindsight) of the drastic rhythmic stiffening that will afflict Schoenberg's later style. Best of all, the fabulous richness in harmony, movement, scoring, of the eight bars after the second burst of riotous mirth and mockery as the closing stages revert to the opening: the extension here into pure six-part singing is among the composer's most exultant beauties; and the hero (for such he is for all his abjection)'s final (for now) collapse – one last colossal *lunge* of aspiration, then extinction, foretells an even more riveting moment of utter defeat – Moses' despair at the end of the later opera. Tragic (in artistic terms) that this extraordinary work is vitiated by its very essence from practicable realization in performance.

The clear goal of these, Schoenberg's most fecund years, the vast visionary oratorio *Die Jakobsleiter/Jacob's Ladder*, to his own text (finished the next year, 1917), worked on intensively into the early 1920s, then abandoned, to be intermittently resumed in hope, relinquished again in despair, for the rest of the composer's life. The extant torso manifests the same glories, the same practical problems, the same limitations, even flaws – greyness, stiffness, formulaic constructivism – as already perceived in passing moments earlier; all these now on the most massive and ambitious scale conceivable.

But meanwhile, something quite different from anything earlier: a complete surprise, wholly diverging from the visionary/idealistic path; and one of its composer's unimpugnable triumphs. *Pierrot lunaire* was written rapidly in spring/early summer 1912, to a commission from a celebrated cabaret *diseuse*. None of the other works of this time was commissioned, and the three most elaborately demanding were not performed for a decade or more, the grandest of all – the *Jakobsleiter* torso – not till well after Schoenberg's death. But *Pierrot* was heard immediately (October the same year), understood (up to a point), appreciated (enough to be repeated fairly often), and exercised widespread and fruitful influence across several cultural boundaries.

Pattern – symmetry and asymmetry – is paramount. The twenty-one poems selected for setting from a German translation of Albert Giraud's French originals are grouped into 'three times seven': each poem, though their metres vary, is thirteen lines long, the first two lines returning identical as the second couplet of the second quatrain; the last line of each last stanza (always five lines long) closes the pattern, with the opening line (already repeated as line seven) unaltered. The brilliantly versatile ensemble (it has become a sort of standard) comprises five players; two woodwinds, two strings, piano. The flute can change to piccolo, the clarinet to bass-clarinet, the violin to viola (the cello doesn't double but can give a convincing similitude of both viola and double-bass). Ingenious deployment of these eight instruments means that every one of the twenty-one numbers is differently scored: not of course using the full forces in each – there are duets, trios, quartets; and the closing melodrama employs all of the available timbres by way of envoi.

Giving *Pierrot* its exact designation – *melodrama* – poses a problem that has never been satisfactorily resolved. What *is* this queer-sounding *Sprechstimme*? The *diseuse* is to speak, not sing: but the vocal part is placed upon the stave with specific pitches as well as rhythms: beautiful pitches too, as was once proved by an ancient BBC Third Programme experiment wherein the piece was sung straight. Endless quasi-solutions to the unanswered problem, from the frankly ludicrous – all squeaks and slides and affected battiness – to more musical renditions that retain a vestige of pitches and contours so lovingly composed but then forbidden. Yet the *outré* – extravagant, histrionic/hysterical, camp, *gamine* – is of the essence in this cabaret/revue/music-hall/end-of-the pier Pierrot-piece, its letter and spirit of *commedia dell'arte* as reimagined by the *fin de siècle*, a preoccupation widespread in the culture of the time from Verlaine onwards, to which Schoenberg's masterpiece is perhaps the most significant contribution. The same programme that broadcast the all-sung performance included a still-more daring experiment, omitting the voice altogether. It revealed a work of wonderfully intricate, rich-wrought chamber-music, as it were Brahms's late Clarinet Trio and Quintet passed through the shot-silk velvet of his last piano-pieces (written some thirty years previous in the same city of Schoenberg's first thirty-seven years): reaching beyond the excoriations of expressionism into a realm of fantastical poetry, often dark, sometimes disquieting, even frightening, then, as often light, whimsical, droll, bizarre, grotesque and parodistic, diaphanous and exquisite – *moonstruck*, as the text has it.

The first septet runs 'moondrunk' from grace, elegance, quicksilver fantasy into areas of morbidity and anguish, albeit as yet relatively playful. The second grows sinister and menacing as expressionism's darker aspects reach the surface – blasphemous Red Mass, fearsome Gallows-Song, macabre Decapitation, excoriating Crucifixion. The third group wholly changes direction – darkness evaporates – almost all (for parody and grotesquery still figure) is lyric, delicate, euphonious, eventually nostalgic and sweetly elegiac – Pierrot the Dandy, sated with sardonicism and sadism, hankers for home – Bergamo: the 'ancient scent' of fairy-tales calls him, the intoxicating allure of the past – in the music itself, major/minor bitter/sweet tonality.

Back now from divertimento lightness, however dark, to the composer's mainstream course – ethical, visionary, auto-expressive, pushing to the extreme edges of the articulable as to the practicable. Even before *Die glückliche Hand* was finished Schoenberg had planned and started an oratorio-symphony on an enormous scale, with Swedenborg (as mediated by Balzac's *Séraphîta*), together with Strindberg's *Wrestling Jacob*, in the background and to the fore texts by Dehmel (again), Tagore, the Bible, and words of his own: all these grappling with the central problem that occupied him all his life, from at least his conversion to Protestantism aged twenty-four (and no doubt before) to the *Modern Psalms* whose text and music he was still working on right up to his death over half a century later – the struggle with God (as of Jacob and the Angel), the ascent (as of Jacob and the Ladder) by which mankind arrives at recognition of Him, unity with Him in Prayer. This enterprise, begun in 1912, abandoned 1914, was extensively quarried for, and found its appropriate form in *Jakobsleiter*, also doomed to remain incomplete – the text written 1915–17, the music never reaching beyond the opening stage, gigantic as it is. There are external causes for its remaining incomplete – his two bouts of military service; just as pressing the internal – the incipient and contradictory demands of new compositional techniques; and, surely, realization at whatever level of consciousness that the vision could not be encompassed.

The text is now his own: gristly home-made philosopho-prose-poetastry. At the Ladder's foot Gabriel, compère, urges humanity onwards and upwards, out of the mire, chaos, strife, of earthly existence. The Unsatisfied, the Doubters, Rejoicers, Indifferent, Apathetic, are all choral: a Protester, One Wrestling, a Chosen One and a Monk, are soloists. All in turn make their plea and are harangued then rejected by the implacable Archangel. His last word to the last candidate, the spiritually complacent Monk, might well be the composer's message to the planet as well as to himself – go forth; utter; suffer: be Prophet and Martyr. Then One Dying begins to speak: she welcomes death with mounting abandon; speech transforms into song, she dissolves in sounds to become a spark of the eternal flame. Her soul-double joins, then the men, even Gabriel himself: the orchestra melts in celestial effulgence –introducing the Interlude intended to link into the work's second part, in text an interminable farrago of jaw-breaking amateur theology, its music unfinished, nay unbegun, to nobody's regret.

No problem with the work's ending here, however unintended. But even *Jakobsleiter* Part I presents real difficulties of style as well as idea. The emanation of burning authenticity has not touched the composer with music nearly so good as its predecessors. It remains a sketch: working it up in full, Schoenberg might have lavished the fabulous inventiveness of the *Orchestral Pieces* and the *Hand*: but the oratorio's more conventional layout would have precluded this. There's a thickening, a straightening out, in the invention itself – Reger, Max Bruch, Brahms, rather than Kandinsky and Scriabin. And the fact that *Jakobsleiter* includes Schoenberg's first investigations towards what will become 12-note serialism foretells the listener's difficulties now imminent.

Before the sticking-point, a delightful farewell glimpse of *Pierrot* in the *Serenade* (1920–23) – all grace and sparkle, complete with mandolin and guitar, except in one duff number, unfortunately on the direct path to what will come. The fourth movement sets for baritone in German a sonnet of Petrarch: each line has eleven syllables; set syllabically this uses eleven notes: the same order is retained throughout the voice-part, the instrumental accompaniment is loosely derived from the same collection, and the result is charmless, stiff, unmemorable. But the Method has been adumbrated: it proves germane for all its primitivity. Tried and tested in ten short movements for solo piano, gathered into two separate sets, opp. 23 and 25 (1920–23). Piquant that op. 25's five numbers contain four Baroque forms – prelude, gavotte with musette, menuet and trio, gigue. The feint at formality by way of a bow to the past will soon swell into an attempt to restore and continue the music of tonality's Teutonic heartland, 'Bach to Brahms', with new-forged technical equipment. Some five years of creative block now loosens: his frustrations are over: Schoenberg, aged fifty-ish, all set to start over again.

Five extra notes

When he made his notorious announcement that 'this day I have made a discovery that will ensure the supremacy of German music for a hundred years to come', it is this grand dynastic hegemony that is invoked. The great Teutonic masters (save Haydn, the Father of every one subsequent to him) are given a characterizing technical tag ('Bach for polyphony', etc.) and accorded their place in this overweening family romance, culminating in the charismatic leader who will consolidate, confirm, continue (and perhaps close). The radical revolutionary becomes the law-enforcing conservative in a new start half-way along the life of a turbulent and domineering personality who can link his new discovery into an artistic calling from On High equally with the perceived regeneration of a country's shattered economy, society, morale. 'Composition with 12 notes related only to one another': an ordering of the pitches, in its four basic shapes – forwards, backwards, upside-down forwards, upside-down backwards – piquant from the man who had so recently revelled in Swedenborg's vertiginous abolition of forwards/backwards for space and time. These basic shapes, transposable to any other pitch, providing material for the entire texture in its every detail of a total composition – melody and counter-melody, contrasting music, accompaniment-figures, decorative elaboration; and, fundamental, its harmony. The total mutual interdependence of all these pitch-constituents, fused vertical/horizontal, as constitutes the glory of baroque/classical/romantic tonality, organically interrelated with a deeper unity emanating from the single nucleus, and free of the 'tyranny' of tonal hierarchy – the cycle of fifths, the mediant relationships, and all the further means whereby a key-note functions as *home*. In 12-note music all pitches are equal and none is more equal than any other.

Compelling in theory and on paper. It's never worked in sound except – a huge concession – when mitigated, adulterated, softened, misunderstood, traduced, by whoever employs it to whatever successful outcome – including, sometimes, by its actual inventor, and, more consistently, by his two most celebrated pupils. Thence the principle spread worldwide down the middle decades of twentieth century, in widening ripples of dissemination and dilution, embracing some exceedingly remote and unlikely victims. Often renewing and recharging the moribund, versatile and fruitful the further it evolved from its chauvinist, doctrinaire starting-point. Paradoxically Schoenberg, the most aggressively antagonistic composer ever, wins when he loses.

But at what cost. For he has also lost the greatest part of what had made most of his oeuvre hitherto so perennially extraordinary and convincing. Hints of grey amid the rainbow gamut have already

been heard: with the discovery and exploitation of the serial technique, pitch-colour is the first sacrificial victim; so too with earlier
moments of rhythmic woodenness and stiffness in the phrasing –
the moment-to-moment spontaneity, the free-associative flux are sacrificed to mechanized motoric energy that constricts rather than
liberates. The main problem – crux of all the others – is *harmony*: the
tensile power yet infinite subtlety whereby horizontal and vertical
intertwine in tonal music to apprehensible aural comprehensibility
for ears untrained in music but simply loving 'the sound it makes', is
ditched – right out of the window – replaced with a dead letter,
unmeasurable by the senses, understandable only in theory.

Take the theme of Schoenberg's *Orchestral Variations* op. 31,
his first large-scale work in the new system (1926–8). The 12-tone
line, eloquent and shapely in itself, is given in all four orderings,
the last in counterpoint with its upside-down mirror: phrasing is
expressive, intervals conjunct; one senses the symmetries without
ticking them off; so far, so good. But these pleasing lines on cellos,
then violins, are harmonized by their complementary notes segmented into chords that cannot relate except by-the-book. Where
Bach-Beethoven-Brahms, writing a variation-work, build upon their
theme's harmonic structure, Schoenberg cannot. As if to prove it, he
provided in a radio talk around the *Variations'* première a 'traditional'
harmonization – very Regeresque, slithy and slithery – to show that
he could do it if he wanted to, but didn't want to any more. By now,
though, he can't do 'traditional' either (the woeful tally of his later
returns to tonality will come in due course). The would-be deeper
bonds between every element of which music is made have been
fatally severed, however logically, in this brief, simple instance of
what prevails almost everywhere in his serial works between the
wars. The way this music is made is not appreciably born, as in
tonality, of its actual substance: the facture is unimpugnable; the
sounds themselves paradoxically arbitrary and haphazard.

Other problems: all twelve notes, constantly in play, makes for
mud, not colour, like mixing the plasticines. Twelve is also too
many: super-chromatic saturation after Wagner certainly needed
sorting and cleansing, but this result is more tangled and satiating

still. Also, perpetually at high tension since so consistently dissonant. This music is in a perpetual frenzy of overloading: tension-
and-release, the in-and-out-take of breath, are not possible when all
notes have equal rights: they are reduced to primitive simplicity –
relaxation goes slower and softer, climax/cadence/conclusion can
only be achieved by dynamics and by piling yet more pitches into
the stew; varieties of density perforce grow crude. And the insoluble
paradox in the contradictions between the baroque and (especially)
the classical forms now revived and predominant. They are *tonal*
forms, from baroque dance and aria to classical sonata and rondo,
including variation and culminating in fugue: tonal processes articulated these procedures through and through: the prevailing neo-
classicism of the interwar decades, ambiguous enough when merely
sporting borrowed costumes from the past, is given a different and
harder twist by Schoenberg. Another paradox: the palpable mastery,
ease, naturalness with which he still composes – buttressed with
characteristic aggressive defensiveness – '12-note music is music as
before but with five extra notes'; 'my music is not modern, just badly
played'; 'I do compose as I did [in *Verklärte Nacht* and the *Gurrelieder*] but you can't see it', etc., etc. The evident fire and intensity – 'I
am composing again with the spontaneity of youth' – there's never a
doubt that in this respect he is the same composer. And last paradox,
the 'islands' of utterly right notes and real beauty in all these works –
a passing chord, a fragment of texture, an expressive contour, a whole
passage – where the ear is convinced and grateful. These places don't
work *because* of the method, but despite it. In realistic terms, 'serialism' has always been implicit in all well-composed music since
Sumer is Icumen In and Notre-Dame conductus; and is innate since
the chromatic scale became well-tempered: never more audibly than
in the two outer limits of Schoenberg's elected ancestry, Bach and
Brahms.

The *Variations* are the climax and consolidation of 12-note serialism's first phase: it had included some smaller pieces not deficient,
here and there, in charm. Op. 31 is *big*: it makes a highly conscious
nod to Old German Mastery, Brahms for the genre (itself with long
classical lineage), Bach invoked with his four-note musical signature,

at pitch, conspicuously haloed in surround sound. (During his years of experiment Schoenberg had orchestrated two Bach chorale-preludes, and in 1928 also comes a resplendently glorious version of the Master's *St Anne* prelude and fugue.) The *Variations*, an ambitious and impressive work, presents a fused mix of solutions and failures that is tricky and challenging to weigh. Whatever its problems, there's nothing insipid about it.

There is wide variety, after an impressionist introduction and the theme: nine variations well contrasted in mood, tempo, texture; they can embrace delicacy and euphony as well as abrasion and aggro – Var. 7 is almost Oriental in liquid arabesque – Pierrot's Bergamo waxes art nouveau, art deco, cubist. But the finale concentrates ever more maniacally the downside of all-chromatic facture: in the presto rush to the terminal cliff-edge, cadence/pitch has all but dis-appeared. The rhetoric, though, is unmistakable – it says 'fuck you: here I stand: I can do no other'. Pardon my German: the composer's is as gross.

The two operas from Schoenberg's interwar years stand so antithet-ical as to seem hardly the work of a single author. *Von Heute auf Morgen/From One Day to the Next* (1928) is his one attempt at contem-porary *moeurs* – '*moderne Menschen*' as the libretto says – a *Zeitoper* to compare with those of the next German generation, Hindemith, Weill, above all the tearaway success of Ernst Krenek's dreadful *Jonny spielt auf* (1926–7): all dance-bands, popular hit-songs, saxo-phones and crooners, sort-of jazz. It also resembles Strauss's *Inter-mezzo*, ahead of the game (1923) in dramatizing a real-life marital blip (Schoenberg's libretto written by his wife under a pseudonym). This bizarre affair is followed by a brief reversion to expressionism in the *Accompaniment to a Film Scene* (1929–30) – *Threatening Danger*; *Fear*; *Catastrophe* – back to *Five Orchestral Pieces*, forward to Holly-wood, where, when he got there, proud composer and canny film producers failed to agree.

He is on course, dead-centre, with *Moses und Aron* (the double A in the latter name avoided so as to achieve the magic twelve letters not the unlucky thirteen) – the magnum opus of Schoenberg's serial music, and maybe of his entire output: the subject he was born to treat – sublime, strong, archaic, deeply troubling and exploratory; and, very important, a given; not his own invention, which tends towards the cranky, the amateur, the clunking, the absurd. It demands to be treated in full. A biblical source provides rock-solid foundation; upon it his ethical/religious/human ideologies and speculations can build rather than founder. The spiritual quest, present from the start, first pursued at length and as such in *Jakobsleiter*, was explicitly continued in a play not intended for music, from the late 1920s – *The Biblical Way*, concerning vain efforts to found a permanent Jewish land in modern Africa. The libretto for *Moses* followed closely – a remix of the same constituents, with the reversals that precipitate the subject from crankiness to permanence: Moses' mission is indeed to found a state-and-place for his race, out of Africa (specifically Egypt) to a promised land as yet undefined and unlocated; set in measurably archaic/historical times with a strong turn towards mythology; and – the vital missing element – the quest to know, discover, be known and discovered by, a new conception of divinity, the One God, father and guide of a Chosen People; and the hero elected and driven to bear the message, to be the vessel and interpreter, to lead the spiritual revolution and the concomitant exodus, from bondage, across perils of sea and desert to the new homeland, where harmony of body and soul is symbolized by milk and honey.

Once the libretto was ready the music followed rapidly, despite hitches and the work's innate difficulties and enormous technical complexity. Acts I and II were complete by early 1932. Act III was barely begun then, and remained a chimera for the next nearly two decades: right up until the composer's death he toyed, fretted, hoped: the self-sufficiency of the two completed acts now seems absolute and crystal-clear, in story, in subject, above all in the score. Let us see how *es muß sein*.

Moses speaks but cannot sing: the vocal impediment mentioned in the biblical account – a halt, a stammer – becomes of enormous symbolical meaning as well as sonorous significance, put against his half-brother Aaron, a lyric tenor of persuasive fluency and charm.

God's voice in the first scene is also a blend of sung and spoken; in the choral representation of the Voice from the Burning Bush six solo voices sing, the six-part chorus speaks. God's Voice calls the Jewish man, so high in the Egyptian hierarchy, to accept the mission to lead his own people out of slavery to their oppressors. It will be given a mandate: it will be hard, but signs and wonders will compel recognition. Moses' opening words show that he already recognizes the divine nature – only; infinite; omnipresent; invisible; inconceivable – and the nature of his task locked into the word Chosen – his people are the chosen race, Moses the chosen one to lead them to freedom in a chosen land; and to reveal to them their own unique God, renewing the race's ancient covenant, restoring the idea of monotheism.

The wonderful music to this scene is, at last, what 12-note composition is *for*: the technique is given a *raison d'être* beyond mere accounting: the mystic numerological glow and shimmer to these chords and their circumambulant textures fuses the superstitious, reverent, other-worldly with the hear-and-now sensual accuracies of the sounds, their production, their assimilation into comprehensibility and communication that truly expresses what it's saying and could be achieved no other way.

It ends with Moses' first intimation of unworthiness: but I cannot utter: thought is given me, not speech. 'Aaron will be your mouth: see, he's approaching; go greet him, and begin.' The brothers meet: the senior insists upon his jaw-breaking crunch of solemnities, the junior translates into fluent eloquent lyricism, turning abstract to sensory, deep to shallow, weighty to lightweight. His realpolitik grasps the immediate upshot: deliverance from the bonds of Pharaoh. The Folk now appear, and Deeds replace Words.

Signs and wonders, visible and conceivable, sorcerer's tricks to astonish, cow, win. Moses' rod transformed into a serpent – the six solo voices from the Burning Bush sing Aaron's name, in warning, in vain: the music wriggles, twists, seethes, hisses, almost visibly. Moses' three enthusiasts renew their faith; the sceptical priest puts a damper on proceedings – your rod persuades us, but can't compel Pharaoh to set us free – again the six solo voices warn, this time wordless. The

Folk waver: Aaron, now firmly in charge, berates their broken spirit and shrunken pride – this won't overcome Pharaoh! – and causes his brother's strong hand to sicken disgustingly into leprosy – again the Folk describe and the music makes one see, hear, smell, the loathsome canker. The miracle of Nile-water into blood carries conviction where impalpable idealism fails. Aaron's eloquence waxes and persists, Moses is near forgotten. Your God will free you, lead you to the land of bounty, fulfilling the ancient covenant: as for Pharaoh, leave him to the clear Nile waters, wherein he will surely drown. The Folk enthusiastically take up the strain, repeating and amplifying the threats and promises, fully satisfied with the new Deity, who has chosen us above all other folk and will make us free! Free! – a huge confident sweep of martial fervour ending Act I in a tremendous positive blaze.

It is separated from Act II by a mysterious Interlude: the Folk, now bemused, anxious, deserted – after successfully escaping Egypt – by their leader, absented up in the mountains; whispers and *Sprechstimme* replace the jubilant choral strains concluding Act I; the orchestra whispers too in a fascinating dusky cobweb of sonority – where is Moses? Where is his God? Act II proper opens before the Magic Mountain: seventy Elders, disaffected by the doubting priest of earlier, voice complaint – we're worse off than in Egypt – what's this inconceivable law from an Invisible God? Aaron pleads for order to be kept: too late – the Elders are swept aside as the Folk rush in in rage, their 'where is Moses?' now violent as they threaten life and limb, calling for their old gods, visible, actual, effectual. Under extreme pressure, and having unwisely intimated that, approached too near, this too-severe new God might have slain his servant, Aaron capitulates: I return you your gods, as you demand: abandon the Inconceivable; your deities are sensory; bring out your gold!

Confidence and high-spirits take over; and thus to the act's centrepiece, a multimedia ultra-colourful sequence of song, dance, tableau, action, in praise of the Golden Calf whose stage-directions suggest old-style Hollywood epics – Cecil B. DeMille's *Ten Commandments* above all (first made 1923, redone 1956 – too early, then too late, for Schoenberg). Lurid and vivid, perhaps best realized by abstention – austere production can imply where literalism fails to thrill – as 'laden camels, asses, horses, porters, wagons, enter from different directions bringing gold, grain, wine and oil, animals for sacrifice: butchers prepare and dance, slaughter and throw the meat to the crowd, who fight over the hunks and consume them raw': but as evening comes on, some is cooked and offered upon the pagan altar, dedicated as burnt offerings to the massive gleaming idol. Miraculous cures and human sacrifices ensue, wanton sensuality, guzzling drinking, riot and debasement, all graphic, to eventual satiation and exhaustion. The orgy spends itself; lassitude and disgust follow; songs and dances recede into quiet consummation, the fires die down, all is dark, still, silent. A distant man's voice cries that Moses descends the Mountain.

The music for this great span of debauchery reverts in colour and sensory immediacy to where such goals had been left, on the completion in 1913 of *Die glückliche Hand*. The 12-note 'discovery' was a call-to-order, a 'method' of ensuring meaningful relationships between the notes after the intoxicating but perilous seas of intuitiveness and arbitrariness. Innately classicizing after its baroque baptism, it seemed doomed to sacrifice some of the things the radical young composer had done best – at their best, with burning genius. Becoming a man and putting away childish things involved relinquishing all that. Listening to serial pieces like the 3rd String Quartet, even the *Orchestral Variations*, one wonders whether it was worth it: listening to the Wind Quintet one is certain it was not. In *Moses* the new system at last yields music as good as its inventor can compose. True from the very opening in the mystic richness of the Burning Bush, present most vividly down the course of Act I in Aaron's specious but exciting miracles, it here bursts into lurid exotic bloom for the Act II spectacle; nor losing the sonorous burnish and rightness in the orgy's hard, bitter aftermath.

Moses is descried: the music goes jagged and 'expressionist' as the Folk stream back in; he enters, anathematizes the pagan Image, which vanishes: the Folk too, after just two bars' lament for their lost gold: within seconds the tumultuous crowds of earlier are replaced by the two brothers, bringing their differences to crisis-point in a theological agon hard to understand or listen to though indispensable to the work's meaning and to its dramatic human trajectory. It was remarkable to see this potential dead-area tingling with involvement, even excitement, in the visually null, musically outstanding production brought by Welsh National Opera to Covent Garden: with fine artists singing and speaking, and intelligent subtitles, the audience palpably rose to the arguments as though it were Wotan and Loge in *Rheingold*, or Wotan and his daughter in the last Act of *Walküre* – as if, indeed, it were a sort of weird love-duet, in a work conspicuously devoid of erotic interest and of any but the tiniest cameo-parts for female voices. Perhaps it *is* a sort of weird love-duet. Certainly, a strong turn-of-the-screw force powers the whole of the brothers' exchange. Aaron wins by sophistries: I followed my inward voice – we thought you dead – the Folk needed what I could give them. I love this Folk, you love only your Idea: and talking of images, are not these Laws you hold in your arms graven images too? Crushed, Moses smashes the stone tablets engraved with the Commandments taken direct from the Only God, and, as at the start, begs to be relieved of his mission – a terrible moment for the rough speaker, immediately palliated by the smooth singer, mellifluous throughout, never more so than now, certain that the Chosen People will remain true to their sacred calling through his simpler, clearer, more assimilable and realistic grasp of the inner laws and their outer embodiment than the Commandments' grim bearer will ever succeed in expressing.

As if to prove it, the Folk begin to sing from backstage, confident in their role, chosen before all others by the Only God, serving him alone, led by him to the plenteous land in fulfilment of his ancient Covenant. They are on the move thither, guided by a pillar of fire: as dawn comes up, the fiery signal becomes a pillar of cloud – God's signs, visible indications of his promises; fulfilment, indeed, of his very existence. To Moses, mere symbols, images, idols. The chorus, with its off-stage marching-band, peaks as the main orchestra falls silent, then in their turn rapidly fade into the distance. Aaron has left to join them. Moses is alone. His impassioned final speech

points the speech/song contrast/conflict at its acutest, so closely following his brother's climactic lyric cantilena. The full orchestral
strings return, however, to sustain eloquence at its highest intensity,
all the violins massed in unison, enormous leaps from their lowest
note to their stratosphere – jagged/dangerous/precipitate/burning, as
the desperate Chosen One berates the God who apparently deserts
and betrays him: will you let it be thus? Shall Aaron, my mouth, get
away with it? So I too, then, have fashioned an image – false, as an
image must be. I am defeated: it was all delusion and madness – here
the violins' highest notes, long-sustained, plunge down, joined by
supporting woodwinds and piano, to link into violas, cellos, basses,
in a vehement collapse five octaves lower, curt and brutal. Silence.
Broken by the last whisper of the disappearing Folk – *Götter*/*Gods*
(they've been boasting that *our* Almighty is mightier than the gods
of Egypt). The orchestra's cavernous bottom is touched by the few
instruments who can sound it (double-bassoon, bass tuba, double-
basses) and Moses' broken sentence is completed – and *can* not and
must not be uttered. Unison violins steal softly in again, wide intervals, long notes, settling on their last for *his* last, the famous 'O Word,
O Word, that I lack' – or, 'that fails me' (both are right). His last act,
words failing, is – as violas and cellos join the long-held unison
violins and they all swell, prolonged, from *p* to *f* and then diminish
to *pp* – to sink to the ground in despair. The Word has failed him
because God gave him no persuasive powers of eloquence; the Word
is lacking: but the Word has in itself failed because it lacks within
it what God promised him it contains: the Word is not the Word of
Truth; the promise is void.

The tragic power of this double-edged ending, so unforgettably
rendered in its music (and after all that preceded) gives the close
of *Moses und Aron* one of the supreme curtains in all opera, shattering as the deaths of Siegmund then Hunding or the destruction of
Klingsor's castle, and much less melodramatic. It is a triumph to
have wrung sublime and profound operatic embodiment from a
subject and its treatment on the face of it so unlikely. Moses' failure
is Schoenberg's triumph: this is what he came into the world to
achieve – Called/Chosen indeed; and with the new-made technical

means that exactly correspond. Regrettably there are only ten Commandments, though Schoenberg the 'Kabbalist' has made his title
consist of twelve letters. But seriously: there is unmistakable self-
identification and autobiographical thrust in this work concerned
with a unique, privileged mission, a new constitution, a spiritual
regeneration, a law-promulgation to lead benighted mankind into
the light; which just as unmistakably is objectified, transcended,
impersonalized, into a great work of art applicable to all sorts and
conditions. 'Someone had to be me': Schoenberg is here with the
Luthers, the Wagners, the Tolstoys, the Nietzsches, the Old Testament Prophets and the Divine Subject of the New.

Act III? Its text gave its author much trouble: to its composer
the music proved so problematic that he could make no headway
despite his preoccupation with it, nagging away for the rest of his
life. It has become commonplace to suggest that this blockage
shields an unconscious intention not to complete the work; that the
devastating close of Act II is final in a more poetic, human, philosophical sense. Perhaps facile, even impertinent; but surely true. The
legends in Jewish tradition concerning the death of Moses, beautiful
and moving as they are, go into strange terrain unconnected with
the brothers' conflict or its possible/impossible resolution: Moses, as
passed down the Christian tradition, is chiefly memorable – after the
Golden Calf and the Commandments – for being forbidden entry
into the Promised Land, permitted only to glimpse it from afar.

Schoenberg's text has only one scene. Aaron, now inexplicably a
prisoner, is further argued with: no new ground is broken beyond
reference to a further miracle, water from the rock, and the daring
suggestion that the Promised Land is yet another deluding image.
Aaron's words diminish, Moses' wax longer and more intractable,
ending with what he's uttered already, an accusation of betrayal.
Some soldiers offer to kill the traitor, but his brother goes on and on,
then tells them to set Aaron free – if he desires it, he can live. When
freed, Aaron drops down dead, and Moses has the last, not clearly
consequential, word – even in the desert you shall be invincible and
reach the goal – Unity with God. The arguments are woolly, especially after the trenchancy manifested earlier: the human situation

shallow as well as unexplained, especially after the subtle symbiosis between the brothers so searchingly explored already; the victory to the man last seen in the abjection of total defeat is hollow and unconvincing in every way. Whatever his motivation, identification, intention, it is not possible to believe that Schoenberg believed himself in his Act III: his inability to set it says as much. Had he somehow managed to fake it (inconceivable!) it would have been the doing of an Aaron: false – wilful and factitious – to the work's *true* close.

After his summa comes Schoenberg's dismissal from his native land, exile to an alien USA with a total reconversion to Judaism and a partial return to tonality. Several oddities from these years: baroque reworkings – a Cello Concerto after Monn (forgotten composer of the early eighteenth century), a Concerto for String Quartet after Handel, precede the move: their baroquerie is so idiosyncratic and extravagant as to offend taste, sense, sensibility – Dada, surreal, for all the profusion of manic invention. Two sizeable original concertos, for violin (1935–6), for piano (1942), preserve and extenuate the claim to inherit the Great German Tradition: the violin concerto is strong and assertive, admitting no amelioration: the piano one is more gracious – its naïve little programme – 'Life was so easy; but suddenly hatred broke out; a serious situation was created; but life goes on' – perhaps personal, perhaps connected with events at large, and so general it could apply to anyone and everything, or no one and nothing. These works are 12-note serial: they lie alongside three tonal efforts, a *Suite for Strings* (1934), *Variation for Wind-Band* (1943), both intended to exercise young American players and instruct them in old European mastery. *Variations upon a Recitative* for organ (1941) embraces the densest polyphony he ever perpetrated, in and out of tonality, a nightmare gargoyle surpassing the worst organ-abominations of Liszt or Reger.

'*On revient toujours* [we always come back] – a longing return to the older style was always vigorous in me, and from time to time I had to yield to that urge.' A more fruitful urge was Schoenberg's formal return to the Jewish faith on reaching Paris from Berlin,

May 1933. His Protestantism of 1898 had been, like Mahler's, a career move necessitated in anti-Semitic Vienna: nor did Schoenberg need the externals to be the ultimate Protestant. His reconversion to Judaism is genuine and will burgeon in the texts and music of his final years. *Kol Nidre* (1938): the legend from the Kabbala tells how God creates light and crushes it into a million sparks that only the faithful can discern: thence the Prayer for Atonement whereby those Jews who've been compelled to renege on their religion can be received back into it – 'all such vows, oaths, promises, pledges, that have estranged us from the sacred task for which we were chosen are hereby annulled'. Perhaps the most persuasive of all the composer's 'returns' to tonality and to belief: certainly, the most moving.

The next five works oscillate between severe restraint and vehement protest. But first, neither: *Prelude to Genesis* (1945), commissioned to launch an epic film covering the Bible complete, closing with wordless chorus loud and bright on wide-spread Cs, distant reminiscence of Haydn's creation of light from chaos. Protest looms fierce in the *Ode to Napoleon Buonaparte* (1942), wherein Byron's scorn for the European conqueror is reapplied to the detested and dreaded Hitler, and the poem's paean to George Washington re-applied to FDR – Joseph the provider in the land of plenty now nurturing the milk and honey of European-Jewish culture. (A fascinating parallel running from *Moses* onward with Thomas Mann's contemporaneous epic *Joseph and His Brothers*.) This repellent piece is wholly eclipsed by *A Survivor from Warsaw* (1947), which deals direct as the *Ode* oblique with the horrors of the age. Format as in *Kol Nidre* – speaker, chorus, orchestra; also focusing upon an ancient Jewish prayer/hymn: and the two works meet from opposite ends technically. In the *Survivor*, pure 12-note writing tending towards a tonal-tinged breakthrough: in *Kol Nidre*, tonality influenced strongly by serial organization. The later work could hardly fail on 'humanitarian' grounds, but there is no emotional blackmail; the excoriating subject-matter is expressed in an inspired unexploitative score that transcends it and turns it into art. *A Survivor* is also cinematic, visual as verbal, both X-rayed and X-flayed with a harsh, edgy, nervously articulated orchestra – shrieking piccolos, brutal trumpet fanfares and tattoos, stamping ostinati, percussion tuned – xylophone – and untuned to the fore. Every aspect of daily abuse and suffering in the Ghetto is vividly evoked, till the accumulated pressure of so many burning fragments coalesces into the unison male chorus, chanting the old prayer so long neglected, the *Shema Yisrael*: Hear O Israel, the Lord thy God is one God – a fine contour, nobly doubled by trombone as a sublimated march, surrounded by a fragmented nimbus of jagged dissonance, broadening into a close of blinding incandescence.

The abstract works are a string trio (1946) and a *Fantasy* (1949) for violin and piano. '*On revient toujours*': the return here is to the rigour of his earliest 12-tone music, but with a new lucidity, and sometimes a new simplicity and sweetness – no longer embattled and didactic – agreeable to diversion and pleasure even when, as in the trio, recounting a near-terminal heart-attack and subsequent hospitalization – the return now still further back to naked expressionism.

To close, the last fruits of the composer's return to the faith of his fathers. *Israel Exists Again!* (unfinished) 1949: *Dreimal tausend Jahre* (1949): *De Profundis* (1950): *Modern Psalms* no. I (unfinished at his death in 1951). Israel was founded as a state in 1948: the old composer was deeply stirred and deeply regretted that age and infirmity prevented his taking up an invitation to visit, and even to head an academy of composition. *Israel Exists Again!* for chorus and orchestra to his own text, typically fervent and clunking – it has always existed, though invisibly . . . and here the fragment breaks off: the music equally characteristic, fervent, clunky – broad-spaced, searingly dissonant, and full of promise. *Dreimal tausend Jahre* is a brief, drab, unaccompanied motet, looking to the restoration after 'thrice a thousand years' of the Temple in Jerusalem – God's return to his own rightful place. The promise of *Israel* is fully fulfilled in *De Profundis*, setting Psalm 130 for six-part chorus *a cappella* in a mix of sung and spoken/shouted vocalization reminiscent of the choral writing in *Moses*, conveying the same naked intensity in compact space, unforgettable in live performance.

Schoenberg returned to his own home-made texts for his final project, a sequence of *Modern Psalms*; twenty-five were completed, further were planned; again so typical – to number them from 151 on, as if the ancient Psalter of his people was not quite sufficient. Such chutzpah is wholly absent from the music he managed for the first, the last he was able to notate, though remaining unfinished. The concern is again pure *Moses*: prayer, addressing oneself to God, and how to; and does He care or even notice; and how to achieve unity with the Only, the Eternal, the Omniscient, Omnipotent, Unimaginable – words virtually identical with Moses' before the Burning Bush. This third, last, shortest, of his religious torsos has a quality all its own: luminous pan-tonal serenity, born of the 12-note row's construction in major and minor thirds, audible throughout even when orchestral texture grows tense and agitated. Speaker and chorus exchange the same words, continuing or alternating: the break-off point is as moving as the drain-out and collapse of onward flow in the unfinished contrapunctus of Bach's *Art of Fugue*, the place where Mozart's *Requiem* gutters away, the anguished scrawls on the unfinished close of Mahler's 10th.

(Re)solving the impasse: Berg and Webern

Schoenberg is denied the Promised Land. His two most celebrated pupils and followers, for whom he is master, leader, guide, both achieve it in fascinatingly complementary fashion. Webern's later work pushes the 12-note method's implications to an extreme – strips, essentializes, isolates, making its construction the audible *raison d'être* of the music. Berg's later work adapts the method to very different ends, never relinquishing either the post-Mahler *Affekt* – rhetoric and emotion at fever-pitch – or the late-tonal language in which it was uttered, embodied, organized.

Webern starts here too: both composers are rooted in Wagner, late Brahms, Wolf, expressionist Strauss, Mahler, and their teacher's own irresistible personality. Thereafter they diverge: one of music's suggestive dichotomies, like Bach/Handel, Wagner/Brahms,

Tchaikovsky/Musorgsky, Strauss/Mahler (and so on to Schoenberg/ Stravinsky – Messiaen/Carter – Tippett/Britten – even Glass/Boulez). Both are localized, with their master's life for the most part, in 'our loved and hated Vienna'; the factitious 'Second Viennese School' linking all three (initially a mere publishers' gimmick, the tag seems to have stuck).

Alban Berg: born Vienna 1885 of a cultivated affluent family: pupil of Schoenberg from 1904; slave to His Master's Voice and its peremptory demands for the rest of his life, yet in his own music achieving a fruitfully independent journey. Marriage 1911. Served reluctantly in the Great War. Financially insecure in later years thanks to post-war inflation. Persistent bad health: *Wozzeck*, premièred 1924, the Second Viennese School's only wider success; its successor, *Lulu*, not quite completed at his death from blood-poisoning 1935.

Anton von Webern: born Vienna 1883 into minor former Austrian aristocracy. Pupil of Schoenberg from 1904. Married 1911; a living made by teaching and conducting: corpus of thirty-one opus-numbered works, plus fragments/incompletions/rejections; barely recognized in his lifetime, posthumously (after his tragic accidental death in 1945) taken up as avant-garde cult.

Putting their works in parallel will clarify their comparable paths (see pp. 725-6).

What both composers are doing in their music, and how it's done, can be *heard*. In their antithetical ways, both reveal a more realistic sense of the listener's perception than their master. Maybe Berg's solution 'betrays' him: Aaron's mellifluous seductive elo-quence, simplifying, even compromising the Message by reaching the Folk's lower instincts, and their hearts. Webern's Way certainly realizes the Idea even beyond the vision of him who 'discovered' it; but it could be that his taking it to such an extreme is equally a mis-understanding, even a betrayal, even a perversion.

Connected with such thoughts, a further complement before trying each composer separately. Their reception, during their life-times and beyond, is just as congruent. *Wozzeck* swept Europe from the start, and thence the world: *Lulu* too, though much later: and the

Alban Berg		Anton von Webern	
1907–8	Piano Sonata op. 1	1908	*Passacaglia* for orchestra op. 1

–'graduation works'–

Alban Berg		Anton von Webern	
		1909	*Five Movements* for string quartet op. 5
			Six Pieces for Large Orchestra op. 6
1910	String Quartet op. 3	1910	*Four Pieces* for violin &
1912	*Altenberglieder* for voice & orchestra		piano op. 7
		1911–13	*Six Bagatelles* for string quartet op. 9
1913	*Four Pieces* for clarinet & piano op. 5		*Five Pieces for Small Orchestra* op. 10
1914–15	*Three Pieces for Orchestra* op. 6	1914	*Three Little Pieces* for cello & piano op. 11
		1915	Song-sets, with piano (op. 12) & with small instrumental
1917–	*Wozzeck* begun		groups (opp. 13–18): in the later sets (opp. 17–19) trying
1922	*Wozzeck* completed		the 12-note technique, alongside Schoenberg's first serial compositions of 1920–23

Schoenberg's first sizeable 12-note work, *Wind Quintet* 1924
from now-abouts both his principal pupils adopt it too.

Alban Berg		Anton von Webern	
1923–5	*Chamber Concerto*	1926–7	String Trio op. 20
1925–6	*Lyric Suite* for string quartet	1927–8	Symphony op. 21
1929	*Der Wein*	1928–30	Saxophone Quartet op. 22
1929–	*Lulu* begun	1931–4	*Concerto for Nine*
	Acts I & II complete		*Instruments* op. 24
	Act III not fully scored		
1935	Violin Concerto	1935	*Das Augenlicht* op. 26
Died 1935		1935–6	*Variations for Piano* op. 27
		1936–8	String Quartet op. 28
		1938–9	First Cantata op. 29
		1940	*Variations* for orchestra op. 30
		1941–3	Second Cantata op. 31
		Died 1945	

Presenting them as complements will clarify their divergencies

Alban Berg
Construction, of fetishistic, almost crazed game-playing, schemes and cyphers beyond any comparable forebears (J. S. Bach, Schumann): complexity, secrets, intimate private meanings:

Its *goal*, ultra-expressivity & total subjectivity, the pre-1914 aesthetic of saturation taken yet farther into a 'decadence of maximalism'. Humane: empathy with life high and low, in all its aspects – 'nothing alien' – supremely evinced in the two operas –

Hence *impurity*: the idiom alludes, quotes, uses & abuses cheap music, popular strains, vulgar marches, American dance-bands. Impure most of all in his adaptation of the 12-note technique: inventive cunning to get it to yield the notes he wants: liaison with the scale, the triad, the arpeggio, with harmonic push-&-pull, if only occasionally with tonality as such: pragmatic – a folksong, a street song, a Bach chorale, a note-row for a violin concerto built around the instrument's open strings.

Anton von Webern
Construction, of ultra-severity & economy, to show the working as essentially – even simply – as possible. No secrets – scaffolding – 'bone-structure': sometimes at the expense of flesh:

Its *goal*, to demonstrate a rarified pantheism – the sacredness of a flower, a leaf, a snowflake, a crystal, a grain of sand, a drop of dew. Not 'human' in the least, though sometimes extremely subjective –

Hence *purity*: no outside stylistic references, quotations, allusions. Even the (neo-)classicism is, unlike his master's, absolutely devoid of idioms & routines. Hence an adaptation of the 12-tone technique so rapid, eager, thoroughgoing. It's *made* for him as not for its inventor. With Schoenberg 12 is too many: chromatic overkill results. Webern's innate frugality essentializes and isolates the total chromatic into small cells, even just the bare intervals.

Berg Violin Concerto is virtually standard repertoire. Despised by the post-war avant-garde as 'the 12-tone Puccini', he has by now found his own permanent level: compare the Strauss/Mahler seesaw. The generation of 1945, equally deploring Schoenberg as failing his own fulfilment, found their way forward from point zero in 'St Anton', who also by now is given a fairer and more balanced estimation. Imitation of either – of all three – is futile. All are 'extremes that have no future' except, as with Wagner, by transformation. Fruitful fertilization runs sideways, not direct, and its richest results can often not be audibly related to their sources.

And a footnote: Schoenberg's veneration for Bach, in orchestrations, in using his musical signature, and throughout the ramifications and workings of the serial principle, has already been mentioned. In Berg and Webern, Bach's presence is just as characteristic as all their other complements and contrasts. Berg has recourse to the Bach chorale in his Violin Concerto as its emotional nub, catharsis, resolution in acquiescence and solace: all is association and *Affekt*. Webern's Bach is for workings, not emotion: he X-rays the six-part ricercar from the *Musical Offering*, when setting it out for orchestra, as though it were one of his own original works – a distilled essence, without grace or charm (albeit a touch of sweetness at the main cadence-points, with the solo violin). The 'back-to-Bach' movement of the interwar decades, represented by Hindemith in Germany and Stravinsky in Paris, is completely different, both between these two and in contradistinction to their Viennese contemporaries.

Thus to the music itself, from their beginnings to their adoption of 12-note technique. Their respective op. 1s already indicate their difference despite the common background, the contemporaneity (1907–8) between the two young Schoenberg-pupils, and the two works' status as 'graduation-pieces': Berg's Piano Sonata rich, romantic, effusive, over-wrought; Webern's orchestral *Passacaglia* disciplined by the process, its clear ancestor the finale of Brahms's 4th Symphony; Bach behind both, though allowing itself some hefty moments of Mahlerian rhetoric, soon to be sublimated out of sight and sound. An acuter link comes with their respective works for string quartet in these years: Berg's sizeable op. 3 (1910); Webern's miniature *Five Movements*, op. 5 (1909) and minuscule *Six Bagatelles* op. 9 (1911–13). Berg's is complex/complicated, dense/demanding beyond the parallels with/inspiration from his master's 2nd Quartet (the one with soprano singing of 'air from other planets'). Webern's *Five Movements* take Schoenberg's other tendency of these times, towards aphorism, fragmentation, splintering of texture and continuity, to new extremes, quite radical whether grinding or delicate, machine-like, inexorable or refined nearly beyond capture, even audibility, ferocious or fugitive: all modes equally precise and compelling. Still more the *Bagatelles*, with his master's famous preface/imprimatur – 'every glance can be stretched into a poem, every sigh into a novel [he might here have intended a sly allusion to Berg, to whose op. 3, and other works later, this certainly applies]: but to express a novel in a single gesture, a joy in a breath . . . such concentration can only be present in proportion to the absence of self-pity' (another sighing glance at the presence of such, sometimes in floods, in Berg?). This preface goes on to wonder how musicians can execute such music and how listeners can receive it – salient considerations in all Webern's work from now on. These split-hair sonorities of the utmost intensity, fragile and disconnected, in the smallest imaginable space yet bursting it with dynamic pressure – range, mode of attack, dynamics all in perpetual extremity – bring to its existence when heard – overheard – *live* – a sort of physicality different in kind to any other composer.

Webern's exiguity is almost self-caricaturing in the *Three Little Pieces* op. 11 for cello and piano (1914), respectively nine, thirteen and ten bars short, and fashioned as much from silence as from sound. He remarked around this time that once the twelve pitches had been heard there seemed nothing more to add. Much later he described uncomprehending reactions to his mature music – 'a high note, a low note, a note in the middle – the music of a madman!' – but this never applies more aptly than to his opp. 9 and 11. An almost comic example is the (relatively) high Bb, the cellist's last note in the second of the *Three Little Pieces* – three short beats in a very fast tempo, *fff crescendo*: in a live context the 'madness' simply doesn't signify; such notes are apprehended in a new way. These cello-pieces are the sparsest instances of all three composers' aphoristic aims in these years – including Webern's own *Four Pieces* for violin and piano op. 7 (1910) and Berg's *Four Pieces* for piano and clarinet op. 5 (1913). The conjunct melodic fluidity, warmth of harmony, fullness of texture and dramatic rhetoric of the Berg undoubtedly will appeal more widely.

Just these qualities prevail, however, in no uncertain manner in Webern's largest work of these times, the *Six Pieces for Large Orchestra* op. 6 for 1909, the year of Schoenberg's seminal *Five Orchestral Pieces*. Berg's set of *Three Pieces for Orchestra* op. 6 closes this venture in 1914–15 – a high plateau of modernist achievement at large and of Viennese expressionism in particular. The two pupils are now operating at the same level as their master, to whom both their works are dedicated: this plateau is exalted common ground; after it the three composers' differences so widen as to preclude comparison. Schoenberg's ambiguity over entitling his *Five* has already been mentioned. Wider programmatic associations in Webern's *Six* only became known long after his death. The gigantic orchestra he employed originally (reduced later in a more realistic revision, more usually played) belies their inward intimacy and secrecy. Here, risking 'madman' literalism, is what one hears.

No. 1: a low flute, caught by a muted trumpet then a horn, separated by two lovely celesta chords; tender three-note phrase of four-part harmony on violas and cellos ('novel in a sigh'); uncurling clarinet and trumpet lines, harp and solo strings in background; sudden surge into full texture, soaring violins, plunging lower strings, between them stammering horns and singing trumpets; as this deflates, the clarinets stutter, a solitary horn remains, with a harp glissando; a single lovely celesta chord, descending five-note phrase on trumpet, repeated, elongated and softer and disappearing; single soft harp harmonics. For the public this first piece 'expresses the expectations of a catastrophe': and the second 'the certainty of its fulfilment' (a clear congruence with Schoenberg's first Orchestral Piece – 'Premonitions'; and fourth – '*Peripetie*'). But privately, the first piece is to express my frame of mind when I was still in Vienna, already sensing the disaster [of his mother's death] yet always maintaining the hope that I would find her still alive. It was a beautiful day – for a moment I firmly believed that nothing had happened. Only during the train journey to Carinthia – the afternoon of the same day – did I learn the truth.

No. 2: This source doesn't detail the second (catastrophe's fulfilment) so closely. An errant bass-clarinet line surrounded by interspersions – single notes, little flurries, brief chords on other instruments, till an upward rearing trombone then tuba break it; agitation, at once followed by slow even contours on flutes over a haze of strings muted and *am Steg* (*sul ponticello*/on the bridge, a soft but harsh nasal timbre); agitation resumes, stuttering brass and strings pizzicato, merging and building to woodwind sighs, brief relief with celesta and strings (now bowed normally) interrupted at once by a dissonant cry, twice, on brass; strings (now unmuted) ascend from bottom to top, high woodwinds wail, low trombones menacingly flutter enforced with percussion; the wailing, extended, cut off this time by a ferocious all wind/brass dissonance intensified with cymbals trilling; the lower percussion three times make a soft limping tattoo; dissonance again; two limps; dissonance, one limp; dissonance again, now snapped off rather than sustained.

No. 3: 'the most tender contrast' says the public note; in the private one, this music 'conveys the impression of the fragrance of the Erica [a kind of heather], which I gathered at a spot very meaningful to me and laid on her bier'. Tender glances on a solo viola, three notes long, then two, over softest-possible chords on trumpets: a solo clarinet recalls the five-note phrase closing the first piece; a solo double-bass, just two notes under softest-possible strings; a delicate seven-note glint, gigue-like, almost naïve, led by glockenspiel; it dies – one more note, echoed by harp; expressive bassoon solo rises, answering solo violin descends, harp softly supports a single eloquent note on solo horn; celesta varies the descent, harp resumes its background, two two-note words for solo trumpet. The whole is an Introduction, as the programme for the public says, to no. 4:

> which I later entitled *marcia funèbre*. Even today I do not under-
> stand my feelings as I walked behind the coffin to the cemetery. I
> only know that I walked the entire way with my head held high,
> as if to banish everything lowly all around. I beg you to under-
> stand me properly – I am myself trying to gain clarity about that
> peculiar state. I have talked to no one as yet about it. The evening
> after the funeral was miraculous. With my wife I went once again
> to the cemetery and there straightened out the wreaths and
> flowers on the grave. Always I had the feeling of my mother's
> bodily presence – I saw her friendly smile, it was a blissful feeling
> that lasted moments. Two summers after that [actually it was
> three] I was at our estate again for [an] extended period; this
> was the time when I wrote these pieces at summer's end. Daily,
> towards evening, I was at the grave – often in deep dusk.

I have let the composer's private confessions run on to the end of the work, not just its celebrated fourth Piece. Unique in Webern's oeuvre for uniform rhythmic pulse, set off for seven bars of un-pitched percussion, very low, near-inaudible at first, on bass-drum rolling, plus tam-tam and two deep bells. Once a regular pulse is perceived, pitches enter – four-note dissonances, all off-beat, passed across woodwind and bass choirs, guttering out after the fourth exchange to sour sustained snarl on four trombones, supporting a solitary piccolo-line anxiously circulating the same few notes. A few more bars' funeral tolling, till a subdued line on low clarinet, succeeded by high horns: the sustained tolling resonance has now dried here into dully emphatic brass punctuation, each short chord hiccoughed-down by the bass drum, instantly damped dead. Horn taken over by trumpet, its long, soft, low, even notes the simplest passage in all Webern. As it closes, the resonance of bells and tam-tam resumes, and a snare-drum enters quietly, swelling to a slight apex crowned with a woodwind glance followed by a loud brass ejacula-tion. Snare-drum again; horns begin a syncopated pronouncement, picked up by full brass group, ever more craggy and minatory, joined eventually by trumpets – a real big-band moment – and then finally with woodwinds too, the same chord, jerkily ejaculating/stammering/spitting in a colossal *tenuto*, till released for one more scrunch, edged now with cymbals and the snare-drum, joining timpani and all the other untuned battery for an all-percussion crescendo to the threshold of pain and over.

Nos. 5 and 6 'are an epilogue: remembrance and resignation'. No. 5 is reflective and annealing: led by an expressive trombone, warmly harmonized in varying colours; oboe answers, then clarinet, a solo cello, a horn, clarinet again, oboe again, flute – tiny phrases, never more than seven notes long after the initial trombone (and the cello has but one, though deeply felt); closed by horn (one note) and harp (curt chord). A deep-rooted high-arched sigh (containing a whole novel) on the strings, a well-tamed lyric tuba, and – breaking the texture of discontinuous continuity – a snatch of jig-like quasi-nursery-rhyme, recalling the similar moment in the third Piece and also here led by the glockenspiel. It fades. Silence. Wide-spaced, beautifully voiced soft chord: inside it a flute-figure, high a-top, a solo violin: the chord is sustained to the end, its lower middle pitches on trombones gently swerving before settling; violin still floats a-top, stilled; a solo trumpet plucks a single note, thrice repeated – the fused *image sonore* trembles into invisibility.

No. 6 retains the same mood – 'remembrance and resignation': eloquent understatements – glance/glimpse/sigh/whisper – on oboe, bassoon with viola solo, horn, trumpet; clarinet underpinned by softly ticking ostinato chord-succession, like the moment towards the close of Schoenberg's 'Premonitions' recalled down the wrong end of a telescope. One of the deep bells from the funeral-toll begins to vibrate, and continues to, as it were, after the piece, and the work, has ended, with violin solo of four notes, overlapped by a solo trumpet (two notes); solo string harmonics (just one); leaving the sonorous space to harp and celesta . . . disappearing . . . only the deep bell *kaum hörbar wahrnehmbar* – scarcely audible.

*

Berg's *Three Pieces* op. 6 also has such moments of 'overhearing' inwardness: it too places its main weight upon a march; and employs gigantic orchestral forces whether to entrance the senses with rarified beauty or to blow its listeners out of their comfort-zones. A principal difference places it apart from the sets by his peers: it's a big work; longer, more architectural, unified symphonically rather than by mood and picture – the influence of Mahler, already half or wholly transmuted *bei* Schoenberg and Webern, remains explicit in Berg, and will so till his dying day. Closer too, though the latest of these works, to the idioms surrounding it in its *own* culture – Zemlinsky, Schreker, Korngold, the expressionist and post-expressionist Strauss – it is lavish, luscious, voluptuous, sensory and sensual; enticing, erotic, extravagant; filled with the allure of cheap music expensively dressed; a thriller. But its thrills are expensive, not cheap. The march has its problems: the first two Pieces are high among the wonders of the epoch.

No. 1: *Praeludium*, is no mere introduction: deep unpitched percussion in overlapping rhythms, impalpably indistinct, is joined by timpani, their pitches gradually clarified and enhanced in the orchestra as the dulled reverberance comes softly together and disappears; a plangent high bassoon tops the static yet crepitating texture now ensuing, capped by a horn, answered by a trumpet – expectant growing and slowing – pause for intake of breath, exhaled on an incredible sonority: over dark neutrality, stratospherically high trombone, soft and noble, intoning four times its *long/short* single note, then just a *long*, before the crepuscular flurry animates and nuclei of themes are discerned, briefly, almost at once cut off by low growling menaces from angry deep brass, strings, harps. Now the movement's main process/progress can commence – a long lyric line, ardent and careening, rich in orchestral doubling and expressive counter-subjects: its unfolding unfurling, ever fuller, peaks in a characteristically drastic climax, collapsing into a ghost funeral march closely influenced by its prototype – the first movement of Mahler's 9th Symphony, still in 1913 a recent revelation of engulfing power. The earlier single-note tattoo for trombone returns, now safely an octave lower on flutes and bassoons: as it fades, violins and

celesta shimmer in a delicious slow, shivering cascade, as yet unexplained and seemingly incongruous: back on course, the expressive
cantilena curves cooling, declining, punctuated by gaps, guttering
down and out, to barely pitched then without pitch except barely
discernible timpani, as the percussion that began the Piece ends it.

Just after the unobtrusive start of no. 2, the mysterious
shivery descent on violins and celesta returns exactly, initiating
Reigen/'Round-dance', a title inevitably bringing up a parallel with
Schnitzler's thus-named drama of 1900 wherein Vienna's conventionalized easy-going sexuality was pinioned for once and for
all. Berg's round-dance is sensual enough – after these introductory frissons are done, a slow voluptuous waltz-tempo sets up: the
real thing, not an idealization as in the last of Schoenberg's *Five
Pieces*. Berg acknowledges the 'potency of cheap music', succumbing to it *con amore*, relishing it with a satiny sheen of lusciousness
surpassing *Rosenkavalier* – another near contemporary (1911) that
everyone would have heard, set in rococo Vienna but evoking, via
Johann Strauss, the praline-coated palaces to be seen all around,
with their boudoirs and secret stairways known only to the chosen
few. The refined opulence of Berg's waltz is *knowing*: the success
of its seductive charm consists precisely in the way it plays upon
its hearers' inner fantasies. Yet there is a simultaneous subversive
aspect – mocking, parodistic, destructive – not so far distant from
the clearly aggressive love/hate of Ravel's Vienna-evocation in *La
Valse* (another contemporary), conventionally seen as prophetic
of the civilization's auto-destruction whose dream of privilege,
elegance, covert sexuality, was embodied in the triple-time dance
whose origins had been so modest, domestic, proletarian, bourgeois, decorous.

This is corn and kitsch of high artistic calibre; comparable in
equivocacy to Strauss, Mahler, Puccini, Rachmaninov's *Symphonic
Dances*, Messiaen's *Turangalîla*: the facture and imagination are such
that cavils and scruples of taste have to be waived. It's the ensuing
March that raises the problems. Perhaps its extravagance can best be
explained – excused – by seeing it as potential theatre-music, a study

for the military strain in *Wozzeck*, already in Berg's mind (though this strain is less extreme in the opera than in the concert-hall).

All the way from soft fragmentary scuffles already spoiling for a fight, via climax upon climax, collapse upon collapse, to the all-hell-of-an-ending: sudden furious upsurge on deep brass, joined by trumpets then all six horns then xylophone; and, in the very final bar, the hair-splitting, ear-splitting single last note at the very last possible split second before the next, non-existent, bar, joined deep beneath by bass of the pitched orchestra at the tritone, plus the bass-drum and the Hammer of Fate borrowed from the finale of Mahler's 6th, already present at each previous climax, now ensuring a well-aimed execution.

Facile – and anyway a commonplace – to link such violence with the world-events overtaking its composition, and the ensuing carnage. But connection cannot be avoided: something in the air even before it happened, universally sensed, and breathed in even by this gentlest, subtlest, most suave, courteous, civilized man, just as the refined, sensitive aesthete Ravel was to intuit and vibrate to in his *valse*, so congruent with Berg's *valse-Reigen*.

Both composers' other early works could be thus lovingly detailed, nuance upon nuance. Berg's *Altenberglieder* (1912) sets five texts originally sent on postcards from the way-out Viennese poet Peter Altenberg: perfection of refinement, ravishingly transporting, sensuously sensitized to capture impalpable inner worlds wherein senses and feelings mingle and fuse in a dapple of sonorous colour. Not without sinew either – the long singing line in the first, the passacaglia of the last. Webern's *Five Pieces for Small Orchestra*, op. 10 (1911–13) achieve a quintessence as individual and flawless. The vast forces of his *Six Pieces* are reduced to four solo woodwinds, three brass, four solo strings, celesta, harmonium, mandolin, guitar, harp, plus percussion – extensive but sparingly used. Every gesture, every breath, can be easily pinpointed – each individual sound is crystal-clear, isolated in silence, quivering with living anticipation, suggestive and inexplicable as Klee at his most poetic: not so much 'a novel in a sigh' as an Alp in an egg-cup.

Complementary ways with serialism

Berg in his *Altenberglieder*, Webern in these *Five Pieces for Small Orchestra*, achieve individuality and perfection within the aura of their master un-oppressed by his heavy shadow. Their devotion to him 'words cannot utter'; or rather, words do utter it, in letters and other documents, and reported speech, whose tone is scarce credible – also discreditable – Schoenberg's dominating stance and expectation of total fidelity, together with performances of endless services, some by no means light; the pupils' grovelling obsequi-ousness, submission, worship, masochistic bending of the knee to kiss the rod and embrace the yoke. What will they do when the Leader announces his personal Reich – the system that guarantees 'the supremacy of German music for a century to come'?

So well-defined already before the war in their complementary natures, it is clear that their adaptation to the 12-note technique will be idiosyncratic, characteristic, tending further to emphasize diffe-rence. Neither could have either composed, or wished to compose, a wind quintet, an orchestral variations, a *Moses and Aaron* à la Schoen-berg: though they are all-obedient, his matter and his manner are equally alien. Rather, each in his own personal take on the method proves its viability and flexibility beyond what was possible, some-times beyond what was acceptable, to its inventor.

Webern's paths can be followed in his successive songs with instruments, from op. 12 to op. 19 (op. 12 has just piano accompani-ment; op. 19 has a small chorus rather than solo voice) from *c*.1915 to *c*.1925. Twenty-eight in all, ranging from freely atonal to trying out the new method to using it strictly, much as in the ten move-ments from the same years of Schoenberg's two piano collections, opp. 23 and 25. Webern's poets remain faithful to the epoch and its culture – Stefan George, Rilke, versions from the Chinese as first used by Mahler and Strindberg, Karl Kraus, a smattering of Goethe. No Maeterlinck or Dehmel, no Altenberg, nothing home-made: and, unique to him, folk-texts, religious texts in Latin as well as German; and, closest in sensibility and in inflexion, Georg Trakl, whose tense, vulnerable personality, colour-infused imagery, concentration, combination of directness and obliquity, are very close to Webern's. Not, however, his cocaine-addiction: Webern can manage what the drug does simply by contemplating a crystal or a flower.

These song-sets make a very special chapter of music: a *ne plus ultra* of rarification, very difficult to perform, to hear, to understand; still near-impenetrable after a hundred years. Lyricism is their heart: their body is spun steel, totally dissonant, exposed without ameliorating in-fill or disguise: nothing palliating, vague, approximate: naked expression. The listener senses that these painful notes, painful sometimes unto excruciation, are exact and right, without knowing why. Every pitch carries conviction of burning fanatical sincerity. There are helpful aids – the increasing use of canon – something to follow; and a single passacaglia – something to stand firm upon: moments of sensory warmth, as in the op. 13 set, closest in its instrumental ensemble to the sound-world of the op. 10 orchestral pieces; or decorative sensitivity, usually in the relatively hedonistic Chinese settings. Maximum contrast, the lacerating cruelty of the Catholic songs, Latin or German, with their bleeding wounds and load of guilt even beyond their prototype, the Sacred Songs from Wolf's Spanish book. The all-Trakl set, *Six Songs* op. 14, makes the best way in: poet and composer at one in new perceptions caught, held, embodied, by new linguistic means. No question of this music's calibre, consistency, integrity, at one with its fascinating technical facture, already developed to a high finish, and now in tandem with their master's masterful 'discovery'. There is no dividing-line; the difference is impossible to hear. By 1926 Webern is ready to take the 12-note method on to a larger canvas (*relatively* larger: this is Webern, not Schoenberg or Berg) in the String Trio op. 20 (1926–7), the first work to break the run of vocal settings over the preceding decade.

Berg's Way is the opposite: not esoteric or introverted (though hardly extrovert: this is Berg, not Strauss or Hindemith) so much as in large structures, implicitly programmatic and sometimes autobiographical, ultra-emotional, in an idiom that refuses to eschew the expressive language of his origins however much the actual facture employs the new technique. His path is marked by just two works of extensive size and enormous complexity, bursting also with subjective content: the *Chamber Concerto* for piano, violin and thirteen wind instruments (1923–5) and the *Lyric Suite* (1925–6) for string quartet. Before them comes the masterpiece that, while taking the expressionist aesthetic to its maximum, bursts its limits, taking the idiom out from its claustrophobic provinciality onto a European then a world stage.

Wozzeck (begun 1917 completed 1922) was from its première (1925) an unexpected success, placing it outside Schoenberg's self-determined stance, and exciting his scorn. Berg's opera sets Georg Büchner's extraordinary play, closely based upon actual events, left chaotic at his death in 1837, with minimal re-arrangement and full retention of its harsh diction. The result is an apparently incongruous mix of advanced sophisticated musical language and possibly wilfully complex schematic construction, with bold presentation of bloody events and frightening exposure of psychosis: yet the incongruities fuse at white heat; heart and head, body and spirit: nothing in the operatic repertoire can compare, though there have been plentiful attempts to emulate. The following account attempts to detach and reattach formalism and content-matter.

Act I: *'Five Character-Pieces'*: scene i) the wretched soldier Wozzeck is giving his Captain his daily shave; we learn something of his circumstances – lives with his mistress Marie and their child. Captain a neurotic teasing bully, given to high-toned moralizing and more than a touch of religious mania, with the Bible to back him up. A baroque *'Suite'*, prelude and its retrograde repeat enclosing four dance-forms separated by two cadenzas. Lurid-coloured Interlude to ii) – open fields; Wozzeck and his mate Andres cutting sticks; Wozzeck in communion with sinister vibrations from nature – apocalyptic visions and hallucinations, a hollow gulf beneath them, a bodiless head rolling along the ground, a Masonic plot, the fiery setting sun threatening judgement: Andres' hunting-song, sane and straight, intercut with Wozzeck's unhinged imaginings: *'Rhapsody on a chord-sequence'* (wonderful chords): distant drumming from the barracks as dark comes on and the world goes dead. Military strains infiltrate the orchestral change of scene and predominate in iii) *'March and Lullaby'*: Marie in her room playing with her little boy, watching the soldiers pass, admiring them, particularly the splendid Drum-Major, to the scorn of her neighbour Margret. Trio of *March* – what fine lads! Irked beyond endurance by Margret's insinuations Marie slams the window shut – the outdoor wind-band racket immediately cut off, replaced by warm-hearted strings: the poor little mite – she lulls him to sleep and falls a-dreaming herself, reverie infiltrated by soldiery: Wozzeck looks in, still disturbed by his vision of total destruction, barely glancing at the child, hurrying off to report for duty, leaving Marie alone and scared. Scene iv) *'Passacaglia on a 12-note theme'* (with twenty-one variations: the reverse digits a numerological pun like Bach's 14/41): Wozzeck and the crazed sadistic Doctor; needing the money he submits as guinea-pig to horrible experiments. Unlike Marie, the Doctor is delighted with the indications of insanity shown by Wozzeck's hallucinations – so vivid do they still remain that we come to believe them too and to share, even identify with, his turbulent inner life – all done by music of incomparably suggestive *tinta*: the passacaglia ends on the Doctor's ecstatic expectations – an hallucination of his own – of immortal fame: deflated by prosaic 'now Wozzeck, show me your tongue again'. Scene v) gives Marie's inevitable fall: a *'Rondo'*; march-music again, creeping though the Interlude/scene-change; in the street outside her dwelling Marie admires the virile attributes of the Drum-Major, for all his fatuous vanity an irresistible force. He's got an eye for her attractions too: he embraces, she fights him off, only inciting him further: her yet-more-determined resistance stiffens his determination; she yields – 'it's all the same' – and takes him indoors. Act I ends on a slow, soft, full-orchestra oscillation with the *Tristan*-chord (desire) included, gradual accelerando and crescendo to a tremendous trill: echoed gapped, very soft, just on flutes and celesta as Act II begins.

(When *Wozzeck* is played without intervals – it's not a long work, lasting less than many single acts in Wagner – the impact of hearing it unbroken in the opera-house – no awkward encounters, no chit-chat, no G&T – is shattering, and Berg's continuity across the acts' ends and beginnings really tells.)

Act II's construction is the least perceptible of the work's

architectural games: a '*Symphony in Five Movements*'. These schemes
are indispensable to the composer: to the listener/viewer they are
perceived only subliminally if at all; the music's surface suffices.
Scene i) is the Symphony's *Sonata*: next morning; Marie dreaming
over the ear-rings her lover gave her – the echo from *ff* to *pp* of
the seduction-music tells all. She tries to quieten the child (who
no doubt witnessed the primal scene) but only scares him with
frightening fairy-tales. Wozzeck appears, at once sees the jewels,
is suspicious, bewails their lot, gives her the money earned from
his two tormentors in Act I, hurries off, leaving her overcome with
shame – 'I could kill myself' – *her* lot too ('I'm a bad lot'). Another
amazing orchestral scene-change – *Salome* concentrated into an
electric thimble – into ii), out in the open, Captain and Doctor
meet in a '*Fantasy and Fugue on three themes*'. The two men plague
each other over their physical symptoms, but join forces when
Wozzeck hurries by, to torment him with hints of his mistress's infidelity, till he bursts out in despair – 'end it all by hanging' – rushes
away, leaving the two to shake their heads in contempt. Now the
Symphony's slow movement, a *largo* using only the instruments
of Schoenberg's *Chamber Symphony*: iii) man and mistress in confrontation, more sideways than head-on: she 'denies all wrong-
doing' – 'better a knife in my body than lay a hand on me – my
father never dared.' To vertiginous swoops and swirls he takes in
the fatal hint – a knife. The ensuing interlude sets up a '*Ländler*',
potent cheap music, transporting to scene iv), a tavern with its on-
stage dance-band: soldiers, maids, prentices outside in the garden;
the prentices, slightly pissed, argue callow metaphysics; Marie and
the Drum-Major dance together amid the throng, Andres joins
with his guitar. They exchange at cross-purposes, the two prentices
resume their drunken discussion, the hunting chorus again: then
an idiot appears, slyly creeping up to Wozzeck, at the side of all
the activity, sniffing out *blood blood blood* – gruesome combination
of the little *Ländler*-band (complete with harmonica) re-tuning
then resuming, and frightful expressionist snarls on muted brass as
Wozzeck, two crucial words lodged in his tormented brain, watches
the sensual rout with abhorrence. The ensuing orchestral

Interlude/change-of-scene blows up the waltz into a thing of apoca-lyptic horror, suddenly curtailed by soft male chorus, wordless – the snoring soldiers in the barracks, Wozzeck among them, moaning in his sleep, his sound imitated by a single suffocated stratospheric double-bass note remembered from Salome at the cistern's-edge panting for her trophy. Scene v), is a *'rondo marziale'* (finale of 'Symphony'): Wozzeck's moaning turns to words as he awakes in anguish, addressing Andres, haunted by the dance rhythms and sights, a knife flickering before his eyes – 'lead us not into tempta-tion'. Enter Drum-Major, drunk and vaunting – 'I'm a *man*; I've got a *woman*: a woman to breed little drum-majors.' On he brags, detailing her charms – who is it? ask your friend Wozzeck! – as he offers a swig from his brandy-bottle. Goaded beyond bearing, Wozzeck fights and is inevitably beaten. Victor lurches out, victim on the floor, as the soldiers fall back to sleep.

The overlap into Act III is inaudible – measured silences – which can be as telling as a musical overlap. The structural background here is *'Six Inventions'*. For i), an 'invention on a theme' with seven variations: Marie and the boy; overcome with guilt and misery, she reads from her Bible – the Woman taken in Adultery, and Jesus' com-passionate refusal to pass judgement. Sung cries of 'Lord God' inter-rupt the speech-song of the sacred text. The boy seems to reproach her; she pushes him away then pulls him to her, telling of the little boy lost, hungry and weeping, all alone in the world. No Franz? – she turns again to the Bible for the story of Mary Magdalene – 'Saviour, you forgave her; forgive me.' Orchestra swells in next interlude to an emotional climax the scene had largely bound in. Curtain up again on a forest-path by a pool at dusk. ii) 'invention on a note' (B♮): Marie and Wozzeck walk together, they sit, he seeks to reminisce – how long since we've been together, how long is still to come? She makes to get up, he pulls her down and kisses her – 'I'd give all Heaven, all Salvation, to kiss you.' She shivers; the night dew falls: 'You will freeze no more'; 'What do you say?' 'Nowt.' The moon rises red, he draws the knife and plunges it into her throat, able to scream its last cry for help as climax of the construction, a high B♮: the note which, persisting throughout the scene, has steadily pulsated deep below, on one drum then two, from the moment when the knife was drawn.

The change-of-scene now is sensational: the same note, now in middle tessitura, swells from a single horn *pppp* to piecemeal incorporation of the entire orchestra at the same pitch-level, reaching over five bars with no other content (the staggered entries are imperceptible) *fff*; curt grinding dissonance, a fateful rhythm on bass drum solo, the basis of next scene – iii), 'invention on a rhythm'. Before it, the B♮ again, now three octaves deep, tutti from the start, this time including timpani and unpitched percussion rolling in crescendo from *ppp* to *fff*, cut off by the jangle of an on-stage out-of-tune piano, playing a frenetic polka clearly built on the rhythm thwacked out just before by the bass drum. A tavern; Wozzeck splurging around to deaden his deed, sloshing back the wine, drowning out the pianist; then as the polka resumes seizing Margret to dance for a moment, instantly desiring to pull her onto his lap – 'you're so hot!' She launches into a sour folksong accompanied by the sour piano; then perceives the blood on his hand. The simple rhythm accumulates inventively across itself as the texture thickens; suspicions mount, Wozzeck's excuses/explanations fail, his self-contradictions accuse him: all the voices take up the cry – human blood! He rushes out, back to the pool, seeking to find the knife and/or to expunge the stain.

Interlude into iv) 'invention on a six-note chord': the same forest path by the pool, under a bloody moon. He searches desperately; cries 'Murder!' stumbles on Marie's corpse – 'why this crimson necklace? like your golden ear-rings, well-earned?'; finds the knife, throws it deeper into the water, hears it sink – the six-note chord fascinatingly interlocked with itself. 'The moon rises bloody red – will it blab my business to the whole world? Too near the edge – they'll find it when swimming or gathering mussels – deeper [he wades in] – deeper – I am bloody, I must wash – no, no, the water is blood – I wash myself in blood' [he sinks from sight and drowns]. As he disappears to sounds of the six-note chord rushing in parallel, like Herod's wind in *Salome* on acid, the Doctor and the Captain pass by – 'Do you hear? The water calls. It's a long time since anybody was drowned: we'd better go. It groans ... there's someone drowning. It's weird ... red moon, grey mist ... There it is again ... softer ... disappeared. Come away quick!' The parallel chords slow up, stagger, deplete, ending up like the croaking of frogs. And now an 'invention on a key', prosaic description for the Interlude that follows, using material from a symphony Berg worked on and left incomplete before the war, now intercalated with motifs from all over the opera. An opinion-divider: for Stravinsky this emotional outpouring is too overt, too breast-beating, underlining and exaggerating, in the end diminishing the pity and terror elsewhere under such restraint that yet speak for themselves. For most, to give what's been curbed, even denied, hitherto its full utterance at last achieves a sublime cath-arsis. Naturally both views are true: and what cannot be missed is Berg's command of post-Mahlerian rhetoric and pathos: the first movement of Mahler's 9th Symphony the immediate model, now strained to maximal limits in this invention on the same key, good old tragic Viennese D-minor. It heaves to its heavy, banged-out climax, and subsides at once into the act's sixth invention – 'on a quaver-rhythm', that of the children's singing-game 'ring-a-ring-a-roses – all fall down'. Scene v): Marie and Wozzeck's little boy is playing with the other children from their street. They all screech the news and scamper off to take a look – 'Hey you, your mother's dead.' Younger than them, he doesn't understand, carries on riding his toy horse, limping tentatively after them as they disappear: gently dissonant ostinato on the jingly 'quaver-rhythm', locking into rocking ostinati, gradually quenched and smothered in a very wide/high/deep-spaced G-D fifth on muted strings, swelling, peaking *mp* with harp, disappearing as the ostinato rocks on for ever and ever.

Though chock-a-block with schemes, devices, formalities, note-games, *Wozzeck* is not a 12-note work; from now I'm concentrating on those that are. If they are! The *Lyric Suite* is noted, among many other striking features, for alternating sections using the new method and sections freely composed (if anything *bei* Berg can be free). And the *Chamber Concerto* also tries the technique this way and that, always Berg's way not Schoenberg's. Among the many devices used in the opera, 12-note structuring figures, comparable to the proto-serial stretches in *Jakobsleiter*. Berg's two wordless works are, in their way, as difficult to understand and enjoy as Webern's song-sets opp. 12–19. Not through rarification: the *Chamber Concerto*'s layout is clear, its idiom expansive, generous, inviting; its tone fervently emotional; its textures athletically virtuoso and exuberant – often any two of these together, sometimes all three. The difficulties are the complexity, the density of busyness, the overload of information, the jungle of over-growth and undergrowth vegetative/animal/avian, as if a 'Douanier' Rousseau were executed by W. P. Frith.

In nightmares begin responsibilities: the sleep of unreason, be it never so fetishistically organized, brings forth Beauty. Everything inspissated, occluded, over-wrought in the near-masterpiece *Chamber Concerto* is righted in the *Lyric Suite* that immediately followed, though its outward complexity and secret inward workings are more forbidding still – let alone what later discoveries have uncovered by way of a world of private significances: the music speaks for itself, as itself, direct, irrespective of all external referents.

With its close contemporaries, Janáček's two and Bartók's middle three quartets, the *Lyric Suite* stands at a polar opposite from the medium as domestic music-making for cultivated amateurs – engaging, decorous, within well-maintained parameters: the Haydn ideal, first stretched then broken by late Beethoven, exploded beyond recovery in these fiendishly difficult virtuoso works that transcend '*Kammermusik*' altogether. Immediately in Berg's back-ground is his master's *Verklärte Nacht* – a symphonic poem now on four not six strings: the *Suite* is also a sort of reverse fulfilment of his fellow-pupil's string-quartet *Six Bagatelles*: 'a novel in a sigh' turned inside-out: Adorno called it an opera without words; and indeed the listener cannot miss the hyper-charged perfervour, the hysterical drama of contrasts and extremes, passage by passage and on the broader scale; will sense the zigzag speeds and moods of the six movements even before consulting programme-note or score. The scissor-succession opens out in antithetical directions from no. 1, *allegretto giovale* to 3, *allegro misterioso* with a *trio estatico*, to 5, *presto delirando*, thrice recurring, separated by two *tenebroso* episodes wherein time and motion freeze. Thus for the wind-up. The wind-down runs no. 2, *andante amoroso*, with *Ländler* insets and a slower 'secret' central trio; 4, *adagio appassionato*; 6, *largo desolato*. Perception of interconnections across all six movements increases on every hearing: most marked, the complete incorporation into the *adagio* (no. 4) of the *trio ecstatico* (no. 3). The listener would sense obscurely that the return of the *misterioso* after the *estatico* seems to be going in reverse; that the *largo* empties out at its approximate centre to quote the opening of *Tristan* would not be missed. The puzzle here is, what can it *mean*? Another quotation is heard in a lull between the passionate climaxes of the *adagio appassionato*: probably unheard in the welter of the first instance, where it is attributed in the score: clearly out in the open when returning, soft, though not perhaps recognized so widely outside its own culture: '*du bist mein eigen, mein eigen*'/'you are my one and only', taken from the *Lyric Symphony* of Zemlinsky, to whom Berg's *Lyric Suite* is dedicated – its very title another homage – and possibly explicable as such.

So much perhaps/possibly/probably! Perhaps/possibly/probably not! What is going on here in this 'latent opera'? Recent discoveries have revealed its characters, if not a plot: as with most secret programmes there is a lady not his wife in the case. Every parameter of the *Suite*'s exceedingly intricate construction involves her and the composer's initials, their respective significant numbers, references to whatever might have transpired and what certainly was *felt* (if only by him, it seems): plus personal touches – affectionate memories and vignettes – thus the 'secret' trio within the *andante amoroso* refers to the lady's children and their games; more grown-up, the spiralling expanding intervals of the *adagio*'s theme as it develops, to the man's mounting masculinity. All this is explicit in the copy of the published score Berg annotated in full to preserve this 'monument to a great love'. A(lexander) von Z(emlinsky) comprehends A-to-B(loke) and H-to-F(rau) (Alban Berg, Hanna Fuchs-Robbetin): all these initial letters (except Z) are notes in music which form thematic material, serial or free: proportions, durations, even metronome marks are multiples of his twenty-three and her ten: and, most important of all, the closing *largo* is a word-by-word setting – voiceless; but the fit so exact that the movement can be convincingly performed with a soprano, like the vocal portions of Schoenberg's 2nd Quartet – of Baudelaire's *De Profundis Clamavi*, rendered into German by Stefan George. *Desolato* indeed: the poem's blank leaden despair is unmatched in any language: 'From the black pit wherein I am sunk I implore your pity: this desolate world, half the year under a sun without heat, the other swathed in night, this sterile land between cruel icy light and dark like primal chaos ... I envy the beasts, lost in senseless sleep, so slow time's spindle winds down and down ...' The citation from *Tristan* comes where the text expands on the land's sterility – no stream, no tree, no field, no flock: characteristically allusive and displacive, Berg is evoking the *oed' und leer* desolation at the start of *Tristan* Act III in his quotation of the opera's very opening, a musical icon known to all.

So what?! What's this to us, who aren't Alban Berg or Hanna Fuchs-Robbetin? The *Lyric Suite* stands firm and disinterested in autonomous integrity, a masterpiece fusing cerebration and emotional utterance all the way from A to Z at the highest level. Knowledge of what prompted it can't add to it; its nature at all points, from *giovale* to *desolato*, can't be mistaken; the needs, desires, fulfilments, disappointments, despairs that go into it and stream out from it are commonplaces of humanity – matters of life and death intermingled with the prosaic and the banal. Fascinating, absorbing, touching, to learn of the intimate small-print codicils born of the composer's extra-marital longings built into the innermost facture of his notes: for just evaluation of his *Lyric Suite* this knowledge takes us up the way from A to B, and back from H to F. Z for Zemlinksy is a mere token.

Comparable games at incomparably greater length and complexity and voltage dominate *Lulu*, the second opera, its third act not quite completed at Berg's death in 1935. *Earth Spirit* and *Pandora's Box*, two plays from the pre-war epoch by Frank Wedekind are welded into continuity with skill and flair, tracing the title-heroine's progress from unknown gutters, via husbands and lovers from every stratum of society, ending in the jungle of Jack London's London and her death at the hands of Jack the Ripper. Berg, with his mania for pattern and symmetry, has shaped this forward-moving trajectory into a vast palindrome, a pyramid, up to the apex, down in parallel descent to the rock-bottom; at the dead-centre the marvellous orchestral interlude is an *actual* palindrome in which going-into-reverse is clearly audible, though the intended patterning of the complicated scenario in a silent movie is rarely even attempted in production.

All this became clearer when the withheld Act III was released after the composer's widow's death in 1976. The skilful realization by Friedrich Cerha was first produced in Paris in 1979: since then *Lulu* is always given in full: rightly of course, but big problems remain. It is a very long piece, consistently set at extremes of complication and strain: to tell the story in full would involve extensive exploration of intermeshing character/action/words/music beyond anything else by any other composer. It is the most consciously planned and elaborated opera ever: All or Nothing: a Monument of Modernism comparable to *Finnegans Wake*, requiring their *all* from Joyce's 'ideal insomniac' readers. Overdetermined intentions are realized in a proliferation of detail overlying extreme cerebral schematization. Yet the upshot is charged with unforeseen visceral directness: it's the boldest opera ever written with regard to daring subject-matter, horrible people, frightful events. The intellectual and emotional demands on its audiences are unparalleled. Yet it is an object of unending fascination, even when mixed with repulsion, and the sheer numbness born of exhaustion at the doubled overload. The horrors and the beauties, the games and the unanswerable ambiguities, are bound cause/effect effect/cause in inseparable interfusion.

There are only two further concert-works. The song-cycle with orchestra *Der Wein* (more Baudelaire à la Stefan George) is a gorgeous bibulous dry-run for *Lulu*. The Violin Concerto interrupted the opera, whose third act was left unpolished and largely un-scored at Berg's death. It takes the general ambience/method/world of the *Lyric Suite* to new levels of ambiguity – a string quartet in the classical line; a Romantic symphonic poem, with protagonist and narrative, crisis and pacification; these with ostensible 'official' identification and occasion; within/behind, an inner testament of private meanings unknown till recent years. More: in its integrated synthesis of the constructivistic with the expressive, of the new serial techniques (plus plentiful games of its own) with the old forms and procedures – of tonality with atonality – it is a key icon of musical modernism's problems and their solutions: the Art of the Future with its heart in the Past.

The Concerto's outer shell is the 'Requiem for an Angel', Manon, daughter of Alma Mahler by Walter Gropius, dying of polio aged eighteen: the first half depicts the lovely young girl, the second her struggle with the disease, its victory, her death, and a grieving elegy culminating in acquiescence and apotheosis. Inside this shell, another: the 'story of a great love' continued from the *Lyric Suite*: AB and HF, though not so omnipresent as before, still participate significantly, amid a barrage of their personal numerology reinforced by the half-crazed numerological theories of Wilhelm Fliess, who persuaded – nay fooled – even Freud for a while. Inside this second shell, a third. Towards the end of Part I, and again as a distant echo at the work's very end, comes a Carinthian folksong (on instruments, no actual singing): the 'official' interpretation saw this as evoking Manon's girlish innocence. Its aura for the composer is quite other, and outside the AB/HF nexus too: the melody belongs to his liberteenage – at seventeen his relationship with a maid at the parental summer house in Carinthia resulted in an illegitimate daughter – Albertine (of course). With its words the song refers obliquely to the situation: Maria, the maid's actual name, doubles with Manon; in the folksong the girl's name is Mizzi, a familiar affectionate for Marie, mistress of Wozzeck and mother of his illegitimate child in Berg's first opera. These three layers of association make the work a palimpsest of inter-tingling intimacy for its composer – deeply touching and human, absolutely germane and yet not indispensable to the listener for total involvement and comprehension. Another ingredient altogether can be easily dispatched: the recent discovery that the work's four-in-one structure – two Parts, each of two sections – hinges upon the 'four F's' – *Frisch*; *Fromm*; *Fröhlich*; *Frei* – which, inter-tangled, make a swastika; their hearty nationalistic connotations were usurped by the Nazi Party. Berg typically reverses the order to cancel them out, a gesture as invisible as inaudible. Yet a further fold, however, is ubiquitous and profound, powerfully repressed and all the more powerful for it: Berg's own death, precognized and almost pre-disposed as he worked desperately against the clock and his terminal illness to compose, as well as the 'angel''s and his 'great love''s, his own Requiem.

These programmes, explicit or secret, underlie the Concerto's unmistakable play of moods – dreamy nostalgia, rustic cheer, ferocious battle with disease and death, lamentation, comfort, apotheosis, fade into distant memory. The idiom is pellucid however rich, its integration of tonal and atonal assured for the ear by the 12-note row's structure upon the solo violin's open strings, fifths filled in with thirds major or minor, the final four notes each a whole-tone apart. Berg here succeeds where his master fails, by fusing inherited techniques, pregnant with use and association, with the new-fangled Method. Culmination, the second part of Part II after the killer virus has seized its prey, a statement of, variations upon, Bach's funeral chorale *Es ist genug* from Cantata 60, *O Ewigkeit, du Donnerwort*. Berg needs the chorale for its words as well as its notes – 'It is enough! Lord, when it please thee, release me: goodnight, world; to my heavenly home I depart in peace; my great sorrow remains behind; it is enough.' This key-phrase famously opens the chorale on four notes a whole-tone apart; returning at the end the words fall into reposeful diatonic cadence: both shapes are used by Berg with compositional virtuosity and deep expressive meaning. After a simple statement of the chorale – its strange opening already imminent in the tail-end of the note-row – variations gradually and continuously expand, increasing in intensity technical and emotional, till the *Höhepunkt* (Climax – marked thus in the score just in case it's missed) – dead-centre rhetorical hit of the utmost pathos. It abates, orchestral violins drop away desk by desk leaving the soloist alone, drifting into a new landscape with echoes of the Catholic Carinthian folksong interlinked with the Protestant chorale, its two four-note shapes for *es - ist - ge - nug* ubiquitous. A flicker of open strings, a wide-voiced added sixth, blandest of consonances, centred on Bb, for Berg and Bach – beautifully manipulated Beatitude, utterly theatrical, courting and avoiding tackiness; the work as a whole opening up new possibilities for Western Music's unique and greatest resource, harmony.

Webern's course after his total commitment to the 12-note method consists of just twelve works, from *c.*1926 to his accidental death in 1945 out on his balcony for an evening smoke at a time when curfew forbade, shot by an American GI. Four are chamber-works, mostly showing the composer at his most unalluring and impenetrable. Not that he presents a jungle of complexity: the opposite – radical elimination of every parameter that isn't structure, building-block, demonstration. The String Trio op. 20 (1926–7) is a big piece by his standards: the dragon at the gate, not without sparkle, as comparison with the String Quartet op. 28 (1936–8) shows. This truly *is* charmless, arid, a demonstration-piece, all scaffolding, in pitches as in its rhythmic structure – all minims and crotchets – rigor mortis. Whereas the Quartet for Saxophone, Clarinet, Violin and Piano op. 22 (1928–30) has real character as well as a sound of its own and a touch of lilt in its rhythms. The *Variations for Piano* op. 27 (1935–6) used to be a favourite showpiece for Webern's technique and aesthetic: insensitively played, wooden notes; sensitively played, a real sense of harmony, even a fluidity, within the rhythmic/durational grids. That Webern remains secretly programmatic even in such music can be ascertained by speculative likelihood: here are his earlier jottings for what eventually becomes the finale of the Saxophone Quartet.

> *Main themes* – I coolness of early spring (Anninger, first flora, primroses, anemones, pasque-flowers). *Secondary* i) cosy warm sphere of highest meadows. II Dachstein, snow and ice, crystal-clear air: ii) Solanella, blossoms of the highest region. III the children in ice and snow: i) repetition of 1st secondary theme (sphere of the alpine roses); ii) repetition of 2nd secondary theme, light, sky: IV *Coda* – outlook into the highest region.

However detached his music might appear, his response to the natural world, informed by his fervent Catholic piety, always lies within – another salient connection with/difference from the equally content-charged Berg. Altogether separate from his fellow-composer and their master, Webern's Nazi-sympathies, which some hostile listeners even manage to locate also in the control-freak discipline of his music. All that can be said in amelioration is that he was hardly alone in his naïve ignorance of the Party's true nature, seeing it rather as a realization of visionary ideals that can *truly* be interconnected with his work – health, sanity, purity, regeneration.

Three orchestral works: Symphony op. 21 (1927–8); *Concerto for Nine Instruments* op. 24 (1931–4); *Variations* op. 30 (1940). 'Orchestral' is relative; never again *bei* Webern the gigantic forces required by the *Six Pieces* of 1909 (their practical reduction – slight – dates from 1928): op. 21 has clarinet and bass clarinet, two horns, harp and strings; op. 24 three solo woodwinds, three solo brass, one violin and one cello – the 'soloist' in this 'concerto' is the piano; op. 30 has four woodwinds, four brass, timpani, celesta and harp, strings. This *Concerto* used to be the ultimate demonstration-piece when analysing the composer's radical and stringent newness. *Everything* 'comes in threes' – the three-note nucleus, three-part chords all the way, unmissable, rammed home in total schematization throughout the fiercely skeletal first movement. The second, slow and unremittingly even in rhythm, reduces the tally to two separated pitches, passed parsimoniously between the seven line-instruments, the keyboard's dyads, and plentiful silences, filling the quota. The finale returns to threes-for-all: two rhythms, one even and emphatic, one gapped and perky, bounce off each other till regularity sets in. Severe jocularity – Mondrian made audible: and the mixture of silences and single-notes in the middle movement can sometime be strangely compelling – one *listens*.

And the Symphony is a wholesale pleasure; one of its composer's best works. Here process and structure, the habitual *raison d'être*, are deployed to appeal to the ear, even the fantasy, as well as the mind. Opening movement a complex double-canon whose intricate workings are laid out across the entire ensemble in *Klang-farben* changes of timbre as exquisitely gauged and balanced as the *Concerto* is raucous and strident. The theme, with seven variations, that follows permits itself something of the continuity of pre-war works – it even employs ostinati: this going athwart the strict palindromic facture of all nine sections – the eleven-bar theme, each eleven-bar variation, and the eleven-bar coda where the elimination of material and texture, the measured silences one can almost hear, achieve eloquence via its denial. The later *Orchestral Variations* themselves come somewhat in between: larger scale, material more complex (or rather less simplified), totally clear and audible without the poetry, even allure, of the Symphony, tending towards the *Concerto*'s look-at-me QED.

Three cantatas for soloists, chorus, orchestra: *Das Augenlicht/Light of the Eye* op. 26 (1935); 1st Cantata op. 29 (1938–9); 2nd Cantata op. 31 (1941–3). Open textures full of air and space, without any of the claustrophobia often oppressive in Webern's purely instrumental music: spare and shining, sometimes jagged and strident (always harsh muted brass, usually *ff*), sometimes on the verge of inaudibility (muted solo strings; harp, celesta, mandolin). A sense of durations, timbres, registers, even silences, being serialized as well as just pitches. A problem with the poet of all three works – Hildegard Jone, a personal friend: she is arch/pious/fey: yet also just what Webern needs – simple vocabulary, concrete metaphors (but not metaphysical), pantheist/evolutionary/organic, yet strong in the Faith, with Catholicism behind and sometimes to the fore. The themes: growth from a cell to full fruition; the inner life; light; love – Charis and charity; Jesus; eternity in a wild flower; bees and birds and buds: all these congruent equivalents for the composer's own compositional concerns as well as expressing his mere pieties and his truly sacred places. There is no need to cringe (though one sometimes does) at this Patience Strong dumb-down of Goethe 'without his folly *re* the Cross'.

Another possible problem, in these works' passages of close harmony: *a cappella* rhythmic unison four-part writing, where the chords are murky and oddly tacky, in marked contradistinction to some very fine harmony all around, and in the late *Variations* too (they belonging with the cantatas as a sadly 'final period'), and to the general fluidity and sparse-inhabited emptiness. *Das Augenlicht* doesn't quite achieve this: not yet the airy suppleness (the *rigid* String Quartet is still to come). The 1st Cantata is very good, the 2nd terrific: its finale, a bouncing/bounding/sprung-rhythm singing Renaissance motet, one of Webern's finest things. In his last months, an intimation of a 3rd, projected before the bitter meaninglessness of his death: it's all Life – Hildegard Jone again: 'Sunlight speak – Up goes the curtain of Night! Through Light the splendour become visible; visible the pillars of being: See, the colours arise!'

Envoi: exquisite lyric essence, gaunt and steely strong yet also fragile as a harebell or a snowflake: extreme – rare beyond rarification – Schoenberg himself asked if 'he went too far?' – a *précieux* 'diamond' (Stravinsky's term) of mannerism, without compare. Utterly impossible as the basis for a new language of music, though this is how Weben was taken in the 1950s. Rather, a 'purifier of the language of the tribe': a perpetual example: not to be imitated: inimitable – but they all did.

Other interwar Germans: Hindemith and Weill

Once widely seen as a major Modern alongside Bartók, Stravinsky, the 'Second Viennese School' – and as a bastion of health and sanity for those of more conservative views of the time – Paul Hindemith has long been in recession. His journey, beneath its apparent sobriety, is puzzling. Born near Frankfurt 1895, early gifted as violinist and in composition – the music of his early youth abounds with energy and invention that sweeps all before it while not sticking in the memory: late Romantic – Brahms/Reger, the non-programmatic side – the other tending towards expressionism in subject-matter, not in idiom. Wartime pieces include the *Lustige Sinfonietta* of 1916, which incorporates mordant poems by Morgenstern – a cheeky reaction to the surrounding horrors, including the recent death of his father in the conflict; so fluent and young-masterly is the current old-master language, sent up rotten, that one feels this twenty-one-year-old can and will do *anything*. Amid copious instrumental works of these years three short theatre pieces stand out: *Das Nusch-Nuschi* (1920) is the least – a puppet-mime parodying the dark doings done direct in *Mörder, Hoffnung der Frauen/Murderer, Hope of Women* the year before, and *Sancta Susanna* the year after. In the first, to a text by painter/poet/lover of Alma Mahler, Oskar Kokoschka, a woman has maimed a man who has abused her; but she still lusts after him, gratifies it, him too; virility restored, he abandons her to die alone. In the second a young nun, inflamed by hints and sights of sexual activity, strips and embraces the naked figure of the crucified Christ in the chapel of her nunnery. Music to match; and in the two operas quite without parody – head-on post-*Elektra* expressionism.

These powerful early curiosities only mentioned because so wholly other from what Hindemith so rapidly brings about, and still stands for as its chief manifestation – the 'Back to Bach' German version of neo-classicism, functional, purposeful, energetic and busy; workmanship to the fore, factured by a worker; absolutely inhuman – no subjectivity; real, objective – an *object*, of use like a lamp, a chair, a teapot: *Sachlichkeit*/objectivity, *Gebrauchsmusik*/music-for-use. The reaction against violent/morbid/subjective content is total: *Sancta Susanna* in 1921, then the series of chamber concertos – Hindemith's 'Brandenburgs' – inaugurating the 180-degree swing commences in 1922; he's twenty-seven, not too late to seek another world.

An outstanding player, viola replacing violin, as soloist and in a famous string quartet; active as teacher, in great demand as composer; copious output, providing, it seems, a sonata and a concerto for every individual instrument, amid substantial orchestral works. Herein lies the problem: mass-production of a standardized product of guaranteed solidity, dependable, infallible, impersonal and boring: for all the energy and expertise yielding little joy, let alone rapture – a work-out at the gym. So it goes for the rest of his life, with a first flush of real distinction *c*.1922 to the mid-1930s before routine sets firmly in.

Another puzzle: it's obvious that Hindemith's new aims and the bluff idiom that bears them will be opposed to the continuing developments alongside in Schoenberg and his greatest pupils.

Hindemith preached impersonality/restraint/objectivity, a musical language to match, firmly grounded in classical practice and built upon tonality/diatonicism/modality, the fundamental acoustic facts of life. It's inevitable that he should deplore atonality even when disciplined and codified into the 12-note method, just as he rejected the subjective expressionism surviving and reviving in the Schoenberg circle's aesthetic. It's 'ironic' that the dead sound of most Hindemith after the mid-1930s, for all the proclamations of acoustic cleanliness, is so comparable to the dead sound of the total-chromatic saturating such contemporary works of Schoenberg as the Violin Concerto and the 3rd and 4th String Quartets. Their ends are the same; their means antithetical; their results equally uncaptivating. Both (sides of the same coin) were great teachers and compelling theorists. Hindemith codified his practice, having practised it first, in a series of rigorous instruction-manuals: theory after the event, and why not? But he then applied this rigour to the handful of inspired works composed earlier, and without question spoilt them – possibly a unique case of 'unjustified criticism' whereby a creator damages his creations in the cause of some supposed 'higher truth'. Though he prohibited performance of the two main victims, the song-cycle *Marienleben* and the opera *Cardillac*, in their original versions, the ban failed: comparison between first and second thoughts is interesting and illuminating.

Though not Jewish, and not practising 'Degeneracy' in artistic style and content after the early shockers (and one saucy piece of stage-nonsense involving a bathroom scene), Hindemith was controversial enough to get into trouble with the Nazis. From this period comes his noblest work, *Mathis der Maler* (1934–5), a full-length opera to his own libretto – very accomplished – based upon the life of Matthius Grünewald and his famous altar-piece; interweaving private and public in a time of social and political upheaval – the Peasants' Revolt, and the role and responsibility of the artist in such troubled times: in the line of *Meistersinger* and *Palestrina* – a worthy successor, though a trifle dull. He emigrated to the USA in 1939, taught at Yale, codified his theory/practice in a would-be update of Bach's *Forty-eight Preludes and Fugues* for piano entitled

Ludus Tonalis (1942) and untiringly provided American orchestras with symphonies and concertos: one of each stands out, the
Concerto for Cello (1940) and the *Symphonia Serena* of 1946. In 1953
he returned to Europe and, for the rest of his life (he died 1963),
he taught, conducted and, of course, composed, much the same as
before, much more of the same. His summa is another full-scale
opera on an elevated moral/ethical theme: *Die Harmonie der Welt*
(1956–7), again to his own text, on the life and work of Johannes
Kepler. It is awfully tedious: high-minded, grey, indigestible. Gratefully back to the vital period and its two principal masterpieces
before they were bowdlerized.

Das Marienleben: Rilke's beautiful poems on the life and death of
the Virgin: fifteen songs in all. The subject-matter released unwonted
tenderness, delicacy, suppleness, in the young Hindemith's typical
idiom, all no-nonsense and cheerful abrasion. There *is* abrasion in
the piano-part here and there; harmony and, particularly, counterpoint can be as harsh as sweet; and the demands on the soprano
are fearsome. Successfully encountered and overcome, the cycle in
its entirety is like a series of medieval emblems, hard as stone, yet
graceful and gracious, vouchsafing the resonance behind/within
of the poet's meditative metaphysical depths. In 1948 the mature
composer took this product of his youth – completed 1923 when
aged twenty-eight – in all its intensity and daring, replacing them,
with a long breast-beating Preface to justify, by middle-aged cir-
cumspection, bland for all its vigour, sententious for all its sagacity:
Polonius instead of the Prince.

Sometimes Hindemith leaves well alone. Two songs are virtually
unaltered, and there's much good material retained in others. Several
are completely re-conceived, notably the centre point 'Wedding
at Cana', where a succinct original becomes a sprawling scherzo/
fugue in which the poem is engulfed rather than set. The 1923 'feck-
lessness' over key centres is replaced by 1948's carefully elaborated
symbolic scheme that fails to register with the hoped-for weight (but
one *does* notice the introduction of quasi-Wagnerian recurrences,
for instance, a bitter dissonance evoking the Crucifixion). Most

disconcerting of all are the two widely separated songs built upon a ground bass (nos. 2 and 13): the bass remains unchanged, above it the polyphonic voices in soprano and piano right hand diverge totally, while making the same general sense. One wonders how the composer could understand the changes as in any way corrective to a fault. And two other songs seem to me so remarkably superior in their first versions as to make one wonder about his artistic sanity. The original 'Birth of Christ' (no. 7) is an exquisite study in parallel and contrary-motion thirds, as if the devotional songs in Wolf's *Spanish Songbook* were transported into the twentieth century; its replacement, a humdrum pastorale that the later Hindemith could and did extrude by the yard. Though 1948 yields a few compensations and very occasional improvements, what Glenn Gould called 'A tale of Two Marienlebens' is a moral model of genius defeated by pedantry worthy of *Die Meistersinger*. Gould also called it 'the greatest song-cycle ever written': characteristically overdoing it (what about Schubert, Schumann, Berlioz, Mahler, for a start?!). But the place of *Marienleben* is high and perennial: performers and listeners able to withstand its formidable price will be richly if stringently rewarded. The original, of course: the revision lies in the scrapyard of history.

The other early masterpiece subjected to treatment more ideological than artistic is the opera *Cardillac* (1926): the two works were to stand together on show-trial; indicted for juvenile error, exemplarily curbed by responsible discipline into maturity. Hoffmann's tale concerning the demoniac master-jeweller so in love with his creations that he can hardly bear to let them go, and can and will commit murder to repossess them; turned into a play mid-nineteenth century; adapted for Hindemith by an old expressionist hand, Ferdinand Lion, who was working simultaneously for another composer on the gruesome old urban-legend of the Golem. The story, the stage-directions, and many locutions in the words themselves, still retain a flavour of the old aesthetic Hindemith was so anxious to replace; yet Lion also strove consciously towards objectivity, stylizing the characters – *the* Daughter, *the* Cavalier, etc. – so that only the principal/title role is named; emphasizing generalities not particulars – *Sachlichkeit* above all, bringing to the fore the linked questions of the artist's debt to society and his duty to his art alone. Such contradictions and tensions between early-Romantic sources and up-to-date treatment might have wrecked the work; resolved, they add to its uncanny power.

The telling and text of Lion's libretto are superb. Hindemith's score lies athwart in fascinating fashion – cool, with inner heat; facture solid and reliable – a bed or wardrobe from Maples or Heals, at the polar opposite from the miracles of costly artifice lying at the heart and vitals of the principal protagonist; uniformly unflagging, proficient, skilful, by a composer and craftsman at the height of his particular powers; always the right thing in the right place, crackling with invention. From this norm, three numbers stand out as *inspired*, even by the old romantic-subjective-expressive ideals he was so eager to escape. But first, the opera's most notorious stretch, the courtship-seduction Pantomime ending Act I: the lovers' canoodlings are accompanied by a dryly delicious double-concerto for two flutes in cool neo-Baroque style, lightly accompanied by chamber-orchestra; as it winds up and disappears, the tutti orchestra crashes in to graphically depict in mime the master-murderer, come to reclaim his precious creation: all over in thirteen bars of shattering cataclysm: not great music, but unforgettable for the incongruity, then the contrast.

Cardillac's aria opening Act II *is* great music – a marvellous invocation for sun and light to penetrate the earth's deepest mines wherein gold lies dormant till surfaced, retrieved, made ductile in its master's hands – the gold he loves. It commences on a heavy thick undertow of all the strings in unison octaves; a tingle of cymbals, the winds in scintillation of staccato well-remembered in Tippett's *Midsummer Marriage* where, at the start of Act II, he evokes the brilliant midday sun on Midsummer day. The scoring shifts – strings on the staccato, then joined by jazz-kit and brasses. All this prelude to elegantly contoured cantilena on saxophone, accompanied by soft intermittent tattoo-figure on brasses, the jazz-kit, also intermittent, an occasional glockenspiel dyad, never-changing, as the demon jeweller invokes sunlight that will wake the sleeping gold. The gaps gradually join in linear cantabile except for the continuing tattoo in the bass, the voice-part even more expansive, till declining to a replay of the opening as he declares his love for his material and resumes fashioning it – the saxophone melody first, then back to the very opening even as the Merchant enters and begins to investigate under pretence of enquiry. Spirit rather than letter of this music returns, varied and enhanced, to close the act. Petty human concerns have interrupted the work: now the master-maker can resume, putting them aside, invoking moonlight now, and the dark clefts wherein the gold sleeps – magnificent strong florid-rhetorical jagged unison line – 'Baroque' new-minted – climaxing on the tattoo-figure hammered out by a near-tutti, continued in the bass as he realizes he's missing an item from his treasury. His agitation mounts to angst, anger, determination to dare all, whatever it may be, to regain his creation: and the act ends in a storm of turbulence as he rages off – final bar a crescendo to *ffff* on timpani and percussion alone: expressionism lives.

Who needs theory after-the-event when the practice is so sufficient? Hindemith's late (1952) revision according to correct musical principles and a more 'responsible' presentation of the artist's place in society involves recasting the text (now by the composer himself), some additional characters, and an extra act incorporating portions of an opera on the Phaeton myth from the 1680s by Lully (shades of *Le Bourgeois gentilhomme*) for its supposed resemblance (I suppose) to the overweening nature of Cardillac's self-esteem and its disastrous fate (but Cardillac is a master; Phaeton is ignorant and foolish). The embargo its composer placed upon his original has rebounded: once no longer enforceable, it has run in reverse – 1926 is always preferred to 1952 when the work is given – rarely enough: it ought to be mainstream repertoire.

And so, perhaps, should *Mathis der Maler*: a fine, thoughtful work whose attitudes, unlike Cardillac's, are unimpugnable – very fine moments, the best extracted in the purely orchestral *Symphony* version, within a structure of stolid solidity, purpose and stance ethical and humane. It comes most vividly to life when panels from

Grünewald's wondrous altar-piece are animated to illuminate the principal action and personages by means of allegory and parallel, and the quiet renunciatory close is almost as moving as that of *Palestrina*, which it so resembles. But much in it doesn't come vividly to life, and there are acres of dead wood. And after it, the all-bran production-line, busy mills grinding out *Sachlichkeit* and *Gebrauchsmusik*. Hindemith's return to Europe after the Second World War was nourished by high hopes of a prominent place in the restoration of a sane and healthy musical culture, at large, and for his own country in particular. The 'Second Viennese School' were all out of favour (and two of them were dead): Bartók had died prematurely: Stravinsky, possibly a spent force, was anyway safely far away in Los Angeles: of the Moderns, Hindemith, in his late fifties, might have seemed to have the field to himself. But the new spirit of *Stunde Null* felt and thought very different: and time has proved unkind, albeit just, in evaluating his initially enormous talent, its brief peak, its long decline into elevated routine. A wry anecdote, possibly apocryphal, can stand as emblem. Touring Germany in the late 1940s, Hindemith invited questions after a presentation of the new Gospel of 'back-to-normality, and it's me': a gaunt figure raised its arm: 'Yes, yes, Doktor Klemperer,' said the flattered composer (they had been closely associated in Klemperer's great Berlin days) – 'you have a question?' 'Where is the toilet?' A characteristic insult better applied to Krenek's *Jonny spielt auf*: more than thirty German productions in its first season (1927), more than twenty foreign productions soon following: a preposterous period-piece, story and music alike, deservedly forgotten except in idle curiosity. The next composer, equally indissoluble to the country, the epoch, the culture, is for keeps.

Kurt Weill; born Dessau 1900, son of the cantor at the city's Synagogue: early musical education locally, then under Humperdinck in Berlin; back there, after brief theatrical experience, to enter Busoni's masterclass. Some early operatic successes before *The Threepenny Opera* (1928), a tearaway hit. This first collaboration with Brecht followed by four others; a revue, *Happy End* (1929); a full-length opera developed out of a brief singspiel of 1927 into the *Rise and Fall of the City of Mahagonny* completed two years later; *Der Jasager* – he who says yes – a *Lehrstück* (teaching-piece) for schools (1930); a ballet with singing, the *Seven Deadly Sins* (1933). Several other stage-works while still in Germany, and an isolated Symphony (1933) of great significance. In 1926 he had married the chanteuse ineffaceably associated with his music, Lotte Lenya; their on/off relationship and sharp reactions to circumstances personal, political, theatrical, charted in their highly flavoured correspondence. Inevitably in trouble with the Nazis after 1933 – Jewish *and* degenerate *and* composing what the Nazis contemptuously termed 'nigger-jazz': they fled, initially to Paris, eventually to New York where he died in 1950 (she lived on till 1981). The American years full of new collaborative ventures for Broadway and Hollywood: mainly musicals – some seven in all – though including an ambitious, idealistic biblical drama *The Eternal Road* and a full-scale grand opera *Street Scene*. The jury's still deliberating on all these and their balance of commercial/cynical with the moral/political commitment of his European oeuvre. Even with the highest motives, did he sell out? Probably not: but on strictly artistic ground there's no indecision whatsoever over the earlier pieces' superior quality.

Early Weill is gritty-grey: Hindemithy, touches of the recent Stravinsky, plenty of his master Busoni (but nothing at all of his first master Humperdinck): none of these are relinquished as base. Colour enters via jazz and American popular music, liberating altogether other strains closer to home – traces of Jewish cantillation and the folkloric side of Mahler's songs, whether sentimental/nostalgic, or vigorous/marching. What's loosened is a melodic genius second to none in the twentieth century: Weill stands with Gershwin and Prokofiev for fertility, potency, expression, catchiness. These marvellous numbers cross boundaries to become equally indispensable to music high and low: 'Mack the Knife' and a few others are international folksongs, universal as Coca-Cola. Weill is also a master of timing-pacing-characterization, parody cheek-by-jowl with elevation, tongue-in-cheek with searching didactic moral intent. Above all – even melody – he is a marvellous harmonist: if you hear talk of tonality being clapped-out/used up, close your eyes and think of Weill and Gershwin.

First hit, *The Threepenny Opera*; first sizeable effort the ambitious *Mahagonny*, its parts greater than its whole; *Happy End*, a non-starter as a show, contains the best songs of all – 'The Bilbao Song', 'The Sailors' Tango', 'The Song of the Hard Nut', 'Hell-Rose Lily', the immortal 'Surabaya Johnny'. In the *Seven Deadly Sins* everything fuses at high temperature and comes out right. Brecht's biting parable whereby each vice in turn can be turned to advantage, is matched by excellent lyrics: Weill's score is tip-top with not a weak link: the chosen format – mime and dance to show the eye, music to tell the ear, fusing into a composite *Gesamtkunstwerk* in the space of forty-five minutes – original and completely successful. The heroine is split into two: 'sisters', yet composite – Anna I who sings, Anna II who mimes, dances and, very occasionally, speaks. Composite, yet tellingly, also across each other – reason and temperance and common sense versus instinct, letting yourself go, foolhardiness. She/They set out from their humble homestead in the sticks to conquer American Capitalism and milk its riches, represented by seven major cities, each one ripe for a cardinal sin. The girl's family is represented vocally by a solo male quartet, remaining back at home, eagerly awaiting news, exhorting from a distance, piously and greedily amassing the shekels, singing in blasphemous inversion of conventional morality, hypocrisy incarnate, the topsy-turvy values grotesquely represented by *Mutter* being the deep bass of the quartet.

This marvellous innovative masterpiece deserves loving account of its every Sin, contained between the sleazy loucheness of the *Prologue* and the bleary seductive *Epilogue* – 'well we did it – here's our little house on the Mississippi' – a warm consonant close after the varied excoriations experienced en route. Highlights are *Anger* and *Lust*. The former involves all the forces in an agitated helter-skelter driven with motoric dynamism from start to finish. The two tenors and two basses sing in overlapping antiphony: It's no go! They don't send us enough, they're spending it on themselves. Anna I takes over with jack-booted authority – we're doing fine! We're in Los Angeles: if we play it right, we'll reach the top. Military/minatory grows brilliant and sparkling, the helter-skelter combining, for a sizeable dance-episode without words, returning at climax for the united Family's chant of their Prayer's salient wish. What ensues is another of Weill's long unfolding Mahlerian melodic contours – compare *Revelge* – underpinned by march-driven accompaniment, as Anna I draws the moral: your righteous anger is futile; learn the lesson – things aren't fair or just, man is a wolf to man, keep your indignation to yourself: and, bitterest of all – he who does no wrong will atone for it here below. The rage informing this music gradually abates as Prudence/Reason/Circumspection gain victory over Impulse/Generosity of spirit. 'So Anna I curbed her anger, urged self-control: you know what happens when you don't.' 'I know it, Anna', says her usually mute mime Sister, as the marvellous arc of melody sinks to the middle of the texture, vital motion retained above, and eventually stays fixed upon the equivocal if tranquil added sixth of the key.

Sloth, *Pride*, *Gluttony*, *Covetousness* must speak for themselves ('oh taste and hear'). Seventh and last comes *Envy*, 'first-born of Hell', mother of the other six. Which are listed in order, each with a harsh brutal encapsulation. Then Anna I, looking contemptuously at her poor envious Double, takes stock in a swinging march-song: we are all born free and can do as we please; but most folks are fools, not knowing why and whither. We're not fools: we've learnt to renounce banal gratifications; we've put the Sins aside in self-sacrifice; and *we* will triumph at the end when *they* are all condemned to nothingness outside the barred gates of virtue's reward. If music can convey simultaneous opposites, here is an instance: the proclamation's triumphalism is utterly subverted by the music's damning finger. Climax as she ceases and the Family renew their Prayer *fortissimo* and everything sinks full and satisfied into the *Epilogue* as described: full circle; the two sisters merge into one: Happy End.

Weill's 2nd Symphony followed closely on the *Seven Deadly Sins* and shares its stylistic idiom in general, and something of the same moral urgency, albeit entirely without programme let alone text. It is a work of masterly assurance, certain of its language and its aims: the almost solitary representative of a tradition that has gone underground and perhaps disappeared entirely – the single instance I can point to as showing the absent centre of a putative twentieth-century musical language. A heavy responsibility indeed: but it is a strong work. It is more concentrated and distinguished (as well as infinitely more attractive) than the 'Brandenburger' works of Hindemith which it sometimes resembles. Unlike Schoenberg's neo-classical works it inhabits the real aural sphere. It has a purposefulness often lacking in Stravinsky's neo-classical scores, which it also resembles and, in places, ante-dates. Its first movement rediscovers, long before the Russian's *Symphony in C*, the cumulative rhythmic and architectural power of an unchanging time-signature; its adagio reconquers the resources of the eight-bar phrase. In all three movements its use of elements from popular song-and-dance music exposes the would-be sophisticated Six as feckless, even inept, and in the satirical 'wrong-note' march in the finale Weill unerringly achieves what in Prokofiev is hit-or-miss, and in Shostakovich miss-and-miss with twenty times the ammunition. It does not attempt the refined harmonic subtlety and melodic thrill of the songs, but nevertheless displays an irresistible harmonic and melodic potency, is formally masterly, and scored (apart from a few miscalculations) with brilliant and direct simplicity. No one else could have done it; it is as unique in its time as in Weill's oeuvre. Was it only a lucky fluke, or might he have gone on from here to create a true lingua franca? It's already abundantly clear from the songs and the *Seven Deadly Sins* above all that he was a master; but there is no further context for this unexpected projection into the exemplary.

The $64,000 question, concerning the calibre of Weill's American work when compared with the European that he so decisively relinquished, is not resolved even by implication. Are the later works inferior? And if so, is the shift in standard knowing, even cynical (in the teeth of his heart-on-sleeve declarations), or genuinely unconscious? Weill's ambition to achieve a 'Broadway opera', inspired by seeing *Porgy and Bess* in 1942, is first realized in part by the Cellini-derived *Firebrand of Florence* (1945), which flopped; and then two years later by *Street Scene*, much more appropriate in its all-American setting and subject. Commercial by necessity, idealistic by choice, they represent the climax of an endeavour that never degenerated into cheapness. The overriding desire to continue working (one tends to forget that he was only thirty-five when he arrived in the States) and the impossibility of hawking around the European corpses (whose life has been so specific to their time and place) are wholly understandable. But something seems askew in the Broadway shows, even as they are now being revived to great acclaim. Common to both is the cultivated craftsmanship that never disgraces the ex-pupil of Busoni, whatever dubious gutter he taps. But the European music burns with an acrid genius so corrosive to liver, lights and life as to make the later, even at its best, seem synthetic and anodyne. From all the output the voice of Lenya is inseparable:

> when I feel this longing for you, I think most of all of the sound of your voice, which I love like a very force of nature, like an element. For me all of you is contained within this sound; every-thing else is only a part of you; and when I envelop myself in your voice, then you are with me in every way.

And here is that voice, 'speaking', in a letter to her husband composed in their idiomatically spelt English:

> I got a very nice letter from Nannerl Huston, with a long para-graph about: how unimportent life is and how wonderful death is. I don't know why, but I get terribly hungry, when I read things like that. So I went to the kitchen and made myself coffee and felt, there is nothing more beautiflil than life.

CHAPTER XIII
France Resumed

Gabriel Fauré

The shape of Fauré's work over a long life – 1845–1924 – is unusual for his epoch; and its nature right athwart it. There are ten substantial chamber-works, all save one either early or late; one full-length opera, *Pénélope*, and one substantial theatrical *spectacle*, *Prométhée*, and a handful of scores to accompany plays, mainly ephemeral, two of distinction: plentiful minor religious music and one major piece, the well-loved *Requiem*. Consistent from first to last is a large body of solo piano-music, mainly in genres familiar from the early Romantics, particularly Chopin and Schumann – thirteen nocturnes, thirteen barcarolles, five impromptus, four *valses-caprices*, nine preludes, eight *piéces brèves*, and a substantial set of variations – never less than impeccable, often delectable, sometimes first-rate: a couple of concertante-works for piano and orchestra are not so special. And a still larger body of *mélodies*: many individual songs of high distinction and six cycles (seven if the three comprising *Poème d'un jour* count as a cycle). Almost nothing written originally for orchestra alone in this epoch of the orchestra's ascendancy, whether gigantic and masterful like Strauss and Mahler, mainstream like Elgar or Sibelius, refined into atmosphere and light like Debussy and Ravel, anatomized and X-rayed like Schoenberg, or blown up into caricature then primitivistic violence as in Stravinsky. With this singular abstention, unique in his time, goes indifference to extremes in every direction all around – of lurid subject-matter, of extravagant extroversions and introversions, the exploration of ever-more intricate nuance in sound, of megalomaniac spiritual states. Fauré writes nocturnes and barcarolles, violin or cello sonatas, etc.), songs with piano, whose impulse is innately and intrinsically absolute: 'music about music', its content 'abstract', though without the chill that these terms might connote.

Yet, paradoxically, this wholly un-experimental un-radical figure – one doesn't want to say conservative, let alone academic, for all his distinguished tenure as head of the Paris Conservatoire – is as bold an extender and eroder of the idiom and grammar of music as any vaunted 'emancipation of the dissonance' or melting away in exotic scales, modes, textures like his younger compatriots. Fauré's long trajectory from the darling of the salons, all politeness and pearls, to an erosion of tonality in its way as devastating as any, comes in an unbroken span, calmly evolving without incident, almost imperceptible till one takes a sounding now and then to measure the extraordinary degree of change and that change's extraordinary nature. I offer here a path – *chemin perfide* – through the work, generalizing mostly, stopping occasionally to particularize: my choices are based entirely upon the pleasure, delight, fulfilment of every desire that this 'master of charms' (as Debussy called him) provides so abundantly. Any other selection altogether would come to just the same conclusions.

To begin, 1st Violin Sonata 1875–6: 1st Piano Quartet 1876–7: works of extraordinary felicity, abundance, ease – Mendelssohnian grace and fluency without his weaknesses: all melody, as if 'development' were a laborious nuisance; forms perfected – shapely, unemphasized but assured; enormous ingenuity hidden within the ease, and passion within the decorum or the playfulness. For this latter, see the scherzo in the sonata – skittish/kittenish gaiety, yet the texture of feathery dexterity can hint, then give fully, broad singing contours which, flowering in the trio, can hint, then divulge, the scherzo's return: for passion within the decorum, see the lovely curvaceous ebbs and flows of the andante, violin and piano right hand answering, echoing, overlapping, combining, launching forth separately, coming together again: amorous intimacy incarnate, though never bursting the bonds as chez Franck.

In the quartet, virility too: the first movement's main theme as powerfully 'masculine' as anything in Brahms, its development as resourceful and fertile in counterpoints, inversions, reaccentuations and reharmonizations. The second subject, initially little more than a wiggle, then grows in both strength and versatility; the keyboard-writing combines Mendelssohnian dash with Lisztian bravura as well as Brahmsian weight; yet the layout for piano and strings always perfectly balanced, and the entity effortless, seamless, continuously surprising. Within the delicate scherzo power lies latent – Schubertian, here; great waves of arpeggio rise out of the whirring momentum and sink back: the trio begins *sotto voce* songful, then swells through key after key, restoring the momentum in combination before scherzo-return, closing in the same cunning enharmonic/near-whole-tone cadence. The adagio begins grave and broad, then opens out into melting lyricism sometimes so rich in chromatic intensity as to resemble turns of phrase in Schoenberg's *Verklärte Nacht* twenty years later. Chez Fauré the impress of *Tristan*, still raw in the Viennese, is tenderly assimilated, almost without a trace of source. The return of the initial *serioso* is now transfigured by this radiant moonlit benediction. And Fauré has no 'finale-problem': tearaway motion, all bounding energy never going rough even when its energy brims over into bigger gesture, nor losing springy songfulness that soon gains ample space in which to bloom. The gestural idea, on strings, now softly punctuates a broadening-out on piano – *moto perpetuo* for a moment abates, resuming as songfulness returns, redistributed among the strings, then initial momentum builds up greater and greater exuberance – no hectoring, no bullying, no coercion – pure *joie de vivre*, whether climactic, or again whispered, then climatic again: a pause – a cadenza – a shy resumption, piano alone, gently vibrating as background to the most exquisitely clever imaginable re-entry of the strings, reintroducing in turn a combination of previous themes that discovers in them possibilities unexplored earlier. Energy again swells, the sails fill with a fresh strong breeze, the small craft skims elegantly, punctually, beautifully, into harbour. Perfect youthful masterpieces as, too, the 2nd Piano Quartet a few years later (1885–6) – by no means a re-run; completely different in every respect save the conspicuous felicity of its ideas and its facture.

    It took Fauré longer to leave the salon in his songs and solo piano music. Never less than charming from the start, but it's some time before they are more. Early gems of *mélodie* – *Lydia*, *Les Roses d'Ispahan*, *Les Berceaux*, from the 1860s onwards, can perhaps best be savoured in the celebrated *Après un rêve* of *c.*1878. In 1887 comes his first setting of Verlaine – *Clair de lune*, soon followed by *Spleen*, then in 1891 *Cinq mélodies de Venise* and in 1892–4 the nine songs of *La Bonne Chanson*, with a prelude in *Prison*: seventeen in all, all supreme, epitomizing the ripe bloom of his maturity before the long voyage into ever stranger and subtler mysteriousness. They make an absorbing comparison with Debussy's Verlaine settings, overlapping in time (*c.*1880–1904) and in choice of six poems. Their subject-area too: Watteau, *commedia dell'arte*, *fêtes galantes* – moonlight/nostalgia/ prettiness, deepening into melancholy/pain/anguish/despair (as essayed also by Ravel in one of his two settings of Verlaine, *Un grand sommeil noir* of 1895, touched on by Fauré in *Prison* the year before). Also amorous indolence, sensuous/sensual hedonism, *La Rose/C'est l'extase*. And young love – both composers' *Green*, and in Fauré's *La Bonne Chanson*, the story of a courtship and its felicitous fulfilment.

Clair de lune: piano steals the show with its long keyboard line evoking menuet continuing almost throughout, into which the singer insinuates the words syllabically, no melody – 'telling of your soul, a landscape of maskers singing and playing, gay but sad – the minor key of love, unable to believe their happiness, so fragile and evanescent.' Now at last the menuet sinks into arpeggio accompaniment, only a ghost of itself here and there, as the voice at last expands into the moonlight, 'sad and lovely, inducing birds to dream and fountains to sob in ecstasy among the statues' – curious little bump of obliquity in the poem, matched by brief cessation of accompaniment before the singer in turn ceases and the menuet resumes and fades. *Spleen*: the famous *il pleure dans mon coeur*, doesn't yield Fauré at his very best – a bit bland and smooth for this hapless cry of a wounded heart, the 'ceaseless grief without cause, neither love nor hate, the pain inexplicable'. *Prison*, however, lacerates with its poised hieratic calm: a view from up high, over the roof into the sky, here so 'clear and blue ... the church bell, the plaining bird ...' Sudden triple outburst – 'my God, life is there, simple and tranquil!

This peaceful sound from the village! What, you who weep without end – say, what have you done with your youth?' The succession of even chords contains within their equality an ache of tormented harmony, masterfully curbed.

The set of five 'Venetian Verlaines' is a summit. As with Debussy's six *Ariettes oubliées* and eight *Fêtes galantes*, no narration, though a strong feeling of affinity and belongingness. *Mandoline* is the lightest: the piano delicately evokes the instrument, occasionally picking up the vocal phrases – now gently florid, now gently curved – serenaders and serenaded exchange faded nothings under the singing branches – 'these same old lovers – their dress, their style, their pleasures'; now the voice is more forward and the outdoor mandolin becomes a salon piano; its left hand sings, its right twice remembers the florid phrases the singer no longer produces – 'the soft blue shadows swirl in an ecstasy of rose-grey moonlight and the mandolin chatters in the breeze – the mandolin of the serenaders and their lovely listeners' – Fauré repeats the opening line and ends on the instrument's little get-ready. Ready for *En sourdine*, deeper into the same terrain without brittleness and detachment: a single lover, the single intimate addressed, a mutuality: inviting her 'to mingle souls, hearts, senses, in the calm of the evening among the trees ... half close your eyes, fold your arms on your breast, dispel purpose ...'; mood and momentum of tranced tranquillity, the piano's even figuration gradually outlining fuller melodic contour in echoing augmentation of the singer's syllabic shapes, more imperative, in the command to half-close the eyes, and so on. Harmony intensifies, the left hand also sings: a fourth stanza lightens for the banishment of purpose, right hand floating higher and independent: *and* ... fifth stanza ... *and* ... the music swells and broadens ... 'when, solemn, the evening darkens the oaks, the nightingale will sing, voice of our despair' – exquisitely understated in a long diminuendo and ascent, ending on a delicately poised proximity of pitches that if simultaneous would be dissonant beyond utterance – here moving to a consonant cadence of comfort without complacence.

Green makes a marked complement/contrast to Debussy's famous setting, all eager springing anticipation, relaxing stage-by-stage into amorous repose. Fauré's keeps the same sober-even measure from start to finish: a pulse like *Après un rêve* whose obvious conventionality mustn't conceal its inner art, arching ebb-and-flow of harmony and enharmony supporting the voice's breathless parlando: 'I bring fruits, flowers, foliage; and my heart, beating only for you; don't destroy them – let my humble gift be sweet to your lovely eyes.' Now the mood moves inward even as momentum goes onward: a tiny hesitation-limp in the piano hints at the lover's impulsive self-effacement even as he presses his presence: 'I arrive still wet with dew – let me repose myself at your feet, let my fatigue dream of its assuagement.' The final stanza exactly repeats the first – 'on your young breast let my head sink, still ringing from your last kisses: let it re-find calm after the kindly tempest: let me sleep awhile, while you too repose' – a wonderful expansion into a near-but-distant key, the tiny internal amorous hesitation four times. *À Clymène* perhaps lowers the stakes, but *C'est l'extase* is 22-caret. Again, a comparison with Debussy's setting, all-hedonistic abandon to glowing sensuous indolence. Fauré's *extase languoureuse* and *fatigue amoureuse* are more (so to speak) functional: the music is in motion; a journey is under way. Against delicate conventional accompaniment, piano intones a descending fourth, voice joins, they shadow each other, enharmonic shifts gleam and slither, the two melodic strands diverge into independence – piano insinuating a motif from *Green*; phrases expand; half-way: continuation more impassioned – 'this self-lamenting spirit, this drowsing lament – isn't it ours? Thine and mine? The humble chant exhaled by this humid night.' Passion spent, subsidence into acquiescent calm, winding down into post-climactic post-melody, eventually post-rhythmic too.

La Bonne Chanson: almost the only great song-cycle, French, German, Austrian, English, of felicity – *bonheur, vie en rose*. Courtship successful, mutual love assured and fulfilled, happiness-everafter. Only Brahms's *Schöne Magelone* can compare; and, of course, Janáček's *Young Man* ends on a glorious high note. The affianced pair meet in an atmosphere of medieval chivalry enveloping the first song – *Une sainte en son auréole* – she is *chatelaîne* as well as saint, all grace and love, in the ancient horn-haunted forests; the virginal blushes of a mother-o'-pearl swan – all that's suggested by her patrician Carolingian name (never divulged). The suave linear accompaniment suggests a string consort – and there is indeed a version for string quintet with piano that perfectly realizes this polyphonic aspect but spoils later songs with redundant infill. After this calm-moving calm, *Puisque l'aube grandit* ripples and surges: 'I will follow your guidance wherever you lead me, towards happiness be the path smooth or stony', then easing into relaxed well-being as he dedicates his songs to her pleasure and wishes for no other Paradise than doing so. *La lune blanche luit dans les bois*: 'it is the hour – the lake reflects the willows, the wind ruffles them, the moon irradiates the woodland scene – oh my belovèd, it is the moment – *l'heure exquise*'; rendered in a rapt barcarolle, lilting in support of arching vocal phrases, climaxing before 'a vast tender appeasement' seems to descend from the joy-intoxicated firmament to hallow the key-phrase as italicized, no longer lilting – even and smooth and ineffably tranquil.

Whether smooth or stony, the path ahead now turns troubled – *J'allais par des chemins perfides* – the easy flow of the first song now agitated with ever-stranger enharmonic ambiguities, false friends, disquieting and treacherous: 'but all will be well, your glance draws me through the night towards the dawn; keep on – love will show the way' – and indeed the first song's material focuses undistorted as this fourth song reunites the pair in joy, in the same key, with the same soft climactic high note, as for *l'heure exquise*. Agitation renews in the fifth: *J'ai presque peur, en vérité* – 'I tremble to think how close, now, we are intervolved; your slightest impulse can send my whole being into disorder.' Pitter-patter of unease; but over a steady bass, and the anxious voice twice punctuated by a *petit phrase* in the piano's right hand that, with the poem's change of mood – 'whatever may be, my hope is boundless, plunged in the supreme happiness of being able to say, again and always, *I love you*', and the setting's change from minor to major and the nervous accompaniment from pitter-patter to lyric arpeggiation – blossoms into curling sprays of melody more melodious than the singer's long-held notes; till he too expands into two nearly-rhyming apostrophes: strong, high, formal – *'que je vous aime'*; then soft, low, intimate – *'que je t'aime'*; a distinction wholly caught in Fauré's music.

The next song, *Avant que tu ne t'en ailles*, alternates several tempi and textures: interior stillness – 'before you, pale morning star, vanish away'; frisky buoyancy high in the piano with an ascendant three-note lark high in the air (though the poem says 'a thousand quails in the thyme'). Its closing hymnic motif is almost immediately incorporated into the joyous turbulence of *Donc, ce sera par un clair jour d'été* – 'the shining summer sun, accomplice in joy, will magnify your beauty': blissful mutuality, then as evening advances, turbulence eases into contentment – 'the stars will look down, smiling on the spouses'. The eighth song, *N'est-ce pas?*, seems to reopen anxious questionings; but the mood is now of calm certainties – 'we will, without fret, follow the path of smiling hope, not caring who knows us or not, enclosed in our love, two nightingales singing together into the night: unconcerned with our fate we move together to the same steps, hand-in-hand, child-like, fused in one in our love – *n'est-ce pas?*' Larks and quails and the hymnic paean to the rising sun combine in the opening strains of the closing song, *L'hiver a cessé* – 'light floods the clear firmament, quickening the saddest heart: the earth renews herself.' Then the music quietens, though its babbling momentum is not stilled – 'I've had spring in my heart the whole year round, and now the return of green, the eternal blue, confirm my love: come summer, come autumn, come winter, every season will ravish me' – a beautiful return of the phrase in *Puisque l'aube grandit* where the poet-lover declares he'll sing for her his ingenuous songs; subsiding at once into further reminiscences further back – to the very first song of all, closing the circle-cycle in a ring of wedded bliss, adamant yet gentle – *'ô Toi que découvre cette fantaisie et cette raison!'* Its music at once palpable and distanced down a long vista of *temps passé*. Nowhere in all music have the surges and ebbs of *bonheur*, at once shy and abandoned, quiveringly sensitive and interior yet unabashed and direct, been so felicitously caught and given voice.

Fauré's output is at its fullest fruition from *c.*1888, with the completion of the *Requiem*, to *c.*1912 and his longest and most ambitious effort *Pénélope*, the opera on the return of Ulysses to his long-suffering wife. As well as more songs complementing and filling out the two perfect Verlaine sets, much piano-music, ranging from the delicious *Huit pièces brèves* to the monumental *Theme and Variations* set, there's another Greek-subject theatre-piece *Prométhée* – noble, dullish; and a grand, isolated, somewhat problematic chamber-work, the 1st Piano Quintet. Rather than any of these I will concentrate upon just three from these years, none monumental, one apparently slight, another certainly occasional, the third a single song three pages long.

Dolly (1893–6): suite of six short movements for the homely medium of piano-duet – two people, four hands, one piano. The humble aim precludes exploration of his stealthily evolving strangeness equally with the size and scope required by the stage-works or the *Requiem*. *Dolly* nevertheless encapsulates in small all Fauré's large range: brio and *élan* in the concluding *Pas espagnol* – his modest contribution to the line of Spanish music in French from Bizet to Ravel: demure coquettish flirtation in the two *valses* – *Mi-a-ou* with the seductive cats, *Kitty-valse* with the delicious young girls: in the opening *Berceuse* the lulling tenderness that used to enchant the nation as signature-tune for 'Listen with Mother': *Tendresse* itself (the fifth piece), touching upon deeper currents, erotic and sensuous; lightened and sublimated in *Le Jardin de Dolly*, the centrepiece. The ideas first-class throughout, the craft perfected, the art consummate, subtle and sometimes exceedingly ingenious – that canon in *Tendresse* – the sidestepping evasions as surprisingly delightful as the delightfully surprising straightforwardness alongside: a flawless miniature world of tact, gentleness, humour, sweetness, without anything cheap, faked, condescending.

In 1889 Fauré provided six numbers for *Shylock*, a mishmash from *The Merchant of Venice*, deservedly forgotten. His score is patchy: its two songs distinctly inferior: but the purely instrumental bits are marvellous; up there with Mendelssohn's *Dream* and Sibelius's *Tempest*, wholly worthy of their Shakespearean inspiration. Omitting the songs, a perfect little orchestral suite: *Entr'acte* (really a *prélude*) alternating bright but gentle fanfare-tune with dulcet amorous strains foretelling what's to come; an *Épithalame* worthy of an English Coronation

without the pomp and flannel, again complementing the public processional with intimate strains from the *Entr'acte*; a spritely *Finale*,
gay and happy, with, within its infectious whirling energy, some of
the composer's most effortlessly elliptical harmonic boldnesses. The
pearl of great price precedes the gaiety – a tiny *Nocturne*, no doubt
mirroring Shakespeare's celebrated 'in such a night . . .', wherein calm
mutual amity is hymned in a long singing arch of melody, heard once,
repeated enhanced and differently directed, peaking with passion
nonetheless intense for being so interiorized: a *hymnus amoris*, sacramental without needing to invoke Novalis, Schopenhauer, or Christianity. If Fauré had written nothing else, these two pages would
declare an unknown master of rare distinction.

So, too, the three pages for voice and piano of *Le Parfum impériss-
able* of 1897. Leconte de Lisle's poem cloaks a strong simple simile
in language of sinuous suggestive tortuosity:

> As, when the sun's flower, the rose of Lahor has, drop by drop of
> its perfumed soul, filled the vial of earthenware, or of crystal, or
> gold, can, drop by drop spread it all upon the burning sand – as,
> when rivers and seas in vain inundate the resonating inner sanc-
> tuary, narrow and enclosed, the divine aroma is safeguarded even
> in breaking, and the happy dust survives, perfume-charged – so
> for the open wound of my heart: you flow thus too, celestial
> ichor – inexpressible, inexplicable love, enflaming me for ever, for
> her! That my love be pardoned, that my ill be blessed – that, by
> mankind's brief hour and time's infinity, my heart be embalmed
> in a perfume that can never perish.

The strong simple single simile – as the shards retain the perfume's fragrance even when the flask is shattered, so my heart, fired
with love, preserves my love's undying essence. Fauré's wonderful setting combines the strength and simplicity, with the sinuous
tortuosity. One bar of even-paced chords on the main key sets it
in motion: as the voice lands on the last syllable of its last word –
immortelle – the same low-positioned tonic sonority is again reached,
and stilled. Between opening and close the home key is touched,

with plain, almost churchy benediction, six times, each with a beautiful sense of safety, fulfilment, familiarity, anything but trite.

So much for the simplicity: between these moments of touching tonic, the deviances of enharmony and curious balm-annealing dissonance grow more and more extreme: always, however, retaining calm placid momentum. At the furthest, one wonders, as well as how the music has got here, how will it ever manage to get back? Wave upon wave, on this minute scale, rises to a positive incandescence of tranquil strangeness before slipping back into the mundane, transfigured by context, stepping-stone to the next adventure. The processes fuse on the climactic note/word *coeur* as the end nears – the key-note/word, that 'should' be the tonic chord, as just prepared, evaded by an evasion yielding one more slither, acutest of all, on the final syllable of *embaumé* – remotest harmony imaginable before the ineffable – *inexprimable* – imperishable – return home in only two beats: surface unruffled, depths deep beyond plummet's sounding, though all contained within the sounds. An image for the composer himself.

The miracle of large-in-small holds the key to Fauré's 'late style', whether small-scale or surprisingly expansive as in the final chamber-works – ellipsis, essentiality, sparingness (recalling Renoir's wife and her cooking, 'I use only the best, but frugally'), self-containment, severity mitigated with generosity, cool with warmth, impersonality and control with inner volatility. His language is never 'atonal'; yet so thoroughgoing in harmonic ambiguity as to erode 'our tired old tonics and dominants' by wholly other means either from contemporaries in Vienna or from Debussy – who actually said these words – close to home. Fauré is older than any, yet in the best of his latest music he is, in his unobtrusive manner, quite as daring.

Sometimes frugality and cool prevail in a greyish pellucid monotone that gives hostages to the immune. Thus with the four later song-cycles, *La Chanson d'Ève* (1910), *Le Jardin clos* (1914), *Mirages* (1919) and *L'Horizon chimérique* (1921): their texts Maeterlinck-and-water (unsparkling), their music odourless and taste-free even as they are models of tastefulness. Then try the 2nd Violin Sonata of 1916–17 or the 2nd Piano Quintet of 1919–21. Vibrant energy courses through their fast movements: purposeful without didacticism in the opening allegros, always clean-limbed, for all their athletic prowess never bulging with muscle-bound heaviness, nor with overkill in the race towards ever-brighter euphoria in their finales. Only the quintet has a scherzo, quicksilver as the young composer's in his two piano quartets more than a quarter-of-a-century earlier, plus the new subtlety of his latest discoveries. And the andantes calmly and effortlessly explore the depths without furrowing the brow or harrowing the soul or invoking the dark forces beneath the girdle: all these are admitted, but contained, sublimated into grace and benignity – a victory for Apollo, a shining contrast to virtually all his contemporaries, in music as in the other arts, in that time of 'the breaking of nations'.

The two late cello sonatas (1917; 1921) don't achieve such perfect equilibrium: the two subsequent chamber-works – the Piano Trio (1922–3) and String Quartet (1923–4) maybe even surpass it. Terminal rarification has set in in the rare beauty of these last works – he died later in 1924 aged seventy-nine. Spareness is taken so far as it can go within the aesthetic, frugality has to perform a miracle of loaves-and-fishes (but the *best* ingredients only!). The mastery is undiminished, and the same energy within the ease, fire within the cool, content within the understatement, are all intact. Within the empty vessel the perfume lingers imperishable.

Claude Debussy

There are composers whose music one knows so well that one scarcely gives it a thought or troubles to listen to it any more. It might be an early passion that's lost its lustre – Mahler, Bartók – or simply a totality perfected in one's mind, a secret garden that one doesn't want to disturb. A mix of both is so with me for Claude Debussy, principal joy of my early teens.

As a small boy I was entranced with the easier piano-pieces of Debussy that I was (sort of) able to play, and thrilled by more grown-up playing of the harder pieces. Rather later I realized that some of these were transcriptions of orchestral works, and began to hoard every sixpence towards buying them on LP – Toscanini's blazing *La Mer* conspicuous among them. The shops' reopening after Christmas was the best time. Loaded with seasonal cash, I could actually afford two or three records in one go. In January 1959 came an unknown Debussy ballet called *Jeux*. My first hearing of this was like first looking into Chapman's *Homer*. Its entire world – the atmosphere, the swoons and sharpness, the shimmer and glow, the refined incandescence of the harmony, inseparable from the astonishing orchestral luminosity – all that adolescent hankerings had vaguely imagined, was realized fully, at a touch, like a dream come true. For the next few days the turntable never stopped, till this life-transforming eighteen minutes had permeated memory and bloodstream.

And at about this time the great Pierre Monteux, already in his eighties when (rather exaggerated rumour had it) given a 100-year contract with the LSO, gave some revelatory Debussy concerts in London. They included an un-staged *Pelléas et Mélisande* (though no *Jeux*, not yet a standard, for all that he'd conducted its première), and to my mind remain unequalled by any later interpreter. Nor has any conductor so well as he managed to overcome the Festival Hall's cruel acoustic, bathing it in the gentle effulgence of a Monet landscape. But – as with the Impressionists indeed – one wearies. Somehow, in spite of manifest mastery and manifold delights, a dimension seems to be missing from this music. As teenage taste moved forward into the abrasive wonders of modernism which owe Debussy so much, and back into the endless riches of music before him, the celebration of hedonism in effects of light and colour appeared insufficient, however consummate.

His repudiations are so wholescale! Despising symphonic dialectic ruled out the classic core from Haydn to Brahms – Beethoven 'le vieux sourd', Mendelssohn 'that elegant notary'; impatience with Romantic subjectivity ruled out most of the epoch from Berlioz to his Austro-German contemporaries – Berlioz a 'monstrosity'; deploring Strauss; walking out of Mahler's conducting his 'Resurrection' *Symphony* in Paris. A taste so largely defined by negatives leaves precious little with which to build an oeuvre that is without question major. What is left? A miscellany of highly flavoured sound-bites that attract this thieving magpie with the sensitive ear and the short attention-span. He loves fragments from nearby: Franck ('It's all pure music, and what's more, it's all exquisite music ... even the discovery of a beautiful new chord could fill his day with joy'), Gounod ('For all his weakness ... a necessity'), Chabrier ('So marvellously endowed by the comic muse'), Fauré ('The play of fleeting curves that is the essence of Fauré's music can be compared to the movements of a beautiful woman without either suffering from the comparison'), Massenet ('His music is vibrant with fleeting sensation, little bursts of feeling and embraces that we wish would last for ever'). All this, taken with Debussy's known delight in Delibes and Lalo, suggests a Frenchness very different from his official endorsement of the eighteenth-century masters and one very close to the origins of his style. Subtract Rameau and Couperin and an *Image* is lost, and a strain in the three sonatas, but *Pelléas* would be very different without Massenet, and, without Franck, Debussy would be unimaginable as he now stands.

Everything else is exotica. Wagner in glowing flecks of colour, though emphatically not in the whole; little touches of Weber and Schumann, bigger of Chopin, still more of Borodin, and most of Musorgsky. All these, and the French sources – including queer little nuggets of his ambiguous friend Satie – are fused and transformed by a seminal experience, gamelan music of Java, encountered in Paris in 1889, that 'make our tonics and dominants seem like ghosts'. Intake from music so crosses over into influence from nature – 'the sound of the sea, the outline of a horizon, the wind in the leaves, the cry of a bird' (as he said) that the two cannot be distinguished.

And all this is inseparable too from his absorption in artefacts visual and verbal, and from his astonishing empathy with remote places and rarified states of the spirit. The still water of *Reflets dans l'eau*, the deep clear well in his opera, the stagnant pool in the first of his late Mallarmé songs – these are at once visual images, places of the mind and moments of sonorous organization. And so it is for the piece evoking a Japanese lacquer depicting goldfish, or a Spanish night sultry with perfumes, or a fresh flaxen-haired girl, or a submerged cathedral, or gardens in the rain, or the faun toying with the memory of the nymphs, and all the familiar list of apparently peripheral picturesqueness. Every one is profoundly contemplated in sound, till, like Keats' Grecian urn, they attain a quasi-religious significance all the more absorbing for the absence of emphasis.

With this kaleidoscope of surprises and incompatibles he made a new way of perceiving musical events. He invented another; all his material existed already, in its own discrete context – but he is totally original. Jettisoning the residue, he isolated just the colours he liked and presented them as objects for reflection in which the appeals to ear and eye are indistinguishable. The way he heard what caught his imagination has become the way everyone hears. He altered music more completely than any other composer: but the message has been so wholly received as to seem by now rather ordinary. Ordinary; like Bach and Mozart; a classic.

Some salient dates for Debussy have already been indicated, discussing his friend Chausson (page 547): others will emerge as the work is explored. The earliest music – late 1870s to around 1887 – comprises many songs and smaller piano-pieces: his poets include Verlaine and a single setting of Mallarmé – signs of future preoccupations: the piano-pieces with their evocation of Watteau via Verlaine in eighteenth-century forms – in the *Suite bergamasque* a menuet and a passepied, in *Pour le piano* a sarabande and toccata, in the *Petite Suite* (for piano-duet) another menuet and a cortège – both solo-works also commence with a *prélude*; and the most familiar number in all this early time – *Clair de lune* from the *Bergamasque* – takes its title too from Verlaine. All this music is sweetly pretty and pretty slight – *deux arabesques* can stand for everything: deftly turned and charming, only once, in the Satie-esque sarabande from *Pour le piano*, prophesying the wonders to come. They begin to show themselves in two complementary and contemporaneous works of the late 1880s; five settings of Baudelaire for soprano and piano; a cantata on Rossetti's *Blessed Damozel*, translated as *La Damoiselle élue*, for principal soprano supported by subsidiary mezzo, with orchestra and female chorus. Enter Wagner: the young Debussy was as intoxicated as any artist of his time and place with the inescapable influence: he visited Bayreuth twice (1888–9) and as an impecunious student earned a precarious living ploughing through the Meister's music-dramas in the salons of the rich, singing all the roles in his husky composer's voice. I was intrigued when, a few years back, his piano-score of *Parsifal*, said to be copiously annotated in his own hand, came up for auction. Inspection at Sotheby's generous showrooms proved disappointing: I'd hoped for appreciative or disapproving exclamations and underlinings – *j'adore cela! formidable! hélas!* etc. – but Debussy's handwriting was confined to putting in the text in French, and by no means complete.

No matter. *La Damoiselle* says it all, evincing unmissable absorption in the large from the start – the character, mood, layout of the opening prelude – to passing flickers of detail, sometimes so closely derived from the small print of Wagner's score rather than its great moments (though these aren't entirely absent) as to be virtually quotations – plagiarisms, even – except – the vital point – that even when literally stolen, Debussy's re-angling casts the sounds in a new light. The result is a homage to *Parsifal* that avoids Wagnerism: pure Burne-Jones, the poem's mawkishness strained through the opera's burning repression of carnality into an area of sublimation, un-ideological, non-allegorical, on a miniature scale, and not eschewing more refined sensualities nearer home (mainly Massenet): a work of singular perfection – its orchestration especially – that maybe he only superseded, never surpassed.

Analogous but rather different, the relationship of the Baudelaire-songs to Wagner's other Romance-opera (it's pretty obvious that Debussy's artistic sensibility couldn't maintain the same quivering rapport with the heroic mythological gigantism of the *Ring*, still less with the interlocking bourgeois/*Junker* craft-based competitive ethos of *Meistersinger*). These wonderful songs are as infused with *Tristan* as the cantata with *Parsifal*: there are indeed a few virtual quotations, with the same magical re-lighting by which near-identical notes somehow sound quite new-heard; but the main impulse here comes from those piano-bashing sessions in the salons of Paris and no doubt at home: the layout of *Tristan*'s orchestral

textures, the most intricate in Wagner's oeuvre, as transcribed
for the pianist's two hands, has informed the most detailed in all
Debussy's; sometimes symphonically developing, always quasi-
orchestral, sumptuous beyond almost anything from his maturity
until touched on again in some of the late études. With *La Damoiselle* Debussy's wonderful ears remember, reproduce, transform, the
orchestra of *Parsifal*: with the Baudelaire-songs his avid, retentive
memory lies in the wonderful fingers of his way with the piano.
Again, one has to say that this achievement was superseded but
never surpassed.

Also from the late 1880s come three sets of further Verlaine
settings with piano, now fully characteristic: the so-called *Ariettes
oubliées* (because published, '*déjà un peu vieilles*', only in 1903); three
songs of 1891; a cycle of three *Fêtes galantes* (1892; a second three,
Fêtes galantes II, followed in 1904, a nostalgic farewell to a favourite terrain): fifteen songs in all, lighter, as befits the poet, than the
Baudelaire-set – exquisite in facture and expression, precious stones
of the French *mélodie*. And by 1904 Debussy's solo-piano output,
slower to take off, had burgeoned in ambition and stature to match,
rival, outdo the *mélodie* in his mature harvest.

But the full extent of his unfolding powers, and originality, is
orchestral, albeit saturated in imagery visual and verbal. *Printemps*
(1887) is a precursor: a lovable piece poised between the salon-idiom
of the earlier piano-music and the late orchestral masterpiece on
the same subject – the first celebrates Botticelli and renaissance; the
second celebrates France in burgeoning strains of joyous delight –
rondes de printemps. The first landmark, however, is *L'Après-midi d'un
faune* (1892–4): the relatively faceless String Quartet of 1894 makes
the point – no literary source to inspire and direct; no pictures,
ditto; dutiful, near-academic, a graduation-piece after the event,
heavily indebted to Franck despite some liberating touches of
gamelan. *L'Après-midi* is quite another matter. Daring and original
not to set Mallarmé's eclogue – impossible anyway, and boring if
it *were* possible – so much as to use it to suggest, evoke, resonate
with impulses, sensations, desires. Attempts to link Debussy's score
phrase-by-phrase with Mallarmé's words are deluded: if proven, so

what? Better to try to capture the evanescent wonder phrase-by-phrase, sounds-in-themselves.

'It fades as one looks at it' – said Busoni. The poet who inspired the piece, hearing what the musician had made of his music-aspiring words, paid tribute thus: 'an illustration presenting no dissonance with my text ... rather, it penetrates far further into the nostalgia and light with subtlety, malaise, richness.' Simpler, Ravel's wish to have this embodiment of pagan sensuality played at his funeral 'because it is perfect'. And let Mallarmé have the last as he'd had the first words:

> Sylvain d'haleine première
> Si ta flûte a réussi
> Ouïs toute la lumière
> Qu' y soufflera Debussy.

(Sylph, if your flute has succeeded with its first breath, listen to all the light with which Debussy will infuse it.)

Before *L'Après midi* was finished, Debussy was already embarked upon *Pelléas et Mélisande*, the background to every foreground completion from 1892 on till its own, in a sudden rush for its première in 1902. The progress of this opera, whose plot is a symbolist gloss upon/dilution of *Tristan*'s, is marked by an ever-more conscious rejection of his previously unabashed Wagnerism, and acknowledgement of a devotion to its aesthetic and stylistic opposite in the songs and *Boris Godunov* of Musorgsky. This realignment can be heard in two song-sets of the *Pelléas* decade: four *Proses lyriques* (1892–3) to his own rather arty texts, music only intermittently engaging; and three *Chansons de Bilitis* (1897) to words by his friend Pierre Louÿs, equally precious but, in their concentration and sureness of tone, conducive to a high point of French *mélodie*, evolving a world of quasi-antique Hellenism, delicately (no. 1) or intensely (no. 2) erotic, wonderfully evoking (no. 3) a Pan/Faun hedonism lost under the snows of a later age.

But the principal achievement after *L'Après-midi* is again

orchestral. The three *Nocturnes* were originally associated with Velásquez, entitled 'studies in grey' or *scènes au crépuscle*, for violin and orchestra, the first with strings only, the second with winds, the third tutti. No trace survives of a concertante in this endeavour of 1894–6: the *Nocturnes* as they now stand (1897–9) draw their visual inspiration from Whistler's Thames-impressions, themselves often entitled with the appellation from music. The pieces are as saturated in things seen as *L'Après-midi* in its unset poem. Debussy's compatriot painter-contemporaries also figure: this is the closest he comes to 'what some fools call Impressionism': the somewhat disingenuous later disclaimer is his own – he preferred 'reality' – 'the sound of the sea, the outline of a horizon, the wind in the leaves, the cry of a bird, set off complex impressions in us; and suddenly one of these memories surfaces, expressing itself in the language of music.' And so far as the particular 'language of music' is concerned here, Musorgsky to the fore: *Nuages* is inconceivable without him in general and one famous passage in particular; the central episode of *Fêtes* an outright replay from *Boris*; and the *Sirènes* have distinctly Russian-Orientalist contours.

'*Nuages* – the immutable sky, the slow melancholy procession of the clouds, fading away in shades of grey softly tinged with white'; the composer's own description; more specifically, born ('suddenly one of these memories surfaces') of the view as he'd crossed the Pont des Arts on a stormy day, clouds driven by the wind, a passing tug sounding its hooter. Procession of even dyads on woodwinds, their memorable pattern taken direct from the third song of Musorgsky's *Sunless* cycle, 'The noisy day is done'. The pattern poises, a cor anglais unmistakably sounds the hooter, texture thins into high soft strings over almost imperceptible drum-roll. Reopening, the dyads doubled in three octaves on divided strings and taken further – debt to Musorgsky already repaid. And so one could continue, catching every sonorous event as it forms and evanesces, gently replaced by the next. All such tiny details, of material, texture, instrumentation, articulation, can be implicitly compared with the painter's palette and the transference of its constituents to the canvas. The result, however, is not so much an impressionist picture in sound – the clouds, the light, the river, the tug – as their translation and transformation into an inward image more symbolic than representational: a model for what Debussy will later achieve in his oeuvre for piano with its wealth of evocative titles. This happens first and clearest with *Nuages*, and is continued in the *Nocturne* that follows.

Fêtes: 'the dancing rhythm with sudden flashes of light; then the procession – a dazzling evanescent vision – crosses and is merged with the festival day with its unchanging background, blending music and luminous dust in a cosmic vibration' – again the composer's own words: the piece also draws upon a surfacing memory, the Bois de Boulogne during holidays, its joyous thronging crowds, the band of the Garde Nationale approaching, appearing, passing out of sight and sound. The central procession comes in three rounds, first only its oom-pah accompaniment, bare fifths on drums, pizzicati cellos and basses, second harp, four bars; for the next four, first harp fills out the chord – by chance the *Tristan*-chord, but the episode *in toto* borrowed lock, stock and barrel from *Boris*: tick-tock, chime, animated figurines – the moment in Act II where the clock strikes the quarter, delighting and distracting the Imperial children, then, fifteen minutes later, intensifying their guilty father's hallucinations. These had been omitted from Rimsky-Korsakov's 'revision'; Debussy can only have known it from the original score. For all that the harmonic base derives from the un-omittable Coronation bells in Act I, this toy-recreation, with its regular pulsation and the miniature fanfares, is as exactly reproduced as the progression from *Sunless* that opens *Nuages*: Debussy the thieving magpie. No shame when the result is so captivating as here – all festive glory as the toys grow vibrant and life-sized.

The Sirens of the third *Nocturne* are represented by a wordless female chorus; their necessity often precludes performance of the triptych complete. Yet there's also a feeling, difficult to define, that this third panel isn't quite up to the first two. '*Sirènes* – the sea and its tireless innumerable movement; then, among waves silvered by the moon, one hears the mysterious siren-song as they laugh and pass on' – Debussy's own words, the picture inspiring a sonorous thesaurus of ripples, wave-formations, water-textures, subtle shifts of lighting within a narrow range from silver to gold.

Debussy's next sea-music, in *Pelléas et Mélisande*, will be finer-toned; and his next orchestral work, *La Mer*, devoted entirely to the sea, is an unequivocal masterpiece. But it's the opera that should come next here: composed alongside *L'Après-midi* and the *Nocturnes*, the longest-sustained effort of his life, central to his outlook, idiom, aesthetic: a ten-year prison sentence, obsessive and claustrophobic, from which the open physical exuberance of *La Mer* is manifestly an escape, mirrored in his personal circumstances – release from a constrictive first marriage, joyous start to a second.

Debussy had probably already read Maeterlinck's play, and considered it for an opera, on its publication in 1892: for sure he attended the first production the next year, and began work at once, with the fourth act, soon rejecting this premature essay – too Wagnerian – and returning to compose the whole from the start, revising Act IV when reached. Work on *Pelléas* occupied him throughout the rest of the decade and into the next: orchestration came last; then – practical necessity as the long-delayed première neared – April 1902 – adding orchestral interludes to enable scene-changes, almost up to the last minute. During the *Pelléas*-years come *L'Après-midi* and the *Nocturnes*, as described, fully achieved in his own idiom: the struggle to achieve the opera was a struggle to overcome Wagner; or rather, the Wagner within himself, so fruitful when directly acknowledged – the *Parsifal* of *La Demoiselle élue*, the *Tristan* of the Baudelaire-songs; so ambiguous, inhibiting, indeed inimical, when taken to the stage. His correspondence of these years bears witness to the urgency of the need to escape the tyranny of 'old Klingsor': the score itself shows the strain. His antidote to the Wagnerian 'poison' was principally Musorgsky: 'You're seeing *Boris* tonight?' he asked some visitors in later years; 'You'll find all *Pelléas* there.' But Strauss, also seeing *Pelléas* when it was safely produced, published, famous, exclaimed, 'But this is all *Parsifal*!' Both views are true: yet Debussy's opera remains unique, without equivalent for all its subsequent influence.

A disinterested observer might as well have said 'it's all *Tristan*'.

Maeterlinck's vague pre-Raphaelite 'Allemonde' lies within a Wagnerian ambience, and the story itself is a variant upon *Tristan*'s: for
externals only: it substitutes for love/death, the metaphysics of night/
day, the profound psychological probing into memory and the inner
life, a generalized gloomy fatalism; and underlying both plots is a
bourgeois tragedy of jealousy and adultery that might have been
treated realistically à la George Sand or even Flaubert. Wagner's
adaptation of the old romance swathes it in soul-reaching metaphysical poetry, Maeterlinck's 'minor Merovingian royalty' enact their
fate in atmospheric, enigmatic ambiguity. Both settings – Ireland/
Cornwall/Brittany, or simply 'Allemonde' – are but vaguely indicated
and might be transposed to other times and places (and in productions nowadays usually are).

Bare organum-like strings immediately establish 'long ago and
far away'. The curtain rises – deep in a forest, a well, a weeping girl:
enter an older man, gruff though not unkind – he's lost too. His
leading questions, her evasive answers; every word articulated with
the utmost sensitivity to speech-inflexions, and, behind the words,
to every unspoken hint and nuance. Leitmotifs employed, fugitive
and intuitive as in Wagner explicit and knowing. He frankly names
himself – Prince Golaud: she shyly confesses – Mélisande. They leave
together – give me your hand – oh don't touch me! No I won't
touch you; but come; the night will be very dark and cold. Tone,
coloration, pace, idiom, manner, all established with understated
restraint: utter newness, yet deep-saturated in its two inspiring
models, German and Russian.

And thus throughout, in every exchange between every personage as they gradually appear – the old king and his consort, the
young half-brother Pelléas; later the little boy – the royal family
of Allemonde with whom the strange young girl becomes fatally
involved. From the consistent norm some highlights stand out.
The close of Act I when the young man and the young girl are left
together on the seashore as night approaches, the wind rises, and
we sense the tiniest *soupçon* of mutual attraction. In Act II their
innocently flirtatious play at the fountain ended by the loss of her
wedding ring (she's now married to Prince Golaud): the close of

the same act when they've been sent by the unconsciously provocative husband to search for it by the seashore, knowing it won't be
there – the dark grotto suddenly lit up by the moon (one of the loveliest four bars in all music) revealing three decrepit paupers asleep,
but of course no ring. These moments reach their apogee early in
Act III, the celebrated scene where Mélisande at an upper turret
window combing her hair lets it loose upon the enraptured Pelléas
below. Thus enlinked, yet separate, their long duet far surpasses their
actual love-duet in the subsequent act. Golaud interrupts both –
first time, he nervily reprimands – stop playing around, you're just
children: second time, sword in hand, murder in heart, soon to be
successfully executed.

Other highpoints all involve the husband as principal focus:
Golaud leading his frightened half-brother through the castle vaults
to reveal the stagnating waters of death lying beneath the daily-
dying life of the inmates above. He means harm but represses it for
now, and the mood lightens as he guides Pelléas up to the sea-terrace
where the air is fresh, waters sparkle, children bathe, noonday bells
ring forth – every texture tried in *Sirènes* essentialized into radiance,
with more than a touch of gamelan in the pentatonic contours and
layered orchestration, harps and glockenspiel prominent, *La Mer*'s
Jeux de vagues on the not-too-distant horizon. Dark counterpart,
Golaud's mounting suspicions, tainted by jealousy of his not-quite-
rival, compelling his little son to spy by night on the not-quite-
lovers: a frightening scene, its music owing equally to Klingsor
goading Kundry, and Boris with his real children, then confronting
the apparition of the child he'd had slain.

All this is classic art: reservations insinuate in the *actual* love-
duet, as mentioned, slightly faded from the start, its violent conclusion taking recourse to corny melodrama, almost cardboard. More
general, a sense that in the last act the atmosphere has slackened.
There are lovely touches, and the dying fall of Mélisande's death is
moving. But the opera's unique calibre lies earlier: an accomplished
Debussy-ist might have managed Act V and much of Act IV. When
Pelléas was in its first season a cult, the young Turks – *Les Apaches*,
Ravel among them – would conduct the most ordinary conversations

in the manner of the *maître*'s masterpiece. Here and there it sounds as though they were still at it.

A graver reservation concerns the orchestral interludes. Debussy is consummate with words even when the temperature lowers, but the interludes, last minute additions, veer between flimsy make-shift and a portentousness alien to the work's triumph of restraint. *Parsifal* predominates everywhere, sometimes barely mitigated by the magical transformation of this source achieved in *La Damoiselle* and surfacing again in *Jeux*. One such place is almost blatant: Richard Strauss was not so wrong.

The sole completed opera was a hard act to follow, in the end impossible. 'I have this curious need to leave my works unfinished' Debussy wrote in a letter of 1909. A scholarly study of his theatrical ventures from the earliest years to the last lists some sixty projects. A famous handful are realized, however unevenly – one opera, three ballets, and the grandiose D'Annunzio *Mysterium*. Some are of course adaptations, usually for dancing, of existing concert-scores. Predictably, there are passing fancies that flicker briefly and go out for ever ('Debussy's score was never started' becomes a familiar formula). Surprising is the large number of apparently serious propositions upon which energies were expended and hopes built – scenarios crafted, texts written and rewritten, contracts signed, money taken, music commenced – ideas that advanced well beyond the impulsive and sometimes, as with the two Poe operas, occupied him to obsession-point over many years, and yet still petered out, *sans issue*. 'Apparently serious' – but for the most part such clear non-starters as to be difficult to reconcile with a Debussy of delicate literary discrimination. There is a remote period charm in the decadent pseuderie of *Les Noces de Sathan*, *Le Chevalier d'or* (a 'Rosicrucian pantomime'), the *Drame Cosmogonique*, *Siddhartha*, *No-ja-li* and so forth. Mixed in with such trash are several themes from great literature – *Eugene Onegin*, *King Lear*, *Don Juan*, *Tristan*, the *Oresteia* all figure. Their incongruity for his purposes must have struck the composer; the *Tristan* at least lingered on for some years, and was publicly announced.

But there *are* some genuine might-have-beens. On the basis of what we know already, the *Axel* project of the late 1880s, the Louÿs collaborations of the 1890s, a piece of pure phantagasm by St-Pol-Roux (1911), would all seem cause for regret. The operatic version of *As You Like It* sounds enchanting (intensest interest 1902–4, but Debussy had considered incidental music back in 1886 and was to again in the last months of his life); while two Valéry projects, a ballet *Orphèe* (*c*.1895) and an opera *Amphion* (*c*.1900), cause a real pang of loss: beautiful and original in conception, beautifully suited to Debussy's sensibility yet suggestive, unlike the Poe-fetishes of later, unhappier years, of drawing from it notes he never otherwise would have sounded. The same goes for the various projects with Victor Segalen. Even the successful exteriorization of *Pelléas* and *Jeux* is shown to be accidental, enhancing these works' aura of fragility and specialness. One senses between the lines what it must have been like, at once blessed and cursed with a vision of some as-yet-intangible relation between music (itself only slowly emerging and of its nature infinitely fugitive) and a stage far removed from the norm of footlights, grease-paint and projection of over-life-sized personality, and then in pursuit of this vision to be caught in a succession of perpetually hopeful collaborations, idealistic, yet ever-more devious as free fancy meshes with expectant impresarios, anxious publishers, aggravated performers, as the failed delivery-dates and broken contracts mount up – all this incurred in pursuit of the pressing need for money to sustain a profoundly uncongenial way of life. The great 'normal' theatre-composers – Mozart, Wagner, Verdi, Strauss, Puccini, Stravinsky, Britten – appear almost vulgar by comparison, not in their commercial acumen so much as the way that their theatrical ventures, however visionary and rarified, are so robustly exteriorized to accord with the status quo.

A few words about the *Mysterium – Le Martyre de Saint Sébastien: Mystère en cinq actes*. The invitation to provide incidental music for D'Annunzio's whole-evening extravaganza on the life and death of St Sebastian arrived late in 1910 for a première the next year. 'Incidental' is not the *mot juste*: the piece is in every respect lavish, and its score continuous, requiring the largest forces, choral and orchestral, that Debussy ever employed, and longer than *Pelléas*. In addition, the genre is hybrid, the taste dubious – the title-role danced and spoken; and by a woman! D'Annunzio's text, lurid and meretricious, makes Maeterlinck for all his mannerism and occasional portentousness appear a model of style and restraint.

Debussy's score was composed at speed: as with his previous theatrical emergency, the orchestral interludes for *Pelléas*, his principal recourse is to the music of *Parsifal*, more appropriate here given its congruity to *Le Martyre* in plot and subject. *Le Martyre* is soaked in Wagner's score. Sometimes the borrowing is flagrant – the sequence where the sexually ambiguous Saint enacts Christ's Crucifixion is substantially a recomposition of the Act I Transformation-music where Amfortas's personal guilt, spiritual anguish, physical torment, rise into the woeful cry of his whole Order. And there are plentiful smaller borrowings, flecks of memory no doubt involuntary yet also compulsive: for all his mockery Debussy hasn't escaped 'old Klingsor', knows it, and maybe, deep down, doesn't want to.

Wholly positive, however, is *Parsifal*'s presence in Debussy's theatrical venture the next year, the ballet *Jeux*, composed for Diaghilev, featuring Nijinsky as dancer, choreographer and author of the scenario. The wondrous creature had created a *succès de scandale* as Debussy's *faune* in 1912; the première of *Jeux* in May 1913 was a flop, utterly overshadowed by the same company/dancer-choreographer's next *succès de scandale*, the première of the *Rite of Spring* later the same month. Stravinsky's masterpiece went on to conquer the world as a concert-work; Debussy's score never made it as a ballet, and only slowly came into its own in the concert-hall – equally a masterpiece: with its near namesake *Jeux de vagues*, right at the crest of the oeuvre, a crown-jewel in Music's Empire.

Nijinsky's scenario is 'idiotic' – Debussy's word in private, omitted in his press-statement: 'in this scenario there is a park, a tennis-court, the chance meeting of two girls and a young man seeking a lost ball, a mysterious nocturnal landscape, and something sinister in the darkening shadows.' Nijinsky's diary equivocates: Diaghilev, it seems, had created the 'plot' for Nijinsky's Faun, and now in *Jeux* wanted to enact his fantasy-life with his real-life lover – two boys and an older man, love-making *à trois*. Nijinsky records his disgust at what could anyway never be represented on-stage – 'Debussy did not like the subject either, but he was paid 10,000 gold francs for this ballet and therefore had to finish it.' Whatever the truth the situation is ambiguous enough to justify the composer's 'something sinister'. But the main mystery is how a scenario so flimsy and vacuous can inspire a major work by a major composer. Somehow, despite the doubts (and notwithstanding the 10,000 gold francs) the music, complex and absolutely fresh, was written quickly and without requiring the collaboration indispensable to getting *Le Martyre* out on time, and had helped with other orchestral projects of these years – the duff ballet-successor *Khamma* (also 1912) and *Gigues* commencing the triptych of *Images*. 'Idiotic' or not, the scenario is followed in every detail by every aspect of the score, from construction in the large to every twist and turn of fine proliferating detail. Listening to *Jeux* following the choreographic instructions is a revelation of the reason why the music is constructed the way it is, the cause of its every gesture and duration and change of colour and mood. Debussy has captured with astonishing success all the subtle fluctuations that his plot and characters demand.

> The curtain rises on an empty park. A tennis ball falls – a young man, dressed for tennis, racquet held high, leaps across the stage, then disappears. From backstage left two young girls appear, timorous and inquisitive. For a moment they seem to look for nothing but a place to exchange their secrets. One dances alone, then the other in her turn; they cease, abashed by the sound of rustling leaves. The young man, backstage left, seems to be hiding and following their movements through the branches – he stops in front of them. They want to run away but he gently leads them back and invites them to start again. He begins to dance – the first girl runs towards him – they dance together. He wants to kiss her – she escapes – he tries again – she again escapes – then yields, and joins him.

And so on. So, what is the substance behind the silliness, the flimsiness, the 'idiocy': the content within the void? It can be elicited by a surprising but undoubted Parsifalian context to his work on the ballet, and then by the music itself. A letter written during the composition gives the clue – 'I'm thinking of that orchestral colour which seems illuminated from behind, so marvellously effected in *Parsifal*!' Whatever his reservations, sometimes childishly resentful, about Wagner's last opera in general, his praise for its orchestral magic is unbounded – 'unique and unexpected, noble and strong ... one of the finest monuments of sound ever raised to the serene glory of music'. It shone as a touchstone, an almost miraculous pre-vision of the new sonorities he sought to recreate as his own. In particular, the area where opera and ballet overlap in setting and in subject: Klingsor's magic garden, populous and odorous with Flower-maidens whose sole purpose is sensuous-sensual seduction of likely male victims, one especially; and the park where the cast is reduced to only three. Wagner's scene, after an introduction in common time, all palpitation, flurry, expectancy, is a waltz-sequence; first all frisk-flirtatious as the handsome virgin-hero appears after doing battle with the girls' lovers; then languid, luscious, amorously caressing, after a brief salvo of animation settling into indolent ease, intensifying with arabesques of melody and gorgeous harmonic and orchestral coloration (fragrance too, in the words) – to all of which he's by no means indifferent. Ever more voluptuous, they proffer their burgeoning charms; then, finally, skittishly alert as they quarrel over his; till, at the last moment, he growing half-angered, Kundry's voice is heard from within their foliage, calling his name, heard for the first time in the opera named after him.

Jeux too is a *valse*-sequence, set within a framework establishing place/time/mood, and with *intermèdes* as the action might require. The waltz-modes are yet more variegated than the Flower-maidens' waltzes; an individual arabesque motif prevails, unmissably remem-bered from source to homage, amid the general wealth of decora-tive vegetative tendrils recalling less explicitly Kundry's seductive wiles in her preceding scene with her (tor)mentor and the subse-quent scene where she deploys them for her victim's destruction; and sometimes moments of unforgettable harmony are repro-duced; all these within the instrumental sonority, that 'orchestral

colour which seems lit from behind' for which Debussy's admiration couldn't be higher.

Differences are also paramount. The Flower-maiden scene is but
a stage in the opera's long allegorical/emblematic/narrative Quest
towards understanding, compassion, healing, integration of carnal
and spiritual in the individual and the community: the ballet has no
such past and future – it hovers at just this stage alone – the Bower
of Bliss, the Garden of Earthly Delights, are never abandoned; its
'moral' (if any) is *carpe diem* – taste and enjoy while you can, now,
while it lasts; pleasure will fade like the flowers, and so will you;
seize the moment. The two works are at opposite poles aesthetically
and goal-wise even as they meet in the garden at the centre. Wagner
is all content, subject, message; Debussy all evasion – 'but of course
[he wrote with regard to *Jeux*'s being *risqué*] in a ballet any hint
of immorality escapes through the feet of the *danseuse* and ends
in a pirouette'. Plot is reduced to a nothing, characters are ciphers,
subject-matter wholly latent. But the score's 'manifest content' –
the rhythmic delicacy, the wonderful harmony, the proliferation of
subtly-suggestive melodic arabesque, the consummate radiance and
liveliness of the orchestra – in a word, the *music* – actually holds,
diffused from depths to surfaces in breathtaking equipoise, the
meaning whose explicit utterance would destroy it. Debussy's extraordinary achievement here is to hold sexual thralldom, the urge to
submit to desire yet the desire to escape, the yearning for redemption, healing, integration – everything so powerful and painful in
Wagner's subject – in lucid suspension. All this content is present
but not presented – there by subtle association with and assimilation of his inspiring source. And Debussy's subject – if one is to
gloss crassly 'something sinister in the darkening shadows' – is sexual
pleasure (im)pure and (un)simple. Here the ballet is fixed where
the opera moves on – no sublimation or renunciation – the real
thing-in-itself, unpalliated and unashamed till the second tennis-
ball bounces onto the stage. Next stop, the *Jardin du sommeil d'amour*
from Messiaen's *Turangalîla* – itself a homage, this one declared in
full, to *Tristan*.

*

Back to the concert-halls for *La Mer* (1902–5): subtitled 'three symphonic sketches'; César Franck resurrected and excelled, an ultimate
fruit of the French cyclic symphony, transformed by Impressionism
and leaping into the twentieth century. The painter in question here
is Debussy's revered Turner; behind him, 'the sea itself': he'd been at
one point in early youth intended for a sailor, and the sea remained a
passion throughout his life. This great work is so deservedly admired
and enjoyed that I must confine myself to generalities. The outer
movements give the lie to Debussy as pale, effete, washy: the first
culminates in a brass chorale ending *fff* before its long diminish
to *p*; to return to its full potency at the end of the third. Between
comes *Jeux de vagues*, 'impressionism' at its zenith, quicksilver volatility of timbres, momentous, flecks and glints, then Tritons blasting
their conches, naiads creating the waves. Barely thematic, a play of
sea-surfaces, till the mighty paragraphs of undertow begin to swell
far beneath, the combination built over an unchanging bass-note,
anchoring a magnificent climax as undertow penetrates middle then
top of the multiple-layered texture, before, as usual, the poetic disappearing close.

   The next orchestral work from this, his most productive period,
is a triptych of *Images* evoking three countries through a partial
employment of their national musics. Debussy is no folklorist, and
only becomes a sort of nationalist later, under pressure of patriotic sentiment when his country is invaded and its culture threatened. *Ibéria* is at the centre of the *Images*, a triple-panel within the
triptych. It's notorious that the composer barely set foot in the Spain
he evokes so often – in many piano-works too – and so marvellously:
and famous, that Manuel de Falla claimed this music captured the
essence and soul of a land as exotic to its composer as the Far East
and the remote past. The scheme, as much poetic as architectural,
is Day; Night; Next Morning. Day – *Par les rues et par les chemins* –
brilliant with guitar-imitations and real castanets, vibrant and open
for the hot dry dusty main views, suggestive and slightly sinister for
the secret alleys and courtyards; with fascinating layered heterophony, round upon round of increasing complexity, issuing in a blaze
of midday fanfares, up to return of opening, down to dusty dusk.

Les parfums de la nuit exactly what it says, languorous and voluptuous, working in snatches of *La Soirée dans Grenade* from the first set
of piano *Estampes* alongside transformed themes from *Les rues et les
chemins* – *Ibéria* too is cyclic; the impress of Franck remains living,
now entirely without any presence of his style and idiom. Gorgeous
parfumé climax, long lingering exhalation, poetic overlap into *Le
Matin d'un jour de fête*, night-bells and evaporating sultriness alternate with reviving vitality – a distant march, its material borrowed
from another Spanishy piano-piece, *La Sérénade interrompue* from
the first book of *Préludes*. Guitars, earlier latent, now explicit – half
the strings must hold their instruments in guitar-position the more
vibrantly to pluck them. Tumult waxes ever brighter and more vivacious, is quelled momentarily by a street fiddler, audibly jeered off:
as animation returns the movement seems somewhat to lose its grip,
grow scrappy and cursory, though the trombone slides in the very
last bars are worth waiting for.

Gigues, preceding *Ibéria* in the triptych, is its perfect complement, cool, rainy, melancholy; its original title was the paradoxical
Gigues tristes. It evokes land- and moodscapes equally unknown to
its composer except in imagination, either Scotland or the north
of England – no one is sure, though the piece's principal material
is undoubted, the Northumbrian reel 'The Keel Row', outlined in a
beautiful slow introduction which, for want of a better word, must
be called 'impressionistic', and subsequently basis of the piece's body,
a march rather chirpy than military. Before it gets going, the *triste*, a
wistful slow *gigue* on oboe d'amore, whose plaintive timbre evokes
bare hills and heather glens under misty wetness. Then the march,
then resumption of slow introduction, to end on a rainy-luminous
major third, all poised for the imminent eruption of dazzling dusty-
dry Spain.

Rondes de Printemps, third in the triptych, is also its principal glory.
The folksong for Debussy's evocation of France is *Nous n'irons plus
au bois*, already used in *Jardins sous la pluie* from the piano *Estampes*:
and the shape, as the title indicates, is a round-dance/rondo, episodic
and kaleidoscopic yet firmly directed in unforced exuberance
towards a clear-defined goal. Before this, lavish variety of textures

from brightness almost raucous to delicacy almost refined out of existence – '*léger et fantasque*', the passages in 15/8 recalling those in *Fêtes*; a moment marked '*avec charme*'; a gently murmurous still centre, '*doux et flottant*', all a-shimmer over softly rocking drums and cello pizzicato, ending in a pentatonic mirage of boundless orchards in their April blossoming. The prevailing mode, though, is of vitality, energy, gaiety, rising sap; a spring-passage at the other end of the spectrum from Stravinsky's *Rite*, all a-quiver with new life.

It was in the year of *Rondes de Printemps* – 1909 – that Debussy's cancer was first diagnosed. Not yet debilitating: nevertheless he is, in his last nine years, under the shadow of death; and despite some triumphs, notably *Jeux*, there is a sense of fatigue, eking out, mannerism, self-repetition, in the music of this time, until the sudden, extraordinary, renewal of powers in his reaction to his country's peril when Germany invaded in 1914. The second book of twelve *Préludes* for piano (1910–13) show the decline: amid some gems and a couple of marvels – *Brouillards*, *La Terrasse des audiences au clair de lune* – lie some makeweights and some pure sillinesses unworthy of a great artist in his prime. So too with another chance-venture, *La Boîte à joujoux*, inspired by his daughter, aged eight in 1913, the year of its composition, that he couldn't trouble to orchestrate for himself. Also of 1913, the three Mallarmé-settings with piano, where one might expect a renewal of empathy: pale and thin after the sumptuous bloom of *L'Après-midi*. By 1914 it could seem that Claude Debussy was a spent force.

So the recovery of 1915 is all the more wonderful – a complete return to top form, with exploration of hitherto undiscovered terrain, in a substantial work for two pianos (June); two chamber sonatas, first of an intended group of six (July); and two books of *Études* for solo piano, six in each (August–September) that codify, surpass, transcend all his previous keyboard output for all its richness and variety. *En blanc et noir*, the two-piano work: energy, edge, power, almost without precedent in the oeuvre and in the central of its three movements doing things he'd never previously attempted. First movement is marked '*avec emportement*' – 'transported' – a

whirlwind torrent of physical drive, a sublimated dance, albeit no
known dance-prototype, suggested rather by the inscription at the
start – who sits tight and doesn't dance confesses basely to some
disgrace: perhaps in this war-urged work an oblique regret that,
sick and aged fifty-three, its composer couldn't expect to join the
fight to defend his invaded *patrie*. The two keyboards assail each
other upwards and downwards, then agree to blend and collabor-
ate as the *emportement* lyricizes; then grows *scherzando*, not without
malice, even impertinence, before four bars' soft oscillation swells
into return of opening, soon taking new directions, sighing, melting,
playful *without* malice, rich and sonorous in fuller chordal textures:
suddenly rudely awoken by their melodic outline only, banged out
in unison by both players – Debussy the Cubist, indeed the Vorticist, edge against edge – snatch of opening now liquidly gentle,
the angry unison again, then its transformation into amorous
suavity that could have come out of *Jeux*, all these boldly juxtaposed
without transitions. Opening idea and texture again, tonally miles
from home and dulcet where before it was hard, cooling into return
of the *scherzando*, completely transformed – whimsical, quizzical,
with cheeky little tootles on piano-as-flageolet. Mellow warmth,
suddenly jeered off by a brief moment marked *strident*, vanishing at
once into the depths of the pianos – soft ostinati; miles above them
the pert tootle of the flageolet, twice almost turning into a parody
of a military bugle (whose serious time will come). Rapid crescendo
and rise from the depths to four terrific bars which must have given
the work its title – Piano 2 in fistfuls of white notes, thrice; in the
gaps, Piano 1 on the black notes, joined for the fourth bar by the
second player, before they plunge together into a recapitulation
of opening, right key, exact at first, soon mounting to *appassionato*
climax on material previously cantabile, remaining *emporté* all the
way to just prior to the end – sudden soft opening – texture, alien
key, rapidly swelling and righting to triumphal close on a *positive*
almost unique in the composer's oeuvre.

Now the negative: elegy, sombre killing-fields; pastorale and
balsam; battle-scene; moment of Victory; pastorale; apotheosis: a
preposterous scenario, its explicit programme, its un-reserve and

obviousness, its potential crassness and tackiness all unsuspected in this of all composers, yet executed with the passion and power of total commitment. The elegy is explicit in the dedication to the memory of a friend 'killed by the enemy March 3 1915', and an epitaph from Villon's *Ballade contre les ennemis de la France*. Dark brooding sonorities underpinned with soft drum-taps; sudden explosion of harsh dissonance; the drums continue soft, their C against sustained F♯; above both, a brave bugle sounds, transformed from tootling tin-whistle in the first movement, swallowed in second dissonance acrid as the first but now very soft. Its bass-note now G♯, but the pastoral ditty above it remains in C – a touch of *gigue triste* on oaten stop, enveloped then in first dissonance, now soft, over its F♯. Now an innocent wisp of neutral rusticity, yielding to calm banks of common chords, serene and salving, so close to Vaughan Williams' evocation of French war-landscapes in his *Pastoral Symphony* as to suggest acquaintance with Debussy's prototype. Returning, the innocent unaccompanied line turns sombre-harmonized, alternating with the cloud-capp'd serenity, then expands into grief contained within cool, then swells into sudden soft bell-sounds, simultaneously high and clear, deep and tolling, backdrop to the *gigue triste*.

Now the battle-scene: deep tolling retained below; the drum-taps return; a snide little sarcasm from *Petrushka* (a work for which Debussy's admiration knew no bounds); dull flurries of smoke, then the high clear bells on top. The menacing enemy nears, furtive, mechanized, ugly – the first line of *Ein' feste Burg*; the sarcastic gesturing grows satirical; more bells, high and low, obscured by billowing smoke, as the chorale's last line is heard, coming closer. The texture busies; amid it, the brave bugle-signal; Boche chorale again, now marked *rude* and coarsely doubled in seconds and sevenths. The fanfare strengthens, the foul atmosphere solidifies into a dissonant tremolo: chorale-lines not actually from the original are stamped out, then its original closing line; smoke billows up into change of key – flats to sharps that can immediately be appreciated by the ear, with a change of momentum and sonority and mood equally appreciable – *joyeux* – as the brave bugle asserts itself: the gallant French army advances with blithe courage to a blinding visionary moment of Victory – the tattoo full and brilliant in C-major again, though the harmony is ambiguous and the second statement already softer than the first, and the moment continues to diminish all the way, down to return of the grieving music, then the bells low and high, and a straightened-out reminiscence of the pastoral-strain, followed by the *gigue triste* itself. Inspired closing bars of apotheosis, grand and severe piled-up thirds in contrary motion, powerful lunging bass, the bugles now trumpets, thrice, and the very end ferociously emphatic.

The third movement is quite different again, an escape from close-up depiction of brutality and its defeat into a world of light and freshness, in hopeful expectation of a future when 'the war to end wars' will eventually end: dedicated '*à mon ami Igor Stravinsky*' and headed with a line from Charles d'Orléans that Debussy had set back in 1908 for *a cappella* chorus – 'Winter thou'rt nowt but a villain'. The gaiety and euphoria of *Rondes de Printemps* are renewed in these pellucidly luminous sounds, all arabesque diaphony.

As remarkable, the twelve *Études* of later the same year and the same creative upsurge. Background here is Debussy's agreement to replace unavailable or unacceptable German editions of the Chopin studies for his French publisher. The war's immediate impact is here reduced to a piece of hack-work whose upshot is anything but hackneyed. His boyhood love of Chopin was rekindled, resulting in a new direction to his body of solo piano music that had begun to show a dispiriting sense of self-repetition in recent years.

The spirit that fires this upsurge is seen plain in a letter of early August 1915 – 'I want to work not so much for myself as to give proof, however small it may be, than even if there were 30 million Boches, French thought will not be destroyed.' As he concluded he wrote to his publisher (on 30 September) 'last night at midnight, I copied out the last notes of the études. Ouf! The most intricate Japanese print is child's play compared with the notation of some of these pages; but I am pleased, it is good work.' And in retrospect, writing to a friend in mid-October, he can say

I was able once again to think in musical terms, which I had not
been able to do over the last year. It is certainly not essential that
I write music, but it is all I am able to do more or less compe-
tently. I must humbly admit to the feeling of latent death within
me. Accordingly I write like a madman or like one who is condemned to die the next morning.

That December came the first operation for cancer, which in spite
of relative success made clear what had not been so before – that
the disease was terminal.

Even the composer himself might be surprised to produce twelve
Études for piano with no extra-musical connotations. After the pretty
salon-pieces of his teens and twenties – a mazurka, a nocturne, a
reverie, two arabesques, etc. – it is predominantly evocative, illustrative, poetic. The trajectory runs via the Watteau–Verlaine-tinted
Suite bergamasque and the harder-edged Baroque recreation of *Pour le
piano*, to the great breakthrough of the *Estampes* (evoking Java, Spain
and Parisian back-gardens under rain), the two sets of *Images* (water,
bells, more Orientalia, including lacquer goldfish), *Children's Corner*
(his daughter's moods and toys), and the two books of *Préludes*
(twenty-four impressions ranging from nature-studies stormy and
serene to character-studies serious and parodistic; places, moods,
landscapes, heather, mist, a Greek vase, a submerged cathedral). Be
the source a postcard from India or Spain, a line from Baudelaire, a
phantasm from myth or Dickens, a reminiscence of the minstrels at
a London music-hall, or the ever-deepening reflections of sound and
light in still water, the result is to render such things into a musical
object that is only rarely superficially pictorial. Rather, Debussy
meditatively penetrates to the essence of what sets him off, achieving a spiritualized rather than a depictive likeness. That this is also
true of his orchestral works from *L'Après-midi d'un faune* through to
Jeux tends to confirm one's sense of this artist as being unfitted for,
uninterested in, abstract musical thought. Or, since all music must
also achieve this whatever else its aim, one could say that, in order to,
he needs to start out from a subject or an object of contemplation.

The exceptions are interesting, and all highly germane to the composer's final efflorescence into études and sonatas: First, the Baroque forms of *Pour le piano* – prelude, sarabande, toccata; from the *Images* come *Mouvement*, another *perpetuum mobile* like the toccata, and *Hommage à Rameau*, another sarabande, this one paying explicit tribute to a great compatriot and predecessor; from the *Préludes*, *Les Tierces alternées*, a real étude *avant la lettre* whose title gives nothing beyond a musico-technical description different from that conveyed by menuet, sarabande, passepied, etc., let alone *Le Vent dans la plaine* or *Des pas sur la neige*!

Not that a complete technical control of the ten fingers is not required for Debussy's wholly evocative pieces. *Jardins sous la pluie* needs perfect arpeggii; *Poissons d'or* could be entitled 'étude for trills, *tremolandi* and decorations'; *La Cathédrale engloutie* an 'étude for opposed sonorities' or '*pour les accords*'. Examples could be multiplied; and virtually every Debussy piano-piece prior to the *Études* is a study in *l'art de toucher le pianoforte*. What is new in the actual studies themselves (though not wholly new, as we've seen) is the severe concentration upon point of execution; technical problems are now isolated from descriptive connotations or intentions, to become their own *raison d'être*. This, and the related matter of treating a single interval, making a piece in order to explore its properties (this, too, not utterly without precedent in his output). Taken together, and with the intensity of these explorations added in, the extreme absorption in (say) repeated notes within staccato and legato, equally with what happens when music is built around fourths – what you can do with a fourth, what a fourth makes you do – the upshot amounts to a new thrust in Debussy's work. It is his summa: where, naturally, there will be nothing whatsoever concerning fugue, canon, variation, sonata. But there will be the quintessence of a long experience of a very particular way with piano textures, with conjunction and repetition and diversification, extension and curtailment, with harmony and colour – with everything that Claude Debussy brought to an output that remains unique whatever the eclecticism of its manifold sources: of, in a word, his style; presented as a sort of codified yet passionate last-minute essence. The unexpected bonus is the music's beauty, emotional

depth, and new-made inventiveness; just when the well had seemed
to run dry, its waters reappear clearer, deeper, charged with the
elixir of life. The immediate background is a resurgence of inventive energy after depression and fallowness and despite illness, in a
context of heightened feeling because of enemy action not just at
large but also at his cultural heart, whose effect is to fire his pride
in his own country and its heritage. Then, more apropos yet, to be
soaked again by accident of war in the Chopin that had delighted
him so as a boy. After dallying between these twin loyalties for the
Études' dedication – he asked his publisher in a letter of 28 August
1915 which of the two, '*si admirables devineurs*' both, it should be,
F. Chopin or F. Couperin? – he plumped eventually for nostalgia
(and, surely, the deeper musical impulse). And inscribed them '*à la
memoire de Frédéric Chopin*'.

Even so, the *Études* are uneven. Here, two indubitable highlights:
Étude viii) *pour les agréments* is the set's most precious jewel. Debussy,
lover of the 'divine arabesque', here gives 'ornament' a whole new
dimension: even for Couperin and Chopin, the *Études*' twin deities,
decoration exists to be applied to underlying contour; for Debussy
its true meaning lies deep within the music's surface. The piece is
volatile and quicksilver beyond all its precedents. Already the first
bar suggests an unwritten blues by Gershwin, and there is both
intuitive cunning and intellectual daring in the rapid succession of
completely different ideas with no kind of 'discourse' between them:
two bars of downward guitar-strum are followed by two of glittering gold cadenza as out of *Poissons d'or*, then by two that might have
come direct from *Reflets dans l'eau*. Then after the first 'flute/viola/
harp' pastorale, an extraordinary three bars of singing bass, murmuring middle yielding to simpler off-beat choral accompaniment
for airy melody high in the treble. This texture yields in turn to
three bars of great intricacy with an almost jazz double-bass left
hand ('*léger et dansant*'); even these three are not continuous texturally, and when, after the curtailed return of the trio-sonata *galan-
terie* the deep bass melody returns from before, its accompaniment
is reimagined in rocking chords, rapidly spread, '*souple et ondoyant*';
the former airy top here briefly joins the bass, and the whole melts

away into a bar of pungent Spanish minstrels, a *sérénade interrom-pue* by two bars of cadenza poised upon the piece's core, nine bars of such lavish opulence and dazzling changes of mode-colour as to leave one breathless with pleasure. This too fades, and the opening eight bars return unchanged, up to the downward guitar-plunge, and the flash of goldfish, now extended into a cadenza which lands us surprisingly but inevitably upon the F major in which the piece had begun, now shining high in the treble (fifths only) and glowing deep in the bass.

Étude xi) *pour les arpèges composées*: an earlier attempt at this étude exists and has been published with a conjectural conclusion by the Debussy scholar and pianist Roy Howat. It is a sweet, pretty piece, but spineless, and completely effaced by the final result, with which it has almost nothing in common. They share only the ultra-refined delicacy of sound; but from the start the replacement is devoted to a purpose – *composed arpeggii* – rather than generalized rippling up and down. The germinating figure is a thrice-repeated right-hand quintuplet, followed in bar 2 by a version as a sextuplet, with added inner melody, against fours in the left hand so fourthy as to seem escaped from the study in fourths. 'Composed arpeggii' – the odd designation turns out to be a study in ornamentation and decoration and their fascinating ambiguity, to complement no. viii) and its *agréments*. Wholly unforetold in the earlier draft is a complete comic-heroic/lyric Spanish scene where we see the young lovers, the elderly husband, the pompous town clerk, the fussing duenna – the most delicious of all Debussy's many such episodes, right through his career from the *Chanson espagnol* of 1883 to the Violin Sonata of 1916–17. Neither Ravel nor Falla would have been capable of such ambiguity and subtlety of shading as these twenty-one bars contain – all the way from *lumineux* to *elegantamente, un poco pomposo* – amorous and chivalric, yet also absurd, satirical with affection and without caricature. After the Spanish intermezzo (which has precious little bearing on '*les arpèges composées*' though sporting two *giocoso* bars encrusted with ridiculously affected '*agréments*') back to liquidity – and indeed the *poissons d'or* flash and gleam in this piece too, more particularly in its first section. Cleverest of all is the delicious final page which manages to fuse *plaza* and plash, alternating bars of both with characteristically volatile elasticity.

Spanishry also figures in two of the three 'Sonatas for various instruments', first half of a projected set of six, then to be followed by an ensemble-piece employing all the combined forces. Their title-pages engraved in pastiche eighteenth-century style, the composer boldly inscribed as '*musicien français*', makes explicit identification with his country in its troubles, though there is no reference to them in actual musical imagery. The dedication is to his wife, and the project is intimate – a stripping down with merciless economy to essentials: as he wrote during work on the sonatas, 'how much has to be explored and discarded before one reaches the naked flesh of emotion!' Once considered evidence of a sad decline, the sonatas' place in estimation and the repertoire is now assured: Debussy is again on to something new for him, which happens to fit well into the changing temperature and aims of the times – the general international move towards cool impersonality, objectivity, classicism, in reaction to the perfervours of music's most excessive epoch.

Yet it has to be admitted that decline is manifest here: from one work to the next the impulse audibly tires, material goes anaemic, the effort forced. The Violin Sonata comes latest (1916–17); its first movement frail, limpid, diaphanous, but as an *invalide*; the ensuing serenade and the whirling finale a second serve from the Spanish-harlequin brew fresher and stronger in the first sonata, for cello. The second, for flute, viola and harp, is almost as fragile. Occasionally the listener senses what its composer means by 'the naked flesh of emotion': more often the sense of 'what must be explored and discarded' prevails. A fuller potential for the unique instrumental combination reaches its surprising and wonderful fruition in the sound-world of Britten's first 'Church Parable' *Curlew River*, wherein sources Japanese, Balinese, European plainsong, fuse into an acoustic amplification of what Debussy had happened upon, with no immediate progeny, a half-century before.

The trio sonata's middle movement is a wraith of a menuet, linking neatly into a living *commedia dell'arte* presence in the Cello

Sonata. This work's principal intonation however is Spanish: grave *risoluto* start, for piano declamatory, then florid for cello; then melancholy for both – almost footsteps in the snow, Bilitis seeking in vain the deserted shrine of Pan and the nymphs: then dry and sandy up to grand return, now shared by both players, of the opening declamation: floridity returns, then melancholy, this latter combining with memory of initial grandeur, disappearing into a perfectly placed *tierce de Picardie*, the movement's sole goal. *Sérénade – Pierrot fâché avec la lune* – droll grotesquerie, volatile and capricious, cousin across the battleground of the lighter vein in Schoenberg's *Pierrot lunaire*: leading direct into the finale. Spanish-ish again – *léger et nerveux*, dry, with guitar-effects, clean and open, its high spirits veiled but unforced, till a brief interpolation – slow, richly sonorous, heart-rending in its sadness: Debussy's words while composing the next sonata apply yet more fully to this place – 'so terribly melancholy that I can't say whether one should laugh or cry. Perhaps both?' Laughter returns with return of animation that can even manage to gather in the *triste* material, before a penultimate moment – cello alone, declamatory – then a precipitate close with guitar-pizzicato.

Triste, too, that Debussy continued to be preoccupied during these years, and right on to the end, with theatrical projects that had no future, though, in the case of the two one-act operas on stories by Poe, a long and hapless past. Two ballet-schemes – Orientalist *No-ja-li* and Verlaine/Watteau *Fêtes galantes* (both overlap from 1912–15) – yielded some musical sketches: and the idea for an opera on *As You Like It*, dating right back to his youth in Rome as Prix-holder, was still active in 1917 only months before his death early the next year. A Debussian Shakespeare-comedy: the very thought is enchanting. 'One doesn't know whether to laugh or to cry. Perhaps both?'

Maurice Ravel

Trying to encapsulate Ravel in a nutshell, the facts, the stereotypes, the questions mutually interact. Exquisite, precious, perfectionist dandy, scion of Swiss engineer/inventor father and a Basque mother:

petit-maître/minor master, or up there with his overlapping compatriots Fauré and Debussy? Ultimate realization of the pursuit of
impersonal facture untainted by self-expression, even recognizable
traits, out of Poe via Baudelaire, who claims complete self-effacement
before the model: imitate – if you have anything of your own to say
it will reveal itself through your unwitting deviation; if not, you
will at least have attended a good school – which *could* result in
pastiche, academicism, frigidity; and does *in fact* produce some of
the most characteristic manners in all the repertoire. Output small
and choice: it will be possible to mention, describe (or at any rate
evoke), evaluate (or at any rate indicate predilections and reservations) virtually every note he wrote.

The earliest pieces can be rapidly dispatched: all small scale –
songs, piano solos, a diptych for two pianos. All, however slight,
are prophetic: *Sérénade grotesque* (1893, aged eighteen) – acrid Spanishry, fierce, sarcastic, *très rude* (his own instruction): 1895 a couple
of songs, one all affectation – *Ballade de la Reine morte d'aimer*, Satie
to the fore; and yet further, the two-piano *Habanera* – Ravel's most
characteristic piece to date (also 1895), good enough to be scored
without alteration as third movement of the *Rapsodie espagnole* some
years later. The *Habanera*'s companion-piece, *Entre cloches*, was not
thus rescued, though bells continue to resonate in several products
of his maturity.

And so it goes: two Mallarmé settings, a sonata for violin and piano
(unobtrusively forgotten, no great loss), a spinning-song, another
song depicting dark depression – *Si morne!* All these will bloom later
in full. The first orchestral piece comes in 1898, aged twenty-three –
Shéhérazade, ouverture de féerie, Borodin and Balakirev at the prow,
Rimsky for the title, the mature orchestral song-cycle of the same
name five years ahead. But 1899 only yields the lugubrious *Pavane pour
une infante défunte*, whose popularity came to embarrass the composer
(he claimed he'd only written it for the evocative title).

The years 1900–1905 counterpoint the droll story of Ravel's
attempts to gain the Prix de Rome – five failures, in varying degrees
of near-miss and utter abasement – with the rapid and steady maturation from precious fragility into work of calibre and stature. The

discrepancy, between prize-seeking obsequiousness and cynicism (the award prestigious; and he needed the money) with tongue-in-cheek mockery and juvenile provocation, makes delicious reading. Alongside such fustian mediocrity as his Prix de Rome cantatas – *Semiramis*, *Myrrha*, *Alcyone*, *Alyssa* – lie intertwined the authentic achievements of Ravel's mid–late twenties. Piano first: 1902 *Jeux d' eau* – Liszt in Chinese, full *utilège* of the shining, tinkly pianism tried out in occasional moments of earlier songs, suddenly perfected with sure sense of shape and direction. The *Sonatine* was completed over the next three years: maybe a tiny bit dinky – the *petit maître* comes into his own here rather than the fulfilment of deeper matter hinted earlier: dejection, rancour, dark sleep, all banished from this impeccable music, utterly characteristic and lovable, but somehow even the *Sérénade grotesque* and the *Menuet antique* have more character, if not more calibre. The set of five collectively entitled *Miroirs* (written coincidently, 1904–5) has everything. i) *Noctuelles* – night-spirits/moths – magic scintillating dissonances, exactly in focus, glinting yet flocculent; its middle section on an octave pedal foreshadowing a night-vision altogether less friendly – *Le Gibet*. ii) *Oiseaux tristes* – *delicatissimo* transcriptions of the birds' almost-speech; unlike the twitterings of Ravel's subsequent birds, *these* little creatures have souls. iii) *Une barque sur l'océan* – all bravura figuration; gorgeous luminosity and swell, rather empty – no harbour – a painted boat upon a painted ocean: not till *Shéhérazade*'s *Asie* will there be a sea-voyage fraught with content. The same reservation applies to iv) *Alborada del gracioso*: this jester's morning serenade goes on too long: the *Sérénade grotesque* intimated it all already, the *Habanera* touched early perfection, and the best Spanishry lies in the future. v) *La Vallée des cloches* – again these bells peal in Chinese! – continues a lifetime's preoccupation, chiming in delicate tintinnabulatory evocation into a trait of the culture, Debussy's Oriental bells yet to come, and Enescu's astonishingly acute capture, on a well-tempered Klavier, of overtones and micro-intervals.

Next, two substantial instrumental works without evocation, or neo-classicism however sideways. Ravel's String Quartet (1902–3) is a problem: he's trying so hard; it feels like a graduation-piece. The gamelan/guitar in the pizzicato parts of the second movement prophesy pleasures to come, the relentless, frenetic busyness of the finale, equally, a persisting difficulty with closing movements never solved in the whole oeuvre. All these negatives turn positive in the *Introduction and Allegro* for solo harp (written to show off an allegedly superior new chromatic instrument) with flute, clarinet and string quartet, of 1905. Forms are free, the material subtly intertwining; textures are often 'orchestral' with felicity and aptness, not strain and un-idiomacy; separate themes are superimposed with delightful spontaneity and real ingenuity, not enforced with look-at-me cleverness; lengths are right, material top-notch. The harp-makers must have been deeply gratified.

Finest bloom of these Prix de Rome years is the other *Shéhérazade*: three songs with orchestra to texts, by the egregiously named 'Tristan Klingsor' (the real man died as recently as 1966), giving Ravel exactly what he needs at this juncture to set him going – exotic/erotic, amorous/sensual, suggestive/ambiguous. *Asie* is the exotic, a veritable dictionary of Oriental wonders. The porcelain sector is especially delectable: we've been here before, in *Jeux deau* and *La Vallée des cloches*: these are better still. So, too, for the sinister sequel, the executioner, the blood and roses, the terrific climax at love and hate – right back to *Un grand sommeil noir* (1895) – which with uncanny rightness lands us again in the ocean-voyage momentum so soft and inviting at the start. And so to the anticlimactic sign-off, the sly self-consciousness of the artifice by which the tale is recounted – itself deflected in turn by five closing bars again renewing the initial magical summons.

La Flûte enchantée: the instrument insinuates the entire second song with a hint of ambiguity – amorous bliss or wistful regret: and ambiguity permeates *L'Indifférent*; he of the title is clearly male, but the sex of the person so urgently addressing him is uncertain – the gentle girl-like eyes, the delicate lines of the face with its downy shadow – 'Enter! Let my wine refresh you! But no, you pass, with a graceful gesture of decline, your haunch so languid and feminine.' The imploring note, all the more urgent for its understatement, aches in the memory as the Being Beauteous passes from view.

*

Interlude: Ravel the idiomatic and sympathetic setter of folksongs, with absolutely sure touch and tone for very diverse originals – the equal in this area of Brahms, Grainger, Britten. His arrangements run to some fifteen: *Cinq mélodies populaires grecques* (1904–6) plus an extra Greek song, *Tripatos*, in 1909. The year after, his entries won 1st Prize in four categories for this kind of endeavour – French, Spanish, Italian, Hebrew (Russian, Flemish and Scottish were not awarded, and only the *Chanson ecossaise* of these extra numbers has survived). Their chief glory, the Hebrew setting, is continued in two further of 1914 – *Kaddish* and *L'Énigme éternelle*, hauntingly inward expressions of empathy, in particular for the supreme prayer of the Jewish rite, as to have one wonder, fruitlessly, at his atheistic rationalism, and indeed his race. A few isolated songs of these years yield little of value – the extreme dissonance of *Les grand vents venus d'outre-mer* (1907) is the most interesting: they serve to put into relief the achievement of the five *Histoires naturelles* (1906). Jules Renard wrote some seventy thumb-nail sketches from bird/animal/insect life in an apparently casual conversational prose peppered with col-loquialisms and throw-aways. Ravel's affinity was clear when friends recognized in his settings the intonations of his own mischievous and idiosyncratic speech. The mix of sensibility and its deflation induced hostility even from the composer's own circle: the alleged offences against decorum are inexplicable now. Behind these mini-masterpieces lie the delectable *Histoires naturelles* (not so called) by his adored Chabrier – little pink pigs, pompous turkeys, chirruping cicadas – and his absorption in Musorgsky's theory and practice of natural declamation as opposed (sometimes literally) to art-and-artificial singing that reaches its apogee in the concurrent compos-ition of *L'Heure espagnole*. It is not unfair to say that Ravel's birds, beasts and insects, like D. H. Lawrence's, are more human than their human characters in opera and novels. Every song is consum-mate in depiction and characterization: the Peacock's vanity, daily expecting his bride, unfurling in vain the glory of his tail (a glorious moment); the Cricket, carefully putting his underground house in order, then hiding within it. The Kingfisher lies at the heart – two pages of rapt wonderment worthy of Traherne or Dürer – 'not a bite [complains the fisherman] – but something better; as I held out my rod, a kingfisher alighted and stood on its tip'. *On ne peut pas plus lent* is the composer's instruction for these exquisitely voiced treble dissonances set against warmer, deeper consonances within a background of silence, proving that music can render kingfisher-blue. Finally, the Guinea-fowl, all rage and spite – music can also render almost-human malice.

Two isolated minor songs of 1907 point in different directions. *Sur l'herbe* sets a Verlaine conversation-piece: its gallantry and coquetry, French vignettes with a Spanish tang, sound like a study for Ravel's operatic comedy of characters, completed in sketch the same year. But *Les grands vents venus d'outre-mer* reverts to Ravel's youthful darkness, going still further in dissonance and angularity: it too bears immediate consequences in a suite of three piano-pieces completed 1908, *Gaspard de la nuit*, whose first movement, however, is *Ondine*, a child of *Jeux d'eau*. The Lisztian model is excelled in this most evanescent depiction of water-droplets ever achieved by music. Aloysius Bertrand's prose-poem – each piece is preceded by an entire source from this remarkable writer from early French Romanticism – gives the water-nymph's own words, promising her mortal admirer wondrous rewards deep down in the lake: 'but as I replied that I loved a mortal girl, sulky and spiteful she wept a few tears, threw a peal of laughter, and vanished in a sudden shower'. The long singing lines within the exquisite figuration foretell dawn in *Daphnis*, commenced the year after *Gaspard* was completed. Second, *Le Gibet*, celebrated feat of technical and compositional challenge exactly equated with atmospheric intensity without compare: Ravel's dark side reaches here its macabre apotheosis. An octave B♭ sounds throughout – the bell from the walls of the distant town as the setting sun reddens the corpse dangled from the gallows. Below it creep dusky hollow fifths; rising into and slightly above it, a plaintive shred of melody. The bell resonates deep as its middle-range continues, and cloud of densely luminous dissonances float within and above – 'darkness visible'. Music that can be felt along the nerves and senses – expressionist impressionism, haunting, compelling, *beautiful* – a flower of evil.

Whereas *Scarbo*, the third piece, is just trying too hard to have your flesh creep! There's an air of *blague* in Ravel's own attitudes – his declared aim to surpass Balakirev's *Islamey* in virtuosity; then his confession that he'd frightened himself here – 'I wanted to write a caricature of romanticism, and maybe succeeded too well'; and that he'd achieved the piano-transcription of a non-existent orchestral original. (He did not, for once, score *Gaspard* himself: subsequent attempts vindicate his abstention – paradox becomes fact.) *Scarbo*, the sinister dwarf scuttling in and out of the arras; reality, or phantasm of disturbed insomniac imaginings? His hideous aspect; his malign menaces: here too, an ancestor – the *Sérénade grotesque* of 1893 – for jerky spasmodic gestural rudeness, snarls, snaps, and a distinctly Spanish flavour. *Scarbo* takes all this about as far as it can go: a remarkable feat of black magic conjury, somehow ludicrous in its very luridness; best when, at last, the dwarf, the pianist, the composer stop showing off and permit an elegant disappearing-act. The black-magic complements the white-notes of Ravel's next piano-work, the altogether unvirtuoso, benign fairy-music of *Ma mère l'Oye*.

However, 1907–8 are predominantly devoted to Spain: both these years' major endeavours feature the land in their very titles – the one-act opera and the orchestral *Rapsodie*, three movements newly composed around the *Habanera* of 1895, unchanged in substance, orchestrated from the original two-piano format with the luminous expertise of *Asie* behind it – still, perhaps, the *Rapsodie*'s finest movement. The others have a whiff of picture-postcard Spain, all surface, whether brilliant, as in the *Feria* finale, or stereotyped languor/erotic as in the first, *Prélude à la nuit*. The comparison would be with Debussy's orchestral triptych *Ibéria*: his *Parfums de la nuit* penetrate deep into the sensuous mystery, his bright festive morning is sharper-etched, and the subtle play of dark alley and thronged thoroughfares in his first section, *Par rues et chemins*, reveal an artist above mere depiction and display. Ravel's Spain is frankly a showpiece – virtuoso orchestral mastery for a virtuoso orchestra and conductor – Bernstein's quip that 'when I do *Rapsodie espagnole* there's not a dry seat in the house' actually befits the nature of the score itself.

L'Heure espagnole also has its abiding questions. Ravel had completed its piano-score before the *Rapsodie*, returning to orchestration in 1909 even after its rejection the previous year (the eventual première 1911). A piece of high-class flim-flam, delightfully improper, expertly engineered by the half-Swiss precisionist conjoined with the half-Basque, perfectly calculated to function – clocks like humans, humans like clocks. Its action is deftly dispatched: the neat sexy equation – dull middle-aged husband, attractive young wife, her two disappointing gallants, the hefty muleteer who gives satisfaction, the games in and out of the man-sized clocks – revealed within the *hour* of the title. Every inflexion, every single- or double-entendre, is caught with witty alacrity. *Music* isn't the aim. Not for nothing that the composer was concerned at this period with a possible instrumentation of Musorgsky's *Marriage*. The parodies are acuter than in his thus-designated efforts '*à la manière de*' Borodin and Chabrier of a few years later. The only let-down is the closing quintet, a *habañera* in which two disgruntled suitors, one stout, one weedy, a well-contented bloke, a well-gratified wife, a complaisant husband well-pleased with such successful sales, draw the moral but fail to adorn the tale with, at the last, a well-rounded number with a memorable tune. *This* is better-served by an oddment for the same years as *L'Heure espagnole*, the *Vocalise en forme de Habanera*: absolutely minor, utterly characteristic – in actual fact composed by Alfredo Casella, Ravel's collaborator in the collections of parodies; the more skilful because he has no voice of his own.

The year of the opera's full score, 1909, sees also the first intimation of his fullest: the scenario and some sketches for a ballet, *Daphnis et Chloé*. Of the year's two finished compositions, one is nugatory – *Menuet sur le nom d'Haydn* (whose centenary fell that year): the other is one of Ravel's most perfect – five movements for piano four-hands, based upon fairy-tales, for children to play: *Ma mere l'Oye/Mother Goose*, after Perrault. Its sophistication makes it hard for children to play, and perhaps to enjoy: as later with Ravel's second opera, child-centred though it be, its pleasures are best appreciated by consenting adults. But only a rare spirit of unsentimental empathy – the polar opposite of the Wordsworthian child – could have managed such unassuming chastity as the *Pavane de la Belle au bois dormant*: spare, austere, every note sensitized, tender beyond words. *Petit Poucet* – little Tom Thumb, wandering the countryside scattering breadcrumbs to know his way home – opens up depths of enfantine poignancy as plangent as Mimi or Butterfly (and at one point rather resemblant). The birds devour the crumbs and little Tom is, presumably, Little Boy Lost. Another miniature world opens up next – *Laideronnette, Impératrice des Pagodes, locus classicus* for 'Orientalism in music' poised between distance/enchantment and ethnomusicological/anthropological fidelity – a recreation of gamelan music from Java and Bali, not so far-reaching as the revelation for the painters of Japanese prints, yet sufficient to occasion Debussy's exclamation that 'it makes our tonics and dominants seem like ghosts'. Next, *Les Entretiens de la Belle et la Bête*. Both are perfectly characterized, she in a supply spare *valse*, once dubbed 'Satie's fourth *Gymnopédie*', he (why is the Beast feminine in French?) by subterranean growling, over which the waltz accompaniment grows quietly menacing; Beauty's anxiety quivers touchingly over the long-sustained growls, which intensify and rise in the most graphic manner to almost meet her in the middle. Now, the magic: the two superimposed – the device so forced and unconvincing back in Ravel's String Quartet, here as right poetically as it is technically adroit. In the fifth and final number, where tender reverence prevails throughout: a slow grave sarabande, Fauré to the fore, *Le Jardin féerique*, warm without cloying to start, rising to crystalline harping high up in both players; the melody exfoliates, descending again to warmer registers, swelling over a two-note carillon to end in a burst of sunlit fanfares overlain with cascades of glissandi: the Sleeping Beauty wakes, Little Tom Thumb is found, Beast is restored by Beauty's compassionate solicitude into Handsome Prince, and they all live happily ever after. Ravel's orchestration follows in 1911: not just of the five original piano-duets; they are now set, differently ordered, into the loose and silly scenario for a ballet. Not surviving as such: its demise entails loss of the composer's most exquisite orchestral imaginings, in links and interludes newly written.

Back to 1910; Ravel's richest time. A long haul – piano-score of *Daphnis* completed; and the *Chants populaires*, as aforementioned. The next year yields a new piano-suite of the highest calibre – *Valses nobles et sentimentales*. Its title conflates those of several Schubert dance-sets; its motto, from Henri de Régnier, might well be Ravel's own – *'le plaisir délicieux et toujours nouveau d'une occupation inutile'*. As also its idiom, utterly characteristic and recognizable from bar one and in every subsequent vicissitude, sentimental or noble, ferocious or dinky, seductive, poignant, fragile, intoxicated, nostalgic. At the première in a concert wherein every item was initially anonymous, it excited derision or outright hostility. Even close friends were fooled. Yet this marvellous music seems best-set of all his output to make friends! Already all right for piano, and in its orchestrated version – no *prélude* or links; absolutely unaltered – it is the most perfect thing he ever achieved. He stations himself before his model – here the furthest in culture and style from any other he employed – and obeys some of its injunctions: most notably, adherence almost throughout to Schubert's regular eight-bar periods, indispensable to the original's strictly functional purpose, music to waltz to. However much Ravel melts the internal phrasing, the base is strong and sure. He then 'deviates' into something purely himself, unbeholden even to his adored and revered Chabrier, whose *Trois valses romantiques* for two pianos are the closest prototype. (He'd played them with a pianist-friend to their composer back in 1893, the year before Chabrier's death.) Much of the language here has become shopsoiled, bargain-basement debased, by later exploitation. To return to source is to be cleansed and purged: the bathwater is perfumed with cultivated and expensive essences, but the perfume is imperishable.

'Hard to *valse* to': the ballet subsequently made in 1912 of this consummate concert-piece – *Adélaïde, ou le langage des fleurs* – was a failure: *La Valse*, intended from the start as a ballet-score, notoriously was rejected by Diaghilev as undanceable. The problem is acute with Ravel's most ambitious completed work, *Daphnis et Chloé*, also intended from the start to be danced: not rejected by Diaghilev but just as truly 'the portrait of a ballet', not the actuality, as its initial lukewarm reception in 1912, followed by more than a century of relative neglect, amply proves. But the other part of Diaghilev's verdict on *La Valse* in 1920 should also be remembered – 'it is a masterpiece, of course'. Where does *Daphnis* most suitably belong? Not the theatre, quite: the concert-hall of course – but this isn't quite right either; all those orchestral players in black and white, the bright lights, the restless audience, that chorus ... With eyes closed, imagining what is evoked by the ears' assiduous attention: this music, like all music, speaks for itself as itself, though its evocative and narrative aims are clear enough.

The Hellenistic pastoral by Longus is easily summarized. Pan the presiding deity; the swain Daphnis and the shepherdess Chloé join votaries at his shrine; also there Dorcon, loutish goatherd, who bullies Daphnis into a dance, and is jeered off as the winner claims his reward, Chloé's fervent embrace. Left alone, the still-innocent swain is approached by an 'older woman', experienced, avid to teach the tyro the *ars amoris*. She fails, though leaving him somewhat troubled. Real trouble – Chloé pursued by pirates, imploring the nymphs' protection in vain, carried off to the pirates' camp. Daphnis, re-entering, finds only her abandoned sandal: he beseeches Pan's aid. At the camp, Chloé is forced to dance for the pirate chieftain. She attempts escape and is recaptured. At this direst moment, sudden uncanny elements are released, flamelets flicker, fantastical creatures leap and bound: terrified by Pan's minions, the pirates scatter. Night gives way to dawn: Daphnis alone, in anguish, till the shepherds return safe with Chloé. The lovers re-enact the story of the god's love for Syrinx; all ends in a celebratory communal dance, generous enough to include a brief solo for the loutish goatherd.

Ravel's score is luxurious, even sumptuous, albeit without the conspicuous waste of near contemporaries in Germany and Austria. He intended, rather, homage to Greece as seen through the eyes of the French eighteenth century: its dances are evoked as Pan's devotees pay their tributes near the start. The shy lovers,

the clumsy rival, the would-be seductress, are all tellingly characterized. The pirates, however, are tame: their music rude, rough, proficient enough but unconvincing – 'homework well done' – *Russian*
homework, specifically Polovtsian via Borodin. Back on course soon
after – the loveliest dawn in all music – long, long arcs of melody,
surrounded with rippling decoration, terrace upon terrace as the
light intensifies, drowning out tweets of birdsong and passing shepherds' pipes, waves of resplendence founded surely upon slow-
changing harmony. Just as celebrated, the flute for Chloé, alone,
then joined by Daphnis as they merge their love with Pan's for
Syrinx. The closing *danse générale* is just the thing. A first version
was rejected by the composer's fastidious perfectionism; five-to-a-
bar replaced more conventional triple-time: the upshot, a replay of
Rimsky's *Scheherazade* easily surpassing the model. At the last and
hugest climax, the motif for the rescued and reunited lovers sings
out broad and warm over continuing Bacchic/Panic momentum –
Balakirev's *Tamara* enlisted to guide the orgy to its goal in unforced
exuberance. *Daphnis* the ballet was no triumph. *Daphnis* the score is
at its best a thing of joy for ever.

From the next year, 1913, come two widely discrepant ventures
having in common only Ravel's discipline/aesthetic of modelling:
by parody – '*à la manière de* . . .'; two contributions to join his friend
Casella's anthology of that title. The minor composer's efforts are
never less than accomplished and, in several instances (Franck;
Debussy; Wagner – and Ravel himself: *Almanzor ou le mariage
d'Adélaïde*) lethal: the better composer's *Borodin* and *Chabrier* remain
relatively feeble. Perhaps he loved both too well: he's certainly 'done'
them both better in his own original pieces.
    The other venture of 1913 is without parallel, except in its context
of music by friends also responding to the same source at the same
time with songs for soprano and a chamber-ensemble, of the utmost
textural refinement, in an idiom so radical as almost to be called
'experimental'. These friends formed *Les Apaches* – wild men, *outré*,
bohemian, connoisseurs of the flagrant, enemies of the routine, the
academic, the establishment – modernists. One of them, the young

Stravinsky, famous after *Firebird* and *Petrushka*, soon to be notorious with *Le Sacre*, returned from Berlin with news of an astounding new sound just encountered there: the vocalist rather speaks than sings; behind her, or rather, integral to the mesh of texture, a small group of instruments, piano predominant, produces endlessly elaborate and inventive enrichment, illustration, enactment, in an idiom whose abandonment of tonality goes way beyond what even *Les Apaches* had achieved, even imagined: Schoenberg's *Pierrot lunaire*. To place your easel before an original not seen, only described, outdoes Ravel's previous provocation: it is 'unsafe', it lives dangerously. The response of all the circle to the news from Berlin forms a precious atoll of extraordinary calibre: Stravinsky's *Three Japanese Lyrics*, Ravel's *Three Poems of Stéphane Mallarmé*, Maurice Delage's *Quatre poèmes hindous* – this almost unknown figure achieves here (and in a thimbleful of other pieces) results worthy of his company. Coincidentally with Ravel's settings, Debussy – no *Apache* – was also engaged at this time setting Mallarmé: they overlap in two poems; a potentially distressing wrangle over rights and priorities was only averted by the younger composer's tact and generosity.

It's not possible to paraphrase Mallarmé at his most arcane, nor to describe Ravel at the extremity of his potential. *Soupir* – Sigh – is relatively comprehensible, a dedication to a muse-figure in melancholy autumnal weather: a white fountain sighs for the unattainable *azur*, mirrored in pools whose stagnant water reflects the dead leaves' agony, where the yellow sun's long ray ploughs a cold furrow. Amazing opening texture of arpeggio harmonics from the string quartet: through this virtually pitchless whittering the voice rises sober and even as the words – the calm sister, the autumn dream – gradually supported by the piano's catching and holding her notes; then the flute, following her line, flowering over and above her as the piano's harmony extends and descends, to bind the *azur* above and its reflection below in a single embrace. At this key-word, half-way through poem and setting, the two clarinets enter, so unobtrusive as to be inaudible, perceptible only when the surrounding texture ceases and they are left exposed. The string quartet now re-enters, playing normally, in rich harmonic jamminess: the woodwinds join; harmony so succulent in its refinement as to be imbibed via the senses by osmosis. These instruments drop away leaving piano alone, tingling wide-spaced dissonances reminiscent of the dangling man in the setting sun from *Gaspard*. The uncanny sound gives way to the modal/pentatonic sound of the opening, without its fluttery momentum: this returns only on the poem's last syllable, two brief flecks over a deep bass; then a final sustained white-note epitome.

Placet futile can also be exemplified, if not explained: a gallant address – '*Princesse!*' – from an epoch of extravagant artificial compliments not so far from Verlaine's *Fêtes galantes*, and his *Sur l'herbe* that Ravel had already set. Mallarmé's poem also has an Abbé, addressing the Princess with hyperbolic conceits, sometimes risqué – 'I won't even figure nude on your Sèvres china': mostly affected and absurd – his succession of comparisons – 'since I can't be your whiskered lapdog, nor lozenge, nor rouge' (etc.) – leads to a whimsical imperative – 'let me be . . .' – held suspended in the setting by many a hesitation – 'let me be . . . the shepherd of your smiles.' Perhaps surprising, Ravel eschews almost wholly the pavane/menuet/forlane that the text invites and Debussy's setting accepts. Instead, the opening invocation is the clearest reference to the sound of *Pierrot lunaire* to be heard in this very different context. Languour reigns for the amorous Abbé's first lines, up to the nakedness denied the Sèvres porcelain. Piano, hitherto silent, plunges in with music at once turbulent and diaphanous, still further complexified two bars later with the woodwinds' entry, while the voice commences and continues her ironic demurs, which, suddenly, go cool not ardent. Equally ironic, the wheedling imperatives – '*nommez nous*' – the royal plural transferred from the royal personage to whom the futile petition is urged, where there comes, after all, a touch of Couperin or Rameau. The image of the shepherd fingering his flute brings this instrument into the insinuating banter: the voice's second '*Princesse!*', and request to herd her smiles, loses the suggestive edge to close on a pure pentatonic disappearing-act – the flick of a fan from three lines earlier, maybe? Not marked when the word was actually heard.

These first two poems are from earlier in Mallarmé's oeuvre: *Surgi de la croupe et du bond* is mature and obscure – the next notable

composer to set such texts will be Boulez. The poet-sylph on the
ceiling gazes down at a vase unbedecked with blooms, unani-
mated by kisses, whose water has dried, a widow in her death-agony,
unconsenting to tell anything of a rose in the shadows. The music
is as gnomic, lapidary, palpable yet fugitive, as the words. A soft
scrunch from pizzicato quartet; a flute solo against tremolandi,
almost back to *Shéhérazade* nine years earlier; upward sprays from
the other flautist, viola, clarinet, downward for piano, upward again
for bass-clarinet, leaving dense harmonic mesh as the voice enters
with crupper and leap of vase's ephemeral glassiness (to wonder-
ingly render the first line). Texture now completely stills save for two
tolling bell-like notes – initially B♭, same as the single bell-toll in *Le
Gibet*; and the remainder of the sonnet is set simply and syllabically.
From '*agonise*' (the vase's endless pain of widowhood) the piano
flutters as well as tolling, the quartet sustains close harmony, each
of the four woodwinds in turn signs off with a curve of melody –
piccolo; clarinet; flute; clarinet again, lower; bass-clarinet – leaving
only the rose in the darkness, these words enveloped in duskily
shining chords over the cello's open bottom string, and a final waft
of harmonics with a splinter of pizzicato. It really is as if Ravel, too,
had heard the first *Pierrot* in Berlin. Perhaps a cul-de-sac; for sure a
jewel precious in both senses.

Next year came the war, and, anyway, a marked change of direction –
1914 shows this orderly artist in a ferment: orchestrating Schumann
and Chopin for dancing, while holding in mind several self-
contradictory major original projects – *La Cloche engloutie* again
(first mooted back in 1906); *Zaspiak-Bat*, a tribute to his Basque
lineage; a *St François d'Assise*; a piano trio. Only this last is realized,
alongside the two Hebrew melodies mentioned earlier, and the start
of a suite of piano-pieces inspired by Couperin, finished three years
later. For now, therefore, only the trio, first pure music of size since
the String Quartet and similarly problematic. The sparer the better;
the two middle movements a distinct success – ingenious, diverting,
profound: no. 2 a *Pantoum* – the Oriental verse-form occasionally
employed by nineteenth-century French poets; no. 3 a *Passacaille*,

whose technical stringencies inhere within his native musical culture. The first movement's initial poise and elegance are often subverted by turbulence seemingly or actually without purpose: the finale's limpid start is deceptive; as it proceeds and concludes, the movement occasions overwriting and underlining unique in Ravel's best period, recalling juvenilia and prophetic of trouble to come, just as the frugality of the second and third foretell his late *style dépouillé* – stripped down (or even flayed); and the difficulties he experienced with the trio as a whole prefigure those dominating the decades after the war.

The years 1915–18 can be swiftly summarized. Too fragile for combat but determined to aid his country however he possibly can, Ravel becomes an ambulance-driver for the French army: and for the French music-lover edits Mendelssohn's piano-works to get them out of the hands of the *sales Boches*: and composes three unaccompanied choruses to his own text. In 1916 he is sick; in 1917 his mother dies – 'the only person he ever loved': he is discharged from service; and the Couperin-suite is completed. In 1918–19 comes *Frontispiece*, a *jeu d'esprit* for piano five-hands (shared between three players). Otherwise, he is scoring away, his own compositions and others'. In 1920 he completes, for solo piano, for two pianos, for full orchestra, the *'poème choreographique' La Valse*, and commences two major projects whose prolonged birth-agonies will from now on be his norm. The wartime yield is understandably meagre: that of his remaining years harder to understand, and sadder.

Le Tombeau de Couperin makes an expressive parallel with Debussy's contemporaneous sonatas, evoking an idealized eighteenth-century civilization as its values, and *la patrie* herself, are invaded with destruction and conquest in view. As with the central panel of Debussy's *En blanc et noir*, though not his sonatas, every movement in Ravel's suite is dedicated to the memory of a friend (one to two brothers) killed in action. His own orchestration (1919) is of course consummate: the piano original contains two numbers unaccountably not scored: the second, a demure and ingenious fugue, the sixth a rampaging toccata; the fifth is yet another menuet (possibly recalling Haydn's well-known plea for something new in this familiar form, and not forgetting Ravel's own menuet on Haydn's name) – a delicate dainty, broadening into almost sarabande-seriousness for its middle musette, upon which the menuet's return is cleverly superimposed: no. 3, a forlane, is delectable – a refined sicilienne, elegantly vagrant, with surprising pressure in the penultimate stretches, before the ultimate extracts further piquant tweaks from the by-now familiar ingredients. Best of all is the first, the *prélude*, a whirl of volatile fluidity, whirling up and down, higher and lower every time, with weightless effervescence; *vif*, the instruction, might well indicate *living* as *fast*: as if there were no war to end all wars at its very threshold.

The three choruses are slight and sweet. *Frontispiece* is a curiosity – experimental, complex, dense, Ravel's closest proximity to modernism, Viennese or Bartókian. Vienna is closer still in *La Valse*, originally titled *Wien* at its inception back in 1914, and on the backburner until the immediate post-war years, concluded at last in 1920. In 1914 it would surely have been modest and innocent, a pendant to the suite of waltzes honouring Schubert. By the end of the war it has swollen into a self-destructive apocalypse. One perceives this palpably: it's innate in the notes, irrespective of what has inevitably been read into it – a counter-blast to Teutonic musical culture (though Austria scarcely figures as such), or the crazed dance of an entire civilization on the edge of a volcano. The *poème* sets scene and epoch – the imperial court towards 1855: 'through breaks in whirling clouds one perceives couples waltzing; the clouds gradually disperse, and one distinguishes a vast hall populous with revolving dancers; the scene progressively lightens, the chandeliers at their brightest at figure B.' So far so good: this is only a fraction of the work's whole; the evocation continues far further; intoxicating oomph and virtuosity, not euphoric and carefree like its model the *Fête polonaise* from Ravel's adored *Roi malgré lui* – a certain hecticness is already sensed, an exaggeration, a latent hysteria as of Empson's poem about a ball in the nineteenth century. A more lyric strain strays in from the *Valses nobles et sentimentales*, counter-weighted with hoofiness alien to that piece even at its most energetic; and one is never wholly freed from those whirling mists, which descend again,

temporarily obliterating the scene into its initial obscurity. Coming
into view once more, things are still brighter, harder, growing lurid,
even garish. Faintness and nausea threaten, one moment seems to
simulate throwing-up with its colossal wallops on tam-tam, big
drum, cymbals, the brass strident as possible on the off-beats, all
the strings smearing up and down in sickening glissandi. Yet nearer
the end the debauched dance ceases for two bars of interrupting
unison that seems to convey repulsion, before animation rekindles,
now expressionistically crazed, nay vile – those trombone slurps! –
before rushing to its percussion-heavy doom, and a brutal final five
notes as of the chopper to chop off your head. 'The portrait of a
ballet, not a ballet,' said Diaghilev. Rather, the brilliant and frightening exteriorization of something demonic and undying at the heart
of an elegant cultivated civilization, disguised as Wien but Parisian
as the can-can; or at the core of an exceptionally sensitive and gifted
individual whose life is now revealed as futile.

Next year (1921) the Parisian moved from the capital to his entran-
cing toybox house and garden Le Belvédère, worked on at a duo
sonata for violin and cello, completed the year following, when he
also orchestrated Musorgsky's *Pictures at an Exhibition* and various
Debussy piano-pieces; managed a brief tribute for violin and piano
to his revered mentor and friend Fauré and a showy showpiece for
the same combination: all the time contemplating Alain-Fournier's
Le Grand Meaulnes – read and loved when it came out during the
war – and Colette's libretto for a one-act opera-ballet with a child,
his mother and plenty of animals and toys. In 1923 comes an isolated
song, *Ronsard à son âme*, and the start on a duo sonata for violin
and piano, not completed until 1927, which also sees another isolated
song, *Rêves*. In 1924 he scored the violin showpiece (*Tzigane*) and
continued the one-acter, whose première occurred the year after. In
1926 he completed a set of three songs with instruments, *Chansons
madécasses*, begun the year before, while 1928 sees a tour in the USA
and the composition of *Boléro*: 1929 the commencement of two
piano concertos, alongside brooding on the possibility of a more
substantial *Jeanne* than the fantail *jeu d'occasion* of 1927, *L'Éventail de*

Jeanne (sardonically marked 'Wagneramente'): *Jeanne d'Arc*. In 1930 the 1st Piano Concerto, for left hand alone, is finished; the next year the one for two hands. In 1932, a projected opera *Morgiane* – return to his youthful relish of the *1001 Nights*; and three brief songs on Don Quixote were begun, completed with strain the next year, when he also attempted the third opera. All the time, now, his health precarious; declining through 1934–35–36: in 1937 an ultimate operation fails: he died that December aged sixty-two.

The bare facts outline the *triste histoire*: the musical harvest can be gathered in by species. Songs first: two miniatures; *Ronsard à son âme*, written for the poet's quatercentenary birthday, setting his version of Hadrian's *animula* – go, little soul ... farewell ... don't trouble my sleep – to something so spare – bare fifths for the piano until just before the close, the voice chaste and austere – as to be gaunt were it not also so tender. Just when the poet sleeps and the music all-but-disappears, a soft-as-possible pile-up of eight fifths summarizes the whole. *Rêves* is equally bare: the poem speaks of memory in surreal disjunctive images – a child's play, a muted voice, eyes softened with love, dreaming among the trees, the noise of departure from some station (the train's hooter vividly imitated) – old dreams 'from the vague land of little things that will die well, good, and wise' – the text as woolly as the music lucid, succinct, every note alive in the simplest of textures – the *style dépouillé* in essence.

These slender offerings are blown sky-high by the *Chansons madécasses*, three songs where the voice is accompanied by flute and cello as well as piano, reminder in part of the *Pierrot*-combination, which Ravel heard live in Paris 1922, after merely hearing *of* it in 1913. Schoenberg's work impresses a strikingly audible thumbprint at the start of the second song and is more imperceptibly perceptible elsewhere. Otherwise the extreme exiguity of the music shows the spareness of *Ronsard* and *Rêves* in their true light – masterly economy, merciless excision, pared to the bare bone – fruitful result of pruning all luxuriance and ornamentation.

Évariste-Desiré de Parny is almost as unreal as Tristan Klingsor or a French Ossian: his so-called translations from the Madegascan appeared in 1787; and they give Ravel just what he needs – plain but rhythmic prose like the *histories naturelles*, subject-matter exotic/ erotic/intimate, in the outer two never so pared-down nor so explicit. It's the middle song that explodes: the violence is startling – cries of *aoua!* added by the composer to Parny's *Méfiez-vous des blancs* – the Blacks' hatred of 'the treacherous Whites who usurped our land, our goals, our women' – a spine-chilling opening, persisting in memory as the music grows soft and velvety though always exuding menace. Remarkable how just three instruments can convey such a range of repressed rage. *Aoua!* re-reached – new tyrants, stronger and more numerous – till disappearing in an echo of the first invasion.

With his last songs and last work, *Don Quichotte à Dulcinée*, Ravel returns to Spain. Slight and touching, belying the immense effort of their composition, the little trilogy presents the Knight of the Doleful Countenance in three aspects. Third and simplest, the toper: a drinking-song toasting happiness. First, the lover, whose extravagant language and exalted sentiments vie with his down-to-earth music, a fetching dance-movement alternating two and three beats in bars of the same length. Middle and best, the warrior, dedicated equally to his Lord and his Lady: Don Quixote invokes Saints Michael and George to guard his honour, the Madonna to protect Dulcinea: a strict plain choral accompaniment to a plain vocal declamation, rising to noble fullness for the dedication of his blade, and declining to a soft Amen. The song's piety is moving – not a scintilla of irony or mockery – till the clatter of drinking blows it all away. There's plenty more Spanishry to come before this, its last defiant salvo.

But first, back some fifteen years to collect the two duo sonatas from the 1920s. Both suffered prolonged gestation, both had a whole movement rejected, both show in various ways Ravel's post-war search for and finding new ways of achieving a naked essentiality ungrateful to lovers of his earlier bloom who lament its sacrifice. The violin–cello duo is certainly a crinkled thing – acrid, rebarbative, acerbic. Dedicated to the memory of Debussy, such qualities seem inappropriate; published initially alongside memorial tributes by inter alia Bartók and Stravinsky, the stringency and aggression are more in tune – the older master vying with the young Turks (now not so young), all of them so indebted to the great Original. There's something flagrant, even delinquent about this work, written, it goes without saying, with mastery of every aspect of the challenging medium. Stravinsky, Bartók, Schoenberg, masters of outrage in their different ways, have not been invoked idly. And this unlovable tour de force is more consistently itself than its successor, the duo sonata for violin and piano. A very variable piece, the first movement's flawless mastery of *la longue ligne*; the second a blues, X-rayed and flayed rather than indolent and sexy; the last-minute substitute finale a cop-out – all vacant virtuosity, pointless busyness, a buzz in a bottle. Here the ingenious recourse to citations from the preceding movements seems 'desperate, not serious'. (And as for *Tzigane*: Ravel has scarcely 'deviated': the ersatz goulash is served up with consummate bravura, and the tongue is firmly in the cheek.)

Of the two simultaneous piano concertos, both so effortful and prolonged in the making, that for left hand alone was completed first and is incontestably the finer. Both take on the kind of challenge that Ravel always invited and flourished on: here, obviously, a full-scale work for solo hand: the technical problems are surmounted, seemingly without strain and with total success. A dark work fundamentally, for all the stretches of bright sunlight: and very Spanish. Black swelling waves, so soft as to be near-inaudible, through which is perceived a shadowy submarine monster groping along the ocean-floor. A three-note descending figure casts a baleful light, head-motif to continuation circulating upon itself: as it declines and falls, the creature comes into clearer focus and eventually surfaces – the Kraken! – a terrific climax, cut off to introduce the soloist's bravura entry, soon settling to presentation, clear-cut and substantial, of the theme hitherto undefined – a Spanish grandee, superb in his pride. The full orchestra takes him up in a magnificent tutti, boiling over at the top, subsiding for soloist in complementary vein – lyrical, reflective, wistful. The orchestra steals in with the Hildago's consort – his beautiful Marquesa. Her growing animation precipitates the work's middle section, a machine-made allegro, initially a jog-trot laced with mirthless laughter. A slither of descending triads, diatonic or chromatic, from the Violin Sonata, plus an imitation of its bluesy smear (remembered by Britten when evoking a steam-train's hooter in his Hardy song-cycle). Now a twinkly contrast-section: then back to jog-trot, here as background for return of the three-note descent from near the concerto's start, elastically extended over the processional *omp-pom omp-pom* – bassoons first, then trombone, then woodwinds; then ever more impassioned, all the violins. The gigue-jog punctuates, on piano first, gradually thickening: then the machine winds down – more mirthless laughter, twinkly middle-section again, soon, this time, accelerating in a scramble to mighty return of the Grandee-Sarabande, now including the soloist with the full orchestra. Its proud climax froths over and down a second time, as before leaving the soloist alone for solo-hand cadenza, a marvel of resource – low figuration, right back to the piece's start – no Grandee, just the three-note descent and its extensions; then the wistful melody, floating atop a mesh of arpeggiation that manages to contain a lower as well as the upper voice. This poetic conjuring-act achieved, re-enter the Hildago, mounting in stately splendour till the orchestra's re-entry brings the work to its grand close. Not quite – its three final spasms are immediately followed by five bars of the allegro – cheeky cock-snooking gesture complete with mirthless laughter, a slurp on the trombones all-but-obliterated by a shattering slap of the tam-tam.

The challenge confronted in the two-hand concerto was, as Ravel purportedly put it, to write 'a *proper* concerto, like Mozart and Saint-Saëns'. History doesn't relate whether he considered he'd succeeded. The first movement alternates cheeky street-strains, resembling his juniors in the Paris of *entre deux guerres*, with equally chic bluesy-strains sent through ever-more seasick vibrancies to precede a vapid cadenza before a jungle/bacchanale/fiesta end. No. 2, however, is special: the piano's long line, poised over deceptively formal/featureless accompaniment, flows grave, serene, sad but not melancholic: it was in fact excogitated painfully, modelled link by link upon the slow movement of Mozart's Clarinet Quintet. The old gibe 'synthetic melody' is actually true in a positive sense for this moving triumph over increasing disabilities. As the piano closes, woodwind soloists answer: acrid new notes insinuate into the soloist's continuation: shadowy suggestions coalesce into a fine climax; from its dissolution the cor anglais sings the opening melody while the soloist's right hand, still over the left's patient accompaniment, decorates with delicate filigree of figuration and scales. The melody reaches a transfiguring key-change before returning home to a plain, simple, exactly right close. Derailed at once by the rude gesture-to-attention commencing no. 3; then toccata-chopping, with shrill noises – ships' hooters? – from woodwinds and trombone, then settling down in facetious earnest to displays alternating perkiness with common-touch vulgarity – a streetwise echo of the aristocratic *Tombeau de Couperin*, the pagan joy of *Daphnis'* closing dance, unmistakable strains from Stravinsky's *Shrovetide Fair* and early Prokofiev. The rude opening gesture returns to punctuate, then to terminate, this cheap affair.

And what can be said about *Boléro*? The composer said it all – 'a piece for orchestra without music' – and recommended that its choreography should be set in a factory. But this one-off is unimpugnable: the melody itself is marvellous; it can certainly bear the number of repetitions within the work, and better than most the number of times it's heard outside it. The crescendo, of timbres and doublings as much as of decibels, is masterly, the sole transfiguring harmonic switch gut-wrenching: to require more would be tactless – *enough* is sufficient.

Far the most sustained yield from the post-war prospect of lowered horizons and blighted fields is Ravel's second one-act opera *L'Enfant et les sortilèges*, to a libretto by Colette specially written for him – he'd never collaborated before. 'Specifically written' suggests what is surely the case – a touch of flattery, even homage, combined with suitedness to a genuinely admired artist's known predilections and strengths: animals, children, toys, magic and *Maman* – even (a long shot) – a portrait of the artist himself as *enfant méchant*. We hear the child before the curtain rises – aimless and shapeless in the pair of oboes' parallel fifths and fourths, oscillating now up now down, the very image of footling – before we see him, 'aged six or seven', doing nothing, his active naughtiness for the moment without object – a solo double-bass's high harmonics strike dissonant pitches and rhythms against the cool unfazed oboes: below both the child sulkily details his boredom. Enter Maman to her characterizing descending fourth. 'You've been a good boy?' No: he's not done any of his assigned homework, only a few nastinesses. He sticks out his tongue when gently reproached. She leaves – 'think of your faults – of your duties – above all, think of your mother's distress.' The moment he's alone, a terrific storm of temper-tantrum, not unlike the first movement of the two-hand concerto: done from the life, climaxing 'I'm naughty and free!'

Now commences the succession of brilliant cameos, memorably droll, piquant, funny, acute, once or twice tender/touching, once cutting deeper, that constitutes the work's principal content. First, the grunting old armchair, then the bench, the couch, the pouffe, *la chaise de paille*, all furniture the child has damaged: then the wrecked clock, condemned to endless, senseless ding-dong-ding. Then one of the score's highlights, the duet of two broken teacups – English/male, Chinese/female, both languages pidgin, their music American, a sleazy dance-band foxtrot: the clever play of superimpositions and combinations is a thing of delight. Next, the fire and her warning – I warm the good, I burn the naughty – watch out! Now a rustic musette for the shepherds and shepherdesses from the wallpaper the boy has stripped, fading nostalgically into the work's first love-duet. Magical pages – *sortilèges* in different intonation – for the boy's infatuation with the Princess from his torn book of fairy-tales: poignant hapless chivalry – 'if I had a sword, I'd defend you'; her reproachful lament – 'alas, my little Prince, you're too feeble – what can you do for me now?' – Ravel's *style dépouillé* bared to 'the naked flesh of emotion'. She sinks into the floor: left bereft, the boy reveals his hitherto unsuspected vulnerability in a desolate little song – simple, unaffected, plangent without sobbing – to 'the heart of the rose and the perfume of the lily'.

The second love-duet will be more disturbing. Before it, another torment, Mad Mathematics, a crinkled old man and his chorus of numbers, torturing the child with horrible sums and conundrums. They subside into nightfall: the moon rises like the ghost of a moonstruck moment in *Pierrot lunaire*: '*Oh ma tête!*' the poor child mutters. Enter the Black Cat, courting his white paramour. This duet is sensual and erotic as the first chaste and wistful: le Noir insinuates, wheedles, urges; la Blanche coquettes, before a graceful and willing submission; the boy watches and hears, fascinated and frightened, as their voices combine in a passionate coil of miaux, leading to he knows-not-what. Every insinuation in the music identifying the felines with Mama and Papa is so well understood that it needn't be spelt out.

The moonlit garden – magical transformation opening out wide serene spaces; but not tranquil for long: the trees groan with the wounds inflicted by the boy's knife, a dragonfly flutters by grieving for the mate the boy had impaled on a pin, a bat flickers about – she too has suffered his wanton cruelty. Evocative backdrop – birds, insects, frogs. None of this, after the trees, is up to the distinction and freshness of earlier – a very 1890s-ish *café chantant* waltz, given an emotional intention it can't carry, as a squirrel escaped from the boy's cage accuses him – 'for my *beaux yeux* you entrap me! See what they reflect – freedom, brotherhood, universal benevolence.' The lonely boy sadly utters two broken syllables *ma-man*: the creatures bristle with hostility and rise against this nasty little human who loves nobody and whom nobody loves. In the fracas the squirrel is wounded: the child bandages its paw. Wondering, the animals desist – 'he dressed the wound, he staunched the blood . . . he's hurt too – what can we do? He called out a word *ma-man* – what does it mean?' They approach the dark house, its lights come up, and a quasi-fugal chorus gently unfolds, largely unaccompanied, calm and even – a new intonation in Ravel's music. Gradually it incorporates the opera's opening, the oscillating oboes on parallel fourths and fifths that had illustrated aimless tedium and incipient malice. Now they lie atop a haze of white-note euphony: they sound the child's Alteration, Reformation, Transformation. The orchestra evaporates, leaving only the oboes: the creatures sing a final tribute, the boy the final word, its syllables now joined – *Maman* – the only person Ravel ever loved.

Eric Satie

Erik Satie, born 1866: paucity of formal musical training; exiguous bohemian early life as *café-chantant* pianist and composer; fascinated by way-out religious impulses and movements, even going so far as to found a Church of his own; on–off friendship with Debussy, who certainly owes him a stylistic debt whatever the uncertainties of their association. Sensing need of further training, turned himself over, aged forty, to his artistic antithesis, d'Indy's Schola Cantorum, managing to graduate to its repressive requirements. As the temperature changed and the coloristic bloom of Debussy, then Ravel faded, Satie's queer, lean/mean parsimony began to come into its own: the new taste embodied in a collaboration with Picasso for Diaghilev, the ballet *Parade* (1917) with its 'Cubist' slant on the 'absolutely modern' – skyscrapers on stage, typewriters, gunshots, sirens in the orchestra, foxtrots and music-hall in the idiom. This new feel foretells the changed air of post-war Paris just as his earlier phase – the 'sweet medieval musician strayed into our century' as Debussy called him – had influenced, even liberated, an earlier generation, including Debussy and especially Ravel. Satie thus all set, in his mid-fifties, to be guide, model, eventually mascot, to the latest musical fashions – cheek and *chic*, Dada, fun, mockery, subversion, Cocteau as master-of-ceremonies, Poulenc as, eventually, its most enduring outcome. Beyond his example for *Les Six*, Satie's obsession with machine-like symmetries, patterning, repetition, quasi-naïve basic materials, and consequent eschewal of complexity, expressiveness and subjectivity in favour of quizzical neutrality, are principal source for the minimalism that swept the world of music from the 1960s on. Something else, however, underlies his present popularity: the bitter-sweet intonations of his *Trois gymnopédies*, endlessly heard in endlessly varied re-instrumentations from the originals for solo piano.

Frugal-sweet can prevail elsewhere – *Trois morceaux en forme de poire* for piano-duet (written to show that he *could* do '*forme*' when he wanted; and seven *morceaux,* not three). More often, whimsicality and conscious absurdity – *Trois véritables préludes flasques* (*pour un chien*), culminating in *Sports et divertissements*, mordant vignettes to accompany his own texts. *Sonatine bureaucratique* after Clementi – nascent 'Cubist' neo-classicism, not lost on Stravinsky. Melancholy detachment – *Pièces froides*; and cool meditation – the *Sarabandes* so beloved (and imitated) by Debussy. Bitterness can also prevail – sarcasm, scarcely veiled contempt and hostility are more frequent than any other mood – *Trois croquis et agaceries d'un gros bonhomme en bois* and *Aperçus désagréables* – culminating in a chorale, also marked *désagréable*, emulated by Stravinsky's sacrilegious parodies in *The Soldier's Tale*; and the infamous *Vexations*, a nasty little crinkle to be played over and over again for so long as pianist or listener can bear it (a rendition on YouTube lasts nearly twelve hours). This teasing aspect not lost on the 'anti-music' of John Cage and subsequent ventures into the outré and absurd.

Undoubtedly Satie's finest half-hour and most representative work is *Socrate* (1920), a sort of opera-cantata in three tableaux, texts taken from several Platonic dialogues, to show aspects of the man and then the manner of his death. Originally composed for four (uncharactered) sopranos with small orchestra, perhaps more essentially heard when given by just one singer (male or female) with piano only, as its composer himself used to. While Satie must intend his instrumentation to make a sound as carefully neutral as his notes, it doesn't really work; balance is odd, individual timbres will not be repressed, and the overall effect is surprisingly coarse. Whereas the piano is the ideal medium – the accompaniment can be played without any loss of detail, and its solemn simplicities realized with uniformity of touch and rhythm. Colour and dynamics can be graded as sparingly as in the music itself, and, above all, harmony sounds clearer. Similarly, to use one voice rather than to 'cast' so undramatic a conception among its 'protagonists' is entirely within the spirit of its particular, peculiar stylization: and the plainer the voice, the stronger the result. In any music that requires vocal bloom to make its full effect this would be disadvantageous. In *Socrate* not a vestige of hedonistic pleasure remains: it is not merely paradoxical to say that the piece is enhanced by the lack of gratification in any parameter, vocal or material. Satie's miracle here, the reverse of Christ's at Cana, is to inebriate his listeners with water alone.

Tableau I: *Portrait of Socrates* is taken from the *Symposium* – an ugly, fat, old Silenus, or a divine intoxicating old flute-player? II: *Banks of the Ilissus*: Phaedrus and his master in casual small-talk, relaxation, pastoral philosophizing. III: *Death of Socrates*: farewell to youth (whom he'd been accused of corrupting); to family and friends; invoking the swan who sings sweet as death nears; thanking the slave who administers the hemlock, quaffing it without a qualm, following its course up his body, discharging his last obligation – a sudden convulsion, closing the dead man's orifices – 'such was our friend's ending, the wisest and justest of mankind.'

Deliberate flat prosaic telling by words, retained exactly in the syllabic monotone, almost without contour and entirely without espressivo, of the voice-part, and the coolly machine-ostinato-patterned accompaniments, neither tonal nor modal, all tensions ironed out of the pitches, yet communicating a version of pathos unique to its composer, in this work especially. 'How many times have I [it's his younger friend and follower Darius Milhaud who speaks] seen, at the end of a performance, tears in the eyes of the audience.' How? By employing a harmonic range entirely without dissonance or suspension. Not *literally* without, of course – he has 'suspended the suspension', frozen anything tense and cadence-needing in his chords so that no move is needed after all, and fixed his added notes so that every chord, whatever its constitution, is 'common'. This norm established, exceptions to it are all the more telling. A simple example is the one touch of acid at the end of *Bords d'Ilissus* when the crickets are mentioned. More complex, the major/minor dissonance towards the end of *Mort de Socrate* when the jailor, following the course of non-sensation from feet to calves, shows the disciples that their master's body is stiffening. These dissonances are at first registered with a pang; then very soon they too are frozen in their turn, to become 'common chords' with all the others. Similarly, the uniformly pedestrian movement and level dynamics become a norm against which any change, however slight, stands out with great intensity. Three times in *Mort de Socrate* a sudden crescendo to *fortissimo* compels the music out of suppression. When (the second time) this is combined with the one disturbing rhythm in the entire work, the result is climactic out of all proportion to its constituents, or even to its place in the narrative. Then at once all is calm and blank again – but we can now see beneath as well as above – and the next time, we see beneath from the beginning. It *is* monotonous, of course; not with the aggravation of *Vexations*; but with its inexorable plainness. Yet its monotony (didn't Satie say that monotony is 'mysterious and profound'?) is varied and alleviated so as to achieve exactly the right balance whereby nothing is actually monotonous, but nothing is exactly interesting either (that too would be wrong); thus the famous closing pages reach a grave limpid pathos 'beyond human feeling', like a simultaneous lowering of the gaze and opening-out of an endless horizon.

Francis Poulenc

Francis Poulenc, born and died Paris (1899–1963), epitomizing the city's spirit of the interwar decades; of its time/place/tone, yet surviving if not transcending it. The public's love of Poulenc has never been in doubt: the intellectuals have been slower to catch on. By now it's obvious that he alone of *Les Six* and its associated culture is destined to last: the apparently slender and silly unobtrusively gains ground by intrinsic quality, concealed at first within pure pleasure, while the portentous, the mediocre, the bogus – Milhaud's *Christophe Colomb*, Tailleferre, Auric, Honegger – sink below the horizon of their time and place. Despite everything, Poulenc remains. And if the qualification suggests surprise, surprise is still what one feels. Far weightier figures than *Les Six* – Schoenberg, Hindemith, Bartók – wax and wane; apparently weighty figures now ascendant – Birtwistle, Shostakovich, Henze – will find their final measure in due course. Poulenc's pendulum is stationary – minor but permanent.

Though not a colossus, his is certainly not a still small voice! Coarse, raucous, titillating, vulgar; bourgeois and well-heeled yet reeking of garlic and gutter, café and circus, *pissoir* and back-alley:

the whiff of incense and the glimpse of stained-glass window
only add piquancy to the succulent mix. By the standards of High
Modernism he's hardly a composer at all. A friend's memorable
remark, that Poulenc's tongue is always in his cheek except when
it's in someone else's, neatly insinuates the technique, or lack of,
whereby, more than any composer before or since, he fabricates
his music by outrageous cribbing. Pastiches or direct quotes from
his favourites – inter alia Mozart, Schumann, Scarlatti, Musorgsky,
Offenbach, Satie, Chabrier, Debussy, Ravel, together with popular
and folk-musics from his native traditions and places – constitute
the entire texture and procedure of his work. The thieving-magpie
approach is itself stolen from the Parisian decades of Stravinsky,
whose 'kleptomania', by contrast so severe and disciplined, nevertheless gave Poulenc an open invitation to his own unbridled
pillage. Stravinsky's *actual* pieces are stolen from most of all – 'you
can tell what Igor's been writing from what Francis writes' (or
words to that effect), said a wag.

The miracle is that the collage – for in no way does he ever try to
synthesize – cannot for a moment be mis-ascribed. Poulenc is always
utterly recognizable, one hundred and ten per cent himself, even
when one is shocked by the petty larceny, before learning to adjust
the cultural focus to admit its frank (he was well-named) delights.
The oeuvre is quite copious, ranging widely in genre and tone.
A ballet, *Les Biches*, sums up more easily than many a portentous
monument the spirit of the 1920s – frivolous, sexy, equivocal. Several
concertos include some incongruous juxtapositions – Gothic horror
and café gaiety (organ); Mozart and Javanese gamelan (two pianos).
But there is not much purely orchestral music, and what there is
is not good. More ambiguous, the stature of the sacred choral pieces
beloved of choristers and audiences alike. The grave, sweet, austerity
of his many unaccompanied motets is moving in its naïve fervour;
but the concert-works with orchestra on religious texts, especially
the ubiquitous *Gloria*, can irritate by the very mix of sanctimony
and vulgarity that gives them their unique smell. The Puritan disapproval which says this isn't how sacred music ought to be is exactly
what's being teased and cajoled into submission that can also be

liberation. The music's vindication is palpable – the *Jongleur de Nôtre-Dame* juggling his balls before the altar, an authentic game equally or more pleasing to the Madonna than suffering seriousness and exalted counterpoint. Heaven forbid that Poulenc perpetrate ersatz-Bach, cod-*Elijah*, off-Messiaen, to realize his religious vision: demotic, sleazy, tacky, can also speak for a full heart. But sometimes it's all just a bit too much. This music seems to lose out from the best of him, to be at once bland yet indecorous, vulgar without the slap 'n' tickle, and often coarsely composed and crudely scored.

Ambiguity becomes definite with Poulenc's most ambitious undertaking, *Dialogues des Carmélites*, an opera concerning Catholic scruples and doubts, set among nuns amid the outside disturbance of the French Revolution. Every listener feels the queasy power of the final scene where the nuns' chorus is depleted, voice by voice, as they reach the terminating clomp of the off-stage guillotine. Here deliberate compositional naffness enacts an extreme situation to unforgettable effect. But the endless preceding stretches are a pious bore: the ultra-tackiness of the subject-matter, together with the actual poverty (not simply frugality) of the musical material, the incongruous mixture of saccharine and asperity, black bread of humility with soft eiderdown of hedonistic comfort, leaves, for once, from this lover of rich food above and below the belt, a really bad taste. Every lover of Poulenc's true muse would instantly swap the nuns for the deliriously silly and utterly inspired *Les Mamelles de Tirésias* ('Tiresias' Tits') with its 'message' – not so silly – to get going, in a world overwhelmed by total warfare (it was composed in 1944) on the job of making babies. This sparkling *divertissement* bids fairest for Poulenc's masterpiece (*and* this un-covertly gay composer fathered an illegitimate daughter two years later: imagine a 'little Miss Britten').

Nevertheless the weight lies mainly in the frailer genres: a varied body of solo piano music; a handful of duo sonatas that, almost uniquely in contemporary music, can exercise the willing amateur as well as the polished professional; they culminate in the ever-green sextet for piano and winds (strings didn't characterize his potential so vividly). And then there is the large output of songs (often composed for Pierre Bernac), far more extensive than those of Debussy or Ravel, let alone the precious handful each by Duparc and Chabrier, to all of whom Poulenc is the deserving heir. Their range of mood, atmosphere, emotions, give him a resonance beyond the *petit maître*. Above all, the love songs, whose finest hour is the Éluard cycle *Tel jour telle nuit*, a surreal recreation of the Heine/Schumann *Dichterliebe* (with Schubert behind both). It shows heightened erotic utterance to be wholly compatible with a musical speech that remains fundamentally within the spirit of light music – elegant, diaphanous, shopsoiled yet transfigured. Like Britten, an inspired accompanist writing for a favoured collaborative artist upon whose distinctive voice every phrase is honed, Poulenc knows his medium through and through. These two have, alone, kept the still small art of *Lieder* alive in songless times.

Spain

A special corner of European music from the late nineteenth/early twentieth century. Hitherto 'Spanish music' had been almost entirely a foreign invention, a branch of the exotic 'Other', Russian from Glinka and Rimsky-Korsakov, then French – *Carmen* and *España*, thence Debussy's frequent incursions and the ubiquity of the strain in Ravel, with his inheritance from his Basque mother. Wholly native roots were first appreciated by Felipe Pedrell (1841–1922), a vital source and father figure for all his younger compatriots; scholar of their country's rich musical past, folkloric and composed (editing Victoria complete and disseminating other old masters). An inspiring teacher; his creative gift not outstanding, though of inestimable value to those who were. It is remarkable that the pattern of his pupils' careers have so much else in common too: some brief biographical and descriptive cameos will show the common trajectory.

Isaac Albéniz – born 1860 – child prodigy pianist (he passed the entrance to the Paris Conservatoire at seven, to be declined on grounds of age!). Adventurous international youth as player – composition-study at Leipzig then Brussels – close contact with

Pedrell, putting him in touch with deeper Spanish roots – glittering European career as pianist/composer. During his years in London, a projected operatic trilogy on Arthurian legends, financed by wealthy English patron (only *Merlin* completed): this post-Wagnerian direction quite wrong for his true gift – brilliant, colourful, virtuoso-pianism Spanishry, its peak the four books of *Iberia* (1905–8), each containing three pieces named after specific locales, and festivals secular or religious. Marvellous though the pianism is, these twelve numbers are more gorgeous still in the orchestrations by his associate Enrique Arbós, who completed five (the others were done by Carlos Surinach, finishing as late as 1955). These supercharged, light-filled vibrating little tone-pictures deserve to be up there with *España*, *Rapsodie espagnole*, *Boléro*. Albéniz lived later in Paris, died 1909.

Enrique Granados – born 1867 – youthful piano-studies in Barcelona – inspiring contact with Pedrell. To Paris 1887 – the Conservatoire not receiving him, took private lessons with one of its professors. Return to Barcelona 1889; further connection with Pedrell; some success with opera, but his more characteristic achievement lies in songs and piano-pieces, particularly *Goyescas* (1911), six miniatures inspired by specific Goya etchings or paintings; later fashioned awkwardly into an opera, best-heard as an enchanting cycle of keyboard-moods, its high-point the celebrated *Maja y el ruiseñor/ The Maiden and the Nightingale*: Granados is only widely remembered for this one lovely flower – it suffices. There might have been more but for his sad end: returning in 1916 from the opera's production in New York the boat was torpedoed; he refusing to abandon his wife, both lives were lost.

Federico Mompou – born 1893, studied piano as a boy in Barcelona: aged nine he heard Fauré play there and never forgot the experience – when he could, reached the Paris Conservatoire, Fauré its head though Mompou studied with others. Returned to Barcelona 1917; 1921 back to Paris, living almost reclusively, admitting no public career either as pianist or composer, gradually amassing a large output of small pieces mainly for his own instrument – on from the intimate aspect of Satie, with Fauré, Debussy, Ravel, Falla, assimilated *in toto*. Its heart came late – four books (1959; 1962; 1965; 1967) of *música callada*/'silent music' – deeply inward and touching (especially in his own coolly rapt recordings) – secret, devotional, concentrated, deceptively simple, wry and sweet – wholly without virtuosity – *spiritual* exercises – 'silent music' indeed – music heard, or overheard, only by its player. Died 1987.

Roberto Gerhard – born 1896, but still in time also to study with Pedrell in Barcelona before breaking the pattern with some five years' work with Schoenberg in Vienna and Berlin – the sole Teutonic element (apart from Albeniz's brief period in Leipzig) in these composers' otherwise wholly Francophile orientations. Back then to Barcelona. The upshot of the Civil War brought him to England 1939; settled in Cambridge till his death 1970. But he remained an unmistakably Spanish composer all the way, even as he evolved from 12-tonerei to become a very self-conscious avant-gardist. The acute hard-edged/metallic sense of pitch and timbre in such later works as the *Concerto for Orchestra* (1965) and the ensemble-pieces characterizing Zodiac-figures – *Leo*, *Libra*, *Gemini* – can recall the bright frugality of the later Falla. And the 1940s, Gerhard's richest period, is pure Spain – two splendid stage-works, ballet on *Don Quixote*, opera on Sheridan's *Duenna*; the marvellous Violin Concerto; the terrific if bombastic 1st Symphony of 1952–3 stands at the cusp.

Manuel de Falla

Manuel de Falla, the most substantial of these composers, also follows their principal trajectory: with variations – he's not Catalan, for a start. Born Cadiz 1876; the city was still a living centre of Andalusian folk-music, vital to Falla's later achievement. Early study of music theory and piano; 1896 to Madrid, livelihood eked out with piano-based chores and writing zarzuelas (five in all). Revelation of Pedrell's absorption in both Spanish popular music and the polyphony of the Golden Age; benefitting too from the older man's awareness of young tendencies from Russia and France. Discovery, 1906, of Louis Lucas' forgotten treatise *L'Acoustique nouvelle*, claimed in later life to be the secret basis of his harmonic thinking. Writing songs and piano-pieces. Two competitions 1904 – for piano-playing, for composition of a one-act opera: Falla won both.

But he never liked Madrid: escape to Paris 1907: Paris in the grip of Spanish fever – *l'heure espagnole* indeed! Ravel engaged on this opera, Albéniz on *Iberia*, Debussy on *Ibéria*. Meets Dukas, always a helpful and revered friend; his compatriots Albéniz and Ricardo Viñes, pianist devoted to the modern impulses. Debussy, to whom Falla owes his deepest debt, was elusive. Needy subsistence; songs and piano-pieces achieving mastery; *La vida breve*, the competition-winning opera, eventually produced after much trouble – Nice 1913, Paris the following year, with success; then Madrid, where he'd returned on the outbreak of war. *El amor brujo*, ballet with song, first version 1915; *Nights in the Gardens of Spain*, orchestral evocations with concertante piano 1916, which also saw the revised *El amor*.

Diaghilev was impressed: a complicated cluster of projects without issue prevented his invitation for Falla to take on some Pergolesi-arrangements – they went instead to Stravinsky, and 'the rest is history'. But Diaghilev did succeed with *Tricorne – The Three-Cornered Hat*, for Massine, décor by Picasso, first version 1917, the fuller revision triumphing in London two years later. In 1920 Falla returns to Spain, settling in Granada. Still needy: two prestigious commissions to the rescue – from Arthur Rubinstein for a major piano-work, *Fantasía Bética* 1919; from the Princesse de Polignac for a theatre-piece, *Master Peter's Puppet-Show*, completed 1922. Friendship with Lorca, serious engagement with the survival and revival of authentic *cante jondo*: many other enterprises and much travel within Spain and abroad – Falla is not yet the reclusive ascetic of later, though his compositions increasingly concentrated and sparse – *Psyché* 1924 (all seven minutes of it); the intense compacted *Harpsichord Concerto* completed 1926. On the other hand, this same year sees the conception of what would have been his mightiest project by far, the would-be vast 'scenic oratorio' *Atlántida*.

In 1936 the Civil War began – Lorca was murdered – the combination precipitates a nervous breakdown: after this Falla's bodily health and spiritual condition are equally fragile, the lifestyle increasingly austere, the absorption in religious devotion almost that of a monk or a mystic. Civil War precedes Global War – with its advent, self-exile to Argentina, initially just for concerts then for permanent residence, isolated and frail, consistently ill both real and hypochondriac (I retain a vivid memory of his house in Granada; the cramped spaces, the cupboard below the stairs where he and his sister took shelter during the bombardments, the narrow single bed, the tiny bath, the medicine-cabinet bristling with every kind of medicine): the lifestyle ever more 'Spanish' in self-denial, the vast *Atlantis*-dream intermittently addressed and, at his death in 1946, far from realized.

'The most substantial' of these Spanish composers: true for the calibre of Falla's oeuvre, but scarcely of its quantity – a tiny handful of intensely wrought music, whose range of idiom and technique, from lush luxuriance to stripped-down austerity, is, even so, surprisingly wide. The *efflorescence* of Albéniz and Granados is reduced to *essence*. Already the *Seven Spanish Folksongs* (finally of 1915) show the process. Product equally of musicological research and compositional resource, lovingly combined with refinement and panache worthy of Ravel's in this area, with the great difference that all this material is native to its composer. Slight and slender, every song varied in approach and treatment, whether heartbroken or mocking, blessing or cursing Love, lulling the baby, or about nothing in particular (the Moorish cloth whereon a spot has fallen, lowering its price).

El amor brujo/*Love, the Sorcerer* develops similar stuff with greater length and elaboration: Candelas the gypsy-girl, obsessed by the memory of a departed lover whose ghost interferes with her new man Carmelo's wooing: another girl is deployed to entice the dead man's spirit (in life he had been unfaithful yet jealous); and faithful new love triumphs. Each brief number is perfected – scene-setting, song of un-requitement, dance of terror as the evil spirit menaces, magic circle of midnight as he is exorcized in the famous Ritual Fire Dance, the will-o'-the-wisp song when the exorcism hasn't fully worked, the seductive Pantomime by which the other girl beguiles the phantom, the concluding Dance of the Game of Love as day breaks, bells ring out, Candelas and her Carmelo conjoin in harmony (and the evil one and his dupe are left, presumably, to their own pleasures).

Nights in the Gardens of Spain is Falla's closest approach to the French-Spanish music so inspiring and liberating for him – Debussy's: for evocative suggestiveness, for sensuous opulence, for letting itself go. Paradoxically it is at the same time more formal both in structure and in genre than Debussy in his prime. A thematically linked triptych of nocturnal reverie, dance, festivity – Alhambra and Córdoba, wholly beguiling, that maybe doesn't add up into a compelling whole. Also true of Falla's longest and most ambitious completed score, the *Three-Cornered Hat*, a showpiece for the Diaghilev company in its post-war years, at its best in self-contained dances comprising the two concert-suites, at its weakest in linking passages for mime and narration.

From now on direct Spanishry in Falla's output is gradually relinquished: the music grows harder and sparer, losing *volupté* and warmth: an essentialization into the inner life of the idiom comparable to Stravinsky's treatment of his Russian folklore after the *amplesse* of the first three Diaghilev-scores. First yield, *Fantasía Bética* (from the Roman name for Andalusia): the comparison in actual keyboard sonority is with Bartók – again a concentration of folkloric material from earlier richness: brittle and pungent, guitar and harpsichord to the fore, somewhat rebarbative till the central intermezzo with its beautiful translation into keyboard terms of the singing voice. More traditionally pianistic, Falla's last piece for *actual* piano, the memorial *hommage* to his friend and champion Dukas on his death in 1935 – grave, serious, plain even in its fullness: but the *Bética* more nearly foretells the keyboard work falling between, the concerto for *actual* harpsichord. And for *actual* guitar the *tombeau* for Claude Debussy, Falla's contribution to a symposium published in 1920 commemorating the great composer's death two years before. Both these *hommages*, with two others, later orchestrated in a suite of *homenajes*, where they probably sound to best advantage.

The next work of size is the theatre-piece *Master Peter's Puppet-Show*. A very original conception derived from Cervantes by the composer himself. Don Quixote, Sancho Panza in attendance, witnesses a puppet-play telling a heroic/romantic episode from the days of Charlemagne. Master Peter presents, his Boy shrills 'roll up, roll up' and sets scene and personages – rescue of Christian Princess Melisendra from Moorish captivity by her knight Gayferos, all preceding well in the teeth of Moorish menaces on Melisendra's chastity, till interrupted briefly but imperturbably, then at increasing length and waxing exasperation by the deluded old Quixote, in the end putting the whole show to rout, and culminating in ardent prayer to his peerless Dulcinea and a paean to the nobility of knight-errantry. This odd little piece, at once fresh and crinkled, radiant and sombre, is a consistent and surprising treat, realizing the precarious conceit more fully than either of its two stage-predecessors their scenarios. And it has some of the best bitonality ever written – genuine friction between alien tonalities, acutely registered and telling – 'right-note' dissonance in the epoch of 'wrong-note music' by even some of its best composers and plenty of its poorest.

Bitonality lives rampant in the *Harpsichord Concerto* (its sonority already exploited in the puppet-piece: Falla indicates piano as alternative but the older instrument is vital to the work's effect). The clash of keys here is terrifying – crude, extreme, ugly, implacable, and absolutely *echt*, unforgiving in the slow middle movement, crackly and acrid in the opening allegro and the closing vivace. These outer movements can sound merely dry: in a good performance (especially that made soon after the première with the composer himself and most of the original five-piece 'orchestra') the crackle (not just that of the recording's date) burns and scrawbs like no other music of the epoch save the Devil's triumphal march in Stravinsky's *Soldier's Tale*. While the middle movement resembles nothing else whatever. Its unlikely performance-indication, *giubiloso ed energico* ('jubilant and energetic'), is complemented by date and festival at its end – *A. Dom. MCMXXVI. in Festo Corporis Christi*: before playing this movement Falla used to 'bend his head, close his eyes, and fold his hands in prayer'. Rapid arpeggiated chords introduce and punctuate a liturgical chant, massively chordal on violin and cello, then put against itself in grinding imitation on all the instruments. Then the Procession – bare-footed, bare-backed flagellants, whipped and blood-flecked, the chant in one key, fully chordal, on the keyboard, against the unchanging tonality of the five other players – an unforgettable sonorous image of unbearable anguish, bodily and spiritual, repeated a little later with the instrumental forces reversed. Between, the movement's only *pianissimo*, like a sigh from the catacombs, without the harpsichord, which crashes in with the second round of torture. Elsewhere, cascades of scales ascending and descending, first time on the keyboard, second on the three woodwinds, third on clarinet only, which *do* seem to justify the *giubiloso*. Another recurring element is the harpsichord's lower register thrice interpolating deep bell-resonances on other notes alien to what's heard on the surface – gnomic wordless sidelines in a movement that, albeit brief, appears enormous, nay endless, in its merciless cruelty yet, amazingly, concludes in an unforced unfeigned blaze of accord. Not till the far-more-exiguous Christian Sonatas of Galina Ustvolskaya is a work of *real* music so reduced (at least Falla's still does *pitches*).

So to the problematic *Atlántida*, easily his largest and most ambitious venture, undertaken however as his lengths contracted, his idiom concentrated and his health failed. *L'Atlántida* – epic poem in Catalan by Jacinto Verdaguer completed 1876 (Falla's initial interest sparked by its fiftieth anniversary 1926) – covers with magnificent scope the myth of the submerged continent, the founding legends of Spain and its evolution from Pagan to Christian, and Columbus's discovery of the New World. The composer adapted the text himself, freely adding and subtracting while retaining the broad shape. Prologue, *Sunken Atlantis*, presents to Columbus (unnamed) as a boy the figure of Atlas, once sustainer of the vault of heaven and ruler over the Garden of the Hesperides where now the ocean rolls, its destruction the punishment meted out by the gods to his overweening sons, the Atlantides. Who then saved Spain? The True God, raising a protective wall of Pyrenees: *Hymnus Hispanicus* in his praise.

Part I is largely completed and wholly coherent. For the remainder, state of story, text, score, grow more and more uncertain and there is precious little of the real Falla in the copious anonymous wasteland. Strangest, the representation of the monster Geryon with his three heads – three male singers, the middle with words that appear just and true; the upper and lower grunt and expectorate in wordless mockery, giving the true words the lie. Strongest, two choruses, hymning first Spain then Barcelona – fierce in sinewy jubilation. But much of the score's devoted realizer's work is a mishmash, including oodles of Debussy and, for the Garden of the Hesperides, more than a whiff of the Flower-maidens from *Parsifal*. The conflicting condition of scores, recordings, descriptions, is as yet impossible to reconcile.

Happier to close this very close figure with two works of finished perfection. Well, not quite: *Homenajes* for orchestra, completed 1938, is a miscellany – four *hommages* to revered fellow-musicians: a fanfare on E(nriques) F(ernández) A(rbós) is a bit nondescript: more surprising the extended finale, the work's only new composing, on themes from Spanish music's father figure, Pedrell, strangely lacks identifying features. No one but Falla could have composed the other two: the achingly poignant tribute to Debussy, quoting from the French master's Spanish works wherein, Falla claimed, Spanish music first disclosed its full potential; and the achingly sombre processional for Dukas, as scored from the piano-original still more sonorous with its heavy soft brass and resonating gong – *spes vitae* its new superscription, the dense elliptical harmony resembling the best music, its opening, in *Atlántida*. And *Psyché* is perfect: flute and harp with string trio accompany the soprano singing a precious little conceit in French by a friend of the composer – after the disastrous disclosure of her lover Cupid's identity, Psyché, rather than to despair, is invited to enjoy the new day in all its spring freshness: a fastidiously wrought miniature of surpassing elegance, matched by the enchanting *very* miniature engraved score with its pastiche mock-heroic dedicatory epistle.

CHAPTER XIV
Russia Resumed

Stravinsky

What strikes the impartial listener confronted with Stravinsky's earliest compositions is their relative paucity of raw talent and their absolute absence of originality. Of all the great Moderns his is the smallest natural gift: there's nothing comparable to Schoenberg's *Verklärte Nacht* and *Gurrelieder*, Bartók's *Kossuth* and *Second Suite*, Berg's *Altenberglieder*, or, nearer to home, the young Rachmaninov, or, from a slightly later birth-date, the rich abundance of the young Hindemith before he curbed it.

Igor Stravinsky, born near St Petersburg 1882, died New York 1971. His first music is dull and dutiful: the Symphony in Eb (1905–7) heavily beholden to Glazunov, with unconvincing Tchaikovskian elements; the four *Études* for piano (1908) to Scriabin and Rachmaninov; the two orchestral pieces – *Scherzo Fantastique* (1907–8) and *Fireworks* (1908) to his teacher Rimsky-Korsakov, with contemporary French touches from Dukas rather than Ravel or Debussy: the *Chant funèbre* in Rimsky's memory (1908), recently recovered after more than a century gone missing, reveals the imprint of his later principal abomination Wagner. (And the middle section of the *Scherzo* is virtually a paraphrase of the Good Friday music in *Parsifal*.) *Faun and Shepherdess* (1907), modest little scena after Pushkin, retains a faded charm: the first act of *Le Rossignol/The Nightingale* (1909), Oriental fairy-tale after Andersen, is on an altogether higher level than any of these others.

But it was *Fireworks* that caught Diaghilev's attention and led eventually to the commission for a full-length ballet on the legend of the Prince, the Monster and the Firebird. Its popularity, as Stravinsky soon superseded his first triumph, came to embarrass him as much as Beethoven had been by his Septet, Wagner by *Rienzi*, Schoenberg by *Verklärte Nacht*. *Firebird* – best relished *in toto* in all its lavish expansiveness rather than in the too-selective suites in the various revampings by which the composer sought to retain endangered royalties for his most frequently played work – remains supreme in Orientalist/nationalist allure and sheer coloristic virtuosity: undercut by another devastating comment, the composer's own, in retrospect – 'I was prouder of the orchestration than of the music.' (Debussy had remarked soon after the première, 'You've got to begin somewhere.')

The immediate upshot of *Firebird*'s immediate success is right on target: *Petrushka* (1911). Every feature of plot and place suits: the Petersburg setting, the outdoor raucousness of the city's Shrovetide Fair, and their cinematic intercutting; then the sinister claustrophobia of the indoor action with its cast of dolls and puppets and their mystic manipulator; above all the rage with which Petrushka's frustration is rendered, originating in a concertante for piano versus orchestra vividly expressing impotent fury, brilliantly adapted for and incorporated into the scenario. All these elicit authentic utterance despite – still – being unoriginal in themselves; the Charlatan's mystic passes are pure Scriabin, the crowd-scenes pure Russian nationalism electrically recharged by startling juxtapositions of tempo and texture, the provocative piano and annihilating orchestra pure Liszt enhanced with Ravel's *Jeux d'eau*; and, prophetic, the Ballerina, object of Petrushka's hapless longing, and his rival the Moor whom she favours, both depicted in cliché-material, dinky-pretty for her, sultry-saturnine for him, tweaked, parodied, dangled in ironic tweezers perfectly rendering straw-filled puppets on their twitching strings. The effect at the ballet's close when interior erupts out into the bustling market-place, and the miniature *crime passionnel* is exposed, Petrushka's humanity flickers into visibility and is flicked out – 'see, only sawdust!' – then reappears as jeering ghost, eternally gibbering, futile as when he was 'alive', is one of the iconic moments in the century's arts at large.

So to the century's most notorious artistic scandal. The clamour dies down: well before its centenary *The Rite of Spring* (1911–13), never fully satisfactory as danced until much later, had been assimilated into the concert repertoire as an unfailing showpiece, bringing orchestras to their knees and audiences to their feet. And truly perceived as the ultimate outcome of nineteenth-century Russian nationalism: a maximalist triumph of folklore (and actual folk-material, long suppressed and denied by its composer, but proven by his sketches and the patient assiduity of scholarship); Glinka's *Kamarinskaya*-method of cycles of ever-enhancing repetition, Musorgsky's rough uncouthness, Rimsky's brilliant polish, at their ultimate; an extreme consummation with – for Stravinsky himself, if not for some ill-advised imitators – no future whatever unless fully assimilated and refashioned. Paradoxical, that this terminal exposition of primitivity – the annual ritual sacrifice of a virgin girl to propitiate the old gods and ensure renewed fertility – is at the same time a thoroughly modern machine empowered with every device of mechanized mass-efficiency, progenitor of subsequent celebrations-in-sound of steam-engines, skyscraper-topped cities, iron foundries, equally with primeval rites set in remote archaic paganism.

And piquant that *Le Sacre* is surrounded in Stravinsky's own contemporary oeuvre by exoticism, Orientalism, delicacy/precious-ness/refinement, at the opposite pole from its colossalism; also by one work of mysterious magnificence virtually unique till divulging surprising relationships with some subsequent descendants. Delicacy and lyricism flourish in two settings of *Balmont Poems* (1911), precious refinement in three ravishing *Japanese Lyrics* (1913), Stravinsky's creative response to the unforgettable impression made by *Pierrot lunaire* at one of its earliest unveilings in Berlin. Chinoiserie *in excelsis* (with an excursus into Japonaiserie for the mechanical nightingale), in the further two acts completing *Le Rossignol* (1913–14). The apparent discrepancy between Act I of 1908 and the immediately post-*Sacre* continuation is, in fact, a felicity. The earlier music is all standard Orientalism, effected with skill and poetry – the Nightingale's *fioriture* – and wit, the absurd courtiers, mistaking frogs for the bird, then their fatuous pleasure when disabused. Blown away by *courants d'air*, virtuoso entry to the modern acts, inventing exoticism to come (notably Messiaen's): the fantastic *marche Chinois* – best Orientalism in all music? – the wooden stiltedness of the mechanical bird, the Scriabin/Szymanowski of the true bird (Roxana from *King Roger* heightened into ecstasy), the ghoulish fanfares characterizing Death: all this (save the Emperor's perhaps slightly perfunctory recovery at hearing the living birdsong) is consummate of its kind: and the three-act totality is beautifully enclosed within a framework, the song of the Fisherman who has observed the story from the side-lines.

The unique work aforementioned is *Zvezdoliki/King of the Stars* (1911–12), setting for chorus and enormous orchestra of Balmont's exalted, vatically obscure poem; dedicated to Debussy and, in its weak second half, revealing indebtedness, albeit in *hommage*, amounting to plagiarism. The first half, however, is strong, daringly stark, its naked major/minor harmony in blocks of antiphonal sonority prophetic of the great work Stravinsky would all-too-soon be dedicating to Debussy's memory; still more, of the *Symphony of Psalms*, setting texts altogether worthy of its still-greater dedicatee, God himself.

The finest fruit of Stravinsky's native culture in his own music, *Svadebka/Les Noces/The Wedding*, ballet with song, was also conceived, and composed in its first form, during these protean years: essentially intact by 1914, held up by uncharacteristic uncertainties over appropriate instrumentation, running through almost contradictory solutions down the next near-decade, its musical substance substantially the same till the definitive final solution of 1923. *Les Noces* is the end of the line for nationalistic Russian folklore, concentrating the impulse with drastic austerity, eschewing all the command of colour and virtuosity paramount in its three predecessors. No orchestra, whether gigantic as first envisaged, or reduced to a pungent cimbalom/dulcimer-sizzling ensemble; no pianolas (a further failed notion): a black/white gamelan of four pianos and percussion tuned or (mainly) unpitched; inevitable and right accompaniment to the voices, choral (mainly) and soloists who represent rather than actually *are* the Bride, the Groom, the Mother, the drunken Guest, the Priest, enacting the timeless wedding-rites. Richard Taruskin's description remains best – 'fundamentally monodic, or heterophonic … departing radically from the norms of traditional Western practice': just as his one-page demonstration encapsulates the work's entire 'musical space' into a single plane of modal/scalic symmetries/asymmetries 'whose intellectual beauty strikes as deep as the work's joyous physicality and the stirring realities within its formalized presentation of the fundamental facts of human continuity', and his hundred-page indication of sources gathers in the rich lore of ritual observance with the same encyclopaedic fervour as Stravinsky's in setting them to sounds. Here – rather than in *The Rite*, now more aptly perceived as the last of its kind – is the refreshing recharge that ensures renewal, be the result for good – Messiaen, Copland, Britten; for fair-to-middling – *Carmina Burana*; for middling-to-poor – minimalism à la Reich and Adams; or for minimalism puny – Glass. Renewal most of all for Stravinsky himself. After *Les Noces* he abandons explicit Russian folklore; but the techniques and habits learnt here remain constant across every later vicissitude right to the end.

Svadebka remains unsolved background to the puzzling diversity of Stravinsky's wartime-work right into the early 1920s: the output varies between insouciantly trivial *jeux d'occasion*, a couple of innovatory theatre-pieces on a reduced platform, and one individual masterpiece, the *Symphonies of Wind Instruments*, as seminal to the subsequent century as is the sung ballet. Trivialities first: eight miniature piano-duets in two sets – a march, waltz and polka with easy second-part for tyro players, the dedicatees respectively Casella, Satie (no tyros) and Diaghilev (who might just have managed the polka's one-bar vamp); the second set, where the tyro takes the top, comprises an andante, Española, Balalaïka, Napolitana and gallop. Little snatches of popular commonplace sarcastically disdained with dissonance/grimace/subversion, cheeky and snide, wickedly delectable. Comparable, the solo piano *Cinq Doigts* (1922), ostensibly for children (beginning with his own), though too full of traps and stretches beyond small hands really to serve the purpose so solicitously achieved in the earlier books of Bartók's *Mikrokosmos*.

On a higher shelf the *Three Pieces for String Quartet* (1914), where caricature certainly plays a part, reflecting in its destructive attitude towards Austro-Germany's most hallowed medium Stravinsky's bitter contempt for Teutonia from his wartime Swiss security (shown in naked crudity in such polemics as *Souvenir d'une marche boche* with its hate-filled quote from Beethoven's 5th Symphony), even as he delights in no. 1 in the sweaty-peasant bagpipes from his native land, and in no. 2 affectionately imitates the appearance and gesticulations of a famous English clown. But no. 3 is altogether other – *cantique* of rapt inward devotion (headed *liturgique* when he subsequently orchestrated it), pertaining to the litanies in the *Symphonies of Wind Instruments*, thence to the *Symphony of Psalms* and on into the religious works of the 1950s and 60s. Also for string quartet, the *Concertino* of 1920 takes the anti-medium textures of *Three Pieces* into better places – a strong astringent piece, as also in a much later full instrumentation. And *Piano-Rag-Music* (1919), among several other such flirtations, is a miracle of witty deconstruction/ reassembly cubism.

Alongside all these (1914–20) come several sets of miniature songs or choruses with a handful of instruments, generically known as *Pribaoutki* – Russian peasant or children's nonsense verses and games, set to notes that even when tender – lullabies for cats – are acrid and crinkly without concession to normal notions of euphony, and remain thus, unassimilated, undigested. An exhilarating dose of salts for palates jaded and sated with pralines and marshmallows, chips off the *Svadebka* block (always in the background, unresolved, all these years). And close-aligned to the two complete theatre-pieces, *Renard* (1915–16) and *L'Histoire du soldat* (1918); more extensive yet still brief and composed of juxtaposed miniatures.

Renard – universal fable of the vainglorious cock, boasting of his prowess among his hens, twice tempted down from his proud perch by the ingratiating fox who's eventually routed and killed by other farmyard animals: a consummate affair, witty in timing, sharp-etched in instrumentation, mordant in characterization: a triumph

of folklore raised into art. *The Soldier's Tale* is more savvy/chic/city-
ish, with its tango, *valse*, ragtime – the piano-duet parodies taken far
further, notably in the chorales that punctuate the kind of sententious inverted moralizing later perfected in Brecht's family-prayers
for Weill's *Seven Deadly Sins*. These chorales flay Bach's euphonious
four-part harmonizations with '*inappétisant*' wrong notes à la Satie,
as if the inadvertent *trouvailles* in this area, when Ballerina and Moor
collide in *Petrushka*, were now elevated to a Principle of Perversity, its
tone unmistakably anti-Hun. The solo violin, property of the Soldier
till gambled to the Devil (the story is again Andersen), is equally
defiant of violin-as-cantabile, and highly prophetic of the works with
which Stravinsky resumes writing for the instrument in the early
1930s: the percussion-only ending as the Devil triumphs without
bothering any further to collect his due, the best tunes, is a striking
success not taken up later – this was left to Varèse. Compared with
Renard, compact and crammed with invention, *L'Histoire* seems a
little dilute and distended: too much speech?

The *Symphonies of Wind Instruments* (1920) brings to the surface
elements, elsewhere only implicit in these years, of the Russian
liturgy. This awkwardly named masterpiece originates in its eventual
goal, the closing chorale, composed for the album of tributes for
Debussy, who'd died in 1918. The impressive fragment might have
remained thus, un-instrumented, an icon of marvellous hieratic
chords, glowing yet freezing, solidifying into stillness. The subsequent forward extrapolation of the eventual work is equally iconic;
with the *Rite*, Stravinsky's most influential score. Not at once: misunderstood, scorned, neglected for decades until its importance
gradually percolated and ramified. A form made of fragments, juxtaposed and sometime superimposed, a mosaic of nuggets up against
each other edge-to-edge, differing in momentum and timbre, woodwinds and brasses in separate choirs, antiphonal and formal; a sublimated re-creation, with no resemblance in actual idiom, of the
liturgy of the Russian Requiem.

Wildly contrasting ingredients hurled at the listener like stones –
shrill high ejaculations with a twiddle; rich, soft, slow chord
repeated long: short; a four-note snatch of hollowed-out chant;

the chord again, long: short, with a brief new continuation; the wondrous single chord again; the four-note chant now extended to six: the chord, long: short; a sort of Amen on two high oboes and cor anglais. So it goes; self-evident, the intercut of sonorities, speeds, characters, timbres, always clear and unambiguous. Now for continuity over fragmentation: continuous interplay of textures, timbres, tempi, startling new voicings, characters ranging from wilful/lugubrious to sharp/spiky, growling low and strident high, lulling and hypnotic or ferocious: a kaleidoscope, the same elements in ever-differing alignments: everything growing, as it were, backwards from the originating chorale, which is at the same time the work's inevitable destination. It is finally given complete, on full forces though still chorically alternating, the harmony at once mercilessly austere and tinglingly juicy; finally, after a silence, the tutti, soft yet permeating. Religious ritual abstracted into sonority.

The paradox of such austerity and gawkiness as a tribute to Claude Debussy! Yet the *Symphonies'* mosaic construction is the logical successor to Debussy's Way, most of all in *Jeux*, whose aesthetic shot-silk suavity and sexy subject-matter are at the most opposite imaginable: it makes one blink to realize that *Parsifal* somehow illuminates both from far, far behind. Far more immediate, the importance for all Stravinsky's ensuing composition of the non-developmental mode of continuity perfected here – albeit rooted in Glinka's *Kamarinskaya*, that mighty 'acorn' – a new way of building a musical journey crucial for many very different kinds of composer in decades to come.

Finally from these diverse and pregnant years, something equally prescient and completely different. Encouraged by the success of two ballets with music arranged from Italian Baroque originals, Diaghilev put to his house-composer a similar project based upon bits and pieces of Pergolesi and his circle, to be danced by Léonide Massine and designed by Picasso. The result, *Pulcinella* (1919–20), is a delight: Stravinsky's part mainly confined to a very inauthentic orchestration of his materials, occasionally venturing more freely, and very occasionally revealing the composer of *The Rite of Spring*. This modest job proved equally an Open Sesame to the future as the *Symphonies*, its consequences more audible and more immediate. 'The epiphany that made all my later music possible,' he wrote in grateful retrospect: as the 1920s dawn and Stravinsky's style takes a new direction, these words are put into deeds.

'Neo-classicism': the interwar decades

The significant and provocative dedication of his brief *opera buffa Mavra* (1921–2) to the memory of Pushkin, Glinka and Tchaikovsky, heralds for Stravinsky a changed stance: explicitly invoking an older Russia – not archaic, primeval, folkloric, pagan – civilized, European, artistic; and implicitly revoking the picturesque coloristic fairy-tale/ legendary legerdemain of Rimsky-Korsakov that had culminated in *Firebird* and exploded in *Le Sacre*. A pity that this tight, light, dry piece – based upon a Pushkin episode wherein the daughter of the house ensures her lover's attendance by having him hired by her mother as their (female) cook, the ruse successful until he's discovered shaving – made few converts to such an important aesthetic transformation. Not until *Apollo* (1927–8) could the switch of idiom be counted lovable; still more the next piece, *Le Baiser de la fée/ The Fairy's Kiss* (1928), where Tchaikovsky's own material is lovingly recomposed. Not for the last time, Stravinsky's previously ardent advocates were disconcerted, or worse, by the volte-face: they were reassured that he was back on the right track when, eventually, in 1923, *Les Noces* reached the stage in its final perfected sonority.

But its musical substance dates back to 1914: Stravinsky's *new* music was just as disconcerting as *Mavra*. The *Octet* for wind instruments (1922–3) delights with its wit and dexterity – 'Baroque' and 'Clementi' (Satie's *Sonatine bureaucratique* recalled) teased into 'Cubism' with flair and fun: the ensuing Piano Concerto with an orchestra only of winds, timpani and double basses (1923–4) remains lumpy, stiff, uningratiating, if imposing; something left out to weather. Upper strings, with their suspiciously expressive cantabile, were backgrounded in *Mavra* and omitted entirely in the *Octet* and the concerto: after this latter a solo-piano phase follows whereby the composer, always exigent and with rather an expensive lifestyle, sought a career for his own idiosyncratic playing: *Sonata* (1924), *Serenade in A* (1925), somewhat dry music though no longer *forbidding*.

Forbidding for sure, the next theatre-piece, *Oedipus Rex* of 1926–7. Upper strings are re-admitted in full, though the sonority's *tinta* remains wind-heavy, with piano and timpani also prominent. Very of-the-epoch to adapt the Sophocles, a story known to everyone; and have Cocteau's skeletal epitome translated into Latin so that familiarity can be kept at arm's length by 'a language turned to stone', and to have the audience furthermore alienated by the dinner-jacketed compère patronizingly introducing each new twist of the trap, with, towards the end, a hint of pity for the wretched protagonist, victim of hubris, his pride crushed, his body violated, his life in 'disaster, ruin, shame' – another victim to the sacrifice – delivered in clipped radio-announcer's accents in the language of wherever the opera is performed (the Latin is obligatory). Then to call it not an opera but an 'opera-oratorio', and have its musical idioms range from Bach to Offenbach – Johann Sebastian for Oedipus' beautiful self-pitying pleas for his people's understanding as destiny begins to close in; Jacques for the final romping chorus describing the off-stage hideosities when the trap is sprung: and including – for Creon – oodles of Handel; for Jocasta almost-parody Verdi: and throwing in Russian church-music, the Hymn closing the first part repeated exact at the start of the second. Seemingly chic as described: in effect the unlikely amalgam comes over with power and authority: catharsis is achieved, guilt of parricide and incest, flaws of superbia, purged and expiated: Oedipus' moment of truth makes one long for how Stravinsky might have risen to an *Antigone* maybe, an *Oedipus at Colonus* surely. (These were left, respectively, to Honegger – forget it; and Enescu, whose contemporaneous *Oedipe* tells the life-story complete in a style and aesthetic drastically antithetical to Stravinsky's; they make an absorbing comparison.)

Strings in all their cantabile beauty are not only reallowed but form the entire sound-body in Stravinsky's next – *Apollo Musagetes* (1927–8) – whose subject is, of course, the birth and celebration of music itself, with grace, balance, proportion, measure. At last pleasure, however strait-laced and disciplined, can be re-admitted too! This lovely score, gracious and yielding, occasionally heroic and dynamic, was very soon to be rechoreographed by Balanchine, their first collaboration in a succession so richly fulfilled subsequently.

But not for the next, *The Fairy's Kiss* (1928), a near-terminal enterprise of the insatiable Ida Rubenstein, which effects for Tchaikovsky in ardent cognizance what he'd done impulsively, with pleasure and detachment, for 'Pergolesi' in *Pulcinella* a decade or so before. Tchaikovsky, though, is Stravinsky's native culture. In what must have appeared to be permanent exile from a homeland abandoned to philistine values comes this homage to the principal ornament of the lost Imperial regime, Tchaikovsky and the ballet. No matter that it is only his minor salon-music that Stravinsky uses as a basis: this allegory of the composer's fate, the kiss of the muse who animates then destroys, is powerful. There's no real plot: the allegory suffices: and the recreation of the master's spirit, so opposite in temperament – all ardour, openness, abandon, as against all wit, control, cool – makes for something unique in Stravinsky's oeuvre and in the epoch's music at large. Most remarkably in the unlikely yet fervent embrace of Tchaikovsky's emotionalism, whereby 'None But the Lonely Heart', a drawing-room throbberama nearing kitsch, is transfigured by the merciless X-raying learnt in Stravinsky's parody-years into a surpassing, utterly un-ironic, expression of longing and loss: an identification across abysses of time and type that testifies to a true bond between the two composers, beyond the mere cultural polemics of Stravinsky's initial embracing an Imperial rather than a populist inheritance. The ensuing Epilogue's frozen-in-time-and-space bleakness doesn't efface this moving tribute to heart-on-sleeve sincerity. And the ballet's earlier scenes are a treasury of invention without compare: Stravinsky the self-confessed 'miser in music' here pours out his gold in plenty.

Just here comes his final work for himself as soloist, the *Capriccio* for piano and orchestra (1928–9), where grace and charm, inspired by Weber, win out against the grim 'wrong-note' Baroque of the earlier concerto. A delight: blown sky-high by Stravinsky's next – the *Symphony of Psalms* (1930), wherein the Paris playboy with a White

Russian past bridges the divide and again realigns himself with what endures and can be resuscitated from across it. The symphony's dedication nicely balances God and Mammon: *'composée à la gloire de Dieu'* and *'dédiée au "Boston Symphony Orchestra" à l'occasion du cinquantenaire de son existence'*. Orchestra again heavily weighted by winds: flutes, oboes, trumpets (with all their doublings) in fives (but eschewing the warmer, more luscious clarinets – too Wagnery/ Brahmsy); deep drums (no other percussion); only low strings; a harp, two pianos: the resulting *Klang* unforgettable from first *secco* chord to last long-sustained wide-voiced soft tutti major third, resonating on in body and spirit well after it has vanished. In between, the three Psalms – Latin again obligatory.

No. 1: prayer arising from depths of lamentation – 'hold not thy peace: for I come as a stranger before thee, and a sojourner as all my fathers were. O spare me a little that I may recover my strength before I go hence and be no more seen': excoriating cry from the pit of abasement, mounting steadily from semitonal wailing to broad beseeching clamour.

No. 2: a double fugue, one instrumental, very Bachian, upon which is superimposed the second, on chorus, somewhat Handelian. The text advocating patience and writing rhymes powerfully with the mood of Eliot's exactly contemporary *Ash Wednesday*:

> Lord I am not worthy
> Lord I am not worthy
> > but speak the word only.

The clamour of No. 1 has been heard, the Lord has raised the patient penitent from the mire, set his feet upon the rocks, ordered his goings, and given him a new song of thanksgiving. 'Many shall see it, shall see it and fear, and shall put their trust in the LORD' (the appellation printed in CAPS throughout the work, and so-to-speak set to CAPS in the music). Not open to doubt that, for all the granitic Byzantine impersonality 'turned to stone', a tone of Vindication is sensed here – 'many shall see it, and fear'. It will not be the last.

So to no. 3, Psalm 150 in its entirety, praising the LORD, in his holiness, in the firmament of his power, in his noble acts, according to his excellent greatness: thence to the instruments of praise – trumpet, lute, harp, strings, pipes: praise him all creatures that have breath: Alleluia. The 'new song', granted in the second Psalm setting, is heard in hypnotic slow stasis over an ostinato ordering its goings, closing the first section with the luminous major third, plus flattened seventh, a quasi-dominant asking for more. Vouchsafed in an energetic propulsive allegro, repeated-note pulsations remembered from Jocasta's muttered *oracula* in *Oedipus*, downward-plunging cascades acknowledged by the composer to be inspired by Elijah's fiery chariot, chatter as of the startled neighbours ending *Mavra*; all these transcending their antecedents. Then cools into stately Baroque sarabande, which locks into rocking slowness and return of opening tempo for praise upon the well-tuned cymbals, upon the loud cymbals (nothing *literal* here, nor for the Psalmist's volume-level). Final section: 'choir' of five trumpets, five oboes, eventually the entire block of winds over the eternal three-note ostinato on pianos, harp, timpani: harmony all-diatonic with added pitches, and chromatic touches that burn without pain; thinning out into the simple opening Alleluia and closing on the calm-shining wide-spaced major third, now without the suggestive dominant seventh, for the last word, DOMINUM, the wonderful work's more permanent dedicatee.

Relaxation into lyricism: the violin is now granted most of its full scope in two major works, the Violin Concerto (1931) and the *Duo Concertant* with piano, completed the following year. The concerto is perhaps the finest fruit of the 'Back to Bach' tendency of these interwar decades, whether German (Hindemith) or else-wise. In its outer movements the cheerful extrovert aggression of the instrument's leading role in *L'Histoire du soldat* is taken to new heights: in the two arias, the spare-spun linear elegance first heard in *Apollo* blooms yet more freely. And the *Duo* is maybe the most perfect embodiment of the epoch's neo-classicism. An Apollonian Tempietto for the Muses, rustic yet aristocratic: two *Eclogues* and closing *Dithyrambe* explicitly Grecian; a (slightly garrulous) *Gigue* explicitly

Baroque; the opening *Cantilène* after initial chatter grandly unfolding into softened 'humanized' aspects of the thrilling granite of the
Symphonies of Winds.

Alongside these two, another major piece of the highest calibre,
again for the composer himself (as with the *Duo*) as co-performer –
the Concerto for Two Pianos (no orchestra) of 1931–5. Its unusually
protracted composition indicates its complexity and density of
thought. Strenuous music: only the second movement, *Notturno*,
delivers charm – in abundance: the first is long and demanding
for all its limpid lucidity: some passages foretell direct the angry
patterns fuelling the *Symphony in Three Movements* a decade later.
And the fourth introduces a mighty figure new to Stravinsky's
pantheon of models and exemplars. The third had consisted of four
variations without initial annunciation of a theme: which emerges
towards the end, to become (after a slow introduction) subject of
a fugue whose high-tension and intervallic stringency recreate the
Große Fuge from Beethoven's *Quartet* op. 130 (the *Fuge* is op. 133). It
leaps and grinds and turns upon itself in *stretto* till peremptorily
slain; to be recast, in inversion and drastically curtailed; a rhetorical
apotheosis, a sudden curt quiet end: a cornerstone of the limited
repertoire for this unlimiting medium.

Stravinsky's next theatre-piece is a hybrid: *Perséphone* (1933–4),
ballet with words – choral; a single solo singer (male) in the role
of narrator-cum-commentator; the protagonist herself (initially Ida
Rubenstein, yet again), who speaks as well as dances. She, and the
work, are encumbered with the high-toned fustian with which Gide
clad the archaic myth, another rite-of-spring whereby a virgin girl
is sacrificed – here not to her death; just for the winter-half of each
year – to ensure ever-renewed regrowth. The embarrassment of its
text and the expense of its requirements make *Perséphone* a rarity
in theatres and concerts. The principal sacrifice is not so much her
maidenhead as the loss of (amid some perfunctory wait-till-ready
noodlings) Stravinsky's freshest and tenderest music.

Another dance-piece follows, unfoist with words sung let alone
spoken, its inspiration a formalized game of poker in three deals –
Jeu de cartes (1936); a witty score packed with parody and some actual

quotations, showing signs of standard manufacture for all its vitality. They materialize more apparent in the little chamber concerto *Dumbarton Oaks*, completed two years later. For the first time the term *epigonic* crosses the mind, listening to this neat, dry music, somehow devoid of 'identifying characteristics' for all its unmistakable traits: and of heart, that its composer would have disdained in theory but had restored in practice, in his own (in)imitable way ever since *Apollo* and *Le Baiser*. This music is growing tired and *routiné*; in need of another recharge; a change of attitude and idiom. The *Symphony in C* stands square on the fault line – biographical too: over the course of its composition the composer relocated to the USA: the work's first two movements are European, its second two American. The 'European' half contains Stravinsky's most explicit homage to Austro-German symphonism, principal model Haydn, Beethoven for the propulsive dynamism: the 'American' finale is, in fact, explicitly Russian in material and sonority; the slow introduction and its later recurrence within the ensuing allegro – the liturgical bassoons recalling the *Symphonies* of winds and of Psalms, and the work's very end, setting previously vigorous momentum into ritual freeze recalls the close of both these and the *Octet*. But the neo-Baroque of the second movement, perfectly factured and poised, can seem cold not cool: and the rhythmic twitches and tweaks of the third seem merely nervy, even insect-like, till the delicious closing two-part invention for a pair of trumpets.

The first sizeable piece of Stravinsky's Second World War output, indicating its acclimatization to a new country, culture, language, is also a symphonic hybrid, whose parts more surely fail to make a whole: this *Symphony in Three Movements* (1942–5) begins thrillingly dynamic, almost à la *Sacre*; then grows scrappy and noodling; the middle movement, made from leftovers/rejects from thwarted attempts by this recent resident of Beverly Hills to secure gainful employment in the studios of Hollywood, is more desultory still; and the finale disintegrates before one's ears, though the perfunctory material is, here and there, highly prophetic of strange, gaunt, sinewy textures and processes to come, particularly in *Agon*. But the

1940s pieces are piecemeal altogether, as scattered and decentralized as those of Stravinsky's Swiss exile in the previous war, without that time's timeless high points. *Danses Concertantes* (1941–2) continues on from the already formula-tending *Jeu de cartes*, and *Scènes de ballet* (1944) concludes this downward journey (though it's also got some interestingly voiced chords and a soppy-heroic trumpet-tune to raise a smile of pleasure). The Concerto in D for strings (1946) really *is* epigonic – it could have been written by an imitator, a parodist, a machine. *Four Norwegian Moods* (1942) and *Babel* (1944) are side-effects of Hollywood's two faces, lucre and art respectively: another, the *Ode* in memory of Koussevitzsky's wife (1943), has, like the symphony, some passages, amid the debris from the cutting-room floor, strikingly prognostic of serial adventures in an unsuspected future only a decade off. Further desperation over finances account for three *jeux d'occasion* between 1942 and 1945: the *Scherzo à la Russe* for Paul Whiteman's band, the *Ebony Concerto* for Woody Herman's, and the *Circus Polka* for a flotilla of young elephant ballerinas.

Three works of superior calibre stand out in this difficult time: the Sonata for Two Pianos (1943–4); the *Mass* for chorus and winds (1944–8); the ballet *Orpheus* (1947). The two-piano work is a refined and winning cousin to the rugged concerto for the same combination; the choral work foretells spirit and, to some extent, idiom of religious music still to come; the dance-piece is both successor and predecessor, central panel of an inadvertent Greek triptych begun with *Apollo* and concluded in *Agon*, all of them to classic choreography by Balanchine. The core-myth of music's powers to sway mankind, beasts, and to persuade the Furies of the Underworld to yield their victim, his Eurydice, back to her lover's care until his carelessness loses her again, this time for ever – another take upon propitiation ensuring renewal, albeit oblique and ambiguous. Unmoving, his back to the audience, Orpheus mourns Eurydice – slow white-note scalic patterns on harp, gradually accumulating sustained white-note harmony on strings; winds twice interpose as friends offer gifts and solicitude. Orpheus dances – decorative solo violin, further ornamented with woodwinds and harp, then strange intermittent fanfare-figures; middle-section of stylized weeping. The rest of the story is told with all Stravinsky's late neo-classical mastery of harmony, voicing, spacing: baleful for the Angel of Death, shining as he leads the hero into the Underworld, acrid for the Furies, weeping when they're placated by his lyre, anguished when they beg for more, again calm when they restore him his bride, amiably wandering as he returns to the surface with her.

Their ensuing *pas de deux* is a touchstone for Stravinsky's notions of what music can legitimately express and where it must hold back. The reunited lovers dance together to long unfolding canta-bile string-line: the middle section reintroduces woodwinds. This central passage disappears via harp and clarinet into a foreshortened reprise of the string cantabile. A sudden lurch in just one bar from *p* to *ff*: in the one bar's silence that follows, Orpheus tears the bandage from his eyes. He's broken the bond: Eurydice dies anew, this time not to be restored. In Stravinsky's aesthetic music *must* and *can* not render such things with pathos, however deeply felt; here the 'refusal to mourn' has all the power gained by repression of direct affect. Orpheus' moment of human weakness receives its consequences: he is torn to pieces by Bacchantes from Hades, in a crackling *vivace*, all jerks and spasms, electric and sparking, initially held in by force, suddenly unleashed with terrifying violence, the *danse sacrale* from *Le Sacre* reborn. The flames gutter out as quickly as they'd blazed up; the closing tableau is short. Apollo appears, seizes the lyre from the dismembered musician, raising him up towards the heavens in strains of his own. The plain white-note texture-and-momentum of the opening returns: superimposed on it now, a beautiful song for two horns in quasi-fugal imitation, against a cantus firmus fas-cinatingly distinct from their warm full sonority – muted trumpet doubled by two solo violins playing *sul ponticello*, an edgy, soured dash of vermouth. The combination is broken off for two bars of neutral dry patterning on harp alone; resumption of sonorous song, still more eloquent, with its drop of acid; harp punctuation again; song plus vermouth, gradually diminishing, joined, for last chord only, by full strings, on a soft dominant seventh without a future: absolutely final.

So to *The Rake's Progress* (1948–51), a full evening three-act opera, by far Stravinsky's longest work, culmination of this period of adjustment and assimilation to a new world and language: culmination too, on a wider view, of the entire neo-classical venture accidentally opened up in 1919–20 by *Pulcinella*, 'theorized' in *Mavra*, and by the later 1920s achieving complete aesthetic and artistic vindication. Last and longest; but is it the best? Despite the opera's universal success, there's a sense that the jury are still out: not merely the avant-garde whose new dawn coincided with the *Rake*'s moribundity (as they perceived it), so much as the general music-lover. Auden's libretto (with Chester Kallman's help) after Hogarth's paintings is an elegant affair, deftly deploying the conventions of number-opera, Mozart and Italian. Some situations are contrived – the '*acte gratuite*' whereby Tom the Rake freely contracts his bizarre marriage to Baba the Bearded Turkish Lady, and the satire upon Universal Benevolence wherein Nick the Tempter gulls his victim into believing he can make bread from stone. Auden sparkles in the brothel-scene with its delectable folksong-like lines for Whores and Roaring Boys, adroitly matched by Stravinsky's rumbustious setting: and rises to eloquent pathos where the wretched Rake, confined to Bedlam, identifies himself with Adonis and seems to himself to command not only his lunatic flunkeys but the return, with his Venus, of spring itself. Venus herself – Anne Trulove – is as one-dimensional as her name; her father's a cipher, Baba a caricature: and the cheap, knowing camp of the Epilogue wherein, beyond its obvious model in *Don Giovanni*, all the cast, including Nemesis and Victim, reappear, remains especially galling after the preceding pathos and tenderness that had raised the work well above its previous level of dry detachment. Not least, in the graveyard scene, where the cod *secco*-recitative harpsichord suddenly acquires sinister metallic menace as Nick and his prey play out their card-game. The scene opens with a prelude for solo string quartet that sounds a new note in the opera and in the oeuvre: a dark lugubrious dissonant affair, putting the stage-direction into sound: 'a starless night. A churchyard. Tombs . . . a new-dug grave . . . a sexton's spade . . . a yew-tree': closest of all the many pre-echoes of Stravinsky's eventual serialism that emerge here and there amid the completely different norms of his 1940s.

Mozart is the model throughout – *Giovanni*, clearly, for plot: equally evident, *Così fan tutte* for actual musical idioms, forms, routines, material; also figuring in the admixture are Donizetti and Bellini, notably in the dulcet trumpet solo as Anne arrives in London to seek out her errant lover; and a nod to the French Baroque in Baba's grand sarabande. Yet much of the score is tired despite unfailing fluency and expertise. There's a curious kinship to Stravinsky's bête noire Strauss in his later operas before *Capriccio* rekindles the spirit levels: a whiff of autopilot, at the close of a chapter begun some thirty years before with such vitality, freshness, audacity.

Stravinsky's serialism

Robert Craft gives a moving account of Stravinsky, early 1952, already weakened by flu, breaking down, weeping, claiming the *Rake* to be his farewell, and after it, to be spent as composer. Renewal is vital, as once before: new blood; new pastures, within them new fat kine for the lean kine to devour. Craft's role in bringing to the old master (nearly seventy at the time of this collapse) awareness of exactly what was needed, is vital. Immediate remedial recourse, to transcribe the *Concertino for String Quartet* of 1920 for twelve instruments. More gradual, to urge the possibilities of serialism: not Schoenberg's – dense/chromatic/intense, burning *expressionismo* whatever its urge towards Brahms: *Webern* the ideal model. Craft, soon to be directing the pioneer recording of Webern's compete oeuvre (1954–6), recognized Stravinsky's innate affinity with the composer's spareness, essentiality, explicit facture out of interval-centred basics. His encouragement of the recording-project was total, and he attended many of the sessions.

The recharge after the breakdown is admixed with two other new sources, apparently incompatible with Webern, in effect just as conducive to revitalizing. First, not new but *old* – the music of the Renaissance (which had also been highly germane to Webern's development), all the way from *ars nova* to Gabrieli, Monteverdi, Schütz. Second, not so much new as radical – the European avant-garde emerging after wartime embargo or sheer unavailability, Webern its icon and guide. Nineteen forty-five is Year One for this proto-French Revolution, whose contempt for interwar neo-classicism and its flirtation with/dependence upon the Past, from Baroque to Tchaikovsky, painfully included Stravinsky's entire output after his own early boldness, centred upon the city wherein his artistic life had mostly passed, their ringleader the youthful Pierre Boulez. Somehow the seventy-year-old Stravinsky succeeded in learning from Webern and the Renaissance and made his peace, by truce and truckle, with the firebrands: how, and with what results, is now tracked through to the death.

The *Cantata* on old English texts, Stravinsky's first composition (1951–2) after finishing the *Rake*, is a mix of fresh and drab. Three poems are alternated with verses from the *Lyke-wake Dirge*, better known from Britten's version in his *Serenade*, set for women's voices and a five-instrument ensemble – two flutes, oboe and cor anglais, solo cello, together with soprano and tenor soloists: spare, hypnotic, cool, in complete contrast to Britten's whip-lash vision. *Ricercar I* sets a lovely lyric for the solo soprano – 'the maidens came': all-diatonic, instinct with canonic imitation: well-balanced by the penulti-mate song, duet for her and solo tenor on *Westron Wind*, a vigorous canon-free scherzo. It's the central *Ricercar II*, 'tomorrow will be my dancing-day', that causes the distress, musical and verbal. This long account of Christ's incarnation, birth, baptism, temptation, perse-cution, betrayal by Judas, trial before Pilate, scourging, crucifixion, harrowing of hell, resurrection, ascent into heaven, is set dead-pan with increasingly twisty canonic structures derived from the initial so-characteristic major/minor wriggle, each new stage of the life-story punctuated by the homophonic refrain 'to call my true love to the dance': an ordeal for the listener as well as the tenor.

More pleasure in the little trio of Shakespeare songs that followed (1953) with flute, clarinet and viola. And more depth in the next work (1954), a setting for tenor and string quartet of Dylan Thomas's 'do not go gentle', his memorial poem for his father, here a memorial on the poet's untimely death (a collaboration between him and Stravin-sky had been mooted). The setting is framed between a Prelude and a Postlude of 'dirge canons', antiphonal between the four strings and four trombones, whose polyphonic material – a five-note 'row' – is more chromatic and its serial usage stricter, producing some strange new harmony, voicing, spacing; highly prognostic in this early 1950s 'pocket' of interims of what will in every sense succeed it.

Alongside these vocal pieces come two instrumental works. The *Septet* (1952–3) is still largely diatonic even when, in its closing gigue, diatonic scales are pressed into modal note-rows: a dried-out affair affording no nourishment except in the central passacaglia, yet a necessary stage to be traversed. The triumph of these years is *Agon* (1953–5), third in the triptych of Greek-inspired ballets; this one, unlike *Apollo* and *Orpheus*, without story and named characters: pure pattern, a contest, a game, in essence a demonstration of dance fused with music. Which sounds forbidding in theory: in practice, as realized by Balanchine's choreography, elaborated in close collab-oration with the music and its creator, one of the genre's summits, supreme in elegance that also marvellously achieves expression – eroticism sublimated into gesture and pose. The score is a synthesis and composite: its initial nub, a little two-trumpet fanfare to open a new theatre; other sources, a manual of dance-movements-and-music from seventeenth-century France; English virginal and lute music from Elizabethan/Jacobean times; and – amazingly – Tchai-kovsky's ballet-idiom drawn through the steel mesh of Webern (or perhaps the other way round: Webern animated with the spirit of Tchaikovsky). A ragbag; adding up to a whole way beyond the sum of its parts. A wonder of elegant, intricate game-playing pattern-making – a fusion of body/mind, eye/ear – that contrives also, perhaps inadvertently, to be oddly moving, somehow; and for sure, exhilarating and very sexy.

After this secular triumph, Stravinsky's remaining music is, with only two exceptions, religious and vocal. There are six such works of size and weight, with a few miniatures in between, and a couple of asso-ciated transcriptions, of Gesualdo and Bach: a final harvest of medi-tation and devotion, principally, though including one last dance/mime endeavour, and concluding – appropriately – with a highly condensed *Requiem*. *Canticum Sacrum* (1955) inaugurates the succession: a symmetrical structure inspired by S. Marco in Venice, for which it was written, to whom it was dedicated. An austere texture, taking use of twelve-note rows further than previously, though festive-diatonic for the Monteverdian opening and close. Special: first an oasis of delicate Webernian fragility spun around the tenor soloist's amorous comparisons – myrrh, honeycomb, milk, wine. Second, the work's central panel devoted to the Cardinal Virtues. *Love* is somewhat grim – more an order than a plea that we love one another. *Hope* is sturdy and steadfast: *Faith* yields the densest thought in Stravinksy's music so far – its revealing text 'I was greatly afflicted'. *Threni* (the Lamentations of Jeremiah) a couple of years later tests the Cardinal Virtues to their limits: a quintessence of penitence and woe, set to a queer, scooped-out sound-world unlike any previous music, gnomic and impressive in its abasement. Amid the low sonorities, grunted and muttering or sustained and resonating, the settings of the Hebrew initials in the *Querimonia* of Jeremiah's Third Elegy shine out with extraordinary radiance – icons through which sunlight passes. Between these two intimidating religious meditations comes by way of diversion, even light relief, the finest of all Stravinsky's transcriptions, an orchestration (1955–6) of Bach's *Canonic Variations* on *Vom Himmel hoch* from its organ-original, for the same forces as the *Canticum*. Bach's wit, ingenuity and beauty are recreated in texture as fresh and new as in any of Stravinsky's 'modernistico' music hereabouts: the extra counter-points and 'wrong notes' are so sure, right and delectable that the ear, when it ventures into serial territory of increasing complexity, can be implicitly trusted.

A Sermon, a Narrative and a Prayer (1960–61): the first is harsh-shining etched, concentrated, yet clear, the *Narrative* (the disciple Stephen's stoning and vision of heaven) a little desultory, recovering form for the third, whose closing alleluias with deep tolling gongs make a distant relative to the *Symphony of Psalms*. But the theatre piece *The Flood* (1960–62) is frankly scrappy, yielding both in fun (Noah's calling the beasts, and in altercation with his wife) and in devotional awe to Britten's community pageant on the same mystery-play. Except for two danced numbers, purely orchestral – galvanic energy for Building the Ark, breathtaking depiction of the world overwhelmed by choking waters. Finally come *Abraham and Isaac* (1962–3) and *Requiem Canticles* (1965–6): the former a tough nut that rewards assiduous attention, thereby revealing not a soft sweet centre – rather, a bitter kernel of concentrated essence from which the tale's harsh moral can eventually be reached, retained, rendered comforting. The latter is, again, patchy: the texted sections (from the Mass for the Dead) can seem makeshift; the instrumental sections, whether scratchily urgent or deliciously cool, are far more characterized and memorable. And the Postlude is unique: three marvellous long-held harmonies – 'the light that never was': separated by successions of calm equal chords fascinatingly voiced on celesta, bells, vibraphone (Stravinsky's first employment of this ambiguously attractive instrument, in this his last work). The long-held harmonies and the processional tintinnabulation are linked and held together by a single horn-note emerging from the one and sustained beneath the other. After the first wondrous harmony, six shining ones; pause; another five (horn always binding): silence: second wondrous harmony; six different shining ones, pause; horn, slightly longer, initiates another five, different: silence: third wondrous harmony; different horn-note emerges, base of just four new shining ones: pause: six more, different again (the differences made by some magical serial rotation): silence: two shorter wondrous harmonies, richer and stranger yet: then the final, even more so, and joined by the trio of tuned percussion just the once. Even though this last was its composer's 'chord of death' the closing *image sonore* is at once on ice yet infused with inner fire and life.

In among these six religious works come two purely instrumental pieces: *Movements* for piano and orchestra (1958–9) and *Variations* (in memory of Aldous Huxley, a dear friend and neighbour in Beverly Hills), of 1963–4. *Movements* is a masterpiece of compression, fleet-footed, volatile, elusive, quicksilver and quick-witted. There are five, each with its own tiny refrain: the whole, eight minutes so fragmented with punctuation and silences, nevertheless comes over as a single entity. Its most sustained sonority comes in the fourth, and this movement's epilogue is the only tutti, surprisingly violent amid the prevailing delicacy. As with the later Webern, every individual sound-gesture could be caught in a descriptive word: let the notes do this for themselves! The *Variations*, at around five minutes, are shorter but appear more substantial because of their weightier orchestra and absence of concertante interplay. There's a slight sense here of 'more of same' where 'more is less' – an unattributed *bon mot* of the times claimed that Stravinsky charges a dollar for every note and 50 cents for each rest. One remarkable exception: variations 2, 4 and 10 are absolutely new – meshes of polyphonic texture in twelve parts, the first on twelve violins, second on ten violas and two double basses, the third for eleven woodwinds and a single horn: an astonishing sound – 'ground glass'. Before the winds' version comes var. 9, a *fugato* for strings strayed in from *Agon*: most memorable is var. 6 – bright chords bounced and sustained thrice, alternating with three grunting trombones: most characteristic of the composer, the work's opening gestures and its closing, devolving down to a single low bass-clarinet note, at once arbitrary yet absolutely right; the knack first discovered in *Petrushka* some fifty years earlier – the experience of a lifetime epitomized in one G♯.

The Age of Stravinsky

'*Aber etwas fehlt*': when one asks oneself what is missing from the twentieth century's predominant composer – its master of divertimento yet an artist of profound religious vision, a daemon of destruction and subversion yet a paragon of order and balance – it lies in the area of *Affekt*; music's ability to 'express everything within us', what used to be called *soul*, *heart*, *warmth* before such squashy terms were evicted with ridicule and contempt. They remain vital to what music can do, what it is *for*, what it *is*. Yet this extraordinary 'inventor of sounds' (as Stravinsky described himself on his passport) gave expression no place in his aesthetic credo and did his damnedest to banish it from his work. It is worth trying to formulate one's reservations responsibly: they must at all times be grounded not in mere piety but true respect for the stature of their subject.

Auden, in his obituary tribute, called Stravinsky the representative artist of modern times. Whatever might be thought as to the claim's universality it is certain that he is the century's crucial composer. There was a seismic shift, and he made it; there was a battle and he has won. He is the air we breathe; or to use a grosser metaphor originating with Stravinsky himself, he inseminated the epoch, and the peculiarities of his physiognomy stamp his descendants unto the third and fourth generation.

His victory is to defeat the long hegemony of the Austro-Germanic musical culture, so mighty, so manifestly holding all the greatest figures from Bach to Brahms (to go no further back or forward) that every other felt itself inferior, subservient or marginal. By the turn of the modern century this tradition was decadent, although astonishingly fecund in its decay. A rating circa 1880 would still have it supreme: Wagner, Brahms, Bruckner, three giants at the height of their powers. Yet decay ran alongside: what is latent in the gods grows explicit in the succeeding demi-gods, the generation of the 1860s – Mahler, Strauss, Wolf – and the 1870s – Reger, Schoenberg. These composers, heirs to a wealth of resources used with complete technical mastery, tend towards excess in all things – length, performing forces, volume (and later, exaggerated brevity, barely audible dynamics from a tiny group of players inside or without an enormous orchestra). Nervous intensity is the expressive goal; head and heart alike are liable to implode with approaching over-cerebration and over-kill. A suitable motto for this era of *espressionismo* is 'means over ends', instantly evinced by its worst period-pieces – *Symphonia Domestica* in which Strauss blares the intimacies of married bed and breakfast to an indifferent audience, for instance, or Mahler's 'Symphony of a Thousand' (about which the young Stravinsky sardonically remarked, having first described its colossal apparatus, 'all this, you see, to prove two plus two equals four'). But whereas Stravinsky had his own pressing reasons to detest Teutonian Romanticism in its terminal agonies, we can enjoy more freely the general stylistic ambience and yield ourselves wholly to the particular strains in it that are supreme of their kind, alongside the bombast and slag.

It was Stravinsky's authentic, instinctive loathing and fear of the endlessly uncoiling python of Teutonic expression that was instrumental in dealing it the *coup de grâce*. His attitude was not merely personal. Contempt and indifference were in the air. Well before the Great War brought explicit anti-Boche sentiment into Debussy's music, he had deplored Germanic formulae, teased Strauss in print, walked out of a Mahler symphony, and writhed in subtle gyrations to escape the seductive wiles of Wagner. Debussy, the living composer to whom Stravinsky acknowledged (for once) his principal debt, had absolutely no use for the Teutonic forms or techniques from Bach to Brahms. Stravinsky's own stance, already formed, was perhaps confirmed by the edgy relationship with Debussy, and surely consolidated by friendship with the more congenial Ravel, younger, and frankly cheeky towards the horrors of the Huns, abominating Beethoven's *Missa Solemnis*, preferring Chabrier to *The Ring*.

Stravinsky's intrinsic compositional gift was mean. What is not meagre is an enormous will to write music. If one is drawn by magnetic ambition to compose but knows one is capable only of featureless mediocrity when composing 'by the book', the solution is to make the book contemptible, out-of-date, no longer worth mastering. Send it up, push it over, burn it, reveal its feet of clay, dance upon its grave. Then do otherwise: *your way*, however perverse; indeed, the more artificial and against the grain and nature of music as currently understood, the better. If you cannot join it, beat it. What Stravinsky could not do, and therefore disdained and subverted, was Teutonia at its apex: Wagner and Brahms. It's true that his immediate cultural enemy is the work of their living descendants, his older contemporaries, Brahms fatty-degenerated into Reger, Wagner dissipated into Mahler and Strauss. But behind them stand the Grandfathers who represented the standard of Germanic music under which he grew up. His comprehensive re-slanting of the way to listen, to hear, the way music ought and ought not to be, the way music intrinsically *is*, is a rejection of the healthy centre as well as its disintegrating edges. Initially polarized in factitious polemic, Brahms and Wagner were revealed by the end of the old century as a complementary unity; they are equal tributaries in forming the composer who came to be seen, with a different kind of absurdity, for the first half and beyond of the new century, as Stravinsky's arch-antithesis: Arnold Schoenberg.

Of the two Teutonic giants, Wagner, on the face of it the more immovable impediment, can in fact be disposed of more easily, by the denigration born of genuine artistic distaste. Cutting Bayreuth down to size was as old as Bayreuth itself; the groundswell of hostility was given intellectual thrust in Nietzsche's polemics of the 1880s, and by 1900 or so, the wave of reaction was a commonplace among Young Turks of the next generation. But Brahms could never be dismissed (like Wagner) as a hyperbolic adulterator of artistic genres who then elevated the poisonous brew into a bogus religion with his own glory inextricably bound in (the substance of Stravinsky's objections, common currency by the time he formulated them thus for his Harvard audience in 1939–40). Brahms is less destructible than Wagner because he presents a smaller target. As the most recent embodiment of the Austro-Germanic continuities, he is subtly pervasive rather than crudely invasive. Brahms can represent the Teutonic type at its most normal – a craftsman and grammarian of musical usage at its peak of culture, learnèd in a language rich in inherited resonance, affiliated to this heritage with unquestioning loyalty, bringing to it, so late in its life, a conscious consummation and subsummation. He gathers in a ripe harvest whose conspicuous emotional warmth is inextricably fused, by mastery of every technical means, with powerful brainwork. The result was criticized in his lifetime and still is – for lapses into cosiness and sentimentality, over-squareness that can become muscle-bound, lack of gaiety and lightness of touch, an un-physicality of movement, especially in the absence of a dance-element (apart from the glutinous Viennese waltz), and for limits of emotional range born of his very reverence for the past, showing that intensive cultivation can, sometimes, have its disadvantages. But, of course, Brahms survives such sniping (of which Stravinsky's own paper dart, deploring the later Schoenberg's stiffness of rhythm 'rooted in the most turgid and graceless Brahms' is a fair specimen), just as Wagner has survived the heftier ammunition turned upon him. Between them they fill out each other's alleged deficiencies, and the composite, with Brahms as the norm and Wagner the perpetually extraordinary, is impregnable. Together, they are the culmination of a musical language that comes with 'instructions' as to how it is to be heard and apprehended; how its listeners are to be moved. This is music as food – nourishment spiritual and ethical, albeit in a medium of almost carnal richness; aimed at the deepest and highest spaces in the hungry human soul.

So what does Stravinsky provide instead? Even now, as his best music from all its long trajectory hardens into core repertoire, it is possible to admire, even to love, while still feeling the absence of some essential constituents. The former virtues of economy, exactness, directness, now feel like constriction; the self-denials (Stravinsky at work – 'fretting, pacing, erasing, muttering *"pas de pitié"* the while') now seem to deny the music's actual substance. Moreover, its accompaniment of vindications, special pleadings, ever-more-bellowing Papal Bulls enjoining order, discipline, submission to the laws of Apollo, tends to drown the exiguous melody. Taken together, they amount to an aesthetic position that deliberately narrows music's scope. It becomes illegitimate for music to be anything other than what he himself happens to be writing. The completeness and rapidity of his early success seem to force him to go beyond a triumph-dance, to require the defeated enemy to embrace the victor's philosophy. And it is this philosophy, located more compellingly within the authority of the composer than in the borrowed mouthpieces uttering his aesthetic prescriptions, that has effected the seismic shift between the Age of Wagner and the Age of Stravinsky.

It would be absurd to tax Stravinsky with an absence of what he can't do, therefore doesn't want to do. What he *can* do, and therefore does want to, and therefore does, and is, are what matter. And in the interaction of positive and negative, definitions arise characterizing the characteristics and qualifying the qualities of the epoch's dominant musician. His muse is double-faced. On one side gaiety and wit prevail; in this he is unique among the twentieth-century masters otherwise angst-ridden to a man. In divertimentos he is elegant, stylish, vivacious, at a pretty consistently high level. But there is nothing trivial in this ideal. The high spirits of a fable like *Renard* or a morality tale like *L'Histoire du soldat* are intellectual as well as playful; the audience is likely to be as exhausted as stimulated by this strenuous entertainment; and the same goes for such later displays of athletic wit as the *Octet* for winds, *Jeu de cartes* and *Agon*, or his last purely instrumental work the orchestral *Variations*. Though shadow-less, the composer's divertimento-side is not shallow; which is the cue for the serious face to appear. Not his most scathing adversary could fail to sense the numinous in Stravinsky. His religious expression is the antithesis of 'Protestant', eschewing any confessional witness to a 'personal' saviour. Breast-beating or wrestling with the angel are equally alien. It speaks, rather, by way of ritual observance, whose profundity resembles the grave accusing indifference of a Byzantine Pantocrator. This aspect, like the divertimento, was present nearly from the start – the first survivor is the third of the *Three Pieces for String Quartet* of 1914 (newly entitled *Cantique* when orchestrated in 1928); it surfaces soon after in the abortive project for a Liturgy-ballet and in the process whereby the *Symphonies of Wind Instruments* symbolically renders the Orthodox Burial of the Dead in memory of its great dedicatee. Gestures like this when similarly placed in otherwise 'secular' works (often enough divertimentos) can be understood by analogy as liturgical, from the end of the *Octet* (again) to that of the *Symphony in C* (1940). The *Symphony of Psalms*, an unimpugnable Byzantine masterpiece, comes at the very middle of the divertimento-era (1930), and the *Mass* (completed in 1948) foretells the final period in which the great majority of pieces are religious in inspiration, though never liturgical in function even when the text is drawn from the Catholic Requiem.

Divertimento and ritual unite in the core of major stage-works where all Stravinsky's principal sources – Russia primitive and sophisticated, Greek mythology, Christian Orthodoxy – reveal a corporate core; for the theme is always a variant upon sacrifice, cleansing, propitiating God, or the gods, or forces of nature, to ensure the continuity of renewed fecundity – *The Rite of Spring* (where a virgin is sacrificed), *Svadebka* (where the victim is maidenhood itself), *Oedipus Rex* (a blinding in order to see clearly, bloody acts to purge evil blood-relations that have corrupted the body-politic), *Perséphone* (the seed must consent to lie annually in the underworld of quasi-death, that it may be reborn each spring and renew the earth as of old). And meanwhile beauty, expelled by the back door for sins of Romantic excess, is admitted in the rational light of noon by the Greek portico hastily run up at the front. The impulse here is Apollonian; the genre is ballet (the core of his oeuvre, providing the idiom for many pieces not originally designated for dancing); the subject, disciplining the body's tensions and aggressions into grace, moving communally in ordered symbolic pattern; an eloquence of bodily gesture rather than an expression of internal feeling, an art of measure and stylization, with strong sympathetic alignment to the rhetoric, figures, metres of verse.

Stravinsky can scarcely be faulted! He effects an enormous liberation and refreshment of the musical language in a large (but not redundant) output. Flawless in facture, delicious in entertainment and diversion, it does not abhor some broader humane themes, and succeeds better than any other of its time with the religious. So how can one complain?

An answer can begin in a round-up of some previous reservations. An early line that can still be heard now and again, especially in England, would see in Stravinsky mainly something cold and clever (a term of disapproval), lacking heart and naturalness, brilliant in colour and energy, short on content, cynically attuned to changing fashion (even when in earlier phases it set the pace) all the way from modernist folklore, via cubist baroque, Verdi, Mozart to neo-Webern. Teutonia's counter-attack has more to it and can command heavier artillery: for instance Adorno, with his notorious dismissal of Stravinsky's classicism as 'music about music'. This is one of those backhanded phrases whose apparent significance melts away the more one thinks about what it might mean and how it might apply. What else is the vast majority of Bach and Haydn (to take only the two clearest instances) but music about music, spun from its own substance, essentially made out of its own processes?

Schoenberg's graphic metaphor of a naked savage sporting a bowler hat suggests better the serious Teuton's contempt for what must seem, from their angle, the merest cod and faking, ineptly executed ('Stravinsky can't hear below middle C'), sprinkled with wrong notes whose function – for grammatically they are functionless – is to provoke outrage: see Schenker, arch-analyst of the true classics, with his contemptuous rage against Stravinsky's alleged crimes against the norms. Or else, mere mockery. Paraphrased, this anti-Stravinsky line says that he is compelled, for lack of grounding in the loamy musical culture of Central Europe, to borrow or steal the material that he then subverts, emptying out meaning, retaining only husks and shards.

Direct refutation of these old charges would be otiose so late in the day. Stravinsky has won, his wrong notes are right, his sub-versions are brilliant, and his way of putting music together from what lies to hand is (almost) everybody's way. And no one, surely, would any more call Stravinsky cold, or fail to feel how he *burns*. Not with *espressionismo appassionato*, of course. His passion is for exactness and order, he burns to consume the waste and to reach the essence, be it of an occasional trifle or a major project. For him the precise delineation of a musical object is an all-sufficing aim. But the husks and shards rejected in the process are those aspects of music that matter most to most of its lovers. Ask any average 'lay' music-lovers what music means to them, and they will almost always grope after something vaguely romantic, inchoate but deeply held, concerning the feelings and the emotions. This is by no means incompatible with strong unconscious recognition of the patterns, the construction, even the grammar, by which musical emotion achieves its aims. But the prime purpose is always this emotion – a fact that the professional musician, especially the academic, tends to forget.

Music's power to move is by no means extra-musical; not only is it absolutely intrinsic – first codified in classical times, most mem-orably encapsulated in the first neo-classical era (Dryden's 'What passion cannot music raise or quell?') – but it is, properly seen, the most important and wonderful thing about it. The 'ignorant' popular

view is not vulgar: it is right; and the entire history of the art has
been towards the locating, defining, releasing, extending, refining, of
'Musick's Empire', giving it ever-fuller scope to embrace and contain
still more of human experience. The endeavour is risky: the incomparable equipoise of affects and causes in Bach, Haydn, Mozart is
endangered by Beethoven's heroicism and pathos even as he also
takes inwardness of expression to unheard-of heights and depths.
The growth of Romanticism throughout the nineteenth century
can be measured in terms of loss and gain, but who, weighing the
wealth of the achievement from Schubert to Berg (say), would care
to count the cost?

Its motto remains 'from the heart, may it go to the heart', attached
by Beethoven to the score of the *Missa Solemnis*. And its view of
music's role is none the less valid for being a bit squashy when put
into words (but words are of course not its medium; it shouldn't
need to be put into words). Music as mental refreshment and spiritual nourishment, solace in loneliness, depression and grief; music
as shaper of fantasy and stuff of dreams; music as joy and sweetness. Also as the coursing of the blood, the surge of the libido, the
free representation of the inner life of the dynamic imagination
even as the outer circumstances of the industrial, the modern, the
technological world contract into complete banality. It is an affair
of the heart, warm, expressive, charged with sensibility in all things
secret and intimate – 'the private parts of the spirit'; or 'music's
smile' (of sentiment not amusement, though amusement is part of
it), expressive of tenderness and delight – the *petit phrase* that, as in
Proust, unlocks the past and, as Cosima Wagner said of her Richard's Porazzi-melody (a fragment of *Tristan*-material unused in the
eventual work), 'brought back the most secret incidents of her soul'.
Music as balsam for aching heart, head, hand; and from this, music
as guide to, or goal of, the deepest places of spiritual searching –
music that not only exposes and forms and stimulates into utterance
the innermost recesses of feeling, but seems to actualize a Platonic
Idea of human existence – thought, feeling, senses – rendered into
palpable reality. And thence to the most devastating and overwhelming effects of ecstasy and intoxication – the power of music to unite

millions as one in a 'Kiss for the whole world' (Beethoven again, but this time setting Schiller).

All this redefines the role of the composer from its earlier incarnations as craftsman or quasi-scientist in humble service to his God. A composer's music is born of the whole person – the physiological constitution, the physical characteristics, the identifying voice, gestures, walk; the individual tempo (why is Rossini naturally allegro, Bruckner adagio?); the personality as revealed in things both trivial (Schoenberg claimed that even the way Mahler tied his cravat was expressive) and vital; the cast of mind and temperament; the intellectual interest; the concerns social, cultural, spiritual, sexual.

Piquantly, Stravinsky is as clear an instance of all this as any composer one can think of – even down to his natty and self-revealing choice of cravats! But he would have outlawed the very idea of the composer as vehicle through which one individual's unique angle upon things, his especial sensitivity, acuity, depth of feeling, is realized by the nature of an equally particular musical gift into musical statements that can be communicated to others, and therefore shared, entered, possessed. And thence back from the composer to his attempted sketch of music's scope. All, all is forbidden: everything that music is able to do more efficaciously not only than any other art but than any other resource known to mankind; what music seems not merely to be *for* (if there has to be a function) but intrinsically to consist *of*: the life of the spirit rendered in sounds, giving wings to cumbersome body and invisible soul, uttering everything that cannot otherwise be uttered, or heard. All this, which those who love music as the world's most precious invention find the most precious of its properties, is ostensibly made illegitimate by the Stravinskian stance which, sweeping all before it, has become the very air we breathe. At first fresh and new, this attitude by now clips the wings and chokes the voice, limiting domains so rich and hard-won, stunting the idea of music in its very essence.

This essence, though permanent and indestructible, is nevertheless at a loss when under attack. Having no defences, it exposes the soft flabby frailty of human nature. Insistence on the soul, the smile, the heart, sounds so woolly! When they are invoked as the measure, silliness, even absurdity, is risked. They've become shaming, so their mocker encounters not resistance, but half-willing collusion from within. For who wants to appear wet and exposed in a posture of abasement? the heart and soul laid bare haven't a leg to stand on! So the attack is bound to hit the spot; embarrassment and self-betrayal are deflected by an affectation of detachment and cynicism. Stravinsky's idiosyncratic stance, born of personal and artistic limitation, has, because of his compositional prowess and the colossal authority born of it, cut music down to his own shape and size and put its larger, less concrete aspects out of court.

The principal weapon is 'irony', a word so ubiquitous nowadays as to merit an attempt at its explosion. Whatever it signified originally – a technical term in Greek drama involving 'speaking by contraries' (Johnson's *Dictionary*) – the idea developed into something both supple and subtle, a play of equivocation that, using the oblique to attain the direct, could penetrate to the core of a character, a situation, a thought, a feeling. Johnson's prime definition – 'a mode of speech in which the meaning is contrary to the words' – is the mere grit on which this pearl of European consciousness formed. But nowadays it is hard to find a term of comparable richness so trivialized and over-worked; it has grown so vague and dilute as to mean virtually nothing. Colloquially it stands for something like 'tongue-in-cheek', odd, coincidental, mildly strange or amusing. Its more 'thinking' use is a careless commonplace in discussion of all the arts, a package containing sarcasm, mockery, parody, pastiche, spoof; disguise by quotation or allusion of the direct statement of explicit feeling and overt engagement; a parrying motion of the reflexes to keep such things at bay; guardedness towards the sublime, the sincere, the heartfelt, the naïve, the ingenuous. Defence against those is certainly required when they're bogus, but defensiveness in the face of the real thing reveals frigidity or cowardice. Thus irony is a bastion against the too-revealing vulnerability of impulse and spontaneity, a satirical instrument poised to mow it down. From this, its development as a desideratum inevitably follows; it builds upon fear, wariness, knowingness, evasion, to congratulate itself upon, even to rejoice in, unfeelingness.

But at the bottom irony has something to hide, and its guilty secret is the unchanging facts of human weakness, the quivering heart, the distresses of hope, desire, love, illusions and delusions, tenderness and feebleness, the corruptions of sympathy and empathy, the corrosion of compassion: all these poor human characteristics, seen with contempt rather than charity. Stripped of the protective armour of 'speaking by contraries', men and women are revealed in all their pathos – human, all-too-human. From which an escape can be found in the elevation of personal authority and *terribilità*, with its impersonal laws, rules, orders, over the hapless incoherence and muddle of humanity en masse. Yet the strength of irony is a false strength; its bristling bastions of defensiveness cannot conceal the internal collapse whereby head, heart, body, hand, are no longer integrated as an organic whole.

What might be called an 'irony' in one of its many debased senses deserves to be reasserted as an evident truth: that music's innate emotional content and message-bearing power can only be achieved through the discipline of construction and technique that the Stravinskian stance claims to be music's sole *raison d'être*. Bach, by common consent the greatest master of pattern and geometry ever known, is also saturated in a language of affective symbolism so harmonically rich as to stand closer to Wagner than to any contemporary or predecessor. Nor can Beethoven and Haydn, the master-builders of development and argument, be charged with emotional dryness, except for brief spells of temporary desiccation before a newly acquired technique has been assimilated and given blood. Contrariwise, the greatest masters of overflowing charged-up expression – Schubert, Bruckner, Wagner – reveal an astonishing power to find formal and grammatical vehicles, even a geometry, for content that, on the face of it, would seem to have no chance of achieving organized utterance. Compared with these, Stravinsky, with a body of work, central to the modern spirit, whose consummate brilliance it would be stupid not to admire and rejoice in, seems exiguous. The sanctions he imposed on the name and nature of music bite most sharply at their source. Running right through his glittering yield is a vein of meagreness, perversity and acid. He has composed into his own music his own anti-musicality.

Of course all great art is born of a collusion between its creator's limitations and strengths, knowing and using both, deriving one from the other. No one manifests this more clearly than Wagner: and Stravinsky exemplifies the old truism equally well. His evident limits are short-windedness; frugality that can turn mean; and orderliness so exaggerated that it can become mere tidiness. But he also gives the truism an unprecedented twist, in his conspicuous absence of a fount of original, primal musical inspiration. Yet even this apparently devastating limitation can be turned to advantage, as can be seen in comparison with related figures more generously endowed by nature: Bartók for instance, a *musikantisch* Brahmsian type at the start, only to arrive by remorseless rigour (in emulation, 'ironically', of Stravinsky himself) at self-made deserts of fearful symmetry; or, still nearer home, Prokofiev, overflowing with natural fecundity, more tuneful, more human, more lovable, but indiscriminate, artistically unscrupulous, self-squandering. Stravinsky, with the careful management that is one of his most genuine traits, makes a shorter talent go further than either.

That the other deficiencies are converted to benefits is easier to discern. Short-windedness becomes the basis for a brusque terseness of articulation and punctuation, a gestural authority, closely related to bodily charisma, unrivalled before or since. This, extended in duration, builds an architecture of interlocking strata and juxtaposed blocks that has become twentieth-century common practice as surely as the polyphony, continuo, sonata (and so forth), of previous epochs. Frugality (or just meanness) and orderliness (or just tidiness) underlie the economy, elegance and precision of every move, and a self-observant self-consciousness permits no smallest detail to pass unexamined, evading cliché, banality and routine even where the stylistic surface makes naughty play with the most used-up materials. Wrong notes become right notes; he has the courage to sound them in the first place, then relish them, sense and appreciate their strange qualities, and stick to them with single-minded obstinacy. Every scrap and nugget of perversity is worked with rigorous concentration till it becomes a new thing with a new validity. All this is personal indeed, with a sharpness of character born of the intelligence, acuteness and sheer peculiarity of the ears, which have gradually become the ears by which the entire era hears. But it is the lack of anything fundamental of his own that twists him into complete originality. He must be less gifted for music than any great composer in its history! The absence of an inner well of spontaneous naturalness compels him to forage, from the Folk, from the Past, from contemporaries senior and junior, making himself up out of whatever he cares to hunt down and devour. A new possibility, technical and stylistic, opens out around his every act of theft, rapine and murder; and the musical world, unto the third and fourth generation, has leapt into the outrage and made itself a home.

Can the deliberate emotional hobbling also be seen as a virtue in reverse? The party defence-line (beginning with his apologists in the 1920s and 30s) is that his anti-*espressivo* becomes an absent presence, wherein the music glows with the repressed strength of what it doesn't care to state full-frontally. Such 'suppressionism' clearly hasn't impeded the consistent energy and vitality of the wit, the gaiety, the ceaseless intellectual curiosity. (Compare Webern, where a comparable tendency towards self-pruning clearly results in self-mutilation.) 'Less is more.' But thinking of lost Teutonia, with its fabulous beauty and depth of expression inseparably fused into its technical glories, and all rendered by the loveliness of its undoubtedly right notes, I'm not so sure. Maybe another swing of the pendulum is due.

Stravinsky effected a much-needed, timely and inevitable purge. He was right by gift, by birthplace and angle upon the art – the primitive onslaught from the East slashing with super-sophisticated weaponry into the bloated body of Austro-Germanic high culture, then piecing together a culture of its own, which substitutes 'inhuman' impersonality and 'merciless' geometry for heredity and warmth, in a series of masterpieces almost arrogantly perfected, celebratory, high-spirited, instinct with religious observance. In all this he is a liberator; yet he is also a constrictor by inhibitions and prohibitions which, arising from individual necessity, harden into Laws as subtly inflexible as those of Schoenberg or Boulez are visibly repressive. In as much as he has permeated twentieth-century usage, one might say – as Addison did of Milton – that 'our language sunk under him'. But this isn't quite right. Our *language* rose like leavened bread. Having purged the bloated body, he refreshed the words of the tribe by a dose of salts, in a music where every element permitted to survive has been newly thought out. But the sacrifice is grave – it amounts to jettisoning what is so indispensable a part of music's gradual entry into the fullness of its powers that the old-fashioned *Musikant* would call it simply music itself. What music is for, what it can do, what it is, have been enormously curtailed by Stravinsky's particular sense of these things, and to the extent that he has become the air we breathe, our *century* has shrunk rather than sunk under his influence into something tighter, smaller, dryer. The age of Wagner choked the art one way; the age of Stravinsky chokes it another. Yet, paradoxically, this limited notion of musical creativity is hitched to a creative drive of colossal force that has changed the general sense of what the art can do.

Prokofiev

Sergei Prokofiev: born 1891, early promise as pianist and at composing – his teachers included Rimsky-Korsakov: early successes included three ballets for Diaghilev (one was not produced). Settled in Paris after the Great War, with international career as pianist and composer. Unwilling at first to embrace his post-Revolutionary homeland, decided eventually to relocate to Russia 1933. Hopes for artistic acclaim and financial reward equally dashed: despite devoting his considerable energies and talents to celebrating Officialdom he fell foul of it; several major projects were stymied, most painfully the heroic-epic opera on *War and Peace* (1941–3): positive fruits of the prodigal's return are two full-length ballets in the Tchaikovsky rather than the Diaghilev line, *Romeo and Juliet* (1938) and *Cinderella* (1945), and classic film-scores for *Lieutenant Kijé* (1933),

Alexander Nevsky (1938) and *Ivan the Terrible* (1944), the first two transformed into successful concert-pieces. A copious and protean composer, fluent in every genre and on every scale: in every possible attitude and idiom too. A puzzle. 'Ironically' his death in 1953 was overshadowed by his oppressor Stalin's on the very same day.

'A puzzle': however much one believes that one is at last getting his measure, Prkfv (as he characteristically shortened his name) will always multiply, surprise, disconcert, evade: there's always another unheard concerto, ballet, opera, Soviet cantata or film-score, as well as countless unfamiliar smaller pieces – songs, piano, chamber. And the range – of subjects, intonations, levels as well as musical idiom – is so diverse. His oeuvre is anything but consistent: his bête noire Stravinsky looks hidebound through all his chameleon changes compared with Prkfv, who apparently houses many incompatible personalities from start to stop. Maybe he, too, is trying on borrowed – stolen – clothes: earlier by choice, from restless curiosity; later, after his disastrous return to the Soviet Union, under compulsion to toe the line and placate, an endeavour doomed to fail precisely because he was innately so perverse and irrepressibly individualistic.

'The contradictions cover such a range.' Affectionate sweetness, syrupy sentiment, itchy sarcasm, provocative aggression, can (un)easily cohabit the same work. With one stroke he inaugurates and perfects in the delicious evergreen *Classical Symphony* (1917) what will become the prevalent international tendency of the two decades following. With him it was in reaction to his horrendous *Ala and Lolly* (1914), a would-be ballet more primitive and shocking than Stravinsky's *Rite*. And adjacent to *Chout* (1920), a ballet more Russian folkloric than *Petrushka* and *Les Noces*, the altogether more genuine and genial *Love for Three Oranges* (1919). Also from this time comes the summit of his glittering Christmas-tree tenderness in the magical 1st Violin Concerto: 'it seems impossible to me to love music and not be captivated by it', said Sviatoslav Richter.

By the 1920s Prkfv had reverted to modernist tactics, with a ballet marking the achievements of Revolutionary Russian industry, and an orchestral work in the same vein: the first movement of this 2nd

Symphony (1924–5) is the ultimate machine-music monster: hearing it is to be rolled out flat while being simultaneously fired up to white-heat amid the deafening racket of an iron-foundry. Yet the second movement already predicates the plasticated lyrical idiom – flattened out, cool not heated, coarsened Tchaikovsky – of the final Soviet period. It is wry to learn that after the première he observed: 'it occurred to me for the first time that I might perhaps be destined to be a second-rate composer.'

And so the contradictions continue: the detached drollery of the 2nd Violin Concerto, the raving insanity of *The Fiery Angel* (diabolic possession in a nunnery), the delectable 3rd Piano Concerto, the earthy warmth of the *Overture on Hebrew Themes*, the grandiose paeans to Soviet triumphs. Mostly he provokes, annoys, frustrates, maddens, disappoints. But he can also hit a target dead-centre to wonderful effect – *Romeo and Juliet*, many numbers within and the sweep and panache of the whole; the magnificent film-scores in their eventual concert-form – stark *Alexander Nevsky*, ever-delicious *Lieutenant Kijé* (piquant that its non-existent hero is embodied by one of the composer's most catchy and characteristic tunes – an allegory of his equivocal personality in general): and the perfection of story-telling in the immortal *Peter and the Wolf* (1936) with its light-touch didacticism for recognizing the instruments of the orchestra comparable only with Britten's equally captivating *Young Person's Guide*.

Unexpected treasures include forty-odd numbers for a project on Pushkin's *Eugene Onegin*, planned with tactful care to complement Tchaikovsky's beloved but very partial opera by restoring the multifaceted complexity – wit, irony, ambiguity, violence – of the original. This venture foundering like so many in his cruel last years, Prkfv recycled some of the music for *Cinderella* and *War and Peace*, wherein (for me if not for its many admirers) droopy longueurs far outweigh occasional flashes of high inspiration. The same goes for a couple of other late operatic efforts, failures though written to succeed within the diktats of time and place: Prkfv is so naturally fecund that even when reluctant, weary, unfired, he can infuse the simplistic characters and plots of *Semyon Kotko* or *The Story of a Real Man* with genuine if intermittent quality. In this placatory phase *Cinderella* truly pleases: for all the ersatz-Imperial, an enchanting score on a subject calculated to bring out the composer's truest gifts. Delightful too is the least aspiring of his later operas, *Betrothal in a Monastery* (polar antipode from madness in a nunnery, based upon the same Sheridan original as Roberto Gerhard's *Duenna* and almost its exact contemporary). But the coarse overkill of his Soviet Symphonies 5, 6 and 7 (1944–52) makes sad listening; and the once celebrated 'Wartime' piano sonatas (1940–44) now sound strained and threadbare.

A peculiar mix: the twentieth century's most inventive and attractive melodist, with a vein of fairy-tale fantasy, sauced by satire and spice, exquisitely applied, matchless in flavour: alongside provocative but pointless aggression, meaningless dissonance, self-defeating busyness, obsessive violence, inane mechanization, gross uncouthness of orchestration, trying the listener's patience to its limits till one cries out for the Wolf and the invisible Lieutenant. The phenomenon still perplexes: Prkfv the Pzl: I can't get him together; nor perhaps could he.

Shostakovich

Dmitri Shostakovich: born 1906; precocity recognized early; the 1st Symphony (aged nineteen) enjoyed European then international success. So long as the new Soviet regime remained open to freedom of expression his art took full advantage: when it began to contract and clamp down he became its victim: then its obedient laureate, till, too celebrated for further denunciation, he was able in the works of his final years (died 1975) to utter the personal subjective content so long suppressed or only present in code and cipher.

The problems of assessing Shostakovich fairly are innate to the oeuvre, inextricably bound into the circumstances of the times and the place: and personal to this writer, who has always cordially detested this music and wondered bemused at its staggering popularity. When I was excited by the wonderful colourists of the early twentieth century he seemed drab; when electrified by high modernism, dowdy and conservative; when settling down into sobriety and formalism, so obviously inferior to the intended comparisons – Bach, Haydn, Beethoven, Mahler.

The gift is enormous. And some of its earliest manifestations, before the troubles, are captivating. Did he ever do better, actually, than that 1st Symphony of 1925? A perfect product of adolescent genius, setting up all his later routines with effervescent freshness and brevity – perky, energetic, hectic, sentimental, tragic – before they set in Soviet cement. Soon follows the freedom and abandon of the years, all-too-few, when the most audacious and extravagant ventures in the arts were still perceived as germane to the revolutionary spirit of the fledgling State and a vital part of its development. The wild constructivism of the next two symphonies still conveys the fervour and the hope; the ballets and theatre-music alongside, the high-spirited jinks. Masterpiece of this time remains *The Nose* (1927–8), wherein Gogol's bizarre and frightening fantasy of the severed member leading its own independent existence is perfectly matched to the music's reckless grotesque extravagance – one of the most over-the-top things ever written; that scene in the Cathedral; that all-percussion interlude preceding the rude eructation of awakening, yawning, stretching, shaving; those balalaikas! That eunuch voice! The fulfilment, with unstinted interest, of what Musorgsky had attempted and failed at with his *Marriage* (also Gogol): and at the same time alert and open to current European advances, principally *Wozzeck*. One can easily imagine a *Dead Souls* from the Shostakovich of c.1930.

Instead, trouble ahead. *The Nose* had already encountered difficulties: they reach the surface in the notorious denunciation of his next opera, *Lady Macbeth of the Mtsensk District* (composed 1930–32, first produced 1934), a huge success till visited by Stalin late the next year and promptly banned from performance. The work's success abroad is explained (claimed *Pravda* at Stalin's prompting) by the way 'it tickles the perverted bourgeois taste with its fidgety screaming neurotic music': at home, offence caused by its subversion of civic/social/family decencies and its flagrant presentation of sexual lust in action. What *Pravda* can't or won't explain is why the opera succeeded so well before it was axed. And was Stalin so wrong? The prevalence of parody and 'wrong-note music', used equally to show frenzied murder and inept policemen as absurd, and above all the massed brass-bands accompanying the guilty adulterous bed, are deeply subversive and offensive and are *meant* to be. Such flaunting provocation serves to heighten the black tragedy of the work's close wherein the heroine's plight opens the vials of compassion without defensive detachment and the camouflage of irony. Unfortunately, Stalin had left the theatre long before the work's ultimate nature had been revealed.

Tragic for Shostakovich as artist that this powerful and authentic piece, representing a marked deepening in idiom as in content, should have been his nemesis: *Lady Macbeth* remained in limbo till its gradual reassessment and acceptance after his death; though the limbo had been filled in part by his later revision as *Katerina Ismailova*, which bowdlerizes the original into prudish gentility. The original remains the high point of his achievement as a whole. Also lost for decades was the 4th Symphony (1935–6), a huge sprawling splurge, prudently withdrawn by its composer before its intended première, which only took place in 1961.

Now come the copious deserts of Shostakovich's maturity. Its first dead-sea fruit the 5th Symphony (1937), a substantial and sustained attempt to toe the line and provide the acceptable, still impressive in its unendearing way: Schoenberg recognized in Shostakovich the authentic 'breath of a symphonist' even in an idiom so remote from his own musical culture wherein 'symphony' is paramount. But thereafter, a sorry tale. Copious fluency in every going genre – symphonies, concertos, chamber-music, choral pieces and songs, ballets and film-scores – even *24 Preludes and Fugues* for solo piano (1951), a monument of piety intended to complement Bach's incomparable *48*, surpassed in dismalness only by Hindemith's gruesome *Ludus Tonalis*, written in the same spirit some nine years before. Within the symphonies the movement-types range between portentous brow-clenching 'seriousness' (the admiring cliché calls it 'brooding'), pseudo-profound 'searchingness'; and hectic, scampering, aggressively manic fast music – scherzi, but no jokes – parodistic high spirits, without mirth, on commonplace material: in between these extremes, vapid light-music devoid of charm and invention. All rhetoric and coercion, exercises or instructions in communal lament and rejoicing, constructed of material undistinguished and unmemorable except when hammered out over and over, and seemingly recycled near-identical from work to work. Forms distended to unearned and unbearable length; rhetoric bullying and hectoring, especially when oppressively would-be deep; orchestration abominable if expert and effective – battleship grey or poster-paint scarlet, both equally covering acres of cardboard. Their low points are the 7th Symphony, the notorious 'Leningrad' (1941), whose popularity in the USA drove Bartók to the wicked parody in his *Concerto for Orchestra* even while it sustained the morale of the besieged city that gives it its name; and the wholly abstract 10th (1953), for the composer's adherents the masterpiece of the cycle, but for me indistinguishably consecrating all the traits detailed here. Far truer, its successor of 1957, the 11th – frankly programmatic – a loose-weave atmospheric fresco depicting scenes (*The Palace Square*), time (*The 9th of January*), moods (*In Memoriam*) and events (*The Tocsin*) from the 1905 Revolution with the resources, and the mastery, of a good film-score: lettering twenty feet high tells the tragic/heroic story to a stunned proletariat with power and honesty, without condescension or dumbing-down – an authentic 'common touch'.

No. 14 (1969) is its opposite – absolutely not for the People: private, introverted, personal: eleven meditations on Death, poems mainly by Lorca and Apollinaire with two brief Rilke-settings to close, all in Russian translation, and one original Russian text mourning the loss to the Muses of a compatriot poet. The two Rilke poems are also elegiac, though the last is set with brittle sarcasm, brief lyricism, and a sudden explosion of furious final protest, raging in vain against Death's Dominion. This close uses both soloists for the only time: elsewhere, they sing separate: for the work is a song-cycle as well as a symphony, its models Britten's sequences devoted to a single theme – Spring; Sleep – Mahler's 'symphony' *Song of the Earth* behind both successors; and Shostakovich's work dedicated to Britten, who directed its English première, and whose earlier idiom, all hard and lean, is often recalled. The orchestra is reduced to strings with percussion – used with violence – and celesta, used with icy chill banishing all association with the Sugar-Plum Fairy. The idiom is stripped naked, whether chilled and wandering, or burning in excoriation – both extremes matching the bitter sarcastic bloodiness of the French and Spanish poems chosen with maximum care to perturb and disturb. This music is merciless: listeners are flayed by punishment born of unflinching truth to experience that hadn't, after all, been crushed into silence by the composer's dutiful truckling to his Masters' commands. A good performance 'in the flesh' of Shostakovich's 14th vindicates every jot of his habitual harshness, meanness, over-emphasis, underlining. The nudity of its desolation, the intemperance of its anger, truly 'make the flesh creep': they couldn't have been effected by any other means. A one-off: a masterpiece of exiguity best left unique: diluted into habit, with ever-diminishing returns, without the once-only justification, in most of the music of his last remaining six years. The final symphony, however – No. 15 of 1971 – is an exception: the machine runs down, lively Rossini and death-announcing Wagner weave in and out, undigested.

In more intimate genres, Shostakovich always excelled: with songs, with piano, with small ensembles, sometimes with orchestra. Chamber-music is another thing. The string quartet, above all – a medium congenial to intimacy and essence – promises to preclude the rant and bombast the large orchestra induces. But in the cycle of fifteen (sometimes, unbelievably, estimated with Beethoven's seventeen) the trajectory of the symphonies is repeated on a smaller scale. The last seven (from no. 9 in 1964 to no. 15 in 1974) make a tally of attrition painful to experience, both for the unmitigated exposure of pain pertaining to the *man*, and the wretched condition of the *art*. His final work (1975) the *Sonata for Viola and Piano* goes beyond any 'late style': it sounds positively – negatively, that is – posthumous – the music of the ghost whose machine has stopped.

What is the basis for Shostakovich's appeal? Honest curiosity as to why and how his audience can be genuinely pleased and rewarded by what is so unequivocally, for the most part, so deficient in rewards and pleasure whether simply diverting or, deeper and more arduous, through surmounting difficulties to face the unbearable and overcome, or succumb to it. His huge appeal survives huge unappealingness. I think it must be based in vicarious identification with oppression and repression by a liberal, cultivated, well-heeled, well-fed, well-housed *bien pensant* intelligentsia whose underlying guilt and discomfort are perfectly attuned to exactly the punishment this music inflicts. The terrible nature of Shostakovich's circumstances mustn't prevent a balanced response to his actual notes. If it does, emotional blackmail is committed, which for all its gratifications involves illusion and delusion – a flattering identification with suffering heroism, a holier-than-thou priggishness in the rush to empathize with tribulations not actually experienced save in imagination. To deplore this is to risk appearing stony-hearted. But what else is there to go on, in works of art, than their artistic calibre – in music, the actual notes? All human experience can be encompassed and expressed in music's actual notes, when they show themselves capable of containing what's entrusted to them. With Shostakovich I submit that the intrinsic quality of most of the oeuvre is not strong enough to carry the weight that has been placed upon it: which suggests in turn that what is required of it is lightweight too, whatever heavy appearances to the contrary.

But 'the disposition of those who are pleased with it must be a great blessing to them'.

A note on Alexander Mossolov

Born 1900; in youth part of the experimentalist artistic ferment characterizing the early phase of the new-born Russia, falling into serious trouble as it turned the other way, eventually re-finding favour, dying in 1973. He is remembered now for the one work – *Iron Foundry* of 1926 – which brilliantly epitomizes a tendency of the times, rhyming with Honegger's hymn to the mighty steam-engine in *Pacific 231*, the *Ballet Mécanique* of George Antheil, the menacing technology of Max Brand's *Maschinist Hopkins*, and, closest to home, the constructivism of Shostakovich's 2nd and 3rd Symphonies. His output mostly period-pieces born of the edge of Stravinsky's work when still a Russian radical: justly forgotten except as curiosities: but in this one case, unjustly. Mossolov's machines, against their background of clanking and whirring, really *sing* their grandly shaped, lusty-potent melody: these machines have hearts, souls and balls. At three and a half minutes *Iron Foundry* would make the perfect encore to any performance of its two great progenitors, *The Rite of Spring* and *The Poem of Ecstasy*.

CHAPTER XV

England

Elgar and Delius interlinked

> The rhetorician would deceive his neighbours,
> The sentimentalist himself...

The lines of Yeats, used by Wilfrid Mellers to characterize and differentiate these two composers whose greatest work lies concurrent from the late 1890s to *c*.1920:

> If Delius ran the risk of being the sentimentalist [by which, surely, Yeats and Mellers mean the Man of Feeling who would place his sentiments primary in life and in art], Elgar always felt the lure of rhetoric ... He accepted Edwardian society as zestfully as Delius rejected it; and although both composers took over the idiom of German romanticism, Delius exploited it to express an egocentric isolation, Elgar to express a social conviction no less purposeful than that of Strauss.

A suggestive start, save the last bit – little or no 'social conviction' in Elgar: on the contrary, the more we know, the more we listen, the undercurrents of pain, alienation, angst, perturbation within the sentimental rhetorician, his self-expression, his 'egocentric isolation', more resemble Mahler than Strauss. Personal effusion, intimacy, secrets and enigmas: Elgar is shot through with such, however public the outward show. And Delius is by no means averse to rhetorical utterance now and then, usually tending towards crashing and bombast. What they have in common is

equally as telling as the obvious differences of technique, intonation, genre.

Above all, pastoral, with an intense response to Nature – 'music
is in the trees for all to pluck', said Elgar – '*Our* Malverns', said his
mother: and both composers ache with nostalgia and transience.
Delius is pantheist through-and-through – his principal subjects
range far wider than Elgar's West Country, to include Florida,
Nordic landscapes, German and French, as well as England. But
both composers do a splendid city-portrait: Elgar's *Cockaigne*,
Delius' *Paris*. Also Testaments of Belief: Elgar's ultra-Catholic oratorios; the greatest, *Gerontius*, at its best when most personal – the
death-chamber, the new-born soul skimming free (pastoral too), the
angel's farewell – not all that far from confessional places in Delius.
His own chorus-and-orchestra monument, the *Mass of Life*, is nonetheless a Credo for being defiantly anti-Christian: it could just as
well declare with *Gerontius* 'firmly I believe and truly', affirming the
Will, the need to be Hard, the abandon to sensuality: the closing
Midnight Song is not so distant from the mystic/pantheist side of
Elgar's later oratorios. Nietzsche's texts are quasi-biblical from the
start: they put Man at the centre just as does *Gerontius*. The Delius
Requiem – a work of wartime dedicated to young artists killed in the
conflict – makes a peculiar private statement of belief and unbelief;
Christianity and Islam are both mocked – Buddha too? – but take
to thyself the love of a good woman, and leave the rest to nature (in
the harsh piece's exquisite close).

And both composers, as Mellers reminds us, are late German
Romantics. Wagner permeates, Strauss excites: for Elgar, Mendelssohn, Schumann, Brahms are major tributaries, and he's alert to
Dvořák, Tchaikovsky and lighter French lyricism. Delius is not so
broad: the symphonic line was not his way, and there's surprisingly
little trace of the new intonations in French music despite his years
in Paris and friendly contact with Ravel. Grieg is an important influence in the aspects of his style that tend counter-Teutonic. But the
solid technical/linguistic idiom of both composers is Germanic: as,
too, the cast of mind and soul. Both enjoyed widespread recognition
in Germany – in the case of Delius well before success in his own

country. His largest concert work, and some smaller, set German texts. And his parentage is pure German.

Elgar, born 1857: father kept a music-shop in Worcester; the boy had the run of the stock, eagerly teaching himself many instruments as well as the fundamentals of composition. Keen participation in local musical activities, writing woodwind divertimentos for his friends, music for dances, and for the nearby lunatic asylum, as well as playing organ in his church and violin in the big choirs-and-orchestra events of the Three Choirs Festival: all this the firm basis of his infallible instrumental know-how later.

Delius, born Bradford 1862 to German parents settled in the city: father a prosperous wool-merchant: the boy was christened Fritz. Early proficiency in music: the business-life intended soon proved uncongenial: aged twenty-two to Florida to cultivate oranges: further musical tuition there, and deep absorption in the lush surroundings and the chalorous Black singing – first-fruit, *Florida Suite* (1886–7). By which time he'd moved to Leipzig for full musical education (compare Elgar, self-taught, taking everything in from practical experience). From Germany Delius lived nearly a decade in Paris and got going as composer – his work more successful in Germany than either London or France. Moved to Grez-sur-Loing 1896 to live with his painter-mistress: they married 1903 and lived there the remainder of their span.

Elgar married 'above him' 1889: all his life he suffered a perceived indignity of class-condescension and the obloquy of his Roman Catholicism. Delius, in contrast, a free-thinker, at home with artists and writers, unfazed by questions of social standing. His bloom-time as composer runs *c.*1901–16 – the operas *A Village Romeo and Juliet*, *Fennimore and Gerda*, the *Mass of Life* setting Nietzsche, *Sea Drift* setting Whitman; *Appalachia*, finest flower of the Florida-memories: best of all, a handful of miniatures for smaller orchestra that achieve flawless beauty.

Elgar's first flush of fulfilment runs down the 1890s in works for the Three Choirs and other choral festivals, from *The Black Knight* (1892), *The Light of Life* and *King Olaf* (both 1896) to *Caractacus* in 1898, which year also saw the *Variations on an Original Theme* (*Enigma*) for orchestra, an immediate hit at home and on the continent. His fullest fruition *c*. 1900–1913: *The Dream of Gerontius* and two further large-scale oratorios; both symphonies; a couple of splendid concert-overtures; the rather overblown Violin Concerto; the masterpiece for strings – *Introduction and Allegro*; and plentiful smaller incidental/occasional pieces in between. This rich harvest coincided with the heyday of England's national and imperial self-confidence: towards its end the skies began to turn sullen and unwelcoming – the première of the 2nd Symphony coolly received in 1911, *Falstaff* two years later rather a flop: these two are arguably his finest achievements.

After the Great War his idiom and vision were out-of-joint with changed times. His last sustained flush of composition comes with three sizeable chamber-works and the Cello Concerto, 1918–19: death in 1920 of the wife who'd steadfastly provided support and inspiration inaugurates sad final years – incidental music, choral miniatures, occasionals, arrangements: principal solace, recording his own works with the developing gramophone technology: a stirring resurgence towards the end in a possible third symphony. The final years of Delius are at once more pathetic and more fulfilled. From around 1920, increasing bodily impairment from syphilis, eventuating by 1925 in paralysis and blindness. Still full of music, with no sense whatever, unlike Elgar, that the wind has changed: moving tale of help in notating his locked-up music from Percy Grainger, and later long association with Eric Fenby, by whose patient and loving aid a retrospective final nosegay of faded romanticism was painfully brought into being.

The two composers met only the once, Elgar visiting chair-bound Delius at Grez in May 1933. The sentimental rhetorician and the rhetorical sentimentalist got on surprisingly well. Both were dead within just a year, Elgar first, February 1934, Delius that June.

Edward Elgar: earlier choral works

Hard to bear is the poignancy of loss, the resentment at waste, induced by so many once-living kinds of music separated by time and change, imprisoned in obsolete genres or superseded beliefs and practices – the Renaissance masque, the Baroque *opéra-ballet*, the fulsome welcome-odes of Purcell, the annual cycle of Bach's church cantatas, the homely circle centred on song, piano *morceau*, four-hand duet . . . Manifestly, much excellent music, sometimes important, sometimes supremely great, is cut off from its deep-nourished roots in a lost context of social, civic, religious usage. A quick glance at the lists on the back of old Novello vocal scores of their hard-core staples (mainly Handel) suffices to reveal the extended wasteland, once teeming with life, of the Victorian oratorio. It would require a combination of monumental pedantry and the imaginative anti-quarianism of a Scott or a Hardy, lightly touched with Betjeman-esque nostalgia, to deal sympathetically with this quaint and often hilarious lost world.

Elgar's compositional growth is firmly grounded in this copious choral culture, its twaddle as much as its masterpieces. His earlier cantatas make a determined bid to join it, his later to raise and enhance it; taken together they cover almost his entire composing life, which coincides with English choral culture at its apogee. While the two last oratorios have never quite gained the safe mainstream, *Gerontius* is unbudgeable. And in more general terms, his reputation has never stood higher in all the years since its first peak in the twentieth century's first decade.

But the pre-*Gerontius* pieces, for the most part clear milestones on a great composer's path to prime-of-life powers, none utterly neg-ligible, some patently inspired, are largely neglected. Perhaps these works are killed by the downside of the once-vigorous culture that produced them; the provincial philistinism memorably lambasted again and again in Shaw's concert-notices of the 1880s and 1890s. Plots are stilted and ludicrous (goes the consensus), texts fustian, the genre in general old-fangled and unworkable. These charges can't be denied but they can be side-stepped: for when was it ever other thus, chez oratorio – or indeed with the generality of texted music from the Baroque onwards?

In this great tradition of pure awfulness Elgar stands firm and square. Take for a start *Gerontius*. How Newman's poem, second in its day for popularity only to *In Memoriam*, nowadays groans, creaks and embarrasses divorced from its setting, and sometimes also as set! Nobody turns a hair, and many are on their knees. Yet this seemingly robust appetite jibs at the Revd Capel Cure, MA, and Shapcott Wensley, and H. A. Acworth, CIE. I don't perceive any marked qualitative distinction between their texts, nor the more 'professional' trash of Longfellow (in his own right or translating Ludwig Uhland), and the sainted Cardinal: nor, when Elgar hits top form, in the music.

The vital thing is the conviction and intensity of the composer's response: when authentically charged up they sweep grotty words before them – as is usual; as is proper. Take again the imperishable *Gerontius*. What matters is the passionate identification with which the composer inhabits the situations, becoming the dying Everyman on his deathbed of pain, or the new-born soul skimming weightless and sin-free; his awed fearfulness before the judgment; his cry of unworthiness; his long, achingly nostalgic withdrawal. Outside of its protagonist, rendered with such unforgettable inwardness, *Gerontius* is in fact a very uneven work; far more so than *King Olaf* and *Caractacus*. If these maybe fall short of the later work's high points, they have less distance to fall into the mawkishness, tawdriness, heaviness, that cumber its flatlands.

This is contentious; what seems to me certain is the earlier works' superior freshness and freedom of idiom and of manner. They are not self-conscious: there's only a harmless hint of the dutiful grand set-piece that makes 'Praise to the Holiest' such a grind, still less (a few touches in *Lux Christi* apart) of the over-artfully-wrought textures and oleaginous claustrophobia of the later oratorios, not to mention *The Music Makers*, where the odour of piety sacred or profane waxes well-nigh unbreathable. They are, within the bounds of their genre and culture, wonderfully exuberant, unaffectedly heartfelt, skilful without ostentation, ardently and generously musical – a vital emanation from a young(ish) composer stretching his wings in an environment spacious enough, surprisingly, to give him the room to.

All this is magnificently manifest in *The Black Knight* (op. 25). The young(ish) composer's ambition is shown by his calling the work's four scenes a 'Symphony for Chorus and Orchestra' (conventional-ized by Novello's into 'Cantata'). It had been tentatively begun in 1889, without commission till the conductor of the Worcester Choral Society tried over the sketches some two years later, and offered to put it on if and when Elgar finished it. The vocal score was ready late 1892, the full score early the next year, and the first perform-ance followed that April. Uhland's ballad (1806), itself drawing on a seventeenth-century reworking of a weird putative happening in early Scottish history, came to Elgar via his own (and his mother's) favourite Longfellow: the source is *Hyperion: A Romance* (1839), wherein the hero improvises this translation from the German for his lady's edification. It tells of the Spring festival at Pentecost, with jousting and trumpets: an unknown knight in sable armour chal-lenges the youthful prince, who is felled at the first blow and can barely rise again from the shock: at a grand ball the same evening the dark stranger asks the princess's hand in a dance: for all his suavity, she grows cold in his arms and her fresh garlands fade: at the subsequent banquet the old king looks on in sad bemusement at the blighted royal couple: the mysterious interloper offers them a cool healing draught – initially restorative, but as the young pair embrace the old king the colour drains from their faces and they wither away: in vain the old man cries to be taken too, and is refused – the grim stranger seeks only youth and beauty – 'Roses in the spring I gather!'

Idiom is chivalric/picturesque, out of Weber and Mendelssohn with plenty of early Wagner and awareness of the mature; touches of Tchaikovsky and Dvořák; for the work's symphonic aspect, muscular Brahmsian warmth. The real Elgar to come is every-where glimpsed – his light music and his serious, his pastoral, his 'dream children', his pomp and circumstance, his occasional lapses and excesses. A comparison that runs all the way would be with Mahler's youthful cantata *Das klagende Lied*. This also grows out of early German Romantic subject-matter and its musical treatment, with *Euryanthe* and *Lohengrin* clear ancestors: to tell in a dreamy hybrid of opera, song-cycle, ballad, a tale of dark destruction, setting proud castle and knightly carouse against a glowing evocation of the natural world. *Das klagende Lied* involves sibling jealousy, lust,

murder and supernatural retribution, wherein everyone and everything is annihilated. Its idiom is folkloric, martial, *singverein*-ish,
together with an extraordinary vein of near-hysteria that gets the
tale's latent morbidity out into the open. Whereas in *The Black
Knight* no one has erred: the dark stain is both external and inexplicable, the style is warm, full, sweet; and yet the ending is equally
bleak. Does Elgar's treatment too-much soften, indeed prettify, its
sable content, or is it the work's genius that the events are told *en
rose*, with such decorum both expressive and technical as, paradoxically, to enhance the sinister effect? Both are works of uncanny, disturbing power. Aesop can be emended: the sun charms the traveller
into discarding his cloak, the wind tears it away: the same object is
achieved by *both*.

From the *Bavarian Highlands* (1895), setting folksongs adapted by
his wife, and *The Banner of St George* (eventually 1897 but essentially
sketched next), can be passed by on the other side: the former dinkily
melodious à la Dvořák; the latter a preposterous Imperial period-
piece where, for once, text and setting join hands in sheer mediocrity. Yet Elgar is learning his craft: *Lux Christi – The Light of Life*
(1896) raises the stakes – his most ambitious work to date: a thoughtful subject (Jesus healing the blind man), occasional moments of
inspiration foretelling *Gerontius* at its best, plentiful over-wrought
pious lethargy foretelling *Apostles* and *Kingdom* at their worst, and
overall, increasing command of span, pacing, expressive range and
the orchestra. But little temptation to linger. And with *King Olaf*
and *Caractacus* we are back on course: in these two as much as in the
Enigma Variations Elgar reaches maturity – stylistic, technical, expressive. *Olaf* reverts to childhood favourite Longfellow. The source this
time is *Tales of a Wayside Inn* (first series, 1863), a neo-Chaucerian
anthology of stories told by characters gathered therein to pass the
time. Jerrold Northrop Moore points out how this particular tale
was especially suited to appeal: it is the Musician's Tale (he a tall lithe
violinist not a thousand miles distant from the young Elgar, living in
'that ideal world / whose language is not speech but song'); telling
of the heroic Norwegian who brought the Christian faith to his
pagan lands before, like Siegfried, being undone by treachery from

within and without through his relations with women; in the end, and beyond his death, only his mother remains faithful. In effect, a combination of the chivalrous Christian hero such as St George, seen in three dimensions not cardboard cut-out, in a setting of saga and romance like *The Black Knight*. Harry Acworth, a Malvern neighbour, was called in to cut and reshape the over-generous original at the composer's behest, adding further explanations, often insufficient, to cover the elisions. The cantata was written to fulfil a request from a choral director who'd admired the Longfellow setting, for an evening-length follow-up. It was composed 1894–6 and received its première at the North Staffordshire Music Festival in October 1896, just six weeks after the first performance of *Lux Christi*. It is Elgar's op. 30, and he was thirty-nine.

Invited in 1897 to produce a new work for the Leeds Festival the following year, Elgar seems to have preferred a symphony (possibly his long-dreamed-of tribute to General Gordon) but the Festival Committee insisted upon a cantata, and the result was *Caractacus*, first performed at Leeds in October 1898. The subject had been semi-formed at the back of his mind. Again the initial impulse came from his mother. Out with her son on the Malverns she'd exclaimed, 'Oh! Ed, look at the lovely old hills, can't we write some *tale* about it?' (the account is her own in a letter to her daughter Susannah, 'Pollie', the composer's younger sister). 'Do it yourself, Mother' was his reply, but despite this appeal she demurred: 'No, I can't, my day is gone by if I ever could' (like mother, like son); yet within a month the subject was focused and ready to go. He'd turned again to Acworth, who this time had to start from scratch with no prototype to build upon, producing at the composer's urging both scenario and versification for a libretto that has been widely regretted ever since, though it suffices as surely for suitable set-ability as it is obviously deficient in narrative clarity, character-depiction and dramatic shapeliness.

Its music, like *King Olaf*'s, abounds in *echt*-Elgarian material of wide-ranging character: at its best, as fine as anything he wrote – jingoistic tub-thumping triumphalism are as native to him as the 'beloved woodlands' more akin to present-day sensibilities. Its corny, stilted narrative sits in complement to his sensitivity for character evinced in the very next opus, the *Enigma Variations*, with its loving encapsulation of friends, family and the composer himself.

Delius to c.1913

Appalachia, Variations on an Old Slave Song for orchestra with chorus and baritone soloist of 1898–1903, finest flower of the unforgettable time Delius spent in Florida. Commences with a clear summons on horns, followed immediately by its soft echo: four bars of gentle sustained harmony, a harp arpeggio, arabesque woodwind flutters. The same again, the echo-horn now shadowed with a flute: a third time, horn-calls now harmonized. Sudden hearty strain, immediately diminishing. Horn-summons a fourth time, given here softly on basses and harps: its sostenuto now continuous, its arpeggios a background to the hearty figure sweetened and placid, conversationally exchanged on solo woodwinds and first horn. An introduction to an Introduction. So too is what follows: lively contrast, a harp plus pizzicato twangle – sort of calypso – rapidly swelling in volume and instrumentation till the full orchestra is involved. Horns, trumpets, trombones successively give out a new contour in octaves, in canon across three octaves, triumphantly capped and crowned by the strings *fff crescendo*. This contour will prove a vital second half of the main theme, whose first half is also foretold here on solo trumpet as the gorgeous outburst of this second Introduction subsides.

Theme at last: the Old Slave Song itself on cor anglais, accompanied in harmony and sonority equally lugubrious; then more open and cheery, solo horn with strings, a trifle faster; faster still, on bassoon and clarinet with a swaying momentum in the strings' accompaniment. *Più vivo* again, fragments only of theme amid joyous leaping fanfares culminating in theme-epitome warmly sung by all the upper strings. The exuberance rapidly stilled in three declining sighing breaths – high woodwinds; trumpets and trombones; horns and bassoons – that will recur later. Now come seven Variations, diversified between hearty, lyrical, lush, gracefully dancing, perkily marching, though they all merge seamless – no relation to classical practice; each, rather, is a free fantazia with elements from the theme, other themes too, floating in and out scarcely varied at all, amid generous independent invention. Yet as they accumulate, a bigger whole evolves, greater than the sum of the parts. Finally, what every listener ardently awaits – the full chorus, singing the Old Slave Song, in full harmony, with its words

> After night has gone comes the day,
> the dark shadows will fade away,
> t'wards the morning lift a voice,
> let the scented woods rejoice
> and echoes swell across the mighty stream,
> and echoes swell ... across ... the mighty stream

set in lush wide-spaced choral texture, the diatonic melody chromatically harmonized from the end of the first line onwards, burgeoning from four to five to six to eight parts. Orchestra re-enters slow and solemn, with occasional deep gong-strokes, a solo violin then a trumpet singing vestige of the Song's opening, the lovely paragraph suspiring in two sighs of *ah!* on all the voices *pppp*. A brief coda gives the entire Song on woodwinds in the minor, dark and melancholy, before turning major for the chorus's re-entry, livelier, led by the solo baritone, marked *populare*: 'O Honey, I am going down the river in the morning' – answered by all the men, then joined by the women for 'Aye! Honey, I'll be gone when next the whippoorwill's a-calling': all this to a new strain not employed in the preceding Variation-fantazias. He continues 'and don't you be too lonesome, love, and don't you fret and cry ...' and now the tempo animates as chorus take up the strain not heard since the second Introduction, miles back upstream, that with retrospect – in every hearing subsequent to the first – seems always to have had its words inherent and inseparable:

> For the dawn will soon be breaking,
> the radiant morn is nigh,
> and you'll find me ever awaiting,
> my own sweet Nelly Gray!

Plus plentiful Heigh-ho and la-la-la as canonic entries fill out the sonority with joyous ebullience, up to climatic return of the morning's uplifted voice, the scented woods' rejoicing, the echoes swelling down the mighty stream. Ends with a beautifully judged retreat – *Ah!* – apotheosis of the breathing sighs heard at several places before, now repeated five times, in gradual-drooping chromatic chords over a firm stable bass-note: on the second *Ah!* horns loudly (re)call the summons that had opened the work; remnants of the frisky phrase from early on also return. After the third *Ah!* the orchestra is left briefly alone; after the fourth and fifth it has the last wordless word – one penultimate sigh, a last gentle frisk, a beautiful very Delian cadence, simple but unusual, exactly right for this deeply evocative work that, subtly, without intention, suggests a vein of compassionate tenderness for troubled humanity not often found in this one-hundred-per-cent egotistical artist.

Sea Drift, also for orchestra with baritone soloist and chorus, this time firmly centred on a text, dates from the next year (1904). The poet is Whitman, second only to Nietzsche in Delius' pantheon: the lyric Whitman, not the brawny boaster: tenderly telling, in free verse, irregular lines, with perfect command of tone and cadence, the love, loss, longing of the he-bird deprived of his mate, as perceived and experienced through the eyes of 'I, a curious boy' in a setting revealed by the first line – 'Once Paumanok' – not so far from the Florida of *Appalachia*. The poem is subtly and suggestively divided between and across the baritone soloist and the full chorus, their roles versatile – narrator, boy, he-bird in joy and grief, and – in the background, suggested not stated – a pantheistic entity: the *sea*, the *sea-winds*, the *breakers tirelessly tossing*, the *moon heavy with love*, the *rising stars*, eventually the *air*, the *woods*, the *fields*.

These two chorus-and-orchestra pieces represent Delius on a large scale and at his best. The full-evening works from the same years don't show so well: the six operas are well-nigh impossible, the *Mass of Life* well-nigh absurd – bombastic, overladen, dictatorial-didactic from the opening invocation to the Will; the injunction *Be thou Hard!* via endless would-be-seductive fa-la-lah-ing, to the Great Bell of Midnight at the close. All these have isolated islands of the *true* Delius – *La Calinda* from his Florida days and *Koanga*, the prelude to *Irmelin*, in *A Village Romeo and Juliet* the 'walk to the Paradise Garden' and the *Tristan*-ending, in the *Mass* the tranced evocation of noon-day stillness in a haze of heat and light. But the *true* Delius scale is small, sometimes miniature – posies, garlands, idylls.

In a Summer Garden (though headed 'Spring 1908'): *echt* from the start; tender woodwind chirrups against a drift of sensitized harmony on strings; livening into chirpiness, thickening into rich chromatic honey; more chordal, then more sparky, calming back into gentle chirruping. Solo horn leads to a sostenuto middle-section – no tune as such, though wholly melodious; fading into shadow, soon energizing, growing rather rampageous – a recurrent Delius weakness – till broad cantabile, cut off at climax, wilting to a halt. The piece's resumption more of an *autumn* garden: some figures from earlier, but no sense of a 'recapitulation' even when the very opening does indeed recur – a mosaic of patches, flower by flower, scent by scent; mood-swings, volatility, mutation within minute durations. Two pangs of ardent aching yearning: penultimate touch of *winter* garden with the soft drum-beats: very end, diaphanous diatonic calm with a solitary bird. Eric Fenby's more technical account is good – Delius has invented 'a new type of prose melody against varying tensions of chromatic harmony'. It applies also to *Summer Night on the River* (1911) – lulling chromatic drift, then longer sustained cantabile, equally non-melody (try memorizing it) as so often, evanescing away on gently croaking dissonances: a gem. As, too, *On Hearing the First Cuckoo in Spring* (1911): a real *tune* here, a Norwegian folksong. Delius benefits with a tune to build on; and every local twinge and squirm of blue-notes in its harmonization is exquisitely judged and right – no slurping; so when the diatonics come, complete with cuckoo, they are refreshed and new. *Brigg Fair* (1907) also gains from its clearly defined folksong, this time from Lincolnshire, collected by Percy Grainger, to whom the piece is appropriately dedicated. Fluttery opening haze; folk-tune straight and robust, growing ever-livelier, even a trifle galumphing: return of haze, now more sustained. Variations – this like *Appalachia* is a sort of variation-set – resume thoughtful: a solemn bell, a touch of *yearn*, easing off, heartening up to a very Graingeresque climax. The bells peal out, then the mood tranquillizes to a solemn processional, almost a cortège, trumpet leading, bells continuing, to rather a coarse tutti. Back to shimmering haze: now gently 6/8 with a lilt and a slurp: now going military, then vivacious, then grandiose and inflated – Delius the Rhetorician, not so far off Elgar and much less good at it – the piece is all but spoilt, till broad, tranquil, echoing coda.

Elgar – the great phase

Elgar's declared technical aim in his first symphony, a 'symphony in two keys'; his declared intent, 'a *massive* hope for the future'. The result was an immediate success – widespread performances, enthusiastically received. Yet the work is both complex and complicated: the first movement, in particular, long and sometimes tortuous. A motto-theme, *nobilmente e semplice*, soft, full of internal echoes and overlaps, then fully scored with ceremonial grandeur, then disappearing like a passing procession. The ensuing allegro bursts with contrasting characters, sometimes at odds with themselves – fiery and public, wistful and private; bombastic 'in your face', remote as if overheard from a great distance; towards the end a terrific climax then a withdrawn recession. Ultimate triumphalism reserved for finale: the interim close is soft, fusing every discrepancy, including, in a beautiful and ingenious cadence, the 'two keys'.

Ingenious too feeble a word for what follows, whereby the second and third movements – an *allegro molto*, an *adagio* – are fashioned from identical material: the stage-by-stage transformation from harum-scarum velocity to ardent songfulness has the listener hanging on by the ears, suspending disbelief even as it is so actually effected – an unparalleled feat. Motto-theme subliminal for all this, resurfacing in many guises to fuel the finale, sweeping all before it, plentiful new ideas alongside, ardour generous, technical prowess unflagging. The confidence is not hollow or flatulent: the composer's massive intention had begun – 'there is no programme beyond a wide experience of human life with a great charity (love)': the invocation is not idle.

The 1st Symphony touched the moment, national then inter-national. The 2nd left its audiences cold, to Elgar's bitter chagrin. Their puzzlement is understandable. This 2nd Symphony is a deeply ambiguous work that undermines itself over and again. As often with Elgar, a hodge-podge: the germ of the slow movement, more lament than cortège, dates back some eight years, a private tribute to a dear friend, here converted into the public memorial to the late King Edward VII pompously engraved at the start of the published score. Before it, a quotation from Shelley – 'rarely, rarely comest thou, Spirit of Delight!' – characterizing the musical motto pervading the symphony's outer movements from the toppling, sur-mounting exuberance of its very opening to the sunset glow of its closing pages. Unmarked in the score, lines from Tennyson's *Maud* where the unnamed hero imagines himself long dead, his heart 'a handful of dust', his bones laid in a shallow grave 'only a yard beneath the street'; and the passing wheels and the horses' hooves 'beat, beat, beat' into his un-dead brain. Even without knowing this association in Elgar's mind there is a naked terror in the rondo-scherzo third movement difficult to reconcile with the work's con-fident opening and roseate close, both on the joy-theme inspired by Shelley.

By contrast every aspect of *Falstaff* is perfectly judged. This masterpiece is a combination of symphony – 'symphonic study in C-minor', provocative and challenging on the title-page; 'as close and inevitable a musical structure as anything since Beethoven' (Tovey) – and narrative-episodic symphonic poem à la *Till Eulenspiegel* and *Don Quixote*. And, like them, a character-study: with the salient dif-ference from them, and any other such, in that the presentation/depiction of the character is given simultaneously from without and within the title-protagonist. It is Falstaff's own person, deeds, desires, delusions – from his own consciousness of his self, his perception of his surroundings and companions, the Prince/then King supremely, but also his drinking-mates and their buxom Hostess, as also the two pastoral interludes where he dreams of his distant slender youth – *and* all these matters perceived from outside, narrating and depict-ing with detachment, albeit vivid and wholly involved. This double

perspective gives the work a complexity, depth, dare one say round-
ness, unique to the genre, wherein it remains unequalled.

To achieve all this an extraordinary wealth of highly characteristic material – thematic, harmonic, rhythmic, instrumental – is
employed: a treasury of generosity lavish as Shakespeare himself.
The narrative can be quickly told: Falstaff and Hal – unmistakable,
the fat knight with many themes, fertile and protean in combination
and transformation; the Prince with just one, never-changing, in two
mirroring halves, the second minor, already so near the start foretelling how the companions' association will terminate. Action: the
Gadshill episode; goings-on, furtive, mysterious, groping – Falstaff
and friends off to waylay a convoy of bullion, the Prince and friends
interrupt, Falstaff and co. routed, he returns to the inn to boast of his
invincibility. It's not perfectly clear what's happening: suffice that the
'symphony' here gets its scherzo and development in one, mischievously inventive with or without programmatic details: and Falstaff's
swelling magniloquence cannot be mistaken. At the Boar's Head,
with an almost visible evocation of Mistress Quickly – palpable,
touchable, swellable, bosomy and corseted, feisty, a thousand per
cent female – Elgar the depicter of friends in the *Enigma* variations
taking this curious gift to an apogee. Her cameo is virtually self-
contained, like the two Intermezzi still to come. After it, Falstaff
declaims with grandeur – equally unmistakable – solo bassoon
(marked 'quasi recit. Full tone, coarse') with grotesque leaps, slurps,
hiccoughs, belches. He's drunk; the company joshes, Quickly averts
trouble, he falls into boozy stupor – unmissable too, the marvellous
and very *poetic* imitation of his snoring.

First Dream-Interlude: 'Jack Falstaff, now Sir John, a boy, and page
to Thomas Mowbray, Duke of Norfolk' says the score. Elgar's own
gloss extends his meaning to the contrast between the gross present
reality and 'what might have been' in this tender/wistful pastorale, as
green, nimble, fragile, fading as the dreamer is uncouth and flabby.

Stern Reality. A summons from London for Falstaff to recruit
soldiers in the West Country. New energy injected via yet more
themes in this already copious work, including a vivid depiction
of the scarecrow army whom he leads into a ridiculous battle. The

raggle-taggle pass out of sight and their theme is transformed into a lyric passage for strings alone, preparing the way for the second pastoral Intermezzo – reeds and a tabor – Justice Shallow's orchard in Gloucestershire. Not *past* as the first: *present* – old men's nostalgic recall, dreaminess alternating with reediness, swathed in rose-tinted self-delusion, rudely broken by news that Prince Hal is now King Henry.

Confident in expectation of greatness, Falstaff heads impetuously to the capital, his boastful theme huge in augmentation in the bass. Near Westminster Abbey, crowd agog, Falstaff among them: we are given all the glow of his genuine ardour for the Boy/Man, as well as the eagerness of his futile hopes. Excitement mounts, interfused with fond memories of old pranks and japes. The Procession comes into view: the royal theme, *grandioso*, always with its answering half in the minor, then its handsome continuing phrases, now getting stuck. Falstaff waddles excitedly up, toppling forward down a fantastic descant/descent over his fat theme, collapsing in fragments as he is rebuffed. A hard three-note proclamation derived from earlier fanfaring now represents stern repudiation – 'I know thee not, old man ...' Bewildered, the old man tries to question, to plead: in vain: the Procession moves on, the repudiation remains, slithering six times chromatically down. Only shards remain, bits and bobs of memory, previous material fragmented, fractured, failing: one moment of pathos too deep for tears could have strayed from Gerontius' death-chamber; the Gloucestershire orchard, the snoring, an infinitely tender-loving recall of the Royal theme, major then minor. Somehow the consciousness rather than the actual scene has shifted to the old man's own deathbed, as recounted by Mistress Quickly: he babbles of green fields, his fingers twitch. The actual death is – we have the composer's word for it – the full stop on a long-held C-major chord played as soft as possible by all the brass instruments, muted. As it disappears, the tambour strikes up, also muffled, swelling from soft to moderately loud and back again – a memory of the orchard turned into the death-rattle. Suddenly a perking-up, main tempo resumed: Falstaff lives, in just one brief characteristic gesture of his principal theme, in a key right athwart

home, ending on the Repudiation, tutti; all the brass, low unmuted
and the tambour loud and fierce, then left alone to disappear *pianissimo*. Silence. One soft bare pizzicato tonic – C for this 'symphonic
study in C-minor', a *major* third at the top of the triad (but one never
hears it).

Delius from c.1914

Three further larger orchestral pieces, one with a wordless chorus,
and one work for texted choir with orchestra, stand out from Delius'
wartime production. The orchestral works are all evocations of
Nordic landscapes, darker than the French and English already
described (let alone the Florida inspirations): sombre, with hints of
fear, awe, menace.

The Song of the High Hills (1914–16) is uneven: strong and
impressive at its finest, coarse, insistent, mechanical at its worst;
delicacy and refinement alongside square or soupy – evocations of
mountain stillness with their vague intimations of disquiet ('the
wide far distance ... the great solitude' written at one point above
the music) are perfectly achieved; but the climaxes – one 'as forte
as possible' – are painfully strained. The entry of the wordless
choir, preceded by a solo tenor on the same contour, is magic for a
moment – expressive, as the composer told his faithful amanuensis, of 'man's coming and going, he knows not why, he know not
where': but their tune is as trite as the Old Slave Song in *Appalachia*
is genuine, and within a few bars the rich choral texture degenerates into a gluey goo of mushy chromatics without Delius' usual ear
for their precise delineation. When the orchestra rejoins and *fff* is
reached, one wants to reach for the sick-bag. Immediately after, the
inevitable decline and fall: then the return of the work's opening
is, again, magical. But soon yet another climax – 'with Exultation',
though the actual sound is gross and strident; and yet another
softening into shimmering withdrawal – a detumescence too far.

Eventyr – 'Once upon a Time' (1917) – is altogether finer: starts
already harsh and grim, and a truly savage episode – 'furiously' –
ends with a first roar of male voices – a 'wild shout': trolls at work

and play. Later the volume even reaches *ffff*: stark plangency, hard edges, a six-note figure on bells (the score also features a xylophone and more unpitched percussion, freely employed – gong, cymbals, tam-tam – than habitual). Flutters; solemn tolling; more flutters; shudders. Then singing solace, a lilting 6/8 swelling into exultance, declining into nostalgia, fluttering and drooping and receding into a quiet close: enigmatic and mysterious; sinister too – those two wild male roars linger in the mind.

North Country Sketches, the same year, is more acrid still – spare, bitter, chill: *Egdon Heath*, Holst's masterpiece of landscape bleakness (composed only ten years later, by another important English composer who died in 1934), the next stop. Again, uneven: 'Autumn' – 'the wind soughs in the trees' evokes rustling creeping shivers in parallel chromatic chords oddly prescient of the storm in the Sibelius *Tempest*-music. 'Winter Landscape' renders cold with a paradoxical glow of inner heat. 'Dance' seems quite out of place here – a cheery piece of 'bad Grainger', mediocre till – too late – its better class of ending. Finally 'The March of Spring': 'woodlands, meadows and silent moors' – disjointed and piecemeal; some pretty lighter stretches with many swings of mood and texture, lost to lumpenness in a truly awful hearty march – 'bad Grainger' again, not rescued by another delicate fadeaway close complete with cuckoo-calls. For Quality Spring in all its aspects from this period try Debussy's *Rondes de printemps* (lyric dancing rapture), Strauss's *Frühlingsfeier* (Dionysiac madness), Stravinsky's *Rite* (primitive sacrificial destruction/renewal), Mahler's *Trunkene im Frühling* (blissful intoxication), Frank Bridge's *Enter Spring* and, of course, Delius' own *First Cuckoo* – five minutes of perfection.

Elgar and Delius c.1918–34

Post-peak: neither composer now shown at his best, with one shining exception. Both turned unexpectedly to chamber-music. Elgar produced three substantial pieces 1918–19, a violin sonata, a string quartet, a piano quintet – overwrought and turgid from this master of the orchestra with next to no experience of smaller forces:

Delius, four sonatas with piano – one for cello, three for violin – which give hostages to the blasphemer. Neither composer is at home here, especially with their lumpy keyboard-writing: the most successful of these seven works is the Elgar String Quartet where the problem doesn't arise.

Delius turned, surprisingly, towards concertos – three in all, a double for violin and cello (slightly earlier, 1915); one for violin (1919); one for cello (1921). All have ineffable, inimitable moments, the better the closer they come to the composer of nature-idylls, French, English, Norwegian: all fall flat on their faces for argument and structure. Happiest is the cello-work – less laboured, more free-flowing, with one memorably typical and lovely strain towards the end. Elsewhere, *un*memorable: they drift by, sometimes waxing unwelcomely noisy (the orchestra for all three includes three trombones and a tuba!), and the listener's attention drifts too. Elgar's Cello Concerto (1919) is the shining exception. This belovèd work fully deserves its status: a wide range of mood, tone, expression, on fresh living material, from heartfelt elegy and nostalgia to unforced heroic rhetoric to lilting pastoral, with Falstaffian roguery and bonhomie, Hal-like mercurial wit, and an economy of lengths and spareness of textures unprecedented in the symphonies and only suggested in the lean lines of the fat *Falstaff*, here reaching the consummation of all his skill, experience, knowledge, in an essentiality that the overdone chamber-works had lost.

The advancing 1920s are sad for both composers; out of phase with changed times whether resentful (Elgar) or indifferent (Delius); out of contact with their inner creative spark – for Delius, the dying embers so painfully elicited with Fenby's sweet solicitude; for Elgar mere scraps, including a fifth *Pomp and Circumstance* march, piquant relict of the land-of-hope-and-glory-days.

Then in 1932 came a commission from the BBC for a third symphony. One of the most stirring operations in English music of recent decades is the rescue-job effected upon this project, not so much uncompleted as almost un-begun. The initial ripples of excited interest have by now died down, leaving a substantial addition on the verge of the repertoire, and permanent gratitude to Anthony Payne, whose carefully formulated 'elaboration' of the sketches is, in fact, a practical act of homage of the most fascinating kind.

His brief – to realize Elgar's fragments (with the family's approval before their copyright ended in 2005, opening the way to possibly less loving, and certainly less skilful hands) – might appear straightforward. What he has actually achieved is far more remarkable: a living simulacrum of a large-scale, late-Romantic/early-modern symphony by one of its greatest masters, using that master's own material (for the most part already existent, albeit patchy), and intuiting his forms and processes (which for the most part did not exist) by analogy or likelihood.

Which is quite different from the, nevertheless comparable, case of symphonic retrieval from the same stylistic epoch – Mahler's 10th. Mahler left a complete scheme of compelling architectural and rhetorical power, with some sections fully worked and scored, some bare and rudimentary, and plenty betwixt and between: a draft to be worked up with his usual intensity of detail. Elgar left, however, no overall shape beyond the indication of the four movements, and a mass of material much of whose place and function was unspecified.

Yet this is how he had always worked. A list of 'ingredients' for both his completed symphonies can still be disconcerting; such discrepant sources – thumbnail sketches of friends or pets, landscapes and mood-scapes, city lights and shadows, grief personal and ceremonial, a facetious entry in a guest book – in some instances dating right back across several decades. If, by chance, the end products hadn't come about, we would doubt that they *could* have. Elgar's processes are the antithesis of organic growth from germinal cells. His diverse materials fuse and synthesize at final rather than primal stage. In so doing they gather many passing inspirations of detailed working, also the wealth of internal relationships that such methods would seem to have ruled out: and, incidentally yet inevitably, the most basic element of all – symphonic form.

So it would possibly have been with the 3rd. Material lay to hand, some comparatively recent (incidental music of 1923 for Laurence Binyon's *Arthur*), some pre-war; and Payne is surely right to sense a renaissance of creative vigour in the attempts to work them together that were cut off by Elgar's final illness. (Hats off for perceiving this so many years back, when the going consensus even among fervent Elgarians, including myself, was negative.) All the same, the symphony's most vital material is its oldest. This is true in a metaphorical sense, because through its every page Payne's (and our) love of the great canonical works constantly shines. And true specifically in that its best music – the very opening, realized in every detail by Elgar himself, including the orchestration – hails from his richest period (1899–1913), being intended originally for *The Judgement*, third in the oratorio-triptych abandoned after *The Kingdom*. Probably because it is imbued throughout with the granitic memorability of this opening stretch, the first movement is the most successful as a whole. The purposeful trajectory carries over some wobbly moments; and many places, notably the return of the second subject, and the entire coda, are wholly convincing, indeed masterly.

Payne excels at codas. By far his hardest task, he explains on the disc setting out the sketches and what he has done with them, was to discover, in the absence of indication, how the complete work should end. His finale convincingly realizes from the start a full Elgarian texture and momentum, made from the work's sparsest sources. Material from the *Arthur* music touches off a vein of chivalry familiar since *Froissart* back in 1890 and reaching its noblest incarnation to depict Prince Hal in *Falstaff* (1913). Mistress Quickly is also present from that wonderful work; later the fat knight himself unmistakably appears, also a reminder of the percussion motif that characterizes his scarecrow army. All this is skilfully woven together without solving the problem of the ending. Payne's answer is to crown the weightiness of the preceding movements by growing darker and more serious. An inspired transition leads to a coda specifically recreating the effect of 'The Wagon (Passes)', the one strong number in the otherwise tedious *Nursery Suite* that Elgar had put together in 1931 for the Princesses Elizabeth and Margaret Rose. Payne's adaptation of the obsessive rhythm to the finale's authentic material is a stroke of empathetic genius. But the two inner movements raise doubts that cannot be stilled. The intermezzo is a droopy sibling of the two *Wand of Youth* suites wherein the ageing composer revisited his boyhood to such touching effect. At earliest hearings the adagio that follows made the deepest impression: closer proximity reveals the weakness within the two principal melodies – a solemn funeral march and a consolatory pastoral vision: their shortcomings and general lack of focus stand in sharp contrast to the confident paragraphing in the slow movements of both completed symphonies, though the dithery character is moving in itself.

The piquant fact that this movement's most convincing passage, the tiny link joining the two main melodies, is entirely Payne's work suggests a whimsical wider resonance. Could 'elaboration' like Payne's be achieved in the absence of an actual original, such as a master's unwritten opus from an epoch of well-loved and understood musical language? Elgar's 4th and Rachmaninov's, Mahler's 11th, a 9th from Sibelius (since his 8th, known to have been completed before being disseminated in marginalia then destroyed, is already a candidate for direct rescue) just for a start, before reaching back to Tchaikovsky, Schumann, Mozart, Monteverdi, Josquin ...? The uncertain idioms of 'difficult' modern music, together with its palpable failure to gain popular acceptance, have much to learn from the enormous sigh of welcome raised by such essentially nostalgic work of reclamation and replication. It might enable many current composers to come clean and dare to write the music that they, too, have secretly preferred all along. It might liberate embargoed knowledge and un-strangulate expressive gold.

Percy Grainger

This picturesque figure doesn't belong neatly anywhere: though he died as late as 1961 he perhaps fits most suitably into a niche in English music alongside his adored Delius. Born Melbourne 1882; early promise as a pianist led him to serious musical studies in Frankfurt 1895. To London from 1901: extensive pioneering trips collecting folksongs in England and Scandinavia – affectionate friendship with Grieg. Hundreds of transcriptions and arrangements of

his and others' discoveries; folksong from all over the world forms
the basis of the greater part of his original composition too. Friendship with Delius, helping him, as the latter's health declined, to elicit
and notate his music before the Fenby era. Moved to the USA 1914;
career as outstanding if eccentric pianist; frustrated and bitter that
his performing rather than his music was most in demand – though
at the same time a handful of delightful miniatures – e.g. *Handel
in the Strand* and *Molly on the Shore* – became popular favourites
across the English-speaking world. Singular versatility and oddness
in every respect – infinitely impulsive, restless, curious, self-obsessed,
frank, in words, music, actions, attitudes: a prophet, albeit unwitting,
of stances towards sex, gender, personality, ethnicity, etc. that would
only be widely aired, and maybe practised, well after his time.

Why and how is Grainger significant? Folksong collections,
arrangements, fantazias, loom largest: his music independent of
these fertile sources tends to be secondary, for all its ambitions and
sometimes daring. But the technical prowess displayed in such
lollipops as the aforesaid *Handel* and *Molly*, the *Mock Morris*, the
Shepherd's Hey and *Country Gardens*, is irresistible. The same techniques applied to comparable material in *Green Bushes*, the *In a
Nutshell* suite, the *Lincolnshire Posy*, extend the scale and the skill –
there's no question that 'this artist knows how to compose'. And
the range is wide and deep – the bright gaiety of *Let's Dance Gay
in Green Meadow* (on a folk-dance-song from the Faroe Islands) to
the searing passion of *Shallow Brown* (on an old sea-shanty). (These
two are included on the marvellous recording directed by Benjamin
Britten.) The polymorphous omniverousness – the world his oyster:
Polynesia/Oceania, Scotland/Ireland/England, Scandinavia, the
USA, the 'India' of Kipling's Jungle Books, the 'Colonials' of his
native Australia – the list is not complete: the free movement across
the epochs, from archaic/medieval to Renaissance and Elizabethan/
Jacobean, to Tchaikovsky and Rachmaninov, Strauss ('*Rosenkavalier*
Ramble') and Gershwin (elaborate fantasy on themes from *Porgy and
Bess* and some marvellous individual song-transcriptions) – equally
prophesy 'world music' and the 'post-modern' free-for-all with styles
and idioms. Grainger was there first and did it better. At the still

centre of the whirligig, J. S. Bach – many transcriptive homages and the heavenly *Blithe Bells* (a loving take on 'sheep may safely graze' that even as it tickles can make the eye trickle). Then the radical experimenter: gems of complex compression worthy of Webern and Blake's 'all heaven in a grain of sand' – the tiny *Sea-Song* and several others: and 'free music' – his laborious and prolonged attempt, long before technology made it possible, then easy, to capture the sounds, motions, patterns of wind and waters, notate them, have them able to be composed-with – Grainger the precursor of *musique concrète*, then electronics, then Spectralism.

He is extraordinarily difficult to see whole. The range and complexity of his activities do not square with the heterogeneous nature of his actual achievement. The creative multiplicity of versions, which makes his output so confusing and rich, dissolves all sense of a practicable oeuvre. He is central to any discussion of folksong, ethnic musics, improvisation, randomness and games, music education and therapy, music's place in the individual body and the body politic, virtuoso pianism and the living arts of transcription and recomposition, and the evolution of mechanical music from player-piano to electro-acoustics. (The list is not exhaustive.) Then there is his bizarre life and personality, which have attracted one of the best musical biographies. John Bird's even tone and the composer's own passion-choked yet lucid voice together ensure that no later writer can ignore such flagrant connection between life and work.

In order to accommodate this composer to the 'mainstream of history', clichés of 'importance' and 'significance' must be dropped. 'Pleasure' is better; meaning not lollipops but the full extent of music's power to move and elevate by means of delight. Every music-lover has their own view; pleasures overlap in small rapports, making a cult, and wide agreements, making a consensus. Deviation from a consensus is risky, even ridiculous. But we should have the courage of our pleasures. I know that Schoenberg is 'greater' and more 'important' and more 'significant' than Gershwin (say), but Gershwin unquestionably gives me more joy and has enriched my musical life more greatly. This is *my* version, neither better nor worse than any other.

On these grounds, which should be the only grounds, Grainger stands high. As the years pass the pleasure remains, while admiration grows for his audacity, his piercing depth of feeling, the strong and beautiful musical facture he everywhere displays. Grainger's extremes and disparities gradually coalesce, and he takes his place among the art's nourishing musical phenomena. 'Parnassus has many mansions.'

Ralph Vaughan Williams

RVW (1872–1958) is the large benign presiding presence in English music from the 1920s to the 1950s; the benignity not incompatible with a severe, even judgemental aspect: both are evoked in Elias Canetti's vivid partial portrait in his unfinished final book of memoirs. Solid Germanic grounding – early chamber-pieces recently exhumed suggest a Parry or a Stanford in the making; Teutonia is later relinquished in favour of Sibelius. His discovery of *Englishness* centres upon folksong – an active collector and arranger from 1904 on; and hymnody – music editor 1906 of the *English Hymnal*; and Tudor church-music – at its heart, Tallis and Byrd. Not Purcell – no Baroque frippery! VW's Baroque is Bach, though never the 'back-to-Bach' of continental composers between the wars: he is anti-modern, for all that he sometimes achieves it. Technically clumping, even now-and-again clumsy (he'd have despised finish and polish as slick), but at all points the execution suffices for the vision. And behind the benefits of his brief lessons with Ravel in 1909 there is an affinity with Debussy, however utterly different their aesthetic, language, means, ends: the pentatonics, parallel triads, streams of cloud-strata beautifully deployed, most of all in the *Pastoral Symphony*, would not be possible without the example of both French masters.

His heart is in the Folk: amateur music-making, above all choral: his principal sources of inspiration the Bible in the Authorized Version (despite being undoubtedly agnostic, probably atheist); Bunyan (*Pilgrim's Progress* a life-long quest); Shakespeare; Blake; Whitman (honorary Englishman). Very prolific – too-much,

too-much-the-same, in an idiom that, once established, is effortlessly fluent, easily becoming facile and predictable. The following
account concentrates upon touchstones only: five greats and a few
semi-greats amid oceans of ascending larks, Greensleeves, Deviants
of Lazarus, Christmas Carol arrangements, and even works of size
and scope like operas and symphonies wherein the vision fails to
burn bright. The five greats put VW's vision among the finest of
its time.

The grandiose *Sea Symphony* (completed 1909) after its terrific
opening grows turgid, bombastic, and not particularly individual: the modest Housman-cycle *On Wenlock Edge* (1909) remains
fresh and free of thickness under Ravel's beneficial influence. VW's
own voice first heard in full – placid, meditative, authoritative – in
the *Fantasia* on a hymn-melody by Thomas Tallis, included in the
English Hymnal four years before: it discovers at one stroke a new
sonority in the layout for double string orchestra, one large one
small, and solo string quartet: the new mode recognized immediately as such from the work's première in Gloucester Cathedral in
1910. The theme softly and subtly suggested in fragments that gradually enrich and combine in alternating choirs of chordal sonority:
middle section rhapsodic as further possibilities of the Tallis are
gradually unfolded; a climax of passionate urgency; further possibilities, more lyrical; a seraphically triumphant close, diminishing into
the reverberant spaces from which the opening had first emerged.

The next symphony is the lovable *London* (completed 1913): the
third makes the central icon of VW's entire output – the *Pastoral*
(1921). For many years this work was apprehended, not without
justice, as embodying the quintessence of the English countryside,
till it emerged that its inspiration is born of the French, as experienced during the composer's wartime service wherein he saw at
close quarters the futility and suffering under the light and dark of
ravaged nature – an exact analogy with the work of the war-artists,
Spencer, Nevinson, the Nash brothers. And this ultimately English
version of pastoral is, paradoxically, the work that shows his clearest
affinity with Debussy and gratitude to Ravel. Unforgettable, the
terraces of slow-flow parallel triads recreated from Debussy's *Nuages*,

and still more akin to similar passages in Debussy's wartime vision of a native landscape at peace, in the pastoral framework of his (non-combatant) battle-scene, the middle movement of *En blanc et noir* for two pianos of 1915, a work that VW probably didn't know. Also shared, the lone trumpet of the *Pastoral*'s slow movement: it seems to be uttering undivulged words, as does the solo voice, soprano or tenor, opening and concluding the finale. The symphony's only 'English' movement is its third; it begins with earthy clodhopping, gentles slightly, to become yet more hobnailed, eventually a parody – no gallant French *paysan*; a burly John Bull: either or both are blown away in the movement's magic-surprise coda, a sudden presto light as a straw in the wind.

The 4th Symphony (1931–4) contrasts totally with its predecessor: VW the pacific ruminator/VW the 'judicial', unsparing and implacable. These complementary masterpieces are the composer's outward limits. The 4th is from first to – especially – last, an almost unmitigated onslaught of grinding tension and dissonance, the coarse, thick, doubled scoring, elsewhere a liability, here part of the work's very nature, indispensable to its effect. Between first and last there, of course, has to be remission. The furious first movement contains oases of calm and ends mysteriously withdrawn. The ensuing slow movement uncurls in singing polyphony, reaches an impassioned climax, not without anger, returns to the long-drawn-out linear texture, ends calm and spent on a gentle flute solo. All hell breaks out with the scherzo, heavily redeploying the four-note motto heard at the symphony's opening: fleet yet clumsy, as if the quicksilver of Holst's 'Mercury' were recast in lead: a trio of stolid, lumpen good-cheer, then back to the boil, a brief die-down, still tense over soft, agitated bass-itch on drums and low strings, *ppp* till sudden swollen rush into finale: initially four-square/forthright; a crude oom-pah – jackboots not clodhoppers; an imbecile tune; a stretch of fatuous high-spirits. All this quietens into withdrawn distances, almost prayerful, recalled from Tallis/Gloucester Cathedral/wartime French pastoral: then the main momentum reheats on main materials, toppling into an *epilogo fugato* on the four-note motto that isn't quite B-A-C-H, at first in long notes in close imitation, the intervals grinding away like some frightful Iron Maiden, incorporating as it develops music from the finale's previous scherzo, as well as the first movement, to helter-skelter stampede over the cliffs of madness; till the concluding page where the plunge is frozen into high/low alternation of the motto, and the terminating brutality of the cadential resolution where the Judge's sentence is executed. 'I don't know if I like it,' said the composer after rehearsals for the première, 'but it's what I meant.'

Several other smaller works are candidates for the Five: the closest runner resembles neither of the great symphonies – the *Mass in G-minor* (1922), most inspired instance of VW's love of vocal polyphony from Tudor and Jacobean England; archaizing with bold directness and no hint of pastiche. *Flos Campi* (1925) is more ambiguous. A concertante for viola, small orchestra and chorus, who only sing without words: the work's nature and mood are given in superscriptions to each movement from the Song of Songs: unwontedly erotic for this composer – *quia amore langueo/*'for I am sick of love'; renewal of spring and desire; seeking the absent lover, 'he whom my soul loveth, but I found him not'; then the lover's cry of longing – 'return, oh Shulamite'; their final mutuality – *pone me ut signaculum super cor tuum/*'set me as a seal on thy heart'. Lovely layered textures, at once dense and shining, for the intermixed playing and singing, with more delicate tincture of coloration than usual in VW, harp and celesta providing the pomegranates: contrasting with spare, free-flow meditations for the viola, sometimes in sweetly-acid dissonant counterpoint with solo woodwinds. The prevailing mood of sensuous or plangent longing has one exception – a hearty march, disconcertingly trite: not the 'army with banners' to whom the lover is compared in Solomon's Song: more vague and implausible – thirty-score valiant men gathered around the sovereign's bed, all bearing swords, 'being expert in war'. This episode breaks the spell with perhaps needed contrast but blots an otherwise lovely piece.

Job, another Old Testament subject more akin to the composer's temperament, would seem to be set for a masterpiece: every constituent is promising – the sublime original, reinterpreted in Blake's etchings, their gestures and groupings realized choreographically:

but somehow this ballet-score (1931) falls short of its mark – VW's Satan is as risible as the demons in *Gerontius*, nor does God or the Sons of the Morning elicit his best tunes. Stronger, the Piano Concerto of 1926–31 in the 'modernist' vein of the 4th Symphony, unwarrant-edly neglected. And the next symphony – No. 5, completed 1943 – is perhaps the best loved of the sequence. A return to his gentle medita-tive aspect with, here, an association with his life-long absorption in *Pilgrim's Progress*. Next comes the 6th (1944–7), a return to his other side and the ferocity of the 4th. Both later works are obliquely respon-sive to their composition in times of phoney, then actual, war, as nos. 3 and 4 had been to the Great War recollected in pastoral tranquillity or in reaction to darkening times: and both seem a bit of a second brew. The only new element is the creepy epilogue to the 6th, conflict concluded, all sides losers, Cold War on the way: an uncanny feeling of bleak, blanched etiolation, hope abandoned, no grace abounding.

But VW is far from spent. There are ten more years of vigorous production, some of it bold, even experimental: notably the 7th Symphony, '*Antartica*' (1952), a huge blow-up of a film-score telling of Scott's heroic/tragic last expedition; and the 8th, a divertimento glinting with 'all the glocks and spiels known to the composer'. Nothing Great is added until the 9th and last (1957), a powerfully summatory gathering-in without replication; a grand farewell. Sad that what he *intended* as his summa, the opera on Bunyan that had preoccupied him all his life (première 1951) is a noble bore. He had left it too late. Its freshest music, the pastoral episode for the *Shep-herds of the Delectable Mountains*, dates from thirty years before; its deepest had been used in the 5th Symphony. Plenty else in the large oeuvre is written on autopilot, and comes out dilute and manner-ist. The Great Five and some near-misses place him in imperishable stone: and his hymn-tunes are among the best ever.

Gustav Holst

Gustav Holst: born 1874: with his close friend Vaughan Williams an ardent collector of folksongs in the years before the Great War:

also ardent, his devotion to teaching – many generations of girls at St Paul's School, Hammersmith, from 1905, and working men and women at Morley College, Lambeth, from 1907, owned his inspiring presence: also like VW an advocate of the dedicated amateur in music: they also shared an early enthusiasm for Whitman, comparable to, though very different from, that of Delius. Unlike VW, Holst was keenly interested in religions archaic and remote, going so far as to teach himself Sanskrit as well as Greek and to translate sacred texts from both for setting to music. Also unlike his friend, alert and positive to modernist contemporaries from the continent – Scriabin, Stravinsky, Schoenberg all palpable in *The Planets*, the neo-classicism of the 1920s in his own output of this time. Always frail, he wore himself out through overwork, dying in 1934.

A smaller figure than his grand contemporary, and unlike him Holst doesn't expand into fuller stature after the First World War. *The Planets* (1914–16), by far his best-known music, says it all: seven powerful characterizations of the Temperaments, iconic and unforgettable, and superbly scored. *Mars, Bringer of War* has become an archetype for brute moronic menace; *Venus, Bringer of Peace*, for cool dulcet suavity; *Mercury, the Winged Messenger*, for quicksilver volatility. *Jupiter, Bringer of Jollity* is less convincing: the jocundity seems a tiny bit forced, though the 'big tune' is as fine as anything comparable by Elgar or VW. Utterly authentic and compelling, the embodiment of weary decay and attrition in *Saturn, Bringer of Old Age*, with its climax as terrifying as that of *Mars* without the relish of bloodlust; and the beautiful solace of its close. *Uranus the Magician* is a second brew from *L'Apprenti sorcier*, and *Neptune the Mystic* can seem like late Scriabin got up in gauze for a Kensington pageant. A slight tendency to smile is diverted by the extra Planet – *Pluto the Renewer*, wittily and poetically concocted as *hommage* by Colin Matthews in 2000; and wiped from the face by recalling *Mars* and *Saturn*.

Some other notable works of Holst, before and after his principal success. Three stand out in particular. *Sāvitri*, a chamber-opera from 1908–9, period of his most intense involvement with Hindu religion and culture that also includes three sets of choral hymns from the *Rig Veda*. This episode from the *Mahābhārata* presents

Death, come to claim her husband Satyavān from his loving wife Sāvitri, her metaphysical struggle to have him restored, Death's defeat, the couple's reuniting, freed from Maya/Illusion – 'for even Death is Maya'. Impressive in its austerity, in complete contradistinction to the prevailing tendency of its date, including Holst's own 'Wagnerian bawling' (his own phrase) that he'd recently overcome and ejected. Strength and emotion lie within restraint: when the music opens up it grows fulsome, and after this the very restraint is limp. The same elements are in play, perfectly balanced, in *Curlew River*, first and greatest of Britten's three church parables nearly half a century on, of which Holst's work is a clear precursor.

He learnt Greek to read, and then make his own version of, a marvellous text from the apocryphal *Acts of John* to set as *The Hymn of Jesus* (1917–19) for chorus and orchestra. Two plainsongs gradually grow into praise of the Trinity; then a series of mysterious paradoxes – 'Fain would I be pierced; and fain would I pierce ... Fain would I eat; fain would I be eaten' (and such); thence an ecstatic devotional dance; then a series of daring, dazzling dissonances – half the choir sliding down semitonally, triad by triad from the other half – representing mystic union: 'to you who gaze, a lamp am I; to you that know, a mirror': wonderful sounds, absolutely out of their time and place, connecting all-unbeknown with such near-contemporary visions as Scriabin's *Mysterium*, Schoenberg's *Jakobsleiter*, Stravinsky's *Zvezdoliki*. All the more disconcerting when Victorian/Edwardian/Georgian England does, after all, intrude towards the end.

Holst believed *Egdon Heath* (1927) to be his best work. Subtitled 'Hommage to Thomas Hardy', with a superscription from *The Return of the Native* that suggests precisely the music's character: 'a place perfectly accordant with man's nature – neither ghastly, hateful, nor ugly; neither commonplace, unmeaning, nor tame; but, like man, slighted and enduring; and withal singularly colossal and mysterious in its swarthy monotony.' The composer had lunched with the novelist during the piece's composition: they'd visited the place together – '[Hardy] is sorry I'm seeing it in summer weather, and wants me to come again in November.' (Alas Hardy died shortly before the première.) With the utmost economy and self-denial these thin strands of sound capture the bleak terrain and the stoical view of life it implies: half-way through, a sad procession seems like an elegy to the lost world – 'England, my England': it alternates with the ghost of a gigue; the vision disintegrates into the mists. Starvation victuals; emaciated and impressive; unwitting ancestor of such later visions of pastoral as Birtwistle's *Silbury Air* and Julian Anderson's *Book of Hours*.

William Walton

Born Oldham 1902: early musical promise, chorister from age ten at Christ Church Oxford; as undergraduate there, taken up by the aristocratic Sitwell siblings, collaborating with Edith on *Façade* (1922), with Osbert on *Belshazzar's Feast* (1931); meanwhile freeing himself from their patronage and realizing his promise in the overture *Portsmouth Point* (1925), Viola Concerto (1929), culminating in 1st Symphony (1931–5) and Violin Concerto (1939). A flair for Occasion comparable with Elgar's produced the *Crown Imperial* march for the 1937 Coronation: his 'war-work' equally patriotic: distinguished film-scores – wartime uplift, e.g. *The First of the Few*; Shakespearean, e.g. *Henry V*; this latter continued into the 1950s, by when his principal energies are concentrated upon the full-scale opera (more after Chaucer than Shakespeare) *Troilus and Cressida* (1948–54). Round about now, permanent expatriation to Ischia. His later harvest consists mainly of successors – to the two string concertos, one for cello (1956); to *Belshazzar*, a *Gloria* and a *Te Deum*; to *Crown Imperial, Orb and Sceptre* for the 1953 Coronation; to *Portsmouth Point* several lighter orchestral pieces; to *Façade* a farcical one-acter *The Bear*; to the 1st Symphony a 2nd (1960): the strongest work of these later years, *Variations on a Theme by Hindemith* for orchestra, has no prototype. Died 1983.

Does Walton quite make Five Greats? *Façade* for sure: a brilliant start, this cheeky riposte to Schoenberg's *Pierrot lunaire*, setting for speaker twenty-one nonsense-texts by Edith Sitwell in three groups of seven like the model. The reciter is unseen, heard through a mouthpiece; the players are concealed too – a sparky handful whose chief difference from the *Pierrot* ensemble is to omit the piano and add percussion, exchanging Schoenberg's often rich Brahmsy textures, sometimes dense with learnèd devices, for jazzy lightness, saxophone to the fore. Song and dance forms prevail; parody, vaude-ville, end-of-the-pier feel. Delirious absurdity of the poems, vibrant with imagery, arch, affected, camp, twee, redolent of the epoch in mockery à la Lytton Strachey of *Eminent Victorian* high seriousness. The music, while hardly cutting deeper, exactly matches spirit and letter, bringing out nuances of hedonism and nostalgia beyond the poet's scope. No sense of a trajectory, however oblique, as in the Schoenberg: just non-sense: and unlike *Pierrot*, written at white heat, *Façade* took several years after its private première to get into final form, and yielded spin-offs in additional numbers and orchestral arrangements without text. After the raucous little introductory fanfare, the twenty-one numbers come in three principal categories: Dance-types; English – *Hornpipe*, *Mariner Man*, *Popular Song* (plus the *Scotch Rhapsody*): and Continental – *Pasodoblé* (tango, the text citing 'oh I do like to be beside the sea-side', but altogether 'Spanish'), *Tarantella*, *Country Dance* (a *Ländler*), *Polka*, *Valse*. American – '*Some-thing lies beyond the scene*' (dance-band), '*Old Sir Faulk*' (fox-trot). Nostalgia, Languour, Luxury, 'Mediterranean' – *En famille*, *Long steel grass*, *Through gilded trellises*, *Lullaby for Jumbo* (alluding to Debussy's in *Children's Corner*), *By the Lake*, *The man from a far countree*. More Mediterranean yet, with a whiff of the erotic/exotic insinuatory à la Firbank – *Black Mrs Behemoth*, *Four in the Morning*. In *Jodelling Song* the 'exotic' is Switzerland: the finale is another tarantella, *Sir Beelze-bub*. 'All are delectable.'

No parody or fancy-dress in the Viola Concerto, evincing imme-diately from first bars and first performance the distinction of style and workmanship that places its composer at one bound in the first league. Tovey saw the calibre at once: 'any concerto for viola must be a *tour-de-force*; but this seems to me one of the most important modern concertos for any instrument, and I can see no limits to what may be expected of the tone-poet who could create it.' The prevailing *tinta* of major/minor ambiguity, richly bitter-sweet, in harmony and melodic contour, for all its initial derivation from Hindemith – who played the solo part at the première and became a life-long friend – establishes Walton's unmistakable mature idiom: a masterpiece of passionate, elegiac, melancholy introspection.

Not so *Belshazzar's Feast*: a monument of metallic cinema-deco glitz, OTT in choral and, particularly, instrumental demands – orchestral brass not inordinate, but requiring two additional brass-bands, antiphonally placed for spatial thrills; and an organ; and tons of percussion. All this celebrates the Feast with barbaric splendour: in a grand March successive pagan deities are characterized in full Technicolor – the Gods of Gold and Silver, of Iron and Wood, of Stone, of Brass (plenty around): then All Together, *Marcia Trionfale*, a sort of recapitulation wherein the chorus narrates, rather than enacting, the King's orders to eat, drink, bring forth princes, vassals, wives, concubines (briefly juicy here rather than savage). The chorus now become pious Israelites, denouncing these false gods who can neither see nor hear, before continuing to narrate – they call for music to extol Belshazzar's glory: then switch back to being Babylonians – 'O King, live for ever': the versatility, prowess, bravura of all this unmatched in all Oratorio. And it has to be said that the Babylonians have the best tunes. After the catastrophe, graphically evoked in full Hammer Horror – the hand, the writing, the judgment (this had already been prophesied at the work's very opening), the single shattering shout of *Slain!* – the chorus of Israelites rejoicing seems set on *Portsmouth Point* for a long while, before broadening into terraces of *Alleluia* and the ejaculatory close. The work's finest music is quite other, in both halves before and after the crunch. Again the Walton of melancholy elegy: in the first half, after the minatory summons, exquisite plangency of the exiles by the waters of Babylon, weeping their loss, hanging their harps upon the willows, compelled by their captors to sing the songs of their conquered country, rising to vows of vengeance burning with pain. And in the second half, where the clamorous rejoicing abates, the chorus again change race to lament the fall of their great city Babylon, destroyed in one hour; growing ravishingly inward for the silencing of her music, for the quenching of the light of the candle that shall shine no more. Then Israelitish noise and motion re-illume till the convulsive end.

The 1st Symphony remains Walton's *chef d'oeuvre*: Tovey's expectations fully fulfilled. The first movement a sustained arc of tension upon tension, edgy nerviness all the gamut from irritable itch to feverish anguish, achieved with masterful control at maximum stretch. And completely original – it used to be said 'Sibelius', but actually not; if beholden at all, a possible origin in a still less Teutonic source, the driving motoric energy of nationalist Russia – *Polovtsian Dances*, Balakirev, Rimsky-Korsakov, as taken further in such French continuations as Debussy's *Fêtes* and the final dance of Ravel's *Daphnis*. All these are all festive and celebratory: Walton's first movement is anything but. In the second – *scherzo 'con malizia'* – analogues are clear. The diabolerie and sarcasms of Prokofiev, the 'malice' and frustrated rage of *Petrushka*: but again, Walton's particular Hell-bent character is all-itself. Closer to home, the driven quality in the scherzo of Elgar's 2nd Symphony, and the terror and claustrophobia of its central episode, emerging from and retreating back into its quicksilver wit. In the slow movement the major/minor coloration of the Viola Concerto expands into a full range of false-relations, with blue-note clashes as American as English, and emotional temperature comparable to Rachmaninov (also the super-plush textural upholstery; always clear and luminous, never clotted as in, say, Bax). A repertoire of small expressive phrases gradually and surely unfurls into large melodic paragraphs never quite repeating, making in effect a single unbroken whole of eloquent intensity.

Walton's problems with his finale were publicized by the performance of the first three movements before it was completed. Early doubts, persisting till relatively recently, claimed that his solution was neither appropriate nor up to calibre. The first three movements are certainly a hard act to follow: they beg for resolution/satisfaction/fulfilment and receive it with interest in the finale: a superb piece of rhetoric, energy, apotheosis (achieved with astonishingly ordinary-sized forces). Walton's ceremonial aspect, later to devolve into the unabashed uplift of the heroic wartime film-scores, is as genuine and unforced as Elgar's: both composers command *nobilmente/grandioso* to the manner born. Between comes the terrific fugue – Hindemith the model, easily surpassed – which releases in ebullient energy the strains set up earlier, culminating in the mighty harmonic wrench at the climax, where percussion is brought in for the first time just in case the moment is missed, though the harmonic timing has done it in itself. Then heroic rhetoric again; an elegiac touch of trumpet solo; the apotheosis; and the grinding savage/exultant closing chords recalling the close of the first movement. Here Sibelius's 5th can be discerned, and *Tapiola* in the preceding passionate string apostrophe. Not a hint of Mahler or Strauss, nor any other Teuton or anyone French. It is *itself*: with VW's 4th, its overlapping contemporary, the greatest instrumental symphonies of any country, not just England, between the wars.

The Violin Concerto, Walton's last major work before the war, is a gorgeous expensive luxury-item – a Cadillac with silver fittings, custom-built for Jascha Heifetz, the composer's Mediterranean side expanded from the languorous numbers in *Façade* via the delicious idyll *Siesta* (unaccountably neglected) in full bloom. Expert, it goes without saying: perhaps a little too knowing in its calculated intention to beguile – in which it certainly succeeds. Opulence and desire to appeal win altogether in *Troilus and Cressida*. Walton's correspondence charting its composition shows his concern to model timing and pacing upon opera's sure-fire winners, mainly Verdi and Puccini. The principal source of the music's actual idiom, however, resonates with Hollywood at its most synthetic, fluent, meretricious. The tight discipline whereby irony, subversion, acridity learnt from his beloved Ravel, Stravinsky, Prokofiev, balance and curb sensuous Romanticism learnt from Rachmaninov, Elgar, Strauss, has slackened: below the svelte surfaces yawns a sleazy abyss – always yearning to embrace its victim – of pure Korngold.

Walton after his most ambitious work remains a bit wobbly: three sizeable pieces stand out from the second pressings of divertimenti and choral numbers. The Cello Concerto can seem like more of the same – the Violin Concerto with vibraphone attachment. The other two pieces are more ambitious. His 2nd Symphony has never yet recovered from its poor initial reception: the time is now ripe. Its first movement is unmistakable – mordant edginess, razor-sharp articulation, volatility, alongside yearning major–minor melodic gestures, expert and fluent though nothing new. The middle movement slow and melancholy, tending now towards gravity and sombreness with moments of fret and bale: a generous passionate climax – no irony let alone 'pornography': the guard is down. The finale *does* offer something new: a passacaglia – ten variations and concluding fugue with accelerating coda – on a 12-note ground. As with Britten and Copland, this experiment with Schoenberg's serialism opens up new ways of hearing and organizing to fertilize wellploughed soil to impressive effect, somewhat vitiated when the very end is invaded by uplift/Coronation bombast; and the final overemphasized G-major sounds unconvincing, unearnt by previous adventures that it doesn't confirm.

More integrated and attractive, *Variations on a Theme of Hindemith* – late-life tribute to the composer who, as violist, had premièred Walton's concerto: a thread from *Mathis der Maler* weaves in and out of the nine continuous variations, becoming explicit in no. 7, the expressive centre, where the score prints within quotationmarks what the music speaks with touching eloquence. Another quotation involving a Teutonic master is not thus signalled, though both conspicuous and incongruous when it occurs. Two such masters in fact – for this is Schoenberg's citation of the B-A-C-H motto in his own *Orchestral Variations*. Walton is again attempting to make his peace with the serialism so universal and seemingly 'necessary' when this and the 2nd Symphony were written – and so charged-up the atmosphere in which both works were so badly received. With Walton the experiment doesn't quite convince – compare the 12-tone variations punctuating and structuring Britten's *Turn of the Screw*, wherein the new and the familiar interpenetrate to mutual advantage. Yet, all in all, the *Hindemith Variations* is a living entity, with new angles and aspects wrought of well-tried shapes and procedures, even in the by-now-expected closing fugue: the coda is particularly pleasing – there's a glow to the sound, of gratitude to the dedicatee and his music, including the theme, that surpasses him in fervour and warmth.

Benjamin Britten

Born 1913: early precocious brilliance as pianist and composer, 1927 composition lessons with Frank Bridge; 1930 Royal College of Music for composition (with John Ireland) and piano; 1932 accredited op. 1 (from a great mass of juvenilia); 1933 first work to manifest real presence – *A Boy was Born*. Incidental music for GPO film unit and left-leaning theatre, 1935–9, including collaboration with Auden, who also put together text for *Our Hunting Fathers* (1936); 1937 life-long association begins with Peter Pears – regular recital-partnership from the next year: *Frank Bridge Variations* (1937): 1939 Britten and Pears remove to the USA; it also sees Violin Concerto and *Les Illuminations*; 1940 *Sinfonia da Requiem* and *Michelangelo Sonnets* – first work actually written on Pears' voice. Encountering E. M. Forster's talk on Crabbe induces an impulse of homesickness; returns to England 1942 with the Koussevitzky commission for *Peter Grimes* in his pocket; on the voyage *A Ceremony of Carols* and *Hymn to St Cecilia*; back home, the *Serenade* (1943) begins to reach the heart of the gift. Registered Conscientious Objector; much devoted music-making, culminating in visit to newly liberated German concentration camps 1945. That year, triumphant première of *Peter Grimes*. Plentiful incidental scores for the new-founded BBC Third Programme: next operatic projects move into chamber-forces – *Rape of Lucretia* (1946) – leading to formation of the English Opera Group the year after – practical, versatile, not requiring large resources and houses, able to tour – first-fruit *Albert Herring* (1947). That year he moves to Aldeburgh, scene of Crabbe and *Grimes*; notion born of a local-based Festival; its first in 1948, still flourishing seventy-plus years on. For English Opera Group a loving realization of *The Beggar's Opera* (1948), and a loving theatre-piece for children, *The Little Sweep* (1949): alongside theatre-works, the *Young Person's Guide to the Orchestra (Variations and Fugue on a Theme of Purcell)*

(1946), *Saint Nicolas* (1948), *Spring Symphony* (1949), many Purcell-realizations, many lovable versions of English folksongs.

Next Grand Operas *Billy Budd* (1951), *Gloriana* (1953): the first possibly Britten's finest hour, the second a notorious fiasco, from which the work took several decades to recover. Further chamber-operas *The Turn of the Screw* (1954), *A Midsummer Night's Dream* (1960); between them a children's pageant, *Noye's Fludde* (1957), and a full-length full-orchestra ballet, *The Prince of the Pagodas*, the year before: all four interspersed with his finest song-cycles with piano – *Winter Words* (Hardy, 1953) and *Six Hölderlin Fragments* (1958), a set with guitar accompaniment *Songs from the Chinese* (1957); and, finest of all, with small orchestra, the *Nocturne* (1958), successor to the *Serenade* of fifteen years earlier. All the time tireless activity organizing the Festival, emerging as a fine conductor and incomparable accompanist to *Lieder, mélodie* and his own song-cycles.

War Requiem (1962); after its huge international impact, a change of direction, in *Curlew River* (1964) – first and best of three church parables (its successors – 1966 and 1968 – successively less successful). Later song-cycles on Blake, Pushkin, Soutar, growing dry and formulaic: the same with cello-suites, a harp suite and other smaller pieces. Penultimate opera, *Owen Wingrave* (1970), initially for television – a pacifist tract short on nourishing music: recovery in the last, *Death in Venice*, three years later. Major heart surgery at that time; after it, performing no longer possible, and further composing virtually 'posthumous'; a flicker of former magic in the suite on English folksongs *A Time there Was* (1974), of former dramatic power in *Phaedra* (1975); a touching farewell to Venice in the 3rd String Quartet the same year; died the next, aged only sixty-three.

Britten's image has greatly changed over the years. The early flowering of his manifestly outstanding gifts took him instantly to the top after the triumph of *Peter Grimes* in 1945, despite the sneers of the Establishment, of which (as usual) he imperceptibly, inescapably became a part, to end up, five months before his too-early death in 1976, a peer of the realm. By then it was the young and snooty who sneered. With the general public, popularity was ardent and unfeigned, and his worldwide following continues to increase.

Yet perception of the man and the music has altered. The earlier image combined Mozartian comprehensiveness with Mendelssohnian facility and brilliance in a vein of mercurial brio, gaiety and dash, and was expressed in a technique too unselfconscious to be fazed by the 'sentimental' problems of modernity. A much-quoted letter of 1942 wherein Auden urges his friend to embrace Chaos over Order, Bohemia over Bourgeois Convention, has become central to these changed perspectives. Since his death a shift of angle, together with biographical 'revelations' as expected, have elicited a dark side to his work, as with his personality. Britten is now perceived as tormented by guilt and angst, revealed most explicitly in the obsessive return again and again to ever-narrowing variants of the same few themes – prejudice, persecution, pacifism and destructiveness, and corruption of innocence even while it is vainly hankered after – culminating in the oblique but unmistakable self-projection of *Death in Venice*.

These opposing perceptions are compatible, even complementary. It is obvious that, between the pastoral opening song of the *Serenade* and the deep serenity of the closing sonnet, and alongside the gay vivacity of the hunting scherzo, lie the sick rose with the canker at its heart and the blood-flecked demonism of the *Lyke-wake Dirge*; and we now appreciate *Peter Grimes* as the representative masterpiece of English 1940s Romantic/Gothic, where Graham Sutherland's thorny forests parted to reveal neo-Grünewald and John Piper was so persistently beset by glowering weather. So to darker matter: exploration of the nexus between desire and destruction in *Billy Budd*, not so much via the stilted villainy of Claggart as in the ambiguous yet unswerving relish with which Billy's own goodness and Vere's justice, fairness and decency all make as surely, and far more convincingly, for the kill. Above all, the twists and feints by which the erotic glamour that dare not speak its name drown out the all-too-complicit innocence in *The Turn of the Screw*; and the exposure of pure naked anguish in that unique fusion of East and West, medieval and serial, strict and floating, *Curlew River*.

That the dark prevails in this complex vision is clear as daylight: that it was always so is confirmed by the higher standing nowadays of such earlier milestones of introspection and pain as *Our Hunting Fathers* and the *Sinfonia da Requiem*.

But concentration on this 'sado-masochist' aspect is now so general that there is a real danger of neglecting the earlier perception, all sweetness, lightness, radiance, exuberance and breathtaking technical ease – the Young Apollo (with prominent nose and receding chin) whose last lovely fling was the fairy music in *A Midsummer Night's Dream*. All this remains, and is the more valuable since such qualities were rare in twentieth-century art at large – particularly in most music concurrent with Britten's peak production and (for me, and I suspect for most of his lovers) compositional prime, *c*.1943–58. *Albert Herring*, the *Spring Symphony*, *The Prince of the Pagodas*, as well as many smaller things (for example, everyone's favourite, the *Hymn to St Cecilia*) are undimmed witness.

I fear that my continuing aversion to the *War Requiem*, his most celebrated success, might seem to put my ardent advocacy of Britten in general at a disadvantage. I would place it with other pieces that don't share its appeal, like the United Nations anthem *Voices for Today* and the pacifist opera *Owen Wingrave*; they are sermons, on poker-work texts of startling simplism – war is bad, peace is good, we must love one another and/or die. Simply on musical grounds (all others are emotional blackmail) this public aspect lacks the sharp memorable inspiration and sheer compositional invention of the authentic masterpieces whose ethical credentials might well be seen as 'incorrect' – all the dark matter already mentioned, and plenty more.

The only view to have sunk below the horizon is the middle course that Britten himself hopefully characterized as his purpose: to be useful – local first, universal last if at all – an impersonal provider like all pre-Romantic composers, and Rossini and Verdi in later times; a sort of superior occasional artist, fulfilling a need with no-nonsense craftsmanship. This has so obviously come true that it hardly seems worth remarking. But however posterity decides, and time winnows grain from chaff in a large output that undoubtedly tends towards self-dilution and self-duplication at its latter end, Britten will surely last through many a further shift of emphasis.

The fourteen stage-works – seven operas, one musical, one ballet, one children's entertainment, one communal pageant, three church parables – are of course the core of Britten's oeuvre, all the way from *Paul Bunyan* of 1941 to *Death in Venice* of 1973 (then *Paul Bunyan* revised the next year). They are easily accessible and often discussed: this account will be brief and generalized. Closely related preoccupations recur bold and clear throughout the span: Grimes the possibly-not-so-innocent outsider, if not sadistic certainly rough, caught up in accidents and coincidences of his own making, ostracized, hounded to suicide: Lucretia certainly innocent, debauched by vaunting male lust, suiciding in noble shame: Albert the bashful virgin, by a single night on the tiles escaping mean small-town virtues and his smothering Mum: Billy the beautiful sailor, trapped by fatality, betrayed by an inner flaw, apex of a suppressed erotic triangle that dare not declare itself direct, strung up on the yard-arm according to The Rules: Gloriana, ageing sovereign, strung between infatuation with attractive, headstrong youth and her duty to her country, her people, her self: Governess, inviting and harbouring forbidden desires via the collusive mediation of her young charges and the fascinating/alluring ghosts: Mother, grief-demented with the loss of her child, only freed from her madness by the apparition of his spirit: Owen, scion of a fighting clan, his courage tested by his conscientious objection, paying the price with his life: Aschenbach, seduced away from discipline, propriety, decorum, by a vision of unattainable beauty, going to pieces physically and morally, dissolving in terminal ecstasy. Only one gets away – the Shakespearean comedy wherein sparring lovers supernatural and mortal are reconciled and all ends mended.

The music for all these is, however, very various: each has its own idiom, pace, sonority: none could be mistaken for any other. The sea-music in the *Grimes* interludes and the wide open sea-spaces of *Budd* feel quite different: so with the supernatural in the *Screw* and the *Dream* – one malign, seductive, destructive; the other diaphanous, delectable, delicious (for all that the celesta figures prominent in both): the succession in *Albert* of satirical small-town vignettes sketched with such fun: *Lucretia* with the sheerly loveliest lyricism in all Britten for the serving-girls with their spinning and their flowers, pitched against the sex-driven fury of Tarquin and the mournful dignity of the violated heroine's lament: in *Gloriana* the expressive contrast between bright/festive/public, and intimate/passionate/private. In all these there is no overlap: the gift is versatile and protean. And *Budd* and *Screw* have between them his most daring and complex music in texture, polyphony, harmony – the naval one the biggest orchestra he ever employed, the spooky one only the thirteen-piece ensemble, but never so brilliant a range of sonority extracted from it. Their boldness best shown in complementary passages of wonderful harmony – the succession of plain triads high/low, loud/soft, the scoring and voicing always altering, representing the wordless/sightless mission where Vere has to tell Billy the inevitable verdict: and the atonal limbo opening the second act of the other, where the two love-bereft ghosts collude in bitter resentment that yet has their quarry in view.

Britten's operatic achievement is large and lasting: that almost all the pieces are core repertoire is the more remarkable because all their themes are so off-centre. The principal absentee is erotic love. The vulgarity of Walton's would-be 'red-blooded heterosexuality' for his *Troilus and Cressida* is, of course, utterly eschewed: repression and suppression are Britten's forte, especially when direct presentation of what fuelled him naturally was not possible; but the fire from that fuel is dim and tepid. The force driving the genre of opera is love in all its varieties from erotic passion to its spiritually directed sublimation, including salient relationships amical and familial – Wotan and his daughter, Eva with her actual father and Sachs her fatherly friend; the Countess and her Count, Susanna and her Figaro; Katya and Boris; Borromeo and Palestrina, Palestrina and his precursors, Moses and his God. In all such places save Ellen's maternal feeling for Grimes and his for her protecting solace, Britten falls short: there's a numbness at the heart of the matter.

Other crucial issues of character and plot are often underdone and sometimes evaded. Early criticisms included Lucretia and Albert, surely vindicated since. But doubts persist with Billy and the two men transfixed by his wondrous innocence and beauty. Both librettists knew that the music's depiction of their villain was dud. Instead of Forster's desired 'passion – love constricted, perverted, poisoned, but nevertheless flowing down its agonised channel; a sexual discharge gone evil', Claggart is, in Crozier's words, a 'boring black-masked villain', diluted from the incomparably stronger prototype of Verdi's Iago. Peter's suicide in *Grimes* is the first of several fudged emotional high points, which arguably include the death of Miles, and certainly the fade-out of *Gloriana* and the denouement of *Owen Wingrave*. These things ramify in such passages as the orgy in *The Burning Fiery Furnace*, the anaemic view of city vice in *The Prodigal Son*, in *Budd* again, the muffled Dionysiac muting towards the end; in Aschenbach's Dionysiac nightmare in Act II of *Death in Venice*.

Britten can't do such things: he is inhibited by gentility and shame. Auden (later) suggests as much, speaking of 'what seemed like Ben's lack of daring, his desire to be the Establishment ... playing safe for amiability as guard against his queerity, but insisting on the innocence of adolescence as if this was a courageous attitude'. For clearly Innocence is far from innocent, and his work at its greatest and its most typical is impelled by a clutch of dark matter, not balanced by a corresponding warmth of libido. (Compare Puccini, who gave both sadism and eroticism their head.) There is no good love music in Britten. The two couples in *A Midsummer Night's Dream* are cardboard; Sid and Nancy in *Herring* are charming cameos; Aschenbach goes on about Tadzio's beauty firing him to new flights of inspiration, but the music remains earthbound. The closest Britten gets is always weird as well as wonderful – such unforgettable inspirations as those purely orchestral chords during which Vere invisibly and inaudibly tells Billy that he must hang; the Ghost and the Governess commingling their passionate voices as the boy through whom alone they can meet dies of the terror they've between them induced. On the evidence of his musical inspiration Britten was more warmly and feelingly stirred by sadism, sacrifice and death than by peace, goodwill, reconciliation and compassion. This should be no cause for regret. We value artists in the end for what they have done best, not for what they 'ought' to have done, and in many instances dark matter is the source of the brightest value.

If Britten 'evaded', 'denied' and 'stopped' it is worth asking what prevented him, and what might have been if he'd flown free. The short answer to what prevented him is the replacement of Auden by Aldeburgh. What might have been is a more fruitful speculation. There were three such chances in his career. In 1955, after *The Turn of the Screw* and its pendant *Canticle III*, Britten told Edith Sitwell (poet of the latter) that he felt 'on the threshold of a new musical world', and that he'd be taking the next winter off to do 'some deep thinking'. And indeed, the ensuing world tour included the revelatory experience of Bali, which fertilized important areas thereafter, and of Japan, source of *Curlew River* and thence of his entire late phase. So this is a growth-point where 'what might have been' actually happened.

Not so the extended emotional range offered in the mid-1960s by two ambitious operatic subjects which both came to grief, *Anna Karenina* and *King Lear*. The excuses for the termination of both projects do not disguise recognition of artistic incapacity. Instead, back to 'innocence' and its dark underside, with boys' voices to the fore, and the drabbest decade in his output, with gritty cello suites, bleak cycles of Blake and Soutar, the steeply diminishing returns of the two church parables that followed *Curlew River*, the lacklustre *Voices for Today* and the feeble *Owen Wingrave*. The third window opens briefly amid this dead patch: a projected ballet which he discussed with unwonted freedom with Sidney Nolan while touring Australia in 1970. He was thrilled by the desert, the light, the Aboriginal boys, and planned to contrast the stifled life and tragic death of an English juvenile with the Rousseau-esque naturalness 'and a kind of *Magic Flute* ending' of the Aboriginal. Though on returning he mentioned the idea to the Covent Garden directorate, Britten had killed this one himself; as the enchanted plane-flight descended, 'he suddenly said "Well, that's the end of that. When I get back to

England I won't be like that any more. My destiny is to be in harness and to die in harness."' Which, indeed, is what happened – harnessed, above all, to long-standing *idées fixes* (*Wingrave* and *Death in Venice* had been in mind since the American years) whose grip was so strong that he could only fantasize, not act, upon anything that transcended them. But, in the end, we possess what was caught rather than what escaped. And it is positive. This is a major composer, after all, not quite the fourth 'B' that his mother was determined he should be, following Bach, Beethoven and Brahms, but a gigantic figure in the pluralist jungle of post-war music, who probably gave more pleasure than any.

His best period remains the astonishingly fertile decade from *Peter Grimes* (1945) to *The Prince of the Pagodas*, with brilliant flashes before and some shafts of genius even as the language grows etiolated, notably the renovatory *Curlew River* (1964) and the valedictory *Death in Venice* (1973) three years before his own. His ultimate importance is, for us now, uninterestingly unknowable compared with what we have enjoyed already, still do and still will.

And after all! To have made public pleasure – in opera above all – out of the deeply screwed-up places of an occluded personality is a triumph of the will that, in a perverse way, surpasses Wagner's, just because of the off-centredness of its subjects. To get international audiences in music's most explicit genre willingly to side with the sadistic visionary against the decent norms, to throb with the ganglings of a gormless youth tied to his mother's apron-strings, to be moved to the marrow as a man pretending to be a monk pretending to be a mad woman twitters away over the boy she has lost, or as an elderly writer of untarnished probity goes to pieces in exaltation and degradation over the boy he has found, is an extraordinary achievement. He spread his obsessions and starvations very wide and very deep.

Britten needs words. Much of his purely instrumental music is scrappy and dried-out in every aspect save that of technique. If not plots and character, then narratives – *Saint Nicolas, Abraham and Isaac, Journey of the Magi, Golden Vanity, Children's Crusade*:

and solo song, the other principal thread throughout the oeuvre from start to finish. Poetry above all induces the gift to flower. Before reaching the main body of cycles and canticles, two works that both employ the word Symphony – *Our Hunting Fathers*, a 'symphonic cycle' with text: *Sinfonia da Requiem*, with no vocal element, its three movements clearly correspondent to titles from the Mass for the Dead.

Both lie dangerously close to the bone, and both caused trouble – no 'playing it safe' (etc.) yet. A work covering human relations with animals, emphatically condemning the chase, is not likely to occasion anything but displeasure at the Norwich Festival 1936! Within a Prologue and Epilogue specially written by Auden come three old poems, also Auden's discoveries, concerning the creatures, hunted or petted: a spell against rats, a lady lamenting her favourite monkey, a roll-call of hawks with their picturesque names, enlisted for the kill and transformed into a Dance of Death. Auden's own eloquent if obscure poems are set to melodious recitative rising to impassioned utterance – in a *Prologue* 'O pride so hostile to our charity', in the *Epilogue* a cry to 'be anonymous', its intensity rarely surpassed in the composer subsequently, operatic or otherwise. *Rats away!* a furious scherzo – *con fuoco* – fleet and skeletal yet heavy and emphatic, demanding needle-sharp precision from the orchestra and giddy virtuosity from the singer. Even when the music quietens it remains stretched skintight, for the parody-liturgy prayer: the final *Amen* a sardonic mutter, almost inaudible, before the rodent-scamper resumes and dissipates. Before this the singer must heave out the dread monosyllable – *Rats!* – interpolated into the dog-Latin no fewer than twelve times. Amid the whirring fragments, high shrill long notes on upper woodwinds and, miles below, a baleful solo tuba – prophetic of fog-horn in *Grimes*, orgiastic nightmare in *Venice*.

Now follows Messalina's lament for her simian 'treasure', painful with its exaggerated plangency framed within a complex tissue of strumming pizzicato ending each time in piercing dissonance introducing anguished ululations from the lady herself, before the poem distances to describe her extravagant woe in simple sobriety till her next direct outcry – *fie, fie, fie*, thirty-three times, from top to bottom of vocal range, guttering out, exhausted, on a regular tolling monotone taken up by the orchestra for extended coda: over the tick-tock, expressive woodwind solos – flute, oboe, clarinet, bassoon (briefly), and finally saxophone. The tick-tock tolling pulse is taken over by the voice's re-entry in the next poem, a virtuoso patter-song of the hawks' names interspersed with onomatopoeic imitations of their calls.

It is a *Totentanz*: a headlong tarantella, hell-bent and blood-flecked, the orchestral textures sometimes baring to the skeleton, filling out into skin, muscle, ligament, though never flesh. 'Pleasure fit for Kings' a salient line lost in the scrabble and scrum: disgust-filled spasms from woodwinds and horns, in a general stance and idiom surprisingly close to the modernist/constructivist Shosta-kovich of the 1920s. Extended orchestral interlude where everything lets rip, climaxing in percussion-break of unhooded violence, ending with vile smear of sliding trombones. The voice, sated, mutters on the same low note as *Amen* in *Rats!*, notoriously conjoining two hawk-names previously wide apart – *German, Jew* – before a final call and disintegrating collapse down pizzicato cellos and basses to link into the *Epilogue*. Silly little figure on xylophone – all bone – with droll harmonization: saxophone eloquent and 'vocal', voice itself dry, simple recitative. The texture gradually fills out to reach the impassioned setting of 'anonymous', then thins into a purely orches-tral close, à la *marcia funèbre*: the trivial tinkly xylophone with its mechanized dissonant accompaniments gradually joined by high singing lines undermined with soft rude interjections on muted brass – Dance of Death transformed into Funeral March, à la sarcas-tic early Prokofiev with a flavour all its own, never to be revisited.

The *Sinfonia da Requiem* overlaps in subject, treatment, idiom, youthful brilliance, virtuosity. The trouble *this* work caused was altogether more hurtful: commissioned to mark the 2600th anni-versary of the Japanese Empire; even in peacetime a tricky propos-ition, and this was 1940. But the centre of the embarrassment was the work's explicit Christian connotations: deemed inappropriate, even insulting; the crisis was averted, and the eventual dedication to the memory of the composer's parents remains valid and permanent.

The liturgical sources are compressed into three linked movements. *Lacrymosa* another cortège, setting forth over deep sustained bass plus heavy drum-beats, the same D as *Amen* and '*whurrett, whurrett, German, Jew*' in *Our Hunting Fathers*.

The first movement is taut and tense, screwed up to breaking-point. No. 2, another scherzo from hell, almost euphoric were it not so disquieting; hunt here, after lamenting trio, swells into march, exploding then imploding; the entire orchestra self-destructs, flying apart like a collapsing machine. From the fragments the third slowly assembles into a berceuse, expands into serene unfolding lines – yearning, aspiring – then thinning away to a gentle expiry. The work as a whole reveals a genius for purely orchestral composition that Britten never followed up.

Except the once – its perfect complement. The *Young Person's Guide to the Orchestra* began as score for a film introducing the orchestral instruments, its evergreen afterlife is a work without words, *Variations and Fugue on a Theme of Purcell*. Superb theme – D-minor again, without hint of *Requiem* – presented six times: full orchestra; woodwinds in F; brasses in E♭; strings in G-minor (guide to tonal relationships too); percussion, the timpani tuned to the dominant, preparatory to grand restatement on full forces in home tonic. Variations for individual instruments now follow, each a perfect encapsulation of timbre and character – flutes and piccolo chirpy and playful, oboes (no cor anglais) expressive and plangent, clarinets (no bass) feline and agile, bassoons strutting then songful (no double-bassoon): all this accompanied only by strings and harp. Strings now to the fore: violins in brilliant *polacca*, then cantabile; violas melancholy, even elegiac; cellos expansive and warm; double-basses gruff, then songful, then gruff turning comic. The accompani-ments for the strings are more varied, and we've been unobtrusively taken through several further tonalities. Strings are again back-ground (which includes cymbal-splashes and gong-strokes) for splendidly bardic harp in its native D♭-major.

So to brasses, ever-deft little cameos of invention exactly captur-ing character – baying horns, tattooing trumpets (with military drum, from this registered Conscientious Objector), trombones and tuba pompous and orotund. The percussion variation is particularly effective: dance accompaniment of dry strings, ritornello for timpani introducing in turn cymbals/bass drum/tambourine; military drum again, with Chinese block; *danse macabre* xylophone; Spanishy casta-nets and sinister gong; three cracks of the whip; then, what every kid has waited for, all together, ending with a special solo for the kitch-en's highest timbre, the triangle, as the *saltarello* rhythm vanishes up the xylophone and the Fugue commences in D-major. Same order as in the *Variations* for fugal entries from piccolo downwards, of a perky subject that might have represented an extra character in *Peter and the Wolf*: down through the woodwinds; down, modu-lating, through the strings; first mini-climax: then soft and sweet for the harp; frothing up for ebullient horns, brilliant trumpets, bullish trombones and tuba: then adroitly set-out for percussion. So to the apotheosis – Purcell grand and slow on brass, fugue-subject sparkling busily above: expectations gratified; end in a blaze of exultant triumph, young Apollo at the helm, smiling all over his sunny countenance: a masterpiece of populism without condes-cension; neat, even elegant, without being finicky; 'educative', even 'improving', without patronizing or dumbing-down: and not a hint of dark, painful places.

Which will tend to loom large as Britten's songs with instru-ments are explored. Not in their first manifestation, *Les Illumin-ations*, setting Rimbaud for high voice and strings. Despite the music's liveliness and the diaphanous grace, the essence of these extraor-dinary words has not been reached. Rimbaud is peculiar, perverse, sinister, suggestive: Alleghanies and Lebanons, the moon howling and burning; the faun softly stirring his right then his left thigh; chariots of silver and bronze, ships of steel and silver; men's faces malformed, leaden, livid, charred: above all, the adored yet frightful body of the Being Beauteous, wounded scarlet and black against the snow. Ravel might have held the key to this savage parade: Britten is trammelled. At home, he rises and flowers. Two song-cycles with small forces: *Serenade* for tenor, horn and strings, *Nocturne* for tenor with strings and seven obbligato instruments: both set an anthology from various English poets across the centuries and styles, chosen à la Auden with Auden-inspired sureness of taste, evoking sleep, night, dreams felicitous or nightmarish, memories and reflections; and, in the *Nocturne*, the dawn of the next day.

Both works speak along their entire span. The *Serenade* covers sweet twilight pastoral, pantheist ecstasy, the hunting gaiety of Diana's court, the rapt calm closing invocation to midnight. Within, the dark places – superb arc of horn melody introducing the tenor's monotone for the sick rose, then both soloists vying to scarify with *This ae nighte*. The whole compressed, or opening out, within the horn's entry from offstage and receding into silence at the close, employing the instrument's natural harmonics, achingly off-tune.

Nocturne takes up where *Serenade* left off: a deeper exploration of the same themes, its darker places more disturbing, its gaiety, lyricism, exultation more buoyant. The dedication to Mahler's widow is absolutely appropriate for this masterpiece of *Nachtmusik*. Each of the eight poems is allocated a different obbligato instrument to partner the tenor, save the first, with strings alone, and the last, where all the forces join to make, in effect, a reduced full orchestra. And the whole plays – sings – continuously, linked by a rocking/breathing figure, long/short, gently binding the entire duration into an entity. The harmony of this motif, initially pure C-major plus added diatonic notes, gradually veiled in overlapping bitonality, is quintessentially Britteny, often imitated but strictly inimitable, unmistakable for any other.

Texts run from Shelley, celebrating the Poet, who transforms sensation into cognition, creating 'forms more real than living man', set to an ardent phrase due for much re-articulation as the work advances; thence to Tennyson's Kraken, a monster from the depths of the ocean and the unconscious (bassoon): thence Coleridge's vision 'by moonlight, in a wilderness' of a beautiful boy, all alone – 'no friend, no loving mother near?' – transparent diaphony with harp. Now to horn, ingeniously imitating the midnight noises of Middleton's text – dinging bell, howling dog, miaowing cat, tweeting nightingale, hooting owl, croaking raven, chirruping cricket, nibbling mouse. Now to the heart of darkness (timpani): Wordsworth's recall of the September Massacres in Paris 1792. Britten's setting recaptures the terror of the *dies irae* in the *Sinfonia* and the *Totentanz* from *Our Hunting Fathers*, climaxing on the declaimed phrase from *Macbeth* – 'sleep no more'. Curiously followed by the *Nocturne*'s only dull number on an unworthy poem of Owen – cor anglais the featured obbligato, a dilute re-brew of *Lucretia*'s post-rape threnody with the same timbre. Enter fresh air, flute and clarinet, for Keats's invocation to Sleep: calibre as well as sustenance and relief from nightmare as a new day dawns. The complete ensemble enters stealthily and piecemeal for prelude to the concluding poem, Shakespeare's Sonnet 43, compacted conceit of sleep/wakefulness, night/day, dark/bright, love/death. Britten's superb setting shows, as never so clearly, the direct influence of his dedicatee's first (and best) husband Gustav Mahler: its sustained intensity recalls most nearly the master's *Kindertotenlieder*. For the concluding couplet the intensity lifts; the dark shadows of paradox and ambiguity recede: the light paradox remains –

> All days are nights to see till I see thee,
> And nights bright days when dreams do show thee me

– set to parlando almost casual after the preceding urgency, delicately punctuated by harp, the breathing/rocking/lulling gradually disappearing up the keys to end in the high C-major whence it had emanated: then one further sonority, ambiguous and insistent to the last – a soft high major third on D♭, avoiding the triteness of an easy resolution, opening up a further magic casement.

As with his adored Schubert and despised Brahms, songs with piano (mostly) figure in Britten's output from first to last, usually composed for the partnership with Pears. Cycles alternate with *Canticles* – fifteen works in all; one for soprano, one for mezzo, one for baritone; the rest for tenor. Pears" is joined by another voice for *Canticle II* telling the story of Abraham and Isaac, and two other voices for *Canticle IV* telling the journey of the Magi; and for *Canticle III* a solo horn. One cycle has guitar not piano accompaniment, and later on, harp takes over, even before heart-surgery prevented the composer's own participation. Poets are wide-ranging and eclectic, involving no less than six languages – as well as English there are French, Italian, German, Russian, Scots. Only the *Songs from the Chinese* employ translations. And also, from first to last, many realizations of Purcell and copious arrangements of folksongs, from the British Isles and France.

Three highlights from this profusion that show, in different ways, an empathetic match of text and music not yet achieved in the *Michelangelo* Sonnets, perhaps; certainly not in the *Donne* Sonnets, where the same reservations apply as with Rimbaud – there's more in these words than this music reaches. Not so with Hardy: *Winter Words* sets eight poems neatly juxtaposed in contrasting moods and genres to make a life-to-death sequence, with a hint of passing seasons: and, after, the implicit question – whether mere oblivion or a glimpse of eternity. *At day-close in November*: impetuous fast waltz, harmony acrid/edgy/bitonal, sweetening for the children who'll never conceive a time before the autumn trees or after they'll have past and gone. Second, the first of three mini-dramas: the lone boy on the midnight train, ignorant of origin or destination. The engine's hooter then the jogging of the carriage ingeniously onomatopoeic; the melisma, twice, on 'journeying' hypnotic. The observer now grows reflective: the imitative figures alternate to accompany thoughts occasioned by the listless lad, ticket stuck in his hat-band – what his past, what future? The next stanza continues to ponder – is he an innocent, floating far above base sinful humanity, in but not of it? The hooter has the last word: questions unanswered. *Wagtail and baby*: comic relief, this satire (Hardy's term) – dry Rossini-like accompaniment for left hand, right hand imitating the bird's erratic motions, as bull, stallion, mongrel fail to faze him, baby watching all three; then, seeing the wagtail fly off in terror as 'a perfect gentleman' nears, 'falls a-thinking'. Witty little number, earning its light place in the human tragi-comedy by contrast not calibre. Human again, *The little old table*, its creaking graphically rendered by sharp little stabs and chirrups learnt from the cricket in Ravel's *Histoires naturelles*: their purpose, to capture a past irretrievably lost – *she* brought it, *she* looked at me, *I* did not understand her impulse; any future owner will never know what hangs upon this droll little sound: times gone and to come again implicit in times present.

Core of the cycle, *The choirmaster's burial*, full-scale scena, in a setting, with persons. The Tenorman tells of the old organist's oft-made request that he be interred to his favourite Psalm-tune *Mount Ephraim*: perhaps he'd hear it as the voices of the 'seraphim' – beautiful melisma on this word, emerging from the plain recitative with which the setting begins, the piano gently outlining the old hymn-tune complete. Now the scena comes to life: functional parlando, the old man's passing reported, and his request, vicar characterized like a character strayed in from *Albert Herring*: it's midwinter, too bitter for outdoor music, a read service *quicker* (rhyming with *vicar* of course): cursory rites, music banished, voice's hasty monotone, piano's dry low scurry. 'But' (the story continues) – ''twas said' – the vicar looked out at dead of next night – and now the piano, picking up a passing earlier mention of lutes, gives *Mount Ephraim* in full, limpid and diaphanous, not a hint of organ-indoors: the voice, threaded freely in and out, describes the angelic band, 'singing and playing' (these words set thrice). The delicate melisma on 'seraphim' re-used for 'the ancient stave' and again for 'the choirmaster's grave'. The seraphic vision fades, the prosaic returns in deliberately plain conclusion perfectly attuned to the tender-loving tact and rightness of the whole episode, now distanced in times past – 'such the Tenorman told, when he had grown old'. *Proud songsters* now, balancing the Wagtail, a rush of springtime euphoria, thrushes and finches by day, nightingales by night – 'brand-new birds of twelve months' growing', formed of grain, earth, air, rain, into shrill exultant life.

Next the third mini-drama: a station-platform, another Lost Boy, this one knowing who he is and what he's about, striking up on his fiddle while the other passengers, a handcuffed convict and his guardian constable, await the train. As the boy plays, the prisoner suddenly bursts 'with grimful glee' into a celebration of liberty: 'this life so free is the thing for me!' – one of life's little ironies at which the officer can only smile and remain silent, 'as if unconscious of what he heard'. And so it goes till the train comes in. With easy cunning the entire piano-part imitates the violin; at first improvisa-tory, then regular for 'the life so free', then again loose and airy, dis-appearing up to the highest possible E – almost audibly a natural harmonic: the whole song could be accompanied by the fiddle – Britten at once poetically apt and precisely practical. The voice is posed across the instrument with scrupulous sensitivity: the scene is *seen*.

The final song is goal as the *Burial* was core. *Before life and after*, a plea for relief from pains bodily and spiritual; mental too – the torments of consciousness, of feeling, itself a disease so inimical to peace and well-being. *Nescience* is the goal: *how long* before its primal rightness can be reaffirmed. *How long?*, the last words, set five times in the dying fall of a single broad-spanned paragraph, voice and piano right hand duetting in overlapping cantabile (not-so-distant model the thus-textured songs in Wolf's Italian collection), over low thick chugging left-hand triads, dogged and almost ugly. The cycle ends on some kind of resolution of this and its previous questions, albeit no answers.

Winter Words is not a collection like a Wolf songbook: it's a genuine cycle à la Schumann's Eichendorff *Liederkreis*, and more intricately interlinked than that work in *poetic* content though not doing its motivic interconnections. My florilège of words and phrases from the poems, with description of the notes, attempts to show how deeply they are interfused, every underlying theme subtly and profoundly rhyming across eight songs on the face of it so mis-cellaneous. One instance – the constable 'as if unconscious of what he heard' leads from the thoughtless children in the first song, via reflections occasioned by the travelling boy, the creaking table, the thoughtful baby, the thoughtless vicar, to the time before conscious-ness troubled life's goodness and the desperate appeal for the balm of its antithesis, nescience. Britten doesn't – can't – do the erotic: here, via Hardy, is what he *can* and *does* do: he bares his heart by indirection, and it beats ardent.

Songs from the Chinese: six translations by Arthur Waley, set for tenor and guitar, inspired as much by Pears as by the artistry of the great Julian Bream. Britten's native scrupulous spareness with his pitches makes the instrument a natural: as with the harp, earlier and subsequently, apparent limitations of range, volume, tuning, are turned to compositional advantage. This cycle is a divertimento after Hardy's bleakness, but not without an undercurrent of melancholy and pessimism. *The Big Chariot* dispels them with vigour – 'don't think about the sorrows of the world': thrice repeated – its first consequence 'you will only make yourself wretched', its second 'or you will never escape from your despair', its third 'you will only load yourself with care': the image of the big dusty vehicle rendered by heavy chords and brilliant passage-work. *The Old Lute* follows, an exquisite meditation on time and decay, evoking ancient memories locked within the antique instrument, 'not appealing to present men's taste', through ingenious self-reflective four-part harmony born of the guitar's innate intimacy and its physical layout, despite a key-signature of four sharps, blown away in a fast tiny coda, all naturals and harmonics, as the bright music of present men's taste twangs deliciously on, off, disappears. *Autumn Wind* an urgent toccata: nature in decline and dispersal, the poet languishes in his lady's absence, perhaps rejection: the folk revel and feast, but sad thoughts come – 'youth so brief, age so sure'. Vigour and youth renewed by the *Herd Boy*, robust against wind and rain, distant then suddenly face-to-face; setting off further sad thoughts symbolized by dark smoke oozing through the thatched roof; wistful yearning perfectly expressed in the ambiguous close. Real *Depression* expressed in the song of that name that follows, picking up previous keywords as in the Hardy cycle – the bonny boy, the jade stops of the old lute, age and decay: 'though my limbs are old, my heart is older yet.' Here the guitar/lute chords – three-thick, then four, then five, finally six – are born directly of the instrument's tuning, layout and the ability to slide up and down the strings, in a slow scotch-snap rhythm also prevailing in the voice-part, combining in an *image sonore*, jade made audible, of its subject, regretful and deploring, sadly and wisely acquiescent. Again, gloom blown away by vigour in the concluding *Dance Song*; warrior-gay, the lament for the Unicorn, his hoofs, his brow, his horn, all mocking melancholy – even the penultimate cry of *Alas!* is jeering. Then the same word again, in a soft mutter,

touches the truth, and the adorable work ends on an upwardly disappearing flurry of harmonics recalling the flute and zither that the
old lute can't manage at the close of its song.

Finally, in this carefully selective survey of Britten the song-writer,
the *Spring Symphony*: large-scale work from its composer's prime.
No story to pertain to the operas' troubled subjects – a lyric song-
cycle with full chorus and a boys' choir as well as the three soloists,
loosely fused into the four-movement frame of the title's second
word, wholly devoted to celebrating its first, in an anthology à la
Serenade, Auden-inspired (though by now – 1949 – Britten had
escaped the poet's immediate domineering personal contact), and
including at its heart an elaborate Auden-setting.

Part I: the *Introduction* one of Britten's finest inventions: an
anonymous sixteenth-century text invokes the sun – 'Shine out' –
and marks the disappearing passage of winter. A few soft bars upon
a skeletal figure articulated by timpani and harps, sustained on gong,
cymbals, pitchless drums high and low, a clicking xylophone, ending
in luminous vibraphone, invite the chorus in to invite the sun out
in all his 'thousand-coloured light'. The percussion makes a link, at
once neatly formulaic and sonorously apt, to every successive event.
Strings first, soft overlapping entries from double-basses to top of
violins, in a haze of tritonal dissonance: vibraphone renews next
choral appeal, extended to banish black winter. Curtailed reminder
of percussion and strings, who freeze upon a unison G six octaves
deep/high. Now the woodwinds' turn – soft wriggling shapes,
oboes first, flutes superimposed, then clarinets two octaves apart,
above and below, then bassoons below, then double-bassoon and
bass-clarinet an octave lower still. No link: chorus straight in, for
imitative – contrapuntal and onomatopoeic – depiction of the grey
wolf's howling, then the halting gait of old age. Vibraphone returns
with next imperative – *shine out!* A snatch of harps and percussion,
immediately receding as low bass to the brass's turn – choked muted
fanfares peaking in suspensions of freezing dissonance, fading for
next choral entry – the quaking fish and his aching feet. Vibraphone
reduced to a mere semitone, a near-inaudible *shine out!* and, what

the movement has led up to and longed for, the spectacular super-imposition of all its materials.

Over the percussion/harp figure, now helped by trombones and tuba, the long string contour, the wiggly woodwinds, the brass fanfares with suspensions, all enter in the same bar and continue simultaneously for another eight – *complexe pas compliqué*, a feat of lucid jungle, tribute to a miraculous ear – with certain places in *Billy Budd* a year or so later, Britten's most spontaneous and unselfconscious alignment with the most advanced edges of 'modern music'. Cut off at its peak, leaving the vibraphone alone to shine out as the chorus, now for the first time *fortissimo*, again invoke the sun: another marvellous line from this fascinating poem – 'the stars in icicles arise' inspires the hard glittering sound that, near the start, the 'thousand-coloured light' then subdued.

The Introduction now eliminates itself with a promise of Spring. Only the Auden-setting at the centre, and the finale, again fully employ the full orchestra: every other song uses a selection. Thus, Spenser's *Merry Cuckoo* for the tenor soloist with just the three trumpets, merrily fanfaring and stuttering, one going muted for the aberrant title-bird. *Spring, the Sweet Spring* (Nashe) is a concerted number, chorus keeping up only salient words, background to all three soloists revelling in song and dance, lambkins frisking, fragrance, piping, young lovers meeting, old wives sunning, and delighting in ingenious bird-imitations between each stanza. So to *The Driving Boy*, introducing the boys' chorus singing Peele's lusty words with chop-cherry woodwinds and a splendidly blaring tuba: the scene distances, high strings steal in, the boys whistle, the solo soprano reflects with words by Clare. Boys now regain foreground with their own instrumentation and music; she and hers float sweetly above – 'a happy boy, a dirty boy, a happy dirty driving boy'. This 'first movement' ends stately and almost solemn: Milton's *Morning Star*, on full chorus and brass, with drums to mark rhythm, and bells, not in the poem but aptly festive for this hymn to welcome the month of whom the Star is harbinger: marked dance-rhythm underlies the choir mainly in sturdy unison for May, bounteous and benign, inspiring mirth, youth, warm desire: brief sonorous climax, rapid fade, wishing the month never to end, and what every listener unconsciously wishes, *both* bells, a semitone apart, very gently struck simultaneously.

Part II is the *Symphony*'s quasi-slow-movement. The contralto soloist leads off with Herrick's *Welcome, Maids of Honour*: a delicate sprinkle of both harps with five solo woodwinds intersperses a rich velvet-piled bank of divided violas, cellos, basses, support for the voice's suave ample line. The Maids serve the Spring: fresh, fair, sweet, surpassing damask roses, but – virgins – doomed to lie alone. Soloist fades sadly away, downwards, the delicate six-note pattern twinkles away upwards, the low strings close on very high harmonics and the absent violins take over, sole accompaniment for exquisite silvery setting of Vaughan's *Waters Above*, continuous wandering undulation *ppp sul ponticello*, swelling into volume and natural tone for salient words – *welcome*; *glad*; *shining sun*. Against this shimmery backdrop, only in one or two parts, the tenor poises long-breathed lyric phrases, perfectly attuned to the radiant inner tranquillity of Vaughan's words as well as their outward imagery – *dew, doves, drink* – inspired by the light spring rain. A♯, an actual or implicit pedal throughout, taken up by initial unison B♭ of the re-entering chorus for Auden's *Out on the Lawn*. Women only, in soaring wordless two-part contour, then taken up by the men. Full winds now enter, underpinned with drum, on a choked diatonic dissonance: as it fades, its internal momentum is continued in an ornamental duet for two soft-tongued instruments, alto-flute and bass-clarinet (as in the grocery-shop, silent and empty, before Albert Herring returns, tiddly after May Day revels), accompaniment to the contralto soloist's ruminations on this 'windless night of June'. The chord returns to punctuate, the chorus returns as ritornello. Another dense chord introduces the next line, with woodwind obbligati now busy and chatty, a pair of oboes, a bassoon-line, after the chord again, half-way, joined by the cor anglais – 'healers, brilliant talkers, eccentrics, silent walkers' – the moon shines indifferent on all. The next lines grow agitated: chord still *ppp*, but sharply iterated; clarinets trill low and continuous, a flute flutters high: only the singer remains undisturbed. Unlike the moon, attendant upon gravity, we, for all our security 'look' – she does so; then down, acquiescent, to 'endure the tyrannies of love'; the men's chorus briefly recalls the wordless ritornellos. And she remains imperturbable – even complacent – rehearsing placidly the menace threatening Eastern Europe, while in trumpets and drums all hell is let loose, cut off sharp by re-entry of choral refrain, now high and loud, women and men in close imitation. It at once diminishes to *pp* and the opening Bb. First choked chord; brief encapsulation of all the woodwinds' preceding duets and trios, as the poem poses the question – what right our freedom, in England, now – and evades it. Ending on the opening, now again *ppp*, wordless as always, perhaps wisely: this brief repair to Britten's tepid pre-war pink doesn't quite convince, any more than the loaded moments, also within the Auden-ambience, of *Our Hunting Fathers* back in 1936.

Part III is the *Symphony*'s scherzo. All ebullition for Barnfield's *When will my May Come?*: upwards-tearing lower strings, descending upper, introducing the tenor, all crowing anticipation. His song mainly accompanied by the two harps – delightful twangling as he proffers his promises, mainly rustic then ending with aristocratic extravagance – a silver well (with golden sands) wherein he can wash his paramour's ivory hands. Last verse more pressing, strings urgently interrupting lover's beseeching – if you don't pity my tears, vows, oaths, what can I do? He ends impetuous again, finally on a dying rise of amorous query, answered in the ensuing duet with soprano. Peele again: strings strum, woodwinds intercurl in sinuous pairs: the soprano has an oboe and flute, the tenor a bassoon and clarinet. Finally, with characteristic ingenuity, the voices overlap in close canon with all four woodwinds intercurling: high-spirited vehemence for the Lovers' Anathemata, given half-way by each in turn, then finally together, in octaves – 'they that do change old love for new, pray gods they change for worse'; and an adroit disappearing-act, up the rope-ladder to nowhere. *Sound the Flute* (Blake) restores good cheer: chorus again, all the brass with the men, all the woodwinds with the women, all the strings with the boys: then all-together-now: welcoming in the Year, not the Season, with rousing brio. Next stop, Summer.

In Part IV, finale, Britten's aim and achievement put the *Spring Symphony* alongside the 'Merrie England' of such interwar works as Vaughan Williams' *Five Tudor Portraits* and Dyson's *Canterbury Pilgrims*. Britten joins the club (so to speak) and enhances it with terrific spirit and flair. In this long extract from Beaumont and Fletcher's *Knight of the Burning Pestle*, the Town-Crier presents May-month to the citizens of London in a three-part continuous structure: *moderato alla valse/allegro pesante*/return of the *valse*. Distant muffled pitchless percussion, and thinnest possible intimation to the dance on pairs of flutes and oboes, in antiphony then together, joined then in three-part overlap by clarinets. Into these pale strains lurches the bucolic woof of a cow-horn on its single C (not counting un-grace notes from below and – just thrice – from above). The tenor sturdily announces, athwart the *valse*-metre, the Festivities: the other two soloists join his invitation to Lovers and Town; the chorus gradually infiltrate; and the allegro bursts in, an energetic toccata, enumerating joys public and private, delicious and occasionally indecorous: the music's rate of gaiety and invention matches the poets'. Their text is split between chorus high and low, the three soloists as a unit, and the boys. The orchestra, sometimes rumbustuous, sometime refined to transparency: a helter-skelter kaleidoscopic Bartholomew Fair of varieties, turning gig-like as the tenor re-assumes the Crier while the two ladies slip off their gowns and assume the motley. Full choral vigour closes the allegro – the lusty youth of London – let it never be said that we can't make riot: terrific crash of unpitched percussion, dying away to return of the uncouth cow-horn and the *moderato alla valse*. The Crier calls for a general dance, the other soloists join him, as the triple time music of the opening resumes low and soft, on chorus too, wordless, gradually rising and swelling till bursting out in full, soloists included with the folk, with splendidly rude accompaniment. The *valse* whirls and billows into brighter keys till – the great moment – duple metre penetrates triple: the boys' choir doubled by four stopped horns give out the ancient round *Sumer is Icumen In*, with its loud cuckoo and promise of new growth in beasts and verdure, man and maid. Spring rounds – though the old melody's endless possibilities for canon aren't used: the single line holds the centre of the surrounding *valse-*polyphony. Summer rounds, joyous and intoxicating – surely the composer's happiest, freest moment – gradually decline; the Crier closes the pageant on a patriotic note; the scene slips from sight and sound; and so, my friends – I – cease. *Crash!*

Michael Tippett

Born London 1905; no settled parental home, here and there abroad, early expected to train as lawyer, but determined upon composition though his training sporadic (all his life he would be accused of 'amateurishness'): the most vital of his musical studies were in strict counterpoint. Slow to mature though composing plentifully, including a full-scale (pre-1st) Symphony (1933–4): only with the 1st String Quartet (1934–5) is a characteristic voice appreciable, only with the Concerto for Double String Orchestra (1938–9) does it enter its Kingdom. Deeply involved before the war in left-wing politics and devoted to his teaching and conducting at Morley College. Humane values tested and expressed in an oratorio, *A Child of Our Time* (1939–41) to his own text (the first of many). Jailed 1943 as Conscientious Objector. Second String Quartet 1941–2, 3rd 1945–6, between them the acknowledged 1st Symphony (1944–5); intertwined, two outstanding song-cycles, *Boyhood's End* (1943) and *The Heart's Assurance* (1950–51): slow growth of a full-scale opera, *The Midsummer Marriage* (1946–52), eventually produced in 1955 to universal bemusement. Nevertheless, from his mid-forties on recognized as a significant composer, even important, even great. Succession of major pieces from what remains his richest period: *Fantasia Concertante on a Theme of Corelli* for strings (1953), Piano Concerto (1953–5), 2nd Symphony (1956–7). Copious talks and writings about music, as well as his own libretti. Next opera, *King Priam* (1958–61), marks a change of direction and shift of style, further explored in a second Piano Sonata (1962) and a Concerto for Orchestra (1962–3), which use material taken direct from *Priam*. Second of the three major oratorios, *The Vision of St Augustine*

(1963–5), third *The Mask of Time* (1980–82); intertwined, the next two operas *The Knot Garden* (1966–9) and *The Ice Break* (1973–6), a Triple Concerto for violin, viola, cello (1978–9) as well as chamber-works and Occasionals. The closing phase included a fifth opera, *New Year* (1986–8), and a concert-aria setting Yeats's *Byzantium* (1988–90): he bowed out with a consciously retrospective farewell in *The Rose Lake* for orchestra (1991–3). Died 1998.

A Child of Our Time and the Double Concerto for Strings have their acknowledged places in the canon. Not so the 1st Symphony, a magnificent work, complex and ambitious, so assured and bold as, already, to deserve standing with VW's 4th and Walton's 1st as the outstanding work in the genre of the time. Tippett here not quite in full bloom: a certain greyness to the pitches, the melodic contours, the harmony; a certain functional drab to the orchestration. None of this impedes the impetuous contrapuntal energy of the two outer movements, less so still in the third, a headlong scherzo, sounding bright and clear a note unknown to British music hitherto – medieval/Pérotin/Renaissance/Monteverdi – brilliant, clamorous, hard-edged dancing rounds, in antiphonal choirs, mainly for winds, led by ebullient trumpets. This scherzo encloses another new intonation in its trio – a fantazia à la Lawes and Purcell for strings alone; soaring, leaping paragraphs of polyphonic song, culminating in ecstasy completely devoid of sensuality. The first movement has touches of the same in the string apostrophes punctuating its otherwise prevailing bristle of developmental contrapuntal energy; much syncopation with jazz as well as Tudor madrigalism behind, Hindemith and neo-classical Stravinsky to the fore. The resulting language is not exactly tonal, but decidedly not atonal: perhaps 'extended diatonicism' can define it best. It figures large in the finale, codifying the first movement's contrapuntal thrust into a terrific double-fugue: first subject all fizz and physicality, second subject long, gentle, singing lines; their gradual infiltration and reconciliation a triumph of intellectual and athletic prowess. The climax of the process is underlined by heavy drum-strokes which, as the texture winds down, continue to puncture, remaining loud as the orchestra self-eliminates; till, victory assured, they too go suddenly soft; then, once more, very soft, leaving behind only a long, sustained unison E on lower strings. That this note, never changing from its entry at the climax, is the movement's dominant, is not the least of this work's masterly know-how: as subtle, by suggestion, as the refusal to end in a blaze of glory is unmissable.

For it is, after all, a wartime work, with a prison-sentence for the composer during its making. Something of this, though completely non-self-expressive, permeates the slow movement – the second – the heart: built upon a ground-bass à la Purcell, a heaving eight-bar figure, strongly marked half-way and at the end by emphatic timpani. These landmarks become anchors as the variations ramify, bristly and complex, hard to 'hear' though always intelligible if the listener, sometimes desperate, holds on to the ground-bass. Immediately recognizable, a stuttering ghost-fanfare for three muted trumpets, echoed by three horns, later taken up at the structure's expressive core by three piccolos, answered by the trumpets again (higher now, so the first oboe needs to take the top part). This flickering hallucinatory vision has been plausibly likened to the uncanny unreality of blackout London in the quiet intervals of the Blitz. Then the process resumes, dense/tense lines, replicated and new-minted, uncoiling over the ground-bass (hold on tight!) up to a dryly clamorous climax; then subsidence – bombed out – onto the last bar of the bass-resolving drum-rhythm. Dark heart of a master-piece that should be a cornerstone of the repertoire.

The year after completing his 1st Symphony Tippett began the long quest to achieve his first opera, shaped from wide eclectic reading, much brooding, and originating in bizarre dreams so remote from the eventual story as to seem incredible. The genesis of *The Midsummer Marriage* dates back to *A Child of Our Time* in the early 1940s. The opera was originally intended as something almost farcical, then as the years darkened, gradually deepened and thick-ened into a comedy in the classical sense – impediments confronted and overcome to eventuate in loving union – illuminated above all by close absorption in the writings of Jung: the reformation only realized over some six years' intensive work.

It is too easy to mock at, or remain baffled by, every aspect of *The Midsummer Marriage* except its music: pretentious with book-learning, laden with quotations, parallels, allusions, its psychology amateur, its plot creaking, its characters stereotyped, its text rife with stilted poetastry. When was it ever otherwise? Opera is 'exotic and irrational' by the oft-quoted definition in Johnson's *Dictionary*. Not to jib at *Rigoletto*, *Trovatore*, *La forza del destino*, then to object to the Tippett is to exercise double-standards. Even Wagner is not immune. And most of all, *The Magic Flute*, Tippett's acknowledged prototype – a mishmash of absurdity, fustian, cliché, whose background events and propulsions are never explained, whose foreground mingles highbrow and low wherein ethical solemnities and popular gags jostle side by side, all in doggerel verse; all in all an illogical amalgam that portends deep truths of Enlightenment and integration – it's all pure Tippett. And despite its theatrical viability, as well of course as its manifest musical worth, there's not yet been a staging fully realizing *Marriage*'s range.

Another acknowledged child of *The Magic Flute*, the Strauss/Hofmannsthal *Die Frau ohne Schatten*, is concerned with the same themes and borrows something of the same patterning, treating them with conscious grandeur in a time of universal war. Tippett's manner is miles away from Strauss, yet both operas borrow – purloin – from the Mozart its basic premise: two couples, Royal and Ordinary, in complementary quest for the fullness of mutual understanding without which their love is incomplete, indeed impossible. In Tippett's version the primeval divide between Man and Woman is signified by the resonant quotation prefacing the score – 'You shall say, I am a child of earth and of starry heaven': his aim is to reconcile the opposition, both for the elevated and the prosaic pair. To the latter is also given the go-ahead to propagate, as in Papageno and Papagena's delightful duet when, ordeals surmounted, they anticipate their happy brood. For the royal couple no such outcome is foretold, any more than for Tamino and Pamina. Rather, they remain above the human-animal purpose of carnality, enthroned in exalted, celestial chastity, though the music graphically endorses the text's injunction to go forth and multiply. This was the message of *Die Frau*, and of another wartime opera at the far end of the spectrum, Poulenc's *Les Mamelles de Tirésias* (1944), ostensibly frivolous, yet urging just the same purpose – '*faisons des enfants!*' – upon a world gone mad with destruction.

So *The Midsummer Marriage*'s language of high and low, its imagery of light and dark, come direct from the Mozart: also its setting in a timeless archaic nowhere – for *Zauberflöte* 'Egypt', for the *Marriage* a kind of ancient Greece crossed with loamy West Country England (or maybe the composer's ancestral Cornwall) with something Pan-like, sylphic, dryadic rustling among the rhododendrons. Both settings centre upon a mysterious Temple with mysteriously authoritative Priests – the cult of Isis and Osiris; something undivulged out of Freud, Jung, *The Golden Bough*, George Bernard Shaw, *Peter Pan*, *The White Goddess*, served by a She-Ancient and a He-Ancient, and diverted by a troupe of antique young dancers. Tippett has no Sarastro to head the priestly cult, nor any equivalent to the Queen of the Night: his male authority-figure is the elevated heroine's father King Fisher: business-suited businessman (though armed with a holster and gun) he stands for the modern world, inhabited also by the lowly couple whose quest is equally valid – his young secretary and her mechanic boyfriend. The name King Fisher indicates another important source, Eliot's *Waste Land*, with all its mytho-poetic apparatus behind it: Lord of the sterile terrain who must be sacrificed to give way for the burgeoning younger up-comers who replace him and restore fertility. Madame Sosostris also makes an important guest-appearance from *The Waste Land*'s machinery, though she also owes something to Erda in *The Ring*. And all this is set, as not in Mozart, Strauss, Poulenc, into a framework of perpetually revolving seasons, whose climax is Beltane Fire at the Midsummer solstice.

I cannot give here a detailed account of plot intertwined with music balancing the earlier description of Tippett's Mozartean prototype. To view only landmarks in this long lavish score by no means implies stretches of routine/humdrum/wait-for-it: the level of the material is innately generous, its riches not exceptional. Act I centres upon the high couple's symmetrical seesaw: Jenifer's ascent – 'for me the light! for you the darkness!' – of the musical staircase to her celestial realm – music of extraordinary exaltation: Mark's descent – 'for you the light! for me the dark!' – into the subterranean cave – music of extraordinary vehemence and power. Thence to their rhyming returns, she charged with fierce chastity, he with priapic rising sap; thus precipitating their agon, reversing their trajectories – he up, she down.

Act II concentrates upon the low couple, to which the agon is now transferred – 'she must leap and he must fall on the longest day of all'. Their sexual struggle is mirrored in the turning of the seasons and the processes, at once cruel and inevitable, that ensure renewed fertility. The music is flawless: within a frame of glorious summer evocation come three Ritual Dances wherein is enacted the yearly cycle.

First dance – *The Earth in Autumn*; the hound (female) hunts the hare (male; Strephon): built over a ground-bass (Tippett's saturation in Purcell to the fore) – tense, gapped, purposeful; bare at first, then busy with volatile flute above, articulate horn in the middle; cunning counterpoint full of internal asymmetries and echoes. The chase ever closer, and more perilous for the quarry, who at last unexpectedly escapes capture, briefly jubilates, and vanishes. Dazzle of sunlight; magic music; then preparation-music exactly as before, for second dance – *The Waters in Winter*.

The water invitingly painted in murky low-lying syncopation supporting a sinuous, continuously undulating chromatic figure on muted violas. Strephon-as-fish lunges to the surface – two clarinets, alternating gurgles with obstreperousness. The otter hunts her prey – rich, almost clogged harmony, tense with eroticism. First attempt thwarted; second round, music as before but tightened up a notch: she's nearer, but still fails. The third, though, is a close thing – the fish gets entangled and only escapes with a wrench – the music vividly says ouch! – and his jubilation is marred by the pain. Dazzle of sunlight, then magic music, exactly as before. The preparation, though, is new. Dancers sow a field of spring corn – graceful singing/ swinging two-part writing – Tippett the madrigalist. It invigorates, and cuts off leaving only a high soft chord on four solo violins, held in stasis, start of third dance – *The Air in Spring*; enchantingly delicate spriteliness, when their chord unsticks, for the four violins – Tippett the Vivaldisto. Strephon-the-bird hops about – syncopated pizzicato bass beneath the violins' continuous play – pecking at the new-sown grain. The trees dance a more lyric strain, the bird looks to them as though his nest lies therein; tries to fly, but a wing is broken – the fish's wrench remembered. He falls to the ground, to recurrence of the plangent distress-music heard when his dance was tripped up in the first dance. He lies helpless, all the twitter ceased: miles above the dark, distressful chord, a solitary piccolo softly trills, then rapidly descends in chromatic scale, joined by other woodwinds as brass chokes upwards – the hawk targeting her helpless victim. The little bird manages to hide, the hawk re-ascends. Round 2 as before, intensified and concentrated, hawk hugely more audible and visible. Round 3 same material yet more compacted and threatening: the hawk nearly gets her prey as the stage darkens to near-blackout under the huge shadow of her wings.*

The Summer of the opera's time and place is reserved for Act III. Before it can crown the year, ugly unfinished business must perforce be concluded. Heavy Father King Fisher produces his strongest weapon, Sosostris, 'famed clairvoyante', who sees past, present and future. Her aria, the work's principal set-piece, begins, perhaps, under-par before rising undoubted to a vision of Jenifer alone in paradisal Elysium. But Mark the Lion approaches 'symbol erect' (concession to the times that every lover of the work cherishes). Heavy Father, aghast, smashes the crystal ball whose truth he cannot bear. Huge ensemble, involving the chorus, young low couple and Ancients to the fore, raises tension but resolves nothing. King Fisher strips the clairvoyante's veils to reveal the high pair in mutual contemplation, light and shadow fused: attempting

---

*   The three stages for each season are not literal repeats: the screw is tightened at each with considerable skill. The three symbolism is important too; and the triple return of identical preparation-music becomes wearing if there isn't more in between. The old concert-version of the *Ritual Dances* used to contain them complete but the Tippett Estate has apparently sanctioned only the shortened version and forbidden the whole, perhaps necessarily for the dancers' stamina.

to destroy the forbidden unity he aims his gun, only to crumple in cardiac arrest. Slight sense of stiltedness blown away by the fourth dance, *Fire in Summer*: unlike the three previous it involves voices. Its first half is the opera's love-duet, as Mark and Jenifer open their voices, silent since Act I: its second is fully choral, with the Ancients thrown in too. Music of springy virility in the duet, lithe and lean in dancing polyphony, the Hindemith in Tippett rescued from dryness into sappy warmth. The lovers sing in canon, Mark leading, doubled by horn, Jenifer following, with oboe and clarinet, a virtuoso flute obbligato fluttering florid above (homage to Mozart): all exultant exuberance, leaping with sprung-rhythm elasticity over a busy bass. The words are a sub-Yeatsian invocation of Zodiac figures with a Zenith and a leaping dog (and the lovers are translated into Shiva and Shakti, if you like that kind of thing). Silence tastebuds, open ears and spirit to this glorious affirmative of the marriage of carnal and spiritual, starry heavens and fruitful earth, triumphant and resplendent when the bull is reached – Taurus/Minotaur – 'whose blood and sperm are all, all, all fertility'. Now the second part – *presto* toccata in the strings, long sustained notes on the chorus, extolling sexual love by which humanity is perpetually renewed, turning into divine love by which God's face is perpetually revealed. The lovers' canon praising Love's transfiguring fire is now led by Jenifer, Mark following: the Ancients have another canon to themselves, invoking the heavenly One, the Two, the Three as Paraclete, making 'symbolic union with the Four', etc. What had Tippett been reading? No matter: the music sweeps all before it as the disparate vocal strands coalesce in cries of 'Wonder! Praise!' and bid all to 'Rejoice exceedingly' – Tippett's beloved Handel to the fore – from the chorus; the lovers' solo voices ricochet even more vertiginous and ecstatic. (The low couple have skedaddled unobserved, no doubt to rise and fall to the serious yet delightful business of propagation.)

Aftermath: all ash and emptiness under cold blanched moonlight. Morning after – 'was it a vision, was it a dream?' – the high couple, united in reality, on the fruitful earth after the starry heavens, ready now for the marriage that had been intended for the day itself.

Apparently prosaic, this moment is in fact cue for the magical score's most magical music. Over a hazy bank of low muted strings four unmuted solo violins begin a lark-ascending canon, all-diatonic, fragile and delicate, tender tendrils of new growth, moving high and low, reaching an enhanced C-major into which a slow chorale-like tune on flute and horn softly intrudes, with gently lively counter-subject, subliminally martial, on clarinets, harp on barcarolle-bass, the four violins remaining translucent and decorative on high. The lovely tapestry is broken off twice by the lovers' voices, off-stage and wordless, then resumed as though uninterrupted. The third break is different – they enter from opposite sides, now dressed for their marriage (no more Shiva and Shakti).

Mark sings first, to music from his very first salutation to Jenifer when she'd refused him. Her acceptance now unwithholding and ardent – love so unbounded it could even embrace her father 'had he lived'. This is Midsummer Day: he proffers the wedding-ring; and for reasons that the head wonders at but the heart feels to be in the right place, exultantly sings some lines of Yeats (from *Lapis Lazuli*): 'All things fall and are built again / And those that build them again are gay.' Their friends, the boys and girls of the chorus, are in happy, hopeful, farewell mode, taking up the same words as the sun also rises: another inspired moment, a very original ending: the earlier soft hint of chorale now waxes into a complete chorale-prelude – its model of course the scene with the two armed men in *The Magic Flute*. Initially still soft, with the clarinet march counter-subject and a busy scamper of violins in four parts; this texture broken off, thrice, in mid-flight, by the chorus singing the same tag from Yeats, receding further each time, also broken off in its turn in different places by the orchestra's resumption of the unfolding chorale-prelude. (The stage-directions don't specify: we presume that Mark and Jenifer leave with their companions.) Each orchestral resumption is louder and fuller-scored: last, a great burst of A-major after white-note neutrality – nine bars of glory: long silence: the same nine bars exactly repeated: long silence: a third time (of course); now curtailed and diminishing to leave behind a high, pure, shining A-major on upper woodwinds, a solo trumpet as bass; joined then by mid-to-lower strings; finally the full brass, soft, long-held with swell and ebb. All things fall and are built again; fruitful earth and starry heavens at one.

How to account for the relatively few performances of this incandescent masterpiece. It's an expensive and difficult work, the chorus part especially taxing; and requiring a first-rate troupe of dancers. Productions have been few and dire in all cases I've seen (and the photos of the first) – abjectly failing to match the Vision's profundity and the music's calibre. The shining exception was a television film directed by Elijah Moshinsky for Channel 4 in 1984, whose imaginative sympathy and inventiveness managed to find convincing visual expression for such puzzles as the He- and She-Ancient and a mystic Sorceress who, when unveiled, turns into a lotus flower containing a pair of lovers. The musical performance was very fine, the dances terrific, and the way in the closing stretch the cameras swept over unrolling landscapes of unbounded bounty, in a way no theatre could manage, quite wonderfully fulfilled the work's theme: the audience is literally and metaphorically *transported* by this marvellous affair. Maybe the original requirements for settings, costumes, actions, are unrealizable: but perhaps the best solution of all might be to respect them and carry them out as closely as possible. We don't change the composer's notes (and only a few of the librettist's solecisms!). Moshinsky's version is the completest endorsement yet achieved of *The Midsummer Marriage*'s unique place in the canon of opera, and particularly in the context of the perilous 1940s and anxious 50s when it was conceived and brought to birth and first seen and heard – the finest musical yield of its time.

The Midsummer Marriage opens Tippett's richest period, with three outstanding works of size amid plentiful smaller things – after which, a drastic change of direction that seems to close an epoch. The 2nd Symphony encapsulates, in particular, everything discovered in the opera, without the difficulties and potential hindrances of text and plot; and here and there suggesting already the new directions to come. An incandescent masterpiece and the bloom-time's most lovable blossom: *Fantasia Concertante on a Theme of Corelli*, third in the line of great English works for multi-divided strings (after Elgar then Vaughan

Williams). Tippett's layout is triple – a full body, a smaller body about half the size, a concertante-group of two solo violins and a single cello. The germinal material from Corelli comes in two tempi, stately and lively: their alternation ever-lengthening with ever-enriching embellishment – sometimes so encrusted that the over-fraught vessel can seem in danger of going under, except that control is so sure – occupies the work's first section. Now come three pages of exquisite intensity; a long-drawn singing line on *all* the cellos below a delicate halo of upper strings: then the line goes high, the accompaniment low: a climax urgent yet ample. All this is prelude to the ensuing Fugue, incorporating as it expands – on the full forces with no antiphony – Bach's own fugue on the Corelli-motif. The writing, initially sober, waxes ever more buoyant, florid, virtuosic, airborne, ecstatic, reaching a vibrant fizz of luminous gold dust on high violins, as the Fugue's subjects return below, broad and strong, culminating in a tense-yet-juicy dissonant scrunch, then declining rapidly into the third section: a Pastorale, gradually revealing its affinity with the slow/fast pattern of the Corelli-material, with ever-freshening embellishments, sometimes delicate sometimes ardent sometimes both – a sort of Grinling Gibbons in sound – and ending bright and clear on Corelli's *vivace*. A homage as much to Purcell as to Corelli on his tercentenary (with Bach in the background). Ian Kemp, Tippett's best biographer, calls it his 'perfect' (not his 'greatest') work: 'of no other can it be said that not a note is out of place, not a moment misconceived or miscalculated': and there are many moments and *millions* of notes.

In which the Piano Concerto, final harvest of *The Midsummer Marriage*, can sometimes get bogged down and lost. The first movement is glorious – a continuous effusion of lyricism that never clogs or cloys: Tippett, inspired by a performance of Beethoven's 4th Piano Concerto, wanted the instrument again to *sing* after half a century of percussive writing. Even when growing strenuous, the midsummer magic born of the opera is never lost. The finale is a complete success too – an enormous gigue, now light and dancing, now heavy and clodhopping though always high-spirited; yielding at one point an ampler cantabile episode, at another a gentle pastorale, at the heart an ardent duo for the soloist and the celesta. It's the

middle movement that occasions worry: slow grinding canons, initially bare, then lost in the soloist's jungle of figuration. Here there
is a sense of misconception and miscalculation, of those millions
of notes being out of place. Enormous relief when the keyboard
ceases and the high strings, hitherto silent, release a flight of impassioned apostrophe: the piano replies with wistful demureness: they
exchange five times, and the soloist has the last word. Back to *Corelli*
and the 2nd Symphony for radiant quintessence.

King Priam, Tippett's second opera and next work of size, stands
upon the cusp of a drastic change, in aim, direction, idiom, technique: a determined effort at self-modernization – in effect,
Stravinskyfication – to attain the opposite of his heretofore effusive
lyrical generosity (though there are, as indicated, hints of what's to
come in the sectional construction of the 2nd Symphony's slow
movement and finale). The means and materials are prevalently
blocks of sound, hard-edged, brusque, brutal – lumps and rocks,
fanfares to the fore, percussion prominent, befitting the compressed
presentation of the archaic/tragic/heroic subject, which, being a
given rather than an original tale, also benefits from such telegrammatic curtness. Priam the centre throughout: his crucial choices
compel all the action and almost all the characters, from the initial
decision to have his infant son Paris killed, and his second decision,
seeing and recognizing the youth (rescued and brought up by a
shepherd) encounter his elder brother Hector, to acknowledge him
and bring him to Troy. Well-known consequence – the ten-year war
sparked by the youth's abduction of Helen, wife of Menelaus, King
of Sparta. In the Greek camp their champion Achilles sulks, refusing
to fight, sending his lover Patroclus to represent him. Patroclus is
slain by Hector, Achilles is roused to revenge, Hector is slain in
turn, Paris has to tell their father, Priam dares visit the triumphant
hero and beg Hector's body for decent burial. The plea is granted.
When in turn Paris slays Achilles, Priam is unmoved, waiting in the
promised expectation of his own death at the hands of Achilles' son.

This tight all-male corps is varied, though not loosened, by
the women. Ingeniously and with meaning the three Goddesses,

between whom Paris had also to exercise choice, are identified with
the three female roles: Athene, wisdom, Hector's wife Andromache;
Hera, devotion to house and home, his mother Hecuba; Aphrodite,
erotic love, Helen. Every personage is given his or her instrumental sonority; thus the orchestra also participates in the events as if
its individual sections were characters – the human mosaic enacted
in the musical construction and the sounds that compose it. The
prevailing *tinta* is warfare; barbarous metallic clangour, absolutely
appropriate, dominates almost throughout. It would grow oppressive if the piece were not so short; despite this suitability, the listener
yearns for and welcomes the moments when the composer yields,
to give his old magic its chance, as in Helen's thrilling account of
her conception – Leda ravished by amorous Zeus in guise of a swan.
Lyricism is granted in Achilles' song, accompanied by guitar, of nostalgia for his lost homeland. And, most strikingly, towards the end –
Hermes, messenger of death, come to let the grieving old monarch
know his end – 'he already breathes an air as from another planet';
and the ensuing hymn to music issuing from 'the mirrored world
within' – for 'mirror upon mirror mirrored is all the show'. Flights
and depths like these mitigate the story's harshness and metallic
fatigue of the score's prevailing sound-world.

As the quotations show, Tippett's own libretto is not averse, even
in this mode of clipped telegrams and anger, to cultural allusions.
There are several notoriously clunky lines: 'Divine go-between, that's
who I am,' Hermes announces: 'Stop the world I want to get off'
(itself a quotation of course) in one of the point-the-finger Brechtian
interludes: 'Prince Hector will want his bath the moment he comes
from fighting' from his wife: 'You are not the founding sort' – Priam
to Paris after he's avenged Hector's death. Such moments no more
spoil the telling than the cod-Eliot and actual Yeats in *The Midsummer Marriage*. Nor do they abate in *The Knot Garden*, Tippett's next
opera. On the contrary, quotation and allusion become more and
more central to his way to expressing *himself*.

Meanwhile, two instrumental works born directly from *Priam's*
idiom, methods and sometimes its actual material. The 2nd Piano
Sonata: a compacted volley of some twenty distinct characters and

speeds, mosaically laid edge-to-edge without interaction, development, trajectory: late product of Stravinsky's *Symphonies of Winds*. Still more so in the immediately ensuing *Concerto for Orchestra*, where the implied next step is boldly taken – to have the discrepant materials superimposed as well as juxtaposed. They all are striking, whether direct from or aligned with music from *Priam* or quite new. The first movement shows matter and manner at its clearest and best. Strings are omitted: woodwinds, brasses, harp, piano, percussion are redistributed in small, self-contained ensembles existing initially in spaces of their own, only gradually beginning to impinge upon each other. The movement finds new juxtapositions and superimpositions all the way to its self-elimination on a quizzical question-mark. Answered by a lento giving strings and harp their turn, still rich and ornate in proximity to Corelli and 'The Air in Spring' from the *Marriage*. But the finale, wherein all the forces join, is a cop-out, over-dependent upon wholesale thefts from *Priam*, the material growing mannered and routine.

Which loom ever-larger as Tippett's later works expand in aim and sometimes size – two further oratorios, three further operas, more symphonies, amid other pieces more plentiful than in earlier years. *The Vision of St Augustine* and *The Knot Garden* are yet nearer the heights than the abyss: the oratorio, setting the key-passage from Augustine's *Confessions*, has marvellous moments, including the vision itself and the dizzying *Engelkonzert* concluding Part I, but elsewhere much is grey, opaque, muddy, or else suddenly brassy, triumphalist, trite. The opera is equally uneven: a play of archetypes and couples detaching in search of the better half, posited upon Shakespeare's *Tempest*, the score a mishmash of acute and flaccid, the libretto often cringe-making.

And so it goes, musical calibre in inverse proportion to ambitions and pretensions. Operatic – *The Ice Break* (Soviet labour camps, USA race-riots); *New Year* (something to do with a spaceship from another planet); 3rd Symphony, reversing the *Ode to Joy* concluding Beethoven's 9th in the light of twentieth-century atrocities; 4th Symphony, cradle-to-grave accompanied by the recorded susurration of a heavy sleeper; *The Mask of Time* essaying deep mighty themes at evening-long length with a characteristic welter of texts embracing sublime and ridiculous. All these works yield moments worthy of the earlier triumphs – in the *Mask* the setting of verses from Shelley's *Triumph of Life* with its shattering depiction of the chariot of time and the havoc in its wake; and the work's closing stretch is truly awesome. The Triple Concerto (for string trio with orchestra) alternates arbitrary pitches, material from stock, gesture without substance, abrasion without purpose, with the singing shapeliness of the slow movement, complete with a touch of gamelan. But *Byzantium*, in prospect a marriage made in heaven – Tippett setting late Yeats – in upshot, pure hell: all histrionic mannerism, taxing the heroic soprano soloist to her limits, tormenting the listener as well as the dolphin-torn sea with its all-too-literal gongs.

Tippett's final work, *The Rose Lake* for orchestra, is a return to personality rather than a continuation of mannerism and habit. Touchingly retrospective – a long glance down the years, recovery (however dilute) of youthful lyricism, this evocation of magical rose-tinted waters from dawn to dusk: some new features too – spare airborne heterophony to contrast with the glowing close harmony on the horns, a soft-edged marimba preferred to the boney xylophone, moments of delicate Orientalist coloration suggesting a late liking for Messiaen, even Takemitsu. As so often before, the end is quizzical.

CHAPTER XVI

USA

Four radicals

Charles Ives

Born in 1874 of old English stock into deepest New England: principal influence for whole life his father, local musician of unconventional fibre, training his son in traditional and unusual music techniques in a fertile ambience of popular demotic Americana – hymns, ragtime, parlour-songs, dance-music, theatre-music, brass-bands – the very stuff of his son's mature output, however transfigured. Studied, more normally, Yale 1894–8: church organist 1889–92; out of sympathy with what it required. Abandoned this 1902 for Insurance, pursued with flair and success for his entire middle life, retiring 1930, while simultaneously composing with ardour and intensity and total isolation some of the most daring musical adventures ever undertaken. Major heart attack 1918: downcast by the Great War and the way his country tended after it; virtual abandonment of composition after *c*.1920. Despite neglect and mockery, began to self-publish writings on music, as well as his music itself; occasional isolated performances in the 1930s of works conceived and written before the war a revelation to younger generations of American modernists: as dissemination and understanding spread it grew clear that his experiments and conceptions, frequently achieving their goal, anticipated many post-war developments in technique and – usually – surpassed them in artistic content.

The packed two-and-a-half decades of compositional activity are fraught with incompletions, alternatives, botches, still being sorted long after his death in 1954. The output's principal categories are songs and choral music, piano and chamber works, and works for orchestra with or without voices. 'Specimen Days' from all these.

SONGS

A continuous production from his teens onward, background to the explosion of major undertakings in his hectic years and often their initiating nucleus. As well as the celebrated self-publication in 1922 of *114 Songs*, many others remained uncollected. Their range is remarkable: sentimental parlour-ditties à la Stephen Foster; scraps of nostalgia, droll humour, whimsies, ribaldries, mostly to his own words; hymn-settings; languid *mélodies* to French texts; sometimes attractive German *Lieder* (including an *Ich grolle nicht* in the teeth of Schumann's); snatches of Latin and Italian; fragments from the English poets – Milton, Cowper, Byron, Keats, Wordsworth, Shelley, Browning, Tennyson, Arnold, Meredith, up to Kipling and *Grantchester*; fragments from American poets – Whittier, Longfellow, Whitman, and plentiful poetastry; pieces of uplift – *Majority*, *Lincoln the Great Commoner*, '*Nov. 2 1920*', as chunky and rebarbative as, elsewhere, soft, dreamy, traditional. Two must represent the whole. They're antithetical: *Remembrance*, a nine-bar miniature, its superscription from Wordsworth – 'the music in my heart I bore / Long after it was heard no more' – exactly fits the composer's own text – 'A sound of a distant horn, o'ershadowed lake is borne, my father's song' – compacted together in a loving evocation of the principal figure in his life: piano on luminous open fifths, delicately grounding into tonic major, voice on lyric horn-call, piano taking it up in canon, broken off at the paternal word to end on a haze of redolent dissonance fading away into past and loss. *General William Booth Enters into Heaven* (1914, but not included in the 1922 *114*): Vachel Lindsay's poem *made* for Ives's gamut of styles as, too, for his concerns religious and humane: hearty and raucous – 'Booth led boldly with his big bass drum'; revival songs – cries of Hallelujah! constantly breaking in; widely variegated intonations for the motley crowds who follow their Salvation Army General, grotesque

and distorted for 'lepers, lurching bravoes, drabs and drug-fiends'
etc., the scum of the cities; flagrant razzmatazz for 'big-voiced lassies'
with their banjos – 'tranced, fanatical, they shrieked and sang "Are
you washed in the blood of the Lamb?"' The riotous procession
quietens as Jesus appears extending his hands in welcome: Booth
notices not, 'but led his queer ones / Round and round' – round
and round the words repeat in spell-bound intoxication: and as
the scum are redeemed, 'clad in raiment new', their crooked limbs
straightened, their blind eyes 'opened on a new sweet world', the
same question – 'Are you washed in the blood of the Lamb?' – is re-
asked: a visionary human-scape worthy of Stanley Spencer. These
two songs, at each edge of Ives's range, contain by implication the
greatness of his art.

CHORAL

From the Steeples and the Mountains (1901): extreme instance of
the composer's experimental daring, at its most mechanized and
complex, devoted to encapsulate a metaphysical challenge – 'from
the Steeples – the Bells! – then the Rocks on the Mountain begin
to shake!' – originating in actual sonorous experience – equidistant
belfries, marching bands. A technical description of this four-minute
piece takes four pages of specialist description in David Nicholls'
excellent book on *American Experimental Music*; here's a summary.
Four sets of bells, two in C-major, treble and bass; one in B-major,
treble; one in Db-major, bass. They enter successively, each sustaining its lowest note while the next descending scale starts; they then
launch into a canon involving elaborate contracting rhythmic
values: this process is now reversed, the values expanding, the pitches
gradually altering into traditional campanological patterns – result,
'extreme polyphonic complexity and motivic duality'. Thus the background: foreground, a single trumpet and a single trombone, initially in aggressive/exultant fanfares before launching their own
canon entirely unrelated to the materials and processes of the bell-
machine, jagged and penetrating, ultra-dissonant, at once ferocious
and celebratory. They now are subjected to an unusual version of

retrograde – bar-by-bar reverse order, each bar in itself as at first time, with free material between each completed phrase. The two simultaneous processes, bells and brass, complete, total madness – the bells, *fff*, jangle and glissade and tremolando on the discrepant major sevenths of their diatonic scales, the two brasses ululate in frenzy, ending in barbaric chromatic yawp, trumpet descending trombone arising, before a sort-of cadence on an octave C as the bells, with a hint of Big Ben, reach sort-of cadences in several sort-of keys. Forty-eight bars, four minutes of ultra-organization sounding like pure Bedlam in a Belfry, yet unforgettably achieving its visual/auditory physical/metaphysical goal. Rather than his *Bell-Tower*, the literary equivalent might be Melville's *Cock-a-Doodle-Do!* Alas Ives never took on Melville, who transcends all the Transcendentalists rolled into one.

PIANO

Amid an output including another sizeable sonata and many smaller things, frequently crucibles for subsequent orchestral pieces, the *Concord Sonata* stands out, for length, difficulty, grandeur of aim, range of idiom and expression, and the sheer hugeness of its reach. It preoccupied Ives continuously from near the start to near the end, originating in an orchestral triptych devoted to some revered New England figures – the Alcotts (from 1904), Emerson (from 1907), Hawthorne (1910): the finale, Thoreau, originates in a song-setting. He tinkered, enhanced, enriched, ever anew – 'this is the only piece which every time I play it or turn to it, seems unfinished.' As indeed it still remains. The upshot, that there can never be an ultimate version, foretells the aleatoric strain in the post-1945 avant-garde. One can hear something of this divine discontent in the unspeakably vivid hilarity and pathos of the fragments recorded by the composer in various sessions 1933–43, where he pounds, bangs, shouts, groans, curses and plays with inimitable idiosyncrasy and freedom.

First movement, *Emerson* – 'America's deepest explorer of the spiritual immensities' – is the most daunting – crag, chunk, crisis, crash, ultra-dissonance, sometimes remitting into clear clean diatonicism,

sometimes contrasting with luminous openness or simple plainness, and for one magic moment joined by a solo viola, towards
the gently shining close after all the enraged ecstatic raving. No. 2:
Hawthorne – 'trying to suggest some of his wilder, fantastical adventures into the half-child-like, half-fairy-like phantasmal realms': a
volatile scherzo, melting down to a recitativo accompanied by soft
black-note clusters, and one climactic all-white, to be played 'by
using a strip of board 14¾ inches long', before deliquescing again
into uncapturable fleetness, then inward hymnody, then a touch
of Ives's favourite band-music, then ragtime, moments of violence,
of withdrawal, of humour, daintiness, further volubility – cascades
ending very soft till sudden, explosive, concluding spasm. No. 3: *The
Alcotts* – a domestic scene, the family at home in Orchard House in
Concord Village itself, suggestive to the composer of 'that common
virtue lying at the height and root of all the Concord divinities'. At
its heart, the 'little old spinet-piano' on which one of the sisters used
to try at Beethoven's 5th – whose opening, already galumphingly
interjected throughout *Emerson*, is used now with pious inwardness (as never in the original) from the very start and thence on,
swelling 'in a gradually excited way' to a massive climax, relaxing
to a sweet parlour-song, opening out into this not-so-good movement's best passage, lyric-free dissonant counterpoint, building
to another over-grandiose climax on Beethoven's iconic four-note
figure. Finale: *Thoreau* – a day in the life of the hermit of Walden
Pond – 'an autumn day of Indian summer': contemplation, activity,
observation, sense-impressions – 'the faint sound of the Concord
bell – "tis prayer-meeting night in the village': dusk – 'the poet's flute
is heard out over the pond . . . is it a transcendent tune of Concord?'
Back to the cabin by moonlight 'with a strange liberty in Nature,
a part of herself'. Perhaps the sonata's best movement, certainly its
most appealing; reclusive and tranquil after the muscle-strain, the
exhausting quicksilver, the torpid sentiment, of its three predecessors, though not eschewing Ives's habitual heat-up-to-boiling-point
followed then by balmy decline and fall, the flute joining, its pastoral
air including the Beethoven notes, ending with their first three, re-
echoed after it's ceased in the piano's almost inaudible close.

Redoubtable: a bit of an ordeal to hear, which can be transformative/transcendental but also can be merely draining. Vindication of its composer's intention is curiously brought about by hearing the extremely accomplished transformation into a *Concord Symphony* by Henry Brant. One'd think the original cries out for orchestral treatment: it indeed does: but then, returning to the piano in all its limitations, strains, cussèdness is to recognize that it must be thus: cussèdness is its blessing, strain its nature, limitations its liberations. Listen again to Charles Ives proving this himself with fistfuls of wrong/right notes, infectious vigour, wild abandon, glee, fury, snatches of irrepressible singing and shouting – a lifeline to New England's greatest son. Then hear his incomparable way, voiceless yet singing, with *The Alcotts* complete – the best case for this movement.

CHAMBER-MUSIC

Many fascinating and successful experiments for various combinations of instruments, as always often overlapping with song and orchestra-movements. Principal landmark the 2nd String Quartet (1911–13): the 1st, from Ives's college-days, a relatively tame affair, fluent and unexceptionable, recognizable only in its use, already, of hymns and popular songs. Odd that its opening fugue on 'From Greenland's Icy Mountains' was adapted virtually unaltered for the third movement of the 4th Symphony, where the new context of undaunted boldness renders it incongruous, even absurd. The 2nd Quartet is a reaction against any such conventionality. He'd had enough of polished gentility in the medium – 'too much of an emasculated art ... the same old even-vibrations, sybaritic apron-strings, keeping music too much tied to the old ladies'. Here is the distinctly nasty antidote to such perceived niceness: i) four men discuss; ii) they argue; iii) they make it up 'then walk up the mountain-side to view the firmament'. This naïve programme is too easily obeyed – alternating banal harmoniousness with truly ugly dissension, parody of sweetness and expressiveness (including an *andante emasculata* – surely unique in music?), a standard Ivesian visionary ending. His own view – 'one of the best things I have' – is hard to endorse: the piece perhaps finds its fulfilment in a later 2nd Quartet – Elliott Carter's, where the idea of four characters in conflict and togetherness is taken to its ultimate.

ORCHESTRAL WORKS

To the mountain-tops: Ives is almost consistently at his greatest in his orchestral works. *The Unanswered Question* and *Central Park in the Dark*, both of 1906, originally intended as a diptych for full strings and a handful of other instruments. The *Question* – 'the perennial question of existence' – is posed by a solo trumpet, repeating the same five-note phrase in two near-identical versions (slightly different rhythmic alignments; and the final pitch varies) seven times: four flutes – 'fighting Answerers' – interject six times, each slightly faster and more insistent, dissonance to the fore; after their fifth and loudest yet they settle on a low soft four-semitone cluster, the trumpet interposing his sixth Question, before skittering off in *presto molto agitando con fuoco* ending in a piercing shriek: then the trumpet's last, still Unanswered. Unmoved and unmoving, constant from start to finish, muted strings hold 'the silence of the Druids' in plain white-note counterpoint, a distant recall of the *Heiliger Dankgesang* in Beethoven's A-minor String Quartet op. 132. The programme is naïve, the metaphysics infantile if sufficient, the music unforgettable.

Central Park is more specific: Ives's note details 'a picture-in-sounds of nature and of happenings that men would hear some thirty or so years ago (before the combustion engine and radio monopolized the earth and air) [Heaven knows how he'd do it a further century and more on], when sitting on a bench in Central Park on a hot summer night': and goes on to recall 'the night sounds and silent darkness', represented by strings, interrupted by the distant Casino, street-singers, late carousers, the El, a parade, news-boys crying next day's papers, pianolas 'having a ragtime war', a street-car, a fire-engine, a runaway cab-horse. 'Again the darkness is heard – an echo over the pond – and we walk home.' As naïve in its pictorialism as *Question* in its 'philosophy', and again realized to perfection in the notes: string backdrop is here harmony not counterpoint – patterned intervallic construction, thirds, fourths, fifths, over a very-slow-moving four-note ground-bass: a clarinet talks, a flute chatters, joined by an oboe, a solo violin floats far above, the piano(la) begins its ragtime, the clarinet repasses; then all three woodwinds plus keyboard liven the tempo, trombone and bassoon lurch in, a second piano sets up a contradictory rhythm, piccolo then trumpet join the scrum, then high and bass drums. They all accelerate all the way, getting completely out of synch, and explode *con fuoco* with a final cymbal-clash. The strings have sustained their slow circulating pattern without break or acceleration or crescendo and are left thus doing when the interruptions break off. It does truly seem, now, that 'the darkness is heard'.

These two brief, linked pieces are perfectly fashioned. Ives's longer orchestral works have their problems, occasionally fundamental, sometimes miraculously (re)solved. The first three symphonies (1898/1900–1902) are 'pre-Ives' – Dvořák and Brahms with hymn tunes and populist elements: then *Robert Browning Overture* (1908–12) is a mixed bag. Also from his maturity come two *Orchestral Sets* that form its crown; then come the fantastic but desperately uneven 4th Symphony and the long-brooded *Universe Symphony*.

And, first, another composite work whose individual numbers come to constitute a symphony – four self-contained tone-pictures evoking *New England Holidays*, in their seasonal festive order. Winter; *Washington's Birthday* (1909) follows a familiar journey – rapt remote stillness, bells, sudden close-up/close-in to raucous barn dance, fade into nostalgic haze of parlour-song. The daring complexity of the metrical and melodic superimpositions beggars belief – the Jew's harp! – the Breughelian relish! Spring; *Decoration Day* (1912): same trajectory – 'O come all ye Faithful', bells, a *sotto voce* processional, suddenly full-frontal in circus garishness; the recession into distance brief then abrupt. Summer; *Fourth of July* (1913) – same trajectory, textures and treatment yet more abandoned, bold aggressive proclamation of popular tunes against raving black mesh of backdrop. Autumn; *Thanksgiving* (1904) – grim severity to commence, hymns, not marches or dances – 'God of our Fathers' – coalescing into a thick grinding jelly, thinning via bells to a delicate flute solo, then tender-loving strings. Sudden lively barn dance, soon eradicated by returning celestial tenderness; a touch of lumpy granitic grandeur introduces the actual choir in a plain hymn against jubilant tintin-nabulation, then the evocation fades away into a golden past with promise of a rosy future as Spring comes round again. In all four *Holidays* it's as though Ives were sonorously 'photographing' the communal festivities from within the epicentre of their hurly-burly activity, while simultaneously seeing/hearing them from a solitary viewpoint over the hill and far away.

First Orchestral Set: Three Places in New England (1903–14). First, *The 'St. Gaudens' in Boston Common (Col. Shaw and his Colored Regiment)*. St Gaudens is the sculptor of the monument to the black soldiers and their commander in the Civil War. Superscription: '. . . the drum-beat of the common-heart / In the silence of a strange and / Sounding afterglow / Moving – Marching – Faces of Souls' – part of a near-nonsensical invocation to Destiny and Freedom. Rapt bitter-sweet strings with fragments of solo woodwinds and occasional shine-twinkle of piano – curiously Delius-y (a radical modernist Delius) – over barely perceptible hint of drum-taps on double basses, whose suggestion of march-music gradually reaches the surface, eventually explicit, building to huge C-major climax, then long exquisite fade into distance.

Second, *Putnam's Camp* – the old military quarters of Revolution-ary times, explored by a young boy a century or so later on a Fourth of July outing, wandering off alone, experiencing a fantasy of men marching, a vision of Liberty as a sorrowful pleading woman, sensing the approach of another band with different tunes and pulse. In-yer-face raucousness of superimposed soldiers' tunes, and curiously debonair snatches of 'trio' amid the gay mayhem. Fade into stasis for the Vision. Ives's gradual insinuation of the alternative march-rhythm is still one of the most celebrated wonders of American – and indeed of all – early twentieth-century music: the combination, and eventual crushing–melding together, remain spine-tingling as the historic fantasy-event passes its 250th anniversary: it culminates in incendiary bedlam and a hard shining all-black-note cluster.

Third, *The Housatonic at Stockbridge*, recalls a walk along the river one summer Sunday morning soon after Ives married his wife, Harmony, with the close proximity of the water and the distant sound of the congregation in church: '...the mists had not entirely left the river and the colors, the running water, the banks and trees, were something that one would always remember.' Intricate, iridescent mesh of decorative figures diatonic and chromatic on upper strings, over deep, slow-moving resonance bass/base, snatches of hymn-tune and song-melody (used later to actually set the poem prefacing this movement in the score – an awful affair by one Robert Underwood Johnson – 'contented river! in thy dreamy realm – the cloudy willow and the plumy elm', etc., etc.). The hymn and the song coalesce into long generous curving contours, the mists rise, the waters sparkle, the cantabile gathers strength and body: its combination heats up into a sustained climax so choking and convulsive one would call it orgasmic were not Ives so decidedly not, even on his honeymoon, an erotic artist.

Three Places is perfect; a masterpiece: the *Second Orchestral Set* (1909 onwards, with as always plentiful re-use of older material) is only a rung or so below. First, *Elegy to Our Forefathers*: Ives's habitual beauteous shining blur, superimposing fragments of tune upon a polyrhythmic/polytonal haze of strings, bells, piano: here, the familiar texture forms the substance of the entire movement. Second, *The Rock-strewn Hills Join in the People's Outdoor Meeting*, provides what the *Elegy* had omitted – a disjunct blues, other dance-strains, jerking over and across each other, ever more syncopated and rude: then cheery extrovert ragtime. Third, *From Hanover Square North, At the End of a Tragic Day, The Voice of the People again Arose*. News of the *Lusitania*'s sinking by a German submarine, May 1915, gradually infiltrating rush-hour crowds in New York City: a nearby organ-grinder's 'In the Sweet By and By' taken up piecemeal by the commuters as the tidings spread. Broader spans than usual, and less dependent on literal use of the demotic source; which, when it bursts in in full is overwhelming – just the one snatch suffices, before the scene fades away into the bye and bye.

The 4th Symphony is Ives's summa, occupying him, in between

other endeavours of the explosion-years, between 1909 and 1916: its
third movement dating back to the 1st String Quartet of 1896. His
programme poses 'the searching questions of "What?" and "Why?"
which the spirit of man asks of life': the first movement asks, the
succeeding three 'are the diverse answers in which existence replies'.
The hymn forming the first movement's goal – 'Watchman, tell us
of the night, what its signs of promise are' actually contains two
Questions – Watchman, what of joy or hope? then – desiring the
Glory-beaming star heralding the Promised day of Israel – dost
thou see its beauteous ray? The entire hymn is sung by the chorus,
clear and sturdy after a rich interweave of other hymnody and
fragments of wholly distinct older pieces, the overall mix serene
and lovely.

Blown away by the 'comedy' (his word) that ensues, in its welter
of quotations – hymns, marches, ragtime and barn-dance, popular
and patriotic songs – what? and why? indeed – superimposed upon
underlying material from the *Hawthorne* movement of the *Concord
Sonata*, now associated with 'The Celestial Railroad,' Hawthorne's
wry/ironic 1843 modernization of *Pilgrim's Progress*, wherein allegorical places and personages from Bunyan are tweaked into their
opposite – the Slough of Despond conveniently bridged, Apollyon
transmogrified into an engine and harnessed to pull the train, the
Hill Difficulty tunnelled, debris from there used to fill up the Valley
of Humiliation, and so forth. At the gently bitter climax, the steam-
ferry across the ultimate River of Death affrights its passengers into
turning back: only two poor pilgrims who've trudged the whole
path on foot, mocked at every stage, can cross to receive welcome
on the far side by a multitude of Shining Ones. A seething maelstrom of polymetric, polytonal superimpositions, with brief remis-
sions of sweet hymnody, a final orgy of noise; one of its composer's
most sensational successes. Complete contrast in the ensuing Fugue,
for Ives here 'an expression of the reaction of life into formalism
and ritualism'. One wonders if this had been his intention back in
1896? An Unanswered Question. Undoubted, the incongruity in its
new context, and the music's dull mediocrity, un-enlivened by poly-
anything, or the ghost of parody; its sole quotation, from Handel,

pious uplift rather than gladsome liberation for all its *Joy to the World*. The finale is on-track again: whatever one may think of the composer's explanation – 'an apotheosis of the preceding content, in terms that have something to do with the reality of existence and its religious experience', this marvellous music takes the listener wordlessly (even when the chorus join, they hum without text) into places that only music can express. A percussion continuo commences, persists throughout, and continues after pitched material – on full orchestra, on humming voices, on a distant 'choir' of solo violins and harp – has come and gone.

The *Universe Symphony* is Ives's furthest fling into the fundamental Questions and into futurity. Sketches date back as far as, possibly 1908, certainly 1911; he continued for a few more years, abandoned it, resumed several times in his long silent 'retirement', and continued to toy with it until shortly before his death. The work remains sketchy and fragmentary, thus joining some other ambitious Unfinisheds, all very different – Bruckner's 9th, Mahler's 10th, Elgar's 3rd. A more direct comparison – again, differences notwithstanding – lies in two exactly contemporary parallels: the overweening reach of Schoenberg's *Jakobsleiter* and Scriabin's *Mysterium* – gigantic conceptions with aims unrealized and unrealizable (and, in Schoenberg's case, also toyed with right up to the end). Ives's ambitions are woolly, portentous and explicit:

> an attempt in tones, every form or position known or unknown (to me) as the eternities are unmeasured, as the sources of universal substances are unknown, the earth, the waters, the stars, the ether, yet these elements as man can touch them with hand and microscope and label them as chemicals and atoms, as the eternal motions, life of things and man, their bulk, their destiny. They are not single and exclusive strains, but incessant myriads, for ages ever and always changing, growing, but in ages ever always a permanence – humans of the earth of a man's lifetime, of life and death and future life – the only known is the unknown, the only hope of humanity is the unseen spirit – what can't be done but what reaching out to do (as we feel like

trying it) is to cast eternal history, the physical universe of all humanity past, present and future, physical and spiritual, to cast them a 'universe of tones'.

Phew!

A recording of a pioneering realization of Ives's sketches indicates orchestras A to G: the Heavens have the first four; the Life-pulse the fifth, the Earth and Rock Formations the sixth, an Earth-chord comes last. All gradually coalesce to embody *Past* – from Chaos, formation of Waters and Mountains: *Present* – Earth and the Firmament, evolution in Nature and Humanity: *Future* – rise of all to the Spiritual. Each orchestra has its own rhythm on mainly unpitched percussion (more than twenty players required). Pitched material is slow to occur and unrecognizable in melodic contour and harmonic character: the entire duration of some forty minutes is a murmurous buzz of soft sonority, overheard rather than heard, without anchor or lighthouse or harbour – a backdrop only. The would-be impressed – in fact, frustrated – listener cries out in vain for a safety-line in the pacific wastes – a hymn-tune, a barn-dance, a snatch of *The British Grenadiers* or the composer's favourite *Columbia, The Gem of the Ocean*. This latest and last of Ives's astounding oeuvre transcends all such worldly aids. Perhaps his final wish concerning it, touching equally in generosity and humility, might yet be fulfilled, if a fearless spirit would dare provide the missing foreground to this suggestive sound-sheet: 'in case I don't get around to finishing this, somebody might like to work out the idea.'

Carl Ruggles

Born 1876 into remote Massachusetts fishing-community; mother sang, boy folk-fiddled: moving nearer to Boston, violinist in theatre-bands, studying music and other subjects, writing songs: 1908 married Charlotte, an accomplished, homely contralto; humble teaching posts: 1912 to New York, remaining there till 1938, gradually achieving his tiny yet mighty oeuvre, endlessly revised and perfected, ceasing altogether after Charlotte's death 1957, turning freer and more fluent to painting. Moved to the country 1943 till his own death 1971.

The yield's first-fruit is lost beyond recall – prolonged work as late as 1923 on an opera after *The Sunken Bell*, the Hauptmann play that fascinated several prominent composers in Europe, including Ravel, only Respighi's taken to fulfilment. Ruggles' first survivor is indeed tiny – *Toys* (1919) – a song with piano for his son Micah's fourth birthday. Father's own text offers the little boy 'painted ships … and floats, way up to the stars'. Shot through with tender affection, these sixteen bars are anything but child-friendly: angular vocal line, many cruel intervals, ending in the stars on a soft high B♮, no melody whatsoever: piano-part intricate and intensely dissonant, albeit luminous and opening out into airborne radiance for the floating upwards. Obvious already that, after a youth replicating the very minor songs of Robert Franz (a German near-contemporary of Schumann who survived to nearly outlive Brahms), this composer, now in his forties, will not brook compromise.

Early 1920s he projected a symphony – *Men/Angels/Sun-treader* – abandoned as such; all these titles used separate and subsequent. First, *Angels* (1921), a brief hymn for six trumpets, arranged later for more conventional brass sextet and for organ: the essence of Ruggles at his gentlest and most ecstatic; the consistently dissonant idiom shines at first, burns up to a white-hot climax, subsides into an altered return of the opening, extended, transfigured, to close on a quiet hypnotic dazzle – sacramental, as if blessing a nuptials celestial not human. Before the other mooted titles reappear comes *Vox clamans in deserto* (1923), three songs (four further were started then abandoned), setting the expected Whitman and Browning and a forgotten poet of the period, one David Meltzer. Browning's *Parting at Morning* – 'Round the cape of a sudden came the sea, / And the sun looked over the mountain's rim: / And straight was a path of gold for him, / and the need of a world of men for me.' Meltzer's *Son of Mine*, cry of a dying father to his absent boy in defiance of their final parting. Whitman's *A Clear Midnight*:

This is thy hour, O soul, thy free flight into the wordless,
Away from books, away from art, the day erased, the
   lesson done,
Thee fully forth emerging, silent, gazing, pondering the
   themes thou lovest best,
Night, sleep, death and the stars.

These deeply self-revealing choices induce Ruggles at his tenderest: *Vox clamans* is his most refined/delicate/intimate work, very
beautiful, no hint of the strain, overreach, musculature, macho-
aggro, defiant exaltation, that characterizes most of his music from
now on.

Like *Men and Mountains*. *Men* dates in its first version back to
1920; first in a triptych completed some years later; second comes
Lilacs, third, *Marching Mountains*. 'Great things are done when men
and mountains meet / This is not done by jostling in the street' –
Blake's words preface the score of *Men*, a 'Rhapsodic Proclamation' which says – shouts – it all: rugged muscular rhetoric, jagged
contours, orchestration thickly doubled though never clotted, dense
chromatic polyphony, high dissonance-level – the first bar *ff crescendo* plus *sffz* brass already throws four simultaneous consecutive minor ninths into your face, 'harmonizing' two melodic notes
three-octaves-reinforced, adding the next two chromatic steps – then
everything rumbles into the deeps, everything always on a short
fuse; one brief passage of plangent lyric intensity, a coruscating
close. *Lilacs*, however, is all lyricism: fragrance redolent and saturated: strings only, thirty bars of supercharged intoxication without
drink or drugs – purified, idealized, angelic: the comparison might
be with Delius at his most rapt, with the temperature turned up.
Marching Mountains sublimates the march-character; less improvisatory, more rhythmic though never regular; grows more emphatic –
a huge boil-up and, unusual *bei* Ruggles, a medium-quiet end of
relative repose. *Portals* (1926) for strings only – 'what are those of the
known, but to ascend and enter the unknown? And what of life but
for death?' – Unanswered Questions from Whitman: again intense,
angular, dissonant lines striving effortlessly up, tumbling heavily

down, alternating with tender *Lilacs* – like pools of reflection and meditation. Which win out in the exquisite close, a twelve-note chord built, note-by-note, into a luminous cloud more Wordsworth than Whitman – 'the light that never was' – even Henry Vaughan, had Ruggles known him.

Sun-treader (late 1920s) – third title from the projected three-movement Symphony, now a free-standing movement, at about fifteen minutes his longest and finest, in effect a symphony com-pressed into one. Its superscription is from Browning – 'Light and Life be thine forever'. Familiar, the jagged vaunting proclamation; new, to have it over thudding drum-beats, recurring twice during the music's course, and a third time, more subdued, near the end. Between, upward-furling florid contours of impassioned chromatic melody/polyphony, stretching strings to the limits of tessitura and brass to the limits of athletic stamina; and vases of delicacy, chamber-music within the enormous orchestra, tender as *Vox clamans*, fragrant as *Lilacs*, till knocked for six by the next tense-wrought climax. 'Dissonant Counterpoint' (the term will soon be defined) at its apogee, sometimes gaunt and naked, sometimes enmeshed in density, always *sounding* – no 'wrong notes' in this perpetual 'total chromatic'. Compare 12-tone Schoenberg with its unresolved pitch-deafness. Ruggles' notes are *right*: he gave every one his 'test of time' – his riposte when a friend, Henry Cowell, wondered at his spending hours and hours bashing out the same chord at the piano.

Which is the instrument for his next: *Evocations* – '4 chants for piano', the first commenced 1934, completed 1937; next two 1940–41; another 1943; tinkering on into the mid-1950s ('the test of time' indeed), after he'd made an orchestration, in which form these gnomic utterances – miniatures characteristically alternating, luminous and opaque, strenuous and assertive, limpid and resonat-ing, are best enjoyed. *Organum* (1944 and onwards) shows him back on terrific form: for full orchestra from the start, all the power and punch of *Sun-treader*, compacted and straightened out; ingredients as before; new, the forthright rhythmic simplicity at the shining moment towards the end and at the succession of fourteen mighty chords, in contrary motion, crescendo, filling out the actual close.

After *Organum* composition dries and painting takes over. Just one more piece, completely otherwise; a four-square hymn in memory of Charlotte the year after her death. Text unspecified: it fits best with 'O God our help in ages past': simple, Quaker-plain, with only the occasional strange passing pang to remind one of his previous idiom, culminating in a scrunch on the tune's highest note that, at first almost offensively eccentric, lingers in the memory as peculiarly apt and just – the 'right wrong note' without Satie's/Stravinsky's *désagréable* sarcasm.

Ruth Crawford

Born 1901: early piano-lessons; to Chicago 1921 to study composition; deep absorption in the music and mysticism of Scriabin; *Music for Small Orchestra*, 1926; *Three Chants*, 1930. Vital impact of Henry Cowell, personally and through his remarkable and influential book *New Musical Resources* (much discussed before its eventual publication, 1930). To New York to study with Cowell's teacher and inspirer Charles Seeger, proponent of 'Dissonant Counterpoint' – a concept and practice so crucial to all the composers in this chapter, whether or not they knew of its formulation, that it requires a brief pause for definition. 'Dissonant Counterpoint' is a development from and complement to the traditions of Western counterpoint culminating in J. S. Bach: it seeks by way of negative regulations – sevenths and ninths instead of octaves, tritones instead of tonic/dominant/subdominant fourths and fifths – to reinvigorate usages perceived to be weary if not indeed moribund. Curiously analogous to and roughly contemporary with Schoenberg's 'composition with 12 tones related only to one another', which also attempted to build upon a past perceived as passé and give it a new lease of life. There's an air of rivalry to Seeger's concept – Europe's version still tradition-bound, the New World's version harbinger of a radical new start.

Ruth Crawford travelled to Europe 1930–31 to make contact with its new impulses: they and *New Musical Resources* and Seeger's teaching produce an immediate and remarkable flowering – *Three Songs* (1930–32), String Quartet (1931), in which year she and Seeger

married: married into a vital, pulsating, modernist scene, politics
to the left, *totalement engagé* – *Two Ricercari* with stridently committed texts – 'music is a weapon in the class struggle'. The couple
moved to Washington 1935: from hence on the radical aims and
idiom divert into a more accessible populist style – folksong-based
pieces and plentiful arrangements for children, including four of her
own. Return to something of her previous impulse in an attempted
synthesis – a *Suite for Wind Quintet* (1952) only a flicker of what
might have been; she died of cancer the next year.

The oeuvre, like Ruggles', is tiny, every item brief, the best of
it dense in specific gravity, potent as radium. A Violin Sonata of
1926 foreshadows – tough, fighting, no holds barred. *Music for
Small Orchestra* (same year) already delivers: the first movement
begins with tolling harp and piano – rocking obsession, over which
suavely expressive melodic lines gradually uncoil and unfurl: the
music breathes, swelling towards top of curve and down; rocking
becomes a wailing bird – piano ostinato, dark cor anglais – silence,
deep tolling: a New World echo of Busoni's *Berceuse élégiaque*. No.
2 begins with bright chirrupy flute solo plus chip-chop accompaniment, acceleration to a stop: chuckling bassoon; over it, rapid accumulation of busier, more complex shapes, rising to genial-machine
climax and cut-off: third go, piano ostinato, then brief dense-shining
chords; end, a wry shrug of the shoulders. The whole completely
assured and itself.

Three Chants – the unaccompanied chorus sing in an invented
language to equivalate to the *Bhagavadgita: To an Unkind God*; *To an
Angel*; *To a Kind God*. Astonishing command of absolutely original
choral textures inspired by the chants, humming, heterophony of
the East, to end on a total-chromatic cluster, prefiguring such diverse
later exploration of vocal magic as Messiaen's *Cinq rechants*, Stockhausen's *Stimmung*, Ligeti's *Lux aeterna*. *Piano Study in Mixed Accents*,
1931: all-unison, its forebear the finale of Chopin's Bb-minor Sonata:
within the unbroken stream of bright brittle octaves, a fiendishly
complex constructivistic scheme, all done in eighty-three seconds.

Three Songs, to poems of Carl Sandburg, come in an odd layout:
to the centre the concertanti, soprano and equally prominent

solo oboe, piano, unpitched percussion ensemble; to the rear, two ostinati groups, one of five winds the other a small string group, which though indicated as optional are really indispensable to the work's unique sonority. *Rat Riddles*: percussion susurrates, scratches, itches; oboe and voice intertwine; the combination bound together by a transparent piano-part. The wind and string ostinati interject almost inaudible cluster-chords never deviating from rhythmic unison, usually one at a time, sometimes in pairs or triplets, just once five in succession. Sandburg's rather fey text – 'Who do you think you are, and why is a rat? Where did you sleep last night, and why do you sneeze on Tuesdays?' – is absorbed in the intricate purposeful texture with its uncanny sense of running on an altogether alien clockwork, detached, even indifferent, even when minatory – 'and why is the grave of a rat no deeper than the grave of a man?' Unanswered riddles: Unanswerable. *Prayers of Steel*: a frightening modernization of 'batter my heart'; 'Lay me on an anvil, O God – let me be the girders, the great nail, holding a sky-scraper together': strange masochistic/masonic urge, transformed into an image of power-wielding rather than victimized suffering. The piano comes in spasmodic quintuplets four octaves thick, the oboe whitters in ugly *moto perpetuo*, the voice utters a tense low-lying parlando, rising only to the two settings of 'great nail' (the entire poem is set twice). The string ostinato now and then, always in octaves; the wind ostinato in intermittent *staccato gruppetti*, the percussion binds all these with regular thud, not loud, broken at the end of the first setting, resumed for the second. A machine that, while geared to render demented disorder, is yet under control grim as the words. *In Tall Grass*: here a performance with only the indispensable concertanti is inconceivable: the insinuating-interlocked oboe/voice/piano, their percussion now gentle – furry, whooshing, swishing – *must* have their ostinati background – a nimbus of strings very high and very low, slowly sliding, breathing in/out by means of their swell and subside of dynamics, rendering 'a buzz and a buzz of the yellow honey-hunters ... blur of wings in the dome of my head ...'; and the winds' long-held middle-tessitura chords swelling and contracting at a slower rate – 'who loses and remembers, who keeps and forgets?' After a time the piano-part activates the oboe jitters, the voice goes low before rising again to intercoil; they sink low together, semitone clashing semitone, as the haze of strings, now only high, breathes in, breathes out, and the triangle almost imperceptibly tings. It's as though not just words and music have been fused into indistinguishability: the same too for soprano and oboe, bank of winds and bank of strings, ensemble of percussion, heat-haze and bees – a mesh at once tight yet airy, evanescent, transparent, weightless.

Crawford's other masterpiece is her String Quartet. First movement all volatility, in high dissonance that sears and convinces; scherzo of quicksilver wit, a modernist/constructivist Mendelssohn; slow movement no line (let alone melody) – the four strings sustain closely adjacent pitches, their swellings and diminishings completely unaligned: intensity mounts to something frightening till the texture snaps and disintegrates under the unbearable pressure; finale another *allegro possibile* descendant of Chopin's Bb-minor Sonata, a whirlwind of fugitive suppressed energy: all in all a monument of rare distinction whose classical stature will some day be universally acknowledged.

The rest is saddening. One ideology replaces another: both were admirable; the American folklore undoubtedly producing more good/pleasure/benefit than the international communism: but as a creator she loses it. What little pertains to her and the music of the century's later 1930s and 40s is but fair-to-middling – the plot went elsewhere: and her resumption, as her family duties lightened, in the Wind Quintet the year before her death, is merely – 'O word of fear' – *worthy*.

Edgard Varèse

Born Paris 1883 but brought up mainly in Burgundy, then back to the capital for schooling; 1895 blown away by Debussy's *L'Après-midi*: intended by tyrannical father for engineer; aged twenty beats him up for maltreating stepmother. Schola Cantorum composition-course under d'Indy, studied fugue with Roussel, early music – a life-long passion – with Bordes: can't tolerate d'Indy, resorts to Conservatoire. Brief association with Rodin, ending in bitter quarrel. 'A man full of sun', also a man of rage and violence, later the principal model for Jean-Christophe, genius-composer of Romain Rolland's eponymous novel. Founds a chorus 1906; 1907 to Berlin after a bad tiff with Fauré at the Conservatoire. Six years in Berlin, friendship with Busoni, helped by Hofmannsthal (an uncompleted opera with him on *Oedipus and the Sphinx*, encouraged by Strauss): two orchestral tone-poems, *Bourgogne* 1908 (performed, then later destroyed); *Gargantua* 1909 (unfinished, and lost with all his other early work in a Berlin fire): attends first *Pierrot lunaire* performance chez Busoni 1912. To Paris briefly 1913, then Prague: back in France, called up for armed service 1915, soon invalided out.

To New York 1916, rapidly in contact with its avant-garde, painters and writers as well as musicians: success as conductor, energetic enterprising efforts on behalf of the radical new currents in his art, contributing mightily to them himself – *Amériques* begun 1918–21; *Intégrales* 1924–5; *Arcana* 1925–7; *Ionisation* 1929–31; *Ecuatorial* 1932–4; *Density 21.5* 1936. After this, nothing completed for nearly twenty years: many projects, more and more ambitious, searching for new means – as yet non-existent – for their realization: *One-all-Alone* and *Espace*, both fragmentary, the sole yield. Anger and frustration the core of this composer's being.* When the means developed after the Second World War, they're arguably too late for Varèse's best as composer: the ear had hardened and maybe the spirit had coarsened too – the 'man full of sun' now eclipsed by dark rancour. *Tuning Up* (1947, incomplete) a *jeu d'esprit*; *Déserts* (1950–54) for winds and percussion with taped interludes; *Poème électronique* (1957–8); *Nocturnal*, again with live and mechanical intermixed (1961 onwards, incomplete at his death 1965).

A miniature preliminary, setting Verlaine's *Un grand sommeil noir* for voice and piano in 1906: sole survivor from Varèse's pre-1920

---

* A suggestive parallel with Percy Grainger, two years older, living within a few miles, devoting his later decades to inventing machines that would capture the sounds of Nature and be capable of performing her 'free music'.

output, a dark-fashioned piece, already individual though not fore-telling things-to-come. They arrive with *Offrandes*, two songs with instrumental ensemble: *Chanson de lá-haut/Song from On-High* (poem by Vincente Huidobro) – an unidentified heroic figure watches the world turn, the sleeping Seine, sounding his clarion across the seas, saluting his Queen of the Polar Dawn, Rose of the Winds (albeit faded by autumn): '*dans ma tête un oiseau chante toute l'année*'. The clairon (trumpet) leads, peremptory/jagged/florid, at one point quoting the *Marseillaise*, at all others already unmistak-ably of its composer. Other winds ejaculatory and fierce or delicate in arabesque, strings subdued and gentle save for a single passage of brusque unison. Voice-part mainly low-key parlando, with one moment of powerful declamation – the clarion over the oceans – and one floating phrase hailing his Queen. Most notable, the inter-mittent backdrop of percussion – six players required for an intricate texture of unpitched crepitation, here still subtle and restrained, in later pieces so shattering: and the marvellous harp-part with glis-sandi that Stravinsky called 'a harp-attack'.

La Croix du Sud/Southern Cross (José Juan Tablada): percussion continuum still more elaborate (eight players required now) though remaining always soft: harp (with only one minuscule exception) used as percussion, letting the lower strings jangle and vibrate against each other: voice more athletic: pitched ensemble without prominent soloist – a tapestry of sustained dissonances with pointil-list dabs of colour and movement: and a smeary splotch of activity – chromatic rushes on lower strings, chromatic glissandi on clarinet and brass. Two near-quotations stand out: a call-to-attention from Varèse's own just-completed *Amériques* and a close recall from the end of the first of Schoenberg's *Five Orchestral Pieces*, evidently a seminal experience. Its actual *text* the least of this fascinating music – jaded sub-Rimbaud, surrealism on the way – grotesque women and animals, margarine advertised in the sky, quinine, the Virgin of Sorrows, the Zodiac revolving in yellow fever, the *tristes tropiques* swathed in rain, a zebra, an isle of departed days 'where the murdered women are waiting': Klingsor/Ravel *Asie* gone futur-istic and rotten. An exquisite fade (with the harp's one glimpse of delicacy); cut off by a chord from hell and the percussion's unique chance to bash almost every instrument loudly – they resonate on, long-held, fading to nothing.

Amériques overlaps *Offrandes*, the huge score begun before and completed the same year (1921), then revised/curtailed/curbed in 1927. Brazen, extravagant, exuberant celebration, over-the-top even in its less extreme revision; the mega-goal of the previous epoch's expansion of the orchestra to its biggest ever. *That* had been devoted to the Old World – the exotic/archaic of *Salome* and *Elektra*, the projection of personality and psychology in later Mahler and expressionist Schoenberg, the primitivism of *Le Sacre*. *Amériques*, as its name implies, salutes the New – modernism, mechanization, technology, ocean liners, skyscrapers. Paradoxical to realize that, despite its eschewing pictorial impressionism, the result is the ultimate outgrowth of what Debussy had sown so subtly in *Nuages* – the Seine, the plume of smoke from the passing tug, the sound of its hooter. Another paradox, that despite its staggering originality, *Amériques*, like *Hamlet*, is 'full of quotations': all the composers here mentioned (except Mahler), and some others, are alluded to or used undisguised; it's a container for what had excited Varèse most in Paris then in Berlin. Spasms, explosions, splurts and splurges, rage and laughter (at one point almost literal – the trombone goes *ha ha ha ha!* with sinister jocularity): what the composer termed 'trajectories of sound'/'interpenetration of sound masses'; sound 'constantly changing shape, direction, speed'. Overall effect, a razzle-rabble on the march, Workers of the (New) World Uniting, May Day Riot, angry or festive, Power to the People: some of the melodic material grossly simplified diatonic noodle-doodle amid the consciously dissonant norms, and just right for the populist aim: flooding the abysses of Manhattan, over-soaring the already crazed traffic – those sirens! – storming Wall Street if not the Bastille, stopping only to guillotine class-traitors. Yet also the wider meaning, new worlds on earth, in space, within the psyche – Varèse later claimed he could have called it 'Himalayas' and might have invoked *Espace* or *Déserts* or *Arcana* as well. And, again, the many moments of calm stasis, rumination – the very opening a cool alto-flute arabesque, constantly recurring as balm for the riot; and, elsewhere, moments of sonorous rapture and *volupté* worthy of *Jeux* or *Daphnis and Chloe*.

The years 1922–5 saw *Hyperprism*, *Octandre*, *Intégrales* – three brief works (respectively about four, seven and ten minutes) for small forces after the length and gigantic orchestra of *Amériques*, going together as an inadvertent triptych, splinters, lumps, rocks from the 'Himalayas', exploring further with similar materials to its more modern/dissonant features, eschewing its vestiges of impressionism and expressionism, atmosphere and evocation; pure sonority now the *raison d'être*, 'scientism' – quasi chemistry, physics, crystallography, geology, necromancy, the alchemist in his laboratory – the prevailing inspiration. Yet the actual *stuff* of the music from the same sources – sinuous unaccompanied lines on solo woodwinds and brasses, full of internal repetition and oft-reiterated; stuttered one-note summons; harmony sometimes close-position chromatic, sometimes all wide sevenths and ninths, sometimes diatonic; spasms of fury and outbursts of exhilaration (*Hyperprism* even retains the 'laughing' trombone for just a split second). No strings save the single double-bass in the *Octandre*. Percussion copious, in dense textures of complex unpitched polyphony, granted full equality with winds (the *Octandre* goes without percussion). *Intégrales* is longest and uses the fullest forces with the greatest variety of intonation: close harmony on its six brasses twice recalls Ruggles' *Angels* without that work's consistent inner rapture: and a Procession momentarily recalls the gross populist tunefulness so conspicuous in *Amériques*.

All three splinters conjoin again for the next work, back to massive orchestra, *Arcana* (1925–7). Varèse's affinity with mystic astrology now explicit in the superscription from Paracelsus:

One star exists, higher than all the rest – the apocalyptic star. The second star is that of the ascendant. The third is that of the elements – of these there are four: thus six stars are established. Besides these there is still another star, that of the Imagination, which begets a new star and a new heaven.

(Compare the programme for Ives's *Universe*.) Same ingredients – spasms, explosions, reiterated chords, fanfares and ejaculations, elements of processional with populace-on-the-rampage, a laughing trombone, a battery of complex percussion. New – more continuous rhythmic drive, from the very start with battering ostinato in the bass, plus drums, recurring throughout as a binding agent; the almost cheeky little ditty on high woodwind plus glockenspiel near the start; a stretch of fast continuity; and the longer stretches of withdrawn stasis, eventuating in a total silence preceding a moment of diatonic apostrophe – C-major – that might have occurred in Harris, Schuman, Copland before dissonance briefly resumes: then another huge silence – 'SILENCE IS TO BE BEATEN' the score instructs the conductor (and it 'sounds' as though the chastisement is harsh) before the final six bars' almost inaudibility – semitones very high and very low, a major seventh in the middle, a clicking insect expiring in the dust – confronting the Seven Stars, mankind are just insects? Compare Ives's asked and unanswered Questions.

Ionisation (1929–31): inevitable, a piece for percussion alone; and brilliantly successful (also, in passing, a relief for once from the inflation, the rhetoric, the deafening if thrilling stridency of his habitual writing for brass and woodwinds). Thirteen players make a polyphonic mesh of pitchless texture from very high to low on skins, wood, metal, whether dry and precisely rhythmic – sometimes so well-defined as almost to be themes – or resonant and sustained on the cymbals and gongs: and a pair of sirens, high/low, in canoodling interaction like a pair of amorous serpents. One of twentieth-century music's great moments when, towards the end, piano, glockenspiel and bells, hitherto silent, enter with clangorous pitches – huge deep clusters on the keyboard, right hand and the other tintinnabulators on luminous clear-cut dissonance, loud and frequent, superimposed upon the clicks, rustles, wailing, tappings, plops, tings, of the pitchless patterning.

Ecuatorial (1932–4) is a knock-out: as if the sonorities Varèse had been born for and preparing for in all the previous pieces – the forceful rhetoric, the overkills, the extremes of volume and dissonance – are now fully attached to what's being uttered. Some features remain familiar: four trumpets, four trombones, the battery of unpitched percussion. Unfamiliar, the important piano-part, wholly new, the important organ-part and the pair of ondes Martenots (originally theramins), picked up on an extended visit to Paris between 1928 and 1933 and specially adapted to his purpose. And, of course, the presence of voices, either a solo bass of enormous charisma or, best, a unison male chorus. Their text is taken from the sacred book of the Mayan people in a Spanish version: the tribe's invocation to their gods, in defeat and exile from their rightful heritance. A précis: Builders and moulders, abandon not your people. Spirit of the sky, give us our posterity: may there be green paths, peace, perfect existence. Masters, procreators, begetters, ancestress of the dawn, let there be germination. [Now much syllabic incantation from the Mayan.] Give existence to our children, let them not come to evil. Give life! Oh force in the sky, in the earth, at the four corners, at the four edges, so long as day still dawns, so long as the tribe shall live. Varèse: 'The title is merely suggestive of the regions where pre-Colombian art flourished. I conceived the music as having something of the same elemental rude intensity of those strange primitive works.' Exactly so: somehow this exceedingly 'cultivated'/'advanced' product of Western science and culture achieves the effect and power of alien ancient unfathomable secret significance – a cult object, sacred to religious beliefs and practice long since lost without trace. The sonority is unique – the queer squealing of the ondes, the oily organ, the absolutely non-European piano, on top of brass and percussion – as though it had been invented for the one work, heard here for the first and only time.

After *Ecuatorial* a last cheep before the long gap: *Density 21.5* for solitary flute – the *density* is that of the platinum from which the instrument is made. The gap: baffled frustration, several grandiose projects, all thwarted, as the composer seeks means, not yet invented, for unrealizable ends. Further years in Europe and New Mexico: black depression and blank sterility as two major efforts failed to stir into life: *The One-all-Alone*, theatre-spectacle, apocalyptic and intergalactic, implicitly dramatizing his own situation and condition: *Espace*, vast choral symphony – 'voices in the sky, as though magic invisible hands were turning on and off the knobs of fantastic radios, filling all space, criss-crossing, overlapping, penetrating each other, splitting up, superimposing, repulsing each other, colliding, crashing . . . I want to encompass everything human, from the most primitive to the farthest reaches of science.' Similarity to the aims of Ives's 4th and *Universe* Symphonies is remarkable: chief difference, Varèse asks no Questions.

As the 1940s advance, the creative juices stir towards projects that can, now, be realized in part, if not in the whole. *Tuning Up* (1947), as reconstructed from scrappy performance-material, is a *jeu d'esprit* parodying any orchestra's standard pre-concert routine – witless and irritating, stuffed with self-quotations (including siren), open A's loud and insistent, a fragment of Beethoven's 7th (in A, geddit?) bellicose and ill-humoured. *Déserts* (1950–54) is on-track. 'They are not only physical deserts of land and sea, mountains and snow, outer space, deserted city streets, but also the distant inner space where man is alone [*One-all-Alone* and *Espace* conjoined into the same phrase] in a world of mystery [*Arcana*] and solitude.' Three orchestral sections are separated by two electronic interludes, fashioned from transformations of percussion and factory-noises. The composed music is cleaner and sparer than heretofore, the jagged aggressive material more in focus and, it must be admitted, considerably less exciting. The second such section builds from isolated notes and fragments of fanfare up to the most horripilating chords even Varèse ever made: then a sense of dialogue – these gestures are listening and responding to each other. The third produces a tiny reminiscence of the old raucous celebratory march mode: mainly silences, however, isolated rattles, bangs, batterings, huge crescendos on single notes, and sometimes moments of complete calm. The electronic interludes are a bit of an embarrassment – clunky 'horror' sound-effects, then risibly 'bodily' – internal tummy-borborygmi, external evacuations, snorts and grunts, expectorations, farts. So it goes.

The *Poème électronique* (1957–8) was written for the Brussels World Fair, where it played within a Pavilion designed by Le Corbusier: a montage of machine-noises, bells, voices, piano, percussion, with pure electronics. The fusion of internal spaces, lighting and the sounds that at last began to fulfil the composer's dreams must have been stirring. Out of any such context (it's wretched that the structure was demolished) the score comes across as meagre and desultory. *Nocturnal* (1961 on: incomplete at Varèse's death, several versions, collected and rescued by his devoted editor) goes back to, and inevitably invites comparison with, *Offrandes* and *Ecuatorial* in its use of surreal/ritualistic text with admix of nonsense-syllables plus sighs/groans/mutters/screams – 'syllables of intensity', he called them. *But* – Anaïs Nin's text is awful: and her composer endorses and underlines her rather than escaping her *Delta of Venus* fly-trap. The man-all-alone, full of sun and space, aspiring to and reaching the Star of Imagination, is fully expressed in the eight great works of the decade-and-a-half from 1918 to 1934.

Four traditionalists

Continuation from Ives, Ruggles, Crawford, Varèse, realizing to the full the potentialities suggested by Cowell's *New Musical Resources*, will be reached in due course. Meanwhile, one playboy, a trio of mainstreamers, all four fairly represented by just one work each; then an American Classic; and a Commercial whose genius surpasses all five put together.

First, the playboy: Virgil Thomson – born Kansas City 1896; studied at Harvard 1920–25, while organist at a Boston church: Paris from mid-1920s 'till the Germans came', initially pupil of Nadia Boulanger, one of the earliest in a succession of gifted American composers – 'every small US town has a dime-store and a Boulanger-pupil' as he remarked (though he didn't mention her younger sister Lili, a composer of rare promise who tragically died in 1918 aged 25). Back home, the most notable native music-critic of his day, acute and witty in praise and prejudice alike. Copious output, including pioneering film-scores: a unique feature, inscribing portraits-in-music, seated in front of his subject as a painter before the model (I sat for him once: the sensation strange, the result unrecognizable). Several operas, including two to libretti by his friend Gertrude

Stein: of these the first, *Four Saints in Three Acts*, survives as a period-piece – 'dated, but in the right way', so redolent of its time/place/spirit as, in the end, coming to represent them, icon of the epoch – composed 1927–8, scored 1933 for its stage-première the next year. He lived on, composing, writing, conversing, entertaining – a pillar of the Chelsea Hotel in NYC – till 1989.

Four Saints in Three Acts – the glorious inappropriateness of the title (there are four Acts and around thirty Saints, sixteen named) appealed to Gertrude; it mirrors the work's creation and the end-product. A 'sequence' of non-events only 'organized' into scenario after text and score were complete. Thomson set all the stage-directions too, 'because they made such lovely lines for singing'. All-black cast in a piece not remotely connected with black life/culture/music: Stein loved Spain, Virgil wholly a child of Missouri Southern Baptists and their cheerful, simplistic hymnody. The collaborators met in the middle, agreeing in admiration of the religious life – consecrated and dedicated, in its spiritual disciplines as in its humdrum daily tasks: into both, high-spirits constantly break in, euphoria and happiness – not, after all, a thousand miles from the daily life and work of Catfish Row, setting of the other famous all-black opera the year after (1935), Gershwin's *Porgy and Bess*. Such (non)-events as take place are introduced with studied inconsequentiality by a *commère* and a *compère*. Act I, festivity on the steps of the cathedral at Ávila; St Teresa and her nuns bustle around with their womanly activities, secular and religious (she is represented by two singers – at least they're both female!). Act II, a rural picnic, wherein Teresa and Ignatius Loyola (in historic fact unknown to each other) direct communal diversions; all present are vouchsafed a vision of a many-mansioned Paradise. Act III, Ignatius and his followers at their manly activities, secular and religious: Teresa and her women come to visit, a storm brews up, Ignatius calms it; all the cast see in the ensuing sunshine a preview of Judgment Day. 'Act IV' is confabulated by collusion between *commère* and *compère*: *She* – how many Acts are there in it?; *He* – Four Acts; *She* – Act Four – set in heaven, for an emphatic ending: *He* – Last Act; *Omnes* – Which is a Fact.

Nonsense incarnadine! *Happy* nonsense, carefree and oddly

touching: the infantine prattle of Stein's text, the knowing naïveté of Thomson's setting, combine to sound a holy hilarity, the jongleur whose innocuous tricks are closer to God than lavish pieties; the Praise of Folly, the Folly of the Cross.

Now the three mainstreamers. Two splendid third symphonies, representative of their composers at their finest, deserving their place with such analogous contemporary achievements as Walton's 1st, Vaughan Williams' 4th, Shostakovich's 5th. First, Roy Harris (1898–1979) of Scotch/Irish/Welsh descent; a farming-boy, truck-driver, delivery-man, self-taught then help from college and encouragement from Arthur Bliss, visiting the US. To Paris for Boulanger, not a success: back home, long busy life, copious composing, support from Koussevitzsky. The extensive catalogue includes many more symphonies: the 3rd (1938) remains the peak, a splendid specimen of purposeful clean-cut energy, sustained throughout its *One Movement* (part of the title) from first to last. Spacious open opening, continuous accelerando till broad coda, grandly sustained sense of growth and momentum, on material apparently naïve, even primitive, yet used with resource and ingenuity. Emancipation of the consonance; alongside the 'dissonant counterpoint' of radical compatriots, and in its complementary way just as radical, with a singing-running fresh-air nature alien to them. His own characterizations of the piece's principal sections – Tragic; Lyric; Pastoral; Dramatic; Tragic again – are bluff, direct and just. 'From the chest (hairy) may it go to the chest.' Nothing else of Harris is nearly so good.

William Schuman (1910–92): youth of baseball, weddings, bar mitzvahs, popular song, then overwhelmed by first contact with classical music at a Toscanini concert 1930, deciding at once to become a composer. Private study with Roy Harris; like him, encouraged by Koussevitzsky; long life of public musical service – president of the Juilliard 1945; many symphonies and a fine big strong violin concerto. The 3rd Symphony of 1941 comes in two Parts. Part I consists of a *Passacaglia*, initially ruminative, growing bolder, then crepuscular and remote under long singing lines, gradually energizing, harmony playing off major/minor simultaneities in a generally diatonic language. Sarabande on trombones under leaping strings, issuing into a *Fugue* with resplendent writing for four trumpets, calming then into tranquillo on woodwinds, animating to terrific timpani battery: chopping strings, brazen horns, all woodwinds and brasses over trombone pedal – virile cowboys/snorting stallions – ending in triumphant blaze of apotheosis.

Part II commences with *Chorale* – placid low strings, trumpet solo, flute solo – a vision of calm pastoral, country cousin of Copland's *Quiet City*: some lovely spacing – violins and cellos doubled three octaves apart, parallel fifths in between, swelling from sweetly serious hymnody to harmony more juicy and gritty, renewing placidity on cor anglais, four stopped horns in two parts, a string sigh, muted trumpets, oboe – as if to demonstrate these timbral affinities and differences, till a sudden thwack inaugurates a concluding *Toccata*, on a snare-drum rhythm gradually taken up by woodwinds with whirling virtuosity. Broader, timpani retaining the rhythm, then more whirling, plus xylophone: then this first section winds down to eloquent cello-recitative including splendid pizzicato strumming: impassioned violins take the eloquence, then the strumming, yet further. Principal momentum now winds up: the side-drum rhythm (like a mainstream response to the same instrument's 'tune' in *Ionisation*) insinuates, insists, dominates, conquers, as it spreads like wildfire throughout the orchestra, long-held notes neighing and snorting inside the stampede, spurred on by furious side-drum rim-shots cracking like pistols, ending in a barrage of the major/minor simultaneity hinted at earlier. All-American exhilaration, energy, uninhibition, captured with enormous flair and skill.

The third is Samuel Barber (1910–81): his background is the exception: US aristocracy, cultivated, elegant, well-educated, holding in his music a Romantic/conservative mainstream. The oeuvre's core is song (himself an accomplished singer); larger works a bit iffy, whether orchestral – centred upon three large-scale concertos – or choral, the piously dull *Prayers of Kierkegaard*; or operatic, the effete *Vanessa*, the overreaching *Antony and Cleopatra*; and all overshadowed by the tasteful saccharine of the ubiquitous *Adagio for Strings*.

Barber hits the spot in *Knoxville: Summer of 1915*, a scena for soprano and orchestra, words from James Agee's prologue to *A Death in the Family*, not quite perfected at his death in 1955 (Barber's setting of 1949 found the text in the *Partisan Review*). This lovely prose-poem lovingly recreates a Tennessee boyhood in a haze of nostalgia, without sentimentality though courting it, with occasional undertones of disquiet, quivering apprehensions of loss, movingly sensitized; all this caught to a quintessence in the setting by his near-contemporary. 'We are talking now of summer evenings in Knoxville Tennessee in the time that I lived there so successfully disguised to myself as a child'; words not set, given at the head of the score, already hinting at whimsy and archness so deftly avoided in what follows. Evening, folks out on their porches rocking and talking; people pass, a horse, a loud automobile, a quiet one – evoked in spare lilting-lulling pastorale, beautifully spaced, the occasional modulation neat and telling. Agitation – momentum and mild acridity – the clang of a streetcar with its off-key bell; tranquillity resumes, deeper than before; 'now is the night one blue dew', to the sweetest modulation yet. These same words set a second time to inaugurate the family's domestic evening activities, scents, sounds – cool tender lyricism burgeons above the almost-always understated vocal line.

The family lie around with the boy, mother a musician, father an artist: he listens to the grown-up talk, 'of nothing in particular, of nothing in at all in particular, of nothing at all' – Gertrude Stein comes to mind, the *faux-naïf* repetition, yet touching and affecting – Barber's setting apparently artless in easy casualness, always flexible and sensitive. A delicate tonal shift within the unbroken momentum as the stars come alive – 'they seem each like a smile of great sweetness' (here and throughout I'm giving the words in their transparent clarity because the music is so perfectly commensurate). Talk among these adults so much larger than him, homely and intimate, culminating in his sense of his mother's goodness, then his father's – here the singer ceases for two bars' intensification on orchestra alone, the harmony edgy with a touch of anguish; the eternal note of sadness is heard, even as they lie on their quilts, on the grass, in the evening, among the night-sounds, under the sweetly smiling stars, Knoxville summer of 1915. So to the most potentially dangerous moment of all; a precarious balancing-act between sentiment and sentimentality, simplicity and *simplesse*, ghastly good taste and the perfect tact of restraint and decorum. 'May God bless my people, my uncle, my aunt, my mother, my good father ... oh remember them kindly in their time of trouble, and in the hour of their taking away': and here alone the orchestra is given its head, heart-on-sleeve, wiping away the unchecked tear; then cooling to return of the opening pastoral pallor, lulling lilt, as the little boy is put to bed by those familiars who love him so 'but will not, oh will not, now [the orchestra swells: ceases] not ever [orchestra bursts its bonds, and immediately retreats: soft resumption] but will not ever tell me who I am'. Last fading phrases of pastorale as the scene diminishes into sleep, closing an episode of Essential Americana authentic as anything transcendent by Ives, heaven-storming by Ruggles, radically extreme by Crawford, burning and joyously angry by Varèse, sexily razzmajazzable by Gershwin, hard-edged and spare by Harris or Schuman or Copland (whose moments of quizzical tenderness in his *Emily Dickinson Songs*, *Knoxville*'s exact contemporary, also perfect this particular vein).

'Commercials'

The next sections take their titles from Edmund Wilson's collection *Classics and Commercials* – beneath the antithesis lie incongruities so surprising between Gershwin and Copland that the two terms could almost be applied the other way round.

It is difficult properly to evaluate George Gershwin, the twentieth century's most popular composer. The most direct comparison is with his compatriots and music for stage and screen: the delights of Irving Berlin, Cole Porter, Richard Rodgers are many and various, and while Jerome Kern can dig deeper, it is evident by now that Gershwin remains unsurpassed in musical substance by these or subsequent musicians in the same line. Talents are more equally matched when he is placed with the three masters of nineteenth-century operetta: Offenbach and Second Empire Paris, Johann Strauss and the palmy days of imperial Vienna, Sullivan and the high-Victorian London whose tone was already Edwardian; thence to Gershwin and glitzy Broadway and Hollywood shows of the 1929s and early 30s. All are period-pieces perfectly evoking the culture from which they sprang, local in inflection, universal in popular appeal, achieving the status of folklore. And then there is the music that, whatever its origins, has become core popular repertoire. Gershwin's concert pieces clearly belong here, and bring him without incongruity into contact with the lighter side of some weighty composers.

Nonetheless these direct comparisons somehow fail to get Gershwin right. He is different, and bigger. How does he stand in relation to the 'serious' achievements of his own epoch? Comparison now becomes sullied by the awkward question of popularity: Gershwin is far more widely enjoyed than even the best-known modern masters whose work, historians agree, has changed the course of music. Consider the century's crucial radical composer, still contentious unto the third and fourth generation, Gershwin's friend and admirer Arnold Schoenberg (they enjoyed tennis-games and painted each other's portraits). At the time of Gershwin's meteoric rise to fame, Schoenberg reorganized musical grammar so drastically that it still hurts. The result remains as unassimilated by the average music-lover as when it was new. Scholars can trace a soundless echo of the performances it receives neither in the concert hall nor, as Schoenberg touchingly wished, on the lips of whistling errand-boys. Other kinds of musical experimentation have also proved generally unacceptable. Is it their progenitors' fault? Is Gershwin better because of his enormous appeal? How is Success weighed against Importance? Such polemically poised questions tend to invite philistine answers, whether culture-bashing or elitist. It is more fruitful to describe the four principal classical composers of recent times who really tried, and managed, to touch the popular pulse. The boldest of these composers is Kurt Weill. Beginning as an 'ivory-tower' artist, he answers the internal call that his music communicate burning social and political issues by adopting features of the American dance music which, in the 1920s, was sweeping across Europe. Unless the cure is to fail, the medicine must reach the malaise, so its taste must attract. Weill's decision to debase his style is responsible and admirable; but his real power lies in the consequent release of a musical allure that corrodes the pill it was intended to coat.

Aaron Copland, though not initially, had become by the early 1930s a 'difficult composer' understood only by a sophisticated minority. His subsequent stylistic simplification shows that the wish to reach a large audience is sincerely compatible with a sensitive response to public events, from Depression through to New Deal. Music greets the Common Man and the career prospers. By rigorous essentialization, with Stravinskian irony and un-Stravinskian warmth, the raw materials of the American past, wild West or plain East, are slanted into a genuine vernacular, soon recognized and treasured as such. Dmitri Shostakovich, however, begins modernistic in the last years when the Soviet State still allows it. Once the Golden Age is over he is told what he ought to write, not by sympathetic vibration with the times but by orders from above. Compulsory accessibility lasts until he is too eminent to be harried, then he returns to the bleak final fulfilment of his youthful subjectivity – which, ironically enough, also touches a popular nerve. Benjamin Britten does not have to de-modernize, when prompted by the atmosphere of England in the late 1930s to 'Advance Democracy', since he was gifted from the start with simplicity of utterance. Rather, it is his achievement in the operas of his prime to turn this directness of appeal towards normalizing highly personal themes, in such a way that they work viably for audiences the world over. The compulsion (whether from without or within) to broaden their styles was beneficial for all these composers. In each case the spirit of the age forced into flower an individual genius for popularity, with enormous benefit to musical culture at large. They contrast interestingly with Prokofiev and Poulenc, the only other comparable art-composers in modern times of manifest stature and popularity, both of them accessible not because of ideology or unconscious opportunism, but because they can't help it.

Gershwin of course is also a 'naïve' composer (in Schiller's sense of being at one with his nature and his gift); there is no political mission and no crisis of style. For low commercial purposes he copiously yields high-calibre music, which, immensely appealing to enormous numbers of people immediately and ever since, is problematic only in the attempt to define and evaluate it.

Having set him in context I want now to start again, this time from the premise that Gershwin is a great composer, and see what follows. The claim is based principally upon the songs from the shows (always provided that his own original harmony is unbowdlerized). His work here is at its most commercial, obedient to the genre with its given lengths, received range of sentiment and level of stylistic suitability. There is no sense that he wants to transgress these conventions, no discrepancy between what is expected of him and what he delights to give. Here he produces his most inventive, intense and distinctive music. So he is, in Hans Keller's phrase, 'a major master of minor forms' (but why should a song be called a minor form?), like, say, the Chopin of the mazurkas or the Wolf of the *Italian Songbook* (for both of whom, as for Gershwin, the basic type is already given), or the Webern or Grainger of tiny forms that they have evolved for themselves. This category, of course, overlaps with the miniature masterpieces of composers who are also masters of 'major' forms – say Bach's smallest chorale-preludes, Schubert's songs, Tchaikovsky's dance numbers, Brahms's late piano pieces. The ideal behind all such music is the intense lyric utterance formalized and distilled, the brief duration filled with ideas both unmistakably personal and worked with a scrupulous precision that explores and expands all their possibilities.

These are exalted comparisons: Gershwin's best songs can sustain them. Insubstantiable claims arise only with his more 'artistic' endeavours. The earlier concert-pieces – *Rhapsody in Blue*, Piano Concerto – contain splendid song-material, many touches of mastery and tons of vitality, but are damaged by formal stiltedness, exposing itself in padding, short-circuiting and overblown rhetoric. That he was growing into bigger sizes is shown by *An American in Paris* (where the working-out between the 'hits' is more inventive); in the *Cuban Overture* and *'I Got Rhythm' Variations*, where the whole is surer but the actual material is less distinctive. Only the *Second Rhapsody* gets the balance right, till its 'applaud loudly now' conclusion. But all in all, Gershwin's concert-works reveal, beneath the bravado, a character both vulnerable and naïve: the best reply to his anxious quest for approval, demonstrated by his insatiable desire for high-class composition-lessons, is Ravel's 'Why be a second-rate Ravel when you can be a first-rate Gershwin?' Which matches another well-known anecdote: asking, in response to Gershwin's request for tuition, what he earned, Stravinsky replied, hearing the figure, '*I* should take lessons from *you*!' As well as Ravel (who handed on the baton to Nadia Boulanger, who also declined), Gershwin solicited help from, inter alia, Varèse, Ibert (!), Glazunov and Cowell. The only acceptance came from Joseph Schillinger, with his notorious 'Method', and in this instance, at last, Gershwin's long serious application – three ninety-minute sessions every week over four years, continuing by mail when he moved from New York to Hollywood, where he also approached Schoenberg. Who could have helped him? What did Gershwin *want*? The closest comparison is Schubert's approach, towards the end of his life, to dry old Sechter for instruction in counterpoint. Yet 'any fool can see' – if not at the time then certainly with hindsight – that, in both cases, here is the melodic, harmonic, contrapuntal, rhythmic Natural who needs nothing further than what he already commands.

Porgy and Bess, also aspiring to approval in one of classical music's most sanctified genres, is in a different league from any of the concert-works. Its inspired fusion of Broadway and Hollywood with Negro Spirituals, Shouts and Blues puts the whole endeavour onto a different plane. For all its manifest lapses it stands with Berg's *Wozzeck* and Britten's *Grimes*, Janáček's *Katya* and Shostakovich's *Lady Macbeth* – the outstanding operas of compassion for the social outcast, breaking down barriers of style, class and race, as discussed earlier.

But if it is to be the songs on which the main claim rests, what about the vulgarity, or downright ignobility, of their content? The subject is almost always romantic love, normative and sentimentalized; the tone oscillates between ardour and wryness, the emotional accent is commonplace. The lyrics, deftly crafted and delicious, hardly plumb the depths; the shows as entities put two-dimensional characters into plots consisting of little more than pretext and containers for set-pieces of song and dance. This is mass entertainment, which must appeal at once, or flop. With two exceptions: *Of Thee I Sing* (1931) and its 1933 sequel *Let 'em Eat Cake*, wherein the music, as diverse, rich, catchy as ever, is formally far more elaborate, the stories more sophisticated and adult, the political satire (hitherto absent) so close to the bone that the later work uncharacteristically failed at first. Written to mock Herbert Hoover's presidency, it proved still more germane to Ronald Reagan's, and the score's advances in sophistication of organization and depth of expression are upheld in the overwhelming profusion of *Porgy* two years later. But even in such confections as *Girl Crazy* and *Lady, Be Good* the musical ideas Gershwin finds are far superior to what is needed. His music seizes the true feeling that underlines every banality, intensifying it, as far as it can bear, with the Russian-Jewish fervour of melody, and especially harmony – which link him, after all, with Weill and, behind him, Mahler – and the physical vitality of rhythm and metre that, more obviously, connect with Copland, and hence Stravinsky.

This suggests that familiar situation where a cheap text on a sublime subject is transfigured by inspired music. But with Gershwin, because he is in tune with his subject and its level of utterance, the usual escape clause is not needed. Low style and content are fully integrated with musical gifts of a very high order; the emotional charge of one of his great love-songs is primal, going to the basis of pleasure more freely and directly than anything else in the whole range of music.

Pleasure! The very word is like a knell, closer-allied to pain than enjoyment, not least in our approach to the advanced culture of twentieth-century music. We sweat through *Lulu*, we fight through *Die Soldaten*, we must rise to *Moses and Aaron* and submit to *Donnerstag* or *The Mask of Orpheus*. Contrariwise, there is shame in the easy enjoyment of uncomplicated music – especially when, like Gershwin's, its sensuality is so frank. Artistic attitudes are still fundamentally puritan: pleasure is guilty, virtue grows as predilection and

appetite are denied, enjoyment is a veneer upon Victorian Improve-
ment. The ways of cultural self-deception are devious, but they all
end in hypocrisy.

Yet real unguarded desire will always, like water, find its level.
Witness the ever-rising reputation of those serious composers – for
instance Puccini, Berg, Tchaikovsky, Mahler, Strauss, Messiaen –
who, in whatever ways, subvert once-received canons of good taste,
compelling our 'lenience' to what had formerly been considered
'weakness'. Gershwin, being so completely commercial and vulgar,
has a harder time. But eventually the directness of his music's appeal
to all that is lowest in us, and the warmth and energy of its expression, dissolve snobbery whether direct or inverted. It is base and
low, richly tasty and utterly tasteless, sexy and juicy – all this with
both passion and tenderness and an ease of manner, a good-humour
and happiness that are out of phase with the general tendency of
modern culture. Everything is on the sleeve and below the belt; no
faked-up seriousness, complexities, anxieties, rebarbarations, abstractions stand in the way of what everyone wants. 'Ain't got no shame,
Doin' what I like to do' (as the chorus sing in *Porgy*). And paradoxically, for all this robust vulgarity, Gershwin's musical means are
remarkably pure. He is one of nature's grammarians, with exactness
in gauging chromatic inflections in tonal contexts surpassed only by
Schubert and Chopin. In all three composers there is a classic simplicity of harmony: a compositional essentialness, as in a Schenke-
rian analysis, lies behind the details and the individual traits of style.
(Regrettable that most commercial arrangements simplify, bowdler-
ize or tart-up his originals.)

Many very different great composers, then, can be mentioned,
either in direct comparison or by oblique affinity, in an attempt to
focus Gershwin's greatness more clearly. They are not demeaned by
the contact, nor is he elevated in ways that do his cause disservice.
His content lies in his notes, and the notes cannot lie. With characteristic naïve pride Gershwin asked Alban Berg why he so loved his
songs; the answer was simply, 'Music is music.'

George Gershwin: born 1898 of Russian-Jewish heritage; early
gifted as pianist, strict musical training piecemeal; learnt his skills

as song-plugger, soon writing songs of his own. From mid-1920s, a string of successes on Broadway, usually setting lyrics by his brother Ira; success in the concert-hall too, from *Rhapsody in Blue* (1924) onwards; the musical shows evolve from stereotypical to sophisticated; *Porgy and Bess* (1935) takes freely from both sides of his growing ambitions, and reaches a higher plane. After this magnum opus, he worked also for films, and died in Hollywood of a brain tumour 1937.

A brief encapsulation of his three closest musical relations. Irving Berlin: born 1888 in Russia, son of a cantor – the family emigrated to New York when he was five, and there he remained till his death at 101, 1989. Though Russian-Jewish by blood, yet in his copious, effortless, long-lived career a principal – *the* principal – inventor of 'America' in popular music: in every intonation – ragtime, waltzes sentimental or silky, patriotic uplift, etc. – a total rightness of touch, recognizable by, identifiable with, the appreciative millions, commercials that immediately became classics – folk-music. A few famous titles convey the whole: 'White Christmas', 'Anything You Can Do', 'There's No Business Like Show Business', 'Alexander's Ragtime Band', 'Cheek to Cheek', 'Puttin' on the Ritz', 'God Bless America'. Tributes from two coevals who owe him so much: Gershwin – 'the greatest songwriter who ever lived'; Jerome Kern – 'Irving Berlin *is* American music'.

So to Kern himself, 1885–1945: more sophisticated and educated musically – 'I have seen him struggling for hours over a modulation' – yet with his finger equally on the popular pulse. Concerned to raise the happy-go-lucky hit-or-miss opportunism of the standard genre, to make score/characters/plots integral and interdependent: its triumph *Show Boat* (1927); Broadway musicals could plausibly be characterized as 'Before *Show Boat*' and 'After *Show Boat*'. A well-known exchange is also germane to the piece's place: 'Here is a story [Kern's lyricist is speaking] laid in China, about an Italian [Marco Polo] and told by an Irishman. What kind of music are you going to write?' 'It'll be good Jewish music,' Kern replied. Thus with *Show Boat*: Kern can identify with all sorts and conditions, colours, genders and ages, from the opening chorus of black stevedores to the jazzy strains when the story reaches the 1920s – most profoundly of all in the immortal 'Ol' Man River'. His human empathy, scarcely touched on chez Berlin or Porter, is matched only by Gershwin in *Porgy and Bess*. Some further famous songs indicate the range and the calibre: from *Show Boat* itself, 'Can't Help Lovin' Dat Man'; 'Bill'; 'Only Make Believe'; from other shows, 'Why Do I Love You?'; 'She Didn't Say Yes'; 'A Fine Romance'; 'I'm Old Fashioned'; 'Smoke Gets In Your Eyes'; 'The Last Time I Saw Paris', et al.

Cole Porter, 1891–1964: well-born and wealthy; not strictly a 'Commercial' – in show-business for the fun and joy. But a hundred per cent professional and extremely accomplished, more particularly as he also composed his own exceedingly deft lyrics. The shows as wholes retain the 'Before *Show Boat*' frothiness, albeit rich in memorable songs. *Kiss Me, Kate* (1948) raises the stakes; ingenious and complex take on *The Taming of the Shrew* (Pirandello not so distant) with sharper insights into its characters' psychology via terrific songs and set-pieces than might have been foreseen from earlier days. Some famous standards – 'Let's Do It'; 'You Do Something To Me'; 'Love For Sale'; 'All Through The Night'; 'Anything Goes'; 'Begin The Beguine'; 'I Concentrate On You'; 'Every Time We Say Goodbye', et al.

'Classics'

Aaron Copland

Copland's music is oddly difficult to encapsulate. The oeuvre is shapely and reasonable, virtually every genre is represented, the talent fully used; its trajectory is clear, from 'Roaring Twenties', via radical 1930s and patriotic 40s to the 50s, where renewed experiment fuses or alternates with demotic American in fine consolidation, succeeded by the spare 60s and, in the 70s, dilution and dearth. Then the sound itself, whatever the stylistic vicissitudes, unfailingly frugal, lucid, exact, so shadowless and unambiguous as to be paradoxically elusive. Expression is not expelled with menacing pitchfork à la Stravinsky nor repressed like Ravel (to take the two composers who make the clearest comparison). Within the hard flat brightness unmistakable for any other music – brazen, clangorous, metallic, glassy, strident, gaunt – lies the equally unmistakable Copland tenderness, oddly wistful (a favourite word), shy, stammering, vulnerable. Beyond both lies the seer, visionary lawgiver, of such places as the declamatory close of the *Symphonic Ode* and *Music for a Great City*. Yet unlike his friend Benjamin Britten, there is no self-expression via choice of subjects, motifs, texts, and unlike Mahler (an unexpected but fruitful influence from very early on), absolutely no musical autobiography.

Copland seems always to have known his own worth and who he was, understanding and embracing his exemplary standing as an all-American professional composer. From the very beginning he evinced the sedulous care that had at the end of a long busy life accumulated 'approximately four hundred thousand items', varying from manuscript scores to trivia and ephemera, all ready for the Library of Congress. His life is a model of integration and balance: like the music, there is nothing in excess, nothing wasted; precise without dryness, tight without costiveness, it flourishes within a harmonious relationship of public and private, conspicuously elegant and sober for all the abandon; devoid of illusory goals, lurching embarrassments, painful agonizings, self-reproaches, guilt and compunction. Even when, some twenty years before his death at ninety, the life's *raison d'être* began to diminish, before ceasing altogether, his attitude was calm and stoical. The depletions and humiliation of 'senile dementia' (this hideous technical term corresponds ill with the personal sweetness that never wavered in domestic contexts, as I and countless others can remember) were worn with the same casual grace with which he habitually dressed, and the same bemused shrug with which anything ugly – the McCarthy persecutions – or painful – the troubles with Victor Kraft and later lovers – had always been accepted and accommodated. The 'boy from Brooklyn' (and not so far behind, from the Pale of Settlement), by dint of high intelligence and innate self-discipline and sheer hard work, extended a slender compositional talent to major importance, to such effect that he can truly be said, with Stephen Dedalus, to be 'forging in the smithy of his soul the uncreated conscience of his race'; in music and, because of the very nature of such an achievement, not just in music alone. Russian by lineage, Jewish, homosexual; yet All-American: the paradoxes are resolved into a calm. Leonard Bernstein (another version of the same mix) characterized Copland's grandeur, delicacy, severity, rage, bite, howl, tenderness, etc., then adds, 'None of which corresponds with the Aaron we loving friends know; it comes to us from some deep mysterious place he never reveals to us except in his music.' The relationship between creator and creation will for ever remain mysterious at best, and ultimately unfathomable. Copland's work, even when so direct, straightforward, transparent, exemplifies this as well as such complex, tortuous figures as Wagner or Schoenberg.

For all the undying popularity of a handful of best-belovèds, Copland's oeuvre predominantly consists of neglected treasure. The first two orchestral works (preceded only by juvenilia and a graduation passacaglia for piano) are remarkable for their assurance. Both are rich in potential for his later course; neither has quite made it into the repertoire. *Grohg* (1922–5) as a venture into Mittel-Europe expressionist Gothic is most uncharacteristic, an extravaganza never to be pursued. But as an exercise in dance-types, scoring and sheer composing, already so surefooted as to have needed only minimal adjustment when, recast as the *Dance Symphony* (1929), it sets the precedent of a lifetime.

The *Organ Symphony* (1924), his first actual commission, is still more prophetic, in actual sonorities, techniques, compositional personality. A withdrawn introductory first movement unobtrusively setting up the material for an obtrusive extrovert finale; between, the scherzo, brilliantly establishing at first go the basic texture, material, momentum of the constructivistic minimalism that began to flourish some fifty years later, in both its simplistic variety (no names) and its compound (as e.g. the layered polyrhythmic heterophony of the earlier David Del Tredici). To have put together such opposites as wilful understatement/brazen rumbunction; to have dared play intricate games with material teetering on the edge of sheer imbecility – required original conception and courageous execution. The Piano Concerto of 1926 sustains a similar provocative stance. The cool irony whereby the naïve on-heat passion of Gershwin's two piano-and-orchestra successes (the *Rhapsody in Blue* of 1924, the Concerto of 1925) is replicated 'in aspic' and bombastic *Schelomo*-schlock placed cheek-by-jowl against splintery desiccation; the wicked exuberance with which 'jazziness' is X-rayed and dangled in tweezers for detached appraisal, evince extraordinary juvenile self-possession, calculated yet unwitting, knowing yet innocent.

And the best work from this Adolescent's Corner, *Music for the Theater* (1925), enjoys superior material and a better attitude to it. Parody, slapstick, ribaldry are more closely tied-in to sheer unawkward affection for the popular models. Its 'withdrawn' music (the central interlude) is also less guarded; and the veiled chorale-like passages in the prologue, returning in the epilogue (both times following on the nervy aggression of the stuttering trumpet summons), prophesy the utter simplicity of such a mature, unstuttering utterance as the prayerful string music just before the end of *Appalachian Spring*. It shows Copland's later homage to the common chord to be no affected *simplesse*, but powerful affective simplicity.

Satire and sentiment adjoin in one of the neglected two pieces for violin and piano (also 1926). *Ukulele Serenade* is an ingenious, good-natured counterpart to the devilish wit of the *Soldier's Tale* dance numbers. The *Nocturne* is something more: warmly expressive in itself, and its principal phrase proves astonishingly pregnant and protean, yielding almost all the material for the summit and masterwork of Copland's early phase, indeed one of his greatest works *tout court*, the *Symphonic Ode* for orchestra (completed in 1929). To the native strains of jazz and vaudeville, boldly stylized in primary colours and modernist cross-cutting, is added an unexpected and crucial element which lifts the music on to its imposing public plinth – the rhetoric, the strenuous ardour, the orchestral sonority (at once piercing yet rounded) and the mighty paragraphing of Mahler. The resulting amalgam is one of the great celebrations of nationality in music. It ought to be up there representing

its country like *Finlandia*, *Vltava*, 'Nimrod', but is a rarity. Despite
the eclecticism, it bellows 'America' from every bar, hard-edged and
metallic or deep-pile-driven with juddering tenths into alluvial
mud. And no special demotic was needed to do this. The Ameri-
canness is bigger than style (and individual in particular place
and time): it is a Proclamation, with *Amériques* and the comparable aspects of Ives and Ruggles, the 3rd Symphonies of Harris and
Schuman (not to mention Dos Passos, Thomas Hart Benton and
other heirs of Whitman), celebrating the great land, its awe-inducing
natural wonders and the mind-boggling upward thrust of its cities,
its vibrant racial crucible, its larger-than-life ideals that culminate in
the notion and the actuality of Freedom. All this, palpable for the
work's admirers, was probably not in its composer's mind. *Ode*, he
said, is not an ode to anything in particular, 'but rather a spirit that
is to be found in the music itself'. Copland steps into this colossal
grandeur with the same cool, quizzical unwitting that produced the
flagrant provocations with which he'd preceded it.

But the grandeur was not the way to the immediate future (and
when it was again specifically called for, it was possibly never again
so convincing). The future had been prefigured in *Vitebsk* (1928),
the excoriating movement for piano trio on older music for the
Jewish dybbuk legend, with its searing quarter-tone cantillation
and skirling folkloric euphoria – Copland's only work to stylize his
ethnic origins rather than his naturalized nationhood. In the next
step the gaunt concentration with which this material is treated
becomes the music's principal subject, by exploration of a set of
pitches on the face of it as abstract as a Bach fugue-subject or a
building motif in Haydn or Beethoven.

These *Piano Variations* (1930) crucially discover that the constructivistic rigours (eventually christened and codified as 'serialism') needn't be slave to a strict ordering of the notes. Rather, the
notes make a pool of pitch-resources, a highly characterized clench
of harmony fused into itself or separated out into intervals forming
a repertoire of shapes, a sonorous image-cluster with the material
and its total potential locked into a nugget of heavy-density plu-
tonium. Which, above all, needn't – or even shouldn't – consist of

all twelve notes. The obsession with the twelve shows a misplaced exhaustiveness hanging-over from the nice artificial compromise of equal temperament, its authoritative canonization by Bach, and the gigantic consequences for Western Music ever since. For composer and listener here, less is more: more memorable, assimilable, audible, manageable, both by the composer who manipulates and by the ear that perceives. This is true whether the aim is to purge the sound of tonal implications, or (implicitly or explicitly) to employ them, or any stage intervening. The fact that Copland's five-note 'series' in the *Variations*, and comparable cluster-clunches in subsequent pieces, do preserve a strong quasi-diatonic/tonal identity – major/minor blues-tang with a predilection for a flattened second and a sharpened fourth – is as seminal for the technique as, more important still, the actual sound with which, some twenty years, a world war and a cultural revolution later, the century's principal diatonicists all began, about the time of Schoenberg's death, to explore however shyly his technical legacy. Their means, and their results, are continually prophesied in Copland's tightest works of the 1930s; Stravinsky, the most significant of them, most particularly. Some passages in the *Short Symphony* (1932–3) take the listener from the Stravinsky-sound of the interwar decades, obviously its main starting-point, to the sound of *Agon* in the mid-1950s; while in the *Symphony*'s version for sextet (1937) the span goes from the sound of *L'Histoire du soldat* (especially in the comparable sonority of the 1919 suite for clarinet, violin, piano) through to Stravinsky's 1953 *Septet* at least. Copland's principal European debt is paid back, obliquely and a-historically, in a fascinating three-way-bind whose detailed unravelling would be worth a doctoral dissertation one of these days. Then, as both composers moved from the later 1950s onwards towards a fuller chromatic serialism, this area of memorable sonic consensuality around the potent major/minor clash diverged totally (though never towards Vienna).

Copland's debt to Mahler survives in the marvellous slow movement of the *Short Symphony* where the long laden lines, burning with un-Stravinskian *Affekt*, are straitened into a searing climax of Mahlerian intensity with un-Mahlerian terseness. Later, Mahler's sweetness and nostalgia, eschewed here, are permitted for moments of all the three famous ballets, flowers in the first movement of the Clarinet Concerto (1947–8) and turns to ice-crystals in *Inscape* (1967). Meanwhile the next important work of the 1930s, *Statements* for orchestra (1933–5), is a study, as the title implies, in varied intonations, wherein sentimental and bombastic rhetoric, and their parody, continue a ghost of the Mahler-lineage. For the audience that relishes the parody-element in early Britten and Shostakovich, *Militant*, *Dogmatic* (with its sly insertion of the theme from the *Variations* in its 'note-row' form) and *Jingo* offer a classier version of this typically 30s mood; *Cryptic* and *Subjective* dig deeper into the 'withdrawn' territory present from the very start; while *Prophetic*, the final *Statement*, reveals a further aspect of Copland as seer, visionary, lawgiver of Mosaic power: this aspect making the climax of Bernstein's tribute quoted earlier.

The pivotal work is *El Salón México*. This is reflected in the protracted composition of a brief, apparently simple portrait of a favoured night-spot via the affectionate deconstruction and cross-copulation of its typical musics – four years, on and off (1932–6, years that included the *Short Symphony* and *Statements*, as well as the odd, somewhat perfunctory 'political' ballet *Hear Ye! Hear Ye!*, a score never revived in the composer's lifetime though, as usual, he frugally re-used its best bits elsewhere). For *El Salón*, despite its modest aim, achieves something bold and new. It might well have seemed like a one-off without issue till its manifest quality was endorsed – for the first time in his career – by a spate of high-level performances, transforming his image from an esoteric specialist addressing a cultivated minority to a national figure poised on the brink of international popularity. Its success, both inner and outer, must have changed the way he viewed his talent and its course.

The great leap forward is the total reliance for every element in a piece upon popular melody, whether as here a *trouvaille* or, as later, sedulously researched for the particular appropriate ends of subject, period and place. Whatever the virtues of his output heretofore, Copland could certainly not be called a melodist. His continuity, for all its command of an un-Stravinskian breadth of paragraph, is equally with Stravinsky made up of small units, ostinatos endlessly reiterated, varied, newly juxtaposed and realigned. Only *Vitebsk* had used given material, a use born of special circumstances, its inspiration in a production of *The Dybbuk*. But the plasticity, suppleness, inventive freedom with which the Mexican tunes are intercut, almost interbred, goes beyond the obvious origin in the opening and closing tableaux of *Petrushka* – almost, in its tender, unsatirical purity, back via Stravinsky all the way to Glinka's *Kamarinskaya*. This loss of personality in an identification with the foreign idiom so selfless that it becomes native, gives the cue for all the later feats of stylization – the Wild West ballets *Rodeo* and *Billy the Kid*, with their ballads, sentimental ditties, dances, etc., and the Gentle East whose hymnody infuses *Appalachian Spring* and *Lincoln Portrait*. And thence the whole range – from loving literal arrangement as in the two sets of *Old American Songs* (particularly loving in the subsequent orchestral version) to the distilled spirit of this language without its letter – the core of his mature style and his most beloved works, the sonorous incarnation of his country.

Thus Copland joins the glorious company of twentieth-century masters who need material given or taken from outside themselves to work on – be it folk-strains from their own immediate culture or from their own or other collectors' wide-wandering ethnic gathering: not because of inferior endowment (the list after all includes Grainger, Bartók and above all Stravinsky) so much as self-formation through some element extra to that self, chiming with what is innate. The salient questions with all such composers are, What is the innate endowment? How far can it go before its limits are reached and/or it runs out of steam? What is right for it, that will provide the juice to recharge the engine and extend the journey? The answers given by Copland's two closest *vraisemblers* to this third question make an absorbing comparison. Ravel's was willing submission to a long succession of models, sometimes as a challenge to his prowess, more often from a sort of amorous wish to merge with and become indistinguishable from the adored original. Stravinsky's was the avid appetite of the lean kine to swallow up the fatness of whole fields of culture, giving him sustenance in the form of plentiful matter to reshape. Both lose themselves to find themselves; Copland too. The difference is the absence in him of any sense of dressing up, disguise, stylistic or technical tour de force. No matter that the boy from Brooklyn with his Paris training and Manhattan career is utterly remote from the Wild West and the quietest East: the gift first revealed in *El Salón México* is for cultural permeation and absorption so easy, natural, total as to disarm all intimations of artificiality. His stylistic and ethnic assumptions are his body, not his clothes. Before, he was only a skeleton (though, remembering the *Variations*, and Cézanne's remark about Monet, one has to add, but what a skeleton!).

The difference between his work employing received material and work free of it can be appreciated at once by comparing the generic attractiveness of a nice, friendly socially serviceable school-orchestra workout, stamped New Deal Americana on every bar, like the *Outdoor Overture* of 1938, with *Billy the Kid* from the same year, with its absolutely specific focus, through its employment of the just-right borrowed material, upon a period, a place, a society in all its moods, from violence to tender elegy, from impersonal landscape to human community. Similarly, the dutiful school-opera of 1936, *The Second Hurricane*, and its resourceful, but ultimately unmemorable, sequence of genres and types, with the ostensibly 'grown-up' grand opera three-acter of 1952–4, *The Tender Land*, where the musical language has been washed through with this artificially invented, wholly naturalized American inflection – glowing, radiant, authentic, saturating the lame text and stilted situations, the two-dimensional characters, the knock-kneed dramaturgy. (Because of all this the orchestral suite, yielding the vision, without embarrassments, in all its freshness, is much preferable.)

The twelve years from Billy to Emily (the *Dickinson Songs* of 1950) are Copland's prime: his most prolific, popular, perfected. The earlier achievement is not surpassed; nor perhaps equalled. (It's interesting that its two high points are both revisited later in life as the prime begins to turn. The *Symphonic Ode*, virtually unheard since its première, recommissioned in 1955 with orchestration at once slightly curbed yet filled out; the *Variations* orchestrated 1957 without change, but compromising the specifically pianistic qualities – resonance and attack – that give the original its unforgettable impact.) The loss, if loss it be, is more than compensated for in the greater maturity, depth and breadth that result from the chosen language's deliberate extension of range and tone.

From now on to the end of his composing life an oscillation principle is loosely in play, whereby each move towards expansive accessibility is counterbalanced by a complementary turn towards meditative, abstracted calm. That *Quiet City* (1939) comes between the two Westerns is fortuitous, since this haunting piece began life in incidental music for a play; but the Piano Sonata (1939–41) is a deliberated study in ascetic withdrawal before the festive raucousness of *Rodeo* (1942). Thus the pure chastity of the Violin Sonata of 1942–3 – Ravel's *style dépouillé* and Sibelius's 'glass of cold water' passed through the Satie-mirror and out the other side (Copland seems here to take up his own challenge, 'I wanted to see how simple I could be without losing my personality') – runs concurrent across 1942–3 with the fabulous acridity, pungency, humour and metrical kick of the *Danzón Cubano* for two pianos, and the celebrated pieces of wartime uplift, *Lincoln Portrait* and *Fanfare for the Common Man*. Unique in their day for attaining imaginative utterance (*Statements*, continued) and with a genuine populist charge unsullied by condescension or vulgarity, whether English Imperial or Soviet bathetic, their purity of diction and severity of technique not only saving them from such pitfalls but preventing the willingly stirred auditor from even thinking about the potential tackiness (except when an over-zealous narrator sends *Lincoln* over the top). This over-schematic view should of course be nuanced by enjoyment of the beautiful use of raucous/quietist contrasts within individual works: in *Rodeo*, the 'corral nocturne' between its extrovert neighbours; in the Piano Sonata the shifting, hesitant, then clangorous scherzo between its 'Quaker' outer movements: a favourite sequence is the passage in *Billy* from night-scene, via gunfight, and Billy's death, to open out again on to the wide empty prairie with which the story began.

The impulse to cleanness, freshness, frankness, simplicity, precision informs both the inward- and the outward-directed music of this time. *Appalachian Spring* (1943–4), still the *locus classicus* (more particularly in the sparer, less shiny sound of the original thirteen-instrument scoring) of a particular hard yet tender, soft yet stringent vision of American Pastoral. This triumph of hard-earned intonation yields a procession of successors, gradually diluting and turning very slightly towards the habitual. Still at the top comes the *a cappella* chorus *In the Beginning* (1947), a model of luminous choral layout that, beneath its appearance of gobbling up the long text of the seven days of creation from Genesis as prosaically as possible, succeeds through sheer wide-eyed straightforwardness in inducing awe at the miracle better than could a more elaborate pose. And the twelve Dickinson songs are a wonderful summa of all the composer's accents, compacted, intensified, deepened: 'nature, death, life, eternity' as he succinctly puts it. The contrasts here of bright/dusty, hard/sweet, burning/melting surpass those within or between any other music of the phase. Take the final succession, from the pounding darkness of the 'funeral in the brain', the plain mellifluous old-world 'organ talk', the sprightly *scherzando* of the trip to heaven so poignantly shading off into wry connivance at the older folks' delusion, to the hallucinatory journey past the playing children, the fertile fields, the setting sun, and then the grave and the timeless consciousness beyond; taking up and into its quietus the cycle's climatic midway setting of the death-vanquishing declamatory *Sleep is Supposed to Be*; its fusion of naked with full, deep calm with brittle bell-like clangour and crashing wide-spaced resonation the quintessence of the Copland vision at its most perfected. Then the vein flows a little perfunctory in the viol-fantasia scherzo centre of the String Nonet (1960), where the reward lies in the gorgeous jammy harmony (new adjectives for this composer) of the slow opening pages and their somewhat protracted return at the end. Finally in the *Duo* for flute and piano (1971) it has grown too dilute for the intensity to hold. Here, at last, the white is too pale.

Meanwhile the adventure with serialism counterpoints the slow decline of pastoralism. One's reaction to this nowadays, long after the 'historical moment' that seemed so imperative has passed, is slightly regretful: not from a doctrinaire standpoint; just because Copland the scrupulous, counting 'the note that costs', mean by instinct, training, experience, simply doesn't seem to need it. But perhaps, as with Stravinsky and Britten, even Poulenc and Frank Martin, there was a sense that a well-practised language required refreshment and surprise. As Copland said, experimenting with 12-tone organization, 'I began to hear chords that I wouldn't have heard otherwise'. It certainly makes a direct link with the earlier phases from which the American adventure – East, West and Latin – had been a detour. But this return to constructivistic modernism has its disadvantages. Put the tingling specificity of the pitches in *Vitebsk* beside the relative unmemorability of the texturally similar Piano Quartet of 1950 (which occasioned the pious remark about new chords); put the compelling inevitability of the *Piano Variations* beside the masterfully laboured gawkiness of the vast architectonic *Piano Fantasy* (1952–7), the nearest approach in these years and in this idiom to compositional summa. Compare above all the glorious overreaching ecstasy of the slow music in the *Symphonic Ode* and the tense athletic exhilaration of its allegro, with the steel-plated rhetoric and allegro-by-rote of equivalent places in *Connotations* (1962). A remarkable acuity of ear has weighed the late work's dense sonorities – Copland would be incapable of the carelessness obscuring much of the century's atonal music before, contemporary with (and persisting). The loss is not of skill, vigour, precision; and an inevitable decline in sheer exuberance is balanced by the bracing challenge of the craggy new crunches and crashes. Yet something difficult to formulate fair-and-square has disappeared from this music; for want of a more ambiguous phrase it could be called inner necessity.

The need is, rather, an aspiration at least partly extra-musical; in the Quartet to align with the then-irresistible serialism; in the *Fantasy* to consolidate and surpass a consummate earlier achievement; in *Connotations* to make the ultimate Statement for a Solemn Occasion. The deficiency is unmissable with a pot-boiler like *Canticle of Freedom* (1955), a second-brew from the fresh leaves of *Lincoln*

Portrait; far harder to distinguish in the three works under discussion; and notoriously divisive with the 3rd Symphony with its dead-central position in his life and output (1944–6). This large, noble score is not just patchy but positively slippery. Its meditative movements (first and third) are withdrawn to the point of secrecy but lack the magic inner concentration of such moods in *Statements* and *Quiet City*, while the high spirits of the intervening scherzo seem, just for once, blatant and patronizing rather than popular and liberating. Then the finale, after the heroic magnificence of the famous *Fanfare* and its equally convincing transformation, after an infamous dissonant crisis, into unexpected pastoral delicacy, steers perilously close to the bombast of a Shostakovich apotheosis without (so far as one can tell) any rumour of (un)mitigating irony.

But another rather deliberated piece, his final work of size and emotional scope, gets together pastoral simplicity and the craggy modernistic, makes a farewell, and effects in its dedication to Charles Ives a *hommage* that elegantly celebrates the past, serves the present and salutes the future – *Night Thoughts* for piano, of 1972. Last thoughts too: after this the music's cessation, long in coming, set in for good (for one can't count the quasi-posthumous gleanings issued during the 1970s and 80s, most of them written well before; and the two *Threnodies* (1971 and 1973) even *sound* like ghosts). 'I must have expressed myself sufficiently. I certainly don't feel tortured or bitter, only lucky to have been given so long to be creative.' Though, as often, this fine stoicism has a slight tinge of the press-release, his grateful admirers can only agree.

To confront Copland as a whole is to focus the gratitude in pleasure, delight and deep simple feeling that Copland evokes, transcending country, race and gender, in the 'common man' whom he has reached, to whom he has given utterance in a 'serious classical' language, complementing the demotic commercial genius of Gershwin, Kern, Berlin, et al. Not, like them, a song on every common man's lips: *speech*, rather, or better, *idiom*; a stylized vernacular invented with scrupulous cunning and *savoir faire* from indigenous folklore. A narrow vein compared with Europe and Russia, more out of books than the living throats of cowboys and Shakers; a sort of Ives (throwing in the West to join the East) that takes a chaos of nostalgic bric-a-brac 'cubisticized' à la Shrovetide Petersburg, and tidied into eminently non-messy lucidity through the Franco-Russian training (Stravinsky), whose combination manages miraculously to avoid genteelizing the natural American flamboyance and razzamatazz. Then the gratitude (pleasure, delight, feeling) of the cognoscenti for the austere, inscaped, unforgivingly essentialized modernist, who composes as if there were not a common man, a leaf of grass, a democratic vista, in sight. Yet this music in its clarity, unambiguity, ineffable physicalization of cerebral intensity, is listener-friendly too, however rebarbative or withdrawn in its refusal to cosset the palate with pralines and the body with cushions. So, in the end neither strain nor wishfulness is needed to hear him integral and integrated – what he always claimed. With Copland, uniquely among the twentieth-century masters, there is 'no problem'.

Aaron Copland: born 1900 in Brooklyn, of Russian-Jewish heritage; early piano then composition lessons in New York; to Paris for three years under Nadia Boulanger. Back home, steady consolidation as composer, vital proactivity as performer, presenter, organizer, educationalist, writer on music. The idiom initially advanced, sometimes flagrant, moving mainstream-wards under New Deal then into Second World War to become a National Treasure in later life, even as the composing renewed the experimental unpopulist directions of his youth. 'Retired' – 'it was like turning off a tap' – with the gradual onset of Alzheimer's: died 1990.

Elliott Carter

Born 1908, Carter was a slow starter. Study with Walter Piston, and in Paris with Nadia Boulanger (yet another). There's a handful of works from the 1930s and 40s; in the later 1940s he's moving into new places, culminating 1950–59 in the breakthrough 1st String Quartet: even after this, composition long remained slow and effortful, yet he was now on course for the subsequent near-six-decades: from the mid-1980s the pace quickens; from around the new century the flood-gates open wide – 2007 yielded nine new works, the year of his centenary saw eleven premières, and he continued to write with vigour until his death in 2012 aged 103.

Nine broad 'periods' can be discerned.

1. ALL-AMERICAN, C.1935 TO THE LATE 1940S

The music of this composer, no longer quite young even as it begins, is marked by a complete lack of distinguishing features, within a common mainstream Euro-North American idiom. Take *Pocahontas*, the ballet of 1936–9: bright brassy upfront music, slightly recalling Walton, with tons of energy, bristling polyphony (à la Hindemith, and with a rather higher rate of dissonance than usual in this style), and Tippett's 1st Symphony. Both composers, unknown to each other, reach an uncannily comparable result. With a crucial difference: whereas the Tippett is often awkward and *sometimes* a little anonymous, the Carter is thoroughly accomplished – nothing crude or amateurish – and *totally* anonymous. Only with the Piano Sonata (1945–6) and, still more, the Cello Sonata (1948) do things really begin to happen. The latter's first movement, composed last, demonstrates with quasi-scientific precision the idea stumbled upon intuitively in the three other movements (not in themselves all that distinctive). Perceiving the obvious discrepancy between dry percussive piano and songful long-sustaining cello, Carter exaggerates rather than resolves it, making the two instruments inhabit their own speeds, characters, material, all going their independent ways in apparently random separation, though in fact carefully controlled. In such easily heard processes lie the origin of every later complexity.

2. BREAKTHROUGH

Over 1950–51 Carter took a year out, living in the Arizona desert, rethinking his music so far, the nature of his gifts and concerns; above all, the authentic experimental-modernist interests of his youth that had had no scope in the atmosphere of New Deal patriotic populism prevailing heretofore. The result, the 1st String Quartet, written during that year of reflection, is a historical landmark: a tremendously impressive breakthrough, in technique, architecture, emotional range and sheer duration. *Deliberate* Americanism is now invoked – no further superficial populist extroversion; rather, conscious alignment with another American line, that of radical innovation. The quartet quotes from the line's founding father Charles Ives in homage; daring theories of Charles Seeger and Henry Cowell are put into practice; the influence of the two other marvellous composers who also embodied such ideas in their real music – Ruth Crawford, Conlon Nancarrow – is palpable (and Nancarrow is also quoted).

Yet even in this magnificent achievement, which for the first time manifests masterful genius rather than talented assiduity, some of the same problems characterizing the earlier work still remain; nor do they ever really disappear in the later. A certain deadness in the pitches, for all their colour often (in general) grey: a certain mechanization in the textures, for all their (often fantastic) decorative elaboration: a certain *willed* quality in the metrical manipulations (for all their liberating brilliance).

At the core of his sound lies what must be called, for want of a better word, *abstraction*: as in painting, when a nude, a still-life, a landscape, becomes a pattern of lines and angles or a smattering of splotts. And behind this, there's the fundamental question of identity. In his earlier, populist music Carter was obviously wearing disguise. In the modernist music that follows, he is, even while realizing his potential with breathtaking success, using camouflage.

3. FIRST PEAK:
VARIATIONS FOR ORCHESTRA, 1953–5

In this fine work we find a surprising recurrence of his earlier All-American vein with its uncharacteristic and under-characterized scores from the 1930s and 40s. Here, a decade or so later, is Carter's *real* response to the American Sublime of Copland's *Symphonic Ode*, Harris's and Schuman's 3rd Symphonies, and before them the same note in Ives, Varèse's *Amériques*, Ruggles' *Sun-treader*: proclamatory, rhetorical, brazen, extrovert, uplifting and positive. The next major work, however – the 2nd String Quartet of 1959 – poses the permanent worries in their acutest form so far. Behind the skittish, volatile, playful surface lies something impenetrable, ungraspable, incomprehensible (save to the academic analyst). Purporting to render 'Characters' in quasi-human situations, as indicated by Ives in his argumentative chamber-pieces, reveals in Carter the fundamental anonymity at the heart of his invention. Each instrument has its interval, its rhythm, its mode-of-attack, etc., in a boring and pious bow to the total serialization from Paris and Germany of ten years before. Yet this insistence upon characterization at all costs draws into sharp focus the fact that, *au fond*, this material has no character all – it is potential, merely; the *materia musica* in embryo; not yet composed into living musical continuum, for all the living intention – in a word, dead.

4. JUNGLE

Now, for the well-disposed music-lover, the problems predominate – even for the 'specialist' as well. Carter's next works are so complex – cerebral – conceptual – as to defy one's most determined efforts at understanding in any but abstract terms. Evidently the product of huge and prolonged labour, they nevertheless enter a hermetic area of non-communication as if in perverse rejection of the brilliant explicitness of the *Orchestral Variations*. The composer has for some of them divulged underlying poetic metaphor or scenario, as if realizing that his enterprise needs such 'extra-musical' assistance. And perhaps such analogies are our best – our *only* – way in. Thus with the *Double Concerto* for harpsichord and piano of 1959–61. Still more with the ensuing Concerto for piano alone (1964–5). What does the willing-and-hopeful hearer actually take in, confronting such maximalist/modernist complexity/complication? The 'jungle' textures are both impressive and oppressive, as is the rapid turnover of flickering volatile activity under the sign of Carter's favoured direction, *fantastico*. The solo piano-writing, often alive in clangour or delicacy, is equally often merely 'rent-a-texture' from the anonymous and parody-able avant-garde. In the second movement (of two) the 'long lines' of the little group of soloists surrounding the solo piano – especially the bass clarinet, later the cor anglais – are astonishing feats of keeping-it-up. But the upshot of all the score's fiendish hyper-maximality – the upshot that can be perceived and enjoyed, that is – appears to be simplistic indeed; the Handful against the Crowd. There's a whiff of decadence here; its working definition in artistic terms, means and ends out of synch, is undeniably fulfilled. A discrepancy so blatant brings Carter into unlikely proximity with Richard Strauss on a bad day, or even with Erich Korngold, albeit, obviously, miles apart in idiom.

5. HIGH PLATEAU

The next major work, the *Concerto for Orchestra*, completed 1969, is a knock-out. Though it remains maximally complex, every difficulty is vindicated, every process and scheme audible, every form and proportion expressive, within a sonority of strikingly physical impact. Messiaen's impromptu private reaction to Carter's music – 'the brain is *formidable*, one questions the *sound*' – is here overturned. And the basis in poetry isn't tacked on as a sort of high literary credential, but richly and sensuously realized by means of the actual notes we hear, and the strenuous processes by which they've been found. This verbal source is directly concerned with Inspiration itself: Carter takes his bearings from Saint-John Perse's epic prose-poem celebrating the great winds that sweep the surface of the globe – north, south, east, west, with all their intercrossed subsidiaries, and all their contrasted attributes. Carter's schema typically turns succession into simultaneity: four different types of texture, scoring, momentum, are continually abutting and intercutting each other, and are often heard superimposed, creating a perpetual play of volatility, density, lightness and weight that seems to evolve before one's very ears.

The grand rhetoric and vivid coloration of the *Orchestral Variations*, lost in the intervening jungle, now re-emerge intensified, subtilized, refined. The language at large has to be called 'athematic' now (in the *Variations* one could still just about hold on to their themes). But Carter's deficiencies in this branch of composition, like his namesake Wagner's deficiencies in shapely conjunct melody, are now obversed to become a source of strength. This high plateau is sustained and broadened in several subsequent pieces of the 1970s. After the *Concerto for Orchestra* a sort of pattern sets in, alternating some of Carter's most immediately appealing scores with some of his most forbidding. Third String Quartet (1971) – hyper-complexity's ultimate: in early performances the four players had to use click-tracks in order to hear their own individual *tactus* rather than what the others were playing audibly – the negation of chamber-music as civilized conversation, though a bracing and impressive experience in itself. *Duo* for piano and violin, 1973; 1974 Quintet for brass – both these begin rebarbative and unrewarding, and remain so after many hearings. *A Mirror on Which to Dwell* (1975) – one of Carter's finest, loved and enjoyed as well as merely admired. *Symphony of Three Orchestras* (1976) – another work admixing superb things with a return to the Jungle and a foretaste of arid deserts to come. *Syringa* (1978) – again flawed and marvellous, this cantata setting John Ashbery for soprano and guitar with ensemble in a style of liquid delicacy that delights, enchants, occasionally ravishes the ear; but combining this (to Ashbery's privately communicated resentment) with a bass soloist furiously declaiming fragments of text from Greek poets, playwrights, philosophers, commenting obliquely on the main poem in English. *Night Fantasies* for piano (1980) – despite its homage to Schumann in title and imagery, this work remains impenetrable after many hearings. The same goes for the Robert Lowell cycle of the subsequent year, *In Sleep, in Thunder*. And the *Triple Duo* (1983) also: and another ultimate of complexity/complication, *Penthode* (1985) wherein, as the title indicates, five separate chamber-groups fight it out till the death. But in 1986 came the life-enhancing *Celebration of Some 100 × 150 Notes*, a triumph of delicate fantasy, combined with steely strength, poetry, wit, speed, volatility, invention; an entire technique and aesthetic concentrated into a three-minute nutshell.

6. SETTLED STATE

The irregular pattern that alternates attractive/colourful/relatively accessible with rebarbative/featureless/fairly repellent persists through the 1990s and beyond, right up to the end, with a gradual tendency towards dryness, even aridity, though the energy never falters. Beneath the compulsive spate real urgency and thrust have diminished: earlier slow effortfulness is replaced with fluency and ease that can approach the mechanical. The old composer at last has his habits, his routines, his chord-book: the machine cranks out bigger works in plenty, surrounded by plentiful smaller things, on a production-line. Missing is Inner Necessity: without this vital impulse, the later Carter can often degenerate into note-spinning, like any Baroque or rococo provider – Telemann, Vivaldi – or their twentieth-century successors Hindemith, Milhaud, Villa-Lobos, Henze, Maxwell Davies.

Much of Carter's output now appears exiguous, for all the intelligence and high facture. Some of these works from the mid-1980s to the mid-1990s are among the ugliest music ever written. Try *Tempo e Tempi* (1988–9) or the Quintet for Piano and Winds (1991), the two principal offenders amid stiff and copious competition. Some miniature Occasionals for one, two or three players are surprisingly simple, light of touch, poetical; take *Esprit rude/esprit doux* (1985) for flute and clarinet: it provides the best way in to introduce the outstanding triumph of Carter's late work, the mighty *Symphonia* completed the next year.

7. LATE PEAK

'I am the prize of flowing hope'; these words head the *Symphonia*; they, and its binding imagery, come from a Latin poem by Richard Crashaw – *Bulla/Bubble* – wherein the world is seen, bright and dark alike, from the insouciant angle of a free-floating iridescence high above. The forty-five-minute totality is divided into three movements: no. 1, *Partita* (1993) – airborne, all-volatile playful flux, reflecting the variety and perpetual change of life on earth below: no. 2,

Adagio tenebroso (1994) – the bubble broods on the world's dark side – vision of waste, ominous/obsessive/bleak; the movement's power reined in till, almost when we've ceased to expect it, comes the shattering climax; after which, total desolation. So to no. 3 *Allegro scorrevole* (1996) – *scorrevole*, 'flowing/fluent/gliding' – a study in delicate deliquescence, as if a zephyr had escaped from the buffeting winds of the *Concerto for Orchestra*; the bubble's wayward weightlessness sings, shines, sparkles, and finally seems to gently burst, leaving not a wrack behind. A judicious *Bulla/Summa* from Bayan Northcott, one of Carter's most consistent champions: 'Against all the minimalism retro-styles, and compromises with commercialism that have marked the music of the last couple of decades, *Symphonia* embodies a comprehensive and uncompromising reaffirmation of the modernist vision.'

8. WHAT NEXT?

The inevitable catch-phrase for Carter as he entered his second century, all guns blazing, was the actual quizzical title for his first foray into opera (1997–8), undertaken when only ninety years of age and breaking remarkable new ground on an extended scale. The scenario and libretto for *What Next?* are pretentious tosh. One wonders how this cultivated composer, well-read in languages ancient and modern, the setter of Ashbery, Bishop, Lowell, Stevens, could have countenanced it for a moment. But the resulting score – all the way from the ferocious car crash with which it starts – is astonishing, wholly transcending the stilted surroundings and situation as opera always has and always will. Quite new for Carter is the effervescent lyricism of the writing for women's voices in ensemble – one would almost say Richard Strauss! Not quite the *Rosenkavalier* trio ... (But then, what is?)

Disconcerting is the virtual absence, from the work of a man in his tenth decade, of any sense that this is 'late music'. One thinks of Fauré, Strauss, Vaughan Williams: distillation, strangeness, the inwardly withdrawing quality, meditation, retrospect, farewell. The closest parallel is of course the Verdi of *Falstaff*, crackling with newness at a mere seventy-nine (and even Verdi then audibly winds down in the *Four Sacred Pieces* that follow his last stage-work). One late Carter score alone seems like the product of a very old man, the song-cycle on Wallace Stevens for soprano and orchestra, entitled *In the Distances of Sleep* composed in 2006. Not all the songs either: some retain and renew the tumult of twenty, thirty, forty years before; notably 'To the Roaring Wind', whose title speaks for itself. But elsewhere there is a reflective warmth and amplitude resonant with long, long experience. And one song goes beyond, into a region of bare austerity unique in this composer of fantastical busyness – (110 × 150 notes on every page). Stevens's beautiful poem 'Re-statement of Romance' concerns human closeness and separateness, both intimate:

> The night knows nothing of the chants of night.
> It is what it is as I am what I am:
> And in perceiving this I best perceive myself
> And you. Only we two may interchange
> Each in the other what each has to give.
> Only we two are one, not you and night,
> Nor night and I, but you and I, alone,
> So much alone, so deeply by ourselves,
> So far beyond the casual solitudes,
> That night is only the background of our selves,
> Supremely true each to its separate self,
> In the pale light that each upon the other throws.

Carter's setting accompanies the voice only with a single line, passed among the strings from infinitely high to the bottom of the double-basses, exactly mirroring the text's mysterious familiarity.

9. AND NOW?

Where will this impressive, important, ultimately unembraceable figure ultimately stand? There's a telling compare-and-contrast relationship with his exact contemporary Messiaen, born just a day earlier. Since the deaths of the composers who have manifestly entered the mainstream of general appreciation – Shostakovich in 1975, Britten in 1976 – the world of 'serious classical music' has by common consent been divided by the twin colossi Messiaen and Carter. Neither woos and wows the masses like minimalism (sacred and secular): both will survive when it recedes.

Messiaen is *probably* the greater composer as he *certainly* is the more accessible, appealing, by now almost popular. The ear for pitch and sonority is flawless, the technique unfaultable. His limitations are twofold: aesthetic, or a matter of taste – if his theology and birdsong leave you cold, you miss what for him is absolutely crucial. The same goes also for the sober technical aspects – the naïve repetitiousness, the absence of counterpoint, the frequent outbursts of material that is merely trite or sheerly vulgar, the circularity of the self-enclosed systems. Balancing all this, the strengths – his sensuous precision and astonishingly vivid accuracy of coloration, and the to-the-jugular nature of his overwhelming conviction and communication.

Carter will never be popular. Appeal is precluded by a fundamental anonymity, greyness, even deadness of the material behind its incessant liveliness. And more still by its incredible difficulties – for players in performing his music, for listeners in perceiving it. These things balance the conceptual/cerebral power, lit up at its best with a vein of poetic fantasy; and the boundless sense of adventure – especially in the domain of rhythm – modulation between momentums and textures, stratifying simultaneity of contrasted characters – a new 'species' of polyphonic possibility.

Put side-by-side, their strengths and limits are remarkably compatible. Each is a master, grand where the other is deficient, and vice versa: merge them into one and there'd be a composer of protean comprehensiveness. After the twentieth-century's first six decades, uniquely churned up by radical innovation splitting the language of music asunder, the combination of Carter and Messiaen would make a late-century synthesis comparable to that in his time of J. S. Bach.

CHAPTER XVII

The Route to Messiaen

French exoticism

A broad outline follows of exoticism and primitivity in music from the mid-nineteenth century and all the way along the twentieth, with culmination – the gigantic conflux of sources – in the oceanic comprehensiveness of Messiaen. The line is mainly French, with a strong initial influx from the Russian nationalists: then, as pre-1914 Paris became the Mecca for many composers desiring to escape the perceived Teutonic tyranny, the field widens to embrace Spain, Eastern Europe, Greece, Latin America, all drawn by the allure of Debussy's impressionism and Ravel's Ravelism. I'll indicate with just a glance some key-works of these two, and other composers covered in detail elsewhere, and halt now and again for vignettes of those who aren't.

First, some French forebears. Exoticism seems to be innate in French culture: a now-forgotten harbinger was Félicien David's orchestral *Le Désert* (1844): Berlioz touches upon the Orient in *L'Enfance du Christ* and *The Trojans*, Delibes sets an entire opera in India (*Lakmé*), Bizet one in Ceylon (*The Pearl Fishers*) and another (*Djamileh*) in Cairo: Saint-Saëns' *Samson and Delilah* is Old Testament Gaza, Franck's *Les Djinns* is Arabia. The Russian sources, so vital to the next French generation, can be focused in two seminal orchestral works – Balakirev's *Tamara* (the Caucasus) and its inferior offspring Rimsky-Korsakov's *Scheherazade* – while the very title, *Islamey*, of Balakirev's influential piano-piece speaks for itself. (Musorgsky, still more seminal for Ravel and Debussy, only touches the Orient vestigially.) Debussy's whole way of working is transformed by encountering the Javanese gamelan. Key later pieces are *Pagodes* and *Et la lune descend sur le temple qui fût* (China); *Poissons d'or* (Japan); *La Terrasse des audiences du clair de lune* (India) and two variously imperfect ballets, *Khamma* ('Egyptian') and *No-ja-li* ('Oriental').

Ravel had already raised the veil upon an entire continent in *Asie*: the other two songs of *Shéhérazade* seem to be more Moroccan/Algerian than Eastern: later, *Laideronnette, Impératrice des Pagodes* (from *Ma mère l'Oye*) is Balinese, the *Mélodies hébraïques* Jewish, the *Chansons madécasses* Madagascan, the tea-crockery in *L'Enfant et les sortilèges* Chinese. Stravinsky, already influenced by France even before moving to Paris and associating with his two seniors in person, incomparably renders China and Japan in *Le Rossignol*. And there's a precious conjunction around 1914 of three song-sets with ensemble directly inspired by his report of something utterly strange he'd just encountered, Schoenberg's *Pierrot lunaire*, as exotic as the Orient though emanating from Belgium via Bergamo and Berlin: the fruits of this encounter are Stravinsky's own *Three Japanese Lyrics*; Ravel's three Mallarmé-settings, and the *Quatre poèmes hindous* by their companion-in-arms Maurice Delage.

Maurice Delage (1879–1961) – virtually unknown and utterly neglected, save the handful of miniatures here mentioned: pupil of Ravel (possibly his only), implausibly claimed lover (brief) of Stravinsky: for sure, with both the leading spirits of *Les Apaches*, set to provoke the Establishment and cultivate the Esoteric. His travels in India and Japan in 1912 produced two miniatures of ravishing refinement to stand alongside his more famous friends' achievements in Radical Exotic.

The *Hindou*s cycle employs diverse texts. *Madras* (actually composed there, and dedicated to Ravel) sets a stanza from India itself, by Bhartrihari: the slender beauty walks alone in the forest, resting from time to time to lift the golden veils covering her breasts; she returns to the moon the rays that bathe her – all sensual/sensuous languor. *Lahore*, also composed where it says, sets a poem of Heine which at first seems incongruous but isn't so – the solitary pine-tree, on its freezing northern mountain, sleeps, dreaming of the solitary palm-tree in the distant East, silent and desolate on its burning rock. Delage ingeniously imitates the Indian sitar by twanging sliding pizzicato; the texture glows gently efflorescent as the East is mentioned: when the poem is done, in sensitive parlando, the soprano is left alone in wordless arabesque melisma till the instruments steal quietly in to support her in her loneliness. *Bénarès – naissance de Bouddha*: this text appears to be the composer's: it announces with suppressed excitement the signs – amassing clouds, gods scattering wondrous flowers and mysterious perfumes – of the imminent birth; the full moon, a holy pearl, suspends above the marble palace guarded by 20,000 elephants like grey hills resembling the grey clouds. *Jeypur*, again written at that city and setting Bhartrihari again, this time dedicated to Stravinsky, once more evokes ardent sensuality as in *Madras* (from whose music it quotes): thinking of her you ache in torment; seeing her your mind fails you; if you touch her reason deserts you; how can one call her well-belovèd? An epitome of desire in nineteen bars. Delage's subsequent *Sept haï-kaïs* are just as special: none larger than a fern-leaf.

Further, more mainstream French Orientalisms include Dukas' ballet *La Péri* (Persian) and d'Indy's ingenious *Istar* – not a ballet (though eminently suited), rather, a sequence of orchestral variations, reversed so that each number is successively less ornate, rich, *clad*, ending with the theme in pure bareness: thus enacting the archaic Assyrian story. The Goddess Istar must rescue her lover from the underworld by removing her garments one by one, beginning with her crown; at the seventh (like Salome) she is completely naked and he is saved.

Albert Roussel, 1869–1937: intended for a mathematician; instead, seven years at sea, including experience of the Far East; returned to Paris to commence musical education, continued at the Schola Cantorum under d'Indy till 1908. Roussel also taught there, his pupils including two ultra-incompatibles, Satie and Varèse. Best known for two ballets – *Le Festin de l'araignée* (1913), *Bacchus et Ariane* (1931); plentiful chamber-music and songs, four symphonies:

his most characteristic manner after the Great War is tough, rough, chewy, rebarbative; powerful if somewhat mechanized, strong on energy, short on charm and suavity.

Roussel belongs here for his opera *Padmâvatî* (1913–18) with its thirteenth-century Rajasthan setting, and for the *Three Evocations* for orchestra (1910–11): no. 1, *Les Dieux dans l'ombre des cavernes*, responds in general to Hindu sacred places, in particular to the caves of Ellora, with fine mystic resonance. No. 2, *Au bords de fleuve sacré* adds chorus and soloists setting a specially written poem praising the sacred river and the holy city, perfumes in the night, blooming lotus, blissful lovers in a fusion of bodily and spiritual less than intoxicating when compared to such near-contemporaries as Szymanowski's *Song of the Night* and Scriabin's *Poem of Ecstasy*, let alone *Turangalîla*-to-come. A less flowery work of the same years remains Roussel's most attractive – *The Spider's Banquet.* Not Oriental for sure but surely both exotic and primeval, inspired by the great etymologist Jean-Henri Fabre, and linking in with another aspect of Ravel, the insects in *Histoires naturelles* a little earlier (1906) and in *L'Enfant et les sortilèges* later: for all these reasons I can't resist its inclusion here.

In a peaceable garden sits *l'araignée*, the spider at the centre of her immense silken web already clogged with trapped victims. She waits patiently to ensnare her next dinner; some ants scuttle off with a fallen rose-petal; she attends to her web; a pair of dung-beetles appear; the ants return to collect another petal; a butterfly flits by, hungrily observed by the greedy spider, who entices the lovely creature into the web, where she dies after a struggle. She's cocooned; the murderess dances in triumph till frightened by an apple falling. Worms want this heaven-sent nourishment but it's guarded by two praying mantises; the cunning worms elude them and penetrate the *pomme*; the mantises squabble in mutual accusation, the ants jeering them on, the spider too: climax – two more victims caught in her web for the spider's banquet – her second victory, diverted by a mayfly effortfully freeing herself from her chrysalis, then liberated for a lively *valse*. As she sinks exhausted, all the other insects applaud with genuine admiration, even *l'araignée*.

The two worms emerge from the apple plump and sated; they invite the mayfly to dance but she's spent – her tiny hour is passed; she gives up the ghost. The spider now prepares to eat, but one mantis, freed by a dung-beetle from the web, polishes her off. Funeral music for the pretty creature and the serial killer; gentle close as twilight enfolds the now-deserted garden, at peace as at the start before the carnage. A trifle: an absurdity: an anomaly also in Roussel's oeuvre as a whole: he's here admitted the charm, delicacy, humour, lightness of touch, that elude him in his more ambitious undertakings.

A fanciful, trumped-up exotic now, crossing here with a later twentieth-century strain, the primitive/primeval. Darius Milhaud, 1892–1974: after study at the Paris Conservatoire and commencing career as composer, he passed two years (1917–19) in Brazil as secretary to the poet Paul Claudel, French consul in Rio. Back in Paris, the centre-pivot of its new musical tone epitomized by *Les Six*, whose best composer by now is clearly Francis Poulenc. Of Milhaud's *c*.440 compositions, enjoying huge repute between the wars and vying with the Brazilian jungle for promiscuous fertility, little survives today. He got it right just the once, in the ballet *La Création du monde* (1923). The action, devised by Blaise Cendrars, derives from a creation-myth according to black African folklore: the music is a mingle – cool neo-Baroque à la 1920s' Stravinsky colliding with vibrant saxophone, jazzy riffs and big-band syncopations. Forms and procedures simple, alternating, lively, laid-back, cool/warm/hot: slight but appealing and memorable: a perfect Period Piece, evoking Rio, New Orleans, New York, Paris more than the jungle whence the world originates, outlasting in its lack of pretension many a more apparently Important statement.

Now an authentic Brazilian, for all his years in Paris and later absorption into a French mainstream: Heitor Villa-Lobos, born Rio 1887, studied at its Conservatório; but principal musical education informal – playing in theatre-bands, exploring the deep inner musical life of his country – native Indian, imposed Portuguese, imported African, with popular city-music, especially the tangos

of Ernesto Nazareth, a delicious Latin-American brother to Scott
Joplin in the US. During the war-years he composed, inter alia,
two symphonic poems for orchestra pantheistically celebrating his
mighty country, became excited by Diaghilev's Ballets Russes on
their Brazilian tour, and befriended Milhaud in his Rio period, who
acquainted him with recent musical trends in Europe. Unappreci-
ated at home he relocated, to Europe in 1923–4, and again in 1927–30
to Paris, where he received acclaim and success. Back home, established at last, a national icon, he poured out music with prolificity
easily surpassing Milhaud's – more than two thousand compositions! After the war many foreign visits; success in the US, rather
less in Europe – out of phase and fashion with the latest directions.
Died 1959.

Principally remembered now for nine *Bachianas Brasileiras*
(1930–45), entwining to often delightful effect the Baroque of Bach
with the popular *choro* of his own culture. This latter genre also
embraces some fourteen pieces of his oeuvre, varying from solo
piano or guitar, via small ensembles, to large orchestra works sometimes including voices. The *Chôros* is the core of his gigantic output;
he invents musical Brazil in his own image – 'I don't use folklore,
I am folklore'. Salient for here, *Amazonas* (1917), one of the two
wartime symphonic poems, evoking the mighty river, the endless
jungle, its fauna and its gods. Splendid in frank exuberance and
uninhibited relish; interlocking ostinati and long looping melodic
lines, interrupted – erupted – by shouts, rumblings, slurps and
burps, eructations and ejaculations, yelps and shrieks, violent thuds,
the whole tapestry gradually co-ordinating into continuity culminating in a mighty smash on the gong, then rapidly disintegrating
in a spasmodic, convulsive close. Gentler episodes feature a viola
d'amore and a 'violinophone', who also participate rather haplessly
in the welter of the tuttis. Villa-Lobos clearly heard and learnt from
what the Diaghilev company brought to Rio. What he couldn't
have heard is what *Amazonas* most resembles, especially when its
material waxes gay, populist, riotous: a Latin-American sibling to
Varèse's contemporary *Amériques*, which salutes and celebrates *both*
Americas, north and south. Messiaen claims Villa-Lobos as one

of his favourite composers: and this is proved by many palpable resemblances.

Charles Koechlin

Charles Koechlin, 1867–1950: intended for an engineer but, after a family tussle, music won. Studied at the Paris Conservatoire from 1890, from 1892 with Massenet, from 1896 with Fauré – his life-long gratitude to and reverence for Fauré repaid with the first biography of the *maître* whom, long before, he'd assisted with the logistics of the massive outdoor *Prométhée* and orchestration of the delicate indoor music for *Pelléas et Mélisande*. Koechlin had also helped Debussy with *Le Martyre de Saint Sébastien* and orchestrated the exotic ballet *Khamma*, so reluctantly undertaken by the hard-pressed composer that he muttered 'write *Khamma* yourself and I'll sign it'. These kindly acts indicate something of Koechlin's nature – disinterested and practical – expanding further into visionary, ideal-istic, open-minded, boundlessly curious, learnèd, an outstanding, utterly unacademic pedagogue, unsurpassed in mastery until sur-passed, in all these respects, by Messiaen himself.

So where does Koechlin stand as *composer*? Another enormous catalogue – some 350 opuses, hugely compromised by dilution, repetition, redundancy, absurdity. Dead central to the theme of this outline is Koechlin's life-long obsession, like Percy Grainger's, with Kipling's *Jungle Books*. An early tribute is three orchestral songs com-pleted 1904, still under the wing but not the letter of Debussy, sump-tuous and evocative in their own right – the song of his mother for the little white seal, the jungle night-song, and the song of Kala Nag the captive elephant hankering for his freedom. Koechlin's princi-pal Kipling inspiration, however, comes in four symphonic poems composed on-and-off until the 1930s, though their roots go back to the earliest years of the century. Naïveté here lies close-proximate to high sophistication, cunning complexity, and an orchestral wizardry second to none – not even Ravel.

The first two, *La Loi de la jungle* and *La Méditation de Puran Bhagat*, are stripped bare beyond simplicity: their material doesn't suffice, except to complement the busy animation and complexity of the other two. *La Course du printemps – The Spring Running –* is the longest, a masterpiece of momentum, chock-a-block with intricate detail, always crystal-clear. The score comes with a verbal scenario that again indicates naïveté: the musical substance is anything but. Enough to grasp the underlying place and time – jungle, night, spring in the air – and human impulse – Mowgli, adolescent on threshold of manhood, jungle-bred, friend of all the creatures and speaking their languages, feeling now the lure of humankind as a poison he must expel even as it is desired and cannot be denied – 'Man goes to Man'. He sorrowfully bids the creatures farewell and runs out the poison till he's drained. In Kipling he returns for a second goodbye and they dismiss him, Balou the Bear, Bagheera the Panther, even Kaa the Python ('it is hard to cast the skin'), with love. In Koechlin the boy/man is left alone under the stars, his heart breaking with the divine beauty revealed to his human spirit, hearing his jungle-companions' last echo, asking himself, What is this great mystery? Why all this? – all this coming more naturally in the composer's French words and transcended utterly by his *notes*. The overall shape comes in four sections: Spring in the jungle; Mowgli himself; the Running; Night. The sounds of nature, the boy's restlessness, the impetuous leaps preceding his first run then his second, are all unmistakable in the course of the music – they *speak*. Fabulous harmony/voicing/spacing of the mysterious bits, fabulous sparkling physical prowess of the running bits: their conjoining as a whole a sort of gloss upon all three Debussy orchestral *images* – an exuberant *ronde de printemps*, and a *gigue*, beset with *sons et parfums de la nuit*, all merged into one, enhanced and extended to an epic scale.

Les Bandar-Log is equally astonishing and open to cavils. The Bandar-Log are monkeys, without *la loi de la jungle*. 'They are outcasts. They have no speech of their own, but use the stolen words which they overhear when they listen, and peep, and wait above in the branches.' So goes Balou's charge, and Kipling's own voice takes over for several pages . . . no memory; vain and frivolous and mocking, filthy and angry, gibbering and nimble, clever and sterile, etc., etc. They capture Mowgli and, 'bounding and crashing and whooping and yelling', bear him away through the treetops. The marvellous story (*Kaa's Hunting*) ends satisfactorily, though the Bandar-Log have the last word: 'Brother, thy tail hangs down behind! This is the way of the Monkey-kind.'

Koechlin's piece doesn't tell the tale: rather, it again evokes the jungle-setting, then depicts the creatures' antics before launching a serious critique of their pretensions – transferred to manifestations in contemporary music which he deplored. Somewhat heavy-handed parodies, the more so for their living context – the translucent shine of the vegetation rendered in Koechlin's unmistakable stacked sliding fifths and a snatch of modal melody. Suddenly the monkeys irrupt from the treetops – at once provocatively gesticulating and finely etched, music of split hairs, astounding in its sharp precision and nervy hilarity. Now come the clunky satires. First *'les mouvements parallèles'* – four stupid long notes, descending in whole-tones, grotesquely scored; then in parallel fifths, then double-speed, then doubled again, and again; parallel tritones initiate second round of same; and so with whole chords: everything separated by gibbering mockery or adulation (one and the same). Next, *'l'Atonal'*: after a grunt then a squeak, a 12-note theme jerkily pronounced by two saxophones; it's taken up all over the orchestra at different speeds, the deliberate stiltedness gradually infiltrated by the virtuoso nimbleness of the monkey-music, yielding briefly to a ravishing oasis – *'doux et féerique'* – wherein the long-suffering jungle sings to itself. The Bandar-Log can't abide this, dismiss it with brusque rudeness, and set up the third satire *'le (pretendu) "Retour à Bach"'*, marked *'lourd, scholastique, austère et sec'* – a ludicrous fugue-subject on double-basses, answered successively by a handful of strings in different keys – Milhaud's mechanized polytonality the target rather than the interwar Bachisms of Stravinsky, Bartók, Hindemith, Villa-Lobos; 'wrong-note music' pilloried; not very funny. Nor is the ensuing *'fugato chromatique'*, its pitches ugly, its scoring grotesque. Yet it takes genuine skill to combine this nasty stuff with the preceding diatonic fugue in all its lumbering gormlessness.

This satire-sequence nearly sinks the piece; but it's saved by what ensues. Sudden hush, very soft, low percussion, gongs and big drum, joined by a harp then both harps; the jungle commences its reply – a Miracle worthy of Puran Bhagat, the apes' idiot material, sterile and futile, gently worked into the mysterious harmonies of the opening. '*C'est la forêt qui chante*', in passages of exalted inner rapture, slowly swelling into outer triumph reminiscent of the Gallic victory over the Huns in Debussy's *En blanc et noir*, which Koechlin would surely have orchestrated if its composer had asked. Thereafter, broader lyricism, a hymn to 'true polytonal and atonal new music': Koechlin is too sage not to discern the deeper reflections beyond the smeared glass of fashion and chic. What happens next is not clear programmatically though musically convincing: it seems that the *singes* can *still* only mock true art, pelt it with filth, and be routed by batteries of percussion (eight players required). Volatile and martial alternate, building to a mighty chord on all the brass – a *rappel à l'ordre*: *la loi de la jungle* reimposed: then the Bandar-Log's precipitate flight (with perhaps a prophetic hint of their terrifying defeat at the end of *Kaa's Hunting*). The empty jungle sings itself to deep wordless sleep.

Olivier Messiaen

No brief sketch could contain the culmination of this trajectory, Olivier Messiaen. Born 1908; father teacher of and translator from English, mother a mystic poetess. Their musically precocious boy (he recalled the 'thunderbolt' of receiving the score of Debussy's *Pelléas* for his tenth birthday) studied at the Paris Conservatoire under several famous organists, with Dukas for composition. Himself an outstanding organist, recognized uncontended from the start, appointed to Paris's La Trinité 1931, holding the post for the rest of his life. Recognition as composer slow and contentious. From the start his music plentiful and characteristic; 1936 aligned with *La Jeune France*, a polemical group opposed to the perceived frivolity of then-prevailing French culture, exemplified in music by Cocteau's endorsement of *Les Six* – away with trivial entertainment, bring back 'sincerity, generosity, artistic conscience'. But polemic not Messiaen's way: he pursued these noble pieties unruffled and alone. In 1937, introduction to the ondes Martenot – a mixed blessing (Stravinsky compared this electronic instrument to a colonic irrigation). That same year, *Poèmes pour Mi* orchestrated from voice-and-piano original from the year before, freshest of his pre-war works. A war-prisoner 1940–41, a time made memorable by the composition and performance in the camp of *Quatuor pour la fin du temps*. On release, appointed Professor of Harmony at the Conservatoire, teaching there till retirement 1971. *Harmony!* He could have been professor of melody, rhythm, timbre, form and process, organ and piano, ethnomusicology – above all of ornithology and theology, his principal passions outside music, all of them ingested into music itself.

A long roster of distinguished and important post-war innovators drawn to the most magnetic musical presence of the day, prominent among them Boulez and Stockhausen. Messiaen himself responded creatively, indeed seminally, to *musique concrète*, and especially to serialism in *Quatre études de rythme* and *Cantéyodjayâ* for piano and the *Livre d'orgue* (all 1948–52). His more particular-to-himself theory, *Technique de mon langage musical* published 1944: his practice blooming in *Visions de l'Amen* for two pianos the year before and *Vingt regards sur l'Enfant Jésus* for solo piano (1944): across the two, *Trois petites liturgies de la présence divine* (1943–4) for voices and orchestra. Three major works follow, diverse in genre, linked by involvement in the *Tristan*-myth: *Harawi*, 'songs of love and death' for soprano and piano (1945); the *Turangalîla Symphony* for colossal orchestra, including concertante piano and ondes Martenot (1946–8); *Cinq Rechants* for twelve solo voices (1948).

The rest of the life-oeuvre is equally prodigal. Several overlapping phases can be distinguished. Birds proliferate – *Réveil des oiseaux* 1953, *Oiseaux exotiques* 1955–6 (both concertante-works for piano and instruments): and the comprehensive *Catalogue d'oiseaux*, thirteen solo piano pieces of 1956–8 (with a few extra later). Synthesis of all these, *Chronochromie* for large orchestra 1959–60. After a venture into Orientalism (Japanese brand) in *Sept haïkaï* (1962), God prevails: *Couleurs de la Cité céleste* (1963): *Et exspecto resurrectionem mortuorum* (1964); both for orchestra; *Méditations sur le Mystère de la Sainte*

Trinité for organ (1967–9); and the vast culmination (for now) of this terrain in the oratorio *La Transfiguration de Notre Seigneur Jésus-Christ* (1965–9). A diversion into pantheistic evocation of natural wonders – *Des canyons aux étoiles* (1971–4) – precedes the ultimate summa/synthesis, where God, Nature (birds above all) and Humanity fuse, the epic drama on *Saint François d'Assise*; it occupied five years from 1975 to 1979, its orchestration only completed in 1983. Messiaen himself wondered if he had anything left to say: his last years produced some smaller works, and also two further colossi, *Livre du Saint Sacrement* (1984) for organ and *Éclairs sur l'Au-Delà* (1987–91) for orchestra. He died the year after completing this last consummatory summa.

The technical manual of 1944 has been amplified by posthumous publication of massive treatises upon every aspect of composition, and the revelation of his voluminous working notebooks. This passionate aficionado of birds was a thieving magpie! Material melodic, harmonic, rhythmic, timbral, sometimes from the most unlikely sources – Rameau, Rossini, Massenet, the 'Second Viennese School', as well as more likely – Musorgsky, Debussy, Ravel, Stravinsky – was incorporated into his own work, usually transformed, sometimes disconcertingly unaltered: Jolivet, Loriod. Unlike Debussy's pillaging then transforming favourite minutiae of Wagner, Messiaen has no guilty evasion. And in both instances the theft, covert or frank, is fully repaid by the originality of the result. In Messiaen's case one of the most unmistakable styles ever heard turns out to be often fashioned quite consistently from borrowed plumage.

This vast achievement has excited loathing at worst, or contempt or mockery, and at the least, sarcasm. His music and his aesthetic invite and have received all four. Selected for more detailed description here are some individual works from each period that clearly transcend cavils of taste, predilection, religious commitment, to win on grounds of their sheer artistic calibre.

Poèmes pour Mi: nine songs for '*grande soprano dramatique*', with piano 1936, marvellously orchestrated the next year. Mi is the affectionate diminutive for the composer's first wife: his own texts for her are saturated with the Psalms and the New Testament, images from nature and private tendernesses, mingled together in home-brew sub-surrealism; without embarrassment – or if any, only ours and easily suppressed, lost in the ardent inspiration of the sounds. No. 1, *Action de grâces*, already contains the *mélange* – sky, water, earth, light, the belovèd's smile, her soul 'filled with love and immortality', her body 'which will germinate for the resurrection', all freely granted her lover in the Blood of the Cross and the Bread of the Stars . . . 'mon Dieu, Alleluia!' This tosh is lost in the rapt ecstasy of the music it inspires, richly serene, opaque yet luminous, occasionally declamatory, more consistently lyrical, climaxing in glorious melisma for the Stars; then a pause for 'mon Dieu'; and the carolling joy of the concluding 'Alleluia'. No. 2, *Paysage*, is brief, built around its repeated first, fourth and eight (last) line *'le lac comme un gros bijou bleu'* – the lake and its surrounding countryside are *her*, of course, invoked with chaste *volupté* and three flickers of light across the waters. No. 3, *La Maison*, is equally brief and interior – we will quit this house, these bodies, to contemplate Truth with bodies renewed in youth, beauty, light – absolutely simple, clear, direct. No. 4 brings the soprano's 'grand dramatic' nature into play for the first time: *Épouvante*/Terror; mocking laughter for clutching memories of dirty earthliness that would hold the lovers back from the life to come; malign diabolic curses as of exorcism, climaxing on burning *désespoir* and vehement resistance to the fiery powers whose anger must be assuaged; closing on expansion of the mocking laughter with which the song began.

Part II (with one exception) restores rapt lyricism. No. 5, *L'Épouse* – a sacramental vision of marriage: 'go where the spirit leads . . . nothing can separate you . . . the wife is the husband's extension as the Church is Christ's.' The music's calm certainty must pardon the unappealing sentiments. No such scruple with No. 6, *Ta voix*: a purling stream of tranquil bliss recalling the *alleluia* from the first song, given delicate little hesitation by subtle rhythmic irregularities underlying the continuous flow. Mi might not care to be likened to the Son, beloved by the Father, and incorporated into the incorporeal Angels to adore the Trinity: but she'd surely treasure the open window, and the spring-bird invoked near the start whose voice has the wordless last word in a free arabesque for flute and piccolo – foretelling millions of birds to come – before the simple close – 'thus would you sing'. No. 7 is the second exception: violent and dramatic, the lovers, conjoined, are now *les deux guerriers*, ironclad, compelled forward, crying for remission, urged forward again, transforming groans to cries of joy as victory nighs – 'you will reach the gates of the city' – ferocious defiant ending for the voice elsewhere silky and velvety. As, again, for No. 8, *Le Collier*/The necklace: raptest love-song of all, an apostrophe to hallowed sensuality – her lover's arms around her neck this morning; my necklace: Debussy's Verlaine-setting *C'est l'extase* elevated into the Song of Songs. No. 9, *Prière exaucée*/Fulfilled prayer: the soprano *dramatique* again, urging Jesus, in tense declamation, to rouse the breast from its bitter solitude: 'Say but the word and my soul will be healed.' This febrile stretch culminates in three loud passionate appeals for Grace. *Grand silence dramatique*. Music resumes fast, light, fluttery: '*carillonne, mon coeur!* – ring out, heart's bell; strike, slap, kling for your King!' Soft bright tattoos and fanfares gradually fill the firmament: 'behold your day of glory and resurrection! [*climax*]: Joy [*leaping melisma*] has returned' – great descending scale in chords slower and slower as it falls, set against clamorous bells, triumphal and touching end to a work lovable beyond its lapses.

No such indulgence needed for *Cinq Rechants*, far the most enjoyable (the best?) of the '*Tristan*-trilogy' (its most massive item, the gargantuan *Turangalîla*, was haughtily dismissed by Stravinsky as *plus d'embarasses que de richesses* – 'little more is required to write such music than a copious supply of ink'). What's required for these five 'madrigals' for twelve solo voices is a fantastic ear and a brilliant imagination. As in *Mi* the texts are the composer's: a farrago of pseudo-Indian from Peru and Equador, Hindu and Sanskrit – e.g. the first and last line of No. 1: '*Hayo kapritama, la li la li la ssaréno*' or the nine-times repeated refrain in No. 4 – '*Niokhamî palalan soukî*'; plus near or actual nonsense, descending into wordless/pitchless click'n'clacks – *tk tk tk* – and explosive expletives – *ha ha ha ha ha*. Messiaen's own French – amateur surrealism again – involves principally the love of Tristan (never named), Yseult (who is) and their confidante/pander Brangien. Other love-legends flicker in and out of consciousness – in No. 1 Orpheus, Barbe-Bleu and his seven doors; in No. 5 the gnomic *'Persée Méduse l'abeille l'alphabet majeur'*. Love and Death are implicit throughout; no Birds; and no Christian Theology.

The form of each *rechant* is given by the term itself, borrowed from the French Renaissance: refrains and couplets interlocked, recurring exact or enriched, sometimes with an Introduction, and a Coda that either repeats it or adds something new; memorably to close No. 3 in new words too – *'Tous les philtres sont bus ce soir.'* Every tiny section is sharply characterized, whether languid with longing, urgent with tension, angrily violent, sinuous or athletic, florid or bare: all are pungent and memorable, whether shaped to intelligibility or vacuity – even the *tk tk* and the *ha ha ha* impinge upon the mind and remain fixed there. Most unforgettable of all, the marvellous burst of twelve-part imitation in No. 3 (on *ha ha ha*), the silence, the spifflicating chord that breaks it (on *yoma* – sung – and *sarî sarî sarî* shouted very fast sixteen times); silence, then the luscious close as all the love-philtres are drained tonight. *Incantation incandescent, ululation extraordinaire* – one can but imitate, trying to convey the impression this tingling music makes, masterpiece of vocal virtuosity only equalled in the century in two antithetical places, the Spirituals in *Porgy and Bess* and the Ligeti *Requiem*.

Turangalîla, that magnificent monstrosity, has become, however unlikely, a favourite orchestral showpiece, its preposterous 'philosophy' swallowed whole with its undoubted thrills. Of course there are marvellous moments, indeed movements: the sheer confidence, mastery, unblenching conjunction of erotic kitsch and genuine erotic fervour can sweep one away: but when the clamour – *'joie du sang des étoiles'* – has faded, one thinks meanly of Stravinsky's 'copious supply of ink'. Alongside this tidal-wave came five dry studies for solo piano – *Quatre études de rythme* and *Cantéyodjayâ* – they proved a fruitful way forward. *Mode de valeurs et d'intensités* and *Neumes rythmiques* (Nos. 2 and 3) are significant historically for their strict formalist construction; not only pitches as in Schoenberg, but durations and silences, as hinted in later Webern, are serialized: also – quite new – dynamics and methods of attack (*l'art de toucher le clavecin*). The impact of these ventures into total serialization on the emergent avant-garde was immediate and universal. Messiaen himself seems to have regarded them quite lightly: they sound more delicate, even delicious, than cerebral – a touch of gamelan, a hint of the exotic as suggested by entitling Nos. 1 and 4 *Île de feu*. The ensuing result for him of this apparent dead-end is to open up his freshest, most appealing music: perhaps his best.

Birds now proliferate again: two quasi concertos, *Réveil des oiseaux* (1953) and *Oiseaux exotiques* (1955–6); and *Catalogue d'oiseaux* (1956–8). *Réveil* is devoted to native songsters and comes with Koechlin-like programming of surpassing naïveté and charm. Midnight: the piano introduces a nightingale, another replies, then a third: silence: other night-birds are heard, on solo violin, piccolo clarinet, piccolo flute, celesta: a low bank of trilling strings: a xylophone. Dawn: dawn-birds awake and begin their chorus, sometimes liquid and florid, sometimes harsh and mechanical, the piano always leading. Momentary flurry subsides: a cuckoo on near-pitchless percussion, a woodpecker on a wood-block, then plenty more. Fragments gradually assemble, lengthen, coalesce, superimpose in a tutti of delirious intricacy, its aerial tracery suddenly cut off by silence: the sun rises. Second start, piano a blackcap: more birds, of the daylight now – catch the purring turtle-dove on three low flutter-tonguing flutes, pearly grey amid the bright metallic twitter. This second half matches, without replicating, the first, in gradual accumulation and superimposition: silence: long blackbird song on solo piano: orchestra resumes in bright fragments, including two robins on celesta and glockenspiel: so to second tutti, much shorter, terminated by a harsh hoopoe. As noon approaches the texture thins into fragments – some new birds, some old friends, bold, shy, amorous, harsh (a carrion crow), mocking/lyrical/exultant, all now characterized only by the piano. Silence: three last tweeting flutters – two chaffinches and a blackbird – on violin: silence: the woodpecker twice: the cuckoo, now in the distance: silence. Naïve yes: but the ear is sophisticated and subtle: there's no pedantry in this celebration of a world newborn every night and morning since *le commencement du temps.*

Oiseaux exotiques performs similar for tropical birds without the support of a temporal frame. Phase 1: The solo piano is here joined only by woodwinds, two horns, a trumpet, and percussion tuned (xylophone, glockenspiel) and unpitched: nineteen players in all. They can make a sense-tingling racket: and the structure is tighter, the textures more complex, than in *Réveil*, built upon a rhythmic underlay of many Hindu and Greek metres – eleven Hindu, eight Greek – an unpitched polyphony upon which the pitched aviary is poised – birds from India, China, Malaysia and the New World; forty-seven species in all, thirty-eight from North America. Messiaen's preface lovingly lists them with vivid descriptions of their colours, markings, and sometimes their character – the Red-whiskered Bulbul 'brown top, white underside . . . a strange rather Mephistophelic head, with a black crest, black moustache, white patch on the cheek and a red patch under one eye': the Indigo Bunting, 'the Blue-bird of Mme d'Aulnoy's fairy-tale, every shade of blue occurs in its plumage – peacock blue, cobalt blue, ultramarine.' *Oiseaux exotiques/ecstatiques*: both adjectives earnt and exemplified in this fantastic jungle of glitter, gleam, vociferation, stridulation, captured with flawless ear and constructed, perfectly proportioned, with a concision, almost elegance, unusual in this composer.

A grand synthesis of birds and rhythmic explorations arrives in the impressive work for large orchestra completed in 1960: *Chronochromie*. Birds domestic and *exotiques*, Alpine rocks and torrents thrown in, a strenuous play of metrical constructivism, fearful symmetry imposed from the forms of choruses in Greek tragedy, are all heterogeneously intermingled to realize the dual meaning of the Greek title Kronos/Time, Kroma/Colour. Eros is absent, Theology too: but God is implicit in the wonder of living creation and purposeful design. Messiaen is at once beneficiary and victim of the strange condition by which sight and sound are inseparable: 'colours which blend like combinations of notes, and which shift and revolve with the sounds'. His acute responses to tints and hues can be compared with Van Gogh's in his letters and the hallucinogenic visions of druggie culture contemporary with, though alien to, the composer's Catholic piety. Both parallels come to mind as one closes one's eyes to see the sounds, listening to *Chronochromie*. The *Introduction* chucks rocks across the orchestral groups, alternating with birdsong, familiar from earlier, and dazzling slurps and gushes illustrating waterfalls and torrential streams. *Strophe I* presents metres and birds against a sustained sound-sheet of twenty-two solo strings – the *Oiseaux exotiques'* tuttis with the sustaining pedal down. *Antistrophe I* frames further birds between a vivacious woodwind ritornello: at the centre, a grand slow hymn, dense harmony in rhythmic unison, followed by vigorous momentum with fiendishly demanding string-writing. *Strophe II* then *Antistrophe II* re-jiggle the kaleidoscope in ever-freshened conjunctions of elements familiar from their predecessors. The *Épôde* is different – eighteen solo strings in an enhanced return to *Réveil des oiseaux* not *Oiseaux exotiques*: only French birds, each individualized by its solo player: a dawn-chorus from which distinct voices emerge into brief prominence then sink back into the fascinating tissue of twittering. The *Coda* balances the *Introduction*: same constituents, re-angled and re-juxtaposed, fading away – again as *Réveil* – till, as *Exotiques*, a formidable/implacable close on all the forces, and the silent beats to be beaten, that complete the symmetry.

I intend frankly to skimp the last thirty or so years of Messiaen's huge oeuvre – skirting the Orient, ducking the next three Theological works, transcending the *Transfiguration*, leaping the Grand Canyon without reaching for the Stars: and though awed by the heights, depths, widths, lengths, of *St François d'Assise*, passing by on the other side as deplored by Notre Seigneur Jésus-Christ in the parable. There's a growing sense of self-recycling in this mounting scale of size and ambition: after completing the stage-work, hugest of all, the composer confessed 'I thought I had said everything': he was surely right. Already in the *Transfiguration* a feeling of autopilot persists, though the confidence and mastery never fail, and the ocean-involving chorales closing each Part have to be heard to be believed. Its contemporary organ-cycle the *Mystère de la Sainte Trinité* tests faith, hope and charity: in its successor, *Livre du Saint Sacrement*, next after *St François*, they can be suspended no longer. Even the composer's late recharge from a first visit to the Holy Sites, then Australia, doesn't refresh habitual idioms and techniques, though the descriptions in his travel-diaries ought to have:

> ...saw the golden whistler and white-naped honey-eater. Marvellous play of light and shade. Giant ferns, four to six metres high, form the undergrowth of the forest, the eucalyptus towering above them. The sunlight strikes marvellously into corners of the forest. Strong scent of eucalyptus. Here and there the enormous trunks of the mountain ash. Saw a grey fantail, Eastern whip-bird, Eastern yellow robin, honeyeater. Large glade of grass flecked with pink. Sun and blue sky through the eucalyptus leaves. Saw the territory of the wombat, a sort of little bear, very powerful. Saw a robin and a white-throated tree-creeper. We walk on a narrow path. To the left is a gorge filled with ferns, to the right a pond – the water is russet-green, reflecting the colours of the landscape.

Thence to the glorious lyre-bird – 'it's big!' – and its nest, its dance, and, climactically, its song – 'three lyre-birds singing together can fill a forest with the trumpeting joyous colours of an entire orchestra.' Yet despite these intoxicating allures, the resulting *Éclairs sur l'Au-Delá* is more more-of-same than renovatory: again, and always, with moments that reveal a great composer.

If the willing listener remains impervious (or positively negative) to Catholic theology, jibs at unreconstructed bigotry, is deaf to (or deafened by) the multicoloured plasticene of the nineteenth-century French grand organ or suffers metal fatigue when assaulted by batteries of xylophone and glockenspiel, is unaroused by schemes of duration, non-retrogradable rhythms, Hindu or Greek metres, etc., and, worse still, indifferent to birdsong; and then, worst of all, repelled by the idiom wherein all these meet, so insistent, pressing, repetitive, cloying, embarrassing; if all these, what survives in Messiaen's enormous body of mainly enormous works whose Excess by no means leads inevitably to the Palace of Wisdom? Can even *St François* sustain the twin roles of foundation and cornerstone?

The opera's unsurpassed level of decibels and redundancies: the little tag representing *la joie* which induces a spasm of embarrassed but unambiguous *hatred* well before its thousandth time of asking: that death-scene for the saint of humility, frugality, simplicity, self-effacement, in a furnace of C-major ...? Trite and banal beyond belief! Yet every one of *St François'* eight tableaux has an unforgettable aura of its own, an intensity, an authenticity: and an inventiveness in the sonorous sphere that truly is awesome, leaving Xenakis or Stockhausen far behind in its accuracy, sureness and daring. The tableau where the saint preaches to the birds has – again – to be heard to be believed. And if one prefers the gentler, more lyrical, perfected shorter pieces – *Poèmes pour Mi* and the *Rechants*; the delicious and ever-tingling *Réveil des oiseaux* and *Oiseaux exotiques*; and reserves undiminished awe for the medium length of *Chronochromie*, and an intellectual fascination for the *Messe de la Pentecôte* and *Livre d'orgue*, it's one's own limits that are tested and found constrictive, not his. In the end, gratitude prevails: *plus de richesses que d'embarras*.

CHAPTER XVIII

The Post-War Avant-Garde

The avant-garde of the immediate post-war years – in particular its three outstanding proponents Boulez, Stockhausen and Nono, once dubbed 'the Holy Trinity' – is by now a matter of history. 'Bliss was it in that dawn to be alive': but was the dawn a sunset in disguise? How do the Trinity, plus other composers associated, the stirring *Stunde Null* ideology, stand some seven decades on? Easily comprehensible, the compelling sense of a necessary new start from a clean slate, rejecting a moribund past, creating a new world. Also comprehensible, nostalgia for the heady days of musical modernism in its heroic early manifestations – Stravinsky, Bartók, Schoenberg and his pupils. Yet Schoenberg himself, Berg more obviously, might be perceived as an aspect of the past's dead hand, aesthetically, technically, in actual idiom. Not so Webern: he became the model for an absolutely fresh start. Virtually unknown earlier – embargoed by the circumstances of performance and publication in the Germany and Austria of the 1930s, even before the war made these impossible – his later work was revealed as virgin soil, a *terra incognita* to which the routes now lay open. For the most gifted and radical of the young composers emerging in the late 1940s Webern is prophet, guide, sage – the 'crystal' in which they were reflected, through which they could see the Promised Land, and hope to inhabit it.

Six staccato vignettes follow, starting with the Trinity, with outlines of the composers' careers and compositions, from which just a handful must suffice for a more detailed description.

Pierre Boulez

First of the Trinity, the Oedipal son, slayer of patriarchal tyranny, 1925–2016. Studied with Messiaen; for nine years music-director for a celebrated theatre-company – extensive conducting-experience, later blooming into an outstanding career alongside his composing – the New York Philharmonic, BBC Symphony Orchestra, Chicago, Cleveland, Vienna and Berlin Philharmonics, London Symphony Orchestra – Bayreuth (*Parsifal* 1967–8 and 1970; the centennial *Ring* 1976) and other opera-houses (notably the première of the complete *Lulu* at the Paris Opèra 1979), and orchestras and ensembles worldwide. Most particularly, the *Ensemble intercontemporain*, which he founded to best realize his superlative standards in his own specialized repertoire. Founder-director, 1977, IRCAM (Institut de recherche et coordination acoustique/musique), which he led for many years. Its handsome government patronage brings out the irony of the aggressive iconoclast embraced by the Establishment: this irony has never been more piquantly enacted. Iconoclast into icon: result, a new tyranny yet more unforgiving and oppressive than what it had toppled. The intelligence fuelling the aggression formidably manifest in extensive polemic lectures and writings, notorious in their day, for his merciless impatient contempt – '*Schoenberg est mort*'; 'blow up all the opera-houses'; Messiaen's 'bordello-music'; any new venture not committed to his own particular brand of avantgarde 'absolutely *useless*'; and much else in the same vein.

Compositional landmarks *du côté de chez Boulez*. Late 1940s/early 1950s the *Flute Sonatina* – 'if this is his sonatina, what on earth will his sonata be?' asked Stravinsky: answer, the 1st and 2nd Sonatas for piano solo, the 2nd in particular a monument of scarifying complexity. Close early association with Cage and Stockhausen, both turning sour later: the famous summer-schools at Darmstadt, cradle of the new, early 1950s; association with Nono and Berio, inter alia. First versions of *Le Soleil des eaux* (fully realized 1965) and *Le Visage nuptial* (only fully achieved late 1980s): *Polyphonie X* and studies in *musique concrète* later withdrawn: *Structures* for two pianos (Book I

1951–2, Book II 1956–61) – talismanic example of 'total serialism' (if not, 'totally useless'). *Le Marteau sans maître* (1952–3, revised 1957) – scintillating breakthrough. The 3rd Piano Sonata (1955–7) introduces chance/*aléa* into the hitherto self-enclosed world of total control.

Two brief *Improvisation*s on Mallarmé texts for soprano and small ensemble 1957, gradually expanding into *Pli selon pli/Portrait de Mallarmé*, a full-evening-length work with enormous orchestral forces, only definitively achieved by 1989. *Éclat* 1965, expanded by 1970 into *Éclat/Multiples*; *Rituel* in memory of fellow composer-conductor Bruno Maderna 1974–5; *Répons* for orchestra and electronics – fruit, at last, of IRCAM's founding intention and lavish technology – 1980–84 (and even so, not definitively finished). Round about now, a series of *Notations* commence – orchestral elaborations of tiny early piano-pieces; 1993 … *explosante-fixe* …; 1998 *sur Incises*; 2006 *Dérive II*; more *Notations* up to VII, with further unrealized at the time of his death.

Simply thus listing, there's an impression of under-achievement: Boulez is a perfectionist, compulsively and ceaselessly revising, extending, elaborating, in the image of *le dieu Mallarmé*, towards an intangible goal perhaps never to be reached. Many incompletions too. There's a self-thwarting urge, an internal conflict, sometimes fruitful sometimes barren, alongside the impulse to create: composition is at once aided and inhibited by the brilliant conducting and the powerful exercise of organizational flair, both these netting their goals with conspicuous success. The gift – the *don* – is undisputable: laser-sharp intelligence, a fabulous ear, a charismatic personality. What's missing? And is the extraordinary phenomenon of Boulez-the-composer a sort of flawless failure? The vulgar title of a cheap biography – *Boulez: Composer, Conductor, Enigma* – poses a problem still unanswered. Some pieces that are fully achieved remain among the most distinguished and memorable music of their time. *Enjoyable*, too: often delectable/ravishing/enchanting: there's a feel for sheer sonority second to none in a culture that has always placed this among its most ardent aspirations. Here, Boulez is the direct heir of Messiaen, and before him, of Ravel and Debussy, and before them, Berlioz and Rameau.

Les Soleil des eaux: the earlier Boulez at his most accessible in this brief cantata for solo soprano, mixed choir, and orchestra, on two poems by René Char telling obliquely of mankind's abuse of nature – chemicals poisoning the water, endangering wildlife, imperilling the fishermen's livelihood – with, by implication, a hint of the self-destruction, *homo homini lupus*, of warfare. The first panel, *complainte du lézard amoureux*/plaint of the lizard in love, evokes nature in a mood of sensuous ease, at peace with itself: the huntsman threatens, but passes; nature sings her song – soprano only; fluent, volatile, delicate, complex – the prismatic coloration of birds, beasts, trees, flowers, grasses, unforgettably caught in textures ranging from strident ferocity to exquisite refinement – the tiny interlude half-way through a delicious next stage on from the lake-surface in Schoenberg's *Five Orchestral Pieces* and the hair-splitting refinement of contemporaneous Webern. Schoenberg in more expressionist vein permeates the second panel *La Sorgue* – the Schoenberg of *Die glückliche Hand* with its intricate intermesh of speech and singing – cries, shouts, mutters, whispers, woven into the dense orchestral tapestry. The eponymous river is the protagonist – 'river punished, river forsaken': expressionism refracted, rendered diaphanous and elegant, Debussy behind it rather than Mahler or Strauss, and Messiaen to the fore without a trace of his sometimes oppressive tackiness. One quivers to every evanescent nuance: then the climax evincing destruction and indestructibility comes with lapidary violence, before gentle subsidence into murmurous bees and a lost horizon.

Le Marteau sans maître/*The Masterless Hammer* – title indicating force and power uncurbed and out of control: sequence of settings for mezzo-soprano alternating with purely instrumental movements, nine in total, for just six players – alto flute, xylorimba, vibraphone, guitar, viola, miscellaneous percussion; a unique ensemble, utterly fresh and original (though inevitably much imitated). The three poems are again by René Char: one is set twice; the instrumental sections are also fully involved with the words in a pattern of symmetries and asymmetries, anticipations, commentaries, epilogues, at once labyrinthine and enticing. First movement, *Avant 'L'Artisanat furieux'* – quartet for the gentler of the six players, no xylophone or percussion; preparing the way for the text's later setting: 2, first commentary on *Bourreaux de solitude*, dropping guitar and adding unpitched percussion: 3, *L'Artisanat furieux* now actually set, for voice and alto flute alone, coolly presenting the words' obscure murderous rage: 4, second commentary on *Bourreaux* – all players save the alto flute just featured in the song before: 5, fragile first setting of *Bel édifice et les pressentiments*, the singer accompanied only by a trio of the softest-voiced instruments for this demented dislocation of human experience, alienation, attrition, loss, disembodiment – 'pure eyes in the woods searching, weeping, an inhabitable head . . .'. More later; for now 6, *Bourreaux de solitude* now set complete to fulfil the two preceding commentaries on it – the work's centrepiece, using all the players for this gnomic enigma – 'the step receded, the walker silenced on the dial of imitation, the pendulum chucks its charge of reflex [as in *reflex action*] granite': 7, *Après 'L'Artisanat'*, light-spun trio for alto flute, vibraphone, guitar: 8, third commentary on *Bourreaux*: 9, second setting of *Bel édifice* – all players, though initially omitting alto flute; the voice abandons words for vocalese; the flute is re-admitted; and three gongs, high/middle/low, make their first appearance – the sole deep sonority in an ensemble otherwise entirely lacking bass. After this moment, a tutti; the singer, still wordless, intermeshed with the instrumentation; an epilogue (not so-named, but this is how it feels) for alto-flute only, supported or overwhelmed by the three gongs, and a final splash of suspended cymbal, its single use in the work. Hoping to convey the fascinating elegance of the 'edifice' which owes the hint of a ghost to *Pierrot lunaire*, purged of that work's macabre black density into a cloud of airy nothings, cat's cradle of sharp glinting pins, needles, bare bodkins.

The sonorous character of *Le Marteau* is absolutely special, extravagant and florid, combative yet fragile, interiorized, subtle, evasive, provocative. The sound used to be mocked as 'plink-plonk': it can now be heard and seen to be the embodiment of its day, as was *L'Après-midi d'un faune* for the 1890s: a strange and potent cocktail of clinking ice-cubes and vermouth/wormwood with bitter olives and luscious sweet stuffs, syrups tinct with cinnamon, blood-flecked;

and maybe a whiff of hashish – certainly a breath of the Orient, gamelan timbres and pattern-making, albeit of fiendish complexity. Overall, endlessly beguiling, at once stimulating and soothing: when the entire delicate/aggressive *édifice* is grounded in the three gongs makes one of modern music's great moments: the unruly hammer has found its master, and can be employed to shape new matter.

Le Visage nuptial : many versions of, radical revisions to, this cantata eventuating in a half-hour work for soprano and contralto soloists, female chorus and massive orchestra, including nine per-cussionists playing some sixty instruments. This ensuing result, rich and expressive beyond anything else in Boulez' oeuvre, is surely his masterpiece. The poems – Char encore, redolent and obscure as always – concern erotic love: 1, *Conduite* introduces; 2, *Sévérité* is all amorous anticipation; 3, the centre, *le visage* itself, the apotheosis of erotic fulfilment; 4, *Evadné*, dialectic between inner voices and the external world; 5, *Post-Scriptum*, tells of the lovers' rupture, their return to two solitudes. The whole, a sort of *Poèmes pour Mi* crossed with *Turangalîla*, without the personal intimacy of the song-cycle or the colossal carnal display of the symphony. And Messiaen is indeed audible here and there (though there's neither theology nor birds): closer, the Stravinsky of *Le Sacre* and *Les Noces*. The sensuous refinement of *Le Soleil des eaux*, and its outbursts of anger, are taken further; the fractured clinking of *Le Marteau* is eschewed. For Boulez is here, uniquely, concerned with *harmony*, often dense and rich; and with rhythmic continuity, sometimes positively motoric. Also with areas of feeling not essayed elsewhere – tenderness, voluptuousness, desire and performance – the central scene is explicitly sexual, the aggro familiar from before here conjoined with luminosity both bright and glowing: and after the climax, regret, nostalgia, elegy – all in an idiom unbeholden to previous models for such moods.

Another candidate for Boulez' masterpiece is *Pli selon pli/Portrait de Mallarmé* – again put together from several smaller sections initially distinct, subject to many elaborations and extensions, resulting in an ambitious composite for large forces with some wonderful new material, notably the mainly orchestral framework, *Don* to commence, *Tombeau* to conclude. Whereas Char served the composer well, Mallarmé can perhaps be seen as his downfall. Pursuit of an impossible perfection has resulted in etiolation, preciousness, even affectation – self-strangulation, like the swan in one of the poems here set, is almost courted. *Don du poème* – the birthpangs of creation, the child pale yet dark, wings plucked yet bloody after a horrible ordeal, yet delivery into blue virginal empyrean – the famous sonnet not set complete, the orchestral fabric, sporadic and luminous, interspersed with words from the three sonnets to follow, as if to offer already the Gift in its entirety. They are all accompanied only by the original slender forces – piano, celesta, harp, bells, percussion tuned and unpitched – though the full orchestra now occasionally punctuates. *Le vierge, le vivace et le bel aujourd'hui* centres upon the image of the swan entrapped in ice – a *blanche agonie* – emblem of the art that has *not* been born, or is mangled before fruition: *Une dentelle s'abolit* – another conflicted whiteness, the lace effaced, the game futile, the hoped-for birth aborted: *À la nue accablante tu* – destruction by volcano or shipwreck, abolition by drowning of the potentially new-born (I'm paraphrasing on postage-stamps the near-inexplicable). Thence to the grand finale, re-admitting the full orchestra in all its seething complexity, building in steady accretions of sonorous convulsion to a coruscating climax; then a masterly withdrawal wherein the poem, previously submerged – *Tombeau* (in memory of Verlaine?) – emerges clear onto its final line: the shallow stream, maligned, of death; set with heroic rhetoric – death-defying.

Boulez' finest yield – *Marteau*, *Pli selon pli*, *Visage* – is never again equalled in all his subsequent oeuvre, increasingly lost to dilutions, reworkings, incompletions, as described. Closest is *Répons* with its build-up on the acoustic instruments to another great late twentieth-century moment, the long-heralded entry of the electronics so lavishly funded by the French government. Here the work originally ended – on a high. Its subsequent continuation dissipates the electro-acoustic charge into whitter and twitter; and these words can fairly describe his later trajectory at large, whatever the moments of wonderful sonic ravishment from a composer of consummate ear. The *Notations* can stand for all – orchestral elaborations of dry little early piano studies, lovingly decorated with the arts of a couturier, a coiffeur, a master pastry-cook, working at enormous expense for the most exclusive clientèle – a definition of decadence. With his awesome gifts and compelling authority, Boulez was the most generously endowed composer of his generation: the unfulfilment – the, as it seems, *refusal* to bring in the harvest – is, in artistic terms, tragic. The 'sunset mistaken for a dawn', so misapplied by Busoni to Debussy's *L'Après-midi*, really *does* apply here.

Stockhausen

Karlheinz Stockhausen, 1928–2007: an early pupil of Messiaen, then close association with the avant-garde crucible of Darmstadt and the pioneering electronic studio of Cologne; the high-point of his ventures into electronics and *concrète* remains the ecstatic *Gesang der Jünglinge* of 1955–6; landmarks before this include such 'total serialist' works as *Kreuzspiel* 1951, *Kontra-Punkte* 1952–3, and the earliest in a succession of *Klavierstücke*, reaching No. X by 1961. By then, launched well into his momentous single-minded, independent journey, fuelled by copious theoretical writings à la Wagner. The trajectory is fantastic: unlike Boulez, Stockhausen brings everything he undertakes to complete fruition, sometimes irrespective of calibre. Some highlights of his high flight: *Gruppen* for three orchestras 1955–7; *Carré* for four orchestras plus four choirs 1959–60; *Kontakte* for tape alone, or with piano and percussion, also 1959–60; *Momente*, for soprano, four vocal groups, electronic organs, brass, percussion, comes in two versions some ten years apart, *c.*1962 and 1972; *Hymnen*, collage with electronics and *concrète* of National Anthems from around the globe 1966–9; its antithesis is *Stimmung* (1968) for six solo voices with electronics – inward, secret, erotic; *Trans* for orchestra and tape 1971; *Inori* ('Adoration'), eventually 1973–4 and, best, for large orchestra and mime; *Tierkreis* 1974–5 – many versions of these twelve pieces evoking the Zodiac.

Already there are indications of grandeur amounting, at the least, to delusive foibles that could be indulged (such as the composer's claim to have been born on Sirius), and at the most to megalomania – in the personality and in the art-works born of it. Unforgettable, Stockhausen's unabashed declaration in a BBC interview that 'I am the most important [or was it, the greatest?] phenomenon in music of the last eight hundred [or was it a thousand?] years.' Such beliefs fuel *Licht* – a seven-evening theatrical cycle for the days of the week: not written in their order – *Donnerstag* came first (1978–80), *Sonntag* last (1998–2003). The Wagner-parallel is obvious: indispensable requirements, a new timescale, a new kind of experience, a comprehensive, oceanic, world-making ambition, a new kind of theatre. Two marked differences: *Licht*, in all its enormous extent, is fabricated from many separate free-standing pieces, commissioned independently and enjoying a life of their own in the concert-hall. The other marked difference, of course, is quality. After the unprecedented colossalism of *Licht* Stockhausen turned to the smaller things in a second cycle, *Klang*, evoking the twenty-four hours of day and night, commenced 2004, uncompleted at his death three years later. The hours he put in comprise Ascension; Joy; Natural Durations; Heaven's Door; Harmonies; Beauty; Balance; Bliss; Hope; Brilliance; Faithfulness; Awakening; Cosmic Pulses; Havona; Orvonton; Uversa; Nebadon; Jerusem; Urantia; Edentia; Paradise. Who could ask for anything more? It is difficult to repress one's doubts. But the strongest elements in this portentous universe are important utterances of their time, and remain so for later.

Earliest is *Gesang der Jünglinge*, wherein a boy-chorister's voice is electronically transformed into a choir of celestial beings serving their ordeal in Nebuchadnezzar's burning fiery furnace, from whence they chant an exultant *benedicite*, praising all creatures that have breath and motion – a classic of the medium, at once exhilarating and touching. A second is *Gruppen*: the physical impact of this stunning conception is best experienced live – the three orchestral *groups* placed so far apart as practicable in a concert-hall, the musical material exchanged in antiphony or set against itself in antipathy, climaxing in the celebrated stretch where the same hair-raising chord is tossed across the spaces at ever-diminishing intervals. One senses in this work Stockhausen's affinity in rhetoric and proportion, as well as scope, to the Austro-German symphony – even, maybe, in affective expression, however latent or sublimated. *Carré*, which seems to promise (four orchestras, each with their own choir) to go yet further in the *Gruppen*-direction, in fact pulls in its horns; a gentle creature – tame – the vocal element confined to phonetics and names personal to the composer: 'I hope this music may evoke a little quietude, depth, concentration . . .' but those pieties result in something oddly neutral, even tedious: *Gruppen* remains thrillingly wakeful. A third classic is *Trans*: equally visceral, and equally spatial – strings divided into two halves, antiphonal at each side of the stage: between them, concealed by a veil permeated with purplish-crimson-violet light, the rest of the orchestra: from each side loudspeakers project, very loudly, the pre-recorded noise of a shuttle passed through a loom, shooting across the space at varying intervals averaging twenty seconds, at one point given its own cadenza like the soloist in a concerto, weaving the tapestry of Fate, of Life and Death, the Loom of Time and its inevitable stop. Simple, indeed simplistic, compositionally crude – it's not 'about' composing, not even about *music* – and unforgettably powerful as an *image sonore* that batters and bruises and burns.

Nono

Luigi Nono, 1924–90: from a wealthy patrician Venetian family; studied at the city's Conservatorio, then to Padua for law, but music won. Committed anti-Fascist, member of the resistance, life-long Communist. In composition, an ideological serialist; married Nuria Schoenberg (the boss's daughter) 1955. Early works an important contribution to what permanently defines the emergent avant-garde, with his own particular slant. *Il canto sospeso* (1955–6) widely seen as marrying Italian rhetoric and directness of expression with the absolutely new, Webern behind it rather than the composer's father-in-law. It remains a monument of its epoch. *Sospeso* – suspended (hanging in suspense): setting letters written by political prisoners awaiting execution, in pointillistic fashion, syllables split across the voices, the orchestra also fragmented note-by-note, choir and instruments treated without distinction. The intolerably moving *meanings* – a young man's 'I die for justice. Our ideas will win'; words from three Greek patriots (later condemned and murdered); a woman's words as the Nazis come to kill her; words of farewell from a young Russian girl to her mother – 'I depart, building faith in a better world for you': all these rendered in long-sustained clusters, disintegrated etiolation, for the soprano soloist great tenderness: the Webern cantatas taken a stage further; and a tranced ghost, in the writing for massed female voices, of *bel canto*, counterpointed with jagged rhetoric, all violence and fury. Nudity prevails: understated close on bare bass-drum-roll diminishing to inaudibility. Stockhausen deplored this harrowing work: he accused it of betraying, even exploiting, the texts. On the contrary, *Il canto* remains one of the very few, from so many comparable art-works, to confront the unspeakable with integrity, with refusal to wring the hands and emote.

Nono never matched it: there's a downward spiral even as his subsequent output aspires higher. *Intolleranza 1960* (the date part of the title, and could be considered movable, season-by-season) – opera of agitprop, Soviet-crude though the musical idiom relentlessly avant-garde. *Sul ponte di Hiroshima* (1962) and *La fabbrica illuminata* (1964) – angry, political, social protest. Rage succeeded by calm – placid, meditative, emptied-out – ... *sofferte onde serene* ... (1976) and *Fragmente-Stille an Diotima* (1980) – Hölderlin 'sung silently': finally the vast, slow, vacant-portentous-boring *Prometeo* (1984–5) – a '*tragedia dell'ascolto*', meditation upon silence paradoxically laid upon the most dynamic of all Greek myths.

The 'Holy Trinity' remains a telling soubriquet for these three composers. One wonders, as the vision dims, who was which. I've already suggested that Boulez is the Oedipal Son who, by his murderous action, inherits the Kingdoms of this World (though his father figures, Messiaen apart, all lay in the past). Stockhausen is clearly both God and Spirit, moving upon the face of the waters, creating *Licht* from dark chaotic primal matter. Nono's role in the equation is harder to place – the angel Gabriel? The ensuing sketches will widen the cameo-scope to embrace some significant avant-garde figures who share few or none of such familial interconnections.

Giacinto Scelsi, 1905–88; elder compatriot of Nono though dying only two years earlier; scion of aristocracy, born to affluence and culture, poet as well as composer. If composition it is! *Four Pieces on a Single Note* (1959) remains his *4'33"* – an ultimate challenge from non-sense to sense. Yet there's a dauntingly large output where experimental transcendental aims – music conceived as spiritual improvisational flux, not to be bound to notation but rather, impulse and intuition, 'automatic writing' – certainly achieve impressive realization in recognizably artistic manner. *Aion* (1961), for orchestra with choral voices singing unidentifiable words, can stand represent-ative. Aion/Eternity: intercrossed with 'Four Episodes in the Life of Brahma' – a single day, long as eternity. Scelsi doesn't – can't, won't – do momentum, rhythm, animation, nor motif/theme/melody. Lumps of sonority are lit from inside, as if a dolmen, a pyramid, a cliff-face, were gradually to develop features and become Sphinx, an Easter Island figure, a mountain-sized Buddha. That 'single note' is bent and split into microtones, and eventually stretched to octaves and fifths, then semitones, sevenths, ninths occasionally accumulat-ing harmony in clusters – slowly, inexorably, mainly low tessitura, very occasionally high, sometimes stratospheric: the primitive aspect of Varèse (especially *Ecuatorial*) in the background, Xenakis in the foreground: magnificently saturnine and numinous. Two other fine associated pieces: *Konx-Om-Pax* (1969), inspired by the Eleusin-ian Mysteries (after completing the trials for becoming a Seer this phrase was pronounced to bid the aspirants proceed on up towards the Light), and *Pfhat* (1974) – 'a flash, and the sky opened'. We have been here before!

Away to pleasure, wit, diversion, with Luciano Berio, 1925–2003: from a musical family; studied at the Milan Conservatorio; first marriage to the mezzo-soprano Cathy Berberian, charismatic inspiration for early vocal pieces; 1952 studied with Dallapiccola in the US. Back in Europe, close association with Darmstadt avant-garde – Boulez, Stockhausen, Ligeti, Kagel among them; explor-ing electronics, later directing them at IRCAM; wide recognition for composition, teaching, exposition (the Charles Eliot Norton Lectures at Harvard, 1993–4), and as conductor. A natural *musikantisch* type, mitigating the high-priestly severity of the 'Holy Trinity' with this quality, as also in the ease, fun, playfulness, that had him dubbed 'the Rossini of the avant-garde'. Such humanization, lack of missionary ideology and sense of historical inevitability, can have a downside: with Berio there are plentiful pretensions of another kind – intellectual, literary, political, social, as well as artistic: chic and fashion can prevail over substance. Equally his eclecticism can be disadvantageous, for all the generosity in repudiating the narrow puritanism of his peers. There are many arrangements, transcriptions, completions, of very variable quality. Best by far the everdelectable *Folk Songs* for the enchanting Cathy Berberian: worst by far the deplorable *Rendering*, cooking up the fragments of Schubert's last symphonic project, smothering them in chromium and plate-glass. In-between, atypically stolid transformation of a Brahms Clarinet Sonata into a concerto, and the pedestrian finale for Puccini's unfinished *Turandot* that aims to rectify its perceived injustice to Women.

Berio's original works centre upon the sequence of *Sequenze* for various solo instruments, fourteen in all from 1958 to 2002, exploring virtuosity, rhetoric, characterization, projection – innately theatrical, feeding into several stage-pieces. There are many works for ensemble and for larger forces; the most ambitious is *Coro* (1977), employing a wide range of folk-material – American Indian south and north, Polynesian, African, Persian, Hebrew, Croatian, Italian from Venice to Sicily – counter-coupled with Pablo Neruda and laid out in complex elaboration for groups of singers interspaced among the reshuffled seating-plan of a very large orchestra. The result is a characteristic welter; a jungle of texture, exciting initially, very soon yielding diminishing returns. In the folksongs less was more: in *Coro* more is less. The ultimate effect is of saturation without focus. This sense of the merely decorative, the brouhaha, the bubbling casserole into which anything goes, prevails in almost all his bigger works, the operas above all (or should I say 'operas'? – for there's an element of modish persiflage concerning genre and nomenclature that could be called pseudish). The mix is heady, the touch light yet masterly, the flair, recklessness, exuberance, generosity especially appealing in an epoch of artistic meanness. Berio manipulates and compères his glittering flim-flam with the compelling allure of a seasoned conjuror. Yet we all know that, *au fond*, it's classy tat – the Christmas window displays in Harrods or Macy's – gorgeous while it lasts, but after Twelfth Night it'll be bundled into the bin. He always makes a good sound – beguiling, versatile, witty, sensuous. If Rossini could recognize the idiom he would surely acknowledge the spirit: but flim-flam is, by definition, destined to obsolescence.

One work only survives its time, perhaps because it mirrors it so well – a period-piece that, as Stravinsky said, 'has dated in the right way' – the celebrated *Sinfonia* of 1967–9. Eight solo voices (originally the Swingles) are employed, and a large orchestra. The voices sing and speak (and mutter, shout, insinuate) a mishmash of texts: from Claude Lévi-Strauss (first movement); a eulogy-elegy for Martin Luther King (second, originally the free-standing *O King*); and others, uncapturable by the naked ear (the fifth and final). Central is the famous third, a fantazia built upon a complete run of the scherzo from Mahler's 2nd Symphony (itself a blow-up of the brief originating song into ongoing phantasmagoria with new central material, apocalyptic or dreamily nostalgic). Upon Mahler, Berio has set a collage of inter-punning quotations – some unrecognizable, tributes to colleagues and friends, Boulez and Stockhausen among them, and a self-quotation – in-jokes; others fugitive and subliminal – violin concertos by Brahms and Berg, pastoral scenes from Beethoven and Berlioz; some inexplicable though titivating – Debussy's *La Mer*, Schoenberg's *Five Orchestral Pieces*; some flagrant – the invasion of Mahler's fabric by a stampeding irruption from the *Rite of Spring*; and wicked – Ravel's *La Valse* transmuting into the waltz from *Rosenkavalier* (thus bringing to the surface Ravel's latent sarcastic intention). A triumph of ingenuity that will outlast its day so surely as it embodies it, as already it has outclassed a thousand less skilful and spirited imitations. (The only element in the palimpsest that dates in the *wrong* way is the further layer of spoken text, poetic or *engagé*.)

*

Codettina: Mauricio Kagel, 1931–2008; Argentine by birth, German by adoption from 1957, famous as an avant-garde jester still more committed to *jeux d'esprit* than Berio. There are some very fine serious works, still undervalued, notably the *Kammersymphonie* and the three *Études* for full orchestra. But he remains best known for his jokes – impish celebrations, in 1970 of Beethoven's bicentenary, in 1983 the 150th birthday of Brahms. He reserved his wittiest effort for the Bach tercentenary of 1985. Claiming that music-lovers, for all their discrepant beliefs or varieties of atheism, are united by faith in Bach, he took the composer's life, as documented both officially and domestically, and presented it in the Lutheran format – recitative, aria, chorus, chorale – as the *St Bach Passion*. The result is more than a *jeu d'esprit*. Unwinding as interminable monotone, it develops the irritating allure of a radio serial which cannot be relinquished in spite of one's wry contempt. Eventually Satie's observation that 'boredom is mysterious and profound' is vindicated once more. In its very prosaicness and lack of uplift this cod-*hommage* succeeds where all versions of the Gospel-proper since Bach's time fail in greater or lesser measure, be it hassocks and harmonium like Stainer's *Crucifixion*, a high-tech modernist con completely divorced from devotional use like Penderecki's *St Luke Passion*, or something between the two, like Arvo Pärt's or Sofia Gubaidulina's *St John Passion* – works of portentous vacuity that, for a time, inherited the earth. Kagel's loving send-up has the odd effect, in the end, of both sincerity and humble devotion: 'Bach is God'.

CHAPTER XIX

'Waifs and Strays'

Land is in sight: before it is reached, a gathering-in; eleven composers of calibre from the early twentieth century to the early twenty-first who don't quite fit the main tracks or categories, and certainly don't make a category of their own. Waifs and strays, odds and sods – cameos only, usually just one representative work each, sometimes a cluster.

Ottorino Respighi, 1879–1936: early attendance at the Bologna Liceo for violin and composition; 1901 study with Rimsky-Korsakov in St Petersburg, and the next year with Bruch in Berlin. Returned to Italy, playing chamber-music, later conducting and teaching, fame and success as composer. Fluent and copious – seven operas (including *The Sunken Bell*, after Gerhart Hauptmann's play of 1896, essayed by many composers of the epoch; only Respighi landed the vision); chamber-pieces; orchestrations of Bach, Rachmaninov, Renaissance airs and dances; among purely instrumental orchestral works, the five lavish evocative tone-poems for which he is most famous – *Fountains of Rome* 1916, *Pines of Rome* 1924, *Roman Festivals* 1928, with *Church Windows* 1925 and *Brazilian Impressions* 1928 carrying him further afield.

Uninhibited extroversion with flawless orchestral technique – the Rimsky-Korsakov skills extended, with bombastic bravura, sweeping all before it: Roman cohorts marching down the Via Appia in *Pines*, crazed Fellini exuberance in *Festivals*: fascistic splendour – 'Axis-music', said Stravinsky, another composer deeply indebted to Rimsky. Further afield, Butantan, the snake-pit in *Brazilian Impressions* (complete with *dies irae*), and the same work's Tropical Nights,

Debussy's *sons et parfums* from *Ibéria* on crystal meth. Alongside such, surprising delicacy and sensibility; most of all in *Fountains*, where these prevail throughout, and still more lovely in the third section of *Pines*, the Gardens of the Janiculum, notorious for including a 78-rpm record of an actual nightingale. Respighi excels equally at 'religious kitsch' – the Catacombs in *Pines*, and all four movements of the underrated *Church Windows* – exquisite refinement of The Flight into Egypt; Archangel Michael battling with and expelling Satan with wild relish; the Transportation of St Clare, tender and true; St Gregory the Great, genuine resplendence, with some of the best bell-renditions in all orchestral music.

I choose here to represent Respighi by this gentler, more lyric aspect: *Deità silvane*; five songs written for tenor and piano in 1917, recast in 1926 with small ensemble, to *fin de siècle* paganistic poems by one Antonio Rubino. *The Fauns* with their goatish lustfulness pursue the fearful yet hopeful nymphs. *Egle* dances amid the verdure: nature's sap rises in 'raucous joy', as yet inexplicit though quivering with anticipation. *Music in the Garden* – intoxicating clash of pagan music, tingling cymbals and flutes, as if nature herself were giving voice. *Acqua* – another *valsette* redolent of mossy maiden-hair and reeds. *Crepuscolo/Twilight* – slow waltz hymning Pan as he lies sleeping: but the old carefree hedonistic times are past, the fountain of pleasure dried; as twilight thickens, joy fades into sad regret. The same subject as the last *Bilitis* song in Debussy's erotic/pagan cycle: a closer comparison, because of Respighi's consummate instrumentation, lies with the precious handful of *exotiques/erotiques* by Ravel, Stravinsky, Delage written in Paris *c*.1913 with *Pierrot lunaire* in the shadows: *Deità silvane*, a late-comer and a stranger, fully worthy of this rarified company.

Luigi Dallapiccola, 1904–75: the family interned in Graz for last years of the Great War: returned to Italy 1921; studied in Florence, which became permanent home: taught at Conservatorio; gradual, eventually general recognition as composer of stature, pioneering in adaptation of Viennese serialism to a Mediterranean aesthetic, owing equally to Schoenberg, Berg and Webern as to his lyric/dramatic

Italian forebears. There are four dramatic works: *Volo di notte* (1937–9); *Il prigioniero* (1944–8); *Ulisse* (1960–68) and the *sacra rapresentazione Job* (1950); two ambitious works for soloists, choir and orchestra, *Canti di prigionia* (1939–41) and *Canti di liberazione* (1955): a small output – pieces without texts or subject-matter; and a precious handful of songs with a handful of instruments.

The two with *Prison* in their titles are both born of the circumstances of their time: the cantata directly, the opera at more distance. The Prayer of Mary Stuart opening *Canti di prigionia* was written in immediate response to hearing Mussolini's broadcast officializing anti-Semitism in Italy, July 1939: the lines from Boethius' *Consolation of Philosophy*, opening a way towards hope, followed a year later: the close, lines from Savonarola, was set off by learning of Hitler's speech promising aerial bombardment of England, and completed by the autumn of 1941: the trilogy's first complete performance, that winter, coincided with the day that Mussolini declared war on the USA. These circumstantial interconnections define but do not delimit the work's *engagement*: the times are past history, provisional and local: the concerns remain permanent and universal.

As, too, the Prisoner opera, its source *Torture by Hope* from Villiers de l'Isle-Adam's *Nouveaux contes cruels* (1888). Dallapiccola's version powerfully conveys the claustrophobia of the dark cell, the priest's insinuating rays of delusory hope, the momentary release into air, light, life, the ultimate betrayals – of the individual, of his beleaguered country, of his faith in God. Yet this fine and noble opera also invites reservations. *Tosca* threatens beyond Dallapiccola's opening gesture: an element of manipulation in the titivation of torture is common to both works. Its antithesis, cool detached formalism, play of devices, constructions, symmetries, derive from suchlike that, perhaps, compromise *Wozzeck*. A closer connection, with *Lulu* too, concerns the discrepancies, sometimes disconcerting, between grim sordid subject-matter and the sumptuous luxuriance it elicits: *Prigioniero*'s lush timbres, voluptuous harmony, sensuous vocal-writing are indulged to the full even when the most intense excruciation is rendered. A whiff of the culinary? Isn't this music simply too beautiful for its purpose? Beautiful it surely is: but is beauty enough, or appropriate, for the piece's *content*?

No such scruples arise from the heart of Dallapiccola's corpus, five miniature sets of lyrics for soprano soloist with small ensembles. Webern's ensemble-songs are the evident model: Webern Italianized, supple, fluent and melodious, graceful and grateful. The *Goethelieder* are slightly stiff, the other sets utterly delectable: three are on archaic Greek poems translated by Salvatore Quasimodo – five by Sappho (1942), two from Anacreon (1945) and six (1943) from Alcaeus, Sappho's contemporary and compatriot. This is 'war-music' in the sense and spirit of Ezra Pound's *Cathay* (1915) – exquisite evocations of a remote time and culture amid bombastic patriotic poetastry purporting to express inexpressible contemporary realities. Unlike Pound, Dallapiccola's other wartime output is wholly engaged with current circumstances. His idyllic pastoral Eros is not ignorant or desperate escapism: it affirms eternal verities from an ivory tower of precious perfection, thoroughgoingly Pagan for all his Catholicism. (It must be said that Eros and Aphrodite inspire the best tunes.)

From the very opening of the first *Sappho* song – hymn to evening, animals returning to rest, son to his mother – a small world of magical sonorities opens out: resonant descending fifths, shapely voice-part answered in canon by flute, sensitized harmonic background spare yet sufficient, sinking back into the opening fifths. In the second, the beauty of the lover Gongila puts all who behold her into a tremble, and Aphrodite herself to shame: flowing liquid lines, mirror-imitations not canons, harmony fuller, instrumentation always gently shining. The third song bids the maidens mourn Adonis: tenser, more explicit emotion grows from initial mournful fragments, the voice grows rhetorical – beat your breasts, rend your garments! For the fourth she grows calm and measured – Cretan women circle round the altar beneath a full moon: long even sostenuto, and a peculiarly delicious choir of three clarinets, heard twice, *'senza colore'* but iridescent as a snakeskin, before the parlando disappearing close. No. 5: 'long have I spoken in dream with Aphrodite' – delicate patterns of fifths on harp, caught by glancing strings and sustained winds: the soprano abandons words, after naming the presiding Goddess, for wordless dialogue with a vocal solo horn.

Technical devices, implicit for *Sappho*, come to the fore for the *Anacreon* set; canons in particular – Dallapiccola's 'liquefied Webern', just as strict but more directly concerned to be mellifluous. The soprano sings of languid Eros, bedecked with flowers, he who commands Men and Gods: one clarinet leads the canon, the voice answers, another clarinet follows, a decorative viola wriggles free: later the voice with her followers also grows more ornate: the piano (here there are only the four players) sustains a minimal background with moments of forthcoming. The stilled mood broken by Eros the destroyer, felling the lover as a tree is felled, casting her into a wintry flood: initial ferocity soon yields to limpid mirror-sonorities; furious again for the torrents, closing in excoriation: Eros denounced. The *Deo Gratias* at the foot of the score seems as inappropriate as its date and place – Florence, 18 April 1945 – double dissociation.

Tōru Takemitsu, 1930–96: born Tokyo, spent early boyhood in China, returned to Japan, education curtailed 1944 by conscription; first entranced by Western music during military service, knowledge extended and deepened during the post-war US occupation; no formal musical training – self-taught, by ear and sensibility, desire and love. Early interest in electronics; equally drawn to its antithesis, Cage's play of indeterminacy and chance: Takemitsu paid a paradoxical tribute – 'it was largely through my contact with John Cage that I came to recognize the value of my own tradition', which became a passion for Japanese instruments, techniques, spiritual works, above all its *drama*. Simultaneous, a close involvement with the European/American avant-garde, and brief personal contact with Boulez.

The real Takemitsu, digesting and sometimes reversing all this, only gradually emerges, into a lake of ultra-lush sonorous loveliness – on from Debussy, Ravel, Messiaen, Boulez' sensuous aspect: French Orientalism borrowed, paid back with interest, from a *real* Oriental. Very prolific – much orchestral and ensemble music: vocal doesn't feature so frequently (though he was planning an opera at the time of his death); some one hundred film-scores (including *Ran*).

The best of all this runs all the way from T to U with consummate finesse: take the orchestral idyll *A Flock Descends into the Pentagonal Gardens* (1977) – masterpiece of contemplative sonority, 'mindless' as some lovely natural phenomenon, a flower, a leaf, a snow-crystal, a humming-bird, a ripple of water or light, a scent/touch/taste. What *doesn't* figure is the composer's declared starting-point, a dream possibly connected with a famous photograph of Duchamp, the back of his hair shaved into a five-pointed star of baldness! Think, rather, of doves, flutterings, caresses – even the moments of violence *kiss*: there's never been anything more sheerly ravishing in all music: even its closest comparisons – Debussy's *Jeux*, Ravel's *Prélude à la nuit*, Syzmanowski's 1st Violin Concerto, Messiaen's *Jardin du sommeil d'amour* pale by comparison. One is lost in a maze – how can such *volupté* be wrought from only twelve notes? But *volupté* is all that this piece does: these other works, and others in this vein, come in a context of contrast and complement. Too much Takemitsu grows tacky, sates, can even induce nausea. But no complaints: the flight from T to U is fantastic as it is.

Still in the sonorous-beauty stakes, Per Nørgård's *Iris* (1967) and *Voyage into the Golden Screen* (from the following year) can hold a candle of pure iridescence. Here, however is a composer – Danish, born 1932 – who runs beyond sheer/mere sonorous loveliness and can be as abrasive as any other modernist except Xenakis. In these two orchestral pieces he is concerned only with beauty, and they beguile all the senses. Both are dream-concatenations of structure and facture with mystic pantheism, issuing from the rainbow, *Iris* directly, the *Voyage* generally. Nørgård employs his 'infinity series', a solution at once practical and poetic to the dead side of 12-note serialism, managing to relocate an ordered total chromatic into the harmonic structure inherent within the way we interpret acoustically. In the second movement of *Voyage* this can almost be *heard*: flutes play a continuous stream of intervallic melody, other instruments join at different speeds and registers on the same line, heterophonic polyphony makes a lucid mesh of harmony, exquisitely calibrated and voiced: all is process, all is poetry. No more than

Takemitsu does Nørgård do *themes*: he takes a shine to a particular intervallic set and sets it spinning into 'infinity'; because he likes it so well and uses it so cunningly, his listeners like it too.

'Infinity' for him extends to interstellar spaces, bringing to mind the unforgettable memory of his ardent presentation at an Aldeburgh lecture some years ago of sounds emanating from Venus – or was it Jupiter or Mars? While we all sat back and doubted, his face lit up in joy at these crackling splurts and sploshes of static from the loudspeakers, purporting to be the Music of the Spheres. More down-to-earth:

> We find clear exact phenomena in nature, in the stars, between the planets and the galaxies. Since the science of the future will more and more be based on harmony – that is, the numbered relations of pitches – music will naturally become fundamental to this science. When the laws of music are found in physics, chemistry, and in nature's principles of growth, when you see, for example, how generously the golden mean occurs in the proportions of all plants, you will understand the common connection between nature and life.

Woolly words, and very much of their time (compare, also, 'I stand with one foot in Western rationalism and one in Eastern mysticism, yet I am a stranger to both. I am, so to speak, on some sort of third point'): yet somehow Nørgård succeeds in informing both spirit and letter of these iridescent rainbows of sound. Died 2025.

(Another vignette from the past: exploring the ins and outs of Bedford with Takemitsu between rehearsals and concert in that dull town, delighting in his sweet quiddities, and telling this devout Christian of Bedford's most famous son and his wonderful *Pilgrim's Progress* (of which Tōru had never heard); happening upon a second-hand bookshop, within it finding a fine copy, complete with Doré's illustrations, purchasing it as a gift, before we relocated to the Town Hall and the audience of five old men and a dog for the London Sinfonietta programme, conducted by Oliver Knussen, containing pieces by all three of us.)

*

Stefan Wolpe, 1902–72: Berlin-born and musically educated, under Schreker and Busoni. Communist and Jew, fled Germany, relocating 1934–8 in Palestine, writing complex 'modern music' for the lost elite, simple stuff for the people. To New York 1938, associating with poets and painters, teaching at Black Mountain in North Carolina. A man of passionate aggressive commitment: in his composition class at Dartington, aged thirteen, I shyly proffered my juvenile Vaughan Williams tinged with Britten, a scared little rabbit before his burning impersonal scorn. A marvellous remark by Elliott Carter encapsulates the vehement personality as it informs his actual music – 'he does everything wrong and it comes out right.' Lots of music, ranging from simple-functional to ultra-complex and rebarbative – mainly, once Wolpe settled in New York, for varied chamber-combinations, wacky, quirky, jazz-inflected, high-spirited. His *Symphony* (completed 1955) and *Enactments* for three pianos (1950–53) between them show all these characteristics. The orchestral work proved so difficult to play that it was not heard whole until a decade after its completion. It remains challenging to performers and hearers – also tremendously rewarding. A breathless, verbless sentence from the composer gives tone, temperature, pace: 'to renew expressiveness: the cold, the shabby, the sudden, the lifeless, the rigid, the confused, the joke, the excessive, the dense, the collapsed, the most general, unlayered, smooth, extraordinary, stratified, intensified, slack, shredded, disorganized, nothing-much, continuous, constantly interrupted, the shock and ever-increasing contrast, the simultaneous and the noise . . .': perhaps all this is the subject of the omitted verb – [all these] 'must be perpetually in play, assaulting the listener to the utmost bounds of what can be borne'. One wouldn't put it past him!

Don't be deceived by the *Symphony*'s simple opening announcement: its innocence is a damn lie. Yet it's worth holding on to this shape as an aural guide through the bristling jungle of the first movement: its very thorns and bites are stimulating; one is carried upon ebullient volatility – Wolpatility. Most particularly in the second movement, a scherzo marked *charged*, wherein abrasion proves quite compatible with *brioso* good humour, athletic and witty. And the finale, marked *alive*, bubbles with jocose vitality. Hard to credit words Wolpe wrote above a passage in the first movement – 'like a kind greeting': those written above a passage in the third – 'utterly sunlike' – certainly apply.

Enactments is analogous to the contemporary work of the musician's New York painter-friends. Also to the distant, then-unknown Conlon Nancarrow (see later) in the complex textures the three-piano medium permits, as in the salty jazziness and the dense polyphony. No. 1, *Chant* – restless and gay: 2, *In a State of Flight* – more restless and nervy still, conflict in-turned rather than outward-directed; activity occasionally solidifies, freezing into marvellous harmony; a coda quiet but bristling with restrained menace: 3, *Held In* – twinkly and harp-like, dulcet dulcimer-sounds produced by small hammers beating or the pianists' fingers twinging the strings; a study in resonances unobtainable on Nancarrow's player-piano. No. 4, *Inception* ; its delicate inwardness continues these novel methods of touching-the-clavecin: the gentle centre before 5 – *Fugal Motions*: eleven-minute homage to Beethoven's *Große Fuge*. Again, as in Nancarrow, unremitting cerebration compatible with, fused into, wit, sparkle, deliciousness. No rhetoric or antiphony or feats of competitive prowess between the three pianos: they whitter to themselves, we overhear: even when the fugal motions grow splintery and cutting-edgy, their nervy gaiety obtains quite other goals from Beethoven's heaven-storming sublimity.

György Kurtág: born 1926, Romanian-Jewish, Hungarian citizen from 1948; studied piano and composition in Paris after the 1956 Uprising. Back in Budapest from 1959, always returning there after extended residencies abroad – Berlin (twice), Holland, Paris again, Bordeaux; increasingly highly rated, as with Ligeti, his country's outstanding musical contemporary. Fastidious perfectionist, in his playing (often duo-partner with his wife, Márta), in his teaching, in his composing – guiding spirits Webern, Kafka, Beckett, with father-figure Bartók omnipresent in the background. A choice hard-wrought oeuvre: at its centre *Játékok/Games*, a compendium of delights, including parodies and transcriptions, for young pianists, carrying on from Bartók's *Mikrokosmos*: for grown-ups, two song-cycles for soprano – *Messages of the Late Mlle Troussova* with ensemble (1976–80) and *Kafka-Fragments* (1985–6) with accompaniment for a solo violin. Both deserve detailed description.

Messages sets texts by Rimma Dalos, a Russian poetess resident in Hungary. This work of fleering emotional nudity is, perversely, clad in textures of intricate refinement whose subtle delicacy intensifies the excruciating states of mind and body the poems express. I can find no clue as to the protagonist, Mlle Troussova: fictional, no doubt; equally indubitably drawn from real-life experience. The twenty-one brief utterances are divided into three unequal sections, each headed with an unset quatrain from other writers.

Lines from Anna Akhmatova prefix Part I – *Loneliness* – the cold has checked her smiles; one hope dies, one more song. So to two of Dalos: no. 1 – 'confined to his cell under the intolerable pressure and heat of unrealized desires a man freezes': unwarmed by a spider's-web of sheer sonorous delight spun of the luxurious ensemble – three solo winds, three solo strings, mandoline/cymbalom/harp/celesta/piano/vibrophone/xylophone, bells and tons of unpitched percussion, all used throughout with extreme delicacy. No. 2 – 'the futile day, full of deceit and disappointment, falls like a guillotine on what crumbs of trust still remain'; the delicate web congeals into still-shining chords, darkly luminous on the plucked and struck instruments; the bowed and blown at first sighing, then joining; the voice-parts broad-sustained lyrico-rhetorico, the chords ever richer and stranger till the entire texture gutters out. Part II – *Somewhat Erotic* – is prefaced by Goethe ('when a will-o'-the-wisp shows you the way, you'd better not take it') as well as Akhmatova continued – 'this new song shall be yielded to jeering laughter, for a long silence is unbearably painful.' The ensuing songs are more than 'somewhat' – eroticism explicit and unbearable in words and music alike: 1 – *Heat*; 'sexual desire burns the entire body, aware of the poison yet desperate to ingest': texture all aflame with nervy itches, mostly soft, sometimes scratchy, culminating in a fantastic peal of hysterical laughter from Mlle T. before her expiring cadenza. No. 2, 'the frenzy of two entwined bodies, abandoned beyond pleasure and enjoyment'; the three winds to the fore, with florid horn-part at once exultant and desperate; the song climaxing in a tapestry of interlocking patterns one can almost *see* as one listens, before the exhausted all-passion-spent end. Rimma Dalos speaks of the male lover's face pale with repressed desire: no repression for 3 – the female lover again – 'why shouldn't I squeal like a pig amid everyone's grunts?' The soprano is now unaccompanied: onomatopoeia would be *de trop* in a work whose imitations are entirely psychological and physiological. As in 4, her wild incitation to bite and be bitten – 'here, there, everywhere': savage florid triumph-dance, with brilliant flourishes on piccolo clarinet, the rest of the ensemble chomping all its teeth.

Part III – *Bitter Experience*; *Joy and Grief*, headed now by a quatrain of Blok adducing the blasphemous delight of smirching sacred places. Which we will now experience for ourselves: 1's complete text runs 'you took my heart on the palm of your hand, which you then carefully turned upside-down' – upside-downed in beautiful sighing texture and harmony recalling the Pool of Tears in Bartók's *Bluebeard*. No. 2 is a tiny encapsulation of the woe and weal combining in love; naked amid such sumptuousness, for voice with cymbalom only. Rich garments resumed for 3: fabulous refinement of fluid detail enclosed within more of the fabulous locked chords – she's enchanted by the many-coloured pebbles he brings her. In 4 suffering resumes – its needle will pierce her. No. 5 is a canon of bitterness – she's calm though knowing of his indifference. Onomatopoeia *does* figure in 6, a contribution to the great tradition of rain-music – autumnal flowers, incessant rain, life drains away; overlapping descending scales, in semitones on celesta and piano, in whole-tones on harp (which can't do consecutive semitones), a blur of sustained harmony on the six winds and strings, the whole poised over deep soft reverberation of four gongs and the tam-tam. Only the cymbalom *ascends* (in whole-tones): the soprano doesn't *sing* – she's required to *miaow*. Ravishing extended coda of simultaneous ascents and descents, harp now rising as cimbalom falls. No. 7 is plain, almost austere – her search for salvation, that can *only* fall and fall. In 8 he vanishes: 'the absences in her memory, the missing times' – close-piled imitations, tense and strained. Excruciating masochism returns in 9 – 'deprived of you, I'm like that woman with severed breast in the bath-house'; creeping susurrations, *porta-menti*, glissandi. Direct appeal in 10 – 'love me, forgive me; my wishes are so simple': the song is indeed marked *semplice*, and makes a brief deep well of euphony in the psychotic context, never more psychotic than 11, the *lex talionis* of love gone terminally sour, and the sheer *shame* of retaliation – spasms of momentum begun, ended, thwarted within, by violently dissonant explosions from the entire pitched ensemble, tingled with the pair of cymbals left to vibrate. In 12 she denies reproach – the delusion was hers alone – a toy who believed herself a heroine: simplest and loveliest song in a cycle where neither quality figures much. No. 13 reverses it within seconds: she *does* reproach; bitterness *will* out in the cloud-burst, here actual; in 14 it's metaphorical – 'the cloud-burst of lustful glances', revealing her metaphorical nakedness, 'stripped to the bone': a fierce affair, almost a marching-song, dynamic and climactic. Anticlimactic, the close in 15 – bathos as well as pathos – 'for all we once did together, it is *I* who pays': absolute simplicity, only horn and bass retained from the full ensemble (an appendix drops the double-bass, hence missing the creepy effect of its expiring glissando down more than an octave of microtones). Unsung/unsaid epilogue, quatrain from Blok again, enjoining Time to extinguish in snow all memory of this night of fire: back to the freezing heat of the very first song in the cycle. It's unclear how far the unset epigraphs and this epilogue are intended to be part of the actual work. Overwhelmingly clear, that this lacerating thing penetrates realms of erotic anguish, making Musorgsky's comparable *Sunless* cycle (a clear ancestor) seem almost cosy by comparison.

The luxuriant and curiously delicious ensemble that swathes Mlle Troussova in tulle and makes her plight not just bearable but almost a thing of joy, is eschewed in *Kafka-Fragments*, where the soprano is accompanied, for a far longer duration, in texts yet more bleak, by only a solo violin. Exposure to these forty aphorisms, one or two relatively extended, mostly telegrammatic, many only a few seconds' worth, is unmitigated. Mlle T. could be someone else – a figure from Berg or Janáček, say: the 'I' here, Kafka himself of course, is 'me'; sometimes humorous, even droll, more often self-flayed and self-mocked, without self-pity let alone external forgiveness. It would suffice simply to indicate titles and texts and leave this astonishing music to effect its 'messages'.

Hans Werner Henze, 1926–2012: studied music until conscription 1944, but soon captured and interned by the British; studies resumed post-war, and attendance at Darmstadt as out-and-out young modernist; work in theatres, later to be the centre of his compositional career. Relocation to Italy 1953, detesting equally the politics and the homophobia of his native Germany. Early successes and a handsome retainer from his publishers enabled him to live continuously in Italy – first on Ischia, neighbour and friend of Walton, then in Naples, eventually on the Alban Hills overlooking Rome. Output copious, fluent, lucrative – all genres, focused mainly upon the stage. Champagne socialist, high on radical chic, life gilded and luxurious even as he empathized with the sweating workers of the world, especially Cuban.

Theatre-music the core – operas, ballets, film-scores, action-pieces, ranging from Incidental to Grand: operatic highlights include *Boulevard Solitude* (after *Manon Lescaut*), *The Prince of Homburg* (Kleist), *Elegy for Young Lovers* and *The Bassarids* (Auden; Auden adapting Euripides), *Der junge Lord* (Ingeborg Bachmann), *The Stag King* (Gozzi), *We Come to the River* (Edward Bond), *The Sailor Who Fell from Grace with the Sea* (after Mishima), *The English Cat* (after Balzac), *Phaedra* (Racine), indicating something of the staggering range. Many vocal works extend it in every direction, from Virgil to Hölderlin to Rimbaud. There are ten symphonies, much other orchestral music, buckets of chamber and instrumental, and an appealing autobiography.

Henze's initial avant-garde affiliation was delusive and temporary: his eclectic versatility couldn't be thus confined. It made him the great white hope for new music in the post-war doldrums. He had all the gifts, without ideology and inhibition: loving and learning from both, he seemed likeliest to heal the unnatural dichotomy polarizing Stravinsky and Schoenberg. He responds to everything in every direction with eager avidity: and he can do it all – the technique is as assured as the range is limitless: a new Richard Strauss, stage-based, with a huge flair for the orchestra, and canny sense of the potential within extremely diverse subjects. *'Aber etwas fehlt.'* What's wrong? I speak as an early-hopeful partisan who once saw Hans Werner Henze as the *Retter der Musik*. How does the best-equipped Champion of his times fail to redeem those gifts? Unhorsed by his dexterity, un-lanced by his assurance, limited by his limitlessness, the stuff comes gushing out, and long before the end of the tournament the fair field is emptied of folk.

Undine (1956–7), full-length ballet for Frederick Ashton and Margot Fonteyn, presents in one generous helping the gifts at their most alluring – entirely decorative divertissement, not a whiff of the subsequent political stridency. The full-evening ballet has few successful manifestations after Tchaikovsky's three glorious masterpieces. Only two – Prokofiev's *Romeo and Juliet* and *Cinderella* – still hold the stage: Britten's *Prince of the Pagodas* offers a marvellous score to a synthetic/ersatz scenario. *Undine* has the benefit of an authentic timeless fairy-tale, the inestimable advantage of fine choreography and a peerless ballerina, and the more recent luck of a complete recording, perfect and loving in every detail, under Oliver Knussen. The composer's own Diary of the ballet's making is an additional pleasure of this venture – characteristically evocative, informative, unassuming, ever-ready to learn and be guided, ever-fluent and reliable in producing the goods. It's charming to picture the process: wintering in London, composing every morning in Battersea, guest of the ballet's *secondo uomo* Tirrenio, Alexander Grant; taking the morning's work every afternoon to Ashton in Kensington, thumping it out at the piano, pulling it apart – 'sheets of notes covered the floor and the furniture; debates, sticking-points, new ideas, changes for the fifth and sixth time . . .'. Like Tchaikovsky with Petipa, Henze obeyed the choreographer's experienced practicalities – 'each scene [of the emerging scenario] was annotated with remarks about length, tempo, metre, even instrumentation – expressed in the form of suggestions or questions.' He at first resisted, before recognizing the rightness of such prescriptions; above all, their 'theatrical instinct that knows exactly how long a situation on the stage, a tempo, a type of sound, can go on, and also how long the dancer's physical strength can be expected to last.'

'Fred was quite pitiless. When I played new stuff, he'd stab me with his finger and say "Give me a tune".' Ashton has put his finger on the one element in which this captivating and fecund score is somewhat deficient. Tchaikovsky is more abundant in melody than any other composer, and Prokofiev isn't so bad either. The fairies at his cradle showered upon the new-born Henze every other gift. It wasn't the best of times for music at large when the commission for a full-evening ballet reached the thirty-year-old. He'd been a bit of an avant-garde-ist, defected from the ivory laboratory and been appropriately anathematized as he sought to widen the stylistic possibilities, heal rancorous if factitious rifts, and reach accessibly to the general music-lover, well before minimalism threw its bargain-basement bridge over the abyss. He was alone: it took courage, strength in the teeth of self-doubt, as well as all his awakening flair, to embark upon two hours' worth of ballet-music. The resulting idiom declares some of its sources direct: Tchaikovsky of course, and behind him Delibes. Foremost Stravinsky: Henze is audibly soaked in the neo-classical scores of the 1940s with their circular melodies, wealth of accompaniment-routines, light-fingered orchestration – *Scènes de ballet*, *Danses concertantes*, *Orpheus* – so despised by Messiaen, the avant-garde following suit. *The Symphony in Three Movements* is especially audible – almost quoted here and there – in *Undine*'s long Act III divertissement, virtually a piano-concerto, also besprinkled with droplets of Prokofiev. Harmony when not Stravinsky-diatonic is Bergish-dilute, residues of expressionism as practised by its most tonally inclined master (also deplored by the more unforgiving avant-garde). Knussen's affectionate observation to the composer during the recording-sessions, 'when in doubt, play a minor triad', induced a wry wince of acknowledgement.

The scenario originates in Friedrich de la Motte Fouqué's classic of early Romanticism (1811) written in German, though the author's ancestry, as his name indicates, is partially French. The tale of the water-sprite and her mortal lover torn between human and supernatural has appealed to musicians ever since: Beethoven was drawn, Hoffmann and Lortzing actually composed their operas, Mendelssohn his *Melusine* overture, Dvořák his *Rusalka*, Ravel and Debussy their respective *Ondines* for piano. The tale is irresistibly appealing for its picturesque setting, the heroine for her touching sentiment. And the music? Henze's skill and invention flow generous and unimpaired along a whole evening, picturesque in hunting, sea-storm, wedding, convulsive when the celebrations are overwhelmed by supernatural oceanic forces, lithe for the hero, fragile for the heroine, mournful for the unhappy end, the human lover sinking lifeless, the infatuated water-nymph sinking down into her native element, till the pathetic tale will, doubtless, begin all over again – *she* being deathless, *he* infinitely replaceable. The score a cabinet of delights, never less than curious, often stirring, sometimes moving, always good on the ear. But does Henze command an unmistakable individual voice? Time will tell.

Two cello concertos from around 1970, contrasting and complementary, one French, the other Polish. The Frenchman is Henri Dutilleux, 1916–2013: of distinguished ancestry; Paris Conservatoire, Prix de Rome 1938, his tenure interrupted by the war. After it, various musical jobs; from 1945 Head of Music at Radio France. A notable teacher: as composer the heir to the same forces that shape Messiaen – native French, early Stravinsky and Bartók; but the outcome is quite different – Dutilleux is soaked in literature and painting rather than theology and birds; and he has no Orient or Exotique. A slow worker, the oeuvre small and choice – an admirer puts it thus: 'Why does he write so little? Because he resigns himself only to the masterpiece. In our age of violence and disruption, his difficult mission is to be a civilized artist, and without ostentatious message to defend a certain elevated conception of beauty.' It is possible that this accolade inadvertently overlooks limitations, even inhibitions, that the 'tasteless'/committed/super-plus Messiaen throws to the winds.

The corpus centres around the orchestra – two Symphonies (1951 and 1959); *Métaboles* (1964); *Timbres, espace, mouvement* (1977); the

Cello Concerto, *Tout un monde lointain* (1970); a Violin Concerto, *L'Arbre des songes* (1985). There are chamber-pieces, including a fine String Quartet, *Ainsi la nuit* (1976) and a few vocal works.

The Cello Concerto's title comes from Baudelaire, in whom the composer had immersed himself over some ten years. Opening movement, *énigme* – 'nature, strange and symbolic': soloist commences in ruminative groping cadenza: orchestra creeps in with delicate subtlety that doesn't preclude power, gradually emanating in a scherzo where light-fingered wit and heavy-handed clunkiness combine: Dutilleux is near-unique in recent times in his ability to write *speed*. *Énigme* effaces itself into 2, *regard* – 'poison flowing from your eyes, your green eyes, lakes wherein my soul trembles, seeing itself in reverse': raptly unfolding cantilena on the cello; orchestra spare, mainly strings, occasional tremblingly lovely passages of woodwinds with a touch of celesta; harmonic mastery throughout, particularly for chorale-like close, close to Messiaen yet quite distinct. No. 3, *houles*/surges – Baudelaire's hymn to hair – 'you hold a sea of ebony, a dazzling dream of sails, of oars, of flames and masts': meditative freedom continuing from the *énigme*, waxing more and more impassioned, involving the full orchestra: rhapsodic eloquence deliquescing into swirls, scratchings, light hammer-strokes, plucks, stutters, then disappearing. No. 4, *miroirs* – lines from Baudelaire's *La Mort des amants* so memorably set complete by Debussy – 'our two hearts will become vast flambeaux, reflecting their double lights in our two spirits, twin mirrors' – which invites a lovely play of reflections. The 'Messiaen moment' again, in a fine expansion upwards/ downwards/outwards from its mid-register start. The work ends with subdued energy, almost easy-going after such raptures and such enervations; No. 5 – a gentle *hymne*.

For more vitality, try *Métaboles*, a riot of well-behaved exhilaration celebrating (in the composer's own words) 'the joy of sound' in a state of metamorphosis/metaphor/metabolism itself ('the sum of the processes by which a particular substance is handled in the living body'): the titles of the five movements – *incantatoire, linéaire, obsessionnel, torpide, flamboyant* – tell the listener all that's needed to enjoy this uplifting piece. Try also *La Nuit étoilée – Timbres/espace/*

mouvement the work's more prosaic title: its poetic is taken from Van Gogh's glorious painting of a starry night.

The Pole is Witold Lutosławski, 1913–94: of distinguished lineage; studied at the Warsaw Conservatory; military service, captured by the Germans, escaped, made living in cafés as pianist – these venues often subterranean outlets for national music forbidden under Nazi occupation. Fled Warsaw just in time to miss its destruction. From 1947 Stalinist domination with its compulsory party-line on musical style. While Lutosławski stayed home and towed the line, his composer-friend Andrzej Panufnik managed to get away. Thaw: from 1956 with the Warsaw Autumn festivals, modernist techniques could gradually be accepted and incorporated. Further political and social disturbances of late 1960s/early 1970s coincide with Lutosławski's richest period as composer, with considerable success in the West. He is principally known for his adoption of aleatory methods – 'vamp till ready' – free play for the performers upon patterns of pitch and rhythm provided by the composer: a method that needs a pluperfect ear to succeed, and can too easily become a facile substitute for the labour of writing precisely what is meant and wanted.

Lutosławski's oeuvre centres upon four symphonies and plenty of music for small ensembles, including some attractive songs. Its general trajectory after the prime years tends towards dilution, routine, mannerism. The Cello Concerto of 1969–70 shows him at his most typical and best. As with the Dutilleux, it commences on the soloist alone, cadenza-like, with whimsical play of a shy repeated note gradually opening out into fantasy, always reinvoking the starting-point; shrill riposte on sardonic brass; soloist resumes teasing, now accompanied by staccato strings; again the sarcastic muted brass; cello now briefly pizzicato, then bowed again; tuned percussion more sensitive than the brass to the protagonist's volatility; brass toccata à la Gabrieli; cello with piano, scurrying then growling, till again quelled by ill-tempered trumpets.

And so it goes – protagonist proteus/chameleon, changes of mood, contour, colour, always mocked and repressed. Never having lost face – usually smiling, even laughing, the cello now grows lyrical and thoughtful – still cadenza-ish – exploiting the entire tessitura from lowest to highest. Orchestral strings respond in a cantabile expressive enough to energize the brass in angry intervention, ending with a buzz of strings and a flurry of piano and percussion, altercating gestures of menace. Soloist shyly tries a few notes, is quashed, keeps at it, always being snubbed and bashed. Orchestra and cello defy each other to comic effect: even bells and whistles can't prevail against the cello's persistence: it grows more and more virtuosic, the orchestra more and more aggressive till at last they give over and give up. Left alone, the soloist sobs low and high, returning eventually to the initial repeated notes, inane message to a world at first hostile, finally indifferent. Excellent fooling, with something Shakespearean in the mix of pathos and farce – *Twelfth Night*; or *Punch and Judy*.

Iannis Xenakis, 1922–2001: early studies in music and engineering/technology cut short in 1940 by the war; radical youthful politics, near-fatal injury in street-fight, death-sentence; fled his native Greece 1947, to Paris; rejected for study by Nadia Boulanger, fell out with other established musicians; but Messiaen saw otherwise – don't study harmony and counterpoint, he advised: you are an architect and a mathematician, 'do them in your music'.

Xenakis took French citizenship; continued his architectural training, with strong theoretical/mathematical bent; worked with Le Corbusier, their collaboration inextricably fusing architecture and sonority in the famous Philips Pavilion at the Brussels Expo '58. The two arts are conceived as aspects of each other; yet alongside the strict disciplines both entail, a growing attraction for Xenakis towards the random – the arbitrary – chance. Electronics, *musique concrète*, serialism; total rigour, counterpointed with stochastic liberty – games, computers, throw of the dice. And humanism and pantheism to compare with Varèse – 'Man is one, indivisible and total. He thinks with his belly and feels with his mind': 'the listener must be gripped, whether he likes it or not ... the sensual shock must be as forceful as hearing a clap of thunder or looking

into a bottomless abyss.' As in the two coruscations chosen to epitomize him here. *Cendrées* (1974) – 'before autumn, before summer,
when the flocculent sky descends to meet the earth, all then is white,
opaline, and can maybe last for ever – not fogs nor dews, but cinders'.
Slithering string glissandi, chorus ululating and howling, bass solo
against grumbling bass orchestra, tenors in ejaculations, furious
bass reiterations: violins skitter and squitter, woodwinds hold long
notes, a flute flutters arabesques, joined by other solo winds: long
section of culmination, voices and strings only in dense tangles: now
empty – a vulpine counter-tenor set against sustained horns: '*sons
fantômes – nuage*'; they alternate, then only the cloud, strings and
winds in antiphony, then aggression, *ppp* and *fff*, in mutual defiance.
More howling ululation, then stammer/stutter on full woodwinds
and brasses, voices too, strings in spasmodic leaps; huge tick-tock,
almost rhythmic, gradually disintegrating; furious brass; but end
with pitchless *nuage*, soft as possible till suddenly loud as possible
on the voices; then them alone, again soft as possible: implacability incarnadine.

Jonchaies (1977): *Bulrushes* – the riotous texture of vegetation huge
on the orchestra, virtually unplayable; nature throttling itself in
convulsive superimposition, as if to reproduce Darwinian survival
of the fittest, order and disorder rampant – *compliqué mais pas
complexe*, for such jungle can only be perceived in one plane. Begins
strings alone, bowed and plucked; percussion introduced intermittently; repeated notes gradually slink upwards in ever-mounting
dynamics to a mighty *fff* involving everyone; then division, regular
and irregularizing, out-of-synch like a mad machine. But this isn't
mechanical à la Birtwistle: it is living, organic, green in tooth and
claw, though only green as rushes grow. Six horns (perhaps impersonating frogs), then all the brass; a bell; a solitary trumpet, bit
by bit ensnaring all the other brasses; a horripilating tutti, banks
of massed sonority whirring and pullulating; beneath this, drum-
thumps; a threatening railway hooter – scything the *jonchaies*?
Combine harvester? Ends shrill and high – two piccolos – last larks
before the sky crashes down? Now, if your stamina survives, try
Nomos Gamma (1969): no subject by which to visualize this music;

just the interplay between ultra-violent and catatonic withdrawal – the raw and the cooked.

Wolfgang Rihm, 1952–2024: incredibly productive – some five hundred works; a pillar of the establishment in his native Germany; idiom a sort of neo-expressionism, generalized and anonymous – what began as concentrated, extreme, ultra-intense, born of inner necessity, now by rote by the mile. That he hits the spot – that he can compose with fire – is shown (in my experience) just the once – *Jagden und Formen*, fifty-five minutes of compelling bravura, worth all the other 497 works put together. For the eventual totality comprises three originally separate pieces, much fiddled-with in various palimpsestuous versions, mashed together to make one in a manner without parallel in music, though frequently found in modern painting and sculpture: first, *Hunted Form* (1995–6); next *Harried Form* (1995–8); third, *Hidden Form* (1995–7). The concept of *Form* is common to all; that the imagery of hunt/pursuit/capture also binds them is obvious from the outset/onslaught. Instrumental forces well below those of a full orchestra – two flutes (also playing piccolos), cor anglais, two clarinet-players (doubling on bass-clarinet and its still-more-serpentine double-bass sibling), one bassoon (doubling on its double); two each of horns, trumpets, trombones, and one bass-tuba; oodles of percussion, tuned and unpitched, in the charge of three executants; piano, harp, guitar; just five strings (two violins, one each of viola, cello, bass); twenty-four players in all – yet the complexity and the decibels they achieve can reach hellish levels: Panic, Rout, Pandemonium, Bedlam, Gaderene-rampage through the forests of expressionist madness and over the cliff into the churning sea. There's nothing like it in all music, even where a wild hunt might make a direct comparison, as in Sibelius and Schoenberg. A near-hour of hell-bent scamper, from the two violins alone at the start to the terrifying tutti of the penultimate chase: even the suddenly vanishing ending is still dominated by echoes of the pursuit. Every instrument is taxed to its limits, often in sinewy unison, or in little choirs whose virtuoso unanimity rivals that on display in the great American dance-bands of the 1940s and puts across a comparable vitality, albeit demented rather than imbued with life-affirming good cheer. The long concertante-part for the cor anglais would seem to be impossible – yet there it is, large as life. In some of the few oases of slow, quiet music, the extreme soft high notes for the principal trombonist sound as though the player who can, just about, negotiate them, will have to be carted off to A&E when the solo is over, if not before it's completed.

A commentator puts the overall journey well:

> the piece develops in the manner of a river that temporarily divides into several branches, allowing islands of rhythmic repose to emerge from time to time. Although apparently left to their own devices, the sounds do not produce a sense of anarchy. In the suspensive areas where the music seems to be held in check, silence figures as a dyke that allows a few drops of water to seep through from a flood-tide on the point of destroying all in its path.

Don't let this put you off! The experience of *Jagden und Formen*, live or on disc, is exhilarating as well as perilous: it lives dangerously and fears nothing: marvellous notes when they can be caught (clearest in the oases) – though the entire work could be imagined as written for percussion alone, its notated pitches are innate and intrinsic to its devastating success.

CHAPTER XX

Contemporary Times

Twenty Brits, one Irishman and an Australian

Next, twenty-two composers – Scotch, Irish, English, Australian – since Britten and Tippett. I must add a personal note here – the list includes friends as well as associates: several were my pupils, and one was my teacher.

First the 'Manchester School' – loose journalistic catch-all for the group of gifted musicians who coincided as students at that city's conservatoire in the 1950s: John Ogdon the pianist, Elgar Howarth the trumpeter and conductor – they also wrote music, though the principal composers are Alexander Goehr, Peter Maxwell Davies and Harrison Birtwistle. These three are quite distinct in idiom and aim: in common as they set out was a defiantly anti-Establishment stance: as is the British way, all three end up as Pillars of it.

Take Alexander Goehr, 1932–2024: born Berlin, son of a Schoenberg-pupil; the family emigrated to England the next year, and after Manchester then study in Paris with Messiaen his career was entirely native Establishment – BBC producer (and in 1987 Reith Lecturer); Professor at Leeds University 1971, at Cambridge 1976–99. Outstanding as an educator in private as well as within institutions: unlike his student confrères, an Intellectual, the compositional output interspersed with thoughtful essays, interviews, *pensées*, charting a journey from Boulezian avant-garde to conservative sobriety rooted in Bach, Brahms, Schoenberg, and strict Palestrina counterpoint. Plentiful orchestral music – landmarks *Little Symphony* and *Metamorphosis/Dance*: plentiful chamber-music, with backbone of five string quartets: two full-scale operas and two triptychs of music-theatre pieces: and much else. Uneven – on a dull day, laborious and inhibited; on a good, communicative expressively as well as cerebrally: the declared intention – composing 'to show that certain notes follow and others don't' – completely overcome by the undidactic impulse to musical pleasure in some of its myriad guises.

As evinced by *The Death of Moses*, an extended dramatic cantata of 1992. Exodus is sparse concerning Moses' death. He has delivered his People from the bondage of Egypt; led them through the Red Sea and across the desert; been granted, face-to-face with the Invisible God, the Tablets of the Law; destroyed them in rage at the folk's regression to idolatry: and, crucially, been denied his own entry to the Promised Land, goal of his mission, permitted to all but him. When and where will he die, and where be buried? A long tradition of conflicting uncertainties, enshrined in a large corpus of Hebrew poetry: one sequence has been especially adapted into English for Goehr by John Hollander. Five soloists take on various roles, the chorus describe and comment, children's voices suggest angelic other-worlds, an instrumental ensemble of thirteen players provides the remarkable sonority that makes the piece so special in its time and beyond.

No. 1, Tears and Fears: unanswered unanswerable riddles: Moses commanded to ascend the high mountain and die. 2: Chorus – to *this* man, with all he has done, shall death not be vouchsafed? Framed by Moses' repeated cry to 'Jochabed my mother'. 3: death is near – where shall I die? My heart is empty, my soul bitter. The chorus enjoin peace, but there is no peace for him. 4: he sees to the ends of the earth and the seas, to the end of his past, to the end of time. The Angels are appalled at what looks like presumption – 'who is he and what can he be?' 5: he rages against his death – why? Because I stammered? *No*, says God – that is not why. Then why? Go up to the mountain that reaches the sky – there you will die; it is ordained. 6: Moses moves around the players and singers – five positions, calling in turn upon the Earth, the Heavens, Sun and Moon, Mountains and Hills, Rivers and Deserts, to intercede with God that he be allowed to see the lovely Promised Land. All refuse: they pray for themselves – they too will be vanquished in their diverse ways. Even God declines – 'You've travelled far enough.' Which leads surely to 7: Moses and his God in colloquy – handsome promises gaining no further ground – you must die, not as all men die; and no man will know the place. 8 provides light relief: a succession of Angels – good (Gabriel, Michael) and wicked (Sammael) tease and tantalize the bamboozled Patriarch. At last God himself answers: he calls Moses' Soul out from his body – come forth, daughter! Moses and his Soul converse – all will be well, she sings; he thanks her for her gracious services: 'and God took Moses, and kissed him on the mouth and took his soul' – the work's simplest passage, and its most beautiful, choir in warm harmony, some instruments support-ing, flutes singing above – 'and God wept then, and the Heavens wept, and the Earth wept'. 9: distinctly comic relief now, children's voices to the fore – 'others tell it differently' – three youths digging a grave – whose? – someone whom God loves, just about your size. Moses jumps in and is hailed by the Angel of Death with salutations of Peace: he responds: bright Angels bury him in darkened ground. 10: the human climax; Jochabed seeks her son in all the five places of his great deeds – Egypt, the Nile, the Red Sea, the Desert, Mount Sinai; none has seen him since he disturbed their tranquillity. She is sung by the counter-tenor soloist (the soprano had been reserved for Moses' Soul): her increasingly urgent questions are movingly expres-sive, florid, plangent, as she moves from place to place. Finally, she cries to the Torah, his greatest deed of all – 'Have you seen my son?' The Book replies, enigmatic and drastic – 'There's no more to say. I've said what I've said, that that will abide.' The brusque words, the music equally, decline comfort, assurance, happy ending, let alone apotheosis. It suffices that Moses be buried in this 'shadowed valley', not the high mountain he'd been promised; and that, implicitly, his Chosen People will pass over, not knowing the place thereof, to enter their inheritance, flowing with milk and honey, that he has brought about.

A wonderful piece, with atmosphere and feeling unlike any other, stemming from the rich tradition of Mosaic mythology on which it draws, and wholly caught in its unique sound-world. Goehr's goal was

'Monteverdi as heard by Varèse'; but there are no stylistic references, and other composers can also be fleetingly glimpsed – Messiaen, Ligeti, Takemitsu, the avant-garde of Boulez and Stockhausen, even moments of Orientalizing Britten and madrigalian Tippett. The instrumental forces – two flutes (with their doublings higher and lower), two saxophones, three trombones, two electronic organs (one doubling celesta), harp, bass-guitar – yield a range from radiant celestial shining silver and steel, via delicate golden decoration and sonorous dense-glowing bronze, copper, brass, to iron roughness, indignation, anger. Whatever the intonation, all is luminous, revealing the work's ultimate source, the Burning Bush in Schoenberg's Moses-opera, several times cited direct in Goehr's score. 'Schoenberg is *my* Moses, and I am one of his people too.'

Peter Maxwell Davies: born 1934; pioneering work, after Manchester, at Cirencester School 1959–62; founded and directed the Fires of London ensemble for instrumental and music-theatre presentations 1970; moved to Orkney the same year, closely identifying with its landscape, people, problems, and founding its Festival. Knighted 1987, Master of the Queen's Music 2004–14, fearless spokesman for the arts and for gay rights, died 2016.

Huge and variegated catalogue all throughout his manifold self-transformations: the student modernist; the frugal carols for Cirencester; the serialist/constructionist; the medieval monk; the identification with the sixteenth-century English master John Taverner (several orchestral fantazias and an opera on his life); the camp entertainer (*The Boyfriend*, foxtrots, *Eight Songs for a Mad King*); the expressionist (*Revelation and Fall*, *The Devils*); the Scots nationalist and defender of local loyalties (*Orkney Wedding with Sunrise* and many others); the Beethoven/Mahler/Sibelius symphonist (ten, eventually!); the Haydn string quartettist ('Naxos Quartets'); the baroque provider ('Strathclyde Concertos'); the all-purpose provider to the people (*Kirkwall Shopping Songs*, *The Turn of the Tide*); the political/social protester ... and more. Nothing quite focuses or gels: huge ambitions or modest aims suffer equally from radical defects of ear that vitiate the musical invention harmonic, melodic, rhythmic, above all timbral. What he can do, at its purest, most authentic, best, is heard in *Worldes Blis* (1969): a gruelling, even horripilating experience, this 'motet for orchestra', subjecting the ancient song to medieval, Renaissance, expressionist, modernist procedures of alarming rigour.

Worldes bliss ne last throwe: worldly joy withers in a moment; mix'd ever with woe and misfortune; when it passes man is stripp'd bare; joy is naught but lamentation. Two twangling harps: slowest, lowest possible orchestral gropings in the dark, gradually animating and rising: we seem to *witness* as much as to *hear* the painful evolution from primal ooze to squirming life, longer prolonged than humanly bearable. Fast, at last – spiky pinpricks: back to growling slow-motion, thickening and quickening into huge intensity and a real allegro. Then the texture suddenly all holes. From now on, everything comes in brief spasms of violent convulsions and sudden cools, till a long, busy, yet emptied-out stretch dominated by the two harps: fast and furious again, the second spasm adding unpitched percussion. 'The road of Excess leads to the palace of Wisdom' – hurricane welter of jabbing splinter, an organ adding to the noise, culminating in chunkier tutti ending on colossal crescendo, subsiding into lento. The title-song commences clearly on tuned percussion: it has imperceptibly permeated all preceding sections, and now reaches the surface – handbells, then glockenspiel, then tubular bells – alchemically transformed; still hard to recognize, even to discern, amid the surrounding chaos: till, suddenly, this is cut off; metallic jangle left to ring clear, with organ and high woodwinds to enhance. Under them, the lower orchestral tutti also imitates bells in deepening thick dissonance of utter black. Four brutal bonks on a vast bass drum; ending on mysterious symbolic soft woodwind chord, fading away into nothing: worldly bliss is naught but woe. *Not* a thing of joy: cold and menacing as an iceberg, and as impressive.

Harrison Birtwistle, 1934–2022: his extensive catalogue dominated by theatre-pieces, consistent throughout (and from 1975 for some years he directed music for the National Theatre, its climax a memorable *Oresteia*); they range from the colossal – *The Mask of Orpheus*

1973–4, *Gawain* 1990, *The Minotaur* 2008 – to the miniature; first and best is in between – *Punch and Judy* 1967. His instrumental music often intimately related to his theatrical in subject-matter and treatment. It is copious in small and large: two landmarks for large orchestra *The Triumph of Time* and *Earth Dances*; some landmarks for small ensemble *Tragoedia*, *Silbury Air*, *Ritual Fragment*; a splendid piece for brass band, *Grimethorpe Aria*: several concertos, and much music for just two, three, four instruments. As time's chariot swings by, a sense that his earlier phase contains Birtwistle's peculiar essence at its primal freshest: later, a sense of self-recycling, almost self-parody, encouraged by many prestigious commissions. Like the later Henry Moore, every big city wants one, and is likely to expect, and receive, 'more of the same'. His 'manner' (sometimes descending to mannerism) ranges from bloody violence to anarchic humour, fragility and surpassing tenderness. He is drawn to machines, clocks, chronometers, to ritual and pattern-making – 'refrains and choruses', symmetries, games of counting – sheep (*Yan Tan Tethera*) or Apostles (*The Last Supper*); formalized religious observation from archaic epochs, usually Greek; landscapes actual or imagined: the sound-world is brutal, assertive – brass by the ton, acres of percussion tuned and untuned, screaming woodwinds, strings to the background, harps employed only for savage attack: yet can also be etiolated, emaciated, pared to the bone. A figure of paradox, the contrasts and contradictions enmeshed tight into the vision which, when realized in full, is convincing and compelling in high degree.

Tragoedia (1965), an ensemble-piece, formalizing the dramatic and metrical constituents of Greek tragedy and poetry into palindromic dance-ritual-sacrifice – epitome of a drama, initially a goat-dance, without plot let alone words, inventing at a stroke the Birtwistle manner as described, and remaining one of its most vivid manifestations. A study for *Punch and Judy*, which followed immediately sometimes employed the same material. This fantastic black farce on traditional popular motifs transcends completely the chic violence and arch wordplay of its libretto: still Birtwistle's finest hour and a half, I believe, whatever the grandeurs to come. But we must move on to catch the great chariot before it lumbers out of sight. *The Triumph of Time* (1972): emblematic moralized landscape-journey for large orchestra, inspired by a Breughel print. Through terrain devastated by destruction, Time drives his chariot, laden with cumbersome world-sphere sporting a clock and hung with symbols of the Zodiac. The vehicle tramples discarded weapons, mangled instruments of arts and crafts, and insignia of professions and callings secular and religious: it is drawn by two clapped-out nags bearing the symbols of sun and moon. Time devours a living child; images of time and death are scattered all about, Death himself follows on a donkey, and the fearsome angel of Fame, borne on an elephant, blasting a trumpet, brings up the rear. All this rendered in a slow drear processional, athematic save for a lamenting contour on cor anglais and a three-note figure, intermittent yet persistent, on saxophone. Gradually a coruscating climax is reached, is cut sharply off, leaving behind only mournful aftermath as the ghastly procession makes for inhabited countryside as yet uncontaminated: a vision of unforgettable baleful power, even magnificence.

More cheerful, the landscape evoked in *Silbury Air* for ensemble (1976–7): Silbury Hill in Wiltshire, a site dated *c.*2400 BC, its purpose unknown – unlike its contemporaries the Pyramids, not a funeral place. The music somehow manages to give function to the enigma – almost inhabitation: a fugitive subliminal 'clog dance' in which we can discern the ghosts of long-lost folk in weird garments practising their arcane mysteries. Positively high-spirited, the next ensemble-work (1977) *Carmen Arcadiae Mechanicae Perpetuum* (note the naughty acrostic): 'perpetual song of mechanical Arcady'. Six musical mechanisms are intercut and superimposed in ever-changing formations – late yield from Stravinsky's seminal *Symphonies of Wind Instruments* – bouncing off and slicing into each other, aggressive and exhilarating, witty, elegant, compact. Thereafter much further, never less than unmistakable, but with that sense of self-repetition, as mentioned. But one recent-ish piece flutters free into an altogether different area – *The Moth Requiem* of 2012. Its sonority is special – twelve solo female voices, constantly re-divided; alto flute; three harps. The origin, a moth caught in the strings of a piano, its mysterious sounds as it tries to escape, are put into a poem by Robin Blaser, whose key-line runs 'the air rings with an earlier unease of the senses'. The complete poem is set briefly, core of a litany of many moth-names in Latin: sometimes suggestive – e.g. *Scopula immorata*, *Depressaria discipunctella*; sometime bizarre – e.g. *Costaconvexa polygrammata*, *Eremobina pabulatricula*; sometimes Latinizing their discoverers' names – *Borkhausenia minutella*, *Kessleria fasciapennella*. *Requiem* because some of these species fly under threat of extinction – there's no reference to the liturgy and its texts – the word suffices; by implication only, it can open up a lane to the land of the dead – flittering ghosts of memory and loss, caught in three harps' twangling strings. The overall *image sonore*, like the creatures themselves, is *multicolore*, clumsy yet fragile, dusty with pollen, *noctuelles*, vulnerable and adorable.

Piquant that the British Establishment can embrace this maverick outsider! Birtwistle, like his old friend Maxwell Davies, received a knighthood (1988) and, like all three of the Manchester Group, was laden with honours and degrees.

Robert Simpson (1921–97), edgy and combative, would surely have spurned such rewards even had they been offered. His career – BBC producer for many years – sober enough: his output as composer almost entirely abstract and instrumental, centred upon eleven symphonies and fifteen string quartets. They come in rapid succession, effortful at first, then increasingly fluent: symphony follows symphony, quartet quartet, without helpful handles – whether incidental, like the nicknames attached to his beloved Haydn's, or germinal subtitles (*Espansiva*, 'Inextinguishable') as with his beloved Nielsen's. Even when there is programmatic inspiration, from cosmology, biology, ecology, it is subsumed into a musical dialectic whose severity is without parallel in the last half century. The result is absolutely radical. Eschewing every blandishment of colour, sensuousness, allusion, it takes its stand on pure process, the construction of shape and form out of the grammar of music's materials. Widely regarded, beginning with himself and his immediate supporters, as conservative, locked in embattled defence of classical tonality,

Simpson's music is no such thing. For, paradoxically, his mature work realizes with single-minded ferocity what is implied by some of the twentieth-century lines he so excoriated – the tight intervallic organization of serial music, the obsessive repetitions of simple figures in Stravinsky, even the athematicism of Boulez and the all-system pattern-making of minimalism. His basic urge, however, remains old-style humanism, man-the-measure, aggressively advocating peace, freedom, justice; and the rhetoric that carries it retains old-style musical tropes – especially those tattooing trumpets and drums! – whose conventional and increasingly machine-made nature is redeemed by such purposeful proportion and direction. If this all sounds more rebarbative than attractive, that is its nature and its essence. Which at its best – at a rough hazard the 'middle period' symphonies nos. 3 to 6, before they begin to grow too long and 'indistinguishable' – surely lies alongside the most valuable music of its time, unflinching in integrity.

At this point a work that fits better here than elsewhere – the one-off Symphony of unflinching integrity by another almost forgotten composer, American by birth, English by adoption – Bernard Benoliel (1943–2017). I recall occasional glimpses of this darkly humorous figure: the inner fire informing his remarkable music was palpable beneath the urbane surface. Might and sinew in an idiom of extreme dissonance that yet does not exclude warmth and richness: the closest parallel is the Ruggles of *Men and Mountains*; behind it, Bruckner at his most granitic: visionary intensity without remission, yet absolutely exact; tight-leashed discipline at the mercy of an acute ear; exclamations/excoriations/ecstasies like only one other in these twenty-one composers, though Simpson sometimes comes close. I've encountered nothing else of Benoliel to match this sole Symphony.

The comparison is Minna Keal, born 1909 of Russian-Jewish stock: she showed early promise, studied composition at the Royal Academy of Music and achieved some recognition, but by 1930 or so gave up music for left-wing politics active and fervent. Earlier work beginning to be rediscovered, she resumed composition in the 1970s with a string quartet, op. 1. Her Symphony, op. 3, was completed 1982 and heard at the 1989 Proms under Oliver Knussen, principal champion of Keal's rediscovery. 'You're never too old to make an impact!' she claimed: which it certainly does, in fighting terms: every detail in my description of the Benoliel Symphony applies here too, so nearly in one case that this radiantly embattled figure began to be nicknamed 'Mrs Ruggles'. She'd not yet encountered his work: when she did she recognized the affinity at once and was delighted. Her Symphony – unpredictable, unlikely – is a masterpiece. Died 1999.

Scenes and Arias, completed 1962, by Nicholas Maw (1935–2009) is a song-scena for three female soloists and large orchestra. This music, with its generous emotional warmth and stylistic freedom, was an ear-opener to a whole generation of younger English composers (myself included) when it first shone through the norms of its time, compulsory serialism, anonymous, grey, costive. The very format – soprano, mezzo, contralto – suggested the forbidden sins of the *Rosenkavalier* trio: the reckless virtuosity of the orchestration also recalled Strauss – a Strauss headily cognizant of Stravinsky and Bartók, Debussy and Messiaen. Above all, for his compatriots, Maw's evident love of, debt to, his immediate native forebears, also at that time pretty much off the officially sanctioned progressivist map: Walton for romantic nostalgia, bravura, nervy energy; Tippett for textural richness; Britten for darkly tinged luminosity (and in fact the writing for the three women in combination owes more directly to the beautiful all-female quartet in *Peter Grimes* than to the *Rosenkavalier* trio). If this barrage of great names indicates vagrant/flagrant eclecticism that has to borrow rather than create anew, just listen! The varied idioms of *Scenes and Arias* fuse into an amalgam quite itself. Most music down the centuries, good, bad, indifferent, is composed of what precedes it, ingested, digested, transformed – a process vividly exemplified here.

Maw's text is an anonymous poem of *c*.1300: the man writes to his lover in five stanzas; she replies in four; Maw doesn't distinguish the sexes. Both employ macaronics; each stanza is marked halfway and to close by rhyming Latin – a formal refrain-pattern giving shape to the prevailing fluidity. Moreover, the English of the epoch is infused with French, language of respectful courtesy, intimacy and tenderness expressed in decorous restraint. But nothing restrains the torrents of erotic ardour the words' musical setting releases: from the very start the curbs are loosened – yearning with languor, then seething with restless desire, always cooling for the chiming Latin. Exaltation and melancholy fuse: when the orchestra is freed from brief interjections to bloom with textless expansion, the creaming lusciousness can be almost too much (again recall the frank physicality of *Rosenkavalier*, and throw in the scarcely-less-carnal voluptuousness of the ostensibly spiritual *Turangalîla*). For all the poem's stanzaic/metrical shapeliness there are no melodies as such: rather, many motifs in constant play across a rich harmonic background deriving from the two chords at the very opening. At the work's dynamic climax, the (very Walton-ish) orchestral interlude soon after Part II (the woman's reply to the man) commences, these two chords oscillate in a kind of gigantic trill. In the closing stretch – *vous êtes ma mort et ma vie* – Maw reveals the structural mettle underlying his volatile surge, in a weighty canonic passacaglia permutating through eleven of its possible twelve transpositions. An inheritance from Schoenberg: for *Scenes and Arias* does not abhor what it escapes from that can enrich its language and its technique. The process reaches culmination and apotheosis on the seminal two chords, and they infuse a slow decline and fall after the voices cease.

This marvellous work opened high windows upon wide skies and extensive landscapes. Maw never again approached, let alone surpassed it. Some of his music close in date shares something of the same calibre: but grandiosity, even megalomania, gradually accrued – the gigantic *Odyssey* (1972–87): then middle-brow/middle-of-the-road commonplaces – *The World in the Evening*, a violin concerto, etc.: then finally a long operatic night of sad tired schlock – *Sophie's Choice* (1999–2002). The facture never less than masterly, but from the costly vessel the essential ichor had evaporated.

As mentioned, *Scenes and Arias* proved liberating for several younger English composers in their attempts to find a way through the prevailing atmosphere and, with luck, discover a voice of their own. Maw himself moved over to a new publishing-venture encouraged, and to some extent funded, by Britten, discontented with the company that had so handsomely championed his earlier triumphs. Faber Music, scion of the distinguished house celebrated for prose and especially poetry, soon developed its own recognizable sound – to such an extent that the two words 'Faber Music' could become a catch-phrase, praising and teasing, a soubriquet – like the 'Euston Road School' and, indeed, Impressionism, in painting – for an entire group of composers published by the imprint and holding much in common, stylistic and aesthetic. Outstanding among them are Colin Matthews, Oliver Knussen, George Benjamin, Thomas Adès, Julian Anderson.

First, though, a rather older figure, comparable in some respects yet lying aslant: Jonathan Harvey (1939–2012). His large and varied output is infused and vitiated by a weakness almost gullible for jejune gleanings from Eastern religions, especially Zen Buddhism, and the vapid pantheistic idealism of Rudolf Steiner: a succession of *Inner Light* and other such pieces fervent with such doctrines, which also infect several large-scale stage-works of ineffable absurdity – the *Inquest of Love* remained unequalled in this respect, until easily surpassed by *Wagner Dream*. Harvey at his truest and best is beautifully exemplified by *Song Offerings* (1985) to texts by Tagore – ravishing finesse, lyricism, spiritualized carnality. And one work touches immortality: *Mortuos plango, Vivos voco* (1980), a direct descendant of Stockhausen's equally timeless *Gesang der Jünglinge*. This prototype subjects the voice of a boy chorister to electronic transformation, changing the single source into a multiple hymn of praise as sung by the children in the furnace, miraculously unharmed by the fiery destruction that would consume them. Harvey's work takes its title from the Latin inscription on a great bell in Winchester Cathedral – 'I lament the dead, I call the living'. To the bell's own voice is added the voice of the composer's son, a chorister at Winchester at the time: the two sources are transformed, intercut, transfused, by electronic means, into a single unforgettable *image sonore*, the most touching nine minutes' music of recent decades.

Colin Matthews; born 1946; collaboration with his composer elder brother David on the revelatory publication of Deryck Cooke's realization of Mahler's 10th Symphony; both brothers also worked as amanuenses to Britten in his final years: later association with the Holst Estate and the Britten/Pears Foundation; enlightened generous commitment to recording contemporary British work. After the Mahler, this expert craftsman has devoted much energy to completing, or adding to, or simply orchestrating, much other music: notably Holst – songs, and an eighth *Planet – Pluto the Renewer*; discarded or unfinished pieces of Britten; Scriabin piano-pieces, Fauré songs; and the complete piano *Préludes* of Debussy. His original compositions are extensive, versatile in all genres save choral and (until 2025) operatic.

Consistent throughout is immense energy and speed: Matthews better than any other composer of these times has confronted and solved the problem of *fast* music, the vital factor, largely missing from the post-war avant-garde and its followers, of gearing sheer speed into journey and structure. All these four works following achieve this dynamic momentum. An early instance, *Fourth Sonata* (1974–5) for orchestra, an intelligent and prescient response to American minimalism – 'a necessary breath of fresh air' (he says) after the restrictions of serialism – before it became a universal cliché: somehow fusing process with expressionism in nearly half an hour of exhilarating athleticism. Two more: *Suns Dance* (1985) – the title consciously ambiguous (and surely intended, too, to refer to his young son – a kind of complement in its hectic course to the gentle interiority of bell and boy in Harvey's *Mortuos plango*), and 'intended to convey a sense of power and energy'. It sure does: momentum continuous and (mostly) frenzied, featuring all its ten players, from shrieking piccolo to grumbling double-bassoon, in turn for a concerto-like structure of vertiginous virtuosity – the horn part, particularly, will have your ears on stalks. Audibly a child of *Silbury Air*, with a profile quite distinct from its parent. *Broken Symmetry* for orchestra (1992) takes the same procedures and sounds to interesting further places – 'music I had wanted to write for many years before I had the confidence to do so', its composer says, oddly, considering the nature of his previous achievement and its irresistible confidence.

The Great Journey (1981–8) is quite different. Its text compacts the account given by Cabeza de Vaca, to Emperor Charles V, of his adventures and misadventures in the New World. The mission was sent in 1527 to Florida; it sought treasure, of course, but encountered only privation: Cabeza's party was reduced to just twelve within a year. He was left for dead, but survived among the Indians. The experience humanized the 'savages' for him as they manifested their own humanity: his dogmatic Christianity was modified by both sides' mutual compassion. After more than six years he met up with three other survivors: together they undertook the Great Journey through the interior, meeting with Spanish settlers 1536. His *Relación* was published 1542, and in an English version in Purchas's *Hakluytus Posthumus, or Purchas his Pilgrimes* in 1625. Matthews' work presents the man himself, solo bass, continuous throughout some fifty minutes' duration, accompanied by a small, vividly characterized ensemble. The four parts – *Shipwreck, Landing, Flight, Return* – render with equal skill terrains, travels, the indigenous musics which have to be imagined, the churchly strains derived from contemporary Spanish/Mexican motets: and also succeed in uttering Cabeza's feelings – droll, desperate, dutiful, defiant; and to touchingly suggest the dawn of regard and assistance across the racial divide.

This is the place to mention another impressive journey-piece: *Aria for Edward John Eyre* by the unfairly forgotten Australian composer David Lumsdaine (1931–2024). Eyre's journal recounts a near-disastrous two-man expedition in 1840–41: narration is shared by the two explorers; a solo soprano is added to an ensemble comparable to Matthews' except for the presence of live electronics; their duration is identical (fifty minutes); they both reach comparable intensity in rendering privation and deliverance.

Dominic Muldowney, born 1952, best known for his work at the National Theatre, is better remembered for some very striking concert-music. Three contrasted concertos can exemplify and typify: latest, longest, least penetrable, for violin – dauntingly complex, orchestra in two halves, each with its own conductor, helped by click-tracks, with occasional sampled sound: there are stretches of visceral distraction, but the simultaneous speeds very soon become imperceptible; in the end the listener is left out – as alas, one senses, the players too, solo violin above all.

Elusiveness and complexity became positives in the other two concertos. Genuine apprehension of simultaneous layers of activity/ speed/idiom/mood interests and excites throughout the Piano Concerto. Its complex structure is built upon Baroque and classical prototypes – chorale prelude, fugue, variations, and a single section of passacaglia: all these cubistically/mosaically splintered and intercut (Stravinsky a prime inspiration): highly ingenious but not clever-clever, neat but not too tidy, sometimes dry but never cold. Formalities are set up then subverted, mocked, teased: textures and moods all volatile – fragile and tender, dreamy and nostalgic; sensuous, even luscious; violent and menacing, refined and coarse; humorous alongside solemn. The constant interplay of idiom, from archaic via Romantic to abrasively modern and lovingly cheapo – *palais de danse valses*, uninhibitedly raucous jazziness – *offers* yet *resists*: there's something evasive/elusive/escaping about all this skill and elegance. The closing stages can epitomize – a melodramatic crunch on the gong, a touch of chorale, then a furtive scuttle to the finishing-post.

If all this sounds a bit much, try the Concerto for Saxophone (the instrument has already figured in the Piano Concerto, with a three-note motif continually in play – a mysterious signal, invitation/initiation into secret hinterlands). This work is more compact and open, fluid and lyrical in warm expressive intimacy, flamboyant and ostentatious in public, flirtatious and accommodating, sensual even unto sleaziness, introvert at heart yet heart on sleeve for wild big-band bravura of the finale, oddly subtitled *danses macabres*, in actual effect exuberant and life-enhancing.

Trevor Wishart, born 1946, a genuine Original, his work idiosyncratic and uncategorizable in techniques as in goals. Its material not standard vocal/instrumental pitched/rhythmized, however radically redeployed. Rather, circumambient noise, landscape, cityscape, industry: above all, the human voice, whether articulate speech or wordless ululation, cries/whispers/mutters/strangulations/howls – 'groans that cannot be uttered'; but can be and *are*. This raw material is then subjected to transforming technology. The upshot at its best is rich and strange – raw and cooked – an adventure in sound. Two titles indicate the principal sources: *Vox* and *Globalalia*. The latter is a triumph of its peculiar facture (as above): the former is, as a whole, compromised by long stretches of vapid pop-song: but the best section, *Anti-Credos*, is Wishart's finest *quart d'heure*. Its closest model is Renaissance vocal polyphony at its pitch of perfection – Palestrina. Not of course for actual idiom: yet one senses a comparable framework of rules and usages that permit, within the strictures, purposeful licence heightening intensity and expression. Expressive here becomes literal rather than, as with all other music, a metaphor: expression – vocal utterance from a human body. Wishart is an unlikely figure amid the 'straight' compatriots gathered here (however different among themselves): I recall him out-and-about central Cambridge during a brief residency, eagerly collecting – 'photographing' – raw material from noises of streets, market, passers-by, from which to produce another vibrant, peculiar *objet sonore*, absorbingly itself, absolutely authentic, as true as what it's fashioned from.

Oliver Knussen, 1952–2018: probably the most innately gifted and musical of all this group of composers; an infant prodigy, conducting the London Symphony Orchestra in his 1st Symphony, aged fifteen. Earlier still, he'd sat in as a twelve-year-old on rehearsals for the première of Britten's *Curlew River* in which his father played double-bass: in his early thirties he became Co-Director of the Aldeburgh Festival for fifteen years: and he lived his latter decades in Snape, just up the road from the Maltings concert-hall and Arts Centre.

The publicity surrounding the symphony's performance traumatized the sensitive youngster; he passed several years in the US, making many vital contacts and a marriage. Back home, his outstanding conducting career took off but slowly: in full flower, Knussen was the finest interpreter of his particular brand of contemporary music that it has ever enjoyed – meticulously precise, crystal-clear, ardently expressive, with the intuitive comprehension of a practising composer endowed with a strong sense of crusade/ mission. Original composition always came with difficulty, and many cherished projects were achieved only in part, or not at all. Yet he was relatively fluent all through the 1970s, with a catalogue of miniature perfections – two cycles setting Georg Trakl, *Rosary Songs* and *Trumpets*; *Océan de Terre* setting Apollinaire; two pieces for ensemble, *Ophelia Dances* and *Coursing* – and two further symphonies, the 2nd also vocal, setting Trakl again, and Sylvia Plath, the 3rd purely orchestral. A mighty handful, miniature or extended; a precious harvest of finesse. Trouble ahead: the first performance of the complete 3rd Symphony in 1979 (its first movement had already been given six years before) was the first of many notorious cliffhangers: even as it now stands, this wonderful piece doesn't fully fulfil its composer's original intentions.

His next phase is dominated by two fantasy operas, for children and consenting adults, written in collaboration with the words and images of Maurice Sendak – *Where the Wild Things Are* (1979–83) and *Higglety Pigglety Pop!* (1984–5). Both were born with effort, subject to endless delays, initially given incomplete, the latter only polished off finally in 1999. Knussen's later compositional path was bestrewn with difficulties even as the conducting and recording and manifold enterprises as educator and promoter made further demands: these activities undoubtedly impeded each other as much as – more than – they mutually illuminated. Larger later pieces – Horn Concerto (1994), Violin Concerto (2002) – seem one-dimensional after the ore-laden sumptuousness of earlier orchestral music. Richer is the *Requiem: Songs for Sue* (2005–6) setting in their original languages a cycle of poems by Dickinson, Machado, Auden, Rilke, in memory of his wife, who had died in 2003. Cause for regret, *Cleveland Pictures* for orchestra, withdrawn after an informal try-out in 2003 for further finish/polish which was never applied. Cause for rejoicing, two brief cycles of 1991–2: *Whitman Settings* with piano, then orchestrated;

Songs Without Voices for ensemble – Whitman also the source, invisibly/inaudibly present by means of 'suppressed vocalization'. Around these this brief selection for a larger-than-life figure must reluctantly be confined.

Wordless first: four fine-etched miniatures for eight players, the first three encapsulating the gist of the absent Whitman lyrics: *Winter's Foil* – winter will melt into softness, life will re-arise: 'the delicate miracles of earth / Dandelions, clover, the emerald grass . . .' and so on: 'with these, the robin, lark and thrush, singing their songs – the flitting bluebird . . .' and Knussen adds a closing cuckoo. *Prairie Sunset* – 'shot gold, maroon and violet, dazzling silver, emerald, fawn / The earth's whole amplitude as nature's multiform power consigned for once to colors . . . colors till now unknown: No limit, confine . . . pure luminous color, fighting the silent shadows, to the last.' *First Dandelion* – '. . . forth from its sunny nook of sheltered grass – innocent, golden, calm as the dawn / The spring's first dandelion shows its trustful face.' It would be perverse – labour lost – to try to catch these words in the volatile play of their non-setting: rather, the music realizes their redolence 'without' the need of illustration, obsequious and redundant. The fourth, *Elegiac Arabesques*, can't be sourced in an absent text – a purely instrumental elegy, eloquent and expressive, in memory of an older composer-friend.

The four actual *vocal* songs are more diverse and ambitious – Whitman at his most searching, quizzical and, at one point, ferocious. *When I Heard the Learn'd Astronomer* queries the proofs, the charts, the applause; the poet abandons the lecture to wander along and gaze up at the stars – all the way from fussy turbulence to mysterious shining spaces. The *Noiseless Patient Spider* ruminates upon 'filament, filament, filament' spun forth from the tireless insect; the poet bethinks himself of his own soul, 'surrounded, detached, in measureless oceans of space', throwing forth gossamer threads to somewhere or nowhere – 'only connect'. Erotic fury for *Dalliance of the Eagles*, the birds' amorous violence – 'clinching interlocking claws . . . Four beating wings, two beaks, a swirling mass tight grappling / In tumbling turning clustering loops, straight downward falling . . .'; graphic; frightening: till the wry close as the pair separate, satiated and quenched – she on her flight, 'he his, pursuing'. Finally, *The Voice of the Rain*, a strange utterance of veiled pantheism – 'the Poem of the Earth'; rain as perpetual renewer born of its own nature, ending on a note of love. To hear these remarkable songs first in their original version for soprano and piano, then in Knussen's orchestration, is to rekindle wonder and love for his infallible skills – a perfect translation from spare wide-spaced resonance, all implication and nuance, to the fully-worked intricacy, *complexe mais pas compliqué*, of a master-craftsman who also, via his poet, has something to say.

The most substantial orchestral work of Knussen's later years is *Cleveland Pictures*, an affectionate take on Musorgsky's *Pictures at an Exhibition*, inspired by artworks in the Cleveland Gallery, three of a mooted seven movements dedicated to some composer-friends featured in these pages. The future of this project remains uncertain at the time of writing: I can only offer preliminary impressions based upon a hearing, and a viewing of the visual sources. I: *Portrait avec Penseur* – 'façades and lake with Rodin' (dedicated to George Benjamin) – placid, dignified slow strings interspersed with snarls on brass, then a sort of chorale interspersed with yelps and cries: placidity wins temporarily but is followed by a nervy wriggling bass-clarinet solo, ever more agitated, and this striking enigmatic number ends with an upsurge of ferocity. Linked by a soft chord straight into – II, Velásquez's *Calabazas* (dedicated to Alexander Goehr). The Prado's portrait of the court jester shows him deformed and grimacing. The Cleveland version is quite other: a skinny figure in black with a white collar, an elegant stick, droll, peaky, smiling face, more graceful than stunted. Knussen paints him in a sparkling scherzo reminiscent of grotesquerie in the Musorgsky, with a touch of Russian folksong for contrast. III is brief – ecstatic soaring strings and an inner throb, responding to Gauguin's *Dans les vagues*, displaying a strapping pink broad-backed female nude with a helmet of auburn hair plunging herself into the surging emerald waters. It serves as link to – IV: *Two Clocks* – 'Tiffany and Fabergé': they're hard to distinguish, in this *very* Musorgskyan number, the suite's moment of lightness; delectable; dedicated to Colin Matthews.

V is its inner core, inspired by Goya's *Saint Ambrose*: a large figure set in dark limbo, mitre and robes glistening white, the open book and the border of the cope of dull golden silk; his eyes ecstatically uplifted, a thick Olly-ish beard. Not exactly a music-making image – more, the *idea* of spiritual inwardness: the music made of it intense and serious, passionate strings recalling, though certainly not citing, Tchaikovsky's *Pathétique*, alternating with pungent winds not a thousand miles from Messiaen. As it proceeds, a feature as unique in Knussen's work as surprising – fragments of plainsong with their Latin texts inscribed – *aeterne rerum conditor* – eternal creator of all; *iam surgit ora tertia* – now the third hour has risen; *Deus creator omnium* – God creator of all (quoted at the end of St Augustine's *Confessions*); *Intende, qui regis Israel* – hear, thou ruler of Israel. VI is missing altogether: it would seem to have been based upon André Masson's *Don Quixote and the Chariot of Death*. VII remains fragmentary: unformed, slowish but sense of inner turbulence, enlivening with nervous edginess before disappearing into the unfinished unknown. Whether or not it has a pictorial source in the Cleveland Gallery will perhaps also remain unknown (it appears to be inspired by Turner's livid view of the fire that destroyed Parliament in 1834). Abundantly clear is this music's calibre: it deserves the future its composer didn't live to acquire.

George Benjamin: born 1960, precociously gifted, study chez Messiaen ('my favourite pupil') at sixteen, then *bei* Goehr at Cambridge, where *Ringed by the Flat Horizon* was premièred by the University orchestra in 1980, reaching the Proms in the same year. It inaugurated an unbroken succession of successes on the Continent and at home, where he has also been a distinguished teacher at the Royal College of Music, then King's College London. Endless awards, culminating (so far) with a knighthood in 2017. The output is small and choice: to date, two operas – *Written on Skin* (completed 2012) and *Lessons in Love and Violence* (completed 2017) and some twenty (to date) works for orchestra and ensemble: the idiom and facture are exquisite – painstakingly careful, scrupulously finished and polished – sometimes almost too finished and polished; even as

the result is compelling (in *Written on Skin*, devastating) the listener
cries out for air to penetrate the sealed chamber.

This reservation, on the highest level, does not apply to *A Mind
of Winter* (1981), where Benjamin's art is heard in concentrated essentialized intensity and freedom – surely the most tingling evocation
of cold ever achieved in music. Wallace Stevens's fifteen lines already
do it in words, wherein the physical effortlessly opens out into the
metaphysical. The listener (in a poem initially concentrated on
the viewer) whose 'mind of winter' transports the scene from 'pine
trees crusted with snow', 'junipers shagged with ice', via the sound
of the wind, of leaves, of the land 'blowing in the same bare place',
to where, 'nothing himself', he beholds 'Nothing that is not there
and the nothing that is'. A bar of silence made audible; swish of suspended cymbal, sliding semitonal clusters on multi-divided violins
leaving exposed, long-sustained A-minor chord on lower strings (the
fusion of non-functional tonality with total atonality is bold and
prescient). Miles above, two soft piccolos, a solitary oboe, a diatonic
cluster on middle-winds, the violins growing fluttery and skittery, a
ghostly trumpet, winds more sustained, clarinets wriggle, the chromatic texture fills out, the A-minor chord remaining below till it
too slides into limbo.

The soprano soloist enters imperceptibly on *One* ... Syllable by
syllable gradually granted (`... must have a mind of winter'), long-
held or light parlando, never melodic as such though acutely sensitive to every passing verbal nuance. *And* ... is equally prolonged
(`...to have been cold a long time'); the same sonic elements remain
in play, constantly re-sifted. The poem's single sentence is poised
upon a near-central semi-colon, carefully observed in the setting
by another pure triad – B-major – vibrant upon woodwinds as the
initial A-minor on strings was recessive. Two horns in off-key fanfare-
figures: another long *and* ... initiates the rest of Stevens's structure
(`... not to think / Of any misery ...'): *misery* is not emoted, the
'sound of the wind' not imitated. 'The listener' – the protagonist –
makes a climax of intensity rather than of dynamics; the A-minor
chord unobtrusively slides in below, this time issuing in a searing
high trumpet solo. What the listener *beholds*, as the sounds recede, is

heard by a queer percussive moment marked 'weird' and sounding it. After this, the varying presences of nothingness are no longer sung cantabile – dry, matter-of-fact: and with her last long note again sustained – the note on which she'd first entered – the soprano gives the clinching *is*. An orchestral epilogue recalls, encapsulates, briefly explodes as if in objection, rapidly disappears into reverberating cymbal-swish and the closing bar of silence-made-audible balancing the silence of the opening – 'the nothing that *is*'. Benjamin's icy gloss on the poem holds its metaphysics in equivocation – no underlining emphases, just the sheer piercing penetration of the terrible cold.

Julian Anderson, born 1967: many overlaps with Benjamin – Westminster School and Cambridge University; the advocacy of Oliver Knussen; till recently Faber Music as publisher; a distinguished teacher; a fruitful saturation in French music from Messiaen, Boulez and IRCAM right through to the Spectralism of more recent years, in Anderson's case extending to employment of electronics that place him successor to Harvey. His sources are disparate. The most important is the diatonic route through the twentieth century from Stravinsky's Russian ballet, blown up by Messiaen and aerated by Dutilleux – a line of colour and vitality, dancing rhythms, hard edges, bright decorative repetition, accommodating itself naturally to older traditions of Orientalism and Espagnolerie, yet wholly compatible with another direction out of Stravinsky taken by Copland, Tippett, Britten.

Angstvoll expressionism, the Central-European route through the twentieth century, is with one exception avoided. Anderson's chromaticism is Scriabinesque (erotic, religious, ecstatic) rather than Schoenbergian (dark, tortuous, claustrophobic). But the postwar avant-garde, equally the child of Vienna, Paris and Petersburg, is fruitfully employed both for its technical discoveries and its sonorous refinements. Ligeti is, of course, omnipresent, and the purely delicious aspects of Boulez are everywhere apparent, also his French successors who have reconciled their *maître* to a rediscovery of natural resonance equally with the possibilities of new technology. Experiments in electro-acoustics and micro-intervals, so often fiddling or painful or both, become chez Anderson a

genuine expressive resource. Add to all this related aspects of Oliver
Knussen, George Benjamin, the early Nicholas Maw – the result is
a dictionary of what most music-lovers who enjoy modern music
at all enjoy most. It amounts to a virtual lingua franca of current
usage, the pure clear sparkling mainstream between a right bank of
the galumphing minimalism and a grey left of deceptively monumental modernism.

Though Anderson's take on these usual suspects is individual, the
element that sharply distinguishes him is his employment of ethnic
musics. Again, this is hardly unique. Most of the composers here
named do so – Stravinsky not the least – and with Ligeti the transformation of native Hungarian/Romanian strains goes alongside a
freedom of appropriation ranging from Polynesia to Central Africa.
With Anderson, however, a figure obtrudes whose attitude is completely other, and absolutely seminal. Percy Grainger, polymorphous
devourer of whatever came his way be it folk-music from Norway,
Lincolnshire, Bali, the Faroe Islands et al., *Porgy and Bess* and *Der
Rosenkavalier*, old music – medieval, Renaissance, Baroque – popular
musics of church, pub, parlour, music-hall, cow-bells, church-bells,
blithe-bells, bell-bottom'd drunken sailors. Grainger's open-armed
liberality surely lies behind Anderson's ability to welcome apparently incompatible musics and induce a personal idiom from
sources so familiar and well-worn. (Though he doesn't 'quote'. A
prevalent tendency since Berio's 1968 *Sinfonia* to expose and exploit
your cultural credentials is conspicuous by its absence.) The best
introduction is probably the *Book of Hours*. It moves from infantine
scale-practice, via bell-ringing, to massive constructivistic tintinnabulation, a sort of Medieval Englysshe Mechanical Pastoral, culminating in one of the very few instances since Varèse that convincingly
incorporates taped music into live performance. When this incandescent clangour subsides, all that's left is the ghost of a gigue half-
remembered from Debussy's *Trio Sonata*, scuttling around like a
torn paper bag on a cold, bleak, moonlit Egdon Heath: 'Silbury
Air' – the influence from Birtwistle palpable.

*

Here closes, for the moment, 'Faber Music', born of Maw's *Scenes and Arias* and Britten's publishing enterprise; gathering in strains from English precursors and from all over: a consensus of shining sonority, finish paramount, perfected in accomplishment; but arguably lacking, for the most part, in the deeper undercurrents of its wider ancestry in late Romanticism and the great early Moderns. Music's fuller expressive and technical range, so comprehensive in all preceding epochs, is not employed.

My final six composers couldn't be more different, from what has preceded, and from each other. Eldest is Brian Ferneyhough: born 1943 in the English Midlands, but has lived, worked, succeeded best abroad – on the Continent then in the US as eloquent embodiment of the international avant-garde, icon of 'new complexity', authoritative and forbidding: 'our king over the water', maybe doomed never to be crowned in his native land (nor even to receive a knighthood). His earlier works became touchstones of fiendish difficulty, to hear and also to play – pieces for solo flute or clarinet laid out on six staves; giving each member of a large orchestra their own individual parts. Sometimes the result could be viscerally communicative as well as cerebrally awesome. Try the three sets of *Carceri d'invenzione* from the 1980s, inspired by Piranesi's beguilingly sinister etchings of vast imprisoning architecture, at once endlessly ramifying and horribly oppressive – Nightmares born of Reason. All are for ensemble: I is dense, busy, opaque, menacing; II, a flute concertante, all legerity and flutter, liquid and volatile, later joined by a vagrant singing horn; III features clarinet, all gesture, florid and histrionic, then becomes a twittering machine with eructating brass and *giocose* unpitched percussion, then develops Gabrieli-like festive virtuosity, then thins to fragments – life gutters out and dribbles away.

I recall well the première of *La Terre est un homme* – disgruntled orchestral players (all eighty-eight of them) claiming (as is their way) that they might be doing anything, or nothing (and probably were) in the surging black welter. Later performances, less fraught, reveal a powerful sonorous embodiment of Roberto Matta's desert painting of the same name and the composer's accompanying description – 'leaden, slowly moving sand and sudden flashes of intensely coloured movement' – Varèse's *Déserts* for the 1980s. More accessible to the air and the spirit, Ferneyhough's 4th String Quartet (1989–90): with solo soprano like its grandfather Schoenberg's 2nd and its uncle, the secretly-vocal finale of Berg's *Lyric Suite*: the *words* – passages from Ezra Pound's *Pisan Cantos* 'deconstructed' by A. N. Other – are frankly immaterial: the *music* for voice equally with the four strings, fuses with Ferneyhough's expected intellectual intensity some unexpected qualities – sensuous rapture, textual deliciousness, emotional warmth. Nothing else in this fearsome figure prepares one for such rewards. (And the opera on the life and death of Walter Benjamin is a disaster!)

Gerald Barry: born 1952 in the Irish Republic: his output principally operatic – *The Intelligence Park* (1981–8); *The Triumph of Beauty and Deceit* (1991–2); *The Bitter Tears of Petra von Kant* (2005); *The Importance of Being Earnest* (2010). His idiom and technique are unique, though there are forebears – medieval and Renaissance constructivism, Baroque figuration and hymnody: and the Stravinsky of the Great War years is seminal – hard little Russian peasant-songs with instruments, motor ostinati in *Les Noces*, the derisive Protestant chorales in *The Soldier's Tale*, above all the ejaculatory gestures and abrasive voicings of the *Symphonies of Winds*. Barry's slant on all these is all his own: clunky aggressive patterning, instrumentation coarse and abrasive, melody naïve and exiguous: all-energy, a workout at some inhuman gym putting the body through torments of stamina seemingly impossible. Yet the paradox: high-spirited, bright, gay, exciting – the strain exhilarates even as it exhausts. All this is already present in *Chevaux-de-frise* for orchestra (1987). The title refers to the fence of sharpened stakes defending a stockade in medieval times, thence a knotty verbal device to impede too-facile reading, or a teasing belt to protect the chastity of its wearer and baffle him who would violate it. Barry responds to all these interlaced meanings with sustained ferocity: sharpened stakes prevent penetration equally of the fortress, the text, the sex: at the same time, perversely, the brio of the music is an invitation.

The same paradox holds for the best of the stage-works, *The Triumph of Beauty and Deceit*: cast of five, all-male – Pleasure, Truth,

Beauty, Deceit, Time: the allegory based on an early (1708) Serenata of Handel – *Trionfo del Tempo e della Verità* (Truth was originally *Disinganno* – disillusion), rewritten for London 1737, and for Barry by Meredith Oakes. Her text is cunning and suggestive, dexterously alluding to the source yet subverting its enlightened certainties into salacious amorality. The allegorical figures – they are not *persons* – interact according to their 'nature' with wit and aplomb and speed, though not precluding moments of repose, even tenderness amid the headlong frenzy. Not since Birtwistle's *Punch and Judy* has extremist mannerism enjoyed such a Triumph. And if this all sounds repellent, hold on tight and be tickled black and blue. But this road is barred by more than a *cheval-de-frise*: *Petra von Kant* took it a stage further, with larger forces and timescale, and diminished returns. *The Importance of Being Earnest* offends real tastefulness as opposed to 'ghastly good taste': Wilde's elegance is submerged, then drowned, in tar, oil, mucus, vomit, shit – a fate worse than Reading Gaol. Barry's opera has enjoyed accolades that reveal more about the donors than they'd care to recognize.

John Tavener, 1944–2013: into the expected native ingredients, a surprising shot of serial Stravinsky – a revelatory moment encountering, aged twelve, the *Canticum Sacrum*. His apparently contradictory delight in Richard Strauss made a rich and promising impression earlier on – *The Whale* (1968): *Celtic Requiem* (1971) – taken up by the Beatles and Benjamin Britten – surely unique. Early drawn to religion, first Catholic, converting to Orthodoxy 1977; saturated in Russian culture with subjects drawn from Tolstoy, Dostoevsky, Akhmatova, as well as the Orthodox liturgy. The combination of fervour and *simplesse* hit the spot nationwide with an anthem for Princess Diana's funeral 1997. Knighthood 2000. Later, dissatisfied with Orthodoxy, he explored Eastern religions – Hindu, Buddhist, Islam – while not abandoning a broader Christian basis.

Rather than *The Veil of the Temple* (2003) – a bit much at seven hours – I've chosen *The Protecting Veil* of some sixteen years earlier, which shows the gift at its purest. The Virgin appeared in the skies to Christians in Constantinople at a time of threat from invading Saracens: she unfolded her veil for protection; the infidels were routed. Salient events in her life – Birth, Annunciation of the birth of her Son, his Incarnation, Lament for him at the foot of the Cross, exaltation at his Resurrection, her own Passing – are enclosed between eventless prelude and epilogue celebrating her radiant beauty and benign potency. The solo cello, singing or muttering almost without break, represents the Virgin herself: she is supported by an orchestra of strings only, used with resource and flair. This music, made from next-to-nothing, runs the expressive/emotional gamut from A to B with unforgettable effect: the very simplicity of its fervour is moving: whatever the listener's religious condition, the heart and spirit are wrapped up, rapt to sacred places way out of the diurnal. Tedium beckons, to be lost in concentration. Sincerity, notoriously 'indispensable but guaranteeing nothing', here ensures a result verging upon the divine.

Robert Saxton, born 1953: after early encouragement from Britten and rather fierce encounters with Elizabeth Lutyens, studied at Cambridge and ended up Professor at Oxford. His earlier music, lovingly championed by Oliver Knussen, covers a range between gentle though not insipid, intense but not burning, its coloration radiant, its goal almost mystical. Three titles can indicate: *Ring of Eternity* (1983); *The Sentinel of the Rainbow* (1984); *The Circles of Light* (1985–6). Another fine piece of this time shares the same qualities despite its neutral title – *Concerto for Orchestra* (1984). Some later works – the opera *Caritas* (after Arnold Wesker), the oratorio *Canticum Luminis* (after mathematical/alchemical text from seventeenth-century England), another opera *The Wandering Jew* (after the timeless legend) – take the same concerns to places at once more elevated and more profound, but arguably lose the freshness of the first flush.

Richard Causton, born 1971: an eclectic musical education, embracing gamelan and electro-acoustics: then a succession of teaching posts, culminating (for the moment) as Professor of Composition at Cambridge. He first attracted favour with *The Persistence of Memory* (1995), after Dalí – deliquescing clocks, time/place/space melting away to beguiling effect. Other early successes are all for ensemble: the large orchestra has proved problematic; there's an edge of protesting perversity, even impracticality, that militates against the vision – *vide Millenium Scenes* and others. The way forward is shown to best advantage in an ambitious cycle of ten songs to poems by Salvatore Quasimodo – *La Terra Impareggiabile/ The Incomparable Land* – written piecemeal over a decade (1996– 2007), further refined down another.

Quasimodo's texts celebrate love and death, time and memory (the usuals!) in intonations ranging from introverted meditation to fresh folksongish simplicity (these two taken from fragments of Sappho). Interest and intensity centre upon the piano part, whether pared to the bone or elaborate with decoration, sometimes fierce, mostly delicate, culminating in two cadenzas in the penultimate song, separating the taste of the new rains, the oscillation of the light and the air, the apprehensions of love with sense of death. The voice part is mainly neutral, its moments of eloquence all the more telling.

Judith Weir, born 1954; studied with Tavener, then at Cambridge with the present writer. Of Scottish parentage though based in England, eventually succeeding Maxwell Davies as Master of the Queen's Music in 2014. Her principal output is stage-works: landmarks *King Harald's Saga* (1979), a delicious affair, all eight roles, male and female, and the entire Norwegian army, are sung unaccompanied (no instruments) by a single soprano; *A Night at the Chinese Opera* (1987); *The Vanishing Bridegroom* (1990); *Blond Eckbert* (1994); *Miss Fortune* (2011): all to her own adroit adaptations from very varied originals, her own texts too: and all successful until the most recent, belying its title even as it opened up promising new territory. Much orchestral, chamber and vocal music; *Music for 247 Strings* (1981) for violin and piano (their combined strings give the 247); *Scotch Minstrelsy* (1982) for voice and piano; *The Art of Touching the Keyboard* (1983); the delectable *Serbian Cabaret* (1984) has sadly fallen victim to political pressures beyond the composer's control. The gem of the pieces for orchestra is *Moon and Star* (1995): its choral component, to a poem of Emily Dickinson, is almost lost in the instrumental spaces. The poet's wide-eyed wit and strangeness exactly fit Weir's art at its quintessential – elusive, deceptively simple, making the familiar oblique and new, whimsical/playful/quizzical without archness, fresh as a bluebell, acute as a thistle. Matching Dickinson's list of oddities – the Lark's Bonnet, the Chamois' Silver Boot, the Antelope's stirrup – by which means she aspires to leap the inter-stellar spaces and join Moon and Star, every isolated pitch, triad, dissonance, and some very juicy close-harmony, are new-minted. Juice becomes jammy in dense superimpositions, clarifying finally in shining remoteness for the *He* – 'more than a Firmament' – that *she* can never reach.

From the diverse times and places of Weir's operas – Norwegian sagas, thirteenth-century China, fairy-tale Germany, Sicilian folklore, and others – I've chosen closer to home – supernatural Scotland: *The Vanishing Bridegroom* interweaves three traditional Highland stories concerning fidelity and betrayal, greed, lapse of time, disap-pearance and renewal, resistance and salvation. Act I: an old man on his deathbed directs his three avid sons towards his legacy; it proves missing – which son knows where? Now a parable – the Bride, her impoverished Lover: her disapproving father forbids the match: she swears fidelity to the man of her heart even as the wedding to the Husband forced upon her is celebrated. The pair flee to the Lover's house: the Husband vanishes, but the Lover has grown cold. A Priest absolves the former vow and enjoins the latter: the forlorn Bride escapes to a Thick Wood (sung by massed female voices). Three Robbers are there, two bad one good – the three sons thus distin-guished? She offers her dowry, the baddies take it, the goodie escorts her home to her legal Groom. Back to the Father's deathbed: asked who did best (morally and/or materially) in the Parable, the eldest son elects the Groom who returned his Bride, the second son the Lover who returned her to her Groom: the youngest unexpectedly supports the two Robbers who got the booty, thus exposing himself (perhaps) as the thief of the legacy/dowry.

Act II: the Bride/Wife with her new-born daughter, praying for the infant's safety, Husband and his Friend echoing. Mysteri-ously the two men are transported to the nearby Hill (which, like the Thick Wood, is presented vocally). Husband allured, Friend appalled: Husband vanishes within. Back at home, the disappear-ance is related: a Policeman accuses the Friend of murder. Back at the Hill, accused and accuser wait while it sings (in dusky Gaelic). Hill and Home alternate, as the child grows through girlhood to womanhood and the men grow old. Husband emerges from the underworld in radiant youthfulness. He sings of the beauty he's experienced within/beneath. The Policeman fades away, the two other men misapprehend each other: 'could you not let me be for one instant?' 'An instant!' – twenty years have passed. They agree on one thing, to seek the Priest and have the baby baptized. But she's now a young woman: the action freezes upon her parents' possible reconciliation . . . into Act III . . . and their daughter sings a folksong as she goes about her task, chorus returning the refrain.

The song concerns a hoped-for Lover/Bridegroom. As it ends a dark stranger unobtrusively obtrudes: he takes over the refrain: her song turns towards uncanny questions – eight in all, beginning 'what is heavier than lead?' and ending 'what is the worst that ever was?' The stranger's answers pile up hyperboles of whiteness in her praise even as the atmosphere darkens: he ends upon a miracle, transforming sheep's droppings into faery gold; and an invitation for her to join him, at sunset this very day, to be his wife. But she's been observing his sinister corporeality – pointed head, queer feet. Her parents reappear – 'what a charming young man . . . what a catch.' Their daughter insists upon the sinister signs – horns on his head? hooves on his feet? The family altercation attracts a passing Priest who at once realizes the wooer's identity. He encloses the girl in a holy circle wherein nothing can harm her. All leave her, enthralled within. The stranger returns to press his suit. The sanctity of her space, though invisible, succeeds: this final Bridegroom can't penetrate it despite his increasingly violent threats. Her runic questions recur, now with their answers, which he ignores while insistently reiterating 'Answer me, answer me!' 'The worst that ever was' is the Devil. Thus named, the stranger is defeated ('he disappears, explodes, or slumps dead to the ground' – this stage-direction can characterize the openness of the whole piece's conception and treatment). The latest Bride is saved, choirs of angels laud her, and the place appears to transform into a shrine. All is presented as fluid and oblique: times, places, personages merge and melt, asymmetrical parallels and reincarnations insinuate. There's no single vantage-point, let alone centre, to the storytelling and enactment – the three panels might even be reordered, though their actual order is sure and compelling. The music expresses and enhances every slant with unfailing subtlety: one experiences every quiver, from sordid and prosaic, up the gamut via desire, fear, celebration and malignity to eventual exaltation, however equivocal: and the pantheistic sonorities of the supernatural Hill are indeed supernatural.

Finally something quite other – Howard Skempton, born 1947, associated in late 1960s with the radical experimental movement focused around Cornelius Cardew and the Scratch Orchestra. His *Lento* for orchestra (1990) enjoyed surprising success, for his output is predominantly for his own instruments, piano and accordion; miniatures of disarming directness and deceptive naïveté, songs and dances, chorales, patterns of figuration, accompaniments, pebbles from the seashore. In the mid-1970s some piano-pieces for left hand only, intended for Britten to play after heart-surgery had impaired his right: most recently (2019) *24 Preludes and Fugues* for piano (both hands), each key taking only one small page and concentrating into it a world of implication. In 2023 a sequel for organ.

The aesthetic, and techniques for realizing it, have ancestry in Satie's enigmatic frugality, Morton Feldman's extreme spareness, John Cage's Zen emptiness. Games and systems operate with paradoxical randomness: and the actual material is of extreme simplicity. This is 'music to play with'. And, as important, 'music to pray to'. The ancestor here is the Catalan composer Federico Mompou and his *musica callada* – 'silent music': severe and pellucid meditations permeated with the spirit of St John of the Cross. Skempton himself has come to resemble an El Greco saint, rapt in contemplation as he performs his own ditties on his accordion. To play for oneself his comparable piano miniatures is to recover the same childlike, though hardly infantine, world, innocent without sentimentality, cognizant yet unknowing. The *notes* are easy to play: hard are the necessary concentration and spiritual purity.

Eight American mavericks and minimalists

John Cage, born 1912, taught by Henry Cowell and Schoenberg, whose verdict: 'not a Composer: an Inventor, of genius' still resonates. Influenced by early theological studies, thence absorption in Indian philosophy, Zen Buddhism, and, principally, the Chinese I Ching, advocating chance to solve Unanswered Questions. All these underlie a quizzical angle upon the nature of compositional art – music 'a purposeless play ... an affirmation of life – not an attempt to bring order out of chaos nor to suggest improvements in creation, but simply a way of waking up to the very life we're living'. Early scores for dance; invention of the 'prepared piano' (initially a one-man substitute for more cumbersome and expensive percussion) whereby alterations and inserted objects to the strings yielded a variegated gamelan of sonorities, always curious and often delightful. For ordinary percussion, a series of *Constructions in Metal* from 1939 on: also from these years some *Imaginary Landscapes* involving the play of multiple radios, their stations twiddled according to the laws of chance. Teaching at the adventurous interdisciplinary Black Mountain College; *Music of Changes.* An iconic encounter with Morton Feldman, leaving together a concert in 1950 overwhelmed by the Webern Symphony and unable to face oncoming Rachmaninov, discovering an immediate and long-lived rapport: 1952 *4'33"* for (silent) solo piano: 1957–8 *Concert for Piano* [audible] *and Orchestra*. The stance taken by these and other pieces, his lectures and writings, his personality and lifestyle, widely beguiling and influential. Moving towards ever-larger-longer Events/Happenings, culminating in *Roaratorio* (1979) on texts from *Finnegans Wake*: died 1992.

Schoenberg's bon mot encapsulates the paradox. *Actual* invention flourishes in the *Constructions* for percussion, tinkly and delicious rather than bashy and assertive as *Ionisation* and the other Varèse works where percussion predominates; and in the *Sonatas and Interludes* for prepared piano, elaborately patterned and attractively delicate. Else-wise, the random, the bizarre, the eccentric, predominate over musical substance: whimsicality and teasing win, overflow of a gregarious, exuberant, generous personality (I recall the utter amiability, benign good-humour, complete absence of assertion, in a long conversation with him back in the early 1980s of which I don't retain a single word). But as *art*, the self-deflection leads to auto-destruction: each manifestation a unique happening that, if it's to happen again, must always be different. And the most (in)famous of all, the notorious 4'33" of silence in three measured movements, heavily protected by its publishers for collection of royalties and punishment of plagiarists, is of course *entirely* conceptual – a joke; trying it on; Zen persiflage. As in the comparable cases of Duchamp's *Fountain* and Malevich's *Black Square*, someone had to make the provocative gesture of defiance whether light-hearted, contemptuous, or indeed quasi-religious. Once done, there's no need to do it again even the once, let alone in a spate of cheap imitations. The skylight has been forced, sun and air flood in, now back to the age-old business of putting notes together – real Invention by real Composers.

Morton Feldman, born 1926 of Russian-Jewish lineage, but an archetypal New Yorker all his life (dying 1987), closely associated with the city's avant-garde poets and (especially) painters as much as or more than his fellow-composers. Early teaching from Wallingford Riegger and Stefan Wolpe: copious output, chamber, vocal, orchestral, miniature to inordinate – a late String Quartet lasts many hours, the listener is invited to dip in, dip out, resume, as nature requires. Which suggests the prevailing intonation of the music itself – meditative/contemplative/ritualistic. Three sweetly faded titles suggest somewhat different – *Madame Press Died Last Week at Ninety*; *I Met Heine on the Rue Fürstenberg*; and a sequence of four movements collectively called *The Viola in My Life* – all these dating from 1970–71: gentle almost whimsical tenderness. His best-known work also dates from the same productive years: *Rothko Chapel*, one of many tributes to friends and peers in the visual and verbal arts. Rather than this, which for me suffers slightly from the aura of ersatz quasi-profundity that all-but scuppers the paintings of its dedicatee, the best representative work for Feldman is a later orchestral piece, *Coptic Light* of 1985. Its inspiring metaphor from weaving is at once tactile, visual and spiritual: fragments of ancient Coptic textile with its dense criss-cross facture, subtle richness of colour, and the religious devotion that goes into its making and its uses.

This half-hour of soft sound for large orchestra is all paradox worthy of seventeenth-century English poetry – opposites yoked in harmony, 'dazzling darkness' reversed into veiled luminescence, through a glass darkly, almost unchanging in apparent monotony alert with minute inner animation, flickering and fluctuating. The actual ingredients are simple yet complex – choked yet translucent wind-chords; a spray of glinting yet feathery piano; quiet irregular pulse-heartbeats on drums that almost speak, nay sing; hints of an actual cantabile on strings, without continuous contour, as though the hymnody of Ives's *Housatonic* were stretched out, then fragmented beyond recognition; and towards the end, quenched gruff barks and growls as though a dog was quietly growling or a cat purring while deep asleep. Indeed, the work's entire texture and nature are those of a *creature* – breathing, stirring, humming, bristling, resettling again into timeless tranquillity, ever the same yet always ever so slightly altering – itself in a trance that emanates from it to enclose all its listeners and even its players. And wonderful *notes*: Feldman's ear is attuned to the sensitivities of pitch, timbre, duration, that Cage has expelled.

Conlon Nancarrow, 1912–1997: keen jazz trumpeter in youth; also good solid training in classical music – couldn't be more so, under Walter Piston and Roger Sessions, composers of high academic credentials. Trouble with officialdom after fighting in the Spanish Civil War; moved to Mexico 1940, stayed, took Mexican citizenship 1956. A handful of earlier small pieces, mainly for piano; but comes into his own with his compositions for player-piano. His live piano-writing was already beginning to transcend the limits of human fingers: acting on a suggestion from Cowell's ever-fertile *New Musical Resources*, that the seemingly impossible could be thus actualized,

Nancarrow adapted the device's primitive mechanics to ever-more sophisticated ends, achieving by the time of his death in 1997 a body of over fifty *Studies* that gained renown well before the acclamation of Ligeti, no less – 'this music is the greatest discovery since Webern and Ives . . . something great and important for all music history! . . . utterly original, enjoyable, perfectly constructed but at the same time emotional!' Handsome indeed, from a composer for whom the same claims can plausibly be made. *Awesome* indeed: to adapt Schoenberg's estimate of Cage, Nancarrow is an Inventor to be sure; yet not just an Inventor – a Composer, of genius. His *musical* invention is coruscating and tumultuous, his ear for pitch, momentum, texture accurate as a chronometer, his command of polyphony comparable to Bach at his most learnèd. The only reservation to Ligeti's accolade is its last word: Nancarrow doesn't 'do' emotion/expression/*Affekt*. The crankiest canon in Bach's *Musical Offering*, the most abstruse numbers in the *Art of Fugue*, are instinct with expression in a gamut of tones from heroic and jubilant to pathetic, even tragic, all fused into the mighty cerebration. Nancarrow is a composer of wit: the intellectual energy fizzes, the physical energy is electric. Nor does the medium, chosen for its unique ability to reproduce his constructions, lend itself to sensuous allure, the sheer succulence of sound: the player-piano *is* a machine, its sonority metallic/staccato/ jangling – clattering – buzzing – tinkling. The *Studies* take this as their unalterable basis, a positive, permitting the hitherto inconceivable by sacrificing every other feature that might mitigate or compromise the goal: a sort of super-harpsichord. And to his Bachian fusion of mind/body/spirit (if not affect) via counterpoint, Nancarrow adds the super-vitality of jazz. Blues are palpable in some earlier *Studies*: as their complexity advances it can seem as if Jelly Roll Morton, Fats Waller, Art Tatum, were jamming away simultaneously at different speeds, in different keys, on different keyboards, on a shared theme provided by some latter-day Baroque potentate. Or as Stravinsky, an earlier and unconnected advocate of the pianola, had enthusiastically found – 'writing for eight, for sixteen, for twenty-two hands'.

Where to enter? No. 21 is the simplest to perceive: in two voices, one beginning high at breakneck velocity, gradually descending and slowing down; the other voice simultaneously does the opposite, beginning low and slow, gradually ascending and accelerating to breakneck velocity: for all the iron construction, ludic, hilarious, life-enhancing. So to 26, a canon in seven octave-doubled voices, all in implacable long semibreves, the motif's occasional silent bars at one point coinciding in all seven parts: the texture thickens into massive block chords, then thins out to the initial simplicity, clearing air and ear. These two *Studies* once passed, we can take on 37, a twelve-part canon, every voice at a different speed. Hold on tight!

Elsewhere the mathematics can be fiendishly forbidding, but aural beguilement, and *interest* (as the visual in Hopkins – 'sometimes a lantern moves along the night / That *interests* our eyes'), are always paramount: this music excites, fascinates, astounds before the schemes that have brought it into being can be 'explained' (if not understood): and they're not really needed at the end either.

After this triple baptism, back to an earlier sequence: 3 comes in five related sections: jazzy sources are close and delicious for the first four – wit, ease, relaxation, indolence – then the fifth tears them apart in a storm of exhilarating superimpositions over a tumultuous boogie-woogie bass. 41 comes in three sections, i) and ii) on separate piano-rolls, iii) the two sounding simultaneously. Here, unusually, the resulting jungle overstrains the listener's powers of perception: *more* is a mess: though, building upon the trust we've by now developed in Nancarrow's uncanny aural precision, we are always willing to give it another go: Ives's robust challenge to 'use your ears like a man' applies; we know from heretofore that Nancarrow's ears are the antithesis of cloth or tin.

Surer ground with three *Studies* of consummate calibre. 24 – 'canon 14/15/16' – explores these minuscule tempi-relationships with an infectious, deceptively casual lope, occasionally breaking out into angry gunfire or jabs of prickling staccato, around a central moment of soft stasis. 25 is longer than most, yet can encompass such mind-bending speeds as 175 notes per second – which gives an effect of resonance rare for a medium whose obvious principal characteristic is dryness. The volatility of textural contrasts here,

from gritty sand-dunes to waterlogged *nymphéas*, makes this piece
a highlight. Another is 33 with its play of short-as-possible staccato
and long-held sostenuto: the canonic structure is so intricate as to
be perhaps too hard to discern; the divine madness of the surface
invention cannot be resisted – interlocked blocks of long and short
disintegrate into delicate-glinted glass splinter, then re-coalesce
into the initial sonority and texture till an impetuous final rush
of dismissal – the shoulders shrug as the machine shuts, composer
and listener relax and laugh – it was all a game: the non-Composer
Cage's words for what he wants music to be – 'an affirmation of
life . . . a way of waking up to the very life we're living' – fulfilled by
a real-Composer: who *also* brings 'order out of chaos', the aim Cage
had denied.

The phenomenon known broadly as minimalism began in the
late 1960s as a hostile reaction to the perceived over-complexity,
artificiality, elitism, tyranny, ugliness, non-appeal, of the ascendant
avant-garde; a healthy desire to replace all this by its antithesis –
liberation, simplicity, popular accessibility, attractiveness. Minimalism's earlier manifestations achieved this aim: such landmarks
as Philip Glass's *Music in Twelve Parts* (1971–4) and *Einstein on the
Beach* (1975) were like fresh air blasting keen and lethal through the
claustrophobic laboratories of the ivory tower. Their characteristics
are indeed minimal: fundamentalist diatonicism – nothing of the
sophistications of tonality, only the basics of scales, arpeggios, other
patterns upon which tonality is built, over a primitive harmonic
base: structure and trajectory made by repetition, without themes
let alone development, and eschewing polyphony – in fact, eschewing just about everything, not merely the hated complexity of the
initial target so much as the main course of Western Music down
its previous centuries of evolution. Thus minimalism is as radical as
the modernist avant-garde, and for comparable reasons: *tabula rasa*,
Stunde Null, a new start. And therefore equally an aspect of modernism itself.

    Not everything had to be rejected. There are clear anteced-
ents, even models, from the past: the elaborate constructivisms of

medieval then early Renaissance music; the play of keyboard figuration in the more showy variation-sets of the English virginalists; tattoos and fanfares from Monteverdi's Venice; Vivaldi's inexhaustible supply of one-dimensional textures and their equally indefatigable enhancement in Bach; ever-inventive accompanimental shapes in Schubert's songs; pattern-making in Liszt's piano-writing; its brilliant transfer to orchestral textures in Wagner, above all in his nature-evocations – water, mists, winds, storms, etc. – in the *Ring*; reiterative motifs and their backgrounds in Bruckner, thence Sibelius; the all-modal heterophony of Stravinsky's *Les Noces* – this work's sonority of pianos, percussions, voices comes very close, and some bits of Copland – the scherzo from his *Organ Symphony*, the *Danzón Cubano* – could have been factured by a signed-up minimalist forty years on.

Nonetheless, a radical new start. That it was welcome is attested by its rapid global acclamation, sweeping away not simply what it sought to replace, but much else too. The central stream of later twentieth-century music, continuing to grow with painful slowness from the century's earlier discoveries, gradually accommodating them, setting the plough to furrow pastures new, was also 'invalidated'. The limitations of the minimalist aesthetic, in techniques and expression and actual content, are obvious enough: no more than the avant-garde is it able to employ anything like music's full range of possibilities. The dose of salts, so salutary at first, soon washed away the baby with the bathwater.

Terry Riley, born 1935: pure California; San Francisco Conservatory then Berkeley; later, frequent visits to India to study its classical music and instruments; also inspired by the ideas and stance of John Cage and the Greats of modern jazz; plenty of play with electronics etc. Large and ongoing catalogue, tending (perhaps deliberately) towards self-duplication and dilution.

Got it absolutely right (just the once) in *In C* (1964) for unspecified instruments, voices too, that happen to be knocking around. Its material, fifty-three tiny modules of extreme simplicity, each with its own pattern – some consist of only one note – though all related to the key of C. One player beats a persistent pulse on this note to keep momentum: any number of other players on their various instruments work their way through the modules at their own speed: the materials interlock, separate yet simultaneous, in unpredictable ways, albeit always relating to the unchanging pitch/pulse of C. Thus every performance is different – in overall length, size of personnel, internal details of relationship: communal, exhilarating, happy, life-enhancing. Percy Grainger had pioneered all this in *Random Round* just before the Great War – a 'join-in-when-you-like round for a few voices and tone-tools backgrounded by a gut-string guitar . . .'. Riley's background is a piano or mallet-instrument, which sets up a regular-iterated C that will persist for the piece's entire length, unswerving except perhaps for little breaks to rest the wrists. It wasn't in the original: suggested by Reich later as a practical aid to keeping the piece together.

Other instruments commence on the first of the fifty-three tiny shapes, three E's making a major third: further instruments follow as they incline: gradually they move onto the 2nd, introducing an F and a little more momentum – rests between modules are as important as their notes: 3rd abandons C, 4th introduces G, 5th is identical, except that its gaps are longer. The 6th changes the feel by being the first long-sustained note, the higher C. Its opposite for 7th, three-note tapping on the lower C again, surrounded by much longer rests. The 8th again long-sustained, G then F. By now the full forces, whatever they may be, are in play – not quite a fugue, nor even a real round, but in its carefree way obeying its own rules. And so it goes: 9th shyly insinuates briefest of all possible B's; 10th ditto, with fewer gaps; 11th a little pattern admitting B as one of the Boys; 12th granting the note sustainment; 13th re-fixating on G. The 14th has four long notes ending on a new one – F♯ – that has the force, not a modulation exactly – of a new feel. The 15th to 21st continue with all six pitches so far vouchsafed in play, 19th hitting high G, highest note so far. The 22nd to 26th are more continuous – upward-rising five-note scale, in triplets, from E to B, wherein A is new and all F's are ♯. The 27th and 28th reintroduce semiquavers; 29th reintroduces long-held notes, and the 30th is a long-held C – result, a pure sustained triad declaring the work's title. The 31st to 34th are fragmented, F♯ replaced by F♮. The 35th is far the most extended and eventful module, containing both patter and sostenuto, the latter embracing the piece's last new note, an as-yet-unheard B♭, which takes tessitura as high as it's going to reach save for the unbroken background C; ♯ and ♮ for F are both in play here; and in context this stretch is positively complex. The 36th to 41st descend towards initial restricted areas as in the near-opening, though A is now firmly part of the game. When the 42nd sustains A B A C the piece could almost be called *In A-minor*, and the 43rd and 44th continue this feel. Then the 45th to 47th slope towards G-ishness; 48th to F; 49th to 53rd concentrate upon F with G and B♭ – pentatonic coloration after earlier tritonal; and the happy machine gradually and gently destructs itself and disappears. Three pitches – C♯, E♭ and A♭ – haven't been heard at all: it's a test of the machine's successful running that to play or sing any of these alien notes at any time during its course is to feel their strangeness – they *are* alien, unneeded, undesired, yet exciting, even dangerous. A one-off, ever-fresh, utterly bewitching, no possible progeny: again, like Duchamp's *Fountain*, or his moustache on the *Mona Lisa*, once it's been done there's no call for another.

Steve Reich, born 1936: a New Yorker; early study of piano, avid for the Baroque, and for drums – avid for jazz. At Cornell music yielded to philosophy – a BA thesis on Wittgenstein. Music now prevailed again – study at Julliard, thence to California for lessons from, inter ali, Berio and Milhaud. Tape-music, tentative serialism, involvement in experimental films, close association and collaboration with Terry Riley. The liberating discovery was *phasing*: taped fragments of speech and music split, spliced, altered in pitch and speed, layered across each other to make heterophony and polyphony: these methods gradually transferred to live performers – playing, singing, speaking, even clapping. Close study of the gamelan and African drumming: founded his own ensemble, devoted to his own oeuvre, himself at the controls. Highlights of this, his best phase (in every sense), include *Music for Mallet Instruments, Voices and Organ* and *Six Pianos* (both 1973); *Music for Eighteen Musicians* (1974); *Music for a Large Ensemble* (1978); *Octet* (1979). The no-nonsense titles indicate the attitude, which begin to change with gradual infiltration of a religious element, recovering his Jewish roots studying biblical cantillation in Israel: an immediate result *Tehillim* – setting of Psalms (1981). *Different Trains* (1988) – telling intercut of happy childhood journeys across the US with contemporaneous journeys for the children of European Jewry. The ethical/religious strain now predominates: the works grow somewhat grandiose and very dark, the fresh initial verve all-but-lost. Portentousness threatens in *The Cave* (1993), a video made with his wife's skills in collaboration, concerning the adjacence in Jerusalem of three great religions, Judaism, Christianity, Islam. *Three Tales* (completed 2003) covers twentieth-century issues, from the Hindenburg catastrophe in 1937 to nuclear weapons and sheep-cloning. After this, a return to pattern-and-process, at which he'd earlier excelled: the best of these (so far) is the *Double Sextet* (2007): a more ambitious venture, *Music for Ensemble and Orchestra* (2018), doesn't quite come off. Earliest phases remain classics of their kind. There's no need for details: no music is more up-front: unambiguous, precisely conceived and executed, its primal purity all surface; its surfaces its depths.

Philip Glass, born 1937, is not in the same league. Once the dose of salts had flushed the system and the baby with it, the vacancy is blatant. The two stage pieces that followed from *Einstein* – *Satyagraha* (1978–9) on the life of Gandhi, *Akhnaten* (1982–3) on the life of the Pharaoh who attempted to alter Egyptian religious belief (the opera is frequently sung in his own tongue) retain something of the impulse that originally compelled the minimalist venture. Thereafter, his output makes a descending spiral of ascending productivity into utter vacuity: other stage-works, symphony upon symphony (twelve so far); plenty of other things, press thick and fast with hapless inanity. Let us pass to something more congenial.

John Adams, born 1947, an Easterner: grandfather ran a dance-hall, father a clarinetist, mother sang with big band – a boyhood highlight, introduction to Duke Ellington after a concert. Jazz and

Broadway his natural environment; but musical education strict and strait – Harvard, with composition under old-style modernists, Kirchner, Sessions, Kim, Del Tredici (still in his Webern-costume). By day a practising classical mainliner, by night a surreptitious relisher of popular strains. The modernistic gradually eroded – helped by the revelation and liberation of Cage's example – and the populistic won. Ten years' teaching at the San Francisco Conservatory (1972–82) and from 1979 music adviser to the San Francisco Symphony. Compositional breakthrough: *Shaker Loops* for strings (1978), *Harmonium* for choir and orchestra (1980–81); and, after a self-questioning gap, *Harmonielehre* (1984–5) – 'a statement of belief in the power of tonality at a time when I was uncertain about its future.' He needn't have worried! Its success in itself as a piece opened up success at large, in appreciation and performance world-wide, making him eventually the most-played 'serious classical' composer of his day.

Exemplified by his first opera, *Nixon in China* (1985–7), based upon the President's visit to Chairman Mao in 1972: the opera, and its associated concert-offshoot *The Chairman Dances*, show at its best what minimalism came into being to effect – distinct outlines, rhythmic vitality, unfailing bounce, orchestra bright and clear; letters in poster-paint colours a mile high for all to see and hear; and a libretto that handles the potentially flammable subject with tact, wit and flair. During *Nixon*'s composition came another minimalist classic, *Short Ride in a Fast Machine* – 'fanfare for orchestra': everything Adams does, at its vital best, in brief compass. Thereafter adventures further afield, mingled with more-of-same. The Chamber Symphony (1992) and Violin Concerto (1993) revert to the mainstream modernistic he'd earlier renounced (the only Schoenbergian feature of *Harmonielehre* is its mischievous title, taken from the master's exhaustive textbook). Big further stage-works continue from *Nixon* without its sure touch, and there's a tendency towards portenousness in their response to major public issues: *The Death of Klinghoffer* (1991) – hijack by Palestinian terrorists; the California Earthquake of 1994; the destruction of the World Trade Center in 2001; Robert Oppenheimer and the human background to the first atomic bomb. The musical idiom is too threadbare to cover such serious stuff.

No need to plunge deeper into these shallow waters. Minimalism – in these three composers taken at its prime – might yet re-attach itself to maximalist ends, thus continuing to enrich mainstream compositional endeavours that don't suffer such limiting labels. 'Musicalism' is the only ism that doesn't become a wasm.

David Del Tredici, 1937–2023. At first sight it seems perverse, even wrong, to bracket this composer with the foregoing (though Riley and Reich are coeval, and Glass is exactly contemporary). A Californian: early ambition to be concert pianist; drawn to composition through attending Milhaud's classes at Aspen, and with Milhaud's encouragement changes course accordingly. Begins as hardline modernist – stiff academic serialism in its Webernian version, with no indication of what's to come save in the intensive deployment of learnèd constructivistic devices. Of that universal plague of pointillist textures factured from three- and four-note cells (the hopeless endeavour to adapt for general purposes what was in fact a personal style of extreme mannerism) very little now survives. The seed has only flourished when falling on soil already half-way or more prepared to receive it – Dallapiccola, Boulez, Ligeti, Kurtág, and, supremely, late Stravinsky. Some of Del Tredici's earlier music belongs in this same rare territory of composers who made a genuine continuity on from Webern's influence.

From around the mid-1960s a twin obsession commences with just two writers, Lewis Carroll and James Joyce, both in their different ways masters of the surreal and the nonsensical (not forgetting the strong presence of the former in the latter's *Finnegans Wake*). But Del T. only employs the traditional Joyce of his little poems. First (after some atypical early settings with piano) comes *I Hear an Army* (1964) for soprano and string quartet; then *Night Conjure-Verse* (1965), two poems for two singers and ensemble; and *Syzygy* (1966) – two further poems – for soprano, and ensemble with prominent solo horn part. Brief break uniquely devoted to a biblical text – *The Last Gospel*, using the opening eighteen verses of John's Gospel, with full orchestra (1967). Carroll sets in the next year with *Pop-Pourri* for soprano, ensemble and rock-group, its texts inter alia the Mock Turtle's song from *Wonderland* and 'Jabberwocky' from the *Looking-Glass*. The *Alice Symphony* follows in 1969: 'rock' becomes 'folk', ensemble becomes orchestra, soprano still reigns, and duration extended – four sections, *Speak Gently/ Speak Roughly* (from the Pig and Pepper episode); the *Lobster Quadrille*; *'Tis the Voice of the Sluggard*; and *Who Stole the Tarts?*, the White Rabbit's deposition before the Court of Hearts – all these from *Wonderland*. Which continues to nourish *Adventures Underground* (1971), for the same forces, comprising the *Pool of Tears* and the *Mouse's Tale*: by now Del T.'s texts include the originals of Carroll's parodies too. *Vintage Alice* (1972) concentrates wholly upon the Mad Hatter's Tea-Party.

All these are still at bottom 'modern music', whatever their use of borrowed material from the past or from the vast accumulation of musical cliché subverted, milked far, far beyond what it's worth, indispensable element in the composer's embrace of his author. But it's in his next – deceptively entitled *Final Alice* (1976) – that this queer composer comes out, after all, as a minimalist, albeit of a very peculiar brand. The material is all cliché, cod-tonal, musical kitsch and debris, the reliance on repetition as wholesale as anything by Glass; yet the techniques remain wholly modernistic/constructivist. The fusion of such incompatibles is all Del T.'s: the flagrancy and tastelessness, the compositional brilliance, the sheer daring were, at the time, a liberation just as lifeenhancing as anything by Reich or Riley with their severe purity. *Final Alice* is decisively nay'd by its successor *Child Alice* (1977–81); soprano as always, and again requiring amplification to withstand the huge orchestra, duration up from just over an hour to well over two. Texts drawn from the prefatory and valedictory poems Carroll appended to his immortal prose and his verse-parodies – 'straight' Victorian poetastry in all its squishy sentimentality, matched by an extension of Del T.'s raw materials into a composite of late Austro-Germanic Romanticism in all its post-Wagnerian degeneration. One movement is purely orchestral – the listener, as well as the soprano, *must* be relieved! – *Happy Voices*, punning title for a seventeen-minute fugal tour de force: it wins all the prizes a caucus-race can offer for speed, sonority, gaiety, verve, every possible contrapuntal device deployed with fantastic compositional virtuosity, culminating à la *Goldberg*s in a *quodlibet* binding together its own varied subjects with themes from elsewhere in the total entity.

Final Alice was already over-the-top; *Child Alice* crumples under its own freight, save for the free-flying fugue: and the later trajectory of this marvellously gifted composer is sad. With the passage of time the lean/mean matter and manner of the earlier work are surely what will survive. *Syzygy* first. The layout places soprano with a solo horn to the fore, with an extended set of tubular bells, in contradistinction to the ensemble of eight woodwinds, two trumpets and six solo strings. Here fearful symmetry reigns supreme, and the title conveys it from the start. Syzygy, the word, so juicy and tongueful simply to pronounce, means something equally succulent to the mind; the term is mainly used in astronomy to signify the conjunction of opposite points in a planetary orbit; further connotations run to any kind of yoking together (including copulation), and comparable devices in metrical structure – a gift to the kind of composer so conspicuously represented by David Del Tredici! *Syzygy*, the piece, is wholly and brilliantly about itself and its own processes. Whether it is equally well-paired with the Joyce poems is a matter of doubt that disappears under the astonishing impact of its structure and the sounds wherein its structures are realized.

Pop-Pourri is similar but more so. Lewis Carroll is perfectly attuned to Del T.'s inclinations, and to the original Lobster Quadrille the composer adds, in the spirit of his title, a layering of discrepant texts that already implies weird reaches of verbal surrealism even before his setting compounds them. (The title's other implication, pop-music, will also soon become raucously apparent.) The framework is Bach's own already way-out harmonization of the choral *Es ist genug* from Cantata 60 (*O Ewigkeit, du Donnerwort*), famous for its crucial role in Berg's Violin Concerto. *There* its emotive *Affekt* is paramount: *Pop-Pourri* launders all that away from the very start, the chorale's first phrase 'it is enough' (always in German), on chorus doubled by brass and snapping pizzicato strings. The soprano speaks an introductory choice – will her bizarre companions offer the Lobster Quadrille or a song from the Mock Turtle? The rock-group slithers in – two saxophones and two electric guitars, all amplified, their material very audibly derived from the chorale's first four notes, a segment of whole-tone scale. Speech turns to singing for the song in praise of turtle soup: the soprano slurps it around, as do the saxophones, all over the guitar bass. The slurps grow distant, strings, now bowed tremolandi, infiltrate whole-tonally, the last vocal phrase – 'beautiful soup!' – hangs in the air to be plucked down from it by bells and choral sopranos initiating the *Litany of the Blessed Virgin Mary*, vivid memory from the composer's Catholic childhood, set in full, at first on the same monotone G spaced across all the choral voices, gradually moving out in whole-tone formations. Wind instruments begin to sputter and snarl, then the choir also grows violent and complex: the loving pious Litany is comprehensively destroyed. Texture now thins, dropping away to shuddering strings, bells on the persistent mono-note: suddenly the Catholic Litany is confronted with a blast of Protestant defiance – the chorale's second phrase, blatantly sung and scored as the first.

Alice now notices a book. She tries to read – a cacophonous shriek from all the woodwinds: she then realizes that, this being Looking-glass Land, the words are backwards. Held up to the mirror they'll make sense – cacophonous shriek played reversed. It's the saga of the Jabberwock, told fit by fit with the utmost bravura vocal, instrumental, compositional; fully responsive to and worthy of Carroll's immortal coinages – first stanza alone invents *brillig/slithy/mimsy* for adjectives, *toves/wabe/borogroves/mome rathes* for nouns, *gyre/gimble/outgabe* for verbs. The *Melodrama* comes in eleven fits: introduction setting the scene; Father's Warning; Son in uffish thought; Jabberwock heard in the distance. So far only the orchestra has accompanied: now the creature appears, the rock-group with it, all its four instruments in frightful burbling glissandi bouncing off the full other instrumental forces at ever-shorter intervals: the soprano, amplified (by necessity) grows berserk: for the battle (the fifth fit) she takes up still fiercer electronic enhancement: sixth and

seventh, the beast's subsiding struggles are at once hilarious and terrifying: its death (eighth) is marked by a colossal wallop on the gong,
whose reverberation continues as the hero returns galumphing back
to his father (ninth); father's question, and his own reply – 'come
to my arms, my beamish boy!' – make a broad-spanned climax for
the soprano before (tenth) she too goes mad with frenzied victory.
Finally (eleventh fit) the opening stanza is repeated, and the hideous
sonic palindrome that opened the writing is heard again to close it.

In crashes *Es ist genug*, its first three phrases now vouchsafed; and
thence to a resumption, at Alice's emphatic request, of the Mock
Turtle's hymn to his beautiful soup, sung *al rovescio* (backwards) just
for fun – its gestures and sonorities so marked that the listener can,
as Berg's palindromes, latch on to such quaint medieval constructivism. As it fades, Alice is abandoned by Turtle and Gryphon. But
perhaps she's comforted by the chorale's complete second strophe
(still in German) – 'My Jesus comes: now oh world, goodnight! I fare
in peace for my house in heaven, my great sorrows remain below: it
is enough.' Soup of the Evening trickles through the gaps, saxes and
electric guitar now joined by a wind-machine, three bells on G's
in different registers chime thirteen at different speeds, chiming in
Italian if they could speak, reaching the climactic thirteen – *tredici* –
together: the composer's own signature, here as, frequently, elsewhere, more audible than B-A-C-H.

Nothing more arbitrary than the conjunctions in *Pop-Pourri*
could be imagined: they make the famous surrealist mantra – 'as
beautiful as the chance encounter on an operating-table of a sewing-
machine and an umbrella' – seem quite commonplace. And it *is*
beautiful: the closing pages, as bells and rock-group softly penetrate Bach's harmony with their clear G's or whole-tone slithers, are
haunting, magical, mesmerizing.

György Ligeti

György Ligeti: born 1923 in Romania, Jewish by race, Hungarian by
nationality: studied at the Liszt Academy in Budapest, then taught

there, composing to the usual Communist prescriptions. Fled after the 1956 uprising, first to Vienna, soon to Cologne for eager catch-up with avant-garde ventures previously prohibited. Contact with Boulez and Stockhausen; Darmstadt and electronic music; all these assimilated speedily and rejected gradually. Austrian citizenship 1968; teaching at Stockholm and Stanford; Professor of Composition at Hamburg 1973–89. Universal recognition as an outstanding composer of his time: dissemination enhanced by use of some pieces in three films by Stanley Kubrick – *2001: A Space Odyssey* (without permission), *The Shining* and *Eyes Wide Shut* (with permission); other films also. Died Vienna 2006.

This bald CV doesn't suffice: though in no sense an autobiographical/confessional composer like Tchaikovsky, Strauss, Mahler, Ligeti's life and personality are intricately and vitally interwoven with his work. Absolutely crucial, such things as the weird childhood dream of a world filled with spidery filaments laden with decaying junk, or the location in juvenile experience of all the sonorous, mechanical, surreal, fantastical, lamenting bases of his future concerns: vivid and unforgettable. Still more, the hair's-breadth survivals – from extinction by Nazis, then Soviets, from call-up to the army (by contracting TB, undoubtedly the lesser evil), amid the hideous annihilation of every close relative save his mother. So to the harrowing privations of study in the ruined Budapest of the late 1940s, easy-going in retrospect compared with the cultural repressions soon after; the tortuous affairs and marriages; the hair-raising account of two chances, not taken, to walk free from East to West Berlin in 1952 (had he succumbed to such delirious temptation he'd have come to live with an uncle in Reigate and the course of English, as well as European, music over the past half-century might well have been very different!).

Over the last four or five decades of 'serious classical music' with its generally perceived marginality to life at large – political, social, sporting, even cultural – and its less definable sense of inner strain and exhaustion, the achievement of György Ligeti increasingly stands out as the best there is and the best that could be done. It's one-dimensional, eccentric even (sometimes) to freakishness, it's exiguous and 'made of nothing' – all these will be discussed and qualified in due course – but as time passes even such radical insubstantiality can be felt to coalesce into a core of integrally musical achievement. Or perhaps, rather, the achievement is a shell around the hollow absence at the centre – in effect (albeit undeliberated) the deepest response – born of acute contact familial, political, racial – to proclamations, whether perfervid or merely despairing, that only silence is decent after such outrages against humanity at large and the once-humanistic language of music.

Who is he up against? Or to put it less crudely, where does he stand in the wider context of music's last half-century or so? After the deaths of the two last composers as yet to have reached genuine universal popularity in the art's most solid and established places, Symphony Halls and Opera Houses – Shostakovich in 1975, Britten the year following – the world has by common consent been divided between Elliott Carter and Olivier Messiaen, two complementary giants born on successive days in 1908. Messiaen died in 1992, Carter in 2012. Both can be set into a wider background involving the general degeneration of the avant-garde that had dominated the ideology of the immediate post-war years – Nono into agitprop then dreamy meditative vacuity, Boulez into delicious decorative flim-flam, Stockhausen into sulky megalomania, Berio into a sort of Autolycus of fun and games. Counterpointed with this, the rise of minimalism from its mostly rather severe and schematic beginnings to pop-like popularity – Reich, Glass, Adams, Pärt, Tavener. Between the fall of high complexity and the ascent of lowly simplicity comes the diminution or disappearance, in some cases justified, of more independent figures who once loomed large – Lutosławski, Penderecki, Schnittke, Tippett, Xenakis, Henze – and the tendency for eminent masters of the next generation – Birtwistle, Nørgård, Andriessen – to deliver in response to their very success a standard product; 'more of the same'. It is in this wider context that Ligeti's oeuvre shines forth. There's no question that the innate talent of a Carter, a Messiaen (and indeed several other of the composers mentioned above) is greater. They have more weight, more content. But, analogous to Stravinsky earlier in the century, Ligeti has exercised his relative parsimony – milked his lean kine – with such intelligence as to acquire exemplary stature. He is an icon of essentiality and intrinsicality, around which or within the whole epoch lies.

He starts out anew, from clean white nothingness: every element is questioned, examined, rejected if found wanting, remade if it passes through the needle's eye. The stringency of his refusals is heroic, and the resultant resumption of basics in works invoking 'melody', 'polyphony', 'étude', 'concerto', 'trio', etc. in their titles is as wholly different from the laboratory frigidity of a *'Polyphony X'*, etc. or the culinary frivolity of an *'Opera'*, or (closer to home and an important influence) the radical quizzicality of a Kagel as it is from neo-classic or neo-Romantic replication, however vital. Not that any of this is eschewed when it can be of use; though it can only be of use when passed through the mesh of the purifying filter.

This fundamentalism aligns him with other highly self-conscious attempts to bring a new sound to birth by returning to music's sources: Monteverdi, *Das Rheingold*, Webern, Reich. The 'next-to-nothing' from which he builds – a single note, a single note repeated in a stutter, a horn-call, a chromatic scale – is drastically simple: but he doesn't footle around getting 'inside' such primal material like, say Scelsi, the Stockhausen of *Inori*, or the Spectralists, but rather proceeds to build purposefully upwards and outwards, reinventing continuity and momentum, sonority and shape, motif/theme/melody/polyphony, the small ensemble, the large orchestra, the piano, the voice, expression *in extremis* whether desperate and apocalyptic or, its equally coruscating mirror-image, farcical and absurdist.

The purity and essentialism go alongside wild eager eclecticism. He is highly suggestible, and open to anything from the arts and sciences that takes his capricious and peculiar imagination. Phase by phase there's a long succession of diverse, often incongruous/incompatible obsessions in a lifetime's trajectory running full circle from the compulsory (yet neither unwilling nor unable) Romanian/Hungarian folklorico of his earliest pieces to its gradual return, less and less reluctant, more and more explicit, in the final concertos and other pieces; via fascination with mechanisms, systems, workings, inside music (electronics, new instrumental resources; bent tunings) or outside (stroboscopes/holograms/fractals/chaos-theory), together with the whole world (literally) of ethno-musical possibilities (with particular emphasis on Balinese gamelan and African drumming); the extremes and grotesques of such visual artists down the centuries as Bosch and Breughel, Goya, Ensor, Saul Steinberg and Escher (not forgetting the eminently un-grotesque Altdorfer, Klimt, Brancusi); and surreal and super-reality and dark Gothic fantasy from Poe, Baudelaire and Jarry to Ionesco and Borges, from Carroll and Lear to Sándor Weöres. Nor does he reject the high culture of music itself, as accounts of his seventeen years' devoted teaching at the Hamburg Conservatoire confirm – the vital importance at various stages (or consistently all the way) of medieval and Renaissance polyphony, of *ars subtilior*, of Bach; of Haydn's quartets ('when having to choose between a more ornate structure and a skeleton, Haydn always chooses the skeleton, never using one more note than he needs'), of Beethoven, Bruckner, Brahms, early Moderns, especially of course Bartók (an early goal, 'Hungarian Modernity' with Bartók as begetter, may be said to be realized in such pieces as the Piano and Violin Concertos); of American experimenters and eccentrics like Harry Partch, Cage, La Monte Young, or the not-so-eccentric Conlon Nancarrow or the wholly sassy Reich; and the subsummation of Romantic piano-textures from Chopin and Schumann to Debussy, Scriabin and Ives. Above all, the gradual convergence from the edges to the centre of his output of the traditional *lamento*-motif, which has pervaded European music since Renaissance times at least, and links Ligeti into the entire mainstream of European art-music at his own characteristically oblique angle and distance.

All this seems hardly starting out from 'clean white nothingness'! Indeed, it would appear to be a mishmash of promiscuity and pretentiousness, not innocent of either trendiness and opportunism, were it not so innate and unaffected, and thence turned to such absolutely musical ends. Moreover, Ligeti wears his eclectic acquisitions lightly: there's no hint of a grand synthesis à la Stockhausen – it's more a cabinet of curiosities: intricate, rare, odd, intriguing, delightful, sometimes moving, always beautiful. Again Stravinsky comes to mind as principal precursor (in the attitude if not the aesthetic); where, rather than a lineage, a self-selected 'portfolio' of favoured individuals or idioms is in play, which he can steal from and use. Compare the complementary giants who, with Ligeti, have out-stood the epoch, Carter and Messiaen: both have a family tree, and build confidently into a well-received and strongly characterized, indeed characterizing, usage – for Messiaen, Musorgsky, Debussy, Ravel, Dukas, the earlier Stravinsky, Koechlin, Villa-Lobos, Jolivet; for Carter, the monuments of high radical modernism, plus Ives, Cowell and Varèse. They confidently inherit considerable sophistication and know-how; they don't have to make their own fortunes. Ligeti, like Alice, snatches whatever he can in a precipitate descent down a bottomless hole. The fact that what he can grab fits his predilections so well is his good luck, thence ours.

At the time of his escape from Hungary in 1956 Ligeti was thirty-three, an accomplished and acknowledged composer of line-toeing populism with a 'bottom drawer' of unacceptably experimental pieces undertaken in almost total ignorance both of his contemporaries and juniors in the West and even of the old generation from whom they took their new bearings and their radical departures. Amid all this Hungarian output prior to his escape, a few works stand out, notable for what is to come, striking and permanent in themselves. *Musica Ricercata* for solo piano (1951–3), a study in restrictions gradually lifting, via, inter alia, an eloquent elegy for Bartók, to encompass a fugue at once totally chromatic and in homage to Frescobaldi (and thence to Bach); and the 1st String Quartet (1953–4), taking the Bartók strain into a constantly metamorphosing fluidity prognostic of the works of his prime. Most significant of all but impossible to pinpoint exactly (because respectively lost and unfinished) are two orchestral attempts, both of 1956 – *Visions*, which eventually evolved over the next four years into *Apparitions*, and *Darkness and Light*, which seems to have struggled, for the moment unsuccessfully, with the technical bases for the 'micro-polyphony' that would culminate in the celebrated *Requiem* completed nearly a decade later.

Meanwhile, as 1957 dawned he was 'destitute but free', and avid to make up for lost time. He made his way to an artistic and technological oasis – Cologne, with Stockhausen and the West-Deutscher-Rundfunk electronic studio, where under the surveillance of one of its pioneers he produced *Glissandi* and *Artikulation*. Drawn thence to Darmstadt, Mecca of the avant-garde, from which ambience comes a verbal analysis of one of Boulez' essays in total serialism, *Structures* Book 1A: a vital stage in a disabusal-process consolidated by the failure to advance with a third electronic piece, realizing that it could succeed better employing conventional orchestra, and confirmed by an essay on 'Metamorphoses of Musical Form' (completed 1960), which quietly disposes *in toto* the purported rationale for total serialization. This same year produced the compositional breakthrough: *Apparitions* (after the now-lost *Visions*); next, *Atmosphères*, also for orchestra. The avant-garde's fundamental negation takes on a positive quality in what its restrictive practices produced by way of reaction.

Next comes a deviation into apparent footling, as Ligeti imbibes from the US the debilitating influence of Cage and the conceptual-pantheistic madness of La Monte Young, from Europe the Zen radicality of Cornelius Cardew and the feebly self-conscious silliness of the Dada group Fluxus. He participates, and learns, as part of un-learning the previous adherence to the wrong direction; his efforts closest to this absurdist aesthetic produce two almost legendary stories: the smoking organ at the (necessarily curtailed) première of *Volumina* in 1962, and the marvellous misalliance between civic cultural respectability and its mischievous debunking with the première of the *Poème symphonique* (the very title indicates the ironic tone) for one hundred metronomes, wherein, not for the last time, he appears cast as a cross between Chaplin's Little Tramp and Harpo Marx.

Riper fruit from this subversive mockery comes with *Aventures* (1962) and its successor *Nouvelles Aventures* (1966), where, with admirable brevity, all human expression is mercilessly detached, put on speed and mounted on pins in an absurdist farrago of inspired zaniness. And, between them and related as charcoal to diamond, comes the *Requiem*, the coruscating apocalyptic masterpiece that (incidentally) proves there *can* be non-banal music after Auschwitz and *must* be – not by onomatopoeic breast-beating, on the contrary, but by means of an intensification of discipline: claustrophobic and indeed overwhelming in its density and seriousness. The path towards such strictness was stony and steep – there'd been two attempts already at the same hallowed text (unrelated musically, it seems). The result eventuality came into being with a mighty conscious effort to organize the post-serial flux and achieve 'correct counterpoint' without ideological madness: rather, the models were Ockeghem, Tallis's forty-part motet, J. S. Bach's *Singet dem Herrn* – glories of medieval, Renaissance, Baroque vocal polyphony – but absolutely without stylistic/historical referents, let alone pastiche. The grinding application of constructivist mechanisms in an edifice of exhaustive and comprehensive pedantry underpins with flawless accuracy, precision, logic, technical grip, an expressive content of desperate expressionist extremity, igniting unforgettable conflagrations.

From such 'darkness visible', radiance and serenity are the residue: *Lux aeterna* for chorus (1966), whose inner voice-line generates another orchestral milestone – *Lontano* (1967), a 'study in opalescence' that stands without peer in the post-war repertory for its seraphic shine and consummate detail of workmanship. (For 'orchestra without percussion' says the title-page, reminding one that the vast majority of comparable music that twinkles, glitters, gleams, shines, glows, from Boulez and Berio to Druckman, Knussen, Benjamin, depends heavily upon its arrays of crotales, glockenspiels, vibraphones, etc. to achieve qualities that Ligeti effects through exactly pitched and voiced counterpoint and total textural precision.)

We are now on the threshold of Ligeti's prime. It begins, however, with the (to me) rather overrated 2nd String Quartet (1968): a mounted specimen of what he has called 'frozen expressionism'; 'as if a pane of glass or sheet of ice separated us from the blazing heat of expression'. Despite the composer's exciting metaphors and his own high endorsement, there's something recalcitrant and wayward in the music itself: it yields less the more one tries. Yet it stands as the forbidding entrance to the pleasure beyond. Amid marginalia like the dinky little pieces for wind quintet, the rather faceless

Ramifications for strings and two further studies for organ (non-self-destructing this time) come the *Chamber Concerto* (1969), *Melodien* for orchestra (1971), then the somewhat paler *Double Concerto* (1972), then, again for orchestra, the triumphant *San Francisco Polyphony* (1973–4). Between these two last lies a fascinating anomaly, *Clocks and Clouds*, whose exploration (inspired by Karl Popper) of 'a scale between precision and imprecision' prophesies preoccupations, techniques, sometimes actual sonorities, of music to come. In itself it doesn't wholly convince: the combination of Day-Glo susurration on the orchestra with pale pink yoghurt on the wordless female voice strikes, for once in this composer, and very surprisingly, a note of tackiness, almost kitsch.

The others, flawless in tone and technique, equally embrace the pleasure-principle and take it to more complex places. Their sheer deliciousness and shared delight in intricate process induce an aural intoxication unique in the epoch – champagne without hangover. The play of textural invention – iridescent, arabesque, witty, mechanical, obsessive, scuttling, whirling, sparkling – is extraordinary. And while Significance, Importance, Seriousness, are on holiday, this music is so good that they are secretly incarnate after all. These pieces tip the scale, for all their apparent weightlessness, against vast loads of *Transfiguration*, *Paradise Lost*, *War Requiem*, *All-Night Vigil*, *Gawain*, nay *Licht* itself. The step-by-step reintroduction of thematicism, melody, polyphony, has been wrought with hard ardent toil at the residual resistance of music itself, the more unyielding because at bay with bared teeth, up the tightest cul-de-sac in all its centuries of evolution. After *Musica Ricercata*, the *Requiem*, *Lontano*, Ligeti has truly earned as well as gained the power to melt adamant into liquid – play of water, flow, surge, plash, the twinkling surface-lights, the luminous depths. The hedonism of his times in California, enhanced by multi-chromatic Klimt rather than monochrome Escher, is explicit in some words, for the première of the San Francisco work in the city it celebrates, that he later deleted from the programme note: 'low clouds sailing slowly from the ocean ... the presence of water and salt everywhere ... student musicians between the red bricks of the old chocolate factory ... the view of the red towers of the Golden Gate ... the turning of the cable car'. But such things, and no doubt more, lie deep within the musical fabric.

An appendix to the California experience comes in a marvellous two-piano work in three movements of 1976: *Monument* celebrates pattern in clangorous overlapping bell-change-ringing: *Self-Portrait with Reich and Riley (with Chopin in the Background)* – to which one could add Schumann – pays explicit homage to the ear-opening liberation of minimalism at its purest and most essential: *Bewegung* (i.e. motion/emotion) is a study in figuration (Liszt in the background?) growing more and more florid till it coalesces and freezes into a chorale. Escher's games with the ambiguities of visual perception are here transformed into sound, with input also from an intellectual teaser of the day, Douglas Hofstadter's *Gödel, Escher, Bach*, plus stroboscopes, holograms, fractals, chaos-theory; a heady froth of influences scientific and artistic that brings us to the verge of the solo piano *Études*.

But before the *Études*, *Le Grand Macabre*, Ligeti's sole opera (despite his long-held hopes, ever after, for an *Alice* and a *Tempest*), far his longest and, in some respects, most ambitious work. Its première in 1978, thirteen years after its inception, opened a critical divide that still persists, aided by a tally of mal-productions culminating in the travesty by Peter Sellars of the 1996 revision (which effects muchneeded tightening up), and the failure to reach the first season of the renovated Covent Garden. The huge expansion of expressive and stylistic range necessitated by an evening-length's work seems to have stretched its composer beyond his natural resources, otherwise so scrupulously obeyed. The scenario, black Gothic apocalyptic farce laced with religious mania, political satire, slapstick drollery and lashings of S&M, is jejeune, pointless, morbid. Invoking Poe, Baudelaire, Jarry, Kafka, Ionesco for its text and Breughel, Bosch, Goya, Ensor, Steinberg for its visuals can't guarantee quality. It seems like a precocious schoolboy lark. The trouble for an English clientèle is the native disposition to mickey-taking, silly voices, dislocated logic, home-made Dada, dead-pan irony implicit in the culture and its linguistic habits, embodied down the generations in *Monty Python*, *The Goon Show*, *Carry On* films, back via classic Victorian nonsense,

Lear and Carroll (*Alice* is said to hover high over the whole conception and execution of Ligeti's piece, but her no-nonsense approach
is sadly absent), through the *Dunciad* to the more aberrant metaphysical poets of the seventeenth century. The result is a wasteland
of onomatopoeia, funny noises, freaky characters, exaggerated situations, that wholly fails to amuse. Elaborated and deliberate Absurd-
ism is just too serious! Ligeti had got the balance exactly right, with
no plot or stage to get in the way, in the twenty minutes or so of
Aventures and its sequel.

Yet of course there are positives. Such things as the bank of dense
harmony when the projected end of the world fails to occur, the
fantastic-grotesque passacaglia upon a rotating 12-note distortion
of the bass to Beethoven's *Prometheus/Eroica* finale, the demented
fioriture for the (female) chief of secret police, burgeon well beyond
their annoyingly perfunctory context. And the consistent strain of
music for the young lovers (originally Spermando and Clitoria,
later bowdlerized into Amando/Amanda) etherealizes their endless
carnal quest into a gentle stream of geometric sweetness made
entirely out of consonant tonal intervals, never thickened beyond
a triad, ravishing in itself, and highly influential – not least upon its
own composer's subsequent thinking. Not to mention its refreshing assistance for the 'neo-tonal' practices of many younger composers whose proclivities Ligeti appears to despise. One of history's
little ironies – the liberator deploring the consequences of what he
himself has opened up.

As several times before, Ligeti was drained after this major effort,
and, as before, regeneration was slow and marked only composition of apparent trivia (two pieces for harpsichord, *Hungarian Rock*
and *Passacaglia ungherese*). Under their camouflage a new direction
gradually took shape. The challenge: no self-replication, no play of
stylistic allusion such as had preponderated in the opera, no 'retro'
or 'neo'; but equally, goodbye to all that avant-garde. All these negatives make a positive in the end. The emergent masterpiece, the
Trio for piano, violin, horn of 1982, is subtitled '*hommage à Brahms*':
behind him, the real figure is Beethoven: a distorted twist of the
horn-call from the *Les Adieux* sonata runs throughout, in and behind

a surface more acquiescent with Bartók than anything in Ligeti since his earliest folkloric idiom. The piece in general is more formal in terms of movement-shape overall and phrase-structure within; and yet more fantastical, capricious, liberated. In the letter, his challenge to himself has been flouted: in the spirit, all is permitted, so long as it can be seen and heard to be renewed.

After two complementary works for unaccompanied voices – settings of Hölderlin (1982) – dense, rich, romantic; and of Weöres (1983) – wacky, rhythmic, exuberant – Ligeti again appears to mark time. Under which apparent hiatus, new life is stirring: since 1980 he had been at work, constantly thwarted, on a piano concerto, which only emerged unscathed in 1988, overlapping with the first book, nos. 1–6, of the *Études* for piano solo, completed in 1985. This venture has been recognized as outstanding since the piece-meal appearance of its individual numbers: with the piano-series of Stockhausen, Messiaen's *Catalogue d'oiseaux* and (a special case) the player-piano studies of Nancarrow (enthusiastically promulgated by Ligeti ever since he first came upon them) the most important body of keyboard music since Debussy, Ravel, Bartók. Many of his recurrent concerns focus here, amid plentiful new influences and congruences scientific, poetic, visual, technical, ethnographical, philosophic. Machine-demonism is taken to new extremes of logical madness (*Désordre*; *Touches bloquées*) or else turns delightfully towards lightness and festivity (*Fanfares*), and a new vein of frank, sensuous, loveliness flowers, now delicate and limpid (*Cordes à vide*; *Automne à Varsovie*), now lush and voluptuous (*Arc-en-ciel*). Scriabin, even Rachmaninov, joins the composers who prove compatible with Ligeti's angle on them. About the Piano Concerto I can't (yet) be so sure. Though it was completed after endless redrafting – 'reformulating his technique yet again from the ground up' – the result is so explicitly Bartókian as to seem like a throwback rather than new terrain. Which need not, of course, be a criticism: more a matter of turning through so many angles that he comes full circle, embraces his youth, returns home and 'knows the place for the first time'.

This feeling prevails in the music completed after, up to the time of his death. Alongside the delicious mellowed-Dada *Nonsense*

Madrigals (1988–93) comes the Violin Concerto (1989–93), then a third, the *Hamburg Concerto* for horn, begun in 1998, which also took its time (it was completed in 2003) and is altogether slighter. It sounds to me like Euro-Ligeti. The same feeling prevails here as for the Piano Concerto: and with Book II of the *Études* (1988–94) self-replication undoubtedly sets in, as, more so still, with Book III. Realignment with earliest roots is still more evident in the *Sonata for Unaccompanied Viola* (1991–4) and the nonsense songs (text again by Weöres) for mezzo-soprano with percussion – the total, fruitful, grateful re-admission of every folk element from his early life and the culture of his several countries. But whatever the reservation over the last phase of his activity, this music is still, by most other contemporary standards, exceptional in compositional prowess, imaginative élan, and sheer ability to yield delicious and diversified sonorous pleasures.

Why is Ligeti an exemplar and an icon unmatched in his time? Throughout an epoch wherein, more than ever before, in music anything goes, aural reality is frequently discounted, the hungry sheep (usually cloned and cloth-eared anyway) look up and are not fed, till, maddened with wind, they stray and scatter straight for the Gadarene cliff, plunging into a warm yet sterile ocean of bogusness, hype, pseudo-significance, vacuous vestiges of religion or bargain-basement mysticism – need I go on? – he has remained true. Not alone, obviously. But the extreme purity of his stance does, nevertheless, put him in a solitary position. He uniquely has been able to combine such severity with a simultaneous ability to get through, out of, beyond, transcending the in-turned ivory ghetto, to enter with absolutely no compromise or traduction a wider sphere of communicable content. The fierce fervour of workmanship justifies his listener in condoning what would without it often be jokey, facetious, merely deflationary, even negative. But they are excellent jokes. And the puffed-up sacred cows need puncturing. And negativity is one of his principal subjects.

Which leads to the nub: that his music is always, even when unquestionably great, a feat of legerdemain. He builds in defiance of gravity from bricks made without straw. Yet these whimsical erections stand and hold – pagodas, lighthouses, follies, dolmens, chapels, *maisons rouges*, bars, even the odd Mendelssohn-Turm, Wittgenstein-Haus, Gaudí apartment-block, San Francisco painted lady, set amid a maze, a cemetery, a funfair. There is a Ligeti landscape, and through it, beneath well-wrought clouds, the rivers flow (even if, à la Escher, the perspectives skew): there is a Ligeti cityscape whose trains run on (idiosyncratic) time and whose clocks run amok: the structures are fantastical to the eye, but eminently functional and surprisingly joyful to inhabit. Yet the oeuvre as a whole is grave, even elegiac, despite its piercing character as entertainment. In the end it's nothing less than music itself that he has confirmed. The on-the-edge nature of his peculiar version of it is like the skeleton to which he claims Haydn always reduces his thought. Music so pared-to-the-bone can sometimes be hard to recognize or acknowledge as still being the real thing. Once it has been, it can make almost every one of its contemporaries seem cluttered, approximate, redundant, rhetorical, fulsome.

Envoi

State-of-the-art, 2025. We have the facts, heterogeneous, contradictory, chaotic as never before. 'Let's fantasize.' Imagine a lingua franca from *c*.2000 on, a common practice for composition, in which every promising discovery of the century before has been assimilated and incorporated, its dead bits ditched, its living rejuvenated; in which composers of every colour, gift, aim, will partake as their nature requires and permits, modifying and adjusting as they may and can and need.

Only another Bach would be able to effect such consolidation and synthesis – a composer whose ear and spirit were open to everything encountered, ancient and contemporary, and whose technique could weld it into unity. Another such is clearly unlikely: the desired aim will be achieved communally, shared by many individual composers, usually very different and by no means working consciously towards such a result. That it will be reached – that it is already under way – I have no doubt whatsoever. Music's empire is infinitely renewable, dying again and again to be again and again reborn, transformed utterly yet paradoxically continuous: ultimately its kingdom is not of this world. How might this music of synthesis/communality/inclusiveness actually *sound*? Not an Esperanto; a genuine lingua franca, a living speech, flexible, resonant, comprehensible and comprehensive. I must try to encircle it. I've heard it, here and there, in drifts, dreams, snatches, hints, in the music of many contemporaries big and small; never realized in full, only in suggestion. Every true composer wants to make a sound that's not been heard before, however – obviously and inevitably – beholden to its sources and influences. Otherwise, why bother? The unmistakable presence of a unique personality is at once starting-point and fulfilling end. What's his, what's hers? What's yours, what's mine? Then what's the commonality, the synthesis, the choral unanimity of the probably incompatible differences that, nevertheless, fuse and blend into a Oneness? Here are some attempts to capture and encapsulate the Unicorn.

Harmony: radiant euphonious atonality, mellifluous but not bland or insipid; astringent, acid, abrasive, aggressive, etc. as needs occasion. A gamut of consonance/dissonance in which every pitch counts – every note perceived as adding to the sense of the sound, even though its 'grammar' is intuitive rather than formalized/'by the book'. The term 'atonal' by no means involves relinquishing tonal triads and other more complex chords built from them, nor their tonal relationships. The music of common practice is still tonal, in no retro-sense: pulls and pushes upwards and downwards remain as expressive and as functional as ever – tonality's long and fruitful accumulation of usages is far too beautiful to be lost. As, also, such relatively recent constructions in interval-based harmony, systematic or empirical, that followed on from the decadence and dissolution of classical tonality. And modes, scales, patterns of pitches, invented in the laboratory or drawn from other musical cultures, once 'exotic', now neighbourly. All these can run alongside each other, intermingling and modifying the composite.

Melody: motif, theme, line, contour – shapely and singing, supple like plainsong or metrical like a nursery-rhyme, and everything in between. Also sharpness, angularity, jaggedness – every aspect of the great innovators' discoveries incorporated and naturalized, from Wagner's 'endless melody' to Stravinsky's pulsating/pounding two-note cells. Above all, long lines – clauses, sentences, paragraphs – contour and momentum of every sort – the sweep of an eagle, the jerky gait of a waddling frog.

Counterpoint: liquid free-flowing 'atonal' (as above) polyphony – melodic strands colliding, combining, fusing, separating: one part splitting into two, three, four – 'micro-polyphony' à la Ligeti; heterophony – many voices spun out of the one part.

Rhythm: the same objectives – consolidation and normalization of previous discoveries in this field, whether on the smallest scale – Stravinsky again – or on the broadest; the 'hyper-metres' in mature

Sibelius: or in such individual wonders of proportional construction as the *monoritmica* in Berg's *Lulu* or the articulation and lyri-
cization of silences in the later Webern, or metric modulation as in
Elliott Carter.

Timbre: liberation of instrumental timbre as an element in itself
as important as any other, if not so fundamental (you can't have an
oboe-timbre without the note it's playing!). All the instruments,
'conventional' and new, sometimes played (where suited) with
unconventional techniques: percussion, pitched and unpitched, just
as significant as any other family in the tribes of sound-producers.

Above all, the universal consequences of the non-Teutonic ways
with *form/shape/journey*; the '*Karaminskaya*-method' as triumphantly
manifest in Debussy's *Jeux*, all shimmer, luminosity, evanescence;
and in Stravinsky's *Symphonies of Wind Instruments*, all hard-edged
geometry, intercut and superimposed by force, reaching an ultimate
effect of liturgical ritual. Thence, direct or oblique, Messiaen, Birtwistle, later Tippett, earlier minimalists. Many other new possibilities
too, not least originating in Teutonia itself – the free self-evolving
'movement', unbeholden to any precedent, at which Schoenberg,
Webern, Berg excelled, whose further potential is limitless.

Processes/schemes/devices/games: the earlier twentieth century is
also exceptionally rich and diverse in all these, often to marvellous
effect – to take but one celebrated example, the interplay of all four,
with a strong sense of shape and journey, and powerful expressive
affect, in Bartók's *Music for Strings, Percussion and Celesta*. The epoch
is also awash with dead ducks who can be left to sink without trace
or regret.

Constructivism, the term covering all the others, culminates in
construction: musical architecture that speaks, that is expressive in
itself; *facture* too, the very make of the material, and the ways it is
fashioned into content irrespective of explicit or implicit *Affekt*, as
supremely in Bach, then Haydn, then Beethoven.

Expression: the inheritance above all of Schubert, Schumann,
Wagner – emotional utterance, what the music is *saying*, what it
means. Nothing is alien to music's powers to evoke and move –
pictorial/atmospheric/verbal/conceptual – *all* can be legitimately

and successfully 'musicalized' – Scriabin managed it with colours; Messiaen with birds. Mysticism and metaphysics and scientisms translate naturally into sonorous structures moving in time: perhaps the future will effect the same for smell, taste, touch? Supercilious suggestion: but the further possibilities for music to conquer are real enough.

And *allusion/quotation/reference* are already omnipresent: from tiny tender origins – Beethoven's *An die ferne Geliebte* in Schumann, Mozart's *Ave verum corpus* in Brahms's 1st Symphony, and suchlike – those practices have virtually become a way of life in the past half-century or so. Not altogether new: involuntary memory has always been operative, imitation and modelling paramount, homages paid: *influence* existed long before plagiarism and 'intellectual property' inhibited the free play of give-and-take at all levels of creativity. These practices can be trivial and cheap. They can also be a great resource in uncovering new realms of expression. Let free association *be* free! But what's borrowed or stolen must be repaid or earnt. Berio's *Sinfonia* is now seen as a classic/seminal instance – a *jeu d'esprit* that devolves into responsibility.

And let's close by going wholly crazy. What do I envisage in a compositional synthesis as the twenty-first century winds on? The *Tristan*-prelude crossed with Beethoven's C♯-minor Quartet and *The Art of Fugue*, tinctured with *Jeux* and laced with the *Five Orchestral Pieces* of Schoenberg, articulated into bodily activity by Stravinsky; heartfelt and direct as Schubert and Tchaikovsky, yet charged with intimacies and secrets as Schumann; sparky as Chabrier, colourful as Ravel, exhilaratingly ferocious as Varèse, gay as Grainger; chalorous as Janáček, mordant as Weill, sexy as Gershwin, cool as Fauré, cheeky as Poulenc, mystic as Messiaen, strange as Enescu; bright and open as Copland, veiled and withdrawn as Feldman; life-affirming as Tippett, death-devoted as Ligeti; somehow referencing the wit/surprise/inwardness of Haydn, and whatever it is that we all call 'Mozartian'. Oh, and not forgetting Brahms, Bruckner, Musorgsky, Wolf, and everyone else. Could go on for ever: but here is a start. And a finish.

Glossary of Musical Terms

Some key words and plenty of passing usages are defined in the main text; here are some others.

a cappella (It.) – 'as in a chapel'; a choir singing without accompaniment.

Affekt (Ger.) – passion/emotion/expression, inherent within melodic contour and harmonic movement.

Alberti-bass – chords broken into continuity, usually as accompaniment in the keyboard's left hand to the right hand's melody.

antiphony – spatial echo question-and-answer between choral groups or instruments. Hence between sections of an orchestra.

buffa (It.) – 'funny'; in opera, the complement to *seria*, serious/elevated.

cabaletta (It.) – closing stretch of an operatic aria, demonstrating vocal brilliance and agility.

cantabile (It.) – expressive song-like phrasing, asked of any instrument by analogy with the singing voice.

cantilena (It.) – a singing contour, on whatever instrument.

cantus firmus (Lat.) – the leading voice in polyphonic textures, mainstay of the others.

chaconne – a succession of harmonies, self-contained, re-employed throughout a section or a movement; basis of its process and construction. See also *passacaglia*.

coda (It.); the 'tail'; the close of a movement wherein its material reaches a final working – peroration, culmination, or even a dwindling of energy.

coloratura (It.) – 'colouring': florid, brilliant, vocal writing, most often for female voice but can also be male.

continuo (It.) – the music's foundation in its bass line, figured with numbers indicating changes in harmony; not notated, but improvised using well-established conventions.

da capo (It.) – 'from the beginning'; frequent in seventeenth- and eighteenth-century instrumental and especially vocal works: after a contrasting middle section the first is repeated, sometimes complete, sometimes reshaped and shortened.

diatonic – see under *scales*.

enharmonic – the same pitch re-interpreted: D♯ becomes E♭ or E♭ becomes D♯, and so forth. On an equal-tuned instrument like the piano, the notes of the two keys are identical; a stringed instrument or a voice can subtly adjust the pitch. Fundamental gear change for all tonal music.

facture – the 'making'; from the broadest architecture to the smallest detail of workmanship.

false relation – major and minor thirds in a triad sounded very near or even simultaneously; a particularly English flavour, culminating in Purcell.

fantasia (It.) – a piece freely composed, improvisatory, fantastical.

figured bass – see *continuo*.

gamelan – traditional music of Java and Bali: an elaborate 'orchestra' of tuned bronze percussion and other instruments, the pitch entirely pentatonic (see *scales*), the rhythmic organization subtle and complex. 'Makes our tonics and dominants seem like ghosts' (Debussy).

gigue – a lively dance of the seventeenth and eighteenth centuries.

hemiola (Gr.) – a shift of accent in triple time, wherein 3 + 3 becomes 2 + 2 + 2.

homophony; polyphony; heterophony – homophony is harmonic/chordal, all the parts moving together alike, making harmony. Polyphony its opposite – free play of independent lines, a texture of counterpoint, whether vocal or instrumental. Heterophony sort of between the two: a principal line shadowed by one or more versions of itself, creating an impression of harmony and counterpoint, not the full actuality.

Klangfarben (Ger.) – 'sound-colour'; splitting a contour, even a harmonic pattern, among varied instrumental timbres. Particularly found in Schoenberg's earlier atonality (see *tonality*), then in Berg and, especially, Webern.

melisma (Gr.) – a pattern of notes sung to a single syllable; thence ornament or decoration.

minuet/menuet – seventeenth- and eighteenth-century dance form, which can enclose a contrasting trio (not necessarily in three parts); from Haydn on, the standard third movement in symphonies and

chamber-works, quickening into scherzo (and trio) with Beethoven
and Schubert.

middle eight – contrasting second section for standard songs in
American musicals – best of all, Gershwin.

modes – see *scales*.

monody – unaccompanied melody; usually vocal, can be instrumental.

motet – originally, any sacred vocal work using texts not heard in the
Mass; thence more general in later times.

musette – eighteenth-century dance-form over a drone-bass.

obbligato (It.) – 'obligatory'; the indispensable instrument or voice in
any texture.

ostinato (It.) – 'obstinate'; a repeated rhythmic pattern that persists with
mounting tension/excitement/obsession.

passacaglia (It.) – goes with *chaconne* (qv); the bass unaltering, or gradually varied, upon which is laid the evolving invention of the upper
parts, often very elaborate above the fundamental support. Cf. *cantus
firmus*.

pentatonic – see *scales*.

recitativo (It.) – quasi speech, natural and free (unmeasured) over
figured bass (qv).

ritornello (It.) – 'return'; recurring passages between sections of early
opera, thence in anthems and purely instrumental works, especially
concertos – the *tutti* (qv) between solo episodes.

sarabande – a seventeenth- and eighteenth-century dance, stately
and serious; associated with mourning, as at the close of Bach's *St
Matthew* and *St John* Passions.

scales – see 'Some Basic Technicalities', pp. 20–26, above. Diatonic: the
major tonal 7-note scale; its minor mode, with chromatic inflections.
Pentatonic: any scale of 5 notes, perhaps most commonly deriving
from the 'circle of fifths' (e.g. C G D A E); pentatonic scales the basis
of archaic music the world over and, in Europe, of plainsong and
folksong. Modes: usually refers to scales (named (Greekly) Dorian,
Phrygian, Lydian, etc.) that emerge when starting a standard major
scale on notes other than the tonic; *modality* giving more individual flavours. Chromatic: all the notes, in semitones. Whole-tone
scale: what it says – equal steps a tone apart, 6 to the octave, eroding
tonality because it contains neither dominant (5th degree) or subdominant (4th). Octatonic: regular pattern of tone/semitone, thrice

repeated within the octave; frequently used in first half of twentieth century, an eroder of stale habits, eventually becoming such itself.

sequence – originally, a free extension of the *Alleluia* in the Mass. Later meaning (still current and frequent), repetition of a figure, a clause, a paragraph, at another pitch; usually higher, indicating a rise of tension and excitement; open to abuse!

sicilienne – delicate, lilting eighteenth-century dance form, originating in Sicily.

simplesse (Fr.) – a usage coined by Matthew Arnold to characterize fake simplicity, disingenuous affectation of natural ease.

Singspiel (Ger.) – opera in the vernacular (German) rather than Italian, the musical numbers separate by speech, not joined by sung *recitativo* (qv). Culminates in Mozart's *Die Zauberflöte* (*The Magic Flute*).

sonata – see 'Some Basic Technicalities', pp. 20–26, above.

tamtam – the biggest, deepest gong.

tesssitura (It.) – the compass of a voice part (high, middle, low), both female – soprano, mezzo-soprano, contralto; and male – tenor, baritone, bass.

tonality – see 'Some Basic Technicalities', pp. 20 –26, above. Its apparent antithesis *atonality* (comprehensively covered in several parts of the main text): implies abolition of diatonic scales as basis of the idiom, to be replaced by 'total chromaticism', that is, all pitches are equal.

tremolo (It.) – vibration (trembling): fast-repeated whirring of the bow (strings); oscillation of the fingers (piano).

trepak (Rus.) – vivacious Cossack dance in duple time.

tutti (It.) – the full forces: of choir, of orchestra, of everyone at once.

zarzuela (Sp.) – light musical comedy, sometimes darker, incorporating speech and improvisation.

Select Bibliography

Hermann Abert, *W. A. Mozart*, tr. Stewart Spencer (Yale University Press, 2007)

John Bird, *Percy Grainger* (Oxford University Press, 1976)

David Cairns, *Berlioz*, Volume I: *The Making of an Artist, 1803–1832* (Allen Lane, 2000)

— *Berlioz*, Volume II: *Servitude and Greatness, 1832–1869* (Allen Lane, 2000)

Robert Craft, *Conversations with Igor Stravinsky* (Faber, 1959)

— *Memories and Commentaries* (Faber, 1960)

— *Expositions and Developments* (Faber, 1962)

— *Dialogues* (Faber, 1963)

— *Themes and Episodes* (Faber, 1967)

— *Retrospectives and Conclusions* (Faber, 1969)

James Hepokoski, *Sibelius, Symphony No. 5* (Cambridge University Press, 2003)

Ian Kemp, *Tippett: The Composer and His Music* (Oxford University Press, 1987)

Wilfrid Mellers, *Man and His Music: The Story of Musical Experience in the West* (Oxford University Press, 1962)

— *Celestial Music?: Some Masterpieces of European Religious Music* (Boydell Press, 2002)

Jerrold Northrop Moore, *Elgar: A Creative Life* (Oxford University Press, 1984)

Charles Rosen, *The Classical Style: Haydn, Mozart, Beethoven* (Faber, 1971)

— *The Romantic Generation* (HarperCollins, 1995)

Julian Rushton, *The Music of Berlioz* (Cambridge University Press, 2001)

Richard Taruskin, *Stravinsky and the Russian Traditions: A Biography of the Works through Mavra*, Volumes I and II (University of California Press, 1996)

— *The Oxford History of Western Music*, Volumes I–VI (Oxford University Press, 2005)

Donald Francis Tovey, *Essays and Lectures on Music* (Oxford University Press, 1949; out of print)

Index